Psychotherapy Relationships That Work

Psychotherapy Relationships That Work

Volume 1: Evidence-Based Therapist Contributions

THIRD EDITION

Edited by John C. Norcross
and
Michael J. Lambert

OXFORD
UNIVERSITY PRESS

OXFORD

UNIVERSITY PRESS

Oxford University Press is a department of the University of Oxford. It furthers
the University's objective of excellence in research, scholarship, and education
by publishing worldwide. Oxford is a registered trade mark of Oxford University
Press in the UK and certain other countries.

Published in the United States of America by Oxford University Press
198 Madison Avenue, New York, NY 10016, United States of America.

© John C. Norcross 2019

Second Edition published in 2011
Third Edition published in 2019

CIP data is on file at the Library of Congress
ISBN 978–0–19–084395–3

3 5 7 9 8 6 4

Printed by Sheridan Books, Inc., United States of America

Dedicated to
Carl R. Rogers and Edward S. Bordin
pioneers in investigating and advancing the therapeutic relationship

CONTENTS

Preface ix
About the Editors xv
List of Contributors xvii

1. Evidence-Based Psychotherapy Relationships: The Third Task Force 1
John C. Norcross and Michael J. Lambert

2. Alliance in Adult Psychotherapy 24
Christoph Flückiger, A. C. Del Re, Bruce E. Wampold, and Adam O. Horvath

3. Alliance in Child and Adolescent Psychotherapy 79
Marc S. Karver, Alessandro S. De Nadai, Maureen Monahan, and Stephen R. Shirk

4. Alliances in Couple and Family Therapy 117
Myrna L. Friedlander, Valentín Escudero, Marianne J. Welmers-van de Poll, and Laurie Heatherington

5. Goal Consensus and Collaboration 167
Georgiana Shick Tryon, Sarah E. Birch, and Jay Verkuilen

6. Cohesion in Group Therapy 205
Gary M. Burlingame, Debra Theobald McClendon, and Chongming Yang

7. Empathy 245
Robert Elliott, Arthur C. Bohart, Jeanne C. Watson, and David Murphy

8. Positive Regard and Affirmation 288
Barry A. Farber, Jessica Y. Suzuki, and David A. Lynch

9. Congruence/Genuineness 323
Gregory G. Kolden, Chia-Chiang Wang, Sara B. Austin, Yunling Chang, and Marjorie H. Klein

10. The Real Relationship 351
Charles J. Gelso, Dennis M. Kivlighan Jr., and Rayna D. Markin

11. Self-Disclosure and Immediacy 379
Clara E. Hill, Sarah Knox, and Kristen G. Pinto-Coelho

12. Emotional Expression 421
Paul R. Peluso and Robert R. Freund

13. Cultivating Positive Outcome Expectation 461
Michael J. Constantino, Andreea Vîslă, Alice E. Coyne, and James F. Boswell

14. Promoting Treatment Credibility 495
Michael J. Constantino, Alice E. Coyne, James F. Boswell, Brittany R. Iles, and Andreea Vîslă

15. Managing Countertransference 522
Jeffrey A. Hayes, Charles J. Gelso, D. Martin Kivlighan, and Simon B. Goldberg

16. Repairing Alliance Ruptures 549
Catherine F. Eubanks, J. Christopher Muran, and Jeremy D. Safran

17. Collecting and Delivering Client Feedback 580
Michael J. Lambert, Jason L. Whipple, and Maria Kleinstäuber

18. What Works in the Psychotherapy Relationship: Results, Conclusions, and Practices 631
John C. Norcross and Michael J. Lambert

Index 647

PREFACE

A cordial welcome to the third edition of *Psychotherapy Relationships That Work*. This book seeks, like its predecessors, to identify effective elements of the psychotherapy relationship and to determine effective methods of adapting or tailoring that relationship to the individual patient. That is, we summarize the research evidence on what works in general as well as what works in particular.

This dual focus has been characterized as "two books in one": one book on relationship behaviors and one book on adaptation methods under the same cover. In this third edition, we physically separate the "two books" into two volumes as the number of chapters and the amount of research have grown considerably over the past decade. This Volume 1 features evidence-based therapist contributions to the relationship; Volume 2 addresses evidence-based therapist responsiveness to patient transdiagnostic characteristics.

Our hope in this book, as with the earlier editions, is to advance a rapprochement between the warring factions in the culture wars of psychotherapy and to demonstrate that the best available research clearly demonstrates the healing capacity of the therapy relationship. Previous editions brought renewed and corrective attention to the substantial research behind the therapy relationship and, in the words of one reviewer, "will convince most psychotherapists of the rightful place of ESRs (empirically supported relationships) alongside ESTs in the treatments they provide" (p. 532). Note the desired emphasis on "alongside" treatments, not "instead of" or "better than."

CHANGES IN THE NEW EDITION

The aims of this third edition of *Psychotherapy Relationships That Work* remain the same as its predecessors, but its sponsorship, format, and editorship differ somewhat. This edition was overseen by a task force co-sponsored by the American Psychological Association (APA) Division of Psychotherapy/Society for the Advancement of Psychotherapy and the APA Division of Counseling Psychology/Society of Counseling Psychology. This edition also boasts a practice-friendlier smaller trim size (the physical size of the book).

We have expanded the breadth of coverage. New reviews were commissioned on the real relationship, self-disclosure, immediacy, emotional expression, and treatment credibility in this volume. Of course, updated meta-analyses were conducted for all returning chapters. As noted, we have expanded the book into two volumes, each now co-edited by a stellar psychotherapy researcher (Michael Lambert on this volume, and Bruce Wampold on Volume 2).

The content of each chapter has also expanded. Five new sections appear in each chapter: landmark studies, results of previous meta-analyses, evidence for causality, diversity considerations, and training implications. These additions help readers appreciate the context of the research evidence and unpack its results, especially for treating diverse clients and training psychotherapy students. Since many of the relationship behaviors in this volume cannot be randomly assigned for clinical and ethical reasons (as discussed in Chapters 1 and 18), the causality section summarizes what can (and cannot) be said about the direct impact of the therapist's relational contributions.

The net result is a compilation of 30, cutting-edge meta-analyses on what works in the therapy relationship (this volume) and what works in adapting that relationship to the individual client and his or her singular situation (the second volume). This new edition, appearing nine years after the last incarnation, offers more practical, bulleted information on clinical practice at the end of each chapter.

PROBABLE AUDIENCES

In planning the first edition of the book more than 20 years ago, we struggled to identity the intended audiences. Each of psychotherapy's stakeholders—patients, practitioners, researchers, educators, students, organizations, insurance companies, and policymakers—expressed different preferences for the content and length of the volume.

We prepared *Psychotherapy Relationships That Work* for multiple audiences but in a definite order of priority. First came psychotherapy practitioners and trainees of diverse theoretical orientations and professional disciplines. They need to address urgent pragmatic questions: We know the therapy relationship is crucial to treatment success, but what exactly has been shown to work? What do we know from the research evidence about cultivating and maintaining the therapeutic relationship? What are the research-supported means of adapting treatment to the individual patient beyond his/her diagnosis?

Our second priority was accorded to the mental health disciplines themselves, specifically those committees, task forces, and organizations promulgating lists of evidence-based practices or treatment guidelines. We hope our work will inform and balance any efforts to focus exclusively on techniques or treatments to the neglect of the humans involved in the enterprise.

Our third priority were insurance carriers and accreditation organizations, many of which have unintentionally devalued the person of the therapist and the centrality of the relationship by virtue of reimbursement decisions. Although supportive of the recent thrust toward research informing practice, we must remind all parties to the therapy relationship that healing cannot be replaced with treating, caring cannot be supplanted by managing. Finally, this book is intended for psychotherapy researchers seeking a central resource on the empirical status of the multiple, interdependent qualities of the therapy relationship.

ORGANIZATION OF THE BOOK

The opening chapter introduces the book by outlining the purpose and history of the interdivisional task force and its relation to previous efforts to identify evidence-based practices in psychotherapy. That chapter also presents the key limitations of our work.

The heart of the book is composed of research reviews on the therapist's relational contributions and recommended therapeutic practices based on that research. It features 16 chapters on relationship elements primarily provided by the psychotherapist. Several chapters, such as Chapter 5, Goal Consensus and Collaboration, and Chapter 11, Self-Disclosure and Immediacy, each cover two closely related relationship behaviors.

The concluding chapter presents our reflections and the Task Force conclusions. The latter includes, inter alia, a list of evidence-based relationship elements and our consensual recommendations, divided into general, practice, training, research, and policy recommendations.

CHAPTER GUIDELINES

Except for the bookends (Chapters 1 and 18), all chapters use the same section headings and follow a consistent structure, as follows:

- Introduction (untitled). Introduce the relationship element and its historical context in several paragraphs.
- Definitions. Define in theoretically neutral language the relationship element and identify highly similar or equivalent constructs from diverse theoretical traditions.
- Measures. Review the popular measures used in the research and included in the ensuing meta-analysis.
- Clinical Examples. Provide several concrete examples of the relationship behavior being reviewed. Portions of psychotherapy transcripts are encouraged here while protecting the privacy of patients.
- Landmark Studies. Walk the reader through two to four landmark studies on the topic (including one qualitative study), describing the design, participants, and results.
- Results of Previous Meta-Analyses. Offer a quick synopsis of the findings of previous meta-analyses and systematic reviews.
- Meta-Analytic Review. Conduct an original meta-analysis of all available studies employing a random effects model. Systematically compile all available empirical studies linking the relationship behavior to distal, end-of-treatment outcome in the English language (and other languages, if possible). Include only actual psychotherapy studies; no analogue studies. Use the Meta-Analysis Reporting Standards as a general guide for the information to include. Perform and report a test of heterogeneity. Report the effect size as both weighted r and d (or other standardized mean difference). Include a fail-safe statistic to address the file-drawer problem and provide a table or funnel plot for each study in the meta-analysis.

- Moderators and Mediators. Present the results of the potential mediators and moderators on the between the relationship element and treatment outcome. Examples include year of publication, rater perspective (assessed by therapist, patient, or external raters), therapist variables, patient factors (including cultural diversity), different measures of the relationship element and treatment outcome, time of assessment (when in the course of therapy), and type of psychotherapy/theoretical orientation.
- Evidence for Causality. Summarize the evidence (e.g., lagged correlations, structural equations, unconfounded regressions, growth curve studies) demonstrating that the relational element may causally contribute to treatment outcome. Is there research evidence for a causal link or strictly for correlational association/prediction?
- Patient Contributions. Address the patient's contribution to the therapeutic relationship and the distinctive perspective he/she brings to the interaction (especially since the meta-analyses pertain primarily to the psychotherapists' contribution to the relationship).
- Limitations of the Research. Point to the major limitations of the research conducted to date. A concise paragraph or two here on future research directions is also welcomed.
- Diversity Considerations. Address how dimensions of diversity (e.g., gender, race/ ethnicity, sexual orientation, socioeconomic status) fare in the research studies and the meta-analytic results.
- Training Implications. Explicate briefly the take-home points of your meta-analysis for clinical educators and supervisors. Mention any training resources or programs that have a proven record of teaching the relationship element to competence.
- Therapeutic Practices. Place the emphasis here squarely on what works. Bullet the practice implications from the foregoing research, primarily in terms of the therapist's contribution and secondarily in terms of the patient's perspective.

ACKNOWLEDGMENTS

Psychotherapy Relationships That Work would not have proved possible without two decades of organizational and individual support. On the organizational front, the board of directors of the APA Division of Psychotherapy consistently supported the interdivisional task force, and the APA Division of Counseling Psychology co-sponsored this iteration. At Oxford University Press, Sarah Harrington and Joan Bossert shepherded these books through the publishing process and recognized early on that they would complement Oxford's landmark *Treatments That Work*. We are particularly appreciative of Oxford's flexibility in copyright matters that have enabled us to disseminate farther these consequential meta-analytic results. Their commitment to spreading this book's knowledge through special journal issues and other practitioner publications, even at the expense of their occasional loss of book sales, is noble and probably unprecedented in publishing circles.

On the individual front, many people modeled and manifested the ideal therapeutic relationship throughout the course of the project. The authors of the respective chapters, of course, were indispensable in generating the research reviews and were generous in sharing their expertise. The Steering Committee of the previous task forces assisted in canvassing the literature, defining the parameters of the project, selecting the contributors, and writing the initial conclusions. We are grateful to them all: Steven J. Ackerman, Lorna Smith Benjamin, Guillermo Bernal, Larry E. Beutler, Franz Caspar, Louis Castonguay, Charles J. Gelso, Marvin R. Goldfried, Clara Hill, Mark J. Hilsenroth, Michael J. Lambert, David E. Orlinsky, Jackson P. Rainer, and Bruce E. Wampold. For this task force and this edition of the book, we thank the following for serving on the Steering Committee:

Franz Caspar, PhD, University of Bern
Melanie M. Domenech Rodriguez, PhD, Utah State University
Clara E. Hill, PhD, University of Maryland
Michael J. Lambert, PhD, Brigham Young University
Suzanne H. Lease, PhD, University of Memphis (representing APA Division 17)
James W. Lichtenberg, PhD, University of Kansas (representing APA Division 17)
Rayna D. Markin, PhD, Villanova University (representing APA Division 29)
John C. Norcross, PhD, University of Scranton (chair)
Jesse Owen, PhD, University of Denver
Bruce E. Wampold, PhD, University of Wisconsin

Last but never least, our immediate families—Nancy, Rebecca, and Jonathon (JCN) and Linda, Ritchie, Hillary, Allison, John, and Chris (MJL)—tolerated our absences, preoccupations, and irritabilities associated with editing this book with a combination of empathy and patience that would do any seasoned psychotherapist proud. We gratefully dedicate this book to our grandchildren for teaching us about the value of loving relationship—Emma, Owen, Ethan, Owen, Wyatt, Dylan, Maddie, Spencer, Zippy, the three Tenzins, Ryan, Luke, Noah, Jessi, and Squishy.

John C. Norcross & Michael J. Lambert

ABOUT THE EDITORS

John C. Norcross, PhD, ABPP, is Distinguished Professor of Psychology at the University of Scranton, Adjunct Professor of Psychiatry at SUNY Upstate Medical University, and a board-certified clinical psychologist. Author of more than 400 scholarly publications, Dr. Norcross has co-written or edited 25 books, including *Clinician's Guide to Evidence-Based Practice in Behavioral Health and Addictions, Self-Help That Works,* the *Psychologists' Desk Reference, History of Psychotherapy, Changeology, Leaving It at the Office: Psychotherapist Self-Care,* 12 editions of the *Insider's Guide to Graduate Programs in Clinical & Counseling Psychology,* and *Systems of Psychotherapy: A Transtheoretical Analysis,* now in its ninth edition. He has served as president of the American Psychological Association (APA) Division of Clinical Psychology, the APA Division of Psychotherapy, Society for the Exploration of Psychotherapy Integration, and on the Board of Directors of the National Register of Health Service Psychologists. Dr. Norcross has received multiple professional awards, such as APA's Distinguished Career Contributions to Education & Training Award, Pennsylvania Professor of the Year from the Carnegie Foundation, and election to the National Academies of Practice. An engaging teacher and clinician, John has conducted workshops and lectures in 30 countries.

Michael J. Lambert, PhD, was Professor of Psychology and held the Susa Young Gates University Professorship at Brigham Young University until his retirement in 2016 after teaching for 45 years in the clinical psychology program. He has been in private practice as a psychotherapist throughout his career. He has edited, authored, or co-authored nine books, most notably the fifth and sixth editions of Bergin and Garfield's *Handbook of Psychotherapy and Behavior Change.* His scholarly contributions include more than 40 book chapters, more than 150 scientific articles on treatment outcome, and over 200 presentations across the world, many of them invited addresses. He is co-author of the Outcome Questionnaire-45, a measure of treatment effects widely used to measure and monitor treatment response during psychotherapy. Among Dr. Lambert's awards are Brigham Young University's highest honor for faculty research (the Maeser Award), the Distinguished Psychologist Award from APA Division 29 (Psychotherapy), the Academic Excellence Award from the Utah Psychological Association, and the Distinguished Career Research Award from the Society of Psychotherapy Research. In recognition of his contributions to psychological science, the University of Jyväskylä, Finland, bestowed him with an honorary doctorate in 2013.

CONTRIBUTORS

Sara B. Austin, BA
Department of Psychology, Simon Fraser
University

Sarah E. Birch, PhD
Department of Child Study, St. Joseph's
College

Arthur C. Bohart, PhD
Department of Psychology, California
State University Dominguez Hills
Counseling Psychology Department,
Santa Clara University

James F. Boswell, PhD
Department of Psychology, University at
Albany, State University of New York

Gary M. Burlingame, PhD
Department of Psychology, Brigham
Young University

Yunling Chang, MS
Department of Educational Psychology,
Texas A&M University

Michael J. Constantino, PhD
Department of Psychological and Brain
Sciences, University of Massachusetts
Amherst

Alice E. Coyne, MS
Department of Psychological and Brain
Sciences, University of Massachusetts
Amherst

Alessandro S. De Nadai, PhD
Department of Psychology, Texas State
University

A. C. Del Re, PhD
Palo Alto Veterans Administration
Medical Center

Robert Elliott, PhD
School of Psychological Sciences &
Health, University of Strathclyde

Valentín Escudero, PhD
Departamento de Psicología,
Universidad de A Coruña (Spain)

Catherine F. Eubanks, PhD
Ferkauf Graduate School of Psychology,
Yeshiva University
Mount Sinai Beth Israel Psychotherapy
Research Program, Mount Sinai
School of Medicine

Barry A. Farber, PhD
Program in Clinical Psychology,
Teachers College, Columbia University

Christoph Flückiger, PhD
Department of Psychology, University of
Zürich, Switzerland

Robert R. Freund, PhD
Department of Counseling and
Psychological Services, SUNY–Oswego

Myrna L. Friedlander, PhD
Department of Educational and
  Counseling Psychology, University at
  Albany/SUNY

Charles J. Gelso, PhD
Department of Psychology, University of
  Maryland

Simon B. Goldberg, PhD
Department of Counseling Psychology,
  University of Wisconsin–Madison VA
  Puget Sound Health Care System–
  Seattle Division

Jeffrey A. Hayes, PhD
Department of Educational Psychology,
  Counseling, and Special Education,
  Penn State University

Laurie Heatherington, PhD
Department of Psychology, Williams
  College

Clara E. Hill, PhD
Department of Psychology, University of
  Maryland

Adam O. Horvath, PhD
Department of Psychology, Simon Fraser
  University

Brittany R. Iles, BS
Department of Psychology, University at
  Albany, State University of New York

Marc S. Karver, PhD
Department of Psychology, University of
  South Florida

Dennis M. Kivlighan Jr., PhD
Department of Counseling, Higher
  Education, and Special Education,
  University of Maryland

D. Martin Kivlighan III, PhD
Department of Psychological and
  Quantitative Foundations, University
  of Iowa

Marjorie H. Klein, PhD
Department of Psychiatry, University of
  Wisconsin

Maria Kleinstäuber, PhD
Department of Psychology, Philipps-
  University, Marburg (Germany)
Department of Psychological Medicine,
  University of Auckland, Auckland
  (New Zealand)

Sarah Knox, PhD
Department of Counselor Education &
  Counseling Psychology
Marquette University

Gregory G. Kolden, PhD
Department of Psychiatry, University
  of Wisconsin School of Medicine and
  Public Health
Department of Psychology, University of
  Wisconsin-Madison

Michael J. Lambert, PhD
Department of Psychology, Brigham
  Young University

David A. Lynch, MPhil
Program in Clinical Psychology,
  Teachers College, Columbia University

Rayna D. Markin, PhD
Department of Education and
  Counseling, Villanova University

Debra Theobald McClendon, PhD
Private Practice, Woodland Hills,
  Utah

Maureen Monahan, MA
Department of Psychology,
    University of South Florida

J. Christopher Muran, PhD
Gordon F. Derner School of Psychology,
    Adelphi University
Mount Sinai Beth Israel Psychotherapy
    Research Program, Mount Sinai
    School of Medicine

David Murphy, PhD
School of Education,
    University of Nottingham

John C. Norcross, PhD
Department of Psychology,
    University of Scranton
Department of Psychiatry, SUNY
    Upstate Medical University

Paul R. Peluso, PhD
Department of Counselor Education,
    Florida Atlantic University

Kristen G. Pinto-Coelho, PhD
Private Practice, Ellicott City, Maryland

Jeremy D. Safran, PhD
Department of Psychology, New School
    for Social Research

Stephen R. Shirk, PhD
Department of Psychology, University
    of Denver

Jessica Y. Suzuki, PhD
Program in Clinical Psychology,
    Teachers College, Columbia University

Georgiana Shick Tryon, PhD
Program in Educational Psychology,
    Graduate School and University
    Center of the City University of
    New York

Jay Verkuilen, PhD
Program in Educational Psychology,
    Graduate School and University
    Center of the City University of
    New York

Andreea Vîslă, PhD
Department of Psychology,
    University of Zurich

Bruce E. Wampold, PhD
Modum Bad Psychiatric Center,
    Norway
Department of Counseling
    Psychology, University of
    Madison-Wisconsin

Chia-Chiang Wang, PhD
Department of Counseling, School,
    and Educational Psychology,
    University at Buffalo

Jeanne C. Watson, PhD
Department of Applied Psychology
    and Human Development,
    University of Toronto

Marianne J. Welmers-van de Poll, MSc
Research Centre Youth Care,
    Windesheim University of Applied
    Sciences

Jason L. Whipple, PhD
Alaska VA Healthcare System

Chongming Yang, PhD
College of Family, Home,
    and Social Sciences,
    Brigham Young University

Psychotherapy Relationships That Work

1

EVIDENCE-BASED PSYCHOTHERAPY RELATIONSHIP: THE THIRD TASK FORCE

John C. Norcross and Michael J. Lambert

Ask patients what they find most helpful in their psychotherapy. Ask practitioners which component of psychotherapy ensures the highest probability of success. Ask researchers what the evidence favors in predicting effective psychological treatment. Ask psychotherapists what they are most eager to learn about (Tasca et al., 2015). Ask proponents of diverse psychotherapy systems on what point they can find commonality. The probable answer, for all these questions, is the *psychotherapy relationship*, the healing alliance between client and clinician.

To value or highlight the therapeutic relationship is not to say that it is "all about" or "only" the relationship. Alas, that is frequently the erroneous conclusion reached in the culture wars in psychotherapy that dramatically pit the treatment method against the therapeutic relationship. Do treatments cure disorders, or do relationships heal people? Which is the most accurate vision for practicing, researching, and teaching psychotherapy?

Like most dichotomies, this one is misleading and unproductive on multiple counts. For starters, the patient's contribution to psychotherapy outcome is vastly greater than that of either the particular treatment method or the therapy relationship (Lambert, 2011, 2013; Wampold & Imel, 2015). The research evidence should keep us mindful and a bit humble about our collective tendency toward therapist-centricity (Bohart & Tallman, 1999; Bohart & Wade, 2013). For another, decades of psychotherapy research consistently attest that the patient, the therapist, their relationship, the treatment method, and the context all contribute to treatment success (and failure). We should be looking at all of these determinants and their optimal combinations.

But perhaps the most pernicious and insidious consequence of the false dichotomy of method versus relationship has been its polarizing effect on the discipline. Rival camps have developed, and countless critiques have been published on each side of the culture war. Are you on the side of the treatment method, the randomized controlled/clinical trial (RCT), and the scientific-medical model? Or do you embrace the therapy relationship, the effectiveness and process-outcome studies, and the relational-contextual model? Such polarizations not only impede psychotherapists from working together but also hinder our provision of the most efficacious psychological services to our patients and the best training to our students.

We hoped that a balanced perspective would be achieved by the adoption of an inclusive, neutral definition of evidence-based practice (EBP). The American Psychological Association (APA; 2006, p. 273) did endorse just such a definition: "Evidence-based practice in psychology (EBPP) is the integration of the best available research with clinical expertise in the context of patient characteristics, culture, and preferences." However, even that definition has been commandeered by the rival camps as polarizing devices. On the one side, some erroneously equate EBP solely with the best available research and particularly the results of RCTs on treatment methods, while on the other side, some mistakenly exaggerate the primacy of clinical or relational expertise while neglecting research support.

Within this polarizing context, in 1999, the APA Division of Psychotherapy commissioned a task force to identify, operationalize, and disseminate information on empirically supported therapy relationships. That task force summarized its findings and detailed its recommendations in the first edition of this book (Norcross, 2002). In 2009, the APA Division of Psychotherapy along with the Division of Clinical Psychology commissioned a second task force on evidence-based therapy relationships to update the research base and clinical practices on the psychotherapist–patient relationship. That second edition (Norcross, 2011), appearing 10 years after its predecessor, did just that.

Our aim for the third task force and in this third edition of the book (now in two volumes) remains to advance a rapprochement between the warring factions and to demonstrate that the best available research clearly supports the healing qualities of the therapy relationship (Volume 1) and the beneficial value of adapting that relationship to individual patients beyond their diagnosis (Volume 2). This third edition expands upon the first two editions, in terms of both the research evidence for relational elements and the number of topics under consideration. These two volumes summarize the best available research and clinical practices on numerous elements of the therapy relationship and on several methods of treatment adaptation. In doing so, our grander goal is to repair some of the damage incurred by the culture wars in psychotherapy and to promote rapprochement between the research and practice communities.

In this chapter, we begin by tracing the purposes and processes of the third interdivisional task force cosponsored by APA Division of Psychotherapy and the APA Division of Counseling Psychology. We explicate the need for identifying evidence-based elements of the therapy relationship and, in a tentative way, offer two models to account for psychotherapy outcome as a function of various therapeutic factors (e.g., patient, relationship, technique). The latter part of the chapter features the limitations of the task force's work and responds to frequently asked questions.

THE THIRD INTERDIVISIONAL TASK FORCE

The dual purposes of the Third Interdivisional APA Task Force on Evidence-Based Relationships and Responsiveness were to identify effective elements of the therapy relationship and to determine effective methods of adapting or tailoring therapy to the individual patient on the basis of transdiagnostic characteristics. In other words, we were interested in both what works in general and what works for particular patients.

For the purposes of our work, we again adopted Gelso and Carter's (1985, 1994) operational definition of the relationship: The *therapeutic relationship* is the feelings and attitudes that therapist and client have toward one another and the manner in which these are expressed. This definition is quite general, and the phrase "the manner in which it is expressed" potentially opens the relationship to include everything under the therapeutic sun (see Gelso & Hayes, 1998, for an extended discussion). Nonetheless, it serves as a concise, consensual, theoretically neutral, and sufficiently precise definition.

We acknowledge the deep synergy between treatment methods and the therapeutic relationship. They constantly shape and inform each other. Both clinical experience and research evidence point to a complex, reciprocal interaction between the interpersonal relationship and the instrumental methods. Consider this finding from a large collaborative study: For patients with a strong therapeutic alliance, adherence to the treatment manual was irrelevant for treatment outcome, but for patients with a weak alliance, a moderate level of therapist adherence was associated with the best outcome (Barber et al., 2006). The relationship does not exist apart from what the therapist does in terms of method, and we cannot imagine any treatment methods that would not have some relational impact. Put differently, treatment methods are relational acts (Safran & Muran, 2000).

For historical and research convenience, the field has distinguished between relationships and techniques. Words like "relating" and "interpersonal behavior" are used to describe *how* therapists and clients behave toward each other. By contrast, terms like "technique" or "intervention" are used to describe *what* is done by the therapist. In research and theory, we often treat the how and the what—the relationship and the intervention, the interpersonal and the instrumental—as separate categories.

In reality, of course, what one does and how one does it are complementary and inseparable. To remove the interpersonal from the instrumental may be acceptable in research, but it is a fatal flaw when the aim is to extrapolate research results to clinical practice (see Gelso, 2005, a special issue of *Psychotherapy* on the interplay of techniques and therapeutic relationship).

In other words, the value of a treatment method is inextricably bound to the relational context in which it is applied. Hans Strupp, one of our first research mentors, offered an analogy to illustrate the inseparability of these constituent elements. Suppose you want your teenager to clean his or her room. Two methods for achieving this are to establish clear standards and to impose consequences. A reasonable approach, but the effectiveness of these two evidence-based methods depends on whether the relationship between you and the teenager is characterized by warmth and mutual respect or by anger and mistrust. This is not to say that the methods are useless, merely how well they work depends upon the context in which they are used (Norcross, 2010).

The task force applies psychological science to the identification and promulgation of effective psychotherapy. It does so by expanding or enlarging the typical focus of EBP to therapy relationships. Focusing on one area—in this case, the therapeutic relationship—may unfortunately convey the impression that this is the only area of importance. We review the scientific literature on the therapy relationship and provide clinical recommendations based on that literature in ways, we trust, that do not degrade the simultaneous contributions of the treatment methods, patients, or therapists to outcome. Indeed, we wish that more psychotherapists would acknowledge the inseparable context and practical interdependence of the relationship and the treatment. That can prove a crucial step in reducing the polarizing strife of the culture wars and in improving the effectiveness of psychotherapy (Lambert, 2013).

An immediate challenge to the task force was to establish the inclusion and exclusion criteria for the elements of the therapy relationship. We readily agreed that the traditional features of the therapeutic relationship—the alliance in individual therapy, cohesion in group therapy, and the Rogerian facilitative conditions, for example—would constitute core elements. We further agreed that discrete, relatively nonrelational techniques were not part of our purview but that a few explicitly relationship-oriented methods would be included. Therapy methods were considered for inclusion if their content, goal, and context were inextricably interwoven into the emergent therapy relationship. We settled on several "relational" methods (collecting real-time client feedback, repairing alliance ruptures, facilitating emotional expression, and managing countertransference) because these methods are deeply embedded in the interpersonal character of the relationship itself. As "methods," they also prove possible to randomly assign patients to one treatment condition with the method (for instance, feedback or rupture repairs) and other patients to a condition without them. Indeed, the meta-analyses on both feedback and repair of alliance ruptures feature mostly randomized controlled trials that permit casual conclusions. But which relational behaviors to include and which to exclude under the rubric of the *therapy relationship* bedeviled us, as it has the field.

How does one divide the indivisible relationship? For example, is *support* similar enough to *positive regard* or *validation* to be considered in the same meta-analysis, or is it distinct enough to deserve a separate research review? We struggled on how finely to slice the therapy relationship. As David Orlinsky opined in one of his emails, "it's okay to slice bologna that thin, but I doubt that it can be meaningfully done to the relationship." We agreed, as a group, to place the research on support in the positive regard chapter, but we understood that some practitioners would justifiably take exception to collapsing these relationship elements. Consideration also had to be given to the existence of research evidence; in what ways have researchers operationalized relationship elements in studies. As a general rule, we opted to divide the research reviews into smaller chunks so that the research conclusions were more specific and the practice and training implications more concrete.

In our deliberations, several members of the steering committee advanced a favorite analogy: the therapy relationship is like a diamond—a diamond composed of multiple, interconnected facets. The diamond is a complex and multidimensional entity. The task force endeavored to separate and examine many of these facets.

We consulted psychotherapy experts, the research literature, and potential authors to discern whether there were sufficient numbers of studies on a particular relationship element to conduct a systematic review and meta-analysis. Three relational elements—therapist humor, self-doubt/humility, and deliberate practice—exhibited initial research support but not a sufficient number of empirical studies for a review. Five new relationship behaviors surpassed our research threshold, and thus we included the real relationship, self-disclosure, immediacy, emotional expression, and treatment credibility in this volume.

Once these decisions were finalized, we commissioned original meta-analyses on the relationship elements (Volume 1) and the adaptation/responsiveness methods (Volume 2). Authors followed a comprehensive chapter structure (provided in the preface) and specific guidelines for their meta-analyses. The analyses quantitatively linked the relationship element (or adaptation method) to psychotherapy outcome. Outcome was primarily defined as distal posttreatment outcomes. Authors specified the outcome criterion when a particular study did not employ a typical end-of-treatment measure. Indeed, the type of outcome measure was frequently analyzed as a possible moderator of the overall effect size.

In these meta-analyses, we continually emphasized the association with and prediction of psychotherapy outcome, instead of process variables or other relationship elements. This emphasis on distal outcomes sharpened our focus on "what works" and countered the partial truth that some of the meta-analyses examining predominantly proximal outcome measures in earlier iterations of the book merely illustrated that "the good stuff in session correlates with other good stuff in session." We have responded to that criticism in this third edition while explicating several consequential process linkages.

The chapters and the meta-analyses therein were peer-reviewed by at least two editors and subsequently underwent at least one revision. In particular, the review established that the meta-analyses adhered to the Meta-Analysis Reporting Standards and reported the requisite information (outlined in the preface).

When the chapters were finalized, a 10-person expert panel (identified in the preface and in Chapter 18) reviewed and rated the evidentiary strength of the relationship element. They did so according to the following criteria: number of empirical studies; consistency of empirical results; independence of supportive studies; magnitude of association between the relationship element and outcome; evidence for causal link between relationship element and outcome; and the ecological or external validity of research. Using these objective criteria, experts independently judged the strength of the research evidence as:

Demonstrably effective,
Probably effective,
Promising but insufficient research to judge,
Important but not yet investigated, or
Not effective.

We then aggregated the individual ratings to render a consensus conclusion on each relationship element. These conclusions are summarized in the last chapter of this volume, as are 25 recommendations approved by all members of the steering committee.

Our deliberations were rarely unanimous, but invariably conducted in a collegial spirit and toward a common goal. Democratic process proves messy and inefficient; science is even slower and painstaking. We relied on expert opinion referencing best practices, professional consensus using objective rating criteria, and, most important, systematic reviews of the research evidence. But these were all human decisions—open to cavil, contention, and future revision.

THERAPY RELATIONSHIP

Recent decades have witnessed the controversial compilation of practice guidelines and evidence-based treatments in mental health. In the United States and other countries, the introduction of such guidelines has provoked practice modifications, training refinements, and organizational conflicts. Insurance carriers and government policymakers increasingly turn to such guidelines to determine which psychotherapies to approve and fund. Indeed, along with the negative influence of managed care, there is probably no issue more central to clinicians than the evolution of evidence-based treatments in psychotherapy (Barlow, 2000; Norcross et al., 2017).

The efforts to promulgate evidence-based psychotherapies have been noble in intent and timely in distribution. They are praiseworthy efforts to distill scientific research into clinical applications and to guide practice and training. They wisely demonstrate that, in a climate of accountability, psychotherapy stands up to empirical scrutiny with the best of healthcare interventions. And within psychology, these have proactively counterbalanced documents that accorded primacy to biomedical treatments for mental disorders and largely ignored the outcome data for psychological therapies. On many accounts, then, the extant efforts addressed the realpolitik of the socio-economic situation (Messer, 2001; Nathan & Gorman, 2015).

At the same time, many practitioners and researchers have found these recent efforts to codify evidence-based treatments seriously incomplete. While scientifically laudable in their intent, these efforts largely ignored the therapy relationship and the person of the therapist. Practically all treatment guidelines have followed the antiquated medical model of identifying particular treatment methods for specific diagnoses: Treatment A for Disorder Z. If one reads the documents literally, disembodied providers apply manualized interventions to discrete disorders. Not only is the language offensive on clinical grounds to some practitioners, but also the research evidence is weak for validating treatment methods in isolation from specific therapists, the therapy relationship, and the individual patient.

Suppose we asked a neutral scientific panel from outside the field to review the corpus of psychotherapy research to determine the most powerful phenomenon we should be studying, practicing, and teaching. Henry (1998, p. 128) concluded that the panel would find the answer obvious, and *empirically validated*. As a general trend across studies, the largest chunk of outcome variance not attributable to preexisting patient characteristics involves individual therapist differences and the emergent therapeutic relationship between patient and therapist, regardless of technique or school of therapy. This is the main thrust of decades of empirical research.

What's missing, in short, are the person of the therapist and the therapeutic relationship.

Person of the Therapist

Most practice guidelines and EBP compilations depict interchangeable providers performing treatment procedures. This stands in marked contrast to the clinician's and client's experience of psychotherapy as an intensely interpersonal and deeply emotional experience. Although efficacy research has gone to considerable lengths to eliminate the individual therapist as a variable that might account for patient improvement, the inescapable fact of the matter is that it is simply not possible to mask the person and the contribution of the therapist (Castonguay & Hill, 2017; Orlinsky & Howard, 1977). The curative contribution of the person of the therapist is, arguably, as evidence based as manualized treatments or psychotherapy methods (Hubble et al., 2011).

Multiple and converging sources of evidence indicate that the *person* of the psychotherapist is inextricably intertwined with the outcome of psychotherapy. A large, naturalistic study estimated the outcomes attributable to 581 psychotherapists treating 6,146 patients in a managed care setting. About 5% of the outcome variation was due to therapist effects, and 0% was due to specific treatment methods (Wampold & Brown, 2005).

Quantitative reviews of therapist effects in psychotherapy outcome studies show consistent and robust therapist effects—probably accounting for 5% to 8% of psychotherapy outcome (Baldwin & Imel, 2013; Barkham et al., 2017; Crits-Christoph et al., 1991; Johns et al., 2019). The Barkham study combined data from four countries, 362 therapists, 14,254 clients, and four outcome measures. They found that about 8% of the variance in outcome was due to the therapist, so-called *therapist effects* (Castonguay & Hill, 2017). Moreover, the size of the therapist effect was strongly related to initial client severity. The more disturbed a client was at the beginning of therapy, the more it mattered which therapist the client saw.

They also reported that to a large degree the middle two thirds of therapists could not be reliably and confidently distinguished from each other based on their clients' outcomes. At the same time, 15% to 20% of therapists could be identified whose clients had distinguishably better outcomes with the same percentages having worse outcomes. These therapist effects appeared stable over time. Of course, therapist effects may well be directly related to relationship factors, such as the therapeutic alliance (Wampold et al., 2017).

Two controlled studies examining therapist effects in the outcomes of cognitive-behavioral therapy prove instructive (Huppert et al., 2001; Project MATCH Research Group, 1998). In the Multicenter Collaborative Study for the Treatment of Panic

Disorder, considerable care was taken to standardize the treatment, the therapist, and the patients to increase the experimental rigor of the study and to minimize therapist effects. The treatment was manualized and structured; the therapists were identically trained and monitored for adherence; and the patients rigorously evaluated and relatively uniform. Nonetheless, the therapists significantly differed in the magnitude of change among caseloads. Effect sizes for therapist impact on outcome measures ranged from 0% to 18%. In the similarly controlled multisite study on alcohol abuse conducted by Project MATCH, the therapists were carefully selected, trained, supervised, and monitored in their respective treatment approaches. Although there were few outcome differences among the treatments, over 6% of the outcome variance (1%–12% range) was due to therapists. Despite impressive attempts to experimentally render individual practitioners as controlled variables, it is simply not possible to mask the person and the contribution of the therapist.

Even when self-help treatments are effectively delivered with minimal therapist contact (e.g., King et al., 2017), their relational context includes interpersonal skill, persuasion, warmth, and even, on occasion, charisma. Self-help resources typically contain their developers' self-disclosures, interpersonal support, and normalizing concerns. Thus, it is not surprising that relation between treatment outcome and the therapeutic alliance in Internet-based psychotherapy is of the same strength as that for the alliance-outcome association in face-to-face psychotherapy (Flückiger et al., 2013, Chapter 2).

The size of therapist effects, 5% to 9% of the outcome, may seem small at first glance, but that is misleading. A Monte Carlo simulation demonstrated just removing the bottom 5% of worst-performing therapists and replacing them with average effective therapists could benefit thousands of clients in the long run (Baldwin & Imel, 2013; Imel et al., 2015). Therapist effects are strong, ubiquitous, and sadly ignored in most guidelines on what works.

Therapeutic Relationship

A second omission in most treatment guidelines and EBPs has been the decision to validate only the efficacy of treatments or technical interventions, as opposed to the therapy relationship or therapist interpersonal skills. This decision both reflects and reinforces the ongoing movement toward high-quality, comparative effectiveness research on brand-name psychotherapies. "This trend of putting all of the eggs in the 'technique' basket began in the late 1970s and is now reaching the peak of influence" (Bergin, 1997, p. 83).

Both clinical experience and research findings underscore that the therapy relationship accounts for as much, and probably more, of the outcome variance as particular treatment methods. Meta-analyses of psychotherapy outcome literature consistently reveal that specific techniques account for 0% to 5% of the outcome variance (e.g., Lambert, 2013; Wampold & Imel, 2015), and much of that is attributable to the investigator's therapy allegiance (Cuijpurs et al., 2012; Luborsky et al., 1999). An early and influential review by Bergin and Lambert (1978, p.180) anticipated the contemporary research consensus: "The largest variation in therapy outcome is accounted for by pre-existing client factors, such as motivation for change, and the like. Therapist personal factors account for the second largest proportion of change, with technique variables coming in a distant third."

Even those practice guidelines enjoining practitioners to attend to the therapy relationship do not provide specific, evidence-based means of doing so. For example, the scholarly and comprehensive review on treatment choice from Great Britain (Department of Health, 2001) devotes a single paragraph to the therapeutic relationship. Its recommended principle is that "Effectiveness of all types of therapy depends on the patient and the therapist forming a good working relationship" (p. 35), but no evidence-based guidance is offered on which therapist behaviors contribute to or cultivate that relationship. For another example, although most treatment manuals mention the importance of the therapy relationship, few specify what therapist qualities or in-session behaviors lead to a curative relationship.

All of this is to say that extant lists of EBPs and best practices in mental health give short shrift—some would say lip service—to the person of the therapist and the emergent therapeutic relationship. The vast majority of current attempts are thus seriously incomplete and potentially misleading, both on clinical and empirical grounds. In this book, we compile the best available research evidence on what works in the psychotherapy relationship and then translate that into specific practice and training guidelines.

EFFECT SIZES

The subsequent chapters feature original meta-analyses on the link between the relationship elements and patient outcome. Insisting on quantitative meta-analyses for all the chapters (with one exception) enable direct estimates of the magnitude of association in the form of effect sizes. These are standardized difference between two group means—say, psychotherapy and a control—divided by the (pooled) standard deviation. The resultant effect size is in standard deviation units. Both Cohen's d and Hedges' g estimate the population effect size.

The meta-analyses in this volume employed the weighted r and its equivalent d or g. Most of the chapters in this volume (but not Volume 2) analyzed studies that were correlational in nature; for example, studies that correlated the patient's ratings of empathy during psychotherapy with their outcome at the end of treatment. The correlational coefficients (r) were then converted into d or g. We did so for consistency among the meta-analyses, enhancing their interpretability among the readers (square r for the amount of variance accounted for), and enabling direct comparisons of the meta-analytic results to one another as well as to d (the effect size typically used when comparing the relative effects of two treatments). In all of these analyses, the larger the magnitude of r or d, the higher the probability of patient success in psychotherapy based on the relationship variable under consideration.

Table 1.1 presents several concrete ways to interpret r and d in healthcare. By convention (Cohen, 1988), an r of .10 in the behavioral sciences is considered a small effect; .30, a medium effect; and .50, a large effect. By contrast, a d of

.30 is considered a small effect; .50, a medium effect; and .80, a large effect. Of course, these general rules or conventions cannot be dissociated from the context of decisions and comparative values. There is little inherent value to an effect size of 2.0 or 0.2; it depends on what benefits can be achieved at what cost (Smith et al., 1980).

Given the large number of factors contributing to patient success and the inherent complexity of psychotherapy, we do not expect large, overpowering effects of any one relationship behavior. Instead, we expect to find a number of helpful facets. And that is exactly what we find in the following chapters—beneficial, small- to medium-sized effects of several elements of the complex therapy relationship.

For example, the authors of Chapter 7 conducted a meta-analysis of 82 studies that investigated the association between therapist empathy and patient success at the end of treatment. Their meta-analysis, involving a total of 6,138 patients, found a weighted mean r of .28. As shown in Table 1.1, this is a medium effect size. The corresponding effect size of d is .58. Both numbers translate into happier and healthier clients; that is, clients with more empathic therapists tend to progress more in treatment and experience greater eventual improvement.

Table 1.1. Interpretation of Effect Size Statistics

d	r	Cohen's Benchmark	Type of Effect	Percentile of Treated Patients[a]	Success Rate of Treated Patients[b]
1.00			Beneficial	84	72%
0.90			Beneficial	82	70%
0.80	.50	Large	Beneficial	79	69%
0.70			Beneficial	76	66%
0.60			Beneficial	73	64%
0.50	.30	Medium	Beneficial	69	62%
0.40			Beneficial	66	60%
0.30			Beneficial	62	57%
0.20	.10	Small	Beneficial	58	55%
0.10			No effect	54	52%
0.00	0		No effect	50	50%
−0.10			No effect	46	48%
−0.20	.10		Detrimental	42	45%
−0.30			Detrimental	38	43%

Adapted from Cohen (1988), Norcross et al. (2017), and Wampold and Imel (2015).

[a] Each effect size can be conceptualized as reflecting a corresponding percentile value; in this case, the percentile standing of the average treated patient after psychotherapy relative to untreated patients.

[b] Each effect size can also be translated into a success rate of treated patients relative to untreated patients; a d of 0.80, for example, would translate into approximately 70% of patients being treated successfully compared to 50% of untreated patients.

ACCOUNTING FOR PSYCHOTHERAPY OUTCOME

What, then, accounts for psychotherapy success (and failure)? This question represents an understandable desire for clarity and guidance, but we raise the question here as a way of putting the research evidence on the psychotherapy relationship into an overall context. Our collective ability to answer in meaningful ways is limited by the huge variation in methodological designs, theoretical orientations, treatment settings, research measures, and patient presentations. Of the dozens of variables that contribute to patient outcome, only a few can be included in any given study. How can we divide the indivisible complexity of psychotherapy outcome?

Nonetheless, psychotherapy research has made tremendous strides in clarifying the question and addressing the uncertainty. Thus, we tentatively offer two models that account for psychotherapy outcome, averaging across thousands of outcome studies and hundreds of meta-analyses and acknowledging that this matter has been vigorously debated for over six decades. We implore readers to consider the following percentages as crude empirical estimates, not as exact numbers.

The first model estimates the percentage of psychotherapy outcome variance as a function of therapeutic factors. The comparative importance of each of these factors is summarized in Figure 1.1. The percentages are based on decades of research but not formally derived from meta-analytic methods. The patient's extratherapeutic change—self-change, spontaneous remission, social support, fortuitous events—accounts for

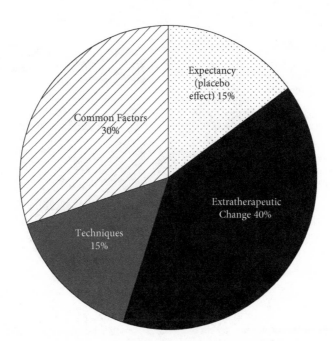

FIGURE 1.1   Percent of improvement in psychotherapy patients as a function of therapeutic factors.

roughly 40% of success. Humans have a tendency to move toward health and to take advantage of opportunities to stabilize themselves.

Common factors, variables found in most therapies regardless of theoretical orientation, probably account for another 30%. The therapy relationship represents the sine qua non of common factors, along with client and therapist factors. Technique factors, explaining approximately 15% of the variance, are those treatment methods fairly specific to prescribed therapy, such as biofeedback, transference interpretations, desensitization, prolonged exposure, or two-chair work. Finally, playing an important role is expectancy, or the placebo effect—the client's knowledge that he or she is being treated and his or her conviction in the treatment rationale and methods. These four broad factors account for the explained outcome variance.

The second model considers all outcome variance in psychotherapy outcome and begins with the unexplained variance, which necessarily decreases the amount of variance attributable to the other factors. As summarized in Figure 1.2, psychotherapy research—and research in any complicated human activity—cannot explain all of the variation in success. To be sure, some of this is attributable to measurement error and fallible methods, but some is also attributable to the complexity of human behavior. Thereafter, we estimate that the patient (including motivation for treatment and severity of disorder) accounts for approximately 30% of the total variance, the therapy relationship for 15%, and the specific treatment method for 10%, and the therapist for 7% (when not confounded with treatment effects). In this model, we assume that

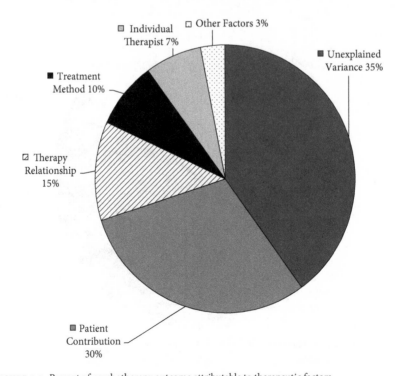

FIGURE 1.2   Percent of psychotherapy outcome attributable to therapeutic factors.

common factors are spread across the therapeutic factors—some pertain to the patient, some to the therapy method, some to the treatment method, and some to the therapist him/herself.

How can psychotherapy outcome be improved? Follow the evidence; follow what contributes to psychotherapy outcome. Begin by leveraging the patient's resources and self-healing capacities; emphasize the therapy relationship and so-called common factors; employ research-supported treatment methods; select interpersonally skilled and clinically motivated practitioners; and match all of them to the patient's characteristics, personality, and world views. This, not simply matching a treatment method to a particular disorder, will maximize success.

The differences between our two models help explain the rampant confusion in the field regarding the relative percentages accounted for by relationships and techniques. The first model presents only the explained variance and separates common factors and specific factors, whereas the second model presents the total variance and assigns common factors to each of the constituent elements. Hence, it is essential to inquire whether the percentages attributable to particular therapeutic factors are based on total or explained variance and how common factors are conceptualized in a particular model.

Despite the differing percentages, the results of both models converge mightily on several take-home points. One: patients contribute the lion's share of psychotherapy success (and failure). Consider the probable outcome of psychotherapy with an adjustment disorder in a healthy person in the action stage versus a chronically mentally ill person presenting in precontemplation/denial. Two: the therapeutic relationship generally accounts for at least as much psychotherapy success as the treatment method. Three: particular treatment methods do matter in some cases, especially more complex or severe cases (Lambert, 2013). Four: adapting or customizing therapy (as illustrated in Volume 2) to the patient enhances the effectiveness of psychotherapy probably by innervating multiple pathways—the patient, the relationship, the method, and expectancy. Five: psychotherapists need to consider multiple factors and their optimal combinations, not only one or two of their favorites.

Consider the results of an unusual meta-analysis of treatments for depression, which illustrate these general patterns. Cuijpers and colleagues (2012) focused on the effects of so-called nondirective supportive therapy (NDST) compared to wait-list control groups, other psychotherapies, and pharmacotherapies. Many psychotherapies have been found effective with depression, but the differences between them are small and unstable. "After more than three decades, most quantitative reviews suggest that the different therapies for depression are equally, or almost equally effective" (p. 281). Cuijpers et al. note that numerous clinical trials have included NDST comparison groups in order to control for common factors that are present across therapies (i.e., the failure to find differences between treatments is because common factors account for improvements, not the specific treatment techniques that are being tested). In these comparisons, NDST contains elements of relationship such as the therapeutic alliance, belief in the treatment, a clear rationale as to why the client has developed the problems, and the like. NDSTs are typically "an unstructured therapy without specific psychological techniques other than those belonging to the basic interpersonal skills of the therapist, such as reflection, empathic listening, encouragement, and helping people to explore and express their experiences and emotions" (p. 281).

The results of 31 psychotherapy trials were examined in the meta-analysis and resulted in an estimate of three elements of change: (1) those due to extratherapeutic factors such as spontaneous remission, client, and community factors (33%); (2) those due to common factors such as therapist, relationship, and expectancy (50%); and (3) those due to specific therapeutic techniques (i.e., the comparison between NDST and other treatments; 17%). The authors suggest caution in relying on these estimates but conclude: "Despite these limitations, this study has made it clear that NDST has considerable effect on mild to moderate depression, that most of the effects of therapy for adult depression is accounted for by non-specific factors, and that the contribution of specific techniques in these patients is limited at best and may in fact be absent for many" (p. 290). Exactly our take-home points.

LIMITATIONS OF THE WORK

A single task force can accomplish only so much work and cover only so much content. As such, we wish to acknowledge publicly several necessary omissions and unfortunate truncations in our work.

The products of the task force probably suffer first from content overlap. We may have cut the "diamond" of the therapy relationship too thin at times, leading to a profusion of highly related and possibly redundant constructs. Goal consensus, for example, correlates highly with collaboration, which is considered in the same chapter, and both of those are frequently considered parts of the therapeutic alliance. Collecting client feedback and repairing alliance ruptures, for another example, may represent different sides of the same therapist behavior, but these too are covered in separate meta-analyses. Thus, to some, the content may appear swollen; to others, the task force may have failed to make necessary distinctions.

Another lacuna in the task force work is that we may have neglected, relatively speaking, the productive contribution of the client to the therapy relationship. Virtually all of the relationship elements in this book represent mutual processes of shared communicative attunement (Orlinsky et al., 2004). They exist in the human connection, in the transactional process, rather than solely as a therapist (or client) variable.

We decided not to commission a separate chapter on the client's contributions; instead, we asked the authors of each chapter to address them. We encouraged authors to attend to the chain of events among the therapist's contributions, the patient processes, and eventual treatment outcomes. This, we hoped, would maintain the focus on what is effective in patient change. (The chapters in Volume 2 examine patient contributions directly in terms of patient characteristics.) Nonetheless, by omitting separate chapters, we may be understandably accused of an omission akin to the error of leaving the relationship out at the expense of method. These volumes may be "therapist-centric" in minimizing the client's relational contribution and self-healing processes.

This limitation proves especially ironic in that the moderator analyses of several meta-analyses indicated the patient's perspective of the relationship proves more impactful to their treatment outcome than the therapist's. The patient's experience of the alliance, cohesion, empathy, and support relate and contribute more to their success than the practitioner's experience. This generally holds, but not invariably, as in emotional expression. There the therapist's observation seems to be more highly associated with better patient success.

Researcher allegiance may have also posed a problem in conducting and interpreting the meta-analyses. Of course, we invited authors with an interest and expertise in a relationship element, but in some cases, the authors might have experienced conflicts of interest due to their emotional, academic, or financial interests. In dozens of implicit ways and explicit decisions, authors may have favored the effectiveness of their scholarly offspring. The use of objective meta-analytic guidelines, peer review, and transparent data reporting may have attenuated any effects of their allegiance, but it remains a strong human propensity in any discipline.

Another prominent limitation across these research reviews is the difficulty of establishing causal connections between the relationship behavior and treatment outcome. The only meta-analyses that contain RCTs capable of demonstrating a causal effect are collecting client feedback and repairing appliance ruptures. (Note that the meta-analyses in Volume 2 were conducted on mostly RCTs and are capable of causal conclusions.) Causal inferences are always difficult to make concerning process variables, such as the therapy relationship. Does the relationship cause improvement or simply reflect it? The interpretation problems of correlational studies (third variables, reverse causation) render such studies less convincing than RCTs where treatments can be controlled. It is methodologically difficult to meet the three conditions needed to make a causal claim: nonspuriousness, covariation between the process variable and the outcome measure, and temporal precedence of the process variable (Feeley et al., 1999). We still need to determine whether and when the therapeutic relationship is a mediator, moderator, or mechanism of change in psychotherapy (Kazdin, 2007).

At the same time as we acknowledge this central limitation, let's remain mindful of several considerations. First, the establishment of temporal ordering is essential for causal inference, but it is not sufficient. In showing that these facets of a therapy relationship precede positive treatment outcome, we can certainly state that the therapy relationship is, at a minimum, an important predictor and antecedent of that outcome. Second, within these reality constraints, dozens of lagged correlational, unconfounded regression, structural equation, and growth curve studies suggest that the therapy relationship probably casually contributes to outcome (e.g., Barber et al., 2000; also see Chapter 2, this volume). For example, using growth-curve analyses and controlling for prior improvement and eight prognostically relevant client characteristics, Klein and colleagues (2003) found that the early alliance significantly predicted later improvement in 367 chronically depressed clients. Although we need to continue to parse out the causal linkages, the therapy relationship has probably been shown to exercise a causal association to outcome. Third, some of the most precious behaviors in life are incapable on ethical grounds of random assignment and experimental manipulation.

Take parental love as an exemplar. Not a single RCT has ever been conducted to conclusively determine the causal benefit of a parents' love on their children's functioning, yet virtually all humans aspire to it and practice it. Nor can we envision an institutional review board (IRB) ever approving a grant proposal to randomize patients in a psychotherapy study to an empathic, collaborative, and supportive therapist versus a nonempathic, cold, authoritarian, disrespectful, and unsupportive therapist. We will say more about casualty in the final chapter in this volume, but for now we warn readers against an either/or conclusion on the ability of the therapy relationship to cause patient improvement.

As with the previous two task forces, the overwhelming majority of research studies analyzed were conducted in Western developed nations and published in English-language journals. The literature searches are definitely improving in accessing studies conducted internationally, but most chapter authors were not able to translate publications in other languages. A prominent and encouraging exception were the authors of the alliance meta-analysis (see Chapter 2), who meta-analyzed studies published in the English, Italian, German, and French languages.

A final interesting drawback to the present work, and psychotherapy research as a whole, is the paucity of attention paid to the disorder-specific and treatment-specific nature of the therapy relationship. It is premature to aggregate the research on how the patient's primary disorder or the type of treatment impacts the therapy relationship, but there are early links. For example, in the treatment of severe anxiety disorders (generalized anxiety disorder and obsessive-compulsive disorder) and substance abuse, the relationship probably has less impact (Flückiger et al., 2013; Graves et al., 2017) than other disorders, such as depression. Specific treatments seem to exhibit a comparable or greater effect size than the therapy relationship in those disorders, but in depression, the relationship appears more powerful. The therapeutic alliance in the National Institute of Mental Health Treatment of Depression Collaborative Research Program, in both psychotherapy and pharmacotherapy, emerged as the leading force in reducing a patients' depression (Krupnick et al., 1996). The therapeutic relationship probably exhibits more impact in some disorders and in some therapies than others (Beckner et al., 2007; Bedics et al., 2015). As with research on specific psychotherapies, it may no longer suffice to ask "Does the relationship work?" but "How does the relationship work for this disorder and this treatment method?"

FREQUENTLY ASKED QUESTIONS

The Third Interdivisional APA Task Force on Evidence-Based Relationships and Responsiveness has generated considerable enthusiasm in the professional community, but it has also provoked misunderstandings and reservations. Here we address frequently asked questions (FAQs) about the task force's goals and results.

• *Are you saying that treatment methods are immaterial to psychotherapy outcome?*

Absolutely not. The research evidence shows that both the therapy relationship and the treatment method make consistent contributions to treatment outcome. It remains a matter of judgment and methodology on how much each contributes, but there is virtual unanimity that both the relationship and the method (insofar as we can separate them) "work." Looking at either treatment interventions or therapy relationships alone is incomplete. We encourage practitioners and researchers to look at multiple determinants of outcome, particularly client contributions.

♦ *But are you not exaggerating the effects of relationship factors and/or minimizing the effects of treatments to set up the importance of your work?*

We think not and hope not. With the guidance of the steering committee members and external consultants, we have tried to avoid dichotomies and polarizations. Focusing on one area—the psychotherapy relationship—in this volume may unfortunately convey the impression that it is the only area of importance. This is certainly not our intention. Relationship factors are important, and we need to review the scientific literature and provide clinical recommendations based upon that literature and especially for impacting training of graduate students. This can be done without trivializing or degrading the effects of specific treatments.

♦ *Isn't your task force just warmed over Carl Rogers?*

No. While Rogers's (1957) facilitative conditions are represented in this book, they comprise only about 17% of the research (3 of 18 meta-analyses) critically reviewed. More fundamentally, we have moved beyond a limited and invariant set of necessary relationship conditions. Monolithic theories of change and one-size-fits-all therapy relationships are out; tailoring the therapy to the unique patient is in.

♦ *The alliance is consistently associated with patient success, but the correlation or effect size is not that large. So it does not seem that the therapy relationship is that powerful after all, right?*

Wrong. Conflating only the therapeutic alliance with the totality of the therapeutic relationship is a pervasive mistake, especially among our cognitive-behavioral colleagues. Look at the book's contents and the 18 meta-analyses; the therapy relationship encompasses considerably more than the alliance alone. In fact, the alliance's correlation coefficient or effect size is not even the largest in this book (see the final chapter for a comparative analysis). Think of the entire relationship, friend, not only the important alliance.

♦ *We are impressed, reading through these chapters how much we now know about what constitutes a good therapeutic relationship but how little we know about training students to create that relationship. What gives?*

What gives, we suspect, is that training invariably lags behind cutting-edge research and practice. Studies must be conducted, published, and aggregated to create a strong evidence base, and only then does it filter down to widespread training. Researchers are enamored with, perhaps even addicted to discovery, but not so much with the implementation of and training of their discoveries (Norcross et al., 2017).

What also probably gives is that experiential training in relationship/helping skills is notoriously more difficult than transmitting academic knowledge in the classroom (Hill, 2014). That's been a recurrent concern and obstacle since Carl Rogers and associates began training their students in person-centered facilitative conditions in the 1960s.

On a positive note, all contributors to this volume addressed training practices for their respective relationship elements and efforts are underway to build training resources based on these meta-analytic results. APA Division of Psychotherapy/Society for the Advancement of Psychotherapy has launched an initiative, Teaching and Learning Evidence-Based Relationships: Interviews with the Experts, in collaboration with the task force. The initiative is directed by Drs. Rayna Markin and Michael Constantino; the videotaped interviews can be found at the division's website (http://www.societyforpsychotherapy.org/teaching-learning-evidence-based-relationships). In the next edition of the book, we will request that contributors describe even more what can be done to develop and train students in these relationship skills.

♦ *An interpersonal view of psychotherapy seems at odds with what managed care and administrators ask of me in my practice. How do you reconcile these?*

We do not reconcile these views, but we hope to influence managed care and behavioral health administrators with the compelling meta-analytic findings in these two volumes.

It is true that a dominant image of modern psychotherapy, among reimbursers and policymakers, is as a mental health treatment. This "treatment" or "medical" model inclines people to define process in terms of method, therapists as providers applying techniques, treatment in terms of number of contact hours, patients as embodiments of mental disorders, and outcome solely as symptom reduction (Orlinsky, 1989).

It is also true that members of the steering committee believe this model to be restricted and inaccurate. The psychotherapy enterprise is far more complex and interactive than the linear "Treatment operates on patients to produce effects." We would prefer a broader, integrative view that aligns with the tripartite EBP model that privileges best available research, clinician expertise, and patient characteristics, cultures, and values. That model incorporates the relational and educational features of psychotherapy, one that recognizes both the interpersonal and instrumental components of psychotherapy, one that appreciates the bidirectional process of therapy, and one in which the therapist and patient co-create an optimal process and outcome (Lambert, 2010).

♦ *Won't these results contribute further to deprofessionalizing psychotherapy? Aren't you unwittingly supporting efforts to have any warm, empathic person perform psychotherapy?*

Perhaps some will misuse our conclusions in this way, but that is neither our intent nor commensurate with our meta-analyses. It trivializes psychotherapy to characterize it as simply "a good relationship with a caring person" or "the purchase of friendship." The research shows an effective psychotherapist is one who employs specific methods, who offers strong relationships, and who customizes both treatment methods and relationship stances to the individual person and condition. That often requires considerable training and experience; the antithesis of "anyone can do psychotherapy."

♦ *Are the task force's conclusions and recommendations intended as practice standards?*

No. These are research-based conclusions that can lead, inform, and guide practitioners toward evidence-based therapy relationships (and, in Volume 2, to responsiveness or treatment adaptations). They are not legal, ethical, or professional mandates.

♦ *Well, don't these represent the official positions of APA Division 29 (Psychotherapy), Division 17 (Counseling Psychology), or the APA?*

No. No. No.

♦ *So, are you saying that the therapy relationship (in addition to the treatment method) is crucial to outcome, that it can be improved by certain therapist contributions, and that it can be effectively tailored to the individual patient?*

Precisely. And this two-volume book shows specifically how to do so on the basis of the research evidence.

CONCLUDING REFLECTIONS

The future of psychotherapy portends the integration of science and service, of the instrumental and the interpersonal, and of the technical and the relational in the tradition of EBP (Norcross et al., 2011). *Evidence-based therapy relationships* align with this future and embody a crucial part of evidence-based practice, when properly conceptualized. We can imagine few practices in all of psychotherapy that can confidently boast that they integrate as well "the best available research with clinical expertise in the context of patient characteristics, culture, and preferences" (APA, 2006) as the relational behaviors and treatment adaptations presented in these two volumes. We are reminded daily that research can guide how to create, cultivate, and customize that powerful human relationship.

Finally, we fervently hope these volumes will indirectly serve another master: to heal the damage incurred by the culture wars in psychotherapy. If our task force is even a little bit successful, then the pervasive gap between the research and practice communities, the treatment method and the therapy relationship contingents, will be narrowed and the insidious dichotomies obliterated. Phrased more positively, psychotherapists from all camps and communities will increasingly collaborate, and our patients will benefit from the most efficacious treatments *and* relationships available.

REFERENCES

American Psychological Association Task Force on Evidence-Based Practice. (2006). Evidence-based practice in psychology. *American Psychologist, 61,* 271–285.

Baldwin, S. A., & Imel, Z. E. (2013). Therapist effects: Findings and methods. In M. J. Lambert (Ed.), *Bergin and Garfield's handbook of psychotherapy and behavior change* (6th ed). New York, NY: Wiley.

Barber, J. P., Connolly, M. B., Crits-Christoph, P., Gladis, L., & Siqueland, L. (2000). Alliance predicts patients' outcome beyond in-treatment change in symptoms. *Journal of Consulting and Clinical Psychology, 68,* 1027–1032.

Barber, J. P., Gallop, R., Crits-Christoph, P., Frank, A., Thase, M. E., Weiss, R. D., & Connolly, M. B. (2006). The role of therapist adherence, therapist competence, and alliance in predicting outcome of individual drug counseling: Results from the National Institute Drug Abuse Collaborative Cocaine Treatment Study. *Psychotherapy Research, 16,* 229–240.

Barkham, M., Lutz, W., Lambert, M. J., & Saxton, D. (2017). Therapist effects, effective therapists, and the law of variability. In L. Castonquay & C. Hill (Eds.), *How and why are some therapists better than others? Understanding therapist effects* (pp. 13–36). Washington, DC: American Psychological Association.

Barlow, D. H. (2000). Evidence-based practice: A world view. *Clinical Psychology: Science and Practice, 7,* 241–242.

Beckner, V., Vella, I., Howard, K. I., & Mohr, D. C. (2007). Alliance in two telephone-administered treatments; Relationship with depression and health outcomes. *Journal of Consulting & Clinical Psychology, 75,* 508–512.

Bedics, J. D., Atkins, D. C., Harned, M. S., & Linehan, M. M. (2015). The therapeutic alliance as a predictor of outcome in dialectical behavior therapy versus nonbehavioral psychotherapy by experts for borderline personality disorder. *Psychotherapy, 52,* 67–77. https://www.doi.org/10.1037/a0038457

Bergin, A. E. (1997). Neglect of the therapist and the human dimensions of change: A commentary. *Clinical Psychology: Science and Practice, 4,* 83–89.

Bergin, A. E., & Lambert, M. J. (1978). The evaluation of outcomes in psychotherapy. In S. L. Garfield & A. E. Bergin (Eds.), *Handbook of psychotherapy and behavior change* (pp. 139–189). New York, NY: Wiley.

Bohart, A. C., & Tallman, K. (1999). *How clients make therapy work: The process of active self-healing.* Washington, DC: American Psychological Association.

Bohart, A. C., & Wade, A. G. (2013). The client in psychotherapy. In M. J. Lambert (Ed.), *Bergin & Garfield's handbook of psychotherapy & behavior change* (6th ed., pp. 219–257). New York, NY: Wiley.

Castonguay, L., & Hill, C. E. (Eds). (2017). *How and why are some therapists better than others? Understanding therapist effects.* Washington, DC: American Psychological Association.

Cohen, J. (1988). *Statistical power analysis for the behavioral sciences* (2nd ed.). Hillsdale, NJ: Erlbaum.

Crits-Christoph, P., Baranackie, K., Kurcias, J. S., Beck, A. T., Carroll, K., Perry, K., ... Zitrin, C. (1991). Meta-analysis of therapist effects in psychotherapy outcome studies. *Psychotherapy Research, 1,* 281–291.

Cuijpers, P., Driessen, E., Hollon, S. D., van Oppen, P., Barth, J., & Andersson, G. (2012). The efficacy of non-directive supportive therapy for adult depression: A meta-analysis. *Clinical Psychology Review, 32,* 280–291.

Department of Health. (2001). *Treatment choice in psychological therapies and counseling.* London, England: Department of Health Publications.

Feeley, M., DeRubeis, R. J., & Gelfand, L. A. (1999). The temporal relation of adherence and alliance to symptom change in cognitive therapy for depression. *Journal of Consulting and Clinical Psychology, 67,* 578–582. https://www.doi.org/10.1037/0022–006X.67.4.578

Flückiger, C., Del Re, A. C., Horvath, A. O., Symonds, D., Ackert, M., & Wampold, B. E. (2013). Substance use disorders and racial/ethnic minorities matter: A meta-analytic examination of the relation between alliance and outcome. *Journal of Counseling Psychology, 60,* 610–616. https://www.doi.org/10.1037/a0033161

Gelso, C. J. (Ed.). (2005). The interplay of techniques and the therapeutic relationship in psychotherapy [Special issue]. *Psychotherapy, 42*(4).

Gelso, C. J., & Carter, J. A. (1985). The relationship in counseling and psychotherapy: Components, consequences, and theoretical antecedents. *Counseling Psychologist, 13,* 155–243. https://www.doi.org/10.1177/0011000085132001

Gelso, C. J., & Carter, J. A. (1994). Components of the psychotherapy relationship: Their interaction and unfolding during treatment. *Journal of Counseling Psychology, 41,* 296–306. https://www.doi.org/10.1037/0022–0167.41.3.296

Gelso, C. J., & Hayes, J. A. (1998). *The psychotherapy research: Theory, research, and practice.* New York, NY: Wiley.

Graves, T. A., Tabri, N., Thompson-Brenner, H., Franko, D. L., Eddy, K. T., Bourion-Bedes, S., & Thomas, J. J. (2017). A meta-analysis of the relation between therapeutic alliance and treatment outcome in eating disorders. *International Journal of Eating Disorders, 50,* 323–340. https://www.doi.org/1002/eat.22672

Henry, W. P. (1998). Science, politics, and the politics of science: The use and misuse of empirically validated treatment research. *Psychotherapy Research, 8,* 126–140. https://www.doi.org/10.1093/ptr/8.2.126

Hill, C. E. (2014). *Helping skills* (4th ed.). Washington, DC: American Psychological Association.

Hubble, M. A., Wampold, B. E., Duncan, B. L., & Miller, S. D. (Eds.). (2011). *The heart and soul of change* (2nd ed.). Washington, DC: American Psychological Association.

Huppert, J. D., Bufka, L. F., Barlow, D. H., Shear, M. K., & Woods, S. W. (2001). Therapists, therapist variables, and cognitive-behavior therapy outcome in a multi-center trial of panic disorder. *Journal of Consulting & Clinical Psychology, 69,* 747–755.

Imel, Z., Sheng, E., Baldwin, S. A., & Adkins, D. C. (2015). Removing very low performing therapists: A simulation of performance-based retention in psychotherapy. *Psychotherapy, 52,* 329–336.

Johns, R. G., Barkham, M., Kellet, S., & Saxon, D. (2019). A systematic review of therapist effects: A critical narrative update and refinement to Baldwin and Imel's (2013) review. *Clinical Psychology Review*.

Kazdin, A. E. (2007). Mediators and mechanism of change in psychotherapy research. *Annual Review of Clinical Psychology*, *3*, 1–27.

King, R. J., Orr, J. A., Poulsen, B., Giacomantonio, S. G., & Haden, C. (2017). Understanding the therapist contribution to psychotherapy outcome: A meta-analytic approach. *Administration Policy In Mental Health*, *44*, 664–680. https://www.doi.org/10.1007/s10488-016-0783-9

Klein, D. N., Schwartz, J. E., Santiago, N. J., Vivian, D., Vocisano, C., Castonguay, L G., . . . Keller, M. B. (2003). Therapeutic alliance in depression treatment: Controlling for prior change and patient characteristics. *Journal of Consulting & Clinical Psychology*, *71*, 997–1006.

Krupnick, J. L., Sotsky, S. M., Simmens, S., Moyer, J., Elkin, I., Watkins, J., & Pilkonis, P. A. (1996). The role of the therapeutic alliance in psychotherapy and pharmacotherapy. *Journal of Consulting and Clinical Psychology*, *64*, 532–539. https://www.doi.org/10.1037/0022-006X.64.3.532

Lambert, M. J. (2010). *Prevention of treatment failure: The use of measuring, monitoring, & feedback in clinical practice.* Washington, DC: American Psychological Association.

Lambert, M. J. (2011). Psychotherapy research and its achievements. In J. C. Norcross, G. R. VandenBos, & D. K. Freedheim (Eds.), *History of psychotherapy* (2nd ed). Washington, DC: American Psychological Association.

Lambert, M. J. (2013). The efficacy and effectiveness of psychotherapy. In M. J. Lambert (Ed.), *Bergin & Garfield's handbook of psychotherapy and behavior change* (6th ed., pp. 169–218). New York, NY: Wiley.

Luborsky, L., Diguer, L., Seligman, D. A., Rosenthal, R., Krause, E. D., Johnson, S., . . . Schweitzer, E. (1999). The researcher's own therapy allegiances: A "wild card" in comparisons of treatment efficacy. *Clinical Psychology: Science and Practice*, *6*, 95–106. https://www.doi.org/10.1093/clipsy/6.1.95

Messer, S. B. (2001). Empirically supported treatments: What's a nonbehaviorist to do? In B. D. Slife, R. N. Williams, & S. H. Barlow (Eds.), *Critical issues in psychotherapy.* Thousand Oaks, CA: SAGE.

Nathan, P. E., & Gorman, J. M. (Eds.). (2015). *A guide to treatments that work* (4th ed.). New York, NY: Oxford University Press.

Norcross, J. C. (Ed.). (2002). *Psychotherapy relationships that work: Therapist contributions and responsiveness to patient needs.* New York, NY: Oxford University Press.

Norcross, J. C. (2010). The therapeutic relationship. In B. L. Duncan, S. D. Miller, B. E. Wampold, & M. A. Hubble (Eds.), *Heart & soul of change in psychotherapy* (2nd ed.). Washington, DC: American Psychological Association.

Norcross, J. C. (Ed.). (2011). *Psychotherapy relationships that work* (2nd ed.). New York, NY: Oxford University Press.

Norcross, J. C., Freedheim, D. K., & VandenBos, G. R. (2011). Into the future: Retrospect and prospect in psychotherapy. In J. C. Norcross, G. R. Vanderbos, & D. K. Freedheim (Eds.), *History of psychotherapy* (2nd ed.). Washington, DC: American Psychological Association.

Norcross, J. C., Hogan, T. P., Koocher, G. P., & Maggio, L. A. (2017). *Clinician's guide to evidence-based practices: Behavioral health and addictions* (2nd ed.). New York, NY: Oxford University Press.

Orlinsky, D. E. (1989). Researchers' images of psychotherapy: Their origins and influence on research. *Clinical Psychology Review, 9,* 413–441.

Orlinsky, D. E., et al. (2004). Process to outcome in psychotherapy. In A. E. Bergin & S. L. Garfield (Eds.), *Handbook of psychotherapy and behavior change* (4th ed.). New York, NY: Wiley.

Orlinsky, D., & Howard, K. E. (1977). The therapist's experience of psychotherapy. In A. S. Gurman & A. M. Razin (Eds.), *Effective psychotherapy: A handbook of research.* New York, NY: Pergamon.

Project MATCH Research Group. (1998). Therapist effects in three treatments for alcohol problems. *Psychotherapy Research, 8,* 455–474. https://www.doi.org/10.1093/ptr/8.4.455

Rogers, C. R. (1957). The necessary and sufficient conditions of therapeutic personality change. *Journal of Consulting Psychology, 21,* 95–103.

Safran, J. D., & Muran, J. C. (2000). *Negotiating the therapeutic alliance.* New York, NU: Guilford.

Smith, M. I., Glass, G. W. V., & Miller, T. L. (1980). *The benefits of psychotherapy.* Baltimore, MD: Johns Hopkins University Press.

Tasca, G. A., Sylvestre, J., Balfour, L., Chyurlia, L., Evans, J., Fortin-Langelier, B., . . . Wilson, B. (2015). What clinicians want: Findings from a psychotherapy practice research network survey. *Psychotherapy, 52,* 1–11.

Wampold, B. E., Baldwin, S. A., Holtforth, M. G., & Imel, Z. (2017). What characterizes effective therapists? In L. Castonquay & C. Hill (Eds.), *How and why are some therapists better than others? Understanding therapist effects* (pp. 37–53). Washington, DC: American Psychological Association.

Wampold, B. E., & Brown, G. S. (2005). Estimating variability in outcomes attributable to therapists: A naturalistic study of outcomes in managed care. *Journal of Consulting and Clinical Psychology, 73,* 914–923.

Wampold, B. E., & Imel, Z. (2015). *The great psychotherapy debate* (2nd ed.). Mahwah, NJ: Erlbaum.

2

ALLIANCE IN ADULT PSYCHOTHERAPY

Christoph Flückiger, A. C. Del Re, Bruce E. Wampold,
and Adam O. Horvath

Authors' Notes. We thank Dianne Symonds for her contribution to the previous meta-analysis (Horvath et al., 2011). We furthermore thank Greta Probst, Laurina Stählin, Rebecca Schlegel, and Chantal Gerl from the University of Zürich for their contributions to this meta-analysis supported by the grant PP00P1_1163702 of the Swiss Science National Foundation. For the present chapter, we used last authorship position for the most senior researcher.

Since our previous review of this literature in 2011, the alliance has continued to be a major focus of the psychotherapy research community. The key words *alliance, helping alliance, working alliance*, and *therapeutic alliance* in PsycINFO resulted in over 2,000 hits in 2000 and generated an additional 5,000 hits in 2010. Our comparable search in early 2017 yielded over 5,000 further items, indicating a several-fold growth in the literature since 2000.

The prominence of the alliance for practitioners and researchers is, in part, based on its important historical roots as well as recent methodological and conceptual innovations. The emphasis on clinical trials in previous decades has failed to clearly elucidate what makes psychotherapy work (e.g., Deacon, 2013; Kazdin, 2009) and has not identified specific treatments that prove more effective than others (Wampold & Imel, 2015). The alliance continues to be one of the most important, if not the most important, factor in psychotherapy success. The impact of the therapist–patient relationship finds broad resonance across psychotherapy orientations.

The continued growth of the alliance literature is probably attributable to the dual facts that (a) research consistently finds a moderate but robust relation between the alliance and outcome across a broad array of treatments (Horvath & Bedi, 2002; Horvath et al., 2011; Horvath & Symonds, 1991; Martin et al., 2000) and (b) the alliance can be assessed in a practical and direct manner. Items such as "I believe my therapist is genuinely concerned for my welfare," "We agree on what is important for me to work on," and "My therapist and I respect each other" can be utilized in many clinical contexts.

In this chapter, we begin with an overview of the origins and definitions of the alliance, its measures, and clinical examples. We provide a meta-analysis of the alliance–outcome literature (1978–2017). The results confirm the robustness of the positive relation between the alliance between therapist and client and psychotherapy outcomes across assessor perspectives, alliance measures, treatment approaches, and countries. We conclude with evidence for causality, limitations of the research, patient contributions, diversity considerations, training implications, and then therapeutic practices.

DEFINITIONS

The term *alliance* (sometimes preceded by *therapeutic, working,* or *helping*) refers to the collaborative aspects of the therapist–client relationship. However, there are non-trivial differences among authors in the precise meaning of the term. As with many other psychological constructs, such as *intelligence,* alliance concepts cover qualities of a broad psychological phenomenon that includes many perspectives and facets. As highlighted in the prior versions of the present chapter (Horvath et al., 2011), one way to grasp the complexity of this concept is by briefly reviewing its history.

Historical Background

The alliance focuses on fundamental considerations of the therapist–client relationship from an interactive perspective: How are decisions about treatment methods made? Who decides therapy goals? What is the quality of the human relationship between therapist and the client?

The concept of the alliance (though not the term itself) originated with Freud (1913). His premise was that all relationships were transference based (Freud, 1912/1958). Early in his writings he struggled with the question of what keeps the analysand in treatment in the face of the unconscious fear and rejection of exploring repressed material. His first formulation suggested that he thought that there was an "analyst" within the client supporting the healing journey (Freud, 1912/1956). Later he speculated about the reality-based collaboration between therapist and client, a conjoint effort to conquer the client's pain. He referred to this process as the unobjectionable or positive transference (Freud, 1927).

Both the importance of the client's attachment to the therapist and his or her ambiguity about this attachment (viz., reality based and conscious versus transferential and unconscious) has echoed throughout the evolution of the alliance. For example, Freud (1925) wrote, "Even the most brilliant results were liable to be suddenly wiped away if my personal relation with the patient was disturbed. . . . The personal emotional relation between doctor and client was after all stronger than the whole cathartic process" (p. 35).

The term *ego alliance* was coined by Sterba (1934), who conceptualized it as part of the client's ego-observing process that alternated with the experiencing (transferential) process. Zetzel (1956) used the term *therapeutic alliance* to refer to the client's ability to use the healthy part of her or his ego to link up or join with the analyst to accomplish the therapeutic tasks. Greenson (1965, 1967) made a distinction between the *working alliance* (i.e., the client's ability to align with the tasks of analysis) and the *therapeutic alliance* (i.e., the capacity of therapist and client to form a personal bond with the therapist; Horvath & Luborsky, 1993).

During the 1970s, efforts were made to detach the alliance from its psychodynamic roots and language to encompass the relational component of all types of helping endeavors. Luborsky (1976) proposed an extension of Zetzel's conceptualization when he suggested that the alliance between therapist and client developed in two phases. The first phase, "Type I alliance," involved the client's belief in the therapist as a potent source of help provided through a warm, supporting, and caring relationship. This level of alliance results in a secure holding relationship within which the work of the therapy can begin. The second phase, "Type II alliance," involved the client's investment and faith in the therapeutic process itself, a commitment to some of the concepts undergirding the therapy (e.g., nature of the problem, value of the exploratory process), as well as a willing investment of herself or himself to share ownership for the therapy process. Although Luborsky's (1976) conceptualization about the therapy process were grounded in psychodynamic theory, his description of the alliance as a therapeutic process was easily applicable to all forms of treatments.

Bordin (1975, 1976, 1989, 1994) proposed a pantheoretical version of the alliance that he called the *working alliance*. His concept of the alliance was based on Greenson's (1965) ideas as a starting point but departed from the psychodynamic premises. Furthermore, the idea of a pan-theoretical model was impacted by Rosenzweig's (1936) identification of common factors across particular orientations. For Bordin, the core of the alliance was a collaborative stance in therapy built on three components: agreement on the therapeutic goals, consensus on the tasks that make up therapy, and a bond between the client and the therapist. He predicted that different therapies would place different demands on the relationship; thus, the "profile" of the ideal working alliance would differ across orientations (e.g., Strunk et al., 2010; Ulvenes et al., 2012; Zickgraf et al., 2016).

A significant consequence of the way the alliance was "reinvented" was that from the beginning the two major voices (Luborsky and Bordin) did not address the boundaries of the alliance and its relations to other parts of the therapeutic relationship. This theoretical ambiguity created a void, which was filled by a number of alliance assessments that were developed more or less in parallel between 1978 and 1986 to empirically explore the role and function of the alliance (Horvath, 2018; Horvath & Luborsky, 1993).

Perhaps the most distinguishing feature of the modern pantheoretical reconceptualization of the alliance is its emphasis on collaboration and consensus (Hatcher & Barends, 2006). In contrast to previous formulations that primarily emphasized the therapist's contributions to the relationship, the therapists' interpersonal effectiveness, or the unconscious distortions of the therapist and client, this new pantheoretical alliance emphasized the active collaboration between the participants. Thus, it highlighted the collaborative parts of therapists as well as clients.

Starting in psychotherapy, the term *alliance* has become increasingly popular in a variety of helping professions, including nursing, social work, medicine (Horvath et al., 2014), and health media (Bickmore et al., 2005). The alliance's emphasis on collaboration is in fortuitous synchrony with the emergent emphasis on the value of collaboration within health services (e.g., Bickmore et al., 2005; Kashe et al., 2017) and medical treatments (e.g., Elwyn, Frosch, Thomson, Joseph-William, Lloyd, et al., 2012).

Recent Alliance Definitions

An increasing number of empirical investigations highlight different aspects of the alliance. In common, however, they assume that the alliance is positively associated with outcome, which is the major focus of the present meta-analytic synthesis.

Psychometric Focus

Some research on the alliance asserts that the alliance is composed of independent elements (facets or components) and attempts to determine to what extent one component may be prioritized in comparison to the other components (e.g., Falkenström et al., 2015; Webb et al., 2011). Other research highlights the alliance as a synergistic assembly of components where the whole is more than the sum of its parts (e.g., goal agreement, task consensus, and bond together produce the therapeutic benefit; e.g., Horvath & Greenberg, 1989).

Longitudinal Unfolding

In contrast to distinct alliance components, some researchers have investigated the alliance as a generalized factor across sessions (e.g., Crits-Christoph, Gibbons et al., 2011; Flückiger et al., 2019). Meanwhile, others have investigated its over-time changes on a session by session basis (e.g., Falkenström et al., 2013; Rubel, Rosenbaum, & Lutz, 2017; Zilcha-Mano et al., 2016).

Participant Perspective

The alliance exists in a transaction (at least a dyadic construct), so different participants understandably experience it differently. The collaborative quality of the alliance highlights all therapy participants, including not only the client and therapist but also partners, group members, and observers. That typically results in simultaneous, interdependent evaluations of the alliance from several participants over time, each representing a particular (e.g., Atzil-Slonim et al., 2015; Kivlighan et al., 2016).

Nested Data Structures

The alliance assessments often are based on multiple nested levels; that is, sessions are frequently nested within patients, patients are nested within therapists, and therapists are nested within clinics. By estimating the proportion of the variance at each level (e.g., Baldwin, Wampold, & Imel, 2007; Dinger et al., 2007) and examining which level contributes most to the overall variability (by not only clients and therapists but also clinics; e.g., Crits-Christoph, Hamilton, et al., 2011), the alliance–outcome association can be unpacked to better understand how it works to increase the benefits of treatment.

For the purposes of this chapter, then, we included all alliance measures so named by the investigator that were used to report an alliance–outcome relation in adult individual psychotherapy. There was no particular definitional restriction to a certain understanding or tradition of the alliance.

MEASURES

What we refer to as the alliance in this meta-analysis is an aggregate based on more than 30 alliance measures, each providing a distinctive operational definition of the concept. The differences among these measures pertain to how the alliance is defined, the source of the data (patient report, therapist report, observer), as well as the time span over which the alliance is sampled.

Consistent with the previous meta-analyses, four measures—California Psychotherapy Alliance Scale (CALPAS; Marmar et al., 1986), Helping Alliance Questionnaire (HAQ; Alexander & Luborsky, 1986), Vanderbilt Psychotherapy Process Scale (VPPS; Suh et al., 1986), and the Working Alliance Inventory (WAI; Horvath & Greenberg, 1989)—accounted for approximately two thirds of the data. In the current search, 73 (69%) of the 105 articles used an inventory that was based on WAI items. Over time, there is a pronounced tendency to use shorter versions of the measures. Each of these four core instruments has been in use for over 30 years and have demonstrated acceptable levels of internal consistency, in the range of .81 to .87 (Cronbach's alpha). Rated (observer) measures tend to report similar inter-rater reliability coefficients.

The shared variance, even among these well-established measures, has been shown to be less than 50% (Horvath, 2009). An investigation of the shared factor structure of the WAI, CALPAS, and HAQ found that "confident collaborative relationship" was the central common theme among them (Hatcher et al., 1996). Items such "My therapist and I respect each other" (WAI patient), "I feel I am working together with the therapist in a joint effort" (HAQ-II patient), "Did you feel that you were working together with your therapist, that the two of you were joined in a struggle to overcome your problems?" (CALPAS patient), and "How productive was this hour?" (VPPS patient) illustrate the shared understanding of the global, heuristic quality of collaboration across measures.

Nonetheless, adding to the diversity of measures is the fact that over time the four questionnaire traditions have evolved. A number of different forms (e.g., short versions, observer versions, translations) of the core measures now thrive. For example, the original HAQ has undergone a major revision (HAQ II; Luborsky et al., 1996) and the two versions of the instrument have in common less than 30% of content; consequently, we coded HAQ and HAQ II as separate measures in our meta-analysis.

In addition, some of alliance research relied on measures related to but not specifically designed to measure the alliance (e.g., Barrett-Lennard, 1978), while in other instances alliance items were combined with other process instruments (e.g., Flückiger et al., 2011; Mander et al., 2013). In some studies, a person might report on a number of different process concepts; for instance, the therapist evaluates empathy and alliance within one scale. The point is that each of the previously mentioned procedures introduces additional variability to the alliance measurement.

The nature of the alliance itself is likely to change over the course of treatment (Tschacher et al., 1998). Therefore, the meaning of a single item across psychotherapy for each person might differ (Beltz et al., 2016). For example, the item "I feel that my therapist appreciates me" may have a qualitatively different meaning at the beginning of a treatment than at a later session when the therapist and client address highly emotional topics. Even though the diversity of the alliance measures likely contributes to the variability of the alliance–outcome relation, it also demonstrates the broadly accepted relevance of diverse ways to assess the collaborative qualities of the dyadic relationship of therapist and client.

CLINICAL EXAMPLES

The alliance represents an emergent quality of mutual collaboration and partnership between therapist and client. As such, it is not the outcome of a particular intervention; its development can take different forms and may be achieved almost instantly or nurtured over a longer period of time (Bordin, 1994) within a responsive, collaborative relationship (Stiles, 2009).

The following dialogue illustrates a realistic conversation about negotiating the clients' collaborative engagement in goal agreement and task consensus, as well as trustful confidentiality at the check-in phase at session three. The client (C) and therapist (T) are discussing a thought diary:

c: I think you are the expert, and therefore I trust you that you can show me the best way to get over my indecisiveness.

т: I really appreciate your openness and trust. At the same time, I believe we need a common understanding about your situation and how we should proceed in your therapy.

c: Well, aren't you going to tell me what I should do?

т: Because [during the last session] we scheduled to take a more precise look at your behaviors and thoughts based on your diary?

c: Well, documentation of situations and thoughts. . . . And all that, sorry to say it, damned silly stuff. [Laugh]

т: Were your thoughts and emotions silly or the structured diary itself?

c: Well, . . . look, I mean a little bit both. . . . You are the therapist and I keep fucking up. So I guess I better start with the documentation. . . . I wish there was a pill or electric shock therapy to . . . it would be easier.

T: I understand that taking a pill or shock might make things easier. At the same time, I am not sure if taking a pill would be a good reason to not take a precise look at your recent situation . . . which basically can be exhausting.

C: I see. Therapy is hard work hard, and, of course, this is not always lot of fun.

T: Well, I understand this "damned silly stuff" is hard work . . . but at the same time, there is also straight-laced humor here . . . right now.

C: Mhmmm . . . It's crazy you know, before I got married I was a pretty wild dog . . . long hair, motorcycles, pretty crazy. Lot of fun!

T: Something like a wild dog that is not fully welcome anymore?

C: Well, I got, let's say "domesticated." . . . You know, married, good job, slick house, kids. . . . Maybe I lost the good parts of my wild side.

T: . . . And the wild side might have something interesting to say . . .

C: I might be a little afraid of my old wild dog. . . . But [with different voice], Doc, basically, my old man was trash, my whole family is trash!

T: You fear that your trashy parts are too negative to let them give a voice?

C: Well, I really fear taking an honest look at this "wild dog" during therapy. At the same time . . . of course . . . I somewhat fear the consequences.

T: I am optimistic that opening the box does not mean destroying all the good things. But, of course, it seems to be important that both of us are careful and honest to bring all the potential consequences to the table.

T: [Pause 10 sec] So, actually, as potential consequence . . . is your wife reading your diaries right now?

C: Well, I thought it would be good to discuss it with her . . . but, I am not sure, if I really should.

T: Ok, I see. Maybe there are different steps here?

In this excerpt, the therapist starts to go forward with his treatment plan, but when he becomes aware of the client's ambivalence, he demonstrates his commitment to explore collaboratively alternatives without losing the therapeutic focus. Clients frequently have a mixture of hopes and worries about therapy. The therapist's challenge in building the alliance is to recognize, legitimize, and work through these conflicts and engage the client in a joint exploration of obstacles.

Some clients, especially in the beginning of treatment, may be somewhat hostile, rejecting, or fearful of treatment or the therapist. The therapist's ability to respond with acceptance and an openness to discuss these challenges is important in establishing the alliance. The following excerpt provides a brief example of such a process at the end of session five (Horvath et al., 2011):

C: [The topic discussed last week] . . . was interesting. . . . But sometimes I can't remember what I talked about from one week to the next.

T: . . . We talked about how difficult it is to imagine how things would be different if . . .

C: [overlap] I sometimes wonder . . . what do therapists do after the session? I mean, . . . do you walk around the block to forget all this craziness? Do you go home and dream about it?

T: Hmm, I . . .

C: [overlap] I mean, it is not like having a discussion with a friend; though goodness knows, I sometimes forget about those too. I think to myself, does he [T] need to hear all of this? How often do I tell you that stuff? I read that Freud sometimes napped behind the couch. . . . Not, mind you, that I think you are falling asleep during our session! But sometimes you look tired. [Laughs] Oh, never mind; this was a useful session. [Looks at the clock] Are we done? [Stands up]

T: So, are you wondering, "What is it in it for him [T]"?

C: I knew you'd say that!

T: Well . . . the therapy relationship is different than other relationships. It is a strange thing to pour one's heart out to someone and then wonder: Did it mean anything to him? What am I to him?

C: Yeah, I guess . . . that's therapy, for you! [stand up again as to go]

T: Not sure if you want to talk about this or go. . . . We still have 10 minutes until the end of our session.

C: Well it is late . . .

T: Interesting that this came up today. And . . . then it's kind of left hanging between us.

C: You mean hit and run? When I don't get something that I want I don't wait for an answer?

T: There was something you wanted . . . from me . . . ?

C: Doesn't take a rocket scientist to figure out. . . . When you were asking "Does it [therapy] work for you" [reference to last week's discussion]," I thought here it comes . . .

T: You mean that I'll quit on you?

C: I know you would not do that. I know you wouldn't. But, I mean, we are talking about this all this time, and I think . . . I talk about it to others too [relates an incident of talking about his marriage to a colleague]. Now I know she [the colleague] feels sorry for me, but of course this doesn't help either. But that's different. Kind of . . . it's not sympathy I need, but sometimes [voice goes shallow, eyes moist]

T: You want from me . . . how I feel personally about . . .

C: [Change of expression; sarcastic] Good fucking time to bring it up!

T: Does this; like this . . . remind . . .

C: You mean do I do this hit and run with [wife]. Yeah. I've been thinking about that. Kind of stupid but interesting; I felt we were really . . . I was telling you something in a way I have not been able to talk about before. Last week, I mean . . . pulled back and felt mixed up when we started. . . . I don't like risking myself as much as I do? Hmm, I guess I went to the right school: "The hit and run academy of motherly love" . . . I am so tired of it. [Pause] . . . I think I am making the connection. . . . [Pause] We got someplace today.

LANDMARK STUDIES

The following landmark research articles have had a lasting impact on the alliance literature.

Latent Communalities across Therapies

The conception of the pantheoretical alliance was fundamentally impacted by Rosenzweig's (1936) conceptualization of common factors across psychotherapy orientations. In his three-page essay, "Some Implicit Common Factors in Diverse Methods of Psychotherapy," Rosenzweig questioned if latent or unrecognized factors common across the psychotherapies are more predictive of outcome than the specific interventions. He proposed three potential candidates for these unrecognized factors: social reconditioning, therapist personality, and formal consistency. Social reconditioning was defined as implicit aspects of the immediate communication within the therapeutic relationship. Interestingly, this factor highlighted the social learning aspects of the immediate psychotherapeutic process, such as the patients talking openly about their concerns and the therapist is genuinely interested to understand the patients' situations. In close connection with the first factor, Rosenzweig highlighted the "stimulating, inspiring" characteristics of a good therapist. Formal consistency during treatment was highlighted: "The patient receives a schema for achieving some sort and degree of personality organization" (p. 414). Moreover, the collaborative quality of the therapeutic learning situation is characterized as "so complex and many-sided in nature" and consists of "an interdependent organization of various factors, all of them dynamically related" (p. 414).

Correlational Meta-Analysis

One of the most impactful products of psychotherapy research lies in the (co)development of meta-analytic methods (e.g., Glass, 1976). Meta-analyses permit a direct and transparent investigation of the generalizability of effects across samples and sometimes measures. Horvath and Symonds (1991) conducted the first meta-analysis of the alliance with psychotherapy outcome. Based on a sample of 24 studies that reported correlations from 20 independent samples (with 980 clients), the omnibus test of the overall alliance–outcome revealed an overall correlation of $r = .26$. That effect size (ES) has proven robust across types of psychotherapies and across decades of research.

The correlations produced by the studies were heterogeneous, and thus the authors examined a broad range of potential moderators to better understand the variability. More specifically, Horvath and Symonds (1991) tested the "halo effect" produced when alliance and outcome were evaluated by the same source (e.g., when both alliance and outcome were evaluated by client). Furthermore, the time of the alliance (early, averaged, late), lengths of treatment, treatment type (psychodynamic, cognitive, eclectic), and the specific alliance measure were examined. Within the same alliance measures, the results were more homogeneous than when effects across the alliance measures were considered, indicating that the measure used has some influence on the alliance–outcome correlation. Other than this result, there was little evidence that the examined moderators impacted the overall alliance–outcome relation. There was also no indication of publication bias based on a contrast between published and unpublished manuscripts.

Horvath and Symonds (1991) concluded, "We think that further progress in this line of inquiry will require the careful examination of the differences as well as the commonalities underlying current research programs and the development of a more integrated perspective of the working alliance. Such effort would likely enhance not only the research thrust but also the clinical usefulness of the construct" (p. 147).

Therapists' Contributions to Alliance–Outcome Relation

Psychotherapy as a socially connected event can be tested using super-nested data structures such as minutes nested within sessions, sessions nested within clients, clients nested within therapists, therapists nested within supervisors, and so forth. Each certainly impacts the process (Hatcher et al., 1995) and outcomes of psychotherapy (e.g., Crits-Christoph et al., 1991; Wampold & Serlin, 2000). Both therapist and client contribute to the alliance, and so the critical question is whether it is the therapist's contribution to the alliance or the client's contribution that best predicts outcome (Baldwin et al., 2007; Del Re et al., 2012; Dinger et al., 2007).

In a sample of 331 clients treated by 80 therapists from the Research Consortium of Counseling and Psychological Services network that included 45 university counseling centers, Baldwin et al. (2007) examined the within and between therapist alliance–outcome correlation measured by the WAI (Horvath & Greenberg, 1989) and the Outcome Questionnaire-45 (OQ-45, Lambert et al., 2004) using mixed effects models. The overall alliance–outcome correlation without consideration of the nested data structure indicated an $r = .24$, which is very close to the estimate produced by meta-analyses (e.g., Horvath et al., 2011). The results, however, indicated that those therapists who generally formed better alliances with their clients had better outcomes: The correlation between the average alliance scores for a therapist and outcome adjusted for pretest scores was .33. On the other hand, the strength of the alliance among clients within one therapist generally were unrelated to outcome ($r = 0.00$). This exemplary study demonstrated that the ability to form an alliance is a therapist characteristic that predicts outcome (Ackerman & Hilsenroth, 2001, 2003).

Alliance in the Society of Psychotherapy Research Collaborative Research Network

The Collaborative Research Network of the Society of Psychotherapy Research (SPR) is an international initiative to investigate the development of psychotherapists across theoretical orientations (Orlinsky & Rønnestad, 2005). As a landmark study within this network, Heinonen et al. (2014) investigated the impact of therapist characteristics with 333 clients and 71 therapists participating in a randomized controlled trial (RCT) of short-term (<21 sessions) and long-term (1–3 years) solution-focused and psychodynamic treatments.

The results indicated that both select therapist's self-reported *professional* characteristics (i.e., currently skillful and efficacious, less frequent experiences of anxiety, boredom, and clinical difficulties) as well as *personal* characteristics (task-oriented and confidential) predicted the formation of better therapist-rated alliances in both short-term and long-term therapies. However, the results also indicated that the client-rated alliances were mostly not predicted by these same therapist characteristics. Heinonen et al. (2014) concluded, "The divergence of therapist and patient viewpoints has implications for therapist training and supervision, as characteristics found detrimental or helpful for the working relationship rated from the perspective of one party may not be predictive of the other therapy participant's experience" (p. 465).

RESULTS OF PREVIOUS META-ANALYSES

Since the initial meta-analysis of Horvath and Symonds (1991), the alliance–outcome correlation has been examined meta-analytically several times (Horvath & Bedi, 2002; Horvath et al., 2011; Martin et al., 2000). The overall correlations varied only slightly over the years (Horvath & Bedi, 2002: $r = .21$, $k = 100$; Horvath et al., 2011: $r = .28$, $k = 190$; Horvath & Symonds, 1991: $r = .26$, number of studies $k = 26$; Martin et al., 2000: $r = .22$, $k = 79$). That suggests stability of the estimate despite accumulating studies, more sophisticated statistical models, and other advances. Moreover, the follow-up articles to the 2011 meta-analysis revealed comparable ESs (Del Re et al., 2012: $r = .27$, $k = 69$; Flückiger, Del Re, Wampold, Symonds, et al., 2012: $r = .29$, $k = 235$). At the same time, each of the meta-analyses revealed relatively large heterogeneity (Horvath et al., 2011: proportion of variability due to true difference among studies $I^2 = 56\%$).

Based on the large amount of heterogeneity in the 2011 sample, four theory-driven moderator analyses were conducted to better understand what hypothesis-driven factors have an impact on the alliance–outcome correlation. Table 2.1 summarizes all of the prior moderator tests. Some moderator analyses were replicated over meta-analyses using slightly different statistical tests (Del Re et al., 2012; Flückiger, Del Re, Wampold, Symonds, et al., 2012; Flückiger, Del Re, et al., 2013; Horvath et al., 2011). Concerning measures, the alliance–outcome correlation appears to be robust across various alliance and outcome measures, perspectives, and treatments (except for the difference between Beck Depression Inventory [BDI] and dropout outcomes), although the moderators did not explain all of the heterogeneity (Horvath et al., 2011). The same source of the alliance and outcome rater (e.g., alliance and outcome evaluated by the client) replicated the absence of a halo effect, replicating the Horvath and Symonds (1991) landmark study.

Three follow-up studies based on the 2011 meta-analysis investigated theory-driven moderators (Del Re et al., 2012; Flückiger, Del Re, Wampold, Symonds, et al., 2012; Flückiger, Del Re, et al., 2013). First, we investigated potential therapist contributions to the alliance–outcome correlation (Baldwin et al., 2007; Dinger et al., 2007) by examining the ratio of clients to therapist, which was a means to examine therapist effects of the alliance–outcome correlation across studies. The results showed that therapist contributions to the alliance predicted outcome, replicating the Baldwin et al.

Table 2.1. Summary of the Investigated Moderators of the 2011 Meta-Analysis

Moderator	Effects on the Overall Correlation	Co-Variability
Impactful moderators		
Outcome measure[a]	BDI > dropout	
Time[a,b]	Early < late[c]/slope	
Researcher allegiance[b]	Alliance investigator[d] > Other	
Therapist effects[e]	Sample-ratio between > within therapists	
SUD clients[f]	% of SUD clients < no SUD	EM clients
Ethnic minority clients[f]	% of EM clients < no minority	SUD clients
Equivalent effects		
Publication source[a]	≈ journal, book, dissertation	
Treatment type[a,b]	≈ CBT, IPT, psychodynamic, SUD treatment	
Alliance rater[a,e]	≈ Client, therapist, observer	
Outcome rater[a,e]	≈ Client, therapist, observer, other	
Disorderspec. outcome[b]	≈ disorder-specific outcome, other outcomes	
Disorderspec. manual[b]	≈ disorder-specific manual, no manual	
RCT design[b,e]	≈ RCT, not RCT	
PS[c]	≈ PS client, not PS client	
Mixed effects		
Alliance measure[a,e]	≈ CALPAS, HAQ, HAQ-II, VPPS, WAI/HAQ < other	

Notes. BDI = Beck Depression Inventory. SUD = substance use disorder. EM = ethnic minority. CBT = cognitive behavioral disorder. IPT= interpersonal therapy. RCT = randomized controlled trial. PS = personality disorder. CALPAS = California Psychotherapy Alliance Scale. HAQ = Helping Alliance Questionnaire. HAQ-II = Helping Alliance Questionnaire II. VPPS = Vanderbilt Psychotherapy Process Scale. WAI = Working Alliance Inventory.
[a]Horvath et al. (2011). [b]Flückiger et al. (2012). [c]Overall test. [d]Alliance assessed early in treatment. [e]Del Re et al. (2012). [f]Flückiger et al. (2013).

finding, a result that persisted when accounting for potential confounds (Del Re et al., 2012). Second, we tested whether the alliance–outcome correlation was impacted by whether the study was an RCT, whether the treatment was a disorder-specific manualization, whether the outcome was a disorder-specific outcome, the allegiance of the researcher to an alliance perspective, and whether the study examined the outcome of cognitive behavioral therapy (CBT) or other treatments. The results indicated that only researcher allegiance modestly impacted the early alliance–outcome correlation (Flückiger, Del Re, Wampold, Symonds, et al., 2012). Third and final, another analysis examined selection bias of ethnic minorities in research samples within treatments for substance abusers. Selection bias was found in the majority of drug treatment research conducted with mostly African American samples, resulting in an artificially lower alliance–outcome correlation for samples with ethnic minorities based on the confound with substance use disorder (SUD) treatments. The same meta-analysis also indicated that very few primary studies reported socio economic status (Flückiger, Del Re, et al., 2013).

META-ANALYTIC REVIEW

Source of Data

To locate new research on the relation between alliance and outcome from March 2010 to April 2017, a search (via EBSCO) of the PsycINFO database and PSYNDEX (for German-language articles) was undertaken using search parameters similar to the prior meta-analyses. The criteria for inclusion in this report were (a) the author referred to the therapy process variable as *helping alliance, working alliance,* or *therapeutic alliance;* (b) the authors provided data of outcome measures at the end of treatment (post-assessment); (c) the data reported were such that we could extract or estimate a value indicating the relation between alliance and outcome; (d) the clients were adults (age >18 years); and (e) manuscripts were written in the English, Italian, German, or French languages. The exclusion criteria included studies not using clinical samples (e.g., analogue data), qualitative studies, and using five or fewer patients.

The flow chart provides an overview of the extraction procedure (Figure 2.1). From the 5,770 articles retrieved dating between 2011 and 2017, we identified 105 new manuscripts that reported an alliance–outcome relation. The integration of the 201 older articles (included in Horvath et al., 2011) resulted in a total of 306 studies based on 295 independent samples. Overall, there are 1,465 reported alliance–outcome relations, representing around 30,000 clients with a mean of 100 clients per study. The 105 new research reports included in the current study are listed in Table 2.2.

The data on which our analysis is based span over four decades (1978–2017) and includes both published ($k = 242$) and unpublished ($k = 53$) studies, independent samples collected in naturalistic settings ($k = 195$), and RCTs ($k = 100$). The number of eligible studies included in this chapter is roughly tripled the size of the data that was available prior to 2000. The growth in the literature over the past decade means not only that there are more studies available for analysis but also that there is a significant increase in the types of therapies, treatment contexts, client problems, and research designs captured by the current meta-analysis. This incremental growth allows finer-graded subgroup analyses.

Statistical Analyses

A random effects-restricted maximum-likelihood estimator was utilized for both univariate and multivariate analyses. This model of analysis is based on the assumption that the studies in this meta-analysis were randomly sampled from a population of studies. All analyses were conducted using the R statistical software packages—ES calculation with the compute.es package (Del Re, 2013), aggregation and univariate methods with the MAd package (Del Re & Hoyt, 2010), and multivariate multilevel meta-analytic methods and meta-analytic diagnostics (i.e., tests for outliers) with the "metafor" package (Viechtbauer, 2010).

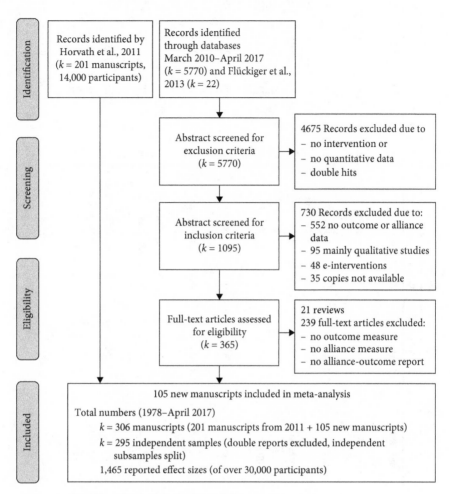

FIGURE 2.1 Flowchart of the included and excluded manuscripts.

In most studies, there were several reported alliance–outcome correlation ESs. To account for the dependencies among the outcomes, a three-level meta-analysis was conducted with ESs at level 1, outcome at level 2, and study at level 3. This procedure takes into account the correlation among within-study measures and thus yields a more precise estimate of the population parameter.

When conducting omnibus and moderator analyses, all correlations were transformed to Fisher's (1924) z for the analyses and then transformed back to r for interpretive purposes. In cases where the primary study reported more than one level of a categorical variable (e.g., reporting both early, mid, and late alliance and outcome correlations), dependencies at the moderator level were accounted for by utilizing a three-level multilevel multivariate meta-analysis, which adds random effects for each study and for each outcome and accounts for hierarchical dependence. These procedures yield estimates that account for covariance between within-study ESs for a fully independent analysis at the moderator level.

Table 2.2. Description of the Data, 2011–2017

Publication	Country	Type	Design	Disorder	Rater	Measure	Time	Rater	Measure	Primary	ES (r =)	ES (d =)	N
Accurso et al. (2015)	US	CBT	RCT	Binge Eating	c	WAI	a	c	EDE	d	0.10	0.2	80
Andrews et al. (2016)	US	Healthy lifestyles intervention	RCT	Psychosis	c/t/o	ARM	e	o/c	Retention/GAF/BDI/BPRS	o	0.02	0.04	211
Applebaum et al. (2012)	US	CBT–phone	RCT	PTSD	c	WAI	e	c	SCL/PTSD symptoms	d/o	0.33	0.7	47
Arnow et al. (2013)	US	CBAS/supportive therapy	RCT	Depression	c	WAI	e	o	HRSD	d	0.45	1.01	224
Auszra, et al. (2013)	Canada	Experiential therapy	RCT	MDE	c	WAI	e	c	BDI	d	0.31	0.65	74
Barnicot, et al. (2016)	UK	DBT	RCT	Borderline	c	STAR	e/a	o	Dropout	o	0.00	0	70
Bedics et al. (2015)	USA	DBT/community treatment	RCT	Borderline	c/t	CALPAS	a	c/o	Suicidality, introject affiliation/HRSD	o	0.08	0.16	101
Bertrand et al. (2013)	Canada	SUD program	Other	SUD	t	CALPAS	e	o	Drug use	d	0.18	0.37	80
Blais et al. (2010)	US	Psychodynamic therapy	Other	Mixed in-patient	c/t	BAM	e	c/o	SOS/amount of trouble/GAF	o	0.04	0.07	20
Bowen & Kurz (2012)	US	MBSR	RCT	SUD	c	WAI	e	c	FFMQ	o	0.41	0.89	32
Brady et al., (2015)	UK	Trauma-focused therapy	RCT	PTSD	o	WAI	e	c	Poor/good responders (PTSD)	d	0.23	0.46	58

Study	Country	Treatment	Design	Disorder		Alliance measure		Outcome measure				N
Brown et al., (2013)	UK	CBT	Other	Anorexia nervosa	c	WAI	m	Dropout/weight gain	o	-0.08	-0.15	65
Burns et al. (2015)	US	CBT	RCT	Chronic pain	c	WAI	e/m	Pain/BDI	d	0.23	0.48	94
Byrd et al., (2010)	US	Counseling	Other	Mixed university sample	c	WAI	e	OQ-45	o	0.45	1.01	66
Calamaras et al. (2015)	US	CBT	RCT	Social anxiety disorder	c	WAI	e	Fear	d	0.05	0.1	62
Carneiro et al. (2011)	Switzerland	Systemic therapy	Other	Mixed university sample	c	WAI	a	OQ-45/satisfaction	c/o	0.55	1.32	10
Carryer & Greenberg (2010)	Canada	Experiential therapy	Other	Depression	c	WAI	e	BDI/SCL/IIP/RSE	d/o	0.25	0.53	38
Carter et al. (2015)	New Zealand	CBT/IPT	RCT	Depression	o	VITAS	e	MADRS	o	0.17	0.34	165
Cavelti et al. (2016)	Switzerland	Community mental health	Other	Schizophrenia	c	STAR	e	Recovered	o/t	0.27	0.55	133
Chao et al. (2012)	US	Various	Other	Schizophrenia (50%)	c	WAI	e	Recovered	c	0.37	0.81	56
Coco et al. (2011)	Italy	Counseling	Other	Mixed university sample	c/t	WAI	e	OQ-45	c	0.21	0.42	65
Constantino et al. (2016)	US	CBAS	RCT	Chronic depression	c	WAI	e	HRSD	o	0.23	0.47	220

(continued)

Table 2.2. Continued

Publication	Country	Type	Design	Disorder	Rater	Measure	Time	Rater	Measure	Primary	ES (r =)	ES (d =)	N
Cook et al. (2015)	UK	SUD program	RCT	SUD	c/t	WAI	e	c	Abstinence	d	0.18	0.36	173
Cooper et al. (2016)	US	Depression	RCT	Depression	o	WAI	e	o	Dropout	o	0.45	1.01	176
Corso et al. (2012)	US	Primary healthcare	Other	Various	c	TBS	e	c	Drug use	d	0.04	0.08	1613
Crameri et al. (2015)	Switzerland	Various	Other	Various	c	HAQ	m	c/t	OQ-45	o	0.15	0.31	260
Crits-Christoph et al. (2011)	US	Various	Other	Depression	c	CALPAS	a	c/o	HRSD/BDI	d	0.38	0.82	45
Crits-Christoph et al. (2011)	US	SUD program	RCT	SUD	c	CALPAS	e/a	c	Global mental health/drug use	d	0.35	0.76	1613
Cronin et al. (2014)	US	Various	Other	Dissociative disorder	c/t	WAI	e	c	PTSD symptoms/SCL/Treatment progress	d/o	0.45	1.01	131
DeSorcy et al. (2016)	US	CBT	Other	Offenders	c	WAI	m	o	Dropout/violence	o	0.07	0.14	423
Doran et al. (2017)	US	CBT/brief relational therapy	Other	Various	c	WAI	a	c	IIP	o	0.31	0.66	47
Ellis et al. (2012)	US	Family-centered treatment	Other	Diabetes	c	BTPS	e	c	Hemoglobin	d	0.22	0.45	72

Study	Country	Treatment	Population		Measure			Outcome					N
Flückiger et al. (2013)	Switzerland	CBT	Mixed university sample	Other	c/t	BPSR	e/a	c	Outcome Composite	o	0.20	0.41	430
Flückiger et al. (2011)	Switzerland	CBT/BWLT	Binge eating	RCT	c	BPSR	e/a	o	Dropout	o	0.48	1.09	78
Gibbons et al. (2010)	US	CM/CBT	Marijuana	RCT	c/t	WAI	e	o	Drug use	d	0.41	0.9	86
Gold et al. (2015)	US	Psychodynamic therapy	Various	Other	c	WAI	m	c	SCL/Improvement	o	0.32	0.68	38
Goldberg et al. (2013)	US	Mindfulness smoking reduction	Smoking	RCT	c	WAI	m	c/o	Abstinence/negative affect/emotion regulation	d/o	0.32	0.68	37
Goldman & Gregory (2010)	US	Dynamic deconstructive therapy	Borderline	RCT	o	WAI	a	c/o	Borderline symptoms/BDI/social support	d/o	0.44	0.98	10
Gullo et al. (2012)	Italy	Counseling	Various	Other	c	WAI	e	c	OQ-45	o	0.18	0.36	32
Gysin-Maillart et al. (2016)	Switzerland	Suicide attempt	Suicidality	RCT	c	HAQ	e	c	BDI/suicidality	d	0.56	1.35	57
Häring et al. (2010)	Switzerland	Psychoanalysis	Various	Other	t	TAB	e	c/o	BDI/IIP	o	0.46	1.03	39
Hartmann et al. (2010)	Germany	Inpatient psychotherapy	Bulimia nervosa	Other	c	HAQ	e	o	Bulimia diagnosis	d	0.00	0	43

(continued)

Table 2.2. Continued

Publication	Country	Type	Design	Disorder	Rater	Measure	Time	Rater	Measure	Primary	ES (r =)	ES (d =)	N
Hartzler et al. (2011)	US	CBT	RCT	SUD	c	WAI	e	c	Drug use/SCL	d/o	0.06	0.11	157
Haug et al. (2016)	Norway	CBT	RCT	Anxiety disorders	c	WAI	e/l	c	late improvement/ GAF/outcome composite	d/o	0.05	0.1	88
Heins et al. (2013)	Netherlands	CBT	Other	Chronic fatigue	c	WAI	e	c	Fatigue symptoms	d	0.11	0.22	183
Hendriksen et al. (2014)	Netherlands	Psychodynamic therapy	RCT	Depression	c	HAQ	m	o	HRSD	d	0.00	0	117
	Canada	Emotion-focused therapy	Other	Depression	c	WAI	e	c	BDI	d	0.20	0.41	30
Hersoug et al. (2013)	Scandinavia	Psychodynamic therapy	Other	Various	c	WAI	m	c/o	Functioning/IIP	o	0.21	0.44	100
Hicks et al. (2012)	Australia	CM	Other	Severe mental illness	c	WAI	m	c	Recovery	o	0.51	1.17	61
Hoffart et al. (2012)	Norway	CBT/IPT	RCT	Social anxiety disorder	c	WAI	m	c/t	Social Phobia Scale	d	0.20	0.41	80
Johansson & Jansson (2010)	Sweden	Psychodynamic therapy	Other	Various	c	HAQ-II	e	c	SCL/IIP	o	0.32	0.68	76
Johansson et al. (2011)	Norway	Psychodynamic therapy	Other	Various	c	WAI	e	c	Functioning/IIP / GAF/SCL	o	0.39	0.84	76
Kaap-Deeder et al. (2016)	Belgium	Treatment as usual	Other	Eating disorder	c	WAI	m	c	Eating symptoms/ body dissatisfaction	d	0.27	0.55	53

Study	Country	Treatment	Design	Disorder	c/t/o	WAI	e	o/c/t	Outcome	d/o			N
Keeley et al. (2011)	US	CBT	Other	Obsessive–compulsive	c/t/o	WAI	e	o/c/t	OCD symptoms	d	0.69	1.92	23
Kirouac et al. (2016)	US	CBT	RCT	SUD	c	WAI	e	c/o	Drug use/SCL	d/o	0.17	0.34	639
Knuuttila et al. (2012)	Finland	SUD program	Other	SUD	c	WAI	e	o	Dropout	o	0.06	0.11	281
Kramer et al. (2014)	Switzerland	CM	RCT	Borderline	c	WAI	e/a	c	OQ-45	o	0.43	0.96	32
Kushner et al. (2016)	Canada	ADM/IPT/CBT	RCT	Depression	c/t	CALPAS	e/l	o/c	HRSD/BDI	d	0.19	0.38	146
Lecomte et al. (2012)	Canada	CBT	RCT	Psychosis	c/t	WAI	a	o/c	Insight/dropout/RSE	d/o	0.37	0.79	35
Leibert et al. (2011)	US	Counseling	Other	Mixed university sample	c	WAI	e	c	OQ-45	o	0.35	0.75	135
Lilja et al. (2016)	UK	MBCT	Other	Depression	c	WAI	a	c	Outcome composite	o	0.28	0.58	40
Lerner et al. (2011)	US	Parent friendship coaching	Other	ADHD parents	c	TPOCS	a	t/o	Parental quality	d	0.36	0.77	27
Lorenzo-Luaces et al. (2014)	US	CBT	RCT	Depression	o	WAI	e	c	BDI	d	0.23	0.47	60
Maher et al. (2012)	US	CBT	RCT	Obsessive–compulsive	c	WAI	e	o	OCD symptoms	d	0.30	0.63	28
Mahon et al. (2015)	UK	Counseling	Other	Mixed university sample	c	WAI	e	o	Dropout	o	0.20	0.41	122

(continued)

Table 2.2. Continued

Publication	Country	Type	Design	Disorder	Rater	Measure	Time	Rater	Measure	Primary	ES (r =)	ES (d =)	N
Maitland et al. (2016)	US	Various	RCT	Various	c	WAI	a	c	Diagnostic screening/fear of intimacy	d/o	0.65	1.7	22
Mallinckrodt & Tekie (2016)	US	Various	Other	Various	c	WAI	m	c	OQ-45	o	0.26	0.54	769
Manne et al. (2010)	US	Cancer counseling	RCT	Cancer	c	WAI	e	c	BDI	o	0.22	0.46	198
Marcus et al. (2011)	US	SUD program	RCT	SUD	c/t	WAI	e	c	Drug use/BDI	d	0.18	0.37	398
Marmarosh & Kivlighan (2012)	US	Counseling	Other	Various	c	WAI	e	c	SCL	o	0.23	0.47	82
McBride et al. (2010)	Canada	IPT	Other	Depression	c	WAI	e	c	BDI	d	0.28	0.58	74
McLaughlin et al. (2014)	US	Prolonged exposure	Other	PTSD	c	CALPAS	a	c	PTBS symptoms/ BDI	d/o	0.38	0.81	116
Mörtberg (2014)	Sweden	CBT	RCT	Social anxiety	c	WAI	e	c	Social Interaction Anxiety Scale	d	0.16	0.32	28
Owen et al. (2013)	US	Counseling	Other	Mixed university sample	c	WAI	a	c	SOS	o	0.29	0.61	91
Pan et al. (2011)	US	CBT	RCT	Phobia	c/t	WAI	e	c/t	Anxiety symptoms/ behavioral approach	d/o	0.51	1.18	30

Study	Country	Treatment	Design	Population		Measure		Outcome				N
Patterson et al. (2014)	US	Counseling	Other	Mixed university sample	c	WAI	e	OQ-45	o	0.38	0.82	132
Pinto et al. (2011)	US	CBT/psychoeducation	RCT	ADHD	t	HAQ-II	e	Retention	o	0.13	0.26	346
Polaschek & Ross (2010)	New Zealand	CBT	Other	Violence	c/o	WAI	m/a	Violence	d	0.10	0.21	50
Ruchlewska et al. (2016)	Netherlands	Community mental health	RCT	Various	t	WAI	e	Readmission	o	0.02	0.04	212
Ruglass et al. (2012)	US	SUD program	RCT	SUD/PTSD	c	HAQ-II	e	Substance use/PTSD symptoms	c/t	0.16	0.33	223
Sasso et al. (2016)	US	CBT	RCT	Depression	o	WAI	e	BDI	d	0.18	0.38	57
Sauer et al. (2010)	US	Counseling	Other	Various	c	WAI	e	OQ-45	c	0.22	0.45	50
Simpson et al. (2011)	US	CBT	RCT	Obsessive–compulsive	c	WAI	e	OCD symptoms	o	0.40	0.87	30
Smerud et al. (2011)	US	Family psychoeducation	Other	Schizophrenia	o	SOFTA	m	Rescue medication/ hospitalization	o	0.06	0.13	28
Smith et al. (2012)	US	IPT/TAU	RCT	Depression	c	WAI	e	BDI	c	0.38	0.82	35
Snippe et al. (2015)	Netherlands	CBT/MBCT	RCT	Depression and diabetes	c	WAI	e/m	BDI	c	0.16	0.32	34
Stiles-Shields et al. (2013)	Australia, US	CBT/supportive therapy	RCT	Anorexia nervosa	c	HAQ	e	BMI/BDI/EDE	c	0.25	0.51	63
Stiles-Shields et al. (2014)	US	CBT	RCT	Depression	c/t	WAI	e	Depression/HRSD	c/o	0.00	0.00	290

(continued)

Table 2.2. Continued

Publication	Country	Type	Design	Disorder	Rater	Measure	Time	Rater	Measure	Primary	ES (r =)	ES (d =)	N
Taber et al. (2011)	US	Counseling	Other	Mixed university sample	c	WAI	e	c	OQ-45	o	0.07	0.15	32
Tschuschke et al. (2015)	Switzerland	Various	Other	Mixed	c	HAQ	e	c	SCL	o	0.15	0.3	81
Turner et al. (2015)	UK	CBT	Other	Eating disorder	c	WAI	e	c	EDE	d	0.24	0.49	94
Ulvenes et al. (2012)	Norway	CBT	RCT	Cluster C	c	HAQ	e	c	SCL	o	0.28	0.58	23
Urbanoski et al. (2012)	US	Various	Other	SUD	c	WAI	m	c	Abstinence/SCL	d/o	0.05	0.11	303
	US	CBT	Other	Partner violence	c	WAI	e/a	o	Physical aggression	d	0.17	0.35	107
Watson et al. (2010)	Canada	CBT/Process experiential	RCT	Depression	c	WAI	a	c	BDI	d	0.53	1.24	66
Watson et al. (2011)	Canada	CBT/Process experiential	RCT	Depression	c	WAI	a	c	BDI/RSE/DAS/IIP/SCL	d/o	0.55	1.33	66
Weck et al. (2013)	Germany	CBT	RCT	Depression	c	HAQ	a	o	Days to relapse	d	0.10	0.2	80
Weck et al. (2015)	Germany	CBT/exposure therapy	RCT	Anxiety	o	HAQ	m	o	OCD symptoms	d	0.17	0.35	68
Weck et al. (2015)	Germany	CBT	RCT	Various	o	HAQ	e	o	Outcome composite	o	0.24	0.49	61

Study	Country	Treatment	Design	Disorder		Alliance measure	Time		Outcome				N
Weck et al. (2016)	Germany	CBT	RCT	Panic	o	HAQ	e	c	Panic symptoms	d	0.29	0.61	84
Weiss et al. (2014)	Isreal	CBT	Other	Panic	c	WAI	e	c	Anxiety sensitivity	d	0.37	0.8	19
Westmacott et al. (2010)	Canada	CBT/process experiential/interpersonal	Other	Schizophrenia (50%)	c/t	WAI	e	c	SCL/GAF	o	0.40	0.87	83
Wheaton et al. (2016)	US	CBT	RCT	Obsessive–compulsive	c	WAI	e	t	OCD symptoms	d	0.10	0.2	37
Xu & Tracey (2015)	US	Counseling	Other	Various	c	WAI	e	c	OQ-45	o	0.28	0.58	638
Zilcha-Mano et al. (2016)	US	CBT/alliance fostering treatment	RCT	Various	c/t	WAI	e	c/t	Problem solved (1 item)	o	0.52	1.22	241

Notes. The descriptions of manuscripts published earlier than 2011 are presented in Horvath et al. (2011). RCT = randomized controlled trials. PTSD = posttramautic stress disorder. MDE = major depressive episode. Treatments: CBT = cognitive behavioral therapy; CBAS = cognitive behavioral analysis system; DBT = dialectic behavioral therapy; MBSR = mindfulness-based stress reduction; BWLT = body weight loss therapy; CM = clinical management; ADM = antidepressant medication; SUD program = substance use disorder program; Rater: c = client; t = therapist; o = observer/other. Alliance measures: WAI = Working Alliance Inventory; ARM = Agnew Relationship Measure; CALPAS = California Psychotherapy Alliance Scale; STAR = Scale to Assess Therapeutic Relationships; VITAS = Vanderbilt Therapeutic Alliance Scale; HAQ = Helping Alliance Questionnaire; HAQ II = Helping Alliance Questionnaire II; TBS = Therapeutic Bond Scale. BPSR = Bern Post Session Report; BTPS = Barriers to Treatment Participation Scale; TPOCS = Therapy Process Observational Coding System–Alliance Scale; SOFTA = system for observing family therapy alliances; TAB = therapeutic working relationship. Time of the alliance assessment: e = early (sessions 1–5); m = mid-treatment (e < m < l); l = late (five last sessions); a = averaged. Outcome measures: EDE = Eating Disorder Examination; GAF = Global Assessment of Functioning; BDI = Beck Depression Inventory; BPRS = Brief Psychiatric Rating Scale; SCL = Symptom Check List–90; HRSD = Hamilton Rating Scale for Depression; SOS = Schwartz Outcome Scale; FFMQ = Facets of Mindfulness Questionnaire; OQ-45 = Outcome Questionnaire–45; IIP = Inventory of Interpersonal Problems–64; RSE = Rosenberg Self-Esteem Scale; MADRAS = Montgomery-Asberg Depression Rating Scale.

Results

The overall weighted average (omnibus) ES, based on 295 independent alliance–outcome relations, was $r = .278$ (95% confidence intervals [CIs; .256, .299], $p < .0001$; equivalent of $d = .579$, 95% CIs [.530, .627]). This ES is identical to what was found in the 2011 meta-analysis ($r = .278$; Horvath et al., 2011). The aggregated ES was computed taking into account the sample size of each study, as well as an adjustment for within-study correlations between outcome measures. The overall ES of .278 indicates the alliance–outcome relation accounts for about 8% of the variability of treatment outcomes.

Our data are based on a search of electronic databases and such public records may be biased in favor of including more published than unpublished material with smaller or negative ESs. We tested the possibility of such bias. The funnel plot (Figure 2.2) is a diagram of standard error on the Y axis and the ES on the X axis. In the presence of bias, the plot would show a higher concentration of studies on one side of the mean than the other. In the absence of publication bias, we would expect the studies to be distributed relatively symmetrically around the aggregated ES. In the funnel plot, there is a slight overrepresentation of $r = 0.00$ results due to the coding rule we used: An alliance–outcome association reported as not significant was coded as $r = 0.00$. With this rule, we intended to be inclusive of studies that were not primarily focused on the alliance–outcome association. There was no indication of publication bias in our sample. As well, we computed how many "hidden" publications with different aggregate ESs would it would take to reduce the overall ES between alliance and outcome to zero. In this data set, the failsafe value was greater than 1,000 (i.e., more than 1,000 studies with zero or negative findings would be required to bring the present alliance outcome relation to zero).

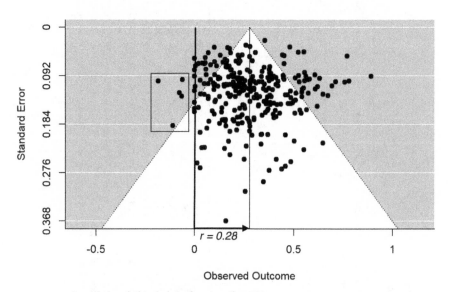

FIGURE 2.2 Funnel plot of all included effect sizes ($k = 295$).

Variability of Effect Sizes

There was a great deal of variability among the ESs associated with the studies, similar to what was found in all but one of the previous meta-analysis (Horvath et al., 2011). The group of alliance–outcome ESs in this study indicates a platykurtic distribution and significant heterogeneity ($Q_{(294)} = 1,017.6$, $p < .0001$; $I^2 = 70.8$, 95% CIs [61.9, 73.1]). I^2 is an index calculated as the percentage of variability due to true differences among ESs (Hedges & Olkin, 1985).

The large I^2 value found in this analysis could be due to several factors including researchers assessing alliance at different points of therapy, the variety of therapy contexts, who rated the alliance and outcome, and the instrument used to measure the alliance. In addition, outcomes were also measured from a variety of perspectives and with diverse instruments, sometimes immediately after treatments, at other times at follow-up. Each of these differences, alone or in combination, could moderate the alliance–outcome relation. In the next sections, the impact of some of these potential moderators are presented. All moderator analyses were adjusted for dependencies of various outcome measures (e.g., simultaneous use of BDI and OQ-45) based on a three-level multilevel multivariate meta-analysis

MODERATORS

We investigated possible moderators of the alliance–outcome relation by examining publication year of the study, treatment type, patient diagnosis, alliance measure, rater of the alliance, time of the alliance assessment, outcome measures, specificity of outcome, source of outcome data, type of research design, and country of study.

Year of Study

We compared the 2011 alliance data set (1978–2011 data, $r_{adjusted} = .26$, $k = 190$) to the more recently collected data (2011–2017 data, $r_{adjusted} = .22$, $k = 105$). The adjusted ES for the new sample was slightly lower than the 2011 data ($r_{difference} = .041$; $p = .041$), perhaps due to the use of abbreviated alliance measures in the newer data or the wide range of included study conditions. The box plot (Figure 2.3) displays the aggregated ESs associated with these outcomes.

Treatment Type

Bordin (1994) argued that the alliance is a significant factor in all types of therapeutic relationships. We tested this claim by examining averaged ESs associated with different psychotherapies. The aggregate ES of each treatment, as identified by the authors of the studies, were not significantly different from each other ($Q_{(6)} = 3.587$): for cognitive behavior therapy ($r_{adjusted} = .20$, $k = 72$), counseling ($r_{adjusted} = .23$, $k = 26$), psychodynamic therapy ($r_{adjusted} = .24$, $k = 57$), humanistic therapy ($r_{adjusted} = .26$, $k = 11$), interpersonal therapy (IPT, $r_{adjusted} = .28$, $k = 9$), and unspecified and eclectic treatments($r_{adjusted} = .24$,

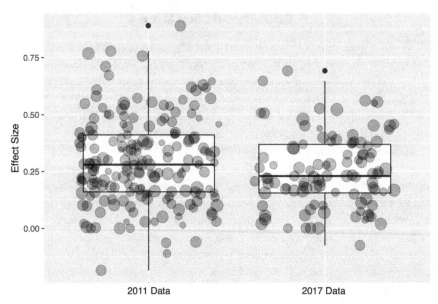

FIGURE 2.3 Comparison of the data published before 2011 (Horvath et al., 2011) and the more recently published data.

$k = 98$). Similar to the 2011 results, the alliance appears to be a pantheoretical factor similarly relevant across treatments.

Patient Diagnosis

Previous research has identified SUD populations with smaller ESs than those of other disorders (Flückiger, Del Re, et al., 2013). We sought to explore the possibility of different alliance–outcome relations among diagnostic groups using the larger sample of studies and a more differentiated grade of clusters. These included anxiety disorders ($r_{adjusted} = .24$, $k = 23$), borderline personality disorder ($r_{adjusted} = .32$, $k = 9$), depression ($r_{adjusted} = .26$, $k = 54$), eating disorders ($r_{adjusted} = .15$, $k = 11$), other personality disorders ($r_{adjusted} = .32$, $k = 5$), posttraumatic stress disorder (PTSD, $r_{adjusted} = .31$, $k = 7$), schizophrenia ($r_{adjusted} = .30$, $k = 12$), SUD ($r_{adjusted} = .14$, $k = 29$), and transdiagnostic samples ($r_{adjusted} = .26$, $k = 107$). The results were consistent with previous research: The SUD population produced smaller alliance–outcome associations than other diagnoses ($Q_{(8)} = 27.958$; $p < .001$). One outlying study (Luborsky, 1985) in which the aggregate ES for this study was very large $r = .78$ was removed from the analysis. In addition, eating disordered populations also had smaller alliance–outcome associations. Moreover, BPD showed large between study differences with correlations ranging from .00 to .78 (e.g., Bedics et al., 2015). Figure 2.4 shows the box plot of results.

Alliance Assessment Measures

Researchers used a wide variety of alliance measures. Within the studies included in the meta-analysis, more than 30 different instruments were utilized. These included

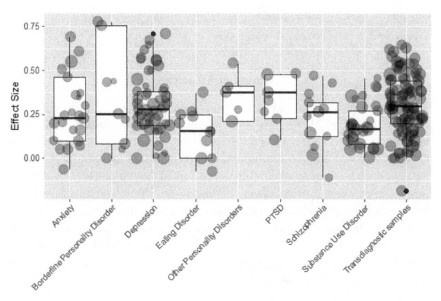

FIGURE 2.4 Alliance-outcome correlation across different clusters of patient diagnoses.

well-established instruments: CALPAS (r_{adjusted} = .22, k = 34), HAQ (r_{adjusted} = .26, k = 33), HAQ-II (r_{adjusted} = .16, k = 8), and WAI (r_{adjusted} = .24, k = 150). We compared the effects for each of the four measures plus a collective category called "other" (r_{adjusted} = .28, k = 71) and a combined category (r_{adjusted} = .20, k = 9) where more than one measure was used but could not be disaggregated. The box plot (Figure 2.5) displays the aggregated ESs associated with these measures. The differences among the effects for different measures were not significant ($Q_{(7)}$ = 7.487; p = .38). However,

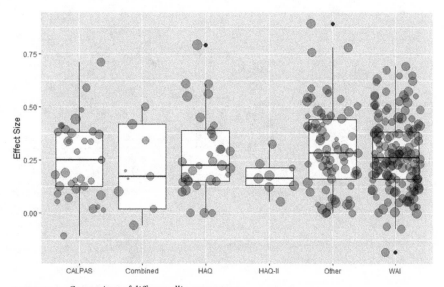

FIGURE 2.5 Comparison of different alliance measures.

variability within each category was large, making it less likely to detect statistically significant differences among these clusters.

Raters of Alliance

The alliance can be rated from four perspectives: clients ($r_{adjusted} = .25$, $k = 223$), observers ($r_{adjusted} = .22$, $k = 66$), other participants such as partners and family members ($r_{adjusted} = .25$, $k = 48$), and therapists ($r_{adjusted} = .22$, $k = 40$). The aggregated ESs associated with each of these perspectives are displayed in Figure 2.6. The omnibus model ($Q_{(3)} = 6.827$; $p = .078$) indicated a trend that the observer rated effects were slightly smaller in comparison to the client rated alliance–outcome correlation (whereas the therapist and other categories did not differ from the client-rated alliance). These findings somewhat differ from previous research (earlier studies did not split the other and observer category) and where the therapists' evaluations indicated a trend toward a lower alliance–outcome association (Horvath & Bedi 2002; Horvath et al., 2011; Horvath & Symonds, 1991).

Time of Alliance Assessment

We examined the impact of the phase of treatment the alliance was assessed by separating the correlations into four categories: early (alliance assessed in sessions one to five; $r_{adjusted} = .022$, $k = 182$); mid (after the fifth session and at least four or more sessions before end-of-treatment; $r_{adjusted} = .21$, $k = 51$); late (within three sessions

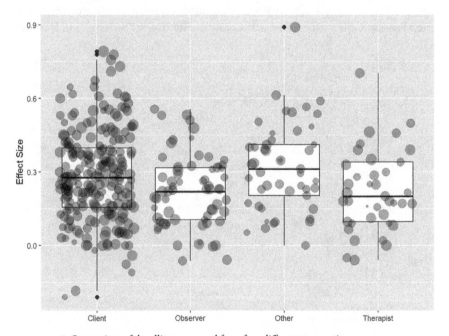

FIGURE 2.6 Comparison of the alliance assessed from four different perspectives.

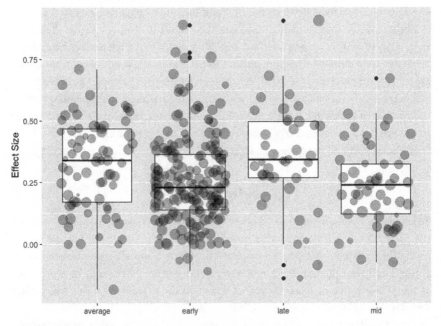

FIGURE 2.7 Time of the alliance assessment by four categories.

of end-of-treatment; r_{adjusted} = .30, k = 41); and averaged (combination of assessment points; r_{adjusted} = .29, k = 73). Figure 2.7 shows the box plot of results. The Q statistic for the overall contrast among these time categories was highly significant ($Q_{(3)}$ = 17.814; p < .001). The result replicates the previous findings (Flückiger, Del Re, Wampold, Symonds, et al., 2012; Horvath et al., 2011) that the relation between alliance and outcome is higher when the alliance is measured late in therapy in comparison to the early alliance assessment (and the other alliance assessments in between these two values). Of course, variables measured at the nearly same time (i.e., proximal variables) typically are more highly correlated than distal variables.

Outcome Measures

As was the case with the alliance measures, a wide range of therapy outcome measures was included in our studies. Thirty-five different outcome assessments were used, which were classified in 11 categories based on the frequency of use (five or more studies; split of depression measures into three categories). The alliance–outcome effects for these 11 classes of measures differed significantly ($Q_{(10)}$ = 24.785; p = .01). The categories and corresponding correlations were the BDI (r_{adjusted} = .28, k = 44), other depression measures (r_{adjusted} = .23, k = 15), dropout (r_{adjusted} = .18, k = 27), global outcome (r_{adjusted} = .30, k = 46), Hamilton Rating Scale for Depression (r_{adjusted} = .26, k = 14), Inventory of Interpersonal Problems (r_{adjusted} = .22, k = 16), OQ-45 (r_{adjusted} = .24, k = 13), other measures (r_{adjusted} = .25, k = 167), risk behavior (r_{adjusted} = .17, k = 35), and Symptom Check List 90 and its shorter versions (r_{adjusted} = .23, k = 58).

The contrast analysis between the BDI and the other categories indicated a statistically significant lower alliance–outcome correlation in dropout or risk behaviors ($r_{\text{difference}}$ = .10 and .11 respectively, $p < .05$). Dropout as a treatment outcome and risk behaviors were almost exclusively utilized in SUD samples. While client termination represents—in one sense—a "hard" outcome index, the SUD samples included in the data were highly variable; clients in these treatments are often volatile and have multiple problems (Flückiger, Del Re, et al., 2013). As a result, individuals might drop out of therapy for a diverse set of reasons, apart from lack of treatment progress. Aside from these effects, all the categories showed high variability within each category.

Specificity of Outcome

Specificity of outcome refers to whether the measure was disorder-specific outcome (r_{adjusted} = .23, $k = 66$) or not (other outcome, r_{adjusted} = .26, $k = 242$). For example, a psychotherapy study of depressed patients might have a specific measure, such as the Eating Disorder Examination questionnaire, and a general symptom measure, such as the SCL-90. Due to relatively higher power in the present data, this small effect was statistically significant ($Q_{(1)}$ = 4.543; $p = .033$) in comparison to the prior meta-analysis (Flückiger, Del Re, Wampold, Symonds, et al., 2012). These results indicate that the alliance is predictive for disorder-specific measures, but predictability may be slightly higher if outcome is assessed based on a broader mental health definition (e.g., World Health Organization, 2014). Moreover, the outcome component of the alliance–outcome relation may integrate patient-centered perspectives on therapeutic change (e.g., Flückiger et al., 2019; Muran et al., 1995).

Sources of Outcome Data

Similar to the measurement of alliance, researchers collect outcome ratings from various perspectives, including clients (r_{adjusted} = .25, $k = 204$), independent observers (r_{adjusted} = .22, $k = 66$), therapists (r_{adjusted} = .29, $k = 34$), and other sources (e.g., dropouts, days of sobriety, rehospitalization; r_{adjusted} = .23, $k = 61$). Figure 2.8 displays the ESs associated with different outcome rating sources. The difference among the alliance–outcome ES obtained by these raters was not statistically significant ($Q_{(3)}$ = 5.885; $p = .117$). The power of these contrasts (the likelihood of finding significant differences among the contrasts) is negatively impacted by the large (more than anticipated) heterogeneity in the data.

Type of Research Design

Previous research has investigated the magnitude of alliance–outcome ES in RCTs (Flückiger, Del Re, Wampold, Symonds, et al., 2012). Our results replicates the finding of no statistically significant differences ($Q_{(1)}$ = .96; $p = .327$) between alliance–outcome effects in RCT (r_{adjusted} = .24, $k = 110$) and other designs (r_{adjusted} = .25, $k = 184$).

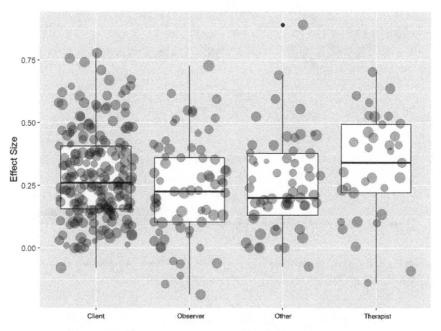

FIGURE 2.8 Comparison of four assessor perspectives of psychotherapy outcome.

Country of Study

There is a broad consensus that psychotherapy is embedded in cultural-specific contexts impacted by language, history, and organization of mental health systems (Asnaani & Hofmann, 2012; Orlinsky & Ronnestad, 2005; Wampold & Imel, 2015). Thus, the country in which a psychotherapy study is conducted might impact the generalizability of the alliance and its relation to outcome across ethnic minorities (e.g., Flückiger, Del Re, et al., 2013; Morales et al., 2018; Owen et al., 2011) and countries (e.g., Falkenström et al., 2019; Wei & Heppner, 2005). Our results indicated there was a statistical trend for differences between countries in the magnitude of the alliance–outcome correlation ($Q_{(9)}$ = 15.78; p = .072). Specifically, Belgium, the Netherlands, and Luxemburg had lower associations in comparison to US samples (BeNeLux countries, $r_{difference}$ = –.11, k = 7). Figure 2.9 displays the heat map of alliance–outcome correlations by country. This figure shows that there is a disproportion of data collection from North America (k = 208), English-speaking countries (k = 21), and European countries (k = 65).

EVIDENCE FOR CAUSALITY

Before responding to this question, one first need to consider some important issues about the nature of causal relationship in therapy: The classic test for causality involves contrasting outcomes with and without the presence of a component/variable in the process. If—all else being equal—the presence of this component produces

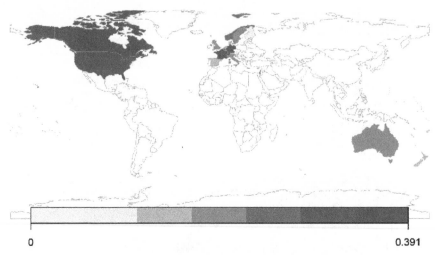

0   0.391

FIGURE 2.9 The international context of studies reporting an alliance–outcome correlation (white: no studies; grey tones: aggregated alliance–outcome correlation).

an effect that is not present in its absence, we infer that the variable has caused the effect. Clearly, removing the alliance from therapy while everything else is held constant is practically impossible and ethically unacceptable. Moreover, research evidence suggests that in psychotherapy multiple, mutuality interactive variables contribute to the changes associated with positive outcome (e.g., Horvath et al., 2011; Norcross & Wampold, 2018). Rather than a single "cause" producing a finite effect, progress, or positive change, therapy process is more accurately understood as the result of interaction of a variety of factors each acting the context of the other (Kramer et al., 2014; Wampold & Imel, 2015). While conceptually we can think of interventions or variables as finite entities (e.g., homework, practice, empathy, interpretation etc.) each having the potential of bring about salutary effect, in clinical practice, all interventions happen in a particular context that includes -among other things- the relational connection between the helper and client (a at least dyadic quality), the timing of the intervention, the place in which therapy unfolds, etc. Each conceptually distinct element in therapy can potentiate or reduce the impact of the others. For example, the impact of offering the client a particular intervention depends not only on the quality of the intervention but weather it was offered responsively "at the right time" and delivered in a form most appropriate for that particular client (e.g., Crits-Cristoph et al., 1988; Grosse-holtforth & Flückiger, 2012; Norcross & Wampold, 2018; Stiles & Horvath, 2017). In this inclusive view of the therapy process, the distinction between causal ingredients and relationship/context becomes less clear and the variety of features of the unfolding processes and dynamic systems of therapy are conceptualized to interact to impact the outcomes synergistically. The degree of effectiveness of an intervention is contingent on the interpersonal dimension, the timing and the capacities, resources and needs of both therapist and client (Horvath, 2018; Stiles et al., 2015).

What research *can* tell us about contribution of the quality of the alliance to positive outcome is twofold: First, meta analytic methods (such as the one we report) can give a reliable estimate of the proportion of variance in outcome that is contingent on the quality of the alliance in general. As noted above, alliance accounts for about 8% of the outcome variance and, while this may not seem like a large proportion, it should be noted that it is not smaller in comparison variances discussed for other well-investigated psychotherapy factors such as treatment methods or therapist effects. And, second, we can answer the question weather the alliance is a surrogate variable standing in for a more basic underlying entity. In this regard, studies have investigated a wide range of possibilities such as: whether the link between alliance and outcomes was a consequence of early gains in therapy, specific to sources of report, kind of treatments, type of outcome measures, phases of therapy, measuring methods, and kind of psychological problems (Crits-Christoph et al., 2006; Flückiger et al., 2012). In each of these investigations (as well as in the current and prior meta-analyses) the results indicate that the alliance indeed makes a real and unique contribution to the therapy process, though the specific ways that the alliance contributes to therapy process likely varies among different kinds of treatments as Bordin (1994) predicted.

Nonetheless, does the alliance actually cause successful treatment outcomes? That question has been investigated and discussed using a variety of advanced empirical models with particular statistical assumptions. For example, several approaches focused on the within-patient, session-by-session prediction during treatment (e.g., Barber et al., 2014; Falkenström et al., 2013; Hoffart et al., 2013; Rubel et al., 2017; Strunk et al., 2010; Tasca & Lampard, 2012; Weiss et al., 2014; Xu & Tracey, 2015; Zilcha-Mano & Errazuriz, 2017). Many of such studies report a significant small to moderate within-patient association between alliance and subsequent outcome variables (e.g., Zilcha-Mano, 2017), even though systematic meta-analyses on these studies are not available at present. One of the more straightforward meta-analytic approaches to answer the causal question lies in the within-study comparison of zero-order alliance–outcome correlations with partial correlations that adjust for intake characteristics and related early symptom change. The partial correlation coefficient is a coefficient used to describe the linear association between X and Y (i.e., alliance and outcome) after excluding the effect of one or more independent factors Z (e.g., intake characteristics, alternative process variables). In the present meta-analysis data, 66 studies reported both coefficients (zero-order alliance–outcome correlations as well as partial correlations). Our results indicated there were no statistically significant differences between zero-order and partial correlations ($Q_{(1)}$ = 1.651; p = .199), indicating that the potential covariates measured did not reduce the magnitude of the alliance and outcome relations (for zero-order correlations r_{adjusted} = .25, for partial-correlations r_{adjusted} = .22).

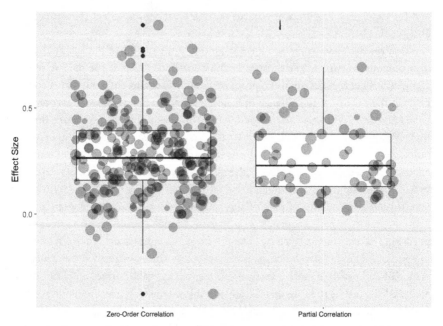

FIGURE 2.10   Comparison of reported zero-order and partial correlations.

These results support the hypothesis that the association between alliance and outcome is not mainly an epiphenomena linked to intake characteristics and related early therapy gains. Figure 2.10 displays the box plot comparing the two categories.

PATIENT CONTRIBUTIONS

The alliance represents a proactive collaboration of clients and therapists across sessions and in moment-to-moment interactions. The alliance is an emergent dyadic quality highlighting the co-contribution and coordination between both patient and therapist. Clearly, from an ethical point of view, all psychotherapy participants have to consent for the overall therapy goals and tasks in a highly confidential setting. Patient proactive engagement is desirable and necessary in the majority of people seeking a psychotherapist. As such, there is no psychotherapy process and outcome without patient contributions (Pope & Vasquez, 2016).

With respect to the alliance, the reviewed research indicates that the therapist makes the largest contribution to the development of the alliance, but certainly the patient contributes to the dyadic relationship. For example, patient trust (Birkhäuser et al., 2017), processing activities (Bohart & Wade, 2013), capacity for attachment and bond (Levy et al., 2018), and social support (Coyne et al., 2018; Levin et al., 2012, Probst et al., 2015) may impact the cooperative quality of the alliance as micro outcome.

Clients' high problem severity may present challenges to the development of the alliance. Personality disorders have been advanced as one notable population with difficult alliances (e.g., Forster et al., 2014). However, personality disordered samples indicate a comparable alliance–outcome association to other diagnostic groups. Our findings show high variability of the alliance–outcome ES in BPD. This variability might go along with unstable emotional states, which might impact the perception of the alliance in single sessions (Bedics et al., 2015; Spinhoven et al., 2007; Ulvenes et al., 2012).

In the current study, we replicated the earlier meta-analytic findings that SUD (Flückiger, Del Re, et al., 2013) and eating disorder (Graves et al., 2017) populations have slightly lower alliance–outcome ESs in adult samples. However, those previous meta-analyses also indicated that the alliance is embedded in a variety of moderating factors such as ethnic minorities in SUD samples and clients' age in eating disorders, highlighting the related psychosocial context within these samples.

LIMITATIONS OF THE RESEARCH

This chapter is based on a quantitative synthesis of the research results. While our team made a sustained effort to seek all the available research on alliance–outcome relation, no meta-analysis is truly exhaustive, and as Figure 2.9 impressively shows, this one is no exception. Given the robust finding of the positive association between alliance and outcome, major changes in the association are not likely in the future, even though there was a slight decrease of the alliance–outcome relation in more recent studies.

A significant challenge for research on the alliance lies in the quantification of potentially different qualities (sometimes called the apples and oranges problem; Schmidt & Hunter, 2014). Given the considerable diversity in what researchers and psychotherapists call the "alliance," we might have collected and summarized different kinds of idiographic and nomothetic understandings. This is a complicated concern, especially in light of the fact that the ESs are quite diverse, albeit positively correlated. A practical response to this challenge is that this chapter provides a "birds-eye view" of the quantitative question: What have researches found about the alliance–outcome relation in individual psychotherapy?

There are also some technical constrains to these analyses. We chose to use independent data. To achieve this, we performed a three-level multivariate meta-analysis. These analyses account for different outcome assessments applied in the primary studies. As a result, the adjusted alliance–outcome correlation was slightly lower in magnitude in comparison to analyses that do not adjust for these potential confounds. In the long run, the use of independent data is statistically justified and provides further evidence that the alliance–outcome ES is far from being zero-correlated even when applying rigorous and conservative statistical models.

In the future, research designs are needed that can test the causal impact of the alliance in psychotherapy outcome. More research is needed in culturally specific samples inside and outside Western countries. More research is also needed that examines the boundary conditions of the alliance measures and their interaction to interpersonal and general process indicators, such as empathy, the real relationship, and corrective experiences.

DIVERSITY CONSIDERATIONS

The relationship between a therapist and a client is embedded in cultural norms, memories, and expectations about the psychotherapist/helper role. Our meta-analysis contained hundreds of studies from North American and European countries but not many from other (maybe less industrialized or "Western") countries. As well, except for substance abuse treatment studies, the percentage of ethnic minority clients appeared low indeed. And hardly any studies reported characteristics of their samples beyond age, gender, and race in terms of sexual orientation, gender identity, and other intersecting dimensions of patient diversity. The same (and even more pronounced) can be said for psychotherapists, where the description of the therapists often only includes the number of therapists.

Except in SUD studies, ethnic minorities are underrepresented and may prove an artifact of the research samples (Barber et al., 1999). Furthermore, SUD samples often used dropout dichotomy (yes/no) as outcome, which may have further diminished the overall outcome association. This is an important finding because it demonstrates that a straightforward focus to categorization systems, such as diagnoses categories or ethnic minority status, without a carful integration of the patients overall psychosocial situation may result in single-edged interpretations. Even though the present meta-analysis is a summary, the present analysis could not disentangle these various psychosocial factors.

TRAINING IMPLICATIONS

Given the consistent correlation between in-therapy alliance and treatment outcome, it seems eminently sensible that mental health professionals could benefit from training to learn how to establish and maintain a strong alliance with their clients. Unfortunately, this is easier said than done.

At present, alliance training in graduate training programs is often nonexistent or, if in existence, the training is not systematic. Reports of clinical and counseling psychology programs in the United States and Canada indicate that systematic training in alliance is desirable and important but relatively rare (Constantino, Morrison, Coyne, & Howard, 2017; Morrison, 2014). The alliance is part of some training and supervision guidelines (American Psychological Association, 2015; Beinart & Clohessy, 2017) and embedded in some therapeutic frameworks (for an overview, see Muran & Barber, 2010). Examples of training programs that prominently focus on the alliance include the relational psychodynamic (Safran & Muran, 2000), humanistic (such as motivational interviewing; Miller & Rollnick, 2012), and cognitive-behavioral (e.g., Kazantzis et al., 2017; Tarrier & Johnson, 2017) approaches.

Three published pilot studies have examined alliance training and investigated its effects on alliance formation (Crits-Christoph et al., 2006; Hilsenroth et al., 2002; Safran et al., 2014). Despite their quasi-experimental design and small samples, these efforts show promise that training can improve a therapist's development of a strong alliance with their clients. Moreover, as the number of studies in this meta-analysis and the integration of the alliance assessments in routine practice clearly attest, the alliance is part of the professional life of many psychotherapy trainees, therapists, and supervisors.

From the meta-analytic results and our collective training experiences, we offer the following training considerations.

- Training can include both long-term (therapy goals, task, bond) as well as short-term perspectives (session goals, task, bond) skills. Alliance training needs coordination at a higher level of abstraction (e.g., coordination of therapy goals and tasks) as well as at an action level (e.g., collaborative communication skills).
- Trainees and their supervisors should be aware that there is no alliance without a psychotherapeutic approach. That is, agreement about the tasks and goal of therapy requires an overall concept of treatment.
- The alliance is part of the individual case formulation. Therapists need to be responsive to patients' individual problems as well as their preferences, abilities and motivational readiness.
- Students can be taught to hold a positive attitude toward receiving participants' honest evaluations of the alliance and of treatment progress.
- Students can be taught to assess the alliance in ways that each participant contributes. Disagreement between therapist assessment and the client assessment is not something negative but instead may be a marker that a discussion of the relationship might prove helpful or necessary (e.g., Atzil-Slonim et al., 2015; Hartmann et al., 2015; Kivlighan et al., 2016).
- Goal and task agreement does not mean that the therapist automatically accepts the patient's goals and tasks, or vice versa. A strong alliance is often a result of negotiation. The shared decisions on treatment goals and tasks should attend ethical considerations.

THERAPEUTIC PRACTICES

The accumulated volume of research on the alliance is impressive. It is certainly among the richest bodies of empirical research on psychotherapy process outcome. Alliance research indicates that collaborative practice has a positive impact on outcome.

- Build and maintain the alliance throughout the course of psychotherapy. That entails creating a warm emotional bond or collaborative attachment with the patient.

- Develop early on in treatment agreement on therapy goals and on respective tasks of patient and practitioner. Those reliably predict therapeutic success.
- Respond to clients' motivational readiness/stage of change and their capabilities during the first sessions of therapy.
- Create wording or therapist slang with a customized quality of inclusiveness and negotiation (e.g., Stiles & Horvath, 2017).
- Collaborate in words and in nonverbal language. Humans detect and perceive nonverbal behaviors—maybe not in every moment but in many moments.
- Address ruptures in the alliance directly and immediately (e.g., Eubanks et al., 2018).
- The alliance of each evaluator (therapist, patient) may be impacted by different social reference groups that may result in divergent alliance ratings. These divergences should be interpreted carefully since they do not have to indicate disagreement.
- Assess regularly from the client's perspective the strength or quality of the alliance. Assessing the alliance in routine practice may help to detect unsatisfactory progress and identify premature terminations. Existing clinical support tools can then help restore the alliance and move patients to improved outcomes (e.g., Lambert et al., 2018; Pinsof et al., 2015; Rise et al., 2012).

REFERENCES

References marked with an asterisk indicate studies included in the meta-analyses.

*Accurso, E. C., Fitzsimmons-Craft, E. E., Ciao, A., Cao, L., Crosby, R. D., Smith, T. L., . . . Peterson, C. B. (2015). Therapeutic alliance in a randomized clinical trial for bulimia nervosa. *Journal of Consulting and Clinical Psychology, 83*(3), 637–642. https://www.doi.org/10.1037/ccp0000021; 10.1037/ccp0000021.supp

Ackerman, S. J., & Hilsenroth, M. J. (2001). A review of therapist characteristics and techniques negatively impacting the therapeutic alliance. *Psychotherapy, 38*(2), 171–185. https://www.doi.org/10.1037/0033-3204.38.2.171

Ackerman, S. J., & Hilsenroth, M. J. (2003). A review of therapist characteristics and techniques positively impacting the therapeutic alliance. *Clinical Psychology Review, 23*, 1–33.

Alexander, L. B., & Luborsky, L. (1986). The Penn Helping Alliance Scales. In L. S. Greenberg & W. Pinsof (Eds.), *The Psychotherapeutic Process: A Research Handbook* (pp. 325–366). New York: Guilford.

American Psychological Association. (2015). Guidelines for clinical supervision in health service psychology. *American Psychologist, 70*(1), 33–46. https://www.doi.org/10.1037/a0038112

*Andrews, M., Baker, A. L., Halpin, S. A., Lewin, T. J., Richmond, R., Kay-Lambkin, F. J., . . . Callister, R. (2016). Early therapeutic alliance, treatment retention, and 12-month outcomes in a healthy lifestyles intervention for people with psychotic disorders. *Journal of Nervous and Mental Disease, 204*(12), 894–902. https://www.doi.org/10.1097/NMD.0000000000000585

*Applebaum, A. J., DuHamel, K. N., Winkel, G., Rini, C., Greene, P. B., Mosher, C. E., & Redd, W. H. (2012). Therapeutic alliance in telephone-administered cognitive–behavioral

therapy for hematopoietic stem cell transplant survivors. *Journal of Consulting and Clinical Psychology, 80*(5), 811–816. https://www.doi.org/10.1037/a0027956

*Arnow, B. A., Steidtmann, D., Blasey, C., Manber, R., Constantino, M. J., Klein, D. N., & Kocsis, J. H. (2013). The relationship between the therapeutic alliance and treatment outcome in two distinct psychotherapies for chronic depression. *Journal of Consulting and Clinical Psychology, 81*(4), 627–638. https://www.doi.org/10.1037/a0031530

Asnaani, A., & Hofmann, S. G. (2012). Collaboration in multicultural therapy: Establishing a strong therapeutic alliance across cultural lines. *Journal of Clinical Psychology, 68*(2), 187–197. doi: https://doi.org/10.1002/jclp.21829

Atzil-Slonim, D., Bar-Kalifa, E., Rafaeli, E., Lutz, W., Rubel, J., Schiefele, A.-K., & Peri, T. (2015). Therapeutic bond judgments: Congruence and incongruence. *Journal of Consulting and Clinical Psychology, 83*(4), 773–784. https://www.doi.org/10.1037/ccp0000015

*Auszra, L., Greenberg, L. S., & Herrmann, I. (2013). Client emotional productivity-optimal client in-session emotional processing in experiential therapy. *Psychotherapy Research, 23*(6), 732–746. https://www.doi.org/10.1080/10503307.2013.816882

Baldwin, S. A., & Imel, Z. E. (2013). Therapist effects: findings and methods. In M. J. Lambert (Ed.), *Bergin and Garfield's handbook of psychotherapy and behavior change* (6th ed., pp. 258–297). Hoboken, NJ: Wiley.

Baldwin, S. A., Wampold, B. E., & Imel, Z. E. (2007). Untangling the alliance–outcome correlation: Exploring the relative importance of therapist and patient variability in the alliance. *Journal of Consulting and Clinical Psychology, 75*(6), 842–852. https://www.doi.org/10.1037/0022-006X.75.6.842

Barber, J. P., Luborsky, L., Crits-Christoph, P., Thase, M., Weiss, R., Frank, A., . . . Gallop, R. (1999). Therapeutic alliance as a predictor of outcome in treatment of cocaine dependence. *Psychotherapy Research, 9*(1), 54–73. doi:10.1080/ 10503309912331332591

Barber, J. P., Zilcha-Mano, S., Gallop, R., Barrett, M., McCarthy, K. S., & Dinger, U. (2014). The associations among improvement and alliance expectations, alliance during treatment, and treatment outcome for major depressive disorder. *Psychotherapy Research, 24*(3), 257–268. doi:10.1080/10503307.2013.871080

*Barnicot, K., Gonzalez, R., McCabe, R., & Priebe, S. (2016). Skills use and common treatment processes in dialectical behaviour therapy for borderline personality disorder. *Journal of Behavior Therapy and Experimental Psychiatry, 52*, 147–156. https://www.doi.org/10.1016/ j.jbtep.2016.04.006

Barrett-Lennard, G. T. (1978). The relationship inventory: Later development and adaptations. *JSAS Catalog of Selected Documents in Psychology, 8*, 68.

*Bedics, J. D., Atkins, D. C., Harned, M. S., & Linehan, M. M. (2015). The therapeutic alliance as a predictor of outcome in dialectical behavior therapy versus nonbehavioral psychotherapy by experts for borderline personality disorder. *Psychotherapy, 52*(1), 67–77. https://www.doi.org/10.1037/a0038457

Beinart, H., & Clohessy, S. (2017). *Effective supervisory relationships: Best evidence and practice.* Hoboken, NJ: Wiley.

Beltz, A. M., Wright, A. G., Sprague, B. N., & Molenaar, P. C. (2016). Bridging the nomothetic and idiographic approaches to the analysis of clinical data. *Assessment, 23*(4), 447–458. https://www.doi.org/10.1177/1073191116648209

*Bertrand, K., Brunelle, N., Richer, I., Beaudoin, I., Lemieux, A., & Ménard, J.-M. (2013). Assessing covariates of drug use trajectories among adolescents admitted to a drug addiction center: mental health problems, therapeutic alliance, and treatment persistence. *Substance Use & Misuse, 48*(1–2), 117–128. https://www.doi.org/10.3109/10826084.2012.733903

Bickmore, T., Gruber, A., & Picard, R. (2005). Establishing the computer–patient working alliance in automated health behavior change interventions. *Patient Education and Counseling, 59*(1), 21–30. https://www.doi.org/10.1016/j.pec.2004.09.008

Birkhäuer, J., Gaab, J., Kossowsky, J., Hasler, S., Krummenacher, P., Werner, C., & Gerger, H. (2017) Trust in the health care professional and health outcome: A meta-analysis. *PLoS ONE, 12*(2), e0170988. https://www.doi.org/10.1371/journal.pone.0170988

*Blais, M. A., Jacobo, M. C., & Smith, S. R. (2010). Exploring therapeutic alliance in brief inpatient psychotherapy: A preliminary study. *Clinical Psychology & Psychotherapy, 17*(5), 386–394. https://www.doi.org/10.1002/cpp.666

Bohart, A. C., & Wade, A. G. (2013). The client in psychotherapy. In M. J. Lambert (Ed.), *Bergin and Garfield's handbook of psychotherapy and behavior change* (6th ed., pp. 219–257). Hoboken, NJ: Wiley.

Bordin, E. S. (1975, September). *The working alliance: Basis for a general theory of psychotherapy.* Paper presented at the Society for Psychotherapy Research, Washington, DC.

Bordin, E. S. (1976). The generalizability of the psychoanalytic concept of the working alliance. *Psychotherapy, 16,* 252–260.

Bordin, E. S. (1989, June). *Building therapeutic alliances: The base for integration.* Paper presented at the Society for Psychotherapy Research, Berkley, CA.

Bordin, E. S. (1994). Theory and research on the therapeutic working alliance: New directions. In A. O. Horvath & L. S. Greenberg (Eds.), *The working alliance: Theory, research, and practice.* (pp. 13–37). New York, NY: Wiley.

*Bowen, S., & Kurz, A. S. (2012). Between-session practice and therapeutic alliance as predictors of mindfulness after mindfulness-based relapse prevention. *Journal of Clinical Psychology, 68*(3), 236–245. https://www.doi.org/10.1002/jclp.20855

*Brady, F., Warnock-Parkes, E., Barker, C., & Ehlers, A. (2015). Early in-session predictors of response to trauma-focused cognitive therapy for posttraumatic stress disorder. *Behaviour Research and Therapy, 75,* 40–47. https://www.doi.org/10.1016/j.brat.2015.10.001

*Brown, A., Mountford, V., & Waller, G. (2013). Therapeutic alliance and weight gain during cognitive behavioural therapy for anorexia nervosa. *Behaviour Research and Therapy, 51*(4–5), 216–220. https://www.doi.org/10.1016/j.brat.2013.01.008

*Burns, J. W., Nielson, W. R., Jensen, M. P., Heapy, A., Czlapinski, R., & Kerns, R. D. (2015). Specific and general therapeutic mechanisms in cognitive behavioral treatment of chronic pain. *Journal of Consulting and Clinical Psychology, 83*(1), 1–11. https://www.doi.org/10.1037/a0037208

*Byrd, K. R., Patterson, C. L., & Turchik, J. A. (2010). Working alliance as a mediator of client attachment dimensions and psychotherapy outcome. *Psychotherapy, 47*(4), 631–636. https://www.doi.org/10.1037/a0022080

*Calamaras, M. R., Tully, E. C., Tone, E. B., Price, M., & Anderson, P. L. (2015). Evaluating changes in judgmental biases as mechanisms of cognitive-behavioral therapy for social anxiety disorder. *Behaviour Research and Therapy, 71,* 139–149. https://www.doi.org/10.1016/j.brat.2015.06.006

*Carneiro, C., Darwiche, J., De Roten, Y., Vaudan, C., Duc-Marwood, A., & Despland, J.-N. (2011). De la clinique à la recherche dans un centre de thérapie de couple et de famille. *Thérapie Familiale: Revue Internationale en Approche Systémique, 32*(1), 101–110. https://www.doi.org/10.3917/tf.111.0101

*Carryer, J. R., & Greenberg, L. S. (2010). Optimal levels of emotional arousal in experiential therapy of depression. *Journal of Consulting and Clinical Psychology, 78*(2), 190–199. https://www.doi.org/10.1037/a0018401

*Carter, J. D., Crowe, M. T., Jordan, J., McIntosh, V. V. W., Frampton, C., & Joyce, P. R. (2015). Predictors of response to CBT and IPT for depression; the contribution of therapy process. *Behaviour Research and Therapy, 74*, 72–79. https://www.doi.org/10.1016/j.brat.2015.09.003

*Cavelti, M., Homan, P., & Vauth, R. (2016). The impact of thought disorder on therapeutic alliance and personal recovery in schizophrenia and schizoaffective disorder: An exploratory study. *Psychiatry Research, 239*, 92–98. https://www.doi.org/10.1016/j.psychres.2016.02.070

*Chao, P. J., Steffen, J. J., & Heiby, E. M. (2012). The effects of working alliance and client-clinician ethnic match on recovery status. *Community Mental Health Journal, 48*(1), 91–97. https://www.doi.org/10.1007/s10597-011-9423-8

*Coco, G. L., Gullo, S., Prestano, C., & Gelso, C. J. (2011). Relation of the real relationship and the working alliance to the outcome of brief psychotherapy. *Psychotherapy, 48*(4), 359–367. https://www.doi.org/10.1037/a0022426

*Constantino, M. J., Laws, H. B., Coyne, A. E., Greenberg, R. P., Klein, D. N., Manber, R., . . . Arnow, B. A. (2016). Change in patients' interpersonal impacts as a mediator of the alliance–outcome association in treatment for chronic depression. *Journal of Consulting and Clinical Psychology, 84*(12), 1135–1144. https://www.doi.org/10.1037/ccp0000149

Constantino, M. J., Morrison, N. R., Coyne, A. E., & Howard, T. (2017). Exploring therapeutic alliance training in clinical and counseling psychology graduate programs. *Training and Education in Professional Psychology, 11*(4), 219–226. https://www.doi.org/10.1037/tep0000157

*Cook, S., Heather, N., & McCambridge, J. (2015). The role of the working alliance in treatment for alcohol problems. *Psychology of Addictive Behaviors, 29*(2), 371–381. https://www.doi.org/10.1037/adb0000058

*Cooper, A. A., Strunk, D. R., Ryan, E. T., DeRubeis, R. J., Hollon, S. D., & Gallop, R. (2016). The therapeutic alliance and therapist adherence as predictors of dropout from cognitive therapy for depression when combined with antidepressant medication. *Journal of Behavior Therapy and Experimental Psychiatry, 50*, 113–119. https://www.doi.org/10.1016/j.jbtep.2015.06.005

Coyne, A. E., Constantino, M. J., Ravitz, P., & McBride, C. (2018). The interactive effect of patient attachment and social support on early alliance quality in interpersonal psychotherapy. *Journal of Psychotherapy Integration, 28*(1), 46–59. https://www.doi.org/10.1037/int0000074

*Corso, K. A., Bryan, C. J., Corso, M. L., Kanzler, K. E., Houghton, D. C., Ray-Sannerud, B., & Morrow, C. E. (2012). Therapeutic alliance and treatment outcome in the primary care behavioral health model. *Families, Systems, & Health, 30*(2), 87–100. https://www.doi.org/10.1037/a0028632

*Crameri, A., von Wyl, A., Koemeda, M., Schulthess, P., & Tschuschke, V. (2015). Sensitivity analysis in multiple imputation in effectiveness studies of psychotherapy. *Frontiers in Psychology, 6*, art. 1042.

Crits-Christoph, P., Baranackie, K., Kurcias, J., Beck, A., Carroll, K., Perry, K., . . . Zitrin, C. (1991). Meta-analysis of therapist effects in psychotherapy outcome studies. *Psychotherapy Research, 1*(2), 81–91.

Crits-Cristoph, P., Cooper, A., & Luborsky, L. (1988). The accuracy of therapists' interpretations and the outcome of dynamic psychotherapy. *Archives of General Psychiatry, 56*, 490–495. https://www.doi.org/10.1080/10503309112331335511

Crits-Christoph, P., Gallop, R., Gaines, A., Rieger, A., & Connolly Gibbons, M. B. (2018). Instrumental variable analyses for causal inference: Application to multi-level analyses of the alliance–outcome relation, *Psychotherapy Research*, doi: 10.1080/10503307.2018.1544724

Crits-Christoph, P., Gibbons, M. B. C., Crits-Christoph, K., Narducci, J., Schamberger, M., & Gallop, R. (2006). Can therapists be trained to improve their alliances? A preliminary study of alliance-fostering psychotherapy. *Psychotherapy Research, 16*, 268–281. https://www.doi.org/10.1080/10503300 500268557

Crits-Christoph, P., Gibbons, M. B. C., Hamilton, J., Ring-Kurtz, S., & Gallop, R. (2011). The dependability of alliance assessments: The alliance–outcome correlation is larger than you might think. *Journal of Consulting and Clinical Psychology, 79*(3), 267–278. https://www.doi.org/10.1037/a0023668

*Crits-Christoph, P., Hamilton, J. L., Ring-Kurtz, S., Gallop, R., McClure, B., Kulaga, A., & Rotrosen, J. (2011). Program, counselor, and patient variability in the alliance: A multi-level study of the alliance in relation to substance use outcomes. *Journal of Substance Abuse Treatment, 40*(4), 405–413. https://www.doi.org/10.1016/j.jsat.2011.01.003

*Crits-Christoph, P., Johnson, J., Gallop, R., Gibbons, M. B. C., Ring-Kurtz, S., Hamilton, J. L., & Tu, X. (2011). A generalizability theory analysis of group process ratings in the treatment of cocaine dependence. *Psychotherapy Research, 21*(3), 252–266. https://www.doi.org/10.1080/10503307.2010.551429

*Cronin, E., Brand, B. L., & Mattanah, J. F. (2014). The impact of the therapeutic alliance on treatment outcome in patients with dissociative disorders. *European Journal of Psychotraumatology, 5*, 22676. https://www.doi.org/10.3402/ejpt.v5.22676

Deacon, B. J. (2013). The biomedical model of mental disorder: A critical analysis of its validity, utility, and effects on psychotherapy research. *Clinical Psychology Review, 33*, 846–861. doi: http://dx.doi.org/10.1016/j.cpr.2012.09.007

Del Re, A. C. (2013). *Compute.es: Compute effect sizes*. R Package Version 0.2-2. Retrieved from http://cran.r-project.org/web/packages/compute.es

Del Re, A. C., Flückiger, C., Horvath, A. O., Symonds, D., & Wampold, B. E. (2012). Therapist effects in the therapeutic alliance-outcome relationship: A restricted-maximum likelihood meta-analysis. *Clinical Psychology Review, 32*, 642–649. http://dx.doi.org/10.1016/j.cpr.2012.07 .002

Del Re, A. C., & Hoyt, W. T. (2010). *MAc: Meta-analysis with correlations*. R Package Version 1.0.5. Retrieved from http://CRAN.R-project.org/package=MAc

*DeSorcy, D. R., Olver, M. E., & Wormith, J. S. (2016). Working alliance and its relationship with treatment outcome in a sample of aboriginal and non-aboriginal sexual offenders. *Sexual Abuse: Journal of Research and Treatment, 28*(4), 291–313. https://www.doi.org/10.1177/1079063214556360

Dinger, U., Strack, M., Leichsenring, F., & Schauenburg, H. (2007). Influences of patients' and therapists' interpersonal problems and therapeutic alliance on outcome in psychotherapy. *Psychotherapy Research, 17*(2), 148–159. https://www.doi.org/0.1080/10503300600865393

*Doran, J. M., Safran, J. D., & Muran, J. C. (2017). An investigation of the relationship between the alliance negotiation scale and psychotherapy process and outcome. *Journal of Clinical Psychology, 73*(4), 449–465. https://www.doi.org/10.1002/jclp.22340

*Ellis, D. A., Berio, H., Carcone, A. I., & Naar-King, S. (2012). Adolescent and parent motivation for change affects psychotherapy outcomes among youth with poorly controlled diabetes. *Journal of Pediatric Psychology, 37*(1), 75–84.

Eubanks, C. F., Muran, J. C., & Safran, J. D. (2018). Alliance rupture repair: A meta-analysis. *Psychotherapy, 55*(4), 508–519. doi: http://dx.doi.org/10.1037/pst0000185

Elwyn, G., Frosch, D., Thomson, R., Joseph-Williams, N., Lloyd, A., . . . & Barry, M. (2012). Shared decision making: a model for clinical practice. *Journal of General Internal Medicine, 27*(10), 1361–1367.

Falkenström, F., Granström, F., & Holmqvist, R. (2013). Therapeutic alliance predicts symptomatic improvement session by session. *Journal of Counseling Psychology, 60*(3), 317–328. https://www.doi.org/10.1037/a0032258

Falkenström, F., Hatcher, R. L., & Holmqvist, R. (2015). Confirmatory Factor Analysis of the Patient Version of the Working Alliance Inventory–Short Form Revised. *Assessment, 22*(5), 581–593. https://www.doi.org/10.1177/1073191114552472

Falkenström, F., Kuria, M., Othieno, C., & Kumar, M. (2019). Working alliance predicts symptomatic improvement in public hospital–delivered psychotherapy in Nairobi, Kenya. *Journal of Consulting and Clinical Psychology, 87*(1), 46–55. doi: http://dx.doi.org/10.1037/ccp0000363

Falkenström, F., & Larsson, M. H. (2017). The working alliance: From global outcome prediction to micro-analyses of within-session fluctuations. *Psychoanalytic Inquiry, 37*(3), 167–178. http://dx.doi.org/10.1080/07351690.2017.1285186

Fisher, R. A. (1924). On a Distribution Yielding the Error Functions of Several Well Known Statistics. *Proceedings of the International Congress of Mathematics, Toronto, 2*, 805–813.

Flückiger, C., Del Re, A.C., Horvath, A. O., Symonds, D., Ackert, M., & Wampold, B. E. (2013). Substance use disorders and racial/ethnic minorities matter: A meta-analytic examination of the relation between alliance and outcome. *Journal of Counseling Psychology, 60*, 610–616. https://www.doi.org/10.1037/a0033161

Flückiger, C., Del Re, A. C., Wampold, B. E., Symonds, D., & Horvath, A. O. (2012). How central is the alliance in psychotherapy? A multilevel longitudinal meta-analysis. *Journal of Counseling Psychology, 59*(1), 10–17. https://www.doi.org/10.1037/a0025749

Flückiger, C., Del Re, A.C., Wampold, B. E., Znoj, H.-J., Caspar, F., & Jörg, U. (2012). Valuing clients' perspective and the effects on the therapeutic alliance—A randomized controlled adjunctive instruction. *Journal of Counseling Psychology, 59*(1), 18–26. https://www.doi.org/10.1037/a0023648

*Flückiger, C., Grosse Holtforth, M., Znoj, H., Caspar, F., & Wampold, B. (2013). Is the relation between early post-session reports and treatment outcome an epiphenomenon of intake distress and early response? A multi-predictor analysis in outpatient psychotherapy. *Psychotherapy Research, 23*(1), 1–13. https://www.doi.org/10.1080/10503307.2012.693773

Flückiger, C., Hilpert, P., Goldberg, S., Caspar, F., Wolfer, C., Held, J., & Visla, A. (2019). Investigating the impact of aggregated early alliance on predicting distress versus subjective change at post treatment. *Journal of Counseling Psychology.* doi: 10.1037/cou0000336

*Flückiger, C., Meyer, A., Wampold, B. E., Gassmann, D., Messerli-Bürgy, N., & Munsch, S. (2011). Predicting premature termination within a randomized controlled trial for binge-eating patients. *Behavior Therapy*, *42*(4), 716–725. https://www.doi.org/10.1016/j.beth.2011.03.008

Forster, C., Berthollier, N., & Rawlinson, D. (2014). A systematic review of potential mechanisms of change in psychotherapeutic interventions for personality disorder. *Journal of Psychology & Psychotherapy*, *4*, 133. https://www.doi.org/10.4172/2161-0487.1000133

Freud, S. (1958). The dynamics of transference [Zur Dynamik der Übertragung]. (J. Starchey, Trans.). In J. Starchey (Ed.), *The standard edition of the complete psychological works of Sigmund Freud* (Vol. 12, pp. 99–108). London, England: Hogarth. (Original work published 1912)

Freud, S. (1913). On the beginning of treatment: Further recommendations on the technique of psychoanalysis [Zur Einleitung der Behandlung—Weitere Ratschläge zur Technik der Psychoanalyse]. In J. Strachey (Ed.), *The standard edition of the complete psychological works of Sigmund Freud* (Vol. 12, pp. 122–144). London, England: Hogarth.

Freud, S. (1927). *The future of an illusion* [Die Zukunft der Illusion]. (W. D. Robson-Scott & J. Strachey, Trans.). London, England: Hogarth.

Freud, S. (1925). *Selbstdarstellung* [An Autobiographical Study]. Wien: Internationaler Psychoanalytischer Verlag.

Gaston, L., Goldfried, M. R., Greenberg, L. S., Horvath, A. O., Raue, P. J., & Watson, J. (1995). The therapeutic alliance in psychodynamic, cognitive-behavioral and experiential therapies. *Journal of Psychotherapy Integration*, *15*, 1–26.

Gibbons, C. J., Nich, C., Steinberg, K., Roffman, R. A., Corvino, J., Babor, T. F., & Carroll, K. M. (2010). Treatment process, alliance and outcome in brief versus extended treatments for marijuana dependence. *Addiction*, *105*(10), 1799–1808. https://www.doi.org/10.1111/j.1360-0443.2010.03047.x

Glass, G. V. (1976). Primary, secondary, and meta-analysis of research. *Educational Researcher*, *5*(10), 3–8.

Gold, S. H., Hilsenroth, M. J., Kuutmann, K., & Owen, J. J. (2015). Therapeutic alliance in the personal therapy of graduate clinicians: relationship to the alliance and outcomes of their patients. *Clinical Psychology & Psychotherapy*, *22*(4), 304–316. https://www.doi.org/10.1002/cpp.1888

Goldberg, S. B., Davis, J. M., & Hoyt, W. T. (2013). The role of therapeutic alliance in mindfulness interventions: therapeutic alliance in mindfulness training for smokers. *Journal of Clinical Psychology*, *69*(9), 936–950. https://www.doi.org/10.1002/jclp.21973

Goldman, G. A., & Gregory, R. J. (2010). Relationships between techniques and outcomes for borderline personality disorder. *American Journal of Psychotherapy*, *64*(4), 359–371.

Graves, T. A., Tabi, N., Thompson-Brenner, H., Franko, D. L., . . . Thomas, J. J. (2017). A meta-analysis of the relation between therapeutic alliance and treatment outcome in eating disorders. *International Journal of Eating Disorders*, *50*(4), 323–340. doi: https://doi.org/10.1002/eat.22672

Greenson, R. R. (1965). The working alliance and the transference neuroses. *Psychoanalysis Quarterly*, *34*, 155–181.

Greenson, R. R. (1967). *Technique and practice of psychoanalysis*. New York, NY: International University Press.

Grosse holtforth, M., & Flückiger, C. (2012). Two kinds of corrective experiences in action: Big Bang vs. Constant Dripping. In: L. G. Castonguay & C. E. Hill (Eds.), *Transformation in psychotherapy: Corrective experiences across cognitive-behavioral, humanistic, and psycho-dynamic approaches.* Washington: APA Books.

Gullo, S., Lo Coco, G., & Gelso, C. (2012). Early and later predictors of outcome in brief therapy: the role of real relationship. *Journal of Clinical Psychology, 68*(6), 614–619. https://www.doi.org/10.1002/jclp.21860

Gysin-Maillart, A., Schwab, S., Soravia, L., Megert, M., & Michel, K. (2016). A novel brief therapy for patients who attempt suicide: A 24-months follow-up randomized controlled study of the Attempted Suicide Short Intervention Program (ASSIP). *Plos Medicine, 13*(3), e1001968-e1001968. https://www.doi.org/10.1371/journal.pmed.1001968

Häring, N., Agarwalla, P., Müller, E., & Küchenhoff, J. (2010). Die emotionale Qualität der therapeutischen Arbeitsbeziehung und ihre Auswirkung auf Prozess und Outcome nach dem ersten Jahr ambulanter Psychotherapien. *Schweizer Archiv für Neurologie und Psychiatrie, 161*(5), 154–165.

Hartmann, A., Orlinsky, D., Weber, S., Sandholz, A., & Zeeck, A. (2010). Session and inter-session experience related to treatment outcome in bulimia nervosa. *Psychotherapy, 47*(3), 355–370. https://www.doi.org/10.1037/a0021166

Hartmann, A., Joos, A., Orlinsky, D. E., & Zeeck, A. (2015). Accuracy of therapist perceptions of patients' alliance: Exploring the divergence. *Psychotherapy Research, 25*(4), 408–419. https://www.doi.org/10.1080/10503307.2014.927601

Hartzler, B., Witkiewitz, K., Villarroel, N., & Donovan, D. (2011). Self-efficacy change as a mediator of associations between therapeutic bond and one-year outcomes in treatments for alcohol dependence. *Psychology of Addictive Behaviors, 25*(2), 269–278. https://www.doi.org/10.1037/a0022869

Hatcher, R. L., & Barends, A. W. (1996). Patient's view of the alliance in psycho-therapy: Exploratory factor analysis of three alliance measures. *Journal of Consulting and Clinical Psychology, 64*, 1326–1336.

Hatcher, R. L., & Barends, A. W. (2006). How a return to theory could help alliance research. *Psychotherapy, 43*(3), 292–299.

Hatcher, R. L., Barends, A., Hansell, J., & Gutfreund, M. J. (1995). Patients' and therapists' shared and unique views of the therapeutic alliance: An investigation using confirmatory factor analysis in a nested design. *Journal of Consulting and Clinical Psychology, 63*, 636–643.

Haug, T., Nordgreen, T., Öst, L.-G., Tangen, T., Kvale, G., Hovland, O. J., . . . Havik, O. E. (2016). Working alliance and competence as predictors of outcome in cognitive behavioral therapy for social anxiety and panic disorder in adults. *Behaviour Research and Therapy, 77*, 40–51. https://www.doi.org/10.1016/j.brat.2015.12.004

Hedges, L. V., & Olkin, I. (1985). *Statistical methods for meta-analysis.* New York, NY: Academic Press.

Heinonen, E., Lindfors, O., Härkänen, T., Virtala, E., Jääskeläinen T., & Knekt, P. (2014). Therapists' professional and personal characteristics as predictors of working alliance in short-term and long-term psychotherapies. *Clinical Psychology and Psychotherapy, 21*, 475–494, doi: 10.1002/cpp.1852

Heins, M. J., Knoop, H., & Bleijenberg, G. (2013). The role of the therapeutic relationship in cognitive behaviour therapy for chronic fatigue syndrome. *Behaviour Research and Therapy, 51*(7), 368–376. https://www.doi.org/10.1016/j.brat.2013.02.001

Hendriksen, M., Peen, J., Van, R., Barber, J. P., & Dekker, J. (2014). Is the alliance always a pre-dictor of change in psychotherapy for depression? *Psychotherapy Research, 24*(2), 160–170. https://www.doi.org/10.1080/10503307.2013.847987

Hersoug, A. G., Høglend, P., Gabbard, G. O., & Lorentzen, S. (2013). The combined predictive effect of patient characteristics and alliance on long-term dynamic and interpersonal functioning after dynamic psychotherapy. *Clinical Psychology & Psychotherapy, 20*(4), 297–307. https://www.doi.org/10.1002/cpp.1770

Hicks, A. L., Deane, F. P., & Crowe, T. P. (2012). Change in working alliance and recovery in severe mental illness: an exploratory study. *Journal of Mental Health, 21*(2), 127–134. https://www.doi.org/10.3109/09638237.2011.621469

Hilsenroth, M., Ackerman, S., Clemence, A., Strassle, C., & Handler, L. (2002). Effects of structured clinician training on patient and therapist perspectives of alliance early in psychotherapy. *Psychotherapy, 39*, 309–323. https://www.doi.org/10.1037/0033-3204.39.4.309

Hoffart, A., Borge, F.-M., Sexton, H., Clark, D. M., & Wampold, B. E. (2012). Psychotherapy for social phobia: How do alliance and cognitive process interact to produce outcome? *Psychotherapy Research, 22*(1), 82–94. https://www.doi.org/10.1080/10503307.2011.626806

Hoffart, A., Øktedalen, T., Langkaas, T. F., & Wampold, B. E. (2013). Alliance and outcome in varying imagery procedures for PTSD: A study of within-person processes. *Journal of Counseling Psychology, 60*(4), 471–482. doi:10.1037/a0033604

Horvath, A. O. (2009, October). *Conceptual and methodological challenges in alliance research: Is it time for a change.* Paper presented at the European Regional Meeting of the Society for Psychotherapy Research, Bozen, Italy.

Horvath, A. O. (2018). Research on the alliance: Knowledge in search of a theory. *Psychotherapy Research, 28*, 499–516. https://www.doi.org/10.1080/10503307.2017.1373204

Horvath, A. O., & Greenberg, L. S. (1989). Development and validation of the Working Alliance Inventory. *Journal of Counseling Psychology, 36*, 223–233.

Horvath, A. O., & Luborsky, L. (1993). The role of the therapeutic alliance in psychotherapy. *Journal of Consulting and Clinical Psychology, 61*, 561–573.

Horvath, A. O., & Symonds, B. D. (1991). Relation between working alliance and outcome in psychotherapy: A meta-analysis. *Journal of Counseling Psychology, 38*, 139–149.

Horvath, A. O., & Symonds, D. (1991). Relation between working alliance and outcome in psychotherapy: A meta-analysis. *Journal of Counseling Psychology, 38*, 139–149. https://www.doi.org/10.1037/0022-0167.38.2.139

Horvath, A. O., Flückiger, C., Del Re, A. C., Jafari, H., Symonds, D., & Lee, E. (2014, June). *The relationship between helper and client: Looking beyond psychotherapy.* Paper presented at the 45th SPR Congress, Copenhagen, Denmark.

Horvath, A., Del Re, A. C., Flückiger, C., & Symonds, D. (2011). The alliance in adult psychotherapy. In J. E. Norcross (Ed.). *Relationships that works* (pp. 25–69). New York, NY: Oxford University Press.

Horvath, A. O., & Bedi, R. P. (2002). The alliance. In J. C. Norcross (Ed.), *Psychotherapy relationships that work: Therapist contributions and responsiveness to patients.* (pp. 37–69). New York, NY: Oxford University Press.

Johansson, H., & Jansson, J.-Å. (2010). Therapeutic alliance and outcome in routine psychiatric out-patient treatment: Patient factors and outcome. *Psychology and Psychotherapy, 83*(2), 193–206. https://www.doi.org/10.1348/147608309X472081

Johansson, P., Høglend, P., & Hersoug, A. G. (2011). Therapeutic alliance mediates the effect of patient expectancy in dynamic psychotherapy. *British Journal of Clinical Psychology, 50*(3), 283–297.

Kashe, S., Lucas, G., Becerik-Gerber, B., & Gratch, J. (2017). Buiding with persona: Towards effective building-occupant communication. *Computers in Human Behavior, 75*, 607–618. https://www.doi.org/10.1016/j.chb.2017.05.040

Kazantzis, N., Dattilio, F. M., & Dobson, K. S. (2017). *The therapeutic relationship in cognitive-behavioral therapy.* New York, NY: Guilford.

Kazdin, A. E. (2009). Understanding how and why psychotherapy leads to change. *Psychotherapy Research, 19*, 418–428. https://www.doi.org/10.1080/10503300802448899

Keeley, M. L., Geffken, G. R., Ricketts, E., McNamara, J. P., & Storch, E. A. (2011). The therapeutic alliance in the cognitive behavioral treatment of pediatric obsessive-compulsive disorder. *Journal of Anxiety Disorders, 25*(7), 855–863. https://www.doi.org/10.1016/j.janxdis.2011.03.017

Kirouac, M., Witkiewitz, K., & Donovan, D. M. (2016). Client evaluation of treatment for alcohol use disorder in COMBINE. *Journal of Substance Abuse Treatment, 67*, 38–43. https://www.doi.org/10.1016/j.jsat.2016.04.007

Kivlighan, D. M., Jr., Hill, C. E., Gelso, C. J., & Baumann, E. (2016). Working alliance, real relationship, session quality, and client improvement in psychodynamic psychotherapy: A longitudinal actor partner interdependence model. *Journal of Counseling Psychology, 63*(2), 149–161. https://www.doi.org/10.1037/cou0000134

Knuuttila, V., Kuusisto, K., Saarnio, P., & Nummi, T. (2012). Effect of early working alliance on retention in outpatient substance abuse treatment. *Counselling Psychology Quarterly, 25*(4), 361–375. https://www.doi.org/10.1080/09515070.2012.707116

Kramer, U., Flückiger, C., Kolly, S., Caspar, F., Marquet, P., Despland, J.-N., & de Roten, Y. (2014). Unpacking the effects of therapist responsiveness in borderline personality disorder: Motive-oriented therapeutic relationship, patient in-session experience, and the therapeutic alliance. *Psychotherapy and Psychosomatics, 83*(6), 386–387.

Kushner, S. C., Quilty, L. C., Uliaszek, A. A., McBride, C., & Bagby, R. M. (2016). Therapeutic alliance mediates the association between personality and treatment outcome in patients with major depressive disorder. *Journal of Affective Disorders, 201*, 137–144. https://www.doi.org/10.1016/j.jad.2016.05.016

Lambert, M. J., Whipple, J. L., & Kleinstäuber, M. (2018). Collecting and delivering progress feedback: A meta-analysis of routine outcome monitoring. *Psychotherapy, 55*(4), 520–537. doi: http://dx.doi.org/10.1037/pst0000167

Lambert, M. J., Morton, J. J., Hatfield, D. R., Harmon, C., Hamilton, S., & Shimokawa, K. (2004). *Administration and scoring manual for the OQ-45.* Wilmington, DE: American Professional Credentialling Services.

*Lecomte, T., Laferriere-Simard, M.-C., & Leclerc, C. (2012). What does the alliance predict in group interventions for early psychosis? *Journal of Contemporary Psychotherapy, 42*(2), 55–61. https://www.doi.org/10.1007/s10879-011-9184-2

*Leibert, T. W., Smith, J. B., & Agaskar, V. R. (2011). Relationship between the working alliance and social support on counseling outcome. *Journal of Clinical Psychology, 67*(7), 709–719. https://www.doi.org/10.1002/jclp.20800

*Lerner, M. D., Mikami, A. Y., & McLeod, B. D. (2011). The alliance in a friendship coaching intervention for parents of children with ADHD. *Behavior Therapy, 42*(3), 449–461. https://www.doi.org/10.1016/j.beth.2010.11.006

Levin, L. Genderson, H. A., & Ehrenreich-May, J. (2012). Interspersonal predictors of early therapeutic alliance in transdiagnostic cognitive-behavioral treatment for adolescents with anxiety and depression. *Psychotherapy*, *49*(2), 218–230. https://www.doi.org/10.1037/a0028265

Levy, K., Kivity, Y., Johnson, B. M., & Gooch, C. V. (2018). Adult attachment as a predictor and moderator of psychotherapy outcome: A meta-analysis. *Journal of Clinical Psychology*, *74*(11), 1996–2013. doi: https://doi.org/10.1002/jclp.22685

*Lilja, J. L., Zelleroth, C., Axberg, U., & Norlander, T. (2016). Mindfulness-based cognitive therapy is effective as relapse prevention for patients with recurrent depression in Scandinavian primary health care. *Scandinavian Journal of Psychology*, *57*(5), 464–472. https://www.doi.org/10.1111/sjop.12302

*Lorenzo-Luaces, L., DeRubeis, R. J., & Webb, C. A. (2014). Client characteristics as moderators of the relation between the therapeutic alliance and outcome in cognitive therapy for depression. *Journal of Consulting and Clinical Psychology*, *82*(2), 368–373. https://www.doi.org/10.1037/a0035994

Luborsky, L. (1976). Helping alliances in psychotherapy. In J. L. Cleghhorn (Ed.), *Successful psychotherapy* (pp. 92–116). New York, NY: Brunner/Mazel.

Luborsky, L., Barber, J. P., Siqueland, L., Johnson, S., Najavits, L. M., Frank, A., & Daley, D. (1996). The revised helping alliance questionnaire (HAq-II). Psychometric Properties. *Journal of Psychotherapy Practice and Research*, *5*, 260–271.

Luborsky, L., McLellan, A.T., Woody, G. E., O'Brien, C. P., & Auerbach, A. (1985). Therapist success and its determinants. *Archive of General Psychiatry*, *42*(6), 601–611.

*Maher, M. J., Wang, Y., Zuckoff, A., Wall, M. M., Franklin, M., Foa, E. B., & Simpson, H. B. (2012). Predictors of patient adherence to cognitive-behavioral therapy for obsessive-compulsive disorder. *Psychotherapy and Psychosomatics*, *81*(2), 124–126. https://www.doi.org/10.1159/000330214

*Mahon, M., Laux, J. M., McGuire Wise, S., Ritchie, M. H., Piazza, N. J., & Tiamiyu, M. F. (2015). Brief therapy at a university counseling center: Working alliance, readiness to change, and symptom severity. *Journal of College Counseling*, *18*(3), 233–243. https://www.doi.org/10.1002/jocc.12017

*Maitland, D. W. M., Petts, R. A., Knott, L. E., Briggs, C. A., Moore, J. A., & Gaynor, S. T. (2016). A randomized controlled trial of functional analytic psychotherapy versus watchful waiting: Enhancing social connectedness and reducing anxiety and avoidance. *Behavior Analysis: Research and Practice*, *16*(3), 103–122. https://www.doi.org/10.1037/bar0000051

*Mallinckrodt, B., & Tekie, Y. T. (2016). Item response theory analysis of Working Alliance Inventory, revised response format, and new Brief Alliance Inventory. *Psychotherapy Research*, *26*(6), 694–718. https://www.doi.org/10.1080/10503307.2015.1061718

Mander, J. V., Wittorf, A., Schlarb, A., Hautzinger, M., Zipfel, S., & Sammet, I. (2013). Change mechanisms in psychotherapy: Multiperspective assessment and relation to outcome. *Psychotherapy Research*, *23*(1), 105–116. https://www.doi.org/10.1080/10503307.2012.744111

*Manne, S., Winkel, G., Zaider, T., Rubin, S., Hernandez, E., & Bergman, C. (2010). Therapy processes and outcomes of psychological interventions for women diagnosed with gynecological cancers: A test of the generic process model of psychotherapy. *Journal of Consulting & Clinical Psychology*, *78*(2), 236–248. https://www.doi.org/10.1037/a0018223

*Marcus, D. K., Kashy, D. A., Wintersteen, M. B., & Diamond, G. S. (2011). The therapeutic alliance in adolescent substance abuse treatment: a one-with-many analysis. *Journal of Counseling Psychology*, *58*(3), 449–455. https://www.doi.org/10.1037/a0023196

Marmar, C. R., Horowitz, M. J., Weiss, D. S., & Marziali, E. (1986). The development of the therapeutic alliance rating system. In L. S. Greenberg & W. M. Pinsof (Eds.), *The psychotherapeutic process: A research handbook* (pp. 367–390). New York, NY: Guilford.

*Marmarosh, C. L., & Kivlighan, D. M. Jr. (2012). Relationships among client and counselor agreement about the working alliance, session evaluations, and change in client symptoms using response surface analysis. *Journal of Counseling Psychology, 59*(3), 352–367. https://www.doi.org/10.1037/a0028907

Martin, D. J., Garske, J. P., & Davis, M. K. (2000). Relation of the therapeutic alliance with outcome and other variables: A meta-analytic review. *Journal of Consulting and Clinical Psychology, 68*(3), 438–450. https://www.doi.org/10.1037/0022-006x.68.3.438

*McBride, C., Zuroff, D. C., Ravitz, P., Koestner, R., Moskowitz, D. S., Quilty, L., & Bagby, R. M. (2010). Autonomous and controlled motivation and interpersonal therapy for depression: Moderating role of recurrent depression. *British Journal of Clinical Psychology, 49*(4), 529–545. https://www.doi.org/10.1348/014466509X479186

*McLaughlin, A. A., Keller, S. M., Feeny, N. C., Youngstrom, E. A., & Zoellner, L. A. (2014). Patterns of therapeutic alliance: Rupture–repair episodes in prolonged exposure for posttraumatic stress disorder. *Journal of Consulting and Clinical Psychology, 82*(1), 112–121. https://www.doi.org/10.1037/a0034696

Miller, R. W., & Rollnick S. (2012). *Motivational interviewing* (3rd ed.). New York, NY: Guilford.

Morales, K., Keum, B. T., Kivlighan, D. M., Hill, C. E., & Gelso, C. J. (2018). Therapist effects due to client racial/ethic status when examining linear growth for client- and therapist-rated working alliance and real relationship. *Psychotherapy, 55*(1), 9–19. doi: 10.1037/pst0000135

Morrison, N. R. (2014). *The state of therapeutic alliance training in clinical and counseling psychology graduate programs* (Unpublished master's thesis). University of Massachusetts, Amherst.

*Mörtberg, E. (2014). Working alliance in individual and group cognitive therapy for social anxiety disorder. *Psychiatry Research, 220*(1-2), 716–718. https://www.doi.org/10.1016/j.psychres.2014.07.004

Muran, J. C., & Barber, J. P. (2010). *The therapeutic alliance: An evidence-based guide to practice.* New York, NY: Guildford.

Muran, J. C., Gorman, B. S., Safran, J. D., Twining, L., Samstag, L. W., & Winston, A. (1995). Linking in-session change to overall outcome in short-term cognitive therapy. *Journal of Consulting and Clinical Psychology, 63,* 651–657. http://dx.doi.org/10.1037/0022-006X.63.4.651

Norcross, J. C., & Wampold, B. E. (2018). A new therapy for each patient: Evidence-based relationships and responsiveness. *Journal of Clinical Psychology, 74*(11), 1889–1906.

Orlinsky, D. E., & Rønnestad, M. H. (2005). *How psychotherapists develop: A study of therapeutic work and professional growth.* Washington, DC: American Psychological Association.

Owen, J., Imel, Z., Tao, K. W., Wampold, B., Smith, A., & Rodolfa, E. (2011). Cultural ruptures in short-term therapy: Working alliance as a mediator between clients' perceptions of microaggressions and therapy outcomes. *Counselling and Psychotherapy Research, 11*(3), 204–212. https://www.doi.org/10.1080/14733145.2010.491551

*Owen, J., Thomas, L., & Rodolfa, E. (2013). Stigma for seeking therapy: Self-stigma, social stigma, and therapeutic processes. *Counseling Psychologist, 41*(6), 857–880. https://www.doi.org/10.1177/0011000012459365

*Pan, D., Huey, S. J., Jr., & Hernandez, D. (2011). Culturally adapted versus standard exposure treatment for phobic Asian Americans: Treatment efficacy, moderators, and predictors. *Cultural Diversity and Ethnic Minority Psychology, 17*(1), 11–22. https://www.doi.org/10.1037/a0022534

*Patterson, C. L., Anderson, T., & Wei, C. (2014). Clients' pretreatment role expectations, the therapeutic alliance, and clinical outcomes in outpatient therapy. *Journal of Clinical Psychology, 70*(7), 673–680. https://www.doi.org/10.1002/jclp.22054

Pinsof, W. M., Zinbarg, R. E., Shimokawa, K., Latta, T. A., Goldsmith, J. Z., Knobloch-Fedders, L. M., . . . Lebow, J. L. (2015). Confirming, validating, and norming the factor structure of systemic therapy inventory of change initial and intersession. *Family Process, 54,* 464–484. https://www.doi.org/10.1111/famp.12159

*Pinto, R. M., Campbell, A. N. C., Hien, D. A., Yu, G., & Gǫrroochurn, P. (2011). Retention in the National Institute on Drug Abuse Clinical Trials Network Women and Trauma Study: Implications for posttrial implementation. *American Journal of Orthopsychiatry, 81*(2), 211–217. https://www.doi.org/10.1111/j.1939-0025.2011.01090.x

*Polaschek, D. L., & Ross, E. C. (2010). Do early therapeutic alliance, motivation, and stages of change predict therapy change for high-risk, psychopathic violent prisoners? *Criminal Behaviour and Mental Health, 20*(2), 100–111. https://www.doi.org/10.1002/cbm.759

Pope, K. S., & Vasquez, M. J. T. (2016). *Ethics in psychotherapy and counseling: A practical guide.* New York, NY: Willey.

Probst, T., Lambert, M. J., Loew, T. H., Dahlbender, R. W., & Tritt, K. (2015). Extreme deviations form expected recovery curves and their associations with therapeutic alliance, social support, motivation and life events in psychosomatic in-patient therapy. *Psychotherapy Research, 25*(6), 714–723. https://www.doi.org/10.1080/10503307.2014.981682

Rise, M. B., Eriksen, L., Grimstad, H., & Steinsbekk, A. (2012). The short-term effect on alliance and satisfaction of using patient feedback scales in mental health out-patient treatment: A randomised controlled trial. *BMC Health Services Research, 12,* 348. https://doi.org/10.1186/1472-6963-12-348

Rosenzweig, S. (1936). Some implicit common factors in diverse methods of psychotherapy. *American Journal of Orthopsychiatry, 6*(3), 412–415. https://www.doi.org/10.1111/j.1939-0025.1936.tb05248.x

Rubel, J. A., Rosenbaum, D., & Lutz, W. (2017). Patients' in-session experiences and symptom change: Session-to-session effects on a within- and between-patient level. *Behaviour Research and Therapy, 90,* 58–66. https://www.doi.org/10.1016/j.brat.2016.12.007

*Ruchlewska, A., Kamperman, A. M., Wierdsma, A. I., van der Gaag, M., & Mulder, C. L. (2016). Determinants of completion and use of psychiatric advance statements in mental health care in the Netherlands. *Psychiatric Services, 67*(8), 858–863. https://www.doi.org/10.1176/appi.ps.201400495

*Ruglass, L. M., Miele, G. M., Hien, D. A., Campbell, A. N., Hu, M.-C., Caldeira, N., . . . Nunes, E. V. (2012). Helping alliance, retention, and treatment outcomes: A secondary analysis from the NIDA clinical trials network women and trauma study. *Substance Use & Misuse, 47*(6), 695–707. https://www.doi.org/10.3109/10826084.2012.659789

Safran, J. D., & Muran, J. C. (2000). *Negotiating the therapeutic alliance: A relational treatment guide.* New York, NY: Guilford.

Safran, J. D., Muran, J. C., DeMaria, A., Boutwell, C., Eubanks-Carter, C., & Winston, A. (2014). Investigating the impact of alliance-focused training on interpersonal process and therapists' capacity for experiential reflection. *Psychotherapy Research*, *24*, 269–285. https://www.doi.org/10.1080/ 10503307.2013.874054

*Sasso, K. E., Strunk, D. R., Braun, J. D., DeRubeis, R. J., & Brotman, M. A. (2016). A re-examination of process–outcome relations in cognitive therapy for depression: Disaggregating within-patient and between-patient effects. *Psychotherapy Research*, *26*(4), 387–398. https://www.doi.org/10.1080/10503307.2015.1026423

*Sauer, E. M., Anderson, M. Z., Gormley, B., Richmond, C. J., & Preacco, L. (2010). Client attachment orientations, working alliances, and responses to therapy: A psychology training clinic study. *Psychotherapy Research*, *20*(6), 702–711. https://www.doi.org/10.1080/10503307.2010.518635

Schmidt, F. L., & Hunter, J. E. (2014). *Methods of meta-analysis: Correcting error and bias in research findings* (3rd ed.). Newbury Park, CA: SAGE.

*Simpson, H. B., Maher, M. J., Wang, Y., Bao, Y., Foa, E. B., & Franklin, M. (2011). Patient adherence predicts outcome from cognitive behavioral therapy in obsessive-compulsive disorder. *Journal of Consulting and Clinical Psychology*, *79*(2), 247–252. https://www.doi.org/10.1037/a0022659

*Smerud, P. E., & Rosenfarb, I. S. (2011). The therapeutic alliance and family psychoeducation in the treatment of schizophrenia: An exploratory prospective change process study. *Couple and Family Psychology: Research and Practice*, *1*(S), 85–91. https://www.doi.org/10.1037/2160-4096.1.S.85

*Smith, P. N., Gamble, S. A., Cort, N. A., Ward, E. A., He, H., & Talbot, N. L. (2012). Attachment and alliance in the treatment of depressed, sexually abused women. *Depression And Anxiety*, *29*(2), 123–130. https://www.doi.org/10.1002/da.20913

*Snippe, E., Fleer, J., Tovote, K. A., Sanderman, R., Emmelkamp, P. M. G., & Schroevers, M. J. (2015). The therapeutic alliance predicts outcomes of cognitive behavior therapy but not of mindfulness-based cognitive therapy for depressive symptoms. *Psychotherapy and Psychosomatics*, *84*(5), 314–315. https://www.doi.org/10.1159/000379755

Spinhoven, P., Giesen-Bloo, J., van Dyck, R., Kooiman, K., & Arntz, A. (2007). The therapeutic alliance in schema-focused therapy and transference-focused psychotherapy for borderline personality disorder. *Journal of Consulting and Clinical Psychology*, *75*(1), 104–115. https://www.doi.org/10.1037/0022-006X.75.1.104

Sterba, R. F. (1934). The fate of the ego in analytic therapy. *International Journal of Psychoanalysis*, *115*, 117–126.

*Stiles-Shields, C., Kwasny, M. J., Cai, X., & Mohr, D. C. (2014). Therapeutic alliance in face-to-face and telephone-administered cognitive behavioral therapy. *Journal of Consulting and Clinical Psychology*, *82*(2), 349–354. https://www.doi.org/10.1037/a0035554

*Stiles-Shields, C., Touyz, S., Hay, P., Lacey, H., Crosby, R. D., Rieger, E., . . . Le Grange, D. (2013). Therapeutic alliance in two treatments for adults with severe and enduring anorexia nervosa. *International Journal of Eating Disorders*, *46*(8), 783–789. https://www.doi.org/10.1002/eat.22187

Stiles, W. B. (2009). Responsiveness as an obstacle for psychotherapy outcome research: It's worse than You think. *Clinical Psychology: Science and Practice*, *16*, 86–91. http://dx.doi.org/10.1111/j.1468-2850 .2009.01148.x

Stiles, W. B., Hill, C. E., & Elliott, R. (2015). Looking both ways. *Psychotherapy Research*, *25*(4), 277–281.

Stiles, W. B., & Horvath, A. O. (2017). Appropriate responsiveness: A key therapist function. In L. Castonguay & C. E. Hill (Eds.), *Therapist effects and therapist effectiveness* (pp. 71–84). Washington, DC: APA Books.

Strunk, D. R., Brotman, M. A., & DeRubeis, R. J. (2010). The process of change in cognitive therapy for depression: predictors of early inter-session symptom gains. *Behaviour Research and Therapy, 48*(7), 599–606. https://www.doi.org/10.1016/j.brat.2010.03.011

Suh, C. S., Strupp, H. G., & O'Malley, S. S. (1986). The Vanderbilt process measures: The Psychotherapy Process Scale (VPPS) and the Negative Indicators Scale (VNIS). In L. S. Greenberg & W. M. Pinsof (Eds.), *The psychotherapeutic process: A research handbook* (pp. 285–323). New York, NY: Guilford.

*Taber, B. J., Leibert, T. W., & Agaskar, V. R. (2011). Relationships among client–therapist personality congruence, working alliance, and therapeutic outcome. *Psychotherapy, 48*(4), 376–380. https://www.doi.org/10.1037/a0022066

Tarrier, N., & Johnson, J. (2017). *Case formulation in cognitive behaviour therapy: The treatment of challenging and complex cases.* London, England: Routledge.

Tasca, G. A., & Lampard, A. M. (2012). Reciprocal influence of alliance to the group and outcome in day treatment for eating disorders. *Journal of Counseling Psychology, 59*(4), 507–517. doi:10.1037/a0029947

Tschacher, W., Scheier, C., & Grawe, K. (1998). Order and pattern formation in psychotherapy. *Nonlinear Dynamics, Psychology and Life Sciences, 2*(3), 195–215.

*Tschuschke, V., Crameri, A., Koehler, M., Berglar, J., Muth, K., Staczan, P., . . . Koemeda-Lutz, M. (2015). The role of therapists' treatment adherence, professional experience, therapeutic alliance, and clients' severity of psychological problems: Prediction of treatment outcome in eight different psychotherapy approaches. Preliminary results of a naturalistic study. *Psychotherapy Research, 25*(4), 420–434. https://www.doi.org/10.1080/10503307.2014.896055

*Turner, H., Bryant-Waugh, R., & Marshall, E. (2015). The impact of early symptom change and therapeutic alliance on treatment outcome in cognitive-behavioural therapy for eating disorders. *Behaviour Research and Therapy, 73*, 165–169. https://www.doi.org/10.1016/j.brat.2015.08.006

*Ulvenes, P. G., Berggraf, L., Hoffart, A., Stiles, T. C., Svartberg, M., McCullough, L., & Wampold, B. E. (2012). Different processes for different therapies: Therapist actions, therapeutic bond, and outcome. *Psychotherapy, 49*(3), 291–302. https://www.doi.org/10.1037/a0027895

*Urbanoski, K. A., Kelly, J. F., Hoeppner, B. B., & Slaymaker, V. (2012). The role of therapeutic alliance in substance use disorder treatment for young adults. *Journal of Substance Abuse Treatment, 43*(3), 344–351. https://www.doi.org/10.1016/j.jsat.2011.12.013

Viechtbauer, W. (2010). Conducting meta-analyses in R with the metafor package. *Journal of Statistical Software, 36*(3), 1–48.

Wampold, B. E., & Imel, Z. E. (2015). *The great psychotherapy debate: The evidence for what makes psychotherapy work.* New York, NY: Routledge.

Wampold, B. E., & Serlin, R. C. (2000). Consequences of ignoring a nested factor on measures of effect size in analysis of variance. *Psychological Methods, 5*, 425–433.

*Watson, J. C., McMullen, E. J., Prosser, M. C., & Bedard, D. L. (2011). An examination of the relationships among clients' affect regulation, in-session emotional processing, the working alliance, and outcome. *Psychotherapy Research, 21*(1), 86–96. https://www.doi.org/10.1080/10503307.2010.518637

*Watson, J. C., Schein, J., & McMullen, E. (2010). An examination of clients' in-session changes and their relationship to the working alliance and outcome. *Psychotherapy Research, 20*(2), 224–233. https://www.doi.org/10.1080/10503300903311285

Webb, C. A., DeRubeis, R. J., Amsterdam, J. D., Shelton, R. C., Hollon, S. D., & Dimidjian, S. (2011). Two aspects of the therapeutic alliance: Differential relations with depressive symptom change. *Journal of Consulting and Clinical Psychology, 79*(3), 279–283. https://www.doi.org/10.1037/a0023252

*Weck, F., Grikscheit, F., Höfling, V., Kordt, A., Hamm, A. O., Gerlach, A. L., . . . Lang, T. (2016). The role of treatment delivery factors in exposure-based cognitive behavioral therapy for panic disorder with agoraphobia. *Journal of Anxiety Disorders, 42*, 10–18. https://www.doi.org/10.1016/j.janxdis.2016.05.007

*Weck, F., Grikscheit, F., Jakob, M., Höfling, V., & Stangier, U. (2015). Treatment failure in cognitive-behavioural therapy: Therapeutic alliance as a precondition for an adherent and competent implementation of techniques. *British Journal of Clinical Psychology, 54*(1), 91–108. https://www.doi.org/10.1111/bjc.12063

*Weck, F., Richtberg, S., Jakob, M., Neng, J. M. B., & Höfling, V. (2015). Therapist competence and therapeutic alliance are important in the treatment of health anxiety (hypochondriasis). *Psychiatry Research, 228*(1), 53–58. https://www.doi.org/10.1016/j.psychres.2015.03.042

*Weck, F., Rudari, V., Hilling, C., Hautzinger, M., Heidenreich, T., Schermelleh-Engel, K., & Stangier, U. (2013). Relapses in recurrent depression 1 year after maintenance cognitive-behavioral therapy: The role of therapist adherence, competence, and the therapeutic alliance. *Psychiatry Research, 210*(1), 140–145. https://www.doi.org/10.1016/j.psychres.2013.05.036

Wei, M., & Heppner, P. (2005). Counselor and client predictors of the initial working alliance: A replication and extension to Taiwanese client-counselor dyads. *The Counseling Psychologist, 33*(1), 51–71, doi: https://doi.org/10.1177/0011000004268636

*Weiss, M., Kivity, Y., & Huppert, J. D. (2014). How does the therapeutic alliance develop throughout cognitive behavioral therapy for panic disorder? Sawtooth patterns, sudden gains, and stabilization. *Psychotherapy Research, 24*(3), 407–418. https://www.doi.org/10.1080/10503307.2013.868947

*Westmacott, R., Hunsley, J., Best, M., Rumstein-McKean, O., & Schindler, D. (2010). Client and therapist views of contextual factors related to termination from psychotherapy: A comparison between unilateral and mutual terminators. *Psychotherapy Research, 20*(4), 423–435. https://www.doi.org/10.1080/10503301003645796

*Wheaton, M. G., Huppert, J. D., Foa, E. B., & Simpson, H. B. (2016). How important is the therapeutic alliance in treating obsessive-compulsive disorder with exposure and response prevention? An empirical report. *Clinical Neuropsychiatry: Journal of Treatment Evaluation, 13*(6), 88–93.

World Health Organization. (2014). *Mental health: A state of wellbeing.* Retrieved from http://www.who.int/features/factfiles/mental_health/en/

*Xu, H., & Tracey, T. J. G. (2015). Reciprocal influence model of working alliance and therapeutic outcome over individual therapy course. *Journal of Counseling Psychology, 62*(3), 351–359. https://www.doi.org/10.1037/cou0000089

Zetzel, E. R. (1956). Current concepts of transference. *International Journal of Psychoanalysis, 37*, 369–376.

Zickgraf, H. F., Chambless, D. L., McCarthy, K. S., Gallop, R., Sharpless, B. A., Milrod, B. L., & Barber, J. P. (2016). Interpersonal factors are associated with lower therapist adherence in cognitive–behavioural therapy for panic disorder. *Clinical Psychology & Psychotherapy, 23*(3), 272–284. https://www.doi.org/10.1002/cpp.1955

Zilcha-Mano, S. (2017). Is the alliance really therapeutic? Revisiting this question in light of recent methodological advances. *American Psychologist, 72*(4), 311–325. https://www.doi.org/10.1037/pst0000094

Zilcha-Mano, S., & Errazuriz, P. (2017). Early development of mechanisms of change as a predictor of subsequent change and treatment outcome: The case of working alliance. *Journal of Consulting and Clinical Psychology, 85*(5), 508–520, doi: http://dx.doi.org/10.1037/ccp0000192

*Zilcha-Mano, S., Muran, J. C., Hungr, C., Eubanks, C. F., Safran, J. D., & Winston, A. (2016). The relationship between alliance and outcome: Analysis of a two-person perspective on alliance and session outcome. *Journal of Consulting and Clinical Psychology, 84*(6), 484–496. https://www.doi.org/10.1037/ccp0000058

3

ALLIANCE IN CHILD AND
ADOLESCENT PSYCHOTHERAPY

Marc S. Karver, Alessandro S. De Nadai, Maureen Monahan,
and Stephen R. Shirk

Increasingly over the past decade, researchers have incorporated measurement of the therapeutic alliance in their research on child and adolescent psychotherapy. This appears to be driven by an attempt to address the field's lack of understanding of how treatments for children and adolescents work. While a number of treatments for youths have been found to be effective in treating a variety of disorders (e.g., Crawford et al., 2018; Glenn et al., 2015; Milrod et al., 2013), there is a great deal of variability in the individual outcomes experienced by those youths who receive treatments (Webb et al., 2014; Wood et al., 2015). Given that youth psychotherapy clients present to treatment with additional engagement challenges relative to adult clients (e.g., not self-referred, lacking insight into difficulties), it is quite logical that the therapeutic alliance would receive a great deal of attention as it may be a critical factor in explaining why youths have such variability in treatment outcomes.

A number of unique developmental considerations make alliance formation more challenging with youth clients. Most prominent is that adult clients choose to attend psychotherapy whereas youth clients in general come to therapy because adults believe that they need it (Barmish & Kendall, 2005). Thus, from the beginning of treatment, therapists are faced with individuals (youths) who may not believe that they actually have a problem (or they blame others in their environment for their problems) and who did not choose to engage in the activity (Clark, 1998). Research on motivation suggests that people are much less likely to change their behavior if they do not acknowledge the existence of a problem and if they do not want to engage in an activity (Bundy, 2004; Lincourt et al., 2002).

Since successful psychotherapy requires active client participation (e.g., self-exploration, practicing skills, homework), engaging youth clients in a strong therapeutic alliance, although challenging, may prove necessary for optimizing therapeutic outcomes. Youth clients may be more likely to resist the initial alliance formation of a psychotherapist and may also be more likely to want to withdraw from therapy once a therapist starts to make change-oriented requests of them (e.g., initiating exposures, challenging cognitions, doing homework; Pekarik & Stephenson, 1988; Reis & Brown, 2006). Faced with these unique engagement challenges, it is not surprising that an increasing number of youth treatment researchers and practitioners are now embracing measurement of the therapeutic alliance and other common factors.

In this chapter, we review the definitions, measures, and examples of the therapeutic alliance in child and adolescent therapy. We also provide landmark studies of the therapeutic alliance with youth clients. In particular, we provide a meta-analytic update on the research evidence showing a relation between the therapeutic alliance and child and adolescent outcomes in psychotherapy. We then examine potential mediators and moderators and explore patient contributions to the therapeutic alliance. The chapter concludes with diversity considerations, training implications, and therapeutic practices on the youth alliance based on the research evidence.

DEFINITIONS

The sheer number of alliance measures in the child and adolescent literature (see Measures section) suggests the absence of a consensual definition of the therapeutic alliance. However, over the past 25 years, two measures, one designed primarily for children, the Therapeutic Alliance Scale for Children–Revised (TASC-R; Shirk, 2003; Shirk & Saiz, 1992), and one for adolescents, the Working Alliance Inventory–Adolescent (WAI–A; Linscott et al., 1993), have emerged as the most frequently used. These two measures are based on different conceptualizations of the therapeutic alliance and provide somewhat different definitions of this construct.

The Therapeutic Alliance Scale for Children (TASC; Shirk & Saiz, 1992) has its conceptual origins in the psychodynamic perspectives of Anna Freud (1946) and John Meeks (1971). Both conceptualized the youth alliance as including two primary components, one involving an emotional connection, called an "affectionate attachment" by Freud, and the other involving collaborative "work" in therapy. As both noted, the alliance is not equivalent to a warm, friendly relationship but rather must include actual collaboration on therapeutic work on problems that need to be addressed. Specifically, the establishment of a positive, trusting relationship is a means to an end; it facilitates participation in the tasks of therapy. Although emotional connection and treatment collaboration/involvement are distinguished, they are both essential components of the therapeutic alliance.

Based on this framework, the alliance with children and adolescents has been defined as a *collaborative bond* (Kazdin et al., 2005; Shirk et al., 2010). A child might enjoy spending time with his or her therapist but resist participating in therapy work (e.g., disclosing thoughts or feelings, learning/trying new coping strategies). Although this pattern might be called a positive relationship, it would not qualify as a positive alliance. Instead, a positive alliance refers to a therapeutic relationship marked by positive emotional connection (e.g., youth feelings toward the therapist of trust, warmth, feeling supported) *and* collaborative involvement in therapeutic work.

The WAI–A (Linscott et al., 1993) draws on the transtheoretical model of the alliance proposed by Bordin (1979). According to this perspective, the alliance is a multidimensional construct composed of three interrelated dimensions: emotional bond between client and therapist, agreement on the goals of therapy, and agreement on the means (tasks) for reaching these goals. DiGiuseppe et al. (1996) proposed that the focus on *agreements* in this model captured the social contractual nature of alliance that is essential for working with older children and adolescents. The fact that youth are typically referred by others (e.g., Yeh et al., 2002) makes the establishment of agreements both difficult and essential for a treatment alliance.

These two prominent perspectives on the youth alliance share the view that the alliance is multidimensional and that a critical dimensional involves an emotional connection or bond between client and therapist. They diverge in their respective emphasis on actual collaboration versus agreements about collaboration and goals ("I work with my therapist . . ." vs. "My therapist and I agree . . .").

However, emerging evidence indicates that both child and adolescent alliance may lack the multidimensional structure found with adults. Factor-analytic studies of multiple alliance measures reveal a unidimensional structure (e.g., Blatt et al., 1996; Ormhaug et al., 2015; Roest et al., 2016; Shelef & Diamond, 2008). From a developmental perspective, it is certainly possible that children and adolescents lack the ability to differentiate alliance components. In contrast, evidence suggests that therapist reports of youth alliance are similar to other adult reports of alliance. For example, DiGiuseppe et al. (1996) found therapist reports of the youth alliance to conform to Bordin's (1979) three-factor structure, and Ormhaug et al. (2015) found a two-factor therapist report of youth alliance with bond and collaboration dimensions.

These findings suggest that therapists distinguish facets of the alliance that are subsumed by general, affective valence among children and adolescents. It is possible, then, that the alliance when assessed from the youth perspective is largely affectively based and primarily centered on the emotional tone of the relationship. Alternatively, it could be the case that prominent measures of child and adolescent alliance do not include items or aspects of the alliance that might be meaningfully distinguished by youth. For example, the bond dimension could attain greater specificity by including items related to being understood (e.g., "My therapist gets what upsets me") or allegiance (e.g., "My therapist usually takes my parents' side in conflicts"). In addition, cognitively relevant dimensions such as credibility (e.g., "My therapist knows how to help me") may be particularly salient to youth. Given that prominent alliance scales have some of their roots in the adult alliance literature, it might be time to revisit our definition of alliance with children and adolescents by taking an inventory of youth descriptions of their therapeutic relationships. Such an approach could illuminate the salient features of youth alliance from a developmentally sensitive perspective.

A second critical distinction between youth and adult alliances is the presence of multiple alliances in youth therapy even when treatment is individually focused. Because children and adolescents often are referred by parents, therapists are faced with establishing and maintaining an alliance with the youth *and* parents or other caregivers. In fact, it is common in the treatment of disruptive or aggressive children for therapists to focus their interventions on parents rather than the identified youth client. In individually focused youth therapy (e.g., internalizing disorders), alliance with parents primarily serves to support child-focused treatment (e.g., transportation, encouragement), but in the case of parent management training or other parent-focused therapies, parents are the active participants in treatment. This raises the question of whether the therapeutic alliance with parents should vary conceptually as a function of parental role in treatment. To date, most research has used parallel measures of youth and parent alliance (Accurso & Garland, 2015; Hawley & Garland, 2008) and has not attempted to differentiate the definition of the parent alliance from the youth alliance.

The presence of multiple alliances in youth therapy is further complicated by potential discrepancies between youth and parent goals for treatment. Unlike adult therapy, youth clinicians are faced with the task of determining whose goals are going to guide treatment. A study of clinic-referred children (Hawley & Weisz, 2003) examined therapist, child, and parent agreement about the most important problems to be addressed in therapy. Amazingly, more than 75% of child, parent, and therapist triads began treatment without agreement on even one target problem. Nearly half failed to agree on one broad problem domain such as aggression versus depression. Curiously, therapists agreed with parents on target problem identification more often than with children regardless of problem type. Of course, the lack of agreement between therapist and youth carries important implications for the alliance; to the degree that alliance entails such agreements, lack of agreement signals a poor alliance, and to the degree that agreement on goals promotes collaboration, disagreement is likely to undermine youth involvement in therapeutic work (Karver et al., 2005). In fact, lack of agreement on goals has been shown to increase the likelihood of premature dropout (Garcia & Weisz, 2002).

In sum, prominent models of youth alliance have drawn on conceptualizations of the alliance as multifaceted. Yet, a growing body of research suggests that the youth alliance, especially when assessed from the youth's perspective, is unidimensional. As a unidimensional construct, youth alliance can be defined as a *collaborative bond* (involving emotional bond and collaborative work) or as a *consensual bond* (involving bond and negotiated agreements).

MEASURES

While 17 different measures have been utilized across the studies in our meta-analysis, two alliance measures, the Working Alliance Inventory (WAI; Horvath & Greenberg, 1989) and the TASC/TASC-R (Shirk, 2003; Shirk & Saiz, 1992), clearly emerged as the most popular in youth treatment studies. The WAI has been used primarily with adolescents and for parent report of youth alliance and the TASC mostly with children and young adolescents. Although the WAI was originally developed for adult therapy, it has been modified for use with adolescents (Linscott et al., 1993). The short version (WAI-S; Tracey & Kokotovic, 1989) of the adult measure (sometimes with some language modification) has been employed most frequently. The WAI measures the quality of the therapeutic relationship across three subscales: bonds, tasks, and goals.

The final item pool for the measure was generated on the basis of content analysis of Bordin's (1979) model of working alliance. Expert raters evaluated items for goodness of fit with the working alliance construct. The WAI-S has been found to have good internal consistency within youth samples (Capaldi et al., 2016; Hawley et al., 2008) and to be highly correlated with observer ratings of the alliance (Karver et al., 2008).

The TASC was developed specifically for child therapy and also was based on Bordin's (1979) model. Two dimensions are assessed: bond between child and therapist and level of task collaboration. Unlike the WAI, task collaboration does not refer to agreements on tasks but to ratings of actual collaboration on tasks such as "talking about feelings" and "trying to solve problems." The therapist version of the TASC involves ratings of the *child's* bond and task involvement rather than the therapist's own. Although items on the bond subscale remain constant, items on the task collaboration scale vary with treatment type to be consistent with cognitive-behavioral (CBT) or psychodynamic tasks. The subscales show good internal consistency and relatively high levels of stability (Shirk et al., 2008). In fact, adequate internal consistency has even been found for youths as young as age five (Klebanoff, 2015). Although therapist and child agreement on bond ratings are medium to strong, agreement is substantially lower for task collaboration (Shirk et al., 2008). The therapist report has been found to be highly correlated with observer reports of the alliance, but youth report on the TASC was only correlated with observational ratings for adolescents and not younger children (McLeod et al., 2017). Overall, across multiple alliance measures, the level of agreement between youth, therapist, and observational reports has typically been fairly low (Fjermestad et al., 2016).

A number of observational measures have appeared in the youth literature in response to the call for objective assessment of the alliance, but none has become the "gold standard." One measure that was developed specifically for child and adolescent therapy and that has been used the most is the Therapy Process Observation Coding System—Alliance Scale (TPOCS-A; McLeod & Weisz, 2005). This observational scale took as its starting point the distinction between bond and task collaboration found in factor analyses of child and therapist reports of alliance (Shirk & Saiz, 1992) and factor analyses of process codes (Estrada & Russell, 1999). Items from a broad range of measures that mapped onto the bond and task dimensions were initially included in the item pool. Expert raters then sorted items into bond or task categories, and the consistently sorted items were retained. The resulting coding system includes eight bond items and six task collaboration items. Bond and task dimensions have been shown to be highly correlated (McLeod & Weisz, 2005), consistent with what has been found with youth self-reports of alliance dimensions, suggesting that alliance as currently measured in the youth treatment field may be a unitary construct. Internal consistency and interrater reliability have been shown to be good across items (Langer et al., 2011; McLeod et al., 2017).

The TPOCS-A has also been found to be highly correlated with youth and therapist report alliance measures (Fjermestad et al., 2012). Thus there is research evidence indicating that the various alliance measures may be examining the same relationship phenomenon, but there is also evidence that suggests that different rater perspectives/measures are picking up on different facets of the alliance.

CLINICAL EXAMPLES

The following verbal interactions derived from a composite of cases reflect features of the therapeutic alliance with young clients.

Example 1

Therapist: So, what is it like when you're feeling really down?

Client: I get like I don't want to talk to anyone. I'm like get away, leave me alone. My dad asks me how I'm doing, and I just say nothing or walk away.

Therapist: You just want some space. You don't want to be pushed.

Client: Exactly.

Therapist: In here, I'm going to ask you a lot about how you are feeling. If you feel like I'm pushing you, is it possible you will not want to talk with me?

Client: I don't think that'll happen because you're not in my face. Talking gets my stress out if I don't get jumped on for what I say. When I'm in a bad mood on the day of our meetings, I look forward to our talking . . . it helps keep me going because I know you get [understand] me. I feel like I can just say what's on my mind . . . and you'll help me feel better.

This first example illustrates a strong emotional bond and positive attachment of a young adolescent toward her therapist. The adolescent's responses suggest that the youth feels understood and supported, trusts the therapist, and is comfortable and looks forward to talking with the therapist. Thus the adolescent talks about thoughts and feelings that are not talked about with others.

Example 2

Therapist: I know that your parents believe that you need to learn skills for talking with your teachers and classmates, but what are your goals for our working together?

Client: Ugh . . . I know how to talk to people! It's just that I get stuck . . . I want to stop worrying . . . that I'll say something wrong . . . and then I just don't say anything . . . and later . . . it's too late . . . and . . . I could have said something okay . . .

Therapist: It sounds like you do know how to talk to others but you'd like some help shifting your focus away from all the things that make you worry and then not say what you think.

Client: Yeah . . . Yeah . . . that's it . . . When I think about what could happen, I become so nervous . . . I just avoid everyone . . . I just want to go walk up to the ins [popular girls] and just be right there talking and not all what if.

Therapist: So, if we could change how much you worry and think about all the negatives and get you more comfortable talking to the people you want to talk to, that would be good for us to work on together?

Client: Definitely, I'm tired of worrying all the time . . . at lunch . . . after school . . .

In this example, the social-contractual goal agreement dimension of the alliance is prominent. Here the adolescent is initially irritated that the parents make an assumption of what the youth needs to address in therapy. The adolescent responds positively to the therapist not assuming that the parents' goals apply to the youth. The adolescent is receptive to the therapist's collaborative goal exploration and comes to an agreement with the clinician on therapeutic goals. It is likely that the youth, perceiving the therapist to be working toward desired goals, will be much more willing to engage in therapeutic activities. This would have been much less likely if the therapist had decided to build a treatment plan based on the parents' goals for the youth.

Example 3

Client: I feel better since we last talked. That stuff we worked on was pretty helpful.

Therapist: That's cool. Great. What stuff did you do?

Client: Like . . . I forgot what it is called . . . like . . . I controlled my temper . . . when I got angry . . . I was like okay like take a deep breath . . . then I walked away.

Therapist: Great. So, stopping and taking a deep breath helped bring your anger down?

Client: Mmhmm.

Therapist: You made a good decision to use your skills. Some people get angry and are like, hey, I'm right, I'm not backing down . . .

Client: If I get up in their face when I'm mad, I end up losing anyway.

Therapist: Losing anyway?

Client: Yeah, I pay for it later. Get in trouble and stuff.

Therapist: So using what we've worked on might have a payoff?

Client: Yeah! It went a lot better this week when I did what we practiced in here.

In this final example, an older child talks with his therapist about using what was taught in session to successfully deal with anger. The client's statements about his behavior reflect the youth and the therapist collaborating on the actual tasks and the youth perceiving those specific tasks to be helpful.

Of course, other features of therapist–youth interactions can reflect the quality of the therapeutic alliance. For example, a child who is unresponsive to therapist questions or who is only willing to talk about topics unrelated to problems or issues that prompted therapy demonstrates behaviorally low levels of connection to the therapist and willingness to collaborate on therapeutic tasks. Similarly, many children will actively participate in games and unstructured play but will avoid talking about concerns or practicing relevant skills in session. Though such children appear to like their therapist, it is not evident that the therapist is viewed as someone who could help with emotional or behavioral problems.

LANDMARK STUDIES

Although clinical interest in the alliance in child and adolescent therapy has a long history, research on the youth alliance emerged notably later than research with adults. A landmark study by Shirk and Saiz (1992) represented the first attempt to operationalize alliance from a developmental perspective. Conceptualizing the alliance as a catalyst for therapy involvement, the original TASC included items related to relational bond, positive or negative orientation to the therapist, and collaboration with the therapist. Items were generated to be relatively easy for children and adolescents to comprehend. An initial evaluation of the child and therapist scales with an inpatient sample of children revealed two dimensions with high internal consistency. Child and therapist ratings of bond were significantly correlated, but reports of collaboration were not. Further, as proposed by the model, emotional bond was significantly associated with collaboration within perspective.

Although not an empirical study, a meta-analysis of relationship variables as predictors of child and adolescent outcomes (Shirk & Karver, 2003) appears to have had an important impact on the growth of alliance studies with youth. One of the most striking findings from this study was the identification of only one study (Eltz et al., 1995) that would have met criterion for inclusion in adult meta-analyses. At the time, a meta-analysis of alliance–outcome relations in individual adult therapy included 79 studies (Martin et al., 2000), clearly indicating the degree to which the alliance had been neglected in child and adolescent therapy research. Notably, few studies used an explicit alliance measure and even fewer that assessed alliance–outcome relations prospectively. Following the publication of this study, research on the child and adolescent alliance accelerated markedly.

A third landmark study explored a central developmental issue regarding the relative contribution of child and parent alliances to varied outcomes (Hawley & Weisz, 2005). In this study of usual care, outpatient therapy, child client ratings of alliance were found to be better predictors of symptom change and other treatment outcomes, while parent ratings were better predictors of treatment continuation. These findings highlighted the potential unique contribution of the parent–therapist alliance to treatment completion.

As in the adult alliance literature, a major question has revolved around whether the alliance is a *cause* or *consequence* of emotional or behavioral change. In the fourth landmark study, direction of effect was evaluated in CBT for child anxiety (Chiu et al., 2009). Alliance and multiple measures of anxiety were assessed at early, mid-, and posttreatment. Early alliance was significantly predictive of symptom change at mid-treatment, but none of the measures of early symptom change predicted mid-treatment alliance. This pattern of results has been replicated in an evaluation of a cross-lagged model of early alliance and early symptom change in CBT for adolescent depression (Labouliere et al., 2017), though a third study showed a pattern of reciprocal associations between change in therapist-reported alliance and change in child-reported anxiety (Marker et al., 2013). Although the foregoing results do not definitively demonstrate the causal role of the alliance, collectively they indicate that the alliance is no mere consequence of symptom change.

Finally, though studies of alliance–outcome relations in youth therapy have increased in recent years, research on therapist strategies or behaviors that facilitate or impede alliance formation is very limited. In a landmark study of adolescent therapy, DiGiuseppe et al. (1996) examined therapist reports of their treatment activities as predictors of adolescent alliance. Results showed that more frequent use of silence, questions about feelings, and interpretations were negatively associated with alliance. This initial study indicated that specific therapist activities might undermine alliance formation, a result that has been replicated in subsequent observational studies of therapist in-session behaviors (cf. Creed & Kendall, 2005; Karver et al., 2006). Alliance-impeding behaviors vary by youth age and treatment type (e.g., pushing the child to talk, failing to acknowledge adolescent expressed feelings). Conversely, a number of behaviors have been shown to facilitate alliance formation such as including the use of collaborative statements with children (Creed & Kendall, 2005) and including rapport-building behaviors such as eliciting relevant information with adolescents (Karver et al., 2006). This line of research is essential for the development of empirically based guidelines for therapists who work with youth.

RESULTS OF PREVIOUS META-ANALYSES

Over the past 15 years, there have been several meta-analytic reviews of the association between the therapeutic alliance and treatment outcome in youth psychotherapy. In the first, Shirk and Karver (2003) reviewed studies examining the associations between any relationship variables and youth treatment outcomes. Only nine of these studies examined the alliance, and, of these nine, only one evaluated the alliance prospectively in individual therapy. The weighted mean alliance–outcome association in those nine studies was $r = .25$. Just a few years later, Karver and colleagues (2006) identified 10 studies that specifically assessed youth alliance (not parent or family alliance) in relation to outcome. A weighted mean correlation of 0.21 was found, but the correlations varied widely across studies ($r = .05–.49$).

Following these early meta-analyses there was an increase in the number of youth treatment studies examining the alliance to outcome relation. Two reviews were conducted in 2011 in an attempt to capture the field's progress in understanding youth treatment processes. Shirk et al. (2011) identified 16 studies that specifically assessed the prospective association between the therapeutic alliance and treatment outcome in individual youth treatment. They found an overall weighted mean correlation of .22, noting that the alliance to outcome relation appeared stronger for children under 12 as opposed to adolescents (although this was not a statistically reliable finding). Alliance measurement later in treatment (either as a late/concurrent measurement, average, or slope) was also more strongly related to treatment outcome than alliance measurement prospectively earlier in treatment (in which alliance measurement would be somewhat less impacted by outcome change that has already occurred; Webb et al., 2011).

Externalizing samples demonstrated a stronger alliance to outcome relation than adolescent and internalizing or substance abusing samples due to the greater variability/challenge in engaging oppositional and disruptive youth. On the other hand, they did not find a difference in the strength of alliance–outcome relations by treatment type (behavioral vs. nonbehavioral) or alliance type (parent vs. youth alliance).

McLeod (2011), utilizing more inclusive study criteria, identified 38 studies assessing the alliance–outcome relation in youth psychotherapy. McLeod found a weaker alliance to outcome association than other meta-analytic reviews ($r = .14$). This finding may have been influenced by a number of methodological factors such as the heterogeneity of the included studies (e.g., parent and family therapy) and the inclusion of outcome measures that were probably more measures of service utilization (e.g., attendance) than client outcomes (e.g., symptoms, functioning).

META-ANALYTIC REVIEW

Since 2011 there has been substantial growth in the number of studies evaluating alliance–outcome relations in child and adolescent therapy, and we next provide an updated meta-analysis of that research evidence. As in our prior 2011 review, our meta-analysis is restricted to child- and adolescent-focused treatments and does not include studies of family therapy (which are reviewed in Chapter 4), includes both prospective and concurrent assessments of alliance and outcome, and also provides an estimate of the association between parent alliance and youth outcome since parents are often included or even the focus (e.g., behavioral treatments) in child and adolescent therapy.

Selection of Studies

We used a four-pronged approach to identify all available studies examining alliance–outcome relations. First, prior reviews of the alliance to outcome association were examined for qualifying manuscripts (McLeod, 2011; Shirk & Karver, 2011). Citations of these articles as well as the articles meta-analyzed in each review were then examined via Google Scholar (referred to as citation tracing) as a means to identify additional manuscripts. Second, the PsycINFO database was searched from 2009 forward to identify articles that have been published since the last major meta-analytic reviews of the therapeutic alliance in child and adolescent therapy. Next, MEDLINE, the Cochrane Database for Systematic Reviews, and Google Scholar were used to search for studies that may have been missed. For these searches, *child, pediatric, youth, adolescent,* and *kid* were used in conjunction with the terms *alliance* or *relationship* and *therapeutic* or *therapy or treatment* or *process*. Fourth, researchers were queried via professional listservs for any unpublished datasets that may be relevant to the current meta-analysis. In addition, authors of published manuscripts describing alliance and outcome data (but lacking data necessary to derive correlations between the constructs) were contacted for additional data.

Inclusion criteria for the current meta-analysis consisted of the following: (a) the study had to include a specific measure explicitly described in the manuscript as an alliance measure; (b) the alliance had to be related to some indicator or measure of distal, continuously measured posttreatment outcome and not another process variable; (c) the study had to be of mental health treatment targeted to an individual youth under age 18 or a parent; (d) the study could not be an analogue study; (e) the study had to be available in English; (f) the study must have included at least 10 participants; and (g) if the study did not directly report a correlation between alliance and outcome, enough information had to be available in the manuscript or via contacting the authors to calculate the effect size. The resulting sample consisted of 43 studies with 3,442 participants.

Coding

Variables were selected for coding because they were relevant to earlier findings and/or they had been coded and analyzed in prior meta-analyses. Some coded variables allowed for examining content/theory-based questions about the alliance while other variables were coded and analyzed to determine any methodological/ study characteristic variables that may have influenced detected alliance–outcome associations. Studies were coded for study design (randomized vs. nonrandomized), study type (efficacy vs. effectiveness vs. alliance-add-on to treatment), type of psychopathology (internalizing, externalizing, mixed, substance abuse, or eating disorders), type of treatment (cognitive-behavioral/behavioral, confounded, or nonbehavioral/unspecified), type of treatment facility (inpatient vs. outpatient), child age (mean and standard deviation), rater of alliance and outcome (child, parent, clinician, observer, other), type of alliance (therapist with youth vs. parent vs. other), timing of alliance measurement (early or middle [during first two-thirds of therapy sessions], late [during the last third of therapy sessions], at termination, posttreatment, or combined), demographics (percentages of females, non-Caucasians, and members of the Hispanic ethnic group), mean child age, and year of study publication.

In cases when studies provided reports from both the total sample as well as subgroups of the same participants on the same measures, subgroups were used in lieu of the total sample, which permits for more precise estimation of moderators while incorporating the same amount of information as the total sample. For studies that provided information about moderators for a larger total sample but not for the reported alliance–outcome correlation or for subgroups, the total sample data point was imputed for the moderator unless there was any reason to believe that the subsample was not representative of the larger sample (e.g., if the overall sample was 50% female, then in the absence of specific subgroup reporting it was assumed that all subgroups were also 50% female). If the mean age was not provided but a range of ages was provided (e.g., 12–18), then the median of the age range was imputed for the mean age. In the case where studies did not report on a moderator variable (e.g., did not report ethnicity data), that study was not included in the moderator analysis for that variable but was included in all other available analyses.

All included studies were double coded by independent raters (as recommended by Buscemi et al., 2005). Discrepancies between raters were resolved by discussions between raters, with a third rater brought in to make a final decision in the case of inability to resolve discrepancies.

Characteristics of Studies

Characteristics of the 43 studies that met inclusion criteria are displayed in Table 3.1. The sample includes 28 published studies and 15 doctoral dissertations. These studies accounted for 311 total effect sizes available for analysis. The mean age of participants for all effect sizes included was 12.38 ($SD = 2.74$). Among these effect sizes (for studies that reported demographics), 54.5% of participants were female, 31.1% were classified as part of a non-Caucasian racial group, and 17.1% were classified in the Hispanic ethnic group. Among these effect sizes, 254 focused on youth–clinician alliance and 56 addressed parent–clinician alliance.

With regard to psychopathology, 155 effect sizes focused on internalizing problems, 72 on externalizing problems, 25 on substance abuse problems, 57 on mixed problems, and only 2 on eating disorders. In terms of types of treatment, 137 effect sizes focused on behavioral therapy (including CBT), 163 focused on nonbehavioral or unspecified treatments, and 11 were confounded (a mix of behavioral and nonbehavioral psychotherapies). For treatment setting, 271 effect sizes focused on outpatient therapy and 40 focused on inpatient therapy.

In terms of methodological features, 165 effect sizes assessed the alliance early or in the middle of treatment, 36 assessed the role of alliance late or at posttreatment, and 110 considered the alliance as it pertained to occurring throughout the entire course of therapy. In considering raters of alliance, 30 effect sizes came from parent report, 150 from child report, 80 from clinician report, and 51 from observer report. In considering raters of treatment outcome, 91 effect sizes pertained to parent reports, 135 to child reports, 56 to clinician reports, and 21 to observer-rated outcome; 4 effect sizes did not fit into any of these categories (e.g., teacher ratings). Regarding study focus, 139 effect sizes came from efficacy studies, 43 from effectiveness studies, and 129 from studies that added alliance measurement to treatment-as-usual. Finally, 138 effect sizes came from randomized controlled trials (RCTs) while 173 effect sizes came from studies that were not RCTs.

Analytic Plan

Because most studies reported results (alliance to outcome relation) as correlations, the product–moment correlation coefficient r was used as our dependent variable. When regression beta coefficients reflected an alliance–outcome relation (e.g., with pretreatment outcome scores and alliance serving as simultaneous predictors of posttreatment

Table 3.1. Summary of Reviewed Studies, Alliance Measures, and Effect Sizes

Study	Patients	Alliance Measure	Overall Study N	Mean Weighted r^a
Abrishami et al. (2013)	Both ages Mixed Problems Confounded	Therapeutic Alliance Scale for Children–Revised	46	−.13
Accurso (2012)	Both ages Mixed Problems Confounded	Therapeutic Alliance Scale for Children	46	.02
Adler (1998)	Both ages Mixed problems Nonbehavioral	Parent Evaluation Questionnaire	92	.23
Anderson et al. (2012)	Adolescent Internalizing Behavioral	Working Alliance Inventory–Short Form	129	.17
Avny (2011)	Both ages Internalizing Behavioral	Therapeutic Alliance Scale for Children Therapeutic Process Observational Coding System	26	.10
Becker (2012)	Both ages Mixed Problems Behavioral	Session Rating Scale 3.0	24	.34
Bhola & Kapur (2013)	Adolescent Internalizing Nonbehavioral	Working Alliance Inventory–Short Form	40	.28
Capaldi et al. (2016)	Adolescent Internalizing Behavioral	Working Alliance Inventory–Short Form	31	.08
Chiu et al. (2009)	Both ages Internalizing Behavioral	Therapeutic Process Observational Coding System	16	.15
Creed (2007)	Both ages Internalizing Behavioral	Therapeutic Alliance Scale for Children Therapist Alliance Building Behavior Scale–Alliance subscale	68	.19
Cummings et al. (2013)	Both ages Internalizing Behavioral	Child's Perception of Therapeutic Relationship	139	.12
Darchuk (2007)	Adolescent Substance Abuse Nonbehavioral	Working Alliance Inventory–Short Form	40	.11

(*continued*)

Table 3.1. Continued

Study	Patients	Alliance Measure	Overall Study N	Mean Weighted r^a
Eltz et al. (1995)	Adolescent Mixed Problems Behavioral	Penn Helping Alliance Questionnaire	38	.08
Fernández et al. (2016)	Adolescent Mixed Problems Confounded	Working Alliance Inventory	20	.63
Forsberg (2011)	Adolescent Eating Disorders Behavioral	Working Alliance Inventory–Observer	78	.05
Hagen & Ogden (2017)	Both ages Externalizing Behavioral	Working Alliance Inventory-Short Form	331	.11
Hogue et al. (2006)	Adolescent Substance Abuse Behavioral	Vanderbilt Therapeutic Alliance Scale–Revised	56	−.06
Hudson et al. (2014)	Both ages Internalizing Behavioral	Child Psychotherapy Process Scale–Alliance	151	.22
Hukkelberg et al. (2013)	Child Externalizing Behavioral	Working Alliance Inventory–Short Form	211	.22
Karpenko (2010)	Adolescent Mixed Problems Confounded	Working Alliance Inventory–Short Revised	116	.45
Karver et al. (2008)	Adolescent Internalizing Confounded	Alliance Observation Coding System Working Alliance Inventory	23	.10
Kazdin et al. (2005)	Child Externalizing Behavioral	Working Alliance Inventory	185	.29
Kazdin et al. (2006)	Both ages Externalizing Behavioral	Therapeutic Alliance Scale for Children Working Alliance Inventory	77	.31
Kazdin & Durbin (2012)	Both ages Externalizing Behavioral	Therapeutic Alliance Scale for Children	97	.46
Kazdin & Whitley (2006)	Child Externalizing Behavioral	Working Alliance Inventory Therapeutic Alliance Scale for Children	218	.26

Table 3.1. Continued

Study	Patients	Alliance Measure	Overall Study N	Mean Weighted r[a]
Keeley et al. (2011)	Both ages Internalizing Behavioral	Therapeutic Alliance Scale for Children–Revised Working Alliance Inventory	22	.49
Kendall (1994)[b]	Both ages Internalizing Behavioral	Child's Perception of Therapeutic Relationship	27	.12
Kendall et al. (1997)[b]	Both ages Internalizing Behavioral	Child's Perception of Therapeutic Relationship	60	.01
Klebanoff (2015)	Both ages Mixed Problems Behavioral	Therapeutic Alliance Scale for Children–Revised	60	.27
Labouliere et al. (2017)	Adolescent Internalizing Behavioral	Alliance Observation Coding System	38	.34
Langberg et al. (2013)	Both ages Externalizing Nonbehavioral	Working Alliance Inventory–Short Form	23	.32
McLeod & Weisz (2005)	Child Internalizing Nonbehavioral	Therapy Process Observational Coding System–Alliance	22	.36
Ormhaug et al. (2014)	Both ages Internalizing Behavioral	Therapeutic Alliance Scale for Children–Revised	52	.15
Ormhaug et al. (2015)	Both ages Internalizing Behavioral	Therapeutic Alliance Scale for Children–Revised	156	.06
Pestle (2012)	Both ages Internalizing Confounded	Child–Therapist Alliance	75	.00
Rabbitt et al. (2016)	Child Externalizing Behavioral	Parent–Therapist Relationship Scales	27	.16
Reyes (2013)	Adolescent Internalizing Behavioral	Therapy Process Observational Coding System for Child Psychotherapy–Alliance	21	.25
Ricketts (2015)	Both ages Internalizing Behavioral	Child's Perception of Therapeutic Relationship	18	.04

(continued)

Table 3.1. Continued

Study	Patients	Alliance Measure	Overall Study N	Mean Weighted r[a]
Roth (2009)	Both ages Mixed Problems Not Specified	Working Alliance Inventory–Short Form	30	.13
Schmit (2015)	Adolescent Mixed Problems Not Specified	Working Alliance Inventory	75	.34
Shirk et al. (2008)	Adolescent Internalizing Behavioral	Therapeutic Alliance Scale for Adolescents	50	.26
Sullivan (2013)	Adolescent Mixed Problems Not Specified	Therapeutic Alliance Quality Scale Session Rating Scale	100	.24
Zorzella et al. (2015)	Child Internalizing Behavioral	Therapeutic Alliance Scale for Children	62	.23

[a]Weights were constructed based on robust variance estimation with a correlated effects model.

[b]Participants from Kendall (1994) and Kendall et al. (1997) were also included in Hudson et al. (2014), with different outcome measures used in Hudson et al. relative to the other two studies. Because the same participants in Hudson et al. were used in these other two studies, correlated effects weighting (which adjusts for the same participants contributing to multiple effect sizes) was arranged so that effect sizes from all three of these studies were considered to be from one sample/study, given that the same participants were reused across studies.

Note. Alliance Observation Coding System (Karver et al., 2003); Child Psychotherapy Process Scale–Alliance (Estrada & Russell, 1999); Child's Perception of Therapeutic Relationship (Kendall et al., 1997); Child–Therapist Alliance (Chorpita & Weisz, 2005); Parent Evaluation Questionnaire (Gaston & Marmor, 1991); Parent–Therapist Relationship Scales (Horvath & Greenberg 1989; Rabbitt et al., 2016); Penn Helping Alliance Questionnaire (Alexander & Luborsky, 1986); Perception of Therapeutic Relationship Scale (Kendall et al., 1997); Relationship with Counselor Assessment (Descutner & Thelen, 1991); Session Rating Scale (Johnson, Miller, & Duncan, 2000); Session Rating Scale 3.0 (Johnson, Miller, & Duncan, 2000); Therapeutic Alliance Quality Rating (Bickman et al., 2012); Therapeutic Alliance Quality Scale (Bickman et al., 2007); Therapeutic Alliance Scale for Adolescents (Shirk, 2003); Therapeutic Alliance Scale for Children (Shirk & Saiz, 1992); Therapeutic Alliance Scale for Children–Revised (Shirk & Saiz, 1992; Shirk, 2003); Therapeutic Process Observational Coding System for Child Psychotherapy (McLeod & Weisz, 2005); Therapy Process Observational Coding System-Alliance (McLeod, 2001); Therapist Alliance Building Behavior Scale–Alliance subscale (Creed & Kendall, 2005); Vanderbilt Therapeutic Alliance Scale–Revised (Hartley & Strupp, 1983); Working Alliance Inventory (Horvath & Greenberg, 1989); Working Alliance Inventory–Observer (Horvath & Greenberg, 1989); Working Alliance Inventory–Short Form (Tracey & Kokotovic, 1989); Working Alliance Inventory–Short Revised (Hatcher & Gillaspy, 2006; Horvath & Greenberg, 1989).

outcome scores), these beta coefficients were converted to *r* (using the procedure suggested by Peterson & Brown, 2005). This procedure allows for nonalliance covariates to be included as predictors. However, if covariates reflected inclusion of multiple treatment groups that could have both impact on outcome and differential relations with alliance, then the beta coefficient corresponding to the alliance–outcome relation was not coded due to the deflating effect on the alliance–outcome relation that would likely be introduced by multicollinearity. Conversions to r were also made for coefficients originating from latent growth models using the same principles as regression betas and from multilevel models (also known as hierarchical linear models or mixed effect models) following procedures delineated in Feingold (2009).

All reported effect sizes were converted to Fisher's Z prior to analysis to normalize the r distribution. Following meta-analytic model estimation, estimates were converted back to r for purposes of reporting, and the overall estimate of r was converted to Cohen's d to aid in interpretation. All conversions between r, Z, and d were performed using formulae provided by Cooper et al. (2009).

To create model estimates, multivariate meta-analysis with robust variance estimation was employed, using inverse variance weighting via a correlated effects model. Multivariate procedures permit the combination of multiple effect sizes from a single study and provide several advantages over univariate meta-analysis. First, multivariate procedures are able to incorporate all relevant data. Because no single measure is consistently employed across a majority of child alliance studies, aggregated effects are multivariate as opposed to univariate, which would not be accounted for by traditional methods. Second, the use of multiple measures from a single study can reduce standard errors for hypothesis tests, increasing statistical power (Riley et al., 2007). Conversely, separate meta-analyses with correlated outcomes (e.g., separate meta-analyses for each proposed level of a moderator) can bias estimates and overestimate variance (Riley, 2009). Third, multivariate meta-analysis permits the comparison of estimates from within-study covariates (e.g., children and parents in a study that reports alliance from both reporters), which is impossible when averaging multiple effect sizes from each study to use univariate meta-analysis. This permits direct comparisons that otherwise would not be possible in a traditional meta-analytic framework.

Meta-analytic procedures were implemented using the R statistical programs (R Core Team, 2017) using the packages Robumeta (Fisher & Tipton, 2017) and metafor (Viechtbauer, 2010). Using these procedures, the experimenter must estimate a within-study correlation, titled ρ. Using functions provided in the Robumeta package, the default when estimating effect sizes was set at $\rho = .8$, and a sensitivity analysis was conducted where parameters were estimated and compared over a range of ρ from 0 to 1 in 0.1 increments.

Because heterogeneity in both methodology and effect sizes among studies is common (Higgins, 2008), a random effects model was employed, which permits increased quality of generalization to future studies on the same topic. To evaluate study heterogeneity, we placed emphasis on the proportion of variability attributable to between-studies heterogeneity (as measured by the I^2 statistic, where such focus on I^2 instead of the traditional Cochran's Q statistic is recommended; Baldwin & Shadish, 2011).

Given that moderators were considered a priori, we calculated effect sizes at multiple levels of hypothesized moderating variables. Theoretical moderators evaluated included treatment type; type of problem treated; and child age, race, ethnicity, and gender. Methodological moderators considered included study design (RCT or not), study type (efficacy, effectiveness, or treatment-as-usual), treatment setting (inpatient vs. outpatient), rater of alliance, rater of outcome, alliance type (youth–clinician or parent–clinician), and time period for which alliance was evaluated (first two-thirds of therapy, termination/posttreatment, or the entire therapy period). All categorical moderators were dummy coded, which permits the estimation of group-specific effect sizes. Categorical moderators with more than two categories were behavioral treatment (for treatment type), efficacy studies (for study type), internalizing disorders (for psychopathology), child ratings (for ratings of alliance and outcomes), youth–clinician alliance (for alliance type), and early alliance (for timing of administration of alliance measure).

We attempted to minimize publication bias first by searching for unpublished studies and then contacting authors who did not provide sufficient information for effect size computation within published articles. It was also assessed via visual inspection of a funnel plot and by Egger's regression test (Egger et al., 1997). Egger's regression test is designed only for univariate analyses; accordingly, we combined effect sizes within studies before running this test. On the funnel plot, effect sizes were plotted on the x-axis and associated standard errors on the y-axis.

Results

The overall mean effect size was $r = .20$ (95% confidence interval [CI] = .15–.24). This result was robust across all possible within-study effect size correlations, with sensitivity analysis finding that estimates of r, associated standard errors, and τ^2 all varied by less than .001 across all tested values of ρ. This overall r translates to a standardized mean difference equivalent of $d = .40$ (95% CI = .30–.50).

This overall effect size was quite similar compared to earlier estimates of the alliance to outcome association ($r = .22$ in Shirk & Karver, 2011; .24 in Shirk & Karver, 2003). This effect remains consistent, despite the fact that the number of studies focusing on the alliance–outcome relation in individual child and adolescent psychotherapy has increased by nearly 50% since the last meta-analysis (Shirk et al., 2011).

Regarding publication bias, visual inspection of the funnel plot (Figure 3.1) reflected probable publication bias. Smaller standard errors were associated with unexpectedly large fluctuations around the overall average effect size, whereas it would be expected that studies with larger standard errors (i.e., usually studies that have smaller sample sizes) would have larger relative fluctuations. No consistent direction of bias was observed in the funnel plot, and Egger's regression test for funnel plot asymmetry was nonsignificant ($z = .60$, $p = .55$). Extreme outliers on the funnel plot had a negligible impact on results; sensitivity analysis found that removing the study associated with these outliers (Fernández et al., 2016) affected the total effect size estimate by less than .01. The extreme outliers represented 2 out of 311 total effect sizes.

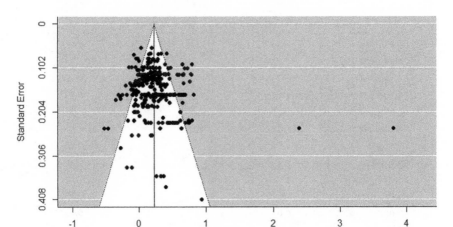

FIGURE 3.1 Funnel plot of observed effect sizes.

MODERATORS AND MEDIATORS

Moderators

As found in prior meta-analyses, a medium-large amount of heterogeneity was observed in effect sizes (I^2 = 69.29%). However, no continuous moderators showed statistically significant prediction of effect sizes, including child age (p = .63), proportion of female participants (p = .99), proportion of non-Caucasian participants (p = .30), proportion of Hispanic participants (p = .66), and year of publication (p = .68).

The effect sizes for moderator levels are presented in Table 3.2. Several categorical moderators showed statistically significant group differences. RCTs (r = .13) showed a smaller alliance–outcome relation relative to non-RCTs (r = .25, p < .01). Relative to internalizing disorders (r = .18), smaller alliance–outcome associations were observed for treatment for substance abuse (r = .01, p = .01) and eating disorders (r = .05, p <. 01).

Mediators

Despite the accumulating evidence for the relation between the therapeutic alliance and outcome in youth treatment, little is known about the mechanism by which this relation occurs. A few researchers have hypothesized mediators, such as greater treatment attendance, greater exposure to active treatment ingredients, greater motivation to change, greater willingness to participate in treatment, greater collaboration and/or involvement in treatment tasks, and greater homework compliance (Chu & Kendall, 2004; Karver et al., 2006; Shirk, 2001; Shirk & Karver, 2006; Shirk & Russell, 1996).

During our literature review, we found six studies (Anderson, et al., 2012; Avny, 2011; Capaldi, 2010; Karver et al., 2008; Shirk et al., 2008; Smith, 2010) that examined

Table 3.2. Estimated Effect Sizes for Categorical Moderators

Moderator	r
Treatment Type	
Behavioral	0.22
Nonbehavioral/Unspecified	0.15
Confounded (both behavioral and nonbehavioral)	0.21
Treatment Setting	
Inpatient	0.17
Outpatient	0.20
Study design	
Randomized controlled trial	0.13
Nonrandomized controlled trial	0.25**
Study Type	
Efficacy	0.18
Effectiveness	0.10
Alliance add-on	0.26
Disorder Type	
Internalizing	0.18
Externalizing	0.24
Substance abuse	0.01*
Mixed problems	0.24
Eating disorders	0.05**
Rater of Alliance	
Child	0.22
Parent	0.21
Clinician	0.21
Observer	0.14
Alliance Type	
Child–Clinician	0.19
Parent–Clinician	0.24
Rater of Outcome	
Child	0.20
Parent	0.18
Clinician	0.28*
Observer	0.15
Other (e.g., teacher)	0.10
Administration of Alliance Measure	
Early (e.g., first two-thirds of therapy)	0.19
Termination/Posttreatment	0.24
Combined (throughout therapy)	0.19

*$p < .05$, **$p < .01$.

Note: The first category in each series of categories is the dummy coded reference group.

potential mediators of the alliance–outcome association in youth therapy. Across these studies, youth therapeutic alliance was found related to plausible mediators such as later compliance with treatment tasks, session attendance, and treatment satisfaction.

Some of these potential mediators such as treatment compliance/participation, homework compliance, and session attendance were also found related to treatment outcomes. However, in none of these studies was mediation of the alliance to outcome relationship found. In many ways, session attendance not being a mediator would not be surprising given that being present for treatment does not necessarily mean that a youth is engaging in that treatment. On the other hand, there has been some evidence of a parent alliance to youth outcome relation mediated by *parental* treatment attendance; however, this finding was underpowered and unreliable. In fact, across the few studies that have searched for mediators, the lack of identification of any reliable mechanisms that may mediate the alliance to outcome relation in youth treatment should be viewed cautiously due to these studies being underpowered with limited samples of participants and therapists and often limited alliance and/or outcome measurement.

EVIDENCE FOR CAUSALITY

Ultimately, to provide compelling causal evidence, experimental designs are required. This is challenging with the therapeutic alliance as one cannot randomly assign the alliance to a select group of therapist–client dyads. The reality is that the alliance is a product of therapist–client interactions. Thus one can only use indirect evidence to support the possibility of a causal relation between the alliance and treatment outcome.

Indirect links have been demonstrated in several studies. For example, several researchers have found that positive change in the alliance over time was associated with greater symptom improvement (Eltz et al., 1995; Sullivan, 2013). A couple of studies have used growth curve modeling to provide evidence that early alliance and/or increasing youth therapeutic alliance is related to use of coping skills and/or rate of youth outcome improvement (Bickman et al., 2012; Hudson et al., 2014). Of course, it is also plausible that growth in outcomes could have led to growth in the alliance over time.

Some researchers have attempted to build some causal support for the alliance by examining it as a mediator between other variables measured earlier in treatment and later treatment outcome. Two studies (Creed, 2007; Darchuk, 2007) found therapist behaviors (collaboration) and client variables (motivation to change, involvement) to respectively predict the therapeutic alliance; neither found support for the alliance as a mediator of a relation to treatment outcome. On the other hand, two other studies (Kazdin & Whitley, 2006; Korchmaros & Stevens, 2014) found the therapeutic alliance to mediate the relation between parental pretreatment social relationships and youth outcomes and to mediate the relation between pretreatment expectations of comfort with a counselor and posttreatment outcome. While it is promising to see evidence of the alliance as a mediator of treatment outcome, these designs are not able to rule out the possibility that early treatment change could be driving the observed relations.

Using methods (e.g., lagged correlations, structural equation/path models) that better address temporal precedence, several researchers have attempted to clarify whether early symptom change predicts the therapeutic alliance or if the therapeutic alliance predicts later symptom change. One study did find early change to have a small predictive relation with later (fourth session) alliance (Reyes, 2013). On the other hand, two studies have provided evidence for the opposite direction, that is, earlier alliance (parent and child reports) being related to later outcome change while controlling for early symptom change (Keeley et al., 2011; Reyes, 2013).

Several researchers have examined autoregressive cross-lagged models to better determine temporal precedence of the alliance and symptom change. The findings have proven mixed. A couple of studies provided support for the unique direction of the alliance (or change in the alliance) predicting outcome change rather than outcome change predicting the alliance (Accurso, 2012; Capaldi et al., 2016). One (Labouliere et al., 2017) found the best support for a parsimonious model of the alliance driving symptom change, with some evidence of bidirectional causality (e.g., Marker et al., 2013), while others (Chiu et al., 2009; Ormhaug et al., 2014) did not find bidirectionality (no prediction of alliance by early symptom change). They found that early alliance predicted mid-treatment change but not final outcome change (which was predicted by mid-treatment alliance).

In conclusion, the studies reviewed provide preliminary causality evidence; however, they cannot be used to determine whether the alliance truly serves a causal role in treatment. Even with evidence of temporal precedence of the alliance relative to symptom change, these designs are still vulnerable to unmeasured variables that may have common influence on the alliance or outcome or both. Probably the only way around these confounds will be studies that experimentally manipulate therapist engagement behaviors, which would be behaviors with evidence for influencing the therapeutic alliance, in either analogue or real-world treatment studies. If the experimental alliance-enhancing condition provided superior treatment outcomes to a control condition, with the alliance serving as a mediator, then this would provide good evidence for the causal role of the therapeutic alliance.

PATIENT CONTRIBUTIONS

Clearly the therapeutic alliance is a bidirectional relationship between a youth and/or parent client and a therapist. The therapist shapes the in-session (and ultimately out of session) behavior of clients, but the therapist's behaviors/efforts toward the client are also shaped by the characteristics that youths and parents bring to therapy. Some characteristics may draw more alliance-enhancing behaviors from a therapist whereas others may push a therapist away.

A growing number of investigations have examined youth factors that contribute to the quality of the therapeutic alliance or the trajectory of alliance change. These youth characteristics potentially provide clinicians with important information that may distinguish between youths who are easier and harder to engage in treatment and thus may need to be engaged differentially to form a successful relationship.

One potent developmental factor is adolescence, viewed as one of the most difficult periods for alliance formation (Castro-Blanco & Karver, 2010; Meeks, 1971). The developmental press toward autonomy, the increasing centrality of peer relationships, and growing doubts about adults' capacity for understanding youth experiences contribute to alliance difficulties. Surprisingly, few studies have examined direct links between developmental stage and youth alliance. Thus far, the limited evidence is mixed with some studies showing more positive alliances among older youth, perhaps reflecting a greater cognitive capacity to understand the usefulness of treatment (Ayotte et al., 2016; Cichocki, 2015) and some studies reporting younger children forming better alliances (Anderson et al., 2012; Figueiredo et al., 2016). Clearly there is more to learn about developmental differences in alliance formation.

The limited research also supports that motivation, willingness to participate in treatment, and lower resistance predict the alliance in youth psychotherapy (Fjermestad et al., 2018; Karver et al., 2005; Shirk & Saiz, 1992). Relatedly, youth positive help-seeking expectancies/credibility beliefs about treatment and/or a potential relationship with a therapist have been found to be related to the alliance (e.g., Christensen & Skogstad, 2009; Eltz et al., 1995; Korchmaros & Stevens, 2014). Conversely, noncooperative youth behavior in-session has been found to predict a worse alliance with the therapist (Creed, 2007).

It is not atypical for youths to make external attributions about their problems, which would make alliance formation challenging with youth with externalizing disorders as they would be more confrontational and less likely to agree with others on the extent, importance, or cause of problems (Gallagher et al., 2010; Shirk & Saiz, 1992). Consistent with this, several studies have found externalizing youths to have the worst alliances while internalizing/distressed youths had the better alliances (Ayotte et al., 2016; Zorzella et al., 2015). Similarly, youths who entered treatment with the most alcohol and illicit drug use, highest distrust of authority, highest levels of defiance, and highest delinquency with low social/cognitive skills, among the most challenging youth populations to engage in treatment because they tend to externalize problems, had the poorest therapeutic alliances formed with their counselors (Bickman et al., 2004; Korchmaros & Stevens, 2014; Simpson, 2008).

Another probable patient contribution is interpersonal functioning (Shirk & Saiz, 1992). Having pretreatment youth social competencies, an agreeable interpersonal style, a stronger relationship with a youth's mother, a stronger sense of security in relationships with caregivers, and higher family and peer support have all been found related to better youth–therapist alliances (e.g., Kazdin & Durbin, 2012; Levin et al., 2012; Reyes, 2013). Severity of interpersonal problems, prior maltreatment, and difficulty with being supportive of others have been found related to greater difficulties in alliance development (Eltz et al., 1995; Reyes, 2013).

Not surprisingly given that alliance formation is a social process, the parent-therapist alliance has been found to have similar interpersonal predictors with maternal social support and parental social relationship variables predicting better parent–therapist alliance (DeVet et al., 2003; Hawley & Garland, 2008; Kazdin & Whitley, 2006). However, more research on potential predictors, such as parental mental health and parental stress, of the parent–therapist alliance is needed (Garland et al., 2014; Karver et al., 2005).

Overall, little research has examined children's social, emotional, peer, biological, and cognitive development and how these characteristics affect and are affected by therapists' perceptions/expectations of youths, therapist behavior, and the alliance formation process. The empirical research on these patient predictors and contributions is lacking.

LIMITATIONS OF THE RESEARCH

The field has yet to come to an agreement on the defining features of the therapeutic alliance with youth. There appears to be a stagnation in the conceptualization of alliance as much of the literature utilizes conceptualizations that are decades old, despite an upsurge in our knowledge about relationships and relationship development. Further, much of the extant alliance literature yields limited variability and high ceiling effects in alliance ratings regardless of respondent (i.e., parent, child, therapist; Garland et al., 2014; Hukkelberg & Ogden, 2013; Liber et al., 2010; Sapyta, 2011). Novel conceptualizations may help in the development of alliance measures that better identify subtleties and consequently more variability in the youth alliance construct. That would then potentially allow for detecting a larger alliance to outcome relation.

In addition, the current research lacks in-depth investigations regarding *how* the alliance works to influence outcomes (Kazdin & Durbin, 2012). Process variables such as treatment adherence and homework compliance are starting points to better understanding the process by which alliance works to improve outcomes. Similarly, more research is needed to support (or refute) the idea that alliance with youth clients serves a causal role in improving therapeutic outcome.

Also lacking in the literature is *how* therapists develop strong alliances with *which* clients. While youth alliance is moderately correlated with therapeutic outcomes, that knowledge serves little practical purpose if psychotherapists do not know the specific steps or behaviors to enhance therapeutic relationships with their clients, especially their tougher cases. As such, determining the specific behaviors to build, enhance, and/or harm the development of the therapeutic alliance with typical youth clients is a priority. Perhaps future research should focus on youths who present to treatment as difficult to engage, as changing the trajectory of their therapeutic alliances has implications for increasing the positive outcomes of youth treatments.

The next set of limitations relate to *when* alliance is being measured. First, there is a dearth of studies that measure alliance and outcome at multiple time points throughout treatment and how the dynamic relation between alliance and outcome might change over time. On a similar note, few studies examine early alliance in relation to early symptom changes and how the nature of this early relationship might have implications for later treatment outcomes.

A limitation of this meta-analysis was that it only included studies written in English. Thus how the alliance relates to outcome in non-English therapies is not necessarily portrayed by the findings of this meta-analysis. In addition, given the relatively small number of studies and the great variability in the treatments across the studies, it is not guaranteed that the findings of this meta-analysis can be generalized to any youth treatment.

A newer limitation of the literature is a lack of reporting information necessary to calculate the correlation between alliance and outcome in some of the more sophisticated studies. Due to the absence of these data, several articles that would have been included in the present study had to be discarded from overall analyses. The majority of these articles utilized newer longitudinal analyses (e.g., hierarchical linear modeling, latent growth modeling), which have less precedence for what to report on and often do not report effect sizes within the test (Feingold, 2009). While it is a step forward to use more advanced methods, the field needs to come to a consensus on data-reporting standards for such analyses to prevent unnecessarily eliminating articles that could be used to better inform the relationship between alliance and outcome.

Additional research is also needed to more closely examine the ongoing dynamic between therapists and youth clients from the beginning of youth treatment. Studies are needed that focus on how clients and their parents present to treatment (potential alliance predictors) and how their characteristics and interpersonal styles interact with therapist characteristics to influence one another's emotions, thoughts, and behaviors. We still know little about how certain youth or parent characteristics may pull for therapist engagement behaviors or if some therapists are more or less capable of engaging youths and their parents who present in different manners to therapy.

Another limitation stems from the fact that much of the current research fails to take a closer look at the therapist, such as therapist characteristics, skill level, internal states, and attitudes toward the client; how these facets contribute to potential alliance-enhancing behaviors; and how these need to be modified relative to stage of therapy, use of different techniques, intended treatment outcome, and/or matching youth or parent characteristics (e.g., youth developmental level) and behaviors. Along these lines, child alliance studies would benefit from embracing the practice of partitioning outcome variance into therapist-related and child-related components, as the current lack of this information obscures the relative contributions of each party.

Finally, more research is needed examining the relations between the therapeutic alliance and other treatment process constructs. It is important to understand the extent of unique and shared variance among alliance and other treatment processes in influencing therapeutic outcomes.

DIVERSITY CONSIDERATIONS

Generalization of the therapeutic alliance research to diverse populations cannot be assumed. Youth and/or parent clients, who differ from their therapists relative to gender, race/ethnicity, sexual orientation, and/or socioeconomic status may have increased difficulty in forming a therapeutic relationship. On the positive side, the moderator analyses in the current meta-analysis found that the effect size for the alliance–outcome association was similar across youth gender and race/ethnicity.

A small number of studies have examined the relation between youth and/or parent demographic characteristics and quality of the therapeutic alliance. The evidence for the most part suggests that female youths may be easier to engage in youth treatment as the majority of studies examining gender and the alliance show that females rate the alliance or alliance improvement more positively than male youth (e.g., Accurso & Garland, 2015; Eltz et al., 1995; Nevid et al., 2017; Zorzella et al., 2015).

The research regarding race/ethnicity has been quite minimal. A handful of studies have found higher therapeutic alliance scores for youth ethnic minority participants as opposed to European American participants (e.g., Hawke et al., 2005; Reyes, 2013; Simpson, 2013). Perhaps when therapists encounter an ethnically diverse youth client, this may cue them to put forth more effort in engaging the youth. At the same time, several studies (e.g., Accurso & Garland, 2015; Garner et al., 2008; Wintersteen et al., 2005) found no race effects relative to the alliance. In sum, the literature on race/ethnicity and the alliance in youth treatment is far too limited.

The literature on socioeconomic status and alliance formation is also quite limited relative to youth treatment. On the one hand, the hardships of living in poverty frequently present additional barriers and stressors that may impair youths' and their parents' ability to prioritize treatment and engage with the therapist (Liebsack, 2016; Shelleby & Shaw, 2014). On the other hand, the experience of extensive environmental stressors may actually increase the incentive for treatment participants to engage with a therapist to acquire needed assistance (Smith et al., 2018). Thus far, there is insufficient evidence of a clear relation between socioeconomic status and the therapeutic alliance.

Similarly, there has been very little research examining the therapeutic alliance in treatment with sexual-minority youths. Some case study (Duarté-Vélez et al., 2010) and survey research (Burckell & Goldfried, 2006) suggests that sexual-minority youth want similar therapist characteristics and behaviors as nonsexual-minority youth: therapists who are flexible, facilitate trust, show understanding of and work toward agreement on goals, affirm characteristics of the youth, and show respect for the youth's culture and as an individual in that culture. More specifically, these youths want therapists who are lesbian, gay, and bisexual (LGB) affirming and are aware of and/or have a personal understanding of the challenges that LBG youth face.

TRAINING IMPLICATIONS

The findings of this meta-analysis continue to support the predictive and clinical value of the therapeutic alliance. It behooves educators and supervisors to ensure that clinicians in training monitor their therapeutic alliances with their youth clients (e.g., providing the TASC after the initial sessions, videotaping therapy sessions) and that they find ways to enhance therapist abilities to engage youth clients and their parents.

Interestingly, while much literature emphasizes the importance of forming a strong alliance with youth clients, there is a notable lack of studies on how to do so. Lamers and colleagues (2016) developed a training program that emphasized how to partner with parents, attend to their positive attributes, and monitor the clinician–parent alliance to enhance the ability of residential treatment team members to engage parents in their youth's treatment. While the intervention showed promise with higher initial alliance relative to a comparison group, the study was limited due to lack of random assignment.

Given the lack of research guidance, we provide our own experience-based guidance on how to train and supervise student clinicians in building and maintaining the therapeutic alliance with youth clients. This training follows the evidence-based steps of behavioral skills training (Miltenberger, 2016). First, trainees learn what the therapeutic alliance is and why it is important. They learn how to recognize indicators of good and poor alliances, and they learn what therapist behaviors are useful for initial alliance building and what behaviors may be helpful for maintaining a good alliance or helping to manage alliance ruptures. Unfortunately, we predominantly utilize adult therapy readings (e.g., Cormier et al., 2016; Poorman, 2003) given that there are relatively few youth readings (e.g., Castro-Blanco & Karver, 2010; Karver & Caporino, 2010) providing guidance on therapeutic alliance formation.

After learning this information, classroom teachers and/or supervisors model sample dialogue that a clinician can use to engage a youth client and/or parent. Following this, trainees participate in various role plays of different therapy situations and receive feedback from their teachers/supervisors that either reinforces correct engagement behaviors or provides corrective feedback to help cue clinicians to utilize potentially more effective engagement behaviors. While this classroom/supervision room based learning is a good early step, ultimately, learning needs to move to actual interaction with clients. Thus we recommend utilizing videotaping of all therapy sessions and collection of self-report alliance data, which can then be reviewed in supervision. These sources of information can then be used (e.g., watching videos in supervision) to provide trainees with further feedback about their use of alliance-enhancing behaviors both initially and throughout treatment.

Taking a closer look at some of the studies within this meta-analysis, an interesting pattern with training implications can be discerned. Notably, smaller alliance to outcome effect sizes were observed for more highly controlled studies. In fact, these studies frequently had clinicians with high alliance scores, thus limiting the variability needed to find a stronger alliance to outcome relation. This raises the question as to why these studies had such high alliance scores. It is possible that the higher quality studies selected higher quality clinicians and that in attempting to provide evidence for their specific psychotherapy, the treatment developers provided better engagement and alliance training to their clinicians. If so, it would prove valuable to explicate what exactly is being taught and how it is being taught and supervised to see if these training methods can be made more broadly available.

THERAPEUTIC PRACTICES

- Create multiple alliances, not only the alliance with the youth. The therapist–parent/caregiver association with treatment outcome is of the same magnitude as the therapist–youth alliance.
- Monitor alliance formation and maintenance over the course of treatment and not just at the beginning of treatment with both the youth and the parents/caregivers. The alliance is related to outcome early in treatment, throughout treatment, and at the end of treatment.
- Consider the measures listed in Table 3.1 for tracking the alliance; specifically, we recommend the TASC-R for youth and the WAI for parents.
- Avoid being overly formal, emphasizing common ground that comes off as inauthentic, "pushing" youth to talk about or overly focusing on emotionally sensitive material, bringing up previous material to discuss before they are ready or too frequently, and criticizing youth clients; these are therapist behaviors that undermine the alliance (Creed & Kendall, 2005; Karver et al., 2008).
- Seek to manifest a friendly disposition (even fun/humorous when appropriate), provide praise, show impartiality (not automatically taking the parental point of view), and demonstrate genuine respect for the youth clients while calmly and attentively eliciting information in an interactive manner about the youth's subjective experience; these are therapist behaviors that promote the alliance. Only gradually address deeper issues after starting on current practical concerns.
- Do not take initial mistrust personally; youths, especially adolescents, are not likely to come to therapy ready to trust a therapist who they often perceive to be another adult authority figure.
- Earn trust and form an alliance by establishing confidentiality, carefully attending (using active/reflective listening methods) to the youth's perspective, showing empathy so that the client feels understood, accepting/validating and seeing value in youth statements, and advocating for the youth and presenting as an ally. Also critical is expressing support for the youth client especially when emotionally painful material is discussed.
- Expect and honor divergent views about treatment goals and how to accomplish them. Formation of a therapeutic alliance with both youth and parent(s) requires the therapist to be open to suggestions/ideas and to collaboratively formulate goals and treatment plans that are responsive to youths and parents.
- Acknowledge parental strengths and collaborate, partner, and set mutual expectations with a youth's caregivers in a relaxed, calm, and not overly formal manner. If parents are not adequately engaged in treatment, they will not bring a youth client even if the youth does have a good relationship with the therapist.
- Socialize the youth to treatment by providing an explicit, consistent, and credible framework for how the planned treatment is supposed to work, orienting the youth to the therapist and client roles in treatment and establishing hopefulness/expectancy that the treatment will be useful in the client's life.

♦ Create a psychotherapy environment in which the youth client feels like a partner in the relationship and maintain flexibility to respond to youth needs even when delivering a manualized treatment. Youth, especially adolescents, are unlikely to remain engaged in treatment if they perceive the therapist to be another adult authority figure who tells them what to do.

♦ Match or adapt alliance-enhancing behaviors and overall approach to a youth client based on his or her developmental level, gender, cultural background, attributional style, readiness to change, treatment preferences, interpersonal skills, and attachment style.

♦ Make adjustments in alliance formation based on parental characteristics (interpersonal skills, level of stress, expectancies on degree of parental involvement in treatment, cultural values) and on any match/mismatch between parent–youth perspectives/goals.

REFERENCES

References marked with an asterisk indicate studies included in the meta-analyses.

*Abrishami, G. F., & Warren, J. S. (2013). Therapeutic alliance and outcomes in children and adolescents served in a community mental health system. *Journal of Child and Adolescent Behavior 1*(2), 1–7.

*Accurso, E. C. (2012). *Therapeutic alliance and outcomes in usual care child psychotherapy* (Doctoral dissertation). Retrieved from https://search.proquest.com/docview/1034733421

Accurso, E. C., & Garland, A. F. (2015). Child, caregiver, and therapist perspectives on therapeutic alliance in usual care child psychotherapy. *Psychological Assessment, 27*(1), 347–352.

*Adler, A. G. (1998). The alliance between child therapist and parent: How it predicts treatment outcome and reflects parent characteristics. *Dissertation Abstracts International: Section B: The Sciences and Engineering, 59*(4-B), 1836.

Alexander, L. B., & Luborsky, L. (1986). The Penn Helping Alliance Scales. In L. S. Greenberg & W. M. Pinsof (Eds.), *The psychotherapeutic process: A research handbook* (pp. 325–366). New York, NY: Guilford.

*Anderson, R. E., Spence, S. H., Donovan, C. L., March, S., Prosser, S., & Kenardy, J. (2012). Working alliance in online cognitive behavior therapy for anxiety disorders in youth: Comparison with clinic delivery and its role in predicting outcome. *Journal of Medical Internet Research, 14*(3), 1–16.

*Avny, S. (2011). *The alliance-outcome association in CBT and usual care for youth depression delivered in community settings* (Master's thesis). Retrieved from http://scholarscompass.vcu.edu

Ayotte, M. H., Lanctôt, N., & Tourigny, M. (2016). How the working alliance with adolescent girls in residential care predicts the trajectories of their behavior problems. *Residential Treatment for Children & Youth, 33*(2), 135–154.

Baldwin, S., & Shadish, W. (2011). A primer on meta-analysis in clinical psychology. *Journal of Experimental Psychopathology, 2*, 294–317.

Barmish, A. J., & Kendall, P. C. (2005). Should parents be co-clients in cognitive-behavioral therapy for anxious youth? *Journal of Clinical Child & Adolescent Psychology, 34*(3), 569–581.

*Becker, T. (2012). *Effectiveness of parent call-in versus e-counseling services in treating pediatric behavior problems uncovered in a primary care medical encounter* (Doctoral dissertation). Retrieved from Proquest. (Order Number 904395036)

*Bhola, P., & Kapur, M. (2013). The development and role of the therapeutic alliance in supportive psychotherapy with adolescents. *Psychological Studies, 58*(3), 207–215.

Bickman, L., Andrade, A. R., Lambert, E. W., Doucette, A., Sapyta, J. & Boyd, A. S. (2004). Youth therapeutic alliance in intensive treatment settings. *Journal of Behavioral Health Services & Research, 31*(2), 134–148.

Bickman, L., Riemer, M., Lambert, E. W., Kelley, S. D., Breda, C., Dew, S., . . . Vides de Andrade, A. R. (2007). *Manual of the Peabody Treatment and Progress Battery* (Electronic version). Nashville, TN: Vanderbilt University.

Bickman, L., Vides de Andrade, A. R., Athy, M. M., Chen, J. L., De Nadai, A. S., Jordan-Arthur, B. L., & Karver, M. S. (2012). The relationship between change in therapeutic alliance ratings and improvement in youth symptom severity: Whose ratings matter the most?. *Administration and Policy in Mental Health and Mental Health Services Research, 39*(1–2), 78–89.

Blatt, S. J., Zuroff, D. C., Quinlan, D. M., & Pilkonis, P. (1996). Interpersonal factors in brief treatment of depression: Further analyses of the NIMH treatment of depression collaborative research program. *Journal of Consulting and Clinical Psychology, 64*, 162–171.

Bordin, E. S. (1979). The generalizability of the psychoanalytic concept of the working alliance. *Psychotherapy: Theory, Research and Practice, 16*(3), 252–260.

Bundy, C. (2004). Changing behaviour: Using motivational interviewing techniques. *Journal of the Royal Society of Medicine, 97*(44), 43–47.

Burckell, L. A., & Goldfried, M. R. (2006). Therapist qualities preferred by sexual-minority individuals. *Psychotherapy: Theory, Research, Practice, Training, 43*(1), 32–49.

Buscemi, N., Hartling, L., Vandermeer, B., Tjosvold, L., & Klassen, T. P. (2005). Single data extraction generated more errors than double data extraction in systematic reviews. *Journal of Clinical Epidemiology, 59*, 697–703.

Capaldi, S. (2010). *The relationship between therapeutic alliance and treatment outcome in prolonged exposure therapy for adolescents with posttraumatic stress disorder* (Master's thesis). Retrieved from http://digitalcommons.pcom.edu/.

*Capaldi, S., Asnaani A., Zandberg, L. J., Carpenter, J. K., & Foa, E. B. (2016). Therapeutic alliance during prolonged exposure versus client-centered therapy for adolescent posttraumatic stress disorder. *Journal of Clinical Psychology, 72*(10), 1026–1036.

Castro-Blanco, D. E., & Karver, M. S. (2010). *Elusive alliance: Treatment engagement strategies with high-risk adolescents*. Washington, DC: American Psychological Association.

*Chiu, A. W., McLeod, B. D., Har, K., & Wood, J. J. (2009). Child-therapist alliance and clinical outcomes in cognitive behavioral therapy for child anxiety disorders. *Journal of Child Psychology & Psychiatry, 50*(6), 751–758.

Christensen, M., & Skogstad, R. S. (2009). *What predicts quality of the therapeutic alliance in a cognitive behavioural treatment for children with anxiety disorders? Therapeutic alliance measured from the patient, therapist and observer perspective* (Unpublished master's thesis). University of Bergen, Norway.

Chorpita, B. F., & Weisz, J. R. (2005). Child-Therapist Alliance. Unpublished measure.

Chu, B. C., & Kendall, P. C. (2004). Positive association of child involvement and treatment outcome within a manual-based cognitive-behavioral treatment for children with anxiety. *Journal of Consulting and Clinical Psychology, 72*(5), 821–829.

Cichocki, B. (2015). The alliance in psychiatric rehabilitation: Client characteristics associated with the initial alliance in a supported employment program. *Work, 5*(4), 811–824.

Clark, M. D. (1998). Strength-based practices- The ABC's of working with adolescents who don't want to work with you. *Federal Probation, 62*(1), 46–53.

Cooper, H., Hedges, L. V., & Valentine, J. C. (Eds.). (2009). *The handbook of research synthesis and meta-analysis*. New York, NY: Russell Sage Foundation.

Cormier, S., Nurius, P. S., & Osborn, C. J. (2016). *Interviewing and change strategies for helpers* (8th ed.). Boston MA: Cengage Learning.

Crawford, E. A., Frank, H. E., Palitz, S. A., Davis, J. P., & Kendall, P. C. (2018). Process factors associated with improved outcomes in CBT for anxious youth: Therapeutic content, alliance, and therapist actions. *Cognitive Therapy and Research, 42*(2), 174–183.

*Creed, T. A. (2007). A mediation model of early predictors of treatment outcome within cognitive-behavioral therapy for children with anxiety disorders: Child involvement, therapist behavior, and alliance. *Dissertation Abstracts International: Section B: The Sciences and Engineering, 68*(3-B), 1919.

Creed, T. A., & Kendall, P. C. (2005). Therapist alliance-building behavior within a cognitive-behavioral treatment for anxiety in youth. *Journal of Consulting and Clinical Psychology, 73*(3), 498–505.

*Cummings, C. C., Caporino, N. E., Settipani, C. A., Read, K. L., Compton, S. N., March, J., . . . Kendall, P. C. (2013). The therapeutic relationship in cognitive-behavioral therapy and pharmacotherapy for anxious youth. *Journal of Consulting and Clinical Psychology, 81*(5), 859–864.

*Darchuk, A. J. (2007). *The role of the therapeutic alliance and its relationship to treatment outcome and client motivation in an adolescent substance abuse treatment setting* (Doctoral dissertation). Retrieved from https://etd.ohiolink.edu

Descutner, C. J., & Thelen, M. H. (1991). Development and validation of a Fear-of-Intimacy Scale. *Psychological Assessment: A Journal of Consulting and Clinical Psychology, 3*(2), 218–225.

DeVet, K. A., Kim, Y. J., Charlot-Swilley, D., & Ireys, H. T. (2003). The therapeutic relationship in child therapy: Perspectives of children and mothers. *Journal of Clinical Child & Adolescent Psychology, 32*(2), 277–283.

DiGiuseppe, R., Linscott, J., & Jilton, R. (1996). Developing the therapeutic alliance in child–adolescent psychotherapy. *Applied and Preventive Psychology, 5*(2), 85–100.

Duarté-Vélez, Y., Bernal, G., & Bonilla, K. (2010). Culturally adapted cognitive-behavior therapy: Integrating sexual, spiritual, and family identities in an evidence-based treatment of a depressed Latino adolescent. *Journal of Clinical Psychology, 66*(8), 895–906.

Egger, M., Smith, G. D., Schneider, M., & Minder, C. (1997). Bias in meta-analysis detected by a simple, graphical test. *British Medical Journal, 315*(7109), 629–634.

*Eltz, M. J., Shirk, S. R., & Sarlin, N. (1995). Alliance formation and treatment outcome among maltreated adolescents. *Child Abuse & Neglect, 19*(4), 419–431.

Estrada, A., & Russell, R. (1999). The development of the Child Psychotherapy Process Scales (CPPS). *Psychotherapy Research, 9*(2), 154–166.

Feingold, A. (2009). Effect sizes for growth-modeling analysis for controlled clinical trials in the same metric as for classical analysis. *Psychological Methods, 14*(1), 43–53.

*Fernández, O. M., Krause, M., & Pérez, J. C. (2016). Therapeutic alliance in the initial phase of psychotherapy with adolescents: Different perspectives and their association with therapeutic outcomes. *Research in Psychotherapy: Psychopathology, Process and Outcome, 19*, 1–9.

Figueiredo, B., Dias, P., Lima, V. S., & Lamela, D. (2016). Working Alliance Inventory for Children and Adolescents (WAI-CA). *European Journal of Psychological Assessment.* [Advance online publication]

Fisher, Z., & Tipton, E. (2017). R Package Robumeta Version 2.0 [Computer software]. Retrieved from https://cran.r-project.org/web/packages/robumeta/index.html

Fjermestad, K. W., Lerner, M. D., McLeod, B. D., Wergeland, G. J. H., Haugland, B. S. M., Havik, O. E., . . . Silverman, W. K. (2018). Motivation and treatment credibility predict alliance in cognitive behavioral treatment for youth with anxiety disorders in community clinics. *Journal of Clinical Psychology, 74*(6), 793–805.

Fjermestad, K. W., Lerner, M. D., McLeod, B. D., Wergeland, G. H., Heiervang, E. R., Silverman, W. K., . . . Haugland, B. S. (2016). Therapist-youth agreement on alliance change predicts long-term outcome in CBT for anxiety disorders. *Journal of Child Psychology & Psychiatry, 57*(5), 625–632.

Fjermestad, K. W., McLeod, B. D., Heiervang, E. R., Havik, O. E., Öst, L. G., & Haugland, B. S. (2012). Factor structure and validity of the therapy process observational coding system for Child Psychotherapy–Alliance Scale. *Journal of Clinical Child & Adolescent Psychology, 41*(2), 246–254.

*Forsberg, S. (2011). *The relationship between therapeutic alliance and treatment outcome in a comparative study of individual and family therapy for adolescent anorexia nervosa* (Doctoral dissertation). Retrieved from Proquest. (Order Number 1433375288)

Freud, A. (1946). *The psycho-analytical treatment of children.* Oxford, England: Imago.

Gallagher, R., Kurtz, S., & Blackwell, S. C. (2010). Engaging adolescents with disruptive behavior disorders in therapeutic change. In D. Castro-Blanco & M. S. Karver (Eds.), *Elusive alliance: Treatment engagement strategies with high-risk adolescents* (pp. 139–158). Washington, DC: American Psychological Association.

Garcia, J. A., & Weisz, J. R. (2002). When youth mental health care stops: Therapeutic relationship problems and other reasons for ending youth outpatient treatment. *Journal of Consulting and Clinical Psychology, 70*(2), 439–443.

Garland, A. F., Accurso, E. C., Haine-Schlagel, R., Brookman-Frazee, L., Roesch, S., & Zhang, J. J. (2014). Searching for elements of evidence-based practices in children's usual care and examining their impact. *Journal of Clinical Child & Adolescent Psychology, 43*(2), 201–215.

Garner, B. R., Godley, S. H., & Funk, R. R. (2008). Predictors of early therapeutic alliance among adolescents in substance abuse treatment. *Journal of Psychoactive Drugs, 40*(1), 55–65.

Gaston, L., & Marmor, C. R. (1991). *Manual of the California Psychotherapy Alliance Scales (CALPAS).* Unpublished manuscript.

Glenn, C. R., Franklin, J. C., & Nock, M. K. (2015). Evidence-based psychosocial treatments for self-injurious thoughts and behaviors in youth. *Journal of Clinical Child & Adolescent Psychology, 44*(1), 1–29.

*Hagen, K. A., & Ogden, T. (2017). Predictors of changes in child behavior following parent management training: Child, context, and therapy factors. *International Journal of Psychology, 52*(2), 106–115.

Hartley, D. E., & Strupp, H. H. (1983). The therapeutic alliance: Its relationship to outcome in brief psychotherapy. *Empirical Studies of Psychoanalytic Theories, 1*, 1–37.

Hatcher, R. L., & Gillaspy, J. A. (2006). Development and validation of a revised short version of the Working Alliance Inventory. *Psychotherapy Research, 16*(1), 12–25.

Hawke, J. M., Hennen, J., & Gallione, P. (2005). Correlates of therapeutic involvement among adolescents in residential drug treatment. *The American Journal of Drug and Alcohol Abuse, 31*(1), 163–177.

Hawley, K. M., & Garland, A. F. (2008). Working alliance in adolescent outpatient therapy: Youth, parent and therapist reports and associations with therapy outcomes. *Child & Youth Care Forum, 37*, 59–74.

Hawley, K. M., & Weisz, J. R. (2003). Child, parent and therapist (dis)agreement on target problems in outpatient therapy: The therapist's dilemma and its implications. *Journal of Consulting and Clinical Psychology, 71*(1), 62–70.

Hawley, K. M. & Weisz, J. R. (2005). Youth versus parent working alliance in usual clinical care: Distinctive associations with retention, satisfaction, and treatment outcome. *Journal of Clinical Child & Adolescent Psychology, 34*(1), 117–128.

Higgins, J. P. (2008). Commentary: Heterogeneity in meta-analysis should be expected and appropriately quantified. *International Journal of Epidemiology, 37*(5), 1158–1160.

*Hogue, A., Dauber, S., Stambaugh L. F., Cecero, J. J., & Liddle, H. A. (2006). Early therapeutic alliance and treatment outcome in individual and family therapy for adolescent behavior problems. *Journal of Consulting and Clinical Psychology, 74*(1), 121–129.

Horvath, A. O., & Greenberg, L. S. (1989). Development and validation of the Working Alliance Inventory. *Journal of Counseling Psychology, 36*(2), 223–233.

*Hudson, J. L., Kendall, P. C., Chu, B. C., Gosch, E., Martin, E., Taylor, A., & Knight, A. (2014). Child involvement, alliance, and therapist flexibility: Process variables in cognitive-behavioural therapy for anxiety disorders in childhood. *Behaviour Research and Therapy, 52*, 1–8.

*Hukkelberg, S. S., & Ogden, T. (2013). Working alliance and treatment fidelity as predictors of externalizing problem behaviors in parent management training. *Journal of Consulting and Clinical Psychology, 81*(6), 1010–1020.

Johnson, L. D., Miller, S. D., & Duncan, B. L. (2000). *Session Rating Scale*. Chicago, IL: Authors.

*Karpenko, V. (2010). *Clinically significant symptom changes in adolescents receiving outpatient community mental health services: Does it relate to satisfaction, perceived change, therapeutic alliance, and improvement in presenting problems?* (Doctoral dissertation). Retrieved from Proquest. (Order Number 746482656)

Karver, M. S., & Caporino, N. (2010). The use of empirically supported strategies for building a therapeutic relationship with an adolescent with oppositional-defiant disorder. *Cognitive and Behavioral Practice, 17*(2), 222–232.

Karver, M. S., Handelsman, J. B., Fields, S., & Bickman, L. (2006). Meta-analysis of therapeutic relationship variables in youth and family therapy: The evidence for different relationship variables in the child and adolescent treatment outcome literature. *Clinical Psychology Review, 26*(1), 50–65.

Karver, M. S., Handelsman, J. B., Fields, S., & Bickman, L. (2005). A theoretical model of common process factors in youth and family therapy. *Mental Health Services Research, 7*(1), 35–51.

Karver, M., Shirk, S., Day, R., Field, S., & Handelsman, J. (2003). *Rater's manual for the Alliance Observation Coding System*. Unpublished manuscript, University of South Florida, Tampa.

*Karver, M. S., Shirk, S., Handelsman, J., Fields, S., Crisp, H., Gudmundsen, G., & McMakin, D. (2008). Relationship processes in youth psychotherapy: Measuring alliance, alliance building behaviors, and client involvement. *Journal of Emotional and Behavioral Disorders, 16*(1), 15–28.

*Kazdin, A. E., & Durbin, K. A. (2012). Predictors of child-therapist alliance in cognitive behavioral treatment of children referred for oppositional and antisocial behavior. *Psychotherapy, 49*(2), 202–217.

*Kazdin, A. E., Marciano, P. L., & Whitley, M. K. (2005). The therapeutic alliance in cognitive-behavioral treatment of children referred for oppositional, aggressive, and antisocial behavior. *Journal of Consulting and Clinical Psychology, 72*(4), 726–730.

*Kazdin, A. E., & Whitley, M. K. (2006). Pretreatment social relations, therapeutic alliance, and improvements in parenting practices in parent management training. *Journal of Consulting and Clinical Psychology, 74*(2), 346–355.

*Kazdin, A. E., Whitley, M., & Marciano, P. L. (2006). Child–therapist and parent–therapist alliance and therapeutic change in the treatment of children referred for oppositional, aggressive, and antisocial behavior. *Journal of Child Psychology & Psychiatry, 47*(5), 436–445.

*Keeley, M. L., Geffken, G. R., Ricketts, E., McNmara, J. P., & Storch, E. A. (2011). The therapeutic alliance in the cognitive behavioral treatment of pediatric obsessive-compulsive disorder. *Journal of Anxiety Disorders, 25*, 855–863.

*Kendall, P. C. (1994). Treating anxiety disorders in children: Results of a randomized clinical trial. *Journal of Consulting and Clinical Psychology, 62*(1), 100–110.

*Kendall, P. C., Flannery-Schroeder, E., Panichelli-Mindel, S. M., Southam-Gerow, M., Henin, A., & Warman, M. (1997). Therapy for youths with anxiety disorders: A second randomized clinical trial. *Journal of Consulting and Clinical Psychology, 65*(3), 366–380.

*Klebanoff, S. (2015). *The therapeutic alliance in cognitive-behavioral therapy for children with autism and anxiety* (Master's thesis). Retrieved from Proquest. (Order Number 1694861568)

Korchmaros, J. D., & Stevens, S. J. (2014). Examination of the role of therapeutic alliance, treatment dose, and treatment completion in the effectiveness of the seven challenges. *Child Adolescent Social Work, 31*, 1–24.

*Labouliere, C. D., Reyes, J. P., Shirk, S., & Karver, M. (2017). Therapeutic alliance with depressed adolescents: Predictor or outcome? Disentangling temporal confounds to understand early improvement. *Journal of Clinical Child & Adolescent Psychology, 46*(4), 600–610.

Lamers, A., Nieuwenhuizen, C., Twisk, J., Koning, E., & Vermeiren, R. (2016). Longitudinal results of strengthening the parent-team alliance in child semi-residential psychiatry: Does team investment make a difference?. *Child and Adolescent Psychiatry and Mental Health, 10*(1), 1–11.

*Langberg, J. M., Becker, S. P., Epstein, J. N., Vaughn, A. J., & Girio-Herrera, E. (2013). Perdictors of response and mechanisms of change in an organizational skills intervention for students with ADHD. *Journal of Child and Family Studies, 22*(7), 1000–1012.

Langer, D. A., McLeod, B. D., & Weisz, J. R. (2011). Do treatment manuals undermine youth–therapist alliance in community clinical practice?. *Journal of Consulting and Clinical Psychology, 79*(4), 427–432.

Levin, L., Henderson, H. A., & Ehrenreich-May, J. (2012). Interpersonal predictors of early therapeutic alliance in a transdiagnostic cognitive-behavioral treatment for adolescents with anxiety and depression. *Psychotherapy, 49*(2), 218–230.

Liber, J. M., McLeod, B. D., Van Widenfelt, B. M., Goedhart, A. W., van der Leen, A. J., Utens, E. M., & Treffers, P. D. (2010). Examining the relation between the therapeutic alliance, treatment adherence, and outcome of cognitive behavioral therapy for children with anxiety disorders. *Behavior Therapy, 41*, 172–186.

Liebsack, B. K. (2016). *Attrition in parent-child interaction therapy* (Doctoral dissertation). Retrieved from Proquest. (Order Number 1864649552)

Lincourt, P., Kuettel, T. J., & Bombardier, C. H. (2002). Motivational interviewing in a group setting with mandated clients: A pilot study. *Addictive Behaviors, 27*(3), 381–391.

Linscott, J., DiGiuseppe, R., & Jilton, R. (1993, August). *A measure of therapeutic alliance in adolescent psychotherapy*. Poster session presented at American Psychological Association convention, Toronto, ON.

Marker, C. D., Comer, J. S., Abramova, V., & Kendall, P. C. (2013). The reciprocal relationship between alliance and symptom improvement across the treatment of childhood anxiety. *Journal of Clinical Child & Adolescent Psychology, 42*(1), 22–33.

Martin, D. J., Garske, J. P., & Davis, M. K. (2000). Relation of the therapeutic alliance with outcome and other variables: A meta-analytic review. *Journal of Consulting and Clinical Psychology, 68*(3), 438–450.

McLeod, B. D. (2011). Relation of the alliance with outcomes in youth psychotherapy: A meta-analysis. *Clinical Psychology Review, 31*(4), 603–616.

McLeod, B. D. (2001). *Therapy Process Observational Coding System for Child Psychotherapy—Alliance scale*. Unpublished manuscript, University of California, Los Angeles.

McLeod, B. D., Southam-Gerow, M. A., & Kendall, P. C. (2017). Observer, youth and therapist perspectives on the alliance in cognitive behavioral treatment for youth anxiety. *Psychological Assessment, 29*(12), 1550–1555.

*McLeod, B. D., & Weisz, J. R. (2005). The Therapy Process Observational Coding System—Alliance scale: Measure characteristics and prediction of outcome in usual care clinical practice. *Journal of Consulting and Clinical Psychology, 73*(2), 323–333.

Meeks, J. E. (1971). *The fragile alliance: An orientation to psychotherapy of the adolescent*. New York, NY: Krieger.

Milrod, B., Shapiro, T., Gross, C., Silver, G., Preter, S., Libow, A., & Leon, A. C. (2013). Does manualized psychodynamic psychotherapy have an impact on youth anxiety disorders? *American Journal of Psychotherapy, 67*(4), 359–366.

Miltenberger, R. G. (2016). *Behavior modification: Principles and procedures* (6th ed.). Boston, MA: Cengage.

Nevid, J. S., Ghannadpour, J., & Haggerty, G. (2017). The role of gender as a moderator of the alliance-outcome link in acute inpatient treatment of severely disturbed youth. *Clinical Psychology & Psychotherapy, 24*(2), 528–533.

*Ormhaug, S. M., Jensen, T. K., Wentzel-Larsen, T., & Shirk, S. R. (2014). The therapeutic alliance in treatment of traumatized youths: Relation to outcome in a randomized clinical trial. *Journal of Consulting and Clinical Psychology, 82*(1), 52–64.

*Ormhaug, S. M., Shirk, S. R., & Wentzel-Larsen, T. (2015). Therapist and client perspectives on the alliance in the treatment of traumatized adolescents. *European Journal of Psychotraumatology, 6*(1), 27705–27714.

Pekarik, G., & Stephenson, L. A. (1988). Adult and child client differences in therapy dropout research. *Journal of Clinical Child Psychology, 17*(4), 316–321.

*Pestle, S. L. (2012). *Alliance after evidence: The impact of youth-therapist alliance on treatment outcome for internalizing youth, over and above protocol effects* (Doctoral dissertation). Retrieved from http://scholarspace.manoa.hawaii.edu/

Peterson, R. A., & Brown, S. P. (2005). On the use of beta coefficients in meta-analysis. *Journal of Applied Psychology, 90*, 175–181.

Poorman, P. B. (2003). *Microskills and theoretical foundations for professional helpers*. Boston, MA: Pearson Education.

R Core Team. (2017). R: A language and environment for statistical computing (version 3.4.2) [Computer software]. Vienna, Austria: R Foundation for Statistical Computing.

*Rabbit, S. M., Carrubba, E., Leeza, B., McWhinney, E., Pope, J., & Kazdin, A. E. (2016). Reducing therapist contact in parenting programs: Evaluation of Internet-based treatments for child conduct problems. *Journal of Child and Family Studies, 25*, 2001–2020.

Reis, B. F., & Brown, L. G. (2006). Preventing therapy dropout in the real world: The clinical utility of videotape preparation and client estimate of treatment duration. *Professional Psychology: Research and Practice, 37*(3), 311–316.

*Reyes, J. M. (2013). *Examining the alliance-outcome relationship: Revers causation, third variables, and treatment phase artifacts* (Doctoral dissertation). Retrieved from http:// digitalcommons.du.edu

*Ricketts, E. J. (2015). *A randomized waitlist-controlled trail of voice over Internet protocol-delivered behavior therapy for chronic tic disorders* (Doctoral dissertation). Retrieved from Proquest. (Order Number 1640769381)

Riley, R. D. (2009). Multivariate meta-analysis: The effect of ignoring within-study correlation. *Journal of the Royal Statistical Society: Series A (Statistics in Society), 172*(4), 789–811.

Riley, R. D., Abrams, K. R., Sutton, A. J., Lambert, P. C., & Thompson, J. R. (2007). Bivariate random-effects meta-analysis and the estimation of between-study correlation. *BMC Medical Research Methodology, 7*(1), 1–6.

Roest, J., van der Helm, P., Strijbosch, E., van Brandenburg, M., & Stams, G. J. (2016). Measuring therapeutic alliance with children in residential treatment and therapeutic day care: A validation study of the Children's Alliance Questionnaire. *Research on Social Work Practice, 26*(2), 212–218.

*Roth, N. P. (2009). *School-based mental health: An examination of individual therapy with rural children and adolescents in the school* (Unpublished doctoral dissertation). University of Kentucky, Lexington.

Sapyta, J. A. (2011). *Evaluating therapeutic alliance longitudinally: Describing therapeutic alliance growth and its implications for outcomes* (Doctoral dissertation). Retrieved from http://etd.library.vanderbilt.edu/

*Schmit, E. L. (2015). *The relationship between working alliance and therapeutic goal attainment in an adolescent inpatient, acute care behavioral hospital* (Doctoral dissertation). Retrieved from Proquest. (Order Number 1680271390)

Shelef, K., & Diamond, G. M. (2008). Short form of the revised Vanderbilt Therapeutic Alliance Scale: Development, reliability, and validity. *Psychotherapy Research, 18*(4), 433–443.

Shelleby, E. C., & Shaw, D. S. (2014). Outcomes of parenting interventions for child conduct problems: A review of differential effectiveness. *Child Psychiatry & Human Development, 45*(5), 628–645.

Shirk, S. R. (2001). Development and cognitive therapy. *Journal of Cognitive Psychotherapy, 15*(3), 155–163.

Shirk, S. (2003, August). *Relationship processes in youth CBT: Measuring alliance and collaboration.* Paper presented at the meeting of the Association for the Advancement of Behavior Therapy, Boston, MA.

Shirk, S. R., Caporino, N., & Karver, M. S. (2010). The alliance in adolescent therapy: Conceptual, operational, and predictive issues. In D. Castro-Blanco & M. S. Karver (Eds.), *Elusive alliance: Treatment engagement strategies with high-risk adolescents* (pp. 59–93). Washington, DC: American Psychological Association.

*Shirk, S. R., Gudmundsen, G., Kaplinski H. C., & McMakin, D. L. (2008). Alliance and outcome in cognitive-behavioral therapy for adolescent depression. *Journal of Clinical Child & Adolescent Psychology, 37*(3), 631–639.

Shirk, S. R., & Karver, M. (2003). Prediction of treatment outcome from relationship variables in child and adolescent therapy: A meta-analytic review. *Journal of Consulting and Clinical Psychology, 71*(3), 452–464.

Shirk, S., & Karver, M. (2006). Process issues in cognitive-behavioral therapy for youth. In P. C. Kendall (Ed.), *Child and adolescent therapy: Cognitive-behavioral procedures* (pp. 465–491). New York, NY: Guilford.

Shirk, S. R., & Karver, M. S. (2011). Alliance in child and adolescent psychotherapy. In J. C. Norcross (Ed.), *Psychotherapy relationships that work: Evidence-based responsiveness* (pp. 70–92). New York, NY: Oxford University Press.

Shirk, S. R., Karver, M. S., & Brown, R. (2011). The alliance in child and adolescent psychotherapy. *Psychotherapy, 48*(1), 17–24.

Shirk, S. R., & Russell, R. L. (1996). *Change processes in child psychotherapy: Revitalizing treatment and research.* New York, NY: Guilford.

Shirk, S. R., & Saiz, C. C. (1992). Clinical, empirical, and developmental perspectives on the therapeutic relationship in child psychotherapy. *Development and Psychopathology, 4*, 713–728.

Simpson, T. P. (2008). *Factors predicting therapeutic alliance in antisocial adolescents* (Master's thesis). Retrieved from http://scholarworks.uno.edu/cgi

Simpson, T. S. (2013). *Trauma-focused involvement in psychotherapy: Relations with therapeutic alliance and symptoms of post-traumatic stress disorder* (Doctoral dissertation). Retrieved from http://digitalcommons.du.edu

Smith, R. (2010). *The impact of therapeutic alliance on outcomes in parent-dyadic interventions* (Doctoral dissertation). Retrieved from https://etd.ohiolink.edu/

Smith, J. D., Berkel, C., Hails, K. A., Dishion, T. J., Shaw, D. S., & Wilson, M. N. (2018). Predictors of participation in the family check-up program: A randomized trial of yearly services from age 2 to 10 years. *Prevention Science, 19*(5), 652–662.

*Sullivan, T. C. (2013). *Validity of session rating scale scores with adolescent clients in a school setting* (Doctoral dissertation). Retrieved from Proquest. (Order Number 1036597251)

Tracey, T. J., & Kokotovic, A. M. (1989). Factor structure of the working alliance inventory. *Psychological Assessment: A Journal of Consulting and Clinical Psychology, 1*(3), 207–210.

Viechtbauer, W. (2010). Conducting meta-analyses in R with the metafor package. *Journal of Statistical Software, 36*(3), 1–48.

Webb, C. A., DeRubeis, R. J., Amsterdam, J. D., Shelton, R. C., Hollon, S. D., & Dimidjian, S. (2011). Two aspects of the therapeutic alliance: Differential relations with depressive symptom change. *Journal of Consulting and Clinical Psychology, 79*, 279–283.

Webb, C., Hayes, A. M., Grasso, D., Laurenceau, J. P., & Deblinger, E. (2014). Trauma-focused cognitive behavioral therapy for youth: Effectiveness in a community setting. *Psychological Trauma: Theory, Research, Practice, and Policy, 6*(5), 555–562.

Wintersteen, M. B., Mensinger, J. L., & Diamond, G. S. (2005). Do gender and racial differences between patient and therapist affect therapeutic alliance and treatment retention in adolescents? *Professional Psychology: Research and Practice, 36*(4), 400–408.

Wood, J. J., McLeod, B. D., Klebanoff, S., & Brookman-Frazee, L. (2015). Toward the implementation of evidence-based interventions for youth with autism spectrum disorders in schools and community agencies. *Behavior Therapy, 46*(1), 83–95.

Yeh, M., McCabe, K., Hurlburt, M., Hough, R., Hazen, A., Culver, S., . . . Landsverk, J. (2002). Referral sources, diagnoses, and service types of youth in public outpatient mental health care: A focus on ethnic minorities. *The Journal of Behavioral Health Services and Research, 29*(1), 45–60.

*Zorzella, K. P., Muller, R. T., & Cribbie, R. A. (2015). The relationships between therapeutic alliance and internalizing and externalizing symptoms in trauma-focused cognitive behavioral therapy. *Child Abuse & Neglect, 50*, 171–181.

4

ALLIANCES IN COUPLE
AND FAMILY THERAPY

Myrna L. Friedlander, Valentín Escudero,
Marianne J. Welmers-van de Poll, and Laurie Heatherington

All psychotherapists need to make a judgment about whether an individual client is ready and motivated for therapeutic work, but therapists conducting couple and family therapy need to concern themselves with each family member's level of motivation and readiness, which often are at odds. For example, not uncommonly, Mother is worried about Daughter's emotional state, whereas Father has no such concerns but fears that Mother's hidden agenda is to portray him as the bad guy. If the therapist does not define the treatment goals and tasks in such a way that everyone can "sign on," or if the therapist is unable to connect empathically with each individual, the treatment may never get off the ground.

Here, then, is the crux of the matter: In concept and in practicality, the working alliance in couple/family therapy (CFT) is both similar to and different from the working alliance in individual psychotherapy. In both treatment formats, therapeutic goals and tasks need to be discussed and agreed upon early on and continually as the process evolves, and in both formats the therapist needs to "click" emotionally with the client(s). Only in conjoint CFT, however, does the therapist need to develop and nurture multiple alliances simultaneously.

The challenge is that these multiple alliances interact with one another in covert as well as overt ways, particularly when family members are in conflict with one another. For example, if Father thinks Mother will lay all the blame for Daughter's troubles on him, he may privately decide to attend the initial session and then be done with it. If Daughter thinks that her parents are using her problems as a way to fight with each other, she may refuse to engage with the therapist in any meaningful way. If Mother expects the therapist to side with her, she may dominate the sessions, which will ultimately backfire if in doing so she further alienates her husband and daughter.

Due to the complexity of balancing multiple working alliances, engagement and retention in treatment figure more prominently in the couple and family literature than in the literature on individual psychotherapy. Although not a common occurrence, sometimes it is the adolescent who brings the family to see a therapist, but ultimately the adult family members are the ones with the power to commit to the treatment or drop out.

Engagement and retention are particularly crucial when conjoint therapy is mandated by one member of the family or by an external authority, such as child protective services. In these cases, the therapist's first objective must be to establish a working relationship with the family aside from the dictates of the mandate so that all family members see the sessions as an opportunity for healing rather than punishment. When the mandate originates within the family itself ("You'll come with me to therapy or else ... I'll leave you ... or You'll be placed in a group home ... or I'll turn you over to the police"), some family members experience the therapy as if they are "hostages" (Friedlander et al., 2006).

These clinical nuances have been studied in ever more sophisticated ways since a seminal article (Pinsof & Catherall, 1986) was published on the working alliance in conjoint couple and family therapy. This original piece took as a point of departure Bordin's (1979) classic model of alliance in individual therapy and expanded it to conjoint treatment. The authors explained that each family member not only creates a personal alliance with the therapist but also observes the unfolding alliances between the therapist and every other family member. Consequently, Client X can report on her own alliance, on her perception of Client Y's alliance with the therapist, and on her sense of the entire family's alliance with the therapist as a "system" or single unit. Moreover, when Client X's alliance is notably stronger than that of Client Y, the alliance is said to be "split." Split alliances can be pernicious, since family members who view their experience with the therapist very differently can wind up being polarized about the value of the therapy itself (Escudero & Friedlander, 2017; Friedlander et al., 2006).

As reflected in the concepts of *therapy hostage* and *split alliance*, measurement of the working alliance in CFT is particularly complex. Researchers have moved beyond the original adaptation of Bordin's (1979) model to capture additional aspects of the alliance unique to CFT, such as each individual's sense of safety with other family members (Friedlander et al., 2006), "split" or "unbalanced" alliances, and family members' alliances with one another (Friedlander et al., 2006; Pinsof, 1994). In recent years, researchers have also discovered how to study alliances as interacting systems, that is, how one family member's alliance with the therapist may predict another family member's view of the therapeutic progress (Friedlander et al., 2012) or final outcome (Anker et al., 2010).

This chapter updates our 2011 meta-analysis of the relation between CFT alliances and clinical outcomes, retention in treatment, and client self-reported improvement (Friedlander et al., 2011a). We begin by offering definitions of alliance and its measurement in CFT, followed by two case examples. We then review the highlights of previous meta-analyses, summarize a handful of landmark studies, and present the results of our updated meta-analysis. In discussing the results of this new analysis, we consider the evidence for causality, for client contributions to the alliance, and for sensitivity to diversity in creating and maintaining CFT alliances. We conclude with training and practice recommendations for enhancing the relational aspects of couple and family therapy.

DEFINITIONS

In the original application of the working alliance to conjoint treatment, Pinsof and Catherall (1986) expanded Bordin's (1979) tripartite conceptualization to distinguish between a client's personal alliance with the therapist, the client's view of other family members' personal alliances with the therapist, and the client's view of the alliance between the therapist and the family as a whole. In this Integrative Psychotherapy Alliance Model, a 3 × 3 matrix crossed the alliance components (*goal, task, bond*) by client perspective (*self, other, group*). Subsequently, the original matrix to include the *within-system alliance*; in CFT this construct refers to (a) the alliance between partners or family members, as well as (b) the alliance between cotherapists or between one therapist and the institution or agency delivering the treatment (Pinsof, 1994). With the addition of the within-system alliance, the revised matrix became 3 (alliance components) × 4 (perspectives) (Pinsof, 1994).

Within this matrix, the *group alliance* construct refers to the working relationship between the therapist and the couple or family as a unit. This group construct is important since it cannot be assumed that the strength or quality of the family unit's working relationship in CFT can be accurately reflected in either the sum or the average of family members' individual alliances with the therapist. In more recent literature, however, what has emerged as more salient than the group–therapist alliance is the allegiance (Symonds & Horvath, 2004) between partners or among family members apart from their collaboration with the therapist (cf. Lambert et al., 2012; Pinsof et al., 2008). This *within-family alliance*, alternately called the family's *shared sense of purpose* (Friedlander et al., 2006), refers to family members' collaboration with each other in therapy. More broadly, the construct reflects family members' agreement on the nature of their problems and the anticipated goals of treatment, as well as the value of working together on these goals in a therapeutic context.

Within-family alliance, or *shared sense of purpose within the family*, is one of four CFT alliance dimensions within the System for Observing Family Therapy Alliances (SOFTA; Friedlander et al., 2006). This conceptual model, which was developed empirically and clinically, contains one dimension that is similar to Bordin's (1979) bond component, *emotional connection to the therapist*. Another dimension, *engagement in the therapeutic process*, refers not only to client–therapist agreement on goals and tasks but also to a family member's sense of optimism that the therapeutic collaboration will lead to change.

The fourth SOFTA dimension, *safety within the therapeutic system*, is unique to the conjoint treatment format. Although feeling safe in therapy applies to a client's experience of individual therapy as well, in conjoint CFT clients are present in the sessions with their partners or other family members. Safety has distinct advantages and disadvantages for family members. Whereas seemingly intractable conflicts can be addressed and potentially resolved with the help of a professional neutral party (the therapist), conflicts sometimes escalate out of hand.

Unfortunately, alliances with the therapist can be compromised when family members feel less safe with each other upon returning home from a session. An adolescent may have found out that her parents are planning to divorce. A woman may have discovered that her partner betrayed her and is planning to leave. A father may have found out that his wife was physically abusing their children while he was out of town. In short, clients' safety in the therapeutic system is intricately linked to the degree to which they "click" emotionally and agree with the therapist—and with other family members—on the goals and tasks of their mutual collaboration (Friedlander et al., 2006).

Recently, the alliance rupture and repair process in the individual psychotherapy literature (e.g., Safran & Muran, 2000) has influenced CFT researchers. In the first published case study of alliance rupture in CFT (Escudero et al., 2012), described more fully later on in this chapter, a rupture was defined as occurring when a split alliance was in evidence or when a client responded to the therapist or to other family members with confrontation or withdrawal behavior. The authors defined a repair as occurring when (a) the family member demonstrates positive alliance-related behavior, (b) therapist and client discuss the rupture directly or indirectly, and (c) they move past it with productive collaboration on the goals or tasks of treatment.

This discussion of CFT alliance definitions would not be complete without mention of some similar of conceptualizations of the alliance construct. That is, whereas both the integrative psychotherapy alliance model and the SOFTA model define the alliance as multidimensional, some authors have studied aspects of the alliance in CFT without necessarily defining them as such. Examples include studies of a couple's agreement on the problems to be addressed in therapy (Biesen & Doss, 2013), a structured intervention to engage reluctant family members in treatment (Szapocznik et al., 1988), and family members' shifts, within a session, from disengagement with one another to sustained, observable engagement in a problem-solving task (Friedlander et al., 1994).

MEASURES

In this section we describe the five most widely used measures in CFT alliance research. Two instruments reflect individual family members' alliances with the therapist, the observational Vanderbilt Therapeutic Alliance Scale–Revised (VTAS-R; Diamond et al., 1996) and the Session Rating Scale Version 3 (SRS V.3.0; Duncan et al, 2003), which is the briefest of all the measures. The other three instruments have specific features that tap into family system dynamics. The Integrative Alliance Scales (Pinsof & Catherall, 1986; Pinsof et al., 2008), with versions for individual, couple (CTAS), and family (FTAS) therapy; the Working Alliance Inventory for individual therapy (WAI; Horvath & Greenberg, 1986, 1989), its short form (WAI-S; Tracey & Kokotovic, 1989), its observer version (WAI-O; Horvath & Greenberg, 1986), and its couples version (WAI-Co; Horvath & Symonds, 2004; Symonds, 1999); and the SOFTA (Escudero & Friedlander, 2017; Friedlander et al., 2006), the only measurement system designed "from the ground up" specifically for CFT, with both observer (SOFTA-o) and self-report (SOFTA-s) versions.

1. **VTAS-R.** To use this measure, trained judges rate a set of items based on their overall perceptions of a session or portion of a session. In the shortened version of the original VTAS (developed to study individual psychotherapy), the item wording was revised on the patient contribution and patient–therapist interaction scales and the therapist contribution scale was dropped (Diamond et al., 1996). However, like the original VTAS, the modified 26-item VTAS-R is highly labor intensive. When factor analyses revealed a single general dimension, the measure was further shortened to five (Shelef & Diamond, 2008) or six items (Robbins et al., 2003). Trained observers rate, for example, "To what extent did the therapist and patient agree upon the goals and tasks for the session?"

2. **SRS V.3.0.** This 4-item visual analog measure is typically administered to clients at the end of a session to provide the therapist with immediate feedback. Since its creation, the SRS has been widely used in systematic progress research (Sparks, 2015). As the questions are generic, the measure has been used to study CFT as well as individual therapy. To complete the measure, clients rate the session by marking a hashed line for each bipolar item, for example, "I did not feel heard, understood, and respected—I felt heard, understood and respected" and "There was something missing in the session today—Overall, today's session was right for me." As the latter item and the title of the measure suggest, the SRS items reflect session impact as well as the working alliance.

3. **CTAS and FTAS.** The content of the Integrative Alliance Scales for individual, couple, and family therapy accounts for the interpersonal dynamics that characterize conjoint therapy. In the original CTAS and FTAS, 29 items assess the therapist's alliances (a) with the respondent (*self*), (b) with other family members (*other*), and (c) with the entire family system (*group*) in parallel client and therapist forms. The measures were subsequently modified (CTASr and FTASr) to assess perceptions of the within-system alliance, which includes within-couple/family and within-therapeutic system (e.g., cotherapists or therapist-supervisor; Pinsof, 1994). A more recent revision of the scales resulted in 12 items per version, called the CTASr-SF and FTASr-SF (Pinsof et al., 2008).

4. **WAI and WAI-Co.** The most widely used measure of alliance in individual psychotherapy, the WAI and its observer form, the WAI-O, have also been used to assess each client's alliance with the therapist in CFT. Specifically adapted to the couple context, the 63-item WAI-Co, has separate scales for client, partner, and couple that tap the emotional bonds (e.g., "The therapist and I trust each other") and therapist/client agreement on tasks and goals. Like the individual WAI, the WAI-Co subscales can be combined to yield a total score. The client form asks for perceptions of the alliance between the therapist and (a) the respondent, (b) the respondent's partner, and (c) the couple as a group. The therapist form asks for perceptions of the alliance with each partner and with the couple as a unit.

5. **SOFTA-o and SOFTA-s.** Developed simultaneously in Spanish and English, the observational and self-report SOFTA measures assess four dimensions of the alliance in CFT, two of which are similar to Bordin's (1979) model: *engagement in the therapeutic process* (client/therapist agreement on goals and tasks as well as active involvement) and *emotional connection to the therapist* (bond between client and therapist). The other two dimensions represent unique aspects of CFT: *safety within the therapeutic system* (e.g., "Client directly asks other family members for feedback about his/her behavior or about herself/himself as a person"), which reflects the individual's sense of comfort participating in therapy with family members and *shared sense of purpose within the family* (e.g., "Family members validate each other's point of view") or the within-system alliance (Friedlander et al., 2006).

In the SOFTA-o, the valence of the 44 verbal and nonverbal indicators reflects clients' favorable or unfavorable thoughts and feelings about the alliance along the four dimensions and therapists' positive and negative behavioral contributions to the alliance, such as, "Therapist expresses interest in the client(s) apart from the therapeutic discussion at hand" and "Therapist defines therapeutic goals or imposes tasks or procedures without asking the client(s) for their collaboration." In both the client and therapist version, trained raters make global ratings on each of the four dimensions based on the tallies of observed therapist behaviors.

In the SOFTA system, parallel self-report measures for client and therapist (SOFTA-s) have 16 items that tap the respondent's perceptions of engagement, connection, safety, and shared purpose. The client version reflects individual perceptions ("The therapist and I work together as a team") whereas the therapist version reflects perceptions of the overall alliance with the family ("The family and I are working together as a team").

In selecting measures, researchers can consider which aspect of the alliance and which perspective is of most importance for their purposes. Aside from the SRS, all of the self-report measures (CTASr/FTASr, WAI-Co, SOFTA-s) have client and therapist versions and assess the alliance between each client and the therapist as well as some system dynamics. In other ways. the self-report instruments differ. Although all measures ask therapists about their alliance with the couple or family as a unit, only the CTASr/FTASr and WAI-Co ask clients to report on the therapist's alliance with their partner or other family members. The VTAS-R and SOFTA-o are observer measures of alliance-related behavior, but only the SOFTA-o requires an identification of positive and negative alliance-related behaviors to inform the raters' overall judgments.

Unlike the VTAS-R, the WAI-O and SOFTA-o have self-report versions that allow researchers to compare client-perceived with observed alliances (cf. Muñiz de la Peña et al., 2009). Finally, the within-couple or within-family alliance can be assessed using either the CTASr/FTASr or the SOFTA-o/SOFTA-s, but the safety aspect of alliance is only measured by the SOFTA instruments.

In the present meta-analysis, we found that these measures yielded different effect sizes for the alliance–outcome association (see Moderators). On the one hand, the measures may be estimating slightly different constructions of the alliance. Alternately, the observer measures, which are behaviorally based, may have greater precision to detect effects. Other explanations cannot be ruled out, however, such as differences in sample composition, type of psychotherapy, and timing of alliance measurement, since study characteristics are confounded with type of alliance measurement.

CLINICAL EXAMPLES

To illustrate how CFT alliances are manifested in practice, we selected two published case studies. Each case had multiple indicators of treatment success as well as repeated self-reported (SOFTA-s) and observed (SOFTA-o) alliances measured over the course of 10 sessions. Both of these relatively brief cases were conducted in naturalistic settings—one in Spain (Escudero et al., 2012) and one in the United States (Friedlander et al., 2014)—with highly experienced family therapists (one man and one woman, respectively). The therapeutic approaches were nonmanualized and broadly systemic in nature. The two families, both living on modest incomes, were seen free of charge in community clinics that conducted family therapy research.

The self-reported alliance and improvement data from the family members and the therapists clearly reflect the alliance concepts discussed earlier in this chapter. Specifically, in the first example, a split alliance and a severe rupture to the within-family alliance (or shared sense of purpose) occurred and were repaired during an early session with a single mother and her adolescent daughter. In the second example, the estranged parents were at an impasse, having different views on the problem and disparate motivations for seeking therapy. This problematic within-family alliance was navigated sensitively by the therapist, who focused on the only problem that all family members agreed upon, namely, the daughter's anger over her parents' estrangement.

A Spanish Family in Crisis

"Rosa" (16 years old) was a troubled youth whose attitude and behavior at home and in school exasperated her mother. By the fourth family session, Rosa had noticeably improved in all areas, in large part due to a strong alliance with the therapist, who had supported her desire to switch schools. At the beginning of the session, however, "Ms. M" responded with sarcasm and intense anger when the therapist challenged her repeated blaming of her daughter and then suggested an individual session to discuss how Ms. M's "personal stressors" might be affecting Rosa and the mother–daughter relationship.

At this point, recognizing the various ruptures (a split alliance, the mother's lack of safety in the session, and the problematic within-family alliance), the therapist asked Ms. M to step out of the room for a brief period (a safety intervention). During his time alone with Rosa, the therapist assessed the strength of their bond in light of the new therapeutic focus he had just proposed to her mother. Upon her return to the session, Ms. M continued to express her anger toward the therapist. In an arrogant and sarcastic tone, she responded to his suggestion that they discuss her personal problems.

Subsequently, the rupture expanded when Ms. M. returned to blaming Rosa for her all problems.

As the session drew to a close, there was no movement toward repair of this severe alliance rupture. When the therapist stood up to leave, he said: "Listen, we have to end this session, but I want you to know something that Rosa and I both agree on: that you are a wonderful and brave person, and it's worth trying to improve." At this, Ms. M. began to cry, explaining that she was at the end of her rope and felt unable to cope with "bad things." She then made her first positive connection statement to the therapist: "'I'm being defensive. It's not you. I appreciate what you do. It's me." Following this comment, the following dialogue took place, reflecting the therapist's empathy with Ms. M:

Psychotherapist: You're feeling a sort of helplessness; you are burned out. Try a little to put all the things that are happening in your life into quarantine.
Ms. M.: I just can't anymore. I can't. I can't. I don't know what to do. What could we do?
Psychotherapist: Let me say this: Rosa needs therapy, YOU need therapy.
Ms. M. (CRYING AND LAUGHING): Yes, we all need therapy. Even our cat needs therapy!
Psychotherapist (HUMOROUSLY, OFFERING HER A TISSUE): Unfortunately, the cat can't come to the hospital!
Ms. M. (SMILING): That's too bad. (Escudero et al., 2012, p. 32)

Next, to repair the within-family alliance rupture, the therapist made several pointed shared purpose interventions by pointing out Ms. M's and Rosa's shared experiences, needs, and feelings. In Session 4, for example, he said:

"Some stress comes from the relationship between you two, from your [Ms. M.'s] problems, then there's Rosa's adolescent stress, and there's stress coming from you, which is normal. . . . You're both in a situation of . . . You're both a lot . . . which is normal because you're a family. . . . I mean it [stress] affects both of you, and that's something you have in common . . . There's an isolation in your family . . . that affects both of you."

Although Session 4 ended on a positive note, the alliance rupture resurfaced in the following session, when Ms. M confronted the therapist about his treatment of her the previous week, indicating her annoyance at his having called her "burned out" in front of her daughter. In response, the therapist apologized: "I shouldn't have said this in front of her, that I was afraid you were burned out."

An American Family at Impasse

"Eleanor" (32 years old) and "Jim" (32 year old) "Beale" had been estranged for a short while due to Eleanor's decision to live with another man while she took some time to consider the future of her marriage. Their daughter "Shawna" (age 12) was extremely angry over the situation; her relationship with her mother was severely strained. Although Jim took responsibility for his part in the couple's problems and desperately wanted Eleanor to return to the family, she refused to allow the marital impasse to be discussed in the therapy.

In the first session, the therapist connected with Shawna about her experience of the family crisis and used a safety intervention to help her express her feelings. By directing her comments only to Shawna, the therapist gave the parents the space to hear their daughter's feelings without being pressured to respond to her negativity:

Jim: She (*looking at Shawna*) got really, really upset one day and just started to scream and yell and say, "I can't handle it anymore," sort of type of thing. And um . . . that kind of gave me a heads up to say things aren't going well with her, there's something not right in the situation, with us as a family. That was actually the day before she left (*points at Eleanor*) um and just . . . I think she's had a hard time dealing with all of this.

Therapist: Let me ask her that . . . (*turns to Shawna*) Is that true? Is that hard?

Shawna: Um yeah.

Therapist: I can imagine it's kinda difficult. [connect *intervention, expressing empathy*]

Shawna: Yeah in the beginning it was bad, but lately it's not so bad. (Friedlander et al., 2014, p. 46)

In the third session, the therapist asked Shawna to step out of the room as a safety intervention that set a boundary between the marital and parental subsystems while she talked with Jim and Eleanor about their opposing motivations and goals for the therapy. Notably, the therapist used her personal bond with each partner in turn:

Therapist: It's a little bit like . . . not a little bit like . . . but a whole lot like grief . . . when there's a death or loss of someone. You know, initially there's sort of a disbelief . . . a shock . . . and certainly just not even taking it in. It's not really real. (*turns to Eleanor*) Obviously for some time before you actually moved, um you had been contemplating this and thinking about it . . . and so it really wasn't so new to you. Um I think . . . I'm hearing that you both are in different places with regard to you know where you're separating with each other. You know . . . For you (*looking at Jim*) there's that hopefulness or wishing or wanting . . . or wanting if only kind of thing. And for you (*looking at Eleanor*), maybe you've got beyond that and you now have recognized that for some reasons that this can't work or is going to work and are able to emotionally be in a place that doesn't hurt quite as much. Am I right? [a connect *intervention, expressing empathy for their struggle*] (Friedlander et al., 2014, pp. 47–48)

In addition, the therapist also used several shared purpose interventions to address the problematic within-couple alliance. These interventions included her perception that, despite their years together, the parents had never really learned to argue productively, to come to a compromise or a resolution. She concluded: "for two really young people . . . you never had a chance to really learn how to be a couple" (Friedlander et al., 2014, p. 49).

In Session 6, when the therapeutic alliances were well established, the therapist encouraged Eleanor and Jim to consider couple therapy after the 10th agreed-upon family session. This renegotiation of the therapy goals and tasks was infused with shared purpose and safety, which followed the therapist's compliment to the couple regarding their improvements in problem-solving (an engagement intervention):

Therapist: So it goes back to what we talked about, and you know we really don't want to get into this couples thing, but it goes back to this whole thing of communication and the difficulties that you've had . . . really being able to say things without you know hurting one another or getting into words [shared purpose intervention, *drawing attention to shared experience*]. . . . And you know, Shawna has kind of learned some of this too, and you know she's practicing [here] and talking about things . . . and she's taken the risk now twice to say some things that really were hard for her to say because she was hurting the two of you. [safety intervention, *acknowledging that therapy involves taking risks*] Okay um, and I guess I'll go so far as to say that you know when you argue like you did the other night and she's still awake, you're really putting her at risk of hurting tremendously, because while she may not have identified as that, she's made very uncomfortable with the ongoing fighting and so um maybe you know it would be really valuable to think more seriously about the two of you having counseling to talk through what needs to be resolved. That is something that couples do. (Friedlander et al., 2014, pp. 49–50)

After this intervention, Eleanor and Jim agreed to continue in couple therapy, which eventually resulted in their reconciliation. It seemed likely that this outcome was due to the clients' trust and bond with the therapist, their progress in understanding one another, and learning how to solve problems respectfully, as well as the therapist's hard work to strengthen the within-family alliance and ensure each person's safety and comfort.

The SOFTA-s alliance questionnaires, the session evaluations, and the outcome data converged to reveal a successful case in which the within-family bonds were severely strained. Notably, analysis of the sessions showed no evidence of a split alliance, possibly because the therapist did not insist that the marital stalemate be addressed in the conjoint family sessions but rather agreed to work with the family on the one mutually agreed-upon goal, to work on the parents' individual relationships with their angry daughter.

LANDMARK STUDIES

In this section, we highlight landmark investigations of the working alliance–outcome relationship unique to CFT. The following is how each landmark investigation took into account the systemic dynamics that characterize conjoint therapy:

1. Robbins and colleagues (2003) were the first to study unbalanced parent–adolescent alliances in relation to dropout versus retention in a research-supported treatment, functional family therapy (FFT). Results were noteworthy in demonstrating the complex nature of studying multiple alliances in relation to outcome in conjoint therapy.

2. Authors of the Norway Couple Project (Anker et al., 2009, 2010; Owen et al., 2014) were the first to investigate client feedback in couple therapy and to analyze clients' self-reported alliances over time using the actor-partner interdependence model (APIM; Kashy & Kenny, 2000). The APIM is ideally suited for studying systemic dynamics due to its ability to identify partner effects (in this case, clients' alliance scores predicting their partners' outcome scores) along with actor effects (e.g., clients' alliance scores predicting their own outcome scores).

3. Lambert and colleagues (2012) conducted the first mixed-methods study of problematic within-system alliances in family therapy "as usual." The objective of this study was to discover, from clients' self-reported and observed behaviors, why this important aspect of the alliance was problematic and, in each of five families (two of whom dropped out), what might have accounted for discrepancies in the clients' willingness to work together toward common goals. Lambert et al. addressed the multidimensional nature of the within-system alliance and commented on how the therapists seemed to have missed several opportunities for repairing ruptures in family members' shared sense of purpose.

Unbalanced Family Alliances

Recognizing the centrality of retaining families in treatment when the identified problem is an adolescent's problematic behavior, a sample of 34 families was used to investigate the alliance–dropout relationship from an archival set of 66 FFT cases seen at the University of Utah (Robbins et al., 2003). For this first investigation of alliance in FFT, the authors selected only those families for whom videotapes of Session 1 were available for analysis, since the first session is considered essential to stimulate the clients' engagement in treatment.

Among the 34 cases were 27 two-parent families and 7 single-parent families in which the head of household was the mother. The adolescents were 20 boys and 14 girls, ages 12 to 18. Families were either self-referred ($n = 18$) or referred by social services, schools, or the juvenile justice system ($n = 16$). The adolescents' presenting concerns included delinquency/violence, drug use, school problems, and family conflict/ communication difficulties. The therapists were 20 female and 14 male graduate students in training who were conducting their first FFT case under supervision.

The 26-item VTAS-R was used to measure the alliance. Three female graduate students served as raters. After extensive training, the raters' mean reliability on 79 videotape segments was intraclass correlation (ICC) = .84. The initial analysis indicated that retention was not significantly predicted by alliance scores averaged across family members. However, the parents' scores were significantly higher than the adolescents' alliance scores. Moreover, in analyzing alliance patterns, dropout was significantly predicted by the parent score minus the adolescent score. Specifically, greater father–adolescent "unbalance" was significantly associated with dropout. The direction of the relation between mother–adolescent unbalance and dropout was similar, but this analysis only approached statistical significance.

The authors concluded that, due to the systemic nature of conjoint family therapy, extrapolation of alliance findings from the individual psychotherapy literature to the family context is not appropriate. Rather, *family role* (mother, father, adolescent) is an essential factor to take into account when studying how early alliances develop in conjoint sessions with adolescents who have behavior problems.

Actor-Partner Alliances Over Time

A large randomized clinical trial (RCT) was used to examine the CFT outcomes of more than 200 White, Euro-Scandinavian couples seen at a government-subsidized family counseling agency in Norway (Anker et al., 2009). In the experimental condition, therapists were provided with both partners' ratings of (a) their psychological functioning on the Outcome Rating Scale (ORS; Miller et al., 2003) at the beginning of each session and (b) the alliance on the Session Rating Scale (described in Measures). At the end of each session, the therapists scored the SRS and then initiated a conversation about the clients' alliance perceptions.

Statistically and clinically significant outcomes were found for the feedback condition at posttreatment as compared with treatment-as-usual. Moreover, these gains were maintained at the six-month follow-up assessment using the Locke Wallace Marital Adjustment Test (Locke & Wallace, 1959). Compared to controls, the experimental couples also reported a significantly lower rate of separation/divorce at follow-up.

In a subsequent article, Anker et al. (2010) reported on the association between family alliances and early change among the 99 experimental couples from the original RCT and 151 couples from another agency that did not take part in the clinical trial. In the full sample (*N* = 250 couples), SRS alliance scores following the initial couple session did not predict outcome at posttreatment. However, the APIM analysis showed that actor and partner alliance scores in the last session did predict outcome. In other words, clients' self-reported functioning at the end of therapy was associated with their own alliance scores (the "actor effect") and with those of their partners (the "partner effect") after the first session. Of note, whereas the actor effect was significantly stronger for the male member of the couple at posttreatment, at follow-up a significant partner effect was found. That is, for both women and men, perceptions of alliance in the first session predicted their partners' marital satisfaction at follow-up.

A subsample of the 118 couples who had completed four or more sessions provided data for a second analysis, which was conducted to determine whether alliance scores would predict final outcomes regardless of early improvement (Anker et al., 2010). Results of the multilevel analysis showed that, controlling for early change in outcome (ORS scores), Session 3 alliance scores on the SRS were unique predictors of outcome at posttreatment (i.e., over and above the contribution of client gender). Notably, men's alliance scores predicted relationship satisfaction early on in therapy, whereas women's alliance scores were more predictive later on.

Finally, researchers conducted a multilevel analysis of 158 couples and 18 therapists who had attended three or more sessions from the original clinical trial (Owen et al., 2014). The purpose of this analysis was to assess variability in outcome due to therapist gender, professional discipline, and clinical experience with couples. Results showed individual therapist effects (8% of the variability in clients' outcomes and 10% of the variability in clients' Session 2 alliance scores). Notably, therapist gender was not significant, but the therapist's (a) alliance quality (averaged client scores) and (b) experience conducting couple therapy accounted for 50% of the variability in outcome.

Problematic Within-Family Alliances

In a mixed-method analysis of five families, multiple sources of data were triangulated: SOFTA-o behavioral observations of the families' shared purpose and the therapists' behavioral contributions to the shared purpose, SOFTA-s scores on shared sense of purpose as reported by each family member, as well as their pre- and posttherapy ratings of target complaints and their written problem descriptions (Lambert et al., 2012). Transcripts of each family's most problematic within-family alliance session were used to understand the therapeutic process based on a qualitative analysis of the verbal interactions (a) between family members and (b) between family members and the therapist.

Sessions from the five cases were selected (from a larger study) if there was evidence of a problematic within-family alliance, operationalized as a negative shared purpose score on the SOFTA-o and a discrepancy in the postsession shared sense of purpose scores of two (or more) family members on the SOFTA-s. The five cases represented diverse family structures, with children ranging in age from 8 to 15.

The data revealed three, interrelated patterns of the within-system alliance. Across cases, clients in three of the families disagreed with each other about the nature of the problem, clients in four of the families disagreed with each other about the goals for therapy, and clients in three of the families disagreed about the value of therapy. The clients' written problem descriptions showed that the within-family disagreements were nuanced. For example, in one case, both the daughter and mother were focused on the father's absence (thus an agreement on the nature of the problem at a general level). However, the mother believed that the father's absence was at the root of her daughter's behavior problems, whereas the daughter blamed her father for leaving and felt angry with him; in other words, mother and daughter had differing views on the necessary focus of therapy. As another example, in two of the families the teenagers indicated a desire to support their single parents, even though they were not at all interested in participating in the therapy.

The therapist data showed that, while all of them appeared to be aware of the weak within-family alliance in their respective cases, they nonetheless focused mostly on individuals, soliciting each person's definition of the problem and goals for treatment.

The researchers pointed out that there were few interventions in which the therapists encouraged family members to interact with each other in alliance-building tasks. These "missed opportunities" included helping family members negotiate a compromise, identifying and encouraging mutual support/caring, and engaging clients to solicit each other's perspectives—in other words, systemic interventions.

In conclusion, the authors suggested that it is necessary not only to build family agreement on the nature of the problem but also to nurture a feeling of emotional connection among family members in coping with their concerns, a sense of "felt unity" or "we're all in this together" *and* to help the clients view conjoint family sessions as a meaningful way to address their problems (Lambert et al., 2012, p. 426). The latter is built when, even in the first session, the work goes beyond information gathering or complaint airing to some kind of progress (even minor) in the clients' feelings of becoming more connected, more understood by one another, or more in tune with each other's perspective.

RESULTS OF PREVIOUS META-ANALYSES

Our 2011 meta-analysis of the alliance–outcome relation in CFT (Friedlander et al., 2011) included 24 studies (excluding dissertations and analogue experiments) with a total of 1,421 clients. In the 17 family and 7 couple therapy investigations, observed and self-reported alliances were predictors of intermediate and distal outcomes as well as retention versus continuation in treatment. In the majority of studies, alliances were observed early in treatment; the handful of investigations that reported multiple administrations of alliance measures typically staggered them (i.e., early, middle, and late in treatment). Half of the studies used observational measures (SOFTA-o and VTAS-R); the most frequently used self-report instruments were the WAI-Co and the CTAS or FTAS.

We conducted the 2011 meta-analysis using a random-effects approach (Hunter & Schmidt, 1990). Correlation coefficients were used for the most part, with conversions to r for studies reporting only t tests. Due to the presence of multiple informants in conjoint therapies, we calculated a meta-analytic statistic within each study to maintain statistical independence.

Across the 24 studies, a weighted aggregate $r = .26$, $z = 8.13$ ($p < .005$); 95% confidence interval (CI) = .33, .20, was found, which is a small to medium effect size (ES), comparable to the $r = .275$ found in a meta-analysis of individual psychotherapy with adults (Horvath et al., 2011). Moreover, observed and self-reported alliances accounted for a substantial proportion of variance in outcomes. An examination of the homogeneity of the couple and family therapy subsamples revealed unaccounted for variability. The observational studies were the most homogeneous, which we speculated might be due to the specific criteria used to measure alliance-related behaviors.

A recent meta-analysis of alliance–outcome in "family-involved treatment" for youth problems included 28 studies with 21 independent samples (Welmers-van de Poll et al., 2018). Inclusion criteria for this meta-analysis differed somewhat from Friedlander et al.'s (2011) meta-analysis in that Welmers-van de Poll et al. included unpublished as well as published studies and excluded (a) studies of family therapy with adult children and (b) studies in which the association between alliance and outcome was reported for individual and family therapy combined. Multilevel models were used to account for within- and between-study variability.

Based on a sample of 2,216 families, Welmers-van de Poll et al. (2018) analyzed three alliance processes: (a) quality of the alliance, (b) split/unbalanced alliances between family members, and (c) improvement as measured either by change scores or by multiple, consecutive measures over time. First, results showed a small but significant association between quality of the alliance and treatment outcome ($r = .183$). The analyses also revealed three significant moderators (alliance timing, type of referral, and age of the problem child). Second, with respect to split alliances, the correlation with outcome in the five studies was nonsignificant, $r = .106$. Finally, for alliance improvement measured over time, the meta-analytic correlation approached significance, $r = .281$.

META-ANALYTIC REVIEW

We conducted two meta-analyses: The major analysis included all CFT studies reporting an association between therapeutic alliances and client outcome. A secondary analysis included studies that specifically reported on the association between outcomes and split or unbalanced alliances, which we studied due to their unique nature and clinical importance.

Locating Studies

As a starting point, we identified all of the couple and family alliance–outcome studies in Friedlander et al. (2011) and in Welmers-van de Poll et al.'s (2018) meta-analysis of 28 studies of conjoint family therapy for youth, with a few additions. To locate additional studies using relevant keywords (e.g., alliance, couple/marital therapy, family therapy), we searched online and through Google Scholar, Wiley Online Library, Eric, Academic Search Premier, PubMed, Medline, PsycInfo, PsycBooks, Web of Science, and ProQuest. For additional CFT studies, we also visually searched every electronic issue (from 2009 to mid-2017) of 11 CFT/systemic journals

Inclusion criteria were CFT published and unpublished English-language studies on alliance (self-reported or observational) in family or couple treatments, treatments-as-usual, group marital therapy, home-based family therapy, and family psychoeducation in which an ES for the alliance–outcome association was available or could be calculated. Outcomes included retention in treatment (vs. premature dropout) as well as mid-treatment improvement and client change. In contrast to Welmers-van de Poll et al. (2018), who only included studies of family therapy with youth, we included studies of couple therapy (with or without children) and family therapy with adult children and their parents/caregivers. Finally, for our secondary analysis of the association between split or unbalanced alliances and outcome, we included studies in which the split was defined through client self-report data and/or by observation of client behavior.

We excluded studies if no intermediate or distal outcome variables were reported (e.g., Heatherington & Friedlander, 1990; LoTempio et al., 2013) or if the study did not distinguish between conjoint family therapy and individual psychotherapy (e.g., Hawley & Garland, 2008). No exclusion criteria were placed on the nature of the samples or the treatment approach.

Sample

Table 4.1 lists the 48 studies in our overall analysis, which reported on 40 independent samples. Table 4.2 presents the studies used in the split alliance analysis. Both tables include information about each study, including the setting, treatment approach, alliance and outcome measures. The weighted mean ES for each individual study appears in the far right column of the table.

The 40 independent samples (32 of family therapy, 8 of couple therapy) reported data on a total of 2,568 families and 1,545 couples. Six of the seven studies (total N = 250 families) in our analysis of split alliance/outcome (see Table 4.2) were also included in the overall meta-analysis; the seventh study, of couple therapy, only tested the association between split alliance and outcome (Bartle Haring et al., 2012).

Coding Procedure and Calculation of Effect Sizes

Prior to the analysis, all studies were coded by the second or third authors using a form based on guidelines provided by Lipsey and Wilson (2001). In doing so, we coded all of the study, sample, and methodological features used for the 21 moderator analyses. When information that was necessary to identify the moderating variables or to calculate an ES was missing, the first author of the study was contacted to obtain this information.

For the 28 studies that were included in Welmers-van de Poll et al.'s (2018) meta-analysis, we used the same coding (with an ICC = .82 for effect sizes) in the present analysis. For the additional studies, the coding was carried out by the second author. Coding difficulties were discussed to consensus by the second and third authors.

To estimate each correlation between alliance and outcome, we calculated Pearson's r. We coded an ES as positive if the correlation was in the expected direction (Diener et al., 2009), that is, higher alliance (or lower split alliance) associated with retention rather than dropout and/or more positive treatment outcomes. Correlations that were not in the expected direction were coded as negative. When a nonsignificant correlation was reported but the information was not sufficient for calculating the ES, we took a conservative approach by assigning a value of zero. This method was used for eight studies (50 effect sizes).

Due to the conjoint nature of CFT, most of the studies had multiple informants (mother, father, child/ren, therapist), measurements, and outcomes. For this reason, we calculated more than one ES per study. In total, we computed 491 effect sizes for the association between alliance (self-reported and observational) and outcome and 31

Table 4.1. Alliance-Outcome Studies in the Meta-Analysis

Study	Treatment Characteristic					Alliance Measurement				Outcome Measurement			Calculation of ES		
	Modality	Problem type	Treatment model	Setting	Referral status	Type	Measure	Time	Rater	Domain	Timing	Rater	N families/ couples	N clients[a]	Wtd. mean ES
Anderson & Johnson (2010)	Couple	Relational distress	Combined Models	C	HS	I	CTASr	M	SR	GT	DT	SR	173	346	.29
Anker et al. (2010)[1]	Couple	Relational distress	Combined models	C	HS	I	SRS	L	SR	GT	DT	SR	250	500	.13
Bachler et al. (2016)	Family	Multi-problem families	TAF	HB	M	I	CP-TAF	Imp	T	GT, IF	EOT	SR	304	n.r.	.36
Bennun (1989)	Family	Mixed	FT	C	HS	I	TS	E	SR	GT, IF	EOT	SR	35	26	.46
Bourgeois et al. (1990)	Couple	Relational distress	FB CBT	C	R	I, WS	CTAS	M	SR	FF	EOT	SR	63	126	.65
Brown & O'Leary (2000)	Couple	Maltreatment by husband	FB CBT	C	R	I	WAI-O	E, M, L	O	GT	EOT	SR	70	140	.54
Chinchilla (2007)[b,2]	Family	Substance use	MDFT	n.r.	Mx	I	VTAS-R	E	O	R, IF	EOT, FU	S, OM	68	66	-.06
Dauber (2004)[b,2]	Family	Substance use	MDFT	n.r.	Mx	I	VTAS-R	E	O	IF	EOT, FU	S	63	61	.41
Escudero et al. (2008)	Family	Mixed	FT	C	HS	I, WS	SOFTA-o	E, M	O	GT	DT	S	37	82	.21
Escudero et al. (in preparation)	Family	Internalizing and externalizing problems	AEFT	C	Mx	I	SOFTA-s	E, M, L	SR	GT	EOT	O, T	44	88	.37

(continued)

Table 4.1. Continued

Study	Treatment Characteristic					Alliance Measurement				Outcome Measurement			Calculation of ES		
	Modality	Problem type	Treatment model	Setting	Referral status	Type	Measure	Time	Rater	Domain	Timing	Rater	N families/ couples	N clients[a]	Wtd. mean ES
Feder & Diamond (2016)	Family	Internalizing problems	ABFT	C	HS	I	VTAS-R	M	O	IF	EOT	S	19	19	.24
Flicker et al. (2008)	Family	Substance use	FFT	C	Mx	I	VTAS-R	E	O	R	EOT	T	86	43	-.05
Forsberg et al. (2014)[3]	Family	Eating disorders	FBT	C	HS	I	WAI-O	E	O	IF	EOT	OM	38	61	.42
Forsberg et al. (2011)[b3]	Family	Eating disorders	FBT	C	HS	I	WAI-O	E	O	IF	EOT	S	38	99	.62
Friedlander et al. (2008)[4]	Family	Mixed	FT	C	R	WS	SOFTA-o	E	O	GT	DT	S	27	n.r.	.45
Friedlander et al. (2012)[4]	Family	Mixed	FT	C	R	I	SOFTA-s	E, M	SR	GT	DT	S	20	36	.46
Glebova et al. (2011)	Couple	Relational distress	FT	C	HS	I	WAI-S	M	SR	FF	DT	SR	195	390	.26
Glueckauf et al. (2002)	Family	Epilepsy with behavioral problems	IFCM or PG	n.r.	R	I	WAI-S	E+M (A)	SR	IE, GT	EOT	F	19	19	.19
Hawley & Weisz (2005)	Family	Mixed	CB MH	C	HS	I	TASC	L	SR	R, IF	EOT	OM, T, SR	65	65	.12

Study	Modality	Problem	Model				Measure								
Hogue et al. (2006)[2]	Family	Substance use	MDFT	n.r.	Mx	I	VTAS-R	E	O	IF	EOT, FU	SR	44	44	-.02
Isserlin & Couturier (2012)	Family	Eating disorders	FBT	C	HS	I, WS	SOFTA-o	E, M, L	O	IF, R	EOT	OM, SR	14	14	.33
Johnson & Talitman (1997)	Couple	Relational distress	EFT	C	R	I, WS	CTAS	E	SR	FF	EOT	SR	32	64	.46
Johnson et al. (2006)[5]	Family	Multiproblem families	HB FT	HB	M	I	FTAS	L	SR	IF	EOT	SR	225	456	.03
Johnson et al. (2002)[5]	Family	Multiproblem families	HB FT	HB	M	I	FTAS	L	SR	IF, FF	EOT	SR	43	45	.19
Keeley et al. (2011)	Family	Internalizing problems	FB CBT	C	HS	I	TASC, WAI	E, M Imp.	SR, T	IF	EOT	SR	23	22	.51
Kim (2007)[b]	Family	Mixed	SFBT	C	HS	I	RRS	E	SR	IF	EOT	SR	25	21	.12
Knobloch-Fedders et al. (2007)[6]	Couple	Relational distress	IPCT	C	HS	I, WS	CTASr	M	SR	FF	DT, EOT	SR	35	80	.39
Kuhlman et al. (2013)	Couple	Depression	FT	C	HS	I	SRS	M	SR	IF	DT, EOT	SR	29	58	.38
Lange et al. (in preparation)	Family	Externalizing problems	MST	HB	M	I	TAM-R	Imp., E, M, L	SR	IF	EOT, FU	SR	848	774	.00
Owen et al. (2014)[1]	Couple	Relational distress	Combined models	C	HS	I	SRS	L	SR	FF	EOT	SR	158	316	.57
Owen et al. (2011)	Couple	Relational distress	PREP	C	HS	I	WAI-S	L	SR	FF	FU	SR	118	236	.19
Pereira et al. (2006)	Family	Eating disorders	FBT	C	R	I	WAI-O	E, L	O	R, IF	EOT, DT	OM	41	36	.18

(continued)

Table 4.1. Continued

Study	Treatment Characteristic					Alliance Measurement				Outcome Measurement			Calculation of ES		
	Modality	Problem type	Treatment model	Setting	Referral status	Type	Measure	Time	Rater	Domain	Timing	Rater	N families/ couples	N clients[a]	Wtd. mean ES
Pinsof et al. (2008)[6]	Couple	Relational distress	IPCT	C	HS	I, WS	CTASr	M	SR	GT	DT	SR	60	120	.29
Quinn et al. (1997)	Family	Mixed	FT	C	HS	I, WS	CTAS	E	SR	GT	EOT	SR	17	34	.59
Quirk et al. (2014)	Couple	Relational distress	PREP	C	R	I	WAI-S	M	SR	FF	EOT	SR	122	244	.27
Raytek et al. (1999)	Couple	Alcohol abuse	MBT	C	Mx	I	VTAS-R	E	T	R	EOT	O	90	180	.37
Rienecke et al. (2016)	Family	Eating disorders	FBT PHP	C, H	HS	I	WAI-S	E, L	SR	R, IF	EOT	O	56	56	.07
Robbins et al. (2006)[2]	Family	Substance use	MDFT	n.r.	Mx	I	VTAS-R	E	O	R	EOT	OM	30	n.r.	.17
Robbins et al. (2008)	Family	Substance use	BSFT	n.r.	n.r.	I	VTAS-R	E	O	R	EOT	OM	31	23	.25
Robbins et al. (2003)	Family	Substance use	FFT	n.r.	Mx	I	VTAS-R	E	O	R	EOT	OM	34	29	-.18
Shelef & Diamond (2008)[7]	Family	Substance use	MDFT	n.r.	Mx	I	VTAS-R(SF)	E, M, L	O	R, IF	EOT	OM, SR	86	68	.23
Shelef et al. (2005)[7]	Family	Substance use	MDFT	n.r.	Mx	I	WAI, VTAS-R	E	SR, O	IE, R	EOT, FT	OM, SR	91	110	.18

Study														
Smerud & Rosenfarb (2008)	Family	Schizophrenia	PG	H	HS	WS	SOFTA-o	M	O	IF	EOT	O	28	n.r.	.74
Sotero et al. (2017)	Family	Mixed	FT	C	Mx	I, WS	SOFTA-o	E, M	O	GT	EOT	T	29	87	.37
Symonds & Horvath (2004)	Couple	Relational distress	n.r.	C	R	I	WAI-co	M	SR	FF	EOT	SR	44	88	.44
Yoo et al. (2016)	Couple	Relational distress	n.r.	C	HS	I	VTAS-R	E, M	O	FF	EOT	R	34	68	.20
Zaitsoff et al. (2008)	Family	Eating disorders	FBT	C	n.r.	I	HRQ	M, L	SR	IF	EOT	SR	40	40	.00

Note. TAF = therapeutische ambulante familienbetreuung; FT = family treatment-as-usual; CtxFT= contextual family therapy; MDFT = multi-dimensional family therapy; AEFT = alliance empowerment family therapy; EFT= emotionally-focused therapy; ABFT = attachment-based family therapy; FFT = functional family therapy; FBT = family behavioral therapy; IPCT= integrative problem-centered therapy; IFCM = issue-specific single-family counseling; PG = multifamily psychoeducational group; CBMH = community-based mental health; PREP = Prevention and Relationship Enhancement Program; HB FT = home-based family therapy; FB CBT = family-based cognitive-behavioral therapy; SFBT = solution-focused brief therapy; FBT PHP = family-based therapy partial hospitalization program; BSFT = brief strategic family therapy; MBT = marital behavioral therapy. C = clinic; HB = home-based; H = hospital; HS = help seeking; R = recruited for the study; M = mandated; Mx = mixed; I = individual client; WS = within-system. CP-TAF = Compliance-Collaboration scale (in the Therapeutische Ambulante Familienbetreuung); TS = therapist scale; VTAS(-R) = Vanderbilt Therapeutic Alliance Scale (-Revised); SOFTA-o/-s = System for Observing Family Therapy Alliances-observer (self-report); SRS = Session Rating Scale; WAI(-S/-O) = Working Alliance Inventory (-short form /observer version); TASC = Therapeutic Alliance Scale for Children; FTAS(r) = Family Therapy Alliance Scale (Revised); CTAS(r) = Couple Therapy Alliance Scale (revised); HAQ = Helping Alliance Questionnaire; TAS = Therapeutic Alliance Scale; RRS = Relationship Rating Scale; HRQ = Helping Relationship Questionnaire; E = early in treatment; M = mid-treatment; L = late in treatment; Imp. = improvement in alliance; A = multiple sessions averaged or added. SR = self-report; T = therapist; O = observer; IF = individual functioning/symptom severity; FF = family/couple functioning; R = retention; GT = goal attainment or therapeutic progress. DT = during treatment; EOT = end of treatment; FU = follow-up; OM = objective clinical log measure (e.g., weight gain); Wtd. = weighted; n.r. = not reported.

[a]Sample sizes and effect sizes are based on the mean of all available reported analyses. [b]Unpublished dissertation. [1,2,3,4,5] Studies with the same numbered superscript used the same or overlapping samples.

Table 4.2. Studies in the Split Alliance/Outcome Meta-Analysis

Study	N (Families/Couples)	N (Clients)	Weighted Mean Effect Size
Bartle-Haring et al. (2012)[a]	72	144	.44
Escudero et al. (in preparation) [a]	44	88	.57
Flicker et al. (2008)[b]	86	43	.02
Kim (2007)[a]	25	n.r.	.27
Forsberg et al. (2014) [b]	38	99	.18
Robbins et al. (2003)[b]	34	n.r.	.33
Robbins et al. (2008)[b]	31	n.r.	.23

Note. Except Bartle-Haring et al. (2012), descriptions of the six other studies appear in Table 4.1.
n.r. = not reported.
[a]Self-reported split alliances. [b]Observer-rated split alliances.

effect sizes for the split alliance/outcome association. Effect sizes on the latter studies (listed in Table 4.2) were analyzed separately.

Statistical Analyses

Although traditional meta-analytic approaches require that the participant samples be independent (Lipsey & Wilson, 2001), we used a multilevel random effects model. This methodology accounts for dependent effect sizes and has been shown to be superior to more traditional meta-analytic approaches when moderators are studied (Van den Noortgate & Onghena, 2003).

The three-level random effects model (with $\alpha = .05$) had the following sources of variance: sampling variance of the observed effect sizes (level 1), variance between effect sizes from the same study (level 2), and variance between studies (level 3). This model was used in our primary and secondary meta-analyses to calculate an estimate of the association between the quality of the alliance and therapeutic outcome as well as an estimate of the association between split/unbalanced alliances and outcome. We also used the three-level model to calculate effect sizes when moderator variables were included in the analysis. Moderators were tested to determine whether the observed variation was explained by sample, study, or methodological characteristics of the studies.

All analyses were conducted using R software (version 3.3.1; R Core Team, 2016) in the *metafor* package. We wrote the R syntax and protocol to model three sources of variance. The *t* distribution was used to test the individual regression coefficients and to calculate confidence intervals. To test moderators consisting of three or more categories, we used an omnibus *F* test of the null hypothesis (i.e., lack of differences between group mean effect sizes). Before conducting the moderator analyses, we centered each continuous variable around its mean and created dummy variables for categorical data. All of the model parameters were estimated using the restricted maximum likelihood method.

Results

The meta-analytic effect sizes for the association between the quality of the alliance and outcome in the couple and family samples together, and the association between split alliances and outcome appear in Table 4.3. Based on the data from 39 independent samples (491 effect sizes), the meta-analytic correlation between level of alliance and outcome was significant, $r = .297$, 95% CI [.223, .351], $p < .001$, $d = .622$. This result indicates that stronger alliances were significantly associated with and predictive of better outcomes. Based on seven independent samples (31 effect sizes), the correlation between split alliance and outcome was also significant, $r = .316$, 95% CI [$-.157$, .458], $p < .001$, $d = .666$, indicating that more split/unbalanced alliances contributed significantly to worse treatment outcomes. These results indicate a medium ES for each analysis.

As shown in Table 4.3, significant percentages of the total variance (all $ps < .001$) between effect sizes was found within (level 2) as well as between studies (level 3). For the alliance-outcome association, level 2 = 35.4%; level 3 = 50.7%. For the split alliance/outcome association, level 2 = 10.4%; level 3 = 40.7%.

Analysis of Publication Bias

To address the file drawer problem (Rosenthal, 1995), we performed a trim and fill procedure (Duval & Tweedie, 2000) to test for indicators of overestimation and underestimation of the true overall ES. A funnel plot with missing effect sizes on the left side of the distribution indicates that the overall ES estimate might be an overestimation of the true effect. In contrast, when the plot indicates missing effect sizes on the right side of the distribution, the overall ES might be an underestimation of the true effect.

We performed trim and fill analyses for the two meta-analyses (alliance–outcome and split alliance–outcome) using all available effect sizes in R in the *metafor* package (Viechtbauer, 2015). As shown in Figures 4.1 and 4.2, both funnel plots showed missing

Table 4.3. Results of the Three-Level Mixed-Effects Meta-Analyses

Analysis	Studies [a]	# ES	Mean r (SE)	95% CI	p	d	% var. (1)	σ^2 (2)	% var. σ^2 (2)	σ^2 (3)	% var. (3)
Alliance/ outcome	39	491	.297 (.036)	.223, .351	<.001	.622	14.0	.029***	35.4	.041***	50.7
Split alliance/ outcome	7	31	.316 (.083)	−.157, .458	<.001	.666	48.9	.009***	10.4	.034***	40.7

Note. SE = standard error; var. = variance; CI = confidence interval.
(1) = level 1; (2) = level 2; (3) = level 3; σ^2 (2) = variance between effect sizes (within studies); σ^2 (3) = variance between studies.
(2) = (between studies).
[a] Number of independent samples (some studies reported on the same sample); # ES = number of effect sizes in the meta-analysis.
*** $p < .001$.

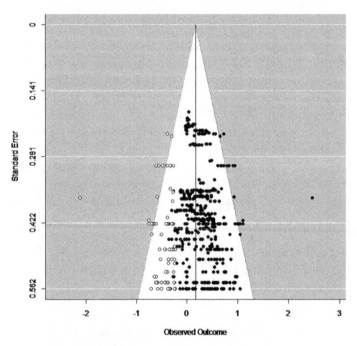

FIGURE 4.1 Trim and fill plot for the alliance-outcome association.

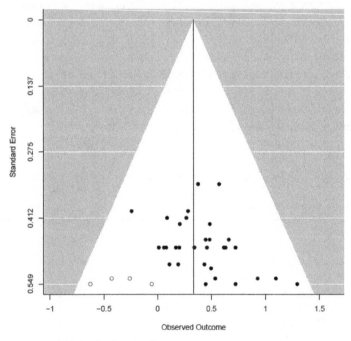

FIGURE 4.2 Trim and fill plot for the split alliance-outcome association.

effect sizes on the left sides of the distribution, indicating that the effect sizes obtained in the two meta-analyses may be overestimating the true effects. Comparisons of confidence intervals revealed that the overall ES for alliance–outcome was significantly smaller after the trim and fill analysis, $r = .167$, $p < .001$. On the other hand, based on the trim and fill analyses, the overall ES for split alliance/outcome did not vary significantly from the originally obtained meta-analytic effect size, $r = .314$, $p < .001$.

MEDIATORS

We located a single study of mediation in our sample (Friedlander et al., 2008). This investigation of 17 low-income families with at-risk children was conducted at a community agency. The purpose of the study was to disentangle first-session alliance-related behavior from mid-treatment progress. The parents' behaviors on two SOFTA dimensions, safety and shared sense of purpose within the family (i.e., the within-system alliance), were observed in Session 1, and parent-rated improvement so far was reported after Session 3.

Results indicated that observers' ratings of the families' shared purpose significantly mediated the relation between parental safety and improvement. In other words, the degree to which parents felt comfortable in the family therapy context in the first session significantly contributed to within-family collaboration in that session, which in turn predicted parent-rated progress after the third session, $p < .05$, $R^2 = .23$, adj. $R^2 = .16$.

Although temporal precedence (Session 1 → Session 3) permitted a degree of causal inference, both alliance predictors were rated in Session 1. For this reason, the authors re-ran the mediation analysis reversing safety and shared purpose variables. The indirect effect was not significant in the alternate analysis, providing support for the conclusion that when parents experience the therapeutic context as safe in the first session, the within-system alliance is enhanced, which in turn facilitates perceived mid-therapy improvement (Friedlander, Lambert, et al., 2008).

MODERATORS

Table 4.4 summarizes the moderator analyses in terms of sample characteristics, treatment characteristics, and methodological characteristics (related to alliance measurement and outcome measurement). For example, under Sample Characteristics, the Problem Type row indicates that 491 effect sizes were analyzed across the 39 samples to determine whether problem type significantly moderated the alliance–outcome correlation. The result was nonsignificant, although both the level 2, or within-study variance (.029), and the level 3, between-study variance (.036), were significant, both ps < .001. In the rows under Problem Type are the analyses for the overall ES for each of seven different problem types (drug abuse, eating disorders, behavior as internalizing/externalizing, etc.); cell values indicate the number of effect sizes analyzed, the mean correlations, and the probability levels. Whereas significant alliance–outcome

Table 4.4. Results of the Moderator Analyses

Moderator	Studies[a]	# ES	Mean r (SE)	95% CI	β (95% CI)	F(df)	p	σ²(2)	σ²(3)
Sample Characteristics									
Problem type	39	491				2.007 (6, 484)	.063	.029***	.036***
Drug abuse	7	114	.190 (.067)**	.060, .314	.022 (−.205, .250)				
Eating disorders	5	116	.203 (.078)**	.053, .344					
Internalizing/externalizing behavior	5	61	.309 (.097)**	.127, .510	.240 (−.205, .250)				
Mixed/diverse	7	73	.249 (.069)***	.116, .371	.083 (−.122, .289)				
Multiproblem families	2	33	.213 (.099)*	.031, .386	.048 (−.258, .354)				
Relational distress	12	92	.330 (.057)***	.227, .426	.180 (.002, .358)*				
Mental illness	1	2	.360 (.131)**	.099, .552	.754 (.217, 1.292)**				
Average age of youth	20	346	.790 (.302)***	.429, .934	−.060 (−.102, −.018)**	7.744 (1, 344)	.006	.038***	.015***
Average age of adults	2	42	.999 (.939)	.289, 1.000	.099 (−.193, −.004)*	4.465 (1, 40)	.041	.004	.270*
% Male youth	19	313	.254 (.084)**	.094, .402	−.160 (−.463, .144)	1.074 (1, 311)	.301	.040***	.030***
% Male adult clients	28	220	.235 (.041)***	.156, .310	.100 (.016, .185)*	5.486 (1, 218)	.020	.011***	.033***
% Clients of color	29	337	.279 (.043)***	.202, .355	−.171 (−.380, −.038)	2.602 (1, 335)	.108	.032***	.019***
% Male therapists	24	258	.310 (.074)***	.172, .435	−.089 (−.480, .303)	−0.198 (1, 256)	.656	.039***	.027***
Referral source	37	479				2.844 (3, 475)	.037	.029***	.036***
Recruited for study	8	83	.400 (.074)***	.272, .514					
Help-seeking	19	241	.335 (.088)***	.235, .405	−.089 (−.262, .084)				
Mandated	2	32	.235 (.138)	−.034, .473	−.184 (−.494, .126)				
Mixed (mandated/help-seeking)	8	123	.137 (.072)*	−.004, .273	−.286 (−.488, −.083)**				
Treatment Characteristics									
Therapy modality	39	491				2.947 (1, 489)	.087	.029***	.038***
Couple therapy	14	104	.359 (.058)***	.257, .453					
Family therapy	25	387	.248 (.043)***	.166, .325	−.124 (−.265, .018)				

	k	N	Estimate (SE)	95% CI	Estimate (95% CI)	F (df)	p		
Therapy model	39	491				7.082 (3, 487)	<.001	.029***	.026***
Structural/functional and multisystemic	7	106	.115 (.065)*	−.012, .238					
Integrating and mixed	19	282	.288 (.040)***	.216, .357	.181 (.037, .325)*				
Attachment and emotion- focused	7	68	.246 (.071)***	.112, .371	.135 (−.053, .324)				
Cognitive-behavioral	6	35	.533 (.083)***	.407, .639	.479 (.273, .685)***				
Treatment integrity	39	491				2.096 (1, 489)	.148	.029***	.040***
Not monitored or reported	16	176	.233 (.054)***	.129, .331					
Monitored	23	315	.327 (.046)***	.245, .405	.103 (−.037, 242)				
Treatment setting	34	387				2.186 (3, 383)	.089	.012***	.037***
Home-based	3	50	.150 (.113)	−.070, .356					
Outpatient clinic	28	297	.355 (.039)***	.287, .420	.220 (−.014, .455)*				
Mixed home-based/clinic	2	23	.244 (.095)**	.062, .410	.098 (−.192, .388)				
Hospital/residential	1	17	.211 (.085)*	.046, .364	−.184 (−.614, .246)				
Alliance Characteristics									
Type	39	491				3.950 (2, 488)	.020*	.029***	.032***
Individual client-therapist	20	267	.230 (.039)***	.157, .301					
Systemic[c]	21	171	.345 (.040)***	.275, .412	.125 (.038, .213)**				
Family members'/partners' scores averaged or added	9	53	.316 (.037)***	.250, .378	.026 (−.058, .110)				
Informant	39	491				1.076 (2, 488)	.342	.029***	.041***
Client self-report	24	262	.279 (.041)***	.204, .351					
Therapist report	14	26	.377 (.078)***	.239, .499	.109 (−.037, .256)				
Observer ratings	15	203	.282 (.052)***	.186, .338	−.003 (−.108, .114)				

(*continued*)

Table 4.4. Continued

Moderator	Studies[a]	# ES	Mean r (SE)	95% CI	β (95% CI)	F(df)	p	σ²(2)	σ²(3)
Alliance Measure	39	491				2.713 (4, 486)	.029	.029***	.035***
FTAS/FTASr	6	62	.379 (.084)***	.229, .511					
WAI/WAI-O/WAI-Co	11	139	.353 (.061)***	.229, .441	−.046 (−.251, .159)				
VTAS/VTAS-R	8	99	.127 (.074)	−.019, .266	−.272 (−.493, −.051)*				
SOFTA-o/SOFTA-s	6	119	.396 (.120)***	.245, .529	.021 (−.216, .258)				
Other	8	72	.214 (.072)**	.073, .342	−.185 (−.402, .033)				
Development of Measure	39	491				0.001 (1, 489)	.981	.029***	.043***
For individual therapy	12	171	.290 (.064)***	.171, .401					
For couple/family therapy	27	320	.289 (.044)***	.208, .365	−.002 (−.154, .151)				
Alliance Construct	39	491				0.490 (5, 485)	.784	.029***	.041***
Bond	5	24	.208 (.077)**	.059, .349	.015 (−.161, .191)				
Goal	3	15	.222 (.090)*	.050, .383	.044 (−.131, .220)				
Task	3	15	.251 (.090)**	.080, .407	.091 (−.131, .220)				
Bond, goal and task (total)	35	339	.293 (.037)***	.225, .358	.131 (−.056, .318)				
Systemic (within and between)	6	44	.330 (.080)***	.184, .462	.092 (−.124, .308)				
Other	2	54	.295 (.099)**	.110, .460					
Alliance timing	39	491				3.3390 (4, 486)	.010	.028***	.040***
Early in treatment	18	235	.236 (.042)***	.158, .313	.077 (−.017, .171)				
Mid-treatment	17	112	.308 (.047)***	−.171, .017	.019 (−.088, .126)				
Late in treatment	9	71	.254 (.057)***	.147, .356	.053 (−.117, .223)				
Improvement in alliance	3	15	.286 (.087)***	.122, .435					
Averaged or added over time	7	58	.423 (.065)***	.312, .522	.210 (.089, .330)***				

Outcome Characteristics

			ES (SE)	CI	Moderator ES (CI)	F			
Outcome domain	39	491				3.052 (3, 487)	.028	.028***	.034***
Individual symptom severity/functioning	19	243	.238 (.041)***	.163, .315					
Parental skills, family/couple functioning	11	78	.388 (.051)***	.300, .471	.166 (.054, .277)**				
Retention versus dropout	11	78	.227 (.050)***	.127, .315	−.018 (−.101, .066)				
Goal attainment/therapeutic progress	12	92	.315 (.051)***	.222, .402	.081 (−.032, .194)				
Outcome informant	39	491				0.228 (3, 487)	.877	.029***	.042***
Client self-report	29	344	.306 (.038)***	.228, .364					
Therapist report	3	11	.321 (.098)***	.133, .482	.027 (−.156, .210)				
Observer ratings	5	33	.272 (.075)***	.124, .396	−.034 (−.177, .109)				
Other[b]	11	103	.267 (.055)***	.165, .364	−.032 (−.133, .069)				
Outcome timing	39	491				2.155 (2, 488)	.117	.029***	.040***
End of treatment	21	293	.287 (.040)***	.213, .357					
Follow-up	16	136	.335 (.044)***	.255, .409	.053 (−.025, .113)				
Mid-treatment	8	62	.205 (.080)**	.080, .325	−.087 (−.222, .048)				

Note. SE = standard error; CI = confidence interval; FTAS = Family Therapy Alliance Scale; FTAS(r) = Family Therapy Alliance Scale (Revised); WAI(-O/-Co) = Working Alliance Inventory (–observer version/–couples version); VTAS = Vanderbilt Therapeutic Alliance Scale; VTAS(-R) = Vanderbilt Therapeutic Alliance Scale (–Revised); SOFTA-o/-s = System for Observing Family Therapy Alliances-observer (self-report). # ES = number of effect sizes in the analysis; σ^2 (2) = variance between effect sizes (within studies); σ^2 (3) = variance between effect sizes (between studies).
[a] Number of independent samples (several studies reported on the same sample). [b] Other = objective clinical log measures (weight gain, days of cannabis use, and attending fewer sessions than scheduled). [c] Includes within-system and therapist-group alliances.
* $p < .05$. ** $p < .01$. *** $p < .001$.

associations were found for each problem type, the overall F test was nonsignificant, indicating no significant difference in alliance–outcome associations based on clients' presenting problem.

Sample Characteristics

In terms of clients, Table 4.4 shows that the average ages of the problem youth (or adult child) and adults participating in the therapy (parents/caregivers or partners in couple therapy) significantly moderated the alliance–outcome association, for youth and adults, although only two studies (reporting on 42 effect sizes) provided the ages of adults. Specifically, correlations were stronger when the targeted child in family therapy was relatively younger and when the adults were relatively older (ages were averaged across clients in each couple or family).

Additionally, correlations between alliance and outcome were significantly stronger by referral source. The association was stronger when clients were either specifically recruited for the study (mean $r = .40$, $p < .001$) or help-seeking (mean $r = .34$, $p < .001$), as compared with involuntary clients or clients who were mandated for treatment (mean $r = .235$, $p > .05$).

Furthermore, adult gender was a significant moderator, indicating stronger correlations between alliance and outcome when the study (sub)sample included relatively more fathers or male partners. Therapist gender (percentage of male therapists in the sample) did not significantly moderate the alliance–outcome association. Aside from male gender, no other therapist variables were sufficiently reported in the various studies to conduct a moderator analysis.

Treatment Characteristics

Table 4.4 shows that therapy modality (couple vs. family) did not significantly moderate the alliance–outcome association. In other words, since the overall meta-analytic ES (.297) was not significantly different for couples (mean $r = .359$) versus families (mean $r = .248$), both $ps < .001$, the alliance–outcome association found in the full analysis was comparable across therapy modalities.

We also tested treatment model as a moderator variable, reasoning that since specific therapeutic strategies are intricately related to alliance development and maintenance (Hatcher & Barends, 2006; Heatherington, Escudero, & Friedlander, 2018), clients' collaborative efforts may differ depending on the therapist's theoretical orientation. In behavioral therapy, for example, both members of a particular couple might respond well to goal setting and homework assignments. In emotion-focused therapy, however, one (or both) of these clients might resist disclosing vulnerable feelings in a treatment setting.

Results showed significant differences in the average alliance–outcome correlation across treatment models, $F(3, 487) = 7.082$, $p < .001$, with 3% of the total variance between effect sizes at both levels 2 (within studies) and 3 (between studies). The strongest correlations emerged for cognitive-behavioral CFT (mean $r = .53$, $p < .001$)

as compared to either attachment/emotionally-focused (mean $r = .246$, $p < .001$) or integrative therapies (mean $r = .288$, $p < .001$). The lowest correlations emerged for structural/functional and multisystemic models (mean $r = .115$, $p < .05$). Despite these differences, the significant correlations indicate that alliance predicted outcome within each of these four major approaches to couple and family work.

Alliance Characteristics

In terms of methodology, Table 4.4 shows three specific alliance characteristics that significantly moderated the alliance–outcome association. First, in terms of the construct itself, a significant difference was found regarding type of alliance measured, $F(2, 488) = 3.950$, $p = .02$. The highest correlation emerged for systemic alliances (within-couple/family and therapist-group; mean $r = .330$) and outcome, as compared to either an individual client's alliance with the therapist (mean $r = .230$) or the sum or average of different family members' alliance scores (mean $r = .316$). Second, in comparing measures of alliance, we found that the SOFTA-o/SOFTA-s yielded significantly greater average effect sizes ($r = .396$) in predicting outcome than other instruments. Third, in terms of timing, adding or averaging alliance scores over multiple time periods emerged as a stronger predictor of treatment outcome (mean $r = .423$) than measuring alliance at a single, fixed point (i.e., early, middle, late, or "improvement").

Outcome Characteristics

Among the three outcome characteristics assessed for moderation (domain, informant, and timing; see Table 4.4), the only significant moderating effect emerged for outcome domain. Specifically, alliance correlated most highly with outcome measures that assessed parental skills or family/couple functioning (mean $r = .39$), as compared to goal attainment or therapeutic progress (mean $r = .32$), retention in treatment versus dropout (mean $r = .28$), and measures of individual symptom reduction (mean $r = .24$).

COMPARISON WITH PREVIOUS META-ANALYSES

The foregoing results are based on 48 studies (which reported on 40 different samples), 15 more than in our previous meta-analytic sample (Friedlander et al., 2011). The present overall ES ($r = .297$) compares favorably to the weighted aggregate r that emerged in the 2011 analysis (.26). As in the 2011 results, the mean ES for the couple therapy studies was not significantly higher than for the family therapy studies.

Comparison of our medium ES for the overall alliance–outcome analysis with the smaller ES for the 28 studies in Welmers-van de Poll et al. (2018) showed a notable difference. This difference may be due to sampling. Whereas the latter analysis only included studies of family therapy with youth, our sample was less restricted in terms of children's ages and included studies that were not available when Welmers-van de Poll et al.'s sample was located. Three of the four additional studies in our sample used the

SOFTA measures of alliance, which in our moderator analyses were significantly more highly correlated with outcome than any of the other alliance instruments.

In 2011, we speculated that an important influence on CFT alliances was the presence of split or unbalanced alliances. In the present analysis, we had sufficient data in seven studies to analyze the association between split alliances and treatment outcome, which showed a medium ES and indicated significantly poorer outcomes when family members' alliances were highly unbalanced.

We tested several moderating factors, as did Welmers-van de Poll et al. (2018). Three variables emerged as significant in both sets of results, notably (a) the timing of alliance (alliance/outcome correlations were greater when alliances were added or averaged over time as compared to a fixed point in time), (b) the average age of youth in the sample (correlations were stronger for families with younger children), and (c) participants' referral source (correlations were stronger for families that voluntarily sought help as compared to those that were involuntary or mandated to treatment).

On the other hand, five significant moderating variables in the present analysis were not significant in the meta-analysis conducted by Welmers-van de Poll et al. (2018): (a) treatment model, (b) type of alliance, (c) alliance measure, (d) outcome domain, and (e) percentage of male clients in the sample. These differences in the two sets of moderator analyses are likely due to the fact that Welmers-van de Poll et al. only sampled family therapy studies, whereas we also included couple therapy studies.

EVIDENCE FOR CAUSALITY

Aside from the one mediation study described earlier (Friedlander, Lambert, et al., 2008) and one cross-lagged panel study (Glebova et al., 2011), we found little evidence for a causal relation between alliance and outcome across the 48 studies.

Two mixed-methods, small N studies (not included in the meta-analysis) provided some evidence to explain how therapist behavior influences clients' alliance-related behavior in good versus poor outcome cases (Friedlander, Lambert, et al., 2008; Sheehan & Friedlander, 2015). Both studies used sequential analyses to test the significance of contingent probabilities in SOFTA-o behaviors. In this model, contingent probabilities (i.e., behavior B significantly following behavior A), are compared with the unconditional probabilities of each type of behavior. When the pattern is statistically significant, behavior A is said to "activate" ("cause") behavior B.

In the first study (Friedlander, Lambert et al., 2008), SOFTA-o behaviors were tracked over time in a good outcome case and a poor outcome case, both of which were seen by the same experienced family therapist. Results showed that, in the good outcome case, clients' positive alliance-related behaviors were activated by the therapist's alliance interventions within a 3-min window 74% of the time. Not only was this sequential pattern less frequent in the poor outcome case (28% of the time), but also the clients responded to the therapists' alliance interventions with negative SOFTA-o indicators 48% of the time. In the second study (Sheehan & Friedlander, 2015), a sequential analysis was conducted to study retention in treatment by comparing the initial sessions of eight families who were seen in brief strategic family. Results showed that the therapists responded with alliance strengthening behavior to clients' negative behavior 61% of the time with the families that stayed in treatment but only 40% of the time with the families that dropped out.

All told, the extant research does not provide strong evidence for causality. The sequential analysis studies nonetheless demonstrate how alliances operate differentially in cases with good versus poor outcomes and how therapists behave so to promote strong alliances with their clients. The discrepant outcomes of cases treated by the same therapists provide some evidence that positive versus negative outcomes are reflected in observable alliance-related processes (Friedlander, Lambert, et al., 2008).

CLIENT CONTRIBUTIONS

Clients' Characteristics

Multiple client characteristics including gender, distress level, and family role figure prominently in the literature on CFT alliances and eventual outcome. In this section, we summarize those client contributions.

In psychotherapy with heterosexual couples, most of the evidence indicates that when it comes to self-reported perceptions of alliance, gender matters (e.g., Glebova et al., 2011; Halford et al., 2016; Knobloch-Fedders et al., 2007). Generally, but not unequivocally (e.g., Heatherington & Friedlander, 1990), male partners' alliance perceptions early in treatment tend to be more strongly associated with outcome than those of their female partners. Notably, one study found that outcomes were enhanced when the man's alliance perceptions exceeded those of his female partner (Symonds & Horvath, 2004). Less frequently, the woman's alliance has been the stronger predictor of outcome, but timing of the alliance measurement also plays a role. Anker et al. (2010) speculated that "[p]erhaps when couples invest longer term commitments to therapy, women's alliances emerge as the more critical, and when couples invest in a shorter term of therapy because of a reluctant partner (usually the man), men's alliance becomes more predictive" (p. 642).

Indeed, in our meta-analysis gender, defined as percentage of male clients in a study's (sub)sample, emerged as a significant moderator variable. Specifically, the correlations between alliance and outcome were stronger when the sample was composed of relatively more fathers or male partners. This finding notwithstanding, gender needs to be considered in light of other, largely unknown factors. In one study (Miller et al., 2015), for example, only the female partner's level of avoidant attachment was associated with (poor) alliance development. As another example, in a study of problem-focused therapy (Biesen & Doss, 2013), gender was not a significant predictor of retention. Rather, when partners viewed their problems similarly before treatment began (one aspect of the within-couple alliance), men as well as women engaged more substantively in the therapeutic process.

Levels of personal and relational distress also play an important role in couples' alliances with the therapist. Maintenance of a strong alliance over the course of couple therapy seems to be negatively associated with the severity of clients' difficulties, including their experience of relational distress in the family of origin (Knobloch-Fedders et al., 2004). As shown in one study, fluctuations in a partner's depressive symptoms from one session to the next were reciprocally associated with fluctuations in the couple's average alliance scores (Kuhlman et al., 2013). Although other authors found no association between individuals' symptoms and alliance development (Knobloch-Fedders et al., 2004; Mamodhoussen et al., 2005), partners who report less dissatisfaction (e.g., Anderson & Johnson, 2010), especially with the sexual aspect of their relationship (Knobloch-Fedders et al., 2004), and who are more trusting of one another (Johnson & Talitman, 1997) seem to have a greater capacity for developing a strong alliance with the therapist, possibly because they begin treatment relatively more satisfied with their relationships (e.g., Knerr & Bartle-Haring, 2010; Symonds & Horvath, 2004).

In family treatment, family role (parent vs. child) is consistently associated with the alliance–outcome relationship. That is, the strength of alliance depends on who is asked or observed. For example, in a study of family therapy for anorexia nervosa, observers' ratings of adolescent alliances (but not parent alliances) predicted early weight gain (Pereira et al., 2006). Rather, the parents' alliance behavior in later therapy sessions was associated with their children's overall weight gain. In an investigation of multidimensional family therapy for adolescent substance abuse, observed (but not self-reported) alliances predicted adolescent outcomes but only when the parent's alliance with the therapist was moderate to strong (Shelef et al., 2005). Additionally, in community based treatment-as-usual (individual sessions with the adolescent paired with conjoint family sessions), adolescents' alliance perceptions predicted their parents' as well as their own ratings of outcome (symptom reduction and family functioning), whereas the parents' alliance perceptions were only associated with their own perspective on outcome (Hawley & Garland, 2008).

Similarly, the adolescents and parents in a study of treatment-as-usual viewed their progress differently in an APIM study (Friedlander et al., 2012). Whereas parents saw improvements when their children rated the alliance positively, the adolescents' views were not associated with those of their parents. Moreover, when adolescents' alliances were strong, they saw their sessions as relatively more valuable, but the parents saw the sessions as considerably *less* valuable when their children's alliance scores were high.

Family role also plays a part in the development of split or unbalanced alliances. As mentioned earlier, although alliances in which the adolescent has a much closer bond with the therapist than does the parent seem to occur just as often as the reverse pattern (Muñiz de la Peña et al., 2009), the type of unbalanced pattern has often been associated with treatment retention. In a study of brief strategic family therapy, for example, unbalanced mother–father alliances and increasingly unbalanced mother–adolescent alliances characterized families that dropped out of (Robbins et al., 2008).

As in couple therapy, family members' levels of personal distress seem to play a role in alliance development. In a study of family therapy for anorexia nervosa, for example, adolescents who had significant weight and eating concerns found it more difficult to establish an alliance with the therapist (Pereira et al., 2006). On the other hand, in a study of multidimensional family therapy, the externalizing versus internalizing nature of the adolescents' problems was not related to alliance development (Shelef & Diamond, 2008).

According to Bowen (1978), adults' personal distress is a reflection of their levels of self-differentiation, which seems to be an influential factor in alliance development. Theoretically, more differentiated adults are able to balance togetherness with aloneness. In one study, parents' perceptions of the family's alliance after Session 3 were associated with their pretreatment differentiation scores (Lambert & Friedlander, 2008). One aspect of differentiation, emotional reactivity, was most closely associated with parents' self-reported safety on the SOFTA-s. Parents who reported less reactivity tended to experience greater comfort in the conjoint therapy context.

More differentiated adults are also able to separate their personal concerns from the concerns of others, notably their children (Bowen, 1978). In the Beale family (described earlier; Friedlander et al., 2014), the parents were able to put aside their marital instability and confusion during the family sessions in order to focus on their daughter's intense distress. In this successful case, the parents' shared concern for their child seems to have allowed each person's alliance with the therapist to develop favorably without ruptures or split alliances. By contrast, in the other case study (Escudero et al., 2012), Ms. M found it particularly difficult to separate her own problems from those of her daughter. It seems likely that Ms. M's apparently poor self-differentiation contributed to the severe within-family alliance ruptures observed in this case.

Finally, in comparisons of observed alliances (on the SOFTA-o) in four sessions with voluntary (self-referred) and involuntary families (referred by a public or private institution service), more positive overall differences were found in Session 1 on all four alliance dimensions, particularly shared purpose and engagement (Sotero et al., 2016). By Session 4, however, only engagement was lower in the involuntary group than the voluntary group.

Clients' Behavior

Just as in individual psychotherapy, the behavior of partners or family members who are most successful in CFT suggests that they feel comfortable, have a trusting emotional bond with their therapists, and stay engaged in the negotiation and renegotiation of therapy goals and tasks as treatment unfolds. In one study, for example, in sessions rated as relatively deeper or more valuable by both clients and therapists, the clients' behaviors reflected a high degree of connection with the therapist, engagement, and safety in the therapeutic process (Friedlander et al., 2010). Family members who demonstrate safety in the therapeutic context with one another tend to be emotionally expressive and vulnerable: they ask each other for feedback; encourage one another to open up or speak frankly; and disclose thoughts, feelings, and memories that may never before have been shared (Escudero & Friedlander, 2017; Friedlander et al., 2006). For parents in particular, safety is closely associated with the family's shared sense of purpose or within-family alliance (cf. Friedlander, Lambert, et al., 2008), the alliance aspect that seems most vital for successful outcomes.

On the other hand, hostility, sarcasm, and prolonged cross-blaming tend to signal a troubled within-family alliance. Of course, in-session family conflict does not always indicate that a therapy session has gone awry. Some clients (and therapists) see therapy sessions as more valuable when conflict is expressed, whereas other clients see the process as more valuable when there is less overt conflict (Friedlander et al., 2010). This variability is likely due either (a) to the nature of the conflict (i.e., whether it is due to dissimilar views on the family's problems or on the value of therapy as a way to resolve those problems) or (b) to the family's general comfort with overt expressions of conflict.

Overall, little is known about adolescent behavior in relation to family therapy alliances. It seems likely that how adolescents behave is highly dependent on the attitudes and behavior of their parents. In the mixed methods study of problematic within-family alliances discussed earlier (see Landmark section; Lambert et al., 2012), the adolescents resisted their parents' attempts at engagement when they disagreed with their parents about the nature of problems or when they felt hostility toward or a lack of connection with their parents. Simply put, clients contribute mightily to the formation of multiple alliances in CFT, and their contribution rivals, if not exceeds, that of the therapist's contribution.

LIMITATIONS OF THE RESEARCH

The findings from this meta-analysis dovetail in most substantive ways with our previous results (Friedlander et al., 2011), strengthening our confidence in the alliance as a strong process variable that predicts treatment retention and couple/family outcomes. That said, there are limitations in the research that raise concern and prompt recommendations for future research.

First, among the 48 studies, double the number (24) in our previous meta-analysis, we found little evidence for causality. To make causal inferences, researchers need to attend to the timing of the alliance measurement and use procedures that establish temporal precedence of the alliance, which is critical for drawing valid conclusions about its causal connection to client outcome (Feeley, DeRubeis, & Gelfand, 1999).

As a group, the 48 studies in the present meta-analysis varied in terms of when the alliance was assessed. While many of the effects emerged in studies of early- or mid-therapy alliances, a sizeable percentage (26%) of the 71 individual effect sizes were based on late-therapy measurements of the alliance (see Table 4.4). Relying solely on late-therapy measurement is problematic, since significant "effects" may not be effects at all but rather a reflection of treatment going well in terms of clients feeling more positively about their collaboration with the therapist (and with each other).

Although we located only a handful of studies on split or unbalanced alliances, a medium ES was found for their association with client outcome. While this meta-analytic finding is intriguing, more research is needed on this topic. In particular, quantitative group studies can be designed to identify client and therapist factors that moderate the split alliance–outcome association, and case studies can be carried out to understand how split alliances may be repaired. Persistent inconsistencies in this line of inquiry have to do with how a split alliance is defined and operationalized, whether and how its severity is assessed, and whether it should be measured once or over several time periods. Among the studies included in our meta-analysis, some researchers defined a split only in terms of the strength of clients' emotional bond with the therapist (e.g., Muñiz de la Peña et al., 2009), whereas other researchers defined a split in all aspects of alliance (i.e., agreement on goals and tasks as well as the bond; e.g., Bartle-Haring et al., 2012). Differing definitions of this phenomenon make it difficult to compare findings across studies.

Another challenge concerns the lack of systems-level analyses. Although use of the APIM model to study couple and family therapy is a recent advance, CFT researchers have yet to come to consensus about how to operationalize the couple or family alliance as a unit. As explained earlier, neither averages nor discrepancies between individual's alliance scores satisfactorily reflect the system-wide alliance.

Future researchers might consider newer methods for analyzing dyadic data that specifically take into account system dynamics: the latent group model (Kivlighan, 2007), the common fate model (Ledermann & Kenny, 2012), and response surface analysis (Shanock et al., 2010). The latent group model "builds off the lay notion that groups and relationships have personalities just like individuals do" (Kivlighan, 2007, p. 425) by determining whether a dyadic unit acts similarly to or differently from its parts (see also Chapter 5 in this volume on group psychotherapy). The common fate model can be estimated through structural equation modeling and combined with APIM. Polynomial regression with response surface analysis (cf. Marmarosh & Kivlighan, 2012) allows researchers to study congruence versus discrepancy in terms of how predictors from two individuals are associated with an outcome variable.

The use of diverse samples in CFT research is still a work in progress, despite greater inclusion in recent years of studies that have sampled sexual-minority clients, low-income clients, and treatment settings outside the United States. More research is needed on the outcomes and processes of building alliances in countries other than Western nations, where most of the present studies were conducted. This recommendation is especially relevant as culturally adapted treatments are developed for clients from collectivist cultures. Do these adaptations enhance the working alliance? If so, will the alliance–outcome associations reported in this meta-analysis hold up across international studies?

Increasing diversity in the characteristics of client samples is a necessary first step toward increasing the formal testing of demographic and individual differences as moderators of the association between alliance and outcome. Overall, significant client moderators in the current meta-analysis were limited to client age, gender, and referral status. Little is known about therapist effects in CFT, although it is possible that clients in conjoint therapies are less concerned than individual clients about their relationship with the therapist and more concerned with how other family members are behaving in therapy (Friedlander, Lambert, et al., 2008).

Moreover, it is not clear *how* the alliance operates over time in relation to other therapy variables. It may be that, regardless of timing, the client's contribution to the alliance is most important, particularly if better functioning clients form satisfactory social relationships (Zilcha-Mano, 2017). Alternately, it may be that early symptom change strengthens the alliance or that a good alliance helps clients feel better but does not in and of itself reduce symptoms.

Methodologies that tease apart the direction of alliance–outcome associations throughout the course of therapy can be the gold standard for answering questions about causality. Even then, it is complicated. When alliances are assessed and "fed back" to therapists after every session, researchers do not know the extent to which the therapists modified their behavior based on the alliance scores or based on discussions with the clients about their treatment progress.

In future studies, rather than assess growth curves across sessions in one variable (alliance) or the other (e.g., improvement-so-far in Friedlander et al, 2012), researchers could use lagged alliance–outcome correlations (e.g., Glebova et al., 2011). Another statistical approach would be to use the Time Varying Effects Model (Tan et al., 2012) to study patterns over time in the correlation between alliance and outcome. It may be, for example, that the association between alliance and outcome reveals strikingly different longitudinal patterns for better and worse outcome cases.

DIVERSITY CONSIDERATIONS

CFT researchers have frequently studied client gender and therapist gender, client race/ethnicity, and socioeconomic status but rarely same-gender couples. Gender is the most frequently studied sociodemographic variable in the CFT alliance literature. Overall, the findings are complex. In studies of heterosexual couple therapy, gender typically yields significant effects. In most studies, but not invariably (cf. Anker et al., 2010), the man's alliance with the therapist was more predictive of outcome than the woman's alliance (e.g., Symonds & Horvath, 2004). Since our previous meta-analysis of the alliance–outcome literature (Friedlander et al., 2011), there has been a significant advance in untangling gender effects using actor–partner and multilevel analyses to study both partners' alliances within the same model. Taken together, these findings are strong enough to have spawned some useful recommendations for the complex task of building alliances in couple therapy.

Unfortunately, however, what we know about the alliance in couple therapy is based on studies with predominantly heterosexual partners. Of the studies included in the present meta-analysis, none was solely with same-sex couples. In the family therapy domain, practice recommendations emerged from a study that compared good and poor therapist–parent alliances in relationship-focused family therapy for the nonaccepting parents of same-sex oriented youth and young adults (Shpigel & Diamond, 2014).

Regarding other client demographics, the current corpus of CFT alliance research includes a number of studies with racially and ethnically diverse US samples, mostly African American, Latino/a, and Euro-American families. Research with predominantly racial/ethnic minority samples is lacking, however, other than a handful of exceptions. The general lack of attention to minority race and ethnicity in the CFT alliance literature is particularly unfortunate since family relationships in collectivist cultures are likely to affect health outcomes in unique ways (Campos & Kim, 2017).

In as much as the CFT alliance literature now includes a considerable range in researchers' nationalities and research locations, it is increasingly diverse in terms of culture and ethnicity. The studies of alliance–outcome associations listed in Table 4.1 were carried out in Austria/Germany, Canada, Finland, Ireland, Israel, the Netherlands, Norway, Spain, and Portugal, as well as in different locations within the United States.

Since poverty is a particularly pernicious family stressor, we were pleased to note that some studies deliberately recruited low-income families (e.g., Friedlander, Lambert, et al., 2008; Quirk et al., 2014). Although many, if not most, samples in the present meta-analysis included single-parent families, we have no information about whether alliances operate similarly in these families as compared with two-parent families. It seems likely that, compared to two-parent families, single heads of household who are coping with problem children may develop qualitatively different relationships with their therapists (Escudero & Friedlander, 2017).

In sum, since our 2011 meta-analysis there has been an encouraging amount of sociodemographic diversity in the CFT alliance literature, particularly geographical diversity, although the extent to which race and ethnicity are being systematically studied lags behind. Still, there are notable gaps in several important aspects of diversity, including sexual-minority couples/families. Generally speaking, research attention to diversity has primarily focused on client characteristics rather than on therapist characteristics or on the demographic composition of the therapist/client system.

TRAINING IMPLICATIONS

Despite the repeated finding that alliance quality significantly predicts CFT outcomes, we located no research on the impact of alliance training on the effectiveness of therapy. In fact, research on alliance training is scarce in individual psychotherapy and almost nonexistent in conjoint CFT. Like others, we believe that these skills can be learned and enhanced in training programs (Karam et al., 2015). Training on alliance building (e.g., Muran & Barber, 2010) can help novice therapists transform negative relational events in session into growth experiences that, in turn, facilitate change (e.g., Crits-Christoph et al., 2006).

Therapists can be taught (didactically) and supervised to evaluate the strength of the alliance based on key observable indicators of engagement, emotional connection, safety, and shared sense of purpose. This skill seems to be learned through clinical experience with couples and families but can also be enhanced through systematic training in recognizing behavioral indicators of alliance. To do so, graduate students can be instructed how to recognize systemic alliances based on the SOFTA model and using the e-SOFTA computer program (Escudero & Friedlander, 2016). In one study, students' knowledge of alliance and observation skills (based on the SOFTA-o) were evaluated pre- and posttraining and compared in terms of accuracy with the knowledge and skills of experienced therapists (Carpenter et al., 2008). The trainees' mean scores on alliance knowledge and observations skills improved significantly.

We recommend a stepwise method for alliance training. First, students are introduced to the therapeutic alliance as a construct, followed by role playing. Evaluation of the training involves assessing students' alliance-related skills with confederates and then with actual clients. The effectiveness of the alliance training program can be evaluated on three levels: conceptualization, observational skills, and executive skills (cf. (Garayoa et al., in preparation).

THERAPEUTIC PRACTICES

- Aristotle said, "The whole is more than the sum of its parts." Based on the results of past and present meta-analyses, the crucial practice point is that strong, balanced therapeutic alliances improve the outcomes of CFT. By *outcomes*, we mean not only final outcomes but also treatment retention, session evaluations, and intermediate (improvement-so-far) results.
- The therapeutic alliance, by definition, is the result of reciprocity between client(s) and therapist. It is essential for therapists to identify markers of clients' receptivity to therapeutic change attempts in the ongoing stream of behavior.
- The alliance–outcome relationship in CFT is decidedly transtheoretical, cutting across theoretical approaches in manualized therapies as well as treatment-as-usual. Therapists can refer to the foregoing review of literature whether they are seeing couples and families in multidimensional family therapy, brief strategic family therapy, structural family therapy, dialogical/narrative therapy, cognitive-behavioral therapy, family-based treatment for eating disorders, emotionally-focused couple therapy, as well as home-based family therapy.
- Our results highlight the need for therapists to develop and closely monitor their alliances with each partner or family member throughout the course of treatment. Despite the normal pull to identify with, or feel a greater affinity to, one partner or family member rather than another, CFT alliances interact, and clients closely observe how their family members are relating to the therapist. It is particularly important not to ignore but rather to pull in quiet or reluctant family members.
- Therapists are advised to be particularly alert to the strength of the alliance within the couple or family unit, since evidence increasingly suggests that it is the most crucial for engagement and retention in treatment as well as for ultimate treatment success. Couples and families who enter CFT with a strong shared sense of purpose seem to have the greatest chance of successful outcomes.
- The within-family aspect of alliance tends to strengthen over time in successful cases. For this reason, it is short-sighted to simply consider each client's alliance separately without being attuned to the within-couple or within-family alliance. Research has shown that even highly experienced therapists tend to use more engagement and connection behaviors to address individual family members and fewer shared

purpose behaviors addressed to the system as a whole, thereby overlooking the quintessential systemic feature of couple and family work.

♦ Identifying family members' shared feelings ("You both describe yourselves as victims of the other") and experiences ("As children, neither of you seems to have gotten what you needed in terms of nurturing from your own parents") and validating their common struggle strengthens the within-family alliance. After doing so, the therapist can suggest overarching goals ("You all seem to want strategies to problem-solve more successfully with one another so that conflict doesn't keep escalating and get out of control" or "We can work together on helping you finding your way back to the close feelings you had for each other at the beginning of your relationship").

♦ Although split alliances occur frequently, therapists can take steps to repair the alliance and prevent dropout. Therapists can be aware, however, that when a client's behavior suggests a mildly split alliance, the family member who views the therapy and/or the therapist most negatively may have more unfavorable feelings than his or her in-session behavior suggests. Focusing on the emotional bond with the disaffected client may prove most helpful in repairing a split alliance.

♦ Even when therapists avoid responding in ways that detract from the alliance, dropout can occur when a therapist fails to use alliance-enhancing responses when a rupture is evident.

♦ When a rupture occurs, such as when a client questions the value of treatment or responds to another family member defensively or sarcastically, the therapist is advised to respond with a deliberate alliance-enhancing intervention to repair the rupture. Examples include indicating that some positive change has already taken place, expressing interest in the client's life apart from the therapeutic concerns, acknowledging that psychotherapy involves taking risks, or emphasizing family members' commonalities or shared experiences.

♦ Parents and children, particularly adolescents, tend to develop different alliances with the therapist. Parents closely observe their children's reactions to the therapeutic process and tend to evaluate improvements based on their assessment of the child's alliance with the therapist, but the reverse is generally not the case. Rather, adolescents tend to be more aware of their own reactions to the therapist than to the reactions of their parents. Thus CFT practitioners will wisely attune to these different developments of the alliance as well as the potentially disparate alliances themselves.

♦ Even mandated and involuntary clients can form strong working alliances in CFT. Therapists can enhance these clients' active involvement by asking, rather than imposing, in-session and homework tasks. Once meaningfully engaged in the therapy process, involuntary clients can benefit considerably.

♦ Therapists are advised to employ safety and emotional connection interventions to enhance the within-family alliance and individuals' levels of engagement in the conjoint treatment process. When engagement is low, the therapist can respectfully (i.e., nondefensively) explore the reasons behind a client's resistance.

♦ With adolescents, therapists can improve a poor alliance by taking a one-down position—avoiding domineering or authoritarian responses. On the other hand, by aligning too strongly with an adolescent, a therapist may unwittingly harm his or her alliance with the parents, particularly if the parents view the treatment only in terms of change in the adolescent and do not expect the therapist to challenge their own behavior.

♦ Therapists typically enjoy the most success in engaging reluctant adolescents by helping them define their personal treatment goals, by presenting themselves as the adolescent's ally, by not challenging their resistance forcefully, and by encouraging the parent(s) to support the adolescent's involvement in the treatment process with empathy and a lack of defensiveness.

♦ With heterosexual couples, a key to success may involve working early on to create a particularly strong alliance with the male partner, particularly if the female partner was the one to initiate the request for help. Later on, it seems important to insure that the female partner continues to be invested in therapy. These patterns are, of course, not universal.

♦ In CFT when there is high emotional reactivity and conflict, possibly the most important safety intervention is either to ask one (or more) clients to step out of the room for a brief period or to conduct alternating sessions with different family subsystems. When parents feel highly unsafe, the therapy has a large chance of resulting in dropout.

♦ Therapists can enhance the alliance by asking clients to complete a brief self-report measure of alliance after each session. It seems likely that when family members provide information about their private experience of the conjoint context, the therapist is better prepared to directly address any alliance strains or ruptures.

♦ In short, each person's alliance matters, and family alliances are not interchangeable. Psychotherapists are strongly advised to recognize that balanced alliances facilitate the therapeutic process and that continual monitoring of the strength of the alliance with each family member and within the family unit is essential for therapeutic success.

REFERENCES

Anderson, S. R., & Johnson, L. N. (2010). A dyadic analysis of the between- and within-system alliances on distress. *Family Process, 49,* 220–235. https://www.doi.org/10.1111/j.1545-5300.2010.01319

Anker, M. G., Duncan, B. L., & Sparks, J. A. (2009). Using client feedback to improve couple therapy outcomes: A randomized clinical trial in a naturalistic setting. *Journal of Consulting and Clinical Psychology, 77,* 693–704. https://www.doi.org/10.1037/a0016062

Anker, M. G., Owen, J., Duncan, B. L., & Sparks, J. A. (2010). The alliance in couple therapy: Partner influence, early change, and alliance patterns in a naturalistic sample. *Journal of Consulting and Clinical Psychology, 78,* 635–645. https://www.doi.org/10.1037/a0020051

Bachler, E., Frühmann, A., Bachler, H., Aas, B. Strunk, G., & Nickel, M. (2016). Differential effects of the working alliance in family therapeutic home-based treatment of multi-problem families. *Journal of Family Therapy, 38,* 120–148. https://www.doi.org/10.1111/1467-6427.12063

Bartle-Haring, S., Glebova, T., Gangamma, R., Grafsky, E., & Delaney, R. O. (2012). Alliance and termination status in couple therapy: A comparison of methods for assessing discrepancies. *Psychotherapy Research, 22,* 502–514. https://www.doi.org/10.1080/10503307.2012.676985

Bennun, I. (1989). Perceptions of the therapist in family therapy. *Journal of Family Therapy, 11*(3), 243–255.

Biesen, J. N., & Doss, B. D. (2013). Couples' agreement on presenting problems predicts engagement and outcomes in problem-focused couple therapy. *Journal of Family Psychology, 27,* 658–663. https://www.doi.org/10.1037/a0033422

Bordin, E. S. (1979). The generalizability of the psychoanalytic concept of the working alliance. *Psychotherapy, 16,* 252–260. https://www.doi.org/10.1037/h0085885

Bourgeois, L., Sabourin, S., & Wright, J. (1990). Predictive validity of therapeutic alliance in group marital therapy. *Journal of Consulting and Clinical Psychology, 58,* 608–613. https://www.doi.org/10.1037/0022-006X.58.5.608

Bowen, M. (1978). *Family therapy in clinical practice.* New York, NY: Jason Aronson.

Brown, P. D., & O'Leary, K. D. (2000). Therapeutic alliance: Predicting continuance and success in group treatment for spouse abuse. *Journal of Consulting and Clinical Psychology, 68,* 340–345. https://www.doi.org/10.1037/0022-006X.68.2.340

Campos, B., & Kim, H. S. (2017). Incorporating the cultural diversity of family and close relationships into the study of health. *American Psychologist, 72,* 543–554. https://www.doi.org/10.1037/amp0000122

Carpenter, J., Escudero, V., & Rivett, M. (2008). Training family therapy students in conceptual and observation skills relating to the therapeutic alliance: An evaluation. *Journal of Family Therapy, 30,* 409–422. https://www.doi.org/10.1111/j.1467-6427.2008.00442.x

Chinchilla, P. (2007). *Comorbidity as a moderator of process-outcome relations in individual and family therapy for adolescent substance abuse* (Unpublished doctoral dissertation). Fordham University, New York, NY.

Crits-Christoph, P., Gibbons, M. B., Crits-Christoph, K., Narducci, J., Schamberger, M., & Gallop, R. (2006). Can therapists be trained to improve their alliances? A preliminary study of alliance-fostering psychotherapy. *Psychotherapy Research, 16,* 268–281.

Dauber, S. (2004). *Treatment focus in individual and family therapy for adolescent substance abuse* (Unpublished doctoral dissertation). Fordham University, New York, NY.

Diamond, G. M., Liddle, H. A., Dakof, G. A., & Hogue, A. (1996). *Revised version of the Vanderbilt Therapeutic Alliance Scale.* Unpublished manuscript, Temple University.

Diamond, G. M., & Shpigel, M. S. (2014). Attachment-based family therapy for lesbian and gay young adults and their persistently nonaccepting parents. *Professional Psychology: Research and Practice, 45,* 258–268. https://www.doi.org/10.1037/a0035394

Diener, M. J., Hilsenroth, M. J., & Weinberger, J. (2009). A primer on meta-analysis of correlation coefficients: The relationship between patient-reported therapeutic alliance and adult attachment style as an illustration. *Psychotherapy Research, 19,* 519–526. https://www.doi.org/10.1080/10503300802491410

Duncan, B. L., Miller, S. D., Sparks, J. A., Reynolds, L. R., Brown, J., & Johnson, L. D. (2003). The Session Rating Scale: Preliminary psychometric properties of a "working" alliance measure. *Journal of Brief Therapy, 3,* 3–12.

Duval, S., & Tweedie, R. (2000). Trim and fill: A simple funnel-plot-based method of testing and adjusting for publication bias in meta-analysis. *Biometrics, 56,* 455–463. https://www.doi.org/10.1111/j.0006-341X.2000.00455.x

Escudero, V., Boogmans, E., Loots, G., & Friedlander, M. L. (2012). Alliance rupture and repair in conjoint family therapy: An exploratory study. *Psychotherapy, 49*, 26–37. https://www.doi.org/10.1037/a0026747

Escudero, V., & Friedlander, M. L. (2016). e-SOFTA: A video-based software for observing the working alliance in clinical training and supervision. In T. Rousmaniere & E. Renfro-Michel (Eds.), *Applications of modern technology in counselor supervision: A practical handbook* (pp. 223–238). Alexandria, VA: American Counseling Association Press.

Escudero, V., & Friedlander, M. L. (2017). *Therapeutic alliances with families: Empowering clients in challenging cases.* New York, NY: Springer. https://www.doi.org/10.1007/978-3-319-59369-2

Escudero, V., Friedlander, M. L., Abascal, A., & Kivlighan, D. M. Jr. (in preparation). *Therapeutic alliances and treatment outcome in a family therapy program based on alliance empowerment.* Manuscript in preparation.

Escudero, V., Friedlander, M., & Heatherington, L. (2011). Using the e-SOFTA for video training and research on alliance-related behavior. *Psychotherapy, 48*, 138–147.

Escudero, V., Friedlander, M. L., Varela, N., & Abascal, A. (2008). Observing the therapeutic alliance in family therapy: Associations with participants' perceptions and therapeutic outcomes. *Journal of Family Therapy, 30*, 194–214. https://www.doi.org/10.1111/j.1467-6427.2008.00425.x

Feder, M., & Diamond, G. M. (2016). Parent-therapist alliance and parent attachment-promoting behaviour in attachment-based family therapy for suicidal and depressed adolescents. *Journal of Family Therapy, 38*, 82–101. https://www.doi.org/10.1111/1467-6427.12078

Feeley, M., DeRubeis, R. J., & Gelfand, L. A. (1999). The temporal relation of adherence and alliance to symptom change in cognitive therapy for depression. *Journal of Consulting and Clinical Psychology, 67*, 578–582.

Flicker, S. M., Turner, C. W., Waldron, H. B., Ozechowski, T. J., & Brody, J. L. (2008). Ethnic background, therapeutic alliance, and treatment retention in functional family therapy with adolescents who abuse substances. *Journal of Family Psychology, 22*, 167–170. https://www.doi.org/10.1037/0893-3200.22.1.167

Forsberg, S. (2011). *The relationship between therapeutic alliance and treatment outcome in a comparative study of individual and family therapy for adolescent anorexia nervosa* (Unpublished doctoral dissertation). Palo Alto University, Palo Alto, CA.

Forsberg, S., LoTempio, E., Bryson, S., Fitzpatrick, K. K., Le Grange, D., & Lock, J. (2014). Parent-therapist alliance in Family-Based Treatment for adolescents with anorexia nervosa. *European Eating Disorders Review, 22*, 53–58. https://www.doi.org/10.1002/erv.2242

Friedlander, M. L., Bernardi, S., & Lee, H. (2010). Better versus worse family therapy sessions as reflected in clients' alliance-related behavior. *Journal of Counseling Psychology, 57*, 198–204. https://www.doi.org/10.1037/a0019088

Friedlander, M. L., Escudero, V., & Heatherington, L. (2006). *Therapeutic alliances with couples and families: An empirically-informed guide to practice.* Washington, DC: American Psychological Association. https://www.doi.org/10.1037/0022-0167.53.2.214

Friedlander, M. L., Escudero, V., Heatherington, L., & Diamond, G. M. (2011a). Alliance in couple and family therapy. In J. C. Norcross (Ed.), *Psychotherapy relationships that work: Evidence-based responsiveness.* (2nd ed., pp. 92–109). New York, NY: Oxford University Press. https://www.doi.org/10.1037/a0022060

Friedlander, M. L., Escudero, V., Horvath, A., Heatherington, L., Cabero, A., & Martens, M. (2006). System for Observing Family Therapy Alliances: A tool for research and practice. *Journal of Counseling Psychology, 53,* 214–225. https://www.doi.org/10.1037/0022-0167.53.2.214

Friedlander, M. L., Heatherington, L., Johnson, B., & Skowron, B. (1994). Sustaining engagement: A change event in family therapy. *Journal of Counseling Psychology, 41,* 1–11. https://www.doi.org/10.1037/0022-0167.41.4.438

Friedlander, M. L., Kivlighan, D. M. Jr., & Shaffer, K. (2012). Exploring actor-partner interdependence in family therapy: Whose view (parent or adolescent) best predicts treatment progress? *Journal of Counseling Psychology, 59,* 168–175. https://www.doi.org/10.1037/a0024199

Friedlander, M. L., Lambert, J. E., Escudero, V., & Cragun, C. (2008). How do therapists enhance family alliances? Sequential analyses of therapist → client behavior in two contrasting cases. *Psychotherapy: Theory, Research, Practice, Training, 45,* 75–87. https://www.doi.org/10.1037/0033-3204.45.1.75

Friedlander, M. L., Lambert, J. E., & Muñiz de la Peña, C. (2008). A step toward disentangling the alliance/improvement cycle in family therapy. *Journal of Counseling Psychology, 55,* 118–124. https://www.doi.org/10.1037/0022-0167.55.1.118

Friedlander, M. L., Lee, H. H., Shaffer, K. S., & Cabrera, P. (2014). Negotiating therapeutic alliances with a family at impasse: An evidence-based case study. *Psychotherapy, 51,* 41–52. https://www.doi.org/10.1037/a0032524

Garayoa, B., Aza, G., Escudero, V. & Muñoz-SanRoque, I. (in preparation). *Efficiency of a training program on alliance-foster skills in family therapy.* Manuscript in preparation.

Glebova, T., Bartle-Haring, S., Gangamma, R., Knerr, M., Delaney, R. O., Meyer, K., . . . Grafsky, E. (2011). Therapeutic alliance and progress in couple therapy: Multiple perspectives. *Journal of Family Therapy, 33,* 42–65. https://www.doi.org/10.1111/j.1467-6427.2010.00503.x

Glueckauf, R. L., Liss, H. J., McQuillen, D. E., Webb, P. M., Dairaghi, J., & Carter, S. S. (2002). Therapeutic alliance in family therapy for adolescents with epilepsy: An exploratory study. *American Journal of Family Therapy, 30,* 125–139. https://www.doi.org/10.1080/019261802753573849

Halford, T. C., Owen, J., Duncan, B. L., Anker, M. G., & Sparks, J. A. (2016). Pre-therapy relationship adjustment, gender and the alliance in couple therapy. *Journal of Family Therapy, 38,* 18–35. https://www.doi.org/10.1111/1467-6427.12035

Hatcher, R. L., & Barends, A. W. (2006). How a return to theory could help alliance research. *Psychotherapy: Theory, Research, Practice, & Training, 43,* 292–299. https://www.doi.org/10.1037/0033-3204.43.3.292

Hawley, K. M., & Garland, A. F. (2008). Working alliance in adolescent outpatient therapy: Youth, parent, and therapist reports and association with therapy outcomes. *Child and Youth Care Forum, 27,* 59–74. https://www.doi.org/10.1007/s10566-008-9050-x

Hawley, K. M., & Weisz, J. R. (2005). Youth versus parent working alliance in usual clinical care: Distinctive associations with retention, satisfaction, and treatment outcome. *Journal of Clinical Child and Adolescent Psychology, 34,* 117–128. https://www.doi.org/10.1207/s15374424jccp3401_11

Heatherington, L., Escudero, V., & Friedlander, M. L. (2018). Where systems theory and alliance meet: Relationship and technique in family therapy. In O. Tishby & H. Wiseman (Eds.), *Developing the therapeutic relationship: Integrating case studies, research and practice* (pp. 257–288). Washington, DC: American Psychological Association.

Heatherington, L., & Friedlander, M. L. (1990). Couple and family therapy alliance scales: Empirical considerations. *Journal of Marital and Family Therapy, 16,* 299–306. https://www.doi.org/10.1111/j.1752-0606.1990.tb00851.x

Hogue, A., Dauber, S., Faw Stambaugh, L., Cecero, J. J., & Liddle, H. A. (2006). Early therapeutic alliance and treatment outcome in individual and family therapy for adolescent behavior problems. *Journal of Consulting and Clinical Psychology, 74,* 121–129. https://www.doi.org/10.1037/0022-006X.74.1.121

Horvath, A. O., Del Re, C., Flückiger, C., & Symonds, D. (2011). Alliance in individual psychotherapy. *Psychotherapy, 48,* 9–16. https://www.doi.org/10.1037/a0022186

Horvath, A. O., & Greenberg, L. S. (1986). The development of the Working Alliance Inventory. In L. S. Greenberg & W. M. Pinsof (Eds.), *The psychotherapeutic process: A research handbook* (pp. 529–556). New York, NY: Guilford.

Horvath, A. O., & Greenberg, L. S. (1989). Development and validation of the Working Alliance Inventory. *Journal of Counseling Psychology, 36,* 223–233.

Hunter, J. E., & Schmidt, F. L. (1990*). Methods of meta-analysis: Correcting error and bias in research findings.* Newbury Park, CA: SAGE.

Isserlin, L., & Couturier, J. (2012). Therapeutic alliance and family based treatment for adolescents with anorexia nervosa. *Psychotherapy, 49,* 46–51. https://www.doi.org/10.1037/a0023905

Johnson, L. N., & Ketring, S. A. (2006). The therapy alliance: A moderator in therapy outcome for families dealing with child abuse and neglect. *Journal of Marital and Family Therapy, 32,* 345–354. https://www.doi.org/10.1111/j.1752-0606.2006.tb01611.x

Johnson, L. N., Ketring, S. A., Rohacs, J., & Brewer, A. L. (2006). Attachment and the therapeutic alliance in family therapy. *American Journal of Family Therapy, 34,* 205–218. https://www.doi.org/10.1080/01926180500358022

Johnson, L. N., Wright, D. W., & Ketring, S. A. (2002). The therapeutic alliance in home-based family therapy: Is it predictive of outcome? *Journal of Marital and Family Therapy, 28*(1), 93–102.

Johnson, S. M., & Talitman, E. (1997). Predictors of success in emotionally focused marital therapy. *Journal of Marital and Family Therapy, 23,* 135–153. https://www.doi.org/10.1111/j.1752-0606.1997.tb00239.x

Karam, E. A., Sprenkle, D. H., & Davis, S. D. (2015). Targeting threats to the therapeutic alliance: A primer for marriage and family therapy training. *Journal of Marital and Family Therapy, 41,* 389–400. https://www.doi.org/10.1111/jmft.12097

Kashy, D. A., & Kenny, D. A. (2000). The analysis of data from dyads and groups. In H. T. Reis & C. M. Judd (Eds.), *Handbook of research methods in social and personality psychology* (pp. 451–477). New York, NY: Cambridge University Press.

Keeley, M. L., Geffken, G. R., Ricketts, E., McNamara, J. P. H., & Storch, E. A. (2011). The therapeutic alliance in the cognitive behavioral treatment of pediatric obsessive-compulsive disorder. *Journal of Anxiety Disorders, 25,* 855–863. https://www.doi.org/10.1016/j.janxdis.2011.03.017

Kim, H. (2007). *Client growth and alliance development in solution-focused brief family therapy* (Unpublished doctoral dissertation). State University of New York at Buffalo.

Kivlighan, D. M. (2007). Where is the relationship in research on the alliance? Two methods for analyzing dyadic data. *Journal of Counseling Psychology, 54,* 423–433. https://www.doi.org/10.1037/0022-0167.54.4.423

Knerr, K., & Bartle-Haring, S. (2010). Differentiation, perceived stress and therapeutic alliance as key factors in the early stage of couple therapy. *Journal of Family Therapy*, *32*, 94–108. https://www.doi.org/10.1111/j.1467-6427.2010.00489.x

Knobloch-Fedders, L. M., Pinsof, W. M., & Mann, B. J. (2004). The formation of the therapeutic alliance in couple therapy. *Family Process*, *43*, 425–442. https://www.doi.org/10.1111/j.1545-5300.2004.00032.x

Knobloch-Fedders, L. M., Pinsof, W. M., & Mann, B. J. (2007). Therapeutic alliance and treatment progress in couple psychotherapy. *Journal of Marital and Family Therapy*, *33*, 245–257. https://www.doi.org/10.1111/j.1752-0606.2007.00019.x

Kuhlman, I., Tolvanen, A., & Seikkula, J. (2013). The therapeutic alliance in couple therapy for depression: Predicting therapy progress and outcome from assessments of the alliance by the patient, the spouse, and the therapists. *Contemporary Family Therapy*, *35*, 1–13. https://www.doi.org/10.1007/s10591-012-9215-5

Lambert, J. E., & Friedlander, M. L. (2008). Relationship of differentiation of self to adult clients' perceptions of the alliance in brief family therapy. *Psychotherapy Research*, *43*, 160–166. https://www.doi.org/10.1080/10503300701255924

Lambert, J. E., Skinner, A., & Friedlander, M. L. (2012). Problematic within-family alliances in conjoint family therapy: A close look at five cases. *Journal of Marital and Family Therapy*, *38*, 417–428. https://www.doi.org/10.1111/j.1752-0606.2010.00212.x

Lange, A. M. C., Van der Rijken, R. E. A., Delsing, M. J. M. H., Busschbach, J. J. V., Van horn, J. E., & Scholte, R. H. J. (in preparation). *Does growth in alliance and therapist adherence predict treatment outcomes in a systemic therapy?* Manuscript in preparation.

Ledermann, D., & Kenny, D. A. (2012). The common fate model for dyadic data: Variations of a theoretically important but underutilized model. *Journal of Family Psychology*, *26*, 140–148.

Lipsey, M. W., & Wilson, D. B. (2001). *Practical meta-analysis*. Thousand Oaks, CA: SAGE.

Locke, H. J., & Wallace, K. M. (1959). Short marital-adjustment and prediction tests: Their reliability and validity. *Marriage and Family Living*, *21*, 251–255. https://www.doi.org/10.2307/348022

LoTempio, E., Forsberg, S., Bryson, S. W., Fitzpatrick, K. K., Le Grange, D., & Lock, J. (2013). Patients' characteristics and the quality of the therapeutic alliance in family-based treatment and individual therapy for adolescents with anorexia nervosa. *Journal of Family Therapy*, *35*, 29–52.

Mamodhoussen, S., Wright, J., Tremblay, N., & Poitras-Wright, H. (2005). Impact of marital and psychological distress on therapeutic alliance in couples undergoing couple therapy. *Journal of Marital and Family Therapy*, *31*, 159–169. https://www.doi.org/10.1111/j.1752-0606.2005.tb01553.x

Marmarosh, C. L., & Kivlighan, D. M. Jr. (2012). Relationships among client and counselor agreement about the working alliance, session evaluations, and change in client symptoms using response surface analysis. *Journal of Counseling Psychology*, *59*, 352–367. https://www.doi.org/10.1037/a0028907

Miller, R. B., Bills, S., Kubricht, B., Sandberg, J. G., Bean, R. A., & Ketring, S. A. (2015). Attachment as a predictor of the therapeutic alliance in couple therapy. *American Journal of Family Therapy*, *43*, 215–226. https://www.doi.org/10.1080/01926187.2015.1034635

Miller, S. D., Duncan, B. L., Brown, J., Sparks, J. A., & Claud, D. A. (2003). The outcome rating scale: A preliminary study of the reliability, validity, and feasibility of a brief visual analog measure. *Journal of Brief Therapy*, *2*, 91–100.

Muñiz de la Peña, C., Friedlander, M. L., & Escudero, V. (2009). Frequency, severity, and evolution of split family alliances: How observable are they? *Psychotherapy Research, 19,* 133–142. https://www.doi.org/10.1080/10503300802460050

Muran, J. C., & Barber, J. P. (2010). *The therapeutic alliance: An evidence-based guide to practice.* New York, NY: Guilford.

Owen, J., Duncan, B., Reese, R. J., Anker, M., & Sparks, J. (2014). Accounting for therapist variability in couple therapy outcomes: What really matters: *Journal of Sex and Marital Therapy, 40,* 488–502. https://www.doi.org/10.1080/0092623X.2013.772552

Owen, J. J., Rhoades, G. K., Stanley, S. M., & Markman, H. J. (2011). The role of leaders' working alliance in premarital education. *Journal of Family Psychology, 25,* 49–57. https://www.doi.org/10.1037/a0022084

Pereira, T., Lock, J., & Oggins, J. (2006). Role of therapeutic alliance in family therapy for adolescent anorexia nervosa. *International Journal of Eating Disorders, 39,* 677–684. https://www.doi.org/10.1002/eat.20303

Pinsof, W. B. (1994). An integrative systems perspective on the therapeutic alliance: Theoretical, clinical, and research implications. In A. O. Horvath & L. S. Greenberg (Eds.), *The working alliance: Theory, research, and practice* (pp. 173–195). New York, NY: Wiley.

Pinsof, W. B., & Catherall, D. (1986). The integrative psychotherapy alliance: Family, couple, and individual therapy scales. *Journal of Marital and Family Therapy, 12,* 137–151. https://www.doi.org/10.1111/j.1752-0606.1986.tb01631.x

Pinsof, W. B., Zinbarg, R., & Knobloch-Fedders, L. M. (2008). Factorial and construct validity of the revised short form Integrative Psychotherapy Alliance Scales for family, couple, and individual therapy. *Family Process, 47,* 281–301. https://www.doi.org/10.1111/j.1545-5300.2008.00254.x

Quinn, W. H., Dotson, D., & Jordan, K. (1997). Dimensions of therapeutic alliance and their association with outcome in family therapy. *Psychotherapy Research, 7,* 429–438. https://www.doi.org/10.1080/10503309712331332123

Quirk, K., Owen, J., Inch, L. J., France, T., & Bergen, C. (2014). The alliance in relationship education programs. *Journal of Marital and Family Therapy, 40,* 178–192. https://www.doi.org/10.1111/jmft.12019

R Core Team. (2016). *R: The R Project for Statistical Computing.* Vienna, Austria: R Foundation for Statistical Computing. Retrieved from www.r-project.org

Raytek, H. S., McCready, B. S., Epstein, E. E., & Hirsch, L. S. (1999). Therapeutic alliance and the retention of couples in conjoint alcoholism treatment. *Addictive Behaviors, 24,* 317–330. https://www.doi.org/10.1016/S0306-4603(98)00085-9

Rienecke, R. D., Richmond, R., & Lebow, J. (2016). Therapeutic alliance, expressed emotion, and treatment outcome for anorexia nervosa in a family-based partial hospitalization program. *Eating Behaviors, 22,* 124–128. https://www.doi.org/10.1016/j.eatbeh.2016.06.017

Robbins, M. S., Liddle, H. A., Turner, C. W., Dakof, G. A., Alexander, J. F., & Kogan, S. M. (2006). Adolescent and parent therapeutic alliances as predictors of dropout in multidimensional family therapy. *Journal of Family Psychology, 20,* 108–116. https://www.doi.org/10.1037/0893-3200.20.1.108

Robbins, M. S., Mayorga, C. C., Mitrani, V. B., Turner, C. W., Alexander, J. F., & Szapocznik, J. (2008). Adolescent and parent alliances with therapists in Brief Strategic Family Therapy™ with drug-using Hispanic adolescents. *Journal of Marital & Family Therapy, 34,* 316–328. https://www.doi.org/10.1111/j.1752-0606.2008.00075.x

Robbins, M. S., Turner, C. W., Alexander, J. F., & Perez, G. A. (2003). Alliance and dropout in family therapy for adolescents with behavior problems: Individual and systemic effects. *Journal of Family Psychology, 17*, 534–544. https://www.doi.org/10.1037/0893-3200.17.4.534

Rosenthal, R. (1995). Writing meta-analytic reviews. *Psychological Bulletin, 118*, 183–192. https://www.doi.org/10.1037/0033-2909.118.2.183

Safran, J. D., & Muran, J. C. (2000). *Negotiating the therapeutic alliance: A relational treatment guide.* New York, NY: Guilford.

Shanock, L. R., Baran, B. E., Gentry, W. A., Pattison, S. C., & Heggestad, E. D. (2010). Polynomial regression with response surface analysis: A powerful approach for examining moderation and overcoming limitations of difference scores. *Journal of Business Psychology, 25*, 543–554. https://www.doi.org/10.1007/s10869-010-9183-4

Sheehan, A. S., & Friedlander, M. L. (2015). Therapeutic alliance and retention in Brief Strategic Family Therapy: A mixed-methods study. *Journal of Marital and Family Therapy, 41*, 415–427. https://www.doi.org/10.1111/jmft.12113

Shelef, K., & Diamond, G. M. (2008). Short form of the Vanderbilt Therapeutic Alliance Scale: Development, reliability, and validity. *Psychotherapy Research, 18*, 433–443. https://www.doi.org/10.1080/10503300701810801

Shelef, K., Diamond, G. M., Diamond, G. S., & Liddle, H. A. (2005). Adolescent and parent alliance and treatment outcome in Multidimensional Family Therapy. *Journal of Consulting and Clinical Psychology, 73*, 689–698. https://www.doi.org/10.1037/0022-006X.73.4.689

Shpigel, M. S., & Diamond, G. M. (2014). Good versus poor therapeutic alliance with non-accepting parents of same-sex oriented adolescents and young adults: A qualitative study. *Psychotherapy Research, 24*, 376–391. https://www.doi.org/10.1080/10503307.2013.856043

Smerud, P. E., & Rosenfarb, I. S. (2008). The therapeutic alliance and family psychoeducation in the treatment of schizophrenia: An exploratory prospective change process study. *Journal of Consulting and Clinical Psychology, 76*, 505–510. https://www.doi.org/10.1037/0022-006X.76.3.505

Sotero, L., Major, S., Escudero, V., & Relvas, A. P. (2016). The therapeutic alliance with involuntary clients: How does it work? *Journal of Family Therapy, 38*, 36–58. https://www.doi.org/10.1111/1467-6427.12046

Sotero, L., Moura-Ramos, M., Escudero, V. & Relvas, A. P. (2017). *When the family doesn't want to come to therapy, is there any hope? A study focusing on outcomes and alliance with (in)voluntary clients.* Manuscript submitted for publication.

Sparks, J. (2015). The Norway couple project: Lessons learned. *Journal of Marital and Family Therapy, 41*, 481–494. https://www.doi.org/10.1111/jmft.12099

Symonds, B. D. (1999). *The measurement of alliance in short term couples therapy* (Unpublished doctoral dissertation). Simon Fraser University, Burnaby, British Columbia.

Symonds, B. D., & Horvath, A. O. (2004). Optimizing the alliance in couple therapy. *Family Process, 43*, 443–455. https://www.doi.org/10.1111/j.1545-5300.2004.00033.x

Szapocznik, J., Perez-Vidal, A., Brickman, A., Foote, F. H., Santisteban, D. A., Hervis, O., & Kurtines, W. M. (1988). Engaging adolescent drug users and their families into treatment: A strategic structural approach. *Journal of Consulting and Clinical Psychology, 56*, 552–557. https://www.doi.org/10.1037/0022-006X.56.4.552

Tan, X., Shiyko, M. P., Li, R., Li, Y., & Dierker, L. (2012). A time-varying effect model for intensive longitudinal data. *Psychological Methods, 17*, 61–77. https://www.doi.org/10.1037/a0025814

Tracey, T. J., & Kokotovic, A. M. (1989). Factor structure of the Working Alliance Inventory. *Psychological Assessment: A Journal of Consulting and Clinical Psychology, 1*, 207–210. https://www.doi.org/10.1037/1040-3590.1.3.207

Yoo, H., Bartle-Haring, S., & Gangamma, R. (2016). Predicting premature termination with alliance at sessions 1 and 3: An exploratory study. *Journal of Family Therapy, 38*, 5–17. https://www.doi.org/10.1111/1467-6427.12031

Van den Noortgate, W., & Onghena, P. (2003). Multi-level meta-analysis: A comparison with traditional meta-analytical procedures. *Educational and Psychological Measurement, 63*, 765–790. https://www.doi.org/10.1177/0013164403251027

Viechtbauer, W. (2015). *Meta-analysis package for R*. Retrieved from http://cran.rproject.org/web/packages/metafor/metafor.pdf

Welmers-van de Poll, M. J., Roest, J. J., Van der Stouwe, T., Van den Akker, A. L., Stams, G. J. J. M., Escudero, V. E., . . . De Swart, J. J. W. (2018). Alliance and treatment outcome in family-involved treatment for youth problems: A three level meta-analysis. *Clinical Child and Family Psychology Review, 21*(2), 146–170. https://www.doi.org/10.1007/s10567-017-0249-y

Zaitsoff, S. L., Doyle, A. C., Hoste, R. R., & le Grange, D. (2008). How do adolescents with bulimia nervosa rate the acceptability and therapeutic relationship in family-based treatment? *International Journal of Eating Disorders, 41*, 390–398. https://www.doi.org/10.1002/eat.20515

Zilcha-Mano, S. (2017). Is the alliance really therapeutic? Revisiting this question in light of recent methodological advances. *American Psychologist, 72*(4), 311–325. https://www.doi.org/10.1037/a0040435

5

GOAL CONSENSUS AND COLLABORATION

Georgiana Shick Tryon, Sarah E. Birch, and Jay Verkuilen

INTRODUCTION

Goals assume great importance in individuals' lives. "Without goals, life would lack structure and purpose" (Emmons, 2003, p. 106). Patients come to psychotherapy with concerns about their life goals and the goals they should work toward in therapy (Michalak & Grosse Holtforth, 2006). Thus, early in treatment, it is vital that clinicians engage patients in a discussion about psychotherapy goals and the activities by which they can be achieved.

Goal consensus between patient and therapist is a key part of treatment success (Bordin, 1979). There is evidence that therapists may not place the same importance on collaborative goal consensus as their patients (Orlinsky et al., 1994); however, therapists should not forgo this valuable asset of the patient's therapeutic experience (DeFife & Hilsenroth, 2011). Unfortunately, practitioners do not always heed this advice. For example, one study (Swift & Callahan, 2009) found that, after the third session, trainee clinicians identified the same two goals as their patients only 31% of the time. One of the purposes of this chapter is to provide a meta-analytic update of the relation between therapist–patient goal consensus and psychotherapy outcome.

Another chapter purpose is to provide a meta-analytic update of therapist–patient collaboration and psychotherapy outcome. Collaboration implies a process of working together, and indeed therapist and patient arrive at goal consensus via the collaborative process. But collaboration is not confined to establishing psychotherapy goals. Practitioners and patients collaborate throughout the course of many types of therapy to effect positive treatment outcomes (Berdondini et al., 2012; Dattilio & Hanna, 2012; Wiseman et al., 2012). In fact, "the strength of collaboration between patient and therapist may have more to do with the effectiveness of the therapy than the particular methods chosen" (Bordin, 1979, p. 255). Therapist and patient make their own contributions to collaboration. Thus in this chapter we conduct two collaboration–psychotherapy outcome meta-analyses: one that examines general collaboration with an emphasis on both patient and psychotherapist contributions and one that assesses only therapist collaboration as it relates to psychotherapy outcome.

In this chapter, we provide definitions and measures of both goal consensus and collaboration, give clinical examples of each, describe three landmark studies, and summarize the results of previous meta-analyses of goal consensus–outcome and collaboration–outcome. After presenting the results of the three meta-analyses (goal consensus–outcome, general collaboration–outcome, and therapist collaboration–outcome), along with their possible moderators, we discuss evidence for causality and limitations of the studies reviewed. The chapter concludes with brief discussions of patient contributions to goal consensus and collaboration, diversity issues in the reviewed research, training implications, and therapeutic practices.

DEFINITIONS

Goal Consensus

Goal consensus is part of the contract between practitioner and patient that outlines their work together. Agreement about goals and the manner in which they will be achieved is the essence of goal consensus. It is a pantheoretical construct that applies to all types of psychotherapy. Similar to our previous meta-analyses (Tryon & Winograd, 2001, 2011), we define goal consensus as (a) patient–psychotherapist agreement on and commitment to goals and the methods by which they will be achieved, (b) patient–psychotherapist agreement on the patient's problem, and (c) the extent to which goals are discussed and clearly specified.

Collaboration

Collaboration is an active process whereby patient and professional work together to achieve treatment goals. "Collaboration between a psychotherapist and a patient occurs at the intersection of the therapeutic relationship and treatment method. Many methods contribute to collaboration, which is then experienced as a respectful, mutual, cooperative relationship" (Kazantzis & Kellis, 2012, p. 133). So, similar to goal consensus, collaboration is a pantheoretical process that applies to all psychotherapies. In keeping with our previous meta-analyses (Tryon & Winograd, 2001, 2011), we define collaboration as "the mutual involvement of psychotherapist and patient in a helping relationship" (Tryon & Winograd, 2011, p. 157).

Related Constructs

Goal consensus and collaboration are sometimes construed as part of the working alliance along with the emotional bond between practitioner and patient (Bordin, 1979). Goal consensus is sometimes considered as part of the therapeutic contract between clinician and patient (Yeomans et al., 1994).

MEASURES

Goal Consensus

The majority of studies in the goal consensus meta-analysis use one of two measures. The 36-item Working Alliance Inventory (WAI; Horvath & Greenberg, 1989), which has forms that patients, clinicians, and observers can complete, was developed to assess the conceptualization of the working alliance as encompassing patient–therapist agreement on the goals and tasks of therapy as well as the formation of an emotional bond (Bordin, 1979). The WAI Goal and Tasks subscales, as well as the Goals and Tasks subscales of the 12-item version of the WAI (WAI-S; Tracey & Kokotovic, 1989) assess patient–practitioner goal consensus more frequently than other measures. The patient form of the WAI has goal and task items such as, "We agree on what is important for me to work on" and "I wish my therapist and I could clarify the goals of our sessions." Related instruments, the Combined Alliance Short Form (CASF)–Patient Version (Hatcher & Barends, 1996) and the CASF–Therapist Version (Hatcher, 1999), each have a Goals and Tasks subscale that mostly consists of Goals and Tasks subscale items from the WAI.

The California Psychotherapy Alliance Scales (CALPAS; Gaston, 1991; Marmar, Gaston, Gallagher, & Thompson, 1989) is also a working alliance measure. The CALPAS Working Strategy Consensus (WSC) subscale assesses patient-therapist goal consensus. WSC "encompasses the patient-therapist similarity of goals; joint effort; and agreement on how people are helped, how people change in therapy, and how therapy should proceed" (Gaston, 1991, p. 69). A typical reverse scored item on the CALPAS WSC patient form is, "Do you feel that you disagree with your therapist about changes you would like to make in your therapy?"

The Goals subscales of the WAI and the CALPAS demonstrate solid reliability. Despite these desirable psychometric properties, some authors (Lambert & Cattani, 2012) are critical of the use of standard working alliance instruments to measure goal consensus. They argue that instruments such as the WAI assess the perception of goal consensus rather than the actual consensus between patient and psychotherapist concerning goals. Other authors (e.g., Busseri & Tyler, 2004) have used idiographic (individually customized) measures unique to each study to assess actual goal agreement between patient and psychotherapist by examining patient-psychotherapist matches on target complaints. However, as with standard instruments, idiographic measures sometimes also assess just the perception of goal agreement, and sometimes consist of only a single item (e.g., Hegel et al., 2002).

Collaboration

The majority of studies in the collaboration–outcome meta-analyses use measures of homework compliance or a CALPAS subscale. "Collaboration research over the last decade has been dominated by studies of behavioral and cognitive behavior therapies and homework compliance" (Lambert & Cattani, 2012, p. 210). So, not surprisingly, the most frequently used indicator by studies in the general collaboration meta-analysis is homework compliance (see Table 5.1). It is generally considered an index of patient collaboration. However, homework assignments are usually generated jointly by both patients and therapists, so patients' homework completion may be a reflection of the general state of patient–therapist collaboration.

The CALPAS subscale Therapist Understanding and Involvement (TUI; Gaston, 1991) is the most frequent measure of psychotherapist collaboration, as reflected in Table 5.1. A typical item from the TUI patient form is, "Did you feel pressured by your therapist to make changes before you were ready?" A TUI item from the therapist form is, "Were your interventions tactful and well-timed?" Other CALPAS subscales, Therapist Positive Contribution and Therapist Negative Contribution (Marmar, Gaston, Gallagher, & Thompson, 1989), also assess psychotherapist collaborative behaviors.

Still another CALPAS subscale, Therapist's Confident Collaboration (TCC; Hatcher, 1999), reflects psychotherapists' collaboration. TCC includes items such as, "I am confident in my ability to help my patient." Composed of CALPAS TCC items and items from the WAI, the Therapist Confident Collaboration subscale of the CASF–Therapist Version (Clemence et al., 2005) is yet another subscale to assess psychotherapist collaboration.

The aforementioned collaboration measures are used frequently. Other instruments to assess collaboration, such as the Contract Rating Scale (Yeomans et al., 1994), the Agnew Relationship Measure—Partnership Scale (Hardy et al., 2001), and the Multiperspective of General Change Mechanisms in Psychotherapy (Mander et al., 2013), appear less frequently in research studies. These measures have subscales that provide information about practitioner and patient negotiation of treatment conditions.

Relation between Measures

The majority of studies that used more than one measure of goal consensus did not report correlations between measures. Correlations for the 11 studies that did report them ranged from .41 to .91. Lower correlations usually occurred between individually customized measures unique to each study, and higher correlations tended to occur between standard measures such as goal and task scales of the WAI.

The majority of studies that used more than one measure of collaboration did not report between measures correlations. All seven studies that reported correlations between collaboration measures used instruments unique to each study. The correlations ranged from .42 to .88.

Just one study (Safran & Wallner, 1991) reported correlations between goal consensus and collaboration measures. The CALPAS Patient Commitment scale correlated .82 with the WAI Goal scale and .74 with the WAI Task scale.

In summary, as expected, different measures of collaboration are positively correlated with each other, as are different measures of goal consensus with each other.

Table 5.1. Frequency Data for Moderator Analyses

Moderator	Goal Consensus (N = 54)		General Collaboration (N = 53)		Therapist Collaboration (N = 21)	
Publication Status		n		n		n
	Published	43	Published	48	Published	17
	$M = .21, SD = .17$		$M = .26, SD = .18$		$M = .29, SD = .21$	
	Not Published	11	Not Published	5	Not Published	4
	$M = .25, SD = .15$		$M = .23, SD = .15$		$M = .27, SD = .15$	
Theoretical orientation	Psychodynamic	6	Psychodynamic	7	Psychodynamic	5
	$M = .24, SD = .17$		$M = .34, SD = .14$		$M = .41, SD = .24$	
	Cog. Beh./Beh.	12	Cog. Beh./Beh.	29	Cog. Beh./Beh.	6
	$M = .29, SD = .21$		$M = .22, SD = .20$		$M = .22, SD = .26$	
	Several	16	Several	12	Several	5
	$M = .18, SD = .14$		$M = .37, SD = .18$		$M = .37, SD = .26$	
	Unspecified	14	Unspecified	3	Unspecified	3
	$M = .23, SD = .14$		$M = .20, SD = .11$		$M = .20, SD = .11$	
	Other	6	Other	2	Other	2
	$M = .15, SD = .17$		$M = .11, SD = .09$		$M = .11, SD = 0$	
Rater	Patient	21	Patient	8	Patient	5
	$M = .23, SD = .16$		$M = .30, SD = .18$		$M = .29, SD = .26$	
	Psychotherapist	7	Psychotherapist	19	Psychotherapist	2
	$M = .41, SD = .13$		$M = .23, SD = .20$		$M = .51, SD = .05$	
	Observer	7	Observer	11	Observer	6
	$M = .28, SD = .12$		$M = .13, SD = .14$		$M = .14, SD = .20$	
	More than One	13	More than One	15	More than One	8
	$M = .17, SD = .16$		$M = .23, SD = .15$		$M = .19, SD = .13$	
	P-T Agreement	6				
	$M = .11, SD = .17$					
Ratings Taken	Early	n 32	Early	n 10	Early	n 7
	$M = .23, SD = 16$		$M = .23, SD = .16$		$M = .23, SD = .18$	
	Mid	0	Mid	6	Mid	4
			$M = .26, SD = .13$		$M = .24, SD = .19$	
	Late	2	Late	10	Late	0
	$M = .45, SD = .24$		$M = .20, SD = .20$			
	Throughout	7	Throughout	19	Throughout	8
	$M = .16, SD = .12$		$M = .29, SD = .19$		$M = .17, SD = .23$	
	Other Times[a]	9	Other Times[a]	4	Unspecified	2
	$M = .15, SD = .16$		$M = .25, SD = .13$		$M = .50, SD = .03$	
	Unspecified	4	Unspecified	4		
	$M = .33, SD = .29$		$M = .49, SD = .08$			

(continued)

Table 5.1. Continued

Moderator	Goal Consensus (N = 54)	n	General Collaboration (N = 53)	n	Therapist Collaboration (N = 21)	n
Publication Status		n		n		n
GC or C						
Measure Taken From	WAI, WAI-S, CASF	29	Homework	26	Homework	0
	$M = .23, SD = .15$		$M = .23, SD = .18$			
	Idiographic Measure	8	CASF	3	CASF	2
	$M = .25, SD = .21$		$M = .31, SD = .11$		$M = .42, SD = .23$	
	CALPAS	8	CALPAS	10	CALPAS	8
	$M = .14, SD = .22$		$M = .38, SD = .25$		$M = .38, SD = .27$	
	Other	9	Other	14	Other	11
	$M = .17, SD = .09$		$M = .22, SD = .15$		$M = .20, SD = .16$	
Percentage Patients of Color	Unreported	23	Unreported	27	Unreported	11
	<=20%	22	<=20%	14	<=20%	6
	$M = .21, SD = .16$		$M = .35, SD = .19$		$M = .41, SD = .25$	
	> 20%	9	>20%	12	>20%	4
	$M = .28, SD = .18$		$M = .20, SD = .15$		$M = .26, SD = .20$	
Percentage Women Patients	Unreported	0	Unreported	2	Unreported	1
	≤50%	13	≤50%	18	≤50%	2
	$M = .22, SD = .23$		$M = .23, SD = .20$		$M = .25, SD = .04$	
	>50%	41	>50%	33	>50%	18
	$M = .21, SD = .15$		$M = .26, SD = .17$		$M = .29, SD = .21$	

Note. Means and standard deviations are reported as weighted correlational effect sizes. Cog. Beh./ Beh. = cognitive-behavioral/behavioral; P-T = patient–therapist; CALPAS = California Psychotherapy Alliance Scale; CASF = Combined Alliance Short Form, WAI = Working Alliance Inventory, WAI-S = Working Alliance Inventory—Short Form.
[a]Times that ratings were taken were unique to each participant.

Further, measures of collaboration are correlated substantially with measures of goal consensus, supporting our decision to consider together both of these facets of the therapeutic relationship in this chapter.

CLINICAL EXAMPLES

The following session transcript concerns "Hope," a 21-year-old college senior and honors student who took a leave of absence from school after being hospitalized for several weeks in a mental health crisis center. A psychotic episode—her first—led to Hope's hospitalization and to a diagnosis of bipolar disorder. Hope recently returned to college on a part-time basis while working toward recovery (Tyron & Winograd, 2011).

The adapted excerpt here is from Hope and her therapist's second session. Elements of goal consensus and collaboration in their interaction are indicated in brackets.

Therapist: Last time we talked about the challenges you've been facing as you return to school and reconnect with friends and family members who know about your recent episode and hospitalization. I gave you a form to use to record some of the thoughts that have been running through your mind when you are around people at school, and some of the ways people act or the things they say that you find upsetting *[therapist collaboration: therapist homework]*.

Hope: Yes, I completed the forms for both of those things *[client collaboration: homework completion]*. I realized that even with people I hardly know, I find myself worrying constantly about whether they know what happened, or if they can just tell by the way I act that I was in the hospital, that I have a mental illness. And when I'm thinking this way, I start to act nervous and insecure, and just find it hard to concentrate.

But when I'm around friends and family members who know about my hospitalization, I feel even worse. They act so differently from the way they acted before my diagnosis. This is what I wrote down: "they either act like I'm made of glass and about to break, or they keep their distance." And I don't know how to get them to just treat me like a regular person again.

Therapist: It sounds to me like some of the people you are close to have disappointed you. You'd like to reconnect with them but aren't sure how to do this. It also sounds to me as though even when people don't necessarily act differently, you are worried that they are seeing you differently, or would see you differently if they knew about your recent life events. This makes it hard to relax around them and focus on your schoolwork.

Hope: Yes, I am quite uncomfortable around other people now, almost all of the time *[patient-psychotherapist goal consensus: congruence on patient problem]*.

Therapist: I also recall that you mentioned being quite isolated.

Hope: Yes, that's true. Since I don't know what to say or how to act, I've started to avoid people. But I don't think spending so much time alone is good for my mood. It doesn't even feel like me. I used to be a really social person *[goal consensus; further congruence on patient problem]*.

Therapist: I was thinking that over the next few sessions, we could work together to come up with ideas about how to talk about your hospitalization and recovery with your friends and family *[collaboration: mutual involvement of patient and therapist in a helping relationship]*. I was also thinking we might try out some relaxation and thought-replacement strategies for when you get anxious around classmates in school.

Hope: I like the sound of that. And I'd also like you to help me experiment with gradually coming out of my shell as I work on getting healthy again *[goal consensus: discussion and specification of goals; collaboration: patient role involvement]*.

LANDMARK STUDIES

This section describes three studies that exemplify research on goal consensus and collaboration in psychotherapy. The first study (Bachelor, 2013) used a correlational design and examined patients' and therapists' views of elements of the working alliance and how they relate to posttherapy outcomes. One hundred seventy-four patients, who had a variety of social and emotional problems, and 131 practitioners, over half of whom were trainees, completed the WAI-S, the CALPAS, and the Helping Alliance Questionnaire (HAQ; Alexander & Laborsky, 1986). Therapists endorsed several theoretical orientations, with the majority endorsing a humanistic orientation. Patients and therapists each completed four outcome measures at the end of therapy.

Participants' WAI-S, CALPAS, and HAQ scores were subjected to a principal component analysis. Patients' scores yielded six factors: collaborative work relationship, productive work, active commitment, bond, disagreement on goals/tasks, and confident progress. Practitioners' scores yielded four factors: collaborative work relationship, client commitment and confidence, therapist confidence and dedication, and client working ability. Thus patients and therapists view elements of the alliance both similarly and differently. A collaborative working relationship emerged as the large first factor for both groups; however, goals and tasks nondisagreement (i.e., goal consensus) was a factor for patients only. Therapists' and patients' scores on each factor demonstrated low to moderate positive correlations with treatment outcomes.

This study provides clear implications for practitioners, indicating that they should be aware that they may view collaboration and goal consensus differently from their patients. To address these discrepancies, therapists can encourage patients to routinely discuss their opinions regarding the patient–therapist relationship. Therapists can also ensure that they and their patients collaboratively identify therapeutic goals and expectations.

The second landmark study (Riberio et al., 2016) used a qualitative research design to investigate how assimilation and collaboration between therapist and client evolve over the course of emotion-focused therapy. Researchers examined the interactions and outcomes of two patient–therapist dyads. Both patients (one man age 24, one woman age 30) had diagnoses of mild to moderate major depressive disorder and were Caucasian. Their therapists were doctoral-level practitioners with extensive clinical experience.

Therapy sessions were transcribed, and trained judges identified the problematic themes (i.e., painful or distressing experiences and memories) expressed during each session. Judges then rated each patient's sessions using the Assimilation of Problematic Experiences Scale (Stiles, 1999), an eight-level scale that describes a sequence of changes in the manner an individual first recognizes, then comprehends, and finally integrates or assimilates problematic experiences into a cohesive self-view.

Trained coders also rated collaboration between therapists and patients throughout the entirety of five therapy sessions representing the beginning (two sessions), middle (two sessions), and end (one session) of treatment using the Therapeutic Collaboration Coding System (Ribeiro et al., 2013). Therapist interventions were coded as either supporting or challenging patient responses described as validation, invalidation, and ambivalence. Raters then described the quality of the overall exchange between patient and practitioner. Patient–therapist exchanges were described as working within or outside of the patient's therapeutic zone of proximal development, which is the area within which a patient can move with the help of the therapist along the assimilation continuum.

The male patient demonstrated some improvement in assimilation, moving from level 0 (avoidance of symptoms) to level 3 (defining the problem); however, he demonstrated little symptomatic improvement on the Beck Depression Inventory–II (Beck et al., 1996) and the Outcome Questionnaire–45.2 (Lambert et al., 1996). In contrast, the female patient showed significant improvement in both outcome assessments and assimilation ratings, moving from avoiding symptom discussions (level 1) in the beginning of psychotherapy to accepting and managing her feelings (level 6) at termination. The transcripts showed that the therapist worked toward actively moving her therapeutic zone toward higher assimilation levels, while the therapist for the male patient worked firmly within the patient's current zone.

These results support the idea that therapeutic goals can and do evolve throughout the course of treatment. During the initial treatment phase, goals typically reflect development of a secure relationship between practitioner and patient. However, in later phases, goals can focus on challenging patients' current conceptualizations and moving toward more integrated and productive ideas.

Finally, a 2005 study (Lingiardi et al., 2005) looked at the relation between early ratings of goal consensus and therapist collaboration and therapy dropout. Patients (31 women, 16 men) and their therapists completed the WSC and TUI subscales of the CALPAS (see Measures section). All patients had personality disorder diagnoses, and 10 (21%) of them prematurely terminated treatment within the first two months. Practitioners were clinical psychologists with at least 10 years' experience who had been trained in the psychodynamic treatment of borderline personality disorders.

Clinicians' WSC and TUI ratings were significantly lower than those of their patients. WSC and TUI ratings were significantly lower when patients dropped out of treatment than when they remained. The results indicated that patient–therapist early treatment goal consensus and early therapist collaborative behaviors are important predictors of patients' continuation in psychotherapy.

RESULTS OF PREVIOUS REVIEWS AND META-ANALYSES

In 2002, we (Tryon & Winograd, 2002) reviewed goal consensus–outcome and collaboration–outcome studies with adult patients published in English in refereed journals before the year 2000. Of the 25 goal consensus–outcome studies reviewed, 68% found a positive relation between goal consensus and psychotherapy outcome on at least one measure completed by patients, psychotherapists, or observers. For the 24 collaboration–outcome studies, 89% had at least one measure of collaboration that related positively to psychotherapy outcome.

In the 2011 volume of *Psychotherapy Relationships That Work*, we (Tryon & Winograd, 2011) reported the results of meta-analyses of 15 studies of goal consensus and adult psychotherapy outcome and 19 studies of collaboration and adult psychotherapy outcome that were published in refereed journals from 2000 through 2009. The goal consensus meta-analysis yielded an effect size of $r = .34$ on a total sample of 1,302 (95% confidence interval [CI] = .23–.45). The collaboration meta-analysis yielded an effect size of $r = .33$ on a sample of 2,260 (95% CI = .25–.42). The effect sizes fall in the medium range, which characterizes "an effect likely to be visible to the naked eye of a careful observer" (Cohen, 1992, p. 156). Based on these meta-analytic results, the second Task Force on Evidence-Based Therapy Relationships concluded that goal consensus and collaboration are probably effective elements of the therapeutic relationship (Norcross & Wampold, 2011).

META-ANALYTIC REVIEW

Inclusion Criteria and Study Selection

The current meta-analyses expanded on the previous reviews and meta-analyses. We included studies written in English of goal consensus and psychotherapy outcome and studies of collaboration and psychotherapy outcome in their respective meta-analyses if they (a) had at least one measure of goal consensus and/or collaboration according to the definitions provided here; (b) involved individual psychotherapy; (c) had at least one measure of psychotherapy outcome; (d) used a group design; (e) involved adult patients (aged 18 years or older); and (f) had a reported effect (r or d), its equivalent (standardized β weight), or other statistic (t or F) that could be converted to an effect.

We conducted searches of the PsycINFO, PsycLIT, Medline, ERIC, and ProQuest Dissertation and Theses Global databases for studies appearing between 1980 and June 2017 using the following terms: patient–therapist goal consensus (9,155 references), patient–therapist collaboration (1,509 references), patient–therapist goal consensus and psychotherapy outcome (1,494 references), patient–therapist agreement and psychotherapy outcome (2,598 references), and patient–therapist collaboration and psychotherapy outcome (1,246 references).

Figure 5.1 provides a flowchart of the search results. Twenty-three of the 84 psychotherapy outcome studies involved in the meta-analyses included measures of both goal consensus and collaboration. The search yielded 54 studies of goal consensus and psychotherapy outcome with a sample size of 7,278; 53 studies of general collaboration and psychotherapy outcome with a sample size of 5,286; and 21 studies of psychotherapist collaboration and psychotherapy outcome with a sample size of 2,081.

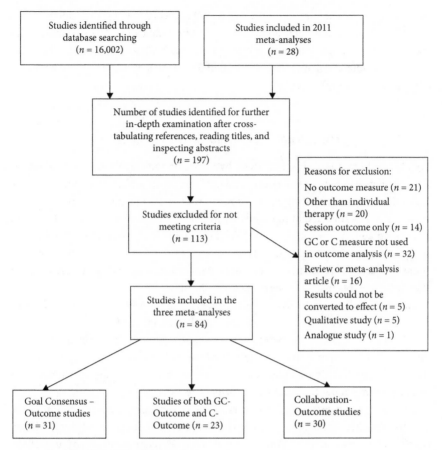

FIGURE 5.1 Flowchart of literature search.

Coding of Study Characteristics and Possible Moderators

For each of the 84 studies, we coded the following and calculated kappa reliability (κ) using GrafPad QuickCalcs software (grafpad.com): study type (goal consensus–outcome, collaboration–outcome, both; κ = .91, standard error [SE] = .04, 95% CI = .83–.99); publication status (published, not published; κ = 1.00); percentage women participants (>50%, ≤50%, not specified; κ = .90, SE = .05, 95% CI = .80–.99); perentage patients of color (>20%, ≤20%, not specified; κ = .92, SE = .04, 95% CI = .85–.99); time of goal consensus or collaboration rating (early, middle, or late in psycho-therapy as well as throughout therapy, other times that are unique to each participant, and unspecified time; κ = .77, SE = .05, 95% CI = .66–.88); rater of goal consensus or collaboration (patient, psychotherapist, observer, more than one of the aforemen-tioned; for goal consensus only, patient–therapist goal agreement; κ = .85, SE = .05, 95% CI = .75–.95); psychotherapy orientation (psychodynamic, cognitive-behavioral/behavioral, several, unspecified, other orientations; κ = .85, SE = .05, 95% CI = .75–.94);

goal consensus/collaboration measure (e.g., WAI, CALPAS, CASF; κ = .89, *SE* = .04, 95% CI = .81–.97); and publication date (κ = 1.00). Publication dates for most of the studies in the meta-analyses were between 1991 and 2010: goal consensus 59% (32 of 54 studies), general collaboration 75% (40 of 53 studies), and therapist collaboration 71% (15 of 21 studies).

Meta-Analytic Estimation of Effect Sizes

We obtained effect sizes for each study by recording the correlation or standardized β weight between outcome measures and goal consensus and/or collaboration measures. Effect sizes were based on either zero-order or partial correlations or beta (β) coefficients. For studies that reported other than correlational statistics, such as *t* and *F*, we used conversion software from Psychometrica (www.psychometrica.de/effect_size.html) to obtain *r* and *d* statistics for each study. In studies with more than one outcome measure of goal consensus or collaboration measure, we averaged correlations or standard β weights to obtain one effect for each study.

All meta-analyses presented were performed using the Metafor 1.9-9 (Viechtbauer, 2010) and the DPPackage 1.1-6 (Jara et al., 2011) packages in R 3.4.0 (R Core Team, 2017). As a general reference, we consulted an edited volume (Cooper et al., 2009) that presents best practices in meta-analysis, and we make reference to chapters from it throughout these analyses. DPPackage 1.1-6 meta-analysis assumes the studies come from an unknown discrete mixture of normal effect sizes.

All effects were converted to a Pearson correlation metric during coding using the Psychometrica software. Because the sampling distribution of the correlation coefficient is dependent on the unknown true correlation, we made use of the Fisher *z* transformation, which is the variance-stabilizing transformation for the Pearson correlation and provides very good transformation to normality (e.g., Borenstein, 2009).

We first fit random effects meta-analysis (Raudenbush, 2009), presenting each outcome's forest plot and effect. We use restricted maximum likelihood (REML) estimation for all models, which is the default in Metafor. As a check against violation of the assumption that θ_i are normal, which can induce bias in the pooled effect size and particularly in its resulting interval estimate, we also run a Dirichlet process prior meta-analysis (e.g., Muthukumarana & Tiwari, 2016).

To assess publication bias, we created a funnel plot as well as computed the regression symmetry test (Egger et al., 1997). To assess influential studies, we used the features provided in Metafor that allow computation of regression-based influence measures (e.g., Cook's *D*, studentized residuals). These measures are based on deleting each study from the total. An influential study is one that alters the outcome of the meta-analysis in a disproportionate way. To account for heterogeneity among the studies, we used random effects meta-regression that adjusts the previously given model for covariates. We employed random effects models for all three meta-analyses.

Goal Consensus Meta-Analysis Results

The pooled effect size for the 54 studies (sample size = 7,278) of goal consensus and psychotherapy outcome on the Fisher z metric was 0.24 ± 0.023 with associated 95% CI of 0.19–0.28. Transformed to the Pearson correlation metric, the point estimate is $r = .24$ with a 95% CI of .19–.28; $d = .49$, 95% CI = .39–.58.

In terms of study heterogeneity, the $I^2 = 66.54\%$, the $H^2 = 2.99$, and Cochran's $Q = 155.54$ on 53 df, $p < .001$. This indicates that there is a considerable amount of heterogeneity in these effect sizes, as is evident from the forest plots in Figures 5.2 (which displays the estimated results from the studies in the analysis) and the cumulative forest plot in Figure 5.3 (which displays estimated study results in chronological order). The funnel plot (see Figure 5.4), which shows study effects to be distributed relatively symmetrically around the aggregated effect size, and the regression symmetry test ($z = 0.81, p > .10$) do not provide evidence for publication bias in the studies in the meta-analysis.

The Dirichlet process prior meta-analysis gives an almost identical effect as for the REML estimates of .24 ± .024 with a 95% credible interval of .18–.29; $d = .49$, 95% CI = .37–.61. A median mixture of four Gaussians is required. Although the REML identifies only one study (Abromowitz et al., 2000) as an outlier, the Dirichlet process identifies this study along with another study (Hegel et al., 2002) as clear outlier studies.

Both outlier studies use only a single item that is unique to each of those studies to measure goal consensus. In contrast, the other studies in the meta-analysis generally use goal consensus measures that have several items and demonstrated reliabilities.

To explore the effect of moderators and potentially account for the observed heterogeneity, we used meta-regression (see Table 5.2 for goal consensus meta-regression coefficients). The estimated $\tau = 0.14$, with $I^2 = 65.00\%$ and $H^2 = 2.86$. The joint test of the moderators suggests that they are not significant: $Q = 20.44$ on 20 df, $p > .1$. Cochran's $Q = 91.44$ on 35 df, $p < .001$, indicating statistically significant remaining heterogeneity. Table 5.2 shows that there was only one individual moderator that was significant at the 5% level (rater 2–therapist). However, with 20 moderators, one false positive would be consistent with Type I errors due to sampling variability so this should be interpreted with caution. Examining the influence statistics for this model, including moderators, does not appear to improve the fit in a meaningful way. In sum, there does not appear to be strong evidence for the effect of the investigated moderators in these data in reducing the heterogeneity. Moderators for each meta-analysis are discussed in more detail next.

General Collaboration Meta-Analysis Results

The meta-analysis of general collaboration and psychotherapy outcome (sample size = 5,286) includes 53 studies that use measures of therapist collaboration and outcome and client collaboration and outcome. We estimated a pooled effect size for general collaboration on the Fisher z metric of 0.28 ± 0.025, for a 95% CI of 0.24–0.34.

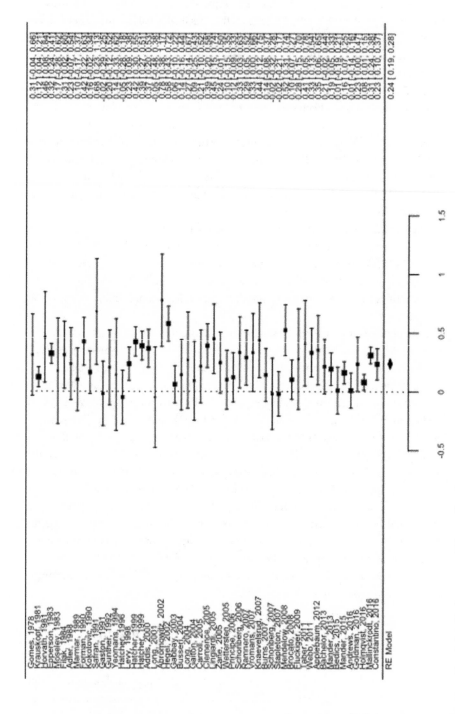

FIGURE 5.2 Forest plot: Goal consensus Fisher z effect sizes.

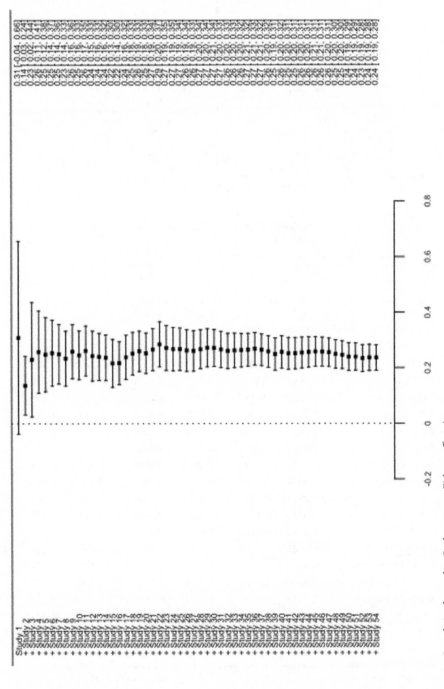

FIGURE 5.3 Cumulative forest plot: Goal consensus Fisher z effect sizes.

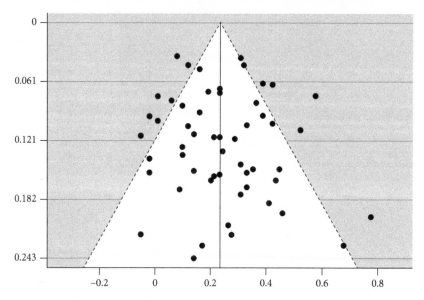

FIGURE 5.4 Funnel plot to assess publication bias: Goal consensus Fisher z effect sizes.

Table 5.2. Meta-Regression Coefficients for Goal Consensus

Factor	Estimate	SE	z Value	p Value	95% CI	
					UL	LL
Intercept	0.1416	0.1110	1.2756	0.2021	−0.0760	0.3591
Cognitive Behavioral/ Behavioral	0.0789	0.0966	0.8167	0.4141	−0.1105	0.2683
As Orientation 3	−0.1145	0.0875	1.3086	0.1907	−0.2859	0.0570
As Orientation 4	−0.0093	0.0906	−0.1027	0.9182	−0.1869	0.1683
As Orientation 5	−0.1288	0.1192	−1.0804	0.2800	−0.3623	0.1048
Rater 2—Therapist	0.2906	0.0901	3.2237	0.0013	0.1139	0.4673
Rater 3—Observer	0.0627	0.0789	0.7955	0.4263	−0.0918	0.2173
Rater 4 >1	−0.0513	0.0654	−0.7845	0.4327	−0.1794	0.0768
P-T Agreement	0.0167	0.0827	0.2017	0.8401	−0.1453	0.1787
Idiographic Measure	−0.0034	0.0863	−0.0391	0.9688	−0.1725	0.0768
CALPAS	−0.0993	0.0820	−1.2114	0.2258	−0.2600	0.0614
Other Measure	−0.0261	0.0727	−0.3583	0.7201	−0.1686	0.1165
Late Rating	0.1148	0.1696	0.6670	0.4984	−0.2176	0.4473
Rating Throughout	0.0606	0.0799	0.7586	0.4481	−0.0960	0.2172
Rating Other Times	−0.0237	0.0674	−0.3514	0.7253	−0.1558	0.1084
Unsp. Rating Time	−0.0369	0.1016	−0.3632	0.7165	−0.2360	0.1622
Not Published	0.1289	0.0738	1.7462	0.0808	−0.0158	0.2735
Of Color ≤20%	0.0601	0.0627	0.9581	0.3380	−0.0628	0.1829
Of Color >20%	0.0310	0.0707	0.4381	0.6613	−0.1077	0.1696
Woman >50%	0.0626	0.0656	0.9545	0.3398	−0.0659	0.1912

Note. SE = standard error; CI = confidence interval; P-T = patient–therapist; CALPAS = California Psychotherapy Alliance Scales.
Orientation 3 = Several. Orientation 4 = Unspecified. Orientation 5 = Other.

The Pearson metric after back-transforming the pooled effect size is $r = .29$ with a 95% CI of $.24-.34$; $d = .61$, 95% CI $= .49-.72$.

For study heterogeneity, the $I^2 = 58.68\%$, $H^2 = 2.42$, and Cochran's $Q = 146.50$ on 51 df, $p < .001$. This indicates that there is a nontrivial amount of heterogeneity in these effect sizes, as is evident from the forest plots (see Figures 5.5 and 5.6). The funnel plot (Figure 5.7) and the regression symmetry test ($z = 1.05$, $p > .10$) do not provide evidence for publication bias in these studies.

Much as is the case with the goal consensus meta-analysis, there appears to be modest nonnormality to the effect size residuals from the random effects model, as is evident from the funnel plot. In this case, the effect sizes have somewhat lighter tails than would be anticipated from the normal distribution but not markedly so. There are three cases with residuals with magnitude larger than 2. Of them, one study (Hatcher, 1999) is identified as influential according to Cook's D, due to its relatively large N.

There are several possible reasons that this study is an influential study. Unlike other studies in the analysis, approximately half of the therapists in the outlier study chose which patients they wanted to rate. It is possible that these therapists chose a patient with whom they had success, thus resulting in a high collaboration–outcome rating. Also, unlike other studies in the analysis, the ratings were completed on ongoing cases after a widely varying number of sessions (2–550) and sometimes years (2 weeks– 18 years). Finally, in contrast to other studies, therapists in the outlier study completed collaboration and outcome measures at the same time.

Using the Dirichlet process prior meta-analysis gives a nearly identical pooled effect as the one just reported, with a mean pooled effect of $.28 \pm .031$ with a 95% credible interval of $.23-.35$; $d = .58$, 95% CI $= .47-.74$, which is slightly wider than that of the REML model that assumes normal study effects. The median model appeared to require a mixture of four normals and it identified the same outlier study (Hatcher, 1999) as before. This result suggests, while there appear to be some nonnormal study effects, the impact on the overall analysis is not substantial.

To assess potential for cumulating evidence over time, we used a cumulative meta-analysis, which is shown in the cumulative forest plot (Figure 5.6). The plot clearly illustrates that, while the early studies did not entirely agree with each other, evidence seems to be largely settling to the aforementioned collaboration effect.

To explore the effect of moderators and potentially account for the observed heterogeneity, we used meta-regression (see Table 5.3 for collaboration meta-regression coefficients). The estimated $\tau = 0.13$, with $I^2 = 53.43\%$ and $H^2 = 2.15$. The joint test of the moderators suggests that they are not significant: $Q = 16.25$ on 20 df, $p = > .10$. Cochran's $Q = 65.92$ on 31 df, $p < .001$, indicating statistically significant remaining heterogeneity. There was only one individual moderator that was significant at the 5% level (unspecified time of collaboration rating taken), but, much as was the case for the goal consensus meta-analysis, one false positive would be consistent with sampling variability. In sum, there does not appear to be strong evidence for the effect of the given moderators in these data in reducing the heterogeneity.

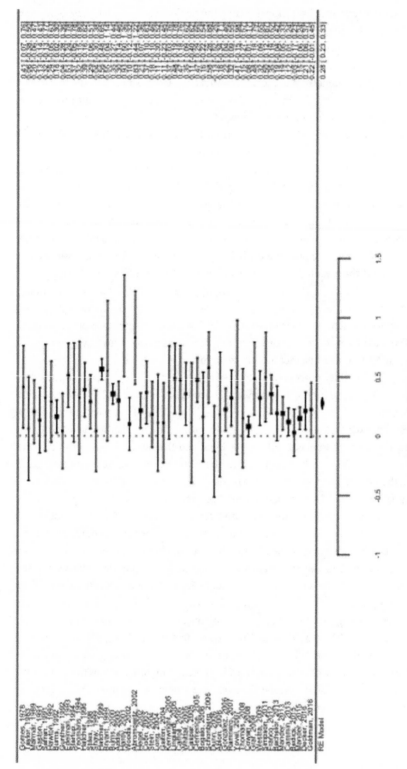

FIGURE 5.5 Forest plot: General collaboration Fisher z effect sizes.

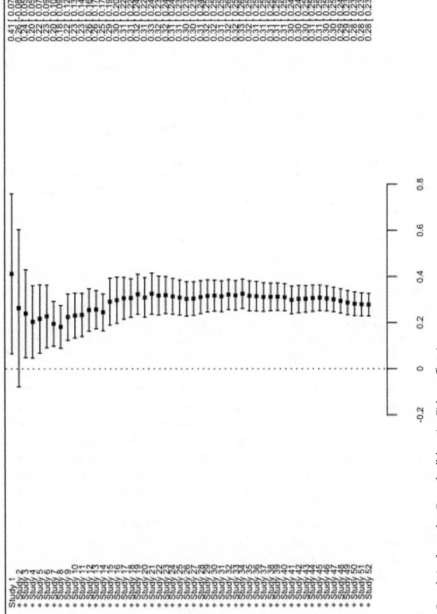

FIGURE 5.6 Cumulative forest plot: General collaboration Fisher z effect sizes.

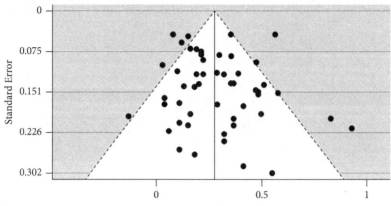

FIGURE 5.7 Funnel plot to assess publication bias: General collaboration Fisher z effect sizes.

Table 5.3. Meta-Regression Coefficients for Collaboration

Factor	Estimate	Std. Error	z Value	p Value	95% CI	
					UL	LL
Intercept	0.3420	0.2054	1.6656	0.0958	−0.0605	0.7445
Cognitive Behavioral/Behavioral	−.2032	0.1675	−1.2130	0.2251	−0.5315	0.1251
Orientation 3	−0.0783	0.1435	−0.5453	0.5856	−0.3595	0.2030
Orientation 4	−0.2437	0.1746	−1.3958	0.1628	−0.5858	0.0985
Orientation 5	−0.0720	0.2309	−0.3117	0.7553	−0.5246	0.3806
Rater 2—Therapist	0.0045	0.1095	0.0409	0.9674	−0.2102	0.2190
Rater 3—Observer	−0.1700	0.1219	−1.3942	0.1633	−0.4090	0.0690
Rater 4—> One	−0.0732	0.1001	−0.7331	0.4647	−0.2693	0.1230
CASF	−0.1532	0.1825	−0.8392	0.4013	−0.5110	0.2046
CALPAS	−0.0471	0.1124	−0.4190	0.6752	−0.2673	0.1731
Other Measure	−0.0624	0.1009	−0.6187	0.5361	−0.2603	0.1354
Mid-Therapy Rating	0.1583	0.1432	1.1054	0.2690	−0.1224	0.4390
Late Rating	0.1037	0.1248	0.8315	0.4057	−0.1408	0.3483
Rating Throughout	0.1615	0.1073	1.5047	0.1324	−0.0489	0.3718
Rating Other Time	0.0648	0.1322	0.4906	0.6237	−0.1942	0.3239
Unspecified Rating Time	0.2995	0.1302	2.3008	0.0214	0.0444	0.5547
Not Published	0.0348	0.1387	0.2512	0.8017	−0.2370	0.3067
Of Color >20%	0.0173	0.1049	0.1654	0.8686	−0.1882	0.2229
Of Color Unreported	0.1034	0.0866	1.1947	0.2322	−0.0662	0.2730
Women > 50%	−.0.0286	0.0754	−0.3560	0.7218	−0.1746	0.1209
Woman Unreported	0.0003	0.1638	0.0016	0.9987	−0.3207	0.3212

Note. CASF = Combined Alliance Short Form; CALPAS = California Psychotherapy Alliance Scales. Orientation 3 = Several. Orientation 4 = Unspecified. Orientation 5 = Other.

Therapist Collaboration Meta-Analysis Results

In keeping with the purpose of this volume to present evidence-based therapist contributions to psychotherapy relationships, we conducted a meta-analysis that focuses on measures of clinicians' collaboration and outcome exclusively. Although therapist collaboration studies are a part of the general collaboration meta-analysis, only measures specific to therapist collaboration were included in this meta-analysis. Table 5.4 describes the 21 studies of therapist collaboration and psychotherapy outcome with a total sample size of 2,081.

The results of the therapist collaboration–outcome meta-analysis proved quite similar to that of the general collaboration–outcome meta-analysis. The pooled effect size on the Fisher z metric is .27 ± .48 with an associated 95% CI of .18–.36. Transformed to Pearson correlation metric the point estimate is .26 with 95% CI of .18–.35; $d = .54$, 95% CI = .37–.75).

For study heterogeneity, $I^2 = 69.02\%$, $H^2 = 3.23$, and Cochran's $Q = 84.64$ on 21 df, $p < .001$. This indicates that there is a considerable amount of heterogeneity in these effect sizes, as is evident from the forest plots (Figures 5.8 and 5.9). The funnel plot (Figure 5.10) and the regression symmetry test ($z = -0.31$, $p > .1$) do not provide evidence for publication bias in these studies.

As is evident from the funnel plot, there appear to be some modest nonnormality to the effect size residuals from the random effects model. In this case, the effect sizes have somewhat lighter tails than would be anticipated from the normal distribution but not markedly so. However, one of the studies (Hatcher, 1999) was deemed influential according to Cook's D; another (Hardy et al., 2001) was close. Both have large and positive residuals, indicating that they have effects larger than would be anticipated from the rest of the studies.

Readers should refer to the general collaboration meta-analysis section for a listing of possible reasons for the influential study (Hatcher, 1999). The other study (Hardy et al., 2001) had a small sample size and low-reliability measures.

To assess the outlier study's (Hatcher, 1999) impact, we refit the model excluding the study's effect. The I^2 is reduced to 52.77% and the estimate of the overall effect decreases slightly, to 0.24. Interpretation of the results would not change.

Using the Dirichlet process prior meta-analysis gives a nearly identical pooled effect as the one just reported, with a mean pooled effect of .27 ± .063 with a 95% credible interval of (.16–.40); $d = .56$, 95% CI =.32–.87, which is notably wider than that of the REML model that assumes normal study effects, reflecting the larger effect of a small number of unusual studies in a smaller overall number of studies. The semi-parametric analysis backs up the analysis that assumes Gaussian effects and identifies the same outlier studies as indicated above.

Summary of Meta-Analytic Results

The goal consensus–outcome, general collaboration–outcome, and therapist collaboration–outcome meta-analyses yielded similar results (ranging from $r = .26$–.29,

Table 5.4. Studies Included in Therapist Collaboration Meta-Analysis

Study	N	% Women[a]	% of Color[b]	Orientation	Rating Taken[c]	Rater	Outcome Measure	C Measure	Effect Size		95% CI for r	
									r	d	LL	UL
Ablon et al. (2006)	17	88	21	Psychodynamic	Mid	O	SCL-90	PPQ	.02	.04	-.47	.05
Bachelor (2013)	75	71	0	Several	Early	C, T	GRS, TCM, PTRS, GAS, PSI	Therapist Confidence & Dedication	.18	.37	-.05	.39
Bedics et al. (2015)	101	100	13	Several	Throughout	C, T	HRSD, IQ, SIQ, SA	CALPAS (TUI)	.03	.06	-.17	.22
Caspar et al. (2005)	18	68	0	Interpersonal	Mid	O	SCL-90, BDI, HRSD,GAF	Plan Analysis	.11	.22	-.38	.55
Clemence et al. (2005)	113	61	2	Psychodynamic	At different times	T	PEI, HRS	CASF-T (TCC)	.47	1.07	.31	.60
Franco (2012)	146	66	39	Unspecified	Mid	C	FUQIC	THDQ	.35	.75	.20	.48
Gaiton (2004)	37	100	59	Several	Early	O	CAPS, IES, CGI, GAS, HRSD, MDUQ, SUI, ASI, CGI-S, Attendance	CALPAS (TUI)	.11	.22	-.22	.42
Gaston et al. (1991)	54	73		Behavioral/CBT	Throughout	C	BDI	CALPAS (TUI)	.13	.26	-.14	.38
Hardy et al. (2001)	24	71		Several	Throughout	C	BDI	CALPAS (TUI)	.73	2.14	.46	.88

Study												
Hatcher (1999)	511	72	4	Several	At different times	T	EID	CALPAS (TUI, TCC)	.51	1.19	.44	.57
Lingiardi et al. (2005)	47	66	0	Psychodynamic	Early	T	Dropout	CALPAS (TUI)	.45	1.01	.19	.65
Long (2004)	26	58		Psychodynamic	Early	T	Dropout	CASF-T (TCC)	.19	.39	–.21	.54
Mander et al. (2013)	202	68		Unspecified	Throughout	C, T	Global outcome (composite of five measures)	MAGCMP	.19	.39	.05	.32
Mander et al. (2015)	447	65		Unspecified	Throughout	C, T	SCL-90, PSQ, IIP, IES	ITPQ	.15	.30	.06	.24
Marmar et al. (1989)	57	75		Several	Early	C	BDI	CALPAS (TUI, TNC)	.08	.16	–.18	.33
Safran & Wallner (1991)	22	50		CT	Early	C	MCMI-D, BDI	CALPAS (TPC, TNC)	.28	.58	–.16	.63
Shaw et al. (1999)	36			CBT	Throughout	O	HRSD, BDI, SCL-90	CTS, CSPRS	.04	.08	–.29	.36
Startup & Edmonds (1994)	25	48		CBT	Early	C	BDI	Therapist collaborative behaviors	.23	.47	–.18	.57
Stiles et al. (1998)	78	53		Several	Throughout	C, T	SCL-90, BDI, IIP, SES, SAS	ARM (PS)	.28	.58	.06	.49

(continued)

Table 5.4. Continued

Study	N	% Women[a]	% of Color[b]	Orientation	Rating Taken[c]	Rater	Outcome Measure	C Measure	Effect Size		95% CI for r	
									r	d	LL	UL
Thomas (2008)	25	84	32	CBT	Early	O	QIDS	Therapist directiveness	.08	.16	−.33	.46
Yeomans et al. (1994)	20	100		Psychodynamic	Early	O	Treatment length	CALPAS (TUI), CRS	.56	1.35	.16	.80

Note. ARM (PS) = Agnew Relationship Measure – Partnership Scale; ASI = Addiction Severity Index; BDI = Beck Depression Inventory; C = client; CALPAS (TCC, TNC, TPC, TUI) = California Psychotherapy Alliance Scale (Therapist Confident Collaboration, Therapist Negative Contribution, Therapist Positive Contribution, Therapist Understanding and Involvement); CAPS = Clinician Administered PTSD Scale; CASF-T (TCC) = Combined Alliance Short Form – Therapist Version (Therapist Confident Collaboration); CBT = Cognitive Behavioral Therapy; CGI = Clinical Global Impression; CGI-S = Clinical Global Impression – Substance Abuse; C Measure = collaboration measure; CI = confidence interval; LL = lower limit; UL = upper limit; CRS = Contract Rating Scale; EID = Estimate of Improvement to Date; FUQIC = Follow-up Questionnaire on Individual Counseling; GAF = Global Assessment of Functioning; GAS = Global Assessment Scale; GRS = Global Rating Scale; CSPRS = Collaborative Study Psychotherapy Rating Scale; CTS = Cognitive Therapy Scale; HRS = Help Received Scale; HRSD = Hamilton Rating Scale for Depression; IES = Inpatient Experience Scale; IIP = Inventory of Interpersonal Problems; IQ = Intrex Questionnaire; ITPQ = Individual Therapy Process Questionnaire; MAGCMP = Multiperspective of General Change Mechanisms in Psychotherapy; MCMID = Millon Clinical Multiaxial Inventory Depression scale; MDUQ = Modified Drug Use Questionnaire; O = observer; PEI = Patients' Estimate of Improvement scale; PPQ = Psychotherapy Process Q-Set; PSI = Psychiatric Symptoms Index; PSQ = Perceived Stress Questionnaire; PTRS = Post-Therapy Rating Scale; QIDS = Quick Inventory of Depressive Symptomatology; SA = Suicide Attempts; SAS = Social Adjustment Scale; SCL-90 = Symptom Check List – 90; SES = Self-Esteem Scale; SIQ = Self Injury Questionnaire; SUI = Substance Use Inventory; T = therapist; TCM = Target Complaints Method; THDQ = Therapist Homework Delivery Questionnaire. Of the 21 correlational effect sizes, 9 (Clemence et al., 2005; Franco, 2012; Gaiton, 2004; Hatcher, 1999; Lingiardi et al., 2005; Long, 2004; Shaw et al., 1999; Stiles et al., 1998; Yeomans et al., 1994) were based on zero-order correlations, and the remaining 12 were derived from partial correlations or partial beta coefficients.

[a]Blank = not reported. [b]Blank = not reported. [c]Time during the course of therapy that collaboration was rated.

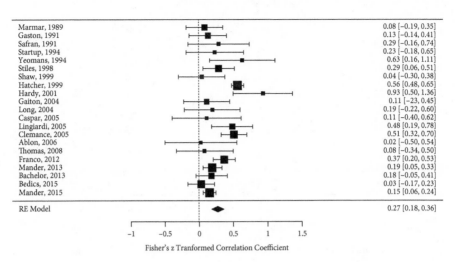

FIGURE 5.8 Forest plot: Psychotherapist collaboration Fisher z effect sizes.

$d = .54-.61$) and medium-sized effects. Meta-regression analyses for goal consensus–outcome and general collaboration–outcome found only one significant moderator each, which could have been due to chance. Results do not appear to be influenced by publication bias or year of publication. The findings are similar to those of previous meta-analyses of goal consensus and collaboration and psychotherapy outcome (Tryon & Winograd, 2002, 2011).

MODERATORS AND MEDIATORS

Table 5.1 presents frequency data and weighted correlational means and standard deviations for variables used in the moderator meta-regressions. Next we summarize the results of those moderator analyses.

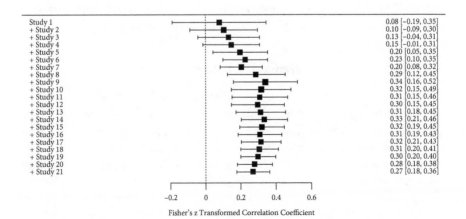

FIGURE 5.9 Cumulative forest plot: Psychotherapist collaboration Fisher z effect sizes.

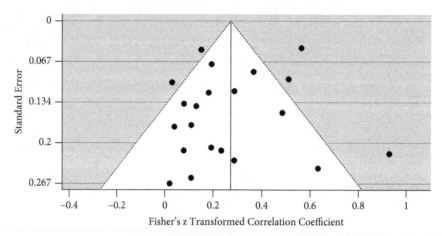

FIGURE 5.10 Funnel plot to assess publication bias: Psychotherapist collaboration Fisher z effect sizes.

Goal Consensus

As indicated, the goal consensus meta-regression (Table 5.2) yielded only one significant moderator (therapist as goal consensus rater). Table 5.1 shows that therapists' perceptions of goal consensus are more highly related to therapy outcome than are those of patients or observers. Table 5.1 specifies smaller goal consensus–outcome effects when goal consensus is rated by several individuals or when studies present patient–therapist goal agreement assessments. The latter occur when psychotherapists and patients separately record problems or target complaints that are then compiled by an outside observer into a measure of convergence or congruence. The larger therapist correlation appears to support the value of therapist ratings; however, because this is the only significant moderator of goal consensus and outcome, we believe that it represents a false positive.

Table 5.1 indicates that most goal consensus studies are published in refereed journals, use the WAI or related inventories to assess goal consensus, rate goal consensus early in psychotherapy, and have samples composed of greater than 50% women. A plurality of studies reported more than one theoretical orientation, patients as raters of goal consensus, but did not report the number of patients of color.

General Collaboration

The general collaboration meta-regression (Table 5.3) yielded only one significant effect (unspecified time of collaboration rating) that we also believe represents a false positive. Table 5.1 shows a large effect between patient–psychotherapist collaboration and treatment outcome when the study does not specify the time at which the collaboration rating was completed. Table 5.1 shows that when rating times are specified, regardless of the period during therapy that ratings are taken, effect sizes are similar and approach a medium effect.

Similar to studies of goal consensus, most studies of general collaboration are published, and women represent the majority of patients. Most studies use cognitive-behavioral or behavioral psychotherapy. Homework completion is the primary collaboration measure, and measurement is taken throughout in a plurality of studies. Therapists represent a plurality of raters. Finally, almost half of the general collaboration studies did not specify the number of patients of color.

Psychotherapist Collaboration

The smaller number of psychotherapist collaboration studies did not permit meta-regression. Table 5.1 shows that, as with the goal consensus and general collaboration research, studies of therapist collaboration are mostly published; women represent more than half the patients; and the number of patients of color is generally unreported. Subscales of the CALPAS and the CASF are frequent psychotherapist collaboration measures. Similar to goal consensus findings, psychotherapist collaboration ratings completed by therapists themselves tend to be more highly related to outcome than are ratings by others, and, similar to general collaboration results, ratings taken at unspecified times are more highly related to outcome than are ratings taken at other times.

Outcome Measures

We did not include outcome measures in meta-regressions, because studies rarely use only one outcome measure ($M = 2.13$, $SD = 1.82$). To obtain an effect for each study, we aggregated the outcome measures and related the aggregate to the goal consensus or collaboration measure. Several measures consistently appeared in the goal consensus and collaboration studies. To examine how these measures relate to goal consensus and/or collaboration singly, we disaggregated them from other outcome measures.

The most common outcome measures for goal consensus were the Beck Depression Inventory, which correlated .29 with goal consensus ($SD = .24$, $n = 1,559$ over 8 studies); therapy retention, which correlated .16 with goal consensus ($SD = .12$, $n = 1,892$ over 11 studies); the Symptom Check List–90 (SCL-90), which correlated .17 with goal consensus ($SD = .13$, $n = 579$ over 4 studies); and the Hamilton Rating Scale for Depression (HRSD), which correlated .20 with goal consensus ($SD = .11$, $n = 537$ over 4 studies).

Common outcome measures for collaboration were the Beck Depression Inventory, which correlated .23 with collaboration ($SD = .16$, $n = 901$ over 15 studies); psychotherapy retention, which correlated .35 with collaboration ($SD = .23$, $n = 1,635$ over 5 studies); the SCL-90, which correlated .16 with collaboration ($SD = .18$, $n = 637$ over 6 studies); and the HRSD, which correlated .14 with collaboration ($SD = .22$, $n = 1,184$ over 11 studies).

EVIDENCE FOR CAUSALITY

Virtually all of the studies in these meta-analyses were correlational in nature, and although they demonstrate positive medium effects between goal consensus and psychotherapy outcome as well as collaboration and psychotherapy outcome, they do not indicate that either goal consensus or collaboration cause a positive treatment outcome, only that they are related to and predict it. For example, the connection between goal consensus and outcome could be caused by other, possibly unassessed, variables.

None of the 54 goal-consensus–outcome studies allow causal interpretations. However, there were two studies that used analyses that suggest causal connections between collaboration and outcome. One study (Burns & Spangler, 2000) used path analyses to determine that homework compliance (a patient collaboration measure) preceded improvement in depressed patients' symptoms rather than symptom improvement leading to increased homework compliance. A dissertation (Franco, 2012) used path analysis to show that psychotherapist homework delivery behavior (a psychotherapist collaboration measure) predicted homework compliance (a patient collaboration measure) that in turn predicted treatment outcome. Results of the other 51 collaboration-outcome studies did not permit causal interpretations.

PATIENT CONTRIBUTIONS

Clinically and theoretically, it does not prove possible to separate patient and practitioner contributions to goal consensus. Both must agree on psychotherapy goals for a consensus to be identified. The meta-analytic result that goal consensus is related to a favorable outcome indicates the importance of patient cooperation in establishing treatment goals.

One way to demonstrate patients' contribution to collaboration is to look at their cooperation in homework completion. Table 5.1 shows that patients' homework completion relates positively to psychotherapy outcome. In addition, two studies (Burns & Spangler, 2000; Franco, 2012) established tentative causal connections between homework completion and psychotherapy outcome.

LIMITATIONS OF THE RESEARCH

Most of the studies in these meta-analyses assessed goal consensus and collaboration at a single time during treatment. In practice, goals change during therapy, meaning goal consensus is ongoing. In similar fashion, patients and practitioners collaborate throughout the course of treatment. Psychotherapy is a dynamic, ongoing process, and research on its relationship elements (such as goal consensus and collaboration) should reflect this reality by assessing them frequently during therapy.

Correspondingly, the vast majority of studies on goal consensus and outcome and collaboration and outcome are correlational, which limits causal conclusions. Studies that use statistical methods, such as growth curves, lagged correlations, and path and structural equation modeling, that permit causal interpretation are needed. When selecting studies for the meta-analyses, we found 32 studies with either goal consensus or collaboration measures that did not use them in outcome analyses. Our meta-analyses might have benefitted from inclusion of the results of these studies. Thus we encourage researchers to relate all study measures to each other. Reporting of participant characteristics has improved over the past 16 years during which we have been reviewing this literature; however, continued improvement is necessary, particularly regarding the reporting of participant ethnicities.

DIVERSITY CONSIDERATIONS

Unfortunately, as Table 5.1 shows, about half of the studies in the meta-analyses did not present patients' race/ethnicity (43% of goal consensus studies, 51% of general collaboration studies, 53% of psychotherapist collaboration studies). Table 5.1 reveals that, when reported, sample sizes for patients of color are generally quite low, representing less than 20% of patients in 71% of goal consensus studies, 63% of general collaboration studies, and 60% of therapist collaboration studies.

The percentages presented in Table 5.1 may or may not be an accurate reflection of the percentages of patients of color and the populations from which they come. The moderator analyses and the statistics for patients of color in Table 5.1 indicate that the effect sizes associated with their responses are in line with other effect sizes in the table. However, given the underreporting of numbers of patients of color, these effects should be interpreted cautiously.

In contrast, Table 5.1 shows that few studies omitted statistics for women patients. Women represent the majority of psychotherapy patients, and the current studies reflect this. When patients' genders are reported, women represent over half of the sample in 80% of goal consensus, 65% of general collaboration, and 90% of psychotherapist collaboration studies. The moderator analyses demonstrate that women patients' ratings are not an influential factor in the goal consensus/collaboration–outcome associations.

TRAINING IMPLICATIONS

Because goal consensus relates to and predicts positive outcomes, trainees can be encouraged to discuss with patients early in therapy their reasons for seeking help and what they hope to accomplish. Research (Swift & Callahan, 2009) cited in the introduction to this chapter suggests that trainees are not always aware of their patients' goals. In addition, the finding (Bachelor, 2013) that goal consensus matters more to patients than to therapists suggests that the latter need to be trained to collaborate with patients to discuss treatment goals and the ways they will work to achieve them. Trainees can also determine what patients have done to ameliorate their concerns, whether they believe the steps they took were helpful, and whether they believe they can work in particular ways.

The results of the collaboration meta-analyses indicate the centrality of team-work in successful psychotherapy. Trainees can learn that patients benefit when both parties work together in a joint effort. They can read the meta-analytic results and discuss their application during classroom interactions. Supervisors are advised to prompt trainees to clarify their statements to patients and ensure that they clearly understand and take into account patients' perspectives. Trainees should be encouraged to respect and honor patients' feelings and wishes through continuing discussion and clarification. Microcounseling skills training (Daniels & Ivey, 2007), reviewing videos of sessions, routine outcome monitoring (described in Chapter 17), and sitting in on sessions conducted by expert psychotherapists can facilitate collaborative process learning.

THERAPEUTIC PRACTICES

The meta-analyses demonstrate positive links between goal consensus and collaboration on the one hand and psychotherapy outcome on the other. The results, based on more than 80 studies and thousands of patients, suggest practices that psychotherapists can employ to enhance patient outcomes.

+ Begin work on the patient's problems only after you and the patient have agreed on treatment goals and the way you will work together to achieve those goals.
+ Share your knowledge with patients by educating them about diagnostic and treatment procedures.
+ Listen to patients and seek their input in the formulation of treatment plans. Do not push your own agendas at the expense of patients.
+ Seek regular feedback, insights, and input from patients regarding their functioning, assessment of psychotherapy, life situation, and desire to change.
+ Provide patients with regular feedback about their progress in psychotherapy.
+ Develop homework assignments that address treatment goals in collaboration with patients. Start with small, easy to accomplish tasks and build to larger ones. Provide homework instructions to patients clearly and perhaps in written form. Get patient feedback on homework and incorporate it.
+ Encourage homework completion. Review homework with patients and discuss their experiences accomplishing it. Make necessary changes in homework assignments to ensure that patients can complete and benefit from them.
+ Be "on the same page" with your patients. Get their feedback to ensure that you are working toward the same goals and that you understand each other throughout treatment.
+ Modify your treatment stance and methods if ethically and clinically indicated in response to patient feedback.
+ Share with patients the results of this research that links their active collaboration with successful treatment outcomes.

REFERENCES

*Ablon, J. S., Levy, R. A., & Katzenstein, T. (2006). Beyond grand names of psycho-therapy: Identifying emprically supported change processes. *Psychotherapy: Theory, Research, Practice, Training, 43,* 216–231. https://www.doi.org/10.1037/0033-3204.43.2.216

*Abromowitz, J. S., Franklin, M. E., Zoellner, L. A., & DiBernardo, C. L. (2002). Treatment compliance and outcome in obsessive-compulsive disorder. *Behavior Modification, 26,* 447–463. https://www.doi.org/10.1177/ 0145445502026004001

*Addis, M. E., & Jacobson, N. S. (2000). A closer look at the treatment rationale and home-work compliance in cognitive-behavioral therapy for depression. *Cognitive Therapy and Research, 24,* 313–326. https://www.doi.org/0147-5916/00/0600-0313

*Adler, J. V. (1988). *A study of the working alliance in psychotherapy* (Unpublished doctoral dissertation). University of British Columbia, Vancouver.

Alexander, L., & Luborsky, L. (1986). The Penn Helping Alliance Scales. In L. Greenberg & W. Pinsof (Eds.), *The psychotherapeutic process: A research handbook* (pp. 325–366). New York, NY: Guilford.

*Andrews, M., Baker, A. L., Halpin, S. A., Lewin, T. J., Richmond, R., Kay-Lambkin, F. J., . . . Callister, R. (2016). Early therapeutic alliance, treatment retention, and 12-month outcomes in a healthy lifestyles intervention for people with psychotic disorders. *Journal of Nervous and Mental Disease, 204,* 894–902. https://www.doi.org/10.1097/ NMD.0000000000000585

*Applebaum, A. J., DuHamel, K. N., Winkel, G., Rini, C., Greene, P. B., Mosher, C. E., & Redd, W. H. (2012). Therapeutic alliance in telephone-administered cognitive-behavioral therapy for hematopoietic stem cell transplant survivors. *Journal of Consulting and Clinical Psychology, 80,* 811–816. https://www.doi.org/10.1037/a0027956

*Bachelor, A. (2013). Clients' and therapists' views of the therapeutic alliance: Similarities, differences and relationship to therapy outcome. *Clinical Psychology and Psychotherapy, 20,* 118–135. https://www.doi.org/10.1002/cpp.792

Beck, A. T., Steer, R. A., & Brown, G. K. (1996). *Manual for the Beck Depression Inventory-II.* San Antonio, TX: Psychological Corporation.

*Bedics, J. D., Atkins, D. C., Harned, M. S., & Linehan, M. M. (2015). The therapeutic alliance as a predictor of outcome in dialectical behavior therapy versus nonbehavioral psycho-therapy by experts for borderline personality disorder. *Psychotherapy, 52,* 67–77. https:// www.doi.org/10.1037/a0038457

Berdondini, L., Elliott, R., & Shearer, J. (2012). Collaboration in experiential therapy. *Journal of Clinical Psychology: In Session, 68,* 159–167. https://www.doi.org/10.1002/jclp.21830

*Bogalo, L., & Moss-Morris, R. (2006). The effectiveness of homework tasks in an irritable bowel syndrome self-management programme. *New Zealand Journal of Psychology, 35,* 120–125.

Bordin, E. S. (1979). The generalizability of the psychoanalytic concept of the working alli-ance. *Psychotherapy: Theory, Research, Practice, Training, 16,* 252–260. https://www.doi. org/10.1037/h0085885

Borenstein, M. (2009). Effect sizes for continuous data. In H. Cooper, L. V. Hedges, & J. C. Valentine (Eds.), *The handbook of research synthesis and meta-analysis* (2nd ed., pp. 221–236). New York, NY: Russell Sage Foundation.

*Brocato, J., & Wagner, E. F. (2008). Predictors of retention in an alternative-to-prison sub-stance abuse treatment program. *Criminal Justice and Behavior, 35,* 99–119. https://www. doi.org/10.1177/0093854807309429

*Bryant, M. J., Simons, A. D., & Thase, M. E. (1999). Therapist skill and patient variables in homework compliance: Controlling an uncontrolled variable in cognitive therapy outcome research. *Cognitive Therapy and Research, 23,* 381–399. https://www.doi.org/10.1023/A:1018703901116

*Burns, D. D., & Nolen-Hoeksema, S. (1991). Coping styles, homework adherence, and the effectiveness of cognitive-behavioral therapy. *Journal of Consulting and Clinical Psychology, 59,* 305–311. https://www.doi.org/10.1037/0022-006X.59.2.305

*Burns, D. D., & Nolen-Hoeksema, S. (1992). Therapeutic empathy and recovery from depression in cognitive-behavioral therapy. *Journal of Consulting and Clinical Psychology, 60,* 441–449. https://www.doi.org/10.1037/0022-006X.60.3.441

*Burns, D. D., & Spangler, D. L. (2000). Does psychotherapy homework lead to improvements in depression in cognitive-behavioral therapy or does improvement lead to increased homework compliance? *Journal of Consulting and Clinical Psychology, 68,* 46–56. https://www.doi.org/10.1037//0022006X.68.1.46

*Burns, J. W., & Evon, D. (2007). Common and specific process factors in cardiac rehabilitation: Independent and interactive effects of the working alliance and self-efficacy. *Health Psychology, 26,* 684–692. https://www.doi.org/10.1037/0278-6133.26.6.684

*Busseri, M. A., & Tyler, J. D. (2004). Client-therapist agreement on target problems, working alliance, and counseling outcome. *Psychotherapy Research, 14,* 77–88. https://www.doi.org/10.1093/ptr/kph005

*Cammin-Nowak, S., Helbig-Lang, S., Lang, T., Gloster, A. T., Fehn, L., Gerlach, A. L., Ströhle, A., . . . Wittchen, H.-U. (2013). Specificity of homework compliance effects on treatment outcome in CBT: Evidence from a controlled trial on panic disorder and agoraphobia. *Journal of Clinical Psychology, 69,* 616–639. https://www.doi.org/10.1002/jclp.21975

*Carroll, K. M., Nich, C., & Ball, S. A. (2005). Practice makes progress? Homework assignments and outcome intreatment of cocaine dependence. *Journal of Consulting and Clinical Psychology, 73,* 749–755. https://www.doi.org/10.1037/0022-006X.73.4.749

*Caspar, F., Grossmann, C., Unmüssig, C., & Schramm, E. (2005). Complementary therapeutic relationship: Therapist behavior, interpersonal patterns, and therapeutic effects. *Psychotherapy Research, 15,* 91–102. https://www.doi.org/10.1080/10503300512331327074

*Clemence, A. J., Hilsenroth, M. J., Ackerman, S. J., Strassle, C. G., & Handler, L. (2005). Facets of the therapeutic alliance and perceived progress in psychotherapy: Relationship between patient and therapist perspectives. *Clinical Psychology and Psychotherapy, 12,* 443–454. https://www.doi.org/10.1002/cpp.467

Cohen, J. (1992). A power primer. *Psychological Bulletin, 112,* 155–159. https://www.doi.org/10.1037/0033-2909.112.1.155

*Constantino, M. J., Laws, H. B., Coyne, A. E., Greenberg, R. P., Klein, D. N., Manber, R., . . . Arnow, B. A. (2016). Change in patients' interpersonal impacts as a mediator of the alliance-outcome association in treatment for chronic depression. *Journal of Consulting and Clinical Psychology, 84,* 1135–1144. https://www.doi.org/10.1037/ccp0000149

*Coon, D. W., & Thompson, L. W. (2003). The relationship between homework compliance and treatment outcomes among older adult outpatients with mild-to-moderate depression. *American Journal of Geriatric Psychiatry, 11,* 53–61. https://www.doi.org/10.1097/00019442-200301000-00008

Cooper, H., Hedges, L. V., & Valentine, J. C. (Eds.). (2009). *The handbook of research synthesis and meta-analysis* (2nd ed.). New York, NY: Russell Sage Foundation.

*Cowan, M. J., Freedland, K. E., Burg, M. M., Saab, P. G., Youngblood, M. E., Cornell, C. E., . . . Czajkowski, S. M. (2008). Predictors of treatment response for depression and inadequate social support—The ENRICHD randomized clinical trial. *Psychotherapy and Psychosomatics, 77*, 27–37. https://www.doi.org/10.1159/000110057

Daniels, T., & Ivey, A. (2007). *Microcounseling: Making skills training work in a multicultural world.* Springfield, IL: Charles C. Thomas.

Dattilio, F. M., & Hanna, M. A. (2012). Collaboration in cognitive-behavioral therapy. *Journal of Clinical Psychology: In Session, 68*, 146–158. https://www.doi.org/10.1002/jclp.21831

*Decker, S. E., Kiluk, B. D., Frankforter, T., Babuscio, T., Nich, C., & Carroll, K. M. (2016). Just showing up is not enough: Adherence and outcome in cognitive-behavioral therapy for cocaine dependence. *Journal of Consulting and Clinical Psychology, 84*, 907–912. https://www.doi.org/10.1037/ccp0000126

DeFife, J. A., & Hilsenroth, M. J. (2011). Starting off on the right foot: Common factor elements in early psychotherapy process. *Journal of Psychotherapy Integration, 21*, 172–191. https://www.doi.org/10.1037/a0023889

*Dunn, H., Morrison, A. P., & Bentall, R. P. (2006). The relationship between patient suitability, therapeutic alliance, homework compliance, and outcome in cognitive therapy for psychosis. *Clinical Psychology and Psychotherapy, 13*, 145–152. https://www.doi.org/10.1002/cpp.481

*Edelman, R. E., & Chambless, D. L. (1993). Compliance during sessions and homework in exposure-based treatment of agoraphobia. *Behaviour Research and Therapy, 31*, 767–773. https://www.doi.org/10.1016/0005-7967(93)90007-H

Egger, M., Davey Smith, G., Schneider, M., & Minder, C. (1997). Bias in meta-analysis detected by a simple, graphical test. *British Medical Journal, 315*, 629–634. https://www.doi.org/10.1136/bmj.315.7109.629

Emmons, R. A. (2003). Personal goals, life meaning, and virtue: Wellsprings of a positive life. In C. L. M. Keys & J. Haidt (Eds.), *Positive psychology and life well lived* (pp. 105–128). Washington, DC: American Psychological Association.

*Epperson, D. L., Bushway, D. J., & Warman, R. E. (1983). Client self-terminations after one counseling session: Effects of problem recognition, counselor gender, and counselor experience. *Journal of Counseling Psychology, 30*, 307–315. https://www.doi.org/10.1037/0022-0167.30.3.307

*Filak, J., & Abeles, N. (1984). Posttherapy congruence on client symptoms and therapy outcome. *Professional Psychology: Research and Practice, 15*, 845–855. https://www.doi.org/10.1037/0735-7028.15.6.846

*Flückiger, C., Caspar, F., Grosse Holtforth, M., & Willutzki, U. (2009). Working with patients' strengths: A microprocess approach. *Psychotherapy Research, 19*, 213–223. https://www.doi.org/10.1080/10503300902755300

*Forman, N. W. (1990). *The nature of trait empathy in clients with chronic pain and their counselors and its impact on the development of the working alliance and outcome* (Unpublished doctoral dissertation). The Ohio State University, Columbus.

*Franco, C. M. (2012). *Client motivation, working alliance and the use of homework in psychotherapy* (Unpublished doctoral dissertation). Florida State University, Tallahassee.

*Gabbay, M., Shields, C., Bower, B., Sibbald, M., King, M., & Ward, E. (2003). Patient-practitioner agreement: Does it matter? *Psychological Medicine, 33*, 241–251. https://www.doi.org/10.1017/S0033291702006992

*Gaiton, L. R. (2004). *Investigation of therapeutic alliance in a treatment study with substance-abusing women with PTSD* (Unpublished doctoral dissertation). Adelphi University, Garden City, NY.

Gaston, L. (1991). Reliability and criterion-related validity of the California Psychotherapy Alliance Scales–Patient Version. *Psychological Assessment, 3,* 68–74. https://www.doi.org/10.1037/1040-3590.3.1.68

*Gaston, L., Marmar, C., Gallagher, D., & Thompson, L. (1991). Alliance prediction of outcome beyond in-treatment symptomatic change as psychotherapy processes. *Psychotherapy Research, 1,* 104–112. https://www.doi.org/10.1080/10503309112331335531

*Goldman, R. E., Hilsenroth, M. J., Gold, J. R., Owen, J. J., & Levy, S. R. (2018). Psychotherapy integration and alliance: An examination across treatment outcomes. *Journal of Psychotherapy Integration, 28*(1), 14–30. https://www.doi.org/10.1037/int0000060

*Gomes-Schwartz, B. (1978). Effective ingredients in psychotherapy: Prediction of outcome from process variables. *Journal of Consulting and Clinical Psychology, 46,* 1023–1035. https://www.doi.org/10.1037/0022-006X.46.5.1023

*Gonzalez, V. M., Schmitz, J. M., & DeLaune, K. A. (2006). The role of homework in cognitive-behavioral therapy for cocaine dependence. *Journal of Consulting and Clinical Psychology, 74,* 633–637. https://www.doi.org/10.1037/0022-006X.74.3.633

*Graf, M. C., Gaudiano, B. A., & Geller, P. A. (2008). Written emotional disclosure: A controlled study of expressive writing homework in outpatient psychotherapy. *Psychotherapy Research, 18,* 389–399. https://www.doi.org/10.1080/10503300701691664

*Gunther, G. J. (1992). *Therapeutic alliance, patient object relations and outcome in psychotherapy* (Unpublished doctoral dissertation). Michigan State University, East Lansing.

*Hardy, G. E., Cahill, J., Shapiro, D. A., Barkham, M., Rees, A., & Macaskill, N. (2001). Client interpersonal and cognitive styles as predictors of response to time-limited cognitive therapy for depression. *Journal of Consulting and Clinical Psychology, 69,* 841–845. https://www.doi.org/10.1037//0022-006X.69.5.841

*Hatcher, R. L. (1999). Therapists' view of treatment alliance and collaboration in therapy. *Psychotherapy Research, 9,* 405–423. https://www.doi.org/10.1080/10503309912331332831

*Hatcher, R. L., & Barends, A. W. (1996). Patients' view of the alliance in psychotherapy: Exploratory factor analysis of three alliance measures. *Journal of Consulting and Clinical Psychology, 64,* 1326–1336. https://www.doi.org/10.1037/0022-006X.64.6.1326

*Hawton, K., Catalan, J., & Fagg. (1992). Sex therapy for erectile dysfunction: Characteristics of couples, treatment outcome, and prognostic factors. *Archives of Sexual Behavior, 21,* 161–175. https://www.doi.org/10.1007/BF01542591

*Hegel, M. T., Barrett, J. E., Cornell, J. E., & Oxman, T. E. (2002). Predictors of response to problem-solving treatment of depression in primary care. *Behavior Therapy, 33,* 511–527. https://www.doi.org/10.1016/S0005-7894(02)80014-4

*Holmqvist, R., Philips, B., & Mellor-Clark, J. (2016). Client and therapist agreement about the client's problem—associations with treatment alliance and outcome. *Psychotherapy Research, 26,* 399–409. https://www.doi.org/10.1080/10503307.2015.1013160

*Horvath, A. O. (1981). *An exploratory study of the working alliance: Its measurement and relation to therapy outcome* (Unpublished doctoral dissertation). University of British Columbia, Vancouver.

Horvath, A. O., & Greenberg, L. S. (1989). Development and validation of the Working Alliance Inventory. *Journal of Counseling Psychology, 36,* 223–233. https://www.doi.org/10.1037/0022-0167.36.2.223

Jara, A., Hanson, T., Quintana, F. A., Müller, P., & Rosner, G. L. (2011). DPpackage: Bayesian semi- and nonparametric modeling in R. *Journal of Statistical Software, 40*(5), 1–30. Retrieved from https://www.jstatsoft.org/article/view/v040i05

Kazantzis, N., & Kellis, E. (2012). A special feature on collaboration in psychotherapy. *Journal of Clinical Psychology: In Session, 68*, 133–135. https://www.doi.org/10.1002/jclp.21837

*Kenwright, M., Marks, I., Graham, C., Frances, A., & Mataix-Cols, D. (2005). Brief scheduled phone support from a clinician to enhance computer-aided self-help for obsessive compulsive disorder: Randomized controlled trial. *Journal of Clinical Psychology, 61*, 1499–1508. https://www.doi.org/10.1002/jclp.20204

*Knaevelsrud, C., & Maercker, A. (2007). Internet-based treatment for PTSD reduces distress and facilitates the development of a strong therapeutic alliance: A randomized controlled clinical trial. *BMC Psychiatry, 7*, 13. https://www.doi.org/10.1186/1471-244X-7-13

*Kokotovic, A. M., & Tracey, T. J. (1990). Working alliance in the early phase of counseling. *Journal of Counseling Psychology, 37*, 16–21. https://www.doi.org/10.1037/0022-0167.37.1.16

*Krauskopf, C. J., Baumgardner, A., & Mandracchia, S. (1981). Return rate following intake revisited. *Journal of Counseling Psychology, 28*, 519–521. https://www.doi.org/10.1037/0022-0167.28.6.519

Lambert, M. J., Burlingame, G. M., Umphress, V., Hansen, N. B., Vermeersch, D. A., Clouse, G. C., & Yanchar, S. C. (1996). The reliability and validity of the outcome questionnaire. *Clinical Psychology and Psychotherapy, 3*, 249–258.

Lambert, M. J., & Cattani, K. (2012). Practice-friendly research review: Collaboration in routine care. *Journal of Clinical Psychology: In Session, 68*, 209–220. https://www.doi.org/10.1002/jclp.21835

*Levy, E. G. (1998). *Therapeutic process in a managed care type setting: The working alliance, pre-treatment characteristics and outcome* (Unpublished doctoral dissertation). University of Texas at Austin.

*Lingiardi, V., Filippucci, L., & Baiocco, R. (2005). Therapeutic alliance evaluation in personality disorders psychotherapy. *Psychotherapy Research, 15*, 45–53. https://www.doi.org/10.1080/10503300512331327047

*Long, J. R. (2001). Goal agreement and early therapeutic change. *Psychotherapy, 38*, 219–232. https://www.doi.org/10.1037/0033-3204.38.2.219

*Long, M. (2004). *Therapeutic alliance in the identification of premature termination from psychotherapy* (Unpublished doctoral dissertation). Adelphi University, Garden City, NY.

*Mallinckrodt, B., & Tekie, Y. T. (2016). Item response theory analysis of Working Alliance Inventory, revised response format, and new Brief Alliance Inventory. *Psychotherapy Research, 26*, 694–718. https://www.doi.org/10.1080/10503307.2015.1061718

*Mander, J., Schlarb, A., Teufel, M., Keller, F., Hautzinger, M., Zipfel, S., . . . Sammet, I. (2015). The Individual Therapy Process Questionnaire: Development and validation of a revised measure to evaluate general change mechanisms in psychotherapy. *Clinical Psychology and Psychotherapy, 22*, 328–345. https://www.doi.org/10.1002/cpp.1892

*Mander, J. V., Wittorf, A., Schlarb, A., Hautzinger, M., Zipfel, S., & Sammet, I. (2013). Change mechanisms in psychotherapy: Multiperspective assessment and relation to outcome. *Psychotherapy Research, 23*, 105–116. https://www.doi.org/10.1080/10503307.2012.744111

*Marmar, C. R., Gaston, L., Gallagher, D., & Thompson, L. W. (1989). Alliance and outcome in late-life depression. *Journal of Nervous and Mental Disease, 117*, 464–472.

Marmar, C. R., Weiss, D. S., & Gaston, L. (1989). Towards the validation of the California Therapeutic Alliance Rating Scale system. *Journal of Consulting and Clinical Psychology, 1*, 46–52.

*Mendelow, C. M. (2008). *Client attachment and goal orientation as predictors of the working alliance in psychotherapy* (Unpublished doctoral dissertation). Fordham University, New York, NY.

Michalak, J., & Grosse Holtforth, M. (2006). Where do we go from here? The goal perspective in psychotherapy. *Clinical Psychology: Science and Practice, 13*, 346–365. https://www.doi.org/10.1111/j.1468-2850.2006.00048.x

*Moseley, D. C. (1978). *The therapeutic relationship and its association with outcome* (Unpublished doctoral dissertation). University of Alberta, Edmonton.

Muthukumarana, S., & Tiwari, R. C. (2016). Meta-analysis using Dirichlet process. *Statistical Methods in Medical Research, 25*, 352–365. https://www.doi.org/10.1177/0962280212453891

Norcross, J. C., & Wampold, B. E. (2011). Evidence-based therapy relationships: Research conclusions and clinical practices. In J. C. Norcross (Ed.), *Psychotherapy relationships that work: Evidence-based responsiveness* (2nd ed., pp. 423–430). New York, NY: Oxford University Press.

Orlinsky, D. E., Grawe, K., & Parks, B. K. (1994). Process and outcome in psychotherapy-noch einmal. In A. Bergin & S. Garfield (Eds.), *Handbook of psychotherapy and behavior change* (4th ed., pp. 270–376). New York, NY: Wiley.

*Principe, J. M., Marci, C. D., Glick, D. M., & Ablon, J. S. (2006). The relationship among patient contemplation, early alliance, and continuation in psychotherapy. *Psychotherapy: Theory, Research, Practice, Training, 43*, 238–243. https://www.doi.org/10.1037/0033-3204.43.2.238

R Core Team. (2017). *R: A language and environment for statistical computing.* Vienna, Austria: R Foundation for Statistical Computing. Retrieved from https://www.R-project.org/

*Ramnerö, J., & Öst, L.-G. (2007). Therapists' and clients' perceptions of each other and working alliance in the behavioral treatment of panic disorder and agoraphobia. *Psychotherapy Research, 17*, 328–337. https://www.doi.org/10.1080/10503300600650852

Raudenbush, S. W. (2009). Random effects meta-analysis. In H. Cooper, L. V. Hedges, & J. C. Valentine (Eds.), *The handbook of research synthesis and meta-analysis* (2nd ed., pp. 295–316). New York, NY: Russell Sage Foundation.

Ribeiro, E. Cunha, C. Teixeira, A. S., Stiles, W. B., Piers, N. Santos, B. Basto, I., & Salgado, J. (2016). Therapeutic collaboration and the assimilation of problematic experiences in emotion-focused therapy for depression: Comparison of two cases. *Psychotherapy Research, 26*, 665–680. https://www.doi.org/10.1080/10503307.2016.1208853

Ribeiro, E., Ribeiro, A. P., Gonçalves, M. M., Horvath, A. O., & Stiles, W. B. (2013). How collaboration in therapy becomes therapeutic: The therapeutic collaboration coding system. *Psychology and Psychotherapy: Theory, Research and Practice, 86*, 294–314. https://www.doi.org/10.1111/j.2044-8341.2012.02066.x

*Safran, J. D., & Wallner, L. K. (1991). The predictive validity of two therapeutic alliance measures in cognitive therapy. *Psychological Assessment, 3*, 188–195. https://www.doi.org/10.1037/1040-3590.3.2.188

*Schönberger, M., Humle, F., & Teasdale, T. (2006). Subjective outcome of brain injury rehabilitation in relation to the therapeutic working alliance, client compliance and awareness. *Brain Injury, 20*, 1271–1282. https://www.doi.org/10.1080/02699050601049395

*Schönberger, M., Humle, F., & Teasdale, T. (2007). The relationship between clients' cognitive functioning and the therapeutic working alliance in post-acute brain injury rehabilitation. *Brain Injury, 21*, 825–836. https://www.doi.org/10.1080/02699050701499433

*Shaw, B. F., Elkin, J., Yamaguchi, J., Olmsted, M., Vallis, T. M., Dobson, K. S., Lowrey, A., . . .
Imber, S. D. (1999). Therapist competence ratings in relation to clinical outcome in cognitive therapy of depression. *Journal of Consulting and Clinical Psychology, 67,* 87–846.
https://www.doi.org/10.1037/0022-006X.67.6.837

*Simpson, H. B., Maher, M. J., Wang, Y., & Bao, Y. (2011). Patient adherence predicts outcome
from cognitive behavioral therapy in obsessive-compulsive disorder. *Journal of Consulting
and Clinical Psychology, 79,* 247–252. https://www.doi.org/10.1037/a0022659

*Stapleton, M. (2007). *The effect of working alliance on client drop-out for persons with
disabilities in state-federal rehabilitation agency* (Unpublished doctoral dissertation).
University of Maryland, College Park.

*Startup, M., & Edmonds, J. (1994). Compliance with homework behavior in cognitive-
behavioral therapy for depression: Relationship to outcome and methods of enactment. *Cognitive Therapy and Research, 18,* 567–579. https://www.doi.org/10.1007/
BF02355669

*Stein, M. D., Solomon, D. A., Herman, D. S., Anthony, J. L., Ramsey, S. E., Anderson, B. J., &
Miller, I. W. (2004). Pharmacotherapy plus psychotherapy for treatment of depression in
active injection drug users. *Archives of General Psychiatry, 61,* 152–159. https://www.doi.
org/10.1001/archpsyc.61.2.152

Stiles, W. B. (1999). Signs and voices in psychotherapy. *Psychotherapy Research, 9,* 1–21.

*Stiles, W. B., Agnew-Davies, R., Hardy, G. E., Barkham, W., & Shapiro, D. A. (1998). Relations
of the alliance with psychotherapy outcome: Findings in the second Sheffield psychotherapy project. *Journal of Consulting and Clinical Psychology, 66,* 791–802. https://www.
doi.org/10.1037/0022-006X.66.5.791

Swift, J., & Callahan, J. (2009). Early psychotherapy processes: An examination of client and
trainee clinician perspective convergence. *Clinical Psychology and Psychotherapy, 16,* 228–
236. https://www.doi.org/10.1002/cpp.617

*Taber, B. J., Leibert, T. W., & Agaskar, V. R. (2011). Relationship among client-therapist per-
sonality congruence, working alliance, and therapeutic outcome. *Psychotherapy, 48,* 376–
380. https://www.doi.org/10.1037/a0022066

*Taylor, L. B., Agras, W. S., Schneider, J. A., & Allen, R. A. (1983). Adherence to instructions
to practice relaxation exercises. *Journal of Consulting and Clinical Psychology, 51,* 952–953.
https://www.doi.org/10.1037/0022-006X.51.6.952

*Thomas, C. R. (2008). *Evaluating the relationship between therapist collaborative behaviors,
homework adherence, and treatment outcome in cognitive behavioral therapy* (Unpublished
master's thesis). University of Texas at Arlington.

Tracey,T. J., & Kokotovic, A. M. (1989). Factor structure of the Working Alliance Inventory.
Psychological Assessment, 1, 207–210. https://www.doi.org/10.1037/1040-3590.1.3.207

Tryon, G. S., & Winograd, G. (2002). Goal consensus and collaboration. In J. G. Norcross
(Ed.), *Psychotherapy relationships that work: Therapist contributions and responsiveness to
patients* (pp. 109–125). New York, NY: Oxford University Press.

Tryon, G. S., & Winograd, G. (2011). Goal consensus and collaboration. In J. C. Norcross
(Ed.), *Psychotherapy relationships that work: Evidence-based responsiveness* (2nd ed., pp.
153–167). New York, NY: Oxford University Press.

Viechtbauer, W. (2010). Conducting meta-analyses in R with the metafor package. *Journal of
Statistical Software, 36,* 1–48. Retrieved from http://www.jstatsoft.org/v36/i03/

*Vromans, L. P. (2007). *Process and outcome of narrative therapy for major depressive disorder
in adults: Narrative reflectivity, working alliance and improved symptoms and inter-personal*

outcomes (Unpublished doctoral dissertation). Queensland University of Technology, Brisbane.

*Webb, C. A., DeRubeis, R. J., Amsterdam, J. D., Shelton, R. C., Hollon, S. D., & Dimidjian, S. (2011). Two aspects of the therapeutic alliance: Differential relations with depressive symptom change. *Journal of Consulting and Clinical Psychology, 79*, 279–283. https://www. doi.org/10.1037/a0023252

*Westra, H. A., Arkowitz, H., & Dozois, D. J. A. (2009). Adding a motivational interviewing pretreatment to cognitive behavioral therapy for generalized anxiety disorder: A preliminary randomized controlled trial. *Journal of Anxiety Disorders, 23*, 1106–1117. https:// www.doi.org/10.1016/j.janxdis.2009.07.014

*Wettersten, K. B., Lichtenberg, J. W., & Mallinckrodt, B. (2005). Associations between working alliance and outcome in Solution-Focused Brief Therapy and brief interpersonal therapy. *Psychotherapy Research, 15*, 35–43. https://www.doi.org/10.1080/10503300512331327029

*Whittall, M. L., Thordarson, D. S., & McLean, P. D. (2004). Treatment of obsessive-compulsive disorder: Cognitive behavior therapy vs. exposure and response prevention. *Behaviour Research and Therapy, 43*, 1559–1576. https://www.doi.org/10.1016/j.brat.2004.11.012

Wiseman, H., Tishby, O., & Barber, J. P. (2012). Collaboration in psychodynamic psychotherapy. *Journal of Clinical Psychology: In Session, 68*, 136–145.

*Woods, C. M., Chambless, D. L., & Steketee, G. (2002). Homework compliance and behavior therapy outcome for panic with agoraphobia and obsessive compulsive disorder. *Cognitive Behaviour Therapy, 31*, 88–95. https://www.doi.org/10.1080/16506070252959526

*Yeomans, F. E., Gutfreund, J., Seltzer, M. A., Clarkin, J. F., Hull, J. W., & Smith, T. E. (1994). Factors related to dropouts by borderline patients: Treatment contract and therapeutic alliance. *Journal of Psychotherapy Practice and Research, 3*, 16–24.

*Yovel, I., & Safren, S. A. (2007). Measuring homework utility in psychotherapy: Cognitive-behavioral therapy for adult attention-deficit hyperactivity disorder as an example. *Cognitive Therapy and Research, 31*, 385–399. https://www.doi.org/10.1007/s10608-006-9065-2

*Zane, N., Sue, S., Chang, J., Huang, L., Huang, J., Lowe, S., Srinivasan, S., . . . Lee, E. (2005). Beyond ethnic match: Effects of client-therapist cognitive match in problem perception, coping orientation, and therapy goals on treatment outcomes. *Journal of Community Psychology, 33*, 569–585. https://www.doi.org/10.1002/jcop.20067

6

COHESION IN GROUP THERAPY

Gary M. Burlingame, Debra Theobald McClendon,
and Chongming Yang

Cohesion is the most popular of several relationship constructs (e.g., alliance, group climate, group atmosphere) in the clinical and empirical literature on group therapy. Over time it has become confusingly synonymous with the therapeutic relationship in group psychotherapy (Burlingame et al., 2002). From the perspective of a group member, relationships are comprised of three structural components: member–member, member–group, and member–leader. From the perspective of the group therapist, relationships include the same three structural components and two additional ones: leader–group and, in the case of a cotherapy, leader–leader. The complexity of these multilevel structures coupled with their dynamic interplay has created an array of competing cohesion instruments and an absence of a consensual definition.

Our intent in this chapter is to define cohesion, present updated meta-analytic findings, and offer group leaders measures and practices to improve the therapeutic relationship in group treatment and, ultimately, treatment outcome. We accomplish this by reviewing the multiple definitions and assessment measures of group cohesion and discussing a measure that may clarify group relationships using two latent factors (quality and structure) that explain common variance among frequently used group relationship instruments. We then provide clinical examples to illustrate the multiple facets of group relationships. We discuss three landmark studies on cohesion and review the findings of our earlier meta-analysis (Burlingame et al., 2011a, 2011b), followed by an updated meta-analytic review of cohesion's relation with treatment outcome. We then explore potential mediators and moderators, evidence for causality, patient contributions, and diversity considerations gleaned from the updated meta-analysis. We conclude by addressing training implications and therapeutic practices.

DEFINITIONS

Definitions of cohesion have traveled a serpentine trail (Bednar & Kaul, 1994; Crouch et al., 1994; Kivlighan et al., 2000) ranging from broad and diffuse (e.g., forces that cause members to remain in the group, sticking-togetherness) to focused (e.g., attractiveness, alliance) and structurally coherent (e.g., tripartite relationship; Yalom &

Leszcz, 2005). Reviewers have pled for definitional clarity: "there is little cohesion in the cohesion research" (Bednar & Kaul, 1978, p. 800). Indeed, instruments tapping group acceptance, emotional well-being, self-disclosure, interpersonal liking, and tolerance for personal space have been used as measures of cohesion (Burlingame et al., 2002). Behavioral definitions have included attendance, verbal content, early termination, physical seating distance, amount of eye contact, and the length of time group members engaged in a "group hug" (Hornsey et al., 2007). The definitional challenges of cohesion are reflected by one team's observation that "just about anything that has a positive valence [with outcome] has been interpreted at some point as an index of cohesion" (Hornsey et al., 2009, p. 272).

Empirical investigations examining the multidimensional structure of cohesion have reported as few as two and as many as five dimensions (Braaten, 1991; Cattell & Wispe, 1948; Griffith, 1988; Selvin & Hagstrom, 1963) with common factors including vertical and horizontal cohesion as well as task and social/affective cohesion.

Ample evidence supports two definitional dimensions of cohesion. The first dimension relates to the structure of the therapeutic relationship in groups and is most often referred to as vertical and horizontal cohesion (Dion, 2000). Vertical cohesion represents a member–leader relationship and refers to a group member's perception of the group leader's competence, genuineness, and warmth. Horizontal cohesion describes a group member's relationship with other group members and with the group as a whole. The second dimension contrasts task cohesion (task performance) or the work of the group with affective or emotional cohesion (interpersonal/emotional support; Griffith, 1988). In task cohesion, members are drawn to the group to accomplish a given task, while in affective cohesion members feel connected because of the emotional support the group affords.

In the chapter, we extend these two dimensions of cohesion (structure and quality) and offer an updated definition and measure to consider. Multiple measures assess the quality of cohesion (e.g., empathy, group climate), but little attention has been focused on how these intersect with the different relationships structures (member–member, member–leader, and member–group) found in group psychotherapy. For instance, group relationship measures assess positive affect. However, some capture members' feelings toward their group (climate), others toward their group leader (alliance), and still others toward other members in the group (cohesion; member–member). This definition is thoroughly discussed in the next section.

MEASURES

Measures of cohesion frequently used in the group psychotherapy research include: Group Climate Questionnaire (GCQ; MacKenzie, 1981, 1983); Cohesion Scale Revised (Lieberman et al., 1973); Group Cohesion (Piper et al., 1983); Group Atmosphere Scale (Silbergeld et al., 1975); Group Environment Scale (GES; Moos, 1986; Moos & Humphrey, 1974); Stuttgarter Bogen (Czogalik & Koltzow, 1987); Therapeutic Factor Inventory (TFI) Cohesion subscale (Lese & MacNair-Semands, 2000); and the Harvard Group Cohesiveness Scale (Budman et al., 1987, 1989). This order of presentation reflects the frequency of use in our meta-analysis; all but the Harvard measure are self-report measures. These eight instruments account for 82% of the measures used in the studies included in our meta-analysis.

Unfortunately, the research has not simultaneously studied two or more cohesion measures in the same study. For instance, of the 15 new studies added to our meta-analysis update (see later discussion), only 3 used two cohesion measures. Two of these studies were validating new measures of cohesion (Group Sessions Rating Scale, Group Entitativity), and the third study never compared the relation between the two cohesion measures (Pisetsky et al., 2015). Thus, of the 15 new cohesion–outcome studies, none have added to our knowledge of how different cohesion measures relate to one another.

Cohesion measures continue to be adapted and created. For example, a new observational measure has been created—the Therapy Process Observational Coding System–Group Cohesion scale (Lerner et al., 2013)—that adds to literature which is dominated by self-report measures. The Group Entitativity Measure–Group Psychotherapy is designed to capture the unity or coherence of the group compared to a group simply being a collection of individual members. The construct comes from social psychology and uses a single-item visual analogue scale that was adapted for clinical groups to simplify assessment of group unity with a user-friendly graphic (Hornsey et al., 2012). A new measure was also recently developed to support feedback to group leaders regarding a member's perception of the relationship. The Group Session Rating Scale (Quirk et al., 2013) is a 4-item alliance measure that was linked to outcome in an initial psychometric study of substance abuse groups but awaits research with other clinical populations.

Table 6.1 summarizes the cohesion measures with the strongest presence in group treatment research. These measures promulgate some of the definitional difficulties outlined in the previous section. For instance, positive aspects of the relationship quality assessed by the measures in Table 6.1 include degree of self-disclosure, inclusion, likability, support, involvement, expressiveness, sense of relatedness, belonging, and trust. Some measures (GCQ, GES) go beyond affective elements and tap the work orientation of the group. Some explicitly address relationship structure (e.g., GCQ = member–group, GC = member–member and member–leader) while others are less clear on which relationship structure members are being asked to assess. Moreover, the absence of studies examining how different measures of cohesion correlate with one another make it impossible to determine if different or similar relationship constructs are being assessed.

Some of these difficulties may be clarified through the Group Questionnaire (GQ; Krogel et al., 2009). The GQ was an outgrowth of our first cohesion chapter (Burlingame et al., 2002), which recognized these definitional and empirical challenges and created a toolkit of group relationship measures (Strauss et al., 2008). The first study (Johnson et al, 2005) created the empirical foundation for the GQ by estimating the correlations of four commonly used measures of the group relationship (group climate, cohesion, alliance, and empathy) from this toolkit. The empirical findings of this study supported three relationship quality factors that capture the affective (*positive bond, negative*

Table 6.1. Cohesion Measures with a Strong Presence in the Cohesion–Outcome Meta-Analysis

Measure	Frequency Used in Meta-Analysis	Common Cohesion Elements Assessed	Unique Elements Assessed
Group Climate Questionnaire (MacKenzie, 1981, 1983)	16	• *Engaged*: degree of self-disclosure, cohesion and work orientation in group • *Conflict*: interpersonal conflict and distrust	• *Avoiding*: degree to which individuals rely on the other group members or leaders, avoiding responsibility for their own change process [a]
Gross (1957) Cohesion Scale Revised (Lieberman et al., 1973)	9	• Group fit, perceived inclusion, attraction to group activities, likability of members, and how well the group works together	
Group Cohesion (Piper et al., 1983)	7	Member–member: • *Positive qualities*: likability, trust, and ease of communication • *Personal compatibility*: attraction, similarity, and desire for personal friendship • *Significance as a group member*: personal importance Member–leader: • *Positive qualities*: likability, trust, attraction, and ease of communication • *Dissatisfaction with leader's role*: discontent with style, communication, and level of personal disclosure • *Personal compatibility*: similarity and desire for friendship	
Group Atmosphere Scale (Silbergeld et al., 1975)	5	• *Group cohesion*: Autonomy, affiliation, involvement, insight, spontaneity, support, and clarity • Aggression	• *Submission*: group conformity • Order, Practicality, and Variety contribute to other aspects of perceived environment. Authors did not define these scales.

Group Environment Scale (Moos, 1986)	3	◆ *Relationships within the group*: cohesion, leader support, and expressiveness ◆ *Personal growth of group members*: independence, task orientation, self-discovery, and anger and aggression ◆ *System maintenance and system change*: order and organization, leader control, and innovation	◆ How the individual is feeling about himself or herself in the group (ex: spontaneous/ hesitant, impulsive/self-controlled, inferior/superior, etc.)
Stuttgarter Bogen (Czogalik & Koeltzow, 1987)	3	◆ *Emotional relatedness*: sense of relatedness with the group (ex: understood/misunderstood, comfortable/ uncomfortable)	
Therapeutic Factors Inventory- Cohesion Subscale (Lese & MacNair-Semands, 2000)	3	◆ Group's investment and commitment perceived by member's sense of belonging and experience of acceptance, trust and cooperation in the group	
Harvard Community Health Plan Group Cohesiveness Scale (Budman et al., 1987)	2	• *Fragmentation vs. global cohesiveness*: withdrawal and self-absorption vs. interest and involvement; mistrust vs. trust; disruption vs. cooperation; abusiveness vs. expressed caring; unfocused vs. focused	• Focuses on the group as a whole. • Observer ratings, rather than self-report.

[a] The GCQ-Avoiding scale has psychometric difficulties (low internal consistency and failure to load onto the factor structures) that have led us to recommend that it should not be scored or interpreted for clinical use (Burlingame et al., 2006; McClendon & Burlingame, 2010).

relationship) and work (*positive work*) facets of the group relationships. It also crossed these quality factors with three structural relationship factors (member–member, member–group, and member–leader) to capture the multiple alliances. A second study (Bormann & Strauss, 2007) collected data from inpatient psychodynamic groups and found the same three relationship quality factors but also found greater support for the structural components (member–member, member–leader, and member–group). A third study reported a similar two-dimensional model that varied by stage of treatment (Bakali et al., 2009). These three studies led to an item-reduction process to identify a subset of "practice-friendly" items that would provide leaders with feedback about the relationship perceptions of group members (Gleave et al., 2017).

The GQ is a 30-item self-report measure of the quality of therapeutic relationship in groups (Burlingame et al., 2017) developed by an international cooperation between the United States and Germany (Strauss et al., 2008). Empirically derived items are responded to by group members using a 7-point, Likert-type scale from 1 (*not true at all*) to 7 (*very true*). The scale assesses three quality subscales: Positive Bond (13 items: e.g., "The group leaders were friendly and warm toward me"; "I felt that I could trust the other group members during today's session"), Positive Work (8 items: e.g., "The group leaders and I agree on what is important to work on"; "The other group members and I agree about the things I will need to do in therapy"), and Negative Relationship (9 items: e.g., "The members were distant and withdrawn from each other"; "There was friction and anger between members"). The measure yields a score for each of the three scales but not a total score. All three subscales have good internal consistency, with Positive Bond ranging from .79 to .92, Positive Work ranging from .85 to .91, and Negative Relationship ranging from .87 to .86 (Chapman et al., 2012; Krogel et al., 2013; Thayer, 2012). The GQ items are organized by three structural dimensions: member–leader, member–member, and member–group. The GQ demonstrates criterion validity, with acceptable correlations with the Working Alliance Inventory, GCQ, TFI, and Empathy Scale (Thayer & Burlingame, 2014). The 30-item GQ factor structure and criterion validity has now been supported in several psychometric studies, which are summarized in Table 6.2.

The three GQ subscales have clarified mixed findings in previous studies, addressed weakness found in other measures, and been used to suggest group composition guidelines (Kivlighan et al, 2017). Indeed, one of the landmark studies described later found that leaders can use GQ feedback to reverse relationship failure in group members. In short, the group relationship literature has begun to move away from a simple correlation between cohesion and outcome measures to providing group leaders with guidelines for group composition along with interventions to reduce relationship failure.

CLINICAL EXAMPLES

The multidimensional complexity of group cohesion makes it impossible to provide a single concrete example. However, our model of the relationship quality and

Table 6.2. Descriptive Information about Group Questionnaire Psychometric Studies

Study	Populations	N	Groups	Instruments
Johnson et al. (2005)	Counseling center; nonclinical	662	120[a]	Group Climate Questionnaire; Therapeutic Factors Inventory; Working Alliance Inventory; Empathy Scale
Bormann & Strauss (2007)	European inpatient	438	67	Group Climate Questionnaire; Therapeutic Factors Inventory; Working Alliance Inventory; Empathy Scale
Bormann et al. (2011)	European inpatient	498	64	Group Questionnaire
Chapman et al. (2012)	Counseling center; SMI inpatient	106	18[a]	Group Questionnaire; Severe Outcome Questionnaire; Outcome Questionnaire 45
Krogel et al. (2013)	Counseling center; nonclinical; SMI inpatient	485	NA	Group Climate Questionnaire; Therapeutic Factors Inventory; Working Alliance Inventory
Thayer (2014)	Counseling center	290	64 [a]	Group Questionnaire; Group Climate Questionnaire; Therapeutic Factors Questionnaire; Working Alliance Inventory
Total		2,479	202 [a]	

Note. NA = not available.

[a] Group membership used in analysis.

Table 6.3. Group Relationship Constructs Conceptually Assessed by Group Questionnaire

Relationship Structure			
Relationship Quality	Member–Member	Member–Leader	Member–Group
Positive Bond	Cohesion	Alliance	Climate
Positive Work	Task/Goals	Task/Goals	None
Negative Relationship	Empathic Failure	Alliance Rupture	Conflict

structure (Table 6.3) provides a practice-friendly framework to recognize therapeutic relationships in group.

We selected a transcript from Session 14 of a 15-session group therapy (Burlingame & Barlow, 1996). The segment begins with a leader acknowledging that the next session will be their last meeting and then probes regarding the work achieved over the course of the group. Group members do not verbally respond to the work probe but instead focus on Positive Bond. The quality and structure categories from Table 6.3 are identified in italics.

Leader to group: This is our next to last session. In thinking about our group I wondered if anyone would care to speak to how they met their goals over the past 14 weeks? *[leader–member/group, Positive Work probe]*

Mary to leader/group: Well . . . I think we've all had fun. I know I have. In fact, we talked after you left last night. We're gonna keep our group going after the last session (smiles at leader.) *[member–group, Positive Work]*

Pete to group: I've had this rotten headache all day . . . it would have been real easy to stay home from almost anything . . . but not from our group. *[member–group, Positive Bond]*

Mary to group: Yeah, today as I thought about coming to group I knew that Steve was going to make me laugh, everybody else in the group is so good to give me their advice and support, and I enjoy everybody so much. *[member–member and member–group, Positive Bond]*

Leader to group: That's great. I really think every single person needs this kind of a positive association, maybe not in a formal setting like this, but somehow or another like this, we need it. We really do. Every human being needs it. *[leader–member/group, Positive Bond]*

The relationship quality and structure model also accounts for the multiplicity of relationships in the group. This two-dimensional model allows a leader to consider multiple aspects of the therapeutic relationship as he or she plans interventions. The following dialogue includes all three relationship structures (member–member, member–leader, and member–group) and begins with a leader probe regarding a conflict that happened at the end of the last group.

Leader to Steve: Steve, you okay? You seemed upset at the end of our last group meeting. *[leader–member, Negative Relationship probe]*

Steve: I need to apologize to you because I was a little bit abrupt with you last week and I . . . thought that was kinda tacky, uh . . . even though I said it was none of you damned business. (Group laughs) . . . But uh, what I meant was I'm not handling it well and, therefore, I can't share anything with you. I have nothing to give (laughs) because I . . . uh, I'm not handling it well. [*member–leader, Negative Relationship*]

Leader: You've done a lot of good work over the past few months but right now you feel like you've got nothing to give—that you're no longer handling it well. [*leader–member, Positive Work*]

Steve: I also feel badly that Susan is not here today. I miss her. [*member–member, Positive Bond*; later interaction will reveal an underlying *member–member, Negative Relationship*] I've been thinking about her and her crisis a great deal, and I almost called you [leader] up to get her phone number. I know we're not supposed to interact outside . . . (Steve goes on to tell the group what he has been thinking about Susan's situation. As they are talking Susan comes into the group and the whole group cheers when she enters.) [*member–member and group–member, Positive Bond*]

Leader to Susan: We wanted you to be here so bad, some of us were thinking that you had a crisis and we were worried. [*leader–member, Positive Bond*] (Susan explains why she is late.)

Steve to Susan: Well, I'm glad you're here . . . because I've been worried about you. (Steve goes on to inquire about Susan's situation and tell her all his thoughts about it. This goes on for quite a while.) [*member–member, Positive Bond*]

Susan to Steve: Thank you. The reason I tore out of work so fast to get here is because I knew I'd get the reception I just got. (Susan starts to cry and group laughs lightly, leader pats Susan on the shoulder and Susan pats Mary on the knee.) [*member–member and member–group, Positive Bond*]

Steve to Susan: I apologize for being abrupt with you last week. That was tactless. I'm sorry. [*member–member, Negative Relationship*]

Susan to Steve: It didn't bother me, but I accept your apology. It means a lot to me that you'd check in with me on that. [*member–member, Positive Bond*]

In this dialogue, Steve is interacting with a notable level of interpersonal risk with the group leader. When Susan arrives, we see multiple levels of Positive Bond, which undoubtedly supports Steve's ability to handle a second Negative Relationship concern from the last session with Susan.

The next segment occurs at the end of the group session with continued evidence of member–group cohesion as another group member reinitiates discussion about continuing to meet after the group has formally ended:

Mary to group: I would like to see us work more on what we discussed last week and that's to continue it all until it finishes. I really am very interested in that . . . for your information . . . sort of a, you know, forming after the group [*member–member and member–group, Positive Work and Positive Bond*]

Susan to Mary (leaning on her shoulder): I don't know if we can live without each other [dramatically]. (Group laughs.) [*member–member, Positive Bond*]

Mary to group: Uh, yeah . . . uh once a month or something like that or whatever . . . I'm easy . . . but just to get together and see how we're doing and talk it over and support each other. [*member–member and member–group, Positive Bond*]

LANDMARK STUDIES

We have noted three important improvements in cohesion–outcome research since our last review. Each of these areas has generated a small number of programmatic studies. For each topic, we have selected exemplary studies—not only methodologically rigorous and creative but also advancing research on the therapeutic relationship. These landmark studies highlight how (a) groups influence a member's perception of cohesion and outcome, (b) member attachment style moderates the cohesion–outcome relationship, and (c) relationship feedback to leaders can reverse deterioration and failure in group members.

Groups Influence Member Cohesion and Outcome

A clinical axiom is that the group as a social microcosm influences members' experience of the therapeutic process and ultimately their treatment outcome. Indeed, some have argued that this is the cardinal therapeutic principle explaining change in group treatment (Yalom & Leszcz, 2005).

The degree to which the group influences its members can be estimated by the intraclass correlation coefficient, which has been viewed as a methodological improvement in group research. When the effect of group's influence is not statistically controlled, group treatment effects can be overestimated (Janis et al., 2016), leading to spurious conclusions. To avoid overestimating the effect of treatment, researchers have recommended controlling for the influence of the group, such as using multilevel models where group is treated as a random factor (Janis et al., 2016). A limitation of our last cohesion–outcome meta-analysis was that most studies did not assess or control for the influence of the group on member's cohesion or outcome scores, which, in turn, could have inflated the effect sizes. Several studies in the new meta-analysis used multilevel models or related statistical practices to control for group influence, which improves the accuracy of the effect sizes we used to update our previous meta-analysis. Unfortunately, even with the updated and improved analysis, no information is provided on how the group affects an individual member because the statistical methods only estimate group influence for aggregated member data.

The actor–partner interdependence model (Kenny & Garcia, 2012) addresses this limitation by providing insight into how a specific group affects individual members. It does so by examining the relation between a member's cohesion score (actor effect) and the aggregated cohesion scores of the remaining group members (partner effect). Past actor–partner research has found that when there is more similarity between an individual member and aggregated member cohesion scores, greater reduction in symptom distress occurs (Lo Coco et al., 2012). This finding has been used to argue for the importance of member conformity to the group norms and the influence of the group on individual members. Although an improvement upon multilevel modeling, interdependence model research is still limited because it cannot determine the direction of influence. In other words, actor–partner similarity could result from the group influencing a member or the member influencing the group.

Our first landmark study enters the landscape here. Gullo and colleagues (2014) tested partner (group) influence by showing that changes in an actor's (group member) cohesion score was longitudinally related to previous partners' cohesion scores. This was done using a cross-lagged analysis that examined the relation between partner (group) cohesion scores from an earlier group session and an actor's (group member) cohesion score at a subsequent group session. After controlling for an actor's earlier cohesion score, if a partner's cohesion score at an earlier session was related to an actor cohesion score at a subsequent session, evidence existed to support that the group was influencing a member's cohesion score. They predicted better outcome when a member's cohesion score was positively influenced by the group (actor–partner relationship) and worse outcome when there was no group influence or no actor–partner similarity.

The study focused on 73 obese or overweight group members who participated in 12-session groups. The therapeutic relationship was assessed at Session 3, 6, and 12 by the Group Cohesion Scale and the California Psychotherapy Alliance Scales–Group (CALPAS-G; Gaston & Marmar, 1994). Pre–post outcome was assessed on an obesity well-being scale and a symptom measure. Small but significant support was found for the partner's perception of the group's cohesion in an earlier session being positively related to a group member's personal cohesion score in a subsequent session. More specifically, for "every unit of change . . . to group as a whole in the previous session, the group member had a .20 change in alliance to the group as a whole in the current session" (Gullo et al., 2014, p. 309). This result suggests that group members changed their perception of cohesion in subsequent sessions to match their group. Moreover, better outcome (less symptom distress) resulted when there was a positive actor–partner cohesion relation, but this effect was even smaller than the actor–partner relation. Interestingly, poorer outcomes were not related to a negative actor–partner relations.

We picked this study as landmark for two reasons. First, it replicates research that has used repeated measures of group relationship to show that increases in cohesion over time can be explained by both the individual member and the influence of the group as a whole. However, this research established correlation; the first of three requirements to causal influence. Second, the Gullo et al. (2014) study constitutes a longitudinal cross-lagged design that addresses the second requirement for a possible causal relation: the group influence preceded member cohesion. The last requirement—ruling out likely confounds—awaits future research. As noted, most of the cohesion literature relies upon a single assessment point that only fulfills the first requirement for causation: covariation. The Gullo et al. study is rare in its attempt to use observational data to begin to build a causal model for group influences on member cohesion.

Attachment Style Moderates the Cohesion–Outcome Link

Two earlier studies determined that member interpersonal style moderated the cohesion–outcome relation (Dinger & Schauenburg, 2010; Schauenburg et al., 2001). Patients who described themselves as "too cold" posted a positive linear cohesion-outcome relation (higher cohesion = better outcome), but patients who described themselves as "too friendly" posted the opposite result. We raised the question, "Could a member's interpersonal style explain past mixed cohesion-outcome findings?" We then answered: "Unfortunately, the jury is out on this question" (Burlingame et al., 2010, p. 123).

Since our last meta-analysis, Tasca and colleagues (2005) have superbly examined how the attachment style of group members might moderate group treatment outcomes and the cohesion-outcome relation. We have selected one of their studies to illustrate this work.

A 16-week group psychodynamic interpersonal psychotherapy (Tasca et al., 2005) was provided to 102 women diagnosed with binge eating disorder. Cohesion was measured weekly via the GCQ and outcomes assessed pre–post therapy (Gallagher, Tasca, Ritchie, Balfour, & Bissada, 2014). Attachment style was assessed using the need for approval subscale of the Attachment Styles Questionnaire (Feeney et al., 1994), and homogenously composed groups were comprised of either high or low attachment anxiety patients. The primary hypotheses were that (a) cohesion would increase over time, (b) cohesion would be higher in the high-anxiety patients at Session 1, (c) rate of cohesion change would be more rapid for the high-anxiety patients, (d) increased cohesion would be related to outcome, and (e) the high-anxiety patients would have a larger cohesion–outcome relation.

Gallagher, Tasca, Ritchie, Balfour, and Bissada (2014) found that cohesion increased over time, but neither the level nor the rate of cohesion change differed between the high- and low-anxiety patients. Surprisingly, increased cohesion was not related to the frequency of binge eating (hypothesis *d*), but this was explained by an interaction with the anxiety condition. Higher cohesion was associated with better binge eating outcomes for the high attachment condition; however, higher cohesion was not associated with better outcomes for the low attachment anxiety condition. High attachment anxiety describes individuals who have a high need for approval. The authors suggest that "experiencing a growing sense of cohesiveness may offer a secure base to those high in attachment anxiety and need for approval, leading to a decrease in the frequency of binge eating" (p. 48).

We selected this study as landmark because it extends and clarifies the earlier findings by repeatedly assessing cohesion, experimentally manipulating attachment anxiety, and clarifying the cohesion–outcome link. The results suggest that patients with greater affiliation needs may benefit most from an increasing affiliative or cohesive group experience, hence the interaction between attachment anxiety and the cohesion–outcome link.

Cohesion Feedback to Leaders Reduces Treatment Failures

Our final landmark study reflects the use of routine outcome monitoring (ROM) in group treatment. ROM systems repeatedly assess clients with an outcome measure, typically on a session by session basis, and then use these data to identify cases at risk for poor outcome. ROM systems are now a recognized evidence-based practice (Wampold, 2015). The feedback and/or alerts provided in a ROM system constitute practice-based evidence and allow clinicians to integrate data in real time to make therapeutic decisions. Unfortunately, until recently, all of the ROM studies have focused on individual and couple therapy.

Four studies testing the effect of ROM systems in group therapy have now been published (Burlingame et al., 2018; Davidsen et al., 2017; Schuman et al., 2015; Slone et al., 2015). However, only one study experimentally tested the independent effect of providing the group leader with feedback on the therapeutic relationship (Burlingame et al., 2018).

Given the supportive evidence for progress feedback, the primary goal of the group ROM study was to hold progress feedback constant and to examine how adding relationship feedback affects relationship deterioration and failure. The group relationship was assessed by the GQ, which provides alerts on relationship deterioration (change alert) from the previous group session on the three quality subscales: Positive Bond, Positive Work, and Negative Relationship. The GQ also alerts therapists when a member's score drops to a relationship failure level (status alert), which was defined as the 10th percentile or lower using population specific norms (Janis et al., 2018). Leaders were trained to immediately intervene when presented with a relationship deterioration alert. In three treatment sites, 430 group members were randomly assigned to one of two experimental arms: therapeutic relationship and outcome feedback (GQ + Outcome Questionnaire-45 [OQ-45]; Lambert et al., 2013) or progress only feedback (OQ-45). Seventeen group leaders simultaneously ran 30 pairs of groups that were randomly assigned to these arms, with 374 members attending 4 or more sessions of a group that typically averaged 12 sessions (average attendance = 9.5 sessions).

Longitudinal change (slope) on relationship and outcome measures revealed that the quality of the therapy relationship significantly increased over time and the patient's distress significantly decreased. When these slopes were correlated, the relationship scores were significantly correlated with the outcome measure with values approximating those reported in our last cohesion–outcome meta-analysis ($r = .25$; 95% confidence interval [CI] = .17–.32).

The study also tested the immediate effect of feedback with a three-session lagged analysis similar to the Gullo et al. (2014) study described earlier. The three-session lag began with a target session that was identified when a member signaled with either a relationship deterioration or failure alert. The analysis then compared the next two sessions on the alerting scale to determine if leaders providing feedback were able to reverse the relationship deterioration and failure compared to their no-feedback groups. Leaders receiving GQ feedback did indeed reverse the course of relationship deterioration within two sessions of receiving an alert.

We chose this study as landmark for two reasons. First, it is the first group ROM study to experimentally test the effect of providing group leaders with relationship feedback in real-time. Second, we selected this study because research has shown group leaders' inability to accurately predict the relationship status of their group members (Chapman et al., 2012). This and additional studies underscore the value of providing relationship feedback since it is one of the best predictors of outcome in group treatment.

RESULTS OF PREVIOUS META-ANALYSES

Our last meta-analysis located 40 studies published across a 40-year span that tested the cohesion–outcome relation. Slightly less than half (43%) of the studies posted a significant correlation between cohesion and client improvement with an average weighted correlation of $r = .25$. Total number of patients in the meta-analysis was 3,323.

Nineteen possible moderators were tested, grouped by four categories: study, leader, member, and group characteristics. Five of these 19 moderators explained between-study variability in the weighted cohesion–outcome correlation.

1. Age of group members was negatively correlated ($r = -.63$) with the cohesion–outcome relation, suggesting that younger members posted higher cohesion–outcome correlations.
2. Leader theoretical orientation produced significantly different correlations: interpersonal ($r = .58$), psychodynamic ($r = -.25$), and cognitive behavioral ($r = .18$).
3. Group structure was relevant: interactive groups that were less structured had a higher correlation ($r = .38$) than problem-specific groups that focused on a common theme.
4. Group size was also relevant: groups with five to nine members posted the highest correlation ($r = .35$) compared to groups with fewer than five members or more than nine ($r = .16$).
5. Group length was a factor: groups lasting between 12 and 19 sessions had higher correlations ($r = .36$) than groups with fewer than 12 sessions ($r = .17$); however, groups with 20 or more sessions posted a similar correlation ($r = .31$) to those in the 12 to 19 range.

We concluded our meta-analysis by noting that the average weighted correlation between cohesion–outcome was comparable to relationship variables studied in individual therapy and that the dominant theoretical orientations all produced significant correlations. Thus cohesion appeared to be an evidence-based process in group treatment.

META-ANALYTIC REVIEW

In our initial meta-analysis (Burlingame et al., 2011a, 2011b) we relied upon five published group therapy meta-analyses to develop inclusion criteria. These criteria included groups that were (a) comprised of at least three members; (b) meeting for the purpose of counseling, psychotherapy, or personal growth, (c) using at least one quantitative measure of cohesion and outcome; (d) producing data that allowed the calculation of effect sizes as weighted correlations; and (e) reported in the English language.

Search Strategy

Our 2011 meta-analysis identified potential articles by searching PsycINFO, MedLine, and Google Scholar for publications between January 1969 and May 2009. A total of 1,506 abstracts were retrieved using the following search terms: group psychotherapy, group therapy, support groups, group counseling, cohesion, group cohesion, cohesiveness, and group climate. Each abstract was reviewed for fit with the inclusion criteria, and, if deemed promising, the article was retrieved and underwent a full text review. A total of 24 articles were included using this method. Next, the reference sections of these 24 articles were reviewed and 42 unduplicated studies were identified and reviewed resulting in 6 studies being included. Finally, six of the most frequently used cohesion measures (GES, Piper's Cohesion Questionnaire Scale, GCQ, Group Atmosphere Scale, Shulz's Cohesion Questionnaire, Gross Cohesion Scale; cf. Table 6.1) across the 30 identified studies were searched using Google Scholar, yielding 1,027 abstracts. Ten additional studies were added, yielding a final data set of 40 studies.

Our updated meta-analysis followed a similar database search using a 2009 to 2016 time frame, which yielded 625 abstracts. These were reviewed using the same inclusion criteria noted earlier with one addition—groups had to last four or more sessions (see Burlingame et al., 2013). We eliminated 560 papers during the screening process and then conducted a full text review of 65 studies. Our previous meta-analysis focused upon estimating effect sizes using studies that assessed cohesion at a single point in time, and we identified 15 studies that fit this analysis. We also identified 12 studies that repeatedly assessed cohesion or studied interactions (for reference, all of these are included in the Landmark Studies section). The reasons for eliminating the remaining 38 papers included the absence of an outcome measure ($k = 14$), no statistical comparison between cohesion and outcome ($k = 9$), focus on alliance instead of cohesion (7), the absence of a therapeutic focus (5), and incomplete data to compute effect size (3).

In all, we identified 55 studies of group therapy, a sample of 6,055 patients, that investigated the cohesion–outcome association. A summary of study characteristics is provided in Table 6.4. The majority of studies were published after 2000 (median of 2005) although a fifth ($k = 12$) were published prior to 1990 capturing several classic papers (e.g., Braaten, 1989; Budman et al., 1989; Roether & Peters, 1972; Yalom et al., 1967). The average group lasted 22 sessions, was comprised of young adults (average age = 36), and was guided by a cognitive-behavioral (CBT), psychodynamic,

Table 6.4. Characteristics of Studies Included in Meta-Analysis

Variable	%	$\underline{N}$
Number of studies		55
Year of publication (median)		2005
Overall number of clients		6,055
Average age of clients		36.0
Average number of sessions		21.8
Theoretical Orientation of Group		
Cognitive/behavioral	35	23
Psychodynamic/existential	23	15
Humanistic/interpersonal/supportive	20	13
Eclectic	6	4
Unknown	15	10
Primary Diagnosis		
Informal	32	17
Anxiety disorder	13	7
Mood disorder	11	6
Substance disorder	8	4
Eating disorder	6	3
Personality disorder	8	4
Medical condition (not somatic disorder)	4	2
Others or unknown	19	10
General psychological distress	26	20
Depression	20	15
Anxiety	18	14
Quality of life/general well being	12	9
Interpersonal problems / relationships	13	10
Self-esteem	7	5
Others	5	4
Country		
North America	46	25
Europe	26	14
Canada	18	10
Australia	11	6
Location		
University counseling center	2	1
Clinic or private practice	7	4
Hospital	36	20
Community mental health center	7	4
Classroom setting	9	5
Others or unknown	38	21
Setting		
Inpatient	18	10
Outpatient	67	37

Table 6.4. Continued

Variable	%	_N_
Mixed or unknown	15	8
Format		
Psychoeducation (structured, didactic instruction, topic-oriented)	9	5
Counseling/therapy (decrease symptoms through therapy)	79	42
Task (group problem-solving, accomplish a goal, non-therapy)	2	1
Support (12 steps, cancer survivor group, Alcoholics Anonymous)	4	2
Analog (pretended group for study, not for real symptoms)	4	2
Mixture of counseling/therapy with task	2	1
Process		
No description in the study	89	47
Described how processes would be enhanced	11	6
Leadership of Group		
Single leader	46	16
Co-led by two leaders	49	17
Mixed (some single and some co-led)	5	2

or humanistic therapist. The vast majority of groups were therapeutic, followed by psychoeducation and support.

Coding and Analysis

We selected and coded 20 variables derived from four main categories: study characteristics, leader characteristics, member characteristics, and group characteristics. Many of these variables have been found to moderate outcome in previous group therapy meta-analyses. The largest numbers of coded variables were associated with the group itself. Specifically, we were interested in the degree of structure and group member interaction associated with the group treatment given the recent emphasis on manual-based treatments. The variables are as follows:

- Five study characteristics: year of publication, attrition, type of cohesion, type of outcome measure, when cohesion was assessed.
- Three leader characteristics: experience, orientation, single leader versus co-led groups.
- Four member characteristics: gender, age, diagnosis, treatment setting.
- Eight group characteristics: specific leader interventions to increase cohesion, groups that allowed greater interaction among members, type of group (psychoeducational, psychotherapy, personal growth), homogeneous (identical or similar diagnoses and presenting problems) versus heterogeneous composition, group size (small, medium, and large groups), session length, treatment setting, and number of group sessions (dose of therapy).

The original meta-analysis used eight raters (one graduate student and seven undergraduate students) trained on a codebook using studies not included in the analysis. They achieved an 85% criterion level of agreement with high interrater reliability (kappa = .73). After achieving this criterion, raters were paired and independently coded the same articles that were contained in the meta-analysis. Complete agreement was required with discrepancies resolved by the graduate student and the senior author. In the update, the senior author (GB) trained a single undergraduate rater using an identical process and the two independently rated articles. Interrater agreement of dually coded articles was very high (97%), and the small number of discrepancies (3%) were resolved by the senior author.

In this analysis, a number of studies used several outcome and cohesion measures, creating multiple cohesion–outcome correlations from a single study. When this occurred, we averaged the values (weighted by n) so that only one correlation per study was included. Following calculation of the aggregate correlation, we examined the degree of heterogeneity in the results across studies using the Q statistic (Berkeljon & Baldwin, 2009). If heterogeneity was found, variability among the study's effect size mean would be higher than what would be expected from sampling error. Thus, when heterogeneity exists, moderator results are ultimately interpreted with more confidence. A random effects model was used; random effects assume that studies are selected from a population of studies and that variability between studies is the result of sampling error. This analytic model is recommended as a more conservative test (Hedges & Vevea, 1998; Lipsey & Wilson, 2001).

Results

Past reviews have concluded that group cohesion demonstrates a positive relation with patient improvement in nearly every published report (Tschuschke & Dies, 1994). Our 2002 narrative review concluded that approximately 80% of published studies demonstrated a statistically significant positive association between group cohesion and treatment outcome (Burlingame et al., 2002).

The results from our meta-analysis (with each study depicted in Table 6.5) paint a more complex picture of the cohesion–outcome association. Slightly more than half (53%, $n = 29$) of the studies posted a statistically significant correlation between cohesion and patient improvement, with an additional three studies having p values in the trend range ($p < .10$). The weighted aggregate correlation for the 55 included studies was statistically significant, $r = .26$ (95% CI = .20–31, $p < .01$), reflecting a moderate effect ($d = .56$) between cohesion and outcome. The 95% CI (.20–.31) for our updated meta-analysis falls within the CI of our previous meta-analysis (.17–.32). Heterogeneity of effect sizes was significant ($Q = 26.84$, $df = 54$, $p < .001$) and high with $I^2 = 79.3\%$, which supports exploration of effect size variance with moderator analyses. However, it is noteworthy that 73% ($k = 11$) of the new studies (identified with an $^+$ in Table 6.5) produced a statistically significant relation compared to 43% reported in our last meta-analysis. This suggests stronger support for the cohesion–outcome relation in more recent research. Thus it is unlikely that the size of the

Table 6.5. Sample Size, Average Weighted Correlations, Cohen's *d*, and Lower/ Upper Limits

Study	Sample Size	Weighted Correlation	Lower Limit	Upper Limit	Cohen's d	Lower Limit	Upper Limit
Antonuccio et al. (1987)	106	.00	−.19	.19	.00	−.39	.39
Beutal et al. (2006)	134	.23**	.07	.39	.48**	.13	.83
Bonsaksen et al. (2013)[+]	80	.19[T]	−.03	.39	.53*	.08	.98
Braaten (1989)	110	.21*	.02	.38	.43*	.06	.80
Budman et al. (1989)	90	.63**	.48	.74	1.61**	1.12	2.10
Crino & Dyokvucic (2010)[+]	27	.17	−.18	.49	.33	−.45	1.11
Crowe & Grenyer (2008)	30	.20	−.17	.52	.40	−.34	1.14
Etlink et al. (2015)[+]	128	.30**	.13	.45	1.62**	1.21	2.03
Falloon (1981)	51	.16	−.13	.41	.32	−.25	.89
Flowers et al. (1981)	16	.56*	.09	.83	1.36*	.18	2.54
Gillaspy et al. (2002)	49	.19	−.10	.44	.38	−.19	.95
Grabhorn, et al (2002)	48	.18	−.11	.44	.37	−.22	.96
Hilbert et al. (2007)	138	.24**	.07	.39	.49**	.16	.82
Hoberman et al (1988)	42	.38*	.08	.61	.81	.16	1.46
Hornsey et al. (2012)[+]	30	.29	−.07	.59	.62	−.14	1.38
Hurley (1989)	374	.70**	.64	.75	1.96**	1.71	2.21
Hurley (1997)	678	.35**	.28	.41	.75**	.59	.91
Joyce et al. (2007)	107	.09	−.10	.28	.19	−.20	.58
Kelly et al. (2015)[+]	124	.28**	.11	.43	.58**	.23	.93
Kipne et al. (2002)	12	.00	−.57	.57	.00	−1.25	1.25
Kirchmann et al. (2009)[+]	289	.25**	.13	.35	.51**	.27	.75
Kivilghan & Lilly (1997)	30	.36*	−.01	.63	.76*	.00	1.52
Lecomte et al. (2015)[+]	66	.43**	.21	.61	.94**	.43	1.45
Levenson & MacGowen (2004)	61	.33**	.09	.54	.70*	.17	1.23
Lipman et al. (2007)	38	.15	−.18	.45	.30	−.37	.97
Lorentzen et al. (2004)	12	.30	−.33	.75	.63	−.64	1.90
MacKenzie & Tschuschke (1993	16	.46[T]	−.05	.78	1.04	−.08	2.16
Marmarosh et al. (2005)	102	.54**	.38	.66	1.27**	.84	1.70
Marziali et al. (1997)	17	.19	−.32	.61	.38	−.64	1.40
May et al. (2008)	132	.18*	.01	.34	.36*	.01	.71
Norton & Kazantzis (2016)[+]	373	.14*	.04	.24	.28*	.08	.48
Norton et al. (2008)	54	.30*	.03	.52	.62	.07	1.17
Oei & Brown (2006)	162	−.03	−.19	.12	−.07	−.38	.24
Ogrodniczuk & Piper (2003)	107	.22*	.03	.39	.45*	.06	.84
Ogrodniczuk (2006)	75	.22[T]	−.01	.42	.44	−.03	.91
Ogrodniczuk et al. (2005)	39	.42**	.13	.65	.94**	.25	1.63
Owne et al. (2013)[+]	126	.30**	.13	.45	.63**	.28	.98
Paulus et al. (2015)[+]	221	.38**	.26	.48	.81**	.54	1.08

(*continued*)

Table 6.5. Continued

Study	Sample Size	Weighted Correlation	Lower Limit	Upper Limit	Cohen's d	Lower Limit	Upper Limit
Petry et al. (2011)[+]	239	.19*	.04	.33	.39**	.14	.64
Pisetsky et al. (2015)[+]	190	.18*	.04	.32	.37*	.08	.66
Quirk et al. (2013)[+]	105	.28**	.09	.44	.58**	.19	.97
Ratto & Hurley (1995)	33	.23	−.12	.53	.48	−.23	1.19
Rice & Tonigan (2012)[+]	66	.20	−.05	.42	.65*	.14	1.16
Rice (2001)	59	.00	−.26	.26	.00	−.51	.51
Roether & Peters (1972)	51	−.18	−.43	.10	−.37	−.94	.20
Rugel & Barry (1990)	28	.10	−.28	.46	.20	−.56	.96
Ryum et al. (2009)	27	.15	−.24	.50	.31	−.47	1.09
Shechtman & Mor (2010)[+]	164	.22*	.02	.41	.16	−.15	.47
Taft et al. (2003)	107	.18*	−.01	.36	.37	−.02	.76
Taube-Schiff et al. (2007)	34	.43*	.10	.67	.94*	.21	1.67
Tschuschke & Dies (1994)	16	.72**	.34	.89	2.06**	.77	3.35
van Andel et al. (2003)	38	.19	−.14	.48	.39	−.28	1.06
Woody & Adesky (2002)	48	.17	−.12	.43	.33	−.26	.92
Wright & Duncan (1986)	27	.13	−.26	.49	.27	−.51	1.05
Yalom et al. (1967)	25	.11	−.30	.48	.22	−.60	1.04
Random effect size		.26**	.20	.31	.56**	.43	.69

[+]new studies. *$p < .05$, **$p < .01$.

correlation was overestimated in our past meta-analysis due to studies that did not control for intragroup dependency since most recent studies statistically controlled for group influence.

Orwin's fail-safe N to address the file-drawer problem estimated that 1,571 studies with a correlation of .01 would be needed to nullify our weighted aggregate correlation of $r = .26$ and 107 studies with a correlation of .1. This seems unlikely since less than 10% of our 55 studies met both criteria. We created a funnel plot with effect sizes, as shown in Table 6.5, to check for publication bias. These were plotted using the standard error as the y-axis. Absence of bias is indicated by a higher number of studies symmetrically falling near the average and within the 95% CI lines.

There is some evidence for heterogeneity with a small but equivalent number of studies falling outside either side of the 95% CI line (Figure 6.1). Interestingly, neither sample size nor cohesion measure explain these heterogeneous effect sizes. Studies with small samples produced both large (Tschuschke & Dies, 1994) and small (Kipnes et al., 2002) estimates. Similarly, the same measure of cohesion produced large (GCQ [Hurley]/GQ [Lecomte et al., 2015]) and small (GCQ [Rice, 2001]/GQ [Kipnes et al., 2002]) effect size estimates. The overall conclusion from 55 studies published across a 50-year span is that there was sufficient precision to produce a robust estimate of the relation between cohesion and outcome.

MEDIATORS AND MODERATORS

Few empirical studies examine moderator or mediator variables for the cohesion–outcome link (Hornsey et al., 2007), although recent studies have started to include them. Mediators have been proposed (e.g., member acceptance, support, self-disclosure, feedback), but there has been little progress in the literature due to the varied definitions and confounds with group cohesion (Hornsey et al., 2007). We have highlighted a few interesting moderators (attachment, group influence) in our landmark studies mentioned earlier. Interestingly, with the additional 15 new studies, one of the five moderators that significantly explained between-study cohesion–outcome differences (Figure 6.1) in our last analysis fell away (group size). Six moderators were found to be significant (type of outcome measure, leader interventions to increase cohesion, theoretical orientation, type of group, emphasis on group interaction, dose or number of group sessions). Each is described in more detail next.

Study Characteristics

Four of the study characteristics (publication year, attrition, cohesion measure, time of cohesion assessment) failed to explain variability in the average weighted cohesion–outcome effect sizes depicted in Figure 6.1. However, type of outcome measure was found to be a significant moderator (Table 6.6; $Q = 24.98$, $df = 9$, $p = < .01$). Higher weighted averages were found on both interpersonal and self-esteem measures (Inventory of Interpersonal Problems, Horowitz, Rosenberg, Baer, Ureno, & Villasenor, 1988; Rosenberg Self-Esteem Scale), but these results are heavily influenced

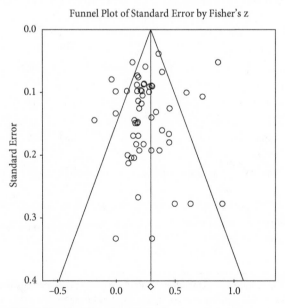

FIGURE 6.1   Funnel Plot of Standard Error by Fisher's Z.

Table 6.6. Weighted Correlations and Ranges by Cohesion and Outcome Measures

	Weight Correlation	Lower Limit	Upper Limit	Z Value	p Value	Times Used
Cohesion Measures						
Group Atmosphere Scale (Silbergeld et al., 1975)	.28	.15	.39	4.30	<.01	5
Group Cohesion (Piper et al., 1983)	.26	.13	.37	4.00	<.01	7
Group Environment Scale (Moos, 1986)	.10	--.06	.25	1.2	.23	3
Stuttgarter Bogen (Czogalik & Koeltzow, 1987)	.55	−.01	.85	1.91	.06	3
Harvard Community Health Plan Group Cohesiveness Scale (Budman et al., 1987)	.41	−.27	.82	1.20	.23	2
Group Climate Questionnaire (MacKenzie, 1981)	.26	.13	.39	3.88	<.01	16
Gross Cohesion Scale (Gross, 1957)	.26	.12	.38	3.54	<.01	9
Therapeutic Factors Inventory–Cohesion subscale (Lese & MacNair-Semands, 2000)	.26	.17	.34	5.35	<.01	3
Outcome Measures						
Outcome Questionnaire (Lambert et al., 2013)	.26	.11	.39	3.32	<.01	2
Inventory of Interpersonal Problems-Circumplex	.30	.21	.39	6.19	<.01	4
Therapy Project List-90 (Braaten, 1989)	.21	.07	.33	3.04	<.01	2
Rosenberg Self-Esteem Scale (Rosenberg, 1965)	.53	.41	.64	7.16	<.01	2
Profile of Mood States (McNair et al., 1981)	.32	.08	.53	2.59	.01	2
Beck Anxiety Inventory (Beck, 1988)	.13	.02	.23	2.65	.02	3
Beck Depression Inventory-II (Beck et al., 1996)	.25	.11	.39	3.32	<.01	11
Symptom Checklist (Derogatis, 1977)	.30	.14	.44	3.70	<.01	13

Note. Test of heterogeneity indicated that effect sizes did not vary significantly across cohesion measures ($Q = 6.10$, $df = 8$, $p = .64$) but varied across different outcome measures ($Q = 24.98$, $df = 9$, $p = < .01$).

by the two student growth group studies (Hurley, 1989; Kivlighan & Lilly, 1997). Thus it remains unclear how these outcome measures might operate in clinical populations, and caution is advised on overinterpreting this moderator. Two measures (Symptom Checklist and Beck Depression Inventory-II) that assess general psychiatric and depressive symptoms, respectively, were used in nearly half (44%) of the studies posting reliable values near the meta-analytic average. Thus the cohesion–outcome relation appears to be well supported when outcome is defined by general psychiatric and depressive symptoms. This conclusion finds further support in weighted correlations for similar measures that were used less frequently (e.g., OQ-45, Profile of Mood States). Moreover, since the Symptom Checklist and the Beck Depression Inventory-II were also two of the most frequently used instruments to evaluate the effectiveness of group psychotherapy, the generalizability to outcome appears sound.

Five cohesion measures produced a statistically significant weighted correlation (Table 6.6), but there were no reliable differences in the size of this correlation between measures ($Q = 6.10$, $df = 8$, $p = .64$). The conclusion to be drawn is that any of these five measures appear to be a reasonable choice for clinicians and researchers alike. However, the GCQ–Engaged continues to dominate the field; with only five-items it is a particularly practice-friendly choice.

Member Variables

None of the member variables (gender, age, diagnosis, treatment setting) explained clinically significant differences in the cohesion–outcome relation. The cohesion–outcome relation continues to be a reliable predictor in both inpatient and outpatient settings ($r = .28$ and $r = .25$, respectively). Furthermore, the positive association of group cohesion and client outcome was demonstrated across all three major diagnostic classifications: Axis I ($r = .22$), Axis II ($r = .44$), and V codes ($r = .29$).

Leader Variables

The majority of studies ($k = 33$) used either single (16) or co-led (17) groups, and there was no difference in weighted correlations for these two types of leadership ($r = .23$ and $r = .25$, respectively). There was a significant difference in the cohesion–outcome relation when examining the theoretical orientation of the group leader ($Q = 9.43$, $df = 4$, $p < .05$). Leaders espousing an interpersonal orientation posted the highest cohesion–outcome relation ($r = .48$, $k = 4$). Other theoretical orientations posted significant but lower values: psychodynamic ($r = .27$, $k = 9$), cognitive-behavior ($r = .22$, $k = 19$), supportive ($r = .22$, $k = 4$), and eclectic ($r = .22$, $k = 3$). In our last meta-analysis, only interpersonal, psychodynamic, and cognitive-behavioral therapies posted statistically significant cohesion–outcome correlations. The addition of 15 new studies to the analysis added two more group approaches, leading to the conclusion that there is sufficient evidence to consider cohesion as an evidence-based relationship factor for groups guided by interpersonal, psychodynamic, cognitive-behavioral, supportive, and eclectic orientations.

Group Variables

In the past, we (Fuhriman & Burlingame, 1994; Burlingame et al., 2004) have suggested that a true test of the cohesion–outcome relation would be to examine studies that emphasized the importance of cohesion as a therapeutic strategy and contrast them with studies that lacked this emphasis. If group cohesion is undervalued or neglected by a group leader, its presence would likely be diminished and perhaps attenuate its association with outcome. We were unable to test this proposition in our last meta-analysis due to an insufficient number of studies reporting this as an explicit focus. With the addition of 15 new studies in this meta-analysis, we were able to test it in this moderator analysis.

Greater attention to cohesion (e.g., group process) was associated with higher weighted correlations ($Q = 6.33$, $df = 1$, $p < .01$). Six studies reported using methods to enhance cohesion: pregroup video tapes (Kivlighan & Lilly, 1997) and in-session interventions to build safety and group cohesion (Lecomte et al., 2015). The difference in correlation was modest but consistent with our previous prediction; the studies focusing on group process interventions had a larger cohesion–outcome value ($r = .40$) compared to the 47 studies (2 studies were unratable on this variable) that did not describe such interventions ($r = .22$).

Another newly identified moderator in this updated analysis was group type ($Q = 19.64$, $df = 5$, $p < .01$). Two analog groups, volunteer members and task group, both produced higher correlations ($r = .58$ and $r = .56$, respectively) than psychoeducation, therapy, and support groups ($r = .22$, $r = .24$, and $r = .25$, respectively). However, correlations for the psychoeducation groups ($k = 5$) and therapy groups ($k = 42$) had a sufficient number of studies to produce reliable correlations. The analog group type correlations, although higher, were based upon only one or two studies each, needing more study to support generalizability. Thus our take-home message from this analysis is that the cohesion–outcome link appears equivalent in psychotherapy, psychoeducation, and support groups. As noted with the analog groups, the support groups also need more study to support generalizability.

Two of the three group moderators from our last meta-analysis continued to be significant. Groups that emphasized greater interaction among group members ($r = .36$, $k = 11$) when contrasted with problem-specific groups ($r = .23$, $k = 42$) comprised of members with similar diagnoses produced higher cohesion–outcome correlations ($Q = 4.29$, $df = 1$, $p < .05$). Dose, or number of group sessions, was also again found to moderate the cohesion–outcome effects ($Q = 7.55$, $df = 2$, $p < .05$). However, there was a change from our last report in regards to number of sessions. In our last analysis, there was no statistically significant difference between groups lasting 13 to 19 and 20 or more sessions, but in the updated meta-analysis there appears to be an association between dose and the cohesion–outcome correlation. Groups lasting 20 or more sessions posted the highest correlation ($r = .41$, $k = 11$), followed by groups lasting 13 to 19 sessions ($r = .27$, $k = 7$) and fewer than 13 sessions ($r = .21$, $k = 27$).

Previously, we found that group size moderated the cohesion–outcome relation with groups containing five to nine members producing the largest correlation. In our update, this difference disappeared with small groups (<5 members) and moderately sized groups (5–9 members) posting equivalent and significant correlations ($r = .37$ and $r = .32$, respectively). However, it is important to note that there was only one study in the small group condition, attenuating our confidence in an equivalence conclusion. Large groups with more than nine members did not produce a statistically significant cohesion–outcome correlation.

EVIDENCE FOR CAUSALITY

Neither our last nor the present meta-analysis provides causal evidence for cohesion affecting outcome since nearly all studies assessed cohesion at a single point in time and then correlated it with outcome. At the same time, a few recent studies address the growth of cohesion over time and then link this growth to changes in outcome. These studies provide some modest support for cohesion growth explaining patient improvement. We use these studies to discuss causality next. In addition, all three studies that we identified as landmark studies address causality, so we also briefly summarize the possible inferences from them.

Temporal Change in Cohesion and Its Relation to Outcome

Repeatedly assessing cohesion over the life of a group is an improvement in the recent cohesion literature since it not only informs us about the pattern of change but also provides a more robust explanation for changes in outcome. We located seven articles that repeatedly assessed cohesion, with most using growth curve modeling (Burlingame et al., 2018; Gallagher et al., 2014; Hornsey et al., 2012; Illing et al., 2011; Lo Coco et al., 2012; Norton & Kazantzis, 2016; Tasca et al., 2013). Five different measures were used across these studies, and all but one study (Lo Coco et al., 2012) found a significant change in slope across time. Without exception, member perception of cohesion increased over time, even in the study that did not demonstrate statistical significance. However, cohesion's temporal relationship to outcome is limited by the fact that four studies assessed outcome at pre- and posttreatment, providing little information about how cohesion and outcome changed together over the course of treatment. Of the remaining three studies that repeatedly assessed outcome and cohesion over the course of treatment, only two (Burlingame et al., 2018; Norton & Kazantzis, 2016) found evidence that cohesion and outcome changed together. Thus caution is warranted until there are more studies that repeatedly assess outcome and cohesion to test if changes in cohesion are simultaneously related to changes in outcome.

Finally, indirect support of this temporal pattern comes from the meta-analytic results showing that dose or the number of sessions moderates the cohesion–outcome correlation; larger doses result in larger correlations. Thus the cohesion–outcome link appears to need sufficient time for group bonding and relationships to build.

Group as Casual Influence on Members

The group as a causal agent in a member's treatment outcome has been asserted as a casual factor for decades by clinical writers (e.g., Yalom & Leszcz, 2005). However, the empirical evidence to support this claim has been correlational. More recently, the group's influence on member perception of cohesion has been studied by more sophisticated statistical models such as APIM or response surface analysis. The consensus from these studies (e.g., Lo Coco et al., 2012; Paquin et al., 2013) is that when members' cohesion scores are more similar to the group average, they show better outcomes. Unfortunately, all of these studies rely upon data aggregated across an entire episode of treatment, making it impossible to test causality.

As reviewed under the Landmark Studies section, the Gullo et al. (2014) study indirectly plumbed causality of cohesion but suffered from a number of limitations. First, the time-lagged assessment in this study still reflects a measured, rather than manipulated, variable. Second, the evidence for causality was weak as demonstrated in the small effects. Third, one of the cohesion measures selected (CALPAS-G) is infrequently used, thus making estimates of its sensitivity to detecting a cohesion–outcome effect less clear. Finally, different theoretical orientations place a greater or lesser emphasis on group dynamics (e.g., interpersonal vs. CBT), and it remains unclear how similar the narrative-autobiographic approach from this study compares to the theoretical orientations noted in our meta-analyses.

Feedback Effect on Relationship Deterioration, Failure, and Outcome

A promising research direction in determining causality since our last review is ROM in group therapy. These studies attempt to impact the therapeutic relationship by manipulating outcome and relationship feedback in group therapy (Burlingame et al., 2018; Davidsen et al., 2017; Slone et al., 2015). Taken together, these studies found that (a) outcome and relationship feedback was associated with better group therapy outcomes and (b) relationship feedback improved cohesion and group process when members were deteriorating or failing.

Implementing feedback informed treatment in groups proves quite different than in individual therapy (Gleave et al., 2017). Group leaders have a more complex therapeutic relationship environment to manage. In our early feedback research (Davies et al., 2008), we learned that group leaders seek a simple color-coded feedback report (Gleave et al., 2017) that can quickly be reviewed before entering a group session.

Table 6.7 displays a sample report from the OQ-Analyst (Lambert, 2015). The report begins with descriptive information about the group, including members

Table 6.7. Weekly GQ/OQ Feedback Report

All GQ alerts are from your last group session/OQ alerts are from the past day or so+

Leader Name: J.M. Barrie

Group ID: 2

Date of Group: 12/5/2015 (Session #11)

Group Members who completed a GQ: Captain Hook, Smee, Wendy, Peter Pan, Tinkerbell, Michael, Lost Boy #1

DID NOT COMPLETE GQ or OQ:

DID NOT ATTEND:

CHANGE ALERTS—based on last group session GQ—NEGATIVE/POSITIVE CHANGE		
	Clients reporting relationship deterioration	Clients reporting relationship improvement
Positive Bond	Peter Pan	None
Positive Work	None	None
Negative Relationship	None	None

STATUS ALERTS—based on last group session GQ—RELATIONSHIP FAILURE/HIGHS		
	Clients at or below the 10th percentile ☹	Clients at or above the 90th percentile ☺
Positive Bond	Peter Pan ☹	Tinkerbell ☺
Positive Work	Peter Pan ☹	Tinkerbell ☺
Negative Relationship	None	Tinkerbell ☺

OQ ALERTS				
	Alert Status	Change from Initial	Initial Score	Most Recent Score
Captain Hook	Red	Reliably Worse	79	129
Smee	Yellow	Reliably Worse	65	81
Wendy	Green	Reliably Improved	65	44
Peter Pan	Yellow	Reliably Worse	72	89
Tinkerbell	White	No Reliable Change	44	47
Michael	Green	Reliably Improved	60	44

Note. GQ = Group Questionnaire; OQ = Outcome Questionnaire.

who did or did not attend the last session as well as those that did not complete the measures. The relationship deterioration (change alert) section immediately follows, listing only members (e.g., Peter Pan) who have deteriorated or improved since the last group session. Members' names in the relationship failure (status alert) section have fallen below the 10th percentile (e.g., Peter Pan) or appear in green if above the 90th percentile (e.g., Tinkerbell). The final section of the report depicts progress alerts for all group members by comparing their most recent OQ-45 administration and baseline (intake) scores with algorithms in the OQ-Analyst. Each member receives either an on-track (green, blue, and white) or not-on-track progress alerts (yellow and red).

PATIENT CONTRIBUTIONS

There is little research on patient contributions to the cohesion–outcome relation. As mentioned, probably the most promising evidence for patient contribution lies in attachment style moderating effect on the size of the cohesion–outcome link. However, three of the articles we cite in the Landmark Studies section (Gallagher, Tasca, Ritchie, Balfour, & Bissada, 2014; Gallagher, Tasca, Ritchie, Balfour, Maxwell, et al., 2014; Tasca et al., 2013) all use data from the same study of 102 binge eating disorder patients, so we are still in need of additional studies testing member attachment style as a moderator. At this point, we cannot know if the need for approval, which appears to make a member more susceptible to the group's influence, is unique to eating disorders (Illing, et al., 2011) or if it is generalizable to other clinical populations.

Similarly, the theoretical orientation used in these studies was a psychodynamic interpersonal group model that emphasizes "group processes . . . such as here-and-now interactions and interpersonal learning to improve the quality of interpersonal interactions" (Gallagher, Tasca, Ritchie, Balfour, & Bissada, 2014, p. 42). One cannot help wonder if group member attachment style would moderate the cohesion–outcome link in a similar fashion with other theoretical orientations (e.g., CBT) that do not place as much emphasis on group processes. Clearly, attachment style's link to interpersonal behavior makes it an ideal candidate for explaining the causal link between cohesion and outcome and for identifying patient contribution to the link.

LIMITATIONS OF THE RESEARCH

The most significant limitation of the cohesion literature is the disparity in how the construct is defined. A summary of the content assessed by the eight primary measures (Table 6.1) used in over 80% of the studies herein reveals some similarity, but major differences in content and the relationship structure are apparent. Differences in how cohesion is defined is further limited by the absence of research that compares how well these measures correlate with one another. Almost all cohesion-outcome studies use a single measure, and the two validity studies noted above compared four different measures making empirical comparisons impossible.

The limited empirical light shed on how different cohesion measures might correlate comes from the psychometric work on the GQ that originally began by comparing the most popular relationship measure (GCQ—16 studies) with the Cohesion subscale of the TFI. Items from the GCQ Engaged subscale and TFI-C loaded on the positive bond factor. Stated differently, the construct validity and criterion validity of cohesion measures are weak.

We also fall short in having sufficient research to establish a strong causal link between cohesion and outcome. The dominant methodology that assesses cohesion once during the life of a group and then correlate it with pre-post differences in outcome is insufficient to make causal inferences. While there is promising research testing the group's effect on member cohesion-outcome, attachment style and relationship feedback, most rely upon a single or small set of studies that limit generalizability. There is an embarrassing paucity of research into the contribution of patient factors and diversity to the cohesion-outcome association. We await research on the effect of therapists, which is hampered in group treatment by the large number of groups needed for each therapist to tease apart therapist from group effects.

Future research to must clarify the similarities and differences between the frequently used cohesion measures. Progress on this is essential, and the careful psychometric research needed will not be glamorous or likely to win professional recognition. However, empirical knowledge about the constructs underlying our measurement tools is a requirement to make meaningful conclusions. The repeated assessment of both cohesion and outcome throughout the course of group treatment is a shortcoming that must be addressed. Two studies over the past decade is insufficient to accrue the empirical foundation to make stronger causal inferences about the effect of cohesion on outcome over time.

The recent research on ROM progress and relationship alerts in group treatment is an exciting development, and we hope to see more of this research in the future. At present, this research has been applied to a limited number of clinical populations: eating disorder (Davidsen et al., 2017), university counseling center (Slone et al., 2015; Burlingame et al., 2018), and brief substance abuse groups with soldiers (Schuman et al., 2015). Extension to other clinical populations is essential, but in doing so it is important for clinicians and researchers alike to capture information about the multiple relationships within a small group, provide the leader with actionable information (so ROM feedback is clinically useful), and provide feedback that can be quickly applied by the group leader. There are clear differences in how ROMs are applied in group treatment; one system, tested by three studies (Schuman et al., 2015; Slone et al., 2015; Davidsen et al., 2017), reviews progress and relationship feedback at the beginning of each session with the entire group, while the OQ-A system provides therapist reports before session (Table 6.7; Burlingame et al., 2018).

DIVERSITY CONSIDERATIONS

There is a paucity of research on the association among diversity, cohesion, and group therapy outcome. In fact, we could not locate a single cohesion-outcome study that addressed diversity. However, there were a handful of alliance studies located in our search ($k = 7$) that were not included in our cohesion meta-analysis. One of these (Walling et al., 2012) looked at how race/ethnicity predicted change in the working alliance for intimate partner violence perpetrators who were treated in CBT groups. Since these findings tap member–therapist alliance, we review them here.

The study investigated the link between group alliance and treatment outcome with men, nearly half (45%) of whom identified with a racial or ethnic minority status (African American, Asian, Hispanic, Native American). They were treated in 16-week, two-hour CBT groups that were racially heterogeneous. Results indicated that the average client group alliance increased over time; however, for therapist-rated alliance, some members increased and others decreased, and when these were aggregated there was no significant temporal trend. Interestingly, race/ethnicity (i.e., minority status compared to Caucasian) was not significantly associated with change in the alliance over time for therapist, but member ratings of alliance showed Caucasian members reporting a significant increase over time with minorities reporting no change (Walling et al., 2012).

Walling et al. (2012) also examined the link between alliance and treatment outcome (change in physical abuse behavior) and found that aggregated client alliance ratings were not related to outcome. However, there was a significant interaction: Caucasians and minority members who grew in group alliance benefitted from treatment, but minority members who reported no growth had poorer outcomes. Interestingly, client ratings of alliance for co-leaders were nearly identical, irrespective of whether the client's race/ethnicity matched or differed from the leader.

The authors understandably interpreted these results within a diversity frame and suggested that changes in the working alliance are "differentially determined by the race/ethnicity of the client" (Walling et al., 2012, p. 188).Since the groups were heterogeneous (minorities ranged from 30%–70%), we wonder if the group influence played the pivotal role. More specifically, research suggests better outcomes for members who conform to the group norms/averages of cohesion. Could an alternative explanation of the race/ethnicity interaction be the member similarity? Could group influence and race/ethnicity factors work in concert? We call for future cohesion–outcome studies that address these and other issues of diversity.

TRAINING IMPLICATIONS

Access to training has been an ongoing difficulty for group leaders. Surveys of 630 psychology, social work, and psychiatry training programs (Fuhriman & Burlingame, 2001) and 422 internship training programs (Markus & King, 2003) indicate widespread consensus that group treatments would increase in use in service delivery systems. Alas, this optimism was not matched by required graduate courses or internship training to prepare students to offer group treatment.

Thus, recognizing limited training opportunities for group leaders in formal academic programs, we offer practical recommendations informed by our meta-analytic findings:

- Clinical educators and supervisors are encouraged to teach group dynamics and their importance in fostering the cohesion–outcome link.
- Trainees require specific training in methods that enhance group cohesion, which in turn is associated with and predictive of favorable treatment outcomes. The most common approach is becoming a clinical apprentice to senior group clinicians, a practice endorsed and used by the American Group Psychotherapy Association.
- There was a clear predictive relation between several measures of cohesion and treatment outcome without differences in their respective abilities to predict outcome, Thus mental health practitioners can adopt a measure with content that

closely matches the goals of their group. (Table 6.1 is a good start point for choosing a measure.)

◆ While some theoretical orientations more naturally focus on group interactions, CBT groups are more problem-focused (Burlingame & McClendon, 2008). Group leaders espousing a CBT orientation are particularly encouraged to study group dynamics and practice fostering member interaction to harness the power of the group.

◆ In the zeitgeist of managed care and professional accountability, many therapists may be receiving feedback, even without knowing how to use that feedback, and may have concerns regarding how that feedback may reflect upon them as clinicians. Training in the use and clinical integration of practice-based evidence, as provided by ROM systems, will probably prove effective in helping therapists improve client outcomes as well as in navigating the tension between their own anxiety about feedback and their growth (McClendon & Burlingame, 2011).

THERAPEUTIC PRACTICES

Our meta-analysis of 55 studies and more than 6,000 group members generates the following therapeutic practices:

◆ Cohesion is reliably associated with and predictive of ($r = .26$, $d = .56$) group outcome. This repeated, robust result argues that group practitioners should seriously consider routinely assessing, monitoring, and enhancing group cohesion for optimal patient outcomes.

◆ Cohesion is certainly involved with patient improvement in groups using cognitive-behavioral, psychodynamic, interpersonal, supportive, and eclectic orientations. Group leaders of all theoretical orientations are encouraged to foster cohesion in its multiple manifestations.

◆ The cohesion–outcome link is strongest when a group leader emphasizes member interaction. Accordingly, group therapists are encouraged to do precisely that.

◆ To conduct a feedback-informed group treatment, the only group relationship measure that has been studied in a randomized clinical trial is the GQ. Group leaders are busy and want quick, easily understood interpretive guidelines such as those available with the GQ (change and status alerts). Thus we currently recommend it for gathering feedback.

◆ There is no difference in the cohesion–outcome link when a group is led by a single therapist or co-led by two therapists, but the cohesion–outcome link is differentially related to leader behavior. When a leader implements specific interventions to support a positive group climate, higher cohesion–outcome correlations result. That research speaks directly to therapists paying attention to the three major relationship structures (member–member, member–leader, and member–group) promoting a positive affective and work relationship and handling conflict when it arises.

◆ Cohesion contributes to group outcome across different settings (inpatient and outpatient) and diagnostic classifications. Thus leaders would be well advised to actively engage in interventions that foster and maintain cohesion regardless of their particular practice setting.

REFERENCES

References marked with an asterisk indicate studies included in the meta-analyses.

*Antonuccio, D. O., Davis, C., Lewinsohn, P. M., & Breckenridge, J. S. (1987). Therapist variables related to cohesiveness in a group treatment for depression. *Small Group Research, 18*, 557–564.

Bakali, J., Baldwin, S., & Lorentzen, S. (2009). Modeling group process constructs at three stages in group psychotherapy. *Psychotherapy Research, 19*, 332–343.

Beck, A. T., Epstein, N., Brown, G., & Steer, R. A. (1988). An inventory for measuring clinical anxiety: Psychometric properties. *Journal of Consulting and Clinical Psychology, 56*, 893–897.

Beck, A. T., Steer, R. A., & Brown, G. K. (1996). *Manual for the Beck Depression Inventory-II.* San Antonio, TX: Psychological Corporation.

Bednar, R. L., & Kaul, T. J. (1978). Experiential group research: Current perspectives. In S. L. Garfield & A. E. Bergin (Eds.), *Handbook of psychotherapy and behavior change* (2nd ed., pp. 769–815). New York, NY: Wiley.

Bednar, R. L., & Kaul, T. J. (1994). Experiential group research: Can the canon fire? In A. E. Bergin & S. L. Garfield (Eds.), *Handbook of psychotherapy and behavior change* (4th ed., pp. 631–663). New York, NY: Wiley.

Berkeljon, A., & Baldwin, S. A. (2009). An introduction to meta-analysis for psychotherapy outcome research. *Psychotherapy Research, 19*(4), 511–518.

*Beutal, M. E., Knickenberg, R. J., Krug, B., Mund, S., Schattenburg, L., & Zwerenz, R. (2006). Psychodynamic focal group treatment for psychosomatic inpatients—with an emphasis on work-related conflicts. *International Journal of Group Psychotherapy, 56*(3), 285–305.

*Bonsaksen, T., Borge, F. M., & Hoffart, A. (2013). Group climate as predictor of short- and long-term outcome in group therapy for social phobia. *International Journal of Group Psychotherapy, 63*, 394–417. https://www.doi.org/1.1521/ijgp.2013.63.3.394

Bormann, B., & Strauß, B. (2007). Gruppenklima, kohäsion, allianz und empathie als komponenten der therapeutischen beziehung in gruppenpsychotherapien—Überprüfung eines mehrebenen-modells. *Gruppenpsychotherapie und Gruppendynamik, 43*, 1–2.

Braaten, L. (1991). Group cohesion: A new multidimensional model. *Group, 15*, 39–55.

*Braaten, L. J. (1989). Predicting positive goal attainment and symptom reduction from early group climate dimensions. *International Journal of Group Psychotherapy, 39*(3), 377–387.

Budman, S. H., Demby, A., Feldstein, M., Redondo, J., Scherz, B., Bennett, M. J., . . . Ellis, J. (1987). Preliminary findings on a new instrument to measure cohesion in group psychotherapy. *International Journal of Group Psychotherapy, 37*, 75–94.

*Budman, S. H., Soldz, S., Demby, A., Feldstein, M., Springer, T., & Davis, M. S. (1989). Cohesion, alliance and outcome in group psychotherapy. *Psychiatry, 52*(3), 339–350.

Burlingame, G. (2010). Small group treatments: Introduction to special section. *Psychotherapy Research, 20*(1), 1–7.

Burlingame, G. M., & Barlow, S. (1996). Outcome and process differences between professional and nonprofessional therapists in time-limited group psychotherapy. *International Journal of Group Psychotherapy, 46*, 455–478.

Burlingame, G., Fuhriman, A., & Johnson, J. (2002). Cohesion in group psychotherapy. In J. C. Norcross (Ed.), *Psychotherapy relationships that work* (pp. 71–87). New York, NY: Oxford University Press.

Burlingame, G., Gleave, R., Beecher, M., Griner, D., Hansen, K., & Jensen, J. (2017). *Administration and scoring manual for the Group Questionnaire—GQ.* Salt Lake City, UT: OQ Measures.

Burlingame, G. M., MacKenzie, K. R., & Strauß, B. (2004). Evidence-based small group treatments. In M. Lambert, A. E. Bergin, & S. L. Garfield (Eds.), *Handbook of psychotherapy and behavior change* (5th ed., pp. 647–696). New York, NY: Wiley.

Burlingame, G. M., & McClendon, D. T. (2008). Review of the book *Cognitive Behavioral Therapy in Groups. International Journal of Group Psychotherapy*, *58*, 133–136.

Burlingame, G. M., McClendon, D. T., & Alonso, J. (2011a). Cohesion in group therapy. In J. C. Norcross (Ed.), *Psychotherapy relationships that work* (2nd ed., pp. 110–131). New York, NY: Oxford University Press.

Burlingame, G. M., McClendon, D. T., & Alonso, J. (2011b). Cohesion in group therapy. *Psychotherapy*, *48*(1), 34–42.

Burlingame, G., Strauss, B., & Joyce, A (2013). Change mechanisms and effectiveness of small group treatments. In M. J. Lambert (Ed.), *Bergin & Garfield's handbook of psychotherapy and behavior change* (6th ed., pp. 640–689). New York, NY: Wiley.

Burlingame, G., Whitcomb, K., Woodland, S., Olsen, J., Beecher, M., & Gleave, R. (2018). The effects of relationship and progress feedback in group psychotherapy using the GQ and OQ-45: A randomized clinical trial *Psychotherapy 55*(2), 116–131.

Cattell, R. B., & Wispe, L. G. (1948). The dimensions of syntality in small groups. *Journal of Social Psychology*, *28*, 57–78.

Chapman, C., Burlingame, G., Gleave, R., Rees, F., Beecher, M., & Porter, G. (2012). Clinical prediction in group psychotherapy. *Psychotherapy Research*, *22*(6), 673–681.

*Crino, N., & Djokvucic, I. (2010). Cohesion to the group and its association with attendance and early treatment response in an adult day-hospital program for eating disorders: A preliminary clinical investigation. *Clinical Psychologist*, *14*(2), 54–61.

Crouch, E. C., Bloch, S., & Wanlass, J. (1994). Therapeutic factors: Interpersonal and intrapersonal mechanisms. In A. Fuhriman & G. M. Burlingame (Eds.), *Handbook of group psychotherapy* (pp. 269–315). New York, NY: Wiley.

*Crowe, T. P., & Grenyer, B. F. S. (2008). Is therapist alliance or whole group cohesion more influential in group psychotherapy outcomes? *Clinical Psychology and Psychotherapy*, *15*, 239–246.

Czogalik, D., & Koltzow, R. (1987). Zur normierung des stuttgarter bogens. *Gruppenpsychotherapie und Gruppendynamik*, *23*, 36–45.

Davidsen, A. H., Poulsen, S., Lindschou, J., Winkel, P., Tróndarson, M. F., Waaddegaard, M., & Lau, M. (2017). Feedback in group psychotherapy for eating disorders: A randomized clinical trial. *Journal of Consulting and Clinical Psychology*, *85*(5), 484–494. https://www.doi.org/1.1037/ccp0000173

Davies, D. R., Burlingame, G. M., Johnson, J. E., Barlow, S. H. & Gleave, R. L. (2008). The effects of a feedback intervention on group process and outcome. *Group Dynamics: Theory, Research, and Practice*, *12*(2), 141–154.

Derogatis, L. R. (1977). *SCL-90: Administration, scoring, and procedures manual-R (revised).* Baltimore, MD: John Hopkins University School of Medicine, Clinical Psychometrics Research Unit.

Dinger, U., & Schauenburg, H. (2010). Effects of individual cohesion and patient interpersonal style on outcome in psychodynamically oriented inpatient group psychotherapy. *Psychotherapy Research, 20*(1), 22–29.

Dion, K. L. (2000). Group cohesion: From "field of forces" to multidimensional construct. *Group Dynamics, 4,* 7–26.

Duncan, B., & Reese, R. (2015). The Partners for Change Outcome Management System (PCOMS): Revisiting the client's frame of reference. *Psychotherapy, 52*(4), 391–401.

*Etlink, E. M. A., Van der Helm, P., Wissink, I. B., & Stams, G. J. M. (2015). The relation between living group climate and reactions to social problem situations in detained adolescents: "I stabbed him because he looked mean at me." *International Journal of Forensic Mental Health, 14,* 101–109.

*Falloon, I. R. H. (1981). Interpersonal variables in behavioural group therapy. *British Journal of Medical Psychology, 54,* 133–141.

Feeney, J., Noller, R., & Hanrahan, M. (1994). Assessing adult attachment. In M. Sperling & W. Berman (Eds.), *Attachment in adults: Clinical and developmental perspectives* (pp. 128–152). New York, NY: Guilford.

*Flowers, J. V., Booraem, C. D., & Hartman, K. A. (1981). Client improvement on higher and lower intensity problems as a function of group cohesiveness. *Psychotherapy: Theory, Research and Practice, 18,* 246–251.

Fuhriman, A., & Burlingame, G. (2001). Group psychotherapy training and effectiveness. *International Journal of Group Psychotherapy, 51*(3), 399–416.

Fuhriman, A., & Burlingame, G. (Eds.). (1994). *Handbook of group psychotherapy: An empirical and clinical synthesis.* New York, NY: Wiley.

Gallagher, M. E., Tasca, G.A., Ritchie, K., Balfour, L., & Bissada, H. (2014). Attachment anxiety moderates the relationship between growth in group cohesion and treatment outcomes in group psychodynamic interpersonal psychotherapy for women with binge eating disorder. *Group Dynamics: Theory, Research, and Practice, 18*(1), 38–52.

Gallagher, M., Tasca, G., Ritchie, K., Balfour, L., Maxwell, H., & Bissada, H. (2014). Interpersonal learning is associated with improved self-esteem in group psychotherapy for women with binge eating disorder, *Psychotherapy, 51*(1), 66–77. Retrieved from http://psycnet.apa.org/doi/1.1037/a0031098

Gaston, L., & Marmar, C. R. (1994). The California Psychotherapy Alliance Scales. In A. O. Horvath & L. S. Greenberg (Eds.), *The working alliance: Theory, research and practice* (pp. 85–108). New York, NY: Wiley.

*Gillaspy, J. A. Jr., Wright, A. R., Campbell, C., Stokes, S., & Adinoff, B. (2002). Group alliance and cohesion as predictors of drug and alcohol abuse treatment outcomes. *Psychotherapy Research, 12*(2), 213–229.

Gleave, R., Burlingame, G., Beecher, M., Griner, D., Hansen, K., & Jenkins, S. (2017). Feedback-informed group treatment: Application of the OQ-45 and Group Questionnaire (GQ). In S. Miller, D. Prescott, & C. Maeschalck (Eds.), *Feedback-Informed Treatment in Clinical Practice: Reaching for Excellence* (pp. 141–166). Washington, DC: American Psychological Association.

*Grabhorn, R., Kaufhold, J., & Overbeck, G. (2002). The role of differentiated group experience in the course of inpatient psychotherapy. In S. P. Shohov (Ed.), *Advance in psychology research* (Vol. 12, pp. 141–154). Hauppeuge, NY: Nova Science.

Griffith, J. (1988). Measurement of group cohesion in U.S. Army units. *Basic and Applied Social Psychology, 9,* 149–171.

Gross, E. F. (1957). *An empirical study of the concepts of cohesiveness and compatibility* (Honors thesis). Harvard University, Cambridge, MA.

Gullo, S., Lo Coco, G., Passagli, C., Piana, N., De Feo, P., Mazzeschi, C., & Kiblighan, D. M. Jr. (2014). A time-lagged, actor-partner interdependence analysis of alliance to the group as a whole and group member outcome in overweight and obesity treatment groups. *Journal of Counseling Psychology, 61*(2), 306–313.

Hedges, L. V., & Vevea, J. L. (1998). Fixed- and random-effects models in meta-analysis. *Psychological Methods, 3,* 486–504.

*Hilbert, A., Saelens, B. E., Stein, R. I., Mockus, D. S., Welch, R. R., Matt, G. E., & Wilfley, D. E. (2007). Pretreatment and process predictors of outcome in interpersonal and cognitive behavioral psychotherapy for binge eating disorder. *Journal of Consulting and Clinical Psychology, 75*(4), 645–651.

*Hoberman, H. M., Lewinsohn, P. M., & Tilson, M. (1988). Group treatment of depression: Individual predictors of outcome. *Journal of Consulting and Clinical Psychology, 56*(3), 393–398.

Hornsey, M., Dwyer, L., & Oei, T. (2007). Beyond cohesiveness: Reconceptualizing the link between group processes and outcomes in group psychotherapy. *Small Group Research, 38,* 567–592.

Hornsey, M., Dwyer, L., Oei, T., & Dingle, G. A. (2009). Group processes and outcomes in group therapy: Is it time to let go of cohesiveness? *International Journal of Group Psychotherapy, 59*(2), 267–278.

*Hornsey, M. J., Olsen, S., Barlow, F. K., & Oei, T. P. S. (2012). Testing a single-item visual analogue scale as a proxy for cohesiveness in group psychotherapy. *Group Dynamics: Theory, Research, and Practice, 16,* 80–9.

Horowitz, L., Rosenberg, S., Baer, B., Ureno, F., & Villasenor, V. (1988). Inventory of interpersonal problems: Psychometric properties and clinical applications. *Journal of Consulting and Clinical Psychology, 56*(6), 885–892.

*Hurley, J. R. (1989). Affiliativeness and outcome in interpersonal groups: Member and leader perspectives. *Psychotherapy, 26*(4), 520–523.

*Hurley. J. R. (1997). Interpersonal theory and measures of outcome and emotional climate in 111 personal development groups. *Group Dynamics: Theory, Research, and Practice, 1*(1), 86–97.

Illing, V., Tasca, G. A., Balfour, L., & Bissada, H. (2011). Attachment dimensions and group climate growth in a sample of women seeking treatment for eating disorders. *Psychiatry, 74*(3), 255–269.

Janis, R., Burlingame, G., & Olsen, J. (2016). Evaluating factor structures of measures used in group research: Looking between and within. *Group Dynamics: Theory, Research and Practice, 20*(3), 165–180. https://www.doi.org/1.1037/gdn0000043

Janis, R., Burlingame, G., & Olsen, J. (2018). Developing a therapeutic relationship monitoring system for group treatment. *Psychotherapy, 55*(2), 105–115.

Johnson, J. E., Burlingame, G. M., Olsen, J. A., Davies, D. R., & Gleave, R. L. (2005). Group climate, cohesion, alliance, and empathy in group psychotherapy: Multilevel structural equation models. *Journal of Counseling Psychology, 52,* 310–321.

*Joyce, A. S., Piper, W. E., & Ogrodniczuk, J. S. (2007). Therapeutic alliance and cohesion variables as predictors of outcome in short-term group therapy. *International Journal of Group Psychotherapy, 57*(3), 269–296.

*Kelly, P. J., Deane, F. P., & Baker, A. L. (2015). Group cohesion and between session home-work activities predict self-reported cognitive–behavioral skill use amongst participants of SMART recovery groups. *Journal of Substance Abuse Treatment, 51*, 53–58.

Kenny, D., & Garcia, R. (2012). Using the Actor-Partner Interdependence Model to study the effects of group composition. *Small Group Research, 43*(4), 468–496. https://www.doi.org/1.1177/1046496412441626

*Kipnes, D. R., Piper, W. E., & Joyce, A. S. (2002). Cohesion and outcome in short-term psy-chodynamic groups for complicated grief. *International Journal of Group Psychotherapy, 52*(4), 483–509.

*Kirchmann, H., Mestel, R., Schreiber-Willnow, K., Mattke, D., Seidler, K., Daudert, E., . . . Strauss, B. (2009). Associations among attachment characteristics, patients' assessment of therapeutic factors, and treatment outcome following inpatient psychodynamic group psy-chotherapy. *Psychotherapy Research, 19*(2), 234–248.

Kivlighan, D., Lo Coco, G, Gullo, S., Pazzagli, C., & Mazzeschi, C. (2017). Attachment anx-iety and attachment avoidance: Member attachment fit with their group and group relationships, *International Journal of Group Psychotherapy, 67*, 223–239.

Kivlighan, D. M., Coleman, M. N., & Anderson, D. C. (2000). Process, outcome, and meth-odology in group counseling research. In S. D. Brown & R. W. Lent (Eds.), *Handbook of counseling psychology* (3rd ed., pp. 767–796). New York, NY: Wiley.

*Kivlighan, D. M., & Lilly, R. L. (1997). Developmental changes in group climate as they relate to therapeutic gain. *Group Dynamics: Theory, Research, and Practice, 1*, 208–221.

Krogel, J. (2009). *The Group Questionnaire: A new measure of the group relationship*. Provo, UT: Brigham Young University.

Krogel, J., Burlingame, G., Chapman, C., Renshaw, T., Gleave, R., Beecher, M., & MacNair-Semands, R. (2013). The Group Questionnaire: A clinical and empirically derived measure of the group relationship. *Psychotherapy Research, 23*, 344–354. https://www.doi.org/1.1080/10503307.2012.729868

Lambert, M., Kahler, M., Harmon, C., Burlingame, G., Kenichi, K., & White, M. (2013). *Administration and scoring manual for the Outcome Questionnaire 45.2*. Salt Lake City, UT: OQ Measures.

*Lecomte, T., Leclerc, C., Wykes, T., Nicole, L., & Baki, A. A. (2015). Understanding process in group cognitive behaviour therapy for psychosis. *Psychology and Psychotherapy: Theory, Research, and Practice, 88*, 163–177.

Lerner, M. D., McLeod, B. D., & Mikami, A. Y. (2013). Preliminary evaluation of an observa-tional measure of group cohesion for group psychotherapy. *Journal of Clinical Psychology, 69*, 191–208.

Lese, K. P., & MacNair-Semands, R. R. (2000). The Therapeutic Factors Inventory: Development of a scale. *Group, 24*, 303–317.

*Levenson, J. S., & Macgowan, M. J. (2004). Engagement, denial, and treatment progress among sex offenders in group therapy. *Sexual Abuse: A Journal of Research and Treatment, 16*(1), 49–63.

Lieberman, M., Yalom, I., & Miles, M. (1973). *Encounter groups: First facts*. New York, NY: Basic Books.

*Lipman, E. L., Waymouth, M., Gammon, T., Carter, P., Secord, M., Leung, O., . . . Hicks, F. (2007). Influence of group cohesion on maternal well-being among participants in a sup-port/education group program for single mothers. *American Journal of Orthopsychiatry, 77*(4), 543–549.

Lipsey, M. W., & Wilson, D. B. (2001). *Practical meta-analysis.* Applied Social Research Methods Series, Vol. 49. Thousand Oaks, CA: SAGE.

Lo Coco, G., Gullo, S., Di Fratello, C., Giordano, C., & Kivlighan, D. M. (2016). Group relationships in early and late sessions and improvement in interpersonal problems. *Journal of Counseling Psychology, 63,* 419–442.

Lo Coco, G., Gullo, S., & Kivlighan, D. M. Jr. (2012). Examining patients' and other group members' agreement about their alliance to the group as a whole and changes in patient symptoms using response surface analysis. *Journal of Counseling Psychology, 59*(2), 197–207.

*Lorentzen, S., Sexton, H. C., & Hoglend, P. (2004). Therapeutic alliance, cohesion and outcome in a long-term analytic group. A preliminary study. *Nordic Journal of Psychiatry, 58,* 33–4.

MacKenzie, K. R. (1981). Measurement of group climate. *International Journal of Group Psychotherapy, 31,* 287–295.

MacKenzie, K. R. (1983). The clinical application of a group climate measure. In R. R. Dies & K. R. MacKenzie (Eds.), *Advances in group psychotherapy: Integrating research and practice* (pp. 159–170). New York, NY: International Universities Press.

*MacKenzie, R. K., & Tschuschke, V. (1993). Relatedness, group work, and outcome in long-term inpatient psychotherapy groups. *Journal of Psychotherapy Practice and Research, 2,* 147–156.

*Marmarosh, C., Holtz, A., & Schottenbauer, M. (2005). Group cohesiveness, group-derived collective self-esteem, group-derived hope, and the well-being of group therapy members. *Group Dynamics: Theory, Research, and Practice, 9*(1), 32–44.

Markus, H. E., & King, D. A., (2003). A Survey of Group Psychotherapy Training During Predoctoral Psychology Internship. *Professional Psychology: Research and Practice, 34*(2), 203–209.

*Marziali, E., Munroe-Blum, H., & McCleary, L. (1997). The contribution of group cohesion and group alliance to the outcome of group psychotherapy. *International Journal of Group Psychotherapy, 47*(4), 475–497.

*May, A. M., Duivenvoorden, H. J., Korstjens, I., Weert, E. V., Hoekstra-Weebers, J. E., Borne, B. V. D., Mesters, I., . . . Ros, W. J. (2008). The effect of group cohesion on rehabilitation outcome in cancer survivors. *Psycho-Oncology, 17,* 917–925.

McClendon, D. T., & Burlingame, G. M. (2011). Has the magic of therapy disappeared?: Integrating evidence-based practice into therapist awareness and development. In R. H. Klein, H. S. Bernard, & V. L. Schermer (Eds.), *On becoming a psychotherapist: The personal and professional journey* (pp. 190–211). New York, NY: Oxford University Press.

McNair, D. M., Lorr, M., & Droppleman, L. F. (1981). *Profile of Mood States manual.* San Diego, CA: Educational and Industrial Testing Services.

Moos, R. H. (1986). *Group Environment Scale manual* (2nd ed.). Palo Alto, CA: Consulting Psychologists Press.

Moos, R., & Humphrey, B. (1974). *Group Environment Scale.* Palo Alto, CA. Consulting Psychologists Press.

*Norton, P. J., Hayes, S. A., & Springer, J. R. (2008). Transdiagnostic cognitive-behavioral group therapy for anxiety: Outcome and process. *International Journal of Cognitive Therapy, 1*(3), 266–279.

*Norton, P. J., & Kazantzis, N. (2016). Dynamic relationships of therapist alliance and group cohesion in transdiagnostic group CBT for anxiety disorders. *Journal of Consulting and Clinical Psychology, 84*(2), 146–155.

*Oei, T. P. S., & Browne, A. (2006). Components of group processes: Have they contributed to the outcome of mood and anxiety disorder patients in a group cognitive-behaviour therapy program? *American Journal of Psychotherapy*, 60(1), 53–57.

*Ogrodniczuk, J., & Piper, W. (2003). The effect of group climate on outcome in two forms of short-term group therapy. *Group Dynamics: Theory, Research, and Practice*, 7, 64–76.

*Ogrodniczuk, J. S., Piper, W. E., & Joyce, A. S. (2005). The negative effect of alexithymia on the outcome of group therapy for complicated grief: What role might the therapist play? *Comprehensive Psychiatry*, 46, 206–213.

*Ogrodniczuk, J. S., Piper, W. E., & Joyce, A. S. (2006). Treatment compliance among patients with personality disorders receiving group psychotherapy: What are the roles of inter-personal distress and cohesion? *Psychiatry: Interpersonal and Biological Processes*, 69(3), 249–261.

*Owen, J., Antle, B., & Barbee, A. (2013). Alliance and group cohesion in relationship educa-tion. *Family Process*, 52(3), 465–476.

Paquin, J., Kivlighan, D., & Drogosz, L. (2013). Person-group fit, group climate and outcomes in a sample of incarcerated women participating in trauma recovery groups. *Group Dynamics: Theory, Research and Practice*, 17(2), 95–109. Retrieved from http://psycnet. apa.org/doi/1.1037/a0032702

*Paulus, D. J., Hays-Skelton, S. A., & Norton, P. J. (2015). There's no "I" in GCBT: Identifying predictors of group-level outcome in transdiagnostic group cognitive-behavioral therapy for anxiety. *Group Dynamics: Theory, Research, and Practice*, 19(2), 63–76.

*Petry, N. M., Weinstock, J., & Alessi, S. M. (2011). A randomized trial of contingency man-agement delivered in the context of group counseling. *Journal of Consulting and Clinical Psychology*, 79(5), 686–696.

*Pisetsky, E. M., Durkin, N. E., Crosby, R. D., Berg, K. C., Mitchell, J. E., Crow, S. J., . . . Peterson, C. B. (2015). Examination of early group dynamics and treatment outcome in a randomized controlled trial of group cognitive behavior therapy for binge eating disorder. *Behavior Research and Therapy*, 73, 74–78.

Piper, W. E., Marrache, M., Lacroix, R., Richardsen, A. M., & Jones, B. D. (1983). Cohesion as a basic bond in groups. *Human Relations*, 36, 93–108.

*Quirk, K., Miller, S., Duncan, B., & Owen, J. (2013). Group Session Rating Scale: Preliminary psychometrics in substance abuse group interventions, *Counselling and Psychotherapy Research*, 13(3), 194–200.

*Ratto, R., & Hurley, J. R. (1995). Outcomes of inpatient group psychotherapy associated with dispositional and situational affiliativeness. *Group*, 19(3), 163–172.

*Rice, A. H. (2001). Evaluating brief structured group treatment for depression. *Research on Social Work Practice*, 11(1), 53–78.

*Rice, S. L., & Tonigan, J. S. (2012). Impressions of Alcoholics Anonymous (AA) group cohe-sion: A case for a nonspecific factor predicting later AA attendance. *Alcoholism Treatment Quarterly*, 30, 40–51.

*Roether, H. A., & Peters, J. J. (1972). Cohesiveness and hostility in group psychotherapy. *American Journal of Psychiatry*, 128(8), 1014–1017.

Rosenberg, M. (1965). *Society and the adolescent self-image*. Princeton, NJ: Princeton University Press.

*Rugel, R. P., & Barry, B. (1990). Overcoming denial through the group: A test of acceptance theory. *Small Group Research*, 21(1), 45–58.

*Ryum, T., Hagen, R., Nordahl, H. M., Vogel, P. A., & Stiles, T. C. (2009). Perceived group climate as a predictor of long-term outcome in randomized controlled trial of cognitive-behavioral group therapy for patients with comorbid psychiatric disorders. *Behavioural and Cognitive Psychotherapy, 37*, 497–510.

Schauenburg, H., Sammet, I., Rabung, S., & Strack, M. (2001). Zur differentiellen bedeutung des gruppenerlebens in der stationaren psychotherapie depressiver patienten. *Gruppenpsychotherapie und Gruppendynamik, 37*, 349–364.

Schuman, D., Slone, N., Reese, R., & Duncan, B. (2015). Efficacy of client feedback in group psychotherapy with soldiers referred for substance abuse treatment. *Psychotherapy Research, 25*(4), 396–407. https://www.doi.org/1.1080/10503307.2014.900875

Selvin, H. C., & Hagstrom, W. O. (1963). The empirical classification of formal groups. *American Sociological Review, 28*, 399–411.

*Shechtman, Z., & Mor, M. (2010). Groups for children and adolescents with trauma-related symptoms: Outcomes and processes. *International Journal of Group Psychotherapy, 60*(2), 221–243.

Silbergeld, S., Koenig, G. R., Manderscheid, R. W., Meeker, B. F., & Hornung, C. A. (1975). Assessment of environment-therapy systems: The Group Atmosphere Scale. *Journal of Consulting and Clinical Psychology, 43*, 460–469.

Slone, N., Reese, R., Mathews-Duvall, S., & Kodet, J. (2015). Evaluating the efficacy of client feedback in group psychotherapy. *Group Dynamics: Theory, Research and Practice, 19*(2), 122–136.

Strauss, B., Burlingame, G., & Bormann, B (2008). Using the CORE-R battery in group psychotherapy. *Journal of Clinical Psychology, 64*(11), 1225–1237.

*Taft, C. T., Murphy, C. M., King, D. W., Musser, P. H., & DeDeyn, J. M. (2003). Process and treatment adherence factors in group cognitive-behavioral therapy for partner violent men. *Journal of Consulting and Clinical Psychology, 71*(4), 812–82.

Tasca, G., Mikail, S., & Hewitt, P. (2005). Group psychodynamic interpersonal psychotherapy: Summary of a treatment model and outcomes for depressive symptoms. In M. Abelian (Ed.), *Focus on psychotherapy research* (pp. 159–188). New York, NY: Nova Science.

Tasca, G. A., Ritchie, K., Demidenko, N., Balfour, L., Krysanski, V., Weekes, K., . . . Bissada, H. (2013). Matching women with binge eating disorder to group treatment based on attachment anxiety: Outcomes and moderating effects. *Psychotherapy Research, 23*(3), 301–314.

*Taube-Schiff, M., Suvak, M. K., Antony, M. M., Bieling, P. J., & McCabe, R. E. (2007). Group cohesion in cognitive-behavioral group therapy for social phobia. *Behaviour Research and Therapy, 45*, 687–698.

Thayer, S. (2012). *The validity of the Group Questionnaire: Construct clarity of construct drift* (Unpublished doctoral dissertation). Brigham Young University, Provo, UT.

Thayer, S., & Burlingame, G. M. (2014). The validity of the Group Questionnaire: Construct clarity or construct drift? *Group Dynamics: Theory, Research, and Practice, 18*, 318–332.

*Tschuschke, V., & Dies, R. R. (1994). Intensive analysis of therapeutic factors and outcome in long-term inpatient groups. *International Journal of Group Psychotherapy, 44*(2), 185–208.

*van Andel, P., Erdman, R. A. M., Karsdorp, P. A., Appels, A., & Trijsburg, R. W. (2003). Group cohesion and working alliance: Prediction of treatment outcome in cardiac patients receiving cognitive behavioral group psychotherapy. *Psychotherapy and Psychosomatics, 72*, 141–149.

*Walling, S. M., Suvak, M. K., Howard, J. M., Taft, C. T., & Murphy, C. M. (2012). Race/ethnicity as a predictor of change in working alliance during cognitive behavioral therapy for intimate partner violence perpetrators. *Psychotherapy, 49*, 180–189.

Wampold, B. (2015). Routine outcome monitoring: Coming of age—with the usual developmental challenges. *Psychotherapy, 52*(4), 458–462.

*Woody, S. R., & Adessky, R. S. (2002). Therapeutic alliance, group cohesion, and homework compliance during cognitive-behavioral group treatment of social phobia. *Behavior Therapy, 33*, 5–27.

*Wright, T. L., & Duncan, D. (1986). Attraction to group, group cohesiveness, and individual outcome: A study of training groups. *Small Group Research, 17*(4), 487–492.

Yalom, I. D., & Leszcz, M. (2005). The *theory and practice of group psychotherapy* (5th ed.). New York, NY: Basic Books.

*Yalom, I., Houts, P. S., Zimerberg, S. M., & Rand, K. H. (1967). Prediction of improvement in group therapy: An exploratory study. *Archives of General Psychiatry, 17*, 159–168.

7

EMPATHY

Robert Elliott, Arthur C. Bohart, Jeanne C. Watson, and David Murphy

Empathy has a long and sometimes stormy history in psychotherapy. Proposed and codified by Rogers and his followers in the 1940s and 1950s, it was initially widely portrayed as primarily a therapist trait and put forward as the foundation of helping skills training programs popularized in the 1960s and early 1970s. Claims concerning its trait-like status and universal effectiveness led to skepticism and then came under intense scrutiny by psychotherapy researchers in the late 1970s and early 1980s. After that, research on empathy went into relative eclipse, resulting in a dearth of research between 1981 and 2000.

Since the late-1990s, however, empathy has again become a topic of scientific interest in clinical, developmental, and social psychology (e.g., Bohart & Greenberg, 1997; Ickes 1997), particularly because empathy, now reconceptualized as an interactional variable, has come to be seen as a key element of the new field of social neuroscience (e.g., Decety & Ickes, 2009). This development has helped relegitimize empathy as a central element of psychotherapy, which has led to an explosion of empathy research in the past 20 years. In fact, interest in empathy has recently rippled into related disciplines such as medicine, where it is now an active topic of investigation in a wide range of medical interventions (from anesthesiology to acupuncture) using a quite diverse array of measures (Pedersen, 2009).

In this chapter, we begin by reviewing definitions and measures of therapist empathy, including the conceptual problem of separating empathy from other relationship variables. We follow this with clinical examples illustrating different forms of therapist empathy and empathic response mode. We move on to describe a range of landmark studies of therapist empathy, including both quantitative and qualitative investigations, followed by a brief review of previous systematic reviews of therapist empathy. The core of our review, however, is a meta-analysis of 82 studies of the relation between therapist empathy and client outcome. In addition to reporting overall effect sizes, we examine a range of moderator variables, such as theoretical orientation and measurement perspectives. After looking at possible mediator variables, we offer a framework for assessing the causal status of the empathy–outcome connection and use this framework to review the evidence. Finally, we explore the role of client contributions and the limitations of the existing evidence base, touching on diversity issues, before moving on to the implications for training and therapeutic practice.

DEFINITIONS

The first problem with researching empathy in psychotherapy is that there is no consensual definition (Batson, 2009; Bohart & Greenberg, 1997; Duan & Hill, 1996; Pedersen, 2009). The problem is compounded when trying to talk about empathy across different fields such as nursing, education, medicine, and psychology. For instance, Bloom (2016) recently wrote a book titled *Against Empathy*, in which he argues that empathy can be destructive in personal relationships, as well as in making moral decisions on a societal level. However, this argument is based entirely on Bloom's definition of empathy, which emphasizes sentimental emotional identification with another.

We begin by synthesizing a range of contemporary dictionary definitions in order to provide a useful working definition:

1. Empathy is interpersonal and unidirectional, provided by one person to another person.
2. Empathy is conceptualized primarily as an ability or capacity and only occasionally as an action.
3. Empathy involves a range of related mental abilities/actions, including
   a. Primarily: Understanding the other person's feelings, perspectives, experiences, or motivations
   b. But also: Awareness of, appreciation of, or sensitivity to the other person
   c. Achieved via: Active entry into the other's experience, described variously in terms of vicariousness, imagination, sharing, or identification.

Several features of this definition can be criticized, for example, that it portrays empathy in outmoded trait-like terms, that it ignores the role of the recipient, that it is too broad, and that it involves a mysterious or potentially misleading process of identification (cf. Bloom, 2016).

Recent neuroscience research on empathy begins to clarify the conceptual confusion. Researchers have made concerted efforts to use a variety of methods ranging from performance tasks, self-report, and neuropsychological assessment to functional magnetic resonance imaging and transcranial stimulation. Research examining the brain correlates of subprocesses of empathy (Decety & Ickes, 2009) extended the initial discovery of "mirror neurons" in the motor cortex of macaque monkeys (e.g., Gallese et al., 1996) to a broader range of affective and perspective-taking components of empathy in humans (Decety & Lamm, 2009). The result of this research has been to deepen and clarify our understanding of therapist empathic processes (Watson & Greenberg, 2009).

The current general view (e.g., Eisenberg & Eggum, 2009) is that empathy can be roughly separated into three major subprocesses, each with specific neuroanatomical correlates. First, there is a more or less automatic, intuitive *emotional simulation* process that mirrors the emotional elements of the other's bodily experience with brain activation centering in the limbic system (amygdala, insula, anterior cingulate cortex) and elsewhere (Decety & Lamm, 2009; Goubert et al., 2009). Second, a more deliberate, conceptual, *perspective-taking* process operates, particularly localized in medial and ventromedial areas of prefrontal cortex and the temporal cortex (Shamay-Tsoory, 2009). Third, there is an *emotion-regulation* process that people use to reappraise or soothe their personal distress when vicariously experiencing the other person's pain or discomfort, allowing them to mobilize compassion and helping behavior for the other (probably based in the orbitofrontal cortex, as well as in the prefrontal and right inferior parietal cortex; Decety & Lamm, 2009; Eisenberg & Eggum, 2009). Both psychotherapy and neuroscience research have repeatedly found that conceptual and emotional elements of empathy do not correlate highly (Duan & Kivlighan, 2005, Hein & Singer, 2010), although in skilled therapists they are likely to coordinate seamlessly and holistically.

Interestingly, the two therapeutic approaches that have most focused on empathy— client-centered therapy and psychoanalytic—have emphasized its cognitive or perspective-taking (Selman, 1980) aspects. That is, they have focused on empathy as *connected knowing* (Belenky et al., 1986), understanding the client's frame of reference or way of experiencing the world. In fact, Carl Rogers talked about empathic understanding, not empathy (Shlien, 1997). By some accounts, 70% or more of Rogers' responses were to felt meaning rather than to feeling, despite the fact that his mode of responding is typically called "reflection of feeling" (Brodley & Brody, 1990; Hayes & Goldfried, 1996; Tausch, 1988). However, understanding clients' frames of reference does include understanding their affective experiences. In addition, empathy and sympathy have typically been sharply differentiated, with therapists such as Rogers disdaining sympathy but prizing empathy (Shlien, 1997). In affective neuroscience terms, this means that therapists in these traditions have often emphasized conscious perspective-taking processes over the more automatic, bodily based emotional simulation processes.

Nevertheless, it is easy to see both processes in Rogers's (1980) definition of empathy:

> the therapist's sensitive ability and willingness to understand the client's thoughts, feelings and struggles from the client's point of view. [It is] this ability to see completely through the client's eyes, to adopt his frame of reference. [p. 85] . . . It means entering the private perceptual world of the other . . . being sensitive, moment by moment, to the changing felt meanings which flow in this other person. . . . It means sensing meanings of which he or she is scarcely aware. (p. 142)

Defined this way, empathy is a higher order category, under which different subtypes, aspects, and modes can be nested. There are different ways one can put oneself into the shoes of the other: emotionally, cognitively, on a moment-to-moment basis, or by trying to grasp an overall sense of what it is like to be that person. Within these subtypes, different aspects of the client's experience can become the focus of empathy (Bohart & Greenberg, 1997). Similarly, there are many ways of expressing empathy, including empathic reflections, empathic questions, experience-near interpretations, empathic conjectures, responsive use of other therapeutic procedures, and a wide range of responsive and carefully tuned nonverbal expressions. Accordingly, empathy is best understood as a complex construct consisting of different acts used in multiple ways.

We distinguish between three main modes of therapeutic empathy: empathic rapport, communicative attunement, and person empathy. First, for some therapists empathy is the establishment of empathic *rapport* and support; this is the definition favored in cognitive-behavioral therapy (CBT). The therapist exhibits a benevolent compassionate attitude toward the client and tries to demonstrate that he or she understands the client's experience, often to set the context for effective treatment. A second mode of empathy consists of an active, ongoing effort to stay attuned on a moment-to-moment basis with the client's communications and unfolding experience. Humanistic and person-centered experiential therapists are most likely to emphasize this form of empathy. The therapist's *communicative attunement* may be expressed in many ways but most likely in empathic responses. The third mode, *person empathy* (Elliott et al., 2003) or experience-near understanding of the client's world, consists of a sustained effort to understand the kinds of experiences the client has had, both historically and presently, that form the background of the client's current experiencing. The question is: How have the client's experiences led him or her to see/feel/think/act as he or she does? This is the type of empathy emphasized by psychodynamic therapists. Of course, empathic rapport, communicative attunement, and person empathy are not mutually exclusive, and their differences are a matter of emphasis.

Many other definitions for empathy have been advanced: as a trait or response skill (Egan, 1982; Truax & Carkhuff, 1967), as an identification process of "becoming" the experience of the client (Mahrer, 1997), and as a hermeneutic interpretive process (Watson, 2001). Many definitions, particularly in the fields of social, developmental, and personality psychology, explicitly include elements of caring, concern, and compassion.

Perhaps the most practical conception, and one that we draw on in our meta-analysis, is Barrett-Lennard's (1981) operational definition of empathy in terms of three different perspectives: (a) the therapist's empathic resonance with the client, (b) the observer's perception of the therapist's expressed empathy, and (c) the client's experience of received therapist empathy.

MEASURES

Reflecting the complex, multidimensional nature of empathy, a confusing welter of measures has been developed across disciplines. During the initial stages of our literature search, many of the abstracts we encountered were of studies on empathy in medicine, nursing, and social and developmental psychology. One of us counted 17 different measures of empathy within the first 100 abstracts reviewed. Following

Barrett-Lennard (1981), most measures of therapist empathy in psychotherapy research fall into three categories: expressed empathy rated by nonparticipant raters, client-rated received empathy, and therapist-rated own empathic resonance. To these can be added a fourth category: empathic accuracy, defined as congruence between therapist and client perceptions of the client (Ickes, 1997; e.g., Duan & Hill, 1996).

In our meta-analysis we have utilized measures of empathy that went beyond rating the mere presence of supposedly empathic therapist response modes such as reflection or paraphrases of the client's words. There is a literature correlating frequency of reflections with outcome, with disappointing results (Orlinsky et al., 2003; Orlinsky & Howard, 1986). Instead, we looked for measures that assessed the quality of therapist empathy. Thus we have focused on studies in which therapists rated their own empathic quality, clients rated their perceptions of how empathic the therapist was, or raters rated the quality of therapists' empathy or studies that attempted to assess empathic accuracy. We note that the scales used to rate the fidelity of motivational interviewing (Moyers et al., 2015) make the same distinction: empathy is rated independently of the number of reflections provided by the therapist.

Observer Ratings

Some of the earliest observer measures of empathy were those of Truax and Carkhuff (1967) and Carkhuff and Berenson (1967). The earliest of these scales asked raters to decide if the content of the therapist's response detracted from the client's response, was interchangeable with it, or added to it; more recent measures focus more globally on activeness, consistency, and depth of empathy. Typically, trained raters listened to 2- to 15-minute samples from session tapes. Samples are usually drawn from the beginning, middle, and/or the end of therapy. Scales such as these do not fully reflect the client-centered conception of empathy as an attitude because they focus narrowly on a particular kind of response, often empathic reflections. Furthermore, the equation of a particular response with empathy has also made these scales less appropriate for measuring empathy in approaches other than client-centered (Lambert et al., 1978). More recent observer empathy measures reflect broader understandings of forms of empathic responding. Watson and Prosser (2002) developed an observer-rated measure of empathy that assesses therapists' verbal and nonverbal behavior and shows convergence validity with client ratings on the Barrett-Lennard Relationship Inventory (BLRI).

In addition, the therapist's general empathy can be rated by others who know or have supervised the psychotherapist. For instance, therapists' empathic capacities can be rated by their supervisors (Gelso et al., 2002). For purposes of our meta-analysis, we grouped together all measures that used external observers.

Client Ratings

The most widely used client-rated measure of empathy is the empathy scale of the BLRI: Other to Self version. Alternative client rating measures have been developed (e.g., Hamilton, 2000; Lorr, 1965; Saunders et al., 1989) as well. Rogers (1957) hypothesized that clients' *perceptions* of therapists' facilitative conditions (positive regard, empathy, and congruence) predict therapeutic outcome. Accordingly, the BLRI, which measures clients' perceptions, is an operational definition of Rogers' hypothesis. In several earlier reviews, including our meta-analysis in the previous editions of this book, client-perceived empathy predicted outcome better than observer- or therapist-rated empathy (Barrett-Lennard, 1981; Elliott et al., 2011; Gross & DeRidder, 1966; Gurman, 1977; Orlinsky et al., 2003; Orlinsky & Howard, 1978, 1986).

Therapist Ratings

Therapist empathy self-rating scales are not as common, but perhaps the most widely used is the BLRI: Myself to Other version. Earlier reviews (Barrett-Lennard, 1981; Gurman, 1977) found that therapist-rated empathy neither predicted outcome nor correlated with client-rated or observer-rated empathy. However, we previously found that therapist-rated empathy did predict outcome but at a lower level than client or observer ratings (Elliott et al., 2011).

Empathic Accuracy

A fourth type of empathy measure uses measures of therapist–client perceptual congruence, commonly referred to as "empathic accuracy" (Ickes, 1997). These typically consist of therapists rating or describing clients as they think the clients would see themselves on personality scales, symptom lists, or within-session experiences and then comparing these to how clients actually rated or described themselves. For instance, one study compared how therapists rated clients on Kelly's Role Repertory Test grid with how clients rated themselves (Landfield, 1971). The measure of empathy is the degree of congruence between therapist and client ratings. This can also be referred to as predictive empathy, because the therapist is trying to predict how clients will rate themselves. This is closer to a measure of the therapist's ability to form a global understanding of what it is like to be the client (person empathy) than it is to a process measure of ongoing communicative attunement.

Recent work on empathic accuracy provides a predictive measure of accuracy of communicative attunement (Ickes, 1997, 2003). This line of research typically employs a tape-assisted recall procedure in which therapists' or observers' moment-to-moment empathy is measured by comparing their perceptions of client experiences to clients' reports of those experiences. For example, researchers (Kwon & Jo, 2012) asked clients to listen to tapes of a session and report on what they were thinking and feeling at various times. Therapists independently listened to the tapes and tried to predict what the clients were thinking and feeling. The degree to which therapist and client agreed was used as a measure of empathic accuracy. Empathic accuracy correlated with counseling outcome .63 ($p < .001$).

Correlations among Empathy Measures

Intercorrelations of empathy measures have generally been modest. Low correlations have been reported between cognitive and affective measures (Gladstein et al., 1987) and between predictive measures and the Barrett-Lennard Relationship Inventory (Kurtz & Grummon, 1972). Other research has found that tape-rated measures correlate only moderately with client-perceived empathy (Gurman, 1977).

These low positive correlations are not surprising when one considers what the different instruments are supposed to be measuring. Trying to predict how a client will fill out a symptom checklist turns out to be quite different from responding sensitively in the session, demonstrating subtle understanding of what the client is communicating, while checking and adjusting one's emerging understanding with that of the client. Similarly, client ratings of therapist understanding may be based on many other things than the therapist's particular skill in empathic reflection. Accordingly, we should not expect different measures of this complex construct to correlate (Gladstein et al., 1987) and could even hypothesize on this basis that using more empathy measure in a study will "dilute" the average association between empathy and outcome. However, Watson and Prosser's (2002) observer measure of empathy did correlate with the BLRI: Other to Self client measure at .66 ($p < .01$).

Confounding between Empathy and Other Relationship Variables

A related concern is the distinctiveness of empathy from other facets of the therapeutic relationship. One early review of more than 20 studies primarily using the BLRI found that, on average, empathy correlated .62 with congruence and .53 with positive regard (Gurman, 1977). Factor analysis of scale-level scores found that one global factor typically emerged, with empathy loading on it along with congruence and positive regard (Gurman, 1977). Others have reported that the empathy scale loaded .93 on a global BLRI factor, with Positive Regard loading .87 and Congruence loading .92 (Blatt et al., 1996). More recently, empathy and the other relationship conditions loaded on a global BLRI factor that accounted for 69% of the variance (Watson & Geller, 2005). Such results suggest that clients' perceptions of empathy are not clearly differentiated from their perceptions of other relationship factors.

On the other hand, empathy did emerge as a separate dimension in reviews of factor analytic studies where specific items were analyzed rather than scale scores (Gurman, 1977). In addition, empathy tends to correlate more highly with the bond component of the therapeutic alliance than with the task and goal components (Horvath & Greenberg, 1986). Thus there is evidence both for and against the hypothesis that the Rogerian triad of empathy, unconditional positive regard, and congruence are distinct variables.

In this regard, we found that many measures of empathy create conceptual confusion by including aspects of both empathy and positive regard. For example, a well-known empathy scale (Burns & Nolen-Hoeksema, 1992), included in our previous meta-analyses, has more items on it dealing with positive relationship qualities in general than it does specific empathy items. We decided in this meta-analysis to include only studies where the "empathy" scale included at least 50% of items we could clearly identify as empathy. Accordingly, we have excluded the Burns and Nolen-Hoeksema instrument from this meta-analysis.

Finally, there is both conceptual and measurement overlap between empathy and other recent relationship constructs such as compassion (e.g., Strauss et al. 2016), presence (Geller et al., 2010), and responsiveness (Elkin et al., 2014). Empathy is typically included as a component in both conceptual and operational definitions of these constructs. Furthermore, in a study of therapists' experience of empathy, compassion was a major component of empathy (Greenberg & Rushanski-Rosenberg, 2002).

In conclusion, empathy is at least partially distinct conceptually from other relationship constructs. However, operationally, things are less clear, with overlap between it and other constructs such as positive regard, congruence, compassion, presence, and responsiveness. In practice, separating empathy out from other relational qualities is a reductionistic fiction, treating relationships as if they were the constituent elements of chemical compounds. Ultimately, we think that it is more useful to treat empathy (and other relationship constructs) as components of a higher order therapeutic relationship.

CLINICAL EXAMPLES

In this section we provide clinical examples of some different types of empathy and specific empathic response modes used to promote in-session client processes and taught in contemporary empathy training (e.g., Elliott et al., 2003; Johnson et al., 2005). We use a running case example to illustrate these.

"Rick" was a 30-year-old unmarried man from a family of unsympathetic high achievers; he had been struggling since his early 20s to break into the movie business. He presented saying that he was anxious and worried much of the time, and at his first appointment he was clearly agitated. At the beginning of treatment, Rick's therapist focused on building *rapport* and trust using empathic understanding responses. *Empathic reflection* responses convey understanding of clients' experiences while *empathic affirmations* are attempts by the therapist to validate the client's perspective. For example:

C1: I'm really in a panic (anxious and looking plaintively at the therapist). I feel anxious all the time. Sometimes it seems so bad, I really worry that I'm on the verge of a psychotic break. I'm afraid I'll completely fall apart. Nothing like this has ever happened to me before. I always felt in charge of myself, but now I can't seem to get any control over myself at all.

T1: So feeling really, really anxious as if you might break down [empathic reflection]— it is just so hard to control and manage it [empathic affirmation].

c2: Yes! I don't know myself anymore. I feel so lost. The anxiety's like a big cloud that just takes over, and I can't even find myself in it anymore. I don't even know what I want, what to trust. . . . I'm so lost.

T2: So you feel so lost, like you don't even know yourself or what you want and need. No wonder you feel lost if it takes over like that. Anxiety can do that, ambushing us and taking over [empathic reflection and empathic affirmation]

c3: (Client tearing up:) Yes, I do feel ambushed and confused (sadly and thoughtfully).

The therapist's empathic recognition provided the client with a sense of being understood, building rapport and fostering a sense of safety that gradually helped the client move from agitation into reflective sadness. To facilitate this the therapist began using more exploratory reflections, which attempted to get at that which was implicit in the client's narratives and help him focus on information that had been in the background but not yet fully articulated, including emerging client experiences. For example:

T 3: And I hear that this leaves you feeling, sort of, sad?

c4: Yes, this is such a familiar feeling. . . . I always felt lost as a kid. Everyone was always so busy—there was no place for me. My siblings were focused on their sports and academic achievements. I was the youngest so I was expected to tag along to their activities even though I hated it. It was so boring!

T4: It sounds almost as if you felt like the odd one out in your family, like you didn't quite fit in somehow? [exploratory reflection]

c5: Yes, very much so. There was so much going on. Mum was always busy with her activities or driving my siblings somewhere. I used to escape with my books and my music.

To further amplify the client's experience the therapist next uses *evocative reflections*, attempts to bring the client's experience alive in the session using rich, evocative, concrete, connotative language, often with a probing, tentative quality. For example:

T5: So you felt forgotten somehow? I have an image of you as a little boy sitting alone in a corner curled up with your book as the people around you rushed to and fro?

c6: Yes, I used to hide away and try to disappear. (Client's voice breaks)

The therapist here is trying to *communicatively attune* in the moment to the client's experience and feel her way into what it must have felt like to be a child in that busy, high-achieving household. The therapist continues to facilitate the exploration of the client's inner experience using *process reflections* and *empathic conjectures*, which go beyond exploratory reflections in that they are attempts to guess or infer what clients might be feeling but have not said out loud yet. They are presented tentatively as hunches grounded in what the client has shared. For example, while watching Rick the therapist noticed that her client's voice shifted and that he looked very sad.

T6: I noticed your voice changed just then [process reflection]. You look very sad; are you? [empathic conjecture] What is happening inside as you recall the busy household? [exploratory question]

C7: I feel like I can't live up to their expectations. Even though I know I've got all this potential, I always feel there is something wrong with me.

T7: So you feel like a failure? [empathic conjecture] Like there is something wrong with you? You are not quite right? [exploratory reflection]

At other times therapists can use *empathic refocusing* responses to offer clients the opportunity to return to an experience they had distanced themselves from. For example:

C8: Yes, that's how it feels when I go home and then it's worse as they pester me about not being married and poke fun at me about my impractical career goals and marginal job waiting table.

T8: So when you're at home, I guess it's just so difficult, but a minute ago I also heard something in you that hangs onto your ambitions and sees yourself as talented and having a lot to offer, is that right? [empathic refocusing response, referring back to C7, delivered as an empathic conjecture]

C9: Yes, that's in there somewhere also, but then it just dissolves.

These examples demonstrate how therapists work to remain *communicatively attuned* to their clients on a moment to moment basis in the session. And as clients continue to share and explore their experiences, therapists begin to develop a sense of *person empathy,* providing a more holistic understanding of their clients' experiences. This more holistic understanding provides some guidance in terms of attending to markers that could become the focus of treatment, for example, unresolved painful relationships or the client's self-criticism.

LANDMARK STUDIES

Quantitative Studies

One of the oldest and most influential of studies on empathy and outcome was conducted by Barrett-Lennard (1962), largely because it was the origin of the most widely used empathy measure, the Empathy subscale of the BLRI. The author adapted and refined an earlier Q-sort measure into parallel client and therapist-perspective self-report measures that included therapist empathic understanding. He provided initial validity and reliability data, using a sample of 35 clients from the University of Chicago Counseling Center. The BLRI was administered to both therapists and their clients after Sessions 5, 15, and 25 and at the end of treatment; outcome was assessed using therapist posttherapy global ratings of degree of client change and an integration of client improvement self-ratings on several pre–post measures of adjustment. All told, six different process–outcome correlations could be calculated, based on dichotomizing clients as more versus less improved; these associations were all in the positive direction and ranged from .16 to .49, with a mean of .42.

Miller and colleagues (1980), in a study of focused versus broad-spectrum behavior therapy for problem drinkers, randomly assigned clients to therapists. Therapists were nine student trainees who received three months of intensive training in basic listening and counseling skills, along with training in the treatment modalities to be delivered. Three raters observed the psychotherapy sessions through one-way mirrors and rated therapists' accurate empathy utilizing a modification of the Truax scales. Ratings were done before outcome data were collected or analyzed. Mean therapist skill ratings were compared to therapists' success rates across clients, and these two were highly related ($r = .82$) in a positive direction. Higher therapist empathy led to greater reductions in problem drinking.

This study also bears on the causality issue, at least on the temporal order of empathy and outcome. The ratings were performed before the outcome data were available. Since clients were randomly assigned to therapists, it seems somewhat implausible that the top-rated therapist on empathy, for instance, just happened to receive 100% of clients who went on to improve the most. Thus this study provides evidence that empathy rated during treatment, or some unmeasured covariate of empathy, occurred before and probably contributed causally to outcome.

Another landmark study in our meta-analysis is Moyers et al. (2016), which had by far the largest number of clients (700) and employed sophisticated multilevel modeling to separate the effects of empathy on outcome both within and between therapists. Drawing on data from the Project COMBINE trial on the effects of motivational interviewing on alcohol problems, outcomes were assessed using drinking behaviors after treatment. Empathy was assessed using an observer measure based on transcripts of session recordings. Between-therapist effects accounted for 11% of the variance in empathy, requiring multilevel modelling to separate out between- and within-therapist components of the association between empathy and outcome.

The effects for empathy were comparatively small. The within-therapist effect picked up differences between clients with whom the therapist was more or less empathic than usual for them; it was statistically significant and equivalent to $r = .15$. The between-therapist effect looked at more trait-like differences in therapist empathy level and was equivalent to $r = .05$, which was not statistically significant. Averaged together in our analysis, these two effects amounted to $r = 10$. Our meta-analysis includes several recent large studies with small effects, mostly but not exclusively from the motivational interviewing literature. These studies involve very brief interventions (often only two sessions) and often include only observer measures of empathy; they may thus represent a different population of studies from the rest of the meta-analysis.

Qualitative Studies

In contrast to the large number of quantitative studies reviewed here, there is relatively little qualitative research on empathy. In the first of a series of three linked qualitative studies, Myers (2000) examined the experience of five female psychotherapy clients.

The focus of the studies was on the process of empathic listening, and interviews were conducted after the therapy had ended. The clients were selected because they had formed a good relationship with their therapist and because they were particularly articulate about their experiences. Myers explicitly acknowledges that no claims of generality can be made from her findings.

Clients participated in a humanistic empathy-based therapy for at least 20 sessions. They were interviewed and also provided written narrative accounts to a series of questions. Interview and written data were content-analyzed for themes. In the first study, three factors characterized empathy: the experience of being understood in contrast to the negative experience of being misunderstood by others, getting feedback from the therapist, and development of a feeling of safety. All clients interviewed reported being listened to as an essential element of their relationship with their therapists.

In the second study (Myers, 2003), the impacts of being empathically listened to and understood were identified. These prominently included an increased sense of personal agency, a redefined sense of self, a renewed sense of being-in-the-world, increased self-acceptance, and increased self-empathy. In the third study (Myers & White, 2010), the clients were interviewed 10 years later. They continued to attribute personal change and growth to being empathically listened to and understood. In particular they noted how they had continued to grow based on their treatment. They emphasized an enhanced sense of personal agency in the form of an increased sense of self-efficacy and greater skill at emotional regulation.

In another landmark qualitative study, MacFarlane and colleagues (2017), Martin and Sterne (1976) interviewed nine clients about their experiences of empathy in psychotherapy. They examined at three features of the empathic experience: (a) clients' phenomenology of empathy, (b) clients' interpretations of the psychotherapists' empathic communication, and (c) clients' perceptions of the utility (e.g., benefits and consequences) of empathy. The nine clients were seen by eight therapists, who were doctoral students in clinical psychology. As in the Myers (2000, 2003) studies, clients were nominated by therapists based on their verbal skills and their ability to report on their experiences. Eight clients were interviewed within 24 hours of a therapy session; the other client was interviewed within 48 hours.

All clients engaged in a two-hour Interpersonal Process Recall interview based on videotapes of their session. Data were analyzed utilizing grounded theory. Three types of empathy emerged: clients' perceptions of therapists' cognitive empathy (a complex combination of therapist attentiveness, asking pertinent questions, reflections, and trying to see things from the client's perspective), emotional empathy (perceptions of therapists' emotional attunement), and client empathy (clients' attunement to the therapist). Two classes of empathy benefits, as perceived by clients, were frequently reported: process-related benefits (how empathy facilitated the therapy process, including impacts like pacing of the session, facilitating openness, helping overcome demographic differences between therapist and client, and facilitating trust) and client-related benefits (improvements in self-understanding, therapist undivided attention as a corrective experience, feeling better, feeling happier). Both of these qualitative studies point to the value of including the client perspective in empathy research and also show how an intensive qualitative examination of the empathic process can begin linking it to client outcome.

RESULTS OF PREVIOUS META-ANALYSES

Major reviews of the empathy literature have occurred since the 1970s. The first major review of the association between therapist facilitative conditions (including empathy) and outcome (Truax & Mitchell, 1971) was later strongly criticized (Lambert et al., 1978) for selective citations of results and numerous methodological failings. Two reviews in the 1970s (Gurman, 1977; Parloff et al., 1978) focused on client perceptions of facilitative conditions and were fairly positive but expressed concern about possible confounds among client-perceived empathy, other facilitative conditions, and client-rated outcome. These focused more broadly on facilitative conditions without attempting to separate out therapist empathy and were either narrative reviews or used box scores to summarize results. Subsequently, Orlinsky and colleagues (1994, 2003) separated out therapist–client mutual empathic resonance and reported strong results using a box score method.

The first meta-analyses to focus specifically on the empathy–outcome literature were the two previous versions of this chapter in 2002 (Bohart et al., 2002) and 2011 (Elliott et al., 2011). Both meta-analyses reported a moderately positive but variable relation between therapist empathy and client outcome. The 2011 meta-analysis was conducted on 57 studies (224 effects) and encompassed a total of 3,599 clients. The average weighted correlation between empathy and outcome was $r = .31$.

META-ANALYTIC REVIEW

In this section we report the results of an updated meta-analysis conducted on available research relating empathy to psychotherapy outcome. We addressed the main question of the overall association between therapist empathy and client outcome. Additionally, we investigated multiple potential moderators of that association: (a) Do different forms of psychotherapy yield different levels of association between empathy and outcome? (b) Does the perspective used to measure empathy predict the level of association between empathy and outcome? (c) Does broad type of client-presenting problem matter for the level of empathy–outcome association? and (d) What other study or sample characteristics predict the level of association between empathy and outcome (i.e., year of publication, sample size, treatment setting, therapy modality and length, therapist experience, type of outcome measure, unit of process)?

Search Strategy

We started with the studies we used in our meta-analyses (Bohart et al., 2002; Elliott et al., 2011) in the two previous editions of this book, which included studies gathered from a wide variety of sources. We then did an inclusive search of PsycInfo for all years, using the search terms:

- "empathy" or "empathic"
- AND "psychotherapy", "counseling" OR "counselling"
- AND "change" OR "outcome*" OR "improvement"
- AND methods: empirical study, quantitative study, treatment outcome, or clinical trial

Screening and Rating of Articles

This search produced 2,222 potential sources, which were then screened systematically as documented in Table 7.1. The inclusion criterion was process outcome research studies relating measured therapist empathy to psychotherapy outcome. The studies

Table 7.1. Prisma Information for Empathy–Outcome Meta-Analysis

Stage	N of Studies Included	N of Studies Excluded	Notes
1. Search Result:	2,222		Date of search: March 3, 2017
2. Abstract screening stage: Possible Empathy → Outcome studies[a]	148	2,074	Not empathy → outcome studies
3. Screening for duplicates	133	15	Including 14 from Elliott et al. (2011)
4. Full text retrieval	99	34	Unable to retrieve full text
5. Full text review and analysis, plus studies carried over from Elliott et al. (2011)	24 + 58 = 82	75	Failed exclusion criteria at full text review or analysis

Note. Results of applying exclusion criteria:

1. Not about psychotherapy/counseling (e.g., training or supervision or empathy in nontherapist populations such healthcare workers in medical encounters) (step 2: 900; step 5: 8)

2. Not research on therapist empathy (e.g., theory articles, clinical case studies; research on client empathy as an outcome) (step 2: 579; step 5: 15)

3. Not process-outcome research on therapist empathy (e.g., measure therapist empathy but do not relate it to client outcome; includes helpful factors studies) (step 2: 433; step 5: 41)

4. n < 5 (e.g., case studies) (step 2: 48; step 5: 0)

5. Analogue studies (i.e., do not involve actual sessions with real clients) (step 2: 54; step 5: 1)

6. Empathy not specifically/explicitly measured (e.g., global Barrett-Lennard Relationship Inventory scores) (step 2: 19; step 5: 16)

7. Sessions <2 (step 2: 9; step 5: 11)

8. Effect size (r or d) not reported or calculable (step 2: 1; step 5: 0)

9. Reviews and meta-analyses (step 2: 12; step 5: 0)

Additional duplicates identified at step 5: 3

needed to report a correlation or sufficient information to calculate one. (Results of applying the exclusion criteria are presented in Table 7.1.) The abstracts of the potential sources were screened by the four co-authors, with a sample of 200 studies to assess reliability. The interrater reliability between original rater and checking rater was kappa = .61, which reflects the difficulty of identifying and agreeing on low baserate events (less than 2% of potential sources were eventually retained for analysis). Accordingly, disagreements were retained for retrieval and further screening. Agreements (n = 13) usually ended up being retained in the final sample used in the meta-analysis (57%), whereas disagreements (n = 14) were almost always dropped (8% retained). This process resulted in 148 sources being retained. Screening for duplicates resulted in dropping 15 sources, 14 of which had been included in the previous version of this meta-analysis, which covered sources through 2008 (Elliott et al., 2011). This process resulted in 133 sources, of which we were able to locate full texts for 99 (most of the dropped sources were doctoral dissertations).

The exclusion criteria were again applied to these 99 full text sources, which were each evaluated by two of the co-authors. Interrater reliability was low (kappa = .45) because of ongoing confusion about whether "therapy" and "outcome" were being studied, whether therapist global facilitative conditions could be counted as measures of empathy, and a lack of clarity in the written reports about the length of brief interventions such as motivational interviewing. All disagreements were therefore discussed to reach consensus, resulting in 24 studies being retained in the analysis. These 24 studies were added to 58 studies that were carried over from Elliott et al. (2011), for a total 82 studies. (See Supplemental Table S1 for summary information about these studies.)

Characteristics of the Studies

Table 7.2 summarizes the 82 studies used in the meta-analysis. For measures of outcome, we included a study as long as there was some assessment of the effects of therapy, even if only at the session level (immediate outcome). There is some conceptual overlap between feeling understood and client satisfaction/session helpfulness, which was used in 19% of studies; we subsequently examined type of outcome measure as a moderator variable. The resulting sample consisted of 290 separate tests of the empathy–outcome association, aggregated into 82 different samples (from 80 studies) and encompassing a total of 6,138 clients, who were seen for an average of 25 sessions.

Estimation of Effect Size

We used Pearson correlations as our main effect size metric in a random effect model. Our strategy was to extract all possible effects. Therefore, we used the following conventions (extensions of those used in Smith et al., 1980) to estimate r: First, if we had a significance level, we converted it to r. If the result was nonsignificant but we had enough information to calculate a t and then convert, we did so. If we had no other information than that the effect was nonsignificant, we set r at zero. If the

Supplemental Table S1. Table of Studies, Sample Sizes, and Effects

Authors	Year	Meta-Analysis Version	N of Clients	N of Effects	r
Barnicot et al.[a]	2014	3	157	2	.010
Barrett-Lennard	1962	1	35	6	.418
Bergin & Jasper	1969	1	24	1	.050
Beutler et al.	1972	1	31	1	.190
Brouzos et al.	2015	3	40	4	.000
Brug et al.	2007	3	142	6	.046
Buckley et al.	1981	1	71	6	.177
Bugge et al.	1985	1	274	1	.574
Bulllmann et al. [PCT]	2004	2	85	1	.330
Bulllmann et al. [CBT]	2004	2	86	1	.410
Cartwright & Lerner	1965	1	28	2	.173
Clark & Culbert	1965	1	10	1	.360
Cooley & Lajoy	1980	1	54	10	.316
Cramer & Takens	1992	2	37	6	.328
Dicken et al.	1977	3	43	9	.080
Dormaar et al.	1989	1	135	3	.000
Duan & Kivlighan	2002	3	57	2	.290
Filak & Abeles	1984	1	50	2	.339
Free et al.[a]	1985	3	57	9	.038
Fretz	1966	1	17	3	.320
Fuertes & Brobst	2002	3	85	1	.570
Fuertes et al.	2006	2	51	2	.529
Fuertes et al.	2007	2	59	2	.214
Gabbard et al.	1986	1	42	12	.218
Garfield & Bergin	1971	1	38	10	.016
Gelso et al.	2002	2	63	2	.235
Gillispie et al.	2005	3	121	2	.050
Goldman et al.	2000	1	38	4	.117
Goodman et al.	2015	3	5	1	.540
Greenberg & Webster	1982	1	31	4	-.046
Gross & DeRidder	1966	1	8	1	.750
Guydish et al.[a]	2014	3	151	2	.238
Hall & Davis	2000	1	162	2	.170
Hamilton	2000	1	132	1	.730
Hansen et al.	1968	1	70	2	.532
Hoffart et al.	2002	2	35	6	.045
Horvath & Greenberg	1981	1	29	3	.141
Kasarabada et al.	2002	3	511	1	.004
Kim et al.	2009	3	61	3	.580
Kolden	1996	3	121	2	.320
Kurtz & Grummon	1972	1	31	42	.069
Kwon & Jo	2012	3	48	1	.613

Supplemental Table S1. Continued

Authors	Year	Meta-Analysis Version	N of Clients	N of Effects	r
Lafferty et al.	1989	1	60	1	.640
Langhoff et al.	2008	2	55	4	.295
Lerner	1972	1	30	4	.165
Lesser	1961	1	22	2	-.292
Lorr	1965	1	320	3	.267
Malin & Pos[a]	2015	3	30	1	.260
Marshall et al.	2002	2	39	2	.400
Marshall et al.	2003	2	41	3	.121
Martin & Sterne	1976	1	143	4	.150
Melnick & Pierce	1971	1	18	1	.450
Miller et al.t	1980	1	41	1	.819
Mitchell et al.	1973	1	120	1	.000
Moyers et al.[a]	2016	3	700	2	.100
Muller & Abeles	1971	1	36	1	.410
Murphy & Cramer	2014	3	62	2	.190
Orlinsky & Howard	1967	1	37	4	.386
Pantalon et al.	2004	2	16	2	.400
Payne et al.	2007	2	6	3	.693
Peake	1979	1	55	2	.196
Rabavilas et al.	1979	1	36	1	.506
Ritter et al.	2002	3	88	3	.250
Roback & Strassberg	1975	1	12	1	.070
Saltzman et al.	1976	1	55	4	.153
Sandberk & Akbaş	2015	3	20	2	.470
Sapolsky	1965	1	16	1	.377
Saunders	2000	1	114	5	.191
Spohr et al.	2016	3	40	2	.230
Staples et al. [Behavior Therapy]	1976	1	30	3	.050
Staples et al. [Psychodynamic Therapy]	1976	1	30	3	.003
Strupp et al.	1969	1	44	1	.330
Thrasher et al.	2006	3	30	1	.480
Truax	1966	1	80	3	.365
Truax et al.	1965	1	40	1	.198
Truax et al.	1966	1	40	5	.332
Truax & Wittmer	1971	1	40	5	.259
Truax et al.	1971	1	116	3	.510
Watson et al.	2014	3	55	7	.370
Wiprovnick et al.[a]	2015	3	59	1	.310
Wisconsin Project (Barrington, 1967; Kiesler et al., 1967; Van der Veen, 1967)	1967	1	12	12	.128
Woodin et al.	2012	3	25	2	.110

Table 7.2. Selected Study Characteristics

Parametric Characteristics:	N	M	SD	Range
Sample size: study/samples	82 samples,	74.9	101.1	5–700
Sample size: clients:	6,138 clients	(median: 42.5)		
Length of therapy (sessions)	61	25.2	37.6	2–228
Effects per study	81	3.6	5.0	1–42
Categorical Characteristics:		Selected Categories		%
Year of publication	82	1961–1980		43
		1981–2000		18
		2001–2016		39
Theoretical orientation	82	Mixed, eclectic, or unknown		60
		Humanistic-experiential		17
		Cognitive-behavioral therapy		15
		Psychodynamic		9
Treatment format	82	Individual		75
Treatment setting	81	Outpatient		83
Client presenting problem	82	Mixed, unspecified		54
Therapist experience level	73	Recent PhD or MD		34
		Master's level		34
Outcome assessment time point	80	Posttreatment		58
Main outcome perspective	69	Client		55
Outcome measure type	61	Symptom ratings		24
		Improvement/recovery		21
		Client satisfaction		19
Main empathy perspective	69	Client (mostly Barrett-Lennard, 1962)		51 / 39
		Observer (mostly Truax & Carkhuff, 1967)		
Empathy measurement unit	80	Therapy to date		53

authors indicated a "nonsignificant trend" but did not report a correlation (e.g., Kiesler et al. [1967] indicated several trends on Minnesota Multiphasic Personality Inventory scales), we estimated the trend by conservatively assigning an effect size of half the size of a significant r.

Coding Procedure and Analyses

As summarized in Table 7.2, we coded multiple features of each study. The following variables were coded: therapy format (individual or group), theoretical orientation, experience level of therapists, treatment setting (inpatient, outpatient), number of sessions (typically the mean), type of problems (mixed/unspecified, depression or anxiety, mild problems, and severe problems such as psychosis or incarceration), source of outcome measure (therapist rating, client rating, objective, and other measures), when outcome was measured (e.g., postsession, posttherapy, follow-up), type of outcome measured (e.g., symptom change, improvement, global), source of empathy measure (objective ratings, therapist, client, therapist–client congruence, trait measure), and unit of measure (e.g., 2- to 5-minute samples, session, therapy to date).

We conducted two sets of analyses: by effects and by studies. First, we analyzed the 290 separate effects to examine the impact of perspective of empathy measurement and type of outcome. Second, study-level analyses averaged individual effects within client samples before further analysis, thus avoiding problems of nonindependence and eliminating bias due to variable numbers of effects reported in different studies (Lipsey & Wilson, 2001). For analyses across studies, including overall effects and moderator variable analyses, we used Fisher's r to z transformation, weighted studies by inverse error ($n - 3$), and analyzed for heterogeneity of effects using Cochrane's Q, and a restricted maximum likelihood (REML) random effects model using Wilson's (2006) macros for SPSS. We also calculated I^2, an estimate of the proportion of variation due to true variability as opposed to random error (Higgins et al., 2003) and fail-safe numbers (vs. $r = .2$).

Results

Probably the single best summary value, as shown in Table 7.3, is the study-level random effects weighted r of .28 (95% confidence interval [CI] of .23–.33), a medium effect size (equivalent to $d = .58$). For analyses of the 290 nonindependent separate effects, average effects were somewhat smaller, at .21 (95% CI = .18–.24; equivalent to $d = .43$). These values were very similar to our previous reviews (Bohart et al., 2002; Elliott et al., 2011) and indicate that empathy generally accounts for about 9% of the variance in therapy outcome. This effect size is on the same order of magnitude as analyses of the relation between the alliance in individual therapy and treatment outcome (i.e., Flückiger et al., Chapter 2, this volume; $d = .57$). Overall, empathy typically accounts for more outcome variance than do specific treatment methods (compare Wampold's [2015] estimate of $d = .2$ for intervention effects).

We also assessed the likelihood of bias, either due to studies with negative effects not being published or to smaller studies with weaker methods producing more favorable results. First, we calculated the fail-safe number, that is, the number of studies with $r = 0$ results required to reduce the weighted effect to a minimum clinically interesting value of $r = .2$ (see Table 7.3). This value was based on 33 studies for the study-level effect of .28; the comparable number for effect level effects was only 12, which means that the effect-level effect is not particularly robust and would drop below the $r = .2$ threshold with only a small number of underreporting null results. Second, we created a funnel plot of the relation between effect size and level of standard error of r (which is a joint function of sample size and effect size). The correlation between standard error of r and effect size was .06, indicating an absence of bias deriving from smaller studies with less precise effects producing larger effects. Further, as can be seen in Figure 7.1, the funnel plot is quite symmetrical, making it unlikely that the

Table 7.3. Empathy–Outcome Correlations: Overall Summary Statistics

	Effect Level (N = 290)	Study Level (N = 82)
N	M (95% CI)	M (95% CI)
Weighted Mean r	.21* (.18–.24)	.28* (.23–.33)
Cochrane's Q	1039.2*	348.68*
I^2	72.2%	76.8%
Fail-safe number	13	33

Note. 95% CI = confidence interval.

* p < .001.

overall effect would be shifted negatively if a larger number of more powerful studies were to be carried out.

Nevertheless, the .28 value conceals statistically significant variability in effects, as indicated by a study-level Cochrane's Q of 348.68 (p < .001); in addition, I^2 was 72%, a large value. Figure 7.1 also attests to the wide variability of effects, even in studies with reasonably large samples and small standard errors. These findings mean that a further examination of possible moderators of the empathy–outcome association is essential (Lipsey & Wilson, 2001). Our sample was large enough to include internal replication of the empathy–outcome association across a range of theoretical orientations in the .21–.30 range (Table 7.4), as well as across observer and client measurement perspectives (Table 7.5) and several client-presenting problems or populations (i.e., depression/anxiety, severe/incarcerated, and mixed/unspecified; Table 7.6).

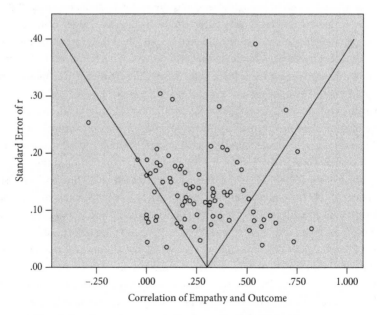

FIGURE 7.1 Funnel plot of empathyoutcome effect by standard error of r.

Table 7.4. Mean Study-Level Effects across Theoretical Orientation

Theoretical Orientation	n	Mean Weighted r	Within Group Q	I^2
Experiential/ Humanistic	14	0.24**	15.32	15.1%
Cognitive-Behavioral	12	0.30**	61.12**	82.0%
Psychodynamic	7	0.21**	5.62	0
Other/Unspecified	49	0.30**	257.08**	81.3%
Between groups Q		1.41 ($df = 3, 78$) (NS)		

Note. Mean correlations and significance tests (vs. null hypothesis $r = 0$) for subgroups calculated using Fisher's z scores and a restricted maximum likelihood random effects model using Wilson's (2006) macros for SPSS. Cochrane's Q tests for heterogeneity were evaluated as a chi-square test under a fixed effect model.

$*p < .05; **p < .01$.

MODERATORS AND MEDIATORS

We divide this section on moderators and mediators into two parts: meta-analytic analyses of potential moderators and therapist mediators.

Moderator Analyses

Although the significant Q and large I^2 statistics point to important moderator variables or sources of heterogeneity, they do not specify what these are. In our previous meta-analyses, we hypothesized that the empathy–outcome association would be larger in humanistic-experiential therapies, such as person-centered. However, we have again found tantalizing evidence that empathy might prove more important to outcome in cognitive-behavioral therapies or other/unspecified treatments than in humanistic or psychodynamic therapies ($p < .05$). None of the pairwise comparisons were statistically significant, possibly because the larger effects are marked by large Q and I^2 statistics indicating other sources of unexplained variability.

We have also replicated the differences we previously found among the empathy measurement perspectives using effect-level analyses (Table 7.5; between-groups

Table 7.5. Mean Within-Study Effects across Empathy Measurement Perspectives

Measurement Perspective	n	Mean Weighted r	Within Group Q	I^2
Observer	102	.21[a]**	347.25**	70.9%
Client	117	.27[a]**	459.35**	74.8%
Therapist	37	.19[a]**	69.19**	48.0%
Empathic Accuracy	34	.01[b]	75.94**	56.5%
Between groups Q		26.11** ($df = 3, 286$)		

Note. See note for Table 7.4. Mean weighted r values that share superscripts do not differ significantly ($p \geq .05$).

$**p < .001$.

Table 7.6. Mean Between-Study Effects across Grouped Client Problem Populations

Client Problem Population	N	Mean Weighted r	Within Group Q	I^2
Severe, chronic, or incarcerated	15	.32**	57.89**	75.8%
Mixed or unspecified	44	.30**	181.5**	76.5%
Depression or anxiety	10	.26**	17.07*	47.3%
Mild, normal, or physical problems	6	.17	7.07	29.3%
Self-damaging activity	7	.19*	15.00*	60.0%
Between groups Q	70.15** (df = 4, 76)			

Note. See note for Table 7.4. Mean weighted *r* values do not differ significantly (p ≥.05).
*p < .05; **p < .01.

Q significant at $p < .001$). Specifically, client measures predicted outcome the best (mean weighted $r = .27$; $n = 117$), slightly better than observer rated measures ($r = .21$; $n = 102$) and therapist measures ($r = .19$; $n = 37$); each of these mean effects was significantly greatly than zero ($p < .001$) but did not differ significantly from each other. In contrast, empathic accuracy measures were unrelated to outcome ($r = .01$; $n = 34$, ns), and were statistically smaller than effects for each of the other three measures ($p < .05$). However, most perspectives were again characterized by large ($I^2 > 50\%$), statistically significant amounts of nonchance heterogeneity. Clarification of the source of this heterogeneity awaits further research; however, for now it seems fair to say that clients' feelings of being understood and observer ratings (and, to a lesser extent, therapist impressions) appear to carry significant weight as far as outcome goes but that empathic accuracy measures do not, in spite of their intuitive appeal.

A new feature here was the analysis of separate effects for client populations grouped into five broad headings (Table 7.6). The largest empath–outcome association was for severe/chronic incarcerated populations, mixed/unspecified, and depressed/anxious. Smaller effects were found for mild/normal/physical problem and self-damaging activities (e.g., substance misuse). (Although the overall between-groups Q showed statistically significant differences, none of the paired comparisons were significant.)

Finally, in Table 7.7, we examined several other variables that might account for some of the heterogeneity of the effect sizes: year of publication, number of effects analyzed in a study, sample size, setting (outpatient vs. inpatient), treatment format (individual vs. group), length of therapy in sessions, therapist experience level, client severity (estimated by scaling client presenting problem/population), globalness of outcome measures (individualized to satisfaction ratings), and size of empathy unit (5 min segment to whole therapy). Using weighted correlations (random effects, REML analyses), only the number of effects reported in a study ($r = -.23$), outcome globality ($r = .32$), and outpatient setting ($r = -.14$) were statistically associated with outcome. Using backwards stepwise regression (random effects, REML), four of these continuous variables significantly predicted effect size ($p < .05$): analyzing fewer effects in a study ($\beta = -.30$), having a smaller sample of clients ($\beta = -.24$), outpatient setting (β

Table 7.7. Weighted Bivariate Associations between Study-Level Effect Size and Selected Continuous Moderator Variables

Predictor	k	r
Year of publication	82	.01
N of effects analyzed in study	82	−.23*
N of clients in study	82	−.15
Setting (1 = outpatient; 2 = inpatient)	81	−.14*
Format (1 = individual; 2 = group)	72	.04
Length of therapy (in sessions)	61	.10
Therapist experience level (6-point scale)	73	−.16
Level of client problem severity (4-point scale)	64	.09
Outcome globality (6-point scale: individualized to satisfaction ratings)	62	.32*
Size of empathy unit (6-point scale)	80	.04

Note. All analyses weighted effects using inverse error (i.e., $n − 3$); random effects analyses followed restricted maximum likelihood model.
*$p < .05$.

= −.31), and outcome globality ($\beta = .28$); together, these four variables accounted for 33% of the variance in effect size.

To sum up our moderator results: First, we found a "more is less" effect. That is, more ambitious (in terms of number of clients) and wider ranging studies (in terms of range of measures) produced smaller effects. Second, for the second time in our series of meta-analyses, we found tantalizing trends that the empathy–outcome association might be larger for CBT than for experiential and psychodynamic clinicians. Third, the client's perception of empathy fares better in predicting outcome than the therapist's. Fourth, using global outcome variables like client satisfaction resulted in larger associations between therapist empathy and outcome, possibly because conceptual confounding between client perceptions of empathy and client ratings of posttherapy satisfaction. Fifth, there was some evidence that the empathy–outcome association was stronger for clients in outpatient settings. Sixth, therapist empathic accuracy did not predict outcome.

In contrast, we found the empathy–outcome association held across a wide range of other variables, both substantive (client-presenting problem/severity, therapy modality) and methodological (year of publication, level/size of unit at which empathy was measured). Findings for therapist experience level and length of therapy were equivocal.

Therapist Mediators

As noted earlier, affective neuroscience researchers have proposed that empathy involves three interlinked skills: affective simulation, perspective-taking, and regulation of one's own emotions (Decety & Jackson, 2004). Supporting this, research has found a relation between various measures of cognitive complexity, such as those of perspective-taking or abstract ability, and empathy in both developmental psychology and psychotherapy (Eisenberg & Fabes, 1990; Henschel & Bohart, 1981; Watson, 2001). With respect to affective simulation and emotion regulation, therapists open to conflictual, countertransferential feelings were perceived as more empathic by clients (Peabody & Gelso, 1982).

The degree of similarity between therapist and client (Duan & Hill, 1996; Gladstein & Associates, 1987; Watson, 2001) also influences the level of empathy. Similarity and familiarity between the target of empathy and the empathizer have been found to be important modulators of empathy in neuroscience research on mirror neurons (Watson & Greenberg, 2009). Another vital factor is therapist nonlinguistic and paralinguistic behavior. This encompasses therapists' posture, vocal quality, ability to encourage exploration using emotion words, and relative infrequency of talking too much, giving advice, and interrupting (Duan & Hill, 1996; Watson, 2001). Other research has shown that responses that are just ahead of the client seem to be more effective than responses that are either at the same level as the client or at a more global level (Sachse, 1990a, 1990b; Tallman et al., 1994; Truax & Carkhuff, 1967). In a qualitative study of clients' experience of empathy, interrupting, failing to maintain eye contact, and dismissing the client's position while imposing the therapist's own position were all perceived as unempathic (Myers, 2000). Conversely, being nonjudgmental, attentive, open to discussing any topic, and paying attention to details were perceived as empathic.

EVIDENCE FOR CAUSALITY

In this chapter we have focused largely on quantitative process–outcome correlational studies in which in-session empathy was used to predict client outcome, generally posttherapy. We have assembled a large and quite broad body of correlational evidence that clearly shows small to medium covariation between these two variables.

What does this covariation mean from a causal point of view? We do not claim that this evidence by itself is sufficient to justify strong and generalizable causal inference that therapist empathy causes client outcome. On the other hand, we would similarly doubt any other single kind of evidence that might be brought to bear on the causal link between these two variables, including randomized controlled trials (RCTs). For us, saying any single kind of evidence is sufficient for making causal inferences is dogma rather than science.

What we advocate instead is a general strategy that logically considers the kind of evidence needed to make generalizable causal inferences. We recommend combining two frameworks for doing so (Cooke & Campbell, 1979; Haynes & O'Brien, 2000). Together, these provide an integrative model of causal inference, consisting of six conditions, all of which we hold are necessary for generalizable causal inference; these fall into three sets of paired conditions (see Box 7.1). Using this framework, we

---

Box 7.1 Causal Inference Conditions for Process--Outcome Correlational Research

Preliminary conditions provide the basis for further investigation:

1. *Precedence*: The hypothesized causal variable must reliably precede the effect variable.

2. *Plausibility*: There must be a plausible explanation ("logical mechanism") for the hypothesized causal relation.

Experimental conditions refer to the validity of claims about the relation (statistical or causal) between variables (independent/causal and dependent/effect):

3. *Statistical Conclusion Validity*: There must be reliable covariation between supposed cause and effect variables.

4. *Internal Validity*: Realistic alternative causes for the observed covariation must be reasonably excluded.

Generalizability/Usability conditions refer to the validity of claims about the general meaning of the causal relationship, that is, the plausibility of generalizing to constructs or real-world situations.

5. *Construct validity*: Reasonable alternative meanings of the cause and effect variables must be ruled out (e.g., social desirability, researcher allegiance).

6. *External Validity*: The generalizability or range of application to relevant real-world settings beyond tightly controlled research settings must be demonstrated.

---

next consider what knowledge claims are currently justified by the available evidence on therapist empathy as a cause of client posttherapy change:

1. **Precedence**: This condition is satisfied when studies measure (a) client outcome at or after the end of therapy and (b) therapist empathy at some earlier point during therapy, which helps us rule out or minimize reverse causation, where for example client early improvement enables therapists to be more empathic. Path analytic or panel correlational designs help us to do this statistically. Assessing therapist empathy independently (e.g., by observer or therapist self-ratings) from client outcome also helps. *In our review, we found statistically significant effects when the precedence condition was satisfied, although they were generally smaller.*

2. **Plausibility**: Regardless of the empirical data, scientists do not accept causal relationships in the absence of a plausible theory linking cause and effect. The best known such theory for the empathy–outcome connection was proposed by Rogers (1957) in his "process equation," which described therapy empathy as one of six conditions needed for personality change. If Rogers' theory now seems overly general, qualitative research studies, such as those we have sampled from here, begin to provide what qualitative researchers (e.g., Corbin & Strauss, 2008) refer

to as a "grounded theory" of the specific ways in which therapist empathy can lead to client outcome. *Based on current theory and emerging qualitative research, we regard this condition as well satisfied.*

3. **Statistical conclusion validity**: This is a necessary but not sufficient condition for causal inference. The credo we were taught, "Correlation does not imply causation," is actually an oversimplification. It would be more accurate to say, "Correlation does not establish causation . . . but it certainly helps." It is also true to say, "Correlation proves causation" in the old-fashioned sense of the word "prove," which originally meant "to put to the test." Most accurately, we can say, "Correlation implies that causation is possible and worth investigating further"; conversely, we can say, "In the absence of attenuating factors and suppressor variables, the absence of correlation rules out causation." *Assessing the statistical covariation between therapist empathy and client outcome was the main focus of our review and is well-supported by our data.*

4. **Internal validity**: Ruling out alternative causes is what RCTs are supposed to be good at; however, the ethical codes that govern psychotherapists forbid them from deliberately practicing in an unempathic manner. Thus alternative strategies must be used. First, it is possible to contrast treatments that explicitly highlight therapist empathy, such as humanistic-experiential psychotherapies (HEPs), with no treatment or other therapies that do not emphasize empathy. A recent meta-analysis (Elliott et al., 2013) of 31 RCTs involving HEPs did just this, finding a weighted standardized difference (d_w) of .81 in comparison to no-treatment or wait-list control groups. In a related meta-analysis, the same authors also analysed 17 RCTs directly comparing Person-centered therapy to CBT, finding statistical equivalence ($d_w = -.10$) between the two treatments. Thus from the experimental evidence we can say that treatments that emphasize therapist empathy are (a) better than no treatment and (b) as effective as CBT. However, this evidence does not tell us what actually brought about change in the treatments studied (see "Construct validity").

That means that a second work-around strategy is needed, as is used in other observational sciences such as astronomy: analyzing and assessing realistic alternative causes (Cook & Campbell, 1979). The most plausible of these internal validity threats are the following:

- **Reverse causation**: Clients who are getting better elicit more empathy from therapists; establishing precedence (see condition 1) can certainly rule this out, as path analysis allows us to do.
- **Third variable causation/selection bias:** Clients who bring more personal resources to therapy are more likely both to improve and to elicit more therapist empathy. Assessing plausible third variables, such as client openness to experience, self-awareness, and greater empathy for the therapist, makes it possible to rule this out.
- **Mortality**: Clients with less empathic therapists may be more likely to drop out of the study, so that their posttherapy data are lost, suppressing possible empathy–outcome effects.

♦ *Compensatory equalization:* Therapists who are less empathic may try to compensate by providing a wider range of more technical interventions, such as self-help resources and homework, also suppressing empathy effects.

The other known internal validity threats (Cook & Campbell, 1979) are unlikely to feature in correlational research or will create conservative biases by increasing error variance; these include instrumentation (rater drift, practice effects), history, maturation, statistical regression, interactions with selection, diffusion/imitation of treatments, compensatory rivalry, and resentful demoralization. This suggests two ideas: (a) In general, internal validity threats are as likely to suppress empathy–outcome associations as to inflate them, and (b) reverse and third variable causation are the only really credible internal validity threats that need to be controlled for in process-outcome research on therapist empathy. This speaks to the importance of moving to more sophisticated causal modeling research; in this update we identified only six such studies, not enough to allow trustworthy conclusions. *We advocate delaying the making of strong claims for therapist empathy as a cause of client outcome until there are enough well-designed causal modeling studies.*

5. **Construct validity:** Although internal validity looms large in debates over correlational data, in our experience the construct validity of the cause and effect variables has proven to be a much more challenging causal condition to satisfy. How do we know that the key causal factor is therapist empathy and not therapist positive regard or even client satisfaction (a weak kind of outcome)? Just because a researcher has labeled his or her instrument "empathy" does not mean that it is in fact what someone else would call empathy as opposed to positive regard, psychological presence, or responsiveness. As we have indicated in this chapter, separating out therapist empathy from other relational conditions is particularly problematic, leading us to conclude (in the spirit of Rogers): *Empathy is a key component of the broader set of therapist offered qualities that clients use to cause themselves to change. In short, we are conceding any claim that therapist empathy uniquely predicts (let alone causes) client outcomes.*

6. **External validity:** *The empathy–outcome association has been demonstrated across a wide range of real-world settings, including different theoretical orientations, treatment settings, client-presenting problems, and therapist experience levels.*

CLIENT CONTRIBUTIONS

As noted, clients contribute to both the experience of empathy and its effects in psychotherapy in several ways. Empathy may be at least as much a client variable as it is a therapist variable. Clients' perceptions of therapist empathy correlate slightly better with outcome than do therapists' or observers' ratings.

Furthermore, there is no particular set of therapist behaviors or techniques that clients identify as "empathic" (Bachelor, 1988). From clients' perspectives, empathy often reflects a global relationship ambiance. This suggests that in part it is clients' *construction* of what happens in therapy that constitutes empathy (Bohart & Byock, 2005).

It is probably more accurate to say that empathy is interactionally constructed (Brodley, 2002; Wynn & Wynn, 2006), which can happen in different ways. First, it matters how clients and therapists mutually perceive one another. In a recent study (Murphy & Cramer, 2014), researchers determined that when therapists and clients were mutually perceiving as experiencing high levels of therapeutic facilitative conditions (including empathy), there was a stronger correlation with outcome. Second, clinical and research experience suggests that the amount of therapist empathy may partly depend on the client and the client's behavior. Early studies (Kiesler et al., 1967) found that levels of empathy were higher with clients who had less pathology and who were brighter but yet were lower in self-esteem. Therefore, the client him- or herself almost certainly influences therapist empathy. Client revelation is an essential link in the cycle of empathy (Barrett-Lennard, 1981). Clients who are more open to and communicate their inner experiencing will be easier to empathize with.

On the other hand, not all clients respond favorably to explicit empathic expressions. One set of reviewers (Beutler et al., 1986) cited evidence that highly sensitive, suspicious, and oppositional patients perform relatively poorly with therapists who are particularly empathic and involved. Another study (Mohr & Woodhouse, 2000) found that some clients prefer business-like rather than warm, empathic therapists. Of course, when therapists are truly empathic they attune to their clients' needs and adjust how and how much they express empathy.

More broadly, different types of empathy may prove hindering or helpful to clients at different times. In alliance ruptures, for example, it is probably useful for therapist empathy to be accompanied and deepened by genuine warmth, openness, and concern for the clients' feelings, rather than defending oneself and blaming the client (also see Safran, Muran, & Eubanks, Chapter 16, this volume).

Keeping in mind the notion of empathy as not only getting inside the skin of the client but getting inside the skin of the relationship (O'Hara, 1984), in some cases the therapist is probably more empathic by not expressing empathy. Martin (2000) notes: "Think of the insensitive irony of a therapist who says, 'I sense the sadness you want to hide. It seems like you don't want to be alone right now but you also don't want somebody talking to you about your sadness'" (pp. 184-185). This response might technically seem empathic, but in fact, at a higher level, it is unempathic and intrusive, because it violates the client's need for interpersonal distance. Variations among clients in desire for and receptivity to different expressions of empathy need further research.

In conclusion, empathy represents a mutual process of shared communicative attunement (Orlinsky et al., 2003). In the sense of the title of this book—"psychotherapy *relationships* that work"—it may well be that we need to think of empathy more as a part of genuine *relationship* and study it as such in its association with outcome, rather than solely as a therapist or client variable.

LIMITATIONS OF THE RESEARCH

Beyond the difficulties in making causal inferences from process–outcome correlations, many reviewers (e.g., Lambert et al., 1978; Patterson, 1984; Watson, 2001) have described a range of problems with research on empathy. In addition to the well-known difficulty of inferring causality from correlational data, these entail (a) the questionable validity of some outcome measures (e.g., client satisfaction); (b) the lack of sensitive outcome measures; (c) the restricted range of predictor and criterion variables; (d) confounds among variations in time of assessment, experience of raters, and sampling methods; and (e) incomplete reporting of methods and results. In fact, these and other problems are not restricted to empathy research but are common to all process–outcome research (Elliott, 2010).

The restricted range of predictor and criterion variables is particularly a problem. In an early and widely cited study (Mitchell et al., 1973), for instance, most of the therapists scored below the minimum level of empathy considered to be effective, and outcome was only modest to moderate in the study. It is not surprising that no significant correlations were found. Furthermore, in a few cases, results were reported as either significant in the positive direction or nonsignificant, possibly disguising weak negative effects. Such reporting practices prove problematic for calculating effect sizes based on limited information, introducing error into calculations.

In this iteration of this meta-analysis, we noted that number of tests of the empathy–outcome association, number of clients, and outcome specificity (vs. global satisfaction) all lowered effect size. This pattern of results suggests a methodologically-driven "more is less" effect (more tests, more participants, more specificity), which needs further investigation.

In the meantime, we believe it is time to move beyond research that simply correlates empathy (and other relationship conditions) with outcome to look at more differentiated questions concerning the measurement of empathy, its manifestation, and its mechanisms of change. It is our view that a mix of research methods is needed to do this, including careful qualitative interview research, detailed discourse analysis on within-session empathy change processes, systematic single-case studies using rich case records, and sophisticated quantitative research using time series and multilevel modeling methods on which to base sound causal inferences.

In attempting to establish a causal relation between empathy and outcome, we advocate a number of statistical procedures that researchers can perform in future studies that offer an alternative to the true experiment with randomization. These include using structural equation modeling and path analysis that each allow tests for variance within causal models in which empathy is represented as an exogenous variable. In structural equation models, empathy is considered a latent construct that is measured by its effect on manifest variables such as outcome. A second alternative is the use of longitudinal data sets with multiple observations of empathy and outcome across the psychotherapeutic process. Panel design using cross-lagged correlations is a method proposed as an adequate test of spuriousness (Kenny, 1975; e.g., Cramer & Takens, 1992). One concern with the cross sectional design in much of current research is that it is not possible to determine whether higher empathy leads to better outcome or vice versa (reverse causation); testing the cross-lagged correlations over time can offer greater security in the claims about the causal nature of the relationship variables on outcomes. By adding at least one additional time point for the assessment of the relationship variables that is synchronized to outcome assessment, the question of causality could be more rigorously addressed in the literature.

DIVERSITY CONSIDERATIONS

Few studies have examined diversity or multicultural competence and psychotherapists' empathy. The development of multicultural competence is required of mental health professionals as reflected in training and accreditation guidelines. It is important for therapists working with diverse populations to be empathic to their clients' specific circumstances as well as the complexities inherent in their social and political locations (Fuertes et al., 2006). This in-depth understanding of clients' specific location within society includes sensitivity to race, oppression, socioeconomic status, gender, sex, and religion as well as other sociopolitical forces. Competent therapists working with diverse populations display high levels of person empathy as well as relational and moment-to-moment empathy for their clients' in-session experiences.

The few studies that have looked at empathy with diverse clients in psychotherapy have examined its relations with working alliance, real relationship, client satisfaction, and intention to follow treatment recommendations. One study highlighted the association between therapists' empathy and clients' satisfaction with the mental health services they were receiving (Gillispie et al., 2005). Clients' overall satisfaction was related to how empathic they perceived their therapists to be and was also positively related to their intent to make use of aftercare. The authors suggest that clients from diverse groups may have a greater need for therapists to be understanding, nonjudgmental, and emotionally supportive during treatment to ensure their participation.

One intriguing study (Fuertes et al., 2007) investigated the relation between multicultural competence, the real relationship (see Chapter 6), and BLRI-E subscale. In this study with AfricanAmerican clients, a positive relation was found between clients' ratings of the real relationship and their experiences of their therapists as empathic. However, it is important not to conflate empathy with multicultural competence, as some studies have shown that the latter is important above and beyond general therapeutic competence and empathy for ethnic-minority clients.

Few studies have looked at gender, socioeconomic status, religion, or oppression specifically with respect to empathy. Nevertheless, researchers have looked at the impact of motivational interviewing on reducing violent abusive behavior in groups of men and women (Woodin et al., 2012). These researchers reported a reduction in both groups' hostile/violent behavior when therapists used more reflections. In addition, a trend toward a reduction in abusive behavior was found with women when counselors showed greater empathy and used open-ended questions. This finding warrants follow-up, as it raises the question of whether men and women respond differently to various types of empathic behaviors. Given the few studies in the area, future research must examine the role of empathy (and other relationship variables) in working with clients from diverse groups.

TRAINING IMPLICATIONS

In the 1940s and 1950s, Carl Rogers and colleagues conducted empathy training in experiential workshops (Kirschenbaum, 2007). They did not just offer didactic instruction on the concept of empathy but conducted live demonstrations and skill practice; over time they also added personal development work. In the 1970s, as part of the initial uncritical enthusiasm for helping skills training, a range of micro-skills programs emerged, with an emphasis on specific therapist behaviors (Danish & Hauer, 1973; Goodman; 1978; Ivey & Gluckstern, 1974). These skill training packages made certain assumptions about the mapping between particular therapist response modes (especially therapist reflection) and higher order concepts such as empathy. As we noted in the Therapist Mediators section, these assumptions soon proved simplistic as research found (a) reflections do not always convey empathy and (b) a wide range of other (especially nonverbal) behaviors can convey empathy.

A meta-analysis of 76 studies of empathy training in the helping professions (Dexter, 2012) produced an overall large (but highly heterogeneous) standardized mean difference effect of .99. That indicates the general effectiveness of a wide range of empathy training methods. Even didactic-only training produced reliable medium-sized effects (standardized mean difference) = .40); however, the combination of didactic and experiential methods produced the largest reliable effect (1.93). Adding feedback and modeling also produced large effects (1.76). In addition, there was a trend toward longer trainings (e.g., longer than 26 hours) having larger effects than briefer trainings (e.g., <5 hrs). These results are consistent with the humanistic-experiential therapy tradition, where substantial amounts of empathy training are a key element of the first year of a training program. This tradition also highlights the value an element not studied in the meta-analysis: personal development work to help students learn about their empathy blocks and blind spots.

In any case, this training meta-analysis points to the value of an extensive, multipronged approach to training empathic therapists. We regret that this level of empathy training is no longer the norm in the training of mental health professionals and are keenly aware of the problems posed by inadequate prior empathy training for therapists trying to learn advanced therapeutic methods. Without the foundational skill and capacity of empathy, much subsequent psychotherapy training rests on shaky ground.

THERAPEUTIC PRACTICES

The most robust meta-analytic evidence is that clients' perceptions of feeling understood by their therapists relate to outcome. As we have shown, empathy is a medium-sized predictor of outcome in psychotherapy. It also appears to be a general predictor across theoretical orientation, treatment formats, and client severity levels. This repeated finding, in dozens of individual studies and now in multiple meta-analyses, leads to a series of clinical recommendations:

- Psychotherapists continuously work to understand their clients and to demonstrate this understanding through responses that address the most poignant aspects of the clients' experience to facilitate clients' tracking of their inner experience in terms of the questions or concerns that they are exploring in therapy.
- The primary task is to be empathically attuned and to understand the import or impact of clients' experiences as opposed to being focused on words and content. Empathic therapists do not parrot clients' words back or reflect only the content of those words; instead, they understand their clients' goals overall as well as their moment-to-moment experiences in the session. Empathy entails capturing the nuances and implications of what people say and reflecting these back to them for their consideration.
- Empathic responses show that therapists continually adjust their assumptions and understandings, attending to the leading edge of client experience so as to facilitate awareness of feelings and perspectives.
- Our meta-analysis determined that clients' reports of therapist empathy best predict eventual treatment outcome. Thus regularly assessing and privileging the client's experience of empathy, instead of trying to intuit whether one's behavior is empathic or not, can be helpful in treatment.
- The meta-analysis also documented that observer ratings of accurate empathy predict outcome. Research has identified a range of useful empathic responses, several of which we presented earlier in the Clinical Examples section.
- Empathy is not only something that is "provided" by the therapist as if it were a medication but is a co-created experience between a therapist who is trying to understand the client and a client who is trying to communicate with the therapist and be understood. Empathy is shown as much in how well the therapist receives, listens, respects, and attends to the client as in what the therapist does or says.
- Empathic therapists assist clients to symbolize their experience in words and track their emotional responses so that clients can deepen their experience and reflexively examine their feelings, values, and goals. Therapists can help clients focus on this inner experience and access as much internal information as possible. To this end, therapists can attend to that which is not said or that which is at the periphery of awareness as well as that which is said and is in focal awareness (Watson, 2001).
- Empathy entails individualizing responses to particular patients. We found significant heterogeneity in the empathy–outcome association, pointing to the value of personalization and clinical judgment. For example, certain fragile clients may find the usual expressions of empathy too intrusive, while hostile clients may find empathy too directive; still other clients may find an empathic focus on feelings too foreign (Kennedy-Moore & Watson, 1999). Effective therapists know when—and when not—to respond empathically. When clients do not want therapists to be

explicitly empathic, truly empathic therapists will use their perspective-taking skills to provide an optimal therapeutic distance (Leitner, 1995), respecting their clients' boundaries.

♦ There is no evidence that accurately predicting clients' own views of their problems or self-perceptions is effective. Therapists should neither assume that they are mind readers nor that their experience of the client will be matched by the client's experience of self. Empathy is best offered with humility and held lightly, ready to be corrected.

♦ Finally, because research has shown empathy to be inseparable from the other relational conditions, therapists are advised to offer empathy in the context of positive regard and genuineness. Empathy will probably not prove effective unless it is grounded in authentic caring for the client. Any one of the conditions without the others would provide a distinctly different interpersonal climate and relationship. We encourage psychotherapists to value empathy as both an "ingredient" of a healthy therapeutic relationship as well as a specific, effective response that promotes strengthening of the self and deeper exploration.

REFERENCES

References marked with an asterisk indicate studies included in the meta-analyses.

Bachelor, A. (1988). How clients perceive therapist empathy—a content-analysis of received empathy. *Psychotherapy, 25*, 227–240. https://www.doi.org/10.1037/h0085337

*Barnicot, K., Wampold, B., & Priebe, S. (2014). The effect of core clinician interpersonal behaviours on depression. *Journal of Affective Disorders, 167*, 112–117. https://www.doi.org/10.1016/j.jad.2014.05.064

*Barrett-Lennard, G. (1962). Dimensions of therapist response as causal factors in therapeutic change. *Psychological Monographs, 76*(43), 1–36.

Barrett-Lennard, G. T. (1981). The empathy cycle: Refinement of a nuclear concept. *Journal of Counseling Psychology, 28*, 91–100.

*Barrington, B. L. (1967). The differential effectiveness of therapy as measured by the Thematic Apperception Test. In C. R. Rogers (Ed.), *The therapeutic relationship and its impact* (pp. 337–352). Madison: University of Wisconsin Press.

Batson, C. D. (2009). These things called empathy: Eight related but distinct phenomena. In J. Decety & W. Ickes (Eds.), *The social neuroscience of empathy* (pp. 3–15). Cambridge, MA: MIT Press.

Belenky, M. F., Clinchy, B. M., Goldberger, N. R., & Tarule, J. M. (1986). *Women's ways of knowing: The development of self, voice, and mind*. New York, NY: Basic Books.

*Bergin, A. E., & Jasper, L. G. (1969). Correlates of empathy in psychotherapy: A replication. *Journal of Abnormal Psychology, 74*, 477–481.

Beutler, L. E., Crago, M., & Arizmendi, T. G. (1986). Research on therapist variables in psychotherapy. In S. L. Garfield & A. E. Bergin (Eds.), *Handbook of psychotherapy and behavior change* (3rd ed., pp. 257–310). New York, NY: Wiley.

*Beutler, L. E., Johnson, D. T., Neville, C. W., & Workman, S. N. (1972). "Accurate empathy" and the AB dichotomy. *Journal of Consulting and Clinical Psychology, 38*, 372–375.

Blatt, S. J., Zuroff, D. C., Quinlan, D. M., & Pilkonis, P. A. (1996). Interpersonal factors in brief treatment of depression: Further analyses of the National Institute of Mental Health

Treatment of Depression Collaborative Research Program. *Journal of Consulting and Clinical Psychology, 64,* 162–171.

Bloom, P. (2016). *Against empathy: The case for rational compassion.* New York, NY: Ecco.

Bohart, A. C., & Byock, G. (2005). Experiencing Carl Rogers from the client's point of view: A vicarious ethnographic investigation. I. Extraction and perception of meaning. *The Humanistic Psychologist, 33,* 187–212.

Bohart, A. C., Elliott, R., Greenberg, L. S., & Watson, J. C. (2002). Empathy. In J. Norcross (Ed.), *Psychotherapy relationships that work* (pp. 89–108). New York, NY: Oxford University Press.

Bohart, A. C., & Greenberg, L. S. (1997). Empathy: Where are we and where do we go from here? In A. C. Bohart & L. S. Greenberg (Eds.), *Empathy reconsidered: New directions in psychotherapy* (pp. 419–450). Washington, DC: American Psychological Association.

Bohart, A. C., & Tallman, K. (1999). *How clients make therapy work: The process of active self-healing.* Washington, DC: American Psychological Association.

Brodley, B. T. (2002). Observations of empathic understanding in two client-centered therapists. In J. C. Watson, R. N. Goldman, & M. S. Warner (Eds.), *Client-centered and experiential psychotherapy in the 21st century: Advances in theory, research and practice* (pp. 182–203). Ross-on-Wye, England: PCCS Books.

Brodley, B. T., & Brody, A. F. (1990, August). *Understanding client-centered therapy through interviews conducted by Carl Rogers.* Paper presented at the annual convention of the American Psychological Association, Boston, MA.

*Brouzos, A., Vassilopoulos, S. P., & Baourda, V. C. (2015). Members' perceptions of person-centered facilitative conditions and their role in outcome in a psychoeducational group for childhood social anxiety. *Person-Centered & Experiential Psychotherapies, 14,* 32–46. https://www.doi.org/10.1080/14779757.2014.965843

*Brug, J., Spikmans, F., Aartsen, C., Breedveld, B., Bes, R., & Fereira, I. (2007). Training dietitians in basic motivational interviewing skills results in changes in their counseling style and in lower saturated fat intakes in their patients. *Journal of Nutrition Education & Behavior, 39,* 8–12. https://www.doi.org/10.1016/j.jneb.2006.08.010

*Buckley, P., Karasu, T. B., & Charles, E. (1981). Psychotherapists view their personal therapy. *Psychotherapy: Theory, Research and Practice, 18,* 299–305.

*Bugge, I., Hendel, D. D., & Moen, R. (1985). Client evaluations of therapeutic processes and outcomes in a university mental health center. *Journal of American College Health, 33,* 141–146.

*Bullmann, F., Horlacher, K. D., & Kieser, B. (2004). *Clarifying as a mediator-variable in person-centered psychotherapy and therapists' gender and therapy-school differences in empathy and positive regard* (Unpublished study). Psychological Institute, University of Heidelberg, Heidelberg, Germany.

Burns, D. D., & Nolen-Hoeksma, S. (1992). Therapeutic empathy and recovery from depression in cognitive-behavioral therapy: A structural equation model. *Journal of Consulting and Clinical Psychology, 60,* 441–449.

Carkhuff, R. R., & Berenson, B. (1967). *Beyond counseling and therapy.* New York, NY: Holt, Rinehart & Winston.

*Cartwright, R. D., & Lerner, B. (1965). Empathy, need to change, and improvement in psychotherapy. *Journal of Consulting Psychology, 27,* 138–144.

*Clark, J. V., & Culbert, S. A. (1965). Mutually therapeutic perception and self-awareness in a T-group. *Journal of Applied Behavioral Science, 1,* 180–194.

Cook, T. D., & Campbell, D. T. (1979). *Quasi-experimentation: Design and analysis issues for field settings.* Chicago: Rand McNally.

*Cooley, E. J., & La joy, R. (1980). Therapeutic relationship and improvement as perceived by clients and therapists. *Journal of Clinical Psychology, 36,* 562–570.

Corbin, J., & Strauss, A. (2008). *Basics of qualitative research: Techniques and procedures for developing grounded theory* (3rd ed.). Thousand Oaks, CA: Sage.

*Cramer, D., & Takens, R. (1992). Therapeutic relationship and progress in the first six sessions of individual psychotherapy: A panel analysis. *Counselling Psychology Quarterly, 5,* 25–36.

Danish, S. J., & Hauer, A. L. (1973). *Helping skills: A basic training program.* New York, NY: Behavioral Publications.

Decety, J., & Ickes, W. (Eds.). (2009). *The social neuroscience of empathy.* Cambridge, MA: MIT Press.

Decety, J., & Jackson, P.L. (2004). The functional architecture of human empathy. *Behavioral and Cognitive Neuroscience Reviews, 3,* 71–100.

Decety, J., & Lamm, C. (2009). Empathy versus personal distress: Recent evidence from social neuroscience. In J. Decety & W. Ickes (Eds.), *The social neuroscience of empathy* (pp. 199–213). Cambridge, MA: MIT Press.

Dexter, V.J. (2012). *Research synthesis with meta-analysis of empathy training studies in helping professions* (Doctoral dissertation). New York University. Retrieved from https://media.proquest.com/media/pq/classic/doc/2696560791/fmt/ai/rep/NPDF?_s=NihQg7jRRnne7H%2FjhvJ2RzN7ybE%3D

*Dicken, C., Bryson, R., & Kass, N. (1977). Companionship therapy: A replication in experimental community psychology. *Journal of Consulting and Clinical Psychology, 45,* 637–646. https://www.doi.org/10.1037/0022-006X.45.4.637

*Dormaar, J. M., Dijkman, C. I., & de Vries, M. W. (1989). Consensus in patient-therapist interactions: A measure of the therapeutic relationship related to outcome. *Psychotherapy and Psychosomatics, 51,* 69–76.

Duan, C., & Hill, C. E. (1996). A critical review of empathy research. *Journal of Counseling Psychology, 43,* 261–274.

*Duan, C., & Kivlighan, D. M. Jr. (2002). Relationships among therapist presession mood, therapist empathy, and session evaluation. *Psychotherapy Research, 12,* 23–37. https://www.doi.org/10.1093/ptr/12.1.23

Egan, G. (1982). *The skilled helper* (2nd ed.). Monterey, CA: Brooks/Cole.

Eisenberg, N., & Eggum, N. D. (2009). Empathic responding: Sympathy and personal distress. In J. Decety & W. Ickes (Eds.), *The social neuroscience of empathy* (pp. 71–83). Cambridge, MA: MIT Press.

Eisenberg, N., & Fabes, R. A. (1990). Empathy: Conceptualization, assessment, and relations to prosocial behavior. *Motivation and Emotion, 14,* 131–149.

Elkin, I., Falconnier, L., Smith, Y., Canada, K. E., Henderson, E., Brown, E. R., & McKay, B. M. (2014). Therapist responsiveness and patient engagement in therapy. *Psychotherapy Research, 24,* 52–66.

Elliott, R. (2010). Psychotherapy change process research: Realizing the promise. *Psychotherapy Research, 20,* 123–135.

Elliott, R., Bohart, A. C., Watson, J. C., & Greenberg, L. S. (2011). Empathy. In J. Norcross (Ed.), *Psychotherapy relationships that work* (2nd ed., pp. 132–152). New York, NY: Oxford University Press.

Elliott, R., Watson, J., Goldman, R., & Greenberg, L. S. (2003). *Learning emotion-focused therapy: The process-experiential approach to change.* Washington, DC: American Psychological Association.

*Filak, J., & Abeles, N. (1984). Posttherapy congruence on client symptoms and therapy outcome. *Professional Psychology: Research & Practice, 15,* 846–855.

*Free, N. K., Green, B. L., Grace, M. C., Chernus, L. A., & Whitman, R. M. (1985). Empathy and outcome in brief focal dynamic therapy. *American Journal of Psychiatry, 142,* 917–921. https://www.doi.org/10.1176/ajp.142.8.917

*Fretz, B. R. (1966). Postural movements in a counseling dyad. *Journal of Counseling Psychology, 13,* 335–343.

*Fuertes, J. N., & Brobst, K. (2002). Clients' ratings of counselor multicultural competency. *Cultural Diversity & Ethnic Minority Psychology, 8,* 214–223. https://www.doi.org/10.1037/1099-9809.8.3.214

*Fuertes, J. N., Mislowack, A., Brown, S., Gur-Arie, S., Wilkinson, S., & Gelso, C. J. (2007). Correlates of the real relationship in psychotherapy: A study of dyads. *Psychotherapy Research, 17,* 423–430.

*Fuertes, J. N., Stracuzzi, T. I., Bennett, J., Scheinholtz, J., Mislowack, A., Hersh, M., & Cheng, D. (2006). Therapist multicultural competency: A study of therapy dyads. *Psychotherapy: Theory, Research, Practice, Training, 43,* 480–490.

*Gabbard, C. E., Howard, G. S., & Dunfee, E. J. (1986). Reliability, sensitivity to measuring change, and construct validity of a measure of counselor adaptability. *Journal of Counseling Psychology, 33,* 377–386.

Gallese, V., Fadiga, L., Fogassi, L., & Rizzolatti, G. (1996). Action recognition in the premotor cortex. *Brain, 119,* 593–609.

*Garfield, S. L., & Bergin, A. E. (1971). Therapeutic conditions and outcome. *Journal of Abnormal Psychology, 77,* 108–114.

Geller, S. M., Greenberg, L. S., & Watson, J. C. (2010). Therapist and client perceptions of therapeutic presence: The development of a measure. *Psychotherapy Research, 20,* 599–610.

*Gelso, C. J., Latts, M. G., Gomez, M. J., & Fassinger, R. E. (2002). Countertransference management and therapy outcome: An initial evaluation. *Journal of Clinical Psychology, 58,* 861–867.

*Gillispie, R., Williams, E., & Gillispie, C. (2005). Hospitalized African American mental health consumers: Some antecedents to service satisfaction and intent to comply with aftercare. *American Journal of Orthopsychiatry, 75,* 254–261. https://www.doi.org/10.1037/0002-9432.75.2.254

Gladstein, G., A., & Associates. (1987). *Empathy and counseling: Explorations in theory and research.* New York, NY: Springer-Verlag.

*Goldman, R., Greenberg, L., & Angus, L. (2000, June). *The York II Psychotherapy Study on Experiential Therapy of Depression.* Paper presented at the annual meeting of the Society for Psychotherapy Research, Chicago, IL.

Goodman, G. (1978). *SASHAtapes: Self-led automated series on help-intended alternatives.* Los Angeles: California Self-Help Center, Department of Psychology, University of California.

*Goodman, G., Edwards, K., & Chung, H. (2015). The relation between prototypical processes and psychological distress in psychodynamic therapy of five inpatients with borderline personality disorder. *Clinical Psychology & Psychotherapy, 22,* 83–95. https://www.doi.org/10.1002/cpp.1875

Goubert, L., Craig, K. D., & Buysee, A. (2009). Perceiving others in pain: Experimental and clinical evidence of the role of empathy. In J. Decety & W. Ickes (Eds.), *The social neuroscience of empathy* (pp. 153–165). Cambridge, MA: MIT Press.

Greenberg, L. S., & Rushanski-Rosenberg, R. (2002). Therapists' experience of empathy. In J. C. Watson, R. N. Goldman, & M. S. Warner (Eds.), *Client-centered and experiential psychotherapy in the 21st century: Advances in theory, research and practice* (pp. 204–220). Ross-on-Wye, England: PCCS Books.

*Greenberg, L. S., & Webster, M. (1982). Resolving decisional conflict by means of two-chair dialogue: Relating process to outcome. *Journal of Counseling Psychology, 29*, 468–477.

*Gross, W. F., & DeRidder, L. M. (1966). Significant movement in comparatively short-term counseling. *Journal of Counseling Psychology, 13*, 98–99.

Gurman, A. S. (1977). The patient's perception of the therapeutic relationship. In A. S.Gurman & A. M. Razin (Eds.), *Effective psychotherapy: A handbook of research* (pp. 503–543). New York, NY: Pergamon.

*Guydish, J., Campbell, B. K., Manuel, J. K., Delucchi, K. L., Thao, L., Peavy, K. M., & McCarty, D. (2014). Does treatment fidelity predict client outcomes in 12-step facilitation for stimulant abuse? *Drug & Alcohol Dependence, 134*, 330–336. https://www.doi.org/10.1016/j.drugalcdep.2013.10.020

*Hall, J. A., & Davis, M. H. (2000). Dispositional empathy in scientist and practitioner psychologists: Group differences and relationship to self-reported professional effectiveness. *Psychotherapy, 37*, 45–56.

*Hamilton, J. C. (2000). Construct validity of the core conditions and factor structure of the Client Evaluation of Counselor Scale. *The Person-Centered Journal, 7*, 40–51.

*Hansen, J. C., Moore, G. D., & Carkhuff, R. R. (1968). The differential relationships of objective and client perceptions of counseling. *Journal of Clinical Psychology, 24*, 244–246.

Hayes, A. M., & Goldfried, M. R. (1996). Rogers' work with Mark: An empirical analysis and cognitive-behavioral perspective. In B. A. Farber, D. C. Brink, & P. M. Raskin (Eds.), *The psychotherapy of Carl Rogers* (pp. 357–374). New York, NY: Guilford.

Haynes, S. N., & O'Brien, W. O. (2000). *Principles of behavioral assessment: A functional approach to psychological assessment.* New York: Plenum.

Hein, G., & Singer, T. (2010). Neuroscience meets social psychology: An integrative approach to human empathy. In M. Mikulincer & P. R. Shaver (Eds.), *Prosocial motives, emotions, and behavior: The better angels of our nature* (pp. 109–126). Washington, DC: American Psychological Association.

Henschel, D. N., & Bohart, A. C. (1981, August). *The relationship between the effectiveness of a course in paraprofessional training and level of cognitive functioning.* Paper presented at annual conference of the American Psychological Association, Los Angeles, CA.

Higgins, J. P. T., Thompson, S. G., Deeks, J. J., & Altman, D. G. (2003). Measuring inconsistency in meta-analyses, *British Journal of Medicine, 327*, 557–560.

*Hoffart, A., Versland, S., & Sexton, H. (2002). Self-understanding, empathy, guided discovery, and schema belief in schema-focused cognitive therapy of personality problems: A process-outcome study. *Cognitive Therapy and Research, 26*, 199–219.

Horvath, A. O., & Greenberg, L. S. (1986). The development of the Working Alliance Inventory. In L. S. Greenberg & W. M. Pinsof (Eds.), *The psychotherapeutic process: A research handbook* (pp. 529–556). New York, NY: Guilford.

*Horvath, A. O., & Greenberg, L. S. (1989). Development and validation of the working alliance inventory. *Journal of Counseling Psychology, 36*, 223–233.

Ickes, W. (2003). *Everyday mind reading: Understanding what other people think and feel.* Amherst, NY: Prometheus.

Ickes, W. (Ed.). (1997). *Empathic accuracy.* New York, NY: Guilford.

Ivey, A. E., & Gluckstern, N. B. (1974). *Basic attending skills: Participant manual.* North Amherst, MA: Microtraining Associates.

Johnson, S. M., Bradley, B., Furrow, J., Lee, A., Palmer, G., Tilley, D. G., & Woolley, S. R. (2005). *Emotionally focused marital therapy workbook.* New York, NY: Brunner Routledge.

*Kasarabada, N. D., Hser, Y., Boles, S. M., & Huang, Y. C. (2002). Do patients' perceptions of their counselors influence outcomes of drug treatment? *Journal of Substance Abuse Treatment, 23,* 327–334. https://www.doi.org/10.1016/S0740-5472(02)00276-3

Kennedy-Moore, E., & Watson, J. C. (1999). *Expressing emotion: Myths, realities, and therapeutic strategies.* New York, NY: Guilford.

Kenny, D. A. (1975). Cross-lagged panel correlation: A test for spuriousness. *Psychological Bulletin, 82,* 887–903.

*Kiesler, D. J., Klein, M. H., Mathieu, P. L., & Schoeninger, D. (1967). Constructive personality change for therapy and control patients. In C. R. Rogers (Ed.), *The therapeutic relationship and its impact* (pp. 251–294), Madison: University of Wisconsin Press.

*Kim, B. S. K., Ng, G. F., & Ann, A. J. (2009). Client adherence to Asian cultural values, common factors in counseling, and session outcome with Asian American clients at a university counseling center. *Journal of Counseling & Development, 87,* 131–142. https://www.doi.org/10.1002/j.1556-6678.2009.tb00560.x

Kirschenbaum, H. (2007). *The life and work of Carl Rogers.* Ross-on-Wye, England: PCCS Books.

*Kolden, G. (1996). Effective processes in early sessions of dynamic psychotherapy. *Journal of Psychotherapy Practice & Research, 5,* 122–131.

*Kurtz, R. R., & Grummon, D. L. (1972). Different approaches to the measurement of therapist empathy and their relationship to therapy outcomes. *Journal of Consulting and Clinical Psychology, 39,* 106–115.

*Kwon, K. I., & Jo, S. Y. (2012). The relationship among counselor experience level, empathic accuracy, and counseling outcome in the early phase of counseling. *Asia Pacific Education Review, 13,* 771–777. https://www.doi.org/10.1007/s12564-012-9235-8

*Lafferty, P., Beutler, L. E., & Crago, M. (1989). Differences between more and less effective psychotherapists: A study of select therapist variables. *Journal of Consulting and Clinical Psychology, 57,* 76–80.

Lambert, M. J., DeJulio, S. J., & Stein, D. M. (1978). Therapist interpersonal skills: Process, outcome, methodological considerations, and recommendations for future research. *Psychological Bulletin, 85,* 467–489.

Landfield, A. W. (1971). *Personal construct systems in psychotherapy.* Chicago, IL: Rand McNally.

*Langhoff, C., Baer, T., Zubraegel, D., & Linden, M. (2008). Therapist-patient alliance, patient-therapist alliance, mutual therapeutic alliance, therapist-patient concordance, and outcome of CBT in GAD. *Journal of Cognitive Psychotherapy, 22,* 68–79.

Leitner, L. M. (1995). Optimal therapeutic distance: A therapist's experience of personal construct psychotherapy. In R. A. Neimeyer & M. J. Mahoney (Eds.), *Constructivism in psychotherapy* (pp. 357–370). Washington, DC: American Psychological Association.

*Lerner, B. (1972). *Therapy in the ghetto.* Baltimore, MD: Johns Hopkins University Press.

*Lesser, W. M. (1961). The relationship between counseling progress and empathic understanding. *Journal of Counseling Psychology, 8,* 330–336.

Lipsey, M. W., & Wilson, D. B. (2001). *Practical meta-analysis*. Thousand Oaks, CA: SAGE.

*Lorr, M. (1965). Client perceptions of therapists: A study of therapeutic relation. *Journal of Consulting Psychology*, 29, 146–149.

Mahrer, A. R. (1997). Empathy as therapist-client alignment. In A. C. Bohart & L. S. Greenberg (Eds.), *Empathy reconsidered: New directions in psychotherapy* (pp. 187–216). Washington, DC: American Psychological Association.

*Malin, A. J., & Pos, A. E. (2015). The impact of early empathy on alliance building, emotional processing, and outcome during experiential treatment of depression. *Psychotherapy Research*, 25, 445–459. https://www.doi.org/10.1080/10503307.2014.901572

*Marshall, W. L., Serran, G. A., Fernandez, Y. M., Mulloy, R., Mann, R. E., & Thornton, D. (2003). Therapist characteristics in the treatment of sexual offenders: Tentative data on their relationship with indices of behaviour change. *Journal of Sexual Aggression*, 9, 25–30.

*Marshall, W. L., Serran, G. A., Moulden, H., Mulloy, R., Fernandez, Y. M., Mann, R. E., & Thornton, D. (2002). Therapist features in sexual offender treatment: Their reliable identification and influence on behaviour change. *Clinical Psychology and Psychotherapy*, 9, 395–405.

Martin, D. G. (2000). *Counseling and therapy skills* (2nd ed.). Prospect Heights, IL: Waveland Press.

*Martin, P. J., & Sterne, A. L. (1976). Post-hospital adjustment as related to therapist's in-therapy behavior. *Psychotherapy: Theory, Research and Practice*, 13, 267–273.

MacFarlane, P., Anderson, T., & McClintock, A. S. (2016), Empathy from the client's perspective: A grounded theory analysis. *Psychotherapy Research*, 27, 227–238.

*Melnick, B., & Pierce, R. M. (1971). Client evaluation of therapist strength and positive-negative evaluation as related to client dynamics, objective ratings of competence and outcome. *Journal of Clinical Psychology*, 27, 408–410.

*Miller, W., Taylor, C., & West, J. (1980). Focused versus broad spectrum behavior therapy for problem drinkers. *Journal of Consulting and Clinical Psychology*, 48, 590–601.

*Mitchell, K. M., Truax, C. B., Bozarth, J. D., & Krauft, C. C. (1973, March). *Antecedents to psychotherapeutic outcome*. NIMH Grant Report 12306. Hot Springs: Arkansas Rehabilitation Research and Training Center.

Mohr, J. J., & Woodhouse, S. S. (2000, June). *Clients' visions of helpful and harmful psychotherapy: An approach to measuring individual differences in therapy priorities*. Paper presented at the 31st annual meeting of the Society for Psychotherapy Research, Chicago, IL.

*Moyers, T. B., Houck, J., Rice, S. L., Longabaugh, R., & Miller, W. R. (2016). Therapist empathy, combined behavioral intervention, and alcohol outcomes in the COMBINE research project. *Journal of Consulting and Clinical Psychology*, 84, 221–229. https://www.doi.org/10.1037/ccp0000074

Moyers, T. B., Manuel, J. K., & Ernst, D. (2015). *Motivational interviewing treatment integrity coding manual 4.2.1* (Unpublished manuscript). Retrieved from https://casaa.unm.edu/download/MITI4_2.pdf

*Muller, J., & Abeles, N. (1971). Relationship of liking, empathy and therapists' experience to outcome in psychotherapy. *Journal of Counseling Psychology*, 18, 39–43.

*Murphy, D., & Cramer, D. (2014). Mutuality of Rogers's therapeutic conditions and treatment progress in the first three psychotherapy sessions. *Psychotherapy Research*, 24, 651–661. https://www.doi.org/10.1080/10503307.2013.874051

Myers, S. (2000). Empathic listening: Reports on the experience of being heard. *Journal of Humanistic Psychology, 40*, 148–173.

Myers, S. A. (2003). Relational healing: To be understood and to understand. *Journal of Humanistic Psychology, 43*, 86–104.

Myers, S. A., & White, C. M. (2010). The abiding nature of empathic connections: A 10-year followup study. *Journal of Humanistic Psychology, 50*, 77–95.

O'Hara, M. M. (1984). Person-centered gestalt: Towards a holistic synthesis. In R. F. Levant & J. M. Shlien (Eds.), *Client-centered therapy and the person-centered approach: New directions in theory, research and practice* (pp. 203–221). New York, NY: Praeger.

Orlinsky, D. E., Grawe, K., & Parks, B. K. (1994). Process and outcome in psychotherapy—noch einmal. In A. E. Bergin & S. L. Garfield (Eds.), *Handbook of psychotherapy and behavior change* (4th ed., pp. 270–378). New York, NY: Wiley.

*Orlinsky, D. E., & Howard, K.I. (1967). The good therapy hour: Experiential correlates of patients' and therapists' evaluations of therapy sessions. *Archives of General Psychiatry, 12*, 621–632.

Orlinsky, D. E., & Howard, K. I. (1978). The relation of process to outcome in psychotherapy. In S. L. Garfield & A. E. Bergin (Eds.), *Handbook of psychotherapy and behavior change* (2nd ed., pp. 283–330). New York, NY: Wiley.

Orlinsky, D. E., & Howard, K. I. (1986). Process and outcome in psychotherapy. In S. L. Garfield & A. E. Bergin (Eds.), *Handbook of psychotherapy and behavior change* (3rd ed., pp. 311–384). New York, NY: Wiley.

Orlinsky, D. E., Rønnestad, M. H., & Willutzki, U. (2003). Process and outcome in psychotherapy. In M. J. Lambert (Ed.), *Bergin and Garfield's handbook of psychotherapy and behavior change* (5th ed., pp. 307–389). New York, NY: Wiley.

*Pantalon, M. V., Chawarski, M. C., Falcioni, J., Pakes, J., & Schottenfeld, R. S. (2004). Linking process and outcome in the community reinforcement approach for treating cocaine dependence: A preliminary report. *American Journal of Drug and Alcohol Abuse, 30*, 353–367.

Parloff, M. B., Waskow, I. E., & Wolfe, B. E. (1978). Research on therapist variables in relation to process and outcome. In S. L. Garfield & A. E. Bergin (Eds.), *Handbook of psychotherapy and behavior change* (2nd ed., pp. 233–282). New York, NY: Wiley.

Patterson, C. H. (1984). Empathy, warmth, and genuineness: A review of reviews. *Psychotherapy, 21*, 431–438.

*Payne, A., Liebling-Kalifani, H., & Joseph, S. (2007). Client-centred group therapy for survivors of interpersonal trauma: A pilot investigation. *Counselling & Psychotherapy Research, 7*, 100–105.

Peabody, S. A., & Gelso, C. J. (1982). Countertransference and empathy: The complex relationship between two divergent concepts in counseling. *Journal of Counseling Psychology, 29*, 240–245.

*Peake, T. H. (1979). Therapist-patient agreement and outcome in group therapy. *Journal of Clinical Psychology, 35*, 637–646.

Pedersen, R. (2009). Empirical research on empathy in medicine—A critical review. *Patient Education & Counseling, 76*(3), 307–322. https://www.doi.org/10.1016/j.pec.2009.06.012

*Rabavilas, A. D., Boulougouris, J. C., & Perissaki, C. (1979). Therapist qualities related to outcome with exposure in vivo in neurotic patients. *Journal of Behaviour Therapy and Experimental Psychiatry, 410*, 293–294.

*Ritter, A., Bowden, S., Murray, T., Ross, P., Greeley, J., & Pead, J. (2002). The influence of the therapeutic relationship in treatment for alcohol dependency. *Drug & Alcohol Review, 21*, 261–268. https://www.doi.org/10.1080/0959523021000002723

*Roback, H. B., & Strassberg, D. S. (1975). Relationship between perceived therapist-offered conditions and therapeutic movement in group psychotherapy with hospitalized mental patients. *Small Group Behavior, 6*, 345–352.

Rogers, C. R. (1957). The necessary and sufficient conditions of therapeutic personality change. *Journal of Consulting Psychology, 21*, 95–103.

Rogers, C. R. (1980). *A way of being.* Boston, MA: Houghton Mifflin.

Sachse, R. (1990a). Concrete interventions are crucial: The influence of the therapist's processing proposals on the client's intrapersonal exploration in client-centered therapy. In G. Lietaer, J. Rombauts, & R. Van Balen (Eds.), *Client-centered and experiential psychotherapy in the nineties* (pp. 295–308). Leuven, Belgium: Leuven University Press.

Sachse, R. (1990b). The influence of therapist processing proposals on the explication process of the client. *Person-Centered Review, 5*, 321–344.

Sachse, R., & Elliott, R. (2001). Process-outcome research in client-centered and experiential therapies. In D. Cain & J. Seeman (Eds.), *Humanistic psychotherapies: Handbook of research and practice* (pp. 83–115). Washington, DC: American Psychological Association.

*Saltzman, C., Leutgert, M. J., Roth, C. H., Creaser, J., & Howard, L. (1976). Formation of a therapeutic relationship: Experiences during the initial phase of psychotherapy as predictors of treatment duration and outcome. *Journal of Consulting and Clinical Psychology, 44*, 546–555.

*Sanberk, I., & Akbaş, T. (2015). Psychological counseling processes of prospective psychological counsellors: An investigation of client-counsellor interactions. *Educational Science: Theory & Practice, 15*, 859–878.

*Sapolsky, A. (1965). Relationship between patient-doctor compatibility, mutual perceptions, and outcome of treatment. *Journal of Abnormal Psychology, 70*, 70–76.

*Saunders, S. M. (2000). Examining the relationship between the therapeutic bond and the phases of treatment outcome. *Psychotherapy, 37*, 206–218.

Saunders, S. M., Howard, K. I., & Orlinsky, D. E. (1989). The Therapeutic Bond Scales: Psychometric characteristics and relationship to treatment effectiveness. *Psychological Assessment: A Journal of Consulting and Clinical Psychology, 1*, 323–330.

Selman, R. I. (1980). *The growth of interpersonal understanding.* Orlando, FL: Academic Press.

Shamay-Tsoory, S. (2009). Empathic processing: Its cognitive and affective dimensions and neuroanatomical basis. In J. Decety & W. Ickes (Eds.), *The social neuroscience of empathy* (pp. 215–232). Cambridge, MA: MIT Press.

Shlien, J. (1997). Empathy in psychotherapy: A vital mechanism? Yes. Therapist's conceit? All too often. In A. C. Bohart & L. S. Greenberg (Eds.), *Empathy reconsidered: New directions in psychotherapy* (pp. 63–80). Washington, DC: American Psychological Association.

Smith, M. L., Glass, G. V., & Miller, T. I. (1980). *The benefits of psychotherapy.* Baltimore, MD: Johns Hopkins University Press.

*Spohr, S. A., Taxman, F. S., Rodriguez, M., & Walters, S. T. (2016). Motivational interviewing fidelity in a community corrections setting: Treatment initiation and subsequent drug use. *Journal of Substance Abuse Treatment, 65*, 20–25. https://www.doi.org/10.1016/j.jsat.2015.07.012

*Staples, F. R., Sloane, R. D., Whipple, K., Cristol, A. H., & Yorkston, N. (1976). Process and outcome in psychotherapy and behavior therapy. *Journal of Consulting and Clinical Psychology, 44*, 340–350.

Strauss, C., Taylor, B. L., Gu, J., Kuyken, W., Baer, R., Jones, F., & Cavanagh, K. (2016). What is compassion and how can we measure it? A review of definitions and measures. *Clinical Psychology Review, 47*, 15–27.

*Strupp, H. H., Fox, R. E., & Lessler, K. (1969). *Patients view their psychotherapy.* Baltimore, MD: Johns Hopkins University Press.

Tallman, K., Robinson, E., Kay, D., Harvey, S., & Bohart, A. (1994, August). *Experiential and non–experiential Rogerian therapy: An analogue study.* Paper presented at the American Psychological Association Convention, Los Angeles, CA.

Tausch, R. (1988). The relationship between emotions and cognitions: Implications for therapist empathy. *Person-Centered Review, 3,* 277–291.

*Thrasher, A. D., Golin, C. E., Earp, J. A. L., Tien, H., Porter, C., & Howie, L. (2006). Motivational interviewing to support antiretroviral therapy adherence: The role of quality counseling. *Patient Education and Counseling, 62,* 64–71. https://www.doi.org/10.1016/j.pec.2005.06.003

*Truax, C. B. (1966). Therapist empathy, warmth, and genuineness and patient personality change in group psychotherapy: A comparison between interaction unit measures, time sample measures, and patient perception measures. *Journal of Clinical Psychology, 22,* 225–229.

Truax, C. B., & Carkhuff, R. R. (1967). *Toward effective counseling and psychotherapy: Training and practice.* Chicago, IL: Aldine.

*Truax, C. B., Carkhuff, R. R., & Kodman, F. Jr. (1965). Relationships between therapist-offered conditions and patient change in group psychotherapy. *Journal of Clinical Psychology, 21,* 327–329.

Truax, C. B., & Mitchell, K. M. (1971). Research on certain therapist interpersonal skills in relation to process and outcome. In A. E. Bergin & S. L. Garfield (Eds.), *Handbook of psychotherapy and behavior change* (1st ed., pp. 299–344). New York, NY: Wiley.

*Truax, C. B., Wargo, D. G., Frank, J. D. Imber, S. D., Battle, C. C., Hoehn-Saric, R., . . . Stone, A. R. (1966). Therapist empathy, genuineness and warmth and patient therapeutic outcome. *Journal of Consulting Psychology, 30,* 395–401.

*Truax, C. B., & Wittmer, J. (1971). The effects of therapist focus on patient anxiety source and the interaction with therapist level of accurate empathy. *Journal of Clinical Psychology, 27,* 297–299.

*Truax, C. B., Wittmer, J., & Wargo, D. G. (1971). Effects of the therapeutic conditions of accurate empathy, nonpossessive warmth, and genuineness on hospitalized mental patients during group therapy. *Journal of Clinical Psychology, 27,* 137–142.

*Van der Veen, F. (1967). Basic elements in the process of psychotherapy: A research study. *Journal of Consulting Psychology, 31,* 295–303.

Wampold, B. E. (2015), How important are the common factors in psychotherapy? An update. *World Psychiatry, 14,* 270–277. https://www.doi.org/10.1002/wps.20238

Watson, J. C. (2001). Re-visioning empathy. In D. Cain & J. Seeman (Eds.), *Humanistic psychotherapies: Handbook of research and practice* (pp. 445–471). Washington, DC: American Psychological Association.

Watson, J. C., & Geller, S. M. (2005). The relation among the relationship conditions, working alliance, and outcome in both process-experiential and cognitive-behavioral psychotherapy. *Psychotherapy Research, 15,* 25–33.

Watson, J. C., & Greenberg, L. S. (2009). Empathic resonance: A neuroscience perspective. In J. Decety & W. Ickes (Eds.), *The social neuroscience of empathy* (pp. 125–138). Cambridge, MA: MIT Press.

Watson, J. C., & Prosser, M. (2002). Development of an observer rated measure of therapist empathy. In J. C. Watson, R. Goldman, & M Warner (Eds.), *Client-centered and experiential psychotherapy in the 21st century: Advances in theory, research and practice* (pp. 303–314). Ross on Wye, England: PCCS Books.

*Watson, J. C., Steckley, P. L., & McMullen, E. J. (2014). The role of empathy in promoting change. *Psychotherapy Research, 24,* 286–298. https://www.doi.org/10.1080/10503307.2013.802823

Wilson, D. B. (2006). Meta-analysis macros for SAS, SPSS, and Stata. Retrieved from http://mason.gmu.edu/~dwilsonb/ma.html

*Wiprovnick, A. E., Kuerbis, A. N., & Morgenstern, J. (2015). The effects of therapeutic bond within a brief intervention for alcohol moderation for problem drinkers. *Psychology of Addictive Behaviors, 29,* 129–135. https://www.doi.org/10.1037/a0038489

*Woodin, E. M., Sotskova, A., & O'Leary, K. D. (2012). Do motivational interviewing behaviors predict reductions in partner aggression for men and women? *Behaviour Research & Therapy, 50,* 79–84. https://www.doi.org/10.1016/j.brat.2011.11.001

Wynn, R., & Wynn, M. (2006). Empathy as an interactionally achieved phenomenon in psychotherapy: Characteristics of some conversational resources. *Journal of Pragmatics, 38,* 1385–1397.

8

POSITIVE REGARD AND AFFIRMATION

Barry A. Farber, Jessica Y. Suzuki, and David A. Lynch

Author Note. We gratefully acknowledge the research assistance provided by Jenna Cohen, Stephanie Fritz, Devlin Jackson, Tao Lin, Amar Mandavia, and Rebecca Shulevitz.

> The deepest principle in human nature is the craving to be appreciated.
> —William James (1890/1981, p. 313)

Over 60 years ago, in what is now considered a classic paper, Carl Rogers (1957) posited that psychotherapists' provision of positive regard (nonpossessive warmth), congruence (genuineness), and empathy were the necessary and sufficient conditions for therapeutic change. Rogers had been developing these views for many years, some of which were expressed as early as 1942 in his seminal work, *Counseling and Psychotherapy.* Still, the publication of the 1957 article catalyzed a shift in the way that many thought about the putative mechanisms of psychotherapeutic change. The prevailing view at the time—and still an enormously influential one, though currently cast in somewhat different (e.g., more evidence-based) terms—was that technical expertise on the part of the therapist, especially in terms of choice and timing of interventions, was the essential discriminating element between effective and noneffective therapy. Under the sway of Rogers' burgeoning influence in the late 1950s and throughout the 1960s, the notion that the relationship was *the* critical factor in determining therapeutic success took hold.

Over the years, a great many studies have attempted to investigate Rogers' claims regarding the necessary and sufficient conditions of therapy. There is, then, a substantial body of research to draw upon in investigating the association between the therapist's positive regard for his or her patients and therapeutic outcome. However, as detailed in this chapter, drawing firm conclusions from these efforts has proven difficult. The problems that typically plague the investigation of complex psychological phenomena have been played out in this area as well: inconsistent findings, small sample sizes, lack of standardized measures, conceptual and statistical overlap among related concepts, and lack of operational definitions of the concepts themselves. In addition, as the Rogerian influence on clinical practice has diminished in the past three to four decades—or, more accurately, has been incorporated into the mainstream with little awareness or explicit acknowledgment (Farber, 2007)—empirical studies based on Rogerian concepts have also waned.

Psychotherapists of varying persuasions, including those from theoretical camps that had traditionally emphasized more technical factors, have increasingly acknowledged the importance of the relationship. Behaviorists and cognitive-behaviorists now suggest that a good relationship may facilitate the provision of their psychological interventions (e.g., Beck, 1995; Leahy, 2008; Linehan, 1993), and many psychoanalytic therapists have shifted their clinical perspective to emphasize "relational" factors (Mitchell & Aron, 1999; Wachtel, 2008).

But even before these relatively recent developments, there is evidence to suggest that Freud's psychoanalytic cases were only successful when he was supportive and positively regarding. As Breger (2009) noted:

> When Freud followed these [psychoanalytic] rules his patients did not make progress. His well-known published cases are failures . . . in contrast are patients like Kardiner and others—cases he never wrote or publicly spoke about—all of whom found their analyses very helpful. With these patients, what was curative was not neutrality, abstinence, or interpretations of resistance, but a more open and supportive relationship, interpretations that fit their unique experiences, empathy, praise, and the feelings that they were liked by their analyst. (p. 105)

This observation suggests that Freud was unaware of, or at least underappreciated, what may well have been the most potent elements of his approach—that along with whatever positive effects accrue as a result of accurate interpretations, psychoanalytic success has arguably always been based substantially on the undervalued ability of the analyst to be empathic and, even more to the point of this chapter, to be supportive and positively regarding of his or her patients.

In this chapter, we review positive regard and discuss how the use of multiple terms (including *affirmation, respect, warmth, support, validation*, and *prizing*) has led to conceptual confusion as well as empirical difficulties in determining the link between this variable and therapeutic outcome. We consider research measures, clinical examples, and landmark studies involving positive regard and affirmation. We then summarize the results of our meta-analysis on the association between therapist positive regard and treatment outcome in psychotherapy. The chapter concludes with diversity consideration, training implications, and therapeutic practices reflective of positive regard and affirmation.

DEFINITIONS

To the extent that the therapist finds himself experiencing a warm acceptance of each aspect of the client's experience as being a part of that client, he is experiencing unconditional positive regard . . . it means there are no conditions of acceptance . . . It means a "prizing" of the person . . . it means a caring for the client as a separate person. (Rogers, 1957, p. 101)

From the beginning of his efforts to explicate the essential elements of client-centered (later termed *person-centered*) therapy, Rogers (1951) focused on positive regard and warmth: "Do we tend to treat individuals as persons of worth, or do we subtly devaluate them by our attitudes and behavior? Is our philosophy one in which respect for the individual is uppermost?" (p. 20). Some of his prominent followers (e.g., Bozarth & Wilkins, 2001) have asserted that positive regard is *the* curative factor in person-centered therapy.

For Rogers, a therapist's provision of positive regard was a crucial counter-balance to the "conditions of worth" typically imposed by parents on their children. Implicit too in Rogers' quote is his disapproval of what he perceived as the arrogance of the psychoanalytic community at that time, including the tendency of its practitioners to accord hierarchical distinctions between themselves and their and patients. Rogers did not believe that anyone, including a therapist, could be more expert or knowledge-able about a client than the client him- or herself. He did not believe that a therapist's neutrality, dispassionate stance, or even intellectual understanding could facilitate a client's growth—no matter how astute the interpretations emanating from such a therapy might be. Instead, he believed that treating clients in a consistently warm, caring, highly regarding manner would inevitably allow them to grow psychologically, to fulfill their potential.

To this day, agreeing on a single phrase to refer to this positive attitude remains problematic. It is most often termed *positive regard,* but early studies and theoretical writings preferred the phrase *nonpossessive warmth*. Some contemporary person-centered theorists continue to prefer the term *unconditional positive regard*. In his famous filmed work with Gloria (Shostrom, 1965), Rogers struggled to find a single phrase to illuminate this concept: it is, he said, "real spontaneous praising; you can call that quality acceptance, you can call it caring, you can call it a non-possessive love. Any of those terms tend to describe it." Some reviews of the research on "acceptance, nonpossessive warmth, or positive regard" (Orlinsky et al., 1994, p. 326) grouped them under the category of *therapist affirmation*. We use the phrase *positive regard* to refer to the general constellation of behaviors encompassed by this and similar phrases.

Further confusing the definition, Rogers' focus on accepting and affirming the client has, from the outset, been conflated with empathy and genuineness. The therapist's attempt to "provide deep understanding and acceptance of the attitudes consciously held at the moment by the client" could only be accomplished by the therapist's "struggle to achieve the client's internal frame of reference, to gain the center of his own perceptual field and see with him as perceiver" (Rogers, 1951, pp. 30–31). Rogers suggested that positive regard (including the component of acceptance) can best be achieved through empathic identification with one's client. In a similar vein, Rogers suggested that the therapist's genuineness or congruence was a prerequisite for his or her experience of positive regard and empathy (Rogers & Truax, 1967).

Additional problems with the concept of positive regard have been identified (e.g., Lietaer, 1984). One is that there may be an inherent tension between this attitude and that of genuineness. That is, therapists' own conflicts, biases, defensiveness, and histories inevitably affect what they can and cannot praise in others. Rogers (1957) asserted that not only did therapists need to provide positive regard but also that clients needed to experience it themselves—truly feel it and believe it. To the extent, then, that a client would perceive a therapist's positively regard as disingenuous, this condition for successful therapy would not be satisfied.

A second, related problem is that it is unlikely that any mental health practitioner can provide constant doses of unconditional positive regard inasmuch as we all reinforce selectively. We reinforce certain actions and not others, and even those actions that we strive to continually reinforce through positively regarding statements or behaviors are subject to the vagaries of our moods or circumstances and the shifting behaviors of those we encounter. Rogers (1957) seems to have understood this:

> The phrase "unconditional positive regard" may be an unfortunate one, since it sounds like an absolute, an all-or-nothing dispositional concept. . . . From a clinical and experiential point of view I believe the most accurate statement is that the effective therapist experiences unconditional positive regard for the client during many moments of his contact with him, yet from time to time he experiences only a conditional positive regard—and perhaps at times a negative regard, though this is not likely in effective therapy. It is in this sense that unconditional positive regard exists as a matter of degree in any relationship. (p. 101)

Positive Regard versus Unconditional Positive Regard

Rogers' multiple attempts to operationalize therapist caring or affirmation have led to a fair amount of confusion. In his 1957 paper, he used the term *unconditional positive regard* and identified two components: *unconditionality* and *regard*. Rogers seemed to emphasize more heavily the *unconditionality* component than the *regard* component, as indicated by sample items he goes on to propose in the same paper: "I feel no revulsion at anything the client says"; "I feel neither approval nor disapproval of the client and his statements—simply acceptance"; "I feel warmly toward the client—toward his weaknesses and problems as well as his potentialities"; "I am not inclined to pass judgment on what the client tells me"; "I like the client." (p. 102). Of these five items, only one ("I feel warmly towards the client") integrates unconditionality with regard, while three items focus exclusively on unconditionality, and only one item ("I like the client") is keyed to regard alone.

In a more fully developed treatise on client-centered theory, Rogers (1959) elaborated on positive regard. He wrote:

> If the perception by me of some self-experience in another makes a positive difference in my experiential field, then I am experiencing positive regard for that

individual. In general, positive regard is defined as including such attitudes as warmth, liking, respect, sympathy, acceptance. (p. 208)

He then offers a definition of unconditional positive regard:

If the self-experiences of another are perceived by me in such a way that no self-experience can be discriminated as more or less worthy of positive regard than any other, then I am experiencing unconditional positive regard for this individual. . . . Putting this in simpler terms, to feel unconditional positive regard towards another is to "prize" him. . . . This means to value the person, irrespective of the differential values which one might place on his specific behaviors. (p. 208)

Here, Rogers offers a single synonym ("prizing") as a stand-in for unconditional positive regard, though that word is now commonly used as an example of the therapist's general positive regard.

Initial efforts to measure Rogers' facilitative conditions distinguished unconditionality from positive regard. As discussed later, the best validated and most commonly used measure of the facilitative conditions, the Barrett-Lennard Relationship Inventory (BLRI; Barrett-Lennard, 1964, 1986) utilized two subscales to assess this construct: Level of Regard, "the overall level or tendency of one person's affective response to another" (Barrett-Lennard, 1986, p. 440) and Unconditionality of Regard, the extent to which "regard . . . is stable" (p. 443). Subsequent research found, however, that the Unconditionality of Regard subscale was less reliable and valid than the other subscales (Barrett-Lennard, 1964; Cramer, 1986). As a result, the Unconditionality of Regard subscale has increasingly been excluded in studies using the other BLRI scales (Level of Regard, Empathic Understanding, and Congruence). Meanwhile, the "Unconditional" specifier has often been dropped from the label of "positive regard," and clinical and research conceptualizations in recent decades have tended to focus more on the "positive regard" strand than the "unconditionality" strand.

Rogers' written and spoken statements consistently maintain that a core feature of positive regard is the therapist's affective attitude toward his or her clients; as noted, he consistently invoked words such as *warmth, liking, affirmation, nonpossessive love,* and *affection* in referring to this facilitative condition. Thus, in making decisions regarding the studies to include in our meta-analysis, we chose to exclude those studies that investigated therapist *respect* and *support*—both these concepts (which were studied as single variables only rarely) have something in common with Rogers' ideas about positive regard, but in our view they omit an essential affective component, a sense of warmth or liking for the client. The same could be said of *validation*—that, conceptually, it lacks an affective element. For example, Linehan's (1993, 1997) attempts to define validation emphasize the concept of acceptance—of communicating to clients that they are heard and seen and that their responses make sense and are understandable within their current life context. Furthermore, as Linehan (1997) has noted, most types and levels of therapist validation within her model reflect communicative activities typically defined as empathic. However—and we are aware that we are drawing subtle distinctions here—therapist validation, according to Linehan (1997), can also be seen as a form of positive regard: "The person, rather than the constructs brought to the interaction by the therapist, is seen and countenanced. Validation used in this sense perhaps comes closest to the meaning of the term 'unconditional positive regard' used by Rogers (1959)" (p. 357). Thus we included *validation* as a term to include in our meta-analysis, specifically when this variable was assessed via a measure (see later discussion) typically used to assess positive regard.

MEASURES

Reading transcripts of Rogers' work (e.g., Farber et al., 1996) makes clear how challenging it is to tease out pure examples of positive regard. Rogers is consistently "with" his clients, testing his understanding, clarifying, and intent on entering and grasping as much as possible the client's experiential world. For these reasons, most research focusing on the effects of therapist positive regard have used measures, typically either the BLRI (Barrett-Lennard, 1964, 1978) or the Truax Relationship Questionnaire (Truax & Carkhuff, 1967), that include items reflecting overlapping relational elements.

The BLRI consists of 64 items across four domains (Level of Regard, Empathic Understanding, Unconditionality of Regard, and Congruence). Eight items are worded positively and eight negatively in each domain; each item is answered on a +3 (yes, strongly felt agreement) to -3 (no, strongly felt disagreement) response format. This instrument can be used by a client, therapist, or external observer. Both Level of Regard and Unconditionality have been used in research studies to investigate the influence of positive regard on the process and outcome of psychotherapy.

Level of Regard, according to Barrett-Lennard (1986), "is concerned in various ways with warmth, liking/caring, and 'being drawn toward'" (pp. 440–441). Positive items include "She respects me as a person," "I feel appreciated by her," and "She is friendly and warm toward me." Representative negative items include "I feel that she disapproves of me," "She is impatient with me," and "At times she feels contempt for me."

Unconditionality of Regard is explained by Barrett-Lennard (1986) in terms of its stability, "in the sense that it is not experienced as varying with other or otherwise dependently linked to particular attributes of the person being regarded" (p. 443). Examples of positively worded items are "How much he likes or dislikes me is not altered by anything that I tell him about myself"; "I can (or could) be openly critical or appreciative of him without really making him feel any differently about me." Examples of negatively worded items are "Depending on my behavior, he has a better opinion of me sometimes than he has at other times"; "Sometimes I am more worthwhile in his eyes than I am at other times."

Truax and Carkhuff (1967) developed two separate instruments for the measurement of Rogers' facilitative conditions. One was a set of scales to be used by raters in their assessment of these conditions as manifest in either live observations or through tape recordings of sessions. There are five stages on the scale that measures

Nonpossessive Warmth. At Stage 1, the therapist is "actively offering advice or giving clear negative regard" (p. 60); at Stage 5, the therapist "communicates warmth without restriction. There is a deep respect for the patient's worth as a person and his rights as a free individual" (p. 66).

The second instrument developed by Truax and Carkhuff (1967), the Relationship Questionnaire, was to be used by clients. This measure consists of 141 items marked "true" or "false" by the client. Of these items, 73 are keyed to the concept of nonpossessive warmth; it is noteworthy, however, that many of these items are also keyed to the other two facilitative conditions (genuineness and empathy). That is, a "true" response on one item may count toward a higher score on more than one subscale. Representative items on the Nonpossessive Warmth scale are "He seems to like me no matter what I say to him" (this item is also on the Genuineness scale); "He almost always seems very concerned about me"; "He appreciates me"; "I feel that he really thinks I am worthwhile"; "Even if I were to criticize him, he would still like me"; and "Whatever I talk about is OK with him."

In addition to these scales, therapist positive regard has been assessed via instruments designed primarily to measure the strength of the alliance. In particular, the Vanderbilt Psychotherapy Process Scale (VPPS) has been used in this manner. The VPPS is "a general-purpose instrument designed to assess both positive and negative aspects of the patient's and the therapist's behavior and attitudes that are expected to facilitate or impede progress in therapy" (Suh et al., 1986, p. 287). Each of 80 items is rated by clinical observers on a 5-point, Likert-type scale either from the actual therapy sessions or from video- or audiotapes of therapy. Factor analyses of these items have yielded eight subscales, one of which, Therapist Warmth and Friendliness, closely approximates positive regard. The specific therapist attributes rated in this subscale include "involvement" (the therapist's engagement in the patient's experience), "acceptance" (the therapist's ability to help the patient feel accepted), "warmth and friendliness," and "supportiveness" (the therapist's ability to bolster the patient's self-esteem, confidence, and hope). Therapist positive regard can also be measured through the Structural Analysis of Social Behavior (Benjamin, 1984), using scores for the Affirming and Understanding cluster. Consistent with Rogers' theorizing about positive regard, this cluster combines elements of warmth and empathy.

Whereas the "bond" component of various alliance measures (e.g., Horvath & Greenberg, 1989; Tracey & Kokotovic, 1989) contains aspects of positive regard phenomena that have been elucidated earlier, its items primarily assume an interaction between patient and therapist that reflects the contributions and characteristics of each. Thus results from studies using alliance measures were not included in our meta-analysis.

A new 43-item measure of positive regard (Psychotherapist Expressions of Positive Regard [PEPR]; Suzuki & Farber, 2016) has been developed. Its factor structure strongly suggests three distinctive components: Supportive/Caring Statements (e.g., "I'm glad you shared that with me"), Unique Responsiveness (e.g., "My therapist remembers the name or details of something or someone I have spoken of in the past"), and Intimacy/Disclosure (e.g., "My therapist has tears in his/her eyes as I relate a sad story"). While each of these factors was shown to be positively and significantly associated with the Working Alliance Inventory-Short Form subscales (Tracey & Kokotovic, 1989), the PEPR measure has not yet been used to examine the relation of positive regard to therapeutic outcome.

CLINICAL EXAMPLES

Arguably, the most cited, if somewhat controversial (Daniels, 2014), example of positive regard comes from Rogers' filmed work with Gloria (Shostrom, 1965). Gloria stated that she wished that her own father would talk to her like Rogers was doing at that moment and then remarked, "Gee, I'd like you for my father." Rogers responded to her, "You look to me like a pretty good daughter." It is a moving moment, one that has been used to illustrate not only positive regard but also corrective emotional experience. The contrast between Rogers' unconditional positive regard and Gloria's father's (presumed) conditions of worth could be seen as catalyzing a corrective experience (Farber et al., 2012), though the absence of any outcome data should temper our confidence in this possibility.

The other examples of positive regard that follow have been purposely drawn from disparate theoretical orientations. Although the therapeutic value of positive regard essentially originated with Rogers, the provision of this facilitative condition can and does occur in the work of practitioners of multiple clinical traditions. Furthermore, clients' ratings of the most affirming therapist behaviors are not restricted to explicit statements reflecting the therapist's valuing of or caring for the client. In one study (Suzuki & Farber, 2016), among the therapist behaviors that clients experienced as most affirming were: "My therapist offers me a new way of understanding a part of myself that I usually view as a weakness"; "My therapist shows she or he is listening through her or his body language"; "My therapist maintains eye contact with me"; "My therapist encourages me to take pride in the things I do well"; and "My therapist speaks to me in a gentle tone of voice." Thus some of the following examples are not prototypical affirming statements but rather therapist words or behaviors that convey an overall attitude of positive regard.

Case Example 1

Client: I can outsmart people. I won't be taken advantage of. I call the shots.
Therapist: It seems important for you to be dominant in every relationship.
Client: Yes. I don't show emotion and I don't put up with it in anyone else. I don't want someone to get all hysterical and crying with me. I don't like it.
Therapist: How did you learn that being emotional is a sign of weakness?
Client: I don't know.
Therapist: What if you meet your intellectual match, if you can't "outsmart" them?
Client: (silence)
Therapist: Okay, what if someone got to you through your feelings?

Client: Last week you did. It bothered me all day.

Therapist: That you were weak?

Client: Yeah.

Therapist: I didn't see you as submissive or weak. In fact, since showing emotion is so difficult for you I saw it as quite the opposite.

In this example, the therapist, primarily psychodynamic in orientation, initially tries to get the patient to open up about his past and discuss his "faulty strategy" of dominating relationships. It appears as if they are about to discuss transference issues. However, the therapist shifts at the end, perhaps intuitively sensing that what would be most effective for this patient (at least at this moment) is a statement of true positive regard. Thus the therapist is affirming, suggesting that she views the client not as weak or submissive but rather the opposite, as perhaps brave for doing something that was difficult for him. This is a good example too of the way in which positive regard can be conveyed through the therapist's offering a new way of understanding what the client perceives as a personal weakness.

Case Example 2

Therapist: You're reading me entirely wrong. I don't have any of those feelings. I've been pleased with our work. You've shown a lot of courage, you work hard, you've never missed a session, you've never been late, you've taken chances by sharing so many intimate things with me. In every way here, you do your job. But I do notice that whenever you venture a guess about how I feel about you, it often does not jibe with my inner experience, and the error is always in the same direction: You read me as caring for you much less than I do. (Yalom, 2002, p. 24).

In this example, Yalom, an existential therapist, offers assumedly accurate feedback to his patient on her interpersonal tendencies (much like a psychoanalytic therapist might do). In doing so, he explicitly conveys the fact that he cares for this patient far more than she imagines to be the case.

Case Example 3

Client: It really hurts when I think about the fact that it is over.

Therapist: Yes, of course it hurts. It hurts because you loved him and it did not work out. It shows, I think, your capacity to love and to care. But it also hurts to have that ability.

Client: I don't think I'll ever feel that way.

Therapist: Right now it may be important for you to protect yourself with that feeling. Perhaps we can look at what you have learned about yourself and your needs and the kind of man who would be right for you.

Client: What do you mean?

Therapist: I mean that you have a great ability to love. But what can you learn about what you need in a man that [Tom] lacked?

Client: I guess I learned not to get involved with a married man.

Therapist: What do you think led you to think you'd be able to handle being involved with a married man?

Client: Well, after my marriage ended, I guess I didn't want to get too attached. So I thought that being involved with someone who is married would keep me from being hurt.

Therapist: Perhaps you've learned that you have such a strong ability to love that you can't compartmentalize your feelings that way. (Leahy, 2001, p. 82)

In this example, Leahy, a cognitive therapist, is consistently empathic ("of course it hurts") and attempts to teach his patient something about herself and her needs and choices (by making a connection between her current behavior and past actions). He also contextualizes his interventions in a supportive, caring way, emphasizing his patient's "strong ability to love."

Case Example 4

Client: I'm just feeling so worn-out and sad.

Therapist (nodding, attentive, maintaining eye contact, and then, after a moment's silence, in a very gentle voice): Tell me more, please. I'd like to really understand what you're going through.

This brief example illustrates the way in which a therapist's body language and the paralinguistic elements of his or her speech can contribute significantly to whatever verbal message is offered to the client. This client feels held and cared about even before the therapist's gentle invitation to share more about his or her situation.

Case Example 5

Client: (smiles) I think I'm having male menopause.

Therapist: (smiles) Okay, but I think you'll need to explain that condition to me.

Client: (laughs) I met this great guy coming out of the supermarket. And we chatted right there on the street and we exchanged phone numbers. He probably won't call. He's a lot younger than I am so I don't think he's really interested, but, hey, I actually had a daylight conversation with an attractive man and he knows my name. Now that's something, huh?

Therapist: Yes, it is. And something different for you.

Client: Yeah, I'm feeling less creature-like. More human these days. Like coming out from under a rock. Oh, I finished my painting . . . the one with the lost boy. I thought about what you said about the boy feeling lost. . . . When I was finishing the painting, I felt like . . . it's almost like you and I came up with that together.

Therapist: I feel that, too. I think that we each contribute to our work here together. The accomplishment of finishing the painting is all yours, though. And talking to a man you find attractive, giving him your name and phone number . . . Sounds well, something commonplace, but not for you. Not in a long time.

Client: I actually surprised myself. It didn't even feel so risky. I just "went with it." He smiled, I smiled back . . .

Therapist: Good. And that was so courageous of you . . .

Client: Yeah, that's me, I guess. My mother used to say that my refusal to not give in irritated the hell out of my father. I'm sure I disappointed him as a son. . . . But sometimes, I'm glad he's gone. I feel guilty thinking and saying it but if I had to choose which parent would go first, I'm not sorry it was him and glad it wasn't my mother. I really still need her.

Therapist: I know. And you know, I want to tell you how much I appreciate your honesty in allowing yourself to think about these things that are sometimes hard to think about.

Client: Thanks. (Pause.) I hope he calls me.

Therapist: I hope so too.

Here, a relationally oriented psychodynamic clinician banters somewhat ("you'll have to explain that condition to me") as a means to be connected and supportive. Moreover, she values her patient's efforts to change ("that was so courageous of you") and gives him credit for the work he's doing in the here-and-now of the clinical setting ("how much I appreciate your honesty").

Case Example 6

Client: Yeah, I don't feel like it's [filling out diary cards every day] for me. I don't want to wake up every day, and go, "Oh, I felt like suicide last Tuesday! Oh my God, I was sad last week!" I don't want to keep remembering!

Therapist: Oh, okay, so you want one of those therapies where you don't remember things?

Client: No, I just don't want to keep bringing it up all the time. "Oh, I was raped on so-and-so date, let me remember what I felt at the time."

Therapist: Yeah, it's so painful to bring up this stuff. Why would anyone want that?

Client: Yeah, exactly!

Therapist: Now here's the dilemma. We could not talk about your problems, and if this would take away your pain and misery, I'd be all for it. On the other hand, if we help you figure out how to tolerate your bad feelings, then you won't have to rely on your pain medicine or resort to thinking of killing yourself when these feelings come up.

Client: But the feelings are horrible! What am I supposed to do, just wave a magic wand to make them go away? You make it sound so easy.

Therapist: It's not easy at all. This is incredibly tough and painful for you, and I also believe you have what it takes to do it. (Adapted from McMain et al., 2001, p. 196)

In this dialogue, a dialectical behavior therapist offers a supportive statement ("I believe you have what it takes to do it") that has much in common with the comments of the relationally oriented therapist in the previous example. Here, the therapist's empathic response ("It's not easy at all") is followed up by a more explicit statement of positive regard.

Case Example 7

Client: I feel like there are people who do care and accept me. I do, but . . .

Therapist: But the person that can't accept and value you, is actually you.

Client: Yes, mostly.

Therapist: It seems the person who is hardest on you is you.

Client: Yes. No one else would be as cruel to me as I am.

Therapist: And make such harsh judgments, you're pretty tough on yourself.

Client: Yes, I wouldn't judge my friends the way I judge myself.

Therapist: No, you're not a very good friend to yourself.

Client: No, I wouldn't treat anyone the way I treat me.

Therapist: Maybe because you can see what is lovable in them, but not in yourself. To you, you're unlovable.

Client: Maybe there are small pieces of me that are lovable.

Therapist: (pause) So there are parts of you that you see as okay, as worthy of being loved.

Client: Yes, I guess. The child in me, the child that struggled and survived. She, I, can still be playful and fun and warm.

Therapist: Those are very wonderful qualities.

Client: She's strong, a survivor.

Therapist: She's a part of you that you can hold on to.

Client: Yes.

Therapist: Do you think she'd judge you so harshly?

Client: No, she loves me.

Therapist: To this special child part of you, none of you is unforgivable.

Client: No, she loves all of me.

In this final example, the client-centered therapist is clearly conveying to the patient that she is worthy of respect and love. The therapist's positive regard for the patient may allow her to begin to view herself as the therapist does. These last few examples are prime illustrations of the multiple aspects of positive regard, including affirmation, trust, understanding, warmth, interest, and respect.

LANDMARK STUDIES

Building on Rogers' early work, including his pioneering emphasis on investigating psychotherapy process and outcome, the large-scale research program led by Truax and colleagues (1966) at the University of Arkansas tested a number of hypotheses about the nature and effects of Rogers' three facilitative conditions. Many of these studies assessed the facilitative conditions collectively rather than singly, comparing differences in outcomes for clients who saw therapists who were "high" in their provision of these conditions (per ratings of outside observers) versus those with therapists in the "low" conditions group. One such study of 40 outpatients found that the group with high ratings on therapist facilitative conditions had 90% global improvement (as assessed on a number of scales completed by patient, therapist, and interviewer), as compared with 50% global improvement for those working with therapists with low scores on the three facilitative conditions (Truax et al., 1966).

The National Institute of Mental Health Treatment of Depression Collaborative Research Program (TDCRP; Elkin et al., 1985), while primarily focused on assessing the comparative effectiveness of four types of psychotherapy provided over 16 weeks, gave rise to a wealth of data on the association of positive regard to psychotherapy outcome. One such study (Rounsaville et al., 1987) focused on the subsample ($n = 35$) of patients in interpersonal therapy and found a positive association between therapist warmth and friendliness as measured by the VPPS and outcome measures (social adjustment, $r = .40$; patient ratings of change, $r = .60$). Other analyses of the TDCRP data have found significant relations between BLRI composite scores (which include but do not parse the specific impact of positive regard) and patient outcomes. For example, Blatt and colleagues (1996) found that patient ratings of the quality of the therapeutic relationship early in treatment, as measured by BLRI total score, contributed significantly to treatment dropout and, for treatment completers, to therapeutic change on a variety of specific (depression, $r = -.15$; social adjustment, $r = -26$) and global (overall symptoms $r = -.22$; global assessment $r = .24$) outcome measures.

Qualitative research on the link between positive regard and therapy outcomes is sparse. In one study (Traynor et al., 2011), the consensus of 20 person-centered practitioners who were interviewed was that in working with clients with psychotic symptoms, unconditional positive regard was especially important. In another qualitative study (Suzuki, 2018), one that relied on consensual qualitative research (Hill, 2012), 15 clients of varied backgrounds and in various forms of therapy were interviewed about their experiences with positive regard in psychotherapy. These clients indicated that positive regard was an essential ingredient in their therapy, strengthening the therapeutic relationship, facilitating personal growth, improving self-esteem and social functioning, and buffering against therapeutic ruptures and the possibility of termination.

RESULTS OF PREVIOUS META-ANALYSES

As part of a comprehensive review of process and outcome in psychotherapy, Orlinsky and Howard (1986) conducted separate reviews of studies evaluating the effects of *therapist support* and *therapist affirmation*. They identified 11 studies that included a support/encouragement variable; within this group of studies they focused on 25 separate findings. Their conclusion: "Although 6 of the 25 are significantly positive findings and none are negative, more than three-quarters show a null association between specific therapist efforts to give support and patient outcome" (p. 326). In addition, the authors identified 94 findings on the association between therapist affirmation (essentially warmth, caring, and acceptance) and outcome, with more than half (53%) demonstrating a significant association between these variables.

Underscoring their emphasis on considering the perspective of raters, they noted that "the proportion of positive findings is highest across all outcome categories when therapist warmth and acceptance are observed from the patient's process perspective" (Orlinsky & Howard, 1986, p. 348). That is, in 30 cases where the patient's ratings of therapist positive regard were used, 20 outcome scores were positively correlated with these ratings (aggregated over the outcome perspectives of patient, therapist, rater, and objective score), and no outcome scores (regardless of the source) were significantly negatively correlated with patient ratings of therapist positive regard.

In 1994 Orlinsky and colleagues studied this general phenomenon under the rubric of *therapist affirmation*, explained by the authors as a variable that includes aspects of acceptance, nonpossessive warmth, or positive regard. They found that 56% of the 154 results reviewed were positive and that, again, the findings based on patients' process perspective (the patient's rating of the therapist's positive regard) yielded even a higher rate of positive therapeutic outcomes, 65%. "Overall," Orlinsky et al. concluded, "nearly 90 findings indicate that therapist affirmation is a significant factor, but considerable variation in ES [effect size] suggests that the contribution of this factor to outcome differs according to specific conditions" (p. 326).

In their review of positive regard for the first edition of this volume, Farber and Lane (2002) highlighted several patterns. First, no post-1990 study reported a negative relationship between positive regard and outcome. Second, the results of the 16 studies analyzed in that chapter were essentially evenly split between positive and nonsignificant effects. That is, 49% (27/55) of all reported associations were significantly positive and 51% (28/55) were nonsignificant. However, the authors noted that the majority of nonsignificant findings occurred when an objective rater (rather than the therapist or patient) evaluated therapeutic outcome. Third, confirming the pattern noted by previous reviewers, Farber and Lane found that when the patient rated both the therapist's positive regard and treatment outcome, a positive association between these variables was especially likely. Last, the effect sizes for the significant results tended to be modest, with the larger effect sizes occurring when positive regard was assessed in terms of its association to length of stay in therapy rather than outcome per se (e.g., Najavits & Strupp, 1994).

Finally, in the previous (second) edition of this volume, Farber and Doolin (2011) analyzed 18 studies. Using a random effects model, they reported an aggregate effect size of $r = .27$ ($p < .000$, $N = 1,067$), indicating that positive regard has a moderate association with psychotherapy outcomes; only two of the studies yielded negative effect sizes. Univariate categorical moderator analyses indicated that the following moderators were significant (i.e., demonstrated significant heterogeneity in their aggregate effect sizes): publication outlet (i.e., journal article vs. dissertation), rater perspective, origin of sample (random vs. convenience sample), measure used to assess positive regard, time in treatment when positive regard was measured, and type (theoretical orientation) of treatment. Notably, they found that the overall effect of positive regard on outcome tended to be higher when the treatment was psychoanalytic/psychodynamic. The authors also noted that as the percentage of racial/ethnic minorities increased in the patient sample, the overall effect size also increased, though this finding only approached significance.

META-ANALYTIC REVIEW

Literature Search and Study Selection

To find studies that documented a relation between positive regard and outcome in psychotherapy, we used the PsycINFO database. Main root terms searched in the title or the abstract were *positive regard, warmth, nonpossessive warmth, therapist affirmation, unconditional positive regard, acceptance, validation,* and *unconditional regard.* All these terms were crossed with *psychotherapy, psychotherapist,* and *psychotherapeutic.* Additional studies were located by running a search with the root term *Barrett-Lennard* since this is the most widely used instrument to assess positive regard. Furthermore, all meta-analyses and review articles yielded by these searches were combed for eligible empirical studies. We generally excluded non-English articles from consideration, with the exception of a few papers that were translated (by a colleague of ours) from German.

The specific inclusion criteria were (a) the study identified positive regard as either unconditional regard, positive regard, warmth, nonpossessive warmth, affirmation, acceptance or validation; (b) positive regard (in any of these forms) was considered as a predictor of outcome in the study; (c) the study reported quantitative outcome data and relevant statistics (e.g., correlations between positive regard ratings and treatment outcome or mean outcome comparisons between groups with differential positive regard ratings) that could be used to calculate effect sizes; and (d) treatment was individual, family, or group psychotherapy.

Our meta-analytic methods allowed for broader inclusion criteria than those used in the previous meta-analysis, which identified only 18 eligible studies. In this iteration, we coded for a variety of treatment variables to investigate whether they had a moderating impact on the relation between positive regard and outcome. Rather than restricting our focus to individual adult psychotherapy, we included 13 studies on family or group treatment and 13 studies that included participants younger than age 18.

Furthermore, in contrast to the previous edition, we did not immediately exclude studies we encountered through the search parameters described previously that looked at positive regard as part of a "composite" factor—typically as part of the constellation of Rogerian facilitative conditions. We obtained disaggregated raw data through correspondence with the authors of three studies, but in most cases this was not possible. Because investigating the facilitative conditions in aggregate is a relatively common practice in both early and more recent studies—a practice justified by the strong intercorrelations among positive regard, empathy, and congruence/genuineness--we included these composite variables with the goal of testing for a moderating effect when positive regard is assessed singly versus in aggregate form. A total of 24 studies using composite scores (typically from the Truax rating scales or BLRI) were included in the meta-analysis. Only those studies where the composite predictor (typically, the three facilitative conditions) was coherently defined with an overall clear relationship to positive regard were included, while studies that aggregated positive regard with an excessively large or unwieldy group of variables were excluded. Finally, we excluded studies that explicitly reported that participants in the low and high facilitative conditions groups did not have significantly different ratings of positive regard.

In addition, we consulted the 2011 chapter to determine which of those 18 studies met our current criteria. One article (Quintana & Meara, 1990) was excluded because it did not explicitly examine the relation between positive regard and therapeutic outcomes. After scanning the literature with these criteria in mind, over 100 studies were selected for review, of which 64 were found to be entirely consistent with these criteria and thus were included in the meta-analysis (Table 8.1).

The characteristics of the studies included are noted in Table 8.2. The study (measurement) characteristics we rated were positive regard measure; whether positive regard was assessed alone or as part of a composite; time of predictor and outcome measurement (early treatment, mid-treatment, late/termination, follow-up, or multiple measurements averaged); rater perspective for predictor and outcome variables (client, therapist, external rater, or combination); and total number of participants.

Characteristics of the sample/treatment that were coded were mean age; percentage of men; percentage of racial/ethnic minorities; nationality (US vs. other); predominant diagnosis (mood/anxiety disorder, severe mental illness, or other); outpatient versus inpatient setting; child versus adult participants; group versus family treatment; and therapy modality (psychodynamic, cognitive behavioral, or mixed/other). The therapist factors coded for this analysis were mean age, percentage of men, and experience level of therapists (trainees vs. non-trainees).

Effect Size Coding

Because the purpose of this meta-analysis was to examine the relation between therapist positive regard and treatment outcome, effects sizes were collected for each analysis that included positive regard and an outcome variable. Since each study reported effects using different types of effect sizes, we converted all effect sizes to Hedges g (per Cooper et al., 2009). When computing Hedges' g, each effect size accounts for the sample size of each study-based analysis; thus Hedges' g offers an unbiased estimator of d since the effect size estimate d tends to have a small overestimation bias that can be removed using a correction formula.

A statistical package available online aided in the statistical analysis for this project (see Del Re, 2010; Del Re & Hoyt, 2010).

Table 8.1. Studies and Effect Sizes Used in the Meta-Analysis Investigating the Effects of Positive Regard on Treatment Outcome

Authors	ES (g)	Year	n	Measure(s)	Format: Sample
Alexander et al.	0.82	1976	21	VPPS	Group/Family: Mixed
Arts et al.	0.33	1994	30; 25	BLRI/Total	Individual: Children
Athay	0.22	1973	150	TRS	Individual: Adults
Bachelor	0.41	1991	45	VPPS	Individual: Adults
Barnicot et al.	0.15	2014	157	BLRI/LR	Individual: Children
Beckham	0.04	1989	32	BLRI/Total	Individual: Adults
Beckham	0.39	1992	55	BLRI/Total	Group/Family: Adults
Bedics et al.	0.41	2012	51	SASB	Individual: Adults
Bell et al.	0.16	2016	85	BLRI/LR; BLRI/U; Total	Individual: Adults
Bennun & Schindler	0.67	1988	35	Other	Individual: Adults
Blaauw & Emmelkamp	0.25	1994	28	Other	Individual: Adults
Blatt et al.	0.20	1996	149	BLRI/Total	Individual: Adults
Brouzos et al.	0.10	2017	56	BLRI/LR; BLR/U	Group/Family: Children
Brouzos et al.	0.10	2015	40	BLRI/LR	Group/Family: Children
Cain	0.53	1973	101; 63	Other	Individual: Adults
Canterbury-Counts	0.13	1989	73	BLRI/LR; BLRI/U	Group/Family: Children
Chisholm	0.50	1998	41	VPPS	Individual: Adults
Conte et al.	0.22	1995	138	1–2 Item Rating	Individual: Adults
Cordaro et al.	1.09	2012	37	VPPS	Mixed: Children
Cramer & Takens	0.34	1992	44	BLRI/Total	Individual: Adults
De Beurs	0.03	1993	31	Other	Individual: Adults
Eckert et al.	0.26	1988	77	1-2 Item Rating	Individual: Adults
Ford	0.45	1978	39	BLRI/Total	Individual: Adults
Garfield & Bergin	0.17	1971	38	TRS	Individual: Adults
Green & Herget	0.55	1991	11	1-2 Item Rating	Group/Family: Mixed
Gustavson et al.	0.12	1994	12	Other	Individual: Adults
Hayes & Strauss	0.27	1998	32	VPPS	Individual: Adults
Hynan	0.55	1990	31	1–2 Item Rating	Individual: Adults
Karpiak & Benjamin	0.16	2004	20	SASB	Individual: Adults
Keijsers et al.	0.37	1991	37	BLRI/Total	Individual: Adults
Keijsers et al.	0.09	1994	60; 53	BLRI/Total	Individual: Adults
Keijsers et al.	0.10	1994	40	BLRI/Total	Individual: Adults
Klassen	0.01	1979	55	BLRI/Total	Individual: Children
Klein	0.36	2001	17; 19;	VPPS	Individual: Adults

Table 8.1. Continued

Authors	ES (g)	Year	n	Measure(s)	Format: Sample
Kolb et al.	0.24	1985	91	BLRI/Total	Individual: Adults
Litter	0.46	2004	47	VPPS	Mixed: Children
Loneck et al.	0.04	2002	39	VPPS	Individual: Adults
Murphy & Cramer	4.96	2010	62	BLRI/LR; BLRI/U	Individual: Adults
Najavits & Strupp	1.23	1994	12; 8	VPPS; SASB; BLRI/ Total	Individual: Adults
Prager	0.16	1970	34; 33; 32	1–2 Item Rating	Individual: Adults
Rabavilas et al.	0.34	1979	36	1–2 Item Rating	Individual: Adults
Reese	0.07	1984	100	BLRI/Total	Individual: Adults
Roback & Strassberg	0.32	1975	24	BLRI/Total	Group/Family: Adults
Rothman	0.54	2007	44; 23; 15	BLRI/U	Mixed: Children
Rousaville et al.	0.43	1987	35	VPPS	Individual: Adults
Ryan & Gizynski	0.51	1971	13	1-2 Item Rating	Individual: Adults
Saunders	0.22	2000	114	Other	Individual: Adults
Saunders et al.	0.16	1989	113	Other	Individual: Adults
Schade et al.	0.67	2015	11	Other	Group/Family: Adults
Schauble & Pierce	2.33	1974	41	TRS	Individual: Adults
Sells et al.	0.30	2006	137	BLRI/LR	Individual: Adults
Staples & Sloane	0.34	1976	17	VPPS	Individual: Adults
Strupp et al.	0.53	1964	44	Other	Individual: Adults
Tillman	0.45	2016	31	BLRI/U; BLRI/LR	Individual: Adults
Truax	0.30	1966	74; 69;63	TRS	Group/Family: Adults
Truax	1.00	1968	30	TRS	Group/Family: Mixed
Truax et al.	0.21	1971	160	TRS	Group/Family: Adults
Truax et al.	0.53	1973	16	TRS	Individual: Children
Turner	0.45	1998	28	Other	Group/Family: Adults
Van der Veen	0.49	1967	15	Other	Individual: Adults
Williams	0.27	1996	50	BLRI/Total	Group/Family: Adult
Williams & Chamberless	0.18	1990	33	Other	Individual: Adults
Zuroff & Blatt	0.16	2006	191	BLRI/Total	Individual: Adults
Zuroff et al.	0.22	2010	157	BLRI/Total	Individual: Adults

Note. $k = 64$. ES = effect size; BLRI/Total = Barrett-Lennard Relationship Inventory, Total; BLRI/ LR = Barrett-Lennard Relationship Inventory, Level of Regard; BLRI/U = Barrett-Lennard Relationship Inventory, Unconditionality; SASB = Structural Analysis of Social Behavior (Affirm/Understand); TRS = Traux Rating Scale; VPPS = Vanderbilt Psychotherapy Process Scale.

Table 8.2. Characteristics of Studies Included in the Meta-Analysis

Sample Characteristic	K	%	Measure Characteristic	k	%
Country			PR Measures[a]		
United States	48	75	Unitary PR Measures	44	69
Other	16	25	BLRI—Level of Regard	8	13
Modality			BLRI—Unconditionality	6	10
Individual tx	48	75	Truax Unconditional Positive Regard Rating Scales	6	10
Group/Family	13	20	VPPS Rating Scales	10	16
Mixed	3	5	SASB—Affirm/ Understand	3	5
Setting			Other PR Measure	14	22
Outpatient	54	84	Composite Measures	22	34
Inpatient	6	10	BLRI—Total score	18	28
Mixed/Other	4	6	Other Composite	5	8
Treatment Orientation					
Psychodynamic	12	19	Outcome Measures[a]		
Cognitive-Behavioral	16	25	Nonspecific[b]	30	47
Mixed/Other	27	42	Specific[c]	46	71
Not Specified	9	14			
Therapist Experience			PR Rater Perspective		
Trainee	20	31	Client	38	59
Non-Trainee	20	31	Therapist	2	3
Mixed	17	27	External Rater	17	27
Not Specified	7	11	Mixed	7	11
			Outcome Rater Perspective		
Patient Age			Client	17	27
Adult	51	80	Therapist	1	2
Child	10	15	External Rater	6	10
Mixed	3	5	Mixed	34	53
Patient Gender			Not Specified	6	10
Majority (>60%) Male	5	8			
Majority (>60%) Female	35	55			
Even split (40%–60%) Male/Female	10	16			
Not Specified	14	22			
Predominant Diagnosis					
Mood/Anxiety Disorder	19	30			
Severe Mental Illness	12	19			
Mixed/Other	22	34			
Not Specified	11	17			

Note. k = 64. PR = positive regard; BLRI = Barrett-Lennard Relationship Inventory; Truax UPR Rating Scales = Truax Unconditional Positive Regard Rating Scales; VPPS = Vanderbilt Psychotherapy Process Scale; SASB = Structural Analysis of Social Behavior
[a] Studies used more than one measure; totals exceed 100%. [b] For example, overall improvement, broad symptom checklist. [c] For example, disorder-specific symptom or area of functioning.

Results

A total of 369 effect sizes within 64 studies, comprising 3,528 patients, were included in the overall analysis. Using a random effects model, the aggregate effect size was $g = .28$, indicating that positive regard has a small association with psychotherapy outcomes. Additionally, the 95% confidence interval (CI) did not include zero (95% CI = 0.25, 0.31), indicating that the effect of positive regard on outcome is significantly different from zero.

To assess whether there was variability among these 64 studies above and beyond what would be expected by chance, a homogeneity test was conducted. Using the homogeneity statistics, Q and I^2 (Hedges, 1982), the assumption that the studies selected were sampled from the same population (i.e., were homogenous) was rejected, (Q ($df = 368$) = 1132.56, $p < .0001$; $I^2 = 67.51\%$). This indicated that there is a large amount of heterogeneity of effects among these studies, suggesting that study factors may be moderating the omnibus effects.

To assess for publication bias or the "file drawer problem," we conducted an Orwin's fail-safe N analysis. The analysis found that a total of 2,049 studies that are not significant at the .05 level would be needed to negate the strength of the aggregated effect. However, the funnel plot of included studies (Figure 8.1) suggests the possibility of publication bias—the substantial asymmetry around the mean may be evidence that included studies disproportionally report elevated effect sizes. The studies that had effect sizes of $g > 1.0$ tended to be published before 1995 and have an n of less than 50, with two exceptions (Cordaro et al., 2012; Murphy & Kramer, 2010).

Since 369 effect sizes were nested within 64 studies, the assumption of independence was managed via stipulating a correlation between outcome measures of .5 (Wampold et al., 1997). To account for this issue statistically, we employed a multilevel random effects meta-analysis in which effect sizes were nested within individual study samples (Konstantopoulos, 2011). This analysis accounted for the fact that some

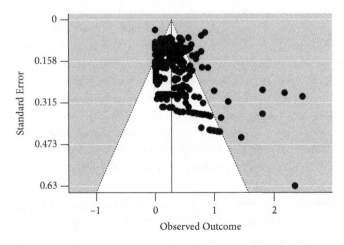

FIGURE 8.1 Funnel plot of studies included in meta-analysis of the effects of positive regard.

studies utilized the same data set to report multiple correlations of positive regard and outcome. Controlling for nesting within samples, the multilevel analysis yielded a larger effect than the random effects model, with an aggregate effect size of $g = .36$ (95% CI = 0.28, 0.44), and the same heterogeneity (Q ($df = 368$) = 1132.56, $p < .001$).

Comparison to Previous Meta-Analytic Results

As noted, the current meta-analysis included a far greater number of studies ($k = 64$) than either the 2011 version ($k = 18$) or the 2002 version of this chapter ($k = 16$). In contrast to the meta-analyses in earlier versions of this volume, the current meta-analysis incorporated studies of positive regard with broader inclusion criteria that investigated child, family, and group psychotherapy, as well as studies that investigated the collective effects of Rogers' three facilitative conditions on therapeutic outcome.

Perhaps as a result of these differences, the current study yielded a smaller effect size; adopting a random effects model, the most recent previous (2011) meta-analysis reported an aggregate effect size of $r = .27$ whereas in this current meta-analysis, g was calculated as .28, a figure that corresponds to nearly double that of r at these lower levels. Furthermore, in the current meta-analysis, for each included study we calculated an effect size for each analysis that associated positive regard with an outcome variable. As a result, nonsignificant findings in secondary or tertiary analyses yielded multiple effect sizes approaching zero. The variability within studies, particularly with the inclusion of all reported findings, contributed to the modest (small) overall effect size of the current meta-analysis. When accounting for the heterogeneity of study data sets, the aggregate effect size increased to $g = 0.36$. This could be indicative of study-level random and systematic error that differentially impact sample characteristics.

MODERATORS

To account for the heterogeneity present in the included studies, we first conducted several univariate categorical moderator analyses. All covariate analyses utilized a restricted maximum-likelihood estimator to generate unbiased estimates of the variance of covariance parameters. To be considered a significant moderator, the factor needed to be both statistically significant in the test for residual heterogeneity (QE) and the test of moderators (QM). As Table 8.3 indicates, the following moderators explained statistically significant heterogeneity of the aggregate effect sizes: therapy format, therapeutic setting, therapist experience level, client diagnosis, and type of outcome measure used. When factors are considered individually (rather than in a multilevel model; see later discussion), positive regard tends to have a more powerful association with psychotherapy outcome in individual therapy, in an outpatient setting, when therapy is performed by trainees, with clients presenting with mood or anxiety disorders (as opposed to severe mental illness), and when outcome is assessed via measures of global or overall symptomatology (as opposed to specific indices of depression or anxiety).

Table 8.3. Statistically significant Univariate Moderators

Moderator Variables	No. of Effect Sizes in Analysis (k)	Effect of Coefficients	95% Confidence Interval [lower bound, upper bound]
Therapy Format			
Individual therapy	369	0.40	[0.32, 0.49]
Group/Family therapy	369	−0.23	[−0.36, −0.10]
Therapeutic Setting			
Outpatient	365	0.41	[0.32, 0.49]
Inpatient	365	−0.30	[−0.44, −0.16]
Therapist Experience			
Trainee	345	0.32	[0.19, 0.44]
Mixed	345	0.27	[0.11, 0.42]
Diagnosis			
Mood/Anxiety Disorder	320	0.41	[0.28, 0.53]
Severe Mental Illness	320	−0.30	[−0.43, −0.17]
Outcome Measure			
Nonspecific Diagnosis	369	0.41	[0.33, 0.49]
Mood/Anxiety Disorder	369	−0.07	[−0.13, −0.01]

Following the univariate moderator analyses, all significant moderators were combined into a multilevel meta-regression model (Table 8.4). The model-building approach was utilized to control for the correlations between moderator variables. The overall test of moderators (QM $(df = 10) = 36.48$, $p < .0001$) indicated that the moderators significantly explained some of the heterogeneity across studies; however, the test of residual heterogeneity suggested that, as a model, the heterogeneity across studies remains high after accounting for the moderators in the model (QE $(df = 288) = 707.33$, $p < .0001$). Since many of the predictor variables are associated (i.e., significantly correlated), the model-building approach corrects for the inflated alpha associated with multiple univariate analyses. When all significant covariates were included in a meta-regression model, only the model's intercept was significant.

Table 8.4. Multilevel Meta-Regression Model with All Significant Univariate Covariates

Parameter	No. of Effect Sizes in Analysis (k)	Statistic	95% Confidence Interval [lower bound, upper bound]	p value
Model	299	0.38	[0.15, 0.61]	$p < 0.01$
Residual Heterogeneity	299	$QE = 707.33$	–	$p < .0001$
Moderators	299	$QM = 36.48$	–	$p < .0001$

EVIDENCE FOR CAUSALITY

Inferring causation inevitably proves to be challenging in all process–outcome analyses. When computing the relation between measures of positive regard and outcomes, virtually all of the effect size conversions within the included studies derived from correlations. Thus causality cannot be established or inferred in this meta-analysis.

Two common methods of approaching causation are temporal analysis and mediation analysis; the analyses conducted here, constrained by the available data, do not meet those standards. When considering the association between positive regard and outcome, it remains a conceptual and measurement challenge to determine whether positive regard influences outcome or whether improved outcomes over the course of therapy modulate positive regard. In reality, both are likely occurring. The potential bidirectionality of this relationship makes inferring causation risky. Since the majority of the included studies investigated the relation of positive regard to more distal outcomes, few studies examined whether this variable serves as a mediator.

To explore the nature of the association of positive regard and outcome, we utilized a multilevel meta-regression. Model-building approaches systematically control for variables that may account for the unexplained variability across and within studies; however, since the majority of the studies included here utilized correlational statistics, interpretations must be made with caution. While this does not and cannot infer causation, it does enable a better understanding of the extent of the relation between positive regard and psychotherapy outcomes and the factors that influence the strength of that relation.

PATIENT CONTRIBUTIONS

The patient's experience of therapist positive regard is the ultimate criterion of its presence. Affirmation succeeds only if it is received as intended, and the client is obviously the primary determinant of that. There is no positive regard without a client, to borrow an analogy from Winnicott (1960). In fact, Rogers (1957) believed that it is only the client's perspective that matters––it is the client's experience of positive regard (or genuineness or empathy) that "counts," and the therapist's belief as to whether he or she has been positively regarding is essentially moot in regard to outcome.

Patient demographics did not emerge as significant moderators in our analyses of the data. In fact, when factors were considered individually (rather than in a multilevel model), only one patient-related characteristic emerged as significant: positive regard was shown to have a more powerful association with psychotherapy outcome with clients presenting with mood or anxiety disorders rather than severe mental illness. This may represent an unfortunate clinical reality—that therapists' provision of positive regard to clients with severe psychopathology does not "work" as well as with clients with mood or anxiety disorders. Rogers (1966) would not have been surprised by this finding; in his work with schizophrenic patients as part of the Wisconsin Project, he theorized that these patients often perceived positive regard as "indifference" and that a more "conditional, demanding attitude," at least in the early stages of therapy, might prove more effective in establishing a good therapeutic relationship (p. 186). On the other hand, the possibility that positive regard is especially potent in working with *less* severely impaired clients is contrary to the perceptions of therapists who were interviewed regarding their perceptions of the nature and value of positive regard (Traynor et al., 2011). Importantly, though, what must be kept in mind is that this finding of a significant contribution of patient severity to the effects of positive regard on outcome no longer emerged when a multilevel model of study characteristics was generated.

Apart from the specific findings of this meta-analysis, it is generally acknowledged that therapists' behavior in sessions is a function, among other things, of the characteristics of their patients. Some patients, including those who are warm, empathic, and disclosing, are more easily liked and likely elicit more affirmation than others. Just as disclosure begets disclosure (Jourard, 1971), it is quite likely that warmth begets warmth. Conversely, demanding, resistant, or angry patients can be difficult to like or affirm. Thus we suspect that those with personality pathologies, especially individuals with borderline, narcissistic, or antisocial disorders, are less likely to consistently evoke positive regard from their therapists.

Another client characteristic that we hypothesize will influence a therapist's tendency to be affirming is the nature of the client's needs at a particular point in session. For example, patients suffering acutely from depression, or dealing with the aftermath of a trauma or loss, may explicitly ask for or more subtly indicate their need for intensive doses of positive regard. These requests may range from "Please tell me I'm going to be okay," to "I really need your support now," to "No one cares about me at all." Another possible factor here is motivational status—that is, a patient's stage of change (e.g., Krebs, Norcross, Nicholson, & Prochaska, 2018). Patients who are more highly motivated to do the work, who appear to be courageous or risk taking, are more likely to evoke their therapist's positive regard.

LIMITATIONS OF THE RESEARCH

Our database was restricted to 64 studies, a relatively small basis for conclusions about a variable that has been part of psychotherapeutic lore for more than 60 years. Although this is a larger number of studies compared to the previous edition (18 studies), we maintained stringent criteria for inclusion into the meta-analysis. It should be noted, however, that some of the studies eligible for inclusion included null results for a subset of the hypotheses tested without reporting adequate information to calculate effect sizes for these tests; as a result, these null results could not be incorporated into the meta-analysis and represent a bias toward significance in our meta-analysis. Moreover, there have been few studies of positive regard within the past 20 years. We believe that the concept of positive regard has not so much gone away in recent years as it has been folded into newer constructs, particularly the therapeutic alliance (see Chapters 2, 3, and 4 in this volume).

Another possible limitation is that positive regard may interact with a specific un-investigated aspect of therapy and that its effects are better understood as a complex product of multiple processes or therapeutic conditions. For example, positive regard might be significantly associated with outcome only when therapist directiveness is low (Orlinsky & Howard, 1978) or, conversely, when therapists frequently assign home-work or are typically challenging or confrontational. The point is that there are too few investigations of the ways in which positive regard may be confounded with other therapist attitudes and behaviors. In a somewhat similar vein, the multiple forms that many "brand name" therapies take (e.g., the many strands and "waves" of cognitive-behavioral therapy) suggest that aggregating multiple varieties of specific therapeutic approaches under a single variable may result in data loss or misleading results.

Finally, the extant research, including our own meta-analysis, has not addressed the question of whether positive regard has different effects on reduction of symptoms (either diagnostic-specific or overall symptoms) in comparison, say, to various, global indices of patient well-being, social adjustment, or happiness, nor do we know the ex-tent to which any beneficial effect of a therapist's provision of positive regard endures beyond the end of treatment.

DIVERSITY CONSIDERATIONS

Participant diversity likely impacts the provision and effects of positive regard in a multitude of ways. Client and therapist demographics (e.g., race, ethnicity, gender, religion, sexual orientation), personal histories, and preferences as well as their in-teraction are all part of diversity considerations. For example, it has been suggested in the clinical literature that therapist expressions of positive regard may be partic-ularly potent when working with stigmatized or marginalized populations, such as sexual-minority youth (Lemoire & Chen, 2005). In an early meta-analysis (Farber & Doolin, 2011), the percentage of racial/ethnic minorities in the sample suggested the same (accentuated) effect, albeit only at a trend level. However, this finding was not replicated in the current meta-analysis.

Due to the inconsistent reporting of patient demographics in our studies, we selected only a small number of demographic variables to include in our meta-analysis—gender composition of clients and therapists and percentage of ethnic minorities among clients. This approach limits the conclusions that can be drawn. While newer studies might be designed to address diversity-related questions, the older studies that comprise the majority of our dataset rarely addressed these matters.

Further, the majority-White composition of psychotherapy practitioners and clients—both in the included studies and in the population as a whole—limits our ability to identify genuine effects for race and ethnicity where they might exist. Only one study included in this meta-analysis sampled a mostly non-White population (Cordaro et al., 2012). A critical mass of studies specifically investigating the conse-quence of positive regard with a more diverse sample of clients will be needed to elu-cidate this issue.

A qualitative investigation of clients' experiences with positive regard (Suzuki, 2018) reported that clients who related easily to their therapists as a result of demographic similarities felt that this rapport facilitated their positive regard. Practitioners working across differences that reinforce a felt differential in power or privilege may need to be especially conscious of the need for and the manner in which they convey positive regard to their clients. Positive regard may be particularly salient in treatment outcome when nonminority therapists work with minority clients. In such cases, the possibility of client mistrust compels greater therapist awareness of the clinical value of consistent provision of positive regard (Sue & Sue, 1999).

TRAINING IMPLICATIONS

The results of our meta-analysis suggest the importance of therapists of all theoretical persuasions adopting an attitude of positive regard toward their clients. The results of recent work on the constituent elements of positive regard (Farber & Suzuki, 2018; Suzuki & Farber, 2016) further suggest that therapists' provision of empathy and positive regard are confounded in the eyes of clients (i.e., that clients perceive empathic reflections as indicative of a therapist's positive regard toward them). Taken together, these findings suggest that while teaching students the value of and means toward effecting a positively regarding attitude toward clients would be valuable in their training, a more comprehensive approach, one that introduces students to the nature and importance of all of Rogers' facilitative conditions, would be of even greater value.

We believe that including Rogers' writings on the facilitative conditions of psychotherapy would contribute greatly to every beginning practica in graduate training programs regardless of the theoretical orientation of that course. We suggest too that practica instructors remind students that practices that encourage therapists to approach patients through a lens of detachment and neutrality, or through exclusively dispassionate, technically driven interventions, are contraindicated by research evidence.

We also believe in the value of clinical supervisors monitoring the quality and consistency of positive regard that supervisees offer their clients. While this may be partially accomplished through supervisory discussions of countertransference (i.e., of therapists' emotional attitudes toward patients), our suggestion here is for supervisors to focus, at least occasionally, on the specific ways in which trainees' acceptance, liking, and caring for their clients have been conveyed (or not) in sessions and what the clinical consequences of these actions have been. As many pundits have remarked, the truth—and perhaps the devil too—is in the details. We believe that supervisors would do well to find out what and why their supervisees convey certain positively regarding attitudes and adopt certain words and phrases but omit others. Such discussion might lead to profitable supervisory discussions regarding the state of the therapeutic alliance and/or the possibility of alliance ruptures within supervisees' caseloads.

Last, viewing *Gloria* is not enough. That is, we imagine that many students' knowledge of Rogers begins and ends with seeing this film. It is a perfectly good introduction to Rogers' work and therapeutic philosophy. "All in all," Rogers says in his post-interview musings that are part of the film (Shostrom, 1965), "I feel good about this interview." But we believe, too, that, based only on viewing this film, many students are left with the wrong impression of what an overall attitude of positive regard truly entails. The senior author's sense in showing this film many times over many years is that burgeoning clinicians have a tendency to reduce Rogers' pervasive acceptance of a person's feelings and experience, including the "deeper core of the person" (Liaeter, 1984, p. 47) to the rendering of a heart-felt compliment (e.g., "You look to me like a pretty nice daughter") or even the adoption of a "nice person" attitude. Watching multiple videos of Rogers' work, reading summaries or transcripts of his sessions (Farber et al., 1996), and/or observing others (e.g., Linehan, 2014) put into practice similar concepts (i.e., validation) are all likely to greatly expand students' understanding of the broad meanings and implications of adopting this attitude into their clinical work.

THERAPEUTIC PRACTICES

The psychotherapist's provision of positive regard or affirmation significantly predicts and relates to therapeutic success. Our meta-analysis indicates a moderate association, suggesting that positive regard is an important but not exhaustive part of the process–outcome equation. Extrapolating from the meta-analysis, we offer the following recommendations for clinical practice:

+ *Provide positive regard in practice.* At a minimum, it "sets the stage" for other mutative interventions and, at least in some cases, may prove sufficient to effect positive change.

   In fact, there is virtually no research-driven reason to withhold positive regard. We are reminded of the oft-heard sentiment in contemporary psychoanalytic circles that one of Kohut's major contributions was to provide a theoretical justification for being kind to one's patients.
+ *Keep in mind that affirming patients serves many valuable functions.* Positive regard strengthens the client's sense of self or agency and belief in his or her capacity to be engaged in an effective relationship. A therapist's positive regard also functions as a positive reinforcer for clients' engagement in the therapeutic process, including difficult self-disclosures, and facilitates growth and resilience.
+ *Avoid the tendency to be content with feeling good about patients; instead, allow yourself to express positive feelings to clients.* The therapist's conveyance of positive regard does not have to translate to a stream of compliments or to a gushing of positive sentiment that may overwhelm or even terrify some clients; rather, it speaks to the need for therapists to communicate a caring, respectful, positive attitude that affirms a client's sense of worth. To many, if not most, clients, the conviction that "my therapist really cares about me" likely serves a critical function, especially in times of stress.
+ *Convey regard through multiple channels.* These entail, inter alia, offering reassuring, caring words; creating positive narratives; active listening; flexibility in scheduling; speaking in a gentle tone of voice; establishing responsive eye contact; and maintaining positive body language.

♦ *Monitor your positive regard and adjust it as a function of particular patients and specific situations.* The research demonstrates that therapists vary in the extent to which they convey positive regard to their patients, and clients vary in the extent to which they need, elicit, and/or benefit from it. We suspect that the inevitable ruptures in the therapeutic alliance (see Chapter 16, this volume) result not only from a therapist's technical errors but also from the therapist's occasional inability to demonstrate minimal levels of positive regard.

REFERENCES

References marked with an asterisk indicate studies included in the meta-analyses.

*Alexander, J. F., Barton, C., Schiaro, R. S., & Parsons, B. V. (1976). Systems-behavioral intervention with families of delinquents: Therapist characteristics, family behavior, and outcome. *Journal of Consulting and Clinical Psychology, 44*(4), 656–664.

*Arts, W., Hoogduin, C. A. L., Keijsers, G., Severeijns, R., & Schaap, C. (1994). A quasi-experimental study into the effect of enhancing the quality of the patient-therapist relationship in the outpatient treatment of obsessive-compulsive neurosis. In S. Borgo (Ed.), *The patient-therapist relationship: Its many dimensions* (pp. 25–31). Rome, Italy: Consiglio Nazionale delle Ricerche.

*Athay, A. L. (1974). *The relationship between counselor self concept, empathy, warmth, and genuineness, and client rated improvement* (Doctoral dissertation). Retrieved from ProQuest Digital Dissertations. (UMI No. 7331254)

*Bachelor, A. (1991). Comparison and relationship to outcome of diverse dimensions of the helping alliance as seen by client and therapist. *Psychotherapy, 28*, 534–549.

*Barnicot, K., Wampold, B., & Priebe, S. (2014) The effect of core clinician interpersonal behaviours on depression. *Journal of Affective Disorders, 167*, 112–117.

Barrett-Lennard, G. T. (1964). *The Relationship Inventory. Form OS-M-64 and OS-F-64 Form MO-M-64 and MO-F-64.* Armidale, New South Wales, Australia: University of New England.

Barrett-Lennard, G. T. (1978). The Relationship Inventory: Later development and applications. *JSAS: Catalog of Selected Documents in Psychology, 8*, 68.

Barrett-Lennard, G. (1986). The Relationship Inventory now: Issues and advances in theory, method and use. In L. S. Greenberg & W. M. Pinsof (Eds.), *The psychotherapeutic process: A research handbook* (pp. 439–476). New York, NY: Guilford.

Beck, J. S. (1995). *Cognitive therapy: Basics and beyond.* New York, NY: Guilford.

*Beckham, E. E. (1989). Improvement after evaluation in psychotherapy of depression: Evidence of a placebo effect? *Journal of Clinical Psychology, 45*(6), 945–950.

*Beckham, E. E. (1992). Predicting patient dropout in psychotherapy. *Psychotherapy: Theory, Research, Practice, Training, 29*(2), 177–182.

*Bedics, J. D., Atkins, D.C., Comtois, K. A., & Linehan, M. M. (2012). Treatment differences in the therapeutic relationship and introject during a 2-year randomized controlled trial of dialectical behavior therapy versus non-behavioral psychotherapy experts for borderline personality disorder. *Journal of Consulting and Clinical Psychology, 80*(1), 66–77.

*Bell, H., Hagedorn, W. B., & Robinson, E. H. (2016). An exploration of supervisory and therapeutic relationships and client outcomes. *Counselor Education and Supervision, 55*(3), 182–197.

Benjamin, L. (1984). Principles of prediction using Social Analysis of Structural Behavior (SASB). In R. A. Zucker, J. Aronoff, & A. J. Rabin (Eds.), *Personality and the prediction of behavior* (pp. 121–173). New York, NY: Academic Press.

*Bennun, I., & Schindler, L. (1988). Therapist and patient factors in the behavioural treatment of phobic patients. *British Journal of Clinical Psychology, 27*(2), 145–151.

*Blaauw, E., & Emmelkamp, P. M. (1994). The therapeutic relationship: A study on the value of the Therapist Client Rating Scale. *Behavioural and Cognitive Psychotherapy, 22*(1), 25–35.

*Blatt, S. J., Zuroff, D. C., Quinlan, D. M., & Pilkonis, P. A. (1996). Interpersonal factors in brief treatment of depression: Further analyses of the National Institute of Mental Health Treatment of Depression Collaborative Research Program. *Journal of Consulting and Clinical Psychology, 64*(1), 162.

Bozarth, J. D., & Wilkins, P. (2001). *Rogers' therapeutic conditions: Evolution, theory and practice. Volume 3: Unconditional positive regard.* Ross-on-Wye, England: PCCS Books.

Breger, L. (2009). *A dream of undying fame: How Freud betrayed his mentor and invented psychoanalysis.* New York, NY: Basic Books.

*Brouzos, A., Vassilopoulos, S. P., & Baourda, V. C. (2015). Members' perceptions of person-centered facilitative conditions and their role in outcome in a psychoeducational group for childhood social anxiety. *Person-Centered & Experiential Psychotherapies, 14*(1), 32–46.

*Brouzos, A., Vassilopoulos, S., Katsiou, P., & Baourda, V. (2017, May). *The group processes in a psychoeducational program for anger management in elementary school students.* Paper presented at the 16th Panhellenic Congress of Psychological Research, Hellenic Psychological Society and Department of Psychology of the Aristotle University of Thessaloniki, Thessaloniki, Greece.

*Cain, D. J. (1973). *The therapist's and client's perceptions of therapeutic conditions in relation to perceived interview outcome* (Doctoral dissertation). Retrieved from ProQuest Digital Dissertations. (UMI No. 7314271)

*Canterbury-Counts, D. (1989). *The impact of the therapeutic relationship on weight loss in a behavioral weight management program* (Doctoral dissertation). Retrieved from ProQuest Digital Dissertations. (UMI No. 8912407)

*Chisholm, S. M. (1998). *A comparison of the therapeutic alliances of premature terminators versus therapy completers* (Unpublished doctoral dissertation). Kent State University, Kent, OH.

*Coady, N. F. (1991). The association between client and therapist interpersonal processes and outcomes in psychodynamic psychotherapy. *Research on Social Work Practice, 1*, 122–138.

*Conte, H. R., Ratto, R., Clutz, K., & Karasu, T. B. (1995). Determinants of outpatients' satisfaction with therapists. *Journal of Psychotherapy Practice and Research, 4*, 43–51.

Cooper, H., Hedges, L. V., & Valentine, J. C. (Eds.). (2009). *The handbook of research synthesis and meta-analysis* (2nd ed.). New York, NY: Russell Sage Foundation.

*Cordaro, M., Tubman, J. G., Wagner, E. F., & Morris, S. L. (2012). Treatment process predictors of program completion or dropout among minority adolescents enrolled in a brief motivational substance abuse intervention. *Journal of Child & Adolescent Substance Abuse, 21*(1), 51–68.

Cramer, D. (1986). An item factor analysis of the revised Barrett-Lennard Relationship Inventory. *British Journal of Guidance and Counselling, 14* (3), 314–325.

*Cramer, D., & Takens, R. J. (1992). Therapeutic relationship and progress in the first six sessions of individual psychotherapy: A panel analysis. *Counseling Psychology Quarterly, 5*, 25–36.

Daniels, D. (2014). "Permanently cheated"—part I. *Contemporary Psychotherapy, 6*(1). Retrieved from www.contemporarypsychotherapy.org/volume-6-no-1-summer-2014/permanently-cheated/

*de Beurs, E. (1993). *The assessment and treatment of panic disorder and agoraphobia.* Amsterdam, The Netherlands: Thesis Publishers.

Del Re, A. C. (2010). *RcmdrPlugin.MAc: Meta-Analysis with correlations (MAc) Rcmdr Plug-in.* R package version 1.0.7. Retreived from http://CRAN.R-project.org/packageRcmdrPlugin.MAc

Del Re, A. C., & Hoyt, W. T. (2010). MAc: Meta-Analysis with correlations. R package version 1.0.6. Retrieved from http://Cran.R-project.org/package=Mac

*Eckert, P. A., Abeles, N., & Graham, R. N. (1988). Symptom severity, psychotherapeutic process, and outcome. *Professional Psychology: Research and Practice, 19*, 560–564.

Elkin, I., Parloff, M. B., Hadley, S. W., & Autry, J. H. (1985). NIMH treatment of Depression Collaborative Research Program: Background and research plan. *Archives of General Psychiatry, 42*(3), 305–316.

Farber, B. A. (2007). On the enduring and substantial influence of Carl Rogers' not-quite-essential nor necessary conditions. *Psychotherapy: Theory, Research, Practice, Training, 44*, 289–294.

Farber, B. A., Bohart, A. C., & Stiles, W. B. (2012). Corrective (emotional) experience in person-centered therapy: Carl Rogers and Gloria Redux. In C. Hill & L. G. Castonguay (Eds.), *Transformation in psychotherapy: Corrective experiences across cognitive behavioral, humanistic, and psychodynamic approaches* (pp. 103–119). Washington, DC: APA Books.

Farber, B. A., Brink, D. C., & Raskin, P. M. (1996). *The psychotherapy of Carl Rogers: Cases and commentary.* New York, NY: Guilford.

Farber, B. A., & Doolin, E. M. (2011). Positive regard. In J. C. Norcross (Ed.) *Psychotherapy relationships that work* (2nd edition) (pp. 168–186). New York, NY: Oxford University Press.

Farber, B. A., & Lane, J. S. (2002). Effective elements of the therapy relationship: Positive regard. In J. Norcross (Ed.), *Psychotherapy relationships that work: Therapist contributions and responsiveness to patients* (pp. 175–194). New York, NY: Oxford.

Farber, B. A., & Suzuki, J. Y. (2018). Affirming the case for positive regard. In O. Tishby & H. Wiseman (Eds.), *Developing the therapeutic relationship: Integrating case studies, research, and practice* (pp. 211–233). Washington, DC: APA Books.

*Ford, J. D. (1978). Therapeutic relationship in behavior therapy: An empirical analysis. *Journal of Consulting and Clinical Psychology, 46*(6), 1302–1314.

*Garfield, S. L., & Bergin, A. E. (1971). Therapeutic conditions and outcome. *Journal of Abnormal Psychology, 77*(2), 108–114.

Gaston, L., Marmar, C. R., Gallagher, D., & Thompson, L. W. (1991). Alliance prediction of outcome beyond in-treatment symptomatic change as psychotherapy processes. *Psychotherapy Research, 1*,104–113.

*Green, R. J., & Herget, M. (1991). Outcomes of systemic/strategic team consultation: The importance of therapist warmth and active structuring. *Family Process, 30*, 321–336.

Gurman, A. (1977). The patient's perception of the therapeutic relationship. In A. S. Gurman & A. M. Razin (Eds.), *Effective psychotherapy* (pp. 503–543). New York, NY: Pergamon.

*Gustavson, B., Jansson, L., Jerremalm, A., & Ost, L. G. (1985). Therapist behavior during exposure treatment of agoraphobia. *Behavior Modification, 9*(4), 491–504.

*Hayes, A. M., & Strauss, J. L. (1998). Dynamic systems theory as a paradigm for the study of change in psychotherapy: An application to cognitive therapy for depression. *Journal of Consulting and Clinical Psychology, 66*, 939–947.

Hedges, L. V. (1982). Estimating effect sizes from a series of independent experiments. *Psychological Bulletin, 92*, 490–499.

Henry, W. P., Schacht, T. E., & Strupp, H. H. (1990). Patient and therapist introject, interpersonal process, and differential psychotherapy outcome. *Journal of Consulting and Clinical Psychology, 58*, 768–774.

Hill, C. E. (Ed.). (2012). *Consensual qualitative research: A practical resource for investigating social science phenomena.* Washington, DC: American Psychological Association.

Horvath, A. O., & Greenberg, A. (1989). Development and validation of the Working Alliance Inventory. *Journal of Counseling Psychology, 36*, 223–233.

*Hynan, D. J. (1990). Client reasons and experiences in treatment that influence termination of psychotherapy. *Journal of Clinical Psychology, 46*, 891–895.

James, W. (1981). *The principles of psychology.* Cambridge, MA: Harvard University Press. (Original work published 1890)

Jourard, S. M. (1971). *The transparent self.* New York, NY: Van Nostrand.

*Karpiak, C. P., & Benjamin, L. S. (2004). Therapist affirmation and the process and outcome of psychotherapy: Two sequential analytic studies. *Journal of Clinical Psychology, 60*(6), 659–676.

*Keijsers, G. P., Hoogduin, C. A., & Schaap, C. P. (1994). Predictors of treatment outcome in the behavioral treatment of obsessive-compulsive disorder. *The British Journal of Psychiatry, 165*, 781–786.

*Keijsers, G., Schaap, C., Hoogduin, K., & Peters, W. (1991). The therapeutic relationship in the behavioural treatment of anxiety disorders. *Behavioural and Cognitive Psychotherapy, 19*(4), 359–367.

*Klassen, D (1979). *An empirical investigation of the Rogerian counseling conditions and locus of control* (Doctoral dissertation). Retrieved from ProQuest Digital Dissertations. (UMI No. DC52536)

*Klein, C. F. (2001). *Clinical process related to outcome in psychodynamic psychotherapy for panic disorder* (Doctoral Dissertation). Retrieved from ProQuest Digital Dissertations. (UMI No, 3024807)

Knox, S., & Hill, C. E. (2003). Therapist self-disclosure: Research-based suggestions for practitioners. *Journal of Clinical Psychology/In Session, 59*, 529–540.

*Kolb, D. L., Beutler, L. E., Davis, C. S., Crago, M., & Shanfield, S. B. (1985). Patient and therapy process variables relating to dropout and change in psychotherapy. *Psychotherapy: Theory, Research, Practice, Training, 22*(4), 702–710.

Konstantopoulos, S. (2011). Fixed effects and variance components estimation in three-level meta-analysis. *Research Synthesis Methods, 2*(1), 61–76.

Krebs, P., Norcross, J. C., Nicholson, J. M., & Prochaska, J. O. (2018). Stages of change and psychotherapy outcomes: A review and meta-analysis. *Journal of Clinical Psychology: In Session, 74*(11), 1964–1979.

Leahy, R. L., (2001). *Overcoming resistance in cognitive therapy.* New York, NY: Guilford.

Leahy, R. L. (2008). The therapeutic relationship in cognitive-behavioral therapy. *Behavioural and Cognitive Psychotherapy, 36*, 769–777.

Lemoire, S. J., & Chen, C. P. (2005). Applying person-centered counseling to sexual minority adolescents. *Journal of Counseling & Development, 83*(2), 146–154.

Lietaer, G. (1984). Unconditional positive regard: A controversial basic attitude in client-centered therapy. In R. F. Levant & J. M. Shlien (Eds.), *Client-centered therapy and the person-centered approach: New directions in theory, research, and practice* (pp. 41–58). New York, NY: Praeger.

Linehan, M. M. (1993). *Cognitive behavioral treatment of borderline personality disorder.* New York, NY: Guilford Press.

Linehan, M. M. (1997). Validation and psychotherapy. In A. Bohart & L. Greenberg (Eds.), *Empathy reconsidered: New directions in psychotherapy* (pp. 353–392). Washington, DC: American Psychological Association.

Linehan, M. (2014). *Three approaches to personality disorders: Dialectical Behavior Therapy* [Video]. Mill Valley, CA: Psychotherapy.net.

*Litter, M. (2004). Relationship-based psychotherapy with court-involved youth: The therapy relationship's effect on outcome. *Dissertation Abstracts International, 65*(12), 4474.

*Loneck, B., Banks, S., Way, B., & Bonaparte, E. (2002). An empirical model of therapeutic process for psychiatric emergency room clients with dual disorders. *Social Work Research, 26*(3), 132–144.

McMain, S., Korman, L. M., & Dimeff, L. (2001). Dialectical behavior therapy and the treatment of emotion dysregulation. *Journal of Clinical Psychology, 57*(2), 183–196.

Meyer, A. E. (1990, June). *Nonspecific and common factors in treatment outcome: Another myth?* Paper presented at the annual meeting of the Society for Psychotherapy Research, Wintergreen, VA.

Mitchell, S. A., & Aron, L. (1999). *Relational psychoanalysis.* New York, NY: Analytic Press.

Mitchell, K., Bozarth, J., & Krauft, C. (1977). A reappraisal of the therapeutic effectiveness of accurate empathy, non-possessive warmth and genuineness. In A. S. Gurman & A. M. Razin (Eds.), *Effective psychotherapy* (pp. 482–502). New York, NY: Pergamon.

Mitchell, K., Bozarth, J., Truax, C., & Krauft, C. (1973). *Antecedents to psychotherapeutic outcome.* NIMH Final Report, MH 12306. Fayetteville: Arkansas Rehabilitation Research and Training Center, University of Arkansas.

*Murphy, D., & Cramer, D. (2010, July). *Mutuality as relational empowerment.* Paper presented at the World Association for Person-Centered and Experiential Psychotherapy and Counselling Symposium, Rome, Italy.

*Najavits, L. M., & Strupp, H. H. (1994). Differences in the effectiveness of psychodynamic therapists: A process-outcome study. *Psychotherapy, 31*, 114–23.

Orlinsky, D. E., Grawe, K., & Parks, B. K. (1994). Process and outcome in psychotherapy— noch einmal. In A. E. Bergin & S. L. Garfield (Eds.), *Handbook of psychotherapy and behavior change* (4th ed., pp. 27–376). New York, NY: Wiley.

Orlinsky, D. E., & Howard, K. (1978). The relation of process to outcome in psychotherapy. In S. L. Garfield & A. E. Bergin (Eds.), *Handbook of psychotherapy and behavior change* (2nd ed., pp. 283–329). New York, NY: Wiley.

Orlinsky, D. E., & Howard, K. (1986). Process and outcome in psychotherapy. In S. L. Garfield, & A. E. Bergin (Eds.), *Handbook of psychological behavior and change* (pp. 311–381). New York, NY: Wiley.

Parloff, M. B., Waskow, I. E., & Wolfe, B. E. (1978). Research on therapist variables in relation to process and outcome. In S. L. Garfield & A. E. Bergin (Eds.), *Handbook of psychotherapy and behavior change* (2nd ed., pp. 233–282). New York, NY: Wiley.

*Prager, R. A. (1971). *The relationship of certain client characteristics to therapist-offered conditions and therapeutic outcome* (Doctoral dissertation). Retrieved from ProQuest Digital Dissertations. (UMI No. b1218412)

Quintana, S. M., & Meara, N. M. (1990). Internalization of therapeutic relationships in short-term psychotherapy. *Journal of Counseling Psychology, 2*, 123–130.

*Rabavilas, A. D., Boulougouris, J. C., & Perissaki, C. (1979). Therapist qualities related to outcome with exposure in vivo in neurotic patients. *Journal of Behavior Therapy and Experimental Psychiatry, 10,* 293–294.

*Reese, L. R. (1984). *A study of patients' perceptions of the psychotherapeutic relationships with the treatment staff at an acute-care community psychiatric facility* (Doctoral dissertation). Retrieved from ProQuest Digital Dissertations. (UMI No. 8502594)

*Roback, H. B., & Strassberg, D. S. (1975). Relationship between perceived therapist-offered conditions and therapeutic movement in group psychotherapy. *Small Group Behavior, 6*(3), 345–352.

Rogers, C. R. (1942). *Counseling and psychotherapy.* Boston, MA: Houghton Mifflin.

Rogers, C. R. (1951). *Client-centered therapy.* Boston, MA: Houghton Mifflin.

Rogers, C. R. (1957). The necessary and sufficient conditions of therapeutic personality change. *Journal of Consulting Psychology, 21,* 95–103.

Rogers, C. R. (1959). A theory of therapy, personality, and interpersonal relationships: As developed in the client-centered framework. In S. Koch (Ed.), *Psychology: A study of a science. Study 1, Volume 3: Formulations of the person and the social context* (pp. 184–256). New York, NY: McGraw-Hill.

Rogers, C.R. (1966). Client-centered therapy. In S. Arieti (Ed.), *American handbook of psychiatry* (Vol. 3, pp. 183–200). New York, NY: Basic Books.

Rogers, C. R. (1986). A client-centered/person-centered approach to therapy. In I. Kutash & A. Wolf (Eds.), *Psychotherapist's casebook* (pp. 197–208). San Francisco, CA: Jossey-Bass.

Rogers, C. R., & Truax, C. B. (1967). The therapeutic conditions antecedent to change: A theoretical view. In C. R. Rogers, E. T. Gendlin, D. J. Kiesler, & C. B. Truax (Eds.), *The therapeutic relationship and its impact: A study of psychotherapy with schizophrenics* (pp. 97–108). Madison: University of Wisconsin Press.

*Rothman, D. B. (2007). *The role of the therapeutic alliance in psychotherapy with sexual offenders* (Doctoral dissertation). Retrieved from ProQuest Digital Dissertations. (UMI No. NR26309)

*Rounsaville, B. J., Chevron, E. S., Prusoff, B. A., Elkin, I., Imber, S., Sotsky, S., & Watkins, J. (1987). The relation between specific and general dimensions of the psychotherapy process in interpersonal psychotherapy of depression. *Journal of Consulting and Clinical Psychology, 55*(3), 379–384.

*Ryan, V. L., & Gizynski, M. N. (1971). Behavior therapy in retrospect: Patients' feelings about their behavior therapies. *Journal of Consulting and Clinical Psychology, 37*(1), 1–9.

*Saunders, S. M. (2000). Examining the relationship between the therapeutic bond and the phases of treatment outcome. *Psychotherapy: Theory, Research, Practice, Training, 37*(3), 206–218.

*Saunders, S. M., Howard, K. I., & Orlinsky, D. E. (1989). The Therapeutic Bond Scales: Psychometric characteristics and relationship to treatment effectiveness. *Psychological Assessment: A Journal of Consulting and Clinical Psychology, 1*(4), 323–330.

*Schade, L. C., Sandberg, J. G., Bradford, A., Harper, J. M., Holt-Lunstad, J., & Miller, R. B. (2015). A longitudinal view of the association between therapist warmth and couples' in-session process: An observational pilot study of emotionally focused couples therapy. *Journal of Marital and Family Therapy, 41*(3), 292–307.

*Schauble, P. G., & Pierce, R. M. (1974). Client in-therapy behavior: A therapist guide to progress. *Psychotherapy: Theory, Research & Practice, 11*(3), 229–234.

*Sells, D., Davidson, L., Jewell, C., Falzer, P., & Rowe, M. (2006). The treatment relationship in peer-based and regular case management for clients with severe mental illness. *Psychiatric Services, 57,* 1179–1184.

Shostrom, E. L. (Producer) (1965). *Three approaches to psychotherapy* (Part 1) [Film]. Orange, CA: Psychological Films.

*Staples, F. R., & Sloane, R. B. (1976). Truax factors, speech characteristics, and therapeutic outcome. *The Journal of Nervous and Mental Disease, 163*(2), 135–140.

*Strupp, H. H., Wallach, M. S., & Wogan, M. (1964). Psychotherapy experience in retrospect: Questionnaire survey of former patients and their therapists. *Psychological Monographs: General and Applied, 78*(11), 1–45.

Sue, D. W., & Sue, D. (1999). *Counseling the culturally different: Theory and practice* (3rd ed.). New York, NY: Wiley.

Suh, C. S., Strupp, H. H., & O'Malley, S. S. (1986). The Vanderbilt Process Measures: The Psychotherapy Process Scale (VPPS) and the Negative Indicators Scale (VNIS). In L. S. Greenberg & W. M. Pinsof (Eds.), *The psychotherapeutic process: A research handbook* (pp. 285–323). New York, NY: Guilford.

Suzuki, J (2018). *A qualitative investigation of psychotherapy clients' perceptions of positive regard* (Unpublished doctoral dissertation). Teachers College, New York, NY.

Suzuki, J. Y., & Farber, B. A. (2016). Towards greater specificity of the concept of positive regard. *Person-Centered and Experiential Psychotherapies, 15*, 263–284.

*Tillman, D. (2016). *The effects of unconditional positive regard on psychotherapy outcome* (Doctoral dissertation). Retrieved from ProQuest Digital Dissertations (10108864)

Tracey, T. J., & Kokotovic, A. M. (1989). Factor structure of the working alliance inventory. *Psychological Assessment, 1*, 207–210.

Traynor, W., Elliott, R., & Cooper, M. (2011). Helpful factors and outcomes in person-centered therapy with clients who experience psychotic processes: Therapists' perspectives. *Person-Centered & Experiential Psychotherapies, 10*(2), 89–104.

*Truax, C. B. (1966). Therapist empathy, warmth, and genuineness and patient personality change in group psychotherapy: A comparison between interaction unit measures, time sample measures, patient perception measures. *Journal of Clinical Psychology, 22*(2), 225–229.

*Truax, C. B. (1968). Therapist interpersonal reinforcement of client self-exploration and therapeutic outcome in group psychotherapy. *Journal of Counseling Psychology, 15*(3), 225–231.

*Truax, C. B., Altmann, H., Wright, L., & Mitchell, K. M. (1973). Effects of therapeutic conditions in child therapy. *Journal of Community Psychology, 1*(3), 313–318.

Truax, C. B., & Carkhuff, R. R. (1967). *Toward effective counseling and psychotherapy: Training and practice*. Chicago, IL: Aldine.

*Truax, C. B., Wittmer, J., & Wargo, D. G. (1971). Effects of the therapeutic conditions of accurate empathy, non-possessive warmth, and genuineness on hospitalized mental patients during group therapy. *Journal of Clinical Psychology, 27*(1), 137–142.

*Turner, S. M. (2007). *Process variables in small-group cognitive therapy for the irritable bowel syndrome* (Doctoral dissertation). Retrieved from ProQuest Digital Dissertations. (UMI No. 9806206).

*Van der Veen, F. (1967). Basic elements in the process of psychotherapy: a research study. *Journal of Consulting Psychology, 31*(3), 295–303.

Wachtel, P. L. (2008). *Relational theory and the practice of psychotherapy*. New York, NY: Guilford.

Wampold, B. E., Mondin, G. W., Moody, M., Stich, F., Benson, K., & Ahn, H. (1997). A metaanalysis of outcome studies comparing bona fide psychotherapies: Empirically, "all must have prizes." *Psychological Bulletin, 122*, 203–215.

*Williams, S. A. (1996). *Therapeutic factors affecting denial change in substance abuse treatment groups* (Doctoral dissertation). Retrieved from ProQuest Digital Dissertations. (UMI No. 9625604).

Williams, K. E., & Chambless, D. L. (1990). The relationship between therapist characteristics and outcome of in vivo exposure treatment for agoraphobia. *Behavior Therapy, 21,* 111–116.

Winnicott, D. W. (1960). The theory of the parent-infant relationship. *International Journal of Psycho-Analysis, 41,* 585–595.

Yalom, I. D., (2002). *The gift of therapy: An open letter to a new generation of therapists and their patients.* New York, NY: HarperCollins.

Zuroff, D., & Blatt, S. J., (2006). The therapeutic relationship in the brief treatment of depression: Contributions to clinical improvement and enhanced adaptive capacities. *Journal of Consulting and Clinical Psychology, 74,* 130–140.

*Zuroff, D. C., Kelly, A. C., Leybman, M. J., Blatt, S. J., & Wampold, B. E. (2010). Between-therapist and within-therapist differences in the quality of the therapeutic relationship: Effects on maladjustment and self-critical perfectionism. *Journal of Clinical Psychology, 66*(7), 681–697.

9

CONGRUENCE/GENUINENESS

*Gregory G. Kolden, Chia-Chiang Wang, Sara B. Austin,
Yunling Chang, and Marjorie H. Klein*

Congruence or genuineness is a relational quality first described and emphasized by Carl Rogers (1957). Research interest in this concept has waxed and waned over the years; however, in the past decade genuineness has begun to reemerge as an important construct in Gelso's conceptualization of the "real relationship" (Gelso et al., 2005; Gelso et al., this volume) and the research generated from this theory.

In this chapter, we define this attribute of the psychotherapy relationship as well as describe prominent measures for its assessment. Throughout the chapter, we use the terms *congruence* and *genuineness* interchangeably. We then provide clinical examples of genuineness and some landmark research studies. We also offer a summary of previous meta-analyses and an original meta-analytic review of its association with psychotherapy outcome. Moderators and mediators of the association between congruence and improvement are investigated and evidence for causality is considered. We conclude the chapter by addressing patient contributions, limitations of the extant research, diversity considerations, and training implications as well as therapeutic practices that might promote congruence and improve psychotherapy outcomes.

DEFINITIONS

The initial definition of congruence or genuineness as applied to the psychotherapy relationship can be found in the writing of Carl Rogers (1957). He proposed that the necessary and sufficient conditions of therapeutic change involved the client being in a "state of incongruence," the client and therapist in "psychological contact" and the therapist as "congruent or integrated in the relationship" while experiencing "positive regard for the client" and "empathic understanding of the client's internal frame of reference" (p. 96). Congruence plays a central role in this framework in that it is a prerequisite for the transmission of empathy and positive regard.

Congruence is comprised of two fundamental elements. First, the therapist is "freely and deeply himself, with his experience accurately represented by his awareness of himself" (Rogers, 1957, p. 97). The therapist is genuinely and mindfully present in interactions with the client, highlighting the importance of personal awareness as well as authenticity. Second, the therapist also has the capacity to skillfully convey this to the client by words and actions. Thoughtful reflection and measured judgment are required of the therapist. Indiscriminant self-disclosure and sharing of thoughts and feelings is clearly not the aim, and the therapist must not engage in deception; such behaviors would be barriers to progress.

In contrast to Rogers' view of congruence as a therapist-offered relational quality, Barrett-Lennard (1962, 2015) highlighted the importance of client experiences. He emphasized the client's perception of congruence as most essential for the outcome of psychotherapy. As such, Barrett-Lennard's work advanced the idea that congruence must be defined according to client perceptions and experiences.

Gelso's (2002) conceptualization of the real relationship in psychotherapy is comprised of two components—genuineness and realism. Genuineness in this framework overlaps with the Rogerian view of congruence and is consistent with early ideas offered by psychoanalytic writers (e.g., Greenson, 1967) in that the real relationship is viewed as undistorted by transferential material. Genuineness is defined as "the ability to be who one truly is, to be nonphoney, to be authentic in the here and now" (Gelso, 2002, p. 37). Moreover, genuineness is related to terms such as authenticity, openness, honesty, non-phoniness (Gelso & Hayes, 1998). In this framework, genuineness includes *both* therapist and patient genuineness in the real therapy relationship. "Genuineness may be seen as the psychotherapy participants' authenticity with each other or the extent to which they are truly themselves as opposed to phony or fake with each other" (Gelso et al., 2012, p. 495). Congruence has both *intrapersonal* and *interpersonal* features; it is a personal characteristic (intrapersonal) of the therapist and patient as well as an experiential quality of the relationship (interpersonal). As such, genuineness is a much broader and more inclusive construct.

Congruence is often not readily grasped and can, at times, seem quite obscure and mysterious. Consider how this relational quality might appear in day-to-day exchanges among others. Workplace manager Smith behaves in a formal, prim and proper, and very focused manner while carrying out her prescribed role of stoically assigning tasks and delivering constructive feedback. Communication is impersonal, direct, clear, and to the point with little emotion; pleasantries are minimal. Supervisees respond in kind. Ms. Smith and her charges interact in a *relationally incongruent* manner.

By contrast, coffee barista Stephanie warmly greets people by their first names, attentively asks about their work today, and openly shares her opinion about a local beer she has recently sampled when she serves a man who she knows enjoys craft beer. Stephanie engages people, mindfully makes contact, and sincerely expresses herself in the brief time it takes to pour and pay for a cup of coffee. Her customers respond similarly. Stephanie and her customers interact in a *relationally congruent* fashion.

In psychotherapy, genuineness or congruence means that both therapists and patients are accessible, approachable, and sincere rather than hidden and obscured behind stereotypical roles. Experiences that are obvious in the encounter are not concealed or shrouded; transparency is paramount but not unbridled. Congruence thus

involves mutual mindful self-awareness and self-acceptance on the part of the therapist and patient, as well as curiosity about the encounter, a willingness to engage, and
the capacity to reciprocally and respectfully share observations.

For Rogers (1957), the congruent therapist "comes into a direct personal encounter
with his patient by meeting him on a person-to-person basis. It means that he is *being*
himself, not denying himself" (p. 101). Similarly, Gelso and Hayes (1998) opine,

> Congruent or genuine therapists are in tune with themselves . . . and although
> they would not be expected to communicate all of their thoughts to their clients,
> rather these therapists display a synchrony between their inner experiences and
> their outer behavior with clients. They are themselves; they do not act phony or
> disingenuous. (p. 119)

Congruence plays such a pivotal role in Rogers' thinking because he views the
problems that patients bring to therapy as a state of *incongruence* and views the therapy
process as promoting congruence, that is, to develop the capacity to approach, recognize, and reflect upon problematic mind states with openness and authenticity rather
than fear and avoidance. Thus therapist congruence models "realness" for the patient, fostering safe and open experiencing, deepening security in the relationship and
resulting in more immediate psychological contact with feelings, thoughts, and urges
(i.e., mindfulness of complex mind states).

Similarly, others within the client-centered and humanistic traditions have
considered congruence/genuineness as the most important of the three Rogerian
therapist-offered facilitative conditions. Lietaer (1993) described genuineness with
an internal and an external facet. The internal facet is comprised of therapists' internal experiencing, when they are aware of their experience with a client (Watson
et al., 1998). The external facet involves therapists' capacity to reveal to the client
aspects of that which they are internally experiencing. This is referred to as transparency. Moreover, transparency explicitly does not involve sharing all aspects of experience; only those aspects of experience fostering growth and healing are conveyed
and only in a climate of empathy. As such, the therapist strives to simultaneously
maintain a personal internally focused connection and an external patient-focused
connection.

In sum, congruence is an aspect of the therapy relationship with two facets, one
intrapersonal and one *interpersonal*. Mindful genuineness, personal awareness, and
authenticity characterize the intrapersonal element. The capacity to respectfully and
transparently give voice to one's experience to another person characterizes the interpersonal component.

MEASURES

Measures of Rogers' facilitative conditions—congruence, positive regard, and
empathy—were developed at the University of Chicago Counseling Center. Halkides
(1958) designed observer-rated scales for each concept. This foundational work was

followed by numerous studies examining the relation between core conditions and patient outcomes (Barrett-Lennard, 1998).

Barrett-Lennard Relationship Inventory

Barrett-Lennard (1959) developed therapist and patient self-report instruments for the facilitative conditions. These measures have become the most recognized and best validated instruments for assessing the core conditions: the Barrett-Lennard Relationship Inventory (BLRI; Barrett-Lennard, 1962). Therapist and patient parallel forms of the BLRI ask the therapist to describe his or her feelings toward the client while in session (e.g., "I am willing to tell him my own thoughts and feelings") or the patient to describe his or her experience of the therapist (e.g., "He is willing to tell me his own thoughts and feelings"). The original 92-item version of the BLRI included five scales: Level of Regard, Empathic Understanding, Unconditionality, Genuineness, and Willingness to be Known. This last scale was merged into the Genuineness/ Congruence scale in the 64-item 1964 revision (Barrett-Lennard, 1978). A shortened, 30-item version of the BLRI was developed later (Gurman, 1973a, 1973b). Table 9.1 presents examples of BLRI items.

Truax Self-Congruence Scale

As Barrett-Lennard was developing and revising the BLRI, Rogers' group at the University of Wisconsin was engaged in scale construction for raters to assess the conditions from audiotape recordings of sessions. Early versions (Gendlin & Geist, 1962; Hart, 1960) were followed by Truax's development of the 1962 Self-Congruence Scale (Rogers et al., 1967) for use in the Wisconsin Schizophrenia Project. Independent observers rate how the therapist "appears" in tape-recorded session samples; Table 9.1 lists the descriptors for the five stages of the Truax (1966b) Self-Congruence Scale. Further revisions of the measure were made for the final ratings of the Wisconsin Schizophrenia Project (Rogers et al., 1967) because of difficulties obtaining acceptable reliability with the Self-Congruence Scale. This modification consisted of a 5-point scale ranging from

> a point where there is obvious discrepancy between the therapist's feelings about the patient and his concurrent communication to the patient (stage 1) to a high point where the therapist communicates both his positive and negative feelings about the patient openly and freely, without traces of defensiveness or retreat into professionalism (stage 5). (Kiesler, 1973, p. 229; see also Rogers et al., 1967, pp. 581–583)

Real Relationship Inventory

Gelso and colleagues (2005, this volume) developed patient and therapist versions of the Real Relationship Inventory (RRI) that included two subscales—Genuineness and

Table 9.1. Rating Scales for Congruence

Congruence Items on the BLRI[a]

Positively Valenced Items

He is comfortable and at ease in our relationship.

I feel that he is real and genuine with me.

I nearly always feel that what he says expresses exactly what he is feeling and thinking as he says it.

He does not avoid anything that is important for our relationship.

He expresses his true impressions and feelings with me.

He is willing to express whatever is actually in his mind with me, including any feelings about himself or about me.

He is openly himself in our relationship.

I have not felt he tries to hide anything from himself that he feels with me.

Negatively Valenced Items

I feel that he puts on a role or front with me.

It makes him uneasy when I ask or talk about certain things.

He wants me to think that he likes me or understands me more than he really does.

Sometimes he is not at all comfortable but we go on, outwardly ignoring it.

At times I sense that he is not aware of what he is really feeling with me.

There are times when I feel that his outward response to me is quite different from the way he feels underneath.

What he says to me often gives a wrong impression of his whole thought or feeling at the time.

I believe that he has feelings he does not tell me about that are causing difficulty in our relationship.

Stages of the Truax Self-Congruence Scale[b]

Stage 1

The therapist is clearly defensive in the interaction, and there is explicit evidence of a very considerable discrepancy between what he says and what he experiences. There may be striking contradictions in the therapist's statements; the content of his verbalization may contradict the voice qualities or nonverbal cues (i.e., the upset therapist stating in a strained voice that he is "not bothered at all" by the patient's anger).

Stage 2

The therapist responds appropriately but in a professional rather than in a personal manner, giving the impression that his responses are said because they sound good from a distance but do not express what he really feels or means. There is a somewhat contrived or rehearsed quality or an air of professionalism present.

Stage 3

The therapist is implicitly either defensive or professional, although there is no explicit evidence.

(*continued*)

Table 9.1. Continued

Stage 4

There is neither implicit nor explicit evidence of defensiveness or the presence of a façade.
   The therapist shows no self-incongruence.

Stage 5

The therapist is freely and deeply himself in the relationship. He is open to experiences
   and feelings of all types—both pleasant and hurtful—without traces of defensiveness
   or retreat into professionalism. Although there may be contradictory feelings, these are
   accepted or recognized. The therapist is clearly being himself in all of his responses,
   whether they are personally meaningful or trite. At stage 5 the therapist need not express
   personal feelings, but whether he is giving advice, reflecting, interpreting, or sharing
   experiences, it is clear that he is being very much himself, so that his verbalizations match
   his inner experiences.

Genuineness items on the RRI-T[c] and RRI-C[d]

My client and I are honest in our relationship. (RRI-T)

My therapist and I had an honest relationship. (RRI-C)

My client and I are able to be genuine in our relationship. (RRI-T)

My therapist and I were able to be authentic in our relationship. (RRI-C)

I hold back significant parts of myself. (RRI-T)

I was holding back significant parts of myself. (RRI-C)

My client shares with me the most vulnerable parts of him/herself. (RRI-T)

I was able to communicate my moment-to-moment inner experience to my therapist.
   (RRI-C)

It is difficult for me to express what I truly feel about my client. (RRI-T)

It was difficult for me to express what I truly felt about my therapist. (RRI-C)

My client genuinely expresses a connection to me. (RRI-T)

My therapist seemed genuinely connected to me. (RRI-C)

Note. BLRI = Barrett-Lennard Relationship Inventory; RRI-T = Real Relationship Inventory–Therapist
form; RRI-C = Real Relationship Inventory–Client form.
[a]Barrett-Lennard (1962). [b]Truax (1966a, pp. 68–72). [c]Gelso et al. (2005). [d]Kelley et al. (2010).

Realism. Items for the RRI were solicited from professional therapists and graduate
students. A pool of 44 items was administered to psychologists with instructions to
rate if they had used that item in their last session with a client. This resulted in a final
scale of 24 items, 12 for Realism and 12 for Genuineness. As noted previously, the
Genuineness subscale is a rating of a broader concept that involves perceptions of the
therapist, the client, and their relationship (see Table 9.1 for examples of these items).

Psychometric Properties of Measures

The reliability of the two most frequently used measures of the core conditions—the
BLRI and the Truax scale—has generally been adequate. Most internal and test–retest

reliability coefficients for the BLRI range between 0.75 and 0.95 with the majority exceeding 0.80 (Barrett-Lennard, 1998). An extensive review reported internal reliability coefficients for congruence ranging from 0.76 to 0.92 with a mean coefficient of 0.89 (Gurman, 1977). On the Truax scale, reliability coefficients for congruence/genuineness ranged from 0.34 to 0.85 with most over 0.65 (Mitchell et al., 1977). The reliability for the RRI in the initial studies using professional and graduate student samples was 0.79 for Realism and 0.83 for Genuineness (Gelso et al., 2005). Confirmatory factor analysis compared one-factor and two-factor solutions; results were slightly more supportive of a single factor, but it was decided to retain the two scales for further study because "the theory from which the measures emanated is embedded in this dual notion" (p. 647). Many recent studies have used the RRI as a single scale and have demonstrated reliability estimates from the mid .80s to the mid .90s for the client version (e.g., Fuertes et al., 2007; Kelley et al., 2010; Kivlighan et al., 2015, Marmarosh et al., 2009) and .80 to .94 for the therapist version (Fuertes et al., 2007; Gelso et al., 2005; Kivlighan et al., 2015; Marmarosh et al., 2009).

CLINICAL EXAMPLES

Therapist Perspectives

The following excerpts are examples of Rogers' description of how his work with individuals with schizophrenia led him to refine the experiential component of client-centered therapy (Rogers et al., 1967). In the first example Rogers explains how he may use his feelings about the difficulty ending a session to provide the "vehicle for therapeutic responding" (p. 389):

> Some of my feelings about him (the patient) in the situation are a good source of responses, if I tell them in a personal, detailed way. . . . One whole set of feelings I have for others in situations comes at first as discomfort. As I look to see why I am uncomfortable I find content relevant to the person I am with, to what we just did or said. Often it is quite personal. I was stupid, rude, hurrying, embarrassed, avoidant, on the spot: I wished I didn't have to go since he wants me to stay. I wish I hadn't hurried him out of the store in front of all those people. Or, "I guess you're mad at me because I'm leaving. I don't feel very good about it either. It just never feels right to me to go away and leave you in here [hospital ward]. I have to go, or else I'll be late for everything I have to do all day today, and I'll feel lousy about that." Silence. "In a way, I'm glad you don't want me to go. I wouldn't like it at all if you didn't care one way or the other." (p. 390)

In reflecting on these moments, Rogers explains that:

> These . . . have in common that I express feelings of mine which are at first troublesome or difficult, the sort I would at first tend to ignore in myself. It requires a kind of *doubling back*. When I first notice it, I have *already* ignored, avoided, or belied

my feelings—only now do I notice what it was or is. I must double back to express it. At first, this seems a sheer impossibility! How can I express this all-tied-up, troublesome, puzzling feeling? Never! But a moment later I see that it is only another perfectly human way to feel, and in fact includes much concern for the patient, and empathic sensitivity to him. It is him I feel unhappy about—or what I just did to him. A very warm and open kind of interaction is created in telling my feelings this way. I am not greatly superior, wiser, or better than the other people in the patient's life. I have as many weaknesses, needs, and stupidities. But the other people in his life rarely extend him this kind of response. (p. 390)

Another example shows how Rogers uses an "openness to what comes next" to increase his sensitivity, even to repair a breach in the interaction. He notes that by being open to what comes next, positive consequences will usually result:

I used to ponder whether I was about to say a right or wrong thing. Then, if it was wrong (as I could tell from the patient's reaction), I would not know what to do. Now I spend moments letting my feelings clarify themselves, but once they feel clear, I no longer wonder so much whether it is right or wrong to express them. Rather, I have open curiosity, sensitivity, and a readiness to meet whatever reaction I will get. This may tell me what I said was "wrong," but all will be well if *now* I respond sensitively to what I have stirred. I now say whatever I now sense which *makes* what I said before "wrong." (p. 391)

A final example illustrates the key role of the therapist's self-experiencing (i.e., mindful awareness) in building mutual congruence:

"We tend to express the *outer* edges of our feelings. That leaves *us* protected and makes the other person unsafe. We say, "This and this (which *you* did) hurt me." We do not say, "This and this weakness of mine *made me* be hurt when you did this and this."

To find this inward edge of my feelings, I need only ask myself, "Why?" When I find myself bored, angry, tense, hurt, at a loss, or worried, I ask myself, "Why?" Then, instead of "You bore me," or "This makes me mad," I find the "why" *in me* which makes it so. That is always more personal and positive, and much safer to express. Instead of "You bore me," I find, "I want to hear more personally from you," or, "You tell me what happened, but I want to hear also what it all meant to you." (pp. 390–391)

Client Perspectives

How is congruence perceived and experienced by the client? One way to capture this is to review the items that a client might endorse in the BLRI as shown in Table 9.1. The client's experience of the highly congruent therapist is that the therapist is fully at ease within the relationship and is openly him- or herself. Being attuned to his or her experience in the moment, the therapist is open to honestly sharing this experience with the client and does not avoid sharing uncomfortable feelings and impressions that are important to treatment. Because of this authenticity and genuineness, the therapist's words accurately capture his or her momentary experience.

Taking this a step further, the RRI–Client version (RRI-C; see Table 9.1) includes perceptions of the interactive therapy relationship: "My therapist and I were able to be authentic in our relationship"; "My therapist and I had an honest relationship." The RRI-C also includes perceptions of self-congruence as reflected in communication of inner experiences to the therapist and/or the awareness of significantly holding back: "I was holding back significant parts of myself"; "It was difficult for me to express what I truly felt about my therapist." Finally, similar to the BLRI, the RRI-C captures the client's observations of therapist congruence: "My therapist was holding back his/her genuine self", "My therapist seemed genuinely connected to me."

Observer Perspectives

A third perspective on genuineness is provided by samples from session transcripts. The following example of Stage 5 high congruence comes from the training material for the Truax (1966a) scale.

c: I guess you realize that, too, don't you? Or do you? (Laughs)

T: Do I realize that? You *bet* I do! Sure yeah—I always wanted somebody to take *care of me*, you know, but I also wanted them to let me do what I wanted to do! Well, if you have somebody taking care of you, then you've got to do what *they* want you to do.

c: That's right. (Pause)

T: So, I never could kind of get it so that I'd have both, you know, *both* things at once: either I'm doing what *I* want to do and taking care of myself or, you know, I used to have somebody taking care of me and then I'd do what *they* wanted to do. And I'd think, "Aw, hell!" It just—never works out, you know.

c: Always somebody there, isn't there? (Laughs)

T: Yeah, just somebody goofing up the works all the time. (Pause) Yeah, if you're dependent on somebody else, you're under their control, sort of.

c: To a certain extent . . .

T: Yeah, that's what I was going to say—yeah, you're right. (Pause). So you just sit around the ward and you read a little bit, and then you go out and play horseshoes and—boy, that sounds like a *drag!* (p. 72)

The next example comes from the transcripts of Carl Rogers's filmed demonstration session with the client "Gloria" (Shostrum, 1966) where he clearly expresses his feeling of closeness to Gloria:

GLORIA: That is why I like substitutes. Like I like talking to you, and I like men that I can respect. Doctors, and I keep sort of underneath feeling like we are real close, you know, sort of like a substitute father.

ROGERS: I don't feel that is pretending.

GLORIA: Well, you are not really my father.

ROGERS: No. I meant about the real close business.

GLORIA: Well, see, I sort of feel that's pretending too because I can't expect you to feel very close to me. You don't know me that well.

ROGERS: All I can know is what I am feeling and that is I feel close to you in this moment.

LANDMARK STUDIES

Rogers Wisconsin Study

Rogers' initial work at the University of Chicago involved studies of the treatment of troubled "normal" individuals, largely college students. His research group began to examine the treatment of hospitalized clients suffering from schizophrenia when he took a joint position in the University of Wisconsin Departments of Psychiatry and Psychology in 1957. Rogers' (1967) edited text *The Therapeutic Relationship and Its Impact: A Study of Psychotherapy with Schizophrenics* summarizes this pioneering work. University of Wisconsin undergraduates were trained to rate audio recordings of therapy sessions using scales developed to measure the three therapist-offered conditions of accurate empathy, positive regard, and congruence. Four-minute samples of the second half of the therapy hour (from Sessions 2 through 15 and every fifth session thereafter) were randomly selected for analysis by three raters. Congruence ratings (averaged across raters) were shown to be reliable in terms of means of the raters ($rkk = .77$) and an estimate of the average intercorrelation of all rater combinations ($rtt = .53$). Results demonstrated that observer-rated therapist congruence was associated with the client's level of experiential involvement in the sessions (i.e., deeper levels of self-experiencing and self-exploration) as well as favorable therapeutic outcome in the form of hospital release time (i.e., greater percentage of time outside of hospital in the year after therapy termination; mean of 89.7 days for high congruence patients compared to 39.8 days for control patients).

The Rogers Wisconsin study is foundational for establishing congruence as a therapist relational element that could be operationalized, observed by raters, and measured in an ecologically valid clinical sample of psychotherapy participants (i.e., hospitalized patients with schizophrenia engaging in psychotherapy with trained professionals). The historical significance of this work for the application of scientific principles to the study of psychotherapy for mental disorders generally, and the specification and examination of Rogerian relational elements in particular, cannot be overestimated.

Barrett-Lennard University of Chicago Study

The premise behind the development of the BLRI is "the view that the *client's experience* of the therapist's response is the immediate locus of therapeutic influence in their relationship" (Barrett-Lennard, 2015, p. 9; see also Barrett-Lennard, 1962). This represents a departure from Rogers' emphasis on therapist experience; clients were counseling center outpatients presenting with a variety of diagnoses and levels of severity. Both therapists and clients completed the BLRI at up to four time points during therapy—after therapy Sessions 1 to 5, at Sessions 15 and 25, and at termination. The sample consisted of 42 clients with 21 different therapists of varying experience levels. "Of the total sample, 30 clients were still in therapy at the 15-interview test point and 26 continued to at least 25 meetings. The length of the therapy ranged from 7 to 96 interviews, with a mean of 33" (Barrett-Lennard, 2015, p. 16).

Reliability coefficients for BLRI congruence were .89 in the client data ($N = 42$) and .94 in the therapist data ($N = 40$) from assessments gathered after the fifth therapy session. Client-rated congruence was the most highly correlated subscale with the BLRI total score ($r = .92$).

Results generally showed that the client's perception of the BLRI relationship elements after five sessions was a significant predictor of change during therapy (as rated by therapists); the direction of therapist-rated elements was positive but failed to reach statistical significance. Specifically, client-rated congruence after five sessions was positively related to therapy outcome. Barrett-Lennard (1962, 2015) hypothesized that perceptions of BLRI relationship elements would be better for clients treated by more experienced therapists; this was supported for the majority of the client ratings including congruence. Examining client- and therapist-rated perceptions together showed that, when client-rated congruence and therapist-rated congruence were both valued highly, therapeutic improvement was more likely to ensue.

The Barrett-Lennard University of Chicago study is foundational for the study of congruence because it established the BLRI as a reliable and valid measure. Most importantly, this study also supported the idea that the client's experiences of congruence mattered and were of value in understanding the mechanisms of change in psychotherapy. In addition, the element of willingness to be known came to be considered an aspect of congruence as a result of the study's findings.

Real Relationship Studies

The *real relationship* is composed to two interrelated elements, *genuineness* and *realism* (see Gelso chapter in this volume). It captures a "component of the relationship, one that goes beyond the work of therapy (i.e., the working alliance) and the unconscious projections and/or distortions of each participant toward the other (i.e., transference-countertransference)" (Gelso et al., 2005, p. 640). The real relationship is the transference-free segment that exists in all human bonds.

Genuineness, in this framework, overlaps considerably with the concept of congruence as conveyed by Rogers (1957) and Barrett-Lennard (1962, 2015) in their seminal work. As such, research examining the real relationship provides more recent foundational work examining congruence/genuineness as a relational change mechanism in psychotherapy. As noted previously, genuineness is viewed as a broader real relationship element that involves the combination of intrapersonal perceptions of genuineness by the therapist and client as well as their interactions (see Table 9.1 for examples of RRI items).

A number of studies have emerged using this conceptual framework. One illustrative study of genuineness using the RRI contrasts clients in brief therapy who continued for eight sessions (i.e., "continuers") with those who completed only three sessions (i.e., early terminators; Gullo et al., 2012). RRI Genuineness scores for clients were associated with treatment success for continuers but not for early terminators. Moreover, for the continuers, the relationship of the overall RRI score (Genuineness and Realism summed) with outcome held when measured both early and later in treatment.

The real relationship studies are foundational for the understanding of congruence because they expand and amplify our understanding of the congruence/genuineness concept. Genuineness is not distinctly a therapist offered condition (Rogers' emphasis) nor solely based on client experience (Barrett-Lennard's emphasis) but an emergent attribute of both participants in the therapy relationship. As such, genuineness is a broader and more inclusive construct in this framework. Regretfully, this approach has had only limited impact on theory and research on congruence as a specific relationship element ($k = 4$ in the current review) due to the obfuscation of congruence/genuineness within the "real relationship" construct; several studies using the RRI did not report information regarding genuineness–outcome associations.

A Qualitative Study with Implications for Congruence

Scnellbacher and Leijssen (2009) offered a case study ($N = 6$) demonstrating the significance of a client's experience of therapist genuineness for therapy progress. According to the authors, therapist genuineness is

> being aware of one's own experience (self-awareness); being emotionally involved in the client's story and the here-and-now interaction, being personally present (self-presence); and being willing to intentionally and verbally reveal personal feelings, thoughts, impressions, experiences, facts, views, values, and methods of working . . . therapeutic genuineness is an inner attitude, a relational experience, and a dynamic process between client and therapist. (p. 208)

Qualitative methods within a multiple case study design were used to describe the extent to which therapists' clinical impressions from the published literature on person-centered and experiential therapies corresponded to the experience of six clients involved in treatment with this approach. Findings suggested that therapist genuineness contributed both directly and indirectly (via the likely mediating influences of empathy, acceptance, and interventions) to therapy outcome. Clients specifically identified self-disclosure as the most prominent indicator of therapist genuineness. Finally, the authors opined that the extent to which genuineness is important for change depends on the specific needs of the individual client. In other words, genuineness can function in various ways depending on the needs of the client; thus it is the fit between client needs and therapist behavior that is most important for progress. These qualitative findings are consistent with research to date and also illuminate ideas for training as well as therapeutic practices.

RESULTS OF PREVIOUS META-ANALYSES

We previously (Kolden et al., 2011a, 2011b) conducted a meta-analysis of the congruence–outcome relation that examined 16 studies (k) representing 863 participants (N) and found effect sizes (ES; r) ranging from –.26 to .69. The weighted aggregate ES for congruence with improvement in psychotherapy was an r of 0.24 or an approximate d of 0.48 ($p = .003$; 95% confidence interval [CI] = .12–.36). The overall ES of r .24 or a d of about .48 is considered a small to medium effect (Cohen, 1988) and accounts for 6% of the variance in treatment outcome.

Kolden et al. (2011a, 2011b) also examined moderators of the congruence–outcome association in the form of measurement-related variables, therapist variables, client variables, and treatment variables. With regard to *measurement perspective*, client-rated outcome ($r = .29$) produced a significantly higher ES than therapist-rated improvement ($r = .07$; $QB = 8.05$, $p < .05$). The *therapist variable* of experience (mean of 7.2 years across five studies) was shown to be positively related to the congruence–outcome ES (B = .05, $p < .01$). The *client variables* education and age (dichotomized teen vs. adult) were also significant moderators of the congruence–outcome ES. As education decreased, the congruence–outcome ES increased (B = –.09, $p < .001$). In addition, the congruence–outcome ES for teens ($r = .42$) was shown to be significantly higher than that for adults ($r = .19$; $Q = 7.15$, $p < .01$). Finally, *treatment variables* of theoretical orientation and format (individual vs. group) were significant moderators of the congruence–outcome ES. For theoretical orientation, studies in a mixed category (described as eclectic, client-centered, or interpersonal; $r = .36$) attained significantly higher effect sizes than those characterized as psychodynamic ($r = .04$; $QB = 8.76$, $p < .01$). With regards to psychotherapy format, group therapy ($r = .36$) obtained a higher congruence–outcome ES than individual therapy ($r = .18$; $QB = 5.55$, $p < .05$).

A more recent meta-analysis (Nienhuis et al., 2018) explored the relation between perceptions of therapist genuineness and the therapeutic alliance. These authors showed a positive association between genuineness–alliance across 13 studies; however, that meta-analysis did not examine the relation with actual treatment outcome.

META-ANALYTIC REVIEW

The research evidence for the relation between therapist congruence or genuineness and psychotherapy outcome has been previously reviewed on at least 13 occasions (in chronological order: Meltzoff & Kornreich, 1970; Truax & Mitchell, 1971; Luborsky et al., 1971; Kiesler, 1973; Lambert et al., 1978; Mitchell et al., 1977; Parloff et al., 1978; Orlinsky & Howard, 1978, 1986; Watson, 1984; Orlinsky et al., 1994; Klein et al., 2002; Kolden et al., 2011a). The consensus of these reviews is that research support for the contribution of congruence to improvement in psychotherapy is *mixed but leaning toward the positive.*

Search Strategy

To identify studies to include in the present meta-analysis, we narrowed our focus to published studies (in English) and dissertation research on individual or group therapy with adults or adolescents (thereby excluding studies of psychotherapy with children). Moreover, we only included studies of actual treatment; analogue studies were excluded. We conducted PsycINFO, PsycARTICLES, and MEDLINE searches using the keywords "congruence," "genuineness," "Barrett-Lennard Relationship Inventory," and "Real Relationship Inventory." In our previous meta-analysis (Kolden et al., 2011a), we identified 25 articles meeting these criteria and 16 were eventually included. For the present review, we identified 31 additional articles.

Inclusion Criteria

To be included in the meta-analysis a study had to present quantitative information adequate to calculate an ES (e.g., a correlation coefficient). Those studies with only a composite score of the therapeutic relationship that included a congruence/genuineness subscale were also excluded, including one (Fuertes et al., 2007) used in our previous review (Kolden et al., 2011a). This procedure resulted in six new articles that were included in our meta-analysis (see Table 9.2). Twenty-five of the 31 identified articles were excluded due to insufficient information. Table 9.2 lists studies included in our meta-analytic review and provides summary information with respect to (a) aggregate ES (for those studies that included multiple reports of congruence–outcome relations), (b) sample size, (c) type and perspective of congruence measure, and (d) type and perspective of outcome measure.

Methodological Decisions

The ES used in this meta-analysis was r, the correlation coefficient for the relation between congruence and outcome. Each study was reviewed and coded by two raters (co-authors Austin and Chang). Discrepancies in original coding were negotiated in a consensus discussion involving the second author. If r was not available or nonsignificant (and not reported), we adopted the strategy of entering zero as the ES (Lipsey & Wilson, 2001).

For studies reporting multiple correlations and using multiple measures, we aggregated within each study by accounting for the dependencies of measures. This aggregation used the correlation matrix among measures if reported. Otherwise, we assumed that the correlation was .50 when the same method was used (e.g., self-report congruence and self-report outcome) and a correlation of .25 when different methods were used (e.g., self-report vs. observation; Gleser & Olkin, 1994). When multiple

Table 9.2. Studies Included in the Meta-Analytic Review

Study	Effect Size (r) s	N	Congruence Measure	Congruence Perspectives	Outcomes Measure	Outcomes Perspectives
Athay (1973)	.24	150	TRQ	Patient	Global	Patient Therapist
Barnicot et al. (2014)#	.25	157	BLRI	Patient	Symptoms	Patient Observer
Buckley et al. (1981)	.06	71	Others	Patient	Symptoms Functioning Self-constructs	Patient
Fretz (1966)	.25	17	BLRI	Patient Therapist	Global	Patient, Therapist
Garfield & Bergin (1971)	−.26	38	Others	Observer	Symptoms, Functioning Global	Patient Observer
Gullo et al. (2012)#	.24	18	RRI-G	Patient Therapist	Global	Patient
Hansen et al. (1968)	.69	70	BLRI Others	Patient Observer	Self-constructs	Patient
Jones & Zoppel (1982)	.10	99	Others	Patient	Symptoms Functioning Self-constructs Global	Patient
Kelley et al. (2010)#	.20	93	RRI-G	Patient	Functioning	Patient
Lo Coco et al. (2011)#	.21	50	RRI-G	Patient Therapist	Global	Patient
Marmarosh et al. (2009)	.41	31	RRI-G	Patient Therapist	Symptoms	Patient
Melnick & Pierce (1971)	.42	18	Others	Observer	Symptoms Functioning Self-constructs	Patient
Ritter et al. (2002)	.21	37	BLRI	Patient	Symptoms Functioning Self-constructs	Patient
Rothman (2007)	.50	44	BLRI	Patient	Functioning Global	Therapist
Staples et al. (1976)	.16	17	Others	Observer	Global	Observer
Tilliman (2016)#	.17	31	BLRI	Patient	Symptoms Functioning	Patient
Truax (1961)#	.20	39	Others	Observer	Functioning	Observer
Truax (1966a)	.38	63	BLRI Others	Patient Observer	Global	Patient
Truax (1971)	−.02	34	TRQ	Patient	Symptoms Functioning Self-constructs	Patient
Truax (1971)	.28	72	TRQ	Patient	Symptoms Functioning Self-constructs	Patient
Truax (1971)	.11	43	TRQ	Patient	Symptoms Functioning Self-constructs	Patient

Note. Congruence Measures: BLRI = Barrett-Lennard Relationship Inventory; TRQ = Truax Relationship Questionnaire; RRI-G = Real Relationship Inventory–Genuineness subscale; Others = other congruence scales/checklists. Outcome Measures: Symptoms = Symptom Check List -90-Revised, Minnesota Multiphasic Personality Inventory most scales, and anxiety, depression, or other psychiatric symptom measures; Functioning = Global Assessment of Functioning Scales and adaptive skills/coping and other functioning scales; Self-constructs = self-concept, self-esteem, self-efficacy, life satisfaction, and psychological well-being scales; Global = a measure focusing on general change without any particular dimension. N = total number of participants per study.

#indicates the studies newly added to this review.

sample sizes were reported within a study, we reported the lowest or most frequently used sample size. Overall, the correlation coefficient from each study was used to calculate an aggregated correlation using a weighted average where the weights were the inverse of variance (Hedges & Olkin, 1985).

A test of homogeneity, using Hedges and Olkin's Q statistic, was conducted to determine if the effect sizes among studies were homogeneous. We adopted a random effects model for determining overall ES since the included studies were quite heterogeneous ($Q = 35.65$, $p < .05$), thus violating the assumptions required for fixed effects ES modeling (e.g., homogeneity of sample, variation in study ES due only to sampling error; Hedges & Vevea, 1998). In addition, random effects modeling allows for greater generalizability. Moreover, if the analysis showed between-study heterogeneity, weighted univariate regression or weighted between-group tests were used to examine moderator variables. Finally, we decided to only investigate potential moderating factors where information was available in at least *five* studies.

Results

Estimates of effect sizes in the 21 studies (k) representing 1,192 patients (N) ranged from $r = -.26$ to .69. The updated weighted aggregate ES for congruence with psychotherapy outcome was $r = .23$ or an estimated d of .46 (95% CI = .13–.32), a small to medium effect (Cohen, 1988) and accounting for approximately 5.3% of the variance in treatment outcome. As compared to our previous review, the aggregated random ES stayed virtually the same from .24 to .23 after deleting one study ($r = .34$ from Fuertes et al., 2007) and adding six studies (with a range of rs from .17 to .25; see Table 9.2). This provides evidence for congruence as a noteworthy facet of the psychotherapy relationship.

Nevertheless, this finding must be interpreted with caution, as publication bias favors significant and positive results. As such, we also conducted a fail-safe N analysis (FSN; Rosenberg, 2005) to examine the robustness of the aggregated results against publication bias. The FSN value for our analyses is 22 (for random effects model), indicating that publication bias did not greatly affect the estimation of aggregated effects (as there were 21 studies included). However, we do not exclude the possibility of the overestimation of the true congruence–outcome relation in psychotherapy.

Conversely, this ES could potentially be an underestimation due to our conservative assumption that treated unreported, nonsignificant results as zero. Moreover, many recent studies using the BLRI and RRI were excluded from the current analyses because global relationship scores were reported from these measures without specification of the congruence/genuineness–outcome correlation. As such, one is left with discomforting uncertainty with regard to the accuracy of the ES estimate for the congruence–outcome relation.

MEDIATORS AND MODERATORS

The finding of heterogeneity of effect sizes among studies ($Q= 36.65$, $p < .05$) led us to examine the extent to which potential mediators and moderators accounted for the variability in magnitude of the congruence–outcome association across the studies. Unfortunately, the studies identified did not provide information sufficient for the consideration of potential *mediators* of the congruence–outcome relationship (i.e., no study examined the mediation of congruence on other factors predicting therapy outcome). However, as noted, weighted univariate regression or weighted between-group tests were used to examine moderator variables. Specifically, we examined potential moderator influences in the form of measurement-related variables, therapist variables, patient variables, and treatment variables. In addition, as noted earlier, we made a methodological decision to investigate only potential moderating factors where sufficient information was available in at least five studies.

Measurement

We found no statistically significant pattern regarding the influence of rater perspective for either congruence or outcome measurement on the congruence–outcome relationship. Moreover, the specific congruence instrument used also did not influence the magnitude of the congruence–outcome relation (aggregated effect sizes ranged from .21 to .32); congruence measures yielded similar results across studies. Among the four types of outcome measures (symptoms, functioning, self-concept/well-being, global), aggregated effect sizes ranged from .16 to .33. Outcome domain was also not a moderator of the congruence–outcome relation.

The density and timing of congruence and outcome measurement was observed to moderate the magnitude of the congruence–outcome relation. Multiple congruence measurement points (weighted $r = .38$, $k =4$) resulted in higher effect sizes than a single measurement point later in treatment or posttreatment ($r = .14$, $k =4$; $QB = 6.12$, $p < .05$). Similarly, studies with pre- and posttherapy measurement of outcomes ($k =10$; weighted $r = .31$) were observed to have a higher aggregated ES than those simply measuring outcomes later or posttherapy ($k =5$; weighted $r = .14$; $QB = 3.48$, $p = .06$). These findings have implications for the design of future studies and are discussed further in the Limitations section later in the chapter.

Two additional measurement-related moderators were also examined: the number of sessions in which congruence was measured (observed range was 2 to 8 sessions; $k = 10$) and the time difference between the measurements of congruence and outcome (unit: number of sessions; range 11 to 24 sessions; $k = 7$). These influences were considered as more studies provided specific information as to when the congruence and outcome measures were administered. Regardless, neither of these variables was found to moderate the congruence–outcome relation.

Therapist Variables

Therapist variables may be another important moderator of the congruence–outcome relationship. Details regarding therapist-relevant information were limited in our previous meta-analytic review (Kolden et al., 2011a, 2011b), but more recent studies provided more specific demographic and education/training characteristics, allowing us to examine their potential moderation on the congruence–outcome relation. Consequently, we investigated five therapist variables: age, clinical experience, licensure status, gender, and license type.

The age of therapists was found to moderate the magnitude of congruence–outcome ES; this was not observed in our Kolden et al. (2011a, 2011b) review. The average age of therapists was 37.2 years, with a range of 28 to 49 and a median of 36. Results from a weighted simple regression analysis indicated a positive relation between the mean age of therapist and the congruence–outcome ES ($B = 0.01$, $p < 0.05$; $k = 6$). Average years of therapist clinical experience across nine studies was 6.4 years (clinical experience ranged from zero years for trainees to 13 years with a median of 5.6 years). Consistent with our previous review, the weighted simple regression analysis indicated a positive relation between therapist clinical experience and the congruence-outcome ES ($B = 0.02$, $p < 0.05$). Finally, in this review we were able to look at therapist licensure status as a moderator of the congruence-outcome relation. Licensed therapists ($r = .27$, $k = 7$) produced significantly higher effect sizes than trainees ($r = -.08$, $k = 3$; $QB = 6.54$, $p < .05$).

Gender (coded as percentage female) and therapist license type (psychologist/counselor vs. a mixed group of licensed therapists) did not moderate the congruence–outcome relation. Therapist minority status was not examined as a moderating influence due to lack of sufficient information as only three studies included this data on therapists.

Patient Variables

Four patient-related variables with information reported in at least five studies were examined for moderation effects: educational attainment, age, gender, and minority status.

Educational attainment, a moderator in our previous meta-analysis (patients with less education were observed to demonstrate a greater congruence–outcome relation) was *not* found to be of significance in our current analyses. This may be explained by the decreasing variation of the effect sizes and years of education among the new studies included in the current analysis (this issue is discussed further in the Limitations section).

As before, patient age as a continuous variable was not a significant moderator of the congruence–outcome relation. In our previous review, we observed that when age was dichotomized as adolescent versus adult, effect sizes for adolescents were significantly higher. We repeated this analysis; however, since only 3 studies included teens (versus 16 including adults), this finding was *not* replicated. This led us to contrast the mean age in studies involving adolescents and college counseling center patients with adult clinical patient samples. We observed a significant difference in the mean age between these groups (20.5 vs. 34.7 years; $t(15) = 4.65$, $df = 15$, $p < .001$). Moreover, studies examining the congruence–outcome relation in younger patients (teens and college counseling center patients; $r = .34$; $k = 9$) attained a significantly higher ES that those using adult clinical psychiatric patients ($r = .18$; $k = 10$; $QB = 5.08$, $p < .05$). Thus it appears that therapist congruence may be more important for outcome in younger patients.

Gender of patients (coded as percentage female) and patient minority status (coded as percentage minority) did not significantly moderate the congruence–outcome relationship.

Treatment Variables

We examined four treatment-related variables for moderation effects: duration, setting, orientation, and format. Therapy duration, the actual number of weeks in treatment, was negatively associated with the congruence–outcome ES ($B = -.001$, $p < 0.05$; $k = 7$). Longer treatment duration was associated with a lower congruence–outcome ES. This finding is not likely to be of importance clinically; nonetheless, it may be a consideration for research design given our earlier findings for density and timing of measurement (i.e., longer treatment duration is associated with greater lags between measurement administrations). This is discussed further in the Limitations section later in the chapter.

The effect sizes among therapeutic settings showed significant differences. School counseling centers ($r = .35$, $k = 8$) had a significantly higher ES than mixed settings (two or more settings; $r = .21$, $k = 5$) and outpatient mental health settings ($r = .06$, $k = 4$; $QB = 9.47$, $p < .05$). This is similar to our previous review, and again this finding is difficult to interpret without resorting to speculation. However, this finding may have more to do with age of patients than characteristics of the setting where therapy was delivered.

Contrary to our previous review, theoretical orientation (psychodynamic vs. a mixed category described as eclectic, client-centered, or interpersonal) was *not* found to moderate the congruence–outcome relation. Similarly, psychotherapy format (group vs. individual), while significant in our previous review, only showed a trend toward a moderating effect on the congruence–outcome association. Group therapy ($r = .32$, $k = 8$) was associated with a higher, but nonsignificant, ES in comparison to individual therapy ($r = .19$, $k = 12$; $QB = 3.47$, $p = .063$).

EVIDENCE FOR CAUSALITY

To infer causality one must consider the evidence for a causal relationship between congruence/genuineness in the therapy relationship and treatment outcome. The overall ES of .23 for congruence to outcome is small to medium; however, one cannot argue for causality from associations alone.

Experimental evidence often provides the most compelling evidence in support of causality as do analyses using lagged correlations, structural equation modeling, and growth curve techniques. Such evidence is not available for the congruence–outcome relation. In our current meta-analysis, 10 studies used pre–post measurement of treatment outcome; the remaining studies used observational designs. Therefore, research evidence at this time is lacking for a strong argument for congruence as a causal contributory element for psychotherapy outcome.

PATIENT CONTRIBUTIONS

Congruence/genuineness is both intrapersonal and interpersonal. It is a personal characteristic (intrapersonal) of the psychotherapist and patient as well as a mutual, experiential quality of the relationship (interpersonal). Thus the patient contribution to congruence refers to both the intrapersonal and the interpersonal qualities of genuineness in the therapy relationship embodied individually by the patient and therapist and experienced by them in interaction.

All of us have needs, preferences, and expectations for relationships; patients bring these to the therapy relationship. One can assume that the *need* for congruence varies across patients as does the *capacity* for genuine experience and participation in relationships. Some patients would like a more congruent therapist and some less. And some patients are more capable of authentic presence to a high degree, others not so much.

A patient who has both the capacity for and greater needs and expectations for congruence is likely to find comfort and satisfaction (an emotional bond) with a highly congruent therapist. These patients require a therapist to be comfortable and at ease; be "real and genuine"; give voice tactfully to what he or she is feeling and thinking; naturally express honest/ authentic impressions; not avoid, hide, hold back, or fail to be direct when the "elephant in the room" requires attention and elaboration. Patients in a congruent therapy relationship learn that it is a safe space, that they are worthy of time and attention, and that they matter as a person with strengths and weaknesses, regrets as well as hopes and dreams. Patient and therapist commitment to truthfulness promotes patient acceptance of problems as well as courage to engage in problem-solving and make changes promoting well-being, symptomatic relief, and enriched functioning.

LIMITATIONS OF THE RESEARCH

Any conclusions drawn from our meta-analysis of congruence–outcome relations must be mindful of the methodological shortcomings of the studies included as well as the search strategy and meta-analytic methods used. Previous researchers have noted the limitations of studies included in our meta-analysis: studies not limited to clients in need of change, low levels or restricted ranges of congruence, different rating perspectives, use of ratings from audiotapes that do not allow nonverbal behaviors to be considered, varying qualifications and/or training of raters, inadequate and variable sampling methods, and small sample sizes (Lambert et al., 1978; Parloff et al., 1978; Patterson, 1984; Watson, 1984). It is also important to consider the limited number of recent studies examining the congruence–outcome association, the lack of any randomized controlled trials investigating the causal impact of congruence, and the observation that the range of effect sizes in the 6 newly identified studies was observed to be smaller when compared to the 16 studies previously evaluated.

Moreover, it is important not to overgeneralize. Positive findings for congruence/ genuineness have appeared primarily in investigations of client-centered, eclectic, and interpersonal therapies. As such, researcher bias (an allegiance effect) is one possible explanation for our results. Additionally, the current moderator analyses underscore the idea that congruence/genuineness may not be a potent change process with all therapists (e.g., younger, less experienced) nor for all patients (e.g., older clinical samples).

Congruence may prove therapeutic for patient change only in the context of the other facilitative conditions, for example, as a precondition for the impact of either empathy or positive regard. Future studies might address this kind of complexity with more sophisticated analytic techniques, such as structural equation modeling. In particular, several recent studies using the BLRI and RRI were excluded from the current analyses because global relationship scores were reported from these measures without specification of the congruence/genuineness–outcome correlation. Thus the congruence–outcome relationship might be quite strong and account for most of the variance in the observed therapy relationship–outcome relation or, alternately, it might be quite small and account for little variance in the therapy relationship–outcome correlation. This is another important matter to be examined and clarified in future research.

While meta-analytic techniques hold great utility for quantitatively integrating and summarizing results across studies, careful consideration is also warranted. Concerns in the present review include quality of studies, comparability of studies, and limited number of studies including the exclusion of 25 due to lack of information sufficient to calculate an ES. Given these limitations, the finding of a small to medium ES in the present quantitative review, and affirmative impressions from our previous qualitative and quantitative reviews (Klein et al., 2002; Kolden et al., 2011a, 2011b), lead us to reaffirm our previous conclusion that the evidence is more supportive of a positive relation between congruence and psychotherapy outcome than appears at first glance. As such, we stand by our observation in our previous review citing Orlinsky and Howard (1978), "If study after flawed study seemed to point in the same general direction, we could not help believing that somewhere in all that variance there must be a reliable effect" (pp. 288–289). A consistent pattern of positive findings is quite unlikely to be explained by study flaws.

DIVERSITY CONSIDERATIONS

Although we observed considerable variability in effect sizes across studies and examined a number of potential moderating influences, much is left to be explained.

The studies did not provide information sufficient for the consideration of potential diversity-related moderators of the congruence–outcome relationship. Patient diversity status (coded as percentage minority; $k = 6$) was not observed to be a significant moderator, and insufficient information was provided in the identified studies to examine therapist diversity status. It will be important for future research to examine a broad array of factors associated with cultural and individual differences including, but not limited to, age, disability, ethnicity, gender, gender identity, sexual orientation, language, national origin, race, religion, and socioeconomic status. Since we are limited in terms of empirical findings for the influence of these factors on the therapy relationship generally, as well as for congruence specifically, we are left to speculate and reflect on ways that diversity considerations might influence congruence/genuineness in psychotherapy.

Cultural background may well influence patient predilection for congruence. Members of divergent cultures often approach psychotherapy in fundamentally different ways than their Westernized counterparts (Patterson, 1996). Culturally sensitive therapy considers patient qualities such as personality, values, political heritage, social structure, and communication style.

For example, the value in Western psychotherapy of autonomy and independence may not hold true for interdependently oriented patients from Eastern or more collectivistic cultures (Tseng, 1999). Research evidence suggests that these patients may prefer a more structured relationship in which the therapist takes on a more formal, directive, and authoritative (i.e., less congruent) role (Sue & Sue, 2003). Accordingly, therapist stances (e.g., openness) or behaviors (e.g., self-disclosure) associated with congruence may be viewed unfavorably by these patients. Other culturally relevant variables, such as congruence match between patient and therapist (Zane et al., 2004) and level of acculturation (Chen & Danish, 2010), may also prove of great consequence in the therapy relationship.

All patients require a therapeutic safe space for genuine and authentic self-reflection where they can give voice to matters guarded most closely. As patient preferences and expectations notably influence treatment outcomes, it will be essential for future research to uncover the extent to which culture and individual differences affect and are affected by congruence.

TRAINING IMPLICATIONS

Congruence has both *intrapersonal* and *interpersonal* features; it is a personal characteristic (intrapersonal) of the therapist and patient as well as an experiential quality of the relationship (interpersonal). Mindful genuineness, personal awareness, and authenticity characterize the intrapersonal element. The capacity to respectfully and transparently give voice to one's experience to another person characterizes the interpersonal component. On the basis of the meta-analytic results and our own training experiences, we recommend the following practices in psychotherapy education and supervision.

- Training programs can first include didactic instruction on congruence/ genuineness as a relational and teachable concept. Graduate training programs have increasingly exposed students to a narrower range of theoretical orientations, and the predominant approach in psychology has been cognitive-behavioral (Heatherington et al., 2013). This has limited the focus of graduate programs on dissemination and training in evidence-based relational elements. We believe that it is crucial that education and training programs revitalize awareness of the congruence concept and give it attention in didactic as well as clinical practicum training activities.

- We advocate developing structured training modules specifically for congruence. Although training models based on Roger's core conditions have been proposed and evaluated (e.g., Carkhuff, 1987), we believe helping skills training provides a more current and relevant approach to the development and evaluation of structured training modules that include didactics, modeling, practice, and feedback (Hill, 2014). Therapists can mindfully *cultivate* the intrapersonal aptitude of congruence. As with all complex skills, this will require knowledge, intent/motivation, and practice. Feedback from peers, supervisors, and perhaps patients (when appropriate) might also enhance the acquisition of the capacity for relational authenticity.

- Therapists can *learn to model* congruence. Congruent responding includes moderated self-disclosure of personal information and life experiences. It could also entail articulation of thoughts and feelings, opinions, pointed questions, and feedback regarding patient behavior. Genuine responses are honest. Congruent responses are not disrespectful, overly intellectualized, or insincere although they may involve irreverence. Genuine therapist responses are cast in the language of personal pronouns (e.g., "I feel . . .," "My view is . . .," "This is how I experience . . ."). Supervision could involve teaching, direct observation, and coaching of these types of skills.

- Patient age appears to be a moderator of the congruence–outcome relation. Therapists could be made aware that congruence may be especially important in younger and perhaps less mature or sophisticated patients (e.g., adolescents, college students, young adults). The congruent therapist tries to communicate acceptance and the possibility of engaging in an authentic relationship as this may not be easily attained in other day-to-day relationships.

- Congruence appears to be a more potent contributor to outcome in psychotherapy offered by older and clinically experienced practitioners. Again, trainee therapists should be made aware of this as an aspirational training goal. Perhaps therapists come to relax the pretense of role-bound formality and give themselves permission to genuinely engage their patients as they gain experience and maturity. As they gain familiarity with treatment delivery, therapists may become less rigid and thus capable of greater degrees of congruence. Moreover, experienced therapists may recognize and more carefully discern a patient's need for relational congruence.

THERAPEUTIC PRACTICES

The research argues that congruence or genuineness should be recognized as an essential psychotherapy relationship element that is consistently associated with and predictive of client change. In closing, we offer a few suggestions for promoting congruence in clinical practice.

- Therapists can aspire to engage genuinely with their patients. This involves acceptance of and receptivity to experiencing with the patient as well as a willingness to use this information in discourse. The congruent therapist is responsible for his or her feelings and reactions and this "ownership of feelings is specified" (Rogers et al., 1967, p. 377). This might include the therapist's thinking out loud about why he or she said or did something. This approach serves a bonding function and also models behavior for the therapy relationship.
- Therapists can encourage genuineness and authenticity by creating a safe space for patients to transparently give voice to their concerns. Other relationship elements, such as warmth, collaboration, and empathy, certainly also play a role.
- Therapists can profitably model congruence in sessions. As noted (in the Training Implications section), a variety of skills (e.g., use of personal pronouns and "I statements") might be brought to bear to accomplish this.
- It is important for practitioners to identify and become aware of their congruence style and to discern the differing patient needs, preferences, and expectations for congruence. Effective therapists will modify and tailor (i.e., match) their congruence style according to patient presentation (Lambropoulos, 2000; Lazarus, 1993).
- The maintenance of congruence requires that therapists be aware of instances when congruence falters. They can these use this awareness as a cue for the need for mindful self-reflection and a return to a more genuine and direct way of relating.

REFERENCES

References marked with an asterisk indicate studies included in the meta-analyses.

*Athay, A. L. (1973–1974). The relationship between counselor self-concept, empathy, warmth, and genuineness, and client rated improvement. (Doctoral dissertation, University of Utah, 1973). *Dissertation Abstracts International, 34*, 3976A.

*Barnicot, K., Wampold, B., & Priebe, S. (2014). The effect of core clinician interpersonal behaviors on depression. *Journal of Affective Disorders, 167*, 112–117.

Barrett-Lennard, G. T. (1959). Dimensions of perceived therapist response related to therapeutic change (Doctoral dissertation). University of Chicago, Chicago, IL.

Barrett-Lennard, G. T. (1962). Dimensions of therapist response as causal factors in therapeutic change. *Psychological Monographs: General and Applied, 76*(43), 1–36.

Barrett-Lennard, G. T. (1978). The Relationship Inventory: Later development and adaptations. *JSAS Catalog of Selected Documents in Psychology, 8*, 68.

Barrett-Lennard, G. T. (1998). *Carl Rogers' helping system: Journey and substance.* Beverly Hills, CA: SAGE.

Barrett-Lennard, G. T. (2015). *The Relationship Inventory: A complete resource and guide.* Walden, MA: Wiley.

*Buckley, P., Karasu, T. B., & Charles, E. (1981). Psychotherapists' view their personal therapy. *Psychotherapy: Theory, Research and Practice, 18,* 299–305.

Carkhuff, R. R. (1987). *The art of helping.* Amherst, MA: Human Resource Development Press.

Chen, J. C., & Danish, S. J. (2010). Acculturation, distress disclosure, and emotional self-disclosure within Asian populations. *Asian American Journal of Psychology, 1*(3), 200–211.

Cohen, J. (1988). *Statistical power analysis for the behavioral sciences* (2nd ed.). Hillsdale, NJ: Erlbaum.

*Fretz, B .R. (1966). Postural movements in a counseling dyad. *Journal of Counseling Psychology, 13,* 335–343.

Fuertes, J. N., Mislowack, A., Brown, S., Gur-Arie, S., Wilkinson, S., & Gelso, C. J. (2007). Correlates of the real relationship in psychotherapy: A study of dyads. *Psychotherapy Research, 17,* 423–430.

*Garfield, S., & Bergin, A. E. (1971). Therapeutic conditions and outcome. *Journal of Abnormal Psychology, 77,* 108–114.

Gendlin, E. T., & Geist, M. (1962). *The relationship of therapist congruence to psychological test evaluations of personality change.* Wisconsin Psychiatric Institute. Brief Research Reports 24. Madison: University of Wisconsin Press.

Gelso, C. J. (2002). Real relationship: The "something more" of psychotherapy. *Journal of Contemporary Psychotherapy, 32,* 35–40.

Gelso, C. J., & Hayes, J. A. (1998). *The psychotherapy relationship: Theory, research, and practice.* New York, NY: Wiley.

Gelso, C. J., Kelley, F. A., Fuertes, J. N., Marmarosh, C., Holmes, S. E., & Costas, C. (2005). Measuring the real relationship in psychotherapy: Initial validation of the Therapist Form. *Journal of Counseling Psychology, 52,* 640–649.

Gelso, C. J., Kivlighan, D. M., Busa-Knepp, J., Spiegel, E. B., Ain, S., Hummel, A. M., . . . Markin, R. D. (2012). The unfolding of the real relationship and the outcome of brief psychotherapy. *Journal of Counseling Psychology, 59*(4), 495–506.

Gleser, L. J., & Olkin, I. (1994). Stochastically dependent effect sizes. In H. M. Cooper & L. V. Hedges (Eds.), *The handbook of research synthesis* (pp. 339–355). New York, NY: Russell Sage Foundation.

Greenson, R. R. (1967). *The technique and practice of psychoanalysis* (Vol. 1). Madison, CT: International Universities Press.

*Gullo, S., Lo Coco, G., & Gelso, C. (2012). Early and later predictors of outcome in brief therapy: The role of real relationship. *Journal of Clinical Psychology, 68*(6), 614–619.

Gurman, A. S. (1973a). Effects of the therapist and patient mood on the therapeutic functioning of high and low-facilitative therapists. *Journal of Consulting and Clinical Psychology, 40,* 48–58.

Gurman, A. S. (1973b). Instability of the therapeutic conditions in psychotherapy. *Journal of Counseling Psychology, 20,* 16–24.

Gurman, A. S. (1977). The patient's perception of the therapeutic relationship. In A. S. Gurman & A. M. Razin (Eds.), *Effective psychotherapy: A handbook of research* (pp. 503–543). Oxford, England: Pergamon.

Halkides, G. (1958). *An experimental study of four conditions necessary for therapeutic change* (Unpublished doctoral dissertation). University of Chicago, Chicago, IL.

*Hansen, J. C., Moore, G. D., & Carkhuff, R. R. (1968). The differential relationships objective and client perceptions of counseling. *Journal of Counseling Psychology, 24,* 244–246.

Hart, J. T. (1960). *A replication of the Halkides study.* Unpublished manuscript, University of Wisconsin, Madison.

Heatherington, L., Messer, S. B., Angus, L., Strauman, T. J., Friedlander, M. L., & Kolden, G. G. (2013). The narrowing of theoretical orientations in clinical psychology doctoral training. *Clinical Psychology Science and Practice, 19,* 362–374.

Hedges, L. V., & Olkin, I. (1985). *Statistical methods for meta-analysis.* Orlando, FL: Academic Press.

Hedges, L. V., & Vevea, J. L. (1998). Fixed- and random-effects models in meta-analysis. *Psychological Methods, 3,* 486–504.

Hill, C. E. (2014). Helping skills training: Implications for supervision. In C. E. Watkins & D. L. Milne (Eds.), *The Wiley international handbook of clinical supervision* (pp. 329–341). West Sussex, England: Wiley.

*Jones, E. E., & Zoppel, C. L. (1982). Impact of client and therapist gender on psychotherapy process and outcome. *Journal of Consulting and Clinical Psychology, 50,* 259–272.

*Kelley, F. A., Gelso, C. J., Fuertes, J. N., Marmarosh, C., & Lanier, S. H. (2010). The Real Relationship Inventory: Development and psychometric investigation of the client form. *Psychotherapy: Theory, Research, Practice, Training, 4,* 540–553.

Kiesler, D. J. (1973). *The process of psychotherapy: Empirical foundations and systems of analysis.* Chicago, IL: Aldine.

Kivlighan, D. M., Gelso, C. J., Ain, S., Hummel, A. M., & Markin, R. D. (2015). The therapist, the client, and the real relationship: An actor-partner interdependence analysis of treatment outcome. *Journal of Counseling Psychology, 62*(2), 314–320.

Klein, M. H., Kolden, G. G., Michels, J., & Chisholm-Stockard, S. (2002). Congruence. In J. C. Norcross (Ed.), *Psychotherapy relationships that work: Therapist contributions and responsiveness to patients* (pp. 195–215). New York, NY: Oxford University Press.

Kolden, G. G., Klein, M. H., Wang, C., & Austin, S. B. (2011a). Congruence. In J. C. Norcross (Ed.), *Psychotherapy relationships that work: Therapist contributions and responsiveness to patients* (2nd ed., pp. 187–202). New York, NY: Oxford University Press.

Kolden, G. G., Klein, M. H., Wang, C., & Austin, S. B. (2011b). Congruence/genuineness. *Psychotherapy, 48,* 65–71.

Lambert, M. J., DeJulio, S. S., & Stein, D. M. (1978). Therapist interpersonal skills: Process, outcome, methodological considerations, and recommendations for future research. *Psychological Bulletin, 85,* 467–489.

Lambropoulos, G. K. (2000). Evolving psychotherapy integration: Eclectic selection and prescriptive applications of common factors in psychotherapy. *Psychotherapy, 30,* 285–297.

Lazarus, A. A. (1993). Tailoring the therapeutic relationship, or being an authentic chameleon. *Psychotherapy, 30,* 404–407.

Lietaer, G. (1993). Authenticity, congruence, and transparency. In D. Brazier (Ed.), *Beyond Carl Rogers: Toward a psychotherapy for the twenty-first century* (pp. 17–46). London, England: Constable.

Lipsey, M. W., & Wilson, D. B. (2001). *Practical meta-analysis.* Thousand Oaks, CA: SAGE.

*Lo Coco, G., Gullo, S., Prestano, C., & Gelso, C. J. (2011). Relation of the real relationship and the working alliance to the outcome of brief psychotherapy. *Psychotherapy, 48*(4), 359–367.

Luborsky, L., Chandler, M., Auerbach, A. H., Cohen, J., & Bachrach, H. M. (1971). Factors influencing the outcome of psychotherapy: A review of quantitative research. *Psychological Bulletin, 75*, 145–185.

*Marmarosh, C., Gelso, C., Majors, R., Markin, R., Mallery, C., & Choi, J. (2009). The real relationship in psychotherapy: Relationships to adult attachments, working alliance, transference, and therapy outcome. *Journal of Counseling Psychology, 56*, 337–350.

*Melnick, B., & Pierce, R. M. (1971). Client evaluation of therapist strength and positive-negative evaluation as related to client dynamics, objective ratings of competency and outcome. *Journal of Clinical Psychology, 27*, 408–411.

Meltzoff, J., & Kornreich, M. (1970). *Research in psychotherapy.* New York, NY: Atherton.

Mitchell, K. M., Bozrath, J. D., & Krauft, C. C. (1977). A reappraisal of the therapeutic effectiveness of accurate empathy, nonpossessive warmth, and genuineness. In A. S. Gurman & A. M. Razin (Eds.), *Effective psychotherapy: A handbook of research* (pp. 503–543). Oxford, England: Pergamon.

Nienhuis, J. B., Owen, J., Valentine, J. C., Black, S. W., Halford, T. C., Parazak, S. E., Budge, S., & Hilsenroth, M. (2018). Therapeutic alliance, empathy, and genuinineness in individual adult psychotherapy: A meta-analytic review. *Psychotherapy Research, 28*, 593–605. https://www.doi:.org/10.1080/10503307.2016.1204023

Orlinsky, D. E., Grawe, K., & Parks, B. K. (1994). Process and outcome in psychotherapy—noch einmal. In A. E. Bergin & S. L. Garfield (Eds.), *Handbook of psychotherapy and behavior change* (4th ed., pp. 270–376). New York, NY: Wiley.

Orlinsky, D. E., & Howard, K. I. (1978). The relation of process to outcome in psychotherapy. In S. L. Garfield & A. E. Bergin (Eds.), *Handbook of psychotherapy and behavior change* (2nd ed., pp. 283–329). New York, NY: Wiley.

Orlinsky, D. E., & Howard, K. I. (1986). Process and outcome in psychotherapy. In S. L. Garfield & A. E. Bergin (Eds.), *Handbook of psychotherapy and behavior change* (3rd ed., pp. 311–384). New York, NY: Wiley.

Parloff, M. B., Waskow, I. E., & Wolfe, B. E. (1978). Research on client variables in psychotherapy. In S. L. Garfield & A. E. Bergin (Eds.), *Handbook of psychotherapy and behavior change* (2nd ed., pp. 233–282). New York, NY: Wiley.

Patterson, C. H. (1984). Empathy, warmth, and genuineness in psychotherapy: A review of reviews. *Psychotherapy, 21*, 431–438.

Patterson, C. H. (1996). Multicultural counseling: From diversity to universality. *Journal of Counseling & Development, 74*, 227–231.

*Ritter, A., Bowden, S., Murray, T., Ross, P., Greeley, J., & Pead, J. (2002). The influence of the therapeutic relationship in treatment for alcohol dependency. *Drug and Alcohol Review, 21*, 261–268.

Rogers, C. R. (1957). The necessary and sufficient conditions of therapeutic personality change. *Journal of Consulting Psychology, 21*, 95–103.

Rogers, C. R., Gendlin, E. T., Kiesler, D. J., & Truax, C. B. (Eds.). (1967). *The therapeutic relationship and its impact: A study of psychotherapy with schizophrenics.* Madison: University of Wisconsin Press.

Rosenberg, M. S. (2005). The file-drawer problem revisited: A general weighted method for calculating fail-safe numbers in meta-analysis. *Evolution 59*(2), 464–468.

*Rothman, D. B. (2007). *The role of the therapeutic alliance in psychotherapy with sexual offenders* (Unpublished doctoral dissertation). University of Manitoba, Winnipeg.

Schnellbacher, J., & Leijssen, M. (2009). The significance of therapist genuineness from the client's perspective. *Journal of Humanistic Psychology, 49*(2), 207–228.

Shostrum, E. L. (Producer). (1966). *Three approaches to psychotherapy* [Film]. (Available from Psychological and Educational Files, Santa Ana, CA)

*Staples, F. R., & Sloane, R. B. (1976). Truax factors, speech characteristics, and therapeutic outcome. *Journal of Nervous and Mental Disease, 163*, 135–140.

Sue, D. W., & Sue, D. (2003). *Counseling the culturally diverse: Theory and practice* (4th ed.). New York, NY: Wiley.

*Tilliman, D. (2016). *The effects of unconditional positive regard on psychotherapy outcome* (Doctoral dissertation). Chicago School of Professional Psychology, Chicago, IL. Retrieved from ProQuest (10108864).

*Truax, C. B. (1961). The process of group therapy: Relationships between hypothesized therapeutic conditions and intrapersonal exploration. *Psychological Monographs: General and Applied 75*(7), 1–35.

*Truax, C. B. (1966a). Therapist empathy, warmth and genuineness and patient personality change in group psychotherapy: A comparison between interaction unit measures, time sample measures, patient perception measures. *Journal of Clinical Psychology, 22*, 225–229.

Truax, C. B. (1966b). *Toward a tentative measurement of the central therapeutic ingredients.* Fayetteville: Arkansas Rehabilitation Research and Training Center and University of Arkansas.

*Truax, C. B. (1971). Perceived therapeutic conditions and client outcome. *Comparative Group Studies, 2*, 301–310.

Truax, C. B., & Mitchell, K. M. (1971). Research on certain therapist interpersonal skills in relation to process and outcome. In A. E. Bergin & S. L Garfield (Eds.), *Handbook of psychotherapy and behavior change* (pp. 299–344). New York, NY: Wiley.

Tseng, W. S. (1999). Culture and psychotherapy: Review and suggested practical guidelines. *Transcultural Psychiatry, 36*, 131–179.

Watson, J. C., Greenberg, L. S., & Lietaer, G. (1998). The experiential paradigm unfolding: Relationship and experiencing in therapy. In L. S. Greenberg, J. C. Watson, & G. Lietaer (Eds.), *Handbook of experiential psychotherapy* (pp. 3–27). New York, NY: Guilford.

Watson, N. (1984). The empirical status of Rogers' hypotheses of the necessary and sufficient conditions for effective psychotherapy. In R. F. Levant & J. M. Schlein (Eds.), *Client-centered therapy and the person centered approach: New directions in theory, research, and practice* (pp. 17–40). New York, NY: Praeger.

Zane, N., Hall, G. N., Sue, S., Young, K., & Nunez, J. (2004). Research on psychotherapy with culturally diverse populations. In M. J. Lambert (Ed.), *Bergin and Garfield's handbook of psychotherapy and behavior change* (5th ed., pp. 767–804). New York, NY: Wiley.

10

THE REAL RELATIONSHIP

Charles J. Gelso, Dennis M. Kivlighan Jr., and Rayna D. Markin

The real relationship in psychotherapy has been scientifically neglected for many decades. However, the idea of a real relationship between therapists and patients has been around for a long time, probably since the beginning of the "talking cure." This element of the therapeutic relationship emerged from psychoanalysis. Freud (1919, 1937) referred to it when he remarked that "not every relation between an analyst and his subject during and after analysis was to be regarded as transference; there were also friendly relations which were based on reality and proved to be viable" (1937, p. 222). Other early psychoanalysts also commented on a personal, non-work connection between the analyst and analysands.

Perhaps the most incisive comment from these early analysts was offered by Anna Freud (1954), when she wrote:

> [W]ith due respect for the necessarily strictest handling and interpretation of the transference, I still feel that somewhere we should leave room for the realization that patient and analyst are two real people, of equal status, in a real relationship with each other. I wonder whether our at times complete neglect of this side of the matter is not responsible for some of the hostile reactions we get from our patients and which we are apt to ascribe to "true transferences" only. (p. 372)

Anna Freud's comment was typical of analysts' views in the sense that the real relationship was seen as the counterpoint to transference. In other words, the word "real" was taken to mean "realistic" in that the real relationship involved each participant perceiving and experiencing the other in ways that befit the other, rather than through the lenses of transference. By contrast, the latter would involve a displacement of past unresolved conflicts with significant others onto the present therapeutic relationship. Thus, when transference was happening, the therapeutic relationship was experienced

351

in a distorted way, whereas the real relationship represented the realistic, nondistorted element of the relationship.

A second key element of the real relationship was highlighted by the psychoanalyst Greenson (1967). This aspect concerned the participants in the analytic dyad being genuine with each other, that is, being themselves in the relationship rather than holding back or being artificial. In this way, the real relationship is connected to the humanistic/experiential therapies that placed genuineness or congruence as the centerpiece of treatment (Perls, 1969; Rogers, 1957). Greenson's conceptualization focused both on realism and genuineness as the key elements of the real relationship. This two-part conception has been a fundamental element of current thought and empirical research on the real relationship (Gelso, 2014; Wampold & Budge, 2012).

Although the real relationship has its roots in psychoanalysis, the current literature focuses on the real relationship as transtheoretical, applying to all theoretical orientations in psychotherapy (Gelso, 2009, 2011; Gelso & Carter, 1985, 1994; Gelso & Silberberg, 2016; Wampold & Budge, 2012). Theoretically, the strength of the real relationship should not vary according the therapist's theoretical orientation, and existing empirical evidence supports this expectation (Gelso, 2011).

DEFINITIONS

Clarifying and extending Greenson's (1967) psychoanalytic conceptualization, the modern transtheoretical definition of the real relationship has been *"the personal relationship between therapist and patient marked by the extent to which each is genuine with the other and perceives/experiences the other in ways that befit the other"* (Gelso, 2009, p. 119; emphasis added). Thus, the real relationship consists of two fundamental elements: *realism,* or realistic perception/experience of the other, and *genuineness.* The more realistically the participants experience and perceive each other, and the more genuine they are with each other, the stronger the real relationship is within the overall therapeutic relationship.

These two elements, realism and genuineness, may be further divided into what has been termed *magnitude* and *valence.* Magnitude refers to how much realism and genuineness exist in the therapeutic relationship, both overall and on a moment-to-moment basis. Valence is a bit more complicated. The real relationship varies on a positive versus negative dimension. Thus, one's genuine and realistic feelings toward another may be negative. For example, the therapist may not like the patient with whom he or she is genuine and who he or she perceives/experiences realistically. In other words, one may have a high magnitude of realism and genuineness vis-à-vis another, but still feel negatively toward the other. Naturally, however, in what may be considered a good or strong real relationship (see below), the participants' feelings for one another would be largely positive.

The additive combination of realism and genuineness, including their valence and magnitude, yields the *strength of the real relationship.* This construct of strength has been its main measure in research studies.

The Who and When

The real relationship is a bipersonal phenomenon, and as such it is contributed to by both the therapist and patient. The therapist contributes by direct self-disclosures of thoughts, feelings, and information, as well as indirectly. For example, the therapist reveals who he or she is not only by what he or she says to the patient but also through the therapist's sense of humor, attire, office décor, facial expressions, body posture, and the like. These all enable the patient to build an image of the therapist as a person. The therapist also contributes to the strength of the real relationship by being genuine and nonphony with the patient, as well as by experiencing/perceiving the patient as he or she is rather than as a projection based on the therapist's past and present unresolved conflicts.

From the patient's side, the enactment of the patient role itself contributes to the formation and development of the real relationship. That is, the real relationship is built and strengthened by the patient's getting in touch with inner experiences and through both verbal and nonverbal self-exploration and communication that share who he or she is. These communications are a part of the patient's genuineness. In addition, the patient contributes to the real relationship through experiencing and perceiving the therapist in ways that befit the therapist. This is not to say that misperceptions, often referred to as transference, will not occur, for better or worse, as described in the following discussion.

Regarding when the real relationship manifests itself and unfolds, it has been theorized (Couch, 1999; Gelso, 2009, 2011, 2014; Greenson, 1967) to be present from the first moment of contact between therapist and patient. Each participant perceives and experiences the personhood of the other immediately, although to probably varying degrees. It has been theorized that as the therapeutic relationship deepens, the strength of the real relationship increases throughout the work (Gelso, 2014). At least two studies on the unfolding of the real relationship support this suggestion (Fuertes, et al., 2013; Gelso et al., 2012)

Interrelated Constructs

Probably all relational constructs are connected to one another. However, for the real relationship, three related constructs are the working alliance, patient transference, and attachment are especially relevant. In addition, both therapist self-disclosure (Chapter 11, this volume) and patient self-disclosure are related to the real relationship. The person-centered concept of therapist congruence (Chapter 10, this volume) is, in certain ways, synonymous with the therapist genuineness element of the real relationship.

The Real Relationship and the Working Alliance

The real relationship and the working alliance have been theorized to be highly interrelated, and they have indeed been referred to as sister concepts (Gelso, 2014).

Beginning with the theoretical work of Greenson (1967), the real relationship was considered more foundational, as it was seen as existing in all relationships from the first moment of contact. The working alliance, on the other hand, was theorized as an artifact of treatment, existing solely for the purpose of getting the work accomplished. Presently, both are more likely to be viewed as occurring from the beginning of treatment, and as highly related, while still separate to the extent that each contributes independent variance in its relation to treatment process and outcome.

The real relationship may be thought of as the personal or person-to-person, non-work connection between two or more persons, whereas the working alliance is the work connection. The working alliance is usually framed as the bond that exists between patient and therapist, the extent of their agreement on the goals of treatment, and their degree of agreement on the tasks that will accomplish those goals (Bordin, 1979). The bond part of the working alliance is particularly overlapping with the real relationship.

The bond that is part of the working alliance is a working bond, that is, the connection between the participants' that directly reflects their therapeutic work (Gelso, 2011, 2014). For example, when the patient communicates his or her confidence in the therapist's skills and competence, or feels a connection to the therapist as an effective professional, that may be considered part of the working alliance bond. Similarly, when the therapist expresses liking of the patient as a patient, this reflects more the working alliance than the real relationship. However, when either of the participants feels a connection to the other on a person-to-person basis, or feels liking or caring for the other as a person, this bond resides more in the realm of the real relationship.

Given the substantial overlap between these two constructs, it has been important to study whether they contribute independently to process and outcome. The empirical findings provide strong support for the real relationship and working alliance as both overlapping and independent elements. Several studies indicate that each contributes independently to the prediction of treatment progress and outcome (see review by Gelso, 2014). In the following text, we extend this research literature by, in addition to reporting the relation between the real relationship and treatment outcome, examining the size of the real relationship working alliance correlation. The purpose of that analysis is to see how much, and under what circumstances, these sister constructs overlap.

Transference and the Real Relationship

Transference entails the patient's perceiving, experiencing, and reacting to the therapist in ways that do not befit the therapist, in ways that are not realistic. Given this fundamental tenet of transference, one can see where it might be viewed as opposite of the real relationship. And, indeed, the real relationship has been theorized by some to be the nontransference element of the therapeutic relationship.

However, most current conceptualizations consider the real relationship as more than merely the opposite of transference (Gelso, 2011, 2014; Wampold & Budge, 2012). First, the real relationship includes two elements, and realism or realistic perception is only one of these two (the other being genuineness). Second, any given session, part of a session, or any single patient expression contains a mixture of transference projections and realistic perception. When the patient is expressing transference-based reactions, he or she is also likely expressing reality-based reactions. A case example of this inevitable mixture follows (Gelso, 2009):

> In my first session following a rather serious surgery, my patient, John, expressed concern by asking "How are you doing today, buddy?" I replied honestly, "I am doing well, thanks." As I began to pursue how some of his concern was transferentially related to the material with which we had been dealing, John replied. "Well, that may be so, but I also was just concerned about you as a person." As I pondered the expression of concern, it seemed clear to me that this single expression was both very rich with transference and very deeply reflective of real relationship. (p. 257)

The real relationship and patient transference, while not opposites, are at least partially and negatively overlapping (e.g., strong real relationship reflects less transference, and vice versa). The research evidence fits this expectation, indicating a small to moderate negative correlation between the two constructs (Gelso, 2014).

Attachment and the Real Relationship

Patients and therapists bring relationship patterns (relationship schema) into their clinical relationship that can enhance or detract from the strength of the real relationship. A key relationship pattern that has received some empirical attention are the attachment patterns of both parties (see Chapter 19 in Volume 2 for more details).

Two dimensions, attachment avoidance and anxiety, are typically used to describe peoples' attachment behaviors and perceptions. Gelso and Hayes (1998) theorized about the role of therapists' and patients' attachment styles in the formation of the real relationship. Specifically, they contended that insecure attachment, low levels of attachment anxiety or avoidance, would be related to a stronger real relationship. In the following discussion, we summarize the research literature on the attachment–real relationship association by reporting the results of a meta-analysis examining the size of the real relationship and attachment correlation.

MEASURES

Only in recent years has empirical research been conducted on the real relationship. A major reason for this slow development is that no reliable measures had been created prior to the mid-1990s. The first measure of the real relationship was developed by Eugster and Wampold (1996), who created patient-rated, eight-item scales of both therapist and patient real relationship. These scales assessed patients' feelings and reactions toward their therapists, as well as patient's perceptions of their therapists' feelings and reactions to them. Eugster and Wampold also developed parallel therapist-rated, 8-item scales of therapist and patient real relationship. The items were identical to the patient-rated items, except they tapped the therapist's views. The items mostly pertain to the genuineness and liking elements of the real relationship, with little attention to the realism element.

Two studies (Eugster & Wampold, 1996; Kelley et al., 2010) found rather modest internal reliability of this measure, with Cronbach's alpha coefficients ranging from the .60s to the mid .70s. Still, the measure did correlate significantly with several other measures to which it theoretically should relate, providing support for its construct and convergent validity. Despite its psychometric limitations, the Eugster and Wampold measure represents a brief, convenient assessment of the real relationship in terms of genuineness and their liking of each other.

Virtually all of the quantitative research on the real relationship since that 1996 study have used two measures that were subsequently developed: the Real Relationship Inventory–Therapist Version (RRI-T; Gelso et al., 2005) and the Real Relationship Inventory–Client Version (RRI-C; Kelley et al., 2010). As implied by their names, the RRI-T taps the therapists' perceptions of the real relationship, whereas the RRI-C assesses the client's perceptions. Both measures consist of a total score and subscale scores for Realism and Genuineness. Within the subscales, items assess the sub-elements of magnitude and valence as previously defined. Furthermore, both the RRI-C and RRI-T examine the rater's assessments of self, other, and the relationship. For example, in the RRI-C, the client rates real relationship items pertaining to himself or herself, the therapist, and their relationship. The valence and magnitude of realism and genuineness combine to yield scores for strength of the real relationship. Solid evidence of reliability and validity of these measures has accumulated since their initial appearance.

The RRI-T and RRI-C have been abbreviated to a 12-item measure, with six items in each of the two subscales, Realism and Genuineness (Hill et al., 2014). Items were derived by the authors selecting the 12 items that they believed best represented the two components within the longer measures. The abbreviated version correlated .91 and .94 with the longer RRI-C and RRI-T, respectively. The shortened RRI has been used in several studies, and support has been found for its reliability and validity (e.g., Kivlighan et al., 2017). This measure would appear to be a good choice when ease of usage is crucial and when the total score is what is being assessed, rather than subscale scores. Examples of items from both the full-length and abbreviated versions of the Client Form are (a) "I had a realistic understanding of my therapist as a person," and (b) "My therapist did not see me as I really am" (negatively stated item). Examples of items from the Therapist Form are (a) "There is no genuinely positive connection between us" (negatively stated item), and (b) "My client's feelings toward me seem to fit who I am as a person."

CLINICAL EXAMPLES

What does the real relationship look like, or how does it manifest, in the psychotherapy hour? The real relationship shows itself at three levels, independent of the therapist's theoretical orientation. At the first level, the real relationship exists in the background of patient–therapist transactions. "It shows itself through the participants' ongoing sensing and understanding of one another and in their feelings toward each other. . . . These inner states simply exist as the therapist and patient explore the patient's inner conflicts and outward behavior about matters other than the relationship" (Gelso, 2011, p. 88). However, the real relationship is expected to come into the foreground when there is a rupture in some aspect of the relationship, when disruptive transferences occur, and when the patient needs the support of a strong real relationship.

At the second level, the real relationship may manifest itself either subtly or explicitly in the behaviors of the participants that reflect realism and genuineness and the valence of these. At the third level, the real relationship can show itself in each and every communication between the participants. This follows Greenson's (1967) suggestion that there is a real relationship aspect in all communications, regardless of how fantastical they may seem.

The psychotherapist can foster the real relationship by sharing aspects of himself or herself and his or her feelings toward the patient. Examples of sharing (from Kasper et al., 2008) occurred between a 51-year-old White male therapist and a 24-year-old White female patient involved in therapy with a 12-session limit. Throughout treatment the therapist expressed a range of feelings in the moment, for example, caring, sadness, disappointment, and connection. One example that highlights the real relationship has to do with the therapist's feelings about the patient's reactions to the forthcoming termination:

Therapist: Last week when we were talking about when we're gonna end and how long we're gonna go. . . . I was sort of wondering what's going in that it doesn't seem like it matters to you one way or the other how long we meet.

Patient: No; actually, the truth of the matter is, like I mean I think I mentioned to you that I would like to go on more than 12.

The patient then goes on to say that she thinks it would be selfish to ask for more sessions. The therapist follows with:

Therapist: So you didn't in some ways wanna hurt me or upset me. For me it hurt, that it felt like it didn't matter [to you] how long [we met].

In subsequent research interviews, the patient expressed to the researchers that because of the therapist's self-disclosure, she felt this was a powerful session resulting in greater closeness and understanding of the impact she has on others.

Another example of deep sharing that is reflective of the real relationship is taken from the 17th and terminating session (from Hill et al., 2008). The therapist is a 55-year-old White heterosexual man and the patient is a 29-year-old African American, lesbian female with long-standing anxiety and depression. This vignette demonstrates how the therapist's genuine sharing facilitates the patient's genuineness:

Therapist: Jo, I respect you so much.

Patient: Do you?

Therapist: I respect you so much. The way you go at these huge issues and face them with such courage . . . the work you've done with me since November has been so hard and so challenging and you have been so strong and capable and successful. I respect your integrity, I respect your courage.

Patient: Thank you, but I'm glad I met *you* because there's no telling if I met with someone else. Not to say that it would have been. . . . It's probably more of a feeling you know, with you than let's say somebody else who is just kind of like "so how do you feel about that?" . . . You really talk about issues and . . . it matters what we talk about in here. I always reflect back and say "Oh that makes sense" or then I'll jot it down. . . .

Therapist: You surprised me right from the get-go, Jo, you just got in the driver's seat and you put your foot on the gas pedal and you went to work. You initiated and you led me and us to such profound conversations at times. It's been a deep sharing.

Patient: Oh, yeah, it really has.

The real relationship may also be fostered by the therapist working with the patient to see the therapist as he or she is. Yalom (2002), for example, describes a case in which he and his patient shared impressionistic notes of each session. The patient idealized Yalom, and Yalom wanted to diminish this idealization so that the patient could seem him realistically. Thus, in Yalom's notes of the sessions that he shared with the patient, he deliberately tried to reveal his most human feelings, including his frustrations, irritations, insomnia, and vanity.

In a more moderate manner, Dr. Patrice Duquette (personal communication, May 2009) provided an example of using the real relationship to help her patient who was suffering from intense anxiety and withdrawal. Duquette is a highly experienced White psychodynamically oriented psychiatrist, and the patient is a 36-year-old White, heterosexual female, who is married and has one child. In the following vignette, Duquette's observations are in parentheses following the patient's verbalizations:

Patient: I can hear myself being tight. I don't want to really feel, don't want to have those feelings. But I don't want to be like this either. (Her mouth is set tight, her forehead is raised and eyes tightened, her voice is very tight and has a cry it in.)

Therapist: Can you feel your throat at all?

Patient: Not really. Can't feel it separate from all the other tightness. Not quite. Don't want to almost. Feels like I can't feel or think, like my brain has just stopped.

Therapist: Try a bit. Can you feel anything? Can you direct your energy, to feel where you are? Can you look at me?

Patient: A little bit. (Tears well up obviously in her eyes, her mouth twists more, her eyes go to an almost vacant look, with her eye contact less intensely focused.) Now I just . . . just . . . it just feels like there is a big gaping hole. (Silence, and she continues looking, but is appearing more frightened by the second.)

Therapist: Stay here. Can you look at me? At me . . . here?

Patient: A little . . . (More tears, eyes are still looking vague and fading.)

Therapist: What do you see? Here? Are you along?

Patient: I see you.

Therapist: (Nods and gestures, as if to say, "More.")

Patient: I can see you (mouth still twisting, patient is limiting her verbal output.)

Therapist: What do you see in me? Can you see my eyes? What do you see?

Patient: That you are present.

Therapist: Who is? Who am I?

Patient: Double D. (Patient chuckles, as if it were a private joke. Therapist recalls that this is how the patient writes her name in her appointment book and smiles slightly in recognition.) Dr. Duquette, that's who you are. (She says this in a firmer voice, with a moment of eye contact. Such moments had come up before in group situations, when I had directed her and others to use my full name by way of fuller recognition of me and our relationships in a given moment.)

Therapist: And so?

Patient: That you see me, care about me, are listening. And that as you see me you are like 99.9% accurate about what you see. (Her voice is settling, she speaks more spontaneously, her eye contact is more directed.)

LANDMARK STUDIES

Research on the real relationship is of recent vintage (although research on one of its elements, therapist genuineness, has existed for many years). The aforementioned Eugster and Wampold (1996) investigation was the first empirical study on the topic. The next study was published nearly a decade later (Gelso et al., 2005) and represented the first instrument development piece, a therapist-completed measure of the real relationship. This measure, along with the subsequent client-completed measure (Kelley et al., 2010), provided psychotherapy researchers with reliable and validated instruments that facilitated empirical efforts. In this section, we summarize the Eugster and Wampold study, the subsequent Gelso et al. investigation, and then a more recent investigation by Kivlighan and colleagues (2017), which represents a multilevel modeling effort separating effects into therapist, client, and session effects. Finally, we mention qualitative work and underscore its near absence.

The First Study

Eugster and Wampold's (1996) study is a landmark because it represents the first empirical study on the real relationship. These researchers surveyed 114 highly experienced therapists and 119 of their patients, using an 8-item measure of the real relationship. Therapists and patients made ratings on a 6-point scale of the quality of the therapist-offered real relationship and the patient-offered real relationship. Four items of the 8-item measure elicited ratings of the self, and four items elicited ratings of the other. Thus, four scores resulted: therapist rating of therapist-offered real relationship (4 items) and patient-offered real relationship (4 items) and patient ratings of patient- and therapist-offered real relationship (4 items each). The researchers developed a battery of nine measures (real relationship was one of these) thought to be relevant to treatment outcome. The criterion was the evaluation of sessions.

Although a range of complex statistical analyses was employed, the simple bivariate correlations with outcome may prove the most revealing. Both therapist and patient ratings of therapist-offered and patient-offered real relationship correlated moderately but uniformly positively with session evaluation (*r*s ranging from .28 to .64). The correlations with session evaluation were especially notable for patient's ratings of their therapist-offered real relationship (*r* = .60) and their own enacted real relationship (*r* = .64). It was also found that patients' and therapists' ratings of the real relationship were significantly associated with patient and therapist ratings of involvement in treatment, comfort, patient progress, therapist expertness, and therapist interpersonal style (e.g., friendliness, empathy, warmth). In essence, this first study demonstrated that the real relationship was a promising variable in terms of its potential influence on treatment outcome, as well as its connection to other important process variables.

Instrument Development

The RRI-T (Gelso et al., 2005) was the first psychometrically sound measure of the real relationship. The results of the instrument-development study for the RRI-T have been described in the Measures section of this chapter. In sum, the RRI-T consisted of 24 items, 12 assessing realism and 12 assessing genuineness. Items were written to tap magnitude and valence within each of the two subscales and to elicit ratings of self (therapist), other (client), and the relationship within realism, genuineness, valence, and magnitude.

In the development of the RRI-T, 130 items were originally written and then, through a series of steps, including the sampling of 80 psychologists, reduced to 24 items. Then 130 psychologists and psychology trainees completed the reduced measure, along with several other measures aimed at assessing the validity of the RRI-T. It was found that RRI-T was significantly related to several measures to which it theoretically should relate (see Measures section), supporting the construct and convergent validity of this instrument. Since the appearance of the RRI-T, all studies of therapist-rated real relationship have employed this measure.

Multilevel Modeling

One of the major steps forward in psychotherapy research has been the development of advanced statistical analyses that can clarify treatment effects. One such technique is often referred to as multilevel modeling, and this technique seeks to determine the independent contribution of different elements (e.g., patient, therapist, treatment, duration) to treatment process or outcome.

In a recent study, multilevel polynomial regression and response surface analysis were used to examine how the real relationship and the working alliance were related to session quality (Kivlighan et al., 2017). Real relationship and working alliance ratings of 2,517 sessions of 144 clients and their 23 therapists were partitioned into therapist-level, client-level, and session-level components. This important study determined how therapy proceeds when the sister concepts of the working alliance and the real relationship are similar or dissimilar from one another in the treatment hour. Multilevel analysis provides a potent method of analyzing these relationships at differing levels.

For both therapists and clients at most levels of analysis (therapist, client, and session), client-rated session quality was highest when both the real relationship and working alliance were strong and lowest when both relational factors were weak. However, for some clients (within a therapist's caseload), session quality across sessions was greatest when working alliance was stronger than the real relationship, whereas for other clients, session quality was best when the real relationship was stronger than the alliance. Within clients, some sessions had the highest quality when working alliance was strongest, whereas other sessions were rated most favorably when the real relationship was strongest. Thus, at both the client and session levels, the most important relational ingredient varied. This finding suggests that therapists need to pay close attention to which relational ingredient is most needed by each client and within each session.

Qualitative work

One limitation of research on the real relationship is the absence of qualitative studies. This is surprising because the construct seems so fitting for qualitative analyses.

There have been some qualitative studies in which implications were drawn for the real relationship. For example, Knox and associates (1997) conducted a qualitative study on 12 psychotherapy patients to determine their views of what were helpful therapist self- disclosures. They found that such disclosures allowed patients to see their therapists as more real and human and influenced clients to be more open and honest. These findings suggest that the genuineness element of the real relationship is strengthened by therapists sharing more about themselves. Similarly, Curtis and colleagues (2004) discovered that psychoanalysts viewed their own analysts' warmth, emotional availability, genuineness, and willingness to explore the patient's feelings about him/her (the analyst) as most helpful. This supports the genuineness aspect of the real relationship. Qualitative work is needed on the real relationship to supplement the quantitative research.

META-ANALYTIC REVIEW

Method

Eligibility Criteria

Because this was the first meta-analysis of the real relationship literature, we included all studies (published and unpublished), regardless of publication date, that reported data allowing calculation of the correlation between the strength of the real relationship and: (a) treatment outcome (pretest–posttest change, treatment progress, and session quality or session outcome), (b) working alliance, (c) transference, and (d) attachment. Pretest–posttest change was defined as studies that used a psychometric instrument (e.g., Outcome Questionnaire-45) that patients completed prior to commencing treatment and at the completion of treatment. For treatment progress, patients and/or therapists assessed the progress to date in their treatment. These progress reports were often, but not always, completed at the conclusion of the patient's treatment. For session quality or outcome, patients reported on the quality or outcome of the session in which the real relationship was assessed. Studies were excluded if they did not have the information necessary to calculate a correlation between real relationship and any of the predictor variables or if the data set was not independent of other studies included in the meta-analysis.

Information Sources

We searched the database PsycInfo for published studies on the real relationship and the pre-identified process and outcome variables. We also contacted researchers known to conduct research on the real relationship for unpublished studies and student theses or dissertations. All except one study were published in English. The exception was a South Korean dissertation in which the key information was translated by the doctoral student.

Search

We used the search term "real relationship" paired with the terms, "therapy/counseling outcome," "session quality/outcome," "treatment progress," "working alliance," "transference," and "attachment."

Study Selection

Titles and/or abstracts of potential studies were independently coded by the third author and two advanced graduate students in counseling psychology. Disagreements were discussed among the coders until a consensus was reached.

Data Collection Process

We developed spreadsheets for coding both study-level and effect size-level data. The second author and an advanced graduate student in counseling psychology independently extracted the targeted data. Disagreements were again discussed and resolved by the two judges. When sufficient data for computing standardized effect sizes were unavailable, study authors were contacted.

Data Items

Along with data necessary for computing standardized effect sizes (Pearson's r), the following data were extracted: (a) type of outcome assessed (see Eligibility Criteria section), (b) sample size, and (c) who (client or therapist) made the ratings.

Summary Measures

The Pearson's correlation coefficient (r) was the effect size measure used in this research. In addition, we report the d for each relationship examined. Methods described by Cooper et al. (2009) were used to compute this effect size and its variance. The Comprehensive Meta-Analysis (v3) statistical software was used to conduct the analyses.

Synthesis of Results

When studies contained multiple effect sizes, we aggregated data within studies and then between studies, based on the specific comparisons from our different analyses. We computed Pearson's r and 95% confidence intervals as summary statistics. The heterogeneity among effect sizes in an analysis was assessed using the Q-statistic (assessing whether between-study heterogeneity exceeds that expected by chance alone). All analyses used random effects models.

For the correlation between real relationship and outcome, type of outcome (pretest–posttest change, treatment progress, or session quality) was assessed as a between-study moderator of the correlation between real relationship and outcome. For the real relationship outcome analysis, within-study moderators included (a) source of the real relationship rating (client or therapist), (b) source of the outcome rating (client or therapist), and (c) rater match (same rater for both real relationship and outcome; e.g., client-rated real relationship and outcome) or different rater for real relationship and outcome (e.g., therapist-rated real relationship and client-rated outcome).

For the correlations between (a) real relationship and working alliance, (b) real relationship and transference, and (c) real relationship and attachment, within-study moderators included (a) source of the real relationship rating (client or therapist), (b) source of the outcome rating (client or therapist), and (c) rater match (same rater for both real relationship and outcome; e.g., client-rated real relationship and outcome) or different rater for real relationship and outcome (e.g., therapist-rated real relationship and client-rated outcome). For the real relationship and transference analysis, type of transference (positive or negative) was an additional within-study moderator. For the real relationship and attachment analysis, attachment dimension (anxiety or avoidance) was an additional within-study moderator.

Risk of Bias across Studies

For each of the analyses that we conducted, we assessed publication bias by visually inspecting funnel plots for asymmetry.

Real Relationship and Outcome Results

Five studies reported the correlation between real relationship and psychotherapy progress, five studies reported the correlation between real relationship and pretest–posttest outcome, and six studies reported the correlation between real relationship and session quality. The omnibus effect size was significant ($r = .38$, 95% CI [.30, .44], $p < .001$, $d = 0.80$, $N = 1,502$ participants). There was significant heterogeneity across the studies ($Q[15] = 31.90$, $p = .007$). The fail-safe N was 759, and the trim-and-fill analysis did not suggest evidence of publication bias. The funnel plot for this analysis is displayed in Figure 10.1. This result shows a moderate association between real relationship and outcome. The real relationship–outcome relation is of a larger magnitude (moderate) than the working alliance–outcome relation (small, $r = .28$), found in a previous meta-analysis (Horvath et al., 2011).

A moderator test was conducted to determine whether the type of outcome assessed was related to the magnitude of the correlation between real relationship and psychotherapy outcome. For this analysis, we created two dummy variables: (a) whether or not the outcome assessed represented progress and (b) whether or not the outcome assessed represented session quality. Therefore, whether or not the outcome assessed was a pretest–posttest change was the reference group. Neither the progress dummy variable (coefficient = 11.69, z-value = .90, $p = .371$) nor the session quality dummy variable (coefficient = .08, z-value = .62, $p = .538$) was significant. Therefore, the type of outcome assessed was not related to the strength of the real relationship outcome correlation.

Study name		Statistics for each study					Correlation and 95% CI
	Correlation	Lower limit	Upper limit	Z-Value	p-Value		
Ain, 2011	0.420	0.188	0.608	3.410	0.001		
Bhatia & Gelso, 2017a	0.290	0.177	0.395	4.897	0.000		
Bhatia & Gelso, 2017b	0.420	0.312	0.517	7.022	0.000		
Eugetsr & Wampold, 1996	0.310	0.134	0.467	3.377	0.001		
Fuertes et al., 2007	0.360	0.114	0.564	2.820	0.005		
Fuertes et al., 2016	0.530	0.303	0.700	4.173	0.000		
Gelso et al., 2005	0.360	0.165	0.528	3.515	0.000		
Gelso et al., 2012	0.730	0.548	0.846	5.800	0.000		
Gullo et al., 2012	0.560	0.263	0.760	3.408	0.001		
Kivlighan et al., 2016	0.230	0.069	0.379	2.781	0.005		
Lee, 2017	0.440	0.230	0.611	3.894	0.000		
Lo Coco et al., 2011	0.230	−0.052	0.478	1.606	0.108		
Markin et al., 2014	0.180	−0.032	0.376	1.668	0.095		
Marmarosh et al., 2009	0.280	−0.004	0.523	1.930	0.054		
Owen et al., 2011	0.300	0.007	0.545	2.006	0.045		
Perez-Rojas, 2015	0.490	0.343	0.614	5.872	0.000		
	0.365	0.321	0.409	14.800	0.000		

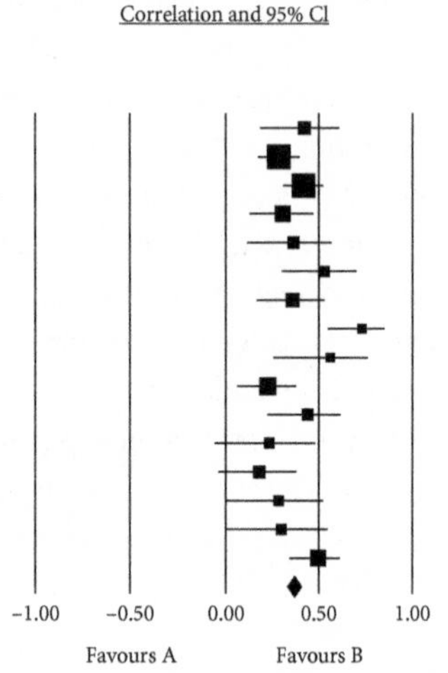

−1.00   −0.50   0.00   0.50   1.00

Favours A   Favours B

Meta Analysis

FIGURE 10.1 Funnel plot of effect sizes and confidence intervals (CI) for the meta-analysis of real relationship and treatment outcome.

Note: The last line of the table is the estimated results (random effects) for the meta-analysis. "Box" size is relative to sample size, with larger boxes indicating a larger sample. "Favors A" indicates a negative correlation whereas "Favors B" indicates a positive correlation.

Within-study moderator tests revealed that (a) who assessed the real relationship (client or therapist) was unrelated to the strength of the real relationship outcome correlation (coefficient = −.09, z-value = −.51, p = .614), (b) who assessed outcome (client or therapist) was unrelated to the strength of the real relationship outcome correlation (coefficient = .20, z-value = 1.33, p = .183), and (c) whether the assessor of real relationship and outcome was the same (e.g., client assessed both real relationship and outcome) or different (e.g., therapist assessed real relationship and client assessed outcome) was unrelated to the strength of the real relationship–outcome correlation (coefficient = −0.18, z-value = −1.19, p = .235). Therefore, rater source did not affect the size of the real relationship–outcome correlation. The role relationship moderator is important because it suggests that single-rater bias does not affect the size of the real relationship–outcome correlation.

Relation with Other Process Variables

As suggested earlier, the real relationship probably interconnects with other key elements of the therapeutic relationship. Below we summarize the meta-analytic results on the association between the real relationship and the working alliance, transference, and attachment style.

Real Relationship and Working Alliance

Nine studies reported the correlation between real relationship and working alliance. The omnibus effect size was significant (r = .58, 95% CI [.51, .64], p < .001, d = 1.42, N = 1,070 participants). There was significant heterogeneity across the studies ($Q[8]$ = 19.67, p = .012; Figure 10.2). The fail-safe N was 4,016, and the trim-and-fill analysis did not suggest evidence of publication bias. This result supports Gelso's characterization of the real relationship and the working alliance as "sister" constructs; medium to large correlation but not identical constructs. The funnel plot for this analysis is displayed in Figure 10.2.

Within-study moderator tests revealed that: (a) who assessed the real relationship (client or therapist) was unrelated to the strength of the correlation (coefficient = −.17, z-value = −1.68, p = .092), (b) who assessed WA (client or therapist) was unrelated to the strength of the real relationship–working alliance correlation (coefficient = .01, z-value = .14, p = .889) but (c) whether the assessor was the same (e.g., client assessed both WA and RR) or different person (e.g., therapist assessed WA and client assessed RR) was related to the strength of the real relationship–working alliance (coefficient = −.52, z-value = −5.02, p < .001). The assessor match explained 54% of the variance in the size of the real relationship–working alliance correlation. When the person was in the same role, the real relationship–working alliance correlation was .83, but when different people assessed real relationship and the working alliance, the real relationship–working alliance correlation was .31. This correlations for the role analysis suggest

Study name	Statistics for Each Study					Correlation and 95% CI
	Correlation	Lower limit	Upper limit	Z-Value	p-Value	
Bhatia & Gelso, 2017a	0.540	0.450	0.619	9.909	0.000	
Bhatia & Gelso, 2017b	0.630	0.549	0.700	11.629	0.000	
Fuertes et al., 2016	0.360	0.099	0.574	2.665	0.008	
Gelso et al., 2005	0.470	0.291	0.617	4.758	0.000	
Kivlighan et al., 2016	0.650	0.544	0.735	9.206	0.000	
Lo Coco et al., 2011	0.450	0.196	0.647	3.323	0.001	
Marmarosh et al., 2009	0.490	0.239	0.680	3.596	0.000	
Owen et al., 2011	0.720	0.541	0.837	5.882	0.000	
Perez-Rojas, 2015	0.670	0.559	0.757	8.881	0.000	
	0.584	0.543	0.622	21.626	0.000	

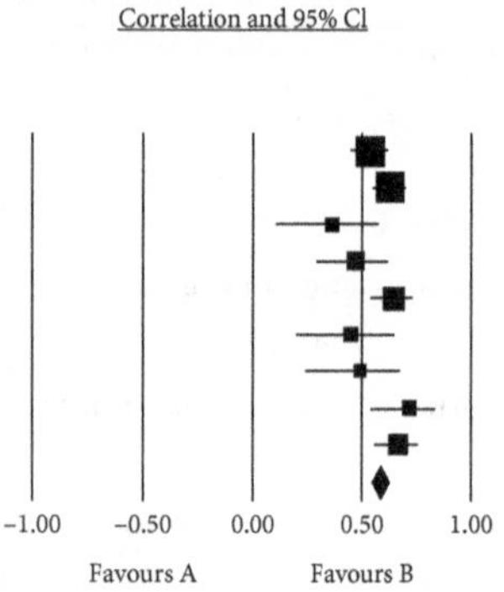

−1.00   −0.50   0.00   0.50   1.00

Favours A   Favours B

Meta Analysis

FIGURE 10.2 Funnel plot of effect sizes and confidence intervals (CI) for the meta-analysis of real relationship and working alliance.

Note: The last line of the table is the estimated results (random effects) for the meta-analysis. "Box" size is relative to sample size, with larger boxes indicating a larger sample. "Favors A" indicates a negative correlation whereas "Favors B" indicates a positive correlation.

that single-rater bias may, under certain circumstances, inflate the size of the real relationship–working alliance correlation.

Real Relationship and Transference

Four studies reported the correlation between real relationship and transference. The omnibus effect size was significant ($r = -.17$, 95% CI [$-.25$, $-.10$], $p < .001$, $d = -.35$, $N = 619$ participants). There was not significant heterogeneity across the studies ($Q[3] = 0.07$, $p = .995$; Figure 10.3). The fail-safe N was 129, and the trim-and-fill analysis did not suggest evidence of publication bias. The real relationship is not the opposite of transference but does evidence a small to moderate negative relationship with transference. The funnel plot for this analysis is displayed in Figure 10.3. Due to the small number of studies, we do not report on any moderator analyses.

Summary and Conclusions

The meta-analytic results show that there is a moderate correlation between real relationship and treatment outcome. This relationship is not moderated by how outcome is assessed or by who does the assessment of the real relationship and outcome; in particular, there is no evidence of single-rater bias inflating the size of the real relationship–outcome correlation. These results confirm the importance of the real relationship and provide support for Gelso's (e.g., 2014) theoretical writings. As previously noted, the real relationship–outcome meta-analytic correlation is larger than the working alliance–outcome correlation. However this size difference needs to be

Study name	Statistics for Each Study					Correlation and 95% CI
	Correlation	Lower limit	Upper limit	Z-Value	p-Value	
Bhatia & Gelso, 2017a	−0.170	−0.283	−0.052	−2.816	0.005	
Bhatia & Gelso, 2017b	−0.170	−0.288	−0.047	−2.692	0.007	
Gelso et al., 2005	−0.170	−0.364	0.038	−1.601	0.109	
Marmarosh et al., 2009	−0.210	−0.466	0.079	−1.430	0.153	
	−0.173	−0.246	−0.097	−4.440	0.000	

−1.00   −0.50   0.00   0.50   1.00

Favours A   Favours B

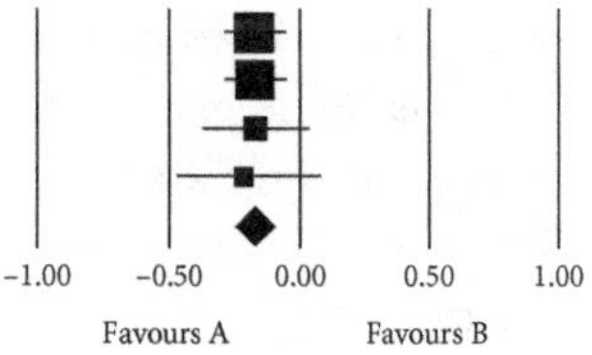

MetaAnalysis

FIGURE 10.3 Funnel plot of effect sizes and confidence intervals (CI) for the meta-analysis of real relationship and transference.

Note: The last line of the table is the estimated results (random effects) for the meta-analysis. "Box" size is relative to sample size, with larger boxes indicating a larger sample. "Favors A" indicates a negative correlation whereas "Favors B" indicates a positive correlation.

placed in context. There have been far more studies reporting the working alliance correlation than studies reporting the real relationship–outcome correlation. Therefore, the working alliance correlation in meta-analyses should be more stable than the real relationship–outcome correlation found in this study.

As previously noted, the real relationship is a component of Gelso's (2014) tripartite model of the therapeutic relationship. As hypothesized in that model, the real relationship and the working alliance should have a moderate to large correlation, and our meta-analytic results confirm this hypothesis. There is evidence that mono-rater bias may inflate the size of the real relationship–working alliance correlation. Therefore, researchers should be careful when interpreting the size of the relationship–working alliance correlation when both ratings are coming from either the client or therapist.

Gelso (2014) argued that the real relationship should not be considered the opposite of transference because the real relationship is not entirely composed of the opposite of distortion (reality). Therefore, he argued that the correlation between the real relationship and transference should be small to moderate and negative. The meta-analytic results support this expectation. Taken together, the results of these three meta-analyses provide support for the propositions that Gelso laid out in his tripartite model of the therapeutic relationship.

PATIENT AND THERAPIST CONTRIBUTIONS

Patient attachment theoretically contributes to the strength of the real relationship. Alas, only four studies reported the correlation between real relationship and attachment. For these studies, a positive effect size indicated that a secure attachment (low attachment anxiety and avoidance) was related to a stronger real relationship. The omnibus effect size was significant ($r = .17$, 95% CI [.06, .28], $p < .0003$, $d = 0.35$,

N = 303 participants). Therefore, a secure attachment relationship was associated with a stronger real relationship. The funnel plot for this analysis is displayed in Figure 10.4.

Both the patient and the therapist bring differing capacity to form a therapeutic relationship in the psychotherapy encounter. These different capacities are embedded in patients' and therapists' relationship histories. As hypothesized, the meta-analytic results of the three available studies show that the anxious and avoidant attachment orientations of both patients and therapists are negatively related to the strength of the real relationship.

Do differences between therapists or differences between clients in their abilities to form and grow real relationships best predict treatment success? There are two parts to this question. First, are some therapists (clients) better than other therapists (clients) in forming real relationships with their clients (therapists) and are these between-therapist (between-client) differences in real relationships related to psychotherapy outcome? Second, if between-therapist and between-client differences are related to outcome, which type of difference is a more important predictor of outcome? Three studies (Kivlighan et al., 2014; Li et al., 2016) examine this important question.

Kivlighan et al. (2015) found that therapists who, on the whole, were rated as having stronger third session real relationships had clients who reported more treatment progress. However, for clients within any single therapist's case load, there was no association between the client's real relationship with their therapist and treatment progress. Although complicated, this difference between therapists as a whole and individual therapists as rated by clients on their caseloads implies that the therapist's contribution to the real relationship and its connection to session progress is stronger than is the patient's contribution.

Kivlighan et al. (2014) reported a similar finding. They found that therapists who, across all of their clients, were rated as having increasing real relationship strength as treatment progressed, had clients who reported a greater decrease in symptoms. Within any given therapist's case load, however, changes (increases or decreases) in

Study name	Statistics for Each Study					Correlation and 95% CI
	Correlation	Lower limit	Upper limit	Z-Value	p-Value	
Fuertes et al., 2007	0.230	−0.028	0.459	1.753	0.080	
Fuertes et al., 2016	0.210	−0.064	0.454	1.507	0.132	
Marmarosh et al., 2009	0.080	−0.209	0.356	0.538	0.591	
Moore & Gelso, 2011	0.160	−0.006	0.317	1.889	0.059	
	0.170	0.056	0.280	2.916	0.004	

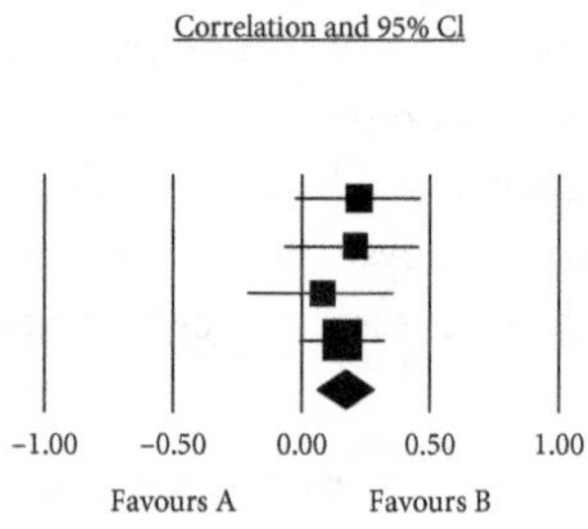

Meta Analysis

FIGURE 10.4 Funnel plot of effect sizes and confidence intervals (CI) for the meta-analysis of real relationship and attachment.

Note: The last line of the table is the estimated results (random effects) for the meta-analysis. "Box" size is relative to sample size, with larger boxes indicating a larger sample. "Favors A" indicates a negative correlation whereas "Favors B" indicates a positive correlation.

client-rated real relationship with their therapist were unrelated to change in client symptoms across treatment. Again, this difference between therapists as a whole and any given therapist's caseload suggests that therapists are more significant contributors than are patients to the role of the real relationship in symptom improvement as treatment progresses.

Another study extended these two investigations by examining between-therapist differences in the dyadic real relationship (Li et al., 2016). Theoretically, the real relationship is a two-person construct with both the therapist and client contributing to the dyad's real relationship. However, most of the research literature treats client and therapist real relationship perceptions as discrete entities.

Researchers (Li et al., 2016) used the common fate model (CFM; Ledermann & Kenny, 2012) to model the dyadic real relationship and to examine how this dyadic real relationship was related to session evaluation. Psychotherapists who, across all of their clients and sessions, had a stronger dyadic real relationships had clients who reported better session evaluations; whereas therapists who across all of their clients and sessions had weaker dyadic real relationships also had clients who reported worse session evaluations. When clients within a therapist's case load reported a stronger dyadic real relationship with their therapist, there was no statistical association with session evaluation.

Taken together, the three statistically sophisticated studies show that between-therapist differences in early real relationship, between-therapist differences in the growth of the real relationship, and between-therapist differences in the dyadic real relationship are better predictors of treatment outcome than between-client differences in the real relationship. That is, in plain English, the individual therapist makes more difference than the individual client when it comes to the real relationship. These studies suggest that researchers should continue to study therapist differences in the real relationship, as they may prove key to successful therapeutic change. For example, what characteristics do some therapists possess that allow them to form and grow stronger real relationships with their clients? Or, what do some therapists do or not do with their clients to form and grow stronger real relationships?

EVIDENCE OF CAUSALITY

It is critical to understand the causal relationships between the real relationship and treatment outcome, but unfortunately there are no purely experimental studies that allow us to draw strong causal inferences. It is difficult, if not impossible, to conduct true experiments in field studies of organismic variables, such as the real relationship. This is so because in the real world of psychotherapy, one cannot ethically assign clients randomly to differing levels of real relationship offered by the same or equivalent therapists. Experiments in the form of laboratory analogues of psychotherapy may allow for causal inferences, and such studies would be a useful addition to the field studies that have been done to date. While laboratory experiments are in themselves not directly relevant to clinical practice, when combined with field studies, this sort of methodological triangulation may allow for meaningful causal inferences.

At the same time, longitudinal field studies have been done, and these do allow for stronger causal statements than cross-sectional correlational investigations. For example, three growth curve studies have provided strong suggestions of causality. All three studies collected client- and therapist-rated real relationship ratings longitudinally and examined how linear change in real relationship was related to treatment outcome.

In one of the studies (Gelso et al., 2012), it was found that linear increases in therapist-rated and client-rated real relationship predicted therapists', but not clients', ratings of treatment progress. Another of these studies (Lee, 2017) found that linear increases in client-rated, but not therapist-rated, real relationship were related to decrease in distress. Finally, the third study (Kivlighan et al., 2014) revealed that when clients of a given therapist reported increasingly strong real relationships, they also experienced decreasing emotional distress.

Taken together, these studies show that an increasing real relationship is related to better treatment outcome. However, there are inconsistencies in findings, depending on who rates the real relationship and who rates outcome. Still, these growth curve studies provide some tentative evidence that change in real relationship is related to better outcomes. It is important, however, for more studies to examine the causal ordering of the real relationship and outcome using other methodological approaches.

LIMITATIONS OF THE RESEARCH

The main limitations of the research conducted to date on the real relationship pertain directly to the few studies that have been conducted. Thus, although the findings of this meta-analysis are highly promising regarding the relation of the strength of the real relationship to differing outcomes (session outcome, treatment progress, and treatment outcome), the number of studies is small, especially for the three outcome types taken separately. More studies are needed associating the real relationship to treatment outcome, both immediately following termination and at follow-up. No studies of which we are aware have been done on the latter.

Similarly, no studies have examined the real relationship in psychotherapies of varying theoretical orientations. Is the real relationship different with therapists who practice psychodynamic, cognitive behavioral therapy, experiential, integrative, and other therapies? Does the relation of the strength of the real relationship to outcome differ for dissonant treatments? What is the relation of real relationship and outcome for brief versus longer-term therapies? Nearly all of what we now know is based on brief treatments, and work on longer treatments is sorely needed.

Another limitation of the research is that nearly all of the studies on real relationship have been conducted by a small number of researchers from a small number of laboratories. It is well documented throughout the history of psychotherapy research that findings emerging from laboratories that espouse the theoretical construct being studied have somewhat different, and usually more favorable, findings than those in which the investigators are not proponents. In the case of the real relationship, nearly all studies have been conducted by those who have theorized about the importance of the real relationship and their colleagues and students. Findings will probably be modified as a larger number of investigators, including those who are not proponents, study this construct and its impact.

We have already lamented the paucity of qualitative research on the real relationship. It would be helpful to study from a qualitative perspective what patients and therapists believe make for a strong real relationship and what they believe weakens it in particular treatments. It would be especially useful to ground these opinions in specific experiences, for example, of patients commenting on their own therapy experiences or of therapists commenting on specific cases. Such work could lead to further refinements in practice, training, and theory.

Because empirical research on the real relationship is still in its early stages, there are many questions that await empirical scrutiny. Among the major ones are:

a. What therapist–patient interactions occur in sessions in which there are stronger and/or more salient real relationships?
b. Which therapist and patient factors facilitate stronger real relationships? Although some such factors have been studied, many therapist and patient factors either require further study or have not been studied at all.
c. How do cultural factors such as race, ethnicity, and sexual orientation relate to the strength and salience of the real relationship?
d. Similarly, what factors, for example, multicultural competence and orientation, may moderate or mediate the relation of such cultural factors and the real relationship?
e. How does the real relationship manifest itself in treatment in other countries? To date, the only other countries in which the real relationship has been studied are Italy (e.g., LoCoco et al., 2011) and South Korea (Eun Ju, 2015), and the findings have been consistent with research in the US.
f. How does the real relationship vary in strength and impact for patients with differing personalities and disorders?

These are but a few of the many questions that may be fruitfully examined in future studies.

DIVERSITY CONSIDERATIONS

Little is known at this point about how diversity, such as race, ethnicity, and sexual orientation, influence the real relationship, or how the strength and salience of the real relationship may moderate or mediate the relation of diversity to treatment outcomes. To date, three studies have examined such factors, and these present intriguing findings.

One such study examined how therapists' multicultural orientation (MCO; values about the salience of cultural factors in the lives of therapists and clients) was associated with the strength of the real relationship, working alliance, and treatment outcome (Owen et al., 2011). One hundred seventy-six clients rated the MCO of their 33 psychotherapists and also rated their working alliances, real relationships, and treatment outcomes. Most central to the present chapter, clients' ratings of the real relationships with their therapists were positively correlated with treatment outcomes for both White ($n = 95$) and racial-ethnic minority ($n = 81$) clients. Also, client ratings of their therapists' MCO indicated that multicultural orientations of therapists were positively associated with ratings of the strength of the real relationship. The greater therapists' MCO in the eyes of their clients, the stronger the real relationship between therapist and client.

In another such study involving 144 clients and their 19 therapists, clients rated some therapists as having stronger real relationships and working alliances with their REM clients, whereas other therapists were seen to have stronger working alliances and real relationships with their White clients (Morales et al., 2018). These differences were independent of the race of the therapists. Nuanced findings such as these may prove valuable as they take us closer to understanding which therapists work best with which clients regarding race and ethnicity.

A third diversity-related study focused on the real relationship with lesbian ($n = 76$) and gay ($n = 40$) clients (Kelley, 2015). The real relationship accounted for significant variance in clients' positive feelings about their therapists above and beyond months in therapy, therapists' helpful and unhelpful therapy practices, and the working alliance. This study offers evidence of the importance of the real relationship in the eyes of lesbian and gay clients.

No studies to date have examined how therapist and/or patient gender bear upon the role of the real relationship. Although virtually all studies on the real relationship break down samples by gender, none of these investigations has actually studied gender and the real relationship. This absence is especially striking in light of the long-standing, replicated findings about differences in men and women in various relational characteristics.

TRAINING IMPLICATIONS

The evidence presented in this chapter suggests that a strong real relationship is an important ingredient of successful psychotherapy. From this, we encourage psychotherapy training programs and psychotherapy supervisors to focus on the real relationship and its strengthening and weakening over time.

Teaching the real relationship to trainees is a complicated endeavor because the concept is often experienced as highly nebulous, nonverbal, and difficult to grasp in concrete terms. In comparison, for example, the working alliance, is more easily explained and tangible to trainees, as it is often defined as agreement on the goals and tasks of therapy and the working relationship. The real relationship (although it has been operationalized for research purposes) is something that must be experienced to be truly known.

We suggest that training in the real relationship consists of both a didactic and experiential component. For example, in practicum and internship classes, readings on the real relationship can be accompanied by students completing a case studies on a patient with whom they have experienced a strong real relationship and one with whom they have experienced a weak one. On a more basic level, it is often helpful to have students think of a relationship in their personal lives in which they shared a high degree of genuineness and have felt truly known, and how this experience, in turn, affected their sense of self and the overall relationship.

Another factor that complicates training students on the real relationship is that it is often difficult for students to separate transference/countertransference reactions from the real relationship and, at the same time, understand that both these phenomena can be true at the same time. That is, client and therapist may be smack in the middle of a transference–countertransference reenactment and at the same time have real and genuine feelings for one another's authentic self. We have found it helpful for supervisors and instructors to share with students their own experiences with patients when it was, for example, difficult for them to separate a countertransference from real relationship reaction to a patient, or when they had a strong feeling of both at the same time. Along these lines, we have seen many trainees unintentionally dismiss patients' feelings toward them as purely transferential, when doing so (although it was partly true) minimized the client's real experience of connection to the therapist. Thus, we believe it a critical part of training to underscore to trainees that the therapeutic relationship is complex and multifaceted, and to use real life case examples as demonstrations.

Lastly, we believe it is essential to teach trainees that while self-disclosure is one avenue toward a strong real relationship, it is not the only avenue, and sometimes taking this road may get you lost. On the one hand, depending on the specific therapeutic situation and the therapist's theoretical orientation, self-disclosure, or therapeutic immediacy, may of course strengthen the real relationship, as the therapist makes himself or herself vulnerable and human and models genuineness and authenticity for the patient. On the other hand, we have seen many trainees rush to self-disclosure out of their own performance anxiety, need to be liked, or confusion over their role and boundaries in the therapeutic relationship. Here, self-disclosure may actually hinder the development of a strong real relationship.

The real relationship may be facilitated by what the therapist says, but it is also a product of who the therapist *is*. It is vital to teach trainees that much of what we communicate to our patients (and vice versa) about who we are is in fact not verbal at all. A useful skill for trainees to develop is to be able to accurately assess the strength of the real relationship. In this regard, the real relationship inventories can be used as a training tool. For example, trainees can watch a therapy session putting themselves in the place of the client or the therapist and rate the session using the real relationship inventory. Trainees can compare ratings and discuss the differences among their ratings. It may be particularly helpful if sessions ratings of the real relationship by the patient and therapist are available for comparison.

THERAPEUTIC PRACTICES

How can practitioners foster and develop a strong real relationship? From one vantage point, the real relationship simply is. The participants in the therapy relationship are whom they are, and nothing can be manipulated to strengthen the real relationship.

The empirical evidence suggests that the real relationship does change across sessions, usually strengthening (Gelso et al, 2012; Kivlighan et al., 2016), but this change may represent a natural evolution that comes about through the participants getting to know each other more deeply. This strengthening may be a result of the similarities between therapist and patient in terms of human qualities, for example, sense of humor, basic interests and values, and sense of attunement to others. When therapist and patient are "part of the same tribe" (Gelso & Silberberg, 2016) in these ways, they more likely take to each other as persons, thus paving the way for a strong real relationship. From a second vantage point, although a portion of the real relationship may simply exist and naturally unfold, there are therapist actions that facilitate a strong real relationship. These include:

- *Seek to grasp empathically the patient and he or sher inner experience.* Evidence indicates that therapist empathy is significantly related to the strength of the real relationship (Fuertes et al., 2007). The therapist's successful understanding of the experience of the patient facilitates the realism element of the real relationship on the therapist's side, and because feeling seen and understood accurately can be so intimate, it fosters the patient's sense of personal connection to his or her therapist. In addition, it is likely that therapist empathy begets the strengthening of empathy in the patient, and patient empathy fosters seeing the therapist as he or she truly is, thus deepening the realism aspect of the real relationship on the patient's side.
- *Manage countertransference.* Fundamental elements of the therapist's effectiveness in managing how his or her own unresolved conflicts bleed into the treatment (managing countertransference) include self-understanding, managing one's own anxiety, and grasping the boundaries between oneself and the patient (see Chapter 15, this volume, on managing countertransference). All of these behaviors serve to deepen seeing the patient as he or she is (rather than as projections of the therapist's issues) and being genuine with the patient. They also, in turn, foster the patient seeing the therapist as he or she is and being genuine with the therapist.
- *Share reactions with the patient.* Although therapist self-disclosure is certainly an imperfect indication of genuineness, it does relate modestly to the strength of the real relationship (Ain, 2008, 2011). Well-timed disclosures (including disclosures of feelings within the therapeutic relationship and about the patient) highly relevant to the patient's needs (rather than the therapist's needs) foster therapist genuineness in the patient's eyes.
- *Explain when not sharing.* Despite the connection of therapist self-disclosure to the real relationship and genuineness, we know from clinical experience and research evidence that therapists can be genuine while being relatively nondisclosing. One of the factors that fosters the patient's perceptions of therapist genuineness when not disclosing involves telling the patient just why the therapist is not disclosing. When the therapist clarifies why he or she is not disclosing, the therapist is, in fact, disclosing at a different level, what might be seen as a meta-level.
- *Be consistent and constant.* At the most fundamental level, the patient's sense that he or she could count on his or her clinician to simply be there, and be there on time,

fosters a sense that the therapist can be personally trusted and that the therapist is genuinely interested in the patient as a person as well as a patient. This seems particularly crucial for patients who are highly vulnerable. In addition, consistency is a key factor in helping the patient trust the therapist as a person, and this includes consistency between the therapist's verbal and nonverbal behavior, as well as between each of these over time. This consistency also provides credibility to the real relationship that the therapist is offering to the patient. It fosters the patient's sense that the therapist can be counted on as a person and is congruent as a person.

ACKNOWLEDGEMENT

We thank Ms. Erin M. Hill and Ms. Jillian Lechner for their editorial and research contributions to this chapter.

REFERENCES

References marked with an asterisk indicate studies included in the meta-analyses.

Ain, S. C. (2008). *Chipping away at the blank screen: Therapist self-disclosure and the real relationship* (Unpublished doctoral dissertation). University of Maryland, College Park.

*Ain, S. C. (2011). *The real relationship, therapist self-disclosure, and treatment progress: A study of psychotherapy dyads* (Unpublished doctoral dissertation). University of Maryland, College Park.

*Baumgartner, S. (1995). *Systematic effects of participant role on evaluation of the psychotherapy session*. Madison: University of Wisconsin.

*Bhatia, A., & Gelso, C. J. (2017). The termination phase: Therapists' perspective on the therapeutic relationship and outcome. *Psychotherapy, 54*(1), 76–87. https://www.doi.org/10.1037/pst0000100

*Bhatia, A., & Gelso, C. J. (2018). Therapists' perspective on the therapeutic relationship: Examining a tripartite model. *Counselling Psychology Quarterly, 31*(3), 271–293.

Bordin, E. (1979). The generalizability of the psychoanalytic concept of the working alliance. *Psychotherapy: Theory, Research and Practice, 16*, 252–260.

*Cooper, H., Hedges, L., & Valentine, J. (2009). *The handbook of research synthesis and meta-analysis* (2nd ed.). New York, NY: Russell Sage Foundation.

Couch, A. S. (1999). Therapeutic functions of the real relationship in psychoanalysis. *The Psychiatric Study of the Child, 54*(1), 130–168.

Curtis, R., Field, C., Knaan-Kostman, I., & Mannix, K. (2004). What 75 psychoanalysts found helpful and hurtful in their own analyses. *Psychoanalytic Psychology, 21*(2), 183–202.

*Eugster, S. L., & Wampold, B. E. (1996). Systematic effects of participant role on evaluation of the psychotherapy session. *Journal of Consulting and Clinical Psychology, 64*(5), 1020–1028.

*Eun Ju, L.(2015). *The unfolding of the real relationship, working alliance and the outcome* (Doctoral dissertation). Sookmyung Women's University,Seoul, South Korea. Manuscript in preparation.

Freud, S. (1919). Lines of advance in psychoanalytic therapy. In J. Stratchy (Ed.), *Standard edition of the complete works of Sigmund Freud* (pp. 157–168). London, England: Hogarth.

Freud, S. (1937). Analysis terminable and interminable. In J. Stratchy (Ed.), *Standard edition of the complete works of Sigmund Freud* (pp. 209–253). London, England: Hogarth.

Freud, A. (1954). The widening scope of indications for psychoanalysis discussion. *Journal of the American Psychological Association, 2*(4), 607–620.

*Fuertes, J. N., Ganley, J., & Moore, M. (2016). *Real relationship, therapist self-disclosure, attachment, and outcome in psychotherapy.* Manuscript submitted for publication.

*Fuertes, J. N., Gelso, C. J., Owen, J. J., & Cheng, D. (2013). Real relationship, working alliance, transference/countertransference and outcome in time-limited counseling and psychotherapy. *Counselling Psychology Quarterly, 26*(3–4), 294–312. https://www.doi.org/10.1080/09515070.2013.845548

*Fuertes, J. N., Mislowack, A., Brown, S., Gur-Arie, S., Wilkinson, S., & Gelso, C. J. (2007). Correlates of the real relationship in psychotherapy: A study of dyads. *Psychotherapy Research, 17*(4), 423–430.

Gelso, C. J. (2009). The real relationship in a postmodern world: Theoretical and empirical explorations. *Psychotherapy Research, 19*(3), 253–264.

Gelso, C. J. (2011). *The real relationship in psychotherapy: The hidden foundation of change.* Washington, DC: American Psychological Association Press.

Gelso, C. J. (2014). A tripartite model of the therapeutic relationship: Theory, research, and practice. *Psychotherapy Research, 24*(2), 117–131.

Gelso, C. J., & Carter, J. A. (1985). The relationship in counseling and therapy: Components, consequences and theoretical antecedents. *The Counseling Psychologist, 13*, 155–243.

Gelso, C. J., & Carter, J. A. (1994). Components of the psychotherapy relationship: Their interaction and unfolding during treatment. *Journal of Counseling Psychology, 41*, 296–306.

Gelso, C. J., & Hayes, J. A. (1998). *The psychotherapy relationship: Theory, research, and practice.* Hoboken, NJ: Wiley.

*Gelso, C. J., & Johnson, D. H. (1983). *Explorations in time-limited counseling and psychotherapy.* New York, NY: Columbia University Press.

*Gelso, C. J., Kelley, F. A., Fuertes, J. N., Marmarosh, C., Holmes, S. E., Costa, C., & Hancock, G. R. (2005). Measuring the real relationship in psychotherapy: Initial validation of the therapist form. *Journal of Counseling Psychology, 52*(4), 640–649.

*Gelso, C. J., Kivlighan, D. M., Busa-Knepp, J., Spiegel, E. B., Ain, S., Hummel, A. M., . . . Markin, R. D. (2012). The unfolding of the real relationship and the outcome of brief psychotherapy. *Journal of Counseling Psychology, 59*(4), 495–506. https://www.doi.org/10.1037/a0029838

Gelso, C. J., & Silberberg, A. (2016). Strengthening the real relationship: What is a psychotherapist to do? *Practice Innovations, 1*(3), 154–163.

Greenson, R. R. (1967). *The technique and practice of psychoanalysis.* New York, NY: International Universities Press.

*Gullo, S., Lo Coco, G., & Gelso, C. (2012). Early and later predictors of outcome in brief therapy: The role of real relationship. *Journal of Clinical Psychology, 68*(6), 614–619. https://www.doi.org/10.1002/jclp.21860

Hill, C. E., Gelso, C. J., Chui, H., Spangler, P. T., Hummel, A., Huang, T., . . . Miles, J. R. (2014). To be or not to be immediate with clients: The use and perceived effects of immediacy in psychodynamic/interpersonal psychotherapy. *Psychotherapy Research, 24*(3), 299–315.

Hill, C. E., Sim, W., Spangler, P., Stahl, J., Sullivan, C., & Teyber, E. (2008). Therapist immediacy in brief psychotherapy: Case study II. *Psychotherapy: Theory, Research, Practice, Training, 45*(3), 298–315.

Horvath, A. O., Del Re, A. C., Flückiger, C., & Symonds, D. (2011). Alliance in individual psychotherapy. *Psychotherapy, 48*(1), 9–16.

Kasper, L. B., Hill, C. E., & Kivlighan, D. M. Jr. (2008). Therapist immediacy in brief psychotherapy: Case study I. *Psychotherapy: Theory, Research, Practice, Training, 45*(3), 281–297.

*Kelley, F. A., Gelso, C. J., Fuertes, J. N., Marmarosh, C., & Lanier, S. H. (2010). The real relationship inventory: Development and psychometric investigation of the client form. *Psychotherapy: Theory, Research, Practice, Training, 47*(4), 540–553.

Kelley, F. A. (2015). The therapy relationship with lesbian and gay clients. *Psychotherapy, 52*, 113–118. http://dx.doi/10.1037/a0037958

*Kivlighan, D. M., Gelso, C. J., Ain, S., Hummel, A.M., & Markin, R. D. (2015). The therapist, the client, and the real relationship: An actor-partner interdependence analysis of treatment outcome. *Journal of Counseling Psychology, 62*(2), 314–320. https://www.doi.org/10.1037/cou0000012

*Kivlighan, D. M., Hill, C.E., Gelso, C. J., & Baumann, E. (2016). Working alliance, real relationship, session quality, and client improvement in psychodynamic psychotherapy: A longitudinal actor partner interdependence model. *Journal of Counseling Psychology, 63*(2), 149–161. https://www.doi.org/10.1037/cou0000134

*Kivlighan, D. M. Jr., Baumann, E. C., Gelso, C. J. & Hill, C. E. (2014). *Symptom change and between therapist and within therapist variability in third session intercepts and linear change slopes for longitudinal ratings of alliance and real relationship.* Paper presented at the meeting of the Society for Psychotherapy Research, Copenhagen, Denmark.

Kivlighan, D. M. Jr., Kline, K., Gelso, C. J., & Hill, C. E. (2017). Congruence and discrepancy between working alliance and real relationship: Variance decomposition and response surface analyses. *Journal of Counseling Psychology, 64*(4), 394–409.

Knox, S., Hess, S. A., Petersen, D. A., & Hill, C. E. (1997). A qualitative analysis of client perceptions of the effects of helpful therapist self-disclosure in long-term therapy. *Journal of Counseling Psychology, 44*(3), 274–283.

Ledermann, T., & Kenny, D. A. (2012). The common fate model for dyadic data: Variations of theoretically important but underutilized model. *Journal of Family Psychology, 26*(1), 140–148.

*Lee, E. J. (2017). *The unfolding of the working alliance, the real relationship and the outcome* (Unpublished doctoral dissertation). Sookmyung Women's University, Seoul, South Korea.

Li, X., Kivlighan, D. M. Jr., Gelso, C. J., & Hill, C. E. (2016, November). *Longitudinal relationships among the real relationship, working alliance and session outcome: A common fate model.* Paper presentedat the 2016 North American Society of Psychotherapy Research Conference, Berkeley, CA.

*Lo Coco, G., Gullo, S., Prestano, C., & Gelso, C. J. (2011). Relation of the real relationship and the working alliance to the outcome of brief psychotherapy. *Psychotherapy, 48*(4), 359–367.

*Marmarosh, C. L., Gelso, C. J., Markin, R. D., Majors, R., Mallery, C., & Choi, J. (2009). The real relationship in psychotherapy: Relationships to adult attachments, working alliance, transference, and therapy outcome. *Journal of Counseling Psychology, 56*(3), 337–350. https://www.doi.org/10.1037/a0015169

Morales, K. S., Keum, B. T., Kivlighan, Jr., D. M., Hill, C. E., & Gelso, C. J. (2018). Therapist effects due to client racial/ethnic status when examining linear growth for client-and therapist-rated working alliance and real relationship. *Psychotherapy, 55*(1), 9–19.

*Owen, J. J., Tao, K., Leach, M. M., & Rodolfa, E. (2011). Clients' perceptions of their psychotherapists' multicultural orientation. *Psychotherapy, 48*(3), 274–282.

*Perez Rojas, A. (2015). *Does the acculturation of international student therapists predict the process of psychotherapy with U.S. clients? An exploratory study* (Unpublished doctoral dissertation). University of Maryland, College Park.

Perls, F. (1969). *Gestalt therapy verbatim*. Lafayette, CA: Real People Press.

Rogers, C. (1957). The necessary and sufficient conditions of therapeutic personality change. *Journal of Consulting Psychology, 21*(2), 95–103.

Wampold, W. E., & Budge, S. L. (2012). The relationship and its relationship to the common and specific factors of psychotherapy. *The Counseling Psychologist, 40*(4), 601–623.

Yalom, I. (2002). *The gift of therapy*. New York, NY: HarperCollins.

11

SELF-DISCLOSURE AND IMMEDIACY

Clara E. Hill, Sarah Knox, and Kristen G. Pinto-Coelho

Therapist use self-disclosure (TSD) and immediacy (Im) has long been controversial. Psychoanalytic theorists (Curtis, 1981, 1982; Greenson, 1967) traditionally urged analysts to remain neutral blank screens, allowing clients to project their material onto the clinician. More recent relational psychoanalysts (Eagle, 2011; Levenson, 2010; McWilliams, 2004), by contrast, have suggested that therapists can facilitate the therapeutic process by disclosing and talking about the relationship. Humanistic theorists (Bugental, 1965; Farber, 2006; Jourard, 1971), having always advocated therapist transparency and genuineness, have typically viewed TSD and Im as curative elements of the therapeutic process. Cognitive therapists (e.g., Beck et al., 1979) traditionally view the use of TSD and Im as beneficial to address problems that arise in the relationship.

In addition to such theoretical propositions, however, we need empirical evidence about the effectiveness of TSD and Im to guide its use. There has been a great deal of research interest in TSD, but much of this literature has been analogue and correlational, making it difficult to draw conclusions about clinical consequences. Research on Im is more recent and has been based on methods relevant to therapy with actual clients, yet this literature has not been subjected to as much review as has the TSD literature (Hill & Knox, 2009). Furthermore, the consequences for the two skills have not been compared. The purpose of the present chapter is therefore to conduct an original qualitative meta-analysis of the extant empirical literature to determine what we know about the clinical consequences of TSD and Im in psychotherapy with actual clients.

DEFINITIONS AND FREQUENCY OF USE

TSD can be defined as "therapist statements that reveal something personal about the therapist" (Hill & Knox, 2002, p. 256). We further narrow this definition to involve a *verbal* revelation about the therapist's life or person *outside of therapy*. We explicitly excluded nonverbal self-disclosures (e.g., a family photo on the desk) because we sought to focus on verbal statements that therapists share with clients. We excluded disclosures within or about the therapeutic relationship because we consider these to be Im (see following discussion). TSDs can be about feelings (e.g., "I get angry when someone pushes in front of me like that"), similarities (e.g., "I also had an anxiety disorder"), insight (e.g., "I realized that I have difficulty forming a relationship because my parents had such a bad relationship"), or strategies (e.g., "I try to eat fruits and vegetables and walk every day"). Therapists use TSD to establish a bond, to help clients feel normal or understood, and to encourage more client disclosure (Hill, 2014). Other terms used to describe this construct include self-revealing disclosures, extra-therapy disclosures, self-disclosing disclosures, and transparency.

Im can be defined as "a discussion of the therapeutic relationship by both the therapist and client in the here-and-now, involving more than social chitchat" (e.g., "It's nice to see you"; Hill Gelso et al., 2014, p. 299; Hill & Knox, 2014) or "any discussion within the therapy session about the relationship between therapist and patient that occurs in the here-and-now, as well as any processing of what occurs in the here-and-now patient-therapist interaction" (p. 188) (Kuutmann & Hilsenroth, 2012). Im occurs when therapists talk about the therapy relationship in the present moment. Im can include asking the client about immediate feelings and thoughts (e.g., "How are you feeling talking about this with me?"), statements of immediate therapist feelings (e.g., "I'm feeling annoyed that you are frequently late for sessions"), drawing parallels with other relationships (e.g., "You mentioned that no one seems to care about you . . . I wonder if you feel that I don't care about you?"), making the covert overt (e.g., "You seem so quiet . . . I wonder how you feel about being here?"), acknowledgments of a breach in the relationship (e.g., "We seem to have reached an impasse"), and attempts to repair ruptures (e.g., "I apologize for saying something offensive to you"). Intentions for Im include encouraging the client to express unstated feelings; attempting to negotiate, enhance, or repair the therapy relationship; and modeling appropriate ways to interact with others during conflict (Hill, 2014). Other terms that have been used to describe this construct include metacommunication, relational events, processing the therapy relationship, discussions about the here-and-now in the here-and-now, in vivo work, and present-focused work.

In both TSD and Im, therapists use themselves as part of the intervention. With TSD, therapists refers to the self outside of therapy sessions; with Im, therapists rely on their own perceptions and reactions within the therapy relationship. In both, therapists may feel vulnerable bringing themselves into the relationship instead of focusing exclusively on the client. When using such methods, therapists are not blank screens in a one-sided relationship, but rather are part of the interaction in a two-sided relationship.

Thus, both interventions are defined rather broadly, can be used for a variety of intentions, and may lead to a range of clinical consequences. Furthermore, both mimic other interventions (e.g., a disclosure of feelings is similar to a reflection of feelings; an inquiry about the relationship is a type of open question). They differ, however, in that TSDs tend to be brief and not generate further discussion (Pinto-Coelho et al., 2016), whereas Im tends to involve a number of interchanges as the therapist and client talk about the relationship (Hill et al., 2014).

In a previous chapter reviewing studies that used the Hill Verbal Response Modes Category System to code therapist interventions, TSD (which included both TSD and Im) was coded in 0% to 4% of all therapist response units (e.g., sentences) of therapy sessions (Hill, 1986). In a multiple case study, eight experienced therapists across a range of theoretical orientations used TSD (including both TSD and Im) in 1% of all therapist response units (Hill et al., 1988). In the three case studies (all with good outcomes) with experienced therapists explicitly selected because they used Im frequently as part of their practice (Hill et al., 2008; Kasper et al., 2008; Mayotte-Blum et al., 2012), Im was used extensively (12%, 34%, and 38%, respectively). In contrast, Im was used 5% of the time by nine psychodynamic-interpersonal doctoral student therapists in 16 cases (Hill et al., 2014), and an average of 5% for one acceptance and commitment therapist with three clients (Berman et al., 2012). In summary, across most of the studies, TSD and Im were typically used infrequently (0% to 5%), but Im was used relatively frequently (12% to 38% of all utterances) by three very experienced therapists who were interpersonally-oriented.

MEASURES

TSD and Im have most often been coded in research as verbal response modes (VRMs). Trained judges code these interventions as present or absent in sentences or speaking turns in taped or transcribed sessions, using clearly defined categories that include TSD/Im (e.g., Hill, 1978; Stiles, 1979). The advantages of this method are that TSD/Im can be clearly identified as present in the session, its context can be investigated, the manner in which it is presented can be assessed, and the observable consequences can be determined. Disadvantages are that agreement among judges is often marginal because it is difficult to distinguish among VRMs. Furthermore, VRMs often do not appear clinically relevant because they focus on grammatical form and ignore intent, quality, or manner of delivery. Additional disadvantages are that coding VRMs requires transcripts and is time consuming. Finally, the inner experiences of therapists and clients cannot be assessed, which is crucial given that clients often conceal negative reactions, and therapists often cannot detect these hidden reactions (Hill et al., 1992, 1993; Rennie, 1994). In addition, we know from personal experience as therapists and supervisors that therapists also hide negative reactions from clients, although such experiences have not been the frequent focus of empirical investigation.

Second, TSD and Im have been assessed by providing clients or therapists with a definition, typically at the beginning of an interview, and having them retrospectively report specific instances of these interventions within sessions or treatments. An advantage of this method is that the inner experiences of clients and therapists can be assessed, and these experiences are often different from those of judges watching the sessions. Thus, these measures probably are more valid because they reflect experiences of the participants in the room. A disadvantage is that bias occurs in retrospective recall, given that feelings and reactions often change over time (e.g., an immediate reaction might be subsequently altered as the client further reflects on the experience during an interview). Furthermore, participants may absorb something different from what the therapist intended (e.g., the therapist may disclose and the client may not experience it as feeling understood). An additional disadvantage is that it is difficult to identify the location in a session when recalled TSD or Im occurred, thus making it challenging to assess the interventions' context and therapists' manner of delivery.

A third type of measure used for assessing TSD and Im has been estimates of how much they occurred during an entire session. In this method, trained judges listen to entire sessions and estimate how frequently or how well the therapist used these interventions. Three widely used session-level measures are the Multitheoretical List of Therapeutic Interventions (McCarthy & Barber, 2009), the Psychotherapy Q-Set (Jones & Pulos, 1993), and the Comparative Psychotherapy Process Scale (Hilsenroth et al., 2005). For example, in the Psychotherapy Q-Set, TSD is assessed by the item "Therapist self-discloses," and Im is assessed by the item "The therapy relationship is a focus of discussion." An advantage of this session-level method is that the relative occurrence of many techniques can be measured in an economical manner since transcripts are not required and coding takes little more than the hour required to watch the session. Disadvantages are that the individual interventions are not identified in sessions, and thus context and manner of delivery cannot be assessed, and it is not possible to identify the specific related clinical consequences. In fact, judges might base their judgments on an overall impression of the therapist's behavior rather than on whether the specific behaviors occurred (e.g., judges may rate that the therapist seemed open and approachable rather than that the therapist made a specific verbal disclosure). Thus, conclusions rely on the subjective assessment of judges who were not in the room and who often respond to the interventions based on their personal histories. Note that these session-level measures can also sometimes be completed after sessions by therapists directly involved in the treatment. Although therapist ratings indeed reflect the inner experiences of one of the participants, recall of specific interventions and consequences would be difficult unless the therapist relied on an audio or video replay to make the ratings.

CLINICAL EXAMPLES

To give readers as sense of how these interventions are used in practice, we provide a few examples. First is a helpful TSD reported during a qualitative interview with a 33-year-old female client who had been seeing her male therapist for 11 years (see next section Landmark Studies for more detail about this study). The client reported that early in their relationship, she had difficulty trusting her therapist and thus encountered difficulty in opening up to him. She expressed confusion about what the relationship should be and often tested her therapist to see whether he would be trustworthy. At times, she needed him to be responsive, and he was not. She did, however, view him as patient, open, and reliable and stated that she felt comfortable with him right away. At the time of the disclosure, she thought he would not be able to understand her struggle with drugs, so she asked him if he had ever tried street drugs. The client believed that the therapist disclosed to her that he had tried street drugs because he had no other recourse and wanted to stop the argument. This disclosure shocked the client ("It stopped the argument cold"), made her rethink her assumptions and stereotypes, enabled her to recognize the benefits of healthy disagreement, and allowed her to use the therapy relationship as a learning ground for other relationships in her life. She thus became more assertive in expressing her needs and opinions rationally. This disclosure also challenged her perspective of her therapist, making him more human and more similar to her, thereby increasing her respect for him, making her feel closer to him, and balancing the relationship: "At that moment, it made him a lot more human than I was feeling at the time . . . and changed the whole perspective immediately . . . and made him sort of a kindred spirit in a way" (Knox et al., 1997, p. 280).

The following example of a helpful Im interaction comes from an investigation of Im events in psychotherapy sessions (Hill et al., 2014). The client was a 32-year-old divorced and remarried man in treatment with a single 27-year-old female therapist. A good example of negotiating the relationship before any problems arise occurred in the intake session, when the therapist asked the client how he felt working with her, given that she was younger and female. He said that it was a little startling, although he knew that younger people had expertise that he did not. The client then asked the therapist how it felt to work with him, given that he was older than she. The therapist said it was different, but she felt they could work at it together. At the end of the intake session, when the therapist again checked in with the client, he said "It was fine and he felt like he could talk to her."

Another example of using Im to address problems as they arise in relationships occurred in session 38, after the client had shared a lengthy story. After the therapist gently challenged the client to talk about his feelings, the client "bristled" because he said he could not express his feelings quickly. The therapist asked if it was okay to ask about the client's reactions, to which the client responded that it was okay but that he would probably "bristle," as had just occurred. In response to a query about what she should do if the client indeed bristled, the client said to "just let it go." After further probing, however, the client admitted that he did not like to be interrupted when telling a story. They agreed to keep track of what was going on between them. These examples illustrate how Im was used regularly and productively throughout this therapy to monitor the relationship.

LANDMARK STUDIES

To illustrate how TSD and Im have been investigated, we highlight three studies. The first study involved an examination of TSD and Im combined, the second was an investigation of TSD, and the third of Im.

A Sequential Analysis of TSD and Im

The Hill et al. (1988) study was important because the unexpected results sparked our current interest in TSD and Im. In this naturalistic study of eight cases of brief psychotherapy, clients and therapists watched videotapes immediately after sessions and rated the helpfulness of each therapist speaking turn. Then, a team of trained judges used transcripts to code what therapists said into VRMs (including TSDs, which were broadly defined as anything the therapist said that was personal, thereby including both TSD and Im). Another team of trained judges coded the client experiencing level in each client speaking turn. TSDs occurred in only 1% of therapist speaking turns, indicating that these interventions rarely occurred.

The authors empirically tested three different methods for examining the effects of therapist interventions: correlations between the frequency of usage of techniques with treatment outcome, correlations between the frequency of usage of techniques with session outcome, and sequential analyses of the immediate effects of techniques in subsequent speaking turns. Not surprisingly, different results were found for these analyses. Frequency of TSD was not significantly related to either session or treatment outcome, although significant results were found in the sequential analyses.

Specifically, when looking across all cases (not accounting for nesting effects), TSD was associated with the highest client helpfulness rating and the highest levels of client experiencing, but the lowest therapist helpfulness rating of all VRMs. Hill et al. (1988) speculated that TSDs may have provided clients with a glimpse that their therapists were human and also had problems, and it might have shifted the power balance so that clients felt less vulnerable. Furthermore, the researchers speculated that the infrequent occurrence of TSD may have made clients value these interventions. The authors speculated that low helpfulness ratings by therapists arose because they felt vulnerable and TSDs were discouraged in training.

Intrigued by these findings, Hill and colleagues (1989) further examined the cases and found that almost all of the TSDs were delivered by three of the eight therapists. In addition, they also discovered that the interventions included within the data set were often quite dissimilar (some were disclosing and others involving, some were reassuring and others challenging). Thus, these findings alerted them that TSD is a broad, ill-defined intervention that is infrequently used, rated as very helpful by clients, and not rated as very helpful by therapists. These provocative findings made them want to learn more about TSD.

A Qualitative Study of Client Perceptions of TSDs

In another study (Knox et al., 1997), 13 adult psychotherapy clients in long-term therapy were interviewed via a semi-structured protocol regarding their experiences with TSD (although the definition provided included both TSD and Im, all of the helpful events involved only TSD). Data were analyzed using consensual qualitative research (CQR). Results indicated that helpful TSDs occurred when clients discussed important personal issues (e.g., discussing difficult adolescent experiences, questioning whether their therapist could understand their struggles), were perceived as intended to normalize or reassure (e.g., to ease the client's feelings about an upcoming medical test), and consisted of disclosures of therapists' personal non-immediate information (e.g., sharing information about childhood vacations and hobbies, revealing having experienced struggles similar to those of the client). The disclosures yielded positive consequences for clients, including insight or a new perspective from which to make changes (e.g., clients began to see solutions to their struggles, or used the perspective offered by the TSD to better communicate with partners), an improved or more equalized therapy relationship (e.g., sensing the therapist as "a kindred spirit"), normalization, and reassurance (e.g., clients understood the universality of their struggles and became less anxious, clients felt less alone and "less crazy").

Knox and colleagues (1997) asked these same clients about unhelpful TSDs, although these data were not published in the original article, 8 of the 13 clients reported that unhelpful TSDs occurred (e.g., client discussing her relationship with her mother and daughter) and also when the therapist did something to upset the client (e.g., therapist frequently fell asleep during client's sessions). The TSDs were perceived by clients as related to the therapist's need or concern (e.g., client believed that therapist was frustrated with client, and perhaps with client's daughter and therapist's own daughter) or intended to normalize/reassure (e.g., therapist sought to normalize client's struggles and help client be less negative about himself). These TSDs consisted of therapists' disclosures about their immediate experiences (e.g., therapist denied falling asleep and explained the appearance of such as his response to painful or intense material), indirect nonverbal TSDs that occurred outside of session (e.g., client saw a sign congratulating the therapist and his wife on their new baby), and TSDs of personal, nonimmediate information about the therapist's family (e.g., therapist shared how she tried to work through similar difficulties with her own daughter). These disclosures yielded negative consequences in terms of clients' negative reactions (e.g., felt placated and hurt, thought therapist was "bullshitting") and a negative impact on the therapy (e.g., client remained upset about the disclosure for a few sessions and felt like leaving therapy).

This study was important because it was the first to investigate TSDs using a qualitative methodology and to study the client perspective. Thus, this study yielded not only new information about TSDs but also provided a new methodology for studying them.

Case Studies of Im in Psychodynamic/
Interpersonal Psychotherapy

Three published case studies of Im in psychotherapy (Hill et al., 2008; Kasper et al., 2008; Mayotte-Blum et al., 2012) set the stage and provided the methodology for a larger multiple case study of Im by Hill et al. (2014). In this latter study, judges tracked the use of Im in 16 cases of open-ended psychodynamic/interpersonal psychotherapy. Judges watched all sessions identified by previous judges as involving Im and verified that, in fact, each of the events involved Im. They then coded each instance for length, initiator, type (negotiation of tasks and goals of therapy, exploration of unexpressed feelings or making the covert overt, drawing parallels between other relationships and the therapy relationship, and attempts to repair ruptures by talking about what is going on between the therapist and client), depth, appropriateness, resolution, and quality (the latter four variables used 5-point scales: 1 = poor, 5 = excellent).

Most immediacy events were initiated by therapists and involved exploration of unexpressed or covert client feelings. The average session had fewer than one immediacy event, and the average event lasted about two minutes. In posttherapy interviews, clients indicated remembering and profiting from Im: They said things like, "Very touched," "Wasn't expecting it," "Felt closer," and "Definitely appreciated." The most typical clinical consequences were clients expressing feelings about the therapist or therapy, the establishment or clarification of boundaries, and clients opening up and gaining insight.

The authors also examined client attachment style as a possible moderator of the results. With clients who were more fearfully than securely attached, Im events were higher in quality, longer, initiated more often by therapists than clients, and more focused on feelings. The authors speculated that therapists had to take more initiative and work more gently with fearfully than with securely attached clients.

This study provides a model of how to study a therapist intervention in multiple cases in a systematic manner. Using a case study approach allows for researchers to include context and data from therapists and clients from post-therapy interviews, along with careful analyses of moment-to-moment interactions. Familiarity with the entire case also allowed researchers to investigate both short-term and longer-term clinical consequences.

RESULTS OF PREVIOUS REVIEWS

In the first edition of this book, Hill and Knox (2002) conducted a narrative review of the analogue and naturalistic studies of TSD. Focusing here on the small section of the review about the consequences of TSD in actual therapy, they concluded that TSD was perceived as helpful with regard to immediate outcome, although the effects on ultimate treatment outcome were unclear. This review was narrative rather than meta-analytic and the majority of the studies reviewed were analogue.

Subsequently, Hill and Knox (2009) provided a narrative review of specific therapist interventions (including Im but not TSD) that are effective for processing the therapeutic relationship. They found that Im was useful for resolving misunderstandings and ruptures in therapy, that clients felt validated and cared for when the therapist expressed positive feelings toward the client, that Im helped with negotiation of the therapy relationship, and that Im facilitated the client having a corrective relational experience, opened up the client to a new type of relationship, and reduced client defenses. The negative effects of Im were rare: Prominent instances included clients feeling puzzled by the intervention, feeling pressured to respond, and feeling awkward and confused about the therapist caring for them beyond the professional bond.

In a narrative review of 14 select studies of psychotherapy, Ackerman and Hilsenroth (2001) found that when TSD reveals too much of therapists' own personal conflicts, it may threaten therapy boundaries and weaken the alliance. No mention was made about the clinical consequences of Im (but to our knowledge, no studies had been published on Im at that time).

More recently, Henretty and colleagues (2014) conducted a meta-analysis of 53 studies comparing TSD to non-TSD. They noted, however, that only 6% of the studies in their data set examined therapy sessions; that is, 94% of the studies were analogue. They did not separate the meta-analytic results for the analogue versus naturalistic studies. Overall, TSD was found to have a favorable impact on clients, with clients having favorable perceptions of disclosing counselors and rating themselves more likely to disclose to them. Because we required in our current meta-analysis that studies had to involve actual psychotherapy sessions (see below), we do not review this meta-analysis further here.

We found no existing meta-analyses that directly addressed our questions about the clinical consequences of TSD and Im. Thus, there is clearly a need for reviewing this literature using more than narrative reviews.

QUALITATIVE META-ANALYTIC REVIEW

Our task was to meta-analytically review the literature on the clinical consequences of TSD and Im in therapy. In this section, we describe the inclusion and exclusion criteria we used to determine which studies to include in the review, our rationale for doing a qualitative meta-analysis (QMA), the procedures used in the QMA, and the results of the QMA.

Inclusion and Exclusion Criteria

In our review, we included only studies published in English. We used four steps to identify possible studies: (a) we included studies identified in earlier reviews; (b) we manually examined the last 15 years of *Journal of Counseling Psychology, Journal of Consulting and Clinical Psychology, The Counseling Psychologist, Psychotherapy Research, Psychotherapy*, and *Counselling Psychology Quarterly*; (c) we searched reference lists of relevant published articles; (d) we conducted several PsycInfo searches using the following terms: disclosure, self-disclosure, self-revealing disclosure, self-disclosing disclosure, extra-therapy disclosure, transparency, immediacy, metacommunication, relational events, therapeutic processes, here and now, and present focus; and (e) we sent a query to the listservs of Society for Psychotherapy Research and Society for Counseling Psychology listservs as well as to specific authors who had conducted research in these areas asking for published or unpublished studies in this area written in English. In terms of unpublished data, we identified and included data about unhelpful TSDs that had not been published in the Knox et al. (1997) article and a study by Pinto-Coelho et al. (2018).

To be included in our pool of studies, TSD and/or Im had to be specifically identified as occurring in psychotherapy sessions using one of two methods: (a) coded by trained judges or (b) clients or therapists were interviewed/surveyed and asked to identify specific TSDs or Ims that they recalled from therapy sessions (see the previous section on Measures for more description). Our rationale was that only if specific TSDs/Ims were identified could their clinical consequences be specifically linked to the methods.

Each study also had to clearly state to how many of the participants the consequences applied (e.g., "78% of the clients reported . . ." vs. a vague statement suggesting that TSD/Im was helpful without identifying for how much of the sample such a statement was true). Relatedly, one sample in Safran and Muran's (1996) multisample study was eliminated because the authors stated that the results applied to 15 sessions, but we could not determine how many cases were involved (and the authors did not remember when contacted for additional information).

We did not require that the clinical consequences be immediate given that the influence of TSD and Im could be evidenced beyond the immediate speaking turn. For example, in a task analyses of the final sample of their study, Safran and Muran (1996) reported that Im started a sequence of events that occurred as a result of the Im and thus seemed connected directly to the Im. Thus, we relied on the investigators' determination that the clinical consequences were related to the TSD/Im interventions.

We excluded studies using analogue designs, in which nonclients (e.g., typically psychology undergraduate students) read a transcript or watched a video portrayal of a therapist offering a TSD or Im and rated how much they liked it or how helpful it would be (e.g., Dowd & Boroto, 1982; McCarthy & Betz, 1978). Although analogue methods allow for clear operationalization of the independent variable, they lack external validity and have questionable relation to the therapy process, given that TSD and Im are offered within the context of a therapeutic relationship (Kushner et al., 1979). We also excluded the Clemence et al. (2012) study of a psychodynamic interview (a single interview designed to test the boundaries of the client's ability to work dynamically) because it was not defined as psychotherapy. Similarly, we excluded studies that asked about general attitudes toward TSD/Im (e.g., preference for using or receiving TSD).

We also excluded correlational studies of the association between the frequency of TSD/Im and session or treatment outcome (e.g., Kuutman & Hilsenroth, 2011; Lingiardi et al., 2011) because there is no reliable way of knowing in correlational studies that the session or treatment outcomes are specifically linked with any specific TSD or Im. It could just as easily be that TSD/Im is used more often when the outcome is good as the other way around. Furthermore, the frequency of any method should not necessarily be related to outcome (Stiles et al., 2015). In other words, a single compelling TSD delivered at exactly the right time would probably prove more helpful than 10 TSDs delivered to a client who does not like them.

We could only examine the clinical consequences when TSD/Im occurred, so we did not include studies about the clinical consequences of TSD and Im not being used when it could have been used. For example, in one study that included both the use and nonuse of Im (Rhodes et al. 1994), we only included the clinical consequences when TSD was used.

Decision to Conduct a Qualitative Meta-Analysis

Because almost all of the studies in the final database of 21 studies used qualitative designs, we could not conduct a quantitative meta-analysis. Therefore, we conducted a QMA (Hill, Knox, & Hess, 2012), converting results from the three quantitative studies into qualitative results so that we could include them in the QMA. Whereas most of the chapters in this book link the therapist behavior/process variable with treatment outcome, we link TSD and Im with more immediate clinical consequences, typically those that occurred within the session. The rationale for this choice is that we would not expect the influence of TSD or Im to be distal or last until the end of treatment; rather, the consequences arise more in the immediate aftermath of the intervention. We suspect that there is a complicated sequence of how interventions fit together within the therapeutic relationship to influence therapy outcome in individual cases, but our task here was examining the more proximal link between the interventions and relatively immediate clinical consequences within sessions.

QMA Procedures

All decisions were made via consensus of the three authors. This consensus procedure involved considerable discussion and checking/rechecking the data to ensure that we were tabulating and interpreting the data as fairly and consistently as possible.

We first recorded clinical consequences (e.g., gained insight) listed as being associated with specific TSDs/Ims for each study. We used the authors' words as much as possible to describe these consequences. Based on the recorded data, we then developed categories of clinical consequences (e.g., enhanced therapy relationship). At this point, we tried to be as thorough and descriptive as possible to capture the nuances of the clinical consequences as stated by the authors.

As a team, we next consensually coded each consequence listed in each study into one of the categories. This coding required extensive discussion since different words were often used to express similar consequences. We revised the categories frequently throughout this process, trying to make them as clear as possible. After all consequences were coded, we went back individually and as a team to check the coding. We collapsed categories that appeared to involve similar constructs, particularly to eliminate categories that seldom occurred. Table 11.1 shows the final list of categories.

We developed several decision rules as we proceeded. First, each clinical consequence could count only once per participant, even if several examples of the consequence were given and different terms were used for the consequences within a given category. Second, when we collapsed categories, we sometimes had the problem that different numbers of participants endorsed examples within categories. Our rule was to use the largest number rather than averaging across examples, because doing so provided the best representation of how many clients fit the overall category. For example, if 9 of 12 participants cited an improved therapeutic relationship, whereas only 7 of the 12 cited an improved alliance (both were placed under the same category), we counted 9 of 12 for the category of enhanced therapy relationship.

A third decision rule emerged because several studies involved single cases, whereas others involved multiple participants. It would not be fair to average across studies, because doing so would assign disproportionally greater weight to those studies with fewer participants. Instead, we counted the number of cases to which each clinical consequence applied in each study as well as tabulated the total number of participants for each study. This approach was straightforward for qualitative studies that provided numbers of participants for each clinical consequence; however, several qualitative studies did not include data regarding exactly how many participants mentioned a specific clinical consequence, but rather only noted whether the findings were general (applied to all or all but one), typical (applied to more than half of the participants), or variant (applied to less than half of the participants). In these cases, we estimated the

Table 11.1. Categories of Clinical Consequences for Therapist Self-Disclosure and
Immediacy

1. Client mental health functioning improved (e.g., decreased symptomatology; increased interpersonal functioning (e.g., enhanced relationships with others outside therapy); improved intrapersonal functioning (e.g., more positive self-image, self-healing), behavioral changes (e.g., stopped drinking, lost weight)
2. Client opened up/explored/experienced feelings
3. Client gained insight
4. Client felt understood, normalized, reassured
5. Client used immediacy
6. Overall helpful (nonspecific) for client
7. Enhanced therapy relationship (clarified tasks of therapy, negotiated boundaries, client had a corrective relational experience, client expressed positive feelings about therapist, repaired rupture in relationship)
8. Impaired therapy relationship (e.g., client felt a lack of clarity about the relationship, role confusion blurred boundaries, rupture)
9. Client had negative feelings/reactions
10. Client openness/exploration/insight was inhibited
11. Overall not helpful (non-specific) for client
12. Negative effects for therapist
13. Overall neutral reactions/no changes for client

number for whom the clinical consequence might apply as falling in the mid range of the frequency grouping (e.g., if a typical finding applied for 7 to 11 participants in a sample of 13, we estimated that the result fit for 9 of the 13 participants).

As previously noted, we converted quantitative findings so that we could compare findings across methods. We used Cohen's (1988) standards for estimating effect sizes ($d > .20$ or $r > .10$ is a small effect, $d > .50$ or $r > .30$ is a medium effect, and $d > .80$ or $r > .50$ is a large effect). We considered a small effect size to be equivalent to a variant finding (less than half of the participants), a medium effect size to be equivalent to a typical finding (more than half), and a large effect size to be equivalent to a general finding (all or all but one of the participants). Thus, in a sample of 30 participants, and using the midpoint of the variant, typical, and general category ranges, a small effect would be assigned a weighting of 9 of the 30 participants, a medium effect would be 22 of 30, and a large effect would be 29 out of 30.

A final decision involved how to include the data for the Hill et al. (1988) study, since the clinical consequences were assessed for all the TSD/Im without accounting for nesting within cases, which means that we could not determine for how many cases the clinical consequences were relevant. Given that Hill et al. (1989), in a follow-up study using the same data set, noted that only three of eight therapists used a substantial number of TSD and Im, we used three rather than eight cases as our indicator of the number of cases.

Tabulation of Results

Table 11.2 presents the data for each study. The first column provides the citation for the study. In the second column, we describe the sample, the type of intervention (TSD or Im), the type of event (positive, negative, mixed), and the method used for data analyses. In the third column, we cite the specific clinical consequences linked with the TSD or Im. Consequences are listed in order of their frequency within each study; if consequences occurred with equal frequency, they are listed in the order they were mentioned in the study. In the fourth column, we present the category into which each consequence was coded. In the fifth column, we note the number of cases for whom the consequence applied divided by the total number of possible cases in that study.

We tallied the results across studies for each clinical consequence. For example, using a hypothetical example of consequence X in four studies: X is mentioned once in a case study (so we coded 1/1), 9 times out of 13 cases in a qualitative study (9/13), zero times in a qualitative study of 15 people (0/15), and a medium effect in a study of 30 (22/30). Thus, we could conclude that, of the 59 participants, 32 (.54 or 54%) experienced consequence X.

A complication arose in considering studies that only examined specific clinical consequences rather than allowing whatever consequences were relevant to emerge. For example, in their experimental study, Barrett and Berman (2001, Study 3) only asked clients to complete measures of symptomatology and liking of the therapist, so their data could not be used to estimate other clinical consequences. For the three studies for which only specific consequences were investigated, we put "na" in the corresponding cells of the table to show that these categories were not assessed in this study and thus not counted.

We determined which clinical consequences occurred most frequently across all studies (see Table 11.3). To determine whether some categories occurred more often than others, we a priori agreed to use Ladany et al's (2012) criterion that categories had to differ by at least 30% to be considered different (e.g., categories that were endorsed 70% vs. 40% would be considered different).

Results

Table 11.3 shows the data for each of the clinical consequences across the 21 studies (total sample of 184 cases) for both TSD and Im. The most frequently occurring clinical consequences when both TSD and Im were included were enhanced therapy relationship (60%, Category 7), improved client mental health functioning (42%, Category 1), client gained insight (38%, Category 3), and overall helpful for client (36%, Category 6). The least frequently occurring clinical consequences were inhibited client openness/exploration/insight (6%, Category 10), and negative effects for therapist (5%, Category 12). Using the 30% difference criterion, the top three consequences all occurred more frequently than the bottom two.

From this analysis, we conclude that the clinical consequences of TSDs and Ims are generally positive, in that the therapy relationship was enhanced, the clients had

Table 11.2. Studies Included in the Qualitative Meta-Analysis

Study	Description of Study[a]	Clinical Consequences	Cate-gory	Number / Total
1. Agnew et al. (1994)	Case study of a good outcome case of 8 sessions of psychodynamic-interpersonal psychotherapy with an adult female client with depression and anxiety and an experienced male therapist; Im; good sessions selected based on alliance ratings; task analysis with judges coding sessions	Developed an understanding of roles and responsibilities, consensus about relationship, renegotiation of relationship	7	1/1
		Explored parallel situations outside therapy, enhanced exploration	2	1/1
		New styles of relating outside of therapy	1	1/1
2. Audet & Everall (2010); Audet (2011)	9 adult clients with a range of diagnoses were interviewed about experiences with TSDs given by therapists from a range of experience levels; therapy ranged from 5 to 100+ sessions and was completed at time of interview; clients selected events but not necessarily positive; qualitative	Positive experiences	6	7/9
		Humanized therapist, enabled client to recognize therapist's fallibility, deformalized therapy, equalized power difference, positively affected therapist's credibility/competence, contributed to atmosphere of comfort/ease, removed client from "hot seat"	7	7/9
		Elicited more openness in relationship, divulged thoughts/feelings that were difficult to relay	2	7/9
		Resonated with client's experiences/psychotherapy needs	4	7/9
		Did not alter client's perceptions of therapist's professional qualities	13	5/9
		Negative experiences, negatively affected therapist's credibility/ competence, minimized therapist's professional role, felt overwhelming	11	4/9
		Client felt discomfort/hesitancy	10	3/9
		Humanized therapist beyond client's preferred boundaries/blurred psychotherapy boundaries	8	2/9

3. Barrett & Berman (2001)	36 adult community clients and 18 doctoral student therapists; therapists increased number of TSDs with one client and decreased TSDs with another client, type of therapy not specified but in a university counseling center; reciprocal TSDs; experimental quantitative with clients rating post-session	Decreased symptomatology, $d = .91$	1	35/36
		Client liked therapist, $d = .94$	7	35/36
4. Bennett et al. (2006)	4 good outcome cases (data from 2 poor outcome cases were not included because they did not involve Im); 16–24 sessions of cognitive analytic therapy with adult clients with borderline personality disorder and experienced therapists; Im; repaired ruptures; task analysis with judges coding enactments in 66 sessions that had an alliance threat (based on alliance ratings) of 4 cases	Exploration and clarification of what was collaboratively felt, understandings were elaborated, doubts and objections were explored, understanding and assimilating warded-off feelings	2	4/4
		Linking and explanation, negotiation (acceptance of link was amplified, further explanation, consensus (association to other events, origins in past), closure	3	4/4
		Consensus (agreement about event)	7	4/4
		New ways of behaving (changes in patterns/aims)	1	4/4
5. Berman et al. (2012)	3 adult female clients with anorexia paired with 1 early-career therapist for 17 sessions of acceptance and commitment therapy; Im; all relational events within treatment; qualitative (CQR), with judges coding therapy sessions	Client increased exploration, expressed feelings, more assertive about voicing negative reactions to therapist	2	3/3
		Client was confused about when it was okay to share feelings, client felt disregarded, client felt forced to recommit to therapy	8	2/3
		Client felt controlled/frustrated	9	2/3
		Therapeutic bond was strengthened	7	1/3
		Client was more assertive about stating needs	5	1/3
		Client gained insight into relational patterns	3	1/3
		Client was less open in expression	10	1/3

(continued)

Table 11.2. Continued

Study	Description of Study[a]	Clinical Consequences	Cate-gory	Number / Total
6. Friedlander et al. (2016)	Case study of a 6-session psychotherapy with an adult female client and an experienced female psychodynamic therapist; Im; positive events (corrective relational experiences); qualitative with judges coding process in session and participant accounts	Client had a corrective experience	7	1/1
		More productive narrative-emotion processes, fewer problem markers	2	1/1
		More change markers (more unexpected outcomes)	1	1/1
		More change markers (discovery storytelling)	3	1/1
7. Hanson (2005)	18 adult clients of unspecified diagnoses currently in open-ended therapy with unspecified therapists were interviewed, although authors indicated only 17 for some analyses; range of events; quantitative and qualitative analyses	Client found TSD/Im helpful, client experienced non-TSD/Im as unhelpful	6	18/18
		Fostered alliance/egalitarian relationship, established credibility	7	18/18
		Damaged alliance, insufficient to repair rupture, client "managed" relationship, relationship was nonegalitarian/inappropriately egalitarian	8	16/17
		Role and skills modeling	1	12/18
		Validated clients and their decisions/actions/reality, normalized, moral solidarity	4	10/18
		Client insight/learning	3	9/18
		Invalidated client, dissonance	9	5/17
		Inhibited client disclosure	10	4/17
		Not useful	13	1/17

Study	Description	Findings		
8. Hill et al. (1988) Hill et al. (1989)	8 adult female anxious clients and 8 experienced therapists (most psychodynamic) for 12 sessions; TSD and Im combined; all TSD/IM events in cases; judges coded interventions and consequences and data analyzed quantitatively. Only 3 of the 8 many TSD/Im, so N is 3 for this table	TSD/Im received highest client helpfulness ratings of all response modes/	6	3/3
		TSD/Im was associated with the highest client experiencing levels	2	3/3
9. Hill et al. (2003)	13 experienced therapists from a range of theoretical orientations were interviewed about their experiences of anger directed at them from adult clients who were mild to moderately impaired; Im; positive events (resolution of client anger events); qualitative (CQR) analyses	Anger typically diminished, client variantly made positive changes (e.g., started going to AA and stopped drinking)	1	9/13
		Therapeutic relationship improved (Variant)	7	4/13
		Neutral/mixed outcomes (Variant)	13	4/13
		Negative outcomes (Variant)	11	4/13
10. Hill et al. (1996)	11 experienced therapists from a range of theoretical orientations were interviewed about their experiences with impasses in long-term psychotherapy with adult clients with a range of diagnoses; Im; negative events (impasses); qualitative (CQR) analyses	Terminated unilaterally (Typical)	11	8/11
		Therapists typically ruminated, tried to figure out what went wrong, had self-doubts about abilities, changed strategies with other Cs as a result of experience, and worried about Cs who quit	12	8/11
11. Hill et al. (2008)	Case study of 1 depressed/anxious adult female client and an experienced interpersonally-oriented male therapist for 17 sessions of psychotherapy; Im; all events included; qualitative (CQR), with judges coding all Im events in therapy sessions	Negotiated therapeutic relationship, established rules, client had a corrective relational experience	7	1/1
		Expressed genuine positive feelings about therapist to therapist	5	1/1
		Opened up and explored deeply	2	1/1
		Client cared more about self, was self-healing, was more genuine, trusted self more in relationships with mother and partners	1	1/1
		Client understood relationships in new way	3	1/1

(continued)

Table 11.2. Continued

Study	Description of Study[a]	Clinical Consequences	Cate-gory	Number / Total
12. Hill et al. (2014)	16 cases of open-ended psychodynamic-interpersonal psychotherapy with adult community clients and doctoral student therapists; Im; all events included; qualitative (CQR) with judges coding all Im events in therapy sessions	Established/clarified boundaries, helped establish therapeutic relationship, client had corrective relational experience, helped repair ruptures	7	11/16
		Negative effects on clients	11	11/16
		Client expressed feelings about therapist/therapy	5	8/16
		Client opened up	2	8/16
		Client gained insight	3	7/16
		No effects, clients said neutral or ambivalent things about I, in interviews	13	4/16
		Client felt validated, cared for	4	2/16
		Changed relationships outside therapy	1	1/16
13. Iwakabe & Conceição (2016)	4 best examples of meta-therapeutic processing selected by originator of accelerated experiential dynamic psychotherapy, clients were all seen by one experienced female therapist; Im (metatherapeutic processing); positive events; qualitative (task analysis) with judges coding events.	Client gained relief (facial expression softened, removed emotional burden)	6	4/4
		Client affirmed self and others (recognized inner strength, had a compassionate view of self and others, let go of criticism and need for control of self/others), client had a sense of peacefulness, client gained greater satisfaction and replenishment, client engaged in new emotional coping strategies	1	4/4
		Client got enlivened (positive and vigorous emotions), client grieved (didn't last long but came from processing and then shifted back to positive)	2	4/4
		Client became aware of self-limiting beliefs and behaviors (identified dysfunctional beliefs and relationship patterns)	3	4/4

14. Kasper et al. (2008)	Case study of an adult female client and an interpersonally-oriented male therapist in 12 sessions of psychotherapy; Im; all events included; qualitative (CQR), with judges coding all Im events in therapy sessions	Client was immediate in 79% of speaking turns after therapist Im, whereas client was immediate in 20% of speaking turns when therapist did not use immediacy; chi-square = 169.75, $p < .001$, client talked about relationship issues that would not have otherwise discussed	5	1/1
		Client involvement was lower during Im events than before, $d = .36$, or higher after immediacy events, $d = .47$	10	1/1
		Client opened up/expressed feelings that did not usually allow herself	2	1/1
		Client felt closer to therapist, client felt cared for by therapist	7	1/1
		Client felt satisfied with session	6	1/1
		Client felt pressured to respond, client felt awkward/vulnerable/challenged/hurt/confused about what immediacy was for, client engaged out of deference to therapist's authority	9	1/1
15a. Knox et al. (1997)	13 adult clients with a range of presenting problems were interviewed about their experiences with therapists from a range of theoretical orientations; TSD; helpful events; qualitative (CQR) with judges coding interview	Therapist was seen as more real, therapeutic relationship was seen as improved/equalized	7	9/13
		Client felt normalized or reassured	4	9/13
		Client gained insight and perspective to make changes	3	8/13
		Client used therapist as a model	1	5/13
		Negative influence on therapeutic relationship and therapy	8	4/13
		Neutral	13	4/13
		Negative influence on therapy	11	2/13

(continued)

Table 11.2. Continued

Study	Description of Study[a]	Clinical Consequences	Cate-gory	Number / Total
15b. Knox et al. (1997)	13 adult clients with a range of presenting problems were interviewed about their experiences with therapists from a range of theoretical orientations; TSDS; unhelpful TSDS (only 9 clients identified unhelpful events); qualitative (CQR) with judges coding interviews. These data were not published.	Negative feelings/reactions	9	8/9
		Negative influence on therapy	11	4/9
		Negative influence on therapy relationship	8	4/9
		Client gained new insight/perspective to make changes	3	4/9
		Therapist seen as more human, relationship improved, equalized therapy relationship	7	4/9
16a. Kronner & Northcut (2015)	8 gay male therapists were interviewed about experiences with an adult, gay, male depressed/anxious client in long-term therapy; TSD (historical, philosophical, and emotional); all events included; qualitative (grounded theory)	Client experienced as positive	6	8/8
		Client experienced as negative	11	6/8
		Client experienced as neutral	13	6/8
16b. Kronner & Northcut (2015)	8 gay male therapists were interviewed about experiences with an adult, gay, male depressed/anxious client in long-term therapy; Im (historical, philosophical, and emotional); all events included; qualitative (grounded theory)	Client experienced as positive	6	8/8
		Client experienced as negative	11	6/8
		Client experienced as neutral	13	5/8
17. Li & Kivlighan (2016)	The first four sessions at a college counseling center with 3 student clients and 3 therapists (2 doctoral interns and one experienced); Im; judges coded therapy sessions and data were analyzed quantitatively for associations between Im and client collaboration	Metacommunication in one speaking turn was associated with increased client collaboration in next speaking turn more in latter half of sessions, standardized beta = .23 (interpret same as r) and when therapist communicates with a tentative, nondominant manner, standardized beta = .12, with some neutrality, standardized beta = .18	2	1/3

Study	Description	Finding		
18. Mayotte-Blum et al. (2012)	Case study of one White adult female client with acute stressors paired with an experienced White male relational psychodynamic therapist in long-term psychodynamic therapy; Im; all events included; judges coded therapy sessions and data were analyzed qualitatively using consensual qualitative research (CQR)	Client had more ability to tolerate and explore deeply painful and shameful feelings	2	1/1
		Client had a new relational experience with therapist	7	1/1
		Client communicated positive feelings (e.g., gratitude) to therapist who she was initially ambivalent about trusting	5	1/1
19a. Pinto-Coelho et al. (in prep)	13 experienced therapists of a variety of theoretical orientations were interviewed; TSD; helpful; qualitative (CQR) analyses of interviews	Deepening of psychotherapy work (exploration)	2	10/13
		Deepening of psychotherapy work (insight)	3	10/13
		Clients stated that TSDs were helpful	6	8/13
		Improved therapeutic relationship, client connected more with therapist, client saw therapist as more human, client idealized therapist less	7	8/13
		Alleviated client negative feelings, increased hope, made changes in life	1	5/13
19b. Pinto-Coelho et al. (2018)	13 experienced therapists of a variety of theoretical orientations were interviewed; TSD: unhelpful (only 11 indicated unhelpful events); qualitative (CQR) analyses of interviews	Therapist had ambivalent feelings about TSD	13	3/13
		Client had negative reactions	9	11/11
		Therapist regretted using TSD, therapist questioned appropriateness of TSD with this client	3	7/11
20. Rhodes et al. (1994)	11 clients were interviewed about misunderstanding but only 5 indicated anything about Im; Im; positive events (resolution of misunderstandings); qualitative (CQR) analyses of interviews	Resolution occurred (general), relationship was enhanced/repaired (general)	7	5/5
		Work continued and client continued to grow (general)	6	5/5

(*continued*)

Table 11.2. Continued

Study	Description of Study[a]	Clinical Consequences	Cate-gory	Number / Total
21. Safran & Muran (1996)	6 cases of 20 session cognitive-interpersonal therapy (no information provided about clients and therapists but assume therapists were experienced): Im; positive events (repaired ruptures); qualitative (task analysis) coding of therapy sessions	Client disclosed about block to discussing rupture, client asserted self, client explored avoidance, client self-asserted	2	6/6
		Client expressed negative feelings about rupture, client explored rupture experience	5	6/6

[a]Description of sample includes theoretical orientation and experience level of therapist and diagnosis of client; type of intervention (TSD or Im); type of events (positive, negative, mixed); and method of analysis (qualitative, experimental).

Note. CQR = consensual qualitative research. TSD = therapist self-disclosure. Im = immediacy.

Table 11.3. Number of Clients in 21 Studies for Whom Clinical Consequences Applied (Categories in Columns and Studies in Rows)

Study	1	2	3	4	5	6	7	8	9	10	11	12	13
1	1/1	1/1	0/1	0/1	0/1	0/1	1/1	0/1	0/1	0/1	0/1	0/1	0/1
2	0/9	7/9	0/9	7/9	0/9	7/9	7/9	2/9	0/9	3/9	4/9	0/9	5/9
3	35/36	Na	na	na	Na	Na	35/36	Na	na	Na	na	na	na
4	4/4	4/4	4/4	0/4	0/4	0/4	4/4	0/4	0/4	0/4	0/4	0/4	0/4
5	0/3	3/3	1/3	0/3	1/3	0/3	1/3	2/3	2/3	1/3	0/3	0/3	0/3
6	1/1	1/1	1/1	0/1	0/1	0/1	1/1	0/1	0/1	0/1	0/1	0/1	0/1
7	12/18	0/18	9/18	10/18	0/18	18/18	18/18	16/17	5/17	4/17	0/18	0/18	1/17
8	na	3/3	na	na	Na	3/3	na	Na	na	Na	na	na	na
9	9/13	0/13	0/13	0/13	0/13	0/13	4/13	0/13	0/13	0/13	4/13	0/13	4/13
10	0/11	0/11	0/11	0/11	0/11	0/11	0/11	0/11	0/11	0/11	8/11	8/11	0/11
11	1/1	1/1	1/1	0/1	1/1	0/1	1/1	0/1	0/1	0/1	0/1	0/1	0/1
12	1/16	8/16	7/16	2/16	8/16	0/16	11/16	0/16	0/16	0/16	11/16	0/16	4/16
13	4/4	4/4	4/4	0/4	0/4	4/4	0/4	0/4	0/4	0/4	0/4	0/4	0/4
14	0/1	1/1	0/1	0/1	1/1	1/1	1/1	0/1	1/1	1/1	0/1	0/1	0/1
15ab	5/22	0/22	12/22	9/22	0/22	0/22	13/22	8/22	8/22	0/22	6/22	0/22	4/22
16ab	0/8	0/8	0/8	0/8	0/8	8/8	0/8	0/8	0/8	0/8	6/8	0/8	6/8
17	na	1/3	na	na	na	na	na	Na	na	Na	na	na	na
18	0/1	1/1	0/1	0/1	1/1	0/1	1/1	0/1	0/1	0/1	0/1	0/1	0/1
19ab	5/24	10/24	17/24	0/24	0/24	8/24	8/24	0/24	11/24	0/24	0/24	0/24	3/24
20	0/5	0/5	0/5	0/5	0/5	5/5	5/5	0/5	0/5	0/5	0/5	0/5	0/5
21	0/6	6/6	0/6	0/6	6/6	0/6	0/6	0/6	0/6	0/6	0/6	0/6	0/6
A	78	51	56	28	18	54	111	28	27	9	39	8	27
B	184	154	148	148	148	151	184	147	147	147	148	148	147
C	.42	.33	.38	.19	.12	.36	.60	.19	.18	.06	.26	.05	.18

A = total number of participants who had this consequence across all studies

B = total number of participants across all studies

C = % of participants who had this consequence across all studies

na = not applicable; because of the design of the study, this consequence was not included and thus could not be found better mental health functioning, and the interventions were overall perceived to be helpful. Furthermore, the negative clinical consequences were minimal. These results are consistent with previous reviews (Hill & Knox, 2002, 2009) but provide a more sophisticated analysis of the findings. It is also interesting to think about the clinical consequences that were not found. None of the studies reported client resistance (e.g., avoidance, interrupting, changing the topic), lack of involvement, direct expression of emotions (e.g., crying, laughter, sighing), or action (e.g., behavior change). The wide range of studies included in this analysis, however, suggests caution in interpreting these results.

MODERATOR ANALYSES

Given the heterogeneity among the 21 studies, we searched for moderator variables that might have influenced the results. Specifically, we had enough data to examine type of intervention (TSD vs. Im) as a moderator. Other possible moderators (perspective, therapist experience level, type of event) were examined more speculatively given the lack of studies.

Type of Intervention

TSD Studies

We located five studies that focused on TSD as a unique skill (not combined with Im), encompassing a total of 99 cases. Table 11.4 shows that the four most frequently occurring clinical consequences were enhanced therapy relationship (64%, Category 7), client gained insight (46%, Category 3), client mental health functioning improved (45%, Category 1), and overall helpful for client (37%, Category 6). The three least frequently occurring clinical consequences were inhibited client openness (5%, Category 10), negative effects for therapist (0%, Category 12), and client used immediacy (0%, Category 5). Using the 30% difference criterion, the top four clinical consequences all occurred more frequently than the bottom three.

These results closely parallel the overall analysis of 21 studies, with the exception that the category of clients using immediacy never occurred in this sample whereas it had in the overall sample (because of the immediacy studies). The clinical consequence of the client disclosing more was never reported in this subsample.

These results should be viewed with caution as there were only five studies focused on TSD. These studies varied in terms of type (reciprocal, historical, philosophical, emotional, unspecified), method of analysis (experimental, phenomenological, grounded theory, CQR), and perspective (client ratings after session, interviews of clients, interviews of therapists).

Table 11.4. Number of Participants in TSD Studies for Whom Clinical Consequences Applied (Categories in Columns and Studies in Rows)

Categ/Study	1	2	3	4	5	6	7	8	9	10	11	12	13
2	0/9	7/9	0/9	7/9	0/9	7/9	7/9	2/9	0/9	3/9	4/9	0/9	5/9
3	35/36	na	na	na	na	na	35/36	na	na	Na	na	na	na
15ab	5/22	0/22	12/22	9/22	0/22	0/22	13/22	8/22	8/22	0/22	6/22	0/22	4/22
16ab	0/8	0/8	0/8	0/8	0/8	8/8	0/8	0/8	0/8	0/8	6/8	0/8	6/8
19ab	5/24	10/24	17/24	0/24	0/24	8/24	8/24	0/24	11/24	0/24	0/24	0/24	3/24
D	45	17	29	16	0	23	63	10	19	3	18	0	18
E	99	63	63	63	63	63	99	63	63	63	63	63	63
F	.45	.27	.46	.25	.00	.37	.64	.16	.30	.05	.29	.00	.29

D = total number of participants who had this consequence for studies involving only TSD

E = total number of participants for studies involving only TSD

F = % of participants who had this consequence for studies involving only TSD

Im Studies

Table 11.5 shows the subsample analyses of the 15 studies that focused on Im as a separate skill, encompassing 78 cases. The three most frequently occurring clinical consequences were enhanced therapy relationship (40%, Category 7), client opened up (40%, Category 2), and overall not helpful (39%, Category 11). The four least frequently occurring clinical consequences were negative feelings/reactions (4%, Category 9), felt understood (3%, Category 4), impaired therapy relationship (3%, Category 8), and openness inhibited (3%, Category 10). Using the 30% difference criterion, the top three clinical consequences all occurred more frequently than the bottom four. Thus, there were mostly positive clinical consequences for the therapy relationship and for the client opening up, but also some negative clinical consequences of not being helpful and the client not feeling understood. As with the data set for TSDs, however, we recommend caution in interpreting these data because of the considerable heterogeneity among the 15 studies in terms of samples, events, and analyses. Fortunately, given that there were 15 Im studies, we could investigate several of the sources of heterogeneity, and we turn next to these subsample analyses.

Specifically, sufficient numbers of studies were available for a comparison of five studies involving task analyses of rupture repairs with six studies involving qualitative analyses of therapist immediacy. Both sets of studies involved judges coding the events. Differences between the two sets of studies were therapist experience level (therapists in the task analyses were all experienced, whereas 16 of the 25 therapists in the qualitative studies were doctoral students and only 9 were experienced) and valence of the events (only positive events were coded in the first set but all events within therapy were coded in the qualitative analyses so that there were both positive and negative events).

Im in task analyses of repaired ruptures. For the 16 cases in the task analyses of repaired ruptures, Table 11.6 shows that the most frequently occurring categories were all positive, including client opening up (100%, Category 2), improvements in client mental health functioning (62%, Category 1), gains in insight (56%, Category 3), client used immediacy (38%, Category 5), and enhanced therapy relationship (38%, Category 7). The least frequently occurring were overall helpful (25%, Category 6), and the remaining categories (all 0%; Categories 4, 8, 9, 10, 11, 12, and 13). Using the 30% difference criterion, the top five consequences all occurred more frequently than the bottom eight.

Hence, there was evidence in all five studies of repaired rupture events for the client opening up, exploring, and experiencing feelings; this appears to be an especially robust finding. Also, clients improved in mental health functioning, used immediacy, and had an enhanced therapy relationship. In these studies, researchers never reported that clients felt understood, reassured, or normalized (a frequent consequence for TSDs), perhaps because Im leads more to client expressiveness than to feeling reassured. Interestingly, judges observed no negative consequences for Im in these

Table 11.5. Number of Participants in Im Studies for Whom Clinical Consequences Applied (Categories in Columns and Studies in Rows)

Categ/Study	1	2	3	4	5	6	7	8	9	10	11	12	13
1	1/1	1/1	0/1	0/1	0/1	0/1	1/1	0/1	0/1	0/1	0/1	0/1	0/1
4	4/4	4/4	4/4	0/4	0/4	0/4	4/4	0/4	0/4	0/4	0/4	0/4	0/4
5	0/3	3/3	1/3	0/3	1/3	0/3	1/3	2/3	2/3	1/3	0/3	0/3	0/3
6	1/1	1/1	1/1	0/1	0/1	0/1	1/1	0/1	0/1	0/1	0/1	0/1	0/1
9	9/13	0/13	0/13	0/13	0/13	0/13	4/13	0/13	0/13	0/13	4/13	0/13	4/13
10	0/11	0/11	0/11	0/11	0/11	0/11	0/11	0/11	0/11	0/11	8/11	8/11	0/11
11	1/1	1/1	1/1	0/1	1/1	0/1	1/1	0/1	0/1	0/1	0/1	0/1	0/1
12	1/16	8/16	7/16	2/16	8/16	0/16	11/16	0/16	0/16	0/16	11/16	0/16	4/16
13	4/4	4/4	4/4	0/4	0/4	4/4	0/4	0/4	0/4	0/4	0/4	0/4	0/4
14	0/1	1/1	0/1	0/1	1/1	1/1	1/1	0/1	1/1	1/1	0/1	0/1	0/1
16b	0/8	0/8	0/8	0/8	0/8	8/8	0/8	0/8	0/8	0/8	6/8	0/8	6/8
17	na	1/3	na	na	na	na	na	na	na	na	na	na	na
18	0/1	1/1	0/1	0/1	1/1	0/1	1/1	0/1	0/1	0/1	0/1	0/1	0/1
20	0/5	0/5	0/5	0/5	0/5	5/5	5/5	0/5	0/5	0/5	0/5	0/5	0/5
21	0/6	6/6	0/6	0/6	6/6	0/6	0/6	0/6	0/6	0/6	0/6	0/6	0/6
G	21	31	18	2	18	18	30	2	3	2	29	8	14
H	75	78	75	75	75	75	75	75	75	75	75	75	75
I	.28	.40	.24	.03	.24	.24	.40	.03	.04	.03	.39	.11	.19

G = total number of participants who had this consequence for studies involving only Im

H = total number of participants for studies involving only Im

I = % of participants who had this consequence for studies involving only Im

Table 11.6. Number of Participants in Im Studies Examining Positive Events (Repaired Ruptures) with Experienced Therapists (Categories in Columns and Studies in Rows)

Categ/ Study	1	2	3	4	5	6	7	8	9	10	11	12	13
1	1/1	1/1	0/1	0/1	0/1	0/1	1/1	0/1	0/1	0/1	0/1	0/1	0/1
4	4/4	4/4	4/4	0/4	0/4	0/4	4/4	0/4	0/4	0/4	0/4	0/4	0/4
6	1/1	1/1	1/1	0/1	0/1	0/1	1/1	0/1	0/1	0/1	0/1	0/1	0/1
13	4/4	4/4	4/4	0/4	0/4	4/4	0/4	0/4	0/4	0/4	0/4	0/4	0/4
21	0/6	6/6	0/6	0/6	6/6	0/6	0/6	0/6	0/6	0/6	0/6	0/6	0/6
J	10	16	9	0	6	4	6	0	0	0	0	0	0
K	16	16	16	16	16	16	16	16	16	16	16	16	16
L	.62	1.00	.56	.00	.38	.25	.38	.00	.00	.00	.00	.00	.00

J = total number of participants who had this consequence for Im studies using task analysis on positive events

K = total number of participants for Im studies using task analysis on positive events

L = % of participants who had this consequence for Im studies using task analysis on positive events

events, perhaps because only exemplar positive events were selected so that researchers could determine mechanisms of change. An alternate explanation is that clients and therapists were not interviewed about these events, and judges may not have been aware of some of their negative reactions.

Im in qualitative investigations of positive and negative events. For the six qualitative studies on the range of Im events (total sample = 25), Table 11.7 shows that the most frequently occurring consequences were client opened up (60%, Category 2), client used immediacy (55%, Category 5), overall not helpful (50%, Category 11), and gains in insight (41%, Category 3). The least frequently occurring categories were improved mental health functioning (9%, Category 1), felt understood (9%, Category 4), impaired therapy relationship (9%, Category 8), openness inhibited (9%, Category 10), used immediacy (5%, Category 6), and negative effects for therapists (0%, Category 13). Using the 30% difference criterion, the top four consequences all occurred more frequently than the bottom six. Thus, the clinical consequences for Im as used by mostly doctoral student therapists-in-training (16 of the 25 therapists) were mostly positive (client opening up, using immediacy, and gaining insight), although there were some negative clinical consequences.

Comparison of subsamples of Im. If we compare the results for the five studies that involved trained judges coding Im as used by experienced therapists in positive events (repaired ruptures) with the results for the 6 studies that examined Im as used by therapists ranging in experience levels in both positive and negative events, again coded by trained judges (Table 11.8, columns 5 and 6), we find three meaningful differences (>30%). Studies examining only positive events had more improved mental health functioning (62% vs. 9%, Category 1), more client opened up (100% vs. 60%, Category 2), and more overall not helpful (0% vs. 50%, Category 11). Thus, it appears (not surprisingly) that studying only positive events (repaired ruptures) in cases with experienced therapists provides a different and more positive perspective on the consequences of Im than does studying a range of positive and negative events with less experienced therapists. We suspect that the experienced therapists in the task analyses also had negative Im events in their cases (as did therapists in Hill et al., 2003, Study 9; and Kasper et al., 2008, Study 14), but these were not included in the studies because the researchers examined only repaired ruptures. Table 11.9 shows the most and least frequently occurring consequences across subsamples.

Comparison of TSD and Im

We also compared the results of the five studies that focused on TSD and the six studies that focused on Im (Table 11.8, columns 3 and 6). Studies in the two subsamples were similar in that all included both positive and negative events, although they varied in other ways (of the TSD studies, two involved client interviews, two involved interviews

Table 11.7. Number of Participants in Qualitative Im Studies Examining Both Positive and Negative Events with Range of Experience Level of Therapists for Whom the Consequence Applied (Categories in Columns and Studies in Rows)

Categ/Study	1	2	3	4	5	6	7	8	9	10	11	12	13
5	0/3	3/3	1/3	0/3	1/3	0/3	1/3	2/3	2/3	1/3	0/3	0/3	0/3
11	1/1	1/1	1/1	0/1	1/1	0/1	1/1	0/1	0/1	0/1	0/1	0/1	0/1
12	1/16	8/16	7/16	2/16	8/16	0/16	11/16	0/16	0/16	0/16	11/16	0/16	4/16
14	0/1	1/1	0/1	0/1	1/1	1/1	1/1	0/1	1/1	1/1	0/1	0/1	0/1
17	na	1/3	na	na	na	na	na	na	na	na	na	na	na
18	0/1	1/1	0/1	0/1	1/1	0/1	1/1	0/1	0/1	0/1	0/1	0/1	0/1
M	2	15	9	2	12	1	5	2	3	2	11	0	4
N	22	25	22	22	22	22	22	22	22	22	22	22	22
O	.09	.60	.41	.09	.55	.05	.23	.09	.14	.09	.50	.00	.18

M = total number of participants who had this consequence for Im studies using qualitative analysis on range of positive and negative events

N = total number of participants for Im studies using qualitative analysis on range of positive and negative events

O= % of participants who had this consequence for Im studies using qualitative analysis on range of positive and negative events

Table 11.8. Summary of Percentages of Clinical Consequences across Different Types of Studies

Category	Overall 21 Studies	5 TSD Studies	15 Im Studies	5 Task Analysis Studies of Positive Im Events	6 Qualitative Studies of Positive and Negative Im Events
1 client mental health functioning improved	42%	45%	28%	62%	9%
2 client opened up	33%	27%	40%	100%	60%
3 client gained insight	38%	46%	24%	56%	41%
4 client felt understood, reassured, normalized	19%	25%	3%	0%	9%
5 client used more Im	12%	0%	24%	38%	55%
6 overall helpful for client	36%	37%	24%	25%	5%
7 enhanced therapy relationship	60%	64%	40%	38%	23%
8 impaired therapy relationship	19%	16%	3%	0%	9%
9 client had negative feelings/reactions	18%	30%	4%	0%	14%
10 inhibited client openness	6%	5%	3%	0%	9%
11 overall not helpful for client	26%	29%	39%	0%	50%
12 negative effects for therapist	5%	0%	11%	0%	0%
13 neutral/no changes for client	18%	29%	19%	0%	18%

Table 11.9. Most and Least Frequently Occurring Consequences of TSD and Im

All 21 Studies	5 TSD Studies	15 Im Studies	5 Studies of Positive Im Events	6 Studies of Positive and Negative Im
Most Frequently Occurring Consequences				
Enhanced therapy relationship (60%)	Enhanced therapy relationship (64%)	Enhanced therapy relationship (40%)	Client opened up (100%)	Client opened up (60%)
Client mental health Improved (42%)	Client gained insight (46%)	Client opened up (40%)	Client mental health improved (62%)	Client used immediacy (55%)
Client gained insight (38%)	Client mental health improved (45%)	Overall not helpful (39%)	Client gained insight (56%)	Overall not helpful (50%)
Overall helpful for Client (36%)	Overall helpful for Client (37%)		Client used immediacy (38%)	Gains in insight (41%)
			Enhanced therapy relationship (38%)	
Least Frequently Occurring Consequences				
Inhibited client openness (6%)	Inhibited client openness (5%)	Negative feelings/ reactions (4%)	Overall helpful (25%) health function (9%) Felt understood (0%)	Improved mental Felt understood (9%)
Negative effects for Therapist (5%)	Negative effects for therapist (0%)	Felt understood (3%)	Impaired therapy relationship (0%)	Impaired therapy relationship (9%)
	Client used immediacy (0%)	Impaired therapy relationship (3%)	Client had negative Feeling/reaction (0%)	Inhibited client openness (9%)
		Inhibited client Openness (3%)	Inhibited client openness (0%)	Client used immediacy (5%)
			Overall not helpful (0%)	Negative effects for therapist (0%)
			Negative effects for Therapist (0%)	Neutral/no changes (0%)

Note. The most and least frequently occurring consequences for each subsample differed by at least 30%

with experienced therapists, and one involved an experimental manipulation with doctoral student therapists; all of the six Im studies involved trained judges coding in-session therapist behaviors and a range of experience levels of therapists). Hence, in addition to differences in findings between samples being due to the type of intervention (TSD vs. Im), differences could be due to differences in the experience level of therapists, research approach (interviews vs. coding of behavior), or perspective (judges, therapists, clients). With these limitations in mind, we tentatively explore differences between the two subsamples.

We found five meaningful differences (>30%). TSD, as compared with Im, resulted in more improved mental health functioning (45% vs. 9%, Category 1), more overall helpful for client (37% vs. 5%, Category 6), more enhanced therapy relationship (64% vs. 23%, Category 7), but less client opened up (27% vs. 60%, Category 10) and less client using immediacy (0% vs. 55%, Category 5). Perhaps the differences in consequences are related to differences in intent. With TSDs, therapists typically focus mostly on clients and use themselves to facilitate more client exploration (e.g., "When I have been in your situation, I felt angry. I wonder if you feel that way."). These TSDs seem likely to foster understanding and better mental health functioning. In contrast, Ims are often used because of problems in the relationship and are likely to reveal underlying stresses (e.g., "I am feeling bored right now, and I wonder what is going on with you?").

Other Possible Moderators

We did not have enough studies in the QMA to perform adequate moderator analyses on other variables. We would be remiss, however, if we did not speculate about other variables that might explain the heterogeneity in the studies.

Perspective

The first potential moderator variable is perspective. We can compare the five studies involving task analyses conducted by trained judges of repaired ruptures with the one study involving interviews with experienced therapists about the resolution of events when clients directed anger at therapists (Hill et al., 2003, Study 9). In contrast to the uniformly positive findings for the task analyses from the perspective of judges, the study of interviewed therapists revealed more (>30% difference) negative consequences (clients were not perceived as having opened up or gained insight, and therapists reported more overall negative and neutral consequences). Although there was only one study of therapists, the results proved markedly dissimilar to findings of any of the task analyses. We suspect that therapists had different (and more negative) reactions than trained judges because of the privileged position of having been present during the events and thus having more awareness of (and vulnerability to) the underlying dynamics.

Therapist Experience Level

Similarly, we do not have enough studies to adequately assess the effects of the experience level of therapists, but one preliminary comparison alerts us to the need for further investigation. Of the six qualitative Im studies, we can compare results between the multiple case study that involved 9 doctoral student therapists with 16 clients (Study 12) with three experienced therapists in single case studies (Studies 11, 14, and 18). All studies involved therapists following a psychodynamic/interpersonal orientation, used a qualitative method (CQR) to analyze data, and examined all events (both positive and negative) that occurred in the cases. In comparison with the student therapists, the experienced therapists had more client opening up (100% vs. 50%, Category 2), client using immediacy (100% vs. 50%, Category 5), overall helpful for client (100% vs. 0%, Category 6), enhanced therapy relationship (100% vs. 69%, Category 7), client had negative feelings/reactions (33% vs. 0%, Category 9), and less overall not helpful (0% vs. 69%, Category 11). Hence, the experienced therapists yielded more positive consequences from Im than did the doctoral student therapists.

Repaired Ruptures versus Impasses

We can also do a preliminary comparison of the results of the task analyses of positive events/repaired ruptures with the results of the single study of impasses (ruptures not repaired; Study 10). The consequences for the repaired ruptures were all positive, whereas the consequences for the impasses were all negative. In particular, the Hill et al. (1996) study was the only study in which negative effects were found for therapists, with therapists ruminating about what went wrong and having doubts about their abilities.

EVIDENCE FOR CAUSALITY

We cannot claim evidence of causality for the data in this QMA. In most studies, our evidence for causality is "soft," in that judges, therapists, or clients (depending on the study) linked the interventions and their clinical consequences. Causality can be claimed for the one experimental study that manipulated TSD (Barrett & Berman, 2001) in the first four sessions of treatment. In an additional two studies (Hill et al., 2008; Li & Kivlighan, 2016), TSD or Im was studied in relation to client behavior in the immediate subsequent speaking turns, but this evidence is still associational, given that factors other than therapist interventions undoubtedly influenced the clinical consequences. In the qualitative studies, the link was made by judgments of trained observers, and again other factors undoubtedly contributed to the clinical consequences.

CLIENT CONTRIBUTIONS

There were not enough studies to investigate client contributions to TSD and Im. A few studies, though, pointed to intriguing possibilities that could be examined in future research. In Berman et al. (2012), the same therapist worked with three clients. One client had much better clinical consequences associated with Im than did the other two, which the authors attributed to this client being more compliant and willing to go along with the therapist's directives. In the Hill et al. (2014) study on Im, client attachment style was investigated as a moderator. With clients who were securely rather than fearfully attached, therapists' immediacy focused more on tasks and ruptures than on feelings, were of lower quality, were initiated more often by clients, and were shorter in length. Thus, it appears that therapists may use different types of Im with different clients, and that client attachment style might partially account for differences. In addition, we suspect that client culture, preferences/expectations, presenting problems, severity of psychopathology, and therapist attachment style would moderate the consequences, but such conclusions await further investigation with larger samples.

LIMITATIONS OF THE RESEARCH

One major limitation is the wide range of interventions included under the umbrella of TSD and Im. TSDs can be about feelings, thoughts, insights, strategies, or similar experiences. Likewise, Ims can involve the therapist sharing feelings about the therapy or the client, the therapist inquiring about the client's feelings or reactions, an attempt to negotiate the relationship, an attempt to encourage the client to talk about unexpressed feelings about the relationship, or an attempt to resolve problems in the relationship. Furthermore, TSDs and Ims are verbal statements accompanied and modified by nonverbal behaviors (e.g., head nods, encouraging gestures, facial expressions) within the context of a therapeutic relationship that may be positive or negative. Thus, neither of these interventions is "pure" or unidimensional, but instead both are multifaceted, and each likely varies according to the specific client, therapist, and context. The implication of this complexity is that different interventions might be combined under the larger umbrella of TSD or Im, and these interventions might be used for different intentions and result in disparate consequences.

A second limitation is that there were only 21 studies included in the QMA. There was wide variation across the studies in terms of type of intervention (TSD vs. Im), type of event selected (positive only, range of positive and negative, negative only), perspective (coding by trained judges, interviews of therapists or clients), and method (experimental, task analysis, CQR). Most studies had inadequate descriptions of the type of therapy (e.g., psychodynamic) involved or the diagnosis/presenting problems of the clients. Thus, not only were there few studies, but the existing studies were quite heterogeneous.

We did not compare the consequences of these interventions with other interventions (e.g., reflections of feelings, interpretations). Hence, we do not know whether the consequences are unusual in any way. Similarly, it is important to realize that therapists do not use TSDs or Im on a random basis, but rather (hopefully) for specific intentions in specific contexts. Different contexts could have led therapists to choose to disclose versus use Im or other interventions. Thus, we do not know if TSD or Im would have proven more effective than other potential interventions. Furthermore, we do not know if therapists based their choice of TSD or Im on some clear markers suggesting that these interventions would be appropriate.

DIVERSITY CONSIDERATIONS

All of the studies were published in English, and most were conducted within the United States. Diversity (e.g., gender, race/ethnicity, sexual orientation, socio-economic status) of clients and therapists was not addressed, and we did not have enough information to include diversity dimensions in the QMA.

A study by Kim and colleagues (2003), not included in our QMA because it in-volved single face-to-face sessions with nonclients, nevertheless sheds some light on this question. East Asian pseudoclients were paired with European American counselors who either used or did not use TSD. Whether or not the therapist disclosed and client adherence to Asian values did not predict session outcome. Disclosures of strategies, however, were perceived by clients as more helpful than disclosures of ap-proval/reassurance, facts/credentials, and feelings. In addition, disclosures that were moderately intimate were rated as more helpful by clients and therapists than those low on intimacy. Although results need to be replicated within other cultures and with larger samples, the researchers suggested that the preference of Asian Americans for disclosures of strategies fits with the Asian cultural emphasis on achievement. These results indicate that inclusion of cultural values and types of disclosures may prove more helpful in future research than simply examining race/ethnicity.

TRAINING IMPLICATIONS

Given the findings that TSD and Im led to mostly positive and some negative consequences, training is needed to help therapists use these interventions com-petently. We would also note that, from our years of experience in training novice therapists, these are among the most difficult skills to learn to use effectively. In fact, doctoral student therapists described self-disclosure and immediacy as difficult, ad-vanced skills that were acquired only after considerable practice (Hill et al., 2015). Much of the challenge in using these skills arises because they require so much of therapists personally, and it is difficult for novice therapists to set boundaries on what is and is not appropriate to share with clients and when to address problems that inev-itably arise in the immediate relationship.

We suspect that role-playing and deliberate practice (e.g., Chow et al., 2015; Goldberg et al., 2016) might prove helpful. In other words, therapists would bring to supervision specific times that they could have used TSD or Im. They then would prac-tice such interventions in a safe, supportive environment. Next, they would attempt to use the interventions in sessions with the target client and watch the videotaped results. By repeatedly practicing with the specific client and with supervisor feedback, trainees may be more likely to use these interventions effectively with that client, and hopefully transfer such learning to future clients.

One study (Spangler et al., 2014), in fact, found that instruction, modeling, feedback, and practice were all effective in helping undergraduates learn to use immediacy, but practice was particularly effective. These findings again demonstrate that novice therapists may need extensive rehearsal in using these skills, perhaps in a number of different formats. Learning Im in a controlled training setting does not mean that trainees can apply Im effectively in a clinical setting. In addition, intriguing qualitative findings in that same study pointed to the influence of culture in affecting students' ability to learn and use Im. For example, students from cultures that discourage direct communication found it more difficult to use Im, whereas students whose families encouraged open and direct communication found it easier to use the skill.

In a recent study (Pinto-Coelho et al., 2018), experienced therapists reported a lack of formal training in TSD. The practitioners suggested that trainers include explicit education about TSD in their curricula. They reported that experiencing successful TSD in supervision, being paired with more experienced therapists (e.g., co-therapy, group therapy), and experiencing TSD or the lack of TSD in their own personal therapy were the most compelling training experiences with TSD. Development of a pre-TSD decision-making tool could assist trainees in deciding when to disclose in a specific situation. Finally, construction of a post-TSD measure could assist therapists in assessing and processing the clinical consequences of the intervention.

THERAPEUTIC PRACTICE

Both TSD and Im typically produced positive clinical consequences for clients, suggesting that therapists might consider using them. Given that previous research (e.g., Hill et al., 1988, 2014), however, has shown that both are relatively infrequent in psychotherapy, we stress the need to use them sparingly for appropriate intentions or reasons.

More specifically, with appropriate and effective TSDs, therapists focus on clients and use themselves to facilitate client exploration, which fosters understanding and better mental health functioning. Therapists might think about disclosing when clients feel alone, vulnerable, and in need of support. To learn that they are not the only ones who have felt lonely or distressed can provide a sense of universality. In addition, the meta-analysis indicates that TSD is typically a "safe" intervention when done skillfully, thoughtfully, and with good timing.

In contrast, therapists often use Im to negotiate the relationship and when there are problems in the relationship. Therapists might thus consider using Im primarily to help clients open up and talk about underlying feelings, especially when negotiating the therapeutic relationship. Talking about the relationship, however, has potential for volatility as problems are illuminated, so therapists will need to be aware of and open to their own and clients' reactions, and prepared to address them.

Of course, therapists using both TSD and Im need to keep the focus on the client rather than using these interventions to satisfy their own needs. The meta-analytic results and clinical experience point to negative client consequences of psychotherapists using self-disclosure for self-gratification, even when rationalized that it was done for therapeutic purposes.

As with all interventions, TSD and Im must be delivered with skill, tact, and appropriate timing. Although no research exists that we know of (although the better results with experienced therapists hints at this), we again emphasize that these potentially powerful interventions must be used with care and expertise.

Based on the literature and QMA in this chapter, we offer the following practice recommendations for TSD:

◆ Be cautious, thoughtful, and strategic about using TSD.
◆ Have a client-focused intention for using TSD.
◆ Evaluate how clients might respond and whether TSD is likely to help clients.
◆ Make sure the therapeutic relationship is strong before using TSD.
◆ Use TSD sparingly.
◆ Keep the disclosure brief with few details.
◆ Disclose resolved rather than unresolved material.
◆ Make the TSD relevant to client material.
◆ Focus on similarities between therapist and client.
◆ Focus on the client's rather than on the therapist's needs.
◆ Turn the focus back to the client after delivering the TSD.
◆ Observe the client's reaction to the TSD.
◆ Assess the TSD's effectiveness and decide whether it would be appropriate to use TSD again with this client.

Regarding Im, one practice implication arises from the findings for repaired ruptures. Given the consistency of results for Im across the five studies of repaired ruptures, it appears that Im is indeed a helpful intervention for repairing and resolving ruptures. The careful task analyses, however, reveal that rather than being a single "one-off" intervention, the therapist and client typically engage in a lengthier processing of the rupture via immediacy. In this respect, Im may initiate a more detailed process between therapist and client.

A second implication from the literature is that therapist immediacy frequently generates increased client immediacy (although TSD was not associated with increased client disclosure). Thus, if therapists want clients to be more immediate, it seems useful for them to be more immediate themselves.

A third implication arises from the finding of both positive and negative consequences for immediacy when not restricted to repaired rupture events facilitated by experienced therapists. These results suggest that Im can be useful for resolving problems in the therapy relationship, but that it also is associated with negative effects. It is not yet clear whether the negative effects were because previous problems were not resolved or whether new problems were created by the inappropriate or ineffective use of Im. Nevertheless, the findings suggest that not all Im is positive, and thus therapists must be attentive to how clients respond. Therapist immediacy typically "raises the temperature in the room" and can be difficult for therapists and clients who are not comfortable having open discussions about the relationship.

Finally, we recommend a number of approaches to help therapists skillfully implement immediacy in routine practice. Therapists can watch videotapes of session segments where Im had positive and problematic consequences, examine their own countertransference needs, and seek consultation to ensure they are acting in the best interests of clients. Engaging in deliberate practice, as noted in the training section, would likely prove useful as well.

REFERENCES

References marked with an asterisk indicate studies included in the meta-analyses.

Ackerman, S. J., & Hilsenroth, M. J. (2001). A review of therapist characteristics and techniques negatively impacting the therapeutic alliance. *Psychotherapy: Theory, Research, Practice, Training, 38*, 171–185. https://www.doi.org/10.1037.0033-3204.38.2.171

*Agnew, R. M., Harper, H., Shapiro, D. A., & Barkham, M. (1994). Resolving a challenge to the therapeutic relationship: A single-case study. *British Journal of Medical Psychology, 67*, 155–170. https://www.doi.org/10.1111/j2044-8341.1994.tb01783.x

*Audet, C. T. (2011). Client perspectives of therapist self-disclosure: Violating boundaries or removing barriers? *Counselling Psychology Quarterly, 24*, 85–100. https://www.doi.org/10.1080/09515070.2011.589602

*Audet, C. T., & Everall, R. D. (2010). Therapist self-disclosure and the therapeutic relationship: A phenomenological study from the client perspective. *British Journal of Guidance & Counselling, 38*, 327–342. https://www.doi.org/10.1080/03069885.2010.482450

*Barrett, M. S., & Berman, J. S. (2001). Is psychotherapy more effective when therapists disclose information about themselves? *Journal of Consulting and Clinical Psychology, 69*, 597–603. https://www.doi.org/10.1037/0022-006X.69.4.597

Beck, A. T., Rush, J. A., Shaw, B. R., & Emery, G. (1979). *Cognitive therapy of depression.* New York, NY: Guilford.

*Bennett, D., Parry, G., & Ryle, A. (2006). Resolving threats to the therapeutic alliance in cognitive analytic therapy. *Psychology and Psychotherapy, 79*, 395–418. https://www.doi.org/10.1348/147608305X58355

*Berman, M., Hill, C. E., Liu, J., Jackson, J., Sim, W., & Spangler, P. (2012). Relational events in acceptance and commitment therapy for three clients. In L. G. Castonguay & C. E. Hill (Eds.), *Transformation in psychotherapy: Corrective experiences across cognitive behavioral, humanistic, and psychodynamic approaches* (pp. 215–240). Washington, DC: American Psychological Association.

Bugental, J. F. T. (1965). *The search for authenticity.* New York, NY: Holt, Rinehart & Winston.

Chow, D. L., Miller, S. D., Seidel, J. A., Kane, R. T., Thornton, J. A., & Andrew, W. P. (2015). The role of deliberate practice in the development of highly effective psychotherapists. *Psychotherapy, 52*, 337–345. https://www.doi.org/10.1037/pst0000015

Clemence, A. J., Fowler, J. C., Gottdiener, W. H., Krikorian, S., Charles, M., Damsky, L., & Johnson, B. (2012). Microprocess examination of therapeutic immediacy during a dynamic research interview. *Psychotherapy, 49*, 317–329. https://www.doi.org/10.1037/a0026090

Curtis, J. M. (1981). Indications and contraindications in the use of therapist's self-disclosure. *Psychological Reports, 49*, 499–507. https://www.doi.org/10.2466/pr0.1981.49.2.499

Curtis, J. M. (1982). Principles and techniques of non-disclosure by the therapist during psychotherapy. *Psychological Reports, 51,* 907–914. https://www.doi.org/10.2466/pr0.1982.51.3.907

Dowd, E. T., & Boroto, D. R. (1982). Differential effects of therapist self-disclosure, self-involving statements, and interpretation. *Journal of Counseling Psychology, 29,* 8–13. https://www.doi.org/10.1037/0022-0167.29.1.8

Eagle, M. N. (2011). *From classical to contemporary psychoanalysis: A critique and integration.* New York, NY: Routledge.

Farber, B. A. (2006). *Self-disclosure in psychotherapy.* New York, NY: Guilford.

Goldberg, S. B., Babins-Wagner, R., Rousmaniere, T., Berzins, S., Hoyt, W. T., Whippple, J. L., . . . Wampold, B. E. (2016). Creating a climate for therapist improvement: A case study of an agency focused on outcomes and deliberate practice. *Psychotherapy, 53,* 367–375. https://www.doi.org/10.1037/pst0000060

Greenson, R. R. (1967). *The technique and practice of psychoanalysis* (Vol. 1). New York, NY: International Universities Press.

*Hanson, J. (2005). Should your lips be zipped? How therapist self-disclosure and non-disclosure affects clients. *Counselling and Psychotherapy Research, 5,* 96–104. https://www.doi.org/10.1080/17441690500226658

Henretty, J. R., Currier, J. M., Berman, J. S., & Levitt, H. M. (2014). The impact of counselor self-disclosure on clients: A meta-analytic review of experimental and quasi-experimental research. *Journal of Counseling Psychology, 61,* 191–207. https://www.doi.org/10.1037/a0036189

Hill, C. E. (1978). Development of a counselor verbal response category system. *Journal of Counseling Psychology, 25,* 461–468. doi:10.1037/0022-0167.25.5.461

Hill, C. E. (1986). An overview of the Hill Counselor and Client Verbal Response Modes Category Systems. In L. S. Greenberg & W. M. Pinsof (Eds.), *The psychotherapeutic process: A research handbook* (pp. 131–160). New York: Guilford.

Hill, C. E., Baumann, E., Shafran, N., Gupta, S., Morrison, A., Peres Rojas, A., . . . Gelso, C. J. (2015). Is training effective? A study of counseling psychology doctoral trainees in a psychodynamic/interpersonal training clinic. *Journal of Counseling Psychology, 62,* 184–201. https://www.doi.org/10.1037/cou0000053

*Hill, C. E., Gelso, C. J., Chui, H., Spangler, P., Hummel, A., Huang, T., . . . Miles, J. R. (2014). To be or not to be immediate with clients: The use and perceived effects of immediacy in psychodynamic/interpersonal psychotherapy. *Psychotherapy Research, 3,* 299–315. https://www.doi.org/10.1080/10503307.2013.812262

*Hill, C. E., Helms, J. E., Tichenor, V., Spiegel, S. B., O'Grady, K. E., & Perry, E. S. (1988). The effects of therapist response modes in brief psychotherapy. *Journal of Counseling Psychology, 35,* 222–233. https://www.doi.org/10.1037/0022-0167.35.3.222

*Hill, C. E., Kellems, I. S., Kolchakian, M. R., Wonnell, T. L., Davis, T. L., & Nakayama, E. Y. (2003). The therapist experience of being the target of hostile versus suspected-unasserted client anger: Factors associated with resolution. *Psychotherapy Research, 13,* 475–491. https://www.doi.org/10.1093/ptr/kpg040

Hill, C. E., & Knox, S. (2002). Self-disclosure. In J. C. Norcross (Ed.), *Psychotherapy relationships that work: Therapist contributions and responsiveness to patient needs* (pp. 249–259). Oxford, England: Oxford University Press.

Hill, C. E., & Knox, S. (2009). Processing the therapeutic relationship. *Psychotherapy Research, 19,* 13–29. doi:10.1080/10503300802326046

Hill, C. E., Knox, S., & Hess, S. (2012). Qualitative meta-analysis. In C. E. Hill (Ed.), *Consensual qualitative research: A practical resource for investigating social science phenomena* (pp. 159–172). Washington DC: American Psychological Association.

*Hill, C. E., Mahalik, J. R., & Thompson, B. J. (1989). Therapist self-disclosure. *Psychotherapy, 26*, 290–295. https://www.doi.org/10.1037/h0085438

*Hill, C. E., Nutt-Williams, E., Heaton, K. J., Thompson, B. J., & Rhodes, R. H. (1996). Therapist retrospective recall of impasses in long-term psychotherapy: A qualitative analysis. *Journal of Counseling Psychology, 43*, 207–217. https://www.doi.org/10.1037/0022-0167.43.2.207

*Hill, C. E., Sim, W., Spangler, P., Stahl, J., Sullivan, C., & Teyber, E. (2008). Therapist immediacy in brief psychotherapy: Case study II. *Psychotherapy: Theory, Research, Practice, Training, 45*, 298–315. https://www.doi.org/10.1037/a0013306

Hill, C. E., Thompson, B. J., Cogar, M. C., & Denman, D. W. III (1993). Beneath the surface of long-term therapy: Therapist and client report of their own and each other's covert processes. *Journal of Counseling Psychology, 40*, 278–281. https://www.doi.org/10.1037/0022-0167.40.3.278

Hill, C. E., Thompson, B. J., & Corbett, M. M. (1992). The impact of therapist ability to perceive displayed and hidden client reactions on immediate outcome in first sessions of brief therapy. *Psychotherapy Research, 2*, 143–155. https://www.doi.org/10.1080/10503309212331332914

Hilsenroth, M. J., Blagys, M. D., Ackerman, S. J., Bonge, D. R., & Blais, M. A. (2005). Measuring psychodynamic-interpersonal and cognitive-behavioral techniques: Development of the Comparative Psychotherapy Process Scale. *Psychotherapy: Theory, Research, Practice, and Training, 42*, 340–356. https://www.doi.org/10.1037/0033-3204.42.3.340

*Iwakabe, S., & Conceição, N. (2016). Metatherapeutic processing as a change-based therapeutic immediacy task: Building an initial process model using a task-analytic strategy. *Journal of Psychotherapy Integration. 26*, 230–247. https://www.doi.org/10.1037/int0000016

Jones, E. E., & Pulos, S. M. (1993). Comparing the process in psychodynamic and cognitive behavioral therapies. *Journal of Consulting and Clinical Psychology, 61*(2), 306–316. https://www.doi.org/10.1037/0022-006x.61.2.306

Jourard, S. M. (1971). *The transparent self.* New York, NY: Van Nostrand.

*Kasper, L., Hill, C. E., & Kivlighan, D. (2008). Therapist immediacy in brief psychotherapy: Case study I. *Psychotherapy: Theory, Research, Practice, Training, 45*, 281–287. https://www.doi.org/10.1037/a0013305

Kim, B., Hill, C. E., Gelso, C. J., Goates, M., Harbin, J., & Asay, P. (2003). Counselor self-disclosure, East Asian American client adherence to Asian cultural values, and counseling process. *Journal of Counseling Psychology, 50*, 324–332. https://www.doi.org/10.1037/0022-0167.50.3.324

*Knox, S., Hess, S. A., Petersen, D. A., & Hill, C. E. (1997). A qualitative analysis of client perceptions of the effects of helpful therapist self-disclosure in long-term therapy. *Journal of Counseling Psychology, 44*, 274–283. https://www.doi.org/10.1037/0022-0167.44.3.274

*Kronner, H. W., & Northcut, T. (2015). Listening to both sides of the therapeutic dyad: Self-disclosure of gay male therapists and reflections from their gay male clients. *Psychoanalytic Social Work, 22*(2), 162–181. https://www.doi.org/10.1080/15228878.2015.1050746

Kushner, K., Bordin, E. S., & Rynan, E. (1979). Comparison of Strupp and Jenkins' audiovisual psychotherapy analogues and real psychotherapy interviews. *Journal of Consulting and Clinical Psychology, 47*, 765–767. https://www.doi.org/10.1037/0022-006X.47.4.765

Kuutmann, K., & Hilsenroth, M. J. (2011). Exploring in-session focus on the patient-therapist relationship: Patient characteristics, process and outcome. *Clinical Psychology and Psychotherapy, 19*, 187–202. https://www.doi.org/10.1002/cpp.743

Ladany, N., Thompson, B. J., & Hill, C. E. (2012). Cross analysis. In C. E. Hill (Ed.), *Consensual qualitative research: A practical resource for investigating social science phenomena* (pp. 117–134). Washington DC: American Psychological Association.

Levenson, H. (2010). *Brief dynamic therapy.* Washington DC: American Psychological Association.

*Li, X., Jauquet, C. A., & Kivlighan, D. M. J. (2016). When is therapist metacommunication followed by more client collaboration? The moderation effects of timing and contexts. *Journal of Counseling Psychology, 63*(6), 693–703. https://www.doi.org/10.1037/cou0000162

Lingiardi, V., Colli, A., Gentile, D., & Tanzilli, A. (2011). Exploration of session process: Relationship to depth and alliance. *Psychotherapy, 48,* 391–400. https://www.doi.org/10.1037/a0025248

*Mayotte-Blum, J. Slavin-Mulford, J., Lehmann, M., Pesale, F., Becker-Matero, N., & Hilsenroth, M. (2012). Therapeutic immediacy across long-term psychodynamic psychotherapy: An evidence-based case study. *Journal of Counseling Psychology, 59,* 27–40. https://www.doi.org/10.1037/a0026087

McCarthy, K. S., & Barber, J. P. (2009). The Multitheoretical List of Therapeutic Interventions (MULTI): Initial report. *Psychotherapy Research, 19,* 96–113. https://www.doi.org/10.1080/10503300802524343

McCarthy, P. R., & Betz, N. E. (1978). Differential effects of self-disclosing versus self-involving counselor statements. *Journal of Counseling Psychology, 25,* 251–256. https://www.doi.org/10.1037/0022-0167.25.4.251

McWilliams, N. (2004). *Psychoanalytic psychotherapy: A practitioner's guide.* New York, NY: Guilford.

*Pinto-Coelho, K. G., Hill, C. E., Kearney, M. S., Sauber, E., Sarno, E. L., Brady, J., ... Thompson, B. J. (2018). *When in doubt, sit quietly: A qualitative investigation of experienced therapists' perceptions of self-disclosure. Journal of Counseling Psychology, 65,* 440–552. doi:10.1037/cou0000288.

*Pinto-Coelho, K., Hill, C. E., & Kivlighan, D. (2016). Therapist self-disclosures in psychodynamic psychotherapy: A mixed methods investigation. *Counselling Psychology Quarterly, 29*(1), 29–52. https://www.doi.org/10.1080/09514070.2015.1072496

Rennie, D. L. (1994). Clients' deference in psychotherapy. *Journal of Counseling Psychology, 41,* 427–437. https://www.doi.org/10.1037/0022-0167.41.4.427

*Rhodes, R., Hill, C. E., Thompson, B. J., & Elliott, R. (1994). Client retrospective recall of resolved and unresolved misunderstanding events. *Journal of Counseling Psychology, 41,* 473–483. https://www.doi.org/10.1037/0022-0167.41.4.473

*Safran, J. D., & Muran, J. C. (1996). The resolution of ruptures in the therapeutic alliance. *Journal of Consulting and Clinical Psychology, 64,* 447–458. https://www.doi.org/10.1037/0022-006X.64.3.447

Spangler, P. T., Hill, C. E., Dunn, M. G., Hummel, A., Walden, T., Liu, J., . . . Salahuddin, N. (2014). Training undergraduate students to use immediacy. *The Counseling Psychologist, 42,* 729–757. https://www.doi.org/10.1177/0011000014542835

Stiles, W. B. (1979). Verbal response modes and psychotherapeutic technique. *Psychiatry, 42,* 49–62.

Stiles, W. B., Hill, C. E., & Elliott, R. (2015). Looking both ways. *Psychotherapy Research, 25,* 282–293. https://www.doi.org/10.1080/10503307.2014.981681

12

EMOTIONAL EXPRESSION

Paul R. Peluso and Robert R. Freund

Emotion is universally regarded as a fundamental part of the human experience. Although there are several theories and approaches to emotion, the development and purpose of emotions are considered to be the result of an evolutionary process designed to help solve tasks in life (Scarantino, 2016; Ekman & Cordato, 2011; Tomkins, 2008). As such, from the beginning of psychotherapy, emotion has been therapeutically significant, whether framed in the pathological presentation of clients or reflected in therapeutic engagement to help clients "solve" their emotional problems.

The nascent research on emotion in psychotherapy, and its contributions to outcomes, has come to the fore only relatively recently (Greenberg, 2016). Yet, the evidence from this research is compelling. Not only does it support the idea that emotion substantially contributes to clinical outcomes but also that it is a foundation of both specific and nonspecific processes tied to clinical efficacy (Greenberg, 2016; Orlinsky & Howard, 1978; Rottenberg & Gross, 2007).

While the notion that emotion influences clinical outcomes may not prove surprising, the mechanics of this influence is far from settled. For example, cognitive-behavioral therapies have not proven that cognitive change is the direct mechanism of treatment success, despite having an effect on outcome (Greenberg, 2016). Instead, the direct mechanism of change may flow through affective expression. What therapists attend to, and how it is processed with clients, play a significant role in determining the influence of emotion. Therefore, in summary:

> helping people overcome their avoidance of emotions, focusing collaboratively on emotions, and exploring them in therapy thus appears to be important in therapeutic change, whichever therapeutic orientation is employed. What is needed now is a more differentiated understanding of how to work with emotion. (Greenberg, 2016, pp. 671–672)

At the same time, not all expressions of emotion are of equal, beneficial value or weight. Attention to the context (whether directed at the therapist, at others, at self) and expression (valence, intensity, timing) of emotional arousal are also guiding factors for the therapist to decide what expression of emotions are going to be facilitative of positive outcomes (Whelton, 2004). Thus, therapist discernment, guided by theoretical orientation, is very important. In fact, many of the "new wave" therapies that stress mindfulness and emotional regulation, pay particular attention to emotional expressions (Sloan & Kring, 2007).

An interesting feature of how emotion impacts treatment outcomes is the mediating influence of the therapeutic relationship (Beutler et al., 2000). In particular, the concept of the working alliance (goals, tasks, and bond) has been found to be a significant factor in whether emotional expression is productive for the therapy (see Chapter 2, this volume; Bordin, 1979). This mediation is likely due to the "productivity" elements of the working alliance. Facilitating emotional expression can be considered a therapeutic task, while deriving meaningful interpretations or resolutions of emotions are the goals of that task (Beutler et al., 2000; Greenberg & Pascual-Leone, 2006; Iwakabe et al., 2000). As such, there is a reciprocal process in which emotional expression can strengthen the therapeutic bond, and a positive bond enables more productive emotional expression in therapy. Hence, the therapeutic relationship plays an important role in dampening or heightening emotion in ways that contribute to psychotherapy outcomes.

A productive relationship can train clients in adaptive means of experiencing and expressing emotion (Greenberg, 2014; Wheaton, 2004). The therapeutic relationship fosters corrective emotional experiences that models affect regulation, which clients can learn over the course of therapy. Psychotherapists of all theoretical orientations work toward creating productive emotional experiences that foster clients' corrective emotional experiences on an attachment- or schema-based level (Greenberg, 2016). At the same time, further research is needed on emotion in psychotherapy that explores how emotional process impacts therapy and how therapy impacts clients' emotional process (Rottenberg & Gross, 2007).

This chapter summarizes the research on the role of emotional expressions on psychotherapy outcome and to advance clinical practices based on that research evidence. We begin by defining the core terms, reviewing common measures of emotion, and summarizing landmark studies. We then look at the research literature related to the expression of emotion by both the therapist and the client, and its relation to treatment outcomes, by conducting meta-analyses. Next, we consider the limitations of the research evidence and diversity considerations. Lastly, we offer some suggestions on ways to incorporate expressions of affect in both the training and practice of mental health professionals.

DEFINITIONS

Because emotion is such an all-encompassing aspect of our existence, defining it can sometimes prove difficult (Scarantino, 2016). From a bioevolutionary perspective, emotions serve a critical species survival purpose by providing information about situations that we consider to be personally meaningful (Ekman, 2007; Scarantino, 2016). This information is used to foster action in the service of one's self care

(Greenberg & Safran, 1989; Rottenberg & Gross, 2007). From this perspective, the intensity of an emotional experience increases with the significance of a perceived experience.

A discrete number of universal emotions, also known as primary emotions, are experienced and expressed the same way regardless of culture, race, or developmental background (happiness, sadness, fear, surprise, disgust, anger) by all human beings. What distinguishes and defines these emotions is that they have a signal, a trigger, or theme; they are linked to specific physiological displays that are unambiguous; and there are likely actions that will result from the emotion (Ekman, 2007). Secondary emotions (such as embarrassment, guilt, and pride) are nuanced and represent contextually influenced feeling states. With all emotions (primary or secondary), cultural and other relevant issues will impact the trigger or theme, the display rules, and the attitudes about each emotion. For example, rules about politeness and rudeness may trigger a display of embarrassment for certain behavior in one culture that they would not trigger in another. At the same time, the physiological display of anger may be universal if specifically triggered, but the degree or intensity to which the anger is displayed will be mediated by the display rules in one culture versus another (Ekman, 2007; Ekman & Cordato, 2011). As a result, they are heavily influenced by intra or interpersonal factors. Additional hallmarks of both primary and secondary emotions include perception of the experience, cognitive appraisal that either prompts or interprets the emotional experience, and some form of physiological expression (Sloan & Kring, 2007; Tomkins, 2008).

Emotion research has a long history, with several scientific "branches" or traditions that defined how emotion has been scientifically studied over the years. There is the feeling tradition (which emphasizes the conscious or subjective sensation of emotion), the motivation tradition (where emotions are distinct motivational states that drive behavior), and the evaluative tradition (where cognitive evaluation or interpretation distinguishes one emotion from the other). However, such a detailed treatment is not appropriate in this chapter (for a thorough review of these, see Scarantino, 2016), while at the same time a concise definition of such a broad and encompassing topic as emotion risks being incomplete, for the purpose of this chapter, we define emotion as a feeling state that "(1) have a well-specified object (i.e., one is angry about something), (2) unfold over seconds to minutes, and (3) involve coordinated changes in subjective experience, behavior, and physiology" (Suri & Gross, 2016, pp. 453–454). This definition is an effective combination or the three traditions, and fit with Greenberg's (2016) description of the expression of emotion in therapy: "[It] does not involve simply venting emotion, but rather overcoming avoidance of, strongly experiencing, and expressing previously constricted emotions" (Greenberg, 2016, p. 674).

Affect and Mood

Affect is a relatively quick experience of emotion; a felt, perceived episode of feeling that is expressed through nonverbal and verbal, as well as cognitive, behaviors (Mozdierz et al., 2014). The presentation of affect is both brief and prominent. During the time that it is experienced, the specific affect remains in the foreground of experience, and it generally is tied to a specific stimuli (Rottenberg & Gross, 2007).

Mood is also experienced through intrapsychic and external means, but it differs from affect in that it can be sustained over extended periods of time, serving as an emotional backdrop to other experiences (Mozdzierz et al., 2014). Additionally, mood is generally not tethered to a specific experience or stimuli; rather, it is a diffuse experience of emotion that colors perception and creates an environment from which affect may sometimes (but not always) emerge (Lempert & Phelps, 2016; Rottenberg & Gross, 2007).

Automatic and Reflective Appraisal

A significant part of how emotion emerges is a result of the appraisal process. There are two identified types of appraisal (Ekman, 2007.) The first, *automatic appraisal*, occurs outside the scope of personal awareness and is a result of the brain processes that detect events that may impact our well-being or survival. Automatic appraisal can prompt quick, gut-reaction responses to events (such as fear upon seeing a predator or shame after exposure to humiliation). *Reflective appraisal*, by contrast, is a more nuanced process and comes from an explicit examination of internal thoughts, or experiences. Emotions that emerge from reflective appraisals help a person to derive meaning from his or her experiences and place the events within a proper cognitive frame or larger narrative context (Ekman & Cordato, 2011).

Productive vs. Negative Emotion

Of relevance to therapeutic interactions is the utility of emotion. Historically, the research on emotion and therapeutic outcomes has been mixed, with some studies indicating positive impact on the therapy and others a negative impact (Greenberg, 2016). This ambiguity has been due in part to the failure of researchers to operationally qualify the kinds of emotion present in the therapy and the way it has been processed. Emotional expression alone does not indicate the content or purpose it serves.

Emotion in therapy can be either productive or unproductive, and therapists must identify hallmarks of both qualities. Intrusive emotions that detract from the goals of the therapy can be seen as unproductive, and therapists can work to help clients regulate or compartmentalize them (Greenberg, 2016; Rachman, 1980). Productive emotions, on the other hand, are consistent with the therapeutic goals established by the client and therapist. They are congruent to the topic of focus and further information processing (Greenberg, 2016; Rachman, 1980; Whelton, 2004).

Alexithymia

Another important phenomenon in exploring emotion in psychotherapy is alexithymia. According to Parker et al. (2003), alexithymia is defined as "a multifaceted construct encompassing difficulty identifying subjective emotional feelings and distinguishing between feelings and the bodily sensations of emotional arousal, difficulty describing feelings to other people, an impoverished fantasy life, and a stimulus bound, externally oriented cognitive style" (p. 277). Individuals with alexithymia tend to demonstrate reactive cognitive processing styles, responding to external stimuli rather than internal experiences (Jordan & Smith, 2017). Alexithymia has been associated with a range of mental health conditions, including trauma disorders, substance use disorders, and mood disorders, and is further associated with interpersonal difficulty (Jordan & Smith, 2017; Ogrodniczuck et al., 2008; Whelton, 2004).

Emotional Processing

Emotional processing refers to how individuals experience, organize, make meaning of, and resolve emotional episodes. Broadly speaking, emotional processing involves identifying and addressing the disruption of an emotional baseline and a return to equilibrium (Greenberg, 2016; Rachman, 1980). Emotional processing involves more than mere exposure to emotional experiences, but rather a dual process of exposure and cognitive activation (Teasdale, 1999). The combination of felt experience and cognitive evaluation allows the individual to make meaning of the emotion, as well as the subject or event that originally triggered the emotional reaction (Teasdale, 1999; Whelton, 2004). Successful emotional processing has been positively correlated with treatment outcomes, as well as positive change within individual sessions (Stalikas & Fitzpatrick, 1995; Town et al., 2017; Whelton, 2004).

Emotional Regulation

Distinct from emotional processing is the means by which individuals manage the experience and expression of their emotions, otherwise known as emotional regulation. Emotional processing refers to the experience and cognitive evaluation of emotion, whereas emotional regulation deals with managing emotional states. According to Suri and Gross (2016), "[e]motion regulation refers to a valuation process that targets another valuation (the one that is generating emotion), assigns this valuation a positive or negative value, and takes action to make the emotion either more or less likely to occur" (p. 453).

MEASURES

A number of measures have been used in clinical research to assess emotions and emotional expression. These measures largely fall into two types: self-report or other-rated. Some measures are theoretically derived (e.g., Achievement of Therapeutic Objectives Scale [ATOS]), while others are more generic or atheoretical (e.g., Emotion Facial Action Coding System [EMFACS]). We will describe several of the most commonly used measures that appeared in our meta-analyses.

The Client Emotional Productivity Scale–Revised (CEPS-R; Auszra et al., 2013) is an observational rating system that differentiates whether clients are experiencing an emotion or they are intellectually discussing an experience of an emotion. Coders assess the degree to which an emotion is processed using several criteria, namely, acceptance, agency, attending, congruence, differentiation, regulation, and symbolization. The client's emotional expression is assigned a categorical weight ranging from zero (mixed/uncodeable) and 1 (nonproductive) to 4 (productive). The authors reported a kappa of .75 for the interrater reliability of an earlier version of the measure (Auszra et al., 2013.)

The Client Expressed Emotional Arousal Scale–III–R (CEAS-III; Machado, 1992; Machado et al., 1999) is a 7-point, Likert-type observational coding system that measures primary emotions: anger, fear, joy, love, sadness, and surprise in psychotherapy (as cited in Warwar & Greenberg, 1999). Scores are anchored to specific intensity levels in the voice or in body movements when clients either acknowledge that they are experiencing an emotion, or when they demonstrate specific action tendencies in response to an emotion. Lower scores (from 1 to 3) are indicative of lower emotional arousal, while higher scores (from 4 to 7) represent higher levels of arousal (Boritz et al., 2011). Inter-rater agreement ranges from .75 to .81 among coders (Warwar & Greenberg, 1999).

The Experiencing Scale (EXP; Klein et al., 1969, 1986) is also an observational coding system that was designed to measure the amount and quality of clients' emotional processing in session. Raters use a 7-point, Likert-type scale to code clients' transcribed statements based on the degree to which a client is aware of their emotional experiences, exploration of these experiences, and the level of reflection on these experiences to achieve problem resolution. Both the content of the client's responses and the mannerisms of expression are considered by raters (Gordon & Toukmanian, 2002; Watson & Bedard, 2006). At the lower end of the scale, clients discuss events or concepts with no reference to themselves or their emotional experiences. At the mid-point (Level 3), clients' discussion of emotional experiences is external to the self or based on external events. At the upper ranges of the scale (Level 7), clients' use their reflections on their emotional experiences as a part of the process for problem-solving (Watson & Bedard, 2006). The EXP has been used extensively in psychotherapy research, demonstrated to be generally related to good treatment outcomes (Orlinsky & Howard, 1978) and has consistently had fair to good interrater reliability for both modal session ratings of sessions (ranging from .65 to .93) as well as peak emotional experiences (.61 to–.93; Gordon & Toukmanian, 2002).

Emotion Facial Action Coding System (EMFACS; Friesen & Ekman, 1984) is an emotion coding system based on the Facial Action Coding System (FACS; Ekman & Friesen, 1978). Unlike FACS, which is a comprehensive system for coding facial actions by categorizing muscle movement of facial muscles, EMFACS measures only movements that are potentially relevant to specific affects (e.g., anger, fear, joy, sadness). These expressions are considered to be universal displays and are not specific to a particular theory or approach to therapy (Ekman, 2007). Coders wishing to use

EMFACS must establish reliability with FACS based on an external testing procedure. As a result, reliability estimates are not generally published. EMFACS is useful for distinguishing several types of smiles (e.g., a genuine smile vs. a "social" or unfelt smile).

The *Achievement of Therapeutic Objectives Scale* (ATOS; McCullough et al., 2003) is a coding system that investigates client behaviors within the context of psychodynamic therapy and other therapies, although many of the constructs are rooted in psychodynamic theory (e.g., "defense reactions"). The key subscales for monitoring clients' emotions are the experience of activating affects (Carley, 2006, as cited in Schanche et al., 2011), which has adequate construct validity ($r = .70$) when compared with the EXP (Klein et al., 1986).

The *Positive and Negative Affect Schedule* (PANAS; Watson et al., 1988) is a self-report of positive and negative emotions. The PANAS contains 20 items, with 10 adjectives measuring positive affect (PA), such as active, enthusiastic, or interested, and 10 adjectives measuring negative affect (NA), such as scared, upset, and irritable (Sloan & Kring, 2007). The PANAS has been used to measure both therapist and client affect in therapy and has shown good psychometric properties. Specifically, the PANAS has shown good discriminant and convergent validity with the PA scale correlating negatively with general distress, depression, and anxiety, while the NA scale was positively correlated with the same measures (Sloan & Kring, 2007). Internal consistency for the PA and NA scales ranged from .84 to .90 and good test–retest reliability (over two months). In addition, PA and NA scores are largely uncorrelated (Sloan & Kring, 2007; Watson et al., 1988).

The *Toronto Alexithymia Scale-20* (TAS-20; Bagby et al., 1994) is a frequently used self-report measure of emotional awareness. The TAS-20 assesses clients' inability to accurately label and identify their emotions. The TAS is a 20-item, 5-point Likert-type scale that ranges from "strongly agree" to "strongly disagree." Sample items include "It is difficult for me to find the right words for my feelings." The TAS-20 has three subscales: difficulty identifying feelings, difficulty describing feelings, and externally oriented thinking. Internal reliability estimates have demonstrated good coefficients for the total score (alpha = .80) and for subscales (ranging from .75 to .78; Sloan & Kring, 2007).

Taken together, these measures tap into either expressed emotions (whether self-rated or other-rated) or perceived affect (in the case of PANAS and TAS-20) in the context of a therapy session. Unfortunately, many these scales have not been used together in studies, so finding interrcorrelations amongst the scales is difficult. However, we were able to find some studies that overlapped some of the measures. For example, Auszra et al. (2013) found small, but significant correlation ($r = .26$) between the CEPSS-R and the CEAS-III, while Rasting et al. (2005) found a robust and negative correlation between TAS-20 total scores and displays of aggressive affect ($r = -.67$) as measured by EMFACS. In addition (as reported in the previous text), the ATOS Experience of Activating Affects subscale and the EXP are highly correlated ($r = .70$). As such, we feel that these instruments adequately (though not perfectly) assess aspects of emotional expression and can be included together for the present meta-analyses.

CLINICAL EXAMPLES

The following case by the first author (Peluso, 2012) concerns "Ashley," a 35-year-old, married mother of two children, working as a medical billing supervisor, who presented to therapy with anxiety and depression. She felt unsupported by her husband of eight years, extended family, and coworkers. In addition, Ashley feels overwhelmed physically, emotionally, and psychologically. As she increased her efforts to be independent and self-sufficient, Ashley realized how little she actually can control. Exhausted, she brings the ambivalence of her desire for control and desire for interdependence with others to treatment.

In the following excerpt, the client's emotional expression is the focus of the interaction. The therapist attends to, and then facilitates, the client's emotional expression to process elements that are contributing to her problems:

TH: And that is why you have to work harder than everybody else? Because you don't want to be cast aside, cast away?

CL: (Slowly) Yeah . . .

TH: I'm noticing your face, your body posture; it seems more subdued. Can you tell me how you are feeling right now?

CL: Sad. I feel sad.

TH: You try and try as hard as you can. You work so hard to do your best, and it still doesn't completely work out.

CL: That's why I got so fed up the other day with the kids. I just felt like it didn't matter what I did nothing was going right. I felt like the house was collapsing on me, and I was trapped underneath.

TH: You've felt this way before? That no matter what you did, nothing would "go right."

CL: Yeah, when I was younger.

TH: Can you tell me what happened then?

CL: Well, I was in third grade and my parents got a divorce.

TH: And that was difficult . . .

In this brief exchange, the therapist attends to and comments on the client's nonverbal expression of emotion. The therapist facilitates identification of her emotional experience and then heightens it through reflection. This emotional processing prompts the client to discuss a formative experience in her childhood when her parents divorced, and she felt like her father replaced her with a new family; she and the therapist elicit her belief that she could be "replaced" in other relationships. This belief evokes a strong feeling of fear, which often drives her to "overfunction" and not ask for help. They subsequently decide together to work in session to prevent her from reacting to her fear of being replaced or discarded.

Later in the session, the client's emotional expression serves as an indicator of her flexibility and readiness for change. Ashley's emotional experience and the therapist's sensitivity to it both contribute to clarifying the boundaries of her resistance and readiness for change.

TH: I heard some hesitation in your voice when I suggested that you needed help.

CL: Yeah, I just cringed inside. I felt a lump in my throat.

TH: What was that lump?

CL: What was it? (Doesn't quite get the question)

TH: Yeah, where do you think it came from?

CL: Fear.

TH: Of needing help?

CL: Yeah, and asking for it.

TH: I see. So just thinking of the possibility of asking for help is enough to bring up the old fear of being replaced?

CL: Uh-huh

TH: So then to move too fast, and for me to say "OK, so tomorrow you are going to ask everyone at home and at work for help" probably isn't going to feel as good, and probably won't work, right?

CL: Probably, yeah.

TH: But you can agree with me that it is a goal to work towards.

CL: Yeah (Slowly)

TH: OK, I heard the hesitation again. How about if we worked on the goal of helping you lower your fear of being replaced? Help you feel less lonely? Would that be better?

CL: Yeah (Nodding)

In this excerpt, the client's nonverbal emotional cues indicate that she is not ready to engage in direct action that would resolve her presenting concerns. This serves as a signal to the therapist to engage in collaborative goal setting with the client in which the long- and short-term goals are within a level of personal challenge that she feels comfortable pursuing. Her emotional response is a large part of this process. At the same time, the therapist processes her emotional experience while encouraging practice in regulating her emotions in comfortable increments. The interaction takes place in the context of the working alliance. which in and of itself, may prove corrective as the client is experiencing "not having it all" and yet not being replaced or abandoned.

LANDMARK STUDIES

In the following section, we provide summaries of two landmark studies. The term "landmark" for the purposes of this chapter is any research that guides other researchers, rather than just historical importance (Ginsberg, 2004). Using this criterion, we selected these articles because they discuss the interplay between appropriate emotional arousal and the therapeutic relationship. They also reflect research that blends self-report data with observational data. Lastly, these studies discuss the interplay between appropriate emotional expression and psychotherapy outcomes.

Carryer and Greenberg (2010) explored the interplay of emotional intensity, time spent in emotional process, the therapeutic relationship, and clinical outcomes in depressed clients. The authors selected 38 clients (14 male, 24 female) with primary diagnoses of depression from a larger pool of over 400 patients. The sample was highly controlled with specific inclusion criteria (e.g., scores on the depression and personality modules of the structured clinical interview, scores on the Beck Depression Inventory [BDI], etc.) as well as exclusion criteria (e.g., suicidality, trauma history, comorbidity with specific disorders that might confound treatment, etc.). The selected clients were treated on average for 17.6 sessions of experiential therapy by clinicians (12 female, 2 male) trained extensively in client-centered and emotion-focused therapy. Following each session, clients completed the Client Working Alliance Inventory (WAI) and therapists completed the Therapist Post Session Questionnaire (TPSQ). Outcome measures were administered to the clients at the pre-, mid-, and post-treatment stages of therapy, as well as at a six-month follow-up (BDI, Symptom Checklist-90-Revised [SCL-90-R], Rosenberg Self-Esteem Scale [RSE], and the Inventory of Interpersonal Problems [IIP]). The researchers used the Client Expressed Emotional Arousal Scale-III-Revised (CEAS) as a process measure to observe levels of client emotional arousal during the therapy.

Three sessions from the latter phase of treatment were selected for analysis, based on prior study designs and data. The individual sessions included in the data set were selected based on therapist perception of client emotion in the TPSQ, as well as the reported content of the session as it related to client goals. In accordance with the manual requirements for the CEAS, blind coders watched each session at one-minute increments, rating the highest level of client emotional arousal within that span; they then identified the peak arousal rating within a five-minute segment. By doing this, raters captured what the authors refer to as "an arousal profile" for each session (Carryer & Greenberg, 2010).

The percentage of higher CEAS scores (4 and 5+, respectively) were correlated with scores from the client's fourth session WAI and several outcome measures. In the CEAS, scores of 4 represent a moderate level of arousal, while scores of 5 or higher indicate high to extreme levels of arousal. The CEAS scores of were correlated with the residual gain scores of the outcome measures. The WAI also correlated significantly with client scores on the BDI; as WAI scores increased, BDI scores decreased ($r = -.376$.) Correlations were also significant for all outcome measures and the CEAS scores of 4 (CEAS 4). With the BDI, CEAS 4 correlated positively, meaning as the frequency of moderate arousal increased, so did the client scores on the BDI ($r = .35$).

The researchers did not find significant linear correlations for the CEAS scores of 5 or higher (CEAS 5+) with any of the measures. After completing scatterplots for the CEAS 5+ and BDI scores, the researchers observed a curvilinear, U-shaped distribution, suggesting that at certain frequencies, CEAS 5+ scores were associated with higher BDI scores, and at other frequencies, with lower scores. To understand this relationship more concretely, the researchers established the mean frequency of CEAS 5+ to reorganize the score frequencies (the CEAS 5+ variable was renamed as HiEmot). The absolute value of scores above and below the mean point allowed the researchers to effectively identify linear relationships with the outcome data. After this transformation, HiEmot was found to significantly correlate with BDI ($r = .504$) and the Global Severity Index of the SCL-90-R ($r = .484$).

Overall, the authors concluded that the nuances of the HiEmot variable added to the explained variance of outcomes (as described by the BDI) accounted for by the WAI. Originally, the WAI accounted for 14% of the outcome variance on BDI scores; adding the HiEmot variable increased the outcome variance to 16%, but only when HiEmot was present in the therapy at a moderate frequency (25%). In the most emotionally intense sessions of therapy, therapist management of client emotional arousal and expression is an important factor in the success of the therapy. Specifically, any more than roughly 25% of the time spent expressing emotion might be counterproductive. However, the presence and expression of emotion (even intense emotion) is still important to the efficacy of the therapeutic endeavor.

In an exploration of how client emotional expression is influenced by therapist interventions, Iwakabe et al. (2000) studied therapy sessions conducted by master clinicians. Similar to the previous study, the researchers wanted to test the limits of emotional intensity of client expression and how that relates to the quality of the working alliance. They also were interested in understanding how therapist interventions produced these emotional expressions, as well as the emotional behaviors that prompted. As such, two distinct questions were explored using individual study designs. In the first study, the researchers looked at the differences in in emotional intensity between high working alliance and low working alliance sessions. The second study was designed to assess the target of client emotional expression (i.e., toward what or who the emotion is directed) as well as whether the therapist interventions were different in the low and high working alliance sessions following a client's emotional expression.

For both studies, the researchers used a sample of 25 audiotaped sessions completed by master therapists (Rogers, Beck, Ellis, and others). These sessions were part of a sample from a previous study. Using an observer-based version of the WAI (Horvath & Greenberg, 1986), the researchers identified the mean working alliance rating for all available sessions ($M = 172.5$, SD $= 36.82$). Four sessions with ratings one standard deviation below the mean (<135.23) and three sessions with ratings one standard deviation above the mean (>208.87) were then selected for inclusion as the high and low WAI groups. A fourth high WAI-rated session was selected that was not fully one standard deviation above the mean, but was closest of the sessions available ($M = 195$). These eight sessions comprised the sample included for analysis in the researchers' two studies.

To address the first question of client emotional intensity differences in high and low WAI sessions, five trained independent raters coded each session using the Strength of Feeling Scale–Revised (SFS). The SFS involves raters scaling the intensity of expressed emotion based on verbally related cues (pitch, speed, loudness, etc.) along a 6-point ordinal scale, where 6 indicates the highest, most unrestricted levels of emotion. For any sequence at a Level 4 intensity or higher, raters selected an identifying emotion from a list of 20 possible emotions. The researchers averaged all of the ratings for each session to acquire a mean intensity score for the expressed emotion in each session (for a total of eight scores). A one-way analysis of the variance indicated that there were no significant differences between the high working alliance sessions ($M = 2.79$,

$SD = .98$) and the low working alliance sessions ($M = 2.68, SD = .99$). They explored the emotions that were most commonly identified in each of the working alliance groups. They reported that in the low working alliance sessions, the most commonly identified emotions were anger, fear, and frustration. In the high working alliance sessions however, joy and sadness were most commonly identified.

The second study involved selecting specific episodes of client emotional expression that the researchers could assess at a process level. Ten judges (blind to the previous research processes) rated segments where clients displayed moderate to intense emotion with transcripts and audio, using the Questionnaire for Emotional Expression Events (QEEE), which was designed by the researchers for the study. The researchers found a significant effect for (high vs. low) working alliance group. With the exception of one dimension (linking client emotion to theme or issue), all items were found to have significant effects (therapist empathy, responsiveness to emotion, voice matching, effectiveness of intervention, self-disclosure, interrupting client emotion, and client elaboration of emotion). Some of the observed trends include high WAI therapists were more empathetic, emotionally responsive, and provided more effective interventions. High WAI therapists were less likely to engage in self-disclosure, or interrupt client emotional expression. Lastly, clients in the high WAI sessions were more likely to engage in emotional elaboration than their low WAI counterparts. Further, the data gathered allowed for models of the episodic process to be created.

Client expressions were noteworthy as well. In the high WAI sessions, client expressions of sadness, anger, and fear were directed at an individual or a situation related to the topic of discussion. Therapists were more likely to acknowledge client emotion and make reflective statements that encouraged continued expression. In the low WAI sessions however, expressions of anger and frustration were more likely to be directed at the therapist. In these sessions, therapists were likely to respond with low empathy toward client expression.

This study, and the described study preceding it, serve as landmarks for psychotherapy research on emotion. The researchers relied on innovative, as well as prior assessment methods, and used both qualitative and quantitative methods to develop unique narratives that connected to prior findings. These creative, yet thorough designs can serve as a guidepost for other psychotherapy researchers who are interested in studying expressions of emotion in therapy.

RESULTS OF PREVIOUS META-ANALYSES

There have only been a few meta-analyses conducted on the relation of emotional expressions and therapeutic outcome. Orlinsky et al. (1994) exhaustively reviewed research on therapy elements that correlated with either process or outcome in therapy. They reported effect sizes for the majority of the reviewed articles but did not synthesize them in a meta-analysis. However, a number of their subcategories yielded articles that were included in the present analysis. For example, in their analysis of client perceptions of the emotional aspects of the therapeutic encounter that impacted outcomes, Orlinsky et al. found that therapist focusing on patient affect was beneficial for outcomes in 50% of the studies surveyed, and paradoxical intention (which is often associated with expressions of emotion) was positively associated with outcomes in 100% of the studies surveyed. Client positive affective response and therapist positive affective response were both associated with outcomes in 100% of the of the studies surveyed. Patient expressiveness was positively associated in 63% of the studies surveyed, but, surprisingly, therapist expressiveness was positively associated in only 44% of the studies surveyed. Lastly, therapist affirmation of the patient was positively associated with outcome in 56% of studies, while patient affirmation of therapist was positively associated 69% of the time, and in studies where there was reciprocal affirmation, it was positively associated 78% of the time.

Diener et al. (2007) examined therapist facilitation of client expression of emotion and clinical outcome in psychodynamic psychotherapy. They reviewed 10 studies that either had external raters of emotional expression or participant (client or therapist) readings of emotion and compared them to either standard measures of outcome (HAM-D, BDI, SCL-90) or posttreatment ratings of outcome. Their analysis yielded in a weighted effect size of $r = .30$, considered to be a medium effect. Based on their reported effect size, they estimated that "therapist facilitation of patient affective experience/expression increased patient success rate from 35% to 65%" (Diener et al., 2007, p. 938). Further, they did not find moderators or mediators, suggesting that facilitating client emotion was associated with treatment success independent of other factors.

Pascual-Leone and Yeryomenko (2017) conducted a more focused meta-analysis investigating client's experiencing, a measure of the "degree of a client's involvement in the exploration of new feelings and meanings in relation to the self" (p. 1). They targeted studies that employed the Experiencing Scale (Klein et al., 1986; see previous discussion for details). They included 10 studies (6 published, 4 unpublished) and reported a small to medium effect size ($r= -.19$ to $= -.29$) relating a client's emotional experiencing to their clinical outcome. According to the researchers, because high scores on several of the outcome measures indicated higher levels of a given symptom, all outcome scores were entered with an inverse sign. Therefore, the higher negative sign should be interpreted as having a greater positive effect on outcome. The type of assessing client outcome (observational vs. self-report) did moderate the results ($-.67$ vs $-.19$, respectively). These results led the researchers to conclude that "client experiencing seems promising as a common factor in psychotherapy" (Pascual-Leone & Yeryomenko, 2017, p. 11).

To our knowledge, there is no comprehensive meta-analysis on the relation of patients' emotional expression to psychotherapy outcome across theoretical orientations and assessment measures. Nor did we locate any systematic reviews of the relation of therapist in-session emotional expression and psychotherapy outcome.

META-ANALYTIC REVIEW

We conducted four meta-analyses of the available research. The first two were on the primary question of expression of emotion and therapeutic outcome: one on the association between therapist expression of emotion and psychotherapy outcome and one on the association between client expression of emotion and psychotherapy outcome. The other two meta-analyses were secondary to the purpose of the chapter and examined the association between client and therapist expressions of emotion and the therapeutic process.

Inclusion Criteria

We searched PsycINFO, MedLine, and Google Scholar using terms like "emotion," "affect," and "therapeutic outcome." We included variations on these terms to refine our search as we identified potential articles. We also reviewed previous meta-analyses for potential articles (Diener et al., 2007; Orlinsky et al., 1994). In many cases, the effect sizes reported in the meta-analyses were recomputed to obtain standard errors and inverse variance weights not previously reported. In the process of reviewing articles, we identified additional articles of interest and continued an iterative process of seeking additional sources of published, unpublished, and in-press articles until the relevant literature was exhausted. All articles were in English and presented actual therapy studies (not analogues). We did not constrain the timeframe for publication, though the majority of articles were published between 1996 and 2017.

Initially, our search yielded 236 articles that showed promise for inclusion in one of the three meta-analyses. Further review and coding by both authors eliminated approximately 170 articles due to a lack of appropriate reporting of statistical findings, a use of retrospective questionnaires asking for recollections (primarily from therapists) after therapy had been concluded, a focus on variables not of interest to the topic (not precisely expressions of affect), or simulated clinical settings (not appropriate for the present review and meta-analysis). An additional constraint put on the analyses by the researchers was to include only articles that studied individual therapy.

In all, the studies considered in the meta-analyses were only/primarily in English, and no unpublished studies or dissertations were included. In terms of participant demographics, only 63% reported therapist demographics. Female therapists outnumbered male therapists by a ratio of over 2:1. Only 60% of the articles reviewed targeted specific therapy types, or reported the therapeutic orientation of the therapists. Of those that did, 44% utilized cognitive-behavioral therapy, 27% utilized emotion-focused therapy, and 30% utilized another therapeutic approach. In terms of client selection, over 60% of the clients were screened for a particular diagnosis, and, of those, an overwhelming number of the articles reviewed for this analysis utilized clients with depression and their expression of emotion in therapy. Approximately 74% were seen in outpatient settings. In addition, only 10% of the articles focused on a specific gender, the majority had both male and female clients. Lastly, the majority of studies did not adequately report ethnicity, and when ethnicity was reported, participants were predominately White/European American.

Preparation of Data

All effect sizes were converted to an r coefficient (if not already reported as one), and then a Fisher's r to z transformation was computed for each effect size. This created a normally distributed sampling distribution and allowed for a more accurate approximation of the standard error and the computation of the inverse variance weight (Borenstein et al., 2009). While the majority of studies reported correlations, several reported other statistics. As a result, these were transformed into r statistics using Rosenthal (1994) and then, following Borenstein et al.'s (2009) recommended procedure, transformed into a Fisher's z. The final average weighted effect size was transformed back into a Pearson's r for interpretation.

If an article had more than one effect size reported, these were averaged (Hunter & Schmidt, 2004). Negative correlations were examined for whether the finding was consistent with improvement (i.e., reduction of symptoms). If the negative correlation indicated improvement, then the sign was reversed and entered as a positive correlation for the purposes of the analysis. However, if the finding indicated that there was a negative effect on treatment outcome, then the negative correlation was entered (or averaged together with other within-study effect sizes).

We employed a random-effects model using procedures from Hedges and Olkin (1985) for each transformed effect size. We computed a weighted effect size, standard error, and inverse variance weight (Borenstein et al., 2009; Diener et al., 2009; Lipsey & Wilson, 2001). Z-tests for significance of the overall weighted mean effect size, as well as Q-statistic and I^2 for testing homogeneity were conducted for all meta-analyses. Lastly, a fail-safe N was calculated, which identifies the number of studies needed to reduce the effect size down to below .10 (as suggested by Diener et al., 2009), which is a minimum threshold for a small effect (Cohen, 1988; Norcross & Lambert, 2011).

Results of Therapist Emotional Expression and Therapeutic Process

We located only six studies on this association, and all six of them related therapist emotional expression to therapeutic process, as opposed to distal, end-of-treatment outcome. We summarize the results of this meta-analysis with the dual forewarning that the number of studies is small and that the results report on an association between emotional expression and process, not outcome.

Table 12.1 summarizes the studies used in this meta-analysis. The average weighted effect size was .27 ($z = 2.717, p. = 0.006$), producing a statistically significant medium effect size (transformed from $r(Z)$ to $r = .26$). The 95% confidence interval (CI) for the weighted effect size ranged from .07 to .46. The equivalent d for this effect would be approximately .54. With a Cohen's d of 0.54, 71% of the treatment group will be above the mean of the control group (Cohen's U_3), 79% of the two groups will overlap, and there is a 65% chance that a person picked at random from the treatment group will have a higher score than a person picked at random from the control group (probability of

Table 12.1. Studies Included in Meta-Analysis of Association of Therapist Emotional Expression and Therapeutic Process Meta-Analysis

Author and Year	Total N	Measures of Emotional Expression	Measures of Therapeutic Process/Relationship	Effect Size[a]
deRoten et al. (2002)	6	Mutual Smiling Episodes	Helping Alliance Questionnaire	.66
Gordon and Toukmanian (2002)	20	The Experiencing Scale	York Therapist Process Measure	0.24
Iwakabe et al. (2000)	8	Questionnaire for Emotional Expression Events Empathy and Responsiveness	Working Alliance Inventory (Observer)	.66
Kivlighan et al. (2014)	74	SEQ Arousal and Positivity	Working Alliance Inventory (Therapist)	.01
Kolden (1996)	62	Therapeutic Procedures Inventory- Revised	Therapy Session Report–Bond	.22
Lingiardi et al. (2011)	60	Psychotherapy Q-sort items	Working Alliance Inventory (Observer)	.50

[a]Effect sizes are averaged when more than one is reported (Diener et al., 2009).

Note. SEQ = Session Evaluation Questionnaire.

superiority). Moreover, to have one more favorable outcome in the treatment group compared to the control group, 5.5 people would need to be treated (Magnusson, n.d.).

Cochrane's Q to check for heterogeneity and failed to reject the null hypothesis ($Q = 9.04$, $df = 5$, $p = .1074$) suggesting that any variability amongst the effect sizes investigated is due to sampling error. However, caution must be taken when interpreting this result due to the small number of studies. We also calculated I^2, which equaled 11.63%, indicating that with a random effects model. There was little variation among the studies due to heterogeneity. The fail-safe N to address the "file drawer" problem. Approximately 10 studies with an effect size of zero would need to be published to bring the weighted mean effect size below .10, or practical significance.

Results of Client Emotional Expression and Therapeutic Process

Twenty articles reported results that were appropriate for analysis on the client's expression of affect and how it relates to the therapeutic relationship or therapeutic process. Table 12.2 for a summary of studies. Again, this meta-analysis reports on the association of emotional expression to therapeutic process, not posttreatment outcomes. The average weighted effect size was .30 ($z = 7.9513$, $p. < 0.000$), which is a statistically significant medium effect size (transformed from $r(Z)$ to $r = .30$). The 95% CI for the weighted effect size ranged from .23 to .38. The equivalent d for this effect would be approximately .63. With a Cohen's d of 0.63, 74% of the treatment group will be above the mean of the control group (Cohen's U_3), 75% of the two groups will overlap, and there is a 67% chance that a person picked at random from the treatment group will have a higher score than a person picked at random from the control group (probability of superiority). Moreover, to have one more favorable outcome in the treatment group compared to the control group, 4.6 people would need to be treated (Magnusson, n.d.).

We also computed Cochrane's Q to check for heterogeneity and failed to reject the null hypothesis ($Q = 22.98$, $df = 19$, $p = .2398$) suggesting that any variability amongst the effect sizes investigated is due to sampling error. We also calculated I^2 which was negative and is conventionally transformed to zero, indicating that with the random effects model, there was no variation due to heterogeneity. Lastly, we calculated a fail-safe N to address the "file drawer" problem. Approximately 45 studies with an effect size of 0 would need to be published in order to bring the weighted mean effect size below .10, or practical significance.

Results of Therapist Emotional Expression
on Treatment Outcome

Thirteen articles reported results that were appropriate for analysis on the therapist's expression of affect and how it relates to the therapeutic outcomes. Table 12.3 presents for a list of articles used in the analysis). The average weighted effect size was .28 ($z = 5.7186$, $p. < 0.000$), producing a statistically significant medium effect size (transformed from $r(Z)$ to $r = .27$). The 95% CI for the weighted effect size ranged from .17 to .35.

Table 12.2. Studies Included in Meta-Analysis on Association of Client Emotional Expression and Therapeutic Process

Author and Year	Total N	Measures of Emotional Expression	Measures of Therapeutic Process	Effect Size[a]
Auszra et al. (2013)	74	Client Expressed Emotional Arousal Scale-III-R; Client Emotional Productivity Scale-Revised	Working Alliance Inventory	.22
Capps et al. (2015)	52	Crying-related Coping Behaviour Categories	Combined Alliance Short Form- Client Version	.00
Carryer and Greenberg (2010)	38	Client Expressed Emotional Arousal Scale-III-R	Working Alliance Inventory - Client Total Score	.37
Castonguay et al. (1996)	30	Experiencing Scale	Working Alliance Inventory (Observer)	.33
Cusack, et al. (2006)	62	Restrictive Emotionality subscale of the Gender Role Conflict Scale; Toronto Alexithymia Scale-20	Working Alliance Inventory–Client	.21
deRoten et al. (2002)	6	Mutual Smiling Episodes	Helping Alliance Questionnaire	.66
Goldman et al. (2005)	35	Experiencing Scale	Working Alliance Inventory	.30
Gordon & Toukmanian (2002)	20	The Experiencing Scale	Levels of Client Perceptual Processing	.25
Hill (1988)	5	Client Reactions (Feelings, Scared and Stuck)	SEQ–Depth; SEQ–Smooth	.72
Iwakabe et al. (2000)	8	Intensity of feeling	Working Alliance Inventory (Observer)	.05
Kivlighan et al. (2014)	74	SEQ Arousal and Positivity	Combined Alliance Short Form– Client Version	.12
Lingiardi et al. (2011)	60	Psychotherapy Q-sort items	Working Alliance Inventory (Observer)	.51
Mallinckrodt (1993)	40	SEQ	Working Alliance Inventory	.20
O'Driscoll et al. (2016)	26	Experiencing Scale	Working Alliance Inventory (Observer)	.49

Study	N	Measure	Working Alliance Inventory	Effect size[a]
Pos et al. (2003)	58	Experiencing Scale;	Working Alliance Inventory	.27
Saunders (1989)	113	Empathic Resonance	Working Alliance Inventory	.57
Town et al. (2012)	57	Immediate Affect Experiencing (I-AES)	Working Alliance Inventory	.30
Ulvenes et al. (2012b)	46	Psychotherapy Q-Sort Items	Helping Alliance Questionnaire	.49
Watson et al. (2011)	66	Experiencing Scale; O-MAR	Working Alliance Inventory	.20
Zingaretti et al. (2017)	55	Client Crying in Session	Working Alliance Inventory -Client	.27
			Total Score	

[a]Effect sizes are averaged when more than one is reported (Diener et al., 2009).

Note. SEQ = Session Evaluation Questionnaire. O-MAR = Observer-Rated Measure of Affect Regulation.

Table 12.3. Studies Included in Meta-Analysis on Association of Therapist Emotional Expression and Psychotherapy Outcomes

Author and Year	Total N	Measures of Emotional Expression	Measures of Therapeutic Outcome	Effect Size[a]
Ablon et al. (2006)	17	Psychotherapy Q Sort	Symptom Checklist	.35
Benecke and Krause (2007)	15	EMFACS (Frequency of Duchenne's Smiles)	SCL-90	.85
Hoyt (1983)	30	Therapist Action Scale Items	Good vs. Poor Session Outcome	.23
Jones et al. (1986)	80	Emotional Intensity	Crisis vs Long-Term Therapy	.22
Kivlighan et al. (2014)	74	SEQ Arousal and Positivity	Reliable Change Index	.08
Kolden (1996)	62	Therapeutic Procedures Inventory- Revised	Mental Health Index (Session 4)	.30
McCarthy et al. (2014)	20	Therapeutic Cycles Model (Positive and Negative Emotional Tone)	Beck Depression Inventory	.00
Merten (2005)	10	EMFACS	Change in List of Complaints (pre–post therapy)	.66
Rasting and Beutel (2005)	20	EMFACS (Reciprocal Emotion)	SCL-90	.95
Rice (1973)	48	Expressiveness-Therapist Vocal Quality	Therapist-Rated Success	.14
Rounsaville et al. (1987)	35	Therapist Warmth/Attitude-Negative	Client-Rated Change	.30
Williams and Chambless (1990)	31	Therapist Rating Scale	Behavioral Avoidance Test	.31
Wogan (1970)	82	Therapist Emotional Climate	Client Rating Scale	.24

[a]Effect sizes are averaged when more than one is reported in a single study (Diener et al., 2009).

Note. EMFACS = Emotional Facial Action Coding System. SEQ = Session Evaluation Questionnaire. Symptom Checklist-90 = SCL-90.

The equivalent d for this effect would be approximately .56. With a Cohen's d of 0.56, 71% of the treatment group will be above the mean of the control group (Cohen's U_3), 78% of the two groups will overlap, and there is a 65% chance that a person picked at random from the treatment group will have a higher score than a person picked at random from the control group (probability of superiority). In addition, to have one more favorable outcome in the treatment group compared to the control group, 5.3 people would need to be treated (Magnusson, n.d.).

We computed Cochrane's Q to check for heterogeneity and failed to reject the null hypothesis ($Q = 17.99$, $df = 12$, $p. = .1158$) suggesting that any variability among the effect sizes investigated is due to sampling error and not some other variable or cause. We also calculated I_1^2 which equaled 10.25%, indicating that with the random effects model, there was very little variation amongst the studies due to heterogeneity. For the fail-safe N calculation, about 23 studies with an effect size of zero would need to be published to bring the weighted mean effect size below .10, or practical significance.

Results of Client Emotional Expression and Treatment Outcome

Forty-two studies reported results that were appropriate for analysis on the client's expression of affect and how it relates to distal treatment outcomes. Table 12.4 summaries these studies. The average weighted effect size was .40 ($z = 10.142$, $p < 0.000$), producing a statistically significant medium-to-large effect size (transformed from $r(Z)$ to $r = .39$). The 95% CI for the weighted effect size ranged from .32 to .48. The equivalent d for this effect would be approximately .85. With a Cohen's d of 0.85, 80% of the treatment group will be above the mean of the control group (Cohen's U_3), 67% of the two groups will overlap, and there is a 73% chance that a person picked at random from the treatment group will have a higher score than a person picked at random from the control group (probability of superiority). Lastly, to have one more favorable outcome in the treatment group compared to the control group, only 3.3 people would need to be treated. (Magnusson, n.d.).

We also computed Cochrane's Q to check for heterogeneity and rejected the null hypothesis ($Q = 86.12$, $df = 41$, $p. < .000$), suggesting that any variability among the effect sizes investigated were due to factors other than sampling error. We also calculated an I^2 of 37%, indicating that there was small-to-medium variation due to heterogeneity. The fail-safe N indicated that approximately 138 studies with an effect size of zero would need to be published in order to bring the weighted mean effect size below .10, or practical significance.

Summary of Meta-Analytic Results

In sum, the results of the four meta-analyses presented here indicate that, in a relatively small number of studies, the association of client emotional expression with other process measures is a positive one. That is, client expression or experiencing emotion modestly predicts a better therapeutic relationship and in-session progress.

Table 12.4. Studies Included in Meta-Analysis on Association of Client Emotional Expression and Psychotherapy Outcomes

Author and Year	Total N	Measures of Emotional Expression	Measures of Therapeutic Outcome	Effect Size[a]
Ablon and Jones (1999)	35	Psychotherapy Q-Sort Items	HRSD; BDI; Global Assessment Scale	.44
Ablon et al. (2006)	17	Psychotherapy Q-Sort Items	Symptom Checklist	.50
Andrews (1990)	45	Affective Experience checklist- Excitement (EX) and Anxiety (AN) Subscale	Interpersonal Checklist	.18
Auszra et al. (2013)	74	Client Expressed Emotional Arousal Scale-III-Revised; Client Emotional Productivity Scale-Revised	BDI; SCL-90-GSI	.19
Benecke & Krause (2007)	15	Duchenne Smile	(FBL–Physical Complaint)	.79
Capps et al. (2015)	52	Crying-related Coping Behaviour Categories	Session Evaluation Questionnaire	.45
Carpenter et al. (2016)	4	Unstoried Emotion–NEPCS	Recovered vs. Unchanged	-.45
Carryer & Greenberg (2010)	38	Client Expressed Emotional Arousal Scale-III-Revised	BDI; SCL-90	.54
Castonguay et al. (1996)	30	Experiencing Scale	BDI, HDRS, GAS	.35
Choi et al. (2016)	9	EE at Beginning, Middle and End of Session	Good vs. poor resolvers of self-criticism	.32
Coady (1991a, b)	9	Communication focused on client affect	Combined outcome factors (Derogatis Symptom Index, Beck Mood Scale, Weissman Social Adjustment Scale)	.32
Coombs et al. (2002)	64	Psychotherapy Q-Sort	BDI; HAM-D	0.5
Cusack et al. (2006)	62	Restrictive Emotionality subscale of the Gender Role Conflict Scale; Toronto Alexithymia Scale-20	General Help-Seeking Questionnaire	.40
Foreman and Marmar (1985)	6	Emphasis on client feelings	Improved vs. Unimproved Clients	.89
Gaston and Ring (1992)	10	Emphasis on Emotion	BDI; HAM-D	.51
Gendlin et al. (1960)	32	1 Item Expression of Feelings vs. talking about Feelings	Therapist rating of client change	.47

Study	N	Measure	Outcome	Effect
Goldfried et al. (1997)	57	Coding System of Therapeutic Focus (CTSF)	Ratings of "High" vs. "Low" Impact	.14
Goldman et al. (2005)	35	EXP (Early and Late)	BDI; SCL-90	.47
Greenberg et al. (2007)	8	Client Expressed Emotional Arousal Scale	Better Outcome vs. Poorer Outcome Rating	.76
Herrmann et al. (2016)	30	Proportion of Primary and Secondary Emotion	BDI (change)	.68
Hill et al. (1988)	5	Client Reactions- Feelings, Scared, Stuck	Average Change Scores (Pre–Post Therapy)	.81
Hilsenroth et al. (2003)	20.5	Rating of Client Affect	SCL-90	.64
Horowitz et al. (1984)	29	Action Checklist	Rating of Improvement	.09
Kivlighan et al. (2014)	74	SEQ Arousal and Positivity	Reliable Change Index	.30
McCullough (1991)	16	Client Affect Responding Following Intervention	Composite Outcome Score	.63
Merten (2005)	32	Emotional Arousal (Early and Late in Session)	BDI; SCL-90	.38
Nergaard and Silberschatz (1991)	34	Shame and Guilt	SCL-90	.43
Pascual-Leone and Greenberg (2007)	34	Experiencing Scale (EXP)	Good vs. Poor Outcome Ratings	.49
Pesale et al. (2012)	73	SEQ- Arousal	GSI-RCI, Client Estimate of Improvement	-.02
Pos et al. (2009)	73	Beginning and Working Phase Emotional Processing	BDI; SCL-90	.34
Pos et al. (2003)	58	Experiencing Scale	BDI, SCL-90	.58
Rasting and Beutel (2005)	20	EMFACS (Reciprocal/Unreciprocal Emotion)	SCL-90	.96
Saunders et al. (1989)	113	Empathic Resonance	Session Quality and Outcome at Termination	.40
Schanche et al. (2011)	48	ATOS (Inhibitory and Activating Affects)	Change in self-compassion	.65
Schauble and Pierce (1974)	41	Owning of Feeling	Successful vs. Unsuccessful Outcome	.74
Scherer et al. (2017)	201	Negative Affect Repair Questionnaire (Emotion Suppression Subscale)	SCL-90-GSI	.01
Taurke et al. (1990)	16	Affect/Defense Ratio	High vs. Low Outcome Rating	.55
Ulvenes et al. (2012b)	46	Psychotherapy Q-Sort Items	SCL-90-GSI	.09

(continued)

Table 12.4. Continued

Author and Year	Total N	Measures of Emotional Expression	Measures of Therapeutic Outcome	Effect Size[a]
Watson and Bedard (2006)	20	Experiencing Scale	BDI, Reliable Change Index	.22
Watson and Greenberg (1996)	30	EXP Scale	Degree of Resolution Scale	.85
Watson et al. (2011)	66	Experiencing Scale; Observer-Rated Measure of Affect Regulation (O-MAR)	BDI; SCL-90	.37
Zweig Bortz et al. (2011)	34	Client Emotional Arousal Scale-III	BDI	.34

[a]Effect sizes are averaged when more than one is reported (Diener et al., 2009).

Note. HRSD = Hamilton Depression Rating Scale. HAM-D = Hamilton Depression Rating Scale. BDI = Beck Depression Inventory. SCL-90-GSI = Symptom Checklist-90-Revised: Global Severity Index. GAS = Global Assessment Scale. NEPCS = Narrative-Emotion Process Coding System. EXP = The Experiencing Scale. FBL = Die Freiburger Beschwerdenliste.

In larger numbers of studies, client expression of affect evidences a medium effect, and in one case (client expression), a medium effect size with distal, end-of-psychotherapy outcomes. While direct evidence of causality cannot be established with the correlational studies included in the present analyses, the probability of superiority analyses, as well as the effect sizes (particularly with client expression of emotion and outcomes) provides strong evidence to continue to pursue this area.

These results generally replicate and extend the previous conclusions of systematic reviews and meta-analyses. The magnitude of the effect sizes observed in the current analysis was similar to both Diener et al. (2007) and Pascual and Yeryomenko (2017). In addition, the present analyses separated client and therapist expressions of emotion, which previous meta-analyses had not done before. Therefore, the present findings provide an extension to previous systematic reviews of the expression of emotion in therapy.

MODERATORS

Because of the significant Q statistics, and the I^2 findings in the studies involving client expression of emotion and treatment outcome, we investigated several potential moderators that might explain the variability.

The first analysis conducted was the rater method for capturing emotion expression in the client. A majority of studies ($k = 36$) used observational methods with coders reviewing either video recordings or transcripts. As a moderator variable, Cochrane's $Q = 28.64$, $df = 35$, $p = .7674$ was not significant. The weighted mean effect size was .45 (95% CI = .38, .53), which was significant ($z = 11.55, p < .000$) and slightly higher than the medium-to-large effect size reported in the previous discussion. The equivalent Cohen's d for this effect would be equivalent to 1.01. In addition, the remaining studies ($k = 6$) used self-report measures from the client. These studies evidenced a lower effect size, .20 (95% CI = .06, .34), which was also significant ($z = 2.93$). The equivalent Cohen's d for this effect would be equivalent to .40. The test for homogeneity was also not significant ($Q = 6.53$, $df=5$, $p = .2578$).

The results of the moderator analysis, particularly the differences in effect size between self-report versus trained observers is noteworthy. Client ratings (given in retrospect, or "after the fact") were an order of magnitude lower than observer's ratings. Often, clients are either unaware of the scope of their emotional expressions after they have passed (and thus rated postsession), or once the emotion is processed appropriately, it no longer has the same relevance or power that it had. This result does not mean that the expression of emotion did not have a facilitative or important effect for the client but that probably the recollection of the strength or importance of it is not as salient after the fact (e.g., the Zeigarnik effect). Also, there may be a delay between the experience of the emotion, its processing, and the eventual clinical outcome. However, for the trained observer watching a videorecording, there may be important cues (facial displays, tone of voice, elements of speech) that observers are able to pick up, that clients in retrospect do not. It is possible that these can offer important clues that therapists can attend and respond to, which may be overlooked if they are not explicitly attuned to them.

In several respects, this moderator result mirrors previous findings on a difference between self-report and observational ratings of client outcomes when compared to a client's observed affect (Pascual-Leone & Yeryomenko, 2017). While client ratings of affect are often a convenient and important source of data, the results of the current meta-analysis provide support that external observational coding can often yield superior results, despite being a time-consuming and costly procedure.

Several other moderator analyses were conducted using diagnosis, theoretical orientation, outcome measure, and use of a treatment manual as potential moderator variables. None of the analyses were significant. This result was similar to Diener et al.'s (2007) findings of no moderator variables. Additional moderator analyses were contemplated (gender of client, gender of therapist, experience level of therapist, etc.), but not enough studies reported these demographic variables to yield a useful analyses, so these were not conducted.

EVIDENCE FOR CAUSALITY

The central question of causality is whether there is evidence beyond association of one observed event and another to establishing a temporal and contingent impact. We did not discover any evidence in the reviewed studies in this chapter. None of the studies employed randomization, nor is that likely to occur for clinical, ethical, and practical reasons in the future. As a result, interpretations based on associations, often seen as a limitation of "common factors" research (Norcross & Lambert, 2011), must remain the best tool available for assessing factors like emotional expression in the therapeutic relationship.

Looking at the potential temporal aspect of the relation between affect expression and clinical outcome, Town and associates (2017) looked at *affect experiencing* (or the bodily arousal of emotion in-session) and measures of symptom distress. They focused on four clients (two "recovered" and two "no change") for whom they had observations of 20 sessions each. Thus, they could correlate session emotional experiencing with final outcomes. For the two clients who showed no change, there was no significant correlations between affect experiencing and outcome, but for the two clients who "recovered" there was a significant, negative correlation between affect experiencing and symptom distress. Put simply, for improved clients, increased affect experiencing preceded a lowering of distress for clients who recovered versus clients who did not make any changes. In addition, higher affect experiencing predicted higher client and therapist ratings of the alliance, for both sets of clients.

Other recent findings (Aafjes-van dorn et al., 2017; Ulvenes et al., 2014) also investigated the temporal effects of clients' affect experiencing in session. In these cases too, the client's sense of self was an important moderating variable and may be a meaningful area of investigation in the future as it relates to clinical outcomes. Taken together, the correlational nature of these studies leave us with inklings of possible causality, but without randomized controlled trials, there is no definitive evidence of a causal effect

CLIENT CONTRIBUTIONS

In our meta-analyses, we found that the association between clients' emotional expression and treatment outcome were consistently stronger than the therapists' emotional expressions. Thus, the client's expressions of affect probably prove more important than the therapist's in relation to treatment outcomes. For example, clients who do not process or "get in touch" with their emotions (alexithymia) tend to do the most poorly in therapist reactions (Ogrodniczuk et al., 2008) and clinical outcomes (McCallum et al., 2003). Although many diagnoses have strong affective components (e.g., depression, anxiety, posttraumatic stress disorder), researchers and therapists over the last few decades have typically privileged changes in behavior as the markers of success. Contemporary researchers have only recently begun to systematically investigate how the emotional expression and experiencing can be considered a reliable indicator of therapeutic progress, on the way to lasting change.

Researchers have found that the therapeutic alliance remained strong in the face of the expression of affect during a difficult session. (Hilsenroth et al., 2003; Kivlighan et al., 2014). Interestingly, many studies have found that *therapist* expression of affect (in particular, crying) was generally rated positively by clients (Blume-Marcovici et al., 2013). In a survey of affect in eating disorder treatments, clients interpreted therapists' crying as positive if they understood the meaning behind the therapists' expression (i.e., an indication that the therapist understands them; Tritt et al., 2015). The client's *perception* of the emotional expression, and the meaning accorded to it, contributes to the effectiveness of the intervention and, of course, to the success of psychotherapy itself.

LIMITATIONS OF THE RESEARCH

Several limitations to the current research should be taken into consideration. One constraint was that only published articles were included in the meta-analyses. This decision eliminated several unpublished doctoral dissertations that may have contributed findings. Another limitation was that only studies published or translated into English were considered. Nonetheless, many studies (at least half) were conducted by European teams. It is highly likely that some additional, high-quality research was not included because they were not in English. Additionally, many articles did not publish complete tables of means and standard deviations or correlation matrices. As a consequence, some effect sizes had to be derived indirectly from the information that was published, and if they could not, they were eliminated from the analysis. The analyses were also constrained to individual therapy. While this was a limitation imposed by the authors to reduce additional variability in the analysis, the consequence of the choice was that studies that investigated affective expressions in groups, couple, and family therapy were ignored.

In recent years, researchers have been using structural equational modeling and MML modeling to conduct statistical analyses, which create challenges for researchers to incorporate them into meta-analyses (Cheung & Chan, 2009; Turner et al., 2009). In addition, approaches that use dynamic systems modeling or other exotic designs (e.g., cross-recurrence qualitative analysis) may also not easily lend themselves to meta-analyses (see Liebovitch et al., 2011; Main et al., 2016; Orsucci et al., 2016 for examples). No doubt, in future iterations of this volume, these approaches may be more easily incorporated.

Perhaps the biggest limitation to the meta-analyses was the relative lack of research on how therapists can facilitate productive expression and processing of emotion in therapy. Ackerman and Hilsenroth (2001) called on researchers to "examine the interpersonal exchanges between the client and therapist. . . . Future researchers should work toward integrating quantitative and qualitative analyses of the interactions between clients and therapists to present a clinically meaningful picture of the data" (p. 184). However, in-depth research into this area is limited. One example of the effective use of facilitating client emotion in therapy was reported by, Capps et al. (2015) in a study of client crying in therapy. They tentatively posited the following sequence between therapist and client:

> First was the presence of an affectively charged (i.e., intense) topic or theme (positive or negative valence). Second, this theme or topic was often relational in nature or had to do with the clients' sense of self (self-efficacy, self-image, self-esteem etc.). Third, this theme, topic or the affective intensity surrounding it may or may not have been conscious or explicitly recognized by the client. Fourth, the therapist directed the client to further attend to, expand on or describe their affective experience, (p. 218)

This sequencing demonstrates the reciprocal nature of the therapeutic endeavor, particularly in the expression, and processing, of emotion. This line of inquiry could lead to a better understanding of the affective sequencing previously mentioned and how these parameters could be altered by therapists to produce more productive outcomes. Given the results of the current meta-analyses, with robust associations between positive outcome and facilitating emotional expression in therapy, it is time to thoughtfully and systematically examine ways that clinicians can best facilitate emotional experiencing.

There are several promising directions for research at the therapist level, client level, and at the measurement level. First, at the therapist level, an investigation of the role of therapist expressions of affect would be salient to discovering the reciprocal pattern of interaction has on clients and in clinical outcomes. This line of research may be particularly useful given the relatively fewer articles on therapist affective influences on therapy outcomes (and even process) in the present meta-analysis, compared with articles that studied client affect. Lastly, we suspect that there might be an element of mediation between how experience and mastery affect the expression of affect and its impact on clinical outcomes (Peluso et al., 2018).

Two broad areas at the client level might prove useful to investigate. The first is diagnosis or symptom clusters. In our review, we found that most articles that studied some form of expression of affect in therapy focused on depression. However, other prevalent clinical diagnoses (e.g., anxiety disorders, personality disorders), and more treatment-resistant syndromes (e.g., posttraumatic stress disorder, substance abuse, eating disorders) may also benefit from an investigation of expressions of affect. The second opportunity is to focus on dispositional aspects of the client and how that mediates expressions of affect. Factors such as personality dynamics, attachment style, "sense of self," and alexithymia (to name a few), may mediate clients' expression of affect, which, in turn, could impact the therapeutic alliance and clinical outcomes.

At the level of measurement, it seems that observational methods (i.e., trained external observers using a coding scheme to identify a phenomenon) provide a rich detailing of the affective exchange between the client and the therapist (Ulvenes et al., 2012a). A major drawback to observational methods is that it is often seen as too time (or labor) intensive to provide meaningful feedback in a timely fashion. This drawback may be ameliorated by advances in affective computing (e.g., facial recognition) that could serve as reasonable analogues to human coders, reducing the lag between a therapy session and processing the transcribed material. Also, recent advances in the use of dynamical systems mathematical modelling (Gelo & Salvatore, 2016; Liebovitch et al., 2011; Peluso et al., 2012) have demonstrated that the therapeutic relationship can be reliably modeled, particularly the affective qualities of it (Leudke et al., 2017). These mathematical models can provide a rich graphical description of the dynamics of the relationship to therapists and researchers alike. Ultimately, this research may determine whether expression of affect is in fact a universal common factor for therapeutic success.

DIVERSITY CONSIDERATIONS

One of the serious drawbacks in the majority of the meta-analyzed studies was the lack of diversity represented by the clients and the therapists. As mentioned previously, when ethnicity was reported (and the majority of studies did not adequately report ethnicity), ethnically White/European American participants predominated. As a result, the generalizability of the findings for non-White populations may be limited. In addition, many authors did not adequately address the *lack* of diversity in the samples. We recommend that researchers in the future seek out more ethnically diverse clinical samples, and implement sampling procedures that would increase the inclusion of participants in empirical studies (Hayes et al., 2016).

Another marker of diversity is gender. In the studies in these meta-analyses, we found that women outnumbered men approximately two to one. This ratio this may accurately reflect women's greater participation in therapy as both therapists and clients, at the same time we are concerned that the perspective of men in therapy may be marginalized. This fact may be particularly salient when it comes to the study of emotion and the differences in its expression by men and women and the role that it plays in therapeutic outcomes or therapeutic processes (e.g., Englar-Carlson & Smart, 2014; Englar-Carlson et al., 2010; Kiselica & Englar-Carlson, 2010).

Lastly, participant age was not sufficiently described in a majority of the articles that were reviewed. There was no way to determine what role, if any, age played in the expression of affect (by either therapist or client) and whether this would have an impact on the therapeutic relationship or clinical outcomes.

TRAINING IMPLICATIONS

Several important implications for training therapists follow from the meta-analytic results reported here. Specifically:

- Students can be trained to attend to the presence or absence of patient emotions. Clients with too much negative emotion or little to no positive emotion may point to insufficient treatment progress and may trigger negative reactions in the therapist, which could impact both the therapeutic alliance and clinical outcomes.
- Students can be trained to helping clients to express, label, and process their emotions as part of therapy (Ogrodniczuk et al., 2008).
- Students will benefit from a thorough grounding in the theory and research of emotion and its display. Recently, Ekman created an online platform (http:// atlasofemotions.org) to display and describe the depth, breadth, and range of affect called the "Atlas of Emotions." In addition, Ekman and colleagues have created online training tools for detecting and decoding subtle displays of affect on the face: the Microexpression Training Tool and the Subtle Expression Training Tool.
- It would prove beneficial to provide training and supervision in the depth of emotion as well as depth of processing in both the therapist and the client. In fact, trainees can familiarize themselves with observer ratings scales, like the EXP as "one way to help train therapists orient to their client's immediate process (whether it be affective or cognitive in nature) and then to deliberately deepen the level of meaning exploration" (Pascual-Leone & Yeryomenko, 2017, p. 12).
- Training can avoid the over-representation of approaches that may have inadvertently privileged cognitions and behaviors at the expense of emotions. Orient trainees to approaches that promote the expression of affect, such as the empty chair technique (Greenberg, 2016), experiential methods, and mindfulness-based approaches (e.g., Acceptance and Commitment Therapy).
- Training therapists not to show or process emotion is probably contraindicated by the meta-analytic results. Several studies have demonstrated that, with a good therapeutic alliance, therapist displays of emotion are typically experienced by clients as respectful and promote a shared sense of meaning (e.g., Blume-Marcovici et al., 2013).
- Clinical supervisors can also emphasize the value of expressions of affect and draw supervisees' attention to moments of affect expression in the client, as well as their own emotional reactions. We recommend that trainees regularly videorecord sessions and review them in supervision.

THERAPEUTIC PRACTICES

The results of the meta-analyses confirmed a definite, solid relation between emotional expression, by both client and therapist, and salutary psychotherapy outcomes. Affect in session is associated with and predictive of client progress. Even without hard evidence of a causal link, we can safely recommend the following:

- First, emotion matters. Practitioners benefit from finding opportunities to facilitate client expression and processing of emotion in therapy, rather than trying to control or even discourage it. The current research reinforces the idea of psychotherapy as a "crucible" (Napier & Whitiker, 1978) that contains the emotionally charged reactions without being compromised by it.
- Recent findings (e.g., Scherer et al., 2017) attest to the negative effect of repressing emotions on therapeutic outcomes. That research and these meta-analyses also suggest that therapists should avoid interpersonal behaviors like criticism, dogmatic interpretations, and inflexibility (among others) that promote defensive affect in clients (Ackerman & Hilsenroth, 2001; Diener et al., 2007).
- At the same time, therapists need not avoid showing emotions, either. Therapists displaying emotion is facilitative of the therapeutic relationship and predicts positive treatment outcomes. In fact, there seems to be a positive correlation between more experienced therapists and displaying emotion (Blume-Marcovici et al., 2013), which may be the result of clinical experience.
- Therapists can consider orienting their clients toward affect as a precursor to clients' experiencing affect, as well placing it in a productive context. Previously, researchers have found that "clients of therapists who emphasized affect experienced greater affect" (Ulvenes et al., 2014, p. 321). Given the current finding of a medium effect size for client expression of affect, this strategy is an important consideration for therapists.
- Therapists can learn and practice emotion coaching, as opposed to emotion dismissing. Emotion needs to be focused on, validated, and worked with directly in therapy to promote emotional change (Greenberg, 2016.)
- Therapists can work towards recreating productive emotional experiences with clients that foster corrective emotional experiences on an attachment-based/schema-based level. In the context of a safe, trusting relationship, these emotional processing skills can be internalized into emotion regulation skills (Town et al., 2017). Facilitating emotional expression becomes one of the "therapeutic tasks," with meaning-making and emotional resolution serving as "therapeutic goals."
- Therapists can construct processes for getting accurate, real-time feedback on emotion in psychotherapy. Possibly the day will come when it can be done automatically in real-time using sensing technology that is calibrated to derive information on emotion. This information will then create a feedback loop to practitioners (either during a session, or immediately after it) that can guide them in tailoring therapy or focusing on certain affective elements that signal progress.

REFERENCES

References marked with an asterisk indicate studies included in the meta-analyses.

Aafjes-van Doorn, K., Lilliengren, P., Cooper, A., Macdonald, J., & Falkenström, F. (2017). Patients' affective processes within initial experiential dynamic therapy sessions. *Psychotherapy, 54*(2), 175–183. http://dx.doi.org/10.1037/pst0000072

*Ablon, J. S., & Jones, E. E. (1999). Psychotherapy process in the National Institute of Mental Health Treatment of Depression Collaborative Research Program. *Journal of Consulting and Clinical Psychology, 67*(1), 64–75.

*Ablon, J. S., Levy, R. A., & Katzenstein, T. (2006). Beyond brand names of psychotherapy: Identifying empirically supported change processes. *Psychotherapy: Theory, Research, Practice, Training, 43*(2), 216–231. https://www.doi.org/10.1037/0033-3204.43.2.216

Ackerman, S. J., & Hilsenroth, M. J. (2001). A review of therapist characteristics and techniques negatively impacting the therapeutic alliance. *Psychotherapy, 38*(2), 171–185.

*Andrews, J. D. (1990). Interpersonal self-confirmation and challenge in psychotherapy. *Psychotherapy: Theory, Research, Practice, Training, 27*(4), 485–504. https://www.doi.org/10.1037/0033-3204.27.4.485

*Auszra, L., Greenberg, L. S., & Herrmann, I. (2013). Client emotional productivity—optimal client in-session emotional processing in experiential therapy. *Psychotherapy Research, 23*(6), 732–746. https://www.doi.org/10.1080/10503307.2013.816882.

Bagby, R. M., Parker, J. D. A., & Taylor, G. J. (1994). The twenty-item Toronto Alexithymia Scale–I. Item selection and cross-validation of the factor structure. *Journal of Psychosomatic Research, 38*(1), 23–32.

*Benecke, C., & Krause, R. (2007). Dyadic facial affective indicators of severity of symptomatic burden in patients with panic disorder. *Psychopathology, 40*(5), 290–295.

Beutler, L. E., Clarkin, J. F., & Bongar, B. (2000). *Guidelines for the systematic treatment of the depressed patient.* New York, NY: Oxford University Press.

Blume-Marcovici, A. C., Stolberg, R., & Khademi, M. (2013). Do therapists cry in therapy? The role of experience and other factors in therapists' tears. *Psychotherapy, 50*(2), 224–234. https://www.doi.org/. 10.1037/a0031384

Borenstein, M., Hedges, L. V., Higgins, J. P. T., & Rothstein, H. R. (2009). *Introduction to meta-analysis.* Chichester, England; New York, NY: Wiley.

Bordin, E. S. (1979). The generalizability of the psychoanalytic concept of the working alliance. *Psychotherapy: Theory, Research, and Practice, 16*(3), 252–260.

*Boritz, T. Z., Angus, L., Monette, G., Hollis-Walker, L., & Warwar, S. (2011). Narrative and emotion integration in psychotherapy: Investigating the relationship between autobiographical memory specificity and expressed emotional arousal in brief emotion-focused and client-centred treatments of depression. *Psychotherapy Research, 21*(1), 16–26. https://www.doi.org/10.1080/10503307.2010.504240

*Capps, K. L., Fiori, K., Mullin, A. S., & Hilsenroth, M. J. (2015). Patient crying in psychotherapy: Who cries and why? *Clinical Psychology & Psychotherapy, 22*(3), 208–220. https://www.doi.org/10.1002/cpp.1879

*Carpenter, N., Angus, L., Paivio, S., & Bryntwick, E. (2016). Narrative and emotion integration processes in emotion-focused therapy for complex trauma: An exploratory process-outcome analysis. *Person-Centered & Experiential Psychotherapies, 15*(2), 67–94. https://www.doi.org/10.1080/14779757.2015.1132756

*Carryer, J. R., & Greenberg, L. S. (2010). Optimal levels of emotional arousal in experiential therapy of depression. *Journal of Consulting and Clinical Psychology, 78*(2), 190–199. https://www.doi.org/10.1037/a0018401

*Castonguay, L. G., Goldfried, M. R., Wiser, S., Raue, P. J., & Al, E. (1996). Predicting the effect of cognitive therapy for depression: A study of unique and common factors. *Journal of Consulting and Clinical Psychology, 64*(3), 497–504. https://www.doi.org/10.1037//0022-006x.64.3.497

Cheung, M. W. L., & Chan, W. (2009). A two-stage approach to synthesizing covariance matrices in meta-analytic structural equation modeling. *Structural Equation Modeling, 16*, 28–53.

*Coady, N. F. (1991a). The association between client and therapist interpersonal processes and outcomes in psychodynamic psychotherapy. *Research on Social Work Practice, 1*(2), 122–138. https://www.doi.org/10.1177/104973159100100202

*Coady, N. F. (1991b). The association between complex types of therapist interventions and outcomes in psychodynamic psychotherapy. *Research on Social Work Practice, 1*(3), 257–277. https://www.doi.org/10.1177/104973159100100303

Cohen, J.(1988). *Statistical power analysis for the behavioral sciences.* New York, NY: Routledge.

*Coombs, M. M., Coleman, D., & Jones, E. E. (2002). Working with feelings: The importance of emotion in both cognitive-behavioral and interpersonal therapy in the NIMH Treatment of Depression Collaborative Research Program. *Psychotherapy: Theory, Research, Practice, Training, 39*(3), 233–244. https://www.doi.org/10.1037/0033-3204.39.3.233

*Cusack, J., Deane, F. P., Wilson, C. J., & Ciarrochi, J. (2006). Emotional expression, perceptions of therapy, and help-seeking intentions in men attending therapy services. *Psychology of Men & Masculinity, 7*(2), 69–82. (https://www.doi.org/10.1037/1524-9220.7.2.69

*de Roten, Y., Gillieron, E., Despland, J., & Stigler, M. (2002). Functions of mutual smiling and alliance building in early therapeutic interactions, *Psychotherapy Research, 12*(2), 193–212.

Diener, M. J., Hilsenroth, M. J., & Weinberger, J. (2007). Therapist affect focus and patient outcomes in psychodynamic psychotherapy: A meta-analysis. *American Journal of Psychiatry, 164*, 936–941.

Diener, M. J., Hilsenroth, M. J., & Weinberger, J. (2009). A primer on meta-analysis of correlation coefficients: The relationship between patient-reported therapeutic alliance and adult attachment style as an illustration. *Psychotherapy Research, 19*(4–5), 519–526.

Ekman, P. (2007). *Emotions revealed, second edition: Recognizing faces and feelings to improve communication and emotional life.* New York, NY: Henry Holt.

Ekman, P., & Cordato, D. (2011). What is meant by calling emotions basic? *Emotion Review, 3*(4), 364–370.

Ekman, P., & Friesen, W. V. (1978). *Manual for the facial action coding system.* Washington, DC: Consulting Psychologists Press.

Englar-Carlson, M., & Smart, R. S. (2014). Positive psychology of gender. In J. T. Pedrotti & L. M. Edwards (Eds.), *Perspectives on the intersection of multiculturalism and positive psychology* (pp. 125–141). New York, NY: Springer Science.

Englar-Carlson, M., Stevens, M. A., & Scholz, R. (2010). Psychotherapy with men. In J. C. Chrisler & D. R. McCreary (Eds.), *Handbook of gender research in psychology* (Vol. 2, pp. 221–252). New York, NY: Springer.

Fahrenberg, J. (1994). *Die Freiburger Beschwerdenliste (FBL).* Göttingen, Germany: Hogrefe.

*Foreman, S. A., & Marmar, C. R. (1985). Therapist actions that address initially poor therapeutic alliances in psychotherapy, *American Journal of Psychiatry, 142*(8), 922–926.

Friesen W., & Ekman P. (1984). *EmFACS 7*. Unpublished manual.

*Gaston, L., & Ring, J. M. (1992). Preliminary results on the inventory of therapeutic strategies. *Journal of Psychotherapy Practice and Research, 1*(2), 135–146.

Gehring, A., & Blaser, A. (1982). *Minnesota Multiphasic Personality Inventory (MMPI)*. Bern, Switzerland: Huber.

Gelo, O. C. G., & Salvatore, S. (2016). A dynamic systems approach to psychotherapy: A meta-theoretical framework for explaining psychotherapy change processes. *Journal of Counseling Psychology, 63*(4), 379–395.

*Gendlin, E. T., Jenney, R. H., & Shlien, J. M. (1960). Counselor ratings of process and outcome in client-centered therapy. *Journal of Clinical Psychology, 16*(2), 210–213.

Ginsberg, H. N. (2004). The Prove It study: Is it really an landmark study or another piece of a very important puzzle? *Clinical Diabetes, 22*(3), 133–134.

*Goldfried, M. R., Castonguay, L. G., Hayes, A. M., Drozd, J. F., & Shapiro, D. A. (1997). A comparative analysis of the therapeutic focus in cognitive-behavioral and psychodynamic-interpersonal sessions. *Journal of Consulting and Clinical Psychology, 65*(5), 740–748. https://www.doi.org/10.1037//0022-006x.65.5.740

*Goldman, R. N., Greenberg, L. S., & Pos, A. E. (2005). Depth of emotional experience and outcome. *Psychotherapy Research, 15*(3), 248–260. https://www.doi.org/10.1080/10503300512331385188

*Gordon, K. M., & Toukmanian, S. G. (2002). Is how it is said important? The association between quality of therapist interventions and client processing. *Counselling and Psychotherapy Research, 2*(2), 88–98. https://www.doi.org/10.1080/14733140212331384867

Greenberg, L. S. (2014). The therapeutic relationship in emotion-focused therapy. *Psychotherapy, 51*(3), 350–357.

Greenberg, L. S. (2016). The clinical application of emotion in psychotherapy. In L. F. Barrett, M. Lewis, & J. M. Haviland-Jones (Eds.), *Handbook of emotions* (4th ed., pp. 670–684). New York, NY: Guilford.

*Greenberg, L. S., Auszra, L., & Herrmann, I. R. (2007). The relationship among emotional productivity, emotional arousal and outcome in experiential therapy of depression. *Psychotherapy Research, 17*(4), 482–493. https://www.doi.org/10.1080/10503300600977800

Greenberg, L. S., & Pascual-Leone, A. (2006). Emotion in psychotherapy: A practice-friendly research review. *Journal of Clinical Psychology: In Session, 62*(5), 611–630.

Greenberg, L. S., & Safran, J. D. (1989). Emotion in psychotherapy. *American Psychologist, 44*(1), 19–29.

Hayes, J. A., McAleavey, A. A., Castonguay, L. G., & Locke, B. D. (2016). Psychotherapists' outcomes with white and racial/ethnic minority clients: First, the good news. *Journal of Counseling Psychology, 63*(3), 261–268.

*Hill, C. E., Helms, J. E., Spiegel, S. B., & Tichenor, V. (1988). Development of a system for categorizing client reactions to therapist interventions. *Journal of Counseling Psychology, 35*(1), 27–36. https://www.doi.org/10.1037//0022-0167.35.1.27

*Hilsenroth, M. J., Ackerman, S. J., Blagys, M. D., Baity, M. R., & Mooney, M. A. (2003). Short-term psychodynamic psychotherapy for depression: An examination of statistical, clinically significant, and technique-specific change. *The Journal of Nervous and Mental Disease, 191*(6), 349–357. https://www.doi.org/10.1097/01.nmd.0000071582.11781.67

Horowitz, M. J., Marmar, C., Weiss, D. S., DeWitt, K. N., & Rosenbaum, R. (1984). Brief psychotherapy of bereavement reactions: The relationship of process to outcome. *Archives of General Psychiatry, 41*, 438–448.

Horvath, A. O., & Greenberg, L. S. (1986). The development of the Working Alliance Inventory. In L. S. Greenberg & W. M. Pinsof (Eds.), *The Psychotherapeutic Process: A Research Handbook* (pp. 529–556). New York: Guilford Press.

*Hoyt, M. F., Xenakis, S. N., Marmar, C. R., & Horowitz, M. J. (1983). Therapists' actions that influence their perceptions of "good" psychotherapy sessions. *The Journal of Nervous and Mental Disease, 171*(7), 400–404.

Hunter, J. E., & Schmidt, F. L. (2004). *Methods of meta-analysis: Correcting error and bias in research findings* (2nd ed.). Thousand Oaks, CA: SAGE.

*Iwakabe, S., Rogan, K., & Stalikas, A. (2000). The relationship between client emotional expressions, therapist interventions, and the working alliance: An exploration of eight emotional expression events. *Journal of Psychotherapy Integration, 10*(4), 375–401.

Iwakabe, S., & Stalikas, A. (1995). *A method for assessing client emotional process in counselling*. Paper presented at the Fourth European Congress of Psychology. Athens, Greece.

*Jones, E. E., Wynne, M. F., & Watson, D. D. (1986). Client perception of treatment in crisis intervention and longer-term psychotherapies. *Psychotherapy: Theory, Research, Practice, Training, 23*(1), 120–132. https://www.doi.org/10.1037/h0085579

Jordan, K. D., & Smith, T. W. (2017). The interpersonal domain of alexithymia. *Personality and Individual Differences, 110*, 65–69.

Kiselica, M. S., & Englar-Carlson, M. (2010). Identifying, affirming, and building upon male strengths: The positive psychology/positive masculinity model of psychotherapy with boys and men. *Psychotherapy: Theory, Research, Practice, Training, 47*(3), 276–287.

*Kivlighan, D. M., Marmarosh, C. L., & Hilsenroth, M. J. (2014). Client and therapist therapeutic alliance, session evaluation, and client reliable change: A moderated actor–partner interdependence model. *Journal of Counseling Psychology, 61*(1), 15–23. https://www.doi.org/10.1037/a0034939

Klein, M. H., Mathieu, P. L., Gendlin, E. T., & Kiesler, D. J. (1969). *The Experiencing Scale: A research and training manual*. Madison: Wisconsin Psychiatric Institute.

Klein, M. H., Mathieu-Coughlan, P., & Kiesler, D. J. (1986). The experiencing scales. In L. Greenberg & W. Pinsof (Eds.), *Psychotherapeutic process* (pp. 21–71). New York, NY: Guilford.

*Kolden, G. G. (1996). Change in early sessions of dynamic therapy: Universal processes and the generic model of psychotherapy. *Journal of Consulting and Clinical Psychology, 64*(3), 489–496. https://www.doi.org/10.1037//0022-006x.64.3.489

Lempert, K. M., & Phelps, E. A. (2016). Affect in decision making. In L. F. Barrett, M. Lewis, & J. M. Haviland-Jones (Eds.), *Handbook of emotions* (4th ed., pp. 98–112). New York, NY: Guilford.

Leudke, A., Peluso, P. R., Diaz, P., Baker. A., & Freund, R. (2017). An analysis of the first session: Measuring affect in the therapeutic relationship to predict dropout and return. *Journal of Counseling and Development, 95*(2), 125–135.

Liebovitch, L. S., Peluso, P. R., Norman, M. D., Su, J., & Gottman, J. M. (2011). Mathematical model of the dynamics of psychotherapy. *Cognitive Neurodynamics, 5*(3), 265–275. https://www.doi.org/10.1007/s11571-011-9157-x

*Lingiardi, V., Colli, A., Gentile, D., & Tanzilli, A. (2011). Exploration of session process: Relationship to depth and alliance. *Psychotherapy, 48*, 391–400. https://www.doi.org/10.1037/a0025248

Lipsey M. W., & Wilson, D.B. (2001). *Practical meta-analysis.* Thousand Oaks, CA: SAGE.

Machado, P. P. P. (1992). *Client's emotional arousal in therapy: Development of a rating scale.* Unpublished manuscript, Psychotherapy Research Project, University of California, Santa Barbara.

Machado, P. P. P., Beutler, L. E., & Greenberg, L. S. (1999). Emotion recognition in psychotherapy: Impact of therapist level of experience and emotional awareness. *Journal of Clinical Psychology, 55*(1), 39–57.

Magnusson, K. (n.d.). Interpreting Cohen's *d* effect size. Retrieved from http://rpsychologist.com/d3/cohend

Main, A., Paxton, A. & Dale, R. (2016). An exploratory analysis of emotion dynamics between mothers and adolescents during conflict discussions. *Emotion, 16*, 913–928.

*Mallinckrodt, B. (1993). Session impact, working alliance, and treatment outcome in brief counseling. *Journal of Counseling Psychology, 40*(1), 25–32. https://www.doi.org/10.1037//0022-0167.40.1.25

McCallum, M., Piper, W. E., Ogrodniczuk, J. S., & Joyce, A. S. (2003). Relationships among psychological mindedness, alexithymia and outcome in four forms of short-term psychotherapy. *Psychology and Psychotherapy: Theory, Research and Practice, 76*, 133–144.

*McCarthy, K. L., Mergenthaler, E., & Grenyer, B. F. (2014). Early in-session cognitive-emotional problem-solving predicts 12-month outcomes in depression with personality disorder. *Psychotherapy Research, 24*(1), 103–115. https://www.doi.org/10.1080/10503307.2013.826834

McCullough, L., Kuhn, N., Andrews, S., Valen, J., Hatch, D., & Osimo, F. (2003). The reliability of the Achievement of Therapeutic Objectives Scale (ATOS): A research and teaching tool for psychotherapy. *Journal of Brief Therapy, 2*, 75–90.

*McCullough, L., Winston, A., Farber, B. A., Porter, F., Pollack, J., Vingiano, W., . . . Trujillo, M. (1991). The relationship of patient-therapist interaction to outcome in brief psychotherapy. *Psychotherapy: Theory, Research, Practice, Training, 28*(4), 525–533.

*Merten, J. (2005). Facial microbehavior and the emotional quality of the therapeutic relationship. *Psychotherapy Research, 15*(3), 325–333. https://www.doi.org/10.1080/10503300500091272

Mozdzierz, G, & Peluso, P. R. (2014). *Principles of counseling and psychotherapy: Learning the essential domains and nonlinear thinking of master practitioners* (2nd ed.). New York, NY: Routledge.

Napier, A. Y., & Whitiker, C. (1978). *The family crucible: The intense experience of family therapy.* New York, NY: HarperCollins.

*Nergaard, M. O., & Silberschatz, G. (1989). The effects of shame, guilt, and the negative reaction in brief dynamic psychotherapy. *Psychotherapy: Theory, Research, Practice, Training, 26*(3), 330–337. https://www.doi.org/10.1037/h0085443

Norcross, J. C., & Lambert, M. J. (2011). Evidence-based therapy relationships. In J. C. Norcross (Ed.), *Psychotherapy relationships that work: Evidence-based responsiveness* (2nd ed., pp. 3–21). New York, NY: Oxford University Press.

*Odriscoll, C., Mason, O., Brady, F., Smith, B., & Steel, C. (2016). Process analysis of trauma-focused cognitive behavioural therapy for individuals with schizophrenia. *Psychology*

and *Psychotherapy: Theory, Research and Practice, 89*(2), 117–132. https://www.doi.org/10.1111/papt.12072

Ogrodniczuck, J. S., Piper, W. E., & Joyce, A. S. (2008). Alexithymia and therapist reaction to the patient: Expression of positive emotion as a mediator. *Psychiatry, 71*(3), 257–265.

Orlinsky, D. E., Grawe, K., & Parks, B. K. (1994). Process and outcome in psychotherapy. In A. E. Bergin & S. L. Garfield (Eds.), *Handbook of psychotherapy and behavior change* (4th ed., pp. 270–376). New York, NY: Wiley.

Orlinsky, D. E., & Howard, K. I. (1978). The relation of process to outcome in psychotherapy. In S. L. Garfield & A. E. Bergin (Eds.), *Handbook of psychotherapy and behavior change: An empirical analysis* (2nd ed., pp. 238–328). New York, NY: Wiley.

Orsucci, F. F., Musmeci, N., Aas, B., Schiepek, G., Reda, M. A., Canestri, L., . . . deFelics, G. (2016). Synchronization analysis of language and physiology in human dyads. *Nonlinear Dynamics, Psychology, and Life Sciences, 20*(2), 167–191.

*Pascual-Leone, A., & Greenberg, L. S. (2007). Emotional processing in experiential therapy: Why "the only way out is through." *Journal of Consulting and Clinical Psychology, 75*(6), 875–887. https://www.doi.org/10.1037/0022-006x.75.6.875

Pascual-Leone, A., & Yeryomenko, N. (2017). The client "experiencing" scale as a predictor of treatment outcomes: A meta-analysis on psychotherapy process, *Psychotherapy Research, 27*(6), 653–665. http://www.doi.org/10.1080/10503307.2016.1152409

Peluso, P. R. (2012). *Principles of counseling and psychotherapy: Learning the essential domains and non-linear thinking of master practitioners* [Video]. Alexandria, VA: Microtraining Associates.

Peluso, P. R., Baker, A. Z., Sauer, A., & Peluso, J. P. (2018). Dynamical Analysis of Therapist-Client Interactions. In U. Strawinska-Zanko & L. Liebovitch (Eds.) *Mathematical Modeling of Social Relationships - What Mathematics Can Tell Us About People* (pp. 51–68). New York, NY: Springer.

Peluso, P. R., Liebovitch, L. S. Gottman, J. M., Norman, M. D., & Su, J. (2012). A mathematical model of psychotherapy: An investigation using dynamic non-linear equations to model the therapeutic relationship. *Psychotherapy Research, 22*(1), 40–55. https://www.doi.org/10.1080/10503307.2011.622314

*Pesale, F. P., Hilsenroth, M. J., & Owen, J. J. (2012). Patient early session experience and treatment outcome. *Psychotherapy Research, 22*(4), 417–425. https://www.doi.org/10.1080/10503307.2012.662607

*Pos, A. E., Greenberg, L. S., Goldman, R. N., & Korman, L. M. (2003). Emotional processing during experiential treatment of depression. *Journal of Consulting and Clinical Psychology, 71*(6), 1007–1016. https://www.doi.org/10.1037/0022-006x.71.6.1007

*Pos, A. E., Greenberg, L. S., & Warwar, S. H. (2009). Testing a model of change in the experiential treatment of depression. *Journal of Consulting and Clinical Psychology, 77*(6), 1055–1066. https://www.doi.org/10.1037/a0017059

Rachman, S. (1980). Emotional processing. *Behavioral Research and Therapy, 18*, 51–60.

*Rasting, M., & Beutel, M. E. (2005). Dyadic affective interactive patterns in the intake interview as a predictor of outcome. *Psychotherapy Research, 15*(3), 188–198. https://www.doi.org/10.1080/10503300512331335039

Rasting, M., Brosig, B., & Beutel, M. E. (2005). Alexithymic characteristics and patient-therapist interaction: A video analysis of facial affect display. *Psychopathology, 38*, 105–111. https://www.doi.org/10.1159/000085772

*Rice, L. N. (1973). Client behavior as a function of therapist style and client resources. *Journal of Counseling Psychology, 20*(4), 306–311. https://www.doi.org/10.1037/h0034805

Rosenthal, R. (1994). Parametric measures of effect size. In H. Cooper & L. V. Hedges (Eds.), *The handbook of research synthesis*. New York, NY: SAGE.

*Roten, Y. D., Gilliéron, E., Despland, J., & Stigler, M. (2002). Functions of mutual smiling and alliance building in early therapeutic interaction. *Psychotherapy Research, 12*(2), 193–212. https://www.doi.org/10.1093/ptr/12.2.193

Rottenberg, J., & Gross, J. J. (2007). Emotion and emotion regulation: A map for psychotherapy researchers. *Clinical Psychology: Science and Practice, 14*, 323–328.

*Rounsaville, B. J., Chevron, E. S., Prusoff, B. A., Elkin, I., & Al, E. (1987). The relation between specific and general dimensions of the psychotherapy process in interpersonal psychotherapy of depression. *Journal of Consulting and Clinical Psychology, 55*(3), 379–384. https://www.doi.org/10.1037//0022-006x.55.3.379

*Saunders, S. M., Howard, K. I., & Orlinsky, D. E. (1989). The Therapeutic Bond Scales: Psychometric characteristics and relationship to treatment effectiveness. *Psychological Assessment, 1*(4), 323–330. https://www.doi.org/10.1037//1040-3590.1.4.323

Scarantino, A. (2016). The philosophy of emotions and its impact of affective science. In L. F. Barrett, M. Lewis, & J. M. Haviland-Jones (Eds.), *Handbook of emotions* (4th ed., pp. 3–48). New York, NY: Guilford.

*Schanche, E., Stiles, T. C., Mccullough, L., Svartberg, M., & Nielsen, G. H. (2011). The relationship between activating affects, inhibitory affects, and self-compassion in patients with Cluster C personality disorders. *Psychotherapy, 48*(3), 293–303.

*Scherer, A., Boecker, M., Pawelzik, M., Gauggel, S., & Forkmann, T. (2017). Emotion suppression, not reappraisal, predicts psychotherapy outcome. *Psychotherapy Research, 27*(2), 143–153. https://www.doi.org/10.1080/10503307.2015.1080875

*Shauble, P. G., & Pierce, R. M. (1974). Client in-therapy behavior: A therapist guide to progress. *Psychotherapy: Theory, Research and Practice, 11*(3), 229–234.

Sloan, D. M., & Kring, A. M. (2007). Measuring changes in emotion during psychotherapy: Conceptual and methodological issues. *Clinical Psychology: Science and Practice, 14*, 307–322. 10.1111/j.1468-2850.2007.00092.x

Stalikas, A., & Fitzpatrick, M. (1995). Client good moments: An intensive analysis of a single session. *Canadian Journal of Counselling, 29*, 160–175.

Suri, G. & Gross, J. J. (2016). Emotion regulation: A valuation perspective. In L.F. Barrett, M. Lewis, & J. M. Haviland-Jones (Eds.), *Handbook of emotions* (4th ed., pp. 453–466). New York, NY: Guilford.

*Taurke, E. A., Flegenheimer, W., McCullough, L., Winston, A., Pollack, J., & Trujillo, M. (1990). Change in patient affect/defense ratio from early to late sessions in brief psychotherapy. *Journal of Clinical Psychology, 46*(5), 656.

Teasdale, J. D. (1999). Emotional processing, three modes of mind and the prevention of relapse in depression. *Behaviour Research and Therapy, 37*, S53–S77.

Tomkins, S. S. (2008). *Affinity imagery consciousness*. New York, NY. Springer. (Original work published 1962–1992)

*Town, J. M., Hardy, G. E., McCullough, L., & Stride, C. (2012). Patient affect experiencing following therapist interventions in short-term dynamic psychotherapy. *Psychotherapy Research, 22*(2), 208–219. https://www.doi.org/10.1080/10503307.2011.637243

Town, J. M., Salvadori, A., Falkenstrom, F., Bradley, S., & Hardy, G. E. (2017). Is affect experiencing therapeutic in major depressive disorder? Examining associations between affect experiencing and changes to the alliance and outcome in intensive short-term dynamic psychotherapy. *Psychotherapy*, *54*(2), 148–158. https://www.doi.org/10.1037/pst0000108

Turner, R. M., Ozmar, R. Z., Yang, M. Y., Goldstein, H., & Thompson, S. G. (2009). Multilevel models for meta-analysis of clinical trials with binary outcomes. *Statistics in Medicine*, *19*, 3417–3432.

Tritt, A., Kelly, J., & Waller, G. (2015). Patients' experiences of clinicians' crying during psychotherapy for eating disorders. *Psychotherapy*, *52*(3), 373–380. https://www.doi.org/10.1037/a00311

Ulvenes, P. G., Berggraf, L., Hoffart, A., Stiles, T. C., Svartberg, M., McCullough, L., & Wampold, B. E. (2012a). Can two psychotherapy process measures be dependably rated simultaneously? Generalizability study. *Journal of Counseling Psychology*, *59*, 638–644.

*Ulvenes, P. G., Berggraf, L., Hoffart, A., Stiles, T. C., Svartberg, M., McCullough, L., & Wampold, B. E. (2012b). Different processes for different therapies: Therapist actions, therapeutic bond, and outcome. *Psychotherapy*, *49*(3), 291–302. https://www.doi.org/10.1037/a0027895

Ulvenes, P. G., Berggraf, L., Wampold, B. E., Hoffart, A., Stiles, T. C., & McCullough, L., (2014). Orienting patient to affect, sense of self, and the activation of affect over the course of psychotherapy with Cluster C patients. *Journal of Counseling Psychology*, *61*(3), 315–324. https://www.doi.org/10.1037/cou0000028

Warwar, S., & Greenberg, L. S. (1999). *Client Emotional Arousal Scale–III*. Unpublished manuscript, York Psychotherapy Research Clinic, York University, Toronto, ON.

Watson, D., Clark, L. A., & Tellegen, A. (1988). Development and validation of brief measures of positive and negative affect: The PANAS scales. *Journal of Personality and Social Psychology*, *54*, 1063–1070. http://www.doi.org/10.1037/0022-3514.54.6.1063

*Watson, J. C., & Bedard, D. L. (2006). Clients' emotional processing in psychotherapy: A comparison between cognitive-behavioral and process-experiential therapies. *Journal of Consulting and Clinical Psychology*, *74*(1), 152–159.

*Watson, J. C., & Greenberg, L. S. (1996). Pathways to change in the psychotherapy of depression: Relating process to session change and outcome. *Psychotherapy: Theory, Research, Practice, Training*, *33*(2), 262–274. https://www.doi.org/10.1037/0033-3204.33.2.262

*Watson, J. C., McMullen, E. J., Prosser, M. C., & Bedard, D. L. (2011). An examination of the relationships among clients affect regulation, in-session emotional processing, the working alliance, and outcome. *Psychotherapy Research*, *21*(1), 86–96.

Whelton, W. J. (2004). Emotional processes in psychotherapy: Evidence across therapeutic modalities. *Clinical Psychology and Psychotherapy*, *11*, 58–71.

*Williams, K. E., & Chambless, D. L. (1990). Relationship between therapist characteristics and outcome of in vivo exposure treatment for agoraphobia. *Behavior Therapy*, *21*, 111–116.

*Wogan, M. (1970). Effect of therapist-patient personality variables on therapeutic outcome. *Journal of Consulting and Clinical Psychology*, *35*(3), 356–361. https://www.doi.org/10.1037/h0030110

*Zingaretti, P., Genova, F., Gazzillo, F., & Lingiardi, V. (2017). Patients' crying experiences in psychotherapy: Relationship with the patient level of personality organization, clinician approach, and therapeutic alliance. *Psychotherapy*, *54*(2), 159–166.

Zweig Boritz, T., Angus, L., Monette, G., Hollis-Walker, L., & Warwar, S. (2011). Narrative and emotion integration in psychotherapy: Investigating the relationship between autobiographical memory specificity and expressed emotional arousal in brief emotion-focused and client-centred treatments of depression, *Psychotherapy Research*, *21*(1), 16–26. doi:10.1080/10503307.2010.504240.

13

CULTIVATING POSITIVE
OUTCOME EXPECTATION

*Michael J. Constantino, Andreea Vîslă, Alice E. Coyne,
and James F. Boswell*

Patients' expectations have long been considered a key ingredient and common factor of successful psychotherapy (e.g., Frank, 1961; Goldfried, 1980; Goldstein, 1960a; Rosenzweig, 1936; Weinberger & Eig, 1999). Influenced by classic social psychological findings that substantiated the influence of expectations on people's perceptions and actions (e.g., Asch, 1946; Kelley, 1950; Secord, 1958), researchers and clinicians became interested in how expectations specifically affect psychotherapy.

In his classic book, *Persuasion and Healing*, Frank (1961) argued that for any therapy to be effective there must be within the patient a mobilization of belief in the ability to improve. According to Frank, patients enter therapy because they are demoralized, and restoring their hope and positive expectation, through whatever means, is a powerful change mechanism. Frank's *remoralization* notion centrally represents an *outcome expectation* (OE), or a patient's belief about the mental health consequences of participating in treatment. Others have since concurred with this perspective (e.g., Kirsch, 1985; Shapiro, 1981), some going so far as to suggest that most psychotherapies are inextricably linked with the fostering of patients' adaptive expectations and the revision of their maladaptive ones (Constantino & Westra, 2012; Greenberg et al., 2006; Kirsch, 1990).

This chapter reports the results of a comprehensive meta-analysis on the association between patients' pre- or early therapy OE and their distal treatment outcome across a variety of psychotherapies and clinical contexts. We also review (a) definitions of OE and similar constructs, (b) common OE measures, (c) clinical examples of OE, (d) several landmark studies, (e) moderators and mediators of the OE–outcome link (the former in the context of the meta-analysis), (f) evidence supporting causality in the OE–outcome association, (g) patient factors related to OE, and (h) limitations of the research base. In concluding, we offer OE-relevant diversity considerations, training implications, and therapeutic practices based on the research results. The overarching goal of the chapter is to leverage the research evidence to assist psychotherapists in understanding and enhancing their patients' OE.

DEFINITIONS

OE reflects patients' personal prognostication about how they will respond to a treatment in which they will, or have begun to, engage (Constantino et al., 2011). In psychotherapy, OE is typically assessed on a continuum of the potential *benefits* of treatment, with rare consideration of plausible expected *negative* effects (Schulte, 2008). OEs may be formed before a patient has contact with a therapist or the treatment, and they may be shaped, or revised, after early exposure to the practitioner and consideration of the treatment rationale. Patients' OE can also change across treatment, as influenced by their own history, therapist actions, relationship dynamics, their ongoing appraisal of the treatment's efficacy, and other contextual variables.

OE is differentiated from constructs such as patients' *treatment expectations*, perceptions of treatment or practitioner *credibility*, treatment *motivation*, therapy *preferences*, and general *hope*. Treatment expectations reflect patients' foretelling beliefs about what will transpire during treatment, including how they and their therapist will behave (role expectations), how they will subjectively experience the therapy (process expectations), and how long therapy will last (duration expectation; Constantino et al., 2011). Credibility captures a patient's perception of how plausible, suitable, and logical a treatment seems, and how competent a practitioner is to carry it out effectively (Devilly & Borkovec, 2000).

Historically, there has been some debate over whether credibility and OE are distinct constructs. On the one hand, OE might develop, at least in part, from how credible a treatment seems (Hardy et al., 1995). Moderately significant correlations between OE and credibility/suitability scales support this perspective (e.g., Constantino et al., 2005; Safren et al., 1997). On the other hand, OE often exists *prior* to having any substantial information about the forthcoming treatment or interaction with the practitioner. Credibility, though, is a perception based on knowledge gained *through* direct experience or observation (Schulte, 2008; Tinsely et al., 1988). Thus, although conceptually related, credibly and OE are now commonly viewed as distinct (see Chapter 14, this volume, for a meta-analysis on the credibility–outcome association).

Motivation, which encompasses patients' desire and readiness for change (see Chapter 10, Volume 2), does not necessarily correspond to positive OE. Patients in distress might be highly motivated to engage in treatment, yet have low expectation or faith that it can actually help them (DeFife & Hilsenroth, 2011; Rosenthal & Frank, 1956). Treatment preferences (see Chapter 6, Volume 2) are distinguishable from OE in that they reflect something valued or desired, which might be distinct from an expected outcome. For example, a patient might prefer working with a same-sex therapist, yet expect that it would be more helpful to work with an other-sex therapist. Finally, although positive OE has sometimes been used synonymously with general hope, it is probably more precisely one subtype of hope that is connected to an anticipated local outcome of a particular treatment (Larsen & Stege, 2010). Hope itself is a broader construct about a personally meaningful and fulfilling future (Stephenson, 1991), which can certainly involve determinants beyond therapy (e.g., faith, physical health, social support network).

MEASURES

Patient expectations were traditionally viewed as nuisance variables requiring control in clinical trials. Hence, expectations were assessed mainly to establish the comparability of beliefs engendered by different treatments, thereby eliminating expectancy effects as rival interpretations of between-group differences (Borkovec & Nau, 1972; Holt & Heimberg, 1990). For these purposes, most expectation measures were brief (in many cases one item only; e.g., Heine & Trosman, 1960) and often study-specific (and thus lacking in psychometric validation; e.g., Barrios & Karoly, 1983). In some cases, the measures were confounded with another belief construct (such as credibility; e.g., Hardy et al., 1995) or even an outcome measure (e.g., Evans et al., 1985). Thus, expectations were long undervalued, with relatively few early studies providing a *primary* test of their predictive therapeutic value (Weinberger & Eig, 1999).

Over the past few decades, however, there has been a renewed interest in expectancies, especially with regard to OE as a pancontextual determinant of improvement. Although researchers have continued to use older measures of OE (for a review of expectancy measurement, see Constantino et al., 2012), several newer measures have been developed and psychometrically validated.

The Credibility/Expectancy Questionnaire (CEQ; Devilly & Borkovec, 2000), derived from an earlier iteration (Borkovec & Nau, 1972), is the most widely used OE measure. This brief, face valid measure is in the public domain, and it can be easily adapted for different disorders and treatments. Based on factor analysis, and using trauma language as an example, the measure includes three items assessing patients' OE ("By the end of the therapy period, how much improvement in your trauma symptoms do you think will occur?"; "At this point, how much do you really *feel* that therapy will help you to reduce your trauma symptoms?"; "By the end of the therapy period, how much improvement in your trauma symptoms do you *feel* will occur?") and three assessing their treatment credibility perceptions ("At this point, how logical does the therapy offered seem to you?"; "At this point, how successful do you think this treatment will be in reducing your trauma symptoms?"; "How confident would you be in recommending this treatment to a friend who experiences similar problems?"). Although some researchers have used the CEQ based on this affective (OE) and cognitive (credibility) distinction, others have more straightforwardly measured OE with the single, face-valid item, "By the end of the therapy period, how much improvement in your trauma symptoms do you think will occur?" (typically rated from 0% to 100%; e.g., Price et al., 2008; Vogel et al., 2006).

The Milwaukee Psychotherapy Expectations Questionnaire (MPEQ; Norberg et al., 2011) is a 13-item measure that has two scales substantiated by factor analysis: OE and treatment expectations. This measure is also fairly brief, face valid, in the public domain, and readily adaptable to most clinical situations. The OE scale includes four items rated from zero (Not at all) to 10 (Very much so): "Therapy will provide me with an increased level of self-respect"; "After therapy, I will have the strength needed to avoid feelings of distress in the future"; "I anticipate being a better person as a result of therapy;" and "After therapy, I will be a much more optimistic person."

Another later-generation scale for assessing patients' OE is the Patients' Therapy Expectation and Evaluation (PATHEV; Schulte, 2008). This 11-item measure consists of three factor-analytically derived subscales: hope of improvement (OE), fear of change, and suitability. The hope of improvement subscale includes four items rated from 1 (absolutely wrong) to 5 (absolutely right): "I'm afraid I can't even be helped by psychotherapy"; "I believe my problems can finally be solved"; "Even with therapy, my problems will not change very much"; and "Actually, I'm rather skeptical about whether treatment can help me."

It is worth noting that the expectancy literature has largely focused on adult populations. However, several measures for younger patients and their caregivers have been developed. These include, for example, the Hopes and Expectations for Treatment Record Form (Urwin, 2007) and the Parent Expectations for Therapy Scale (Nock & Kazdin, 2001).

CLINICAL EXAMPLES

A patient's psychotherapy OE is a cognition regarding a probable future experience resulting from treatment. It centers on the current "answer" to some variation of the question: "To what extent do I believe this treatment will alleviate my suffering?" Thus, OE is owned and determined by the patient, and the clinical examples presented in this section represent this ownership. Later, we review research on, and provide clinical examples of, how therapist behavior might influence patients' OE.

A patient's OE can be positive (e.g., "I have faith that I can do the work and feel better"), lacking (e.g., "I can't imagine ever feeling better, even after this therapy"), negative ("I fear that I will feel worse if I go through with this"), or ambivalent (e.g., "Well, I am willing to give it a shot, but I'm just not sure this will work"; "I have been depressed for a long time"). A patient's OE, regardless of its valence, could also prove unrealistic (e.g., "I expect to become a whole new person, unrecognizable from my current flawed self"). Of course, patients' general hopes and their current treatment OE may conflict. For example, a patient might have a desperate wish to feel emotional relief (e.g., "I hope to feel like my old self"), yet have what he or she deems a more reality-based outcome prediction (e.g., "Therapy might not help me completely"; "I will never fully be what I used to be").

OE is also affected by context, including perhaps most powerfully one's own learning experience. For example, a male patient might have had a positive therapy outcome with an older female therapist in the past, which gives him greater faith in the success of a new therapy course if it is recommended with this same therapist or with a different therapist with salient similarities (e.g., gender, age, theoretical orientation).

OE probably interacts with treatment expectations. For example, a patient might generally have a high OE prior to therapy and also expect therapy to focus exclusively on early childhood (a treatment expectation). Upon meeting a well-regarded therapist who tends to work from a here-and-now, problem-oriented perspective, this patient's OE might diminish.

Fortunately, psychotherapists can often responsively frame their approach in accord with the patient's treatment expectations, thereby persuading the patient's OE to become more positive. For example, the practitioner might say,

> In discussing your current problems and relationships, we will likely see traces of these same problems and patterns from your earlier life. People learn many things early on that have a lasting influence on their present thoughts and feelings. Although I often lean toward discussing the here-and-now, your childhood will be important information, and I suspect we will learn something quite useful from connecting past to present. How does this sound to you?

LANDMARK STUDIES

Interest in the topic of how expectations, broadly defined, affect psychotherapy has been around for over 60 years (e.g., Frank, 1958; Goldstein, 1960a, 1960b; Greenberg, 1969; Strupp, 1970; Strupp & Bloxom, 1973). Studies from the early era focused on patient and therapist expectations, different types of expectations (e.g., for treatment process, for the practitioner's personality), different outcomes (e.g., treatment duration, perceptions of the practitioner), and different designs (e.g., correlational associations, examinations of outcome in placebo conditions representing *indirect* tests of prognostics beliefs).

One study was compelling in establishing the potential facilitative effect of OE as a pantheoretical factor. In a secondary analysis of the high-profile National Institute of Mental Health Collaborative Treatment of Depression program (Elkin et al., 1989), researchers found that more positive patient OE (assessed at baseline) was associated with both the likelihood of complete response and lower depression at posttreatment across all four treatment conditions: cognitive-behavioral therapy (CBT) interpersonal psychotherapy, imipramine with clinical management (CM), and placebo with CM (Sotsky et al., 1991).

Despite research suggesting a link between what people expect and what they experience in psychotherapy, experimental attempts to *influence* expectations have been scarce outside of the landmark work on pretreatment role-induction (RI) strategies. Hoehn-Saric and colleagues (1964) developed a RI interview to socialize patients to the nature of treatment before engaging in it. The interview had four components: (a) a general description of therapy, (b) a description of expected patient and therapist behavior, (c) preparation for common therapy occurrences (e.g., resistance), and (d) a suggestion that therapy would likely help within four months. Patients who did versus did not receive the RI interview attended more sessions, evidenced more favorable observer-coded in-session behavior, and demonstrated better outcome from both patient and therapist perspectives. With this design, though, the beneficial effects of the RI interview could not be isolated to any given component; thus, the causal effect of patient OE on outcome remained unknown.

Qualitative research on the OE–outcome connection has been virtually nonexistent. The most advanced qualitative research has centered on patients' retrospective accounts of how therapy did or did not differ from the expectancies (mostly of the treatment type) that they reported at pretreatment. For example, researchers in one study interviewed patients following four sessions of motivational interviewing (MI), which was delivered as a pretreatment to CBT for generalized anxiety disorder (GAD; Marcus et al., 2011). Grounded theory analyses revealed that patients' experience of MI was discrepant from what they expected but in a positive way. In particular, patients thought that the MI clinicians, with their emphasis on empathy and autonomy support, created a safe place to explore their complex feelings about change.

Expanding on this work, in several additional qualitative studies from this team, patients articulated that discrepancies in expected versus experienced process, consistent with MI principles, were corrective relational experiences (Khattra et al., 2017; Macaulay et al., 2017). In particular, patients valued the shift, facilitated by MI, toward heightened control, self-efficacy, and empathic connection, which differed from the expectation that treatment would prove more directive and require compliance. Although this line of research does not explicitly center on OE and outcome, it does support the aforementioned notion that many, if not most, psychotherapies attempt to facilitate patients' adaptive expectations and revise their maladaptive ones (Constantino & Westra, 2012; Greenberg et al., 2006).

There have been several landmark narrative reviews of expectancy–outcome associations (including OE specifically; Arnkoff et al., 2002; Greenberg et al., 2006; Noble et al., 2001). These syntheses have largely supported the empirical promise with regard to the facilitative effect of positive patient OE (greater belief in the degree to which treatment will be helpful). However, the results of the studies reviewed were far from unanimously positive, and the methods (and their quality) across studies varied, which made it difficult to determine the consistency or magnitude of the OE effect across treatment contexts. This question, though, was addressed in the first meta-analysis of the OE–outcome correlation reported in the previous edition of this book (Constantino et al., 2011).

RESULTS OF PREVIOUS META-ANALYSIS

Our team searched the literature for articles published in English through 2009. We included articles reporting empirical research on clinical samples receiving psychotherapy intended to last at least three sessions. The articles also needed to report a bivariate association between patient-reported pretreatment or Session 1 OE and a posttreatment mental health outcome (not explicitly referenced as a long-term follow-up). Based on these criteria, we analyzed the aggregate OE–outcome association across 8,016 patients from 46 independent samples.

The meta-analysis revealed a small, but significant association between more positive early OE and more adaptive mental health outcomes (weighted $r = 0.12$, $p <$ .001, 95% confidence interval [CI] .10 to .15). Expressed as Cohen's (1988) d, the effect size was 0.24. There were no moderating effects on the OE–outcome association of presenting diagnosis, theoretical orientation, treatment modality, research design, or publication date. A test of homogeneity revealed significant heterogeneity between samples, which was not surprising given the different research designs, instruments, and eras.

To address potential publication bias, we also calculated a fail-safe N to determine the number of nonsignificant file drawer studies (of independent samples) that would be required to attenuate the results to an effect less than $r = 0.10$. The fail-safe N was 9; that is, about nine additional samples would need to have an average OE–outcome r of .00 to bring the weighted mean r below .10. Thus, we suggested some caution in interpreting these initial meta-analytic findings. Although the meta-analysis had its limitations, it was the first comprehensive, aggregated analysis of the magnitude of the OE–outcome effect, which empirically substantiated the clinical importance of patient OE.

META-ANALYTIC REVIEW

In this section, we present an update to our original meta-analysis on the association between patient pre- or early-therapy OE and treatment outcomes. Specifically, we added studies published after the previous review and examined additional moderators.

Search and Inclusion Procedures

We first conducted a PsycINFO database search for all references published after December 2009 (the endpoint of our original search) and through June 2017 (the endpoint of our current search). Our specific search term sequence was *expecta** (note that * includes any derivation with this root) AND *psychotherapy* OR *therapy* OR *counsel** AND *patient* OR *client* AND *outcome**. We also activated the following search options: "peer-reviewed"; "English"; "population group: human"; "exclude dissertations"; and "methodology: empirical study, quantitative study, longitudinal study, treatment outcome, follow-up study, prospective study, clinical trial, retrospective study, brain imaging, mathematical model, meta-analysis, field study, experimental replication." This database search yielded 596 references.

We then searched PubMed with the same search sequence, also activating the following search "builder" options: "English"; "species: human"; and "article types: classical article, clinical study, clinical trial, comparative study, controlled clinical trial, corrected and republished article, journal article, meta-analysis, multicenter study, observational study, pragmatic clinical trial, randomized controlled trial, validation studies." This additional search yielded 634 references. Finally, we hand-searched the 2017 issues of 16 clinical journals (to ensure that we did not miss any reports because of a publication lag before appearing in PsycINFO or PubMed). These hand searches revealed no additional reports. Thus, the total initial search yielded 1,230 references.

Next, we reviewed the abstracts of all references and applied the inclusion/exclusion criteria below to create a candidate list. To be included in the meta-analysis, references had to (a) report a published empirical analysis; (b) include a clinical sample; (c) include at least one treatment that was referenced as a form of therapist-delivered psychotherapy (as opposed to, for example, self-help intervention or bibliotherapy) for a mental health problem that was designed to last three or more sessions; (d) include a measure of patients' *own* pretreatment or Session 1 OE; (e) include at least one posttreatment mental health outcome variable (broadly defined) not explicitly referenced as a *follow-up* occasion; and (f) report a statistical test of the relation between OE and outcome in a psychotherapy condition. References were excluded if they (a) reported expectations other than for *early prognosis of treatment outcomes*; (b) only inferred OE from tests of placebo or of similar, but distinct, constructs, such as treatment expectations, credibility perceptions, treatment motivation, therapy preferences, or general hope; (c) only assessed OE retrospectively; or (d) manipulated OE. (Studies that manipulated OE, given their experimental vs. correlational nature, were the subject of a second search, which we describe later in the Evidence for Causality section.)

Based on these criteria, 106 references were selected from the abstract reviews. We fully read these candidates and ruled out another 79 at this stage. Thus, we fully coded 27 references for study characteristics. In the case of references that included multiple studies on distinct samples, we coded these samples separately. In the few cases in which references that included multiple treatment arms reported OE–outcome associations separately by arm, we treated these treatment conditions as independent samples. In one study, the researchers examined the OE–outcome association separately for distinct diagnostic subgroups, which we also coded as separate samples. For analyses from distinct articles that examined data from the same sample, we coded them as one unique sample. For four articles reporting on four independent samples, we discovered that despite researchers reporting effects from an empirical analysis, they did not provide sufficient information to transform unstandardized regression coefficients to standardized coefficients, which, as noted in the following text, was required for our aggregated analysis. Thus, we were forced to remove these four samples from our final count. With these parameters and actions, the total number of *independent samples* from the included references from 2009 to 2017 was 30.

When we conducted the original meta-analysis (Constantino et al., 2011; $k = 46$), we excluded samples testing *only* multivariate effects because of the difficulty obtaining accurate estimates of comparable effects across samples (Lipsey & Wilson, 2001). The inclusion of other variables in the model equations means that even when standardized effects (such as standardized regression coefficients) are reported, the parameters being estimated differ depending on which variables are included. In addition, there was generally insufficient information available to calculate standard errors of these estimates and, consequently, to determine accurate inverse variance weights for the meta-analysis. However, for the present update, we included studies that reported only multivariate effects given more sophisticated methods for converting effect sizes (see the following Data Analysis section). With this change in method, we went back and included eight additional samples published prior to 2009 (i.e., samples that had been excluded in the original meta-analysis).

Also for this updated meta-analysis, we used more precision in coding whether researchers were analyzing OE, credibility, both, or when they were fully confounded. Unfortunately, the literature is rife with this particular construct confound given that the most commonly used instrument for both (the CEQ) can produce a total score that is often used as a predictor but unfortunately conflates two distinct patient beliefs. Our guiding decision for the present meta-analysis was to *include* references for which researchers either clearly measured OE (unconfounded by credibility), or where they clearly referenced OE as their independent variable, even if they measured it poorly (e.g., with the CEQ total score). In the latter case, we coded the OE measure as "poor." We *excluded* references for which researchers (a) conceptualized OE and credibility synonymously, (b) acknowledged reporting on a meta-belief variable (a compound OE/credibility variable), or (c) clearly referenced credibility as their independent variable. In the latter case, the study was included in the separate credibility meta-analysis (see Chapter 14, this volume).

With this updated precision in coding OE, we removed two studies that had been originally included in the previous version of this meta-analysis. We also discovered that two references that were coded in the original sample as contributing two different independent samples had, in fact, analyzed data on the same sample. For the present analysis, we recoded these references as one independent sample.

Thus, the total number of independent samples on which we conducted our updated meta-analysis was 81 (extracted from 72 references). In some samples, researchers assessed OE with more than one measure and/or at both baseline and Session 1. Furthermore, in many studies, researchers assessed multiple treatment outcomes. In these cases, we coded all relevant OE–outcome associations.

Data Analyses

The correlation coefficient, r, was the measure of choice to assess the effect size for most analyses of an independent sample included in the meta-analysis. Some researchers assessed effects (i.e., 65 effect sizes from the total of 209 analyses before aggregation) using other statistical measures (e.g., partial correlations, standardized and unstandardized regression coefficients, coefficient of determination, chi-square). In these cases, the statistical values were converted to r (Bowman, 2012; Del Re & Hoyt, 2010). We set effect sizes to zero that were either not described or simply reported as nonsignificant.

Many references reported multiple effect sizes from multiple measures of OE, multiple time points of OE assessment, and/or multiple measures of outcome. To avoid favoring samples for which researchers calculated multiple effects for any of these scenarios, and violating the assumption of independent samples, we aggregated the reported effect sizes from each independent sample (Del Re & Hoyt, 2010). This aggregation procedure accounted for the intercorrelation among within-study outcome measures, which was imputed as $r = .50$ (Del Re & Hoyt, 2010; Hunter & Schmidt, 2004; Wampold et al., 1997). Additionally, because several samples include multiple OE measures, they fall into more than one category for a variable that we examined as a sample-level moderator. This is problematic in that the use of more than one categorical variable within a sample introduces dependency in the data, which could potentially bias the results. To mitigate this problem, we randomly selected from the relevant samples one level for the categorical moderator of OE measure used (Hunter & Schmidt, 2004).

Because it was possible that not all effect sizes were normally distributed and sample variance may have been dependent on an unknown population effect, we first used Fisher's r to z transformation before including the sample effect sizes in our meta-analysis (see Cooper et al., 2009). We then conducted a random-effects model, which provides an inference about the average effect in the entire population of studies from which the included samples are assumed to be a random selection (Viechtbauer, 2010). In computing the overall effect (with no moderators), we weighted the independent effects by their sample size. In testing potential moderators of the aggregated effect, we used a mixed-effect model. For interpretive purposes, we converted the weighted mean effect size back to r.

We assessed the heterogeneity of effects among our included samples using the Q and I^2 statistics (Higgins & Thompson, 2002). A significant Q statistic indicates heterogeneity, which justifies subsequent moderator analyses. I^2 is computed as a percentage, which reflects the proportion of variability in effect sizes that is due to true differences among the studies versus chance. To identify publication bias, we tested asymmetry based on rank correlation (Begg & Mazumdar, 1994) and regression tests (Egger et al., 1997). Furthermore, we examined a funnel plot using trim and fill procedures (Duval & Tweedie, 2000). We conducted all analyses using the R statistical software packages for meta-analysis "MAc" (Del Re & Hoyt, 2010), "metafor" (Viechtbauer, 2010), and "compute.es" (Del Re, 2013).

Descriptive Statistics

The meta-analysis included 12,722 patients across the 81 independent samples (range = 9 to 3,998 patients per sample). For the 64 samples (79%) for which age was reported, the mean, weighted by sample size, was 37.5 years (sample mean range = 12.0 to 70.5 years). For the 63 samples (78%) for which sex was reported, 56 included both males and females, 4 included only females, and 3 included only males. For each of the 35 samples (43%) for which race was reported, the majority of patients (> 60%) were white. Table 13.1 presents the aggregated effect sizes of the OE–outcome relation per each independent sample included in the meta-analysis. We coded the direction of the effect such that positive rs indicate that higher OE related to more favorable outcomes, whereas negative rs indicate that higher OE related to more negative outcomes.

Table 13.1. Study Characteristics and Average Weighted Effects for Samples Included in the Meta-Analysis

Source for Independent Sample	Treatment (Type/Modality)	Expectancy Measure	ES (r)	Sample N
Abouguendia et al. (2004)	Mixed/Group	SS	.33	98
Barrios and Karoly (1983)	Mixed/Individual	SS	.13	30
Basoglu et al. (1994)	CBT/Individual	SS	.00	154
Belsher et al. (2012)	NR/NR	SS	.13	776
Bisno et al. (1985)	CBT/Group	SS	.04	47
Bloch et al. (1976)	NR/Group	SS	.38	21
Borkovec and Costello (1993)	CBT/Individual	CEQ	.32	54
Borkovec et al. (2002)[a]	CBT/Individual	CEQ	.13	67
Buwalda and Bouman (2008)	O/Group	SS	.07	112
Callahan et al. (2009)	CBT/Individual	SS	.08	40
Calsyn et al. (2003)	O/NR	SS	.31	65
Chambless et al. (1997)	CBT/Group	CEQ	.21	64
Clark et al. (1999)	CBT/Individual	CEQ	.50	27
Cohen et al. (2015)	CBT/Combined	CEQ	.17	391
Collins and Hyer (1986)	NR/NR	SS	.11	3998
Constantino et al. (2005)	Mixed/Individual	SS	.13	186
Crits-Christoph et al. (2004)	PD/Individual	SS	.16	64
Dearing et al. (2005)	CBT/Mixed	SS	.14	190
Devilly and Borkovec (2000)—Study 3	Mixed/Individual	CEQ	.08	11
Evans et al. (1985)	CBT/Group	SS	.33	90
Gaudiano and Miller (2006)	O/Group	CEQ	.26	61
Goldstein (1960b)	NR/Individual	SS	.00	15
Goossens et al. (2005)	Mixed/Individual	CEQ	.15	171

(continued)

Table 13.1. Continued

Source for Independent Sample	Treatment (Type/Modality)	Expectancy Measure	ES (r)	Sample N
Greer (1980)	NR/Individual	PPEI	-.47	47
Heins et al. (2013)	CBT/Individual	SS	.40	217
Holtforth et al. (2011)	CBT/NR	PATHEV	.27	159
Hundt et al. (2013)	Mixed/Individual	CEQ	.20	103
Johansson et al. (2011)	PD/Individual	SS	.28	100
Joyce et al. (2003)	Mixed/Individual	SS	.22	120
Karzmark et al. (1983)	NR/NR	SS	.03	77
Lax et al. (1992)	CBT/Individual	SS	-.25	49
LeBeau et al. (2013)	CBT/Individual	CEQ	.07	84
Leibert and Dunne-Bryant (2015)	NR/Individual	TES	-.28	81
Lewin et al. (2011)	CBT/Individual	SS	.40	48
Lipkin (1954)	EXP/Individual	SS	.16	9
Lorentzen and Høglend (2004)	PD/Group	SS	.21	59
Martin et al. (1976)	NR/NR	PPEI	.19	46
Mathews et al. (1976)	CBT/Individual	SS	.20	36
McConaghy et al. (1985)	CBT/Individual	SS	.54	10
Meyer et al. (2002)	Mixed/Individual	AAE	.22	151
Moene et al. (2003)	O/Individual	SS	.32	20
O'Malley et al. (1988)	INT/Individual	SS	.44	35
Persson and Nordlund (1983)	Mixed/Individual	SS	.18	24
Price and Anderson (2012)	CBT/Mixed	CEQ	.19	67
Price et al. (2008)	CBT/Individual	CEQ	.55	72
Price et al. (2015)	CBT/Individual	CEQ	.28	116
Richert (1976)	NR/Individual	SS	.13	26

Study	Treatment/Format	Measure		N
Rosmarin et al. (2013)	CBT/NR	CEQ	.27	159
Schindler et al. (2013)	CBT/Individual	SS	.00	70
Schoenberger et al. (1997)	CBT/Group	CEQ	.12	56
		SS		
Serafini et al. (2015)—Sample 1	Mixed/NR	SS	.01	193
Serafini et al. (2015)—Sample 2	Mixed/NR	SS	.33	193
Shaw (1977)	CBT/Group	SS	.79	16
Smeets et al. (2008)—Sample 1	CBT/Combined	CEQ	-.10	57
Smeets et al. (2008)—Sample 2	Problem solving CBT + PT/Combined	CEQ	.09	54
Snippe et al. (2015)—Sample 1	CBT/Individual	CEQ	.31	46
Snippe et al. (2015)—Sample 2	CBT/Individual	CEQ	.29	45
Spinhoven and ter Kuile (2000)	Mixed/Individual	SS	.27	164
Steinmetz et al. (1983)	CBT/Group	SS	.35	70
Stern and Marks (1973)	CBT/Individual	SS	.00	16
Sukhodolsky et al. (2017)	CBT/Individual	SS	.16	248
ter Kuile et al. (1995)	CBT/Individual	SS	.35	156
Tollinton (1973)	NR/NR	SS	.59	30
Tremblay et al. (2009)	CBT/Group	CEQ	-.32	47
Tsai et al. (2014)	CBT/Group	OES	-.28	65
Van Minnen et al. (2002)—Sample 1	CBT/Individual	CEQ	.19	43
Van Minnen et al. (2002)—Sample 2	CBT/Individual	CEQ	.19	37
Vannicelli and Becker (1981)	NR/Combined	SS	.15	76
Vogel et al. (2006)	CBT/Individual	SS	-.35	37
Warden et al. (2010)—Sample 1	NR/Mixed	ABC	.12	502

(continued)

Table 13.1. Continued

Source for Independent Sample	Treatment (Type/Modality)	Expectancy Measure	ES (r)	Sample N
Warden et al. (2010)—Sample 2	NR/ Mixed	ABC	.07	381
Warden et al. (2010)—Sample 3	NR/ Mixed	ABC	.03	426
Webb et al. (2014)	CBT/Combined	CEQ	.41	89
Webb et al. (2013)—Sample 1	CBT/Combined	CEQ	.20	420
Webb et al. (2013)—Sample 2	CBT/Combined	CEQ	.15	94
Webb et al. (2013)—Sample 3	CBT/Combined	CEQ	.26	26
Webb et al. (2013)—Sample 4	CBT/Combined	CEQ	.05	36
Wenzel et al. (2008)	CBT/Individual	AAE	.30	28
Westra, Constantino, and Aviram (2011)	CBT/Individual	CEQ	.27	38
Westra, Constantino, Arkowitz et al. (2011)	CBT/Individual	ACES	.58	32
Yoo et al. (2014)	NR/Individual	ECS	.30	284

Note (alphabetized within sections). Treatment Type: CBT = predominantly cognitive and/or behavioral therapy; EXP = predominantly humanistic/experiential therapy; INT = predominantly interpersonal/relational therapy; Mixed = different patients received different treatments (none predominant, or >60%); NR = not reported; O = predominantly other therapy; PD = predominantly psychodynamic therapy; PT = physical therapy; *Treatment Modality:* Combined = patients who received more than one treatment modality; Mixed = different patients received different modalities (none predominant, or >60%); NR = not reported; *Expectancy Measure:* ABC = Anticipated Benefits of Care; ACES = Anxiety Change Expectancy Scale; ECS = Expectation for Counseling Success; AAE = Attitudes and Expectations Questionnaire single expectancy item; CEQ = Credibility/Expectancy Questionnaire or modified version (including Borkovec & Nau's [1972] version); OES = Outcome Expectancy Scale; PATHEV = Patients' Therapy Expectation and Evaluation; PPEI = Patient Prognostic Expectancy Inventory; SS = study specific expectancy measure; TES = Treatment Expectancy Scale; *Outcome Types:* GAD = generalized anxiety disorder; OCD = obsessive compulsive disorder; PTSD = Posttraumatic Stress Disorder; *ES* = weighted effect size (coefficients coded such that positive rs indicate that higher outcome expectation related to more favorable outcomes, whereas negative rs indicate that higher outcome expectation related to more negative outcomes).

[a] Data from the Borkovec et al. (2002) trial were also analyzed in the second study/sample reported in the Devilly and Borkovec (2000) article; thus we treated the effect size data reported in both Devilly and Borkovec (Study 2) and in Borkovec et al. as being drawn from one independent sample.

Results

The overall effect of the meta-analysis ($k = 81$) was $r = 0.18$ (95% CI = 0.14, 0.22), indicating a small, but significant positive effect. Expressed as Cohen's (1988) d, the effect size was 0.36. There was significant heterogeneity in the effect sizes ($Q = 237.99$, $p < .001$; $I^2 = 76\%$, CI = 69% to 87%), indicating that one or more study-level moderators might explain such variability of effects across the independent samples.

The test of asymmetry indicated that publication bias was not present in the included studies ($p > .36$). We also generated a funnel plot, presented in Figure 13.1. The trim and fill procedure (Duval & Tweedie, 2000) estimated that the number of missing studies (i.e., studies on the left side of the plot representing a more negative effect than the weighted mean effect) needed to attain complete symmetry is 17. Even after including these studies in the meta-analysis, the OE–outcome effect remained positive and statistically significant ($r = 0.12$; $k = 98$; 95% CI = 0.07, 0.17).

MODERATORS

There were three significant moderators of the OE–outcome association. First, for every unit increase in age (continuous variable), there was a .006 decrease in the association between OE and outcome ($Q(1) = 4.44$; $p = .03$), indicating that the OE–outcome link was weaker as patients get older. Second, the OE–outcome association was stronger in samples that used either existing measures with extensive psychometric data ($k = 34$) or measures created specifically for a given study (which thus had no prior psychometric data; $k = 36$) compared to existing measures without extensive prior psychometric data ($k = 11$), $Q(2) = 6.94$, $p = 0.03$. Finally, the OE–outcome association was

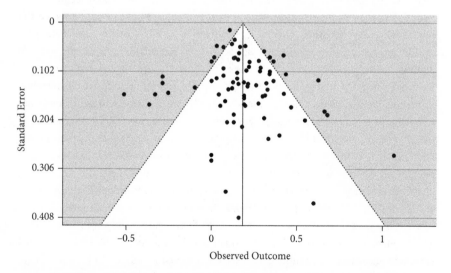

FIGURE 13.1 Funnel plot to assess publication bias in the reporting of the expectations–outcome effect sizes. The vertical bar represents the weighted mean effect size. The black dots represent the studies included in the analyses.

stronger in samples when the practitioner used either a treatment manual ($k = 46$) or a mixture of manualized and nonmanualized treatment ($k = 13$) compared to studies where no manual at all was used ($k = 22$), $Q(2) = 8.53, p = 0.01$.

Additional moderator analyses proved statistically nonsignificant. Specifically:

- Presenting diagnosis, $Q(3) = 0.95, p = 0.57$, coded as mood ($k = 18$), anxiety ($k = 26$), substance abuse ($k = 5$), and other ($k = 81$)
- Treatment orientation, $Q(1) = 0.98, p = 0.32$, coded as cognitive-behavioral ($k = 47$) or other ($k = 34$)
- Treatment modality, $Q(2) = 0.57, p = 0.75$, coded as individual ($k = 43$), group ($k = 12$), or other ($k = 26$)
- Research design, $Q(2) = 0.83, p = 0.66$, coded as comparative clinical trial ($k = 37$), open trial ($k = 16$), or naturalistic setting ($k = 25$)
- Publication date, $Q(2) = 0.16, p = 0.92$, coded as before 2000 ($k = 27$), from 2000 to 2009 ($k = 24$), and from 2009 to 2017 ($k = 30$)
- Participants' sex, $Q(1) = 0.27, p = 0.61$, treated continuously as proportion of females
- Homogeneous versus heterogeneous sample, $Q(2) = 3.37, p = 0.18$, coded as homogenous ($k = 62$), heterogeneous sample ($k = 10$), and cannot tell ($k = 3$)
- OE measurement quality, $Q(1) = 1.96, p = 0.16$, coded as good/moderate ($k = 40$) or poor ($k = 39$)

MEDIATORS

Although the meta-analytic results demonstrate that patients' OE correlates with more favorable treatment outcomes, there remains less information on the specific ways in which OE operates. Nonetheless, several mediator studies have been conducted that point to several promising *candidate* mechanisms of the OE–outcome association.

The most promising candidate, in terms of a replicated indirect effect, is the quality of the patient–therapist alliance. Multiple studies of different treatments have demonstrated that more positive patient pre- or early-treatment OE relates to more positive experiences of the alliance, which, in turn, relates to better outcomes (Abouguendia et al., 2004; Gaudiano & Miller, 2006; Johansson et al., 2011; Joyce et al., 2003; Meyer et al., 2002; Vîslă et al., 2016; Yoo et al., 2014). This consistent indirect effect squares with goal theory (e.g., Austin & Vancouver, 1996), which suggests that people will devote more resources to achieve a goal if they believe that they have a chance of attaining it. In this case, patients who have a more positive OE (compared to a more pessimistic OE) are probably more likely to engage in a collaborative working relationship with their therapist, which, in turn, fosters clinical improvement.

Of course, it is unlikely that alliance quality is the sole mechanism through which OE exerts its ameliorative influence. In fact, additional mediator studies have begun to highlight other candidate mechanisms. In one study, depressed patients with more optimistic baseline OE reported more effective behavioral and cognitive skill usage, which, in turn, related to lower depression (Webb et al., 2013). Another study of CBT for anxiety found that more positive patient baseline OE related to greater patient homework compliance, which, in turn, related to lower subsequent anxiety (Westra et al., 2007). However, several other studies have failed to find an indirect effect of OE on outcome through homework compliance (LeBeau et al., 2013; Snippe et al., 2015).

Another study demonstrated a serial indirect pathway in group CBT for depression; that is, more favorable patient baseline OE related to higher early alliance quality, which, in turn, related to more favorable OE reported *after* alliance measurement, which, in turn, predicted fewer posttreatment interpersonal problems (Vîslă et al., 2016). Hence, Vîslă and colleagues' study demonstrated that alliance and OE can have a bidirectional influence. This "reverse" connection is also supported by a study that demonstrated that patient-reported alliance ruptures in CBT for GAD were associated with more negative postrupture patient OE (Westra et al., 2011). Thus, not only does OE help promote initial engagement in an effective therapy relationship, but the experience of that relationship can influence one's belief in the personal efficacy of the treatment.

OE can also *be* a candidate mechanism of *other* process-outcome relations. In one serial mediator study focused on CBT for GAD, more effective therapists were rated as more competent in delivering CBT techniques, which, in turn, associated with more favorable subsequent patient OE, which, in turn, related to better outcome (Westra, Constantino et al., 2011). In another study, better early alliance quality related to more favorable subsequent patient OE, which, in turn, associated with fewer posttreatment interpersonal problems (Vîslă et al., 2016).

As robust mediators are discovered, researchers can manipulate OE prospectively to determine whether such manipulation causally affects the mediator and, in turn, the outcome. With such causal designs, mediator variables can be "upgraded" to causal mechanisms. For example, therapists could be randomly assigned to provide versus not provide persuasion methods for increasing patient OE. If such methods causally influenced better alliance quality that, in turn, promoted better outcome, then alliance would become a causal mechanism of the OE–outcome effect (Kraemer et al., 2002).

EVIDENCE FOR CAUSALITY

The meta-analytic evidence provides correlational, not causal, evidence for OE's association with patient outcomes. Although we suspected, based on previous reviews (both meta-analytic and narrative), that no studies had designed manipulations to causally affect patients' OEs *in treatment-seeking clinical samples*, we nonetheless conducted a separate search (in PsycINFO and PubMed, respectively) to ensure that no such experiments had been completed in recent years. As expected, these searches revealed no experiments testing strategies to causally enhance patients' OE to improve treatment efficacy.

As noted, the existing experimental research relates to the use of pretreatment socialization/preparation strategies aimed to heighten treatment response. As we reviewed previously in the Landmark Studies section, Hoehn-Saric et al.'s (1964) RI interview represents a classic preparation, with evidence of the RI as a whole (which includes one component targeting facilitation of OE) causally improving patient outcomes.

Despite no *direct* evidence for OE's causal effect on posttreatment outcomes, there is *indirect* evidence for causality in the temporal direction of the OE–outcome link. OE, when typically measured at baseline or early treatment, by nature precedes the assessment of treatment outcome, which an important prerequisite for causality. Going a step further, we are aware of one study (Brown et al., 2014) that examined the lagged association between OE and outcome over time in CBT, medication, medication + CBT, or treatment-as-usual. Across the treatments, the authors found that the model testing more favorable OE as a predictor of better next session outcome was a better fit to the data than outcome levels predicting subsequent OE. These results point to OE being a facilitative factor, as opposed to being solely a byproduct of experiencing improvement.

Relying on the established positive correlation between OE and treatment improvement, some researchers have conducted lab-based experiments with clinical analogue participants to examine whether certain interventions can causally affect individuals' OE. Although outside of a psychotherapy context, such studies provide preliminary information as to how a clinician might facilitate more positive OE in their patients. In a series of such analogue studies, researchers made multiple alterations to an audiorecorded delivery of a treatment rationale to test their effect on participants' postrationale OE (Kazdin & Krouse, 1983). Participants reported more positive OE when the rationale did (vs. did not) include (a) a description of the treatment as "prestigious" (i.e., being novel and supported with empirical research worldwide), (b) vignettes of past successful cases, (c) technical jargon, and (d) a description of the treatment's broad focus on affect, cognition, and behavior.

In another study with audiorecorded treatment rationales delivered to undergraduates, the rationales were manipulated for treatment focus (behavioral only vs. broad), number of techniques to be used (few vs. many), and length of treatment description (i.e., the number of words used by the clinician). Participants postrationale OE was more positive when the rationale was moderate in length (i.e., 250 words) as opposed to briefer or longer (Horvath, 1990). The author argued that a moderate length rationale might be most helpful in facilitating OE in that it is brief enough to comprehend but has enough information to be persuasive.

Another study tested the influence of specific OE persuasion methods, culled from the literature (including the analogue studies just reviewed), on OE (Ametrano et al., 2017). Specifically, undergraduates with elevated social anxiety were randomized to watch a videorecorded rationale of CBT for social anxiety with or without the infusion of OE persuasion methods (i.e., using hope-inspiring statements, highlighting the research support for CBT for social anxiety, using technical jargon, and highlighting the broad effects of CBT on affect, cognition, and behavior). All participants across both conditions reported a significant increase in their OE for changing their anxiety and their confidence in using the CBT exposure techniques effectively. However, despite a manipulation check showing that participants were attending to the OE persuasion methods, there was no difference between the conditions on these belief variables. The authors underscored the likely potency of clear rationale delivery on participant OE (also seen in another analogue study of OE change from pre- to post-CBT rationale exposure; Ahmed & Westra, 2009) but noted that the integrated OE strategies likely lacked sufficient salience above and beyond the general rationale effects.

PATIENT CONTRIBUTIONS

It is clinically important to understand factors that contribute to patients' positive expectations. OE relates not only to more positive distal outcomes but also to more proximal pretreatment variables like adaptive therapy attitudes (e.g., Vogel et al., 2005, 2008) and a higher likelihood of following through with treatment (e.g., Norberg et al., 2011; Swift et al., 2012). The more clinicians understand factors that affect patient OE, the more likely they can respond effectively to this cognition at treatment's outset. To date, the research on patient contributions, which is relatively scarce, has centered on three classes of patient variables: demographic, contextual, and clinical.

Regarding demographic variables, women more than men have reported higher OE in the context of college counseling (Hardin & Yanico, 1983). In another study, older adults about to participate in group therapy for depression reported higher baseline OE than younger adults (Tsai et al., 2014). Regarding contextual variables, patients with versus without prior therapy experience reported more positive OE in advance of group therapy (MacNair-Semands, 2002). Also, among young adults being treated for substance abuse, greater satisfaction with prior treatment correlated with more optimistic OE for the current treatment (Tran & Bhar, 2014).

In terms of clinical variables, presenting symptom severity has been the most studied patient correlate of patient baseline or early-treatment OE. Several studies have demonstrated that more severe global symptoms relate to more pessimistic OE (e.g., Connolly Gibbons et al., 2003; Elliott et al., 2015). Various symptoms (e.g., depression, substance abuse) have also shown negative relations with OE (e.g., Cohen et al., 2015; Constantino et al., 2014; Smeets et al., 2008). Finally, outpatients reporting greater levels of general hope also reported more optimistic therapy-specific OE (Goldfarb, 2002; Swift et al., 2012), as have patients with more psychological mindedness—having an introspective understanding and making psychological attributions for behavior (Beitel et al., 2009).

Although the literature reviewed has illuminated several potential correlates of patient baseline or early-treatment OE, there are mixed results, little replication of significant findings, and few examinations of the relative strength of associations between the patient factors and OE. Addressing these limitations, one study prospectively examined, with socially anxious undergraduates, the associations among OE and patient characteristics that had been supported as significant correlates in at least one prior study (Constantino, Coyne et al., 2017). In the multivariate analysis, the researchers found that only psychological mindedness had a main effect; more versus less psychologically minded individuals reported more optimistic OE. Subgroup analyses indicated that for participants with prior therapy experience, only satisfaction with that experience associated with more positive OE.

In the previously reviewed studies, we are referring to "patient contribution" as a specific, between-*patient* correlational effect, as this type of analysis represents the current state of the literature. However, to differentiate between-*patient* and between-*therapist* factors that contribute to OE development, or to the OE–outcome correlation, researchers will need to parse these two (Constantino, Boswell et al., 2017). There are between-therapist differences in their average patient's OE (Vîslă et al., in press), and next-step research can examine therapist-level predictors of such differences. This type of research will illuminate both patient *and* therapist contributions to OE, with therapist determinants providing the most useful information to tailor practice and training to influence patients' expectancies.

LIMITATIONS OF THE RESEARCH

Several limitations characterize our present meta-analysis. First, because we retained all studies that met our a priori criteria (in the service of comprehensiveness), the analysis contained studies of varying quality. However, to the extent that the more recent studies included improved methodology, publication year was not a moderator. Second, reflecting the state of the literature, we did not differentiate OE measured at baseline, before any contact with a therapist, or OE measured following Session 1, after minimal contact with a therapist. Third, as detailed earlier, there are few data to support a direct causal relation between positive OE and favorable treatment outcomes. Finally, we included only studies in the English language.

Several limitations also characterize the OE literature. First, OE has been primarily measured as a relatively static construct, often only assessed at baseline or early treatment. However, studies have indicated that OE changes as patients move beyond treatment's early stages. For example, in one study, patients rated treatments as less credible and reported lower OE when assessed after Session 4 compared to Session 1 in group CBT. The authors concluded, "Credibility and outcome expectancy erode when exposed to treatment reality" (Holt & Heimberg, 1990, p. 214), perhaps as patients become more cynical before experiencing much progress. Others have suggested that prognostic OE might prove too high and unrealistic at treatment's start, thus requiring time to rework their unrealistic nature (Greer, 1980). As previously reviewed, OE can also become more positive after exposure to a treatment rationale (e.g., Ametrano et al., 2017), and when measured across a longer period through a course of therapy. OE is malleable, thus limiting the empirical and clinical utility of static or single assessments.

Second, studies designed to test strategies that causally enhance patients' OE to improve treatment efficacy remain virtually nonexistent. To us, conducting such randomized trials (in both controlled and naturalistic settings) is the most pressing next-wave research to legitimize further the scientific footing and trainability of the transdiagnostic OE (Constantino, 2012). Progressing from correlational to experimental evidence will allow clinicians to harness and capitalize more fully on this patient factor.

Finally, research examining what therapists can do specifically to cultivate positive patient OE remains in its infancy, with the findings to date almost exclusively drawn from analogue samples. To move OE from being passively "owned" by the patient to one that can be affected by the practitioner, more research is needed with clinical samples. For now, we consider OE an empirically supported predictor of treatment outcome that therapists need to assess and respond to sensitively.

DIVERSITY CONSIDERATIONS

Few studies on OE have explicitly addressed dimensions of diversity; in fact, we only had sufficient data to examine sex as a patient moderator representing a diversity domain. As noted, sex had no effect on the OE–outcome association. Clearly, much more research is needed to understand better how patient multicultural identities might influence OE.

Clinically, we suspect that intersecting multicultural identities do matter in shaping prognostic beliefs about psychotherapy and, either directly or indirectly, treatment outcomes. A case study highlighted how a patient's initially low OE appeared not to emanate from a hopeless outlook but rather from a mismatch between his cultural beliefs about the etiology and amelioration of psychological difficulties and the change mechanisms of the offered treatment (Goodwin et al., 2018). The patient's beliefs about change mechanisms were rooted deeply in his religious views, which was the most salient facet of his cultural identity. In discussing this case, the authors described a missed opportunity to explore collaboratively the patient's faith, as the therapist instead doubled his efforts to champion the therapeutic model. Not surprisingly, this cultural misstep led to the patient canceling his next two sessions. After reflecting on his insensitivity, the therapist reported that he repaired the relationship rupture and ultimately instilled more optimism in the patient about the treatment's efficacy.

As illustrated in this case, dimensions of diversity are inexorably tied to patients' belief about their treatment and practitioner, and these dimensions require the therapist to maintain a meta-level, multicultural orientation. Such an orientation has been described as involving both cultural humility (openness, curiosity, and a suspension of cultural preconceptions), and clinical responsivity to opportunities to explore a patient's cultural identities (Owen et al., 2016).

TRAINING IMPLICATIONS

The present meta-analysis demonstrates a stronger correlational effect of OE on treatment outcome than its predecessor (Constantino et al., 2011). To us, this result increases the scientific credibility of formerly ill-named nonspecific factors like OE (Constantino, 2012). Thus, there is sufficient information to incorporate systematically OE-fostering strategies into clinical training. To us, clinical training should privilege the notion that common and specific factors play together on the same psychotherapy field.

We envision training that starts with an efficient overview of the research on OE, including the present meta-analysis, associated moderators, and patient contributions. Clinicians can then be trained to assess OE and track it over time in appreciation of

OE being malleable. Training can target verbal assessment, first, with questions about psychotherapy in general (e.g., "How much do think that psychotherapy can help you address your concerns?") and, second, with questions centered on the proposed treatment (e.g., "Now that you have heard how I tend to work with people, do you expect that this will be helpful?"). Training can also teach practitioners how to use and score brief measures that are easily adapted to clinical contexts and whose administration can be easily repeated (e.g., the OE subscale of the CEQ or MPEQ, respectively). Moreover, practitioners can assess more subtle markers of lowered OE (e.g., resisting the therapist's direction, missing sessions).

Whatever the markers, practitioners can then be trained to respond contextually when OE is low or unrealistic (whether discovered in response to an explicit question or as revealed by a routine measure). Specifically, trainings in such responsiveness could emphasize the importance of departing from a priori treatment plans when markers of low (or lowered) OE arise. In this vein, practitioners may want to initially respond with foundational clinical support tools, like empathy and validation. Second, clinicians can be trained to respond with specific expectancy enhancement strategies. These more formal interventions can be learned through modular trainings of evidence-based expectancy enhancement strategies (with the practices described in the following Therapeutic Practices section). We envision these trainings being delivered through efficient platforms (e.g., 45-minute in-services, Web-based trainings), with the strategies being actionable in the clinician's subsequent sessions.

THERAPEUTIC PRACTICES

Drawing on the best available research evidence, we outline several practice suggestions to help therapists cultivate and respond to their patients' OE.

- Assess explicitly patient OE verbally or through a brief measure prior to, and early in, treatment. This allow therapists to verify and validate their patients' beliefs.
- Use prognostic risk information from OE to attend closely to therapeutic relationship quality for at-risk patients. Recall that low early OE places patients at risk for lowered OE following an alliance rupture (Westra et al., 2011). Therapists might help prepare patients for relationship tensions, while simultaneously inviting explicit discussions of them (with a direct connection to treatment beliefs): "I suspect that there will be times when we disagree about your treatment. In fact, I may even upset or disappoint you. If this happens, I hope you will share your experience with me, so that we can discuss it head on and work together to adjust our plan to something that you believe in."
- Assess patient transdiagnostic characteristics that might promote low OE, perhaps especially for patients who are less psychologically minded. This will help clinicians forecast patient negative beliefs indirectly, as a complement to direct OE measurement. In the case of low psychological mindedness, cases can be made to incorporate more biological treatments or approaches consistent with a given cultural identity that may not focus on introspection and self-other exploration/ understanding.

- Use persuasion tactics regarding the likely efficacy of psychotherapy, especially when delivering a treatment rationale. For example, clinicians can mention that the treatment is prestigious, supported by research across the world, and focused broadly on feelings, cognitions, and behaviors. They can also intersperse vignettes of past successful cases and use some technical jargon, as these persuasion tactics increase OE.
- Be especially affiliative and supportive with low early patient OE, as research suggests that such a stance promotes better outcomes for these initially pessimistic patients (Constantino et al., 2007). Moreover, for these patients, it is important to not outpace their beliefs by trying to convey more optimism in the work than they are ready to accept (Ahmed & Westra, 2008). A clinician might warmly say, "I can hear in your voice how change does not seem possible right now, even with therapy. This must be terribly upsetting. Can you help me appreciate what this experience is like for you?"
- Tread lightly and empathically in using strategies to enhance OE. Make a concerted effort to use hope-inspiring statements that neither too quickly threaten a patient's beliefs or sense of self, nor promise an unrealistic degree or speed of change. Rather, such statements can be more general, such as, "It makes sense that you sought treatment for your problems" or "Your problems are exactly the type for which this therapy can be of assistance." The therapist can also express confidence and competence in such statements as, "I am confident that working together we can deal effectively with your depression," while maintaining a sense of understanding that the patient might not fully believe this statement at the outset.
- Personalize OE-enhancing statements based on patient experiences or strengths. For example, a therapist can state, "You have already conquered two major hurdles in admitting to yourself that you have a problem and in seeking help, which is not easy to do. This suggests a motivation and desire to change, despite any questions you might have about whether you *can* change." Importantly, clinicians can preserve patient autonomy in their attempts to effect their OE: "I could be wrong, and please tell me if I am, but you strike me as someone who can really accomplish things that you put your mind to."
- Offer a nontechnical review of the research findings on the intended treatment. For depressed patients, for example, a clinician could say, "Much research has shown that people in interpersonal psychotherapy for their depression tend to get significantly better than people who deal with their problems on their own."
- Check in regularly on patient OE and respond accordingly. For example, if a depressed patient has developed unrealistically high expectations after a few sessions, the therapist can provide positive feedback to reinforce self-efficacy and also remind the patient that depression can be recurrent, thus bringing his or her OE more in line with the nature of the disorder. On the other hand, if a patient expresses diminished hope about treatment, the clinician can help him or her retrieve past successes to at least partially bolster future-oriented inspiration (in the context of empathy and validation of the current demoralization).
- Be especially attentive to patient OE when working with younger patients, as OE has a stronger association with outcome. It seems especially important for young

patients to predict at the outset that a treatment can be efficacious. Perhaps an older generation can be more tolerant of uncertainty at the outset, thus having a higher likelihood of deriving benefit from therapeutic action even if initially skeptical.

• Be attentive to patient OE when delivering a manualized treatment, as OE has a stronger association with outcome as per the present meta-analysis. It seems critical for a patient to expect that a packaged treatment will work for him or her.

REFERENCES

References marked with an asterisk indicate studies included in the meta-analyses.

*Abouguendia, M., Joyce, A. S., Piper, W. E., & Ogrodniczuk, J. S. (2004). Alliance as a mediator of expectancy effects in short-term group psychotherapy. *Group Dynamics: Theory, Research, and Practice, 8*, 3–12. https://www.doi.org/10.1037/1089-2699.1.3

Ahmed, M., & Westra, H.A. (2008, September). *Impact of counselor warmth on attitudes toward seeking mental health services.* Paper presented at the meeting of the North American Chapter of the Society for Psychotherapy Research, New Haven, CT.

Ahmed, M., & Westra, H. A. (2009). Impact of a treatment rationale on expectancy and engagement in cognitive behavioral therapy for social anxiety. *Cognitive Therapy and Research, 33*, 314–322. https://www.doi.org/10.1007/s10608-008-9182-1

Ametrano, R. M., Constantino, M. J., & Nalven, T. (2017). The influence of expectancy persuasion techniques on socially anxious analogue patients' treatment beliefs and therapeutic actions. *International Journal of Cognitive Therapy, 10*, 187–205.

Arnkoff, D. B., Glass, C. R., & Shapiro, S. J. (2002). Expectations and preferences. In J. C. Norcross (Ed.), *Psychotherapy relationships that work: Therapist contributions and responsiveness to patients* (pp. 325–346). New York, NY: Oxford University Press.

Asch, S. E. (1946). Forming impressions of personality. *Journal of Abnormal and Social Psychology, 41*, 258–290.

Austin, J. T., & Vancouver, J. B. (1996). Goal constructs in psychology: Structure, process, and content. *Psychological Bulletin, 120*, 338–375. https://www.doi.org/10.1037/0033-2909.120.3.338

*Barrios, F. X., & Karoly, P. (1983). Treatment expectancy and therapeutic change in treatment of migraine headache: Are they related? *Psychological Reports, 52*, 59–68. https://www.doi.org/10.2466/pr0.1983.52.1.59

*Basoglu, M., Marks, I. M., Swinson, R. P., Noshirvani, H., O'Sullivan, G., & Kuch, K. (1994). Pre-treatment predictors of treatment outcome in panic disorder and agoraphobia treated with alprazolam and exposure. *Journal of Affective Disorders, 30*, 123–132. https://www.doi.org/10.1016/0165-0327(94)90040-X

Begg, C. B., & Mazumdar, M. (1994). Operating characteristics of a rank correlation test for publication bias. *Biometrics, 50*, 1088–1101. https://www.doi.org/10.2307/2533446

Beitel, M., Hutz, A., Sheffield, K. M., Gunn, C., Cecero, J. J., & Barry, D. T. (2009). Do psychologically minded clients expect more from counselling? *Psychology and Psychotherapy: Theory, Research and Practice, 82*, 369–383. https://www.doi.org/10.1348/147608309X436711

*Belsher, B. E., Tiet, Q. Q., Garvert, D. W., & Rosen, C. S. (2012). Compensation and treatment: Disability benefits and outcomes of U.S. veterans receiving residential PTSD treatment. *Journal of Traumatic Stress, 25*, 494–502. https://www.doi.org/10.1002/jts.21747

*Bisno, B., Thompson, L. W., Breckenridge, J., & Gallagher, D. (1985). Cognitive variables and the prediction of outcome following an intervention for controlling depression. *Cognitive Therapy and Research, 9*, 527–538. https://www.doi.org/10.1007/BF01173006

*Bloch, S., Bond, G., Qualls, B., Yalom, I., & Zimmerman, E. (1976). Patients' expectations of therapeutic improvement and their outcomes. *American Journal of Psychiatry, 133*, 1457–1460. https://www.doi.org/10.1176/ajp.133.12.1457

*Borkovec, T. D., & Costello, E. (1993). Efficacy of applied relaxation and cognitive-behavioral therapy in the treatment of generalized anxiety disorder. *Journal of Consulting and Clinical Psychology, 61*, 611–619. https://www.doi.org/10.1037/0022-006X.61.4.611

Borkovec, T. D., & Nau, S. D. (1972). Credibility of analogue therapy rationales. *Journal of Behavior Therapy & Experimental Psychiatry, 3*, 257–260. https://www.doi.org/10.1016/0005-7916(72)90045-6

*Borkovec, T. B., Newman, M. G., Pincus, A. L., & Lytle, R. (2002). A component analysis of cognitive-behavioral therapy for generalized anxiety disorder and the role of interpersonal problems. *Journal of Consulting and Clinical Psychology, 70*, 288–298. https://www.doi.org/10.1037/0022-006X.70.2.288

Bowman, N. A. (2012). Effect sizes and statistical methods for meta-analysis in higher education. *Research in Higher Education, 53*, 375–382. https://www.doi.org/10.1007/s11162-011-9232-5

Brown, L. A., Wiley, J. F., Wolitzky-Taylor, K., Roy-Byrne, P., Sherbourne, C., Stein, M. B., . . . Craske, M. G. (2014). Changes in self-efficacy and outcome expectancy as predictors of anxiety outcomes from the CALM study. *Depression and Anxiety, 31*, 678–689. https://www.doi.org/10.1002/da.22256

*Buwalda, F., & Bouman, T. (2008). Predicting the effect of psychoeducational group treatment for hypochondriasis. *Clinical Psychology & Psychotherapy, 15*, 396–403. https://www.doi.org/10.1002/cpp.602

*Callahan, J., Aubuchon-Endsley, N., Borja, S., & Swift, J. (2009). Pretreatment expectancies and premature termination in a training clinic environment. *Training and Education in Professional Psychology, 3*, 111–119. https://www.doi.org/10.1037/a0012901

*Calsyn, R., Morse, G., Yonker, R., Winter, J., Pierce, K., & Taylor, M. (2003). Client choice of treatment and client outcomes. *Journal of Community Psychology, 31*, 339–348. https://www.doi.org/10.1002/jcop.10053

*Chambless, D. L., Tran, G. Q., & Glass, C. R. (1997). Predictors of response to cognitive-behavioral group therapy for social phobia. *Journal of Anxiety Disorders, 11*, 221–240. https://www.doi.org/10.1016/S0887-6185(97)00008-X

*Clark, D. M., Salkovskis, P. M., Hackmann, A., Wells, A., Ludgate, J., & Gelder, M. (1999). Brief cognitive therapy for panic disorder: A randomized controlled trial. *Journal of Consulting and Clinical Psychology, 67*, 583–589. https://www.doi.org/10.1037/0022-006X.67.4.583

Cohen, J. (1988). *Statistical power analysis for the behavioral sciences* (2nd ed.). Mahwah, NJ: Erlbaum.

*Cohen, M., Beard, C., & Björgvinsson, T. (2015). Examining patient characteristics as predictors of patient beliefs about treatment credibility and expectancies for treatment outcome. *Journal of Psychotherapy Integration, 25*, 90–99. https://www.doi.org/10.1037/a0038878

*Collins, J. F., & Hyer, L. (1986). Treatment expectancy among psychiatric inpatients. *Journal of Clinical Psychology, 42*, 562–569. https://www.doi.org/10.1002/1097-4679(198607)42:4<562::AID-JCLP2270420404>3.0.CO;2-4

Connolly Gibbons, M. B., Crits-Christoph, P., de la Cruz, C., Barber, J. P., Siqueland, L., & Gladis, M. (2003). Pretreatment expectations, interpersonal functioning, and symptoms in the prediction of the therapeutic alliance across supportive-expressive psychotherapy and cognitive therapy. *Psychotherapy Research, 13,* 59–76. https://www.doi.org/10.1093/ptr/kpg007

Constantino, M. J. (2012). Believing is seeing: An evolving research program on patients' psychotherapy expectations. *Psychotherapy Research, 22,* 127–138. https://www.doi.org/10.1080/10503307.2012.663512

Constantino, M. J., Ametrano, R. M., & Greenberg, R. P. (2012). Clinician interventions and participant characteristics that foster adaptive patient expectations for psychotherapy and psychotherapeutic change. *Psychotherapy, 49,* 557–569. https://www.doi.org/10.1037/a0029440

*Constantino, M. J., Arnow, B. A., Blasey, C., & Agras, W. S. (2005). The association between patient characteristics and the therapeutic alliance in cognitive-behavioral and interpersonal therapy for bulimia nervosa. *Journal of Consulting and Clinical Psychology, 73,* 203–211. https://www.doi.org/10.1037/0022-006X.73.2.203

Constantino, M. J., Boswell, J. F., Coyne, A. E., Kraus, D. R., & Castonguay, L. G. (2017). Who works for whom and why? Integrating therapist effects analysis into psychotherapy outcome and process research. In L. G. Castonguay & C. E. Hill (Eds.), *Why are some therapists are better than others? Understanding therapist effects* (pp. 309–323). Washington DC: American Psychological Association. https://www.doi.org/10.1037/0000034-004.

Constantino, M. J., Coyne, A. E., McVicar, E. L., & Ametrano, R. A. (2017). The relative association between individual difference variables and general psychotherapy outcome expectation in socially anxious individuals. *Psychotherapy Research, 27,* 583–594. https://www.doi.org/10.1080/10503307.2016.1138336

Constantino, M. J., Glass, C. R., Arnkoff, D. B., Ametrano, R. M., & Smith, J. Z. (2011). Expectations. In J. C. Norcross (Ed.), *Psychotherapy relationships that work: Evidence-based responsiveness* (2nd ed., pp. 354–376). New York, NY: Oxford University Press.

Constantino, M. J., Manber, R., Ong, J., Kuo, T. F., Huang, J., & Arnow, B.A. (2007). Patient expectations and the therapeutic alliance as predictors of outcome in group CBT for insomnia. *Behavioral Sleep Medicine, 5,* 210–228. https://www.doi.org/10.1080/15402000701263932

Constantino, M. J., Penek, S., Bernecker, S. L., & Overtree, C. E. (2014). A preliminary examination of participant characteristics in relation to patients' treatment beliefs in psychotherapy in a training clinic. *Journal of Psychotherapy Integration, 24,* 238–250. https://www.doi.org/10.1037/a0031424

Constantino, M. J., & Westra, H. A. (2012). An expectancy-based approach to facilitating corrective experiences in psychotherapy. In L. G. Castonguay & C. E. Hill (Eds.), *Transformation in psychotherapy: Corrective experiences across cognitive, behavioral, humanistic, and psychodynamic approaches* (pp. 121–139). Washington, DC: American Psychological Association.

Cooper, H., Hedges, L. V., & Valentine, J. C. (Eds.). (2009). *The handbook of research synthesis and meta-analysis.* New York, NY: Russell Sage Foundation.

*Crits-Christoph, P., Gibbons, M., Losardo, D., Narducci, J., Schamberger, M., & Gallop, R. (2004). Who benefits from brief psychodynamic therapy for generalized anxiety disorder? *Canadian Journal of Psychoanalysis, 12,* 301–324.

*Dearing, R., Barrick, C., Dermen, K., & Walitzer, K. (2005). Indicators of client engagement: Influences on alcohol treatment satisfaction and outcomes. *Psychology of Addictive Behaviors, 19,* 71–78. https://www.doi.org/10.1037/0893-164X.19.1.71

DeFife, J. A., & Hilsenroth, M. J. (2011). Starting off on the right foot: Common factor elements in early psychotherapy process. *Journal of Psychotherapy Integration, 21,* 172–191. https://www.doi.org/10.1037/a0023889

Del Re, A. C. (2013). compute.es: Compute effect sizes. R package version 0.2–2. Retrieved from http://cran.r-project.org/web/packages/compute.es

Del Re, A. C., & Hoyt, W. T. (2010). MAc: Meta-analysis with correlations. R package version 1.0.5. Retrieved from http://CRAN.R-project.org/package=MAc

*Devilly, G., & Borkovec, T. (2000). Psychometric properties of the Credibility/Expectancy Questionnaire. *Journal of Behavior Therapy and Experimental Psychiatry, 31,* 73–86. https://www.doi.org/10.1016/S0005-7916(00)00012-4

Duval, S., & Tweedie, R. (2000). Trim and fill: A simple funnel-plot–based method of testing and adjusting for publication bias in meta-analysis. *Biometrics, 56,* 455–463. https://www.doi.org/10.1111/j.0006-341X.2000.00455.x

Egger, M., Smith, G. D., Schneider, M., & Minder, C. (1997). Bias in meta-analysis detected by a simple, graphical test. *British Medical Journal, 315,* 629–634. https://www.doi.org/10.1136/bmj.315.7109.629

Elkin, I., Shea, M. T., Watkins, J. T., Imber, S. D., Sotsky, S. M., Collins, J. F., . . . Parloff, M. B. (1989). National Institute of Mental Health Treatment of Depression Collaborative Research Program: General effectiveness of treatments. *Archives of General Psychiatry, 46,* 971–982. https://www.doi.org/10.1001/archpsyc.1989.01810110013002

Elliott, K. P., Westmacott, R., Hunsley, J., Rumstein-McKean, O., & Best, M. (2015). The process of seeking psychotherapy and its impact on therapy expectations and experiences. *Clinical Psychology & Psychotherapy, 22,* 399–408. https://www.doi.org/10.1002/cpp.1900

*Evans, R. L., Smith, K. M., Halar, E. M., & Kiolet, C. L. (1985). Effect of expectation and level of adjustment on treatment outcome. *Psychological Reports, 57,* 936–938. https://www.doi.org/10.2466/pr0.1985.57.3.936

Frank, J. D. (1958). Some effects of expectancy and influence in psychotherapy. In J. H. Masserman & J. L. Moreno (Eds.), *Progress in psychotherapy* (Vol. 3, pp. 27–43). New York, NY: Grune and Stratton.

Frank, J. D. (1961). *Persuasion and healing: A comparative study of psychotherapy.* Baltimore, MD: Johns Hopkins University Press.

*Gaudiano, B., & Miller, I. (2006). Patients' expectancies, the alliance in pharmacotherapy, and treatment outcomes in bipolar disorder. *Journal of Consulting and Clinical Psychology, 74,* 671–676. https://www.doi.org/10.1037/0022-006X.74.4.671

Goldfarb, D. E. (2002). College counseling center clients' expectations about counseling: How they relate to depression, hopelessness, and actual-ideal self-discrepancies. *Journal of College Counseling, 5,* 142–152. https://www.doi.org/10.1002/j.2161-1882.2002.tb00216.x

Goldfried, M. R. (1980). Toward the delineation of therapeutic change principles. *American Psychologist, 35,* 991–999. https://www.doi.org/10.1037/0003-066X.35.11.991

Goldstein, A. P. (1960a). Patient's expectancies and non-specific therapy as a basis for (un) spontaneous remission. *Journal of Clinical Psychology, 16,* 399–403. https://www.doi.org/10.1002/1097-4679(196010)16:4<399::AID-JCLP2270160416>3.0.CO;2-E

*Goldstein, A. P. (1960b). Therapist and client expectation of personality change in psychotherapy. *Journal of Counseling Psychology, 7,* 180–184. https://www.doi.org/10.1037/h0043998

Goodwin, B. J., Coyne, A. E., & Constantino, M. J. (2018). Extending the context-responsive psychotherapy integration framework to cultural processes in psychotherapy. *Psychotherapy, 55*(1), 3–8.

*Goossens, M. B., Vlaeyen, J. S., Hidding, A., Kole-Snijders, A., & Evers, S. A. (2005). Treatment expectancy affects the outcome of cognitive-behavioral interventions in chronic pain. *Clinical Journal of Pain, 21*, 18–26. https://www.doi.org/10.1097/00002508-200501000-00003

Greenberg, R. P. (1969). Effects of pre-session information on perception of the therapist and receptivity to influence in a psychotherapy analogue. *Journal of Consulting and Clinical Psychology, 33*, 425–429.

Greenberg, R. P., Constantino, M. J., & Bruce, N. (2006). Are expectations still relevant for psychotherapy process and outcome? *Clinical Psychology Review, 26*, 657–678. https://www.doi.org/10.1016/j.cpr.2005.03.002

*Greer, F. L. (1980). Prognostic expectations and outcome of brief therapy. *Psychological Reports, 46*, 973–974. https://www.doi.org/10.2466/pr0.1980.46.3.973

Hardin, S. I., & Yanico, B. J. (1983). Counselor gender, type of problem, and expectations about counseling. *Journal of Counseling Psychology, 30*, 294–297. https://www.doi.org/10.1037/0022-0167.30.2.294

Hardy, G. E., Barkham, M., Shapiro, D. A., Reynolds, S., Rees, A., & Stiles, W. B. (1995). Credibility and outcome of cognitive-behavioural and psychodynamic-interpersonal therapy. *British Journal of Clinical Psychology, 34*, 555–569. https://www.doi.org/10.1111/j.2044-8260.1995.tb01489.x

Heine, R. W., & Trosman, H. (1960). Initial expectations of the doctor-patient interaction as a factor in continuance in psychotherapy. *Psychiatry, 23*, 275–278.

*Heins, M. J., Knoop, H., & Bleijenberg, G. (2013). The role of the therapeutic relationship in cognitive behaviour therapy for chronic fatigue syndrome. *Behaviour Research and Therapy, 51*, 368–376. https://www.doi.org/10.1016/j.brat.2013.02.001

Higgins, J., & Thompson, S. G. (2002). Quantifying heterogeneity in a meta-analysis. *Statistics in Medicine, 21*, 1539–1558. https://www.doi.org/10.1002/sim.1186

Hoehn-Saric, R., Frank, J., Imber, S., Nash, E., Stone, A., & Battle, C. (1964). Systematic preparation of patients for psychotherapy: I. Effects of therapy behavior and outcome. *Journal of Psychiatric Research, 2*, 267–281. https://www.doi.org/10.1016/0022-3956(64)90013-5

Holt, C. S., & Heimberg, R. G. (1990). The Reaction to Treatment Questionnaire: Measuring treatment credibility and outcome expectancies. *The Behavior Therapist, 13*, 213–214, 222.

*Holtforth, M. G., Krieger, T., Bochsler, K., & Mauler, B. (2011). The prediction of psychotherapy success by outcome expectations in inpatient psychotherapy. *Psychotherapy and Psychosomatics, 80*, 321–322. https://www.doi.org/10.1159/000324171

Horvath, P. (1990). Treatment expectancy as a function of the amount of information presented in therapeutic rationales. *Journal of Clinical Psychology, 46*, 636–642. https://www.doi.org/10.1002/10974679(199009)46:5<636::AID-JCLP2270460516>3.0.CO;2-U

*Hundt, N. E., Armento, M. A., Porter, B., Cully, J. A., Kunik, M. E., & Stanley, M. (2013). Predictors of treatment satisfaction among older adults with anxiety in a primary care psychology program. *Evaluation and Program Planning, 37*, 58–63. https://www.doi.org/10.1016/j.evalprogplan.2013.01.003

Hunter, J. E., & Schmidt, F. L. (2004). *Methods of meta-analysis: Correcting error and bias in research findings* (2nd ed.). Thousand Oaks, CA: SAGE.

*Johansson, P., Høglend, P., & Hersoug, A. G. (2011). Therapeutic alliance mediates the effect of patient expectancy in dynamic psychotherapy. *British Journal of Clinical Psychology, 50*, 283–297. https://www.doi.org/10.1348/014466510X517406

*Joyce, A. S., Ogrodniczuk, J. S., Piper, W. E., & McCallum, M. (2003). The alliance as mediator of expectancy effects in short-term individual therapy. *Journal of Consulting and Clinical Psychology, 71,* 672–679. https://www.doi.org/10.1037/0022-006X.71.4.672

*Karzmark, P., Greenfield, T., & Cross, H. (1983). The relationship between level of adjustment and expectations for therapy. *Journal of Clinical Psychology, 39,* 930–932. https://www.doi.org/10.1002/1097-4679(198311)39:6<930::AID-JCLP2270390618>3.0.CO;2-G

Kazdin, A. E., & Krouse, R. (1983). The impact of variations in treatment rationales on expectancies for therapeutic change. *Behavior Therapy, 14,* 657–671. https://www.doi.org/10.1016/S0005-7894(83)80058-6

Kelley, H. H. (1950). Warm-cold variable in first impressions of persons. *Journal of Personality, 18,* 431–439. https://www.doi.org/10.1111/j.1467-6494.1950.tb01260.x

Khattra, J., Angus, L., Westra, H., Macaulay, C., Moertl, K., & Constantino, M. (2017). Client perceptions of corrective experiences in cognitive behavioral therapy and motivational interviewing for generalized anxiety disorder: An exploratory pilot study. *Journal of Psychotherapy Integration, 27,* 23–34. https://www.doi.org/10.1037/int0000053

Kirsch, I. (1985). Response expectancy as a determinant of experience and behavior. *American Psychologist, 40,* 1189–1202. https://www.doi.org/10.1037/0003-066X.40.11.1189

Kirsch, I. (1990). *Changing expectations: A key to effective psychotherapy.* Pacific Grove, CA: Brooks/Cole.

Kraemer, H. C., Wilson, G. T., Fairburn, C. G., & Agras, W. S. (2002). Mediators and moderators of treatment effects in randomized clinical trials. *Archives of General Psychiatry, 59,* 877–883. https://www.doi.org/10.1001/archpsyc.59.10.877

Larsen, D. J., & Stege, R. (2010). Hope-focused practices during early psychotherapy sessions: Part I: Implicit approaches. *Journal of Psychotherapy Integration, 20,* 271–292. https://www.doi.org/10.1037/a0020820

*Lax, T., Basoglu, M., & Marks, I. M. (1992). Expectancy and compliance as predictors of outcome in obsessive-compulsive disorder. *Behavioural Psychotherapy, 20,* 257–266. https://www.doi.org/10.1017/S0141347300017237

*LeBeau, R. T., Davies, C. D., Culver, N. C., & Craske, M. G. (2013). Homework compliance counts in cognitive-behavioral therapy. *Cognitive Behaviour Therapy, 42,* 171–179. https://www.doi.org/10.1080/16506073.2013.763286

*Leibert, T. W., & Dunne-Bryant, A. (2015). Do common factors account for counseling outcome? *Journal of Counseling and Development, 93,* 225–235. https://www.doi.org/10.1002/j.1556-6676.2015.00198.x

*Lewin, A. B., Peris, T. S., Bergman, R. L., McCracken, J. T., & Piacentini, J. (2011). The role of treatment expectancy in youth receiving exposure-based CBT for obsessive compulsive disorder. *Behaviour Research and Therapy, 49,* 536–543. https://www.doi.org/10.1016/j.brat.2011.06.001

Lipsey, M. W., & Wilson, D. B. (2001). *Practical meta-analysis.* Thousand Oaks, CA: SAGE.

*Lipkin, S. (1954). Clients' feelings and attitudes in relation to the outcome of client-centered therapy. *Psychological Monographs, 68*(1), 1–30. https://www.doi.org/10.1037/h0093661

*Lorentzen, S., & Høglend, P. (2004). Predictors of change during long-term analytic group psychotherapy. *Psychotherapy and Psychosomatics, 73,* 25–35. https://www.doi.org/10.1159/000074437

Macaulay, C., Angus, L., Khattra, J., Westra, H., & Ip, J. (2017). Client retrospective accounts of corrective experiences in motivational interviewing integrated with cognitive behavioral therapy for generalized anxiety disorder. *Journal of Clinical Psychology: In Session, 73,* 168–181. https://www.doi.org/10.1002/jclp.22430

MacNair-Semands, R. (2002). Predicting attendance and expectations for group therapy. *Group Dynamics: Theory, Research, and Practice, 6,* 219–228.

Marcus, M., Westra, H. A., Angus, L., & Kertes, A. (2011). Client experiences of motivational interviewing for generalized anxiety disorder: A qualitative analysis. *Psychotherapy Research, 21,* 447–461. https://www.doi.org/10.1080/10503307.2011.578265

*Martin, P. J., Sterne, A. L., Claveaux, R., & Acree, N. J. (1976). Significant factors in the expectancy-improvement relationship: A second look at an early study. *Research Communications in Psychology, Psychiatry & Behavior, 1,* 367–379.

*Mathews, A. M., Johnston, D. W., Lancashire, M., Munby, M., Shaw, P. M., & Gelder, M. G. (1976). Imaginal flooding and exposure to real phobic situations: Treatment outcome with agoraphobic patients. *British Journal of Psychiatry, 129,* 362–371. https://www.doi.org/10.1192/bjp.129.4.361

*McConaghy, N., Armstrong, M., & Blaszczynski, A. P. (1985). Expectancy, covert sensitization and imaginal desensitization in compulsive sexuality. *Acta Psychiatrica Scandinavica, 72,* 176–187. https://www.doi.org/10.1111/j.1600-0447.1985.tb02592.x

*Meyer, B., Pilkonis, P. A., Krupnick, J. L., Egan, M. K., Simmens, S. J., & Sotsky, S. M. (2002). Treatment expectancies, patient alliance, and outcome: Further analyses from the National Institute of Mental Health Treatment of Depression Collaborative Research Program. *Journal of Consulting and Clinical Psychology, 70,* 1051–1055. https://www.doi.org/10.1037/0022-006X.70.4.1051

*Moene, F., Spinhoven, P., Hoogduin, K., & Dyck, R. (2003). A randomized controlled clinical trial of a hypnosis-based treatment for patients with conversion disorder, motor type. *International Journal of Clinical and Experimental Hypnosis, 51,* 29–50. https://www.doi.org/10.1076/iceh.51.1.29.14067

Noble, L. M., Douglas, B. C., & Newman, S. P. (2001). What do patients expect of psychological services? A systematic and critical review of empirical studies. *Social Science & Medicine, 52,* 985–998. https://www.doi.org/10.1016/S0277-9536(00)00210-0

Nock, M. K., & Kazdin, A. E. (2001). Parent expectancies for child therapy: Assessment and relation to participation in treatment. *Journal of Child and Family Studies, 10,* 155–180. https://www.doi.org/10.1023/A:1016699424731

Norberg, M. M., Wetterneck, C. T., Sass, D. A., & Kanter, J. W. (2011). Development and psychometric evaluation of the Milwaukee Psychotherapy Expectations Questionnaire. *Journal of Clinical Psychology, 67,* 574–590. https://www.doi.org/10.1002/jclp.20781

*O'Malley, S. S., Foley, S. H., Rounsaville, B. J., Watkins, J. T., Sotsky, S. M., Imber, S. D., & Elkin, I. (1988). Therapist competence and patient outcome in interpersonal psychotherapy of depression. *Journal of Consulting and Clinical Psychology, 56,* 496–501. https://www.doi.org/10.1037/0022-006X.56.4.496

Owen, J., Tao, K. W., Drinane, J. M., Hook, J., Davis, D. E., & Kune, N. F. (2016). Client perceptions of therapists' multicultural orientation: Cultural (missed) opportunities and cultural humility. *Professional Psychology: Research and Practice, 47,* 30–37. https://www.doi.org/10.1037/pro0000046

*Persson, G., & Nordlund, C. L. (1983). Expectations of improvement and attitudes to treatment processes in relation to outcome with four treatment methods for phobic disorders. *Acta Psychiatrica Scandinavica, 68,* 484–493. https://www.doi.org/10.1111/j.1600-0447.1983.tb00956.x

*Price, M., & Anderson, P. L. (2012). Outcome expectancy as a predictor of treatment response in cognitive behavioral therapy for public speaking fears within social anxiety disorder. *Psychotherapy, 49*, 173–179. https://www.doi.org/10.1037/a0024734

*Price, M., Anderson, P., Henrich, C., & Rothbaum, B. (2008). Greater expectations: Using hierarchical linear modeling to examine expectancy for treatment outcome as a predictor of treatment response. *Behavior Therapy, 39*, 398–405. https://www.doi.org/10.1016/j.beth.2007.12.002

*Price, M., Maples, J. L., Jovanovic, T., Norrholm, S. D., Heekin, M., & Rothbaum, B. O. (2015). An investigation of outcome expectancies as a predictor of treatment response for combat veterans with PTSD: Comparison of clinician, self-report, and biological measures. *Depression and Anxiety, 32*, 392–399. https://www.doi.org/10.1002/da.22354

*Richert, A. J. (1976). Expectations, experiencing and change in psychotherapy. *Journal of Clinical Psychology, 32*, 438–444. https://www.doi.org/10.1002/1097-4679(197604)32:2<438::AID-JCLP2270320250>3.0.CO;2-J

Rosenthal, D., & Frank, J. D. (1956). Psychotherapy and the placebo effect. *Psychological Bulletin, 53*, 294–302.

Rosenzweig, S. (1936). Some implicit common factors in diverse methods of psychotherapy. *American Journal of Orthopsychiatry, 6*, 412–415. https://www.doi.org/10.1111/j.1939-0025.1936.tb05248.x

*Rosmarin, D. H., Bigda-Peyton, J. S., Kertz, S. J., Smith, N., Rauch, S. L., & Bjorgvinsson, T. (2013). A test of faith in God and treatment: The relationship of belief in God to psychiatric treatment outcomes. *Journal of Affective Disorders, 146*, 441–446.

Safren, S. A., Heimberg, R. G., & Juster, H. R. (1997). Clients' expectancies and their relationship to pretreatment symptomatology and outcome of cognitive-behavioral group treatment for social phobia. *Journal of Consulting and Clinical Psychology, 65*, 694–698. https://www.doi.org/10.1037/0022-006X.65.4.694

*Schindler, A., Hiller, W., & Witthöft, M. (2013). What predicts outcome, response, and drop-out in CBT of depressive adults? A naturalistic study. *Behavioural and Cognitive Psychotherapy, 41*, 365–370. https://www.doi.org/10.1017/S1352465812001063

Schoenberger, N. E., Kirsch, I., Gearan, P., Montgomery, G., & Pastyrnak, S. L. (1997). Hypnotic enhancement of a cognitive behavioral treatment for public speaking anxiety. *Behavior Therapy, 28*, 127–140. https://www.doi.org/10.1016/S0005-7894(97)80038-X

Schulte, D. (2008). Patients' outcome expectancies and their impression of suitability as predictors of treatment outcome. *Psychotherapy Research, 18*, 481–494. https://www.doi.org/10.1080/10503300801932505

Secord, P. F. (1958). Facial features and inference processes in interpersonal perception. In R. Taguiri & L. Petrillo (Eds.), *Person perception and interpersonal behavior* (pp. 300–315). Stanford, CA: Stanford University Press.

*Serafini, K., Decker, S., Kiluk, B. D., Añez, L., Paris, M. J., Frankforter, T., & Carroll, K. M. (2015). Outcome expectations and associated treatment outcomes in motivational enhancement therapy delivered in English and Spanish. *The American Journal on Addictions, 24*, 732–739. https://www.doi.org/10.1111/ajad.12301

Shapiro, D. A. (1981). Comparative credibility of treatment rationales: Three tests of expectancy theory. *British Journal of Clinical Psychology, 21*, 111–122. https://www.doi.org/10.1111/j.2044-8260.1981.tb00504.x

*Shaw, H. (1977). A simple and effective treatment for flight phobia. *British Journal of Psychiatry, 130*, 229–232. https://www.doi.org/10.1192/bjp.130.3.229

*Smeets, R. M., Beelen, S., Goossens, M. B., Schouten, E.W., Knottnerus, J. A., & Vlaeyen, J. S. (2008). Treatment expectancy and credibility are associated with the outcome of both physical and cognitive-behavioral treatment in chronic low back pain. *Clinical Journal of Pain, 24,* 305–315. https://www.doi.org/10.1097/AJP.0b013e318164aa75

*Snippe, E., Schroevers, M. J., Tovote, K. A., Sanderman, R., Emmelkamp, P. G., & Fleer, J. (2015). Patients' outcome expectations matter in psychological interventions for patients with diabetes and comorbid depressive symptoms. *Cognitive Therapy and Research, 39,* 307–317. https://www.doi.org/10.1007/s10608-014-9667-z

Sotsky, S. M., Glass, D. E., Shea, M. T., Pilkonis, P. A., Collins, J. F., Elkin, I., . . . Moyer, J. (1991). Patient predictors of response to psychotherapy and pharmacotherapy: Findings in the NIMH Treatment of Depression Collaborative Research Program. *American Journal of Psychiatry, 148,* 997–1008. https://www.doi.org/10.1176/ajp.148.8.997

*Spinhoven, P., & ter Kuile, M. M. (2000). Treatment outcome expectancies and hypnotic sus-ceptibility as moderators of pain reduction in patients with chronic tension-type headache. *International Journal of Clinical and Experimental Hypnosis, 48,* 290–305. https://www.doi.org/10.1080/00207140008415247

*Steinmetz, J. L., Lewinsohn, P. M., & Antonuccio, D. O. (1983). Prediction of individual out-come in a group intervention for depression. *Journal of Consulting and Clinical Psychology, 51,* 331–337. https://www.doi.org/10.1037/0022-006X.51.3.331

Stephenson, C. (1991). The concept of hope revisited for nursing. *Journal of Advanced Nursing, 16,* 1456–1461.

*Stern, R., & Marks, I. (1973). Brief and prolonged exposure: A comparison in agoraphobia patients. *Archives of General Psychiatry, 28,* 270–276.

Strupp, H. H. (1970). Specific vs. nonspecific factors in psychotherapy and the problem of control. *Archives of General Psychiatry, 23,* 393–401. https://www.doi.org/10.1001/archpsyc.1970.01750050009002

Strupp, H. H., & Bloxom, A. L. (1973). Preparing lower-class patients for group psycho-therapy: Development and evaluation of a role-induction film. *Journal of Consulting and Clinical Psychology, 41,* 373–384. https://www.doi.org/10.1037/h0035380

*Sukhodolsky, D. G., Woods, D. W., Piacentini, J., Wilhelm, S., Peterson, A. L., Katsovich, L., . . . Scahill, L. (2017). Moderators and predictors of response to behavior therapy for tics in Tourette syndrome. *Neurology, 88,* 1029–1036. https://www.doi.org/10.1212/WNL.0000000000003710

Swift, J. K., Whipple, J. L., & Sandberg, P. (2012). A prediction of initial appointment attend-ance and initial outcome expectations. *Psychotherapy, 49,* 549–556. https://www.doi.org/10.1037/a0029441

*ter Kuile, M. M., Spinhoven, P., & Linssen, C. G. (1995). Responders and nonresponders to autogenic training and cognitive self-hypnosis: Prediction of short- and long-term success in tension-type headache patients. *Headache: The Journal of Head and Face Pain, 35,* 630–636. https://www.doi.org/10.1111/j.1526-4610.1995.hed3510630.x

Tinsely, H. E. A., Bowman, S. L., & Ray, S. B. (1988). Manipulation of expectancies about counseling and psychotherapy: Review and analysis of expectancy manipulation strategies and results. *Journal of Counseling Psychology, 35,* 99–108. https://www.doi.org/10.1037/0022-0167.35.1.99

*Tollinton, H. (1973). Initial expectations and outcome. *British Journal of Medical Psychology, 46,* 251–257.

Tran, D., & Bhar, S. (2014). Predictors for treatment expectancies among young people who attend drug and alcohol services: A pilot study. *Clinical Psychologist, 18,* 33–42. https://www.doi.org/10.1111//cp.12009

*Tremblay, V., Savard, J., & Ivers, H. (2009). Predictors of the effect of cognitive behavioral therapy for chronic insomnia comorbid with breast cancer. *Journal of Consulting and Clinical Psychology, 77,* 742–750. https://www.doi.org/10.1037/a0015492

*Tsai, M., Ogrodniczuk, J. S., Sochting, I., & Mirmiran, J. (2014). Forecasting success: Patients' expectations for improvement and their relations to baseline, process, and outcome variables in group cognitive-behavioural therapy for depression. *Clinical Psychology and Psychotherapy, 21,* 97–107. https://www.doi.org/10.1002/cpp.1831

Urwin, C. (2007). Revisiting "what works for whom?": A qualitative framework for evaluating clinical effectiveness in child psychotherapy. *Journal of Child Psychotherapy, 33,* 134–160. https://www.doi.org/10.1080/00754170701431370

*van Minnen, A., Arntz, A., & Keijsers, G.P.J. (2002). Prolonged exposure in patients with chronic PTSD: Predictors of treatment outcome and dropout. *Behaviour Research and Therapy, 40,* 439–457. https://www.doi.org/10.1016/S0005-7967(01)00024-9

*Vannicelli, M., & Becker, B. (1981). Prediction outcome in treatment of alcoholism: A study of staff and patients. *Journal of Studies on Alcohol, 42,* 938–950. https://www.doi.org/10.15288/jsa.1981.42.938

Viechtbauer, W. (2010). Conducting meta-analyses in R with the metafor package. *Journal of Statistical Software, 36,* 1–48. Retrieved from http://www.jstatsoft.org/v36/i03/

Vîslă, A., Constantino, M. J., Newkirk, K., Ogrodniczuk, J. S., & Söchting, I. (2016, August). The relation between outcome expectations, therapeutic alliance, and outcome among depressed patients in group cognitive-behavioral therapy. *Psychotherapy Research.* Advance online publication. https://www.doi.org/10.1080/10503307.2016.1218089

Vîslă, A., Flückiger, C., Constantino, M. J., Krieger, T., & Grosse Holtforth, M. (2018). A multilevel analysis of patient characteristics and the therapist as predictors of depressed patients' outcome expectation over time. *Psychotherapy Research.* Advance online publication. http://www.doi.org/10.1080/10503307.2018.1428379

*Vogel, P. A., Hansen, B., Stiles, T. C., & Gotestam, K. G. (2006). Treatment motivation, treatment expectancy, and helping alliance as predictors of outcome in cognitive behavioral treatment of OCD. *Journal of Behavior Therapy and Experimental Psychiatry, 37,* 247–255. https://www.doi.org/10.1016/j.jbtep.2005.12.001

Vogel, D. L., Wade, N. G., & Hackler, A. H. (2008). Emotional expression and the decision to seek therapy: The mediating roles of the anticipated benefits and risks. *Journal of Social and Clinical Psychology, 27,* 254–278. https://www.doi.org/10.1521/jscp.2008.27.3.254

Vogel, D. L., Wester, S. R., Wei, M., & Boysen, G. A. (2005). The role of outcome expectations and attitudes on decisions to seek professional help. *Journal of Counseling Psychology, 52,* 459–470. https://www.doi.org/10.1037/0022-0167.52.4.459

Wampold, B. E., Mondin, G. W., Moody, M., Stich, F., Benson, K., & Ahn, H. (1997). A meta-analysis of outcome studies comparing bona fide psychotherapies: Empirically, "all must have prizes." *Psychological Bulletin, 122,* 203–215.

*Warden, D., Trivedi, M., Carmody, T., Gollan, J., Kashner, T., Lind, L., . . . Rush, A. (2010). Anticipated Benefits of Care (ABC): Psychometrics and predictive value in psychiatric disorders. *Psychological Medicine, 40,* 955–965. https://www.doi.org/10.1017/S003329170999136X

*Webb, C. A., Beard, C., Auerbach, R. P., Menninger, E., & Björgvinsson, T. (2014). The therapeutic alliance in a naturalistic psychiatric setting: Temporal relations with depressive symptom change. *Behaviour Research and Therapy, 61*, 70–77. https://www.doi.org/10.1016/j.brat.2014.07.015

*Webb, C. A., Kertz, S. J., Bigda-Peyton, J. S., & Björgvinsson, T. (2013). The role of pretreatment outcome expectancies and cognitive-behavioral skills in symptom improvement in an acute psychiatric setting. *Journal of Affective Disorders, 149*, 375–382. https://www.doi.org/10.1016/j.jad.2013.02.016

Weinberger, J., & Eig, A. (1999). Expectancies: The ignored common factor in psychotherapy. In I. Kirsch (Ed.), *How expectancies shape experience* (pp. 357–382). Washington, DC: American Psychological Association.

*Wenzel, A., Jeglic, E., Levy-Mack, H. J., Beck, A. T., & Brown, G. K. (2008). Treatment attitude and therapy outcome in patients with borderline personality disorder. *Journal of Cognitive Psychotherapy, 22*, 250–257. https://www.doi.org/10.1891/0889-8391.22.3.250

*Westra, H. A., Constantino, M. J., Arkowitz, H., & Dozois, D. J. A. (2011). Therapist differences in cognitive-behavioral psychotherapy for generalized anxiety disorder: A pilot study. *Psychotherapy, 48*, 283–292. https://www.doi.org/10.1037/a0022011

*Westra, H. A., Constantino, M. J., & Aviram, A. (2011). The impact of alliance ruptures on client outcome expectations in cognitive behavioral therapy. *Psychotherapy Research, 21*, 472–481. https://www.doi.org/10.1080/10503307.2011.581708

Westra, H. A., Dozois, D. J., & Marcus, M. (2007). Expectancy, homework compliance, and initial change in cognitive-behavioral therapy for anxiety. *Journal of Consulting and Clinical Psychology, 75*, 363–373. https://www.doi.org/10.1037/0022-006X.75.3.363

*Yoo, S., Hong, S., Sohn, N., & O'Brien, K. M. (2014). Working alliance as a mediator and moderator between expectations for counseling success and counseling outcome among Korean clients. *Asia Pacific Education Review, 15*, 271–281. https://www.doi.org/10.1007/s12564-014-9320-2

14

PROMOTING TREATMENT CREDIBILITY

Michael J. Constantino, Alice E. Coyne, James F. Boswell,
Brittany R. Iles, and Andreea Vîslă

Patients' belief in the credibility of a healthcare treatment and practitioner is often conceptualized as a common factor of effective psychotherapy (Strong, 1968). Drawing on social psychological research that established credibility as a key determinant of influence (e.g., Hovland & Weiss, 1951; Hovland et al., 1953; Kelman & Hovland, 1953), therapy can be likened to a social influence process whereby therapists establish themselves as professionally credible by embodying expertness, trustworthiness, and attractiveness (the latter reflecting being likeable and similar to the patient; Strong, 1968). Subsequently, therapists leverage established credibility to foster desired attitude and behavior change in their patients.

Whereas Strong's (1968) *social influence theory* focused on patient-perceived *therapist* credibility, his conceptualization of practitioner expertness also encompassed the provision of a problem and treatment framework that a patient finds logical and personally suitable, which can form perceptions of *treatment* credibility. Following this distinction, credibility research to date has largely been split, focusing either on patients' perception of the therapist or their perception of the treatment. Regarding the therapist, studies consist primarily of experimental manipulations designed to increase patients' perception of their provider's credibility (see Hoyt, 1996, for a meta-analytic review), though with no direct tests of its association to clinical outcomes. In this case, change in patient credibility perception is the dependent variable. Regarding the treatment, credibility studies have primarily examined the correlation between patient credibility perception (as the independent variable) and patient treatment outcomes. In fact, in our review of empirical studies that tested the credibility–outcome association, we found no studies centered on *therapist* credibility.

Accordingly, this chapter reports the results of the first comprehensive meta-analysis of the association between patients' early-therapy perception of *treatment* credibility and their posttreatment outcome across varied psychotherapies and clinical contexts. We also review (a) definitions of treatment credibility and similar constructs, (b) common measures of treatment credibility, (c) clinical examples of treatment credibility perception, (d) several landmark studies, (e) moderators and mediators of the treatment credibility–outcome association (the former in the context of the meta-analysis), (f) evidence supporting causality of the association, (g) patient factors contributing to their treatment credibility perception, and (h) limitations of the research base. In concluding, we offer diversity considerations, training implications, and therapeutic practices related to patient-perceived treatment credibility. Throughout the chapter, we leverage the research evidence to provide guidance on how psychotherapists can promote treatment credibility.

DEFINITIONS

Patient-perceived treatment credibility represents, on a continuum of negative to positive, a personal belief about a treatment's logicalness, suitability, and efficaciousness (Devilly & Borkovec, 2000). Unlike true baseline characteristics with which patients present to treatment, this perception can only be formed after learning something about, or having some experience with, the intervention, though this exposure can be minimal (Hardy et al., 1995; Schulte, 2008; Tinsely et al., 1988). Patient-perceived treatment credibility can also shift over the course of psychotherapy based on further exposure to the rationale, ongoing appraisals of improvement, therapist actions, relational exchanges, and other contextual factors (Hardy et al., 1995; Mooney et al., 2014).

Treatment credibility is differentiated from other patient constructs such as perceived therapist credibility, *outcome expectation, treatment expectations,* and treatment *preferences.* Therapist credibility refers to a patient's belief about a given practitioner's ability to help, often conceptualized as expertness, trustworthiness, and attractiveness (Strong, 1968). Conceptually, patient perception of treatment and therapist credibility might often align; for example, if a patient perceives a therapist as high in expertness, he or she may also believe the treatment approach, whatever it may be, to be logical and likely efficacious. It is also plausible that a patient could perceive a specific treatment to be suitable yet simultaneously perceive the therapist delivering it to be untrustworthy and unattractive (e.g., unlikeable and/or unrelatable). Presently, though, the association between treatment and therapist credibility beliefs remains largely theoretical as, to our knowledge, no studies have assessed their empirical association or their potentially distinct contributions to treatment outcomes. As noted, the present chapter focuses on perception of treatment credibility for which research linking this belief to outcome does exist.

Outcome expectation reflects patients' prognostic beliefs about the personal efficacy of a planned or current treatment (see Chapter 13, this volume). There has been a historical debate over the distinctness of patients' treatment credibility belief and their outcome expectation, with some arguing that the credibility belief may be at least a partial determinant of one's prognostic outcome expectation (Constantino et al., 2012; Hardy et al., 1995). Supporting this view, patients' treatment credibility belief and their outcome expectation are often positively correlated to a moderate degree (e.g., Ametrano et al., 2017; Constantino et al., 2005, 2014). Moreover, research has demonstrated that the provision of a logical and compelling treatment rationale (components of treatment credibility perception) can increase patients' outcome expectation postrationale delivery (e.g., Ametrano et al., 2017).

Although moderately correlated, important distinctions remain between treatment credibility and outcome expectation. Whereas treatment credibility can be formed only after some exposure to the intervention, patient outcome expectation can, and often does, exist *before* patients interact with their practitioner or receive any substantial information about the forthcoming treatment (Chapter 13, volume 2). Moreover, treatment credibility and outcome expectation each explains a unique portion of variance in patient outcomes (Mooney et al., 2014; Smeets et al., 2008).

Treatment expectations reflect patients' projections about what will happen during treatment, including how they and their therapist will behave (role expectations), how they will subjectively experience the therapy (process expectations), and how long therapy will last (duration expectation; Constantino et al., 2011). Such expectations also differ from perception of treatment credibility in that they can be formed prior to interacting with a psychotherapist or gaining some direct information about, or experience with, the treatment. Further, whereas treatment credibility perception is evaluative, treatment expectations can be uncritical.

Finally, psychotherapy preferences reflect characteristics of the treatment or practitioner that a patient desires (see Swift, Callahan, & Cooper, volume 2), which may differ from what a patient finds credible. For example, although patients may prefer to engage in a nondirective, supportive therapy, they might actually find the rationale for a directive, problem-solving therapy more credible. Hence, there can be internal tension between what patients prefer and what they believe will prove most helpful.

MEASURES

Historically, patient-perceived treatment credibility was primarily viewed as a nuisance variable requiring matching on, or statistical control of, in comparative clinical trials. Such control was considered vital for demonstrating that between-group differences in treatment efficacy were due to the treatments' specific mechanisms instead of differences in patients' ostensibly extraneous beliefs about the treatments (Kazdin, 1979; Kazdin & Wilcoxon, 1976). Underscoring that this rival interpretation might be especially likely in placebo control conditions, researchers found, not surprisingly, that analogue participants perceived the rationales for bona fide treatments as significantly more credible than the rationales for therapy placebos (Borkovec & Nau, 1972). Consequently, the authors concluded that researchers should regularly assess and control for patients' treatment beliefs in clinical trials as a means to mitigate the inherent belief inequality.

When heeding this call, the vast majority of researchers have used some derivation of the five-item credibility measure that Borkovec and Nau (1972) developed in their influential study. Importantly, though, this scale did not differentiate between patient perception of treatment credibility and their outcome expectation, thereby confounding these two related, but distinct, constructs (Devilly & Borkovec, 2000; Hardy et al., 1995). Additionally, as most early studies were assessing credibility as a covariate, few tested a priori hypotheses about the potential therapeutic effects of patients' treatment credibility belief. Thus patient-perceived treatment credibility has long been an undervalued construct, including when compared to other belief constructs like outcome expectation. Only recently has treatment credibility begun to receive more attention as a pantheoretical creator or correlate of patient improvement, perhaps partly facilitated by the development of a psychometrically sound measure that distinguishes treatment credibility from outcome expectation—the Credibility/Expectancy Questionnaire (CEQ; Devilly & Borkovec, 2000).

The CEQ is by far the most widely used measure of treatment credibility. In fact, in our present meta-analytic review, the CEQ was the only measure used outside of measures developed for specific studies. This six-item measure has been shown in factor analysis to capture the two factors of treatment credibility and outcome expectation, with each subscale possessing three unique items (Devilly & Borkovec, 2000). This brief measure is in the public domain and can be easily adapted for use with different clinical populations and treatments.

Using depression as an example, the three credibility items are "At this point, how logical does the therapy offered seem to you?"; "At this point, how successful do you think this treatment will be in reducing your depressive symptoms?"; and "How confident would you be in recommending this treatment to a friend who experiences similar problems?" The three outcome expectancy items are "By the end of the therapy period, how much improvement in your depressive symptoms do you think will occur?"; "At this point, how much do you really *feel* that therapy will help you to reduce your depressive symptoms?"; and "By the end of the therapy period, how much improvement in your depressive symptoms do you *feel* will occur?" As evidenced by these items, perception of treatment credibility might represent more of a cognitive reaction to the proposed treatment, whereas outcome expectation might represent more of a hybrid cognitive and affective response.

CLINICAL EXAMPLES

A patient's perception of treatment credibility can be thought of as a patient's current "answer" to some variation of the question: "To what extent does this therapy make sense to me as a way to get better?" As a perception that patients fully own, it can begin as positive and absolute (e.g., "This treatment makes total sense to me; it is exactly what I need to feel better"), positively valenced (e.g., "This approach makes pretty good sense for potentially reducing my depression"), negatively valenced ("I just don't see how talking about the relation between my thoughts and feelings could help my depression; to me, it's a chemical imbalance"), negative and absolute (e.g., "No, thank you, this treatment is a sham"), or ambivalent (e.g., "I can see how early relationship patterns might impact my current relationships, but I'm not sure that understanding those patterns would be enough to get me out of this depressive funk").

Credibility perception can and does shift after the patient gains more experience with the treatment. For example, patients may perceive a treatment as more credible if they begin to make progress on completing treatment tasks (e.g., "Now I can see that how I think about things does precede my mood, so maybe focusing on changing my thoughts *is* a way to help me feel better"). Alternatively, patients' initially positive credibility perception might decrease over time if they are not experiencing symptom relief (e.g., "This treatment seems stupid; I've spent all this time trying to change my thoughts, and I just feel worse and worse").

It is also likely that patient-perceived treatment credibility is influenced by one's history. If a patient previously found psychodynamic therapy to be effective in reducing her distress, then she might perceive a new course of it as a more credible option than cognitive-behavioral therapy (CBT). Also, patients' treatment credibility perception is likely influenced by their personal beliefs about the etiology of mental health problems. For example, a patient who strongly believes that mental health problems originate from early childhood experiences, might find a here-and-now, problem-oriented therapy to be less credible than a therapy that aligns with his or her etiological beliefs (e.g., interpersonal, attachment-based approaches). In such cases, therapists could offer a more conceptually aligned treatment, or perhaps it would be sufficient to tailor their original treatment rationale to fit better with patient-specific etiological beliefs (e.g., "You know what, early experiences *are* formative, both for who we become and the problems we have. Although my approach does try to address current problems, I absolutely need you to help me understand how these problems were rooted in your childhood. My sense is that it all matters, so to speak. What are your thoughts?").

Herewith are two additional examples of psychotherapists trying to promote their patients' credibility beliefs about psychotherapy early in treatment. At the outset, a therapist may try to make a treatment sound logical and compelling: "In the context of describing your depression, you have noted a long history of relationship disappointment. Consistent with this, I use an interpersonal approach to treatment that emphasizes the importance of relationship support and quality for improving mood. This seems like a good fit; do you agree?" Therapists can also try to parlay early improvement into continued change: "Last session you experienced your anxiety eventually decreasing when staying in contact with a threatening activity. This is the essence of exposure and response prevention, and I expect that you will continue to see additional improvements with more practice."

LANDMARK STUDIES

Even though landmark investigations sometimes confounded the measurement of credibility and expectancy, these formative studies privileged patient credibility belief as a distinct variable worthy of investigation and informative for practice. One highly influential study was Borkovec and Nau's (1972) analogue research showing that the rationales of placebo control treatments were perceived as less credible than those of authentic therapies. This study also pioneered credibility measurement. The researchers established both a reason (to eliminate a rival explanation for between-group effects) and a means (a systematic measure) to attend to credibility perception in comparative psychotherapy research. In fact, as previously noted, most subsequent studies examining patient-perceived treatment credibility have used either a derivation of the five-item credibility and expectancy measure developed by Borkovec and Nau, or its subsequent iteration (the CEQ; Devilly & Borkovec, 2000).

One of the earliest studies to test the direct association between patient-perceived treatment credibility and treatment outcome compared systematic desensitization to two control treatments for analogue patients with speech anxiety (Kirsch & Henry, 1977). The researchers found that patients' treatment credibility rating accounted for a significant portion of outcome variance, whereas treatment group did not. Interestingly, the treatment groups did not significantly differ in perceived credibility following rationale delivery, suggesting that the lack of between-group outcome differences was not a function of differential credibility perceptions. Rather, the authors argued that perception of credibility may instill more positive outcome expectation, which, in turn, may function as mechanisms of change, irrespective of treatment type.

Another influential study found that in depressed patients receiving either short-term CBT or psychodynamic-interpersonal psychotherapy (PI), patient perception of credibility increased comparably in both conditions from pretreatment when patients received a brief written description of CBT or PI, to after Session 1 (Hardy et al., 1995). Additionally, more favorable post-Session 1 credibility perception (termed *emergent credibility*) was associated with better outcomes in both treatments, whereas initial, pre-treatment credibility perception was correlated with more favorable outcome in PI but not CBT. Importantly, though, these findings held only for short-term PI and CBT (8 sessions) but not for their longer versions (16 sessions). It is also worth noting that Hardy et al. used the original version of the CEQ (Borkovec & Nau, 1972), which confounded credibility and outcome expectation, again underscoring this salient problem plaguing the literature. Limitations notwithstanding, the Hardy et al. study provided some of the first empirical evidence drawn from a clinical sample that (a) treatment credibility perception can change after patients are exposed brief to therapy descriptions, (b) exposure to different bona fide psychotherapies can prompt similar increases in and levels of patient-perceived credibility, and (c) more positive treatment credibility belief can relate to more positive outcomes, at least in shorter-term approaches.

Following these promising findings, the treatment credibility literature was muddied by a study that examined the predictive validity of the updated CEQ (Devilly & Borkovec, 2000). These researchers found that when the significance level was corrected for family-wise error rates, the credibility subscale was unrelated to any treatment outcomes assessed across three separate samples. Yet, the CEQ credibility subscale has continued to be the most widely used measure, including in more recent studies examining patient-perceived treatment credibility as a pantheoretical correlate of improvement. With the mixed findings and inconsistent measurement, the clinical relevance of patient-perceived credibility remains unclear, which underscores the need for the present meta-analysis.

Qualitative research on patient-perceived treatment credibility is rare, with most existing work focused on exploring the suitability of specific treatments for patients with particular mental disorders. For example, one analogue study explored socially anxious primary care patients' initial credibility and suitability beliefs following exposure to cognitive bias modification (CBM), a computer-based treatment (Beard et al.,

2012). Some participants implied that they would find CBM more credible if they saw "evidence that treatment works" (p. 625), such as testimonials, graphs, and research data (Beard et al., 2012). Additionally, one patient highlighted the importance of treatment credibility for achieving positive outcomes, stating that "people have to have confidence in your method of helping them" (p. 625). Low credibility perception also emerged as a potential barrier to seeking treatment, with some participants reporting difficulty imagining how a computerized treatment could help with their social anxiety. Although difficult to generalize to clinical samples and face-to-face therapist contact, these findings do suggest that patient-perceived treatment credibility may be one factor that patients weigh when choosing a mental health treatment and forecasting its personal efficacy.

We are aware of only one qualitative study focused on perceived treatment credibility in a clinical sample (McCracken et al., 2014). In this feasibility study of group acceptance and commitment therapy (ACT) for chronic pain, the authors conducted posttreatment interviews broadly focused on the acceptability and effectiveness of ACT and administered a form asking participants to report their perception of ACT credibility and suitability. Most patients found the treatment credible, but about 20% did not. Qualitative analysis of the interview data revealed that the low credibility ratings may have resulted from a lack of buy-in to the treatment rationale and tasks. For example, one patient stated, "I went again to the second session and again I thought 'what on earth is all this about?' I couldn't relate to any of what he was talking about. It all seemed wishy-washy" (p. 319). The authors also reported that some older participants expressed that the treatment was not speaking their language, raising the possibility that credibility belief may differ as a function of age. Of course, more research is needed, both quantitative and qualitative, to understand possible determinants of patient-perceived treatment credibility and how this belief influences psychotherapy outcomes.

META-ANALYTIC REVIEW

Treatment credibility has long been considered an efficacious common factor in psychotherapy, but there have been no systematic reviews of the credibility–outcome association. In this section, we present the first original meta-analysis of the relation between patients' early-therapy perception of treatment credibility and their treatment outcomes. Additionally, we examined the moderating influence of several patient variables: presenting diagnosis, age, and sex. We also examined the potential moderating influence of the following contextual variables: treatment orientation, treatment modality, research design, date of report publication, and manualized versus nonmanualized treatment.

Search and Inclusion Procedures

We first conducted an extensive PsycINFO database search of published references using the following search term sequence: *credibility* OR *suitability* OR *therapist expert** (note that * includes any derivation with this root) AND *treatment* OR *psychotherapy*

OR *therap** OR *counsel** AND *patient* OR *client* AND *outcome**. We also activated the following search options: "peer-reviewed"; "English"; "population group: human"; "exclude dissertations"; "methodology: empirical study, quantitative study, longitudinal study, treatment outcome, follow-up study, prospective study, clinical trial, retrospective study, brain imaging, mathematical model, meta-analysis, field study, experimental replication." This database search yielded 1,255 references.

We then searched PubMed with the same search sequence as PsycINFO, also activating the following search "builder" options: "English"; "species: human"; "article types: classical article, clinical study, clinical trial, comparative study, controlled clinical trial, corrected and republished article, journal article, meta-analysis, multicenter study, observational study, pragmatic clinical trial, randomized controlled trial, validation studies." This search yielded 677 references. Finally, to ensure that we did not miss any reports because of the time lag before appearing in the online databases, we hand-searched the 2017 issues of 16 clinical journals, which revealed 24 additional reports. Thus the total initial search (PsycINFO + PubMed + hand search) yielded 1,956 references.

We next reviewed the titles and abstracts of all references yielded, applying the following inclusion/exclusion criteria to create a candidate list. To be included, references had to (a) report a published empirical analysis; (b) use a clinical sample; (c) include at least one treatment referenced as a form of therapist-delivered psychotherapy for a mental health problem that was designed to last three or more sessions; (d) include a measure of patients' *own* pretreatment, Session 1, or Session 2 rating of perceived treatment and/or provider credibility; (e) include at least one posttreatment mental health outcome variable (broadly defined) not explicitly referenced as a *follow-up* occasion; and (f) report a statistical test of the relation between credibility and outcome in a psychotherapy condition. References were excluded if they (a) reported credibility assessment other than for early perception of *treatment* or *practitioner*; (b) only inferred credibility belief from tests of placebo or of similar, but distinct, constructs, such as outcome expectation, treatment expectation, or therapy preferences; (c) only assessed early patient-perceived credibility retrospectively; or (d) manipulated credibility belief.

In selecting studies, we also attended to whether studies measured credibility, outcome expectation, or both and whether these constructs were fully confounded. Given that the most commonly used instrument for measuring both credibility belief and outcome expectation (the CEQ) can produce a total score, which fully conflates these two constructs, the literature is rife with this particular shortcoming. For the present meta-analysis, we *included* references for which the researchers either measured credibility unconfounded by outcome expectation or where they clearly and consistently referenced credibility as their intended predictor variable, even if they measured it poorly (e.g., with the CEQ *total* score). In the latter case, we coded the credibility measure as "poor." We *excluded* references for which the researchers (a) conceptualized credibility belief and outcome expectation synonymously, (b) acknowledged reporting on a meta-belief variable (e.g., a composite credibility/outcome expectation variable), or (c) clearly referenced outcome expectation as their independent variable (even if it was confounded with credibility). In the latter case, the study was included in the separate outcome expectation meta-analysis (see Chapter 13, this volume).

Based on these criteria, we selected 105 references to review in full. Based on these reviews, we ruled out another 80 that did not satisfy our inclusion and exclusion criteria. Thus we fully coded 25 references for study characteristics. When references included multiple studies on separate samples, we coded these samples separately. Additionally, when references that included multiple treatment arms reported credibility–outcome associations separately by arm, we treated these treatment conditions as independent samples. With these actions, the total number of *independent samples* from the included references was 32.

For six articles reporting on eight independent samples, we discovered that despite the researchers reporting effects from an empirical analysis, they did not provide sufficient information to transform unstandardized regression coefficients to standardized coefficients, which, as noted in the following discussion, was required for our aggregated analysis. Thus we were forced to remove these eight samples from our final count. Within these parameters, the total number of independent samples was reduced to 24 (extracted from 19 references). In some samples, researchers examined correlations between patient-perceived treatment credibility and multiple treatment outcomes. (In no samples were multiple treatment credibility measures used.) In these cases, we coded all relevant credibility–outcome associations.

Data Analyses

The correlation coefficient, r, was the measure of choice to assess the effect size for most analyses within a given independent sample included in the meta-analysis. Some researchers assessed effects (i.e., 28 effect sizes from the total of 64 analyses before aggregation) using other statistical measures (e.g., partial correlations, standardized regression coefficients, coefficient of determination, chi-squared). In these cases, the statistical values were converted to r (Bowman, 2012; Del Re & Hoyt, 2010). We set effect sizes to zero that were not described or were reported as nonsignificant.

Many references reported multiple effect sizes from (a) multiple time points of treatment credibility assessment and/or (b) multiple measures of outcome. To avoid favoring samples for which researchers calculated multiple effects for any of these scenarios, and violating the assumption of independent samples, we aggregated the reported effect sizes from each independent sample (Del Re & Hoyt, 2010). This aggregation procedure accounted for the intercorrelation among within-study outcome measures, which was imputed as $r = .50$ (see Del Re & Hoyt, 2010; Hunter & Schmidt, 2004; Wampold et al., 1997).

Because it was possible that not all effect sizes were normally distributed, and sample variance may have been dependent on an unknown population effect, we first used Fisher's r to z transformation before including the sample effect sizes in our meta-analysis (see Cooper et al., 2009). We then conducted a random-effects model, which provides an inference about the average effect in the entire population of studies from which the included samples are assumed to be a random selection (Viechtbauer, 2010). In computing the overall effect, we weighted the independent effects by their sample size.

In testing potential moderators of the aggregated effect, we used a mixed-effect model. For interpretive purposes, we converted the weighted mean effect size back to r. We assessed the heterogeneity of effects among our samples using the Q and I^2 statistics (Higgins & Thompson, 2002). A significant Q statistic indicates heterogeneity, which justifies subsequent moderator analyses. I^2 is computed as a percentage, which reflects the proportion of variability in effect sizes due to true differences among the studies versus chance. To identify publication bias, we tested asymmetry based on rank correlation (Begg & Mazumdar, 1994) and regression tests (Egger et al., 1997). Furthermore, we examined a funnel plot using trim and fill procedures (Duval & Tweedie, 2000). We conducted all analyses using the R statistical software packages for meta-analysis "MAc" (Del Re & Hoyt, 2010), "metafor" (Viechtbauer, 2010), and "compute.es" (Del Re, 2013).

Descriptive Statistics

The meta-analysis included 1,504 patients across the 24 independent samples (range = 21 to 165 patients per sample). For the 20 samples (83%) for which age was reported, the mean, weighted by sample size, was 40.8 years (sample mean range = 16.1 to 72 years). For the 21 samples (87%) for which sex was reported, 18 included both males and females, 1 included only females, and 2 included only males. For each of the 14 samples (58%) for which race was reported, the majority of patients (> 60%) were White.

Table 14.1 presents the aggregated effect sizes of the treatment credibility–outcome relation per each independent sample included in the meta-analysis. We coded the direction of the effect such that positive rs indicate that higher treatment credibility perception related to more favorable outcomes, whereas negative rs indicate that higher treatment credibility perception related to more negative outcomes.

Results

The overall association between treatment credibility and treatment outcome ($k = 24$) was $r = 0.12$ (95% confidence interval [CI] = 0.04, 0.20), indicating a small, but significant positive effect. Expressed as Cohen's (1988) d, the effect was 0.24. There was significant heterogeneity in the effect sizes ($Q = 58.16, p < .01; I^2 = 57\%$, 95% CI = 35%–85%), indicating that one or more study-level moderators might explain such variability of effects across the independent samples.

The test of asymmetry indicated that publication bias was not present in the included studies ($p > .39$). Moreover, trim and fill procedure (Duval & Tweedie, 2000) estimated that the number of missing studies (i.e., studies on the left side of the plot representing a more negative effect than the weighted mean effect) needed

Table 14.1. Study Characteristics and Average Weighted Effects for Samples Included in the Meta-Analysis

Source for Independent Sample	Treatment (Type/Modality)	Treatment Credibility Measure	Outcome Types	ES (r)	Sample N
Andersson et al. (2012)	CBT/Group	CEQ	Pain and Impairment	.83	21
			Quality of Life		
Borge et al. (2010)	Mixed/Combined	CEQ	Social Anxiety	.25	80
Borkovec & Costello (1993)	CBT/Individual	CEQ	Anxiety	.00	55
			Severity		
			Worry		
			Depression		
Borkovec & Mathews (1988)	Mixed/Individual	CEQ	Anxiety	.00	30
			Depression		
			Fear		
Borkovec et al. (2002)a	CBT/Individual	CEQ	Functioning	.11	76
			Anxiety		
			Worry		
			Depression		
Carter et al. (2015)	Mixed/Individual	CEQ	Depression	.33	165
Cook et al. (2013)—Sample 1	CBT/Group	CEQ	Nightmares	−.20	124
			Sleep Quality		
Cook et al. (2013)—Sample 2	CBT/Group	CEQ	Nightmares	.11	124
			Sleep Quality		
Devilly and Borkovec (2000)—Study 3	Mixed/Individual	CEQ	Anxiety	.00	22
			Depression		
			Distress		
			PTSD symptoms		

(continued)

Table 14.1. Continued

Source for Independent Sample	Treatment (Type/Modality)	Treatment Credibility Measure	Outcome Types	ES (r)	Sample N
Espejo et al. (2016)	CBT/Group	CEQ	Anxiety and Depression	-.06	58
Jordan et al. (2017)	NR/NR	SS	Premature Termination	.30	56
Mooney et al. (2014)	Mixed/Individual	CEQ	Anxiety	.24	117
			Depression		
Norton et al. (2008)	CBT/Group	CEQ	Anxiety	.10	54
Ramnero & Ost (2004)	CBT/Individual	CEQ	Improvement	-.03	73
Smeets et al. (2008)—Sample 1	CBT/Combined	CEQ	Improvement	-.10	57
Smeets et al. (2008)—Sample 2	Problem solving CBT & PT/ Combined	CEQ	Improvement	.28	59
Smith et al. (2013)	CBT/Group	CEQ	Response	.16	48
Söchting et al. (2016)	CBT/Group	SS	Anxiety	.11	65
			Depression		
			Interpersonal Problems		
			Quality of Life		
Thompson-Hollands et al. (2014)	CBT/Individual	CEQ	Anxiety	.03	29
			Depression		
			Work and Social Adjustment		
Twohig et al. (2010)—Sample 1	CBT/Individual	CEQ	OCD Symptoms	.00	41
Twohig et al. (2010)—Sample 2	CBT/Individual	CEQ	OCD Symptoms	.00	38
Westra et al. (2011)	CBT/Individual	CEQ	Worry	.32	32

| Zaitsoff et al. (2008)—Sample 1 | Family-based treatment/Family | SS | Binge and Purge Frequency | .00 | 41 |
| Zaitsoff et al. (2008)—Sample 2 | Supportive therapy/Individual | SS | Binge and Purge Frequency | .00 | 39 |

Note (alphabetized within sections). Treatment Type: CBT = predominantly cognitive and/or behavioral therapy; Mixed = different patients received different treatments (none predominant, or >60%); NR = not reported; *Treatment Modality:* Combined = patients who received more than one treatment modality; Mixed = different patients received different modalities (none predominant, or >60%); NR = not reported; *Treatment Credibility Measure:* CEQ = Credibility/Expectancy Questionnaire or modified version (including Borkovec & Nau's [1972] version); SS = study specific treatment credibility measure; *Outcome Types:* GAD = generalized anxiety disorder; OCD = obsessive-compulsive disorder; PTSD = posttraumatic stress disorder; *ES* = weighted effect size (coefficients coded such that positive *rs* indicate that higher treatment credibility perception related to more favorable outcomes, whereas negative *rs* indicate that higher treatment credibility perception related to more negative outcomes).

[a] Data from the Borkovec et al. (2002) trial were also analyzed in the second study/sample reported in the Devilly and Borkovec (2000) article; thus we treated the effect size data reported in both Devilly and Borkovec (Study 2) and in Borkovec et al. as being drawn from one independent sample.

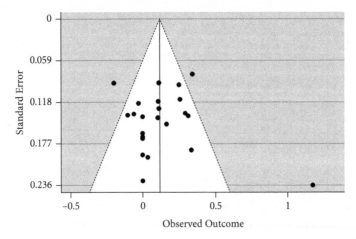

FIGURE 14.1 Funnel plot to assess publication bias in the reporting of the credibility–outcome effect sizes. The vertical bar represents the weighted mean effect size. The black dots represent the studies included in the analyses.

to attain complete symmetry was zero. After visually examining the funnel plot (see Figure 14.1), we observed a study (Andersson et al., 2012) presenting an effect size exceeding 2 standard deviations above the average effect size. After excluding this study from our analysis, the overall weighted effect decreased, but remained significant, $r = 0.10$ (95% CI = 0.03, 0.17). Similarly, the heterogeneity also decreased ($I^2 = 43\%$), but remained significant ($Q = 37.93$, $p = .008$). Therefore, we decided to conduct the moderation analyses on all 24 samples.

MODERATORS

There were no statistically significant moderating effects on the credibility–outcome association for any of the eight potential moderators that we evaluated. The results were:

- Patient presenting diagnosis [$Q(2) = 2.53$, $p = 0.28$], coded as mood ($k = 2$), anxiety ($k = 15$), and other ($k = 7$)
- Patient age [$Q(1) = 1.40$, $p = 0.24$], treated continuously
- Participant sex [$Q(1) = 3.62$, $p = 0.06$], treated continuously as proportion of females
- Treatment orientation [$Q(1) = 1.21$, $p = 0.27$], coded as cognitive-behavioral ($k = 16$) or other ($k = 8$)
- Treatment modality [$Q(2) = 0.67$, $p = 0.71$], coded as individual ($k = 11$), group ($k = 9$), or other ($k = 4$)
- Research design type [$Q(1) = 1.23$ $p = 0.27$], coded as comparative clinical trial ($k = 18$) or open trial ($k = 5$)
- Publication date [$Q(1) = 1.65$, $p = 0.20$], treated continuously
- Treatment manual used [$Q(2) = 0.03$, $p = 0.98$], coded as yes ($k = 18$), no ($k = 3$), and cannot tell ($k = 3$)

That is, the patient-perceived credibility link to treatment outcome was fairly consistent and robust across each of these patient, treatment, and research dimensions.

MEDIATORS

Although correlational data (including from the present meta-analysis) suggest that patients' early-therapy credibility perception relates to more favorable posttreatment outcomes, there remains little information on the mechanisms through which treatment credibility operates. In this section, we review the most commonly *proposed* mechanisms and indirect evidence for them. We also review the one study that formally tested a mediator of the credibility–outcome association, as well as the few studies that point to perceived credibility serving as a mediator of other variables' effects on outcome.

Some have argued that perceived treatment credibility may influence patients' outcome expectation, which could in turn promote more improvement (e.g., Hardy et al., 1995). Supporting this view, patient credibility belief and outcome expectation tend to be moderately correlated (Cohen et al., 2015; Constantino et al., 2014; Devilly & Borkovec, 2000; Mooney et al., 2014). Moreover, several analogue studies have demonstrated that the provision of a logical and compelling treatment rationale (components of treatment credibility perception) can increase patients' postrationale outcome expectation (e.g., Ahmed & Westra, 2009; Ametrano et al., 2017). Despite this indirect evidence, we are unaware of any studies that have formally tested patient outcome expectation as a mediator of the treatment credibility–outcome association.

Additionally, we are unaware of any studies that have systematically tested the directionality of the outcome expectation–treatment credibility link. Such research will be particularly important given that these two patient variables likely exert reciprocal influences on each other; for example, whereas the aforementioned analogue studies suggested that credibility belief can promote subsequent outcome expectation, other research has demonstrated that pretreatment outcome expectation associates with subsequent treatment credibility perception (assessed early in the course of treatment; Mooney et al., 2014). Future research is needed to determine whether these two patient beliefs act in sequence to impact patient outcomes, and, if so, which belief variable precedes the other and under which conditions.

Others have suggested that patient-perceived treatment credibility may facilitate the formation of a stronger therapeutic alliance, which in turn predicts treatment outcomes (e.g., Söchting et al., 2016). Although several studies have supported the association between higher perception of treatment credibility and more positive therapeutic alliance (e.g., Horvath & Greenberg, 1989; Söchting et al., 2016; Westra et al., 2011), the one study that formally tested the full mediational pathway failed to detect an indirect effect of credibility on outcome through the alliance (Söchting et al., 2016). Consequently, this particular mediational pathway requires further testing.

Some have also posited that patient-perceived treatment credibility may *be* a mediator of other variables' effects (e.g., treatment condition) on outcome (e.g., Kirsch &

Henry, 1977). In the one study of which we are aware that tested credibility as a mediator, the authors found that the association between greater baseline symptom severity and reliable change at posttreatment was mediated by increases in treatment credibility perception in CBT for generalized anxiety disorder (Newman & Fisher, 2010). Although it is unusual to consider baseline severity as akin to a "causal" predictor variable, this study demonstrated that credibility perception (although confounded in this study with outcome expectation) can change during treatment and that such change relates to improvement.

EVIDENCE FOR CAUSALITY

With our search criteria, we found no studies that manipulated patient-perceived treatment credibility to determine its causal relation to posttreatment outcome in psychotherapy for clinical samples. To us, conducting such randomized trials in both controlled and naturalistic contexts (the latter being especially pertinent given that no credibility studies included in the present meta-analysis were conducted in naturalistic settings) is a pressing next-wave research agenda. Progressing from correlational to experimental evidence would allow clinicians to harness and capitalize more fully on this common, transdiagnostic patient factor.

Although no *direct* evidence exists for a causal effect between treatment credibility and psychotherapy outcome, there is some *indirect* evidence in the temporal direction of that link inherent in the studies in the present meta-analysis. Namely, patient-perceived treatment credibility, when measured early in treatment, precedes the assessment of posttreatment outcome, which is an important prerequisite for causality. Moreover, such early credibility measurements are less likely to be confounded by early symptom change, though there is some evidence that improvement in the first few sessions relates to patients' subsequent early treatment credibility perception (Mooney et al., 2014). Yet, when these researchers controlled for symptom change prior to the measurement of treatment credibility, there remained a significant positive association between credibility and posttreatment improvement. As this is a single study, future research testing the ongoing temporal relation between treatment credibility perception and improvement on a lagged, session-by-session basis is sorely needed.

In recognition of higher patient-perceived credibility correlating with more favorable posttreatment outcome, some researchers have conducted experiments or quasi-experiments, with analogue or nontreatment samples to examine if the presentation of different treatment rationales can causally affect individuals' credibility belief (Borkovec & Nau, 1972; Frövenholt et al., 2007; McGlynn & McDonell, 1974; Rokke et al., 1990; Tompkins et al., 2017; Wong et al., 2003). The results of these studies have been equivocal, with most showing either that participants perceived genuine therapies as equally credible, or specific subgroups of participants reported differential credibility perception that have yet to be replicated. These results square with the relatively few actual psychotherapy studies that have tested for differential credibility perception among treatment arms and generally found no differences (e.g., Hardy et al., 1995; Kirsch & Henry, 1977; Smeets et al., 2008).

Finally, one analogue study focused on experimentally manipulating *therapist behaviors* as predictors of participants' perception of *treatment* credibility (Dowell & Berman, 2013). The researchers found that greater therapist eye contact and forward trunk lean were associated with greater participant-perceived treatment credibility. However, these same therapist behaviors were also associated with better participant-perceived alliances and therapist empathy, which suggests that these therapist behaviors function as predictors of several positive psychotherapy variables in general, as opposed to being unique determinants of treatment credibility.

PATIENT CONTRIBUTIONS

Given the now-established link between psychotherapy success and patient-perceived treatment credibility, it is important to identify factors that contribute to this belief. Such identification will help clinicians respond effectively. In this section, we review the literature on patient factors that correlate with their early perception of treatment credibility. This research is relatively scarce and has largely centered on patients' demographic and clinical characteristics.

Regarding demographic variables, results have been mixed. In a large study of individuals receiving either cognitive or psychodynamic therapy for various disorders, patient age and education were negatively associated with perceived treatment credibility (Mooney et al., 2014). However, other studies have failed to replicate these findings (Constantino et al., 2014; Smeets et al., 2008). In a study of physical therapy (PT), CBT, and PT + CBT for chronic low back pain, female patients reported higher perception of session one treatment credibility than male patients (Smeets et al., 2008). This finding was replicated in a large sample of patients being treated in a partial hospitalization program (Cohen et al., 2015). However, other studies have failed to find treatment credibility differences between male and female patients (Constantino et al., 2014; Söchting et al., 2016).

Although several studies have failed to find an association between employment status and treatment credibility (Cohen et al., 2015; Constantino et al., 2014; Mooney et al., 2014), in the study of treatments for chronic low back pain (Smeets et al., 2008), patients who were working at least part-time reported higher credibility belief than either those without a job or those who were on full leave or disability. The discrepancy between these findings may be due to the differential relevance of employment status in these studies; that is, work status may be more accurately considered as an indicator of severity than as a demographic variable in a sample of patients with chronic pain, as opposed to other presenting conditions where work status may be less related to the pathology.

Regarding clinical variables, symptom severity has been the most studied correlate of treatment credibility, with mixed results. Two studies found that more severe global (Constantino et al., 2014) and specific (i.e., depression; Cohen et al., 2015) baseline symptom severity relate to lower credibility perceptions, but other studies have failed to replicate this association (Smeets et al., 2008; Söchting et al., 2016). In a study of patients who received either cognitive or psychodynamic therapy, greater early symptom reduction was associated with more positive perception of treatment credibility, whereas baseline symptom severity was not (Mooney et al., 2014). These results suggest that patients may adjust their beliefs about a treatment over time in response to how that treatment is progressing. Finally, the study of applied PT, CBT, and PT + CBT for chronic low back pain showed that patients who reported less catastrophic thinking and more internal control of their pain reported more positive treatment credibility belief, even controlling for other significant credibility correlates (i.e., gender and work status; Smeets et al., 2008).

In sum, existing research has not yielded consistent patterns of specific patient contributions to credibility. Early trends suggest that greater severity (measured in various ways) may render patients less likely to perceive a treatment as credible, perhaps due to greater levels of hopelessness or pessimism. Fortunately, though, early symptomatic improvement may boost the credibility of a given treatment, potentially providing practitioners with a way to combat the lowered credibility perceptions patients with more severe symptoms may hold. Yet, much remains to be learned about patient prognosticators of credibility beliefs and all present trends require replication.

LIMITATIONS OF THE RESEARCH

The present meta-analysis had several limitations. First, in the service of comprehensiveness, we retained all studies that met our inclusion criteria, which resulted in the inclusion of studies of variable quality. Although the majority of studies were rated as being of overall high quality (75.0%), some were rated as moderate (12.5%) and poor (12.5%) quality. Second, of the 24 samples in our meta-analysis, we coded 3 (12.5%) as using *poor* and 4 (16.7%) as using *moderately poor* treatment credibility measures. Problems included, but were not limited to, the use of one-item, study-specific scales and measures that confounded treatment credibility with another construct (e.g., outcome expectation). Third, there were some reports that met our inclusion criteria but failed to provide enough information to extract or transform effect sizes into the standardized coefficients required for our aggregate analyses. In these cases, as discussed already, we had to exclude these samples, which lowered the overall k. Fourth, two-thirds of the meta-analyzed studies used CBT, thus neglecting the majority of psychotherapies employed in routine practice. Finally, the positive weighted effect may have been inflated by an outlier sample for which the specific effect size was more than 2 standard deviations above the aggregated weighted effect size across all included samples. However, even after excluding this outlier, the overall weighted effect remained significant.

Beyond these methodological and statistical limitations of the present meta-analysis, other problems characterize the treatment credibility literature as a whole. First, the manner in which credibility has been typically operationalized and measured in studies rarely aligns with the original conceptualization of psychotherapy credibility as a broad construct that can be parsed into at least two perceptions—of the *treatment* and of the *therapist* (Strong, 1968). One could argue that the historical undervaluing of the therapist credibility construct, relative to treatment credibility, may mirror the psychotherapy field as a whole; that is, the field has tended to focus on developing evidence-based treatments that can be delivered similarly by *any* practitioner. In fact, only recently have individual *therapist effects* become a primary research interest, and an alternative way of couching evidence-based practice in the form of *who (vs. what) works for whom* (Constantino et al., 2017). To us, given that comparisons between bona fide treatments yield virtually no outcome differences, whereas differences between practitioners account for a modest, though relatively consistent, portion of outcome variance (Wampold & Imel, 2015), it is likely that patient-perceived *therapist* credibility would have a greater potential than *treatment* credibility to influence outcome directly.

Second, we found no published studies that manipulated treatment credibility to determine its causal relation to outcome in psychotherapy for clinical samples. Third, treatment credibility has been assessed almost exclusively as a static construct very early in therapy, despite the fact that evidence suggests that perception of treatment credibility is malleable (Hardy et al., 1995; Newman & Fisher, 2010) and can be influenced by prior experiences like symptom reduction (Mooney et al., 2014). Finally, research examining what therapists can do specifically to foster more positive patient credibility belief remains virtually nonexistent, with the one study of this kind having been conducted with an analogue sample (Dowell & Berman, 2013).

To move the treatment credibility construct from a static belief that is fully possessed by the patient to a dynamic variable that can be modified over time by the treatment, psychotherapist, and dyad, more research is needed, especially with clinical samples. For now, we consider treatment credibility an empirically supported *correlate* of posttreatment outcome that therapists need to assess and respond to sensitively when indicated. Although the research can give some guidance as to *how* best to respond to differing levels of treatment credibility (as reviewed below in the therapeutic practices section), more evidence on how therapists directly influence treatment credibility in a way that transmits to positive outcome continues to be needed to strengthen evidence-based *practice*.

Future research will test the ongoing temporal relation between treatment credibility perception and improvement on a lagged, session-by-session basis. Such research could clarify, for example, whether there is something akin to a critical period early in therapy during which the success of interventions aimed at symptom change may have particular power over patients' credibility perception, which could, in turn, have a lasting impact on patients' ultimate outcomes. Additionally, when credibility research advances, it has the potential to guide therapists in generating more positive treatment credibility across all of their patients, regardless of their treatment approach. Existing studies have largely treated patient-perceived treatment credibility as a static characteristic that is determined by the interplay between pre-existing patient characteristics and a particular treatment's early presentation. Again, we know little about the specific factors (patient, therapist, and dyadic) that have an active causal bearing on the development of, and perhaps change in, patients' treatment credibility belief. In short, future research is sorely needed to determine treatment credibility enhancement strategies that therapists can use across theoretical orientations.

DIVERSITY CONSIDERATIONS

Few treatment credibility studies have addressed patients' multicultural identities, which has resulted in a literature with little measurement of, or variability in, such diversity dimensions. Consequently, in the present meta-analysis we had sufficient data to examine only sex as a patient-level diversity moderator. As noted, sex had no moderating effect on the treatment credibility–outcome association, though this finding is far from definitive given the small number of studies. More research is clearly needed to understand better how patient multicultural identities might systematically affect the influence of treatment credibility on clinical outcomes, including in aggregate form in a meta-analysis.

As noted earlier, two studies found that female patients reported higher credibility than male patients (Cohen et al., 2015; Smeets et al., 2008), though other studies failed to find this difference (Constantino et al., 2014; Söchting et al., 2016). Moreover, a few studies have examined patients' racial or ethnic identities as predictors of treatment credibility, though in all cases the associations were not significant (Cohen et al., 2015; Constantino et al., 2014; Mooney et al., 2014). However, given that these studies treated race and ethnicity as categorical variables, they fall prey to the well-documented limitations of obscuring important within-group variability and neglecting more salient culturally-based beliefs (Betancourt & Lopez, 1993). Hence, it would be premature to conclude that these cultural identities have no bearing on treatment credibility.

Addressing these limitations in one analogue study of Asian Americans, participants who reported low levels of white identity perceived cognitive therapy (CT) as more credible than time-limited dynamic psychotherapy (TLDP), whereas participants reporting high levels of white identity perceived the two treatments as similarly credible (Wong et al., 2003). Additionally, the researchers found that participants with more independent self-construals perceived CT as more credible than TLDP, whereas individuals with less independent self-construals perceived the two treatments as similarly credible. The authors posited that both of these findings may result from a correspondence between the participants' cultural beliefs and the treatments' different putative change mechanisms. Specifically, CT may appeal to Asian Americans with low levels of White identity given its emphasis on changing negative thoughts, which aligns with a valued Eastern coping style of modifying internal responses to one's environment. Similarly, the authors argued that Asian Americans who endorse highly independent self-construals may find CT's cognitive mechanism more credible than TLDP's central focus on relationships.

These findings highlight the potential of cultural identities to influence patients' credibility perception, which could inform treatment selection. However, as such research is in its infancy, and focused solely on analogue samples, more systematic work is needed.

TRAINING IMPLICATIONS

Our meta-analysis revealed a small but significant positive association between patients' treatment credibility and distal treatment outcomes. This link further legitimizes credibility as a patient variable that requires consideration in evidence-based practice and clinical training. We believe that training programs should place more emphasis on common, pantheoretical factors that predict psychotherapy success and therapist responsivity to them, including credibility.

Specifically, training could start with an overview of the research on credibility, including the present meta-analysis and patient contributions to credibility perceptions. Practitioners can then be trained to assess patient-perceived credibility and to interpret the data (whether verbal or quantitative) as one of many predictive analytics. Such measurement should be conducted very early in treatment, but also repeatedly, as the research demonstrates that credibility shifts with time. Training can focus first on teaching clinicians to engage in routine verbal assessment of credibility beliefs about the proposed treatment following rationale delivery (e.g., "Now that you've heard more about my approach to treating depression, I'm wondering how logical targeting negative thinking as a way to improve your mood seems to you?") and second on teaching practitioners how to use and score brief, easily adaptable and repeatable measures (e.g., the credibility subscale of the CEQ) that facilitate the tracking of patient credibility over time. Additionally, practitioners could be trained to assess subtle process markers of low (or lowered) credibility perceptions (e.g., resistance to the therapist's direction, homework noncompliance).

Regardless of the specific markers, practitioners can then be trained to respond in ways that reduce the likelihood of further harm to the credibility of a given approach and maximize the likelihood of a shift toward a more adaptive credibility belief (Constantino et al., 2013). Specifically, responsivity trainings could emphasize the importance of departing from a priori treatment plans when markers of low beliefs in the credibility of such plans emerge.

Such departures could involve two primary steps. First, practitioners may want to respond with foundational clinical skills like empathy, validation, and evocation to gain a clearer understanding of a patient's in-the-moment waning credibility belief. Second, clinicians may respond with credibility enhancement strategies once a patient feels heard and validated. The exact nature of these strategies will depend on the specific cause of a patient's reduced credibility revealed through the first step.

We envision these more formal interventions as being disseminated through modular trainings of credibility enhancement strategies (with the specific practices described in the next section). These trainings could be delivered efficiently (e.g., 45-minute trainings, web-based trainings), with the focus on delivering strategies that could be immediately implemented by practitioners. Such *if-then* modular teachings would be an overlay that would introduce evidence-based marker recognition and therapist responses into a clinician's armamentarium.

Finally, to the extent that perception of the therapist matters, either on par with, or perhaps even more strongly than, perception of the treatment, modular trainings can also be designed to help clinicians present themselves as a credible helper, not just the intervention. And if the ability to foster higher credibility ends up being a determinant of treatment outcomes, then training should be informed by the best-performing therapists; that is, we can learn from those therapists who consistently promote the highest credibility across patients.

THERAPEUTIC PRACTICES

Drawing on the best available evidence, we outline several practice suggestions to help therapists effectively promote and therapeutically respond to their patients' credibility belief.

- Assess the patient's treatment credibility (verbally or through a brief measure) early in, and across, treatment. This will provide therapists with prognostic information, as well as a fuller understanding of the match between the treatment and the patient's belief system.
- Enter regularly into a dialogue about what patients do and do not find compelling about a treatment rationale/plan: "I know that I have discussed *my belief* that people's current problems can be a function of early, and now dated, relationship patterns, but I wonder how logical that seems to you? I would not want you simply to comply with my perspective on therapy. Does this relational approach seem to suit you? Let's discuss your questions or concerns."
- Assess as well patient-perceived *therapist* credibility. A clinician might say, "I know that the treatment itself seems to suit you, but I wonder if you have any feeling about me being the one to deliver it? Sometimes people find that a therapist could be more or less suitable, and it is important that we not assume that all therapists are created equal. I genuinely invite you to discuss any reactions to me that you might have at this time, or at any time for that matter."
- Be aware of any patient characteristics that might promote or detract from treatment credibility. This will help clinicians forecast patient negative beliefs indirectly, as a complement to direct credibility measurement.
- Speak in a way that sounds logical and compelling when delivering a treatment rationale. The key is to influence the patient's belief system (not simply deliver a rationale as per a theory-specific "script"). In many ways, promoting credibility belief is individual- and context-based, and therapists should not hold back on trying various means to make a treatment sound personally logical, suitable, and efficacious.
- Tend to patients' verbal and nonverbal indictors that the rationale is understandable, persuasive, and interesting. Although therapists may believe that they are giving a textbook description of, say, behavioral activation for depression, a perplexed look can tell a thousand words; in this case, that behavioral activation may be unconvincing to that particular patient at that particular time. Or, at a minimum, how you are describing it may require more clarity, or a different tact.
- Be responsive when patient-perceived treatment credibility is low. If what a patient finds suitable and efficacious about a treatment differs vastly from the treatment

being proposed or delivered, the clinician may offer a different treatment. To the extent that this credibility perception also links to the particular practitioner, the different treatment could also involve a referral to a different psychotherapist. Another responsiveness strategy could involve maintaining some core elements of a given treatment, but being more flexible in the delivery: "It seems like you are not buying the idea of between-session homework. You know what, that's fine. Perhaps such assignments are not essential for you. And even if we did end up believing that more practice is needed on certain ideas and skills, we could do those together in session . . . perhaps even meeting with each other more frequently. How does that sound?"

◆ Enhance patient credibility by identifying explicit things that patients do find credible and assimilating them into psychotherapy: "I see that the idea of antidepressant medication is important to you. Let's look into that together as a complement to our talk-based sessions. Agreed?"

◆ Try to promote, early, palpable symptom improvement, as the research suggests that such improvement influences treatment credibility. Although symptom remission may not prove the only or ultimate goal of treatment, some early "relief" tactics prove useful in influencing credibility.

◆ Mind your posture, as there is preliminary evidence that greater therapist eye contact and forward trunk lean associate with greater treatment credibility, as well as other adaptive processes (alliance quality, perceived therapist empathy).

REFERENCES

References marked with an asterisk indicate studies included in the meta-analyses.

Ahmed, M., & Westra, H. A. (2009). Impact of a treatment rationale on expectancy and engagement in cognitive behavioral therapy for social anxiety. *Cognitive Therapy and Research, 33*, 314–322. https://www.doi.org/10.1007/s10608-008-9182-1

Ametrano, R. M., Constantino, M. J., & Nalven, T. (2017). The influence of expectancy persuasion techniques on socially anxious analogue patients' treatment beliefs and therapeutic actions. *International Journal of Cognitive Therapy, 10*, 187–205.

*Andersson, G., Johansson, C., Nordlander, A., & Asmundson, G. J. (2012). Chronic pain in older adults: A controlled pilot trial of a brief cognitive-behavioural group treatment. *Behavioural and Cognitive Psychotherapy, 40*, 239–244. https://www.doi.org/10.1017/s1352465811000646

Beard, C., Weisberg, R. B., & Primack, J. (2012). Socially anxious primary care patients' attitudes toward cognitive bias modification (CBM): A qualitative study. *Behavioural and Cognitive Psychotherapy, 40*, 618–633. https://www.doi.org/10.1017/S1352465811000671

Begg, C. B., & Mazumdar, M. (1994). Operating characteristics of a rank correlation test for publication bias. *Biometrics, 50*, 1088–1101. https://www.doi.org/10.2307/2533446

Betancourt, H., & López, S. R. (1993). The study of culture, ethnicity, and race in American psychology. *American Psychologist, 48*, 629–637. https://www.doi.org/10.1037/0003-066X.48.6.629

*Borge, F.-M., Hoffart, A., & Sexton, H. (2010). Predictors of outcome in residential cognitive and interpersonal treatment for social phobia: Do cognitive and social dysfunction moderate treatment outcome? *Journal of Behavior Therapy and Experimental Psychiatry,* *41,* 212–219.

*Borkovec, T. D., & Costello, E. (1993). Efficacy of applied relaxation and cognitive-behavioral therapy in the treatment of generalized anxiety disorder. *Journal of Consulting and Clinical Psychology, 61,* 611–619.

*Borkovec, T. D., & Mathews, A. M. (1988). Treatment of nonphobic anxiety disorders: A comparison of nondirective, cognitive, and coping desensitization therapy. *Journal of Consulting and Clinical Psychology, 56,* 877–884. https://www.doi.org/10.1037/0022-006X.56.6.877

Borkovec, T. D., & Nau, S. D. (1972). Credibility of analogue therapy rationales. *Journal of Behavior Therapy and Experimental Psychiatry, 3,* 257–260. https://www.doi.org/10.1016/0005-7916(72)90045-6

*Borkovec, T. D., Newman, M. G., Pincus, A. L., & Lytle, R. (2002). A component analysis of cognitive-behavioral therapy for generalized anxiety disorder and the role of interpersonal problems. *Journal of Consulting and Clinical Psychology, 70,* 288–298. https://www.doi.org/10.1037/0022-006X.70.2.288

Bowman, N. A. (2012). Effect sizes and statistical methods for meta-analysis in higher education. *Research in Higher Education, 53,* 375–382. https://www.doi.org/10.1007/s11162-011 9232-5

*Carter, J. D., Crowe, M. T., Jordan, J., McIntosh, V. V., Frampton, C., & Joyce, P. R. (2015). Predictors of response to CBT and IPT for depression; the contribution of therapy process. *Behaviour Research and Therapy, 74,* 72–79.

Cohen, J. (1988). *Statistical power analysis for the behavioral sciences* (2nd ed.). Mahwah, NJ: Erlbaum.

Cohen, M., Beard, C., & Björgvinsson, T. (2015). Examining patient characteristics as predictors of patient beliefs about treatment credibility and expectancies for treatment outcome. *Journal of Psychotherapy Integration, 25,* 90–99. https://www.doi.org/10.1037/a0038878

*Cook, J. M., Thompson, R., Harb, G. C., & Ross, R. J. (2013). Cognitive-behavioral treatment for posttraumatic nightmares: An investigation of predictors of dropout and outcome. *Psychological Trauma: Theory, Research, Practice, and Policy, 5,* 545–553.

Constantino, M. J., Ametrano, R. M., & Greenberg, R. P. (2012). Clinician interventions and participant characteristics that foster adaptive patient expectations for psychotherapy and psychotherapeutic change. *Psychotherapy, 49,* 557–569. https://www.doi.org/10.1037/a0029440

Constantino, M. J., Arnow, B. A., Blasey, C., & Agras, W. S. (2005). The association between patient characteristics and the therapeutic alliance in cognitive-behavioral and interpersonal therapy for bulimia nervosa. *Journal of Consulting and Clinical Psychology, 73,* 203–211. https://www.doi.org/10.1037/0022-006X.73.2.203

Constantino, M. J., Boswell, J. F., Bernecker, S. L., & Castonguay, L. G. (2013). Context-responsive integration as a framework for unified psychotherapy and clinical science: Conceptual and empirical considerations. *Journal of Unified Psychotherapy and Clinical Science, 2,* 1–20.

Constantino, M. J., Boswell, J. F., Coyne, A. E., Kraus, D. R., & Castonguay, L. G. (2017). Who works for whom and why? Integrating therapist effects analysis into psychotherapy outcome and process research. In L. G. Castonguay & C. E. Hill (Eds.), *Why are some therapists are better than others? Understanding therapist effects* (pp. 309–323). Washington DC: American Psychological Association. https://www.doi.org/10.1037/0000034-004

Constantino, M. J., Glass, C. R., Arnkoff, D. B., Ametrano, R. M., & Smith, J. Z. (2011). Expectations. In J. C. Norcross (Ed.), *Psychotherapy relationships that work: Evidence-based responsiveness* (2nd ed., pp. 354–376). New York, NY: Oxford University Press.

Constantino, M. J., Penek, S., Bernecker, S. L., & Overtree, C. E. (2014). A preliminary examination of participant characteristics in relation to patients' treatment beliefs in psychotherapy in a training clinic. *Journal of Psychotherapy Integration, 24,* 238–250. https://www.doi.org/10.1037/a0031424

Cooper, H., Hedges, L. V., & Valentine, J. C. (Eds.). (2009). *The handbook of research synthesis and meta-analysis.* New York, NY: Russell Sage Foundation.

Del Re, A. C. (2013). compute.es: Compute effect sizes. R package version 0.2–2. Retrieved from http://cran.r-project.org/web/packages/compute.es

Del Re, A. C., & Hoyt, W. T. (2010). MAc: Meta-analysis with correlations. R package version 1.0.5. Retrieved from http://CRAN.R-project.org/package=MAc

*Devilly, G. J., & Borkovec, T. D. (2000). Psychometric properties of the credibility/expectancy questionnaire. *Journal of Behavior Therapy and Experimental Psychiatry, 31,* 73–86. https://www.doi.org/10.1016/S0005-7916(00)00012-4

Dowell, N. M., & Berman, J. S. (2013). Therapist nonverbal behavior and perceptions of empathy, alliance, and treatment credibility. *Journal of Psychotherapy Integration, 23,* 158–165. https://www.doi.org/10.1037/a0031421

Duval, S., & Tweedie, R. (2000). Trim and fill: A simple funnel-plot–based method of testing and adjusting for publication bias in meta-analysis. *Biometrics, 56,* 455–463. https://www.doi.org/10.1111/j.0006-341X.2000.00455.x

Egger, M., Smith, G. D., Schneider, M., & Minder, C. (1997). Bias in meta-analysis detected by a simple, graphical test. *British Medical Journal, 315,* 629–634. https://www.doi.org/10.1136/bmj.315.7109.629

*Espejo, E. P., Castriotta, N., Bessonov, D., Kawamura, M., Werdowatz, E. A., & Ayers, C. R. (2016). A pilot study of transdiagnostic group cognitive-behavioral therapy for anxiety in a veteran sample. *Psychological Services, 13,* 162–169.

Frövenholt, J., Bragesjö, M., Clinton, D., & Sandell, R. (2007). How do experiences of psychiatric care affect the perceived credibility of different forms of psychotherapy? *Psychology and Psychotherapy: Theory, Research and Practice, 80,* 205–215. https://www.doi.org/10.1348/147608306X116098

Hardy, G. E., Barkham, M., Shapiro, D. A., Reynolds, S., Rees, A., & Stiles, W. B. (1995). Credibility and outcome of cognitive-behavioural and psychodynamic-interpersonal therapy. *British Journal of Clinical Psychology, 34,* 555–569. https://www.doi.org/10.1111/j.2044-8260.1995.tb01489.x

Higgins, J., & Thompson, S. G. (2002). Quantifying heterogeneity in a meta-analysis. *Statistics in Medicine, 21,* 1539–1558. https://www.doi.org/10.1002/sim.1186

Horvath, A. O., & Greenberg, L. S. (1989). Development and validation of the Working Alliance Inventory. *Journal of Counseling Psychology, 36,* 223–233. https://www.doi.org/10.1037/0022-0167.36.2.223

Hovland, C. I., Janis, I., & Kelley, H. H. (1953). *Communication and persuasion.* New Haven, CT: Yale University Press.

Hovland, C. I., & Weiss, W. (1951). The influence of source credibility on communication effectiveness. *Public Opinion Quarterly, 15,* 635–650.

Hoyt, W. T. (1996). Antecedents and effects of perceived therapist credibility: A meta-analysis. *Journal of Counseling Psychology, 43*(4), 430–447. https://www.doi.org/10.1037/0022-0167.43.4.430

Hunter, J. E., & Schmidt, F. L. (2004). *Methods of meta-analysis: Correcting error and bias in research findings* (2nd ed.). Thousand Oaks, CA: SAGE.

*Jordan, J., McIntosh, V. W., Carter, F. A., Joyce, P. R., Frampton, C. M., Luty, S. E., . . . Bulik, C. M. (2017). Predictors of premature termination from psychotherapy for anorexia nervosa: Low treatment credibility, early therapy alliance, and self-transcendence. *International Journal of Eating Disorders, 58*(8), 979–983. https://www.doi.org/10.1002/eat.22726

Kazdin, A. E. (1979). Nonspecific treatment factors in psychotherapy outcome research. *Journal of Consulting and Clinical Psychology, 47*, 846–851. https://www.doi.org/10.1037/0022-006X.47.5.846

Kazdin, A. E., & Wilcoxon, L. A. (1976). Systematic desensitization and nonspecific treatment effects: A methodological evaluation. *Psychological Bulletin, 83*, 729–758. https://www.doi.org/10.1037/0033-2909.83.5.729

Kelman, H. C., & Hovland, C. I. (1953). Reinstatement of the communicator in delayed measurement of opinion change. *Journal of Abnormal and Social Psychology, 48*, 327–335.

Kirsch, I., & Henry, D. (1977). Extinction versus credibility in the desensitization of speech anxiety. *Journal of Consulting and Clinical Psychology, 45*, 1052–1059. https://www.doi.org/10.1037/0022-006X.45.6.1052

McCracken, L. M., Sato, A., Wainwright, D., House, W., & Taylor, G. J. (2014). A feasibility study of brief group-based acceptance and commitment therapy for chronic pain in general practice: Recruitment, attendance, and patient views. *Primary Health Care Research and Development, 15*, 312–323. https://www.doi.org/10.1017/S1463423613000273

McGlynn, F. D., & McDonell, R. M. (1974). Subjective ratings of credibility following brief exposure to desensitization and pseudotherapy. *Behaviour Research and Therapy, 12*, 141–146. https://www.doi.org/10.1016/0005-7967(74)90110-7

*Mooney, T. K., Connolly Gibbons, M. C., Gallop, R., Mack, R. A., & Crits-Christoph, P. (2014). Psychotherapy credibility ratings: Patient predictors of credibility and the relation of credibility to therapy outcome. *Psychotherapy Research, 24*, 565–577. https://www.doi.org/10.1080/10503307.2013.847988

Newman, M. G., & Fisher, A. J. (2010). Expectancy/credibility change as a mediator of cognitive behavioral therapy for generalized anxiety disorder: Mechanism of action or proxy for symptom change? *International Journal of Cognitive Therapy, 3*, 245–261. https://www.doi.org/10.1521/ijct.2010.3.3.245

*Norton, P. J., Hayes, S. A., & Springer, J. R. (2008). Transdiagnostic cognitive-behavioral group therapy for anxiety: Outcome and process. *International Journal of Cognitive Therapy, 1*, 266–279.

*Ramnerö, J., & Öst, L. (2004). Prediction of outcome in the behavioural treatment of panic disorder with agoraphobia. *Cognitive Behaviour Therapy, 33*, 176–180. https://www.doi.org/10.1080/16506070410031691

Rokke, P. D., Carter, A. S., Rehm, L. P., & Veltum, L. G. (1990). Comparative credibility of current treatments for depression. *Psychotherapy: Theory, Research, Practice, Training, 27*, 235–242. https://www.doi.org/10.1037/0033-3204.27.2.235

Schulte, D. (2008). Patients' outcome expectancies and their impression of suitability as predictors of treatment outcome. *Psychotherapy Research, 18*, 481–494. https://www.doi.org/10.1080/10503300801932505

*Smeets, R. M., Beelen, S., Goossens, M. B., Schouten, E. W., Knottnerus, J. A., & Vlaeyen, J. S. (2008). Treatment expectancy and credibility are associated with the outcome of both physical and cognitive-behavioral treatment in chronic low back pain. *The Clinical Journal of Pain, 24*, 305–315. https://www.doi.org/10.1097/AJP.0b013e318164aa75

*Smith, A. H., Norton, P. J., & McLean, C. P. (2013). Client perceptions of therapy component helpfulness in group cognitive-behavioral therapy for anxiety disorders. *Journal of Clinical Psychology, 69*, 229–239.

*Söchting, I., Tsai, M., & Ogrodniczuk, J. S. (2016). Patients' perceptions of treatment credibility and their relation to the outcome of group CBT for depression. *Archives of Psychiatry and Psychotherapy, 18*, 7–15. https://www.doi.org/10.12740/APP/66485

Strong, S. R. (1968). Counseling: An interpersonal influence process. *Journal of Counseling Psychology, 15*, 215–224. https://www.doi.org/10.1037/h0020229

*Thompson-Hollands, J., Bentley, K. H., Gallagher, M. W., Boswell, J. F., & Barlow, D. H. (2014). Credibility and outcome expectancy in the unified protocol: Relationship to outcomes. *Journal of Experimental Psychopathology, 5*, 72–82.

Tinsely, H. E. A., Bowman, S. L., & Ray, S. B. (1988). Manipulation of expectancies about counseling and psychotherapy: Review and analysis of expectancy manipulation strategies and results. *Journal of Counseling Psychology, 35*, 99–108. https://www.doi.org/10.1037/0022-0167.35.1.99

Tompkins, K. A., Swift, J. K., Rousmaniere, T. G., & Whipple, J. L. (2017). The relationship between clients' depression etiological beliefs and psychotherapy orientation preferences, expectations, and credibility beliefs. *Psychotherapy, 54*, 201–206. https://www.doi.org/10.1037/pst0000070

*Twohig, M. P., Hayes, S. C., Plumb, J. C., Pruitt, L. D., Collins, A. B., Hazlett-Stevens, H., & Woidneck, M. R. (2010). A randomized clinical trial of acceptance and commitment therapy versus progressive relaxation training for obsessive-compulsive disorder. *Journal of Consulting and Clinical Psychology, 78*, 705–716.

Viechtbauer, W. (2010). Conducting meta-analyses in R with the metafor package. *Journal of Statistical Software, 36*, 1–48. Retrieved from http://www.jstatsoft.org/v36/i03/

Wampold, B. E., & Imel, Z. E. (2015). *The great psychotherapy debate: The evidence for what makes psychotherapy work* (2nd ed.). New York, NY: Routledge.

Wampold, B. E., Mondin, G. W., Moody, M., Stich, F., Benson, K., & Ahn, H. (1997). A metaanalysis of outcome studies comparing bona fide psychotherapies: Empirically, "all must have prizes." *Psychological Bulletin, 122*, 203–215. https://www.doi.org/10.1037/0033-2909.122.3.203

*Westra, H. A., Constantino, M. J., Arkowitz, H., & Dozois, D. A. (2011). Therapist differences in cognitive–behavioral psychotherapy for generalized anxiety disorder: A pilot study. *Psychotherapy, 48*, 283–292. https://www.doi.org/10.1037/a0022011

Wong, E. C., Kim, B. K., Zane, N. S., Kim, I. J., & Huang, J. S. (2003). Examining culturally based variables associated with ethnicity: Influences on credibility perceptions of empirically supported interventions. *Cultural Diversity and Ethnic Minority Psychology, 9*, 88–96. https://www.doi.org/10.1037/1099-9809.9.1.88

*Zaitsoff, S. L., Doyle, A. C., Hoste, R. R., & le Grange, D. (2008). How do adolescents with bulimia nervosa rate the acceptability and therapeutic relationship in family-based treatment? *International Journal of Eating Disorders, 41*, 390–398.

15

MANAGING COUNTERTRANSFERENCE

Jeffrey A. Hayes, Charles J. Gelso, D. Martin Kivlighan,
and Simon B. Goldberg

Author Note. We are grateful to Andrea M. Samayoa-Sosa and Erin Hill for gathering and organizing data for the meta-analyses in this chapter.

The concept of countertransference (CT) is nearly as old as psychotherapy itself. Like so many fundamental constructs in psychotherapy, the term was originated by Freud, shortly after the turn of the 20th century. The first recorded use of the term can be found in a letter from Freud to Jung in June 1909. Upon learning of an affair that Jung had with one of his patients, Freud wrote:

> I myself have never been taken so badly, but I have come very close to it a number of times and had a narrow escape. I believe that only grim necessities weighing on my work, and the fact that I was ten years older than yourself when I came to psychoanalysis, have saved me from similar experiences. But no lasting harm is done. They help us to develop the thick skin we need to dominate "counter-transference," which is after all a permanent problem for us; they teach us to displace our own affects to best advantage. (Haynal, 1993, p. 362)

Although Freud did not write extensively about CT, it was clear that he viewed it as problematic. For example, Freud (1910) commented, "We have begun to consider the counter transference, which arises in the physician as a result of the patient's influence on his unconscious feelings, and have nearly come to the point of requiring the physician to recognize and overcome this countertransference in himself" (pp. 144–145). This view of CT as detrimental was likely a major influence in the field's neglect of the topic for many decades. It became something to be done away with rather than material worth examining. The good psychotherapist was, in fact, seen as capable of maintaining objectivity and keeping her or his personal conflicts out of the work. During those early days, one might even say that CT attained the status of a taboo topic.

Beginning in the 1950s, conceptions of CT began to change. Countertransference was increasingly viewed as an inevitable aspect of psychotherapy that could have positive or negative effects, depending on how the therapist dealt with it.

Around this same period, the first empirical studies on CT also emerged (e.g., Cutler, 1958; Fiedler, 1951). From then on, there has been a steady increase of clinical and theoretical writing on CT. As is so often the case, however, empirical efforts lagged behind theoretical work, although studies did appear occasionally.

The likely culprits for the slow pace of research were twofold. First, CT originated from and was firmly embedded in psychoanalysis, a discipline containing a decidedly anti-empirical bent and an opposition to the simplification that can manifest in scientific research. Second, and perhaps more telling, the construct itself is awesomely complex, encompassing hidden components of the therapist's personality, painful aspects of his or her past, and occasionally shameful thoughts, feelings, and behaviors in response to the patient. Add to these the definitional ambiguity that seems to be a part of virtually all high-level constructs, and the conditions were ripe for a paucity of research on CT.

In recent years, however, significant changes have occurred in conceptualizations and research on CT. It has been theorized to be a key part of all therapy relationships, and propositions have been offered about its operation across virtually all theoretical orientations and treatment formats (e.g., Brown, 2001; Ellis, 2001; Kaslow, 2001; Rudd & Joiner, 1997). In addition, laboratory analogue studies have sought to reduce this abstract construct to scientifically manageable proportions and have paved the way for clinically meaningful studies, both qualitative and quantitative (Hayes, 2004).

In this chapter, we review empirical research on CT, its management, and its relation to psychotherapy outcome. Our review incorporates psychotherapy studies conducted within all research traditions, including case studies and qualitative research, but the meta-analyses consist solely of quantitative data extracted from empirical studies. We begin the review by describing varying conceptions and definitions of CT and then examine research as it bears upon the question of the effects of CT and its management on psychotherapy outcome.

DEFINITIONS

Three conceptions of CT have been most prominent over the years: the *classical*, the *totalistic*, and the *complementary* views (Epstein & Feiner, 1988). The classical definition, originated by Freud (1910), posits that CT is the therapist's unconscious, conflict-based reaction to the patient's transference. Unresolved conflicts, typically from the therapist's early childhood, are triggered by the patient's transference and are manifested by the therapist in one way or another. These manifestations may be affective, behavioral, somatic, or cognitive and are seen as interfering with treatment. Although Freud thought that CT played a significant role in treatment, he did not write extensively about it, and the construct received relatively little attention among scholars for several decades after the term was first introduced. The totalistic conception of CT originated in the 1950s and has been developed further over the years (Heimann, 1950; Kernberg, 1965; Little, 1951). According to this conception, CT refers to and is synonymous with *all* of the therapist's reactions to the patient. All reactions are important, all should be studied and understood, and all are placed under the broad umbrella of CT. This definition legitimized CT and made it an object of the therapist's self-investigation and use. Accordingly, as the totalistic view gained ascendancy, CT was considered more and more as potentially beneficial to the work, if therapists studied their reactions and used them to advance their understanding of patients and patients' impact on others, including the therapist.

The view of CT as an inevitable reaction to the patient overlaps with the third conception: CT as a complement or counterpart to the patient's style of relating. This conception was developed in interpersonal, relational, and object relations theory (e.g., Anchin & Kiesler, 1982; Butler et al., 1993; Levenson, 1995; Strupp & Binder, 1984). According to the complementary conception, the patient exhibits certain "pulls" on the therapist. For example, the patient who has an oppositional style will tend to generate oppositional thoughts and feelings in the therapist. The well-functioning therapist, however, does not act out *lex talionis* ("an eye for an eye, a tooth for a tooth"), even though it is a justifiable and even predictable reaction. The good therapist, instead, restrains her or his "eye for an eye" impulse and seeks to understand what the patient is doing to stir up these reactions.

An Integrative Definition

In the scholarly literature, as well as in everyday clinical dialogue, these three definitions of CT are all used. The problem is that it is often unclear which of the three, or which combination, is intended at any given time. Beyond ambiguity of usage, each of the three views of CT possesses fundamental limitations. The classical view is overly restrictive in several ways: It construes CT in strictly negative terms; it ignores the nearly inevitable reactions of the therapist tied to powerful "pulls" by the patient; and its focus is almost exclusively on transference, which unfortunately reinforces the view by some therapists that CT occurs only in psychodynamic therapy. The totalistic position, in its attempt to encompass all of the therapist's reactions, may render the concept of CT scientifically meaningless. If all of a therapist's reactions are CT, then there are no therapist reactions that are not CT, and the need for the term *countertransference* is eliminated; one can simply refer to therapist reactions. However, there are varying kinds of therapist reactions, and it is helpful to identify their sources (e.g., preoccupation with a suicidal patient seen earlier in the day; preoccupation with a sick child at home; empathic sadness related to a patient's grief over the loss of a spouse; boredom in response to a patient's grief over the loss of a spouse owing to the therapist's conflicts regarding death). It seems clinically and theoretically useful to distinguish these various therapist reactions, and we favor reserving the term *countertransference* for reactions that stem from the therapist's unresolved personal problems.

The complementary conception is limited in its focus on CT as "pulls" that the patient evokes in the therapist. This focus does not sufficiently account for the therapist's own personality, background, interpersonal style, culture, and the like. It is possible, from the complementary perspective, for the therapist to blame the patient for the therapist's own reactions (e.g., "The patient made me lose my temper"). From our perspective, the therapist's reactions are always the therapist's responsibility. Some patients are notoriously difficult to work with (e.g., those with extremely poor impulse control, addicts who continually generate excuses for their ongoing substance use, adolescents who don't want to be in therapy but whose parents require them to be). Despite the challenges of working with these patients, an expert therapist recognizes that his or her reactions ultimately stem from within and can be profitably examined.

Whereas each of the common conceptions of CT is seriously limited, all three point to important elements of and factors related to CT. From our perspective, then, an integrated definition of CT best includes learnings from all three conceptualizations (Gelso & Hayes, 1998, 2007). We thus define CT as *internal and external reactions in which unresolved conflicts of the therapist, usually but not always unconscious, are implicated.* All of the therapist's reactions are important and worthy of investigation, clinically and empirically, but the definition of CT must be narrower than the totalistic one if it is to be scientifically useful and clinically meaningful. Our conception of CT is similar to the classical in its focus on the therapist's unresolved conflicts as the source of CT, but it is different in that CT is seen as a potentially useful phenomenon if the therapist successfully understands his or her reactions and uses them to help understand the patient. It also differs from the classical conception in the sense that CT is not only a reaction to the patient's transference; it may be a reaction to many factors, both internal and external.

Thus, in seeing CT as both a hindrance and a potential aid to treatment, an integrative definition picks up on the two thematic constructs that have been intertwined, like a double helix (Epstein & Feiner, 1988), throughout the history of thought about CT. In addition, like the totalistic position, our integrative definition suggests that CT is inevitable. This is so because all therapists have unresolved conflicts and unconscious "soft spots" that are touched upon in working with other human beings. Furthermore, we suspect that in many or even most cases in which the therapist's intense reaction is a "natural" response to the patient, therapist unresolved conflicts are implicated. Finally, like the complementary view, an integrative conception of CT does not solely focus on the therapist's reaction to the patient's transference. Rather, it incorporates the therapist's reaction to both transference and nontransference material presented by the patient. The latter includes the patient's personality style, the actual content that the patient is presenting, and even the patient's physical appearance (Hayes, Nelson et al., 2015).

Furthermore, the integrative definition allows for a conceptualization of CT within a variety of theoretical orientations (whereas the classical definition, for instance, is limited to a psychoanalytic perspective). For example, within a cognitive framework, the therapist's CT reactions may take the form of automatic thoughts (e.g., "I should do better") and may evoke self-schemas (e.g., "I am no good"). Alternatively, CT reactions may be conceptualized in humanistic terms, such as when the therapist's conditions of worth are called into play (e.g., "I am worthless because I am not helping this client"). From a feminist perspective, some CT manifestations can be viewed as a reflection of the therapist's socialization process. For example, a therapist raised in an environment in which derogatory beliefs about a cultural group were espoused may find herself or himself reacting negatively to a client who is from that culture. Thus, despite the psychoanalytic origins of CT, and the classical view in particular, CT may—and probably should—be regarded as a pantheoretical construct. No theory "owns" CT, just as no therapist is immune to it.

Two Key Distinctions

Despite the definitional inconsistency, most empirical studies on CT use a definition that involves the therapist's unresolved conflicts as the origin and some characteristic of the patient as the trigger for CT. Before reviewing this research, however, a few additional distinctions need to be made.

Chronic CT versus Acute CT

Acute CT includes therapist responses occurring "under specific circumstances with specific patients" (Reich, 1951, p. 26). In these particular moments, the therapist's needs take precedence over the client's needs. For example, the therapist may subtly reinforce the client's submissive interpersonal behavior due to his or her momentary need to be highly in control. Alternatively, the therapist may stop listening because the patient's material is touching on a painful and unresolved conflict in the therapist that he or she wishes to avoid. In contrast, chronic CT reflects a habitual and pervasive need of the therapist, such that is has become part of his or her personality structure. The practitioner, for example, may be consistently over-nurturing of clients, owing to long-standing conflicts related to the therapist's own history of a lack of intimacy in relationships. Or the therapist may tend to engage in conflict with most of his or her clients, as a result of unresolved aggressive tendencies, or he or she may be highly active and directive with most patients because of discomfort with his or her own passivity. Although there may be patient triggers for chronic CT reactions, the trigger itself is less significant than is true for acute CT. A wide range of patients, and therapy events, will trigger CT that is on the chronic side. In this sense, chronic CT is a "reaction waiting to happen."

CT as Internal State versus Overt Expression

As an internal state, CT may be manifested emotionally, cognitively, and somatically. For example, on a cognitive level, CT may take the form of daydreams, fantasies, and failure to accurately recall therapy-related events. Emotional, somatic, and cognitive CT reactions may range from quite unpleasant to highly pleasant, and with varying degrees of intensity. Anxiety, it might be noted, is a likely cue to the presence of CT, as it indicates that the therapist perceives some form of threat (Gelso & Hayes, 1998). In terms of overt behavior, CT generally has been studied in terms of the therapist's withdrawal, underinvolvement, or avoidance of the client's material or, at times, as overactivity and overinvolvement (Gelso & Hayes, 2007). CT behavior in this respect is seen as hindering because it involves the therapist's prioritizing and acting in accordance with his or her needs without consideration of the best interest of the patient. There are times, however, when CT behavior may be beneficial—for example, in alerting the therapist to the fact that something is awry and requires attention. Deviations from the therapist's baseline activity level, for instance, may be an indicator of underlying conflictual CT feelings (Kiesler, 2001).

Internal CT, on the other hand, is more often seen as potentially helpful in that it can be attended to before it translates into counter-therapeutic behavior. If therapists understand their inner reactions and how they relate to the patient's inner life and behavior, then this understanding may aid the therapist in working with the patient.

MEASURES

In accordance with the previously discussed clinical realities, CT reactions have been operationalized in behavioral, cognitive, somatic, and affective terms (Fauth, 2006). Behaviorally, the most common indicators of CT have been therapists' avoidance of and withdrawal from personally threatening client material. For example, therapist avoidant reactions are those that inhibit, discourage, or divert session content, such as ignoring or mislabeling affect, changing topics, or allowing prolonged silences (Bandura et al., 1960). Positively valenced behavioral manifestations have also been explored in the research literature, and examples include therapists' overinvolvement with their clients (Gelso et al., 1995), or therapists meeting their own needs by excessively nurturing their clients (Hayes et al., 1998; Hayes, Nelson, et al., 2015).

Cognitively, CT has been operationalized as therapists' perceptual distortions of clients and inaccurate recall of what clients discussed in session (e.g., Fauth & Hayes, 2006; Fiedler, 1951; Hayes & Gelso, 1993; McClure & Hodge, 1987). On a somatic level, a measure called the Body-Centered Countertransference Scale has been developed by a team of Irish researchers, and they have found that common visceral CT reactions include therapists' sleepiness, muscular tension, and headaches (Booth et al., 2010).

Affectively, the most common marker of CT is therapists' in-session anxiety, and it has commonly been measured by the State Anxiety Inventory (e.g., Hayes & Gelso, 1993, 2001). Research has explored additional affective CT manifestations, including pleasant feelings, such as hope, happiness, and excitement, as well as unpleasant feelings, such as fear, worry, anger, sadness, and disappointment (e.g., Fauth & Hayes, 2006; Friedman & Gelso, 2000; Hayes et al., 1998; Hayes, Nelson, et al., 2015). Much of the research on emotional CT reactions has used an instrument called the Therapist Appraisal Questionnaire (Fauth & Hayes, 2006), which is a postsession, Likert-type measure of a therapist's affect while working with a client.

Psychotherapists' management of their CT reactions has been measured primarily with the Countertransference Factors Inventory (CFI; Van Wagoner et al., 1991) and several updated versions, all of which focus on five therapist qualities theorized to facilitate CT management: self-insight, conceptualizing ability, empathy, self-integration, and anxiety management. These factors do not reflect what a therapist actually does to manage CT but they are more generally considered to be characteristics that are positively associated with CT management. The original version of the CFI contained 50 items, and subsequently a 27-item version, the CFI-Revised, was developed by selecting only those items with high content validity (Hayes et al., 1991). On both versions of the instrument, therapists are rated on a 5-point, Likert-type scale regarding the extent to which they possess the five qualities thought to facilitate CT management. Typically, these ratings are provided by clinical supervisors of therapist-trainees. A therapist self-report version of the CFI exists, but studies have not supported the validity of its scores. Internal consistency estimates for four subscales on the CFI and CFI-R tend to exceed .80; the internal consistency for self-insight tends to range from .60 to .80 (Gelso & Hayes, 2007).

In terms of the factors that comprise the instrument, therapist *self-insight* refers to the extent to which the therapist is aware of his or her own feelings, including CT feelings, and understands their basis. Therapist *self-integration* refers to the therapist's possession of an intact, basically healthy character structure. In the therapy interaction, such self-integration manifests itself as a recognition of interpersonal boundaries and an ability to differentiate self from other. *Anxiety management* refers to therapists allowing themselves to experience anxiety and also possessing the internal skill to control and understand anxiety so that it does not bleed over into their responses to patients. *Empathy*, or the ability to partially identify with and put one's self in the other's shoes, permits the therapist to focus on the patient's needs despite difficulties he or she may be experiencing with the work and the pulls to attend to his or her own needs. Also, an empathic ability may be part of a larger sensitivity to feelings, including one's own CT feelings, which in turn ought to prevent acting out of CT (Peabody & Gelso, 1982; Robbins & Jolkovski, 1987). Finally, *conceptualizing ability* reflects the therapist's ability to draw on theory in the work and grasp the patient's dynamics in terms of the therapeutic relationship.

Recently, a 22-item instrument called the Countertransference Management Scale was developed to directly assess management of CT during a therapy session (Perez-Rojas et al., 2017). Factor analyses of 286 supervisors' ratings of supervisees yielded two subscales: Understanding Self and Client, and Self Integration and Regulation. Evidence of convergent and criterion-related validity was provided through correlations with measures of theoretically relevant constructs, namely, therapist CT behavior, theoretical framework, self-esteem, observing ego, empathic understanding, and tolerance of anxiety. This instrument appears to have considerable promise as a direct measure of the extent to which therapists manage their CT reactions in sessions.

CLINICAL EXAMPLES

A case example may illustrate the ways in which therapist reactions that are "normal" and understandable can be, and often are, tinged by the therapist's own conflicts. The case involved a therapist-trainee in her fourth practicum of a doctoral training program, who was supervised by one of the authors and who by every indication appeared to have extraordinary potential as a therapist. In the early part of her work with a

20-year old male patient, she experienced ongoing strong irritation, and she reacted to the patient in a controlled and muted manner. For his part, the patient was an angry, obsessional young man who had many borderline features. He negated the therapist's attempts to help him understand how he contributed to his ongoing problems with women, and he denied that therapy could have any impact. Also, he usually challenged or denied the therapist's observations about what he might be feeling. Clearly the therapist's emotional reactions were "natural," given the patient's negativity and hostility. Yet the therapist's reactions were also due to her own unresolved conflicts about not being good enough, about fearing that she could not take care of others sufficiently, and about her excessive fears of her supervisor's evaluation of her. As she came to understand these concerns, her irritation with the patient lessened, and she empathically grasped the frightening emotions that were underlying much of his negativity.

An example of more blatant CT comes from one of the authors' own experiences as a therapist. The therapist's father had struggled with alcoholism throughout his adult life, and he had recently died from cirrhosis of the liver caused by alcohol abuse. Prior to his father's death, the therapist had undergone several months of individual therapy to deal with his father's impending death, and the personal therapy was largely successful in resolving his competing feelings of anticipatory grief and anger at his father.

Several weeks after his father's death, the therapist met for the first time with a male client who was approximately his father's age. The man was seeking therapy for help with marital difficulties, persistent procrastination problems, and stress related to finances. The therapist's own father had faced similar challenges in his later years, all of which the therapist viewed to be caused and exacerbated by his father's drinking. During the initial session, the therapist conducted a fairly standard intake assessment, asking questions about the client's symptoms and functioning in a variety of areas. When asked about his alcohol use, the client remarked that he drank on a daily basis, often alone, and could not recall the last day he had not had a drink. Toward the end of the session, the therapist indicated that he thought psychotherapy would be helpful in addressing the client's marital, financial, and procrastination problems. The therapist then told the client, in a rather cold and punitive tone, that he had a substance abuse problem and that this would need to be addressed at the outset. The client neither agreed nor disagreed that he suffered from substance abuse, but he remarked that that was not why he sought treatment. The therapist grew irritated with the man and restated his position. They set an appointment for the following week, and the client was never seen nor heard from again.

In this instance, the therapist's lingering feelings of anger toward his own father regarding his alcoholism were taken out on the client, who although similar to the therapist's father in many ways, was an undeserving recipient of the therapist's confrontational and unempathic stance. The fact that the client did not return for a second session is hardly surprising in retrospect, although it took the therapist a considerable amount of reflection to understand what had transpired and to decrease the likelihood that future clients would bear the brunt of unresolved conflicts he had with his father.

LANDMARK STUDIES

In the first—and still the largest—qualitative investigation of CT, 127 interviews were conducted with eight experienced therapists who had been identified as experts by their peers (Hayes et al., 1998). Each therapist treated one patient for 12 to 20 sessions, and interviews were conducted with therapists after each session. Therapists identified CT as operative in fully 80% of the 127 sessions, and it appeared that CT was prominent in each case. Such findings support the proposition that CT is a universal phenomenon in therapy, even when defined from a narrower (i.e., integrative) rather than totalistic perspective. The findings also run counter to the myth that good therapists do not experience CT (Spence, 1987).

From the qualitative data, a structural model emerged concerning the origins, triggers, manifestations, effects, and management of CT (see Hayes, Nelson, et al., 2015, for a follow-up qualitative study that provided additional findings pertaining to this model). As regards the effects of CT on treatment outcome, the data contained evidence for both hindering and facilitative effects. For example, one therapist was too immersed in her unresolved conflicts related to strength and independence to connect with her dependent client and help the client work through her problems. On the other hand, another therapist was able to make use of her CT-based needs to nurture and be a good parent by appropriately supporting and being patient with her client. The researchers reflected upon what determines whether CT will be facilitative or hindering and offered the idea that "the more resolved an intrapsychic conflict is for a therapist, the greater the likelihood that the therapist will be able to use his or her countertransference therapeutically" (Hayes et al., 1998, p. 478).

In the first published study that examined the relations among CT reactions, their management, and client improvement, 20 cases of psychotherapy were examined utilizing a variety of measures (Hayes et al., 1997). Treatment duration ranged from 4 to 20 weeks with an average of 8 weeks. The therapists were 20 psychology doctoral students, each of whom was seeing clients in a university training clinic. Two sets of supervisors participated in the study. The students' former supervisors provided ratings of students' CT management abilities on the CFI-R. The students' current supervisors observed every session live and then rated CT behavior afterward. Supervisors, therapists, and clients all completed parallel forms of a measure of client improvement at the conclusion of treatment. Results indicated that former supervisors' ratings of therapists' self-integration and empathy were negatively related to CT behavior. CT behavior was not significantly related to client improvement, and this held true across all ratings of client improvement (i.e., supervisors', therapists', and clients'). Post hoc analyses revealed that, whereas CT behavior was unrelated to client improvement in cases with good outcome, CT behavior strongly predicted client improvement in cases with poor outcome. The authors speculated that in the cases with positive outcomes, the working alliance may have been strong enough to mitigate the effects of CT behavior; in cases with poorer outcome, however, a weaker alliance may have been present such that the effects of CT behavior directly influenced outcome. Limitations of the study included a small number of cases, which hampered the statistical power to detect effects, and the use of a single-item measure of CT behavior.

RESULTS OF PREVIOUS META-ANALYSES

The small but growing number of studies on CT has only recently made it possible for meta-analytic work to be conducted in this area. Meta-analyses have focused on summarizing findings in three domains: (a) the association between CT reactions and psychotherapy outcome (i.e., are CT reactions predictive of poorer outcomes?); (b) the relationship between CT reactions and CT management (i.e., are CT management factors associated with fewer CT reactions?); and (c) the association between CT management and psychotherapy outcome (i.e., does successful management of CT tend to predict better outcome?).

With regard to the relation between CT reactions and psychotherapy outcome, data from 10 studies indicated that the 2 were significantly and inversely related, as expected, though only slightly so ($r = -.16$, Hayes et al., 2011). The implication here is that, while CT reactions are generally unfavorable, their effects account for only about 2% to 3% of the variability in outcome. That being said, correlations between frequency of CT reactions and measures of psychotherapy outcome do not take into account the potency of any one display of CT behavior, which can have damaging effects that are difficult to reverse. Furthermore, the fact that CT reactions can cause clients to drop out of therapy, as evidenced in the earlier clinical example in this chapter with the alcoholic client, would not be captured in studies that only measured outcome at or following termination. But as stated earlier, CT reactions—both internal and external—can be potential sources of insight into the client and one's relationship with the client (Hayes & Cruz, 2006). Therefore, it is perhaps not surprising that the magnitude of the correlation between CT reactions and outcome was not larger than .16.

On the whole, the evidence has accumulated to support a conclusion, though perhaps somewhat overstated, in a review of CT literature offered more than 40 years ago:

> Perhaps the most clear-cut and important area of congruence between the clinical and quantitative literatures is the widely agreed-upon position that uncontrolled countertransference has an adverse effect on therapy outcome. Not only does it have a markedly detrimental influence on the therapist's technique and interventions, but it also interferes with the optimal understanding of the patient. (Singer & Luborsky, 1977, p. 449)

The more recent quantitative body of work suggests that therapists do not have to be perfect. They can have unwanted reactions to clients. Psychotherapy sessions, and patients, can and often do withstand these reactions, particularly when the working alliance is strong and when therapists subsequently understand, and perhaps even self-disclose, their reactions to clients (Ham et al., 2013; Myers & Hayes, 2006; Yeh & Hayes, 2011).

The previous meta-analyses on CT management provide partial insight into why this might be so. On the one hand, evidence from 11 studies suggests that CT management factors play little to no role in mitigating actual CT reactions ($r = -.14$, $p = .10$; Hayes et al., 2011). On the other hand, in seven studies, these same CT management factors were strongly associated with better psychotherapy outcomes ($r = .56$; Hayes et al., 2011). The small number of studies on which this conclusion rests must be kept in mind, however, and it is likely that the magnitude of the association would be smaller with additional studies included in a meta-analysis. With these findings as a foundation, we now turn our attention to results from our updated meta-analytic work.

META-ANALYTIC REVIEW

Eligibility Criteria

We included all studies (published and unpublished) that reported data allowing calculation of the correlations between CT reactions or CT management with psychotherapy outcome. Studies reporting data allowing calculations of the correlation between CT reactions and CT management were also included. Studies that reported data on CT reactions that were not related to psychotherapy outcome were excluded. As noted earlier in the chapter, there are multiple definitions for CT that vary in the type of reactions that can be considered CT. The definitions range from restrictive (such as the classical view of CT) to all-inclusive (the totalistic view).

The purpose of the meta-analysis was to consider unique contributions to the psychotherapy endeavor that are due to CT and its management that are distinct from psychotherapists' general reactions to clients. Because the totalistic view considers all therapist reactions to clients to be CT, the inclusion of studies that used that definition might have resulted in a meta-analysis about therapist reactions in general, rather than conclusions about CT specifically. For the same reason, the inclusion criteria did not allow for studies on general therapist reactions or emotional responses, as those do not meet our definition of CT. In some cases, CT was defined by an article's authors using the totalistic view, but was then operationalized as nontotalistic, often because of the particular measure that was chosen. In these cases, the studies would be considered for inclusion, as the phenomenon being studied was consistent with our working definition of CT.

Psychotherapy outcomes exist on a continuum from immediate to distal. Immediate outcomes pertain to the effects of or on a given phenomenon within the therapy hour, whereas distal outcomes address the effects of treatment on indices of client functioning or well-being at the end of treatment. The latter includes outcomes assessed at various points after termination (e.g., follow-up studies of varying lengths). In between immediate and distal outcomes reside a wide range of what might be called proximate outcomes—those outcomes that pertain to a given session or series of sessions, as well outcomes that are presumed to be the way station for more distal outcomes (e.g., change in patient experiencing may be seen as proximal to change in level of psychopathology, itself a more distal outcome). A striking feature of the empirical CT literature is the paucity of studies seeking to connect CT and its management to more distal outcomes. Most research on CT and its management focuses on immediate or proximate outcomes. Thus, each of the meta-analyses that are reported in this chapter examine whether the timing of the outcome (e.g., proximal vs. distal) moderated the findings.

Information Sources and Search Procedures

We searched the following databases: EBSCO, PsycInfo, and Google Scholar. We used the search terms "countertransference," "countertransference management," "therapy," "outcome," "relationship," "reaction," "working alliance," "session quality," and "management." Titles and abstracts of potential studies were independently coded by two advanced undergraduate students. Disagreements were discussed with the senior author. A total of 70 citations were retrieved. Following the application of the exclusion criteria, 36 studies were retained for analysis representing 2,890 participants.

Data Collection Process

Standardized spreadsheets were developed for coding both study-level and effect size-level data. Data were extracted independently by the second author and one of the same undergraduate students who coded the titles and abstracts of studies. Disagreements were again discussed with the senior author. When sufficient data for computing standardized effect sizes were unavailable, study authors were contacted.

Data Points

Along with information necessary for computing standardized effect sizes, the following data were extracted: (a) authors, (b) whether the study was published or unpublished, (c) year study was published (or conducted, in the case of unpublished studies), (d) journal in which study was published (or if it was an unpublished dissertation), (e) predictor variables, (f) criterion variables, (g) sample size, (h) ethnicity of participants, (i) age of participants, (j) CT rater type, (k) r values (l) whether hypothesis was confirmed, and (m) one-tailed p values.

Summary Measures

The effect size measure that was calculated was Pearson's correlation coefficient (r). Standard methods were used to compute this effect size and its variance (Cooper et al., 2009). The random effects meta-analyses were conducted using the R statistical software package and the "metaphor" and "Mac" packages (Del Re & Hoyt, 2010; Viechtbauer, 2010).

Synthesis of Results

When multiple outcome variables were reported in a single study, data were aggregated first within-studies using the MAc package and then between studies, based on the comparison of interest (and using the commonly employed assumption that outcomes within study are correlated at $r = .50$; Wampold et al., 1997). Summary statistics were computed as Pearson's r along with 95% confidence intervals (CIs). Heterogeneity was systematically assessed using the I^2 (measuring the proportion of between-study heterogeneity) and the Q-statistic (assessing whether between-study heterogeneity exceeded that expected by chance alone). Random effects analyses were used.

Additional analyses tested the timing of outcome assessment as a moderator of the correlation between either CT reactions or CT management and outcome. Outcome timing was coded as proximal if outcome assessment reflected the outcome of a given session (e.g., session depth) and distal if outcome assessment reflected the outcome following the conclusion of treatment (e.g., at termination). Due to the small number of studies in each of the meta-analyses, other potential moderating variables were not examined.

We assessed publication bias by visually inspecting funnel plots for asymmetry within the comparison of interest. In addition, primary models were reestimated using trim-and-fill methods that account for the asymmetric distribution of studies around an omnibus effect (Viechtbauer, 2010).

Meta-Analytic Results

CT Reactions and Psychotherapy Outcome

A total of 14 studies, summarized in Table 15.1, reported the correlation between CT reactions and psychotherapy outcome. The omnibus effect size was significant ($r = -.16$, 95% CI $= -.30, -.03$; $p = .02$, $d = -.33$, $N = 973$ participants), indicating that more frequent CT reactions were associated with poorer psychotherapy outcomes.

The magnitude of this relationship is the same as reported in a previous meta-analysis examining CT reactions and outcome (Hayes et al., 2011), despite the more recent meta-analysis including four additional studies and more than 200 additional participants. Thus, the size of the association is likely fairly reliable and suggests that the effects of CT reactions on psychotherapy outcomes, though small, can be detected.

There was significant heterogeneity across studies ($I^2 = 75.49\%$, $Q[13] = 42.17$, $p < .001$). Evidence suggestive of publication bias was detected in the trim-and-fill analysis. After four studies were imputed to account for the asymmetric funnel plot, the correlation between CT and psychotherapy outcome was no longer significant ($r = -.07$, 95% CI $= -.21, .07$; $p = .308$, $d = -0.14$). A moderator test was conducted to determine whether the timing of outcome assessment (i.e., proximal vs. distal) impacted the magnitude of the correlation between CT and psychotherapy outcome. There was no evidence that this was the case ($Q[1] = 2.16$, $p = .142$).

Table 15.1. Summary of Studies Relating Countertransference Reactions to Outcome

Authors	Year	Publication	Predictor	Criterion	N	Ethnicity (% White)	Age (mean years)	CT rater type	$|r|$	r variance	hypothesis confirmed	p value (1-tailed)
Bandura et al.	1960	JConsult Psy	Approach-avoidance	Hostility	12 TH, 17 CL	not reported	not reported	Observer	0.53	0.03	+	0.04
Yeh and Hayes	2011	PTRPT	Self-awareness TH disclosure	CL rated TH quality & session quality	116 Raters	88	21	Observer	0.38	0.01	+	0.00
Williams and Fauth	2005	PR	Self-awareness	Session eval	18 TH, 18 CL	94 TH, 75 CL	36 TH, 22 CL	TH	0.37	0.04	+	0.07
Hayes, Riker et al.	1997	PR	CT behavior	CL improvement	20 TH, 20 CL	80 TH, 85 CL	31 TH, 25 CL	TH and Sup	0.33	0.04	+	0.08
Ligiéro and Gelso	2002	PTRPT	Negative CT	Working alliance	50 TH	70	not reported	TH	0.32	0.02	+	0.01
Bhatia & Gelso	2017	CPQ	ICB	Session outcome	269 TH	92	not reported	TH	0.18	0.004	+	0.01
Rossberg et al.	2010	CompPsy	FWC-58	SCL-90R	11 TH, 71 CL	not reported	32 CL, 41 TH	TH	0.29	0.03	+	<.05
Westra et al.	2012	PTRPT	Relevance to CL REACT	CRC	4 TH, 30 CL	TH n/a, 57 CL	TH n/a, 40 CL	TH	0.48	0.02	+	0.003
Cutler	1985	Jconsult Psyc	Relevance to TH of CL problem	Task vs ego responses	2 TH, 5 CL	not reported	not reported	Observer	0.24	0.22		0.30
Myers and Hayes	2006	PTRPT	CT	Session quality	224 Raters	89	20	Observer	0.04	0.004		0.28
Kim	2013	Diss	Race of CL and TH, CT, racial bias (TAQ)	GAF, prognosis	56 TH, 56 CL	70	32	TH	0.11	0.02		0.01
Rosenberger and Hayes	2002	JCP	Approach-avoidance	BSI, WAI, Session quality	1 TH 1 CL	100 TH 100 CL	34 TH 21 CL	Observer	0.06	0.99		0.86
Mohr et al.	2005	JCP	CT behavior	Session quality	27 TH, 88 CL, 12 Sup	not reported	not reported	Sup	0.04	0.01		0.37
Hayes, Yeh et al.	2007	J Clinical Psy	Unresolved grief	TH empathy, WAI-S, SEQ	69 TH, 69 CL	89 TH, 93 CL	54 TH, 47 CL	TH	0.03	0.01		0.40

CT Management and Psychotherapy Outcome

Nine studies (Table 15.2) reported the correlation between CT management and psychotherapy outcome. The omnibus effect size was significant ($r = .39$, 95% CI = .17, .6; $p < .001$, $d = .84$, $N = 392$ participants), evidencing a medium to large-medium effect size. This finding indicates that better CT management was associated with larger gains in psychotherapy outcome.

As with the findings pertaining to CT reactions and outcome, there was significant heterogeneity across studies ($I^2 = 88.55\%$, $Q[8] = 101.45$, $p < .001$). Evidence suggestive of publication bias was detected in the trim-and-fill analysis. After three studies were imputed to account for the asymmetric funnel plot, the correlation between CT management and psychotherapy outcome remained significant ($r = .51$, 95% CI =.30, .72; $p < .001$, $d = 1.20$).

A moderator test examined whether the association between CT management and outcome varied depending on when outcome was assessed. There was no evidence that this was the case ($Q[1] = 2.28$, $p = .131$).

CT Management to CT Reactions

A total of 13 studies (Table 15.3) reported the correlation between CT management and CT reactions. The omnibus effect size was significant ($r = -.27$, 95% CI = −.43, −.10; $p = .001$, $d = -.55$, $N = 1{,}394$ participants), indicating better CT management was associated with fewer CT reactions. There was once again significant heterogeneity across studies ($I^2 = 91.20\%$, $Q[12] = 244.43$, $p < .001$). Unlike in the two previous meta-analyses, there was no evidence of publication bias.

EVIDENCE FOR CAUSALITY

These meta-analytic findings are consistent with previous meta-analytic results and prevailing clinical wisdom, but the research has not matured to the point where causal statements can be made with confidence. The meta-analyses report on correlations or association, not casual links. Experimental studies regarding training in CT management are in planning stages, and these will advance the field's knowledge toward causal inference in this area.

We believe the time has arrived for more sophisticated tests of CT reactions, their management, and psychotherapy outcome than has been the case previously. The establishment of large practice-research networks (e.g., McAleavey et al., 2015) likely will facilitate such research, although therapists—who traditionally have been reluctant to engage in CT research (Fauth, 2006)—must still be willing to participate in such studies.

Table 15.2. Summary of Studies Relating Countertransference Reactions to Countertransference Management

	Perez-Rojas et al	Gelso et al	Robbins and Jolkovski	Forester	Kholocci	Hayes, Riker, Ingram	Peabody and Gelso	Fatter and Hayes	Williams et al	Williams and Fauth	Latts and Gelso	Hofsess and Tracey	Friedman and Gelso
Authors													
Year	2017	1995	1987	2001	2008	1997	1982	2013	2003	2005	1995	2010	2000
Publication	PTRPT	JCP	JCP	Diss	Diss	PR	JCP	PR	PTRPT	PR	PTRPT	JCP	JClinical Psy
Predictor	CT Management Scale	CFI	Self-awareness; Use of theory	Body awareness	Mindfulness	CFI-R	Therapist empathy	Meditation experience, mindfulness, and self-differentiation	Self-awareness	Self-awareness	Self-awareness; Use of theory	CFI	CFI-R
Criterion	CT Behavior	Cognitive, affective, behavioral CT	Withdrawal of involvement	Vicarious traumatization	CT Questionnaire	CT Index; Avoidance	CT behavior	CT management	Private self-consciousness	Negative stress	Avoidance	Experiences with CT	Inventory of CT Behavior
N	286 Sup	68 TH	58 TH	96 TH	203 TH	20 TH 20 CL	20 TH 20 CL	78 Sup 100 TH	301 TH	18 TH 18 CL	47 TH	35 TH 12 Sup	149 Sup
Ethnicity (% White)	87	56	91	60	90 TH 80 CL	80 TH 85 CL	not reported	81 TH 78 Sup	92	94 TH 75 CL	25	54 TH 67 Sup	91
Age (mean years)	56	not reported	29	39	42 TH 40 CL	31 TH 25 CL	not reported	not reported	51	36 TH 22 CL	29	28 TH 38 Sup	49
CT rater type	Sup	TH and Observer	Observer	TH	TH	TH, Sup, and Observer	Observer	Sup	TH	TH	Observer	TH	Sup
$|r|$	.66	.04	.04	.10	.15	.18	.24	.28	.29	.43	.45	.57	.59
r variance	.002	.01	.02	.01	.005	.05	.05	.01	.003	.04	.01	.01	.003
Hypothesis confirmed	+							+	+	+	+	+	+
p value (1 tailed)	.001	.40	.38	.17	.19	.22	.15	.05	.04	.00	.00	.00	.00

Table 15.3. Summary of Studies Relating Countertransference Management to Outcome

Authors	Latts	Van Wagoner et al.	Peabody and Gelso	Ryan et al.	Gelso et al.	Williams and Fauth	Fauth and Williams	Rosenber-ger and Hayes	Leidenfrost
Year	1996	1991	1982	2012	2002	2005	2005	2002	2015
Publication	Diss	PTRPT	JCP	PR	JClinPsy	PR	JCP	JCP	Diss
Predictor	CFI	CFI	Openness to CT feelings	KIMS	CFI	Self-awareness	Self-awareness	CFI-R	CFI-R
Criterion	TH effectiveness	TH excellence	TH empathy	SCL-90, IIP	CL outcome	Session eval	TH helpfulness	BSI, Session quality, alliance	CL Outcome (Schwartz Outcome Scale)
N	77 TH 77 sup	122 TH	20 TH-CL pairs	26 TH 26 CL	32 TH 15 Sup 63 CL	18 TH 18CL	17 TH 17 CL	1 TH 1 CL	9 Sup TH 50
Ethnicity (% White)	69 TH 74 Sup	not reported	not reported	35 CL TH not reported	not reported	94 TH 75 CL	65 TH 82 CL	100 TH 100 CL	89 Sup 90 TH
Age (mean years)	29 TH 41 Sup	48	not reported	not reported	29 TH Sup not reported CL not reported	36 TH 22 CL	24 TH 22 CL	34 TH 21 CL	not reported
CT MGMT rater type	Sup	Observer	Observer	TH	Sup	TH	TH	Observer	Sup
Hypothesis confirmed	+	+	+	+	+			+	+
|r|	.89	.55	.42	.18	.39	.18	.17	.38	.002
r variance	.001	.004	.04	.04	.01	.06	.06	.73	.02
p value (1-tailed)	.00	.00	.03	.01	.01	.25	.00	.03	>.05

PATIENT CONTRIBUTIONS

Although CT is fundamentally a function of the therapist's own conflicts and vulnerabilities, there are some features of clients that serve to activate or provoke CT reactions. Thus, we believe that CT is best understood in terms of an interaction between the therapist's unresolved conflicts and aspects of the client that touch upon or stir up the therapist's conflicts (Gelso & Hayes, 2007; Hayes, 1995; Hayes, Nelson, et al., 2015). We refer to this interplay between therapist and client characteristics as the CT Interaction Hypothesis (Gelso & Hayes, 2007). Consistent with this hypothesis, the research does not support the view that there are common client characteristics that universally provoke CT (e.g., Hayes & Gelso, 1991, 1993; Robbins & Jolkovski, 1987; Yulis & Kiesler, 1968). Instead, CT has a decidedly subjective nature to it, and this makes sense given therapists' idiosyncratic histories, conflicts, and vulnerabilities (Fauth, 2006; Kiesler, 2001). The perfectionistic, self-critical client may evoke CT reactions in the therapist who struggles with his or her own perfectionism and may not prove at all difficult for the therapist who is not a perfectionist. As a result, it is incumbent upon therapists to understand themselves, their own inner workings, and to know what types of clients will likely provoke their CT reactions. As the inscription above the temple at Delphi said, "Know thyself."

LIMITATIONS OF THE RESEARCH

Although the empirical literature on CT management is promising, this line of work is in its early stages. In this section, we review the limitations of the extant literature and provide a few useful directions for CT research.

Perhaps the most serious limitation to the research at the present time is the dearth of studies that link CT and its management to distal treatment outcomes. As a result, the link between CT behavior and treatment outcome is a tenuous one. Effects of CT and its management on outcome may be inferred from the data. However, there is precious little *direct* empirical support for such conclusions. In other words, it seems obvious that if CT contributes to avoiding a patient's feelings, recalling the content of sessions inaccurately, and becoming overinvolved in the patient's problems, then it is a good bet that its effects on the treatment outcome are adverse. Further, if CT behavior is negatively related to sound working alliances and to supervisors' evaluations of treatment effectiveness, then it also seems safe to suggest that uncontrolled CT is harmful to psychotherapy. At the same time, we could locate only one study (Hayes et al., 1997) seeking to connect CT behavior to treatment outcomes beyond immediate or proximate outcomes, and the results of that study only partially support the link of CT to outcome.

Clearly, research is needed on how CT and its management are related to treatment outcome, not only in terms of main effects (relating aspects of both to outcome) but also in terms of the conditions under which CT affects outcome. For example, does the effect depend upon patient qualities (e.g., personality, culture, severity and type of disturbance), therapist qualities (competence, experience, self-awareness), and the qualities of CT itself (positive vs. negative, CT feelings vs. CT behavior, mild vs. extreme CT)? Also of interest are the ways in which CT may directly versus indirectly influence outcome. For example, it may be that degree of CT in a given therapy directly affects the working alliance, which in turn directly influences outcome. In this instance, CT may not directly relate to outcome, but instead affects outcome *through* its influence on alliance. Path analytic models might be fruitfully applied to CT research to examine such direct and indirect effects.

Because of the relatively small number of studies in each of the meta-analyses, the magnitudes of the effects detected are likely to change as research accumulates in this area. That being said, it is unlikely that the directions of the relations are going to change. The data support the theoretical suppositions that CT reactions negatively affect therapy outcomes and that successful CT management enhances therapy outcomes. Another limitation of the current research literature is that all of the studies that have been conducted to date focus on individual therapy. The empirical literature is silent on CT and its management in group, couple, and family therapy, although we suspect that these would be fertile areas for future research endeavors.

DIVERSITY CONSIDERATIONS

The CT literature has addressed culture to only a small degree, most notably in the areas of sexual orientation and gender. In a pair of studies examining CT in response to clients of various sexual orientations, therapist-trainees' verbal responses to clients exhibiting relational and sexual problems, contrary to expectation, did not reflect greater CT when these clients were gay (Hayes & Gelso, 1993) or lesbian (Gelso et al., 1995) than when they were heterosexual. However, these trainees' levels of homophobia predicted avoidance of client material in their responses to gay and lesbian, but not heterosexual, clients.

In the aforementioned Gelso et al. (1995) study, there was also some indication that therapist gender interacted with sexual orientation. When responding to a lesbian client, female therapists exhibited greater CT than males, whereas when responding to a heterosexual client, male and female therapists did not differ in their displays of CT. Interestingly, the measure of CT that differentiated male and female therapists when interacting with lesbian and heterosexual clients was the accuracy of recall of sexual words that the client expressed. Female therapists had a poorer recall of the number of sexual words than did male therapists when responding to lesbian clients (but not heterosexual clients). These findings are part of a small but important body of literature on the complex ways in which gender relates to CT (Gelso & Hayes, 2007; Latts & Gelso, 1995).

There is an obvious need for research on CT reactions that may stem from other aspects of the client's or the therapist's culture, such as religion, disability status, age, ethnicity, and race. As regards the latter, recent research has found differential therapist effectiveness as a function of client race and ethnicity (e.g., Hayes, Owen, et al., 2015; Hayes et al., 2015, 2016, 2017). We suspect that culture-related CT reactions are a culprit in these therapist effects (Gelso & Mohr, 2001).

TRAINING IMPLICATIONS

Virtually all of the research on CT management to date has focused on therapist characteristics that are theorized to facilitate the management of CT reactions (e.g., self-insight, clinical experience, self-integration). In fact, early reviewers of the CT literature concluded that, "more experienced and competent therapists tend to be aware of their countertransference feelings and are more able to prevent them from influencing their behavior with their patients" (Singer & Luborsky, 1977, p. 449). Aside from possessing certain qualities such as clinical experience or awareness, however, the research literature does not provide much knowledge about what therapists actually can *do* to manage their CT (for exceptions, see Baehr, 2005; Fatter & Hayes, 2013; Millon & Halewood, 2015).

Recently, this question has begun to be addressed by a team of researchers from New Zealand and Australia who have developed a method for training therapists to manage their CT by engaging in reflective practice (Cartwright et al., 2014, 2015, 2018). *Reflective practice* refers to the examination of one's own covert and overt experiences to enhance learning and professional development (Bassot, 2016; Bradley, 2011). A fundamental assumption inherent in reflective practice is that experience alone is insufficient to facilitate growth; rather, intentional and focused contemplation about one's experience is necessary (Irving & Williams, 1995). Furthermore, reflection must go beyond the description and analysis of a situation. It must also include the framing of a problem, an attempt to understand its causes, and the generation of action plans to try to solve problems (Johns, 2009). Using the principles of reflective practice, clinical psychology students at several universities have been taught to identify their CT reactions to patients and write about them in a weekly log. A model is used to help students frame and understand their CT reactions, and this same model serves as a guideline for students' written reflections.

The value of reflective practice in managing CT is reflected not only in research that demonstrates the negative effects of CT on psychotherapy outcome but also in studies indicating that novice therapists struggle to manage their CT (Hill et al., 1996; Williams & Fauth, 2005). Research indicates that students rate training as helpful in increasing their awareness and understanding of CT (Cartwright et al., 2014). At the same time, following didactic training, students express relatively little confidence about their ability to successfully manage CT in the future (Cartwright et al., 2015, 2018). The fact that students do not expect their increased understanding and awareness of CT to translate into effective CT management strategies suggests that a revision is needed to the content or format of the training that is provided, or to the nature of students' reflective practice.

We have begun to engage in training in which students receive feedback on their written reflections to support and guide exploration of their personal CT reactions. Ideally that feedback would occur in clinical supervision, but supervision typically contains an evaluative component. That is, supervisors are responsible for determining the quality of the clinical services that students provide, typically provide a written evaluation of a student that influences a student's grade in a course, and may even negatively affect a student's progress toward graduation or obtaining a license to practice psychology. Therefore, students often will not disclose CT reactions to their supervisors out of fear of negative consequences (Shafranske & Falender, 2008). It would be possible, however, for students to keep an electronic log and receive feedback from a therapist who is not in an evaluative capacity. A study to that effect is underway at present by the lead author of the chapter.

Fortunately, the medium to large effect size in our meta-analysis on CT management and psychotherapy outcome suggests that training efforts may lead to improved treatment outcomes. Our own training emphasizes the five management factors of self-insight, anxiety management, self-integration, empathy, and conceptualizing ability. Some of these characteristics, such as self-insight and self-integration, are most likely to be developed outside of a formal training context (e.g., in the therapist's own therapy). The remaining factors can be cultivated in supervision, wherein the therapist's specific reactions to particular clients can be examined, ideally in the context of a relationship that is perceived by the trainee to be supportive.

Such training and supervision experiences need not, and should not, be limited to graduate students; managing CT is not a skill that a therapist learns "once and for all" at a certain stage in their professional development. Effective CT management requires an ongoing commitment and willingness to examine one's psychological health, one's reactions to clients, one's current motivations for conducting therapy, and the effects of one's clinical practice on one's life, for starters. We have found that peer supervision for experienced psychotherapists can be an invaluable forum for exploring these matters.

THERAPEUTIC PRACTICES

The meta-analytic evidence points to the likely conclusions that the acting out of CT is typically harmful, though not necessarily irreparably so, and that CT management typically proves helpful to patient outcomes. From these general conclusions, a number of specific clinical practices can be recommended.

- The effective therapist must work at not acting out on internal CT reactions.
- The five CT management factors appear to be useful for understanding and controlling CT manifestations. Self-insight seems particularly important to cultivate, and continually so. A therapist must take seriously Socrates' advice to "know thyself" or else risk having unknown aspects of the self undermine one's work with a client. "We should be the constant objects of our own observation, looking for any intense feelings about patients, and being vigilant about what the next instant will be in which our unconscious may betray us" (Robiertello & Schoenwolf, 1987, p. 290).
- Practice the demanding task of honest, impartial, and persistent self-observation. Self-awareness fosters an understanding of others, and our own blind spots can interfere with our empathy for and insight into others.

- Therapists should work on their own psychological health, including healthy boundaries with patients. Self-integration, along with self-insight, allows the therapist to pay attention to how the client is affecting the therapist and why. Such understanding is the first step in the process of arriving at ways in which CT may be useful to the work. When the therapist seeks to understand internal conflicts that are being stirred by the patient's material, the therapist also considers how this process may relate to the patient's life outside the consulting room—to both the patient's earlier life and current life. Then the therapist may be in a good position to devise responses that will be helpful to the patient.

- Self-integration underscores the importance of the therapist resolving major conflicts, which in turn points to the potential value of personal therapy for the psychotherapist (Geller et al., 2005). Personal therapy for the therapist seems especially important when dealing with chronic CT problems. Although the evidence supports the view that CT occurs in a high percentage of sessions, it seems obvious that chronic CT problems need to be dealt with by the therapist, and that personal therapy is a likely vehicle for such resolution.

- Clinical supervision, for experienced therapists as well as trainees, is another key factor in understanding and managing CT and in using it to benefit clients. Of course, it is helpful if supervisors themselves actively conduct psychotherapy to remain sensitive to the realities and challenges posed by CT.

- An area that must be addressed in clinical practice is how the therapist should deal with CT that has already been acted out in the work. In addition to the need for the therapist to understand that indeed he or she was acting out personal conflicts, some research points to the value of the therapist's admission that a mistake was made and that it was the therapist's conflicts that were the primary source (e.g., Hill et al., 1996; Myers & Hayes, 2006). Therapists need not go into detail about their problems, for doing so more often than not serves therapists' needs more than the patient's. Yet the admission does appear to benefit the work—if a strong working alliance is in place (Yeh & Hayes, 2011)—and to diminish potential impasses.

- Therapists are likely to benefit from engaging in a regular and sustained meditation practice. Meditation promotes emotion regulation (Davis & Hayes, 2011) and has been found in both qualitative and quantitative research to benefit CT management (Baehr, 2005; Fatter & Hayes, 2013).

- Finally, therapists should practice self-care, including getting enough sleep, limiting the number of patients one sees, spending time with friends, eating healthily, exercising regularly, and focusing on the rewards of conducting therapy. These behaviors are associated with practitioner resilience and ultimately better psychotherapy outcomes (Norcross & VandenBos, 2018).

REFERENCES

References marked with an asterisk indicate studies included in the meta-analyses.

Anchin, J. C., & Kiesler, D. J. (Eds.). (1982). *Handbook of interpersonal psychotherapy.* New York, NY: Pergamon.

Baehr, A. (2005). *Wounded healers and relational experts: A grounded theory of experienced therapists' management and use of countertransference.* (Doctoral dissertation). Retrieved from ProQuest Dissertations and Theses database (UMI No. 3148636)

*Bandura, A., Lipsher, D. H., & Miller, P. E. (1960). Psychotherapists' approach-avoidance reactions to patients' expressions of hostility. *Journal of Consulting Psychology, 24*, 1–8.

Bassot, B. (2016). *The reflective practice guide: An interdisciplinary approach to critical reflection.* New York, NY: Routledge/Taylor & Francis.

Booth, A., Trimble, T., & Egan, J. (2010). Body-centred countertransference in a sample of Irish clinical psychologists. *The Irish Psychologist, 36*, 284–289.

Bradley, E. F. (2011). Review of reflective practice in counselling and psychotherapy. *British Journal of Guidance & Counselling, 39*, 104–106.

Brown, L. S. (2001). Feelings in context: Countertransference and the real world in feminist therapy. *Journal of Clinical Psychology, 57*, 1005–1012.

Butler, S. F., Flasher, L. V., & Strupp, H. H. (1993). Countertransference and qualities of the psychotherapist. In N. E. Miller, L. Luborsky, J. P. Barber, & J. P. Docherty (Eds.), *Psychodynamic treatment research: A handbook for clinical practice* (pp. 342–360). New York, NY: Basic Books.

Cartwright, C., Barber, C., Cowie, S., & Thompson, N. (2018). A trans-theoretical training for post-graduate psychology students designed to promote understanding and management of countertransference. *Psychotherapy Research, 28*(4), 517–531.

Cartwright, C., Rhodes, P., King, R., & Shires, A. (2014). Experiences of countertransference: Reports of clinical psychology students. *Australian Psychologist, 49*, 232–240.

Cartwright, C., Rhodes, P., King, R., & Shires, A. (2015). A pilot study of a method for teaching clinical psychology trainees to conceptualise and manage countertransference. *Australian Psychologist, 50*, 148–156.

Cooper, H., Hedges, L. V., & Valentine, J. C. (Eds.). (2009). *The handbook of research synthesis and meta-analysis.* New York, NY: Russell Sage Foundation.

*Cutler, R. L. (1958). Countertransference effects in psychotherapy. *Journal of Consulting Psychology, 22*, 349–356.

Davis, D. M., & Hayes, J. A. (2011). What are the benefits of mindfulness? A practice review of psychotherapy-related research. *Psychotherapy, 48*, 198–208.

Del Re, A. C., & Hoyt, W. T. (2010). MAc: Meta-analysis with correlations. R package version 1.0. 5. Retrieved from http://CRAN.R-project.org/package=MAc

Ellis, A. (2001). Rational and irrational aspects of countertransference. *Journal of Clinical Psychology, 57*, 999–1004.

Epstein, L. & Feiner, A. H. (1988). Countertransference: The therapist's contribution to treatment. In B. Wolstein (Ed.), *Essential papers on countertransference* (pp. 282–303). New York, NY: New York University Press.

*Fatter, D. M., & Hayes, J. A. (2013). What facilitates countertransference management? The role of meditation, mindfulness, and self-differentiation. *Psychotherapy Research, 23*, 502–513.

Fauth, J. (2006). Toward more (and better) countertransference research. *Psychotherapy, 43*, 16–31.

Fauth, J., & Hayes, J. A. (2006). Therapists' male gender role attitudes and stress appraisals as predictors of countertransference behavior with male clients. *Journal of Counseling and Development, 84*, 430–439.

*Fauth, J., & Williams, E. N. (2005). The in-session self-awareness of therapist-trainees: Hindering or helpful? *Journal of Counseling Psychology, 52,* 443–447.

Fiedler, F. E. (1951). On different types of countertransference. *Journal of Clinical Psychology, 7,* 101–107.

*Forester, C. (2001). Body awareness: An aspect of countertransference management that moderates vicarious traumatization. *Dissertation Abstracts International, 61,* 5561.

Freud, S. (1957). Future prospects of psychoanalytic therapy. In J. Strachey (Ed.), *The standard edition of the complete works of Sigmund Freud* (Vol. 11, pp. 139–151). London, England: Hogarth. (Original work published 1910)

*Friedman, S. C., & Gelso, C. J. (2000). The development of the Inventory of Countertransference Behavior. *Journal of Clinical Psychology, 56,* 1221–1235.

Geller, J. D., Norcross, J. C., & Orlinsky, D. E. (Eds.). (2005). *The psychotherapist's own psychotherapy.* New York, NY: Oxford University Press.

*Gelso, C. J., Fassinger, R. E., Gomez, M. J., & Latts, M. G. (1995). Countertransference reactions to lesbian clients: The role of homophobia, counselor gender, and countertransference management. *Journal of Counseling Psychology, 42,* 356–364.

Gelso, C. J., & Hayes, J. A. (1998). *The psychotherapy relationship: Theory, research, and practice.* New York, NY: Wiley.

Gelso, C. J., & Hayes, J. A. (2007). *Countertransference and the therapist's inner experience: Perils and possibilities.* Mahwah, NJ: Erlbaum.

*Gelso, C. J., Latts, M., Gomez, M., & Fassinger, R. E. (2002). Countertransference management and therapy outcome: An initial evaluation. *Journal of Clinical Psychology, 58,* 861–867.

Gelso, C. J., & Mohr, J. J. (2001). The working alliance and the transference/countertransference relationship: Their manifestation with racial/ethnic and sexual orientation minority clients and therapists. *Applied and Preventive Psychology, 10,* 51–68.

Ham, C. C., LeMasson, K. D. S., & Hayes, J. A. (2013). Recovering substance abuse counselors' lived experiences related to the use of self-disclosure. *Alcoholism Treatment Quarterly, 31,* 348–374.

Hayes, J. A. (1995). Waking a sleeping dog: Countertransference in group psychotherapy. *International Journal of Group Psychotherapy, 45,* 521–535.

Hayes, J. A. (2004). The inner world of the psychotherapist: A program of research on countertransference. *Psychotherapy Research, 14,* 21–36.

Hayes, J. A., & Cruz, J. M. (2006). On leading a horse to water: Therapist insight, countertransference, and client insight. In L. G. Castonguay and C. E. Hill (Eds.), *Insight in psychotherapy* (pp. 279–292). Washington, DC: American Psychological Association.

Hayes, J. A., & Gelso, C. J. (1991). Effects of therapist-trainees' anxiety and empathy on countertransference behavior. *Journal of Clinical Psychology, 47,* 284–290.

Hayes, J. A., & Gelso, C. J. (1993). Counselors' discomfort with gay and HIV-infected clients. *Journal of Counseling Psychology, 40,* 86–93.

Hayes, J. A., & Gelso, C. J. (2001). Clinical implications of research on countertransference: Science informing practice. *Journal of Clinical Psychology, 57,* 1041–1051.

Hayes, J. A., Gelso, C. J., & Hummel, A. M. (2011). Managing countertransference. In J. C. Norcross (Ed.), *Psychotherapy relationships that work* (2nd ed., pp. 239–258). New York, NY: Oxford University Press.

Hayes, J. A., Gelso, C. J., VanWagoner, S. L., & Diemer, R. (1991). Managing countertransference: What the experts think. *Psychological Reports, 69,* 139–148.

Hayes, J. A., McAleavey, A. A., Castonguay, L. G., & Locke, B. D. (2016). Psychotherapist effects with White and racial/ethnic minority clients: First, the good news. *Journal of Counseling Psychology, 63,* 261–268.

Hayes, J. A., McCracken, J. E., McClanahan, M. K., Hill, C. E., Harp, J. S., & Carozzoni, P. (1998). Therapist perspectives on countertransference: Qualitative data in search of a theory. *Journal of Counseling Psychology, 45,* 468–482.

Hayes, J. A., Nelson, D. L., & Fauth, J. (2015). Countertransference in successful and unsuccessful cases of psychotherapy. *Psychotherapy, 52,* 127–133.

Hayes, J. A., Owen, J., & Bieschke, K. J. (2015). Therapist differences in symptom change with racial and ethnic minority clients. *Psychotherapy, 52,* 308–314.

Hayes, J. A., Owen, J., & Nissen-Lie, H. A. (2017). The contributions of client culture to differential therapist effectiveness. In L. G. Castonguay and C. E. Hill (Eds.), *Therapist effects: Toward understanding how and why some therapists are better than others* (pp. 159–174). Washington, DC: American Psychological Association.

*Hayes, J. A., Riker, J. B., & Ingram, K. M. (1997). Countertransference behavior and management in brief counseling: A field study. *Psychotherapy Research, 7,* 145–154.

*Hayes, J. A, Yeh, Y., & Eisenberg, A. (2007). Good grief and not-so-good grief: Countertransference in bereavement therapy. *Journal of Clinical Psychology, 63,* 345–356.

Haynal, A. (1993). Slaying the dragons of the past or cooking the hare in the present: A historical view on affects and in the psychoanalytic encounter. *Psychoanalytic Inquiry, 13,* 357–371.

Heimann, P. (1950). Countertransference. *British Journal of Medical Psychology, 33,* 9–15.

Hill, C. E., Nutt-Williams, E., Heaton, K. J., Thompson, G. B. J., & Rhodes, R. H. (1996). Therapist retrospective recall of impasses in long-term psychotherapy: A qualitative analysis. *Journal of Counseling Psychology, 43,* 201–217.

*Hofsess, C. D., & Tracey, T. J. G. (2010). Countertransference as a prototype: The development of a measure. *Journal of Counseling Psychology, 57,* 52–59.

Irving, J. A., & Williams, D. I. (1995). Critical thinking and reflective practice in counselling. *British Journal of Guidance & Counselling, 23,* 107–114.

Johns, C. (2009). *Becoming a reflective practitioner* (3rd ed.). Hoboken, NJ: Wiley-Blackwell.

Kaslow, F. W. (2001). Whither countertransference in couples and family therapy: A systemic perspective. *Journal of Clinical Psychology, 57,* 1029–1040.

Kernberg, O. (1965). Notes on countertransference. *Journal of the American Psychoanalytic Association, 13,* 38–56.

*Kholocci, H. (2008). An examination of the relationship between countertransference and mindfulness and its potential role in limiting therapist abuse. *Dissertation Abstracts International, 68* (9-B), 6312.

Kiesler, D. J. (2001). Therapist countertransference: In search of common themes and empirical referents. *Journal of Clinical Psychology, 57,* 1053–1063.

*Kim, S. S. (2013). Affective cultural countertransference reactions to Asian American clients: A mixed-methods exploratory study. *Dissertation Abstracts International, 73.*

*Latts, M. G., & Gelso, C. J. (1995). Countertransference behavior and management with survivors of sexual assault. *Psychotherapy, 32,* 405–415.

*Leidenfrost, C. M. (2015). Therapist countertransference management and therapy outcome in a naturalistic setting. *Dissertation Abstracts International, 76.*

Levenson, H. (1995). *Time-limited dynamic psychotherapy.* New York, NY: Basic Books.

*Ligiéro, D., & Gelso, C. J. (2002). Countertransference, attachment, and the working alliance: The therapist's contribution. *Psychotherapy, 39*, 3–11.

Little, M. (1951). Countertransference and the patient's response to it. *International Journal of Psychoanalysis, 32*, 32–40.

McAleavey, A. A., Lockard, A. J., Castonguay, L. G., Hayes, J. A., & Locke, B. D. (2015). Building a practice-research network: Obstacles faced and lessons learned at the Center for Collegiate Mental Health. *Psychotherapy Research, 25*, 134–151.

McClure, B. A., & Hodge, R. W. (1987). Measuring countertransference and attitude in therapeutic relationships. *Psychotherapy, 24*, 325–335.

Millon, G., & Halewood, A. (2015). Mindfulness meditation and countertransference in the therapeutic relationship: A small-scale exploration of therapists' experiences using grounded theory methods. *Counselling & Psychotherapy Research, 15*, 188–196.

*Mohr, J. J., Gelso, C. J., & Hill, C. E. (2005). Client and counselor trainee attachment as predictors of session evaluation and countertransference behavior in first counseling sessions. *Journal of Counseling Psychology, 53*, 298–309.

*Myers, D., & Hayes, J. A. (2006). Effects of therapist general self-disclosure and countertransference disclosure on ratings of the therapist and session. *Psychotherapy, 43*, 173–185.

Norcross, J. C., & VandenBos, G. R. (2018). *Leaving it at the office: A guide to psychotherapist self-care* (2nd ed.). New York, NY: Guilford.

*Peabody, S. A., & Gelso, C. J. (1982). Countertransference and empathy: The complex relationship between two divergent concepts in counseling. *Journal of Counseling Psychology, 29*, 240–245.

*Perez-Rojas, A. E., Palma, B., Bhatia, A., Jackson, J., Norwood, E., Hayes, J. A., & Gelso, C. J. (2017). The development and initial validation of the Countertransference Management Scale. *Psychotherapy, 54*, 307–319.

Reich, A. (1951). On countertransference. *International Journal of Psychoanalysis, 32*, 25–31.

*Robbins, S. B., & Jolkovski, M. P. (1987). Managing countertransference feelings: An interactional model using awareness of feeling and theoretical framework. *Journal of Counseling Psychology, 34*, 276–282.

Robiertello, R. C., & Schonewolf, G. (1987). *101 common therapeutic blunders: Countertransference and counter-resistance in psychotherapy*. Northvale, NJ: Jason Aronson.

*Rosenberger, E. W., & Hayes, J. A. (2002). Origins, consequences, and management of countertransference: A case study. *Journal of Counseling Psychology, 49*, 221–232.

*Rossberg, J. I., Karterud, S., Pedersen, G., & Friis, S. (2010). Psychiatric symptoms and countertransference feelings: An empirical investigation. *Psychiatry Research, 178*, 191–195.

Rudd, M. D., & Joiner, T. (1997). Countertransference and the therapeutic relationship: A cognitive perspective. *Journal of Cognitive Psychotherapy, 11*, 231–250.

*Ryan, A., Safran, J. D., Doran, J. M., & Muran, J. C. (2012). Therapist mindfulness, alliance and treatment outcome. *Psychotherapy Research, 22*, 289–297.

Shafranske, E. P., & Falender, C. A. (2008). Supervision addressing personal factors and countertransference. In C. A. Falender & E. P. Shafranske (Eds.), *Casebook for clinical supervision: A competency-based approach* (pp. 97–120). Washington, DC: American Psychological Association.

Singer, B. A., & Luborsky, L. (1977). Countertransference: The status of clinical versus quantitative research. In A. S. Gurman & A. M. Razin (Eds.), *Effective psychotherapy: A handbook of research* (pp. 433–451). New York, NY: Pergamon.

Spence, D. (1987). *The Freudian metaphor*. New York, NY: Norton.

Strupp, H. H., & Binder, J. L. (1984). *Psychotherapy in a new key: A guide to time-limited dynamic psychotherapy*. New York, NY: Basic Books.

*VanWagoner, S. L., Gelso, C. J., Hayes, J. A., & Diemer, R. (1991). Countertransference and the reputedly excellent psychotherapist. *Psychotherapy, 28*, 411–421.

Viechtbauer, W. (2010). Conducting meta-analyses in R with the metaphor package. *Journal of Statistical Software, 36*, 1–48.

Wampold, B. E., Mondin, G. W., Moody, M., Stich, F., Benson, K., & Ahn, H. (1997). A meta-analysis of outcome studies comparing bona fide psychotherapies: Empirically, "all must have prizes." *Psychological Bulletin, 122*, 203–215.

*Westra, H. A., Aviram, A., Connors, L., Kertes, A., & Ahmed, M. (2012). Therapist emotional reactions and client resistance in cognitive behavioral therapy. *Psychotherapy, 49*, 163–172.

*Williams, E. N., & Fauth, J. (2005). A psychotherapy process study of therapist in-session self-awareness. *Psychotherapy Research, 15*, 374–381.

*Williams, E. N., Hurley, K., O'Brien, K., & de Gregorio, A. (2003). Development and validation of the Self-Awareness and Management Strategies (SAMS) scales for therapists. *Psychotherapy, 40*, 278–288.

*Yeh, Y., & Hayes, J. A. (2011). How does disclosing countertransference affect perceptions of the therapist and the session? *Psychotherapy, 48*, 322–329.

Yulis, S., & Kiesler, D. J. (1968). Countertransference response as a function of therapist anxiety and content of patient talk. *Journal of Consulting and Clinical Psychology, 32*, 414–419.

16

REPAIRING ALLIANCE RUPTURES

Catherine F. Eubanks, J. Christopher Muran, and Jeremy D. Safran

The growing literature on the therapeutic alliance (Chapters 2, 3, 4, this volume) underscores the importance of building a strong working relationship with patients. In some therapeutic approaches, the alliance is a central focus (e.g., Safran & Muran, 2000), while in other therapies, the alliance is regarded as a necessary but insufficient condition for positive outcomes (e.g., Beck, 2011). However, across therapies, there are moments when the alliance needs to be more figure than ground to keep the therapy alive: when there is a rupture in the alliance.

In this chapter, we review the growing literature on alliance ruptures and the processes involved in repairing them. We begin by offering definitions of alliance ruptures and a summary of measures used to detect them. We provide clinical examples of ruptures and discuss landmark studies in the rupture literature. We also present meta-analytic findings on the relation of alliance ruptures and repairs to outcome and the impact of alliance rupture resolution training on outcome. The chapter concludes with diversity considerations, training implications, and therapeutic practices on research-informed methods to repair ruptures in the working alliance.

DEFINITIONS

Much of the alliance rupture literature draws on Bordin's (1979) conceptualization of the *alliance* as composed of (a) agreement between patient and therapist on the goals of treatment, (b) collaboration between patient and therapist on the tasks of treatment, and (c) an affective bond between the patient and therapist. A *rupture* is a deterioration in this alliance, manifested by a disagreement between the patient and therapist on the goals, a lack of collaboration on tasks, or a strain in the emotional bond (Eubanks-Carter et al., 2010; Safran & Muran 2000). Although the term *rupture* may connote a dramatic breakdown in the therapeutic relationship, many studies of alliance ruptures also regard subtle tensions and minor misattunements as markers of ruptures. A number of other terms have been used in the literature to describe problems or difficulties in the alliance. These include weakenings (e.g., Lansford 1986), threats (e.g.,

Bennett et al., 2006), misattunements (e.g., Beebe & Lachmann, 2002), challenges (e.g., Agnew et al., 1994), and impasses (Hill et al., 1996; Safran & Muran 2000). Alliance ruptures are also related to constructs such as ambivalence and resistance (e.g., Hara et al., 2015; Chapter 17, countertransference; see Muran [2019] for a review).

Ruptures can be organized into two main subtypes: withdrawal and confrontation ruptures (Harper, 1989a, 1989b; Safran & Muran, 2000). In withdrawal ruptures, the patient moves away from the therapist and the work of therapy, for example, by avoiding the therapist's questions or by hiding his or her dissatisfaction with therapy by being overly appeasing. In confrontation ruptures, the patient moves against the therapist, by expressing anger or dissatisfaction with the therapist or treatment, or by trying to pressure or control the therapist. Ruptures can also include elements of both withdrawal and confrontation.

A rupture is generally deemed to be repaired or resolved when the patient and therapist resume collaborating on the work of therapy with a strong affective bond. Strategies for resolving alliance ruptures include *direct* strategies, which involve the therapist and patient explicitly acknowledging the rupture, and *indirect* strategies, whereby the rupture is resolved without being explicitly acknowledged. Resolution strategies can also be characterized according to whether they are *immediate* strategies, focused on repairing the rupture expeditiously and returning to or changing the therapeutic task the dyad was engaged in prior to the rupture, or *expressive* strategies that aim to shift the focus of the therapy session to exploring the rupture and the patient's needs or concerns that underlie it.

MEASURES

Most studies of alliance ruptures and repairs rely on naturalistic observation of these phenomena in psychotherapy via the use of direct self-report methods, indirect self-report methods, or observer-based methods (Eubanks-Carter et al., 2010). Direct self-report methods involve asking patients and therapists to report on the occurrence of ruptures and rupture resolutions. For example, in a study comparing the efficacy of an integrative relational therapy, cognitive therapy, and short-term dynamic therapy with personality-disordered patients (Muran et al., 2005), patients and therapists completed the Post-Session Questionnaire (PSQ: Muran et al., 1992) following each session.

The PSQ includes self-report, single-item indices of ruptures and rupture resolution that the participant answers using a 5-point, Likert-type rating scale ranging from "not at all" to "very much." Specifically, the participant is asked to complete the following: (1a) "Did you experience any tension or problem, any misunderstanding, conflict, or disagreement, in your relationship with your [therapist or patient] during the session? (1b) If yes, please rate how tense or upset you felt about this during the session; (2a) To what extent did you find yourself and your [therapist or patient] overly accommodating or overly protective of each other? Or to what extent did you feel you were making nice or smoothing things over? Or to what extent did you feel you were holding back or avoiding something? (2b) If yes, please rate how tense or upset you felt about this during the session; (3) To what extent was this problem addressed in this session? (4) To what degree do you feel this problem was resolved by the end of the session?"

With indirect self-report methods, fluctuations in alliance scores are interpreted as ruptures and repairs (Eubanks-Carter et al., 2012). For example, in a sample of 79 clients receiving either cognitive-behavioral therapy (CBT) or psychodynamic-interpersonal therapy for depression, the researchers identified V-shaped rupture-repair episodes using criteria based on shape-of-change parameters calculated for each patient's profile of self-reported alliance scores on the Agnew Relationship Measure (Agnew-Davies et al., 1998). Patients with rupture-repair episodes averaged larger gains than the rest of the sample, suggesting that the process of resolving ruptures contributes to good outcome. A potential future direction for this type of research would be to track fluctuations using measures like the Alliance Negotiation Scale (Doran et al., 2012), which focuses on clients' and therapists' abilities to negotiate disagreements in therapy and thereby maps more closely onto the rupture concept than traditional alliance measures.

Both direct and indirect self-report methods rely on patients' and therapists' ability and willingness to report problems in the alliance. Consistent with the finding that patients generally report higher alliances than therapists (e.g., Tryon et al., 2007), most studies of alliance ruptures find that patients report fewer ruptures than therapists, which raises the possibility that patients may be unaware of or uncomfortable acknowledging some ruptures. Table 16.1 summarizes the frequency of alliance ruptures in 21 studies using various measures.

In addition, evidence from qualitative studies (e.g., Hill, 2010) points to the difficulties therapists can have identifying that a rupture has taken place. Withdrawal ruptures, which are usually subtler and perhaps less emotionally charged for the therapist than confrontation ruptures, may be particularly difficult for therapists to recognize (Eubanks, Burckell, et al., 2018). Observer-based methods may identify ruptures that patients and therapists are unaware of or uncomfortable acknowledging. Another important advantage of observer-based methods is that they can identify ruptures that occur and are then resolved within one session; alliance fluctuations within a session may not be captured by studies of alliance fluctuations across sessions.

The most frequently used observer-based measure of ruptures is the Rupture Resolution Rating System (3RS; Eubanks et al., 2015), which yields ratings of withdrawal ruptures, confrontation ruptures, and therapist attempts to resolve ruptures. Coders rate the frequency of rupture markers and resolution strategies in five-minute intervals. Table 16.2 lists the withdrawal markers, confrontation markers, and resolution strategies assessed by the 3RS. Once coders have completed the frequency ratings, they make summary ratings of the extent to which rupture markers and resolution strategies made a clinically meaningful impact on the alliance, the extent to which ruptures were resolved over the course of the session, and the extent to which the therapist contributed to ruptures in the session. The 3RS has demonstrated good to excellent interrater reliability (intraclass correlations ranging from .73 to .99) for both

Table 16.1. Prevalence of Alliance Ruptures

Study	N	Method	Frequency of Ruptures
Botella et al. (2008)	181 patients	Indirect self-report (WAI)	54% of patients
Chen et al. (2018)	84 patients	Indirect self-report (BPSR)	3.2% of sessions
Colli and Lingiardi (2009)	16 patients	Observer-based (CIS)	Indirect ruptures: 100% of sessions
			Direct ruptures: 43% of sessions
Coutinho et al. (2014)	38 patients	Observer-based (3RS, score ≥3)	Withdrawal ruptures: 17% of sessions.
			Confrontation ruptures: 12% of sessions
Eames & Roth (2000)	30 patients, Sessions 2–5	Indirect self-report (WAI)	7% of sessions
		Direct self-report, patient	19% of sessions
		Direct self-report, therapist	43% of sessions
Eubanks et al. (2018)	42 patients, Session 6	Observer-based (3RS, score ≥3)	Withdrawal ruptures: 74% of sessions
			Confrontation ruptures: 43% of sessions
Gersh et al. (2017)	44 patients, Session 3	Observer-based (3RS)	53% of sessions
Gülüm et al. (2018)	48 patients	Indirect self-report (WAI)	25% of patients
Haugen et al. (2017)	32 patients	Indirect self-report (CASF)	Rupture-repair sequences: 37.5% of cases
Kramer et al. (2009)	50 patients	Indirect self-report (HAq)	42% of patients
Larsson et al. (2018)	605 patients	Indirect self-report (WAI)	25% of patients
Lipner et al. (2018)	73 patients	Indirect self-report (WAI)	84% of patients
Marmarosh et al. (2015)	22 therapists, Session 8	Direct self-report, therapist	50% of sessions
McLaughlin et al. (2014)	82 patients	Indirect self-report (CALPAS)	46% of patients
Muran et al. (2009)	128 patients, Sessions 1–6	Direct self-report, patient	37% of cases
		Direct self-report, therapist	56% of cases

Study	Sample	Measure type	Rupture frequency
Sommerfeld et al. (2008)	5 patients, 151 sessions	Direct self-report, patient	42% of sessions
		Observer-based (judges)	Withdrawal ruptures: 50% of sessions
			Confrontation ruptures: 69% of sessions
			Any rupture: 77% of sessions
Stiles et al. (2004)	79 patients	Indirect self-report (ARM)	Rupture-repair sequences: 21.5% of cases
Strauss et al. (2006)	25 patients	Indirect self-report (CALPAS)	Rupture-repair sequences: 56% of cases
Westra et al. (2011)	38 patients	Indirect self-report (CALPAS)	42% of patients
Wiseman and Tishby (2017)	67 patients, Sessions 5, 15, 28	Direct self-report, patient	40% of cases; 35% of cases; 48% of cases
		Direct self-report, therapist	72% of cases; 62% of cases; 55% of cases
Zilcha-Mano and Errázuriz (2017)	166 patients	Indirect self-report (WAI)	51.2% of patients

Note. Rupture frequencies are based on patient self-report unless otherwise noted. ARM = Agnew Relationship Measure; BPSR = Bern Post Session Report; CALPAS = California Psychotherapy Alliance Scale; CASF = Combined Alliance Short Form; CIS = Collaborative Interaction Scale; HAq = Helping Alliance Questionnaire; 3RS = Rupture Resolution Rating System; WAI = Working Alliance Inventory.

Table 16.2. Rupture Resolution Rating System Rupture Markers and Resolution Strategies

Withdrawal Rupture Markers

Denial	Patient withdraws from the therapist/work of therapy by denying a feeling state that is manifestly evident, or denying the importance of interpersonal relationships or events that seem important and relevant to the work of therapy.
Minimal response	Patient withdraws from the therapist by going silent or by giving minimal responses to questions or statements that are intended to initiate or continue discussion.
Abstract communication	Patient avoids the work of therapy by using vague or abstract language.
Avoidant storytelling and/or shifting topic	Patient tells stories and/or shifts the topic in a manner that functions to avoid the work of therapy.
Deferential and appeasing	Patient withdraws from the therapist and/or the work of therapy by being overly compliant and submitting to the therapist in a deferential manner.
Content/affect split	The patient withdraws from the therapist and/or the work of therapy by exhibiting affect that does not match the content of his/her narrative.
Self-criticism and/or hopelessness	The patient withdraws from the therapist and the work of therapy by becoming absorbed in a depressive process of self-criticism and/or hopelessness that seems to shut out the therapist and to close off any possibility that the therapist or the treatment can help the patient.

Confrontation Rupture Markers

Complaints/concerns about the therapist	Patient expresses negative feelings about the therapist.
Patient rejects therapist intervention	Patient rejects or dismisses the therapist's intervention.
Complaints/concerns about the activities of therapy	Patient expresses dissatisfaction, discomfort, or disagreement with specific tasks of therapy such as homework assignments or in-session tasks such as empty chair or imaginal exposure.
Complaints/concerns about the parameters of therapy	Patient expresses concerns or complaints about the parameters of treatment, such as the therapy schedule or the research contract.
Complaints/concerns about progress in therapy	Patient expresses complaints, concerns, or doubts about the progress that can be made or has been made in therapy.
Patient defends self against therapist	Patient defends his/her thoughts, feelings, or behavior against what he/she perceives to be the therapist's criticism or judgment of the patient.
Efforts to control/pressure therapist	Patient attempts to control the therapist and/or the session, or the patient puts pressure on the therapist to fix the patient's problems quickly.

Table 16.2. Continued

Resolution Strategies

Within the context of a rupture, the therapist clarifies a misunderstanding.

Within the context of a rupture, the therapist changes tasks or goals.

Within the context of a rupture, the therapist illustrates tasks or provides a rationale for treatment.

Within the context of a rupture, the therapist invites the patient to discuss thoughts or feelings with respect to the therapist or some aspect of therapy.

Within the context of a rupture, the therapist acknowledges his/her contribution to a rupture.

Within the context of a rupture, the therapist discloses his/her internal experience of the patient-therapist interaction.

Therapist links the rupture to larger interpersonal patterns between the patient and the therapist.

Therapist links the rupture to larger interpersonal patterns in the patient's other relationships.

Therapist validates the patient's defensive posture.

Therapist responds to a rupture by redirecting or refocusing the patient.

---

the frequency ratings and the summary ratings (Coutinho, Ribeiro, Sousa, et al., 2014; Eubanks, Lubitz, et al., 2018).

Research suggests that the 3RS identifies more ruptures than self-report measures (Coutinho, Ribeiro, Sousa, et al., 2014). However, as there is not yet a gold standard for assessing ruptures, it is impossible to say whether the 3RS is more sensitive than self-reports or is overidentifying ruptures.

At this point, there is some support for the predictive validity of the 3RS. A study that used the 3RS to compare early sessions from patients who completed 30-sessions of CBT to patients who dropped out prematurely found significantly more confrontation rupture markers in dropout cases and significantly more rupture resolution in completer sessions (Eubanks, Lubitz, et al., 2018). A study that used the 3RS to compare early sessions of three good and three poor outcome cases of dialectical behavior therapy for borderline personality disorder found unrecovered clients had a higher frequency of withdrawal ruptures than recovered clients and that withdrawal ruptures tended to persist across sessions despite therapists' attempts at rupture resolution (Boritz et al., 2018). The authors suggested that withdrawal ruptures in this clinical population may pose a particular challenge for therapists.

Several additional observer-based measures assess ruptures in the alliance. One is the Collaborative Interaction Scale (CIS; Colli & Lingiardi, 2009), which assesses both patients' and therapists' positive and negative contributions to the alliance and has demonstrated good interrater reliability. In a validation study (Colli et al., 2017), the CIS identified more alliance ruptures and fewer collaborative processes in a sample of patients with personality disorders as compared to a sample of patients without personality disorders. The observer-based version of the System for Observing Family Therapy Alliances (Friedlander et al., 2006; Chapter 4, this volume), a measure of the alliance in family treatment that has demonstrated good interrater reliability and validity, includes negative client and therapist alliance-related behaviors that could be considered markers of ruptures (e.g., "client comments on the therapist's incompetence or inadequacy"). The Therapeutic Collaboration Coding System (Ribeiro et al., 2013), which assesses whether the therapeutic dyad is working within an optimal zone between the client's actual and potential developmental levels, includes codes for client responses that overlap with ruptures, such as disagreeing with the therapist's intervention, shifting the topic, and nonmeaningful storytelling. An additional observer-based measure that bears similarities to rupture measures is the coordination scale (Westerman et al., 1995). Coordination refers to how well a patient relates his or her contributions in a therapeutic exchange to the therapist's contributions and to the patient's own contributions at other points in time.

As noted, the field has not yet identified a gold standard for measuring ruptures and repairs. This is due to both the nascent stage of this area of research and the complex nature of rupture phenomena. For example, given that ruptures can be emotionally challenging for patients and therapists, self-reports of ruptures are limited by participants' ability and willingness to detect and report problems in the alliance. Observer-based measures are limited by the fact that observers are not participants in the therapeutic relationship and therefore may miss how hurt, misunderstood, or distant the patient or therapist feels. Given these differences in perspective, it is not surprising that limited reliability has been found between observer and self-report measures of ruptures (e.g., Coutinho, Riberio, Sousa, et al., 2014).

Given the probable complex association between ruptures and outcome—namely that ruptures can contribute to poor outcome if unresolved and to good outcome if successfully repaired—establishing predictive validity via links to outcome is not straightforward. Researchers have argued that rupture and repair processes can extend across multiple sessions (e.g., Safran & Muran, 2000); hence, a comprehensive assessment of rupture repair would entail applying both self-report measures and observer-based coding to every therapy session, which is labor intensive. It is also possible that observable markers of ruptures and successful repair processes may vary by treatment or patient or therapist population, which would complicate comparisons of measures across different samples. Additional research comparing and refining different methods of rupture and repair detection is necessary to build greater consensus on the optimal ways to measure these phenomena.

CLINICAL EXAMPLES

Psychotherapists can use immediate resolution strategies in an effort to get treatment back on course, or they can use more expressive strategies that focus on exploring the rupture if they are aware of its occurrence. Research comparing these types of strategies is currently lacking, but, based on our clinical experience, we would argue that neither type of strategy is inherently better—the choice depends on the clinical situation. In the following example (see www.therapeutic-alliance.org/confrontation-3.html), a client confronts the therapist with a complaint about the thought record she was asked to do for homework. The client (C) already keeps a journal and is upset that the therapist wants her to record her experiences in a different way. The therapist (T) validates the client's concerns, tracks the client's movement between confrontation and withdrawal, and ultimately chooses to respond to the rupture by changing the homework task.

T: And so, when I asked you to fill this thought record out, I get the feeling like, it's almost kind of offensive? *Therapist acknowledges that she has contributed to the rupture by saying something that offends the patient. Therapist invites patient's thoughts and feelings about the rupture.*

C: Yeah, well, it's like you didn't think how I was writing my anxiety down was good enough. You gave me this form like I was a child or something. It's like something I did in elementary school. Like why would I have to write this form if I'm already writing it down? *Patient complains about the activity and the therapist, patient defends self (confrontation markers).*

T: So I guess I'm wondering, right, you know, we could talk about a couple different options. I mean, we could talk about—you could continue to do the kind of journaling you've been doing, we could modify the form in some way, we could try an experiment of trying the form. I mean, I know that you're wary of it, you have concerns about it, reservations about it, but I am wondering it would be worth an experiment to try it.

Therapist introduces possibility of changing the task.

C: I mean, I guess I could try it again. I don't know, I don't think it's really going to help, but if I have to try it again, I'll try it again. *Patient complains about activity (confrontation marker); patient is somewhat deferential and appeasing (withdrawal marker).*

T: Well, you don't have to. I mean, many patients who have used it have found it very useful, and actually the fact that it's so simple makes it easier to do quickly, which for many people is an advantage. But I can appreciate that maybe for you it's different. *Therapist provides a rationale for the task and validates the patient's position.*

C: I mean, yeah, I guess I could give it a go. I'll try next time. *Patient is deferential and appeasing (withdrawal marker).*

T: But how are you feeling now? Because I don't want you to, I don't know, sort of give in to kind of get me off your back, you know? *Therapist invites patient's thoughts and feelings about the rupture.*

C: I mean, I just don't know this is going to go anywhere. And so sometimes it feels like I either have to do it your way, or I should just quit this treatment all together. *Patient complains about the activity and the therapist; patient pressures the therapist (confrontation markers).*

T: Do you have any thoughts or ideas about what you would like to be doing, or how you think we should be working together? *Therapist invites patient's thoughts and feelings.*

C: I mean, what if I just give you my journal? What if I make copies of the pages in my journal each week, and you read that instead of these stupid forms you keep giving me? *Patient complains about the activity (confrontation marker).*

T: I'm willing to try that. I think that could be really useful. I'd be interested to see what you've been writing in your journal. *Therapist changes the task.*

In the next vignette (see www.therapeutic-alliance.org/mixed-3.html), a therapist employs more expressive resolution strategies that lead to recognition of how his patient's underlying wish and fear of being an empowered woman emerged in the interaction. A patient begins a session sharing her excitement about seeing a popular performer make a provocative gesture on television in front of millions of viewers. The therapist (T) says that he did not see the performance. The patient (P) responds with a confrontation:

P: Yeah, I should have expected this from you . . . you don't care about the things that matter . . . to me.

T: So . . .

P: Not happy with you.

T: Can you say that a little more . . .

P: NO!

T (Pause). You know I'm really hesitant to say anything right now. *Therapist metacommunicates about his internal experience.* Can I ask what's going on? *Therapist explores patient's immediate experience.*

P: Umm, I feel, I feel a little shaky, I feel a little, like, startled.

T: Can you say a little bit more about the shakiness?

P: I mean, you just got a taste of, it's kind of, the kind of anger that I have . . . I don't think I wanted you to see that.

T: I get the sense that I disappointed you in some way, and I do want to talk about that more, but I want to focus right now on the shakiness, and my sense of you feeling uncomfortable about expressing your anger and your disappointment. *Therapist acknowledges disappointment and then focuses on anxiety.*

P: I mean, I don't know what happens next when I feel like I want to apologize, but I felt really hurt, too. Umm, I think maybe I'm mostly embarrassed. I was out of control so quickly, so out of . . . it's not the kind of, in the real world that's not the kind of behavior, I guess . . . I don't . . . it gets in my way sometimes, I'm sure you can imagine. It's really the frustrating thing about . . .

T: I guess, I have a sense of fear of its impact on me, and how I see that, is that fair?

P: When we started working together, remember, you, that was, you had to consider, it made sense. It was some of the things that I shared about myself, how I can be difficult. And, umm, but I think that, I don't want to lose this, this work together.

T: So, help me, I don't want to put words in your mouth. I have the sense that you're afraid it was too much? And that I might reject you, because of that reaction?

P: I don't know the rules, but if it was my, if I was running this show, I don't know that I would tolerate that, that sort of that like direct anger from a patient.

T: So some concern that it's too much, but I do have a sense that I disappoint you, there's a sense of hurt. Can you say more about that aspect of it? *Therapist returns to disappointment.*

P: I feel, I felt, I feel, sometimes that you maybe don't notice some of the things that are important to me that I share, or how important they are. And, and that was an important story to me . . . I think it reminded me of times that I feel that you are caring about me, the way that, maybe not, taking me seriously enough or something. *Patient expresses underlying wish.*

T: I get that, I get that. Are you willing to go into how that all of that was important to you, at this point?

P: Something about the, the just audacity, something about the, the just, seemed like almost spontaneous—I know it's planned, but the fact she could be so bold, and then, there's no shame about it afterward. That's just very, I see her as a very empowered woman, and I think that, that's pretty cool.

T: Yeah.

P: I don't know if I could do that, or get away with it.

T: I get the significance of it, but I get also the anxiety about it too, the impulse to be like, that strong, and I have a sense that that just played out between the two of us. Does that make sense? *Therapist recognizes patient's wish—and fear.*

P: Yeah.

LANDMARK STUDIES

A number of pivotal studies in the rupture literature have applied the task analysis paradigm to develop and test models of the rupture resolution process. We begin with a review of several of these studies and then summarize two randomized controlled trials (RCTs, both included in the subsequent meta-analysis) examining the effect of ruptures and repair on psychotherapy outcome.

Task analysis combines quantitative and qualitative research methods to construct a model and then progressively refines that model based on empirical data (e.g., Rice & Greenberg, 1984; Safran et al., 1988). In a series of task-analytic studies, Safran and Muran (1996; Safran et al., 1990, 1994) developed a four-stage model of the rupture resolution process: (a) the therapist recognizes and draws the patient's attention to the rupture; (b) the patient and therapist explore the rupture collaboratively; (c) if the patient becomes uncomfortable exploring the rupture, the therapist encourages an exploration of the patient's avoidance maneuvers and their function; and (d) the therapist and patient focus on clarifying the patient's core relational wish or fear that underlies the rupture.

In confrontation ruptures, there is typically a progression from feelings of anger, to feelings of disappointment with the therapist, to becoming aware of feelings of vulnerability and the wish to be seen and nurtured. The resolution of withdrawal ruptures usually involves moving from qualified to increasingly clearer expressions of self-assertion, as the patient is able to tell the therapist what he or she needs. Rupture repairs will often involve cycling between these stages multiple times, and efforts to resolve one rupture may lead to additional ruptures as the patient and therapist negotiate their respective needs for agency and relatedness.

Several task analyses have refined models of resolution in different treatments and with different populations. All the models have supported an association between resolving alliance ruptures and good outcome, but they differ in several ways, prominently including whether ruptures are best addressed directly or indirectly by the therapist. Task analyses of rupture repair in interpersonal-psychodynamic therapy with depressed patients (Agnew et al., 1994), cognitive analytic therapy with patients with borderline personality disorder (Bennett et al., 2006; Daly et al., 2010), and emotion-focused therapy with couples (Swank & Wittenborn, 2013) all feature acknowledgment and collaborative exploration of the rupture as the initial steps in the resolution process. However, task analyses of CBT for depression (Aspland et al., 2008) and CBT for borderline personality disorder (Cash et al., 2014) concluded that direct acknowledgement of the rupture was not necessary. In these models, therapists resolved ruptures by responsively changing the topic of discussion or the therapy task toward the patient's concerns—for example, by letting go of the next item on the therapist's agenda to explore the issue that was most salient for the client at that moment.

Several RCTs have now examined the impact of rupture repairs on psychotherapy outcome. One of these compared the efficacy of an integrative relational therapy, cognitive therapy, and short-term dynamic therapy with personality disordered patients (Muran et al., 2005). Patients and therapists completed the Post-Session Questionnaire (Muran, et al., 1992) after every session. In this treatment study, higher rupture intensity as reported by both patients and therapists was associated with poor outcome on measures of interpersonal functioning, and failure to resolve these ruptures was predictive of dropout (Muran et al., 2009).

Another pivotal study established the probable causal role of rupture repairs on client outcome. The study of 84 clients seen in a university outpatient clinic (Chen et al., 2018) identified alliance ruptures based on fluctuations in patient alliance ratings across sessions and also examined changes in therapist alliance ratings as an index of therapist recognition of ruptures. Therapist perception of a rupture in one session was positively associated with clients' alliance ratings in the next session, even when no rupture occurred according to client ratings. The researchers also found an interaction between therapist recognition of ruptures and ratings of client functioning, such that ruptures were linked to decreases in subsequent client reports of functioning when therapists did not recognize the rupture, but when therapists recognized the rupture, client ruptures were unrelated to subsequent client functioning. These findings provide evidence that therapist recognition of ruptures is a critical component of successful rupture resolution and positive outcome.

RESULTS OF PREVIOUS META-ANALYSIS

In our prior review of the alliance rupture literature (Safran et al., 2011), we conducted two meta-analyses. The first examined studies of the relation between the presence of rupture-repair episodes and treatment outcome. This analysis of three studies that identified ruptures and repairs based on fluctuations in alliance scores yielded a moderate effect size ($r = .24$, $z = 3.06$, 95% confidence interval [CI] = .09–.39, $p = .002$, $N = 148$), indicating that the presence of rupture-repair episodes was positively related to good outcome. The second meta-analysis examined the impact of rupture resolution training or supervision on patient outcome in eight studies. Both pre–post ($r = .65$, $z = 5.56$, 95% CI = .46–.78, $p < .001$, $N = 217$) and group contrast effect sizes ($r = .15$, $z = 2.66$, 95% CI .04–.26, $p = .01$, $N = 343$) revealed that rupture resolution training was associated with significant patient improvement.

META-ANALYTIC REVIEW

We again conducted two meta-analyses: One focused on alliance ruptures, repairs, and outcome, and the second focused on rupture resolution training.

Search Strategies

In an effort to capture all relevant studies, including studies we may have missed in our prior review, we set fewer limits on our literature search. We did not limit our search to studies published in English, nor to studies of only individual therapy with adults. In addition to the primary systematic search described here, which was conducted by the first author, supplementary searches were conducted by the second author and by an advanced graduate student. The contributions of these additional searches are noted.

The primary search involved a computerized search of the PsycINFO database. Using the search terms *alliance* and *rupture, alliance patterns,* and *alliance* (must be mentioned in the abstract) and *outcome,* a list of 1,749 peer-reviewed publications was generated on July 24, 2017. Removal of duplicates resulted in 1,700 publications. We also conducted a PsycINFO search of publications that cited our prior meta-analysis in both forms in which it was published (Safran et al., 2011a, 2011b). This yielded an additional 159 studies, resulting in a total of 1,859 publications. Finally, to ensure that we included studies that have been published in advance form online but had not yet appeared in a journal volume or in PsycINFO, we conducted a search of advance online publications in the journal *Psychotherapy Research* and identified five additional publications. The independent searches of the second author and the graduate research assistant yielded 15 additional studies.

The abstracts of these publications were inspected for studies meeting the following criteria: (a) the publication must concern the alliance in psychotherapy (as opposed to other settings such as primary medical care or schools); (b) the publication must be an empirical study with quantitative measures of treatment or session-level outcome, not a review or theoretical paper; and (c) the study must investigate either alliance ruptures, identified using quantitative criteria, or rupture resolution training, which must feature a specific focus on helping therapists manage alliance ruptures and include a comparison group.

To capture all studies of alliance fluctuations that can be identified as ruptures and repairs, we also included any study with multiple (three or more) measurements of the alliance across therapy, even if that study did not specifically use the term *rupture* in the title or abstract. Our hope was to capture studies that identified ruptures but possibly used other terms (e.g., alliance weakenings) to describe them. We chose a minimum of three alliance measurements because this is necessary for identifying a V-shaped high-low-high pattern. In cases in which we could not tell from the abstract whether or not the alliance was rated at least three times, we erred on the side of inclusivity and selected the study.

These cumulative selection processes yielded 388 studies that underwent full-text review. Based on this review, 17 studies were selected for inclusion in the meta-analyses, and 371 studies were rejected. Reasons for rejection were as follows: the study did not include a quantitative measurement of ruptures or rupture resolution training (339); the study did not link rupture-repair or rupture resolution training to outcome (17); the study used the same dataset as another study in the meta-analysis (5); the study was a task analysis or case study (6); the study provided rupture resolution training but lacked a bona fide comparison group (3); and the study did not report information needed to calculate effect sizes (1).

Coding Studies

We received additional data necessary for calculating effect sizes from the authors of five studies. In addition, we utilized data obtained previously from the author of one of the studies included in our prior meta-analysis (Safran et al., 2011). Finally, we included data from two studies that were in preparation (Eubanks, Lubitz, et al., 2018, Lipner et al., 2018) and were conducted by our research team. These two studies had 10 overlapping cases, so effect sizes were recalculated excluding those 10 cases from Lipner et al. (2018) to ensure that no cases would be included twice in the meta-analysis. In sum, our search efforts yielded 11 studies that were selected for inclusion in the meta-analysis of ruptures, repairs, and outcome and 6 studies for the analysis of rupture resolution training.

Studies that met inclusion criteria were coded for the following: descriptive study information and sample characteristics including type of treatment, length of treatment, prevalence of personality disorder diagnoses in the sample, method used to measure alliance ruptures and repairs, timing of measurement of alliance ruptures and repairs, number of patients, number of therapists, comparison groups, frequency of ruptures and repairs in the sample, and data for the calculation of effect sizes. All studies were coded by the first author, and 58% of randomly selected studies were coded by an additional coder, either the second author or a graduate research assistant. Coders showed a high level of agreement (95.4%) across all variables. Differences were resolved through discussion and consensus.

Data Analysis

Effect sizes were recalculated for all studies. Standardized mean differences were calculated based on means and standard deviations or F ratios provided in the articles or directly from the authors. These standardized mean scores were then converted into r and d effect sizes. When studies reported more than one measure of treatment outcome, effect sizes were calculated for each outcome measure and then averaged to form one effect size per study. Comprehensive Meta-Analysis Version 3.3.07 was used for all analyses using random effect models.

When studies reported findings for more than one comparison group, we selected one comparison group to focus on. Specifically, for the analysis of ruptures, repairs, and outcome, some studies compared patients with rupture-repair episodes to patients without rupture-repair episodes, thereby lumping together patients with unrepaired ruptures and patients with no ruptures. Other studies distinguished between repaired, unrepaired, and no rupture groups. To highlight the clinical importance of repairing a rupture over against leaving it unrepaired, we chose to focus on the comparison between repaired and unrepaired ruptures. However, we also ran analyses comparing patients with repaired ruptures to patients with no ruptures and report those findings here.

For the analysis of six studies of rupture resolution training, two of the studies compared three different training conditions: Bambling and associates (2006) compared alliance process-focused supervision, alliance skill-focused supervision, and no supervision; and Muran and associates (2005) compared an alliance-focused integrative treatment model, brief relational therapy (BRT), to a CBT and to a short-term dynamic therapy. As the majority of studies compared a more process-focused approach to addressing alliance ruptures to non-alliance-focused conditions, we selected the comparison between process-focused supervision and no supervision from Bambling et al. for inclusion in the meta-analysis. Given that more studies in the meta-analysis examined the addition of alliance-focused training to a CBT treatment than a psychodynamic treatment, we chose to select the comparison between BRT and CBT from the Muran et al. (2005) study. In addition, we did not include Stevens et al. (2007), which was in our prior meta-analysis, because that dataset is a subset of the dataset in another, included study (Muran et al., 2005, 2009).

Results: Ruptures, Repairs, and Outcome

We examined the association between alliance rupture-repair and outcome in the 11 studies that provided sufficient data for this analysis. These studies, involving 1,314 patients, consisted of investigations of the relation between rupture resolution (measured by self-report or observer coding) and outcome (operationalized as completion of therapy vs. premature dropout or as change in symptom measures from intake to termination), studies that compared the outcomes of patients with rupture-repair episodes to patients who did not have rupture-repair episodes, and studies that compared the outcomes of patients with rupture-repair episodes to patients with ruptures that were not repaired. Figure 16.1 summarizes the effect sizes of these studies.

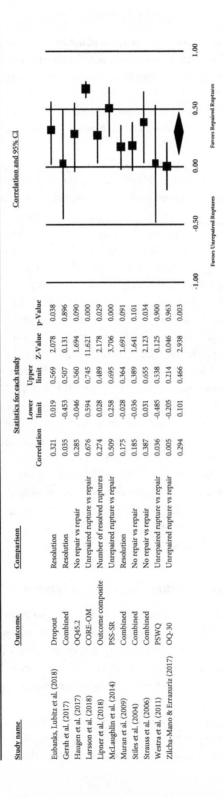

| Study name | Outcome | Comparison | Statistics for each study | | | | | Correlation and 95% CI |
			Correlation	Lower limit	Upper limit	Z-Value	p-Value	
Eubanks, Lubitz et al. (2018)	Dropout	Resolution	0.321	0.019	0.569	2.078	0.038	
Gersh et al. (2017)	Combined	Resolution	0.035	-0.453	0.507	0.131	0.896	
Haugen et al. (2017)	OQ45.2	No repair vs repair	0.285	-0.046	0.560	1.694	0.090	
Larsson et al. (2018)	CORE-OM	Unrepaired rupture vs repair	0.676	0.594	0.745	11.621	0.000	
Lipner et al. (2018)	Outcome composite	Number of resolved ruptures	0.274	0.028	0.489	2.178	0.029	
McLaughlin et al. (2014)	PSS-SR	Unrepaired rupture vs repair	0.509	0.258	0.695	3.706	0.000	
Muran et al. (2009)	Combined	Resolution	0.175	-0.028	0.364	1.691	0.091	
Stiles et al. (2004)	Combined	No repair vs repair	0.185	-0.036	0.389	1.641	0.101	
Strauss et al. (2006)	Combined	No repair vs repair	0.387	0.031	0.655	2.123	0.034	
Westra et al. (2011)	PSWQ	Unrepaired rupture vs repair	0.036	-0.485	0.538	0.125	0.900	
Zilcha-Mano & Errazuriz (2017)	OQ-30	Unrepaired rupture vs repair	0.005	-0.205	0.214	0.046	0.963	
			0.294	0.101	0.466	2.938	0.003	

FIGURE 16.1 Rupture repair and outcome effect sizes.

The meta-analysis yielded an effect size of $r = .29$, $d=.62$, $z = 2.94$, 95% CI = $.10-.47$, $p = .003$, indicating a statistically significant, moderate relation between rupture resolution and positive patient outcome. The *fail-safe N* was 180. (As noted, given that some studies included comparisons across three types of cases—repaired ruptures, unrepaired ruptures, and no ruptures—we also ran the analysis using the comparison of patients with rupture-repair episodes to patients with no ruptures, and obtained similar results, $r =. 24$, $d = .50$, $z = 4.33$, 95% CI = $.13-.34$, $p < .001$).

There was significant heterogeneity across the mean weighted effect sizes, $Q(10) = 62.95$, $p < .001$, $I^2 = 84.12$. We examined a number of potential moderators that might explain this variability.

Patient Characteristics

Some research has found that patients with personality disorders report greater rupture intensity than patients without personality disorders (Tufekcioglu et al., 2013). We examined the impact of patient personality disorder diagnosis in two ways. First, we grouped studies according to whether the majority of patients in the sample had a personality disorder diagnosis or not and found that those groups did not differ significantly, $Q(1) = .23$, $p = .63$. Second, we entered percentage of patients with a personality disorder diagnosis as a continuous variable in a meta-regression and again found that personality disorder diagnosis was not a significant moderator, $Q(1) = .1.76$, $p = .18$.

Therapist Characteristics

Some studies in the sample included trainee therapists, while others included experienced therapists. We examined therapist experience as a moderator by grouping studies according to whether they used a majority trainee sample of therapists or not and found that studies employing primarily trainees did not significantly differ from studies of more experienced therapists, $Q(1)= .03$, $p = .86$. We also used a meta-regression to examine the ratio of the number of patients to the number of therapists (see Del Re et al., 2012) and found that this was not a significant moderator, $Q(1) = .00$, $p = .94$.

Treatment Characteristics

We grouped studies according to whether the treatment was more closely aligned with CBT or with psychodynamic therapy and found no significant differences, $Q(1) = .60$, $p = .444$. We also examined the length of the treatment protocol via meta-regression and found that it was not a significant moderator, $Q(1) = .02$, $p = .88$. Given that several of the studies in this sample were from our own research team, we also compared studies from our research team to studies by other researchers and did not find a significant difference, $Q(1) = .22$, $p = .64$.

Methods for Identifying Ruptures

Finally, we compared the effect sizes for studies that identified ruptures directly (e.g., via self-report or observer coding) to those that measured ruptures indirectly (via fluctuations in alliance scores) and did not find a significant difference, $Q(1)= .75, p= .39$. We also examined whether studies used an observer-based measure of ruptures or not and found that this was not a significant moderator, $Q(1) = .10, p = .75$. We grouped studies according to whether or not they compared rupture-repair cases to cases without rupture repair and found that this was not a significant moderator, $Q(1)=.09, p= .76$.

We examined the timing of rupture measurement by comparing the effect sizes of studies that examined ruptures early in treatment to studies that examined ruptures across the entire treatment. This comparison approached significance, $Q(1) = 3.33, p =.07$. Studies that measured ruptures and repairs early in treatment had a weaker relationship between rupture-repair and outcome, $r =.13, z = 1.90, p = .06$, than studies that identified ruptures and repairs across therapy, $r = .38, z = 3.13, p = .002$. This finding suggests that, as one might expect, measuring ruptures and repairs closer to the end of treatment results in a stronger relationship between rupture-repair and outcome. The timing of rupture measurement is particularly important because when ruptures are measured early, it is impossible to know whether they were later resolved.

Results: Rupture Resolution Training and Patient Outcome

Our second meta-analysis examined the impact of rupture resolution training or supervision on patient outcome. This encompassed six studies and approximately 276 trainee/supervisees. The effect sizes of these studies are shown in Figure 16.2. The aggregated correlation was $r =.11, d =.22, z = 1.08$, 95% CI = $-.09–.30, p = .28$, suggesting that rupture resolution training did not have a significant impact on patient outcomes in the present sample. Of course, with a larger number of studies and greater power, such a modest effect may have proven statistically significant, as it was in our previous meta-analysis.

Mean weighted effect sizes across the six studies were significantly heterogeneous, $Q(5) = 17.19, p = .004, I^2 = 70.92$. Thus we examined several potential moderators (patient, trainee/therapist, and training characteristics) that might explain this variability.

Patient Characteristics

When we grouped studies according to whether the majority of patients in the sample had a personality disorder diagnosis or not, we found a difference in effect size approaching significance, $Q(1) = 3.31, p = .07$. We entered the percentage of patients in the study with a personality disorder diagnosis as a continuous variable in a meta-regression and found that personality disorder diagnosis was a significant moderator, $B= -.007, SE = .0021$, 95% CI = $-.0106,- -.0024, z = -3.12, p = .002$. The greater the

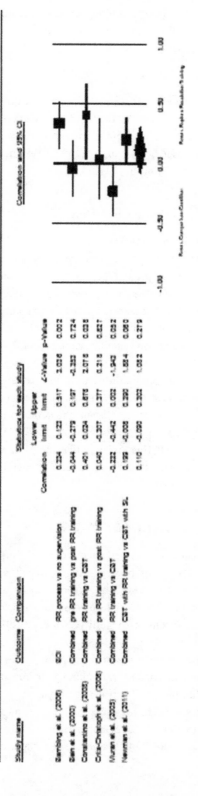

FIGURE 16.2 Rupture resolution training and outcome effect sizes.

percentage of patients with personality disorder diagnoses, the smaller the correlation between rupture resolution training and patient outcome.

Trainee Characteristics

The ratio of the number of patients to the number of therapist trainees was not a significant moderator, $Q(1) = .21, p = .64$. As some studies had different therapist trainees in the rupture resolution condition than in the control condition, while other studies had the same therapist trainees in both conditions, we also examined this variable as a possible moderator. It was not significant, $Q(1) = .12, p = .73$.

Training Characteristics

When we grouped studies according to whether the rupture resolution training condition was more closely aligned with CBT or with psychodynamic therapy, we found a significant difference, $Q(1) = 13.57, p < .001$. For more CBT treatments, rupture resolution training was associated with better patient outcome, $r = .28, z = 3.96, p < .001$. For more psychodynamic treatments, the association between rupture resolution training and outcome was lower and not statistically significant, $r = -.12, z = 1.36, p = .17$.

The length of the treatment was also a significant moderator, $B = -.03, SE = .007, 95\%$ $CI = -.04 - -.01$, $z = -3.86, p = .0001$, such that the briefer the treatment, the stronger the correlation between rupture resolution training and patient outcome. However, when we entered both theoretical orientation and treatment length into the same meta-regression, neither predictor was significant (theoretical orientation: $B = .07, SE = .22, 95\% CI = -.36 - .51, z = .34, p = .74$; treatment length: $B = -.02, SE = .01, 95\% CI = -.05 - .005, z = -1.60, p = .11$). This indicates that these variables share variance, which is consistent with the fact that CBT in this set of studies was generally shorter than the psychodynamic treatment.

EVIDENCE FOR CAUSALITY

To date, the research literature on alliance ruptures and repairs is primarily correlational, demonstrating associations between rupture repair and better outcome. Increasingly sophisticated strategies such as lagged analyses to examine relations between therapist and patient alliance and outcome ratings over time are yielding stronger evidence for causality. One such study (Chen et al., 2018) was described in the Landmark Studies section.

There have been creative efforts to find stronger evidence for a causal connection between rupture resolution and outcome by examining the impact of alliance-focused treatment or training within therapeutic dyads, thereby controlling for many patient and therapist characteristics. An evidence-based case study of an adapted form of BRT for patients with anorexia (Satir et al., 2011) employed an ABCB design (no treatment-BRT-behavior change treatment-BRT) to compare the rupture resolution-focused approach to behavior change treatment within one therapeutic dyad. The patient's caloric intake increased during rupture resolution episodes, which only occurred during the alliance-focused periods of the study.

A recent study (Muran et al., 2018) assessed the additive effect of alliance focused training (AFT) on CBT for personality disorders. To control for therapist and patient individual differences, as well as the possibility that any improvements in therapeutic process could be due to therapist trainee maturation, a multiple baseline design was used. Therapists began conducting a case in CBT with CBT supervision. Therapists were randomly assigned to switch from CBT supervision to AFT after either 8 or 16 sessions. This design permitted identification of changes in interpersonal process as measured by the Structural Analysis of Social Behavior (Benjamin, 1974) following the switch from CBT to AFT. As predicted, after switching from CBT to AFT, therapist trainees demonstrated decreases in blaming behaviors (e.g., criticizing the patient) and directiveness (e.g., directing the patient how to behave), and patients demonstrated complementary decreases in dependent behaviors (e.g., following, accepting, and relying on the direction of the other). Both therapists and patients demonstrated increases in expressiveness (e.g., disclosing, expressing one's innermost self) and affirming behaviors (e.g., understanding the other, providing emotional support, and encouraging autonomy) following the switch from CBT to AFT. Analyses indicated that several of the changes in therapist behavior were linked to positive treatment outcome.

PATIENT CONTRIBUTIONS

As bidirectional processes, alliance ruptures and their repair obviously involve patients; without patients, there is no rupture or repair. Increased incidence or intensity of alliance ruptures has been linked to patient's preoccupied attachment style (Eames & Roth, 2000), having a personality disorder diagnosis (Coutinho, Ribeiro, Fernandes, et al., 2014; Tufekcioglu et al., 2013), core conflictual relationship themes involving negative views of self and other (Wiseman & Tishby, 2017), and ambivalence about change (Hunter et al., 2014). In our second meta-analysis, the greater the percentage of patients with personality disorders, the smaller the correlation between rupture resolution training and patient outcome.

However, there is little to no research on how patients contribute to rupture repairs. A qualitative study of clients' retrospective recall of times when they felt misunderstood by their therapists (Rhodes et al., 1994) found that client assertion of negative feelings, rather than therapist exploration, was the first step in the process of repair. The authors noted that this study was based solely on patients' perspectives and that therapists may view the repair process differently. More research is needed to identify how patients facilitate the resolution of alliance ruptures.

Based on our experience with rupture repair research and training over the past 35 years, we believe that patients best suited to contribute to such repairs are those who are highly motivated for treatment and/or who feel that they have a strong bond with the therapist. Rupture resolution can be a challenging and uncomfortable process; patients have to be committed to the therapy and/or the therapist in order to tolerate their anxiety and actively engage in addressing a rupture. In addition, patient qualities such as psychological mindedness and relative nondefensiveness prove facilitative.

DIVERSITY CONSIDERATIONS

The studies included in our meta-analytic reviews did not examine the role of diversity in the occurrence of alliance ruptures, repairs, or rupture resolution training. The theoretical and clinical literature on alliance ruptures (e.g., Muran, 2007) has noted that differences between patients and therapists in gender, race, religion, sexual orientation, and socioeconomic class can contribute to alliance ruptures, but the research has not yet systematically addressed these questions.

Metacommunication can help therapists to disentangle themselves from a rupture and gain the distance and perspective they need to recognize and explore how differences between themselves and their patients are contributing to a problem in the alliance. For example, a young White female therapist becomes frustrated as she tries to help her older African American male patient identify how his cognitive biases shape his perception of a recent experience at work. The therapist metacommunicates to the patient that she feels they are locked in a power struggle and asks if they can explore what is happening between them. By stepping out of the conflict over the therapeutic task, the therapist is able to reflect on her feelings of frustration. The therapist realizes that she felt that her patient was dismissing her in a patronizing manner, a feeling that she had experienced before in interactions with some older male colleagues. At the same time, as she listens to the patient's view of their interaction, she realizes that she had failed to appreciate the patient's experience with racism at his workplace; she was inadvertently recreating this experience in therapy by being yet another White person who invalidated his perspective.

Some researchers specifically refer to microaggressions, or disrespectful, insulting, dismissive communications about another individual's cultural group, as cultural ruptures (e.g., Hook et al., 2017). A survey of clients at a university counseling center (Owen et al., 2010) found that female clients' perceptions of microaggressions were related to lower alliance ratings and poorer therapy outcome. A similar study (Owen et al., 2014) of racial and ethnic minority clients at a university counseling center found that 53% of clients reported experiencing microaggressions from their therapist in the course of treatment, and in most cases (76%) the microaggression was not discussed. Clients who reported that they discussed the microaggression experience with their therapists had alliance scores comparable to clients who did not perceive microaggressions. A survey of lesbian, gay, and bisexual clients found that 21% reported that their therapist was either dismissive of their sexual orientation or viewed it as a problem (Kelley, 2015). These studies underscore the need for all therapists to be attuned and responsive to cultural ruptures. The nascent research also highlights the potential value of drawing on rupture resolution strategies to address and explore cultural ruptures (Gaztambide, 2012; Spengler et al., 2016).

LIMITATIONS OF THE RESEARCH

The alliance rupture literature has grown since our previous meta-analyses (Safran et al., 2011); however, its primary limitation continues to be its relatively small size. There are many studies that include a single rating of the alliance, as if the alliance were a stable trait in treatment. However, the alliance has both state and trait-like components (Zilcha-Mano, 2017), which necessitates study designs that assess alliance ruptures and repairs throughout treatment.

Our literature search underscored the many missed opportunities for alliance rupture research. As a case in point, our full-text article search yielded over 200 studies that measured the alliance at three or more time points but did not examine the possibility of alliance ruptures. The increased use of measurement of the alliance and outcome at every session as well as observer-based measures of alliance ruptures will provide opportunities to garner stronger evidence of causality by examining how alliance ruptures and repairs in one session, or in one part of a session, may be linked to changes later in treatment.

Studies reporting lower rates of patient-reported ruptures raise concerns that patients may be reluctant to report problems in the alliance, while high rates of observer-reported ruptures raise concerns that observers may be over-coding ruptures (see Table 16.1). More research using multiple measures of ruptures (observer and self-report) across multiple time points in therapy will also help the field to reach consensus about how best to define and operationalize ruptures and repairs. Greater diversity of patient and therapist samples will also increase our understanding of the factors that contribute to ruptures and their repair.

Alliance ruptures present research challenges because they are both obstacles and opportunities: unresolved ruptures are associated with poor outcome, but repaired ruptures are associated with good outcome. Researchers must keep this distinction in mind. Research designs that only measure ruptures early in treatment without determining whether they were later resolved, and designs that fail to distinguish between patients with unrepaired ruptures and patients with no ruptures, can generate misleading findings about the association between alliance ruptures and outcome.

As a future direction, the increased use of routine outcome monitoring systems that assess alliance and outcome at every session (e.g., Chapter 13, this volume) provide a valuable opportunity for tracking the development and resolution of ruptures across therapy. Feedback systems that provide clinical support tools for addressing alliance ruptures can be used to examine the effectiveness of therapist efforts to repair alliance ruptures.

Another important direction is more research on therapists' contributions to alliance ruptures. Therapist characteristics such as attachment style (Marmarosh et al., 2015) and relational patterns (Wiseman & Tishby, 2017) impact therapist reports of ruptures. Therapist and patient characteristics interact to shape the development of alliance ruptures. For example, a systematic case study (Schattner et al., 2017) comparing good and poor alliance cases seen by the same therapist found that in the good alliance case, the therapist's relational needs for intimacy and closeness met the patient's needs for recognition and support. In the poor alliance case, the therapist's and patient's relational patterns were in opposition to each other, with the therapist pursuing closeness while the patient perceived his efforts as intrusive.

Finally, additional research developing task-analytic models and testing them with quantitative studies will clarify which resolution strategies are most effective for specific patients and psychological treatments. Models developed in different therapy traditions can also generate new ways of addressing alliance ruptures that are unique to particular approaches. For example, a task analysis of couple therapy (Swank & Wittenborn, 2013) included the strategy of addressing a rupture with one patient by checking in with the patient's partner to understand his/her experience of the rupture and access empathy for the patient experiencing the rupture.

TRAINING IMPLICATIONS

Although our meta-analysis found limited evidence for the impact of rupture resolution training on patient outcome, there is promising evidence that alliance-focused training can lead to improvements in how therapists interact with patients (Muran et al., 2018). A critical component of alliance-focused training is increasing therapist awareness of ruptures; generally, therapists cannot resolve ruptures that they cannot recognize. As noted, therapist recognition of ruptures has been associated with improvements in client functioning, even when therapists identify ruptures that clients did not (Chen et al., 2018).

Ruptures can be emotionally challenging experiences for therapists, so supervisors need to build a strong supervisory alliance to create a safe space for trainees to share and explore their experiences of ruptures (Eubanks-Carter et al., 2015). Supervisors can model responsiveness to ruptures that emerge in the supervisory alliance, particularly as subtle, passive withdrawal in response to perceived supervisor criticism may be more common than direct confrontation (Friedlander, 2015).

Moderator analysis revealed that rupture resolution training was particularly valuable for cognitive-behavioral therapists, many of whom may not have received explicit training in processing relationship dynamics with their patients. We recommend rupture resolution training for all therapists but propose that it may be especially important for therapists with less experience and training in negotiating the therapeutic alliance.

We would argue that the aim of alliance-focused training is not to teach therapists a prescription of exactly how to handle a rupture but rather to equip them with skills that prepare them to derive their own personalized solutions to specific ruptures when they arise. Therapists need to recognize ruptures, tolerate the difficult emotions they evoke, and respond to their patients in an empathic, genuine, flexible way. The training techniques we use to facilitate these skills include videotape analysis of rupture moments, awareness-oriented role plays, and mindfulness training. Videotape analysis should focus on closely attending to moments of rupture and encouraging trainees to become more aware and accepting of what they were experiencing during the rupture.

Awareness-oriented role plays in which trainees take turns playing the roles of patient and therapist can help them to become more aware of feelings that were contributing to the rupture and to actively engage with any concerns they have about addressing the rupture with the patient. We encourage trainees to develop mindfulness practices, and we incorporate mindfulness exercises into supervision sessions to enhance trainees' ability to attend to the here and now with an attitude of curiosity and nonjudgmental acceptance. In addition to these key features, alliance-focused training can also include readings, watching tapes of experienced therapists, and training in process measures such as the 3RS.

THERAPEUTIC PRACTICES

The research reviewed in this chapter demonstrates that alliance rupture repair is associated with positive outcome. Next we describe research-supported practices for addressing and repairing ruptures in the alliance.

- Be attuned to indications of ruptures in the therapeutic relationship. Be alert to the presence of markers of confrontation ruptures, in which patients express dissatisfaction or hostility, as well as more subtle markers of withdrawal, which may take the form of patients evading or appeasing the therapist in an effort to move away from the therapist or the work of therapy.
- Acknowledge the rupture directly, and openly and nondefensively invite patients to explore their experience of the rupture. If the bond is not strong enough for a direct exploration of the rupture, or if direct exploration would take the focus away from a therapeutic task that needs to be prioritized to alleviate symptoms that are causing the patient great distress, then address ruptures in an indirect, immediate manner by responsively changing the tasks or goals of therapy in the direction of the patient's concerns.
- Empathize with patients' expression of negative feelings about the therapist or the therapy. Validate them for broaching a difficult and potentially divisive topic in the session.
- Accept responsibility for one's own participation in the rupture, and do not blame patients for misunderstanding or failing to comply with the therapist's wishes.
- Consider linking ruptures in session to interpersonal patterns in the patient's life outside of sessions to engage a patient who is withdrawing from a focus on the rupture. At the same time, be alert to the possibility that you—and your patients—may feel pulled to link the rupture to other relationships to escape a painful exploration of how the therapist is disappointing the patient.
- Anticipate that ruptures can evoke feelings of confusion, ambivalence, incompetence, and guilt in some therapists. Develop your abilities to recognize, tolerate, validate, and empathically explore your own negative feelings so that you can do the same for your patients.

REFERENCES

References marked with an asterisk indicate studies included in the meta-analyses.

Agnew, R. M., Harper, H., Shapiro, D. A., & Barkham, M. (1994). Resolving a challenge to the therapeutic relationship: A single case study. *British Journal of Medical Psychology, 67*, 155–170. https://www.doi.org/10.1111/j.2044-8341.1994.tb01783.x

Agnew-Davies, R., Stiles, W. B., Hardy, G. E., Barkham, M., & Shapiro, D. A. (1998). Alliance structure assessed by the Agnew Relationship Measure (ARM). *British Journal of Clinical Psychology, 37*, 155–172. https://www.doi.org/10.1111/j.2044-8260.1998.tb01291.x

Aspland, H., Llewelyn, S., Hardy, G. E., Barkham, M., & Stiles, W. (2008). Alliance ruptures and rupture resolution in cognitive-behavior therapy: A preliminary task analysis. *Psychotherapy Research, 18*, 699–710. https://www.doi.org/10.1080/10503300802291463

*Bambling, M., King, R., Raue, P., Schweittzer, R., & Lambert, W. (2006). Clinical supervision: Its influence on client-rated working alliance and client symptom reduction in the brief treatment of major depression. *Psychotherapy Research, 16*, 317–331. https://www.doi.org/10.1080/10503300500268524

Beck, J. S. (2011). *Cognitive behavior therapy: Basics and beyond* (2nd ed.). New York, NY: Guilford.

Beebe, B., & Lachmann, F. M. (2002). *Infant research and adult treatment: Co-constructing interactions. Infant research and adult treatment: Co-constructing interactions*. New York, NY: Analytic Press/Taylor & Francis.

*Bein, E., Anderson, T., Strupp, H., Henry, W. P., Schacht, T. E., Binder, J., & Butler, S. (2000). The effects of training in Time-Limited Dynamic Psychotherapy: Changes in therapeutic outcome. *Psychotherapy Research, 10*(2), 119–132. https://www.doi.org/10.1080/713663669

Benjamin, L. S. (1974). Structural analysis of social behavior. *Psychological Review, 81*, 392–425. https://www.doi.org/10.1037/h0037024

Bennett, D., Parry, G., & Ryle, A. (2006). Resolving threats to the therapeutic alliance in cognitive analytic therapy of borderline personality disorder: A task analysis. *Psychology and Psychotherapy: Theory, Research, and Practice, 79*, 395–418. https://www.doi.org/10.1348/147608305X58355

Bordin, E. (1979). The generalizability of the psychoanalytic concept of the working alliance. *Psychotherapy: Theory, Research and Practice, 16*, 252–260. https://www.doi.org/10.1037/h0085885

Boritz, T., Barnhart, R., Eubanks, C. F., & McMain, S. (2018). Alliance rupture and resolution in dialectical behavior therapy for borderline personality disorder. *Journal of Personality Disorders, 32*, 115–128.

Botella, L., Corbella, S., Belles, L., Pacheco, M., Gömez, A. M., Herrero, O., . . . Pedro, N. (2008). Predictors of therapeutic outcome and process. *Psychotherapy Research, 18*, 535–542. https://www.doi.org/10.1080/10503300801982773

Cash, S. K., Hardy, G. E., Kellett, S., & Parry, G. (2014). Alliance ruptures and resolution during cognitive behaviour therapy with patients with borderline personality disorder. *Psychotherapy Research, 24*(2), 132–145. https://www.doi.org/10.1080/10503307.2013.838652

Chen, R., Atzil-Slonim, D., Bar-Kalifa, E., Hasson-Ohayon, I., & Refaeli, E. (2018). Therapists' recognition of alliance ruptures as a moderator of change in alliance and symptoms. *Psychotherapy Research, 28*(4), 560–570. https://www.doi.org/10.1080/10503307.2016.1227104

Colli, A., Gentile, D., Condino, V., & Lingiardi, V. (2017). Assessing alliance ruptures and resolutions: Reliability and validity of the Collaborative Interactions Scale–revised version. *Psychotherapy Research.* [Advance online publication] https://www.doi.org/10.1080/10503307

Colli, A., & Lingiardi, V. (2009). The Collaborative Interactions Scale: A new transcript-based method for the assessment of the therapeutic alliance ruptures and resolutions in psychotherapy. *Psychotherapy Research, 19,* 718–734. https://www.doi.org/10.1080/10503300903121098

*Constantino, M. J., Marnell, M. E., Haile, A. J., Kanther-Sista, S. N., Wolman, K., Zappert, L., & Arnow, B. A. (2008). Integrative cognitive therapy for depression: A randomized pilot comparison. *Psychotherapy: Theory, Research, Practice, Training, 45,* 122–134. https://www.doi.org/10.1037/0033-3204.45.2.122

Coutinho, J., Ribeiro, E., Fernandes, C., Sousa, I., & Safran, J. D. (2014). The development of the therapeutic alliance and the emergence of alliance ruptures. *Anales de Psicología, 30*(3), 985–994. https://www.doi.org/10.6018/analesps.30.3.168911

Coutinho, J., Ribeiro, E., Sousa, I., & Safran, J. D. (2014). Comparing two methods of identifying alliance rupture events. *Psychotherapy, 51*(3), 434–442. https://www.doi.org/10.1037/a0032171

*Crits-Christoph, P., Gibbons, M. B., Crits-Christoph, K., Narducci, J., Schramberger, M. & Gallop, R. (2006). Can therapists be trained to improve their alliances? A preliminary study of alliance-fostering psychotherapy. *Psychotherapy Research, 16,* 268–281. https://www.doi.org/10.1080/10503300500268557

Daly, A.-M., Llewelyn, S., McDougall, E., & Chanen, A. M. (2010). Rupture resolution in cognitive analytic therapy for adolescents with borderline personality disorder. *Psychology and Psychotherapy: Theory, Research and Practice, 83*(3), 273–288. https://www.doi.org/10.1348/147608309X481036

Del Re, A. C., Flückiger, C., Horvath, A. O., Symonds, D., & Wampold, B. E. (2012). Therapist effects in the therapeutic alliance–outcome relationship: A restricted-maximum likelihood meta-analysis. *Clinical Psychology Review, 7,* 642–649. https://www.doi.org/10.1016/j.cpr.2012.07.002

Doran, J. M., Safran, J. D., Waizmann, V., Bolger, K., & Muran, J. C. (2012). The Alliance Negotiation Scale: Psychometric construction and preliminary reliability and validity analysis. *Psychotherapy Research, 22*(6), 710–719. https://www.doi.org/10.1080/10503307.2012.709326

Eames, V., & Roth, A. (2000). Patient attachment orientation and the early working alliance: A study of patient and therapist reports of alliance quality and ruptures. *Psychotherapy Research, 10,* 421–434. https://www.doi.org/10.1093/ptr/10.4.421

Eubanks, C. F., Burckell, L. A., & Goldfried, M. R. (2018). Clinical consensus strategies to repair ruptures in the therapeutic alliance. *Journal of Psychotherapy Integration, 28*(1), 60–76.

*Eubanks, C. F., Lubitz, J., Muran, J. C., & Safran, J. D. (2018). *Rupture Resolution Rating System (3RS): Development and validation. Psychotherapy Research.* Advance online publication. doi: 10.1080/10503307.2018.1552034

Eubanks, C. F., Muran, J. C., & Safran, J. D. (2015). *Rupture Resolution Rating System (3RS): Manual.* Unpublished manuscript, Mount Sinai-Beth Israel Medical Center, New York.

Eubanks-Carter, C., Gorman, B. S., & Muran, J.C. (2012). Quantitative naturalistic methods for detecting change points in psychotherapy research: An illustration with alliance ruptures. *Psychotherapy Research, 22,* 621–637. https://www.doi.org/10.1080/10503307.2012.693772

Eubanks-Carter, C., Muran, J. C., & Safran, J. D. (2010). Alliance ruptures and resolution. In J. C. Muran & J. P. Barber (Eds.), *The therapeutic alliance: An evidence-based approach to practice and training* (pp. 74–94). New York, NY: Guilford.

Eubanks-Carter, C., Muran, J. C., & Safran, J. D. (2015). Alliance-focused training. *Psychotherapy, 52,* 169–173. https://www.doi.org/10.1037/a0037596

Friedlander, M. L. (2015). Use of relational strategies to repair alliance ruptures: How responsive supervisors train responsive psychotherapists. *Psychotherapy, 53,* 214–225. https://www.doi.org/10.1037/a0037044

Friedlander, M. L., Escudero, V., Horvath, A. O., Heatherington, L., Cabero, A., & Martens, M. P. (2006). System for observing family therapy alliances: A tool for research and practice. *Journal of Counseling Psychology, 53*(2), 214–225. https://www.doi.org/10.1037/0022-0167.53.2.214

Gaztambide, D. J. (2012). Addressing cultural impasses with rupture resolution strategies: A proposal and recommendations. *Professional Psychology: Research and Practice, 43*(3), 183–189. https://www.doi.org/10.1037/a0026911

*Gersh, E., Hulbert, C. A., McKechnie, B., Ramadan, R., Worotniuk, T., & Chanen, A. M. (2017). Alliance rupture and repair processes and therapeutic change in youth with borderline personality disorder. *Psychology and Psychotherapy: Theory, Research and Practice, 90*(1), 84–104. https://www.doi.org/10.1111/papt.12097

Gülüm, I. V., Soygüt, G., & Safran, J. D. (2018). A comparison of pre-dropout and temporary rupture sessions in psychotherapy. *Psychotherapy Research, 28*(5), 685–707. https://www.doi.org/10.1080/10503307.2016.1246765

Hara, K. M., Westra, H. A., Aviram, A., Button, M. L., Constantino, M. J., & Antony, M. M. (2015). Therapist awareness of client resistance in cognitive-behavioral therapy for generalized anxiety disorder. *Cognitive Behaviour Therapy, 44*(2), 162–174. https://www.doi.org/10.1080/16506073.2014.998705

Harper, H. (1989a). *Coding guide I: Identification of confrontation challenges in exploratory therapy.* Sheffield, England: University of Sheffield.

Harper, H. (1989b). *Coding guide II: Identification of withdrawal challenges in exploratory therapy.* Sheffield, England: University of Sheffield.

*Haugen, P. T., Werth, A. S., Foster, A. L., & Owen, J. (2017). Are rupture–repair episodes related to outcome in the treatment of trauma-exposed World Trade Center responders? *Counselling and Psychotherapy Research, 17*(4), 272–282. https://www.doi.org/10.1002/capr.12138

Hill, C. E. (2010). Qualitative studies of negative experiences in psychotherapy. In J. C. Muran & J. P. Barber (Eds.), *The therapeutic alliance: An evidence-based guide to practice* (pp. 63–73). New York, NY: Guilford.

Hill, C. E., Nutt-Williams, E., Heaton, K. J., Thompson, B. J., & Rhodes, R. H. (1996). Therapist retrospective recall of impasses in long-term psychotherapy: A qualitative analysis. *Journal of Counseling Psychology, 43,* 207–217. https://www.doi.org/10.1037/0022-0167.43.2.207

Hook, J. N., Davis, D., Owen, J., & DeBlaere, C. (2017). Cultural humility and the process of psychotherapy. In J. N. Hook, D. Davis, J. Owen, & C. DeBlaere (Eds.), *Cultural humility: Engaging diverse dentities in therapy* (pp. 91–112). Washington, DC: American Psychological Association. https://www.doi.org/10.1037/0000037-005

Hunter, J. A., Button, M. L., & Westra, H. A. (2014). Ambivalence and alliance ruptures in cognitive behavioral therapy for generalized anxiety. *Cognitive Behaviour Therapy, 43,* 201–208. https://www.doi.org/10.1080/16506073.2014.899617

Kelley, F. A. (2015). The therapy relationship with lesbian and gay clients. *Psychotherapy, 52*, 113–118. https://www.doi.org/10.1037/a0037958

Kramer, U., de Roten, Y., Beretta, V., Michel, L., & Despland, J.-N. (2009). Alliance patterns over the course of short-term dynamic psychotherapy: The shape of productive relationships. *Psychotherapy Research, 19*, 699–706. https://www.doi.org/10.1080/10503300902956742

Lansford, E. (1986). Weakenings and repairs of the working alliance in short-term psychotherapy. *Professional Psychology: Research and Practice, 17*(4), 364–366. https://www.doi.org/10.1037/0735-7028.17.4.364

*Larsson, M. H., Falkenström, F., Andersson, G., & Holmqvist, R. (2018). Alliance ruptures and repairs in psychotherapy in primary care. *Psychotherapy Research, 28*(1), 123–136. https://www.doi.org/10.1080/10503307.2016.1174345

*Lipner, L., Muran, J. C., Safran, J. D., & Eubanks, C. F. (2018). *Identifying alliance ruptures and their relationship to outcome using control charts.* Manuscript in preparation.

Marmarosh, C. L., Schmidt, E., Pembleton, J., Rotbart, E., Muzyk, N., Liner, A., . . . Salmen, K. (2015). Novice therapist attachment and perceived ruptures and repairs: A pilot study. *Psychotherapy, 52*(1), 140–144. https://www.doi.org/10.1037/a0036129

*McLaughlin, A. A., Keller, S. M., Feeny, N. C., Youngstrom, E. A., & Zoellner, L. A. (2014). Patterns of therapeutic alliance: Rupture–repair episodes in prolonged exposure for posttraumatic stress disorder. *Journal of Consulting and Clinical Psychology, 82*, 112–121. https://www.doi.org/10.1037/a0034696

Muran, J.C. (Ed.). (2007). *Dialogues on difference: Diversity studies on the therapeutic relationship.* Washington, DC: APA Books.

Muran, J. C. (2019). Confessions of a New York rupture researcher: An insider's guide and critique. *Psychotherapy Research, 29*(1), 1–14. https://www.doi.org/10.1080/10503307.2017.1413261

Muran, J. C., Safran, J. D., Eubanks, C. F., & Gorman, B. S. (2018). The effect of alliance-focused training on a cognitive-behavioral therapy for personality disorders. *Journal of Consulting and Clinical Psychology, 86*(4), 384–397.

*Muran, J. C., Safran, J. D., Gorman, B. S., Samstag, L. W., Eubanks-Carter, C., & Winston, A. (2009). The relationship of early alliance ruptures and their resolution to process and outcome in three time-limited psychotherapies for personality disorders. *Psychotherapy: Theory, Research, Practice, Training, 46*, 233–248. https://www.doi.org/10.1037/a0016085

Muran, J. C., Safran, J. D., Samstag, L. W., & Winston, A. (1992). *Patient and therapist postsession questionnaires, Version 1992.* Newark, NJ: Newark Beth Israel Medical Center.

*Muran, J. C., Safran, J. D., Samstag, L. W., & Winston, A. (2005). Evaluating an alliance-focused treatment for personality disorders. *Psychotherapy: Theory, Research, Practice, Training, 42*(4), 532–545. https://www.doi.org/10.1037/0033-3204.42.4.532

*Newman, M. G., Castonguay, L. G., Borkovec, T. D., Fisher, A. J., Boswell, J. F., Szkodny, L. E., & Nordberg, S. S. (2011). A randomized controlled trial of cognitive-behavioral therapy for generalized anxiety disorder with integrated techniques from emotion-focused and interpersonal therapies. *Journal of Consulting and Clinical Psychology, 79*(2), 171–181. https://www.doi.org/10.1037/a0022489

Owen, J., Tao, K. W., Imel, Z. E., Wampold, B. E., & Rodolfa, E. (2014). Addressing racial and ethnic microaggressions in therapy. *Professional Psychology: Research and Practice, 45*(4), 283–290. https://www.doi.org/10.1037/a0037420

Owen, J., Tao, K., & Rodolfa, E. (2010). Microaggressions and women in short-term psycho-therapy: Initial evidence. *The Counseling Psychologist, 38*(7), 923–946. https://www.doi.org/10.1177/0011000010376093

Rhodes, R., Hill, C., Thompson, B., & Elliot, R. (1994). Client retrospective recall of resolved and unresolved misunderstanding events. *Journal of Counseling Psychology, 41,* 473–483. https://www.doi.org/10.1037/0022-0167.41.4.473

Ribeiro, E., Ribeiro, A. P., Gonçalves, M. M., Horvath, A. O., & Stiles, W. B. (2013). How collaboration in therapy becomes therapeutic: The therapeutic collaboration coding system. *Psychology and Psychotherapy: Theory, Research and Practice, 86,* 294–314. https://www.doi.org/10.1111/j.2044-8341.2012.02066.x

Rice, L. N., & Greenberg, L. S. (1984). *Patterns of change: Intensive analysis of psychotherapy process.* New York, NY: Guilford.

Safran, J. D., Crocker, P., McMain, S., & Murray, P. (1990). The therapeutic alliance rupture as a therapy event for empirical investigation. *Psychotherapy: Theory, Research and Practice, 27,* 154–165. https://www.doi.org/10.1037/0033-3204.27.2.154

Safran, J. D., Greenberg, L. S., & Rice, L. N. (1988). Integrating psychotherapy research and practice: Modeling the change process. *Psychotherapy, 25,* 1–17. https://www.doi.org/10.1037/h0085305

Safran, J. D., & Muran, J. C. (1996). The resolution of ruptures in the therapeutic alliance. *Journal of Counseling and Clinical Psychology, 64,* 447–458. https://www.doi.org/10.1037/0022-006X.64.3.447

Safran, J. D., & Muran, J. C. (2000). *Negotiating the therapeutic alliance: A relational treatment guide.* New York, NY: Guilford.

Safran, J. D., Muran, J. C., & Eubanks-Carter, C. (2011a). Repairing alliance ruptures. In J. C. Norcross (Ed.), *Psychotherapy relationships that work* (2nd ed., pp. 224–238). New York, NY: Oxford University Press.

Safran, J. D., Muran, J. C., & Eubanks-Carter, C. (2011b). Repairing alliance ruptures. *Psychotherapy, 48,* 80–87. https://www.doi.org/10.1037/a0022140

Safran, J. D., Muran, J. C., & Samstag, L. W. (1994). Resolving therapeutic alliance ruptures: A task analytic investigation. In A. O. Horvath & L. S. Greenberg (Eds.), *The working alliance: Theory, research, and practice* (pp. 225–255). New York, NY: Wiley.

Satir, D. A., Goodman, D. M., Shingleton, R. M., Porcerelli, J. H., Gorman, B. S., Pratt, E. M., . . . Thompson-Brenner, H. (2011). Alliance-focused therapy for anorexia nervosa: Integrative relational and behavioral change treatments in a single-case experimental design. *Psychotherapy, 48,* 401–420. https://www.doi.org/10.1037/a0026216

Schattner, E., Tishby, O., & Wiseman, H. (2017). Relational patterns and the development of the alliance: A systematic comparison of two cases. *Clinical Psychology & Psychotherapy, 24,* 555–568. https://www.doi.org/10.1002/cpp.2019

Sommerfeld, E., Orbach, I., Zim, S., & Mikulincer, M. (2008). An in-session exploration of ruptures in working alliance and their associations with clients' core conflictual relationship themes, alliance-related discourse, and clients' postsession evaluation. *Psychotherapy Research, 18,* 377–388. https://www.doi.org/10.1080/10503300701675873

Spengler, E. S., Miller, D. J., & Spengler, P. M. (2016). Microaggressions: Clinical errors with sexual minority clients. *Special Issue: Clinical Errors, 53*(3), 360–366. https://www.doi.org/10.1037/pst0000073

Stevens, C. L., Muran, J. C., Safran, J. D., Gorman, B. S., & Winston, A. (2007). Levels and patterns of the therapeutic alliance in brief psychotherapy. *American Journal of Psychotherapy, 61*, 109–129.

*Stiles, W. B., Glick, M. J., Osatuke, K., Hardy, G. E., Shapiro, D. A., & Agnew-Davies, R. (2004). Patterns of alliance development and the rupture-repair hypothesis: Are productive relationships U-shaped or V-shaped? *Journal of Counseling Psychology, 51*, 81–92. https://www.doi.org/10.1037/0022-0167.51.1.81

*Strauss, J. L., Hayes, A. M., S.L., J., Newman, C. F., Brown, G. K., Barber, J. P., . . . Beck, A. T. (2006). Early alliance, alliance ruptures, and symptom change in a nonrandomized trial of cognitive therapy for avoidant and obsessive-compulsive personality disorders. *Journal of Consulting and Clinical Psychology, 74*(2), 337–345. https://www.doi.org/10.1037/0022-006X.74.2.337

Swank, L. E., & Wittenborn, A. K. (2013). Repairing alliance ruptures in emotionally focused couple therapy: A preliminary task analysis. *American Journal of Family Therapy, 41*(5), 389–402. https://www.doi.org/10.1080/01926187.2012.726595

Tryon, G. S., Blackwell, S. C., & Hammel, E. F. (2007). A meta-analytic examination of client-therapist perspectives of the working alliance. *Psychotherapy Research, 17*(6), 629–642. https://www.doi.org/10.1080/10503300701320611

Tufekcioglu, S., Muran, J. C., Safran, J. D., & Winston, A. (2013). Personality disorder and early therapeutic alliance in two time-limited therapies. *Psychotherapy Research, 23*(6), 646–657. https://www.doi.org/10.1080/10503307.2013.843803

Westerman, M. A., Foote, J. P., & Winston, A. (1995). Change in coordination across phases of psychotherapy and outcome: Two mechanisms for the role played by patients' contribution to the alliance. *Journal of Consulting and Clinical Psychology, 63*, 672–675. https://www.doi.org/10.1037/0022-006X.63.4.672

*Westra, H. A., Constantino, M. J., & Aviram, A. (2011). The impact of alliance ruptures on client outcome expectations in cognitive behavioral therapy. *Psychotherapy Research, 21*(4), 472–481. https://www.doi.org/10.1080/10503307.2011.581708

Wiseman, H., & Tishby, O. (2017). Applying relationship anecdotes paradigm interviews to study client–therapist relationship narratives: Core conflictual relationship theme analyses. *Psychotherapy Research, 27*(3), 283–299. https://www.doi.org/10.1080/10503307.2016.1271958

*Zilcha-Mano, S., & Errázuriz, P. (2017). Early development of mechanisms of change as a predictor of subsequent change and treatment outcome: The case of working alliance. *Journal of Consulting and Clinical Psychology, 85*, 508–520. https://www.doi.org/10.1037/ccp0000192

Zilcha-Mano, S. (2017). Is the alliance really therapeutic? Revisiting this question in light of recent methodological advances. *American Psychologist, 72*(4), 311–325. https://www.doi.org/10.1037/a0040435

17

COLLECTING AND DELIVERING
CLIENT FEEDBACK

Michael J. Lambert, Jason L. Whipple, and Maria Kleinstäuber

Thousands of clinical trials and naturalistic studies have now been conducted on the effects of psychotherapy. Reviews of this research have shown that about 75% of those who enter treatment in clinical trials show benefit (Lambert, 2013). This finding generalizes across a wide range of disorders except for severe biologically based disturbances, such as bipolar disorder and schizophrenia, in which the impact of psychological treatments is secondary to the symptomatic improvement from psychoactive medication.

Meta-analyses of psychotherapy studies support the previous conclusions and provide a numerical index for overall treatment effects. Early applications of meta-analytic methods to psychotherapy (e.g., Smith et al., 1980) addressed whether or not psychotherapy was effective and provided an estimate of the size of the effect. An average effect size of .85 standard deviation units was found based on 475 studies comparing treated and untreated groups. This indicates that, by the end of treatment, the average treated person is better off than 80% of the untreated control sample. Subsequent meta-analytic findings (e.g., Shadish et al., 1997) have consistently supported the conclusion of the benefit of treatment over control for a broad variety of disorders and have determined that some disorders (e.g., phobias, panic) respond to treatment more easily than others (e.g., obsessive-compulsive disorder; Lambert, 2013).

An often ignored but critical consideration in psychotherapy is the degree to which it is not helpful or even harmful. An estimated 5% to 10% of adult clients participating in clinical trials leave treatment worse off than they began (Lambert, 2013). In routine care, the situation is frequently more problematic. Outcomes for more than 6,000 clients treated in routine practice settings suggest that clients did not fare nearly as well as those in clinical trials, with only about one-third showing improvement or recovery (Hansen et al., 2002).

The situation for child psychotherapy in routine care is even more sobering. The small body of outcome studies in community-based, usual-care settings yields a mean effect size near zero (Weisz et al., 1995, 1999), yet millions of youths are served each year in these systems of care (National Advisory Mental Health Council, 2001. In a comparison of children being treated in community mental health (N = 936) or through managed care (N = 3,075), estimates of deterioration were 24% and 14%, respectively (Warren et al., 2010).

There is no doubt that the deterioration some clients experience during the time they are in treatment is causally linked to therapist activities (Lambert et al., 1977). Certainly, a portion of clients are on a negative trajectory at the time they enter treatment, and the deteriorating course cannot be stopped. Even so, positive as well as negative client change can be affected by therapist actions and inactions. For example, some clients are prevented from taking their own lives because of effective practices, even if they do not otherwise show progress.

Although client and environmental contributions to negative outcomes explains deterioration in many cases, there is also variability in rates across individual psychotherapists. Some therapists hardly have a single client who deteriorates and others experience consistently high rates (Baldwin & Imel, 2013; Okiishi et al., 2003). Research reviews find that the major contribution of therapists to negative change is usually found in the nature of the therapeutic relationship, with rejections of either a subtle or manifest nature being the root cause (e.g., Safran et al., 2005). Research on negative outcomes often finds little of the negative change is attributed to misapplication of therapeutic techniques, while relationship factors instead loom large across treatment formats (e.g., couple, family, group, individual) and theoretical orientations (Lambert et al., 1977).

In efforts to reduce negative outcomes, methods have been proposed that involve regularly monitoring and tracking client progress with standardized self-report scales throughout the course of treatment and providing clinicians with this information before psychotherapy ends (Lambert et al., 2001; Newham et al., 2010). As contextualized feedback theory suggests (Sapyta et al., 2005), the value of monitoring and systematic feedback through session-by-session assessments hinges on the degree to which the information provided goes beyond what a clinician can observe and understand about client progress without such information. The feedback must bring value added beyond the psychotherapist's understanding of a client's well-being.

Unfortunately, clinicians tend to hold overly optimistic views of their clients' treatment progress in relation to measured change (Walfish et al., 2012). Clinicians frequently overlook negative changes and experience difficulty accurately gauging the final benefit clients will receive during treatment, particularly with clients who are failing to improve. For example, even when therapists were provided with the base rate of deterioration in their clinic (8%), and were asked to rate each client at the end of every session (on the likelihood of final treatment failure as well as if the client was worse off at the current session than at intake), they rated only 3 of 550 clients as predicted failures and seriously underestimated worse functioning for a significant portion of clients (Hannan et al., 2005). In addition, a retrospective review of case notes of clients who had deteriorated during treatment found infrequent mention of worsening, even when its degree was dramatic (Hatfield et al., 2010).

Such results are not surprising, given psychotherapist optimism about how many of their clients will experience a positive outcome (routinely estimating an 85% improvement rate in their own practice; Walfish et al., 2012), the complexity of people, and a treatment context that calls for considerable commitment and determination on the part of the therapist, who exercises very little control over the client's life circumstances and personal characteristics. A client's response to treatment is, especially in the case of a worsening state, a likely place where outside feedback might have the greatest chance of impact.

Helping psychotherapists become aware of negative patient change and discussing such progress in the therapeutic encounter are much more likely when formal feedback makes them aware of risk within a particular case. Such feedback helps the client communicate his/her progress and alerts the practitioner to the possible need to adjust treatment (e.g., address problems in the therapeutic relationship, reorient the treatment plan). By contrast, for clients who are progressing well in treatment, progress feedback delivered to therapists is not expected to help psychotherapists be more responsive or effective.

The American Psychological Association (APA, 2006) has recommended routine outcome monitoring be a part of effective psychological services because certain methods of monitoring have been shown to enhance client outcome. Two systems have been listed in the Substance Abuse and Mental Health Administration's National Registry of Evidence-based Programs and Practices (www.nrepp.samhsa.gov/). These two outcome monitoring systems have been the most widely studied with regard to their impact on an individual client's psychotherapy outcome: The OQ-System (Lambert et al., 2013) and the Partners for Change Outcome Management System (PCOMS; Duncan & Miller, 2008; Prescott et al., 2017). Both systems (with adult and the related child outcome measures) can be demonstrated online or installed on a clinician's desktop (www.oqmeasures.com; www.heartandsoulofchange.com; www.pcoms.com). These two Routine Outcome Monitoring (ROM) or Patient Reported Outcome Measurement (PROM) are the subject of the current review and analysis.

This chapter reports the results of systematic and meta-analytic review of the effects of these two feedback systems aimed at improving the outcomes of psychological treatments across varied psychotherapies and clinical contexts. We also review (a) definitions of feedback practices, (b) measures of progress and outcome, (c) clinical examples of feedback informed care, (d) several landmark investigations, (e) mediators and moderators of feedback effectiveness, (f) evidence supporting causality of the interventions, (g) patient factors contributing to effectiveness, and (h) limitations of the research base. In concluding, we review diversity considerations, training implications, and recommended therapeutic practices for collecting and delivering progress feedback.

DEFINITIONS

In many situations, performance and feedback are intertwined and obvious; in others (such as in psychotherapy), a degree of blinding occurs, such that the association is not so temporally connected and the effects of working with a client are harder to discern, making it much more difficult for the therapist to be maximally responsive to the client. The rationale behind collecting and delivering client feedback is based on common sense. If we get information about what seems to be working and, more important, what is not working, our responsiveness to clients will improve.

Many outcome management systems that provide progress feedback have been developed and implemented in clinical settings worldwide. Although the specific procedures employed in each system vary, their common features involve monitoring of client mental health functioning throughout the course of treatment and sharing the client's progress with clinicians (and clients), who can use these data to adjust their behavior as indicated. Such procedures have become known as ROM or PROM.

Howard and colleagues probably developed the first system in the mental health arena using the COMPASS Treatment Outcome System (Lueger et al., 2001). In Germany, researchers (Kordy et al., 2001) developed a computer-assisted, feedback-driven psychotherapy quality management system. In the United Kingdom, the Clinical Outcomes in Routine Evaluation (CORE) system is widely used (Barkham et al., 2001), while a different system is in use in Australia (Newham et al., 2010). Some systems have emphasized the administrative use of data for the improvement of systems of care, rather than feedback to therapists during the course of psychotherapy to improve outcome for the individual client. Administrative use allows managers of mental health services to examine the periodic and final outcome of treatments and compare outcomes to appropriate benchmarks. Now we review the two systems, beginning with the Outcome Questionnaire-45 (OQ-45).

OQ PSYCHOTHERAPY QUALITY MANAGEMENT SYSTEM

Measures

The OQ-45 (Lambert et al., 2013) is a 45-item, self-report measure designed for repeated administration throughout the course of treatment and at termination with adult clients. The OQ was conceptualized and designed to assess three domains of client functioning: symptoms of psychological disturbance (particularly anxiety and depression), interpersonal problems, and social role functioning. Consistent with this conceptualization of outcome, the OQ-45 provides a total score, based on all 45 items, as well as Symptom Distress, Interpersonal Relations, and Social Role subscale scores. Each of these subscales contains some items related to the positive quality of life of the individual (well-being). Higher scores on the OQ-45 are indicative of greater levels of psychological disturbance.

Research has indicated that the OQ-45 is a psychometrically sound instrument, with strong internal consistency (Cronbach's alpha = .93), adequate three-week test–retest reliability (r = .84), and strong concurrent validity estimates ranging from .55 to .88 when the total score and the subscale scores were correlated with scores from the Minnesota Multiphasic Personality Inventory-2, Symptom Checklist-90-Revised (SCL-90-R), Beck's Depression Inventory, Zung Depression Scale, Taylor Manifest Anxiety Scale, State-Trait Anxiety Inventory, Inventory of Interpersonal Problems, and

Social Adjustment Scale, among others (Lambert et al., 2013). The OQ-45 items have been shown to be sensitive to changes in multiple client populations over short periods of time while remaining relatively stable in untreated individuals (Vermeersch et al., 2000, 2004). In addition, evidence from factor analytic studies suggests it measures an overall psychological distress factor as well as factors consistent with the three subscales (Bludworth et al., 2010; De Jong et al, 2007; Lo Coco et al., 2008). In short, the OQ-45 is a brief measure that provides clinicians with a mental health vital sign. A similar OQ measure has been developed for use with children (http://www.oqmeasures.com).

A core feature of outcome management systems is the prediction of treatment failure. To improve outcomes of clients who are responding poorly to treatment, such clients must be identified before termination, and ideally, as early as possible in the course of treatment. The OQ-System plots a statistically generated expected recovery curve for differing levels of pretreatment disturbance and uses this as a basis for identifying clients (starting with the second encounter) who are not making expected treatment gains and are at risk for a poor treatment outcome. Expected treatment response was based on over 11,000 clients who received treatment in a variety of routine care clinical settings (including private practice). Patient progress was modeled over time using hierarchical linear models based on their OQ-45 intake scores. Expected treatment response are available at every possible starting score (except for seldom occurring extreme scores) and at each session of care (up to 20 sessions) using a large number of clients at each intake score (Finch et al., 2001). The OQ-Analyst also provides an alternative prediction system based on rational cut-offs to cross-validate the statistical system, if clinicians prefer.

The accuracy of the signal-alarm system has been evaluated in several empirical studies of treatment-as-usual (Ellsworth et al., 2006; Lambert, Whipple, Bishop, et al., 2002; Lutz et al., 2006; Percevic et al., 2006; Spielmans et al., 2006). It has been found to predict final deterioration in 85% to 100% of cases and to recognize such cases early in the treatment process. Although it generates false positives (i.e., cases it identifies as off-track who ultimately do not deteriorate), its ability to predict treatment failure far exceeds a clinician's ability to do so (Hannan et al., 2005).

A sample feedback report from the OQ-Analyst is displayed in Figure 17.1. This report displays a client's progress at the ninth session of psychotherapy in relation to a horizontal line at a score of 64/63 marking normal functioning, and a solid dark line displaying the expected treatment response. Most important is the "Red" alert signal in the upper right hand corner, which indicates that this client is responding so poorly to therapy that he or she is predicted to prematurely terminate or leave treatment having deteriorated.

In conjunction with identifying deteriorating cases, the OQ-Analyst also provides a method for directing clinician problem-solving with at-risk cases. Overall, this is known as the Clinical Support Tool (CST; Lambert, Bailey, et al., 2015). The CST is composed of a problem-solving decision tree that systematically directs a clinician's attention to factors that have been shown to be consistently related to client outcome. The CST decision tree is provided in Figure 17.2. As can be seen in the example of the failing case, it directs a therapist's attention to several treatment features, starting with

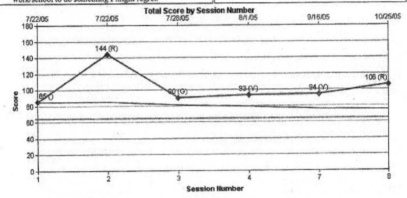

Name:	news, brad **ID:**		Alert Status:	**Red**

Session Date: 10/25/2005 **Session:** 8

Clinician: lambert, m **Clinic:** Clinic A

Diagnosis: Unknown Diagnosis

Algorithm: Empirical

Most Recent Score: 106

Initial Score: 85

Change From Initial: Reliably Worse

Current Distress Level: High

Most Recent Critical Item Status:

8. **Suicide** - I have thoughts of ending my **Frequently** life.
11. **Substance Abuse** - After heavy **Frequently** drinking, I need a drink the next morning to get going.
26. **Substance Abuse** - I feel annoyed by **Frequently** people who criticize my drinking.
32. **Substance Abuse** - I have trouble at **Sometimes** work/school because of drinking or drug use.
44. **Work Violence** - I feel angry enough at **Sometimes** work/school to do something I might regret.

Subscales	Current	Outpat. Norm	Comm. Norm
Symptom Distress:	61	49	25
Interpersonal Relations:	26	20	10
Social Role:	19	14	10
Total:	106	83	45

Graph Label Legend:
(R) = Red: High chance of negative outcome   (Y) = Yellow: Some chance of negative outcome
(G) = Green: Making expected progress   (W) = White: Functioning in normal range

Feedback Message:
The patient is deviating from the expected response to treatment. They are not on track to realize substantial benefit from treatment. Chances are they may drop out of treatment prematurely or have a negative treatment outcome. Steps should be taken to carefully review this case and identify reasons for poor progress. It is recommended that you be alert to the possible need to improve the therapeutic alliance, reconsider the client's readiness for change and the need to renegotiate the therapeutic contract, intervene to strengthen social supports, or possibly alter your treatment plan by intensifying treatment, shifting intervention strategies, or decide upon a new course of action, such as referral for medication. Continuous monitoring of future progress is highly recommended.

REMINDER: THE USER IS SOLELY RESPONSIBLE FOR ANY AND ALL DECISIONS AFFECTING PATIENT CARE. THE OQ-A IS NOT A DIAGNOSTIC TOOL, AND SHOULD NOT BE USED AS SUCH. IT IS NOT A SUBSTITUTE FOR A MEDICAL OR PROFESSIONAL EVALUATION. RELIANCE ON THE OQ-A IS AT USER'S SOLE RISK AND RESPONSIBILITY. (SEE LICENSE FOR FULL STATEMENT OF RIGHTS, RESPONSIBILITIES & DISCLAIMERS)

FIGURE 17.1 Outcome Questionnaire-Analyst screen shot illustrating feedback report of client progress provided to therapist.

the therapeutic alliance, motivation, social support, negative life events, diagnostic formulation, and need for medication referral.

A second measure, the Assessment for Signal Cases (ASC; Lambert, Bailey, et al., 2015), was developed to assist clinicians in going through the decision tree. It was based on the observation that progress feedback was helpful, but that a significant number of off-track clients were still not improving. The ASC is a 40-item client self-report scale aimed at assessing the therapeutic alliance, motivation, social support,

Clinical Support Tools Decision Tree

Not-On-Track Feedback Cases

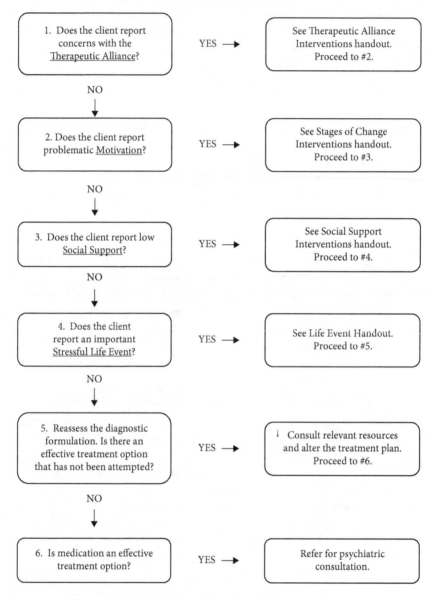

FIGURE 17.2 Clinical Support Tool (CST) problem-solving decision tree.

and negative life events. Rather than a total score, the ASC feedback to clinicians is provided for each assessment domain. The therapeutic alliance scale consists of 11-items drawn from longer popular alliance measures (e.g., "My therapist seems glad to see me"). Motivation consists of 9 items that were drawn from lengthier measures of this construct (e.g., "Honestly, I really don't understand what I can get from therapy").

Eleven social support items were drawn from the published literature and focused on close relationships (e.g., "I could talk about my problems with my family"). The 9-item life-events scale was drawn from the literature on deterioration and includes common loses and disruptions (e.g., "I felt rejected or betrayed by someone"). The subscales have adequate reliability and validity and, like the OQ-45, it is brief and suitable for routine use in ongoing treatment.

Several studies have examined which areas of functioning were most frequently noted as problematic on the ASC (White et al., 2015). Off-track clients frequently reported alliance problems, mainly in their agreement with therapeutic tasks, but other domains were also problematic, especially social support. In fact, about one third of not-on-track (NOT) clients reported problems internal to psychotherapy (alliance and motivation), one third had problems mainly external to therapy (social supports and life events), and the remaining one third had problems spread across all four areas assessed by the ASC. This pattern suggests that it is not sufficient to attribute treatment failure to the alliance solely because factors external to the therapeutic relationship are likely causes of negative outcome as well.

The OQ-Analyst is an on-line software application that facilitates real-time electronic feedback for clinicians (and clients). Once a client takes the OQ-45, commences treatment, and completes a psychotherapy session, the signal-alarm system generates feedback regarding the client's progress. If it is off-track, the ASC is administered, and the CST is used to help clinicians problem-solve with these clients. Figure 17.3 presents a sample feedback report of the ASC. Items that fall below an empirically based cut-off score (about one standard deviation below the mean rating on the item by clients in normative samples) are brought to the therapist's attention. This is also true of subscales. For example, therapists can be notified if the therapeutic alliance, as a whole, is problematic, but also if it is the bond, in particular, that is problematic, while the task and goal consensus are not. Therapists suggest to us that problematic individual items are most helpful in problem-solving. It should also be noted that the OQ-Analyst provides intervention suggestions when problems are identified.

Clinical Example

The psychotherapist, a 62-year-old male, had been seeing a 22-year-old female undergraduate ("Jane") at a university counseling center for 12 sessions of psychotherapy. The client originally complained of anxiety, indecisiveness, and excessive worry about her academic performance, her academic major, and her boyfriend who had recently proposed to her. Her measured treatment progress had been steady and positive with the most recent signal indicating she was functioning in the "normal" range. As a result, she and her therapist had cut back the frequency of their sessions with the goal of bringing the therapy to an end.

In the time between sessions, the client had taken her fiancée to visit her family, who were farmers in a rural area of a nearby state. She was not expecting approval from them because in almost all ways he was nothing like their fantasies of her choice for a partner (preferably someone who would help with the farm). Early in her dating

Name:	C-OQ45, GEORGE, R	ID:	MRN0101
Session Date:	12/25/2006	Session:	1
Clinician:	Clinician, Bob	Clinic:	TX Dallas Clinic
Diagnosis:	Unknown Diagnosis		
Instrument:	ASC		

Subscales	Current Scores	Alerts
Theraputic Alliance:	39	RED
Social Support:	36	
Motivation:	30	RED
Life Events:	29	

Display Interventions Handout

Theraputic Alliance: RED
It is advisable that you address your relationship with the client. Please click 'Display Interventions Handout' button for more information.

1. I felt cared for and respected as a person.	Neutral
2. I felt my therapist understood me.	Neutral
3. I thought the suggestions my therapist made were useful.	Neutral
4. I felt like I could trust my therapist completely.	Slightly Agree
9. My therapist seemed to be glad to see me.	Neutral
10. My therapist and I seemed to work well together to accomplish what I want.	Slightly Disagree
11. My therapist and I had a similar understanding of my problems.	Strongly Disagree

Social Support:

15. I got the emotional help and support I needed from someone in my family.	Strongly Disagree
16. There was a special person who was around when I was in need.	Neutral
21. I felt connected to a higher power.	Strongly Disagree

Motivation: RED

It is advisable that you address your client's motivation in therapy. Please click 'Display Interventions Handout' button for more information.

23. I wonder what I am doing in therapy; actually I find it boring.	Slightly Agree
26. I had thoughts about quitting therapy; it's just not for me.	Slightly Agree
27. I don't think therapy will help me feel any better.	Neutral
28. I have no desire to work out my problems.	Strongly Agree
31. I am in therapy because someone is requiring it of me.	Neutral

Life Events:

32. I had an interaction with another person that I found upsetting.	Strongly Agree
38. I had health problems (such as physical pain).	Strongly Agree

FIGURE 17-3 Representative ASC feedback report.

relationship she was not especially upset by their reaction to him because she realized it would be a shock.

About four weeks after the visit to her family, Jane's measured treatment progress took a strong turn for the worse, and the OQ-Analyst feedback report flagged her as a client at-risk for treatment failure (red alarm). Upon signaling as off-track, the OQ-Analyst administered the ASC to her. The alliance scale of the ASC indicated that the therapeutic relationship was quite strong with regards to her affective bond, agreement on treatment goals, and agreement on the focus of therapy sessions. She felt certain that therapy would prove helpful if she actively participated, according to her answers on the motivations scale. However, she indicated on the social support scale that she was experiencing great difficulty in her family relationships. The therapist was prepared to discuss her negative change and its causes, particularly what had happened in her social support network.

The client (C) began the next session looking uncomfortable, but with a covering smile:

C: I am wondering if you would consider giving me your opinion about something? In this binder, I have several wedding dresses that I want to show you. I would like your opinion about which one you think is the best for me.

T (inner reaction: Immediate surprise and a sense of shock—what in the world would make Jane think an old guy like me would have a valid opinion on wedding dresses; thought #2 wow, she is really avoiding the work of therapy): Jane, I am surprised by your request. How come you are asking me of all people?

C (Immediately breaking into tears. minutes pass): Every time I call my mom to talk about the wedding details, she immediately says, "Are you sure you want to get married?" She will say anything to sew doubt in me and she won't help me make decisions or support me in any way. Every time we talk about the wedding details we end up in a big fight. I need her help and support, not a fight.

Near the end of an emotional session, the therapist makes a suggestion:

T: I can see that this conflict with your folks is getting much worse as the wedding date approaches and that you are thinking of writing them out of your life. Do you think they would drive down here and join us in a session?

C: Yes, I do. But they will be coming in hopes to convince you that he is not a good match and to see if you'll talk some sense into me.

T: Let's talk about how to make it work for you and how we can organize the meeting. . . .

This is a good example of how progress feedback with alarm-signal, the CST, and ASC feedback work together to narrow a therapist's focus, in this case to change from individual therapy to a family intervention. The ASC indicated the client's problem had moved from an internal concern satisfactorily treated with individual therapy to an external stressor concerning the family of origin and clients' response to it. Thus, in response to feedback results and in collaboration with the client, they decided to address family stress in conjoint family sessions. In this case the ASC (according to the therapist) helped him change the focus of therapy to most quickly alter the crisis at hand.

PARTNERS FOR CHANGE OUTCOME MANAGEMENT SYSTEM

Measures

The PCOMS (Duncan & Miller, 2008; Prescott et al., 2017) is a ROM system that employs two ultra-brief scales (4 items each). The Outcome Rating Scale (ORS; Miller et al., 2003) focuses on mental health functioning, modeled after the domains of outcome measured by subscales of the OQ-45 (Lambert et al., 2013). The Session Rating Scale (SRS; Duncan & Miller, 2008) is designed to assess the therapeutic alliance. Because of its brevity, this system is clinician friendly and allows ratings of mental health status and therapeutic alliance to be typically collected in the presence of the therapist. This facilitates discussion of assessment results by the client and therapist in session. The PCOMS provides a rating of the helping relationship at every session, whereas the OQ-System only assesses therapeutic alliance factors (and motivation, social support, and life events) with off-track cases (http://www.whatispcoms.com).

The ORS uses a visual analog scale that requires clients to rate their functioning on four items (subjective well-being, interpersonal relations, social functioning, and overall sense of well-being). The test–retest correlations among nonclinical samples range from .49 to .66 with high international consistency (Cronbach's alpha = 0.93; Miller & Duncan, 2003). Correlations between the ORS and OQ-45 over four waves of repeated administrations among 86 nonclinical individuals ranged from .53 to .69. It appears these two measure share just a moderate amount of common ($r^2 = .28$ to $r^2 = .48$).

The ORS incorporates expected trajectories of client change based on Bayesian inference, the initial score, and the change at a given session in relation to the initial score (Miller et al., 2005). Consistent with the recommendations given in the administration and scoring manual of the ORS, clients are classified as being at risk, or not progressing, if they fail to improve five (or more) ORS points by the third session. Identification of at-risk clients can be generated by employing Web-based software that "calculates trajectories of change at the 25th, 50th, and 75th percentile levels" based on a large archival ORS database (Anker et al., 2009, p. 697). Clients whose ORS score at the third session fall below the 50th percentile mark of the expected trajectory of progress based on individual response are identified as at risk. Unfortunately, the accuracy of identifying cases at risk for treatment failure has not been cross-validated (Schuskard et al., 2017)

The therapeutic relationship as measured by the SRS is based on the concept of the therapeutic alliance by Bordin (1979) and the construct termed "client's theory of change." These interrelated alliance theories emphasize three aspects of the helping relationship: the affective bond, agreement on tasks during sessions, and consensus on treatment goals. Miller and colleagues (2005) developed three items to rate these constructs and a fourth item that provides an overall rating of the relationship. Concurrent validity of the SRS and Helping Alliance Questionnaire-II is .48, with each item correlation ranging from .39 to .44 with the total score. Like most alliance measures, the SRS correlates moderately with other measures. As Fluciger and colleagues (Chapter 2, this volume) point out, this level of agreement is not uncommon even among longer, well-established alliance measures. Use of the SRS encourages discussion between therapist and client about client perceptions of the therapeutic relationship, thus possibly identifying ways to improve it.

Clinical use of the ORS and the SRS is gaining in popularity, and a growing number of published studies have examined the psychometric properties of these measures and the effects of PCOMS on treatment outcome. Figure 17.4 provides a hypothetical example of feedback to both clinician and client for a case falling under benchmark predictions. ORS scores are graphically portrayed in comparison with the 50th percentile trajectory, which is based on the client's intake score. In research and practice, the use of the ORS and SRS is characteristic of ROM practices except that, in addition to client progress, the helping relationship is also the subject of feedback. Joint use encourages the client and practitioner to discuss treatment options to avert a negative outcome when there seems to be a problem in either domain.

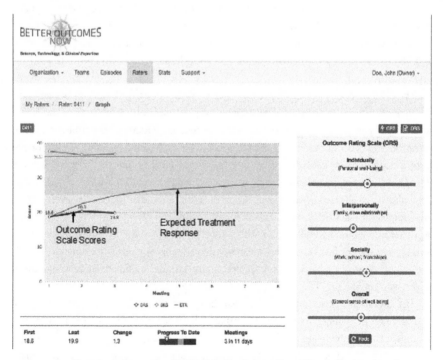

FIGURE 17.4 Hypothetical example of PCOMS feedback for a client falling below benchmark predictions.

Clinical Example

The following excerpt is adapted from Duncan and Reese (2015, p. 395) and provides an example of a therapist (T) introducing the ORS to a client in session:

T: I like to start with this brief form called the Outcome Rating Scale, which provides a snapshot of how you are doing right now. It serves as an anchor point so we can track your progress and make sure that you get what came here to get and if you're not, we can regroup and try something else. It's also a way to make sure your perspective of how you are doing stays central. Would you mind doing it for me?

What I do is I just measure this up. Its four 10-cm lines and gives a score from zero to 40 and I just pull out this ruler and add up the scores, and then I will tell you about what this says and you can tell me whether it is accurate or not. . . . Okay, you scored a 19.8. This scale, the Outcome Rating Scale, has what's called a cut-off score of 25, and people who score under 25 tend to be those who wind up talking to people like me, they're looking for something different in their lives. You scored about the average intake score of persons who enter therapy, so you've come to the right place. And it's not hard to look at this and see pretty quickly that it's the family/close relationships part you are struggling with most right now. Does that make sense?

C: Yes, definitely.

T: So, what do you think would be the most useful thing for us to talk about?

C: Well, I am in the middle of divorce and struggling with figuring this out. . . .

T: If I am getting this right, you said that you are struggling with the divorce, specifically about why it happened and your part in it so you are looking to explore this and gain some insight into what, perhaps, was your contribution. You marked the Interpersonally Scale the lowest (Therapist picks up the ORS). Does this mark represent this struggle and your longing for some clarity?

C: Yes.

T: So, if we were able to explore this situation and reach some insights that resonate with you, do you think that it would move that mark to the right?

C: Yes, that is what I am hoping for and what I think will help me. I know I was not perfect in the relationship, and I want to understand my part. I already know his part!

LANDMARK STUDIES

We have selected two landmark investigations among the OQ studies and two from the PCOM studies.

OQ Landmarks

The Harmon and associates (2007) study was chosen as a landmark because it was the fifth in a series of studies that investigated the effects of feedback on client outcome. It used findings from the earlier studies to examine and possibly replicate the effects of feedback with alarm-signals, the effects of adding direct client feedback using written messages and graphs, and separately measuring the effects of CSTs, all in relation to an archive treatment-as-usual (TAU) group. A total of 1,705 consecutive clients were invited to participate in the study and of those, 1,374 gave consent. A TAU group was formed among clients who were randomly assigned to TAU in three earlier studies (N = 1445; Lambert et al., 2001, 2002; Whipple et al., 2003). The use of this control was necessitated by the fact that by the time Harmon did her work the clinic had implemented the OQ feedback system for all clients. The effective N for this study therefore became 2,819 individuals.

Of the 1,374 new clients, 687 were randomly assigned to the therapist feedback group (TFb) and 687 to the patient/therapist feedback (PT/TFb) group. In the TFb group, 166 clients went off-track with 88 being randomly assigned to CST feedback and 78 no CST feedback. Of the 687 clients randomly assigned to PT/TFb, 203 went off-track with 100 randomly assigned to receive CST feedback and 103 to receive no CST feedback. Combing the off-track cases from the two arms of the study resulted in 188 clients whose therapists received CST feedback and 181 clients whose therapists did not.

The major questions addressed in this study were: Does adding direct, formal client feedback to therapist feedback enhance outcomes? Does adding CSTs enhance outcomes compared to no CST feedback with off-track cases?

Results for both on-track and off-track clients (NOT) indicated that both groups of clients fared statistically significantly better in the feedback conditions compared to TAU, but that direct client feedback provided no additional benefit compared to therapist feedback only. This finding suggested that in the case of both clients who progress well during psychotherapy and those who do not adding direct client feedback using formal reports was not helpful. In addition, the effects of using CST feedback with NOT clients showed that it enhanced outcome compared with no CST feedback (d = .31). When compared with the TAU control, the effect was even larger (d = .73), a moderate-sized effect. This study strengthened the evidence that using CST feedback helps clinicians problem-solve when cases are at-risk of treatment failure.

The Simon and associates (2013) study was also selected as a landmark by virtue of applying feedback methods in a specialty hospital that treated eating disordered patients. Routine care in this hospital setting included a long list of interventions and activities, delivered up to a 30-day stay (M = 10.86 days). The patients received intensive assessment and treatment planning, biweekly individual psychotherapy, daily group psychotherapy, family counseling, nutrition counseling, monitoring by a dietitian, medication (90% of clients), and a semiweekly 12-step group. They additionally participated weekly in music, art, dance, yoga, and movement therapies.

The psychotherapists were licensed professionals with an average of 10 years of experience who had a variety of theoretical orientations. Neither the clinical director nor the psychotherapists initially believed that feedback-assisted treatment would enhance the effectiveness of services, but agreed to participate at the urging of the executive director of the hospital. None of the therapists had experience in using the feedback methods based on the OQ-Analyst, but received two hours of training which oriented them to accessing clinician reports on their computer and interpreting sample reports.

Additionally, group supervision was offered by a member of the research team on a weekly basis. It was aimed at discussing any problems therapists were having understanding clinician reports and CST feedback with cases who went off-track.

In this study, 141 consecutive clients were invited to participate at intake, 137 of them consented to the study, and 133 completed it (64 in TAU and 69 in feedback). Patients were randomly assigned to either the feedback group or TAU within each therapist, so that the same therapists delivered both feedback and the control condition. Clients met criteria for a variety of eating disorders with bulimia (43%) being most common. About 41% of the clients met criteria for three or more disorders, with about 75% meeting criteria for a major depression. Patients reported an eating disorder on average for 11 years prior to admission and were, on average, 26 years of age. Approximately 53% of clients were identified as going off-track during their stay in the hospital, suggesting a rough course of improvement.

Progress feedback reports with alarms indicating off-track status were provided weekly, with the CST report administered at the first time a client became an at-risk case in the feedback condition. TAU clients completed the OQ but reports were withheld from therapists and clients in this condition.

Results indicated that patients on the whole reported large gains during their stay in the hospital. The pre–post effect size for TAU was $d = 1.15$, while that of the feedback group was $d = 1.41$. As measured by the OQ-45, the change in the feedback group took them from the 99th percentile of the normal population at the inception of treatment to the 82nd percentile at the end of treatment. That pattern indicated that they remained, even after treatment, 1.5 standard deviations above the average person in their mental health functioning.

The feedback group had better post-treatment functioning than the TAU group. The between group effect at post-treatment was $d = .36$. Examining the treatment response of patients classified as NOT, progress feedback plus the use of CST feedback resulted in 53% of these clients meeting criteria for clinically meaningful change (Jacobson & Truax, 1991) while this was true for only 29% of those who received TAU. The rate of deterioration was small and equal in both groups. This pivotal study demonstrated that, even in an intensive treatment environment, with many interventions aimed at having a positive effect on client functioning, the effects of formally monitoring client progress and using clinical problem-solving tools proved helpful. This appeared to be the case even though therapists had reservations about the value of this evidence-based practice.

PCOM Landmarks

Anker et al. (2009) conducted a randomized controlled trial investigating the effects of the PCOMS feedback on clients in couple therapy at a community family clinic. Of the 906 Norwegian individuals who initially sought couple therapy, 410 individuals (205 couples) met the inclusion criteria and were randomly assigned to feedback condition or TAU ($n = 103$ in feedback and $n = 102$ in TAU). Therapists were licensed psychologists, social workers, and psychiatric nurses who provided eclectic therapy using a variety of therapeutic approaches (solution-focused, narrative, cognitive-behavioral, humanistic, and systemic therapy). The average number of sessions was 4.75 (SD = 2.71) in the feedback group and 4.45 (SD = 2.73) in the TAU group.

The researchers found that feedback did enhance treatment outcome. The between-group effect size was d = .50 on posttreatment ORS scores. Clinical significant change was examined at the couple level rather than by individual client level. This meant that both members of a couple needed to meet the same criteria for classification. Based on these criteria, 66% of couples in the feedback group and 50% of couples in the TAU were included in the analyses. Of those included in the analysis, the authors reported 51% of couples in the feedback condition achieved either clinically significant change or reliable change, while 2% deteriorated. In contrast, 23% of couples in the TAU group reached either clinically significant change or reliable change and 4% experienced deterioration. With regard to marital adjustment, feedback was found to be somewhat helpful. The posttreatment d between groups was .29, lower than outcome based on the ORS.

This pivotal study demonstrated that feedback enhances treatment outcomes for couple therapy, whereas all previous studies had examined the effects of feedback on individual therapy. In addition this study included a follow-up to see if the results were maintained, which is unusual in feedback research. As well, the results suggested that ROMs can be successfully employed in countries outside the United States, presuming that the intervention is implemented with fidelity.

In the follow-up arm of the study, Anker and colleagues (2009) found that a higher percentage of at-risk couples in the feedback group responded favorably to treatment than those in TAU (29% vs. 9%). Partial support for the social validity of the feedback effect was suggested in the authors' report that, among those who responded to a six-month follow-up (149 couples out of 205 couples), the feedback group had a lower rate of separation or divorce (18.4%) than TAU (34.2%), which indicates the couples in TAU had approximately 1.9 times higher probability of separation or divorce (relative risk = 1.86) than those in the feedback condition. It is noteworthy that this study was replicated in the United States by Reese et al. (2010).

In another landmark study involving the PCOMS, Schuman and associates (2015) studied 263 active duty soldiers referred for substance abuse treatment who were assigned randomly to either a group therapy feedback condition (n = 137) or TAU group (n = 126). The study is important because it examined feedback effects for substance abusing clients as well as group psychotherapy. Soldiers were self-referred or mandated to treatment by their commanding officers (direct supervisor) and met criteria for substance abuse or dependence. There were 10 therapists (civilian employees), and each led 1 of 10 groups. Therapists had no formal PCOMS training. Therapist alerts were based on PCOM cut-off scores of 25 for normal functioning and scores of 5 or more indicating reliable change (progress in the lower 25 percentile). Each group was open and comprised of approximately one-half feedback and one-half TAU clients. There were 8 to 12 clients per group. Clients were not informed of experimental/control assignment. Only five sessions were provided and studied with outcome data based on last group attended or at the fifth session. The type of psycho-therapy was based on clinician preference: cognitive-behavioral, interpersonal, psy-chodynamic, or solution-focused.

The ORS was completed by clients prior to each session by entering responses on a computer. The scoring was not shared with the client unless the therapist chose to do so. Therapists were given progress graphs at the conclusion of each group session, but were left to their own with regards to taking clinical actions.

Results indicated that clients in the feedback condition vis-à-vis TAU achieved sig-nificantly greater improvement on the ORS ($d = .28$), higher rates of clinically signifi-cant change, higher rates of "success" by their commanding officers and clinicians, and attended more sessions. Deterioration rates were high but not different across groups (feedback = 14.6%, TAU = 11.9%). With regards to clinically significant change, there was a statistically significant difference in the percentage of those who did not change (36.5% vs. 49.2%, for feedback and TAU, respectively). The feedback group attended significantly more sessions. Therapists (who were not blind to study condition) rated feedback clients as having a good to fair outcome 116/138 (84%) compared to TAU controls 76/124 (61%). Commanding officers (who were blind to treatment assign-ment) rated 82% of soldiers as having a satisfactory outcome in the feedback condi-tion, while just 51% of controls were viewed this way.

In short, PCOMS feedback strengthened the outcomes of group therapy on a variety of measures. It did so despite any formal feedback training for the group therapists. And it did so for brief therapy (five sessions) with recalcitrant addictive disorders.

We hope these landmark studies and the preceding clinical examples gives the reader a working model of how two popular and researched ROM/PROM methods offer client/therapist feedback in psychotherapy. We now turn to a review of research on the general effects of feedback for modifying behavior, applications across health-care setting, and those more specifically targeting mental health outcomes.

RESULTS OF PREVIOUS META-ANALYSES

Human Performance

In an early meta-analysis on the general effects of feedback on human performance, researchers found a small to medium effect size ($d = .41$) for interventions utilizing feedback compared to no feedback About two thirds of individuals receiving feedback performed better than those who received no feedback (Kluger & DeNisi, 1996). Most of the studies examined in this meta-analysis were analogue situations involving motor performance, puzzle solutions, memory tasks, and the like, rather than clinical prac-tice. Nevertheless, this review did suggest that a broad array of feedback interventions (both on aspects of performance and feedback on outcome) consistently improve per-formance, and encourages the idea that certain types of feedback will enhance prac-titioner ability to help their clients. This meta-analytic research also began to identify specific factors that make feedback more or less effective.

Healthcare

In a meta-analysis focused on healthcare, Sapyta (noted in Sapyta et al., 2005) examined 30 randomized clinical trials conducted in community settings that assessed the effectiveness of client health status feedback to health professionals. The nature of feedback interventions and methods of their delivery varied, from giving general practice physicians depression or anxiety screening information about their clients to repeatedly providing clinicians with their clients' mental health status feedback. The average client in the feedback group was better off than 58% of the control group ($d = .21$, a small effect). Similarly, a more recent review of feedback to healthcare professionals about their client's functioning provided only weak evidence of effectiveness (Boyce & Browne, 2013), especially when it was limited to sharing screening information on a single occasion within primary care.

Carlier and colleagues (2016) examined the effects of feedback in randomized clinical trials in both physical and mental health settings. In more than half the studies (63%), the authors found that the experimental group receiving feedback interventions demonstrated better outcomes than control groups who did not get the intervention. In this review, among the 70% of the studies that were conducted in mental health settings, feedback had superior outcomes on at least one measure of mental health functioning compared to TAU.

Psychotherapy

A meta-analysis of 12 studies focused directly on mental health status feedback in psychotherapy (Knaup et al., 2009). The researchers found a statistically significant, albeit small effect ($d = .10$) for progress feedback across a broad range of feedback methods and clinical populations. This analysis suggested that the effects of feedback across all clients may prove short lived, although few studies had follow-ups. The results also suggested that procedures for delivering feedback matter, with some having greater effects than others. This analysis of feedback effects very likely underestimated the effects of feedback by including studies that used questionable methods and procedures.

Kragelch and associates (2015) provided a review of 172 studies, 27 of which could be organized into five types of feedback procedures. The large number of feedback studies identified highlights the wide array of ROM/PROM possibilities, but unfortunately the majority of identified methods did not provide data on their effects on patient outcome. Only 11 studies were formalized and provided quantitative client-reported outcome measurement. They reported that 9 of the 11 studies showed positive results with the remaining two partially positive. This review sorted studies into various designs based on the degree of intensity of feedback methods. The results suggested that formal guidelines for clinician–client discussion of feedback was most highly associated with improved psychotherapy outcome.

A recent meta-analytic review on feedback was published for the Cochrane database of systematic reviews (Kendrick et al., 2016). This review considered studies of PROMs for improving treatment for mental health disorders in primary care, psychological therapy, and multidisciplinary mental health settings. The review employed strict standards for study inclusion and excluded studies that used CSTs to enhance clinician problem-solving with NOT cases. Such studies tend to have the largest effect size, and their exclusion reduces the overall effect size. This review found weak evidence for feedback, particularly when the measure of client mental health functioning was used for screening purposes, a finding consistent with other reviews (e.g., Gondek et al., 2016). Of 16 feedback studies with specific mental health populations in outpatient settings, 6 studies showed positive results for feedback. The researchers noted that even the studies deemed appropriate for review in the meta-analysis had many methodological flaws. Based on their review, the authors "could not draw any firm conclusions" about the effects of routine monitoring of clients with common mental health disorders using client-reported outcome measures. This meta-analysis is at odds with other reviews of the effects of feedback, possibly because they maintained restrictive methodological standards for reviewing studies (such as the degree of blinding of those delivering and receiving feedback, something that is impossible to implement; see also Davidson et al., 2015).

In contrast to the Cochrane review, Fortney and colleagues (2017) analyzed 51 articles that examined the effects of feedback to practitioners delivering either medication or psychotherapy for mental disorders. They concluded that virtually all randomized clinical trials with frequent and timely feedback of client-reported symptoms to the practitioner significantly improved patient outcomes. They reported evidence for the acceptability of such procedures to both clinicians and clients as well as the feasibility of implementation on a large scale. The authors also noted some ineffective approaches, which included one-time screening, infrequent assessment, and feedback of information from outside the context of the clinical encounter. Aggregated symptom ratings also provided information to therapists that could help them improve their individual performance as well as performance at the clinic level.

The interested reader may also wish to read the narrative review published by Gondeck and associate (2016). They were much more positive in their evaluation of feedback methods than Kendrick et al. (2016), concluding that most of the 27 studies examined showed positive benefits.

OQ and PCOMS

Finally, four previous meta-analytic reviews have been conducted on outcomes using the specific methods under review in this chapter (OQ-System and PCOMS). The first meta-analysis included just three studies, all based on the OQ-45 (Lambert et al., 2003). As these studies were included in the next meta-analysis, a summary is not provided here.

The second meta- and mega analysis of six studies examined the effects of the OQ-45 (Shimokawa et al., 2010). These researchers combined raw data from the six original studies on the OQ-System since they were all conducted by the same research group. Results indicated that progress feedback with at-risk cases had a reliable treatment effect on such cases, which was even larger when the CST feedback was applied with clients predicted to deteriorate. The findings demonstrated that the feedback interventions reduced deterioration rates from about 20% in at-risk clients to 6% while doubling the rate of reliable/clinically significant changed clients. These findings were impressive because clients were assigned randomly to feedback or treatment-as-usual within the same therapist (i.e., the same therapist provided therapy to both feedback cases and no feedback cases). This meta-analysis also confirmed that the effects of progress feedback were limited to NOT clients (NOT, at-risk, predicted treatment failure clients), which constituted about 20% to 30% of the case load. In these studies, progress feedback was seen an intervention for preventing treatment failure rather than one that was likely to be useful across all clients.

In the previous edition of this book, we expanded the meta-analysis to include three studies of the PCOMS (Lambert & Shimokawa, 2011). That meta-analysis focused on the effects on NOT clients of progress feedback, client/therapist feedback, and clinical support tools. When the NOT clients whose therapists received progress feedback were compared with NOT clients whose therapists did not receive feedback, the average client whose therapist received feedback was better off than approximately 70% of clients in the no-feedback condition offered by the same clinicians (routine care). In terms of the clinical significance at termination, 9% of the NOT cases receiving feedback deteriorated while 38% achieved clinically significant improvement. In contrast, among clients whose therapists did not receive feedback, 20% deteriorated while 22% experienced clinically significant improvement. When the odds of deterioration and clinically significant improvement were compared, results indicated that those in the feedback group had less than half the odds of experiencing deterioration (odds ratio [OR] = 0.44, 95% confidence interval [CI] = 0.23–0.85), while having approximately 2.6 times higher odds of experiencing at least reliable improvement (OR = 2.55, 95% CI = 1.64–3.98).

The studies that called for formal written/graphic feedback to clients as well as to clinicians, compared to no feedback (TAU) controls, revealed an effect size of posttreatment OQ scores of g = 0.55, 95% CI = 0.36–0.73— an effect very similar to that of the therapist-only feedback group.

When the outcome of clients whose therapist received feedback and the ASC/ CSTs was compared with that of the TAU clients, the effect size was medium to large, g = 0.70, 95% CI = 0.52–0.88. These results indicate that the average client in the CST feedback group, who stayed in treatment to experience the benefit of this intervention was better off than 76% of clients in treatment as usual. The rates of deterioration (6%) and clinically significant improvement (53%) among those receiving CSTs in addition to progress feedback was quite dramatic compared to TAU. The clients whose therapists used CSTs had less than a fourth the odds of deterioration, OR = 0.23, 95% CI = 0.12–0.44, while having approximately 3.9 times higher odds of achieving clinically significant improvement, OR = 3.85, 95% CI = 2.65–5.60. The previous findings from the original OQ-based feedback studies indicate that three forms of feedback in the OQ-System (progress feedback, client/therapist feedback, clinical support tools) proved effective in enhancing treatment effects for clients at risk of leaving therapy worse off than when they started treatment.

In the fourth review, Duncan and Reese (2015) examined the outcomes of six studies that used the PCOMS. In evaluating the evidence, they concluded: "RCT's demonstrate a significant advantage of PCOMS over TAU. Clients in feedback conditions achieved more pre-post treatment gains, higher percentages of reliable and clinically significant change, faster rates of change, and were less likely to drop out" (p. 393). The meta-analysis reported later in this chapter includes all six of these studies.

In brief summary, the past meta-analytic reviews on the variety of ROM/PROM methods highlight considerable variability in their average effect on patient outcomes. The bulk of evidence supports application of some ROM/PROM methods in routine care, particularly for at-risk patients. Rather than providing a broad review of all methods, the current meta-analysis considers the two most studied ROM/PROM systems. Since many methodological differences exist between the OQ-System and PCOMS (e.g., dependent measure of outcome), we conduct separate meta-analyses.

SYSTEMATIC AND META-ANALYTIC REVIEW

There are four important differences between the OQ-System and the PCOMS. The first concerns the nature of the dependent measures. The OQ-45 asks clients to rate 45 specific aspects of functioning, such as sleep, sexual satisfaction, loneliness, conflicts at work, suicidal thoughts, substance abuse, and the like, each on a 5-point scale. The ORS asks clients to rate four general questions about their functioning. Although meta-analysis converts different scales into a standard metric (effect size or standardized mean difference [SMD]), it cannot overcome the fundamental differences in what is being measured, be that general functioning or specific complaints. Accordingly, in this chapter, separate meta-analyses were conducted on the studies that used the OQ-System and PCOMS (ORS + SRS).

Another important difference is that the OQ-System was designed to enhance the outcome of clients predicted to experience treatment failure, not helping all clients. This is consistent with feedback theory, which suggests feedback will prove helpful when there is a discrepancy between therapists' perception of client treatment response and measured treatment response (Sapyta et al., 2005). In contrast, the PCOMS assumes progress feedback will be helpful for all clients in a clinician's caseload.

The third difference concerns what the feedback systems offer the clinician and client. The PCOMS includes not only progress feedback with alarms (through the ORS) but therapeutic alliance (SRS) feedback from all clients at most sessions. The OQ-System presents alliance, motivation, social support, and negative life event information to the clinician (i.e., the CST, including intervention suggestions) only if a client goes off-track. Accordingly, in this chapter, meta-analytic findings are reported separately for the total sample as well the subsample of not on track samples with regards to the OQ-system and for the total sample only with regards to the PCOMS because outcomes of NOT clients are not consistently reported in PCOMS studies. To reiterate, NOT clients are those who the OQ-Analyst identifies as yellow or red cases if at any time during psychotherapy they reach the cut-score justifying at risk for leaving treatment as "deteriorated."

The fourth key difference between these outcome systems is that they have different methods of identifying "at-risk" cases. The rates of at-risk cases reported in the PCOMS studies are considerably higher (36% to 84%) than studies based on the OQ-System (11% to 56%). High rates of signal alarm cases may diminish the impact of warning systems on clinicians and the likelihood that they can focus greater attention on such cases. The large number of NOT cases identified in PCOMS research leaves relatively few on track clients to be examined in the meta-analysis separately from not on track clients.

Inclusion Criteria and Search Strategy

Electronic databases such as Medline, PsycINFO, PsycEXTRA, Google Scholar, past reviews, and hand searches were used to identify studies that were of mental health outcomes and feedback using either the OQ-System or the PCOMS. Search terms included: Outcome Questionnaire-45; OQ-45; OQ-System; OQ-Analyst; Outcome Feedback; Progress Feedback; Routine Outcome Monitoring; PROM; Client Feedback; Feedback Informed Psychotherapy; Treatment Monitoring; Outcome Rating Scale; Session Rating Scale; Partners for Change Outcome Management System.

The systematic review included studies which met all of the following eligibility criteria: (a) use of OQ-System or PCOMS for providing mental health feedback, (b) the intervention was provided to a mental health sample (without restrictions on diagnoses), (c) the intervention provided was a recognizable psychotherapy (e.g., cognitive behavior therapy, psychodynamic therapy, eclectic psychotherapy) with no restrictions on treatment setting or modality (individual, group, couple), and (d) patients were assigned (not necessarily randomly) either to a psychotherapy with feedback condition or to a psychotherapy without feedback (TAU) condition. To be included in the meta-analysis, the study needed to report client outcomes and test statistics needed for calculating SMDs and ORs at the end of treatment. We limited our literature search to studies published in English-language journals. There were no restrictions regarding the date of publication.

Outcome Measures and Computation of Effects

We collected the mean score, standard deviation, and number of participants at endpoint in the experimental and TAU conditions from each original study to calculate a SMD with a 95% CI for each single original trial. Conventions according to Cohen (1992) were applied to interpret the SMD: values > 0.00 to < 0.30 are considered very small; values ≥ 0.30 and < 0.50 are considered to be small effects; values ≥ 0.50 and < 0.80 are moderate; and values ≥ 0.80 are considered to be large.

For computing treatment effects based on dichotomous data, which means in this meta-analysis to contrast the rates and odds of client deterioration and significant improvement between feedback groups and TAU, we collected the number of clients who deteriorated or improved (see definition in the following discussion) and total sample size at endpoint in the experimental and TAU conditions and calculated an OR with a 95% CI for each single trial (a 95% CI that includes 1.0 indicates nonsignificance of the OR).

A key element in psychotherapy research is operationalizing positive and negative outcome for the individual client. Jacobson and Truax (1991) offered a methodology by which client changes on an outcome measure can be classified in the following categories: recovered, reliably improved, no change, or deteriorated. There are two necessary pieces of information needed to classify these client outcomes: a Reliable Change Index (RCI), and a normal functioning cut-off score. Our analysis of deterioration rates, reliable change, and clinically significant change in this chapter are based on the work of Jacobson and Truax (1991).

Clinical and normative data were analyzed by Lambert and colleagues (2013) to establish an RCI and a cut-off score for the OQ-45. The RCI obtained on the OQ-45 was 14 points, indicating that client changes of 14 or more points on the OQ-45 can be considered reliable (i.e., not due to measurement error). The cut-off score for normal functioning on the OQ-45 was calculated to be 63, indicating that scores of 64 or higher are more likely to come from a dysfunctional population than a functional population, and scores of 63 or lower are more likely to come from a functional population than a dysfunctional population. Support for the validity of the OQ-45's reliable change and cut-off score has been reported (Beckstead et al., 2003; Lunnen & Ogles, 1998).

Based on the same methods developed by Jacobson and Truax (1991), Miller and Duncan (2004) reported the RCI and clinical cut-off scores for the ORS. A change of 5 points or greater in either direction in comparison to the pretreatment ORS score is considered a reliable change. The clinical cut-off score used in studies examining the effects of the ORS was 25 points. However, these clinical significance classification cutoff scores were not applied in every study of the ORS. OQ-System cut-off scores and those based on the PCOMS have not been cross-validated with each other so their comparability is unknown.

Specifically, when examining the odds of deterioration, we dichotomized clients into either the deterioration group or nondeterioration group and then calculated the odds ratio of deterioration for a given comparison. Similarly, when comparing the odds of improvement in two groups, the OR was calculated as the odds of improvement versus those of nonimprovement (e.g., no change, deterioration). We defined a priori that in case two or more studies being eligible for inclusion were available we would perform a meta-analysis. The SMDs or ORs of each single original trial were weighted by the generic inverse variance method (GIVM) offered by Review Manager 5.3 (Review Manager, 2014). According to the GIVM the effect estimate of a single, original trial receives a weight that is equal to the inverse of the variance of the effect estimate (i.e. one divided by the standard error squared; Higgins & Green, 2011). Based on the assumptions of a random-effects model these single weighted effects were aggregated across all available studies to a total, weighted SMD or respectively with a 95% CI (Higgins & Green, 2011).

In case of multiple progress feedback arms in one trial (e.g., one arm with progress feedback plus CST and one arm with progress feedback only), we combined the groups to create a single pair-wise comparison (Higgins & Green, 2011). For the determination of heterogeneity of the aggregated single effects, we applied the Q statistic which has a chi square distribution (Hedges & Olkin, 1985). The problem with this test is its low power, which means that while statistically significant results may indicate problems with the homogeneity of the results, a nonsignificant test statistic does not necessarily indicate heterogeneity. It is therefore recommended to use a p-value of .10 to determine statistical significance (Higgins & Green, 2011). Additionally to the Q-statistic we apply the I^2-statistic to quantify the percentage of variability in effect estimates that is due to heterogeneity rather than sampling error. We used conventions of interpretation that were defined by Higgins and Green (2011). An I^2 index of 50% to 90% indicates substantial levels and an I^2 of 75% to 100% considerable levels of heterogeneity. All meta-analytical calculations were done with the Review Manager 5.3 (Review Manager, 2014). Following the recommendations of the Cochrane Collaboration (Higgins & Green, 2011), we provided a funnel plot as well as a test of funnel plot asymmetry based on linear regression (Egger et al., 1997) to check for a publication bias.

Systematic and Meta-Analytic Review of the OQ-System

Characteristics of Included Studies

Table 17.1 summarizes the 15 included studies examining the OQ-System that fulfilled the inclusion criteria. This represents a doubling of the available evidence from the earlier edition of this book (Lambert & Shimokawa, 2011), and includes studies published after the 2011 version of this book. Three older dissertations that never made their way into publication (Trideau, 2000; Copeland, 2007; Truitt, 2007) were identified in the literature search but were excluded from this meta-analysis due to such serious implementation flaws that their results were suspect (e.g., small ns precluded hypothesis testing with inferential statistics). One study (De Jong et al., 2012) fulfilled the criteria of our systematic review, but it did not provide the necessary statistics to be included in the meta-analysis.

The evidence base for feedback, in contrast to the other relationship factors considered in this two-volume book, is based on experimental studies. With the exception of two studies (Harmon et al., 2007; Slade et al., 2008) using an archival TAU group, all the included studies assigned clients to either receive psychotherapy as usually delivered (TAU) or to receive that same psychotherapy enhanced by some type of progress feedback. In short, we are reporting experimental rather than correlational evidence.

Each of the OQ studies in the meta-analysis required about one year of daily data collection and evaluated the effects of providing feedback about each client's improvement using progress graphs and warnings about clients who were not demonstrating expected treatment responses (signal-alarm cases). A primary question in these

Table 17.1. Clinical Trials Examining the Effects of Progress Monitoring with Alarm Signals and Clinical Support Tool Feedback Using the OQ-45[a]

Study	N Total	N Total Fb/TAU	N NOT (% of N total)	N NOT Fb/TAU	Therapy Setting[b]/Mental Disorders[c]	Country	Significant Effect	CST[d]	Total sample Fb vs. TAU			NOT sample Fb vs. TAU		
									SMD [95% CI]	OR [95% CI] Deterioration	Improvement	SMD [95%CI]	OR [95% CI] Deterioration	Improvement
Amble et al. (2015)	259	144/115	na	na/na	OP-I/mix	N	Yes	No	0.33 [0.09, 0.58]	0.62 [0.24, 1.62]	1.51 [0.90, 2.51]	na	na	na
Crits-Christoph et al. (2012)	304	165/139	116 (38.16%)	54/62	SA-I/SA	USA	Yes	Yes	0.27 [−0.15, 0.70]	na	na	0.47 [−0.16, 1.10]	na	na
De Jong et al. (2012)	413	207/206	67 (16.22%)	na/na	OP-I/mix	NL	No/Yes	No	na	na	na	na	na	na
De Jong et al. (2014)	475	331/144	na	na/na	OP-I/mix	NL	No	No	na	0.98 [0.48, 1.99]	1.17 [0.79, 1.73]	na	na	na
Grizzell et al. (2016)[e]	30	15/15	na	na/na	Voc Rehab-G/mix	USA	No/Yes	Yes	−0.16 [0.56, −0.87]	na	na	na	na	na
Hansson et al. (2013)	262	188/186	72 (19.25%)	37/35	OP-I/mix	S	No	No	0.03 [−0.18, 0.23]	na	na	na	na	na
Harmon et al. (2007)[f]	2,819	1,374/1,445	655 (23.23%)	369/286	CC-I/mix	USA	Yes	Yes	0.17 [0.09, 0.24]	na	na	0.33 [0.18, 0.49]	1.13 [0.75, 1.71]	3.83 [2.62, 5.61]

(continued)

Table 17.1. Continued

Study	N Total	N Total Fb/TAU	N NOT (% of N total)	N NOT Fb/TAU	Therapy Setting[b]/Mental Dis-orders[c]	Coun-try	Significant Effect	CST[a]	Total sample Fb vs. TAU	NOT sample Fb vs. TAU		
Hawkins et al. (2004)	306	70/64	101 (33.01%)	69/32	OP-I/mix	USA	Yes	No	0.13 [−0.16, 0.43]	na	0.44 [0.08, 2.31]	2.14 [0.88, 5.17]
Lambert et al. (2001)	609	307/302	66 (10.84%)	35/31	CC-I/mix	USA	Yes	No	0.08 [−0.08, 0.24]	0.44 [−0.05, 0.93]	0.21 [0.04, 1.09]	1.80 [0.53, 6.10]
Lambert et al. (2002)	1,422	528/492	240 (16.88%)	116/124	CC-I/mix	USA	Yes	No	0.21 [0.09, 0.33]	0.42 [0.17, 0.68]	0.72 [0.39, 1.36]	2.17 [1.19, 3.97]
Probst et al. (2013) Probst et al. (2014)	252	134/118	43 (17.06%)	23/20	IP-IG/Som	DE	Yes	Yes	na	0.23 [−0.37, 0.84]	na	na
Simon et al. (2012)	370	na/na	207 (55.95%)	109/98	OP-I/mix	USA	Yes	Yes	na	0.12 [−0.16, 0.39]	0.49 [0.19, 1.30]	1.68 [0.91, 3.09]
Simon et al. (2013)	133	69/64	71 (53.38%)	33/38	IP-IG/ED	USA	Yes	Yes	0.30 [−0.05, 0.64]	1.41 [0.23, 8.72]	1.38 [0.65, 2.93]	na

Slade et al. (2008)[g]	3,920	2,475/ 1,445	983 (29.79%)	697/286	CC-I/mix	USA	Yes	Yes	na	na	na	0.37 [0.23, 0.51]	na	na
Whipple et al. (2003)	1,339	499/482	278 (20.76%)	147/131	CC-I/mix	USA	Yes	Yes	0.02 [−0.11, 0.14]	na	0.28 [0.05, 0.52]	0.55 [0.28, 1.08]	**1.94 [1.16, 3.24]**

[a]This summary excludes the results of three unpublished doctoral dissertations with serious implementation problems and very small Ns (Trudeau, 2001; Copeland, 2007; & Truitt, 2011). [b]Therapy settings of included studies: CC = college counseling center clients; OP = outpatient clinics; SA = substance abuse clinics; IP = inpatient treatment setting; Voc Rehab = vocational rehabilitation clients; I = individual psychotherapy; G = group psychotherapy; IG = individual & group psychotherapy. [c]Mix = sample comprised clients with different mental disorders; SA = substance abuse disorder clients; ED = eating disorder clients; Som = clients with psychosomatic disorders. [d]Study used Clinical Support Tools (CST) as well as progress feedback. [e]In the Fb condition all clients received CST (but not only the NOT-clients as it was done in the other trials including CST). [f]Includes archival TAU sample (N=1,445) consisting of TAU samples from Lambert et al. 2001, Lambert et al. 2002 and Whipple et al. 2003. [g]Includes archival TAU sample (N=1,445) and archival Fb-sample (N=1,374) from Harmon et al. 2007.

Note: Fb = Feedback group, TAU = Treatment as usual, NOT = Not-on-Track cases (predicted treatment failure), na = number of clients/data not available (were not reported in the original study report), NL = Netherlands, S = Sweden, DE = Germany, N = Norway.

studies was: Does progress feedback with alarm signals about clients' progress improve psychotherapy outcomes compared to treatment without feedback (i.e., treatment as usual)? In some studies the effects of CSTs were studied and the question was: Will the use of CST further enhance at-risk client outcome compared to progress feedback alone and compared to TAU.

The 15 studies in the current systematic review expand upon the original research findings, which were largely conducted in a single university counseling center in the United States. The newer studies examined outcomes across several European countries (Germany, Netherlands, Norway, and Sweden), as well as within inpatient and additional outpatient settings. The current review includes studies of the OQ-System with substance abusing individuals, eating disordered inpatients, psychosomatic inpatients, a vocational rehabilitation sample, additional outpatient samples, and application with group psychotherapy. This expansion of countries, settings, and patient populations is an important development in feedback research.

The total number of clients in the 15 studies was 8,649, of whom 1,958 were NOT cases. In contrast to clinical trials of specific treatments for specific disorders in which strict inclusion criteria make samples highly selective and ns hover around 30 to 50 clients, feedback research on the OQ-System has much larger samples per study. Of the 15 studies reported in Table 17.1, 3 (Amble et al., 2015; De Jong et al., 2014; Grizzell et al., 2016) did include a separate analysis of outcomes for NOT clients. The average number of NOT cases per study was 242 (2,899/12), although some studies had more than one feedback condition, shrinking the number per group to a smaller number depending on the number of experimental groups.

The mean percentage of NOT clients within the 12 studies that reported this number was 31.2% with a range of 11% to 56%. This suggests considerable variability in the portion of patients off-track. The cause of this variability is unknown, but the nature of the client population and the nature of treatment are probably both explanatory. For example, the study with the highest rate of NOT clients (56%) was a hospital-based, outpatient clinic in which most patients were referred from an inpatient stay, had a long history of dysfunction and prior treatment. Outpatients in this particular clinic were unlikely to receive weekly psychotherapy. Their psychotherapy was more likely to occur every three weeks due to clinic policy (this also resulted in delayed feedback). These clients were quite disturbed when they entered treatment and received a less than optimal psychotherapy dosage due to a policy decision outside of their therapists' control.

In contrast, the studies conducted in a university counseling center (Harmon et al., 2007; Lambert et al., 2001, 2002; Slade et al., 2008; Whipple et al., 2003) had a NOT proportion ranging from 11% to 30%. The counseling center clients within this setting started treatment with less disturbance, were younger, often receiving their first episode of care, and met with their therapist on a weekly basis. In routine care it may be difficult to anticipate the portion of individuals who will signal as off-track. Practitioners can anticipate a similar percentage of NOT cases using the OQ-Analyst's algorithms.

As seen in Table 17.1, one study (Grizzell et al., 2016) was seriously underpowered with an n prior to randomization of 30 clients. These vocational rehabilitation clients were randomly assigned to either cognitive-behavioral group therapy plus progress feedback and CST feedback, or cognitive-behavioral group therapy without feedback. The small n in experimental and control groups was further reduced when client outcomes were examined separately for on-track and NOT cases. Thus, the portion of NOT cases and their outcomes could not be analyzed and were not reported in publication of the study. The other 14 studies in this systematic and meta-analytic review started with a minimum of 133 clients and, in most cases, had hundreds of clients assigned into TAU or feedback conditions.

Pattern of Statistically Significant Findings

The usual standard for concluding that one treatment is superior to another is that of a statistically significant (reliable) superiority of one over the other. Of the 15 identified studies, 11 (73%) found a statistically significant difference between the NOT feedback group and the NOT TAU control on the primary outcome variable (OQ-45). If the single underpowered study is excluded from this analysis, 79% (11/14) of studies reported a statistically significant effect for feedback compared to TAU within a therapist's caseload. The practical implication of this finding is that clinics and practitioners are highly likely to find implementing feedback in routine care will reliably enhance client outcomes for NOT clients (i.e., about one third of their case load). The size of this treatment effect and its clinical significance will now be addressed.

Meta-Analyses and Effect Sizes

The meta-analysis showed that the progress feedback intervention out performed treatment as usual in the total sample by a very small but statistically significant effect at the end of treatment (SMD = 0.14, 95% CI = 0.08–0.20). There was consistency in the data ($Q(9) = 11.38$, $p = .250$; $I^2 = 21\%$). Although not statistically significant, the OR show a tendency that Fb in contrast to TAU reduced the number of clients who deteriorated (OR = 0.87, 95% CI = 0.51–1.50; $Q(2) = 0.86$, $p = .650$; $I^2 = 0\%$) and increased the number of improved clients at the end of therapy (OR = 1.30, 95% CI = 0.97–1.73; $Q(2) = 0.64$, $p = .730$; $I^2 = 0\%$). These odds ratios have to be interpreted cautiously because they are both, for deterioration as well as improvement rates, based on only three studies. Results are summarized and depicted in Figure 17.5.

The effects identified in the total sample are larger when effect sizes are calculated with data only from clients who were designated as NOT clients (see summary in Figure 17.6). The effect of the feedback (Fb) intervention was larger and reached significance with a weighted effect size of 0.33 (95% CI = 0.25–0.41). The heterogeneity Index ($Q(7) = 3.79$, $p = .800$; $I^2 = 0\%$) indicated absolute homogeneity in the data. Consistent with this finding, the ORs show a significantly reducing effect of Fb, in contrast to TAU, on the rate of clients who deteriorated (OR = 0.61, 95% CI = 0.46–0.81; $Q(5) = 2.47$, $p = .780$; $I^2 = 0\%$) and a significantly increasing effect on the number of improved clients (OR = 1.89, 95% CI = 1.50–2.37). Both kinds of analyzed OR data demonstrated high consistency ($Q(5) = 0.49$, $p = .990$; $I^2 = 0\%$).

Study or Subgroup	TAU Mean	TAU SD	TAU Total	Feedback group Mean	Feedback group SD	Feedback group Total	Weight	Std. Mean Difference IV, Random, 95% CI
Amble 2015	84.6	25.1	115	75.5	28.6	144	5.7%	0.33 [0.09, 0.58]
Crits-Christoph 2012	66.63	25.07	43	59.9	24.13	43	2.1%	0.27 [−0.15, 0.70]
Grizzell 2016	58.6	31.94	15	63.53	29.37	15	0.8%	−0.16 [−0.87, 0.56]
Hansson 2013	88.9	16.6	186	88.5	15.3	188	8.1%	0.03 [−0.18, 0.23]
Harmon 2007 (1)	61.68	23.88	1445	57.65	24.43	1374	30.1%	0.17 [0.09, 0.24]
Hawkins 2004	69.33	23.42	64	66.03	25.18	137	4.1%	0.13 [−0.16, 0.43]
Lambert 2001	65.12	22.28	302	63.33	23.78	307	11.9%	0.08 [−0.08, 0.24]
Lambert 2002	61.74	24.53	492	56.84	22.48	528	17.2%	0.21 [0.09, 0.33]
Simon 2013	69.5	20.69	64	61.87	29.49	69	3.1%	0.30 [−0.05, 0.64]
Whipple 2013	58.56	23.38	482	58.15	22.25	499	16.9%	0.02 [−0.11, 0.14]
Total (95% CI)			**3208**			**3304**	**100.0%**	**0.14 [0.08, 0.20]**

Heterogeneity: $Tau^2 = 0.00$; $Chi^2 = 11.38$, $df = 9$ ($P = 0.25$); $I^2 = 21\%$

Test for overall effect: $Z = 4.35$ ($P < 0.0001$)

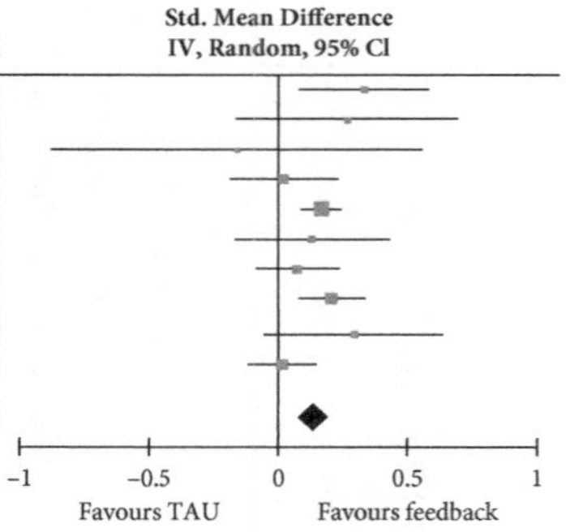

Footnotes

(1) The TAU group in this study is an archival control group composed of TAU group of the studies by Lambert 2001, Lambert 2002, Whipple 2003.

Study or Subgroup	Feedback group Events	Feedback group Total	TAU Events	TAU Total	Weight	Odds Ratio IV, Random, 95% CI
Amble 2015	8	144	10	115	32.0%	0.62 [0.24, 1.62]
De Jong 2014	27	331	12	144	59.0%	0.98 [0.48, 1.99]
Simon 2013	3	69	2	64	9.0%	1.41 [0.23, 8.72]
Total (95% CI)		**544**		**323**	**100.0%**	**0.87 [0.51, 1.50]**
Total events	38		24			

Heterogeneity: $Tau^2 = 0.00$; $Chi^2 = 0.86$, $df = 2$ ($P = 0.65$); $I^2 = 0\%$

Test for overall effect: $Z = 0.49$ ($P = 0.62$)

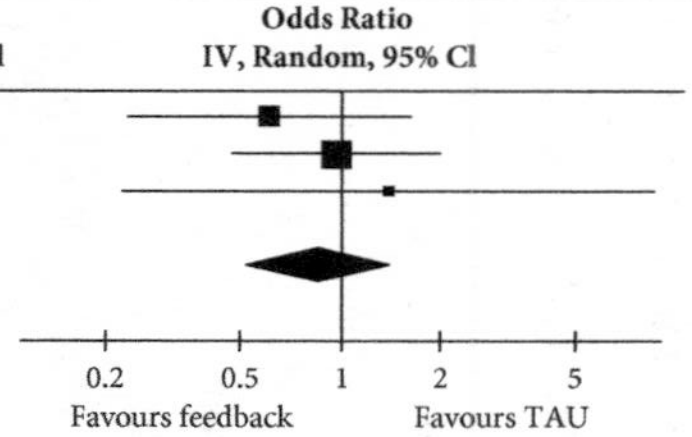

Study or Subgroup	Feedback group Events	Feedback group Total	TAU Events	TAU Total	Weight	Odds Ratio IV, Random, 95% CI
Amble 2015	60	144	37	115	31.4%	1.51 [0.90, 2.51]
De Jong 2014	169	331	68	144	53.8%	1.17 [0.79, 1.73]
Simon 2013	51	69	43	64	14.7%	1.38 [0.65, 2.93]
Total (95% CI)		**544**		**323**	**100.0%**	**1.30 [0.97, 1.73]**
Total events	280		148			

Heterogeneity: $Tau^2 = 0.00$; $Chi^2 = 0.64$, $df = 2$ ($P = 0.73$); $I^2 = 0\%$

Test for overall effect: $Z = 1.77$ ($P = 0.08$)

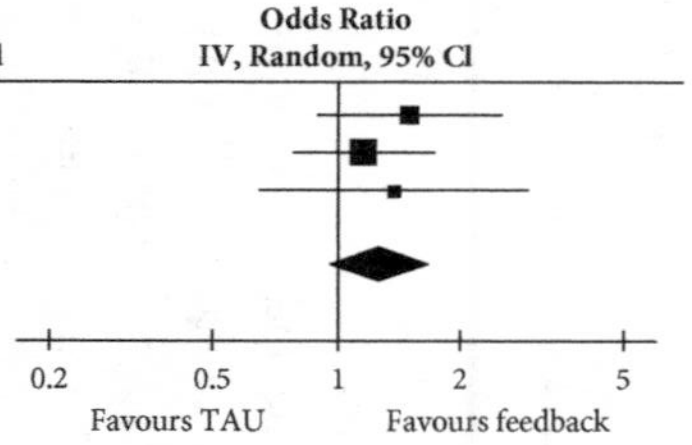

FIGURE 17.5 Forest plot of the comparison progress feedback versus treatment as usual (TAU): Outcome Questionnaire-45 sum score (standard mean difference), cases of deteriorated clients (odds ratio), and cases of improved clients (odds ratio).

Study or Subgroup	TAU Mean	SD	Total	Feedback Group Mean	SD	Total	Weight	Std. Mean Difference IV, Random, 95% CI
Crits-Christoph 2012	85.5	25.8	19	73.3	25	21	1.7%	0.47 [−0.16, 1.10]
Harmon 2007 (1)	80.17	20.74	286	72.99	22.39	369	27.7%	0.33 [0.18, 0.49]
Lambert 2001	83.13	18.92	31	74.57	19.81	35	2.8%	0.44 [−0.05, 0.93]
Lambert 2002	83.72	21.05	124	73.87	25.34	116	10.2%	0.42 [0.17, 0.68]
Probst 2014	98.65	25.46	20	92.57	25.4	23	1.8%	0.23 [−0.37, 0.84]
Simon 2012	83.75	18.48	98	81.62	17.99	109	9.0%	0.12 [−0.16, 0.39]
Slade 2008 (2)	80.17	20.74	286	72.15	22.04	697	34.8%	0.37 [0.23, 0.51]
Whipple 2003	76.11	20.26	131	69.88	23.38	147	11.9%	0.28 [0.05, 0.52]
Total (95% CI)			995			1517	100.0%	0.33 [0.25, 0.41]

Heterogeneity: Tau^2 = 0.00; Chi^2 = 3.79, df = 7 (P = 0.80); I^2 = 0%
Test for overall effect: Z = 7.96 (P < 0.00001)

Std. Mean Difference IV, Random, 95% CI (scale −2, −1, 0, 1, 2; Favours TAU — Favours feedback)

Footnotes
(1) The TAU group in this study is an archival control group composed of TAU group of the studies by Lambert 2001, Lambert 2002, Whipple 2003.
(2) This study shares the archival TAU group and partly the Fb group with the study Harmon 2007.

Study or Subgroup	Feedback Group Events	Total	TAU Events	Total	Weight	Odds Ratio IV, Random, 95% CI
Harmon 2007 (1)	56	369	61	286	48.7%	0.66 [0.44, 0.99]
Hawkins 2004	3	69	3	32	2.8%	0.44 [0.08, 2.31]
Lambert 2001	2	35	7	31	2.9%	0.21 [0.04, 1.09]
Lambert 2002	21	116	29	124	19.8%	0.72 [0.39, 1.36]
Simon 2012	7	109	12	98	8.2%	0.49 [0.19, 1.30]
Whipple 2003	17	147	25	131	17.6%	0.55 [0.28, 1.08]
Total (95% CI)		845		702	100.0%	0.61 [0.46, 0.81]
Total events	106		137			

Heterogeneity: Tau^2 = 0.00; Chi^2 = 2.47, df = 5 (P = 0.78); I^2 = 0%
Test for overall effect: Z = 3.48 (P = 0.0005)

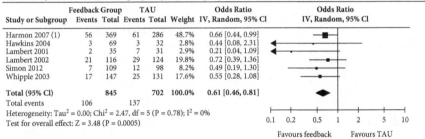

Odds Ratio IV, Random, 95% CI (scale 0.1, 0.2, 0.5, 1, 2, 5, 10; Favours feedback — Favours TAU)

Footnotes
(1) TAU group in this study = archival control group composed of TAU group of studies by Lambert 2001, Lambert 2002, Whipple 2003.

Study or Subgroup	Feedback Group Events	Total	TAU Events	Total	Weight	Odds Ratio IV, Random, 95% CI
Harmon 2007 (1)	120	369	60	286	41.2%	1.82 [1.27, 2.60]
Hawkins 2004	34	69	10	32	6.8%	2.14 [0.88, 5.17]
Lambert 2001	9	35	5	31	3.5%	1.80 [0.53, 6.10]
Lambert 2002	37	116	22	124	14.5%	2.17 [1.19, 3.97]
Simon 2012	37	109	23	98	14.1%	1.68 [0.91, 3.09]
Whipple 2003	58	147	33	131	20.0%	1.94 [1.16, 3.24]
Total (95% CI)		845		702	100.0%	1.89 [1.50, 2.37]
Total events	295		153			

Heterogeneity: Tau^2 = 0.00; Chi^2 = 0.49, df = 5 (P = 0.99); I^2 = 0%
Test for overall effect: Z = 5.41 (P < 0.00001)

Odds Ratio IV, Random, 95% CI (scale 0.2, 0.5, 1, 2, 5; Favours TAU — Favours feedback)

Footnotes
(1) TAU group in this study = archival control group composed of TAU group of studies by Lambert 2001, Lambert 2002, Whipple 2003.

FIGURE 17.6   Forest plot of the comparison progress feedback versus treatment as usual (TAU) for clients who are not on track (NOT): Outcome Questionnaire-45 sum score (standard mean difference), cases of deteriorated clients (odds ratio), and cases of improved clients (odds ratio).

Of the eight studies in which the CST was added to the progress feedback, six studies (Crits-Christoph et al., 2012; Harmon et al., 2007; Probst et al., 2014; Simon et al., 2013; Slade et al., 2008; Whipple et al., 2003) provided sufficient data for calculating a total, weighted SMD. We identified a moderate weighted effect size of .49 (95% CI = 0.25–0.73) for the comparison between the Fb+CST condition and the TAU condition in the NOT sample. The OR analyses showed a significant benefit of CST-Fb on the rate of deteriorating clients (OR = 0.37, 95% CI = 0.22–0.63) as well as on the rate of improving clients (OR = 2.40, 95% CI =1.73–3.35). Effect sizes based on the Fb+CST vs. TAU comparisons in the NOT group are substantially larger compared to the effect sizes based on Fb versus TAU comparisons in NOT group (OQ-45 total score: $SMD_{Fb+CST \text{ vs. } TAU}$ = .49 vs. $SMD_{Fb \text{ vs. } TAU}$ = .33; rate of deteriorated clients: $OR_{Fb+CST \text{ vs. } TAU}$ = .37 vs. $OR_{Fb \text{ vs. } TAU}$ = .61; rate of improved clients: $OR_{Fb+CST \text{ vs. } TAU}$ = 2.40 vs. $OR_{Fb \text{ vs. } TAU}$ = 1.89).

We created a funnel plot for the 10 studies that compare an OQ-based Fb intervention with TAU in the total sample and that were entered in the meta-analysis (see Figure 17.5). This funnel plot (see Figure 17.7, Panel A) indicates asymmetry and a publication bias. The funnel plot shows that the effect estimates of the single trials mainly have a low standard error and are close to the total SMD of 0.14. The sole study

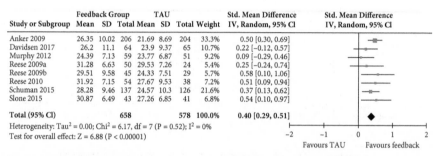

FIGURE 17.7 Forest plot of the comparison progress feedback versus treatment as usual (TAU) in the total sample: Outcome Rating Scale (ORS) sum score (standard mean difference), cases of deteriorated clients (odds ratio), and cases of improved clients (odds ratio:

Note. Extracted data for effect size calculation are based on ORS sum score except for the study by Janse et al., 2016, which used the Global Severity Index of the Symptom Checklist-90.

(Grizzell et al., 2016) that deviates from the pattern had the smallest sample size and accordingly a high standard error. The test of the funnel plot asymmetry confirms the graphic result and the publication bias with an intercept of 6.01 (90% CI = 1.99–10.03), which significantly deviates from zero (p = .039). However these results have to be interpreted carefully. This kind of publication bias analysis assumes that a publication bias is indicated if no studies with low sample sizes (or high standard error) and more extreme effects are included in the meta-analysis. However it is common that progress feedback studies have large sample sizes. Therefore effect sizes from most of these studies have a small standard error. Thus the results of the current funnel plot analysis could underlie a statistical artifact.

This finding is consistent with our earlier meta-analysis in the second edition of this volume (Lambert & Shimokawa, 2011). Overall, the results of examining effect sizes across the published studies suggest a very small effect of .14 for feedback on the whole sample, a larger effect (.33) for feedback on NOT clients, and a still larger effect (.49) when CSTs are provided to therapists. The pattern of results are similar to our previous meta-analysis, but the average effect sizes for each condition are slightly lower.

These findings are also consistent with contextualized feedback theory (Reimer et al., 2005). Feedback will prove most effective when it provides psychotherapists not only with novel information about client treatment progress, but also problem-solving strategies and concrete suggestions for actions to be considered when clients are not making expected progress.

Conclusions Related to Null Findings

Researchers design studies hoping to find a statistically significant difference between an experimental group and a control group if one exists and thus a failure to find a difference needs some exploration. Several trends emerge when considering the OQ studies with null findings. Three dissertation studies that were identified in the literature were not included in this meta-analysis because they had implementation and statistical problems (Copeland, 2007; Trideau, 2000) such that treatment effects could not be tested. A small sample size was also a problem in the Grizzell et al. (2016) study, which was included in the meta-analysis.

In the OQ-System, the clients of interest are those who the algorithms identify as off-track. This will typically be about 31% of clients in each group but will vary in relation to the general disturbance level of the sample, with more disturbed clients producing a higher portion of off-track cases. Hypothetically, one would need to have 200 clients in each group in order to compare the resulting 50 NOT clients within each group if 25% go off-track. Among studies with null findings, only De Jong et al. (2012, 2014) and Hansson et al. (2013) were adequately powered. Such problems raise concerns about the file drawer problem, suggesting that some studies are left out of the review.

Null results are also more likely to occur when therapists are not provided with continuous feedback over the entire course of psychotherapy but at sparse times. The sooner a therapist becomes aware that a client is NOT, the sooner a therapist can re-spond to clients whose progress is doubtful. This is important in clinical practice as well as in testing the effects of feedback in research studies.

Delivering feedback to therapists has become rather easy to accomplish but it does not necessarily follow that therapists will even open their computers before seeing a client. An advantage of the PCOMS method is that therapists actually administer measures in session, although in practice they may fail to do so. Noncompliance with feedback practices has been a significant problem in some studies (e.g., De Jong et al., 2012) and is likely in routine care unless the therapist is committed to implementing this evidence-based practice.

Systematic and Meta-Analytic Review of the PCOMS

Characteristics of Studies

Nine studies, based on eight articles studying the effects of the PCOMS, were identified in our search. This represents a threefold increase from the second edi-tion of this book. These studies are summarized in Table 17.2, which provides the number of clients included in each study, but not the number of NOT clients. In contrast to studies with feedback based on the OQ-45, studies of PCOMS published results mainly focused on all clients, not just off-track clients. In addition, Table 17.2 specifies the sample/setting of the study, if the difference between the experimental group and control group was statistically significant, and the size of the treatment effect.

Studies of the PCOMS intervention share many of the same design features as the OQ-System especially by studying feedback within routine care with clients who are randomly assigned from consecutive cases who are seeking care. The results of the studies are expected to be generalized to those who are in routine care rather than se-lective samples typically reported in randomized clinical trials. As seen in Table 17.2, the total number of clients in the nine studies of PCOMS was 2,272 with a mean per study of 252. An outlier study, with regards to its sample size (Janse et al., 2017), in-cluded 1,006 clients of the 2,272, giving it excessive weight. When this study is removed the mean number of clients per study is reduced to 158 clients, typically divided into either feedback or TAU conditions.

Pattern of Statistically Significant Findings

Across the nine studies, six (67%) reported a statistically significant difference between feedback and TAU conditions. This finding suggests most of the time researchers designed and implemented studies showing a reliable difference favoring PCOMS feedback over treatment as usual. The practical implication of this finding is that clinics and practitioners are highly likely to find implementing PCOMS will reliably improve many clients outcomes.

Table 17.2. Clinical Trials Examining the Effects of PCOMS Progress Monitoring and Alliance Feedback Using the ORS and SRS

Study	N Total[a]	N Fb/TAU	Therapy Setting[b]/ Mental Disorders[c]	Country	Significant Effect	SRS[d]	Total Sample Fb vs. TAU SMD [95% CI]	OR [95% CI] Deterioration	Improvement
Anker et al. (2009)	410	206/204	OP-COP/mix	N	Yes	No	0.50 [0.30, 0.69]	0.36 [0.10, 1.22]	3.96 [2.27, 6.90]
Davidsen et al. (2017)	159	80/79	ED-G	DK	No	Yes/No	0.22 [-0.12, 0.57]	na	na
Janse et al. (2017)[f]	1006	461/545	OP/mix	NL	No	Yes	0.001[e]	1.20 [0.75, 1.91]	2.83 [1.08, 7.43]
Murphy et al. (2012)	110	59/51	CC -I/mix	IRL	No	No	0.09 [-0.29, 0.46]	0.49 [0.11, 2.17]	0.78 [0.36, 1.71]
Reese et al. (2009)	74	50/24	CC-I/mix	USA	Yes	Yes	0.25 [-0.24, 0.74]	0.29 [0.05, 1.88]	3.38 [1.17, 9.78]
Reese et al. (2009)	74	45/29	OP-I/mix	USA	Yes	Yes	0.58 [0.10, 1.06]	1.30 [0.11, 15.05]	2.83 [1.08, 7.43]
Reese et al. (2010)	92	54/38	OP-COP/mix	USA	Yes	Yes	0.51 [0.09, 0.94]	0.68 [0.16, 2.91]	3.99 [1.65, 9.65]
Schuman et al. (2015)	263	137/126	SA-G/SA	USA	Yes	No	0.37 [0.13, 0.62]	1.26 [0.62, 2.59]	1.50 [0.92, 2.46]
Slone et al. (2015)	84	43/41	CC-I/mix	USA	Yes	Yes	0.54 [0.10, 0.97]	0.95 [0.13, 7.09]	3.37 [1.34, 8.45]

[a]The study N = the total sample. [b]CC = college counseling center clients; OP = outpatient clinics; I = individual psychotherapy; COP = couples therapy. [c]mix = sample comprises clients with different mental disorders; SA = substance abuse disorder clients; ED = eating disorder clients. 4 = Study used Outcome Rating Scale (ORS) and the Session Rating Scale (SRS). 4 = when data for calculating SMD/OR were not available the effect size reported by the authors of the original report is provided (however the 95% CI is usually not provided in the original study reports). 4 = effect sizes are based on the outcome Global Severity Index of the Symptom Checklist-90.

Note. COP = couples—410 G = group therapy. SMD = standardized mean deviation; 95% CI = 95% confidence interval. OR = odds ratio. na = number of clients/data not available (were not reported in the original study report). N = Norway. IRL = Ireland. DK = Denmark. NL = Netherlands.

Meta-Analyses and Effect Sizes

Our meta-analytic calculations show that PCOMS feedback (Fb) shows a statistically significant and small benefit (according to Cohen's criteria, effect > .30, < .50) in comparison to the TAU in the total sample (SMD = 0.40, 95% CI = 0.29–0.51). Results of the included studies are highly consistent ($Q(7) = 6.17$, $p = .520$; $I^2 = 0\%$).

Similar to the OQ-System in the total sample, PCOMS feedback does not have a significant benefit in contrast to TAU on reducing the number of deteriorating clients (OR = 0.97, 95% CI = 0.70, 1.36; $Q(7) = 6.55$, $p = .480$; $I^2 = 0\%$). However, in contrast to TAU, the feedback showed a significantly beneficial effect on the number of improved clients (OR = 2.11, 95% CI = 1.29, 3.44) with regards to the total sample. The results have to be interpreted cautiously, however, because the heterogeneity of the effects is large ($Q(7) = 33.85$, $p < .001$; $I^2 = 79\%$). Findings are depicted in Figure 17.8.

The higher heterogeneity levels found in the data from the PCOMS studies suggest that the size of treatment effect is not uniform across studies. Similar to the OQ-System, the clinical results may vary as a function of client, clinician, and/or method variations. Within this set of nine studies, four were conducted outside of the United States (Anker et al., 2009; Davidsen et al., 2017; Janse et al., 2017) and three of these did not show an advantage for feedback.

For example, Janse and colleagues (2017) studied the effects of progress feedback using the PCOMS with clients undergoing behavior therapy in Dutch outpatients ($N = 1006$) in a single mental health organization. Assignment to treatment condition was not random, with 545 clients receiving TAU and 461 receiving feedback. Treatment was provided for an average of 13 sessions (range 1 to 55). Not all therapists participated in both phases of the study: Some therapists left during the first phase, and some therapists joined the organization during the second phase. Fifty-six percent of the therapists participated in both conditions of the study. As is typical in PCOMS research, the paper and pencil versions of the ORS and SRS were used with clients

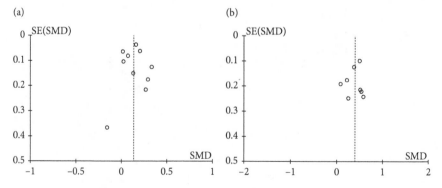

FIGURE 17.8 Funnel plot for studies included to a meta analysis of the comparison between progress feedback versus treatment as usual in the total sample with regards to *a) the OQ score (10 studies) and (b) the Outcome Rating Scale (ORS) score (8 studies) at the end of therapy (SE = standard error of the effect estimate; SMD = standard mean deviation of a single trial).

completing the ORS at the beginning of the session and the SRS at the end of the session. Both measures were immediately scored by the therapist in session, entered into the progress graph, and discussed with the client. Because progress in the first five sessions can be predictive of treatment outcome, therapists were advised that progress should occur during this first phase of therapy and, if it did not occur, to discuss the lack of progress with their client.

Perhaps the most important difference in this study compared with those that had a positive effect was that final outcome was measured using the Symptom Checklist-90 rather than the ORS. To check whether therapists used the feedback from the ORS/SRS during treatment, 89% of the client files in the feedback condition were physically verified (11% of the files were not available anymore) for the presence of completed questionnaires and summary graph, as well as mention of the feedback in the session reports. Of these client files, 77% showed that feedback was used by the therapist. This makes it unlikely that the null results were due to implementation problems, an observation that is bolstered by the finding that feedback led to greater treatment efficiency (an average of two fewer sessions) in the feedback group.

We created a funnel plot for the 8 studies that compared a PCOMS-based Fb intervention with TAU in the total sample and that were entered in the meta-analysis (see Figure 17.8). This funnel plot (see Figure 17.7, Panel B) indicates asymmetry and a publication bias. The funnel plot shows that the effect estimates of the trials all have a low standard error and are close to the total SMD of .40. The test of funnel plot asymmetry confirms the graphic result and the publication bias with an intercept of 3.22 (90% CI = 1.46–4.98) which significantly deviates from zero ($p = .024$).

In sum, aggregated findings from the nine studies indicate that the PCOMS rests on a growing empirical base that boosts confidence in its use as a ROM. Practitioners can expect that PCOMS feedback will enhance client outcomes with an average effect size of SMD = .40 and 95% confidence it will be between .29 and .51. Nevertheless, as our summary shows (Table 17.2), there is considerable heterogeneity in results ranging from SMD = .00 to .58. At this point in time, there are not enough studies to quantitatively analyze the mediators and moderators of outcome, so one is left to speculate as to the causes of seeming discrepancies.

The effect size estimate based on this review is lower than that based on the first three studies examined in earlier meta-analyses (Duncan & Reese, 2015; Lambert & Shimokawa, 2011). This is largely due to the newer studies having smaller effects but also because several new studies failed to find a statistically significant effect for feedback. Despite this, classification of each client's individual change through the Jacobson and Truax (1991) method suggests use of the PCOMS substantially reduces the number of clients classified as "not changed" at termination. These clients are found to change enough to be considered reliably improved when the PCOMS is used.

Conclusions Related to Null Findings

A study that failed to find a statistically significant difference favoring feedback was published by Davidsen and associates (2017). This study tested the effects of client feedback on eating disordered clients undergoing weekly outpatient group psycho-therapy. One hundred fifty-nine clients were randomly assigned to a feedback group (n = 80) or a TAU control (n = 79). Treatment duration was set for 20-25 sessions. The study took place in Copenhagen, Denmark. The ORS and Group SRS were used as feedback measures. Treatment outcome was assessed with the Eating Disorder Examination Interview, ORS, SCL-90, Sheehan Disability Scale, and the Self-Harm Inventory. No feedback effect on any of the measures reached statistical significance. Nor did the effect of feedback on group attendance show any difference between the experimental and control conditions.

The failure to find an effect for feedback may have been due to the use of inde-pendent measures of pre- post change, as in the Janse et al. (2017) study. However, no treatment effect was attained when the ORS was used as the measure of outcome. The authors also studied therapist ratings of the usefulness of the feedback. They re-ported that they could find little evidence that the therapists found it useful or took actions based on the feedback when the client was at risk for deterioration. For ex-ample, referrals within the care unit for provision of additional clinical services were not higher. Thus, this study may have failed due to a lack of enthusiasm on the part of therapists with regards to PCOMS feedback. Similar concerns were raised about OQ feedback in the de Jong et al. (2012) study, which reinforces the importance of proper implementation of ROM/PROM practices.

The study authors suggested that failure could be a result of applying PCOMS in the Danish system of care that restricts flexibility in treatment protocols. That would make it difficult for clinicians to modify treatment as might be expected after receiving individualized feedback that a client was off-track. The authors noted that clinicians felt they had insufficient time to discuss progress or relationships based on the feedback.

Across the 9 studies, 6 (67%) reported a statistically significant difference between feedback and TAU conditions. Several of the studies that failed to find an effect were conducted outside the USA, while all the studies done in the USA found an effect. This raises questions about cross-cultural application and implementation of the methods. Studies done in the USA were conducted by those associated with the development of the intervention and were knowledgeable about how to train therapists, provide supervision, and implement the intervention. A possible cross-cultural problem is undermined by the study by Anker et al (2009) which was conducted in Norway and reported one of the largest effect sizes favoring PCOMS feedback. As further research emerges it may become clearer if null findings arise in cross-cultural applications. The jury is still out on this issue.

The null studies were also prone to be studies that were more recent and that used outcome measures other than the ORS. Future research is needed to determine if there are circumstances or client samples where PCOMS feedback is unlikely to work. The bulk of evidence shows that positive outcomes with the PCOMS have been found across treatment formats (individual, group, and couple treatment) and a wide variety of psychological dysfunctions, including substance abuse.

EVIDENCE FOR CAUSALITY

The research evidence supporting ROM/PROM feedback systems is based on controlled experiments. Clients have been randomly assigned (with several exceptions) to either feedback-assisted psychotherapy or a treatment-as-usual comparison group often offered by the same therapist. Thus, the meta-analytic results provide causal evidence for the salubrious effects of these two feedback systems.

At the same time, a great deal of research needs to be conducted before the specific mechanisms of change are identified. The OQ-System presumably works by supplying therapists with novel information that corrects overly optimistic judgements of client treatment response, by increasing therapist interest and attention to these poorly responding clients, and by assessing what may be causing failure and suggestions for altering treatment. The PCOMS presumably works by increasing client-therapist collaboration through discussing both treatment progress and the working alliance across the entire caseload of clinicians.

OQ-System research has attempted to sort out which aspects of treatment are active (causing) the change by separately studying therapist-only progress feedback, therapist feedback plus direct formal client feedback, or by offering problem-solving strategies with suggestions for treatment modifications and various combinations of these practices. PCOMS research has not yet tried to separate the effects of progress feedback and therapeutic alliance feedback in causing client improvement. Neither system has examined process variables to determine if the mechanisms of change are consistent with their underlying theory of change.

PATIENT CONTRIBUTIONS

We do not know from this meta-analysis the extent to which client variables are particularly important in ROM/PROM. One persistent finding in the OQ-System is that effects are largely limited to clients who have problematic responses to treatment early in psychotherapy. These clients are likely to be more disturbed when compared to other clients, before therapy begins. Initial degree of disturbance increases the likelihood they will run into difficulties but not the likelihood that they will have a positive treatment outcome.

In the PCOMS this does not seem to be the case. PCOMS feedback appears to work across the entire caseload regardless of initial level of disturbance.

Across the 24 studies examined in this review, patient diagnosis does not seem to exert much influence with regards to feedback effects. At the same time, the impact of diagnosis has not been carefully studied, and diagnoses have usually been made by the treating clinician without the benefit of using standardized and reliable methods. We know from the published studies that a portion of patients do not respond to feedback methods, but have no knowledge of the extent to which this is a function of patient variables, therapist factors, or something connected to the nature of the feedback.

LIMITATIONS OF THE RESEARCH

Major limitations of feedback research include the small number of studies evaluating effectiveness, the limited number of researchers responsible for the findings reviewed here, and the sole reliance on single self-report measures. An especially salient limitation across almost all the studies reviewed here is that the same measure was used to track progress and to quantify end of treatment outcome. Although it would be ideal to assess mental health status at the beginning and end of treatment using several standardized measures, this was rarely done and as a result effect sizes reported here may be inflated. Limiting our literature search to the English language may mean we missed valuable studies. The researcher's allegiance effect (Luborsky et al., 1999) is probably operating in the meta-analyses as well. The developers of the respective feedback systems have been directly involved or indirectly consulting on the majority of the published studies considered here. Future research needs to be conducted across a wider range of treatment settings and client populations, thus illuminating the limits of these practices and clarifying the factors that maximize client gains.

The majority of studies were conducted without external grant funding. This has limited the degree of control exerted in this research and also decreased its internal validity. For example, with adequate funding willing therapists could have been selected and paid for implementing feedback. Such therapists could have been provided with more extensive training on effective delivery of feedback and some even screened out of a study if they did not meet fidelity criteria or high delivery standards. There is evidence across studies that many therapists were reluctant to participate. Greater funding would also provide financial compensation to patients for their participation in research, such as completing assessments beyond those routinely used, collecting follow-up data, and other features of well-controlled experiments. Feedback studies require rather large clinics or multicenter trials to ensure adequate sample sizes.

A positive consequence of the paucity of external funding for feedback studies is that they largely occur in naturalistic clinical settings, thus enhancing their external or environmental validity. The results reported in this systematic and meta-analytic review probably come close to those that will be found in routine adoption of ROM/PROM where psychotherapists, some quite resistant, will be asked to change the way they usually practice with patients. Additional studies are needed in which clients are randomly assigned to receive feedback from therapists trained in ROM/PROMS versus therapists who are not trained in these methods.

DIVERSITY CONSIDERATIONS

The research reported in this review has not focused on patient diversity, including their gender, race/ethnicity, age, sexual orientation, SES, and other intersecting cultural dimensions. Nor do the small number of studies permit moderator analyses that could potentially identify the degree to which ROM/PROM practices may prove differentially effective with some patients. The samples studied are reflective of the communities that they came from and have included individuals from a wide range of ethnicities and socioeconomic classes. Still, in the absence of data, we do not know empirically whether some types of clients benefit more or less from feedback.

ROM/PROM methods are dependent on an individual's provision of valid self-reports of mental health functioning. Not being able to read at a fifth-grade level, follow directions, and enter data using a computer present special challenges to some patients. Feedback methods may also increase the burden felt by some patients in ROM/PROM research compared to treatment-as-usual.

TRAINING IMPLICATIONS

These meta-analytic results provide rather convincing evidence that, at least, these two evidence-based ROM/PROMs can be fruitfully adopted in routine care although not inevitably. They can also be introduced routinely into clinical training. Professional bodies have already recognized and recommended ROM/PROMs, as a best practice in routine care (APA, 2006) and in competency-based supervision (Association of State & Provincial Psychology Boards, 2015). Unfortunately, most faculty have not had formal training or experience with ROM/PROM, and few supervisors incorporate progress feedback with a focus on predicted treatment failures into their supervisory practices. Given this state of the field, the evolution towards including ROM/PROMs into supervision and training programs will probably be a slow process (Boswell et al., 2015).

Obstacles to implementation of ROM/PROMS in clinical settings include: financial burden (no reimbursement for use of ROM/PROMS); differing needs of multiple stakeholders; turnover in clinical staff; training costs and sustainability; time burdens (administering, scoring, interpreting, providing feedback to client, etc.); philosophical reservations (e.g., perception that self-report scales are superficial and untrustworthy); fear/mistrust (of external control and management); and uncertainty regarding how data will be utilized and/or compared with colleagues; Boswell et al., 2015). Several strategies can be employed by individual therapists and/or institutions to improve integration of ROM/PROMS (e.g., transparency and clarity regarding ROM, establishing benchmarks, providing formal training, employing local champions) but none of these has been adequately tested to examine their effects.

Several formal attempts to improve clinician attitudes towards ROM/PROMS have been undertaken. For example, Willis and colleagues (2009) studied the attitudes of 96 clinicians towards ROM/PROMS before and after training. Attitudes toward feedback were predominantly positive at baseline and significantly more positive following training. They attributed improvement to the fact that training included using ROM with patients. They concluded that generating positive clinician attitudes is the first step toward improving the processes and effectiveness of ROM/PROMS but that controlled trials with a follow up of clinicians' behavior are needed to determine whether the early changes in attitude are maintained and reflected in routine practice.

Another study (Edbrooke-Childs et al., 2016) examined the effects of two training methods (1-day & 3-days in length) in order to study therapist perception and use of ROM/PROMS in a child treatment system. Their efforts were based on an on-line tool they created, and training to use it. Pre- and post- testing suggested that therapist attitudes became more positive regardless of training length and remained positive. A significant aspect of training that proved most helpful was actual use of the measure with their own clients and subsequent discussion of individual cases.

Training in the feedback methods reviewed here can begin with clinical faculty agreeing on a measure/method and encouraging their training clinic and practicum sites to adopt that method. Second, training can be initiated through a brief (2 to 4 hour) workshop in which participants (faculty, students, and training site personnel) are presented with a didactic on the rationale for the methods, outcome/tracking measure characteristics, the advantages of actuarial versus clinical prediction, and empirical evidence of effects on clients. Following presentation of this information, participants need to have experience using the software and gaining access to clinician and patient feedback reports. Following this, sample reports can be used to model and practice responding to patient questions. It is especially important to introduce the measure to patients in such a way that they are motivated to accurately report their functioning on a weekly basis and also explore reasons for feeling worse.

The training can be quite limited. Research suggests that clinicians, once alerted to the fact that a particular patient is at risk of treatment failure, can problem-solve with that patient. Clinicians need only reflect on the fact that the patient is off-track, administer and use the CST, or discuss the case in supervision. Thus, training does not need to include how to change psychotherapy, but how to access and understand clinical reports. Too many possibilities exist for training to address all the possible causes of deterioration.

Training in feedback methods can take between two and 20 hours. We recommend that training include practice delivering feedback. We also recommend that psychotherapists learning these methods use feedback with half their cases while not using it with the other half. They are frequently surprised and impressed to discover that feedback substantially enhances outcome in their own case load.

THERAPEUTIC PRACTICES

The research evidence supports the use of routinely and formally monitoring the mental health of clients as they undergo a course of psychotherapy using either of the ROM/PROM methods reviewed here. Specifically:

- Employ real-time progress feedback to compensate for clinicians' limited ability to accurately detect client worsening in psychotherapy. Despite evidence that psychotherapists are not alert to treatment failure (e.g., Hannan et al., 2005; Hatfield et al., 2010), and strong evidence that clinical judgments are usually inferior to actuarial methods for making predictions, therapists' over confidence in their clinical judgment stands as a barrier to implementation of monitoring and feedback systems.
- Do so with adults, adolescents, and possibly children. As well as across treatment formats (individual, couple, group) and clinical settings.

- Examine the feedback alerts and reports as vital signs of patient progress, not as a reflection of one's ability as a mental health practitioner. De-shaming practitioners will probably enhance use of the reports; indeed, the failure of some studies to support the value of ROM/PROM has been linked to therapist failure to look at the feedback reports.

- Explicit discussion with patients and problem-solving with at-risk cases to provide additional clinical benefits, such as administering the ASC and using CSTs. As suggested by the general literature on feedback, and the evidence presented here, problem-solving tools prove helpful to off-track clients.

- Use either the OQ System or the PCOMS depending upon the practitioner's or clinic's particular needs. The PCOMS proves quicker, less expensive, but less comprehensive assessments that probably exert greater effects than the OQ System for all patients (effect size of .40 vs. .14 in the present meta-analysis). The OQ System offers more comprehensive assessments and more clinical support tools, but more can prove more expensive and time consuming in probably exerting greater identification of and assistance with patients at risk for deterioration or treatment failure.

- Use ROM/PROM methods with an alarm that identifies clients who are at-risk of treatment failure and thereby focus attention on such cases. Outcomes can, at times, be further enhanced if formal feedback, progress graphs and messages, are provided to both the therapist and the client. The weight of evidence, especially coming from PCOMS studies, suggests direct feedback to clients and therapists is the better practice. In OQ System studies that include a therapist-only feedback condition, therapists decide if and when to discuss the feedback with their clients or to problem-solve on their own.

- Benefit for the client accrues if therapists administer the ASC and uses CSTs to guide their problem-solving with at-risk cases. Brief assessment of the therapeutic alliance, motivation, social supports, and life events plus suggestions for their modification strengthen feedback effects. Research suggests that about one third of off-track clients have problems within the therapeutic encounter, one third have problems outside of the therapeutic encounter, mainly with poor or failing social supports, and the final one third have problems across all assessed areas (White et al., 2015).

- Use electronic versions of feedback systems that expedite and ease practical difficulties. Adding monitoring measures to busy practices can prove a barrier to implementation. Fortunately, the ultra-brevity of the PCOMS and OQ-Analyst software provide instantaneous feedback to clinicians, including on-line solutions. The PCOMS takes only a few minutes in sessions, while if the client takes the OQ-45 immediately prior to the scheduled psychotherapy session, electronic feedback is available to the therapist prior to beginning that session and takes just minutes to absorb.

- Use feedback particularly with circumstances and clients in which treatment progress is limited. The effectiveness of feedback varies as a function of the degree of discrepancy between therapists' views of progress and measured progress (Sapyta et al., 2005); the greater the discrepancy, the more likely feedback will be helpful.

Feedback about poor progress is expected to have a greater impact than feedback indicating positive progress. Bring into the recipient's (therapist's) awareness the discrepancy between what is thought and what is "reality," thereby prompting corrective action.

REFERENCES

References marked with an asterisk indicate studies included in the meta-analyses.

American Psychological Association Presidential Task Force on Evidence-Based Practice. (2006). Evidence based practice in psychology. *American Psychologist, 61*, 271–285. https://www.doi.org/10.1037/0003-066X.61.4.271

*Anker, M. G., Duncan, B. L., & Sparks, J.A. (2009). Using client feedback to improve couple therapy outcomes: A randomized clinical trial in a naturalistic treatment setting. *Journal of Consulting & Clinical Psychology, 77*, 693–704.

Association of State & Provincial Psychology Boards. (2015). *Supervision guidelines for education and training leading to licensure as a health service provider*. Retrieved from www.asppb.net/resource/resmgr/Guidelines/Final/Supervision_Guidelines.pdf

Barkham, M., Margison, F., Leach, C., Lucock, M., Mellor-Clark, J., Evans, C., . . . McGrath, G. (2001). Service profiling and outcomes benchmarking using the CORE_OM: Toward practice-based evidence in the psychological therapies. *Journal of Consulting & Clinical Psychology, 69*, 184–196.

Beckstead, D. J., Hatch, A. L., Lambert, M. J., Eggett, D. L., Goates, M. K., & Vermeersch, D. A. (2003). Clinical significance of the Outcome Questionnaire (OQ-45.2). *The Behavior Analyst Today, 4*, 79–90.

Bludworth, J., Tracey, T. J. G., & Glidden-Tracey, C. (2010). The bi-level structure of the Outcome Questionnaire-45. *Psychological Assessment, 22*, 350–355.

Bordin, E. S. (1979). The generalizability of the psychoanalytic concept of the working alliance. *Psychotherapy, 16*, 252–60.

Boswell, J. F., Kraus, D. Miller, S. D., & Lambert, M. J. (2015). Implementing routine outcome monitoring in clinical practice: Benefits, challenges, and solutions. *Psychotherapy Research, 25*, 6–19.

Boyce, M. B., & Browne, J. P. (2013). Does providing feedback on client-reported outcomes to healthcare professionals result in better outcomes for clients? A systematic review. *Quality of Life Research, 22*, 2265–2278.

Carlier, I. V., Meuldijk, D., Van Vliet, I. M., Van Fenema, E., Van der Wee, N. J., & Zitman, F. G. (2016). Routine outcome monitoring and feedback on physical and mental health status: Evidence and theory. *Journal of Evaluation in Clinical Practice, 18*, 104–110. https://www.doi.org/10.1111/j.1365-1365-2753.2010.01543.x

Cohen, J. (1992). A power primer. *Psychological Bulletin, 112*, 155–159. https://www.doi.org/10.1037/0033-2909.112.1.155

Copeland, B. T. (2007). *Outcome and process measure feedback as they effect therapy outcome* (Doctoral dissertation). George Fox University, Tacoma, WA.

*Crits-Christoph, P., Ring-Cruz, S., Hamilton, J. L., Lambert, M. J., Gallop, R., McClure, B., . . . Rotrosen, J. (2012). A preliminary study of the effects of individual client-level feedback in outpatient substance abuse treatment programs. *Journal of Substance Abuse Treatment, 42*, 301–309.

*Davidsen, A. H., Paulsen, S. Lindschou, J., Winkel, P., Trondardson, M., & Lau, M. (2017). Feedback in group psychotherapy for eating disorders: A randomized clinical trial. *Journal of Consulting & Clinical Psychology, 85*(5), 484–494. https://www.doi.org/10.1037/ccp0000173

Davidson, K., Perry, A., & Bell, L. (2015). Would continuous feedback of client's clinical outcomes to practitioners improve NHS psychological therapy services? Critical analysis and assessment of quality of existing studies. *Psychology and Psychotherapy: Theory, Research and Practice, 88*, 21–37.

De Jong, K., Nugter, M. A., Polak, M. G., Wagenborg, J. E. A., Spinhoven, P., & Heiser, W. J. (2007). The Outcome Questionnaire (OQ-45) in a Dutch population: A cross-cultural validation. *Clinical Psychology & Psychotherapy, 14*, 288–401.

*De Jong, K., Timman, R., Hakkaart-van Roijen, L., Vermeulen, P., Kooiman, K., Passcher, J., & Van Busschbach, J. (2014). The effect of outcome monitoring feedback to clinicians and clients in short and long-term psychotherapy: A randomized controlled clinical trial. *Psychotherapy Research, 24*(6), 629–639. https://www.doi.org/10.1080/10503307.2013.871079

*De Jong, K., Van Sluis, P., Nutger, A., Heiser, W. J., & Spinhoven, P. (2012). Understanding the differential impact of outcome monitoring: Therapist variables that moderate feedback effects in a randomized clinical trial. *Psychotherapy Research, 22*(4), 464–474.

Duncan, B. L., & Miller, S. D. (2008). The Outcome and Session Rating Scales: The revised administration and scoring manual, including the Child Outcome Rating Scale. Chicago, IL: Institute for the Study of Therapeutic Change.

Duncan, B. L., & Reese, R. J. (2015). The Partners for Change Outcome Management System (PCOMS): Revisiting the client's frame of reference. *Psychotherapy, 52*, 391–401.

Edbrooke-Childs, J., Wolpert, M., & Deighton, J. (2016). Using Patient-Reported Outcome Measures to Improve Service Effectiveness (UPROMISE): Training clinicians to use outcome measures in child mental health. *Administration and Policy in Mental Health and Mental Health Services Research, 43*(3), 302–308.

Egger, M., Smith, G. D., Schneider, M., & Minder, C. (1997). Bias in meta-analysis detected by a simple, graphical test. *British Medical Journal, 315*, 629–634.

Ellsworth, J. R., Lambert, M. J., & Johnson, J. (2006). A comparison of the Outcome Questionnaire-45 and Outcome Questionnaire-30 in classification and prediction of treatment outcome. *Clinical Psychology & Psychotherapy, 13*, 380–391.

Finch, A. E., Lambert, M. J., & Schaalje, B. G. (2001). Psychotherapy quality control: The statistical generation of expected recovery curves for integration into an early warning system. *Clinical Psychology & Psychotherapy, 8*, 231–242.

Fortney, J. C., Unzer, J., Wrenn, G., Pyne, J. M., Smith, G. R., Schoenbaum, M., &Harbin, H. T. (2017). A tipping point for measurement-based care. *Psychiatric Services, 68*(2), 179–188.

Gondek, D., Edbrooke, J., Childs, Finks, E., Deighton, J., & Wolpert, M. (2016). Feedback from outcome measures and treatment effectiveness, treatment efficiency, and collaborative practice: A systematic review. *Administration and Policy in Mental Health, 43*, 325–343.

*Grizzell, S., Smart, J., Lambert, M. J., & Fargo, J. (2016). The use of feedback in group counseling in a state vocational rehabilitation setting. *Journal of Applied Rehabilitation Counseling, 47*(4), 10–19.

Hannan, C., Lambert, M. J., Harmon, C., Nielsen, S. L., Smart, D. W., Shimokawa, K. . . . Sutton, S. W. (2005). A lab test and algorithms for identifying clients at risk for treatment failure. *Journal of Clinical Psychology: In Session, 61*, 155–163.

Hansen, N. B., Lambert, M. J., & Forman, E. V. (2002). The psychotherapy dose-response effect and its implications for treatment delivery services. *Clinical Psychology: Science and Practice, 9*, 329–343.

*Hansson, H., Rundberg, J., Osterling, A., Ojehagen, A., & Bergland, M. (2013). Intervention with feedback using Outcome Questionnare-45 (OQ-45) in a Swedish psychiatric outpatient population. A randomized clinical trial. *Nordic Journal of Psychiatry, 67*(4).

*Harmon, S. C., Lambert, M. J., Smart, D. W., Hawkins, E. J., Nielsen, S. L., Slade, K., & Lutz, W. (2007). Enhancing outcome for potential treatment failures: Therapist/client feedback and clinical support tools. *Psychotherapy Research, 17*, 379–392.

Hatfield, D., McCullough, L., Plucinski, A., & Krieger, K. (2010). Do we know when our clients get worse? An investigation of therapists' ability to detect negative client change. *Clinical Psychology & Psychotherapy, 17*, 25–32.

*Hawkins, E. J., Lambert, M. J., Vermeersch, D. A., Slade, K., & Tuttle, K. (2004). The therapeutic effects of providing client progress information to therapists and patients. *Psychotherapy Research, 14*, 308–327.

Hedges, L. V., & Olkin, I. (1985). *Statistical methods for meta-analysis*. San Diego, CA: Academic Press.

Higgins, J. P. T., & Green, S. (Eds.). (2011). *Cochrane handbook for systematic reviews of interventions 5.1.0*. The Cochrane Collaboration. Retrieved from www.cochrane.org.

Jacobson, N. S., & Truax, P. (1991). Clinical significance: A statistical approach to defining meaningful change in psychotherapy research. *Journal of Consulting & Clinical Psychology, 59*, 12–19.

*Janse, P. D., De Jong, K., Van Dijk, M. K., Hunschmaekers, G. J. M., & Verbraak, M. J. P. M. (2017). Improving the efficiency of cognitive-behavioural therapy by using formal client feedback. *Psychotherapy Research, 27*, 525–538.

Kendrick, T., El-Gohhary, M., Stuart, B., Gilbody, S., Churchill, R. Aiken, L., . . . Moore, M. (2016). Routine use of patient reported outcome measures (PROMs) for improving treatment of common mental disorders in adults. *Cochrane Database of Systematic Reviews*. https://www.doi.org/10.1002/14651858.CDO11119.pub2

Kluger, A. N., & DeNisi, A. (1996). The effects of feedback interventions on performance: A historical review, a meta-analysis, and a preliminary feedback intervention theory. *Psychological Bulletin, 119*, 254–284.

Knaup, C., Koesters, M., Schoefer, D., Becker, T., & Puschner, B. (2009). Effect of feedback of treatment outcome in specialist mental healthcare: Meta-analysis. *The British Journal of Psychiatry, 195*, 15–22.

Kordy, H., Hannöver, W., & Richard, M. (2001). Computer-assisted feedback-driven quality management for psychotherapy: The Stuttgart-Heidelberg model. *Journal of Consulting & Clinical Psychology, 69*, 173–183.

Krageloh, C. U., Czuba, K. J. Phty, M., Billington, D. R., Kersten, P., & Siegert, R. (2015). Using feedback from client-reported outcome measures in mental health services: A scoping study and typology. *Psychiatric Services, 66*, 224–241. https://www.doi.org/10.11/appi.ps.201400141

Lambert, M. J. (2013). The efficacy and effectiveness of psychotherapy. In M. J. Lambert (Ed.), *Bergin & Garfield's handbook of psychotherapy and behavior change* (6th Ed., pp. 169–218). New York, NY: Wiley.

Lambert, M. J., Bailey, R. J., White, M., Tingey, K. M., & Stevens, E. (2015). *Clinical Support Tool Manual—Brief Version-40*. Salt Lake City, UT: OQMeasures.

Lambert, M. J., Bergin, A. E., & Collins, J. L (1977). Therapist induced deterioration in psycho-therapy clients. In A. S. Gurman & A. M. Razin (Eds.), *Effective psychotherapy: A handbook of research* (pp. 452–481). New York, NY: Pergamon.

Lambert, M. J., Hansen, N. B., & Finch, A. E. (2001). Patient-focused research: Using patient outcome data to enhance treatment effects. *Journal of Consulting & Clinical Psychology, 69*, 159–172.

Lambert, M. J., Kahler, M., Harmon, C., Burlingame, G. M., Shimokawa, & White, M. M. (2013). *Administration and scoring manual: Outcome Questionnaire OQ®-45.2.* Salt Lake City, UT: OQMeasures.

Lambert, M. J., & Shimokawa, K. (2011a). Collecting client feedback. In J. C. Norcross (Ed.), *Psychotherapy relationships that work* (2nd ed., pp. 203–223). New York, NY: Oxford University Press.

Lambert, M. J., & Shimokawa, K. (2011b). Collecting client feedback. *Psychotherapy, 48*(1), 72–79. https://www.doi.org/10.13140/2.1.4480.5123

Lambert, M. J., Whipple, J. L., Bishop, M. J., Vermeersch, D. A., Gray, G. V., & Finch, A. E. (2002). Comparison of empirically derived and rationally derived methods for identifying clients at risk for treatment failure. *Clinical Psychology & Psychotherapy, 9*, 149–164.

Lambert, M. J., Whipple, J. L., Hawkins, E. J., Vermeersch, D. A., Nielsen, S. L., & Smart, D. W. (2003). Is it time for clinicians to routinely track client outcome? A meta-analysis. *Clinical Psychology: Science & Practice, 10*, 288–301.

*Lambert, M. J., Whipple, J. L., Smart, D. W., Vermeersch, D. A., Nielsen, S. L., & Hawkins, E. J. (2001). The effects of providing therapists with feedback on client progress during psy-chotherapy: Are outcomes enhanced? *Psychotherapy Research, 11*, 49–68.

*Lambert, M. J., Whipple, J. L., Vermeersch, D. A., Smart, D. W., Hawkins, E. J., Nielsen, S. L., & Goates, M. (2002). Enhancing psychotherapy outcomes via providing feedback on client progress: A replication. *Clinical Psychology & Psychotherapy, 9*, 91–103.

Lo Coco, G., Chiappelli, M., Bensi, L., Gullo, S., Prestano, C., & Lambert, M. J. (2008). The fac-torial structure of the Outcome Questionnaire-45: A study with an Italian sample. *Clinical Psychology & Psychotherapy, 15*, 418–423.

Luborsky, L., Diguer, L. Seligman, D. A., Rosenthal, R., Krause, E. D., Johnson, S., . . . Schweizer, E. (1999). The researcher's own therapy allegiance: A "wild card" in comparisons of treat-ment efficacy. *Clinical Psychology: Science & Practice, 6*, 95–106.

Lueger, R. J., Howard, K. I., Martinovich Z., Lutz, W., Anderson, E. E., & Grissom, G. (2001). Assessing treatment progress of individual clients using expected treatment response models. *Journal of Consulting & Clinical Psychology, 69*, 150–158.

Lunnen, K. M., & Ogles, B. M. (1998). A multiperspective, multivariable evaluation of reliable change. *Journal of Consulting & Clinical Psychology, 66*, 400–410.

Lutz, W., Lambert, M. J., Harmon, S. C., Tschitsaz, A., Schurch, E., & Stulz, N. (2006). The prob-ability of treatment success, failure and duration- what can be learned from empirical data to support decision making in clinical practice? *Clinical Psychology & Psychotherapy, 13*, 223–232.

Miller, S. D., & Duncan, B. L. (2004). *The Outcome and Session Rating Scales: Administration and scoring manual.* Chicago, IL: Institute for the Study of Therapeutic Change.

Miller, S. D., Duncan, B. L., Brown, J., Sparks, J. A., & Claud, D. A. (2003). The Outcome Rating Scale: A preliminary study of the reliability, validity, and feasibility of a brief visual analog measure. *Journal of Brief Therapy, 2*, 91–100.

Miller, S. D., Duncan, B. L., Sorrell, R., & Brown, G. S. (2005). The Partners for Change Outcome System. *Journal of Clinical Psychology: In Session, 61*, 199–208.

*Murphy, K. P., Rashleigh, C. M., & Timulak, L. (2012). The relationship progress between progress feedback and therapeutic outcome in student counselling: A randomized control trial. *Counselling Psychology Quarterly, 25*, 1–18.

National Advisory Mental Health Council. (2001). *Blueprint for change: Research on child and adolescent mental health. A report by the National Advisory Mental Health Council's Workgroup on Child and Adolescent Mental Health Intervention Development and Deployment.* Bethesda, MD: National Institutes of Health/National Institute of Mental Health.

Newham, E., Hooke, G. R., & Page, A. C. (2010). Progress monitoring and feedback in psychiatric care reduces depressive symptoms. *Journal of Affective Disorders, 117*, 139–146. https://www.doi.org/10.1016/jad.2010.05.003

Percevic, R., Lambert, M. J., & Kordy, H. (2006). What is the predictive value of responses to psychotherapy for its future course? Empirical explorations and consequences for outcome monitoring. *Psychotherapy Research, 16*, 364–373.

Okiishi, J. Lambert, M. J., Eggett, D., Nielsen, S. L. Dayton, D. D., & Vermeersch, D. A. (2006). An analysis of therapist treatment effects: Toward providing feedback to individual therapists on their clients' psychotherapy outcome. *Journal of Clinical Psychology, 62*, 1157–1172.

Prescott, D. S., Maeschalck, C. L., & Miller, S. D. (2017). *Feedback-informed treatment in clinical practice: Reaching for excellence.* Washington, DC: American Psychological Association.

*Probst, T., Lambert, M. J., Dahlbender; R. W., Loew, T. W., & Tritt, K. (2014). Providing patient progress feedback and clinical support tools to therapists: Is the therapeutic process of patients on-track to recovery enhanced in psychosomatic in-patient therapy under the conditions of routine practice? *Journal of Psychosomatic Research, 76*, 477–484.

*Propst, T., Lambert, M. J., Loew, T., Dahlbender, R. Gollner, R., & Tritt, K. (2013). Feedback on client progress and clinical support tools for therapists: Improved outcome for clients at risk of treatment failure in in-client psychosomatic therapy? *Journal of Psychosomatic Research, 75*, 255–261.

*Reese, R. J., Norsworthy, L., & Rowlands, S. (2009). Does a continuous feedback system improve psychotherapy outcome? *Psychotherapy: Theory, Research, Practice, Training, 46*, 418–431.

*Reese, R., Toland, M., Slone, N., & Norsworthy, L. (2010). Effect of client feedback on couple psychotherapy outcomes. *Psychotherapy, 47*, 616–630.

Review Manager. (2014). RevMan Version 5.3 [Computer program]. Copenhagen, Denmark: Nordic Cochrane Centre, Cochrane Collaboration.

Riemer, M., Rosof-Williams, J., & Bickman, L. (2005). Theories related to changing clinician practice. *Child and Adolescent Psychiatric Clinics of North America, 14*, 241–254.

Safran, J. D., Muran, J. C., Samstang, L. W., & Winston, A. (2005). Evaluating alliance-focused intervention for potential treatment failures: A feasibility and descriptive analysis. *Psychotherapy: Theory, Research, Practice, Training, 42*, 512–531.

Sapyta, J., Riemer, M., & Bickman, L. (2005). Feedback to clinicians: Theory, research, and practice. *Journal of Clinical Psychology, 62*, 145–153.

*Schuman, D. L., Slone, N. C., Reese, R. J., & Duncan, B. (2015). Efficacy of client feedback in group psychotherapy with soldiers referred for substance abuse treatment. *Psychotherapy Research, 25*(4), 396–407. https://www.doi.org/10.1080/19503307.2014.900875

Schuskard, E., Miller, S. D., & Hubble, M. A. (2017). Feedback-informed treatment: Historical and empirical foundations. In D. S. Prescott, C. L. Maeschalck, & S. D. Miller (Eds.),

Feedback-informed treatment in clinical practice: Reaching for excellence. Washington, DC: American Psychological Association.

Shadish, W. R., Matt, G. E., Navarro, A. M., Siegle, G., Crits-Christoph, P., Hazelrigg, M. D., . . . Weiss, B. (1997). Evidence that therapy works in clinically representative conditions. *Journal of Consulting & Clinical Psychology, 65,* 355–365.

Shimokawa, K., Lambert, M. J., & Smart, D. W. (2010). Enhancing treatment outcome of clients at risk of treatment failure: Meta-analytic and mega-analytic review of a psychotherapy quality assurance system. *Journal of Consulting & Clinical Psychology, 78,* 298–311.

*Slade, K., Lambert, M. J., Harmon, S. C., Smart, D. W., & Bailey, R. (2008). Improving psychotherapy outcome: The use of immediate electronic feedback and revised clinical support tools. *Clinical Psychology & Psychotherapy, 15,* 287–303.

*Slone, N., Reese, R. J., Mathews-Duval, S., & Koder, J. (2015). Evaluating the efficacy of client feedback in group psychotherapy. *Group Dynamics: Theory, Research, and Practice, 19*(2), 122–136.

Smith, M. L., Glass, G. V., & Miller, T. L. (1980). *The benefits of psychotherapy.* Baltimore, MD: Johns Hopkins University Press.

Spielmans, G. I., Masters, K. S., & Lambert, M. J. (2006). A comparison of rational versus empirical methods in prediction of negative psychotherapy outcome. *Clinical Psychology & Psychotherapy, 13,* 202–214.

Trudeau, L. S. (2000). *Effects of a clinical feedback system on client and therapist outcomes in a rural community mental health center* (Unpublished doctoral dissertation). Iowa State University, Ames.

Truitt, K. G. (2011). *Modeling treatment outcomes in eating disorders: Does therapist feedback support individually tailored service allocation?* (Unpublished doctoral dissertation). Loma Linda University, Loma Linda, CA.

Vermeersch, D. A., Lambert, M. J., & Burlingame, G. M. (2000). Outcome Questionnaire: Item sensitivity to change. *Journal of Personality Assessment, 74,* 242–261.

Vermeersch, D. A., Whipple, J. L., Lambert, M. J., Hawkins, E. J., Burchfield, C. M., & Okiishi, J. C. (2004). Outcome Questionnaire: Is it sensitive to changes in counseling center clients? *Journal of Counseling Psychology, 51,* 38–49.

Walfish, S., McAlister, B., O'Donnell, P., & Lambert, M. J. (2012). An investigation of self-assessment bias in mental health providers. *Psychological Reports, 110*(2), 639–644. https://www.doi.org/10.2466/02.07.17

Warren, J. S., Nelson, P. L., Mondragon, S. A., Baldwin, S. A., & Burlingame, G. M. (2010). Youth psychotherapy change trajectories and outcome in usual care: Community mental health versus managed care. *Journal of Consulting & Clinical Psychology, 78,* 144–55.

Weiss, B., Catron, T., Harris, V., & Phung, T. M. (1999). The effectiveness of traditional child psychotherapy. *Journal of Consulting & Clinical Psychology, 67,* 82–94.

Weisz, J. R. (2004). *Psychotherapy for children and adolescents: Evidence-based treatments and case examples.* New York, NY: Cambridge University Press.

Weisz, J. R., Donenberg, G. R., Han, S. S., & Weiss, B. (1995). Bridging the gap between laboratory and clinic in child and adolescent psychotherapy. *Journal of Consulting & Clinical Psychology, 63,* 688–701.

*Whipple, J. L., Lambert, M. J., Vermeersch, D. A., Smart, D. W., Nielsen, S. L., & Hawkins, E. J. (2003). Improving the effects of psychotherapy: The use of early identification of treatment failure and problem solving strategies in routine practice. *Journal of Counseling Psychology, 58,* 59–68.

White, M., Lambert, M. J., Bailey, R. J., McLaughlin, S. B., & Ogles, B. M. (2015). Understanding the Assessment for Signal Clients as a feedback tool for reducing treatment failure. *Psychotherapy Research*, *25*(6), 724–734. https://www.doi.org/10.1080/10503307.2015.1009862

Willis, A., Deane, F. P., & Coombs, T. (2009). Improving clinicians' attitudes toward providing feedback on routine outcome assessments. *International Journal of Mental Health Nursing*, *18*, 211–215.

18

WHAT WORKS IN THE PSYCHOTHERAPY RELATIONSHIP: RESULTS, CONCLUSIONS, AND PRACTICES

John C. Norcross and Michael J. Lambert

Having traversed multiple meta-analyses in the foregoing chapters and arrived at the end of this volume, we present here the formal conclusions and recommendations of the Third Interdivisional Task Force. Those statements, approved by the 10 members of the Steering Committee, refer to the work in both this volume on therapy relationships and the second volume on treatment adaptations or relational responsiveness. These statements reaffirm and, in several instances, extend those of the earlier task forces (Norcross, 2002, 2011). We then conclude with some final thoughts on what works, and what does not work, in the therapy relationship.

CONCLUSIONS OF THE INTERDIVISIONAL TASK FORCE ON EVIDENCE-BASED RELATIONSHIPS AND RESPONSIVENESS

- The psychotherapy relationship makes substantial and consistent contributions to patient outcome independent of the specific type of psychological treatment.
- The therapy relationship accounts for client improvement (or lack of improvement) as much as, and probably more, than the particular treatment method.
- Practice and treatment guidelines should explicitly address therapist behaviors and qualities that promote a facilitative therapy relationship.
- Efforts to promulgate best practices and evidence-based treatments without including the relationship and responsiveness are seriously incomplete and potentially misleading.
- Adapting or tailoring the therapy relationship to specific patient characteristics (in addition to diagnosis) enhances the effectiveness of psychological treatment.

- Adapting psychological treatment (or responsiveness) to transdiagnostic client characteristics contributes to successful outcomes at least as much as, and probably more than, adapting treatment to the client's diagnosis.
- The therapy relationship acts in concert with treatment methods, patient characteristics, and other practitioner qualities in determining effectiveness; a comprehensive understanding of effective (and ineffective) psychotherapy will consider all of these determinants and how they work together to produce benefit.
- The following list summarizes the Task Force conclusions regarding the evidentiary strength of (a) elements of the therapy relationship primarily provided by the psychotherapist and (b) methods of adapting psychotherapy to patient transdiagnostic characteristics.

	Elements of the Relationship	Methods of Adapting
Demonstrably Effective	Alliance in Individual Psychotherapy	Culture (race/ethnicity)
	Alliance in Child & Adol. Psychotherapy	Religion/Spirituality
	Alliances in Couple & Family Therapy Collaboration	Patient Preferences
	Goal Consensus	
	Cohesion in Group Therapy	
	Empathy	
	Positive Regard and Affirmation	
	Collecting & Delivering Client Feedback	
Probably Effective	Congruence/Genuineness	Reactance Level
	Real Relationship	Stages of Change
	Emotional Expression	Coping Style
	Cultivating Positive Expectations	
	Promoting Treatment Credibility	
	Managing Countertransference	
	Repairing Alliance Ruptures	
Promising but Insufficient Research	Self-Disclosure	Attachment Style
	Immediacy	
Important but Not Yet Investigated		Sexual Orientation
		Gender Identity

- The preceding conclusions do *not* constitute practice or treatment standards but represent current scientific knowledge to be understood and applied in the context of the clinical evidence available in each case.

RECOMMENDATIONS OF THE INTERDIVISIONAL TASK FORCE ON EVIDENCE-BASED RELATIONSHIPS AND RESPONSIVENESS

General Recommendations

1. We recommend that the results and conclusions of this Task Force be widely disseminated to enhance awareness and use of what "works" in the psychotherapy relationship and treatment adaptations.
2. Readers are encouraged to interpret these findings in the context of the acknowledged limitations of the Task Force's work.
3. We recommend that future task forces be established periodically to review these findings, include new elements of the relationship and responsiveness, incorporate the results of non-English language publications (where practical), and update these conclusions.

Practice Recommendations

4. Practitioners are encouraged to make the creation and cultivation of the therapy relationship a primary aim of treatment. This is especially true for relationship elements found to be demonstrably and probably effective.
5. Practitioners are encouraged to assess relational behaviors (e.g., alliance, empathy, cohesion) vis-á-vis cut-off scores on popular clinical measures in ways that lead to more positive outcomes.
6. Practitioners are encouraged to adapt or tailor psychotherapy to those specific client transdiagnostic characteristics in ways found to be demonstrably and probably effective.
7. Practitioners will experience increased treatment success by regularly assessing and responsively attuning psychotherapy to clients' cultural identities (broadly defined).
8. Practitioners are encouraged to routinely monitor patients' satisfaction with the therapy relationship, comfort with responsiveness efforts, and response to treatment. Such monitoring leads to increased opportunities to reestablish collaboration, improve the relationship, modify technical strategies, and investigate factors external to therapy that may be hindering its effects.
9. Practitioners are encouraged to concurrently use evidence-based relationships *and* evidence-based treatments adapted to the whole patient as that is likely to generate the best outcomes in psychotherapy.

Training Recommendations

10. Mental health training and continuing education programs are encouraged to provide competency-based training in the demonstrably and probably effective elements of the therapy relationship.

11. Mental health training and continuing education programs are encouraged to provide competency-based training in adapting psychotherapy to the individual patient in ways that demonstrably and probably enhance treatment success.

12. Psychotherapy educators and supervisors are encouraged to train students in assessing and honoring clients' cultural heritages, values, and beliefs in ways that enhance the therapeutic relationship and inform treatment adaptations.

13. Accreditation and certification bodies for mental health training programs are encouraged to develop criteria for assessing the adequacy of training in evidence-based therapy relationships and responsiveness.

Research Recommendations

14. Researchers are encouraged to conduct research on the effectiveness of therapist relationship behaviors that do not presently have sufficient research evidence, such as self-disclosure, humility, flexibility, and deliberate practice.

15. Researchers are encouraged to investigate further the effectiveness of adaptation methods in psychotherapy, such as to clients' sexual orientation, gender identity, and attachment style, that do not presently have sufficient research evidence.

16. Researchers are encouraged to proactively conduct relationship and responsiveness outcome studies with culturally diverse and historically marginalized clients.

17. Researchers are encouraged to assess the relationship components using in-session observations in addition to post-session measures. The former track the client's moment-to-moment experience of a session and the latter summarize the patient's total experience of psychotherapy.

18. Researchers are encouraged to progress beyond correlational designs that associate the frequency and quality of relationship behaviors with client outcomes to methodologies capable of examining the complex causal associations among client qualities, clinician behaviors, and psychotherapy outcomes.

19. Researchers are encouraged to examine systematically the associations among the multitude of relationship elements and adaptation methods to establish a more coherent and empirically based typology that will improve clinical training and practice.

20. Researchers are encouraged to disentangle the patient contributions and the therapist contributions to relationship elements and ultimately outcome.

21. Researchers are encouraged to examine the specific moderators between relationship elements and treatment outcomes.

22. Researchers are encouraged to address the observational perspective (i.e., therapist, patient, or external rater) in future studies and reviews of "what works" in the therapy relationship. Agreement among observational perspectives provides a solid sense of established fact; divergence among perspectives holds important implications for practice.

23. Researchers are encouraged to increase translational research and dissemination on those relational behaviors and treatment adaptations that already have been judged effective.
24. Researchers are encouraged to examine the effectiveness of educational, training and supervision methods used to teach relational skills and treatment adaptations/ responsiveness.

Policy Recommendations

25. The APA Society for the Advancement of Psychotherapy, the APA Society for Counseling Psychology, and all divisions are encouraged to educate its members on the benefits of evidence-based therapy relationships and responsiveness.
26. Mental health organizations as a whole are encouraged to educate their members about the improved outcomes associated with higher levels of therapist-offered evidence-based therapy relationships, as they frequently now do about evidence-based treatments.
27. We recommend that the APA and other mental health organizations advocate for the research-substantiated benefits of a nurturing and responsive human relationship in psychotherapy.
28. Finally, administrators of mental health services are encouraged to attend to and invest in the relational features and transdiagnostic adaptations of their services. Attempts to improve the quality of care should account for relationships and responsiveness, not only the implementation of evidence-based treatments for specific disorders.

WHAT WORKS

The process by which the preceding conclusions on which relationship elements are effective require elaboration, as these characterizations tend to be the most frequently cited findings of the three Task Forces. These conclusions represent the consensus of expert panels composed of 10 judges who independently reviewed and rated the research evidence. They evaluated the meta-analytic evidence for each relationship element according to the following criteria: number of empirical studies, consistency of empirical results, independence of supportive studies, magnitude of association between the relationship element and outcome, evidence for causal link between relationship element and outcome, and ecological or external validity of research. The panel classified relationship elements as "demonstrably effective," "probably effective," "promising but insufficient research to judge," "important but not yet investigated," or "not effective." The experts' ratings were then combined to render a consensus. In this way, we added rigor and consensus to the process.

The 10 experts on the Steering Committee of the third task force, in alphabetical order, were

Franz Caspar, PhD, University of Bern
Melanie M. Domenech Rodriguez, PhD, Utah State University
Clara E. Hill, PhD, University of Maryland
Michael J. Lambert, PhD, Brigham Young University
Suzanne H. Lease, PhD, University of Memphis
James W. Lichtenberg, PhD, University of Kansas
Rayna D. Markin, PhD, Villanova University
John C. Norcross, PhD, University of Scranton
Jesse Owen, PhD, University of Denver
Bruce E. Wampold, PhD, University of Wisconsin

Table 18.1 summarizes the meta-analytic associations between the relationship elements and psychotherapy outcomes. As seen there, the expert consensus deemed nine of the relationship elements as demonstrably effective, seven as probably effective, and one as promising but insufficient research to judge. We were impressed by the skepticism and precision of the panelists (as scientists ought to be). At the same time, we were heartened to find the evidence base for all research elements had increased, and in some cases substantially, from the second edition (Norcross, 2011). We were also impressed by the disparate and perhaps elevated standards against which these relationship elements were evaluated.

Compare the evidentiary strength required for psychological treatments to be considered demonstrably efficacious in two influential compilations of evidence-based practices. The Division of Clinical Psychology's Subcommittee on Research-Supported Treatments (http://www.div12.org/PsychologicalTreatments/index.html) requires two between-group design experiments demonstrating that a psychological treatment is either (a) statistically superior to pill or psychological placebo or to another treatment or (b) equivalent to an already established treatment in experiments with adequate sample sizes. The studies must have been conducted with treatment manuals and conducted by at least two different investigators. The typical effect size of those studies was often smaller than the effects for the relationship elements reported in this book. For listing in SAMHSA's National Registry of Evidence-based Programs and Practices (http://www.nrepp.samhsa.gov), which will be soon discontinued, only evidence of statistically significant behavioral outcomes demonstrated in at least one study, using an experimental or quasi-experimental design, that has been published in a peer-reviewed journal or comprehensive evaluation report is needed. By these standards, practically all of the relationship elements in this volume would be considered demonstrably effective if not for the requirement of a randomized clinical trial, which proves neither clinically nor ethically feasible for most of the relationship elements.

In important ways, the effectiveness criteria for relationship elements are more rigorous. Whereas the criteria for designating treatments as evidence based relies on only one or two studies, the evidence for relationship elements discussed here are based on comprehensive meta-analyses of many studies (in excess of 40 studies in the majority of meta-analyses), spanning various treatments, a wide variety of treatment settings, patient populations, treatment formats, and research groups. The studies used

Table 18.1. Summary of Meta-Analytic Associations between Relationship Components and Psychotherapy Outcomes

Relationship Element	# of Studies (k)	# of Patients (N)	Effect Size — r	d or g	Consensus on Evidentiary Strength
Alliance in Individual Psychotherapy	306	30,000+	.28	57	Demonstrably effective
Alliance in Child and Adolescent Therapy	43	3,447	.20	40	Demonstrably effective
Alliances in Couple and Family Therapy	40	4,113	.30	62	Demonstrably effective
Collaboration	53	5,286	.29	61	Demonstrably effective
Goal Consensus	54	7,278	.24	49	Demonstrably effective
Cohesion in Group Therapy	55	6,055	.26	56	Demonstrably effective
Empathy	82	6,138	.28	58	Demonstrably effective
Positive Regard and Affirmation	64	3,528	.28		Demonstrably effective
Congruence/Genuineness	21	1,192	.23	46	Probably effective
The Real Relationship	17	1,502	.37	80	Probably effective
Self-disclosure and Immediacy	21	≈ 140	NA	NA	Promising but insufficient research
Emotional Expression	42	925	.40	85	Probably effective
Cultivating Positive Expectation	81	12,722	.18	36	Probably effective
Promoting Treatment Credibility	24	1,504	.12	24	Probably effective
Managing Countertransference	9	392 therapists	.39	84	Probably effective
Repairing Alliance Ruptures	11	1,318	.30	62	Probably effective
Collecting and Delivering Client Feedback	24	10,921	.14	−.49[a]	Demonstrably effective

NA = not applicable; the chapter employed qualitative meta-analysis that does not produce effect sizes.

[a] The effect sizes depended on the comparison group and the feedback method; feedback proved more effective with patients at risk for deterioration and less effective for all patients.

to establish evidence-based treatments are, however, clinical trials, which are often designated as the "gold standard" for establishing evidence. Nevertheless, these studies are often plagued by confounds, such as researcher allegiance, cannot be blinded, and often contain bogus comparisons (Luborsky et al., 1999; Mohr et al., 2009; Wampold et al., 2010; Wampold et al., 2017). The point here is not to denigrate the criteria used to establish evidence-based treatments but to underscore the robust scientific standards by which these relationship elements have been operationalized and evaluated. The evolving standard to judge evidence-based treatment is now moving away from the presence of an absolute number of studies to the presence of meta-analytic evidence (Tolin et al., 2015), a standard demonstrated repeatedly in this volume.

Consider as well the strength or magnitude of the therapy relationship. Across thousands of individual outcome studies and hundreds of meta-analytic reviews, the typical effect size difference (d) between psychotherapy and no psychotherapy averages .80 to .85 (Lambert, 2010; Wampold & Imel, 2015), a large effect size. The effect size (d) for any *single* relationship behavior in Table 18.1 ranges between .24 and .80. The alliance in individual psychotherapy (Chapter 2, this volume), for example, demonstrates an aggregate r of .28 and a d of .57 with treatment outcome, making the quality of the alliance one of the strongest and most robust predictors of successful psychotherapy. These relationship behaviors are robustly effective components and predictors of patient success. We need to proclaim publicly what decades of research have discovered and what hundreds of thousands of practitioners have witnessed: The relationship can heal.

It would probably prove advantageous to both practice and science to sum the individual effect sizes in Table 18.1 to arrive at a total of relationship contribution to treatment outcome, but reality is not so accommodating. Neither the research studies nor the relationship elements contained in the meta-analyses are independent; thus the amount of variance accounted for by each element or construct cannot be added to estimate the overall contribution. For example, the correlations between the person-centered conditions (empathy, support/warmth, congruence) and the therapeutic alliance are typically in the .50s and as high as .70 (Nienhuis et al., 2016; Watson & Geller, 2005). Many of the studies within the adult alliance meta-analysis (Chapter 2, this volume) also appear in the meta-analyses on collaboration and goal consensus (Chapter 5, this volume), perhaps because a therapeutic alliance measure, subscale, or item was used to operationalize collaboration. Unfortunately, the degree of overlap between all the measures (and therefore relationship elements) is not available but bound to be substantial (Norcross & Lambert, 2014). Whether each relationship element is accounting for the same outcome variance or whether some of the elements are additive remains to be determined.

We present the relationship elements in this book as separate, stand-alone practices, but every seasoned psychotherapist knows this is certainly never the case in clinical work. The alliance in individual therapy and cohesion in group therapy never act in isolation from other relationship behaviors, such as empathy or support. Nor does it seem humanly possible to cultivate a strong relationship with a patient without ascertaining his or her feedback on the therapeutic process and understanding the therapist's countertransference. In volume 2 of the book, which focuses on adaptation methods such as stage of change, reactance level, culture, preferences, and the like, adapting treatment to a patient characteristic rarely occurs in isolation from other elements, such as forming a collaborative relationship with the patient. All of the relationship elements interconnect as we try to tailor therapy to the unique, complex individual. In short, while the relationship elements and adaptation methods featured in this two-volume book "work," they work together and interdependently.

In any case, the meta-analytic results in this book probably underestimate the true effect due to the responsiveness problem (Kramer & Stiles, 2015; Stiles et al., 1998). It is a problem for researchers but a boon to practitioners, who flexibly adjust the amount and timing of relational behaviors in psychotherapy to fit the unique individual and singular context. Effective psychotherapists responsively provide varying levels of relationship elements in different cases and, within the same case, at different moments. This responsiveness tends to confound attempts to find naturalistically observed linear relations of outcome with therapist behaviors (e.g., cohesion, positive regard). As a consequence, the statistical relation between therapy relationship and outcome cannot always be trusted and tends to be lower than it actually is. By being clinically attuned and flexible, psychotherapists ironically make it more difficult in research studies to discern what works.

The profusion of research-supported relationship elements proves, at once, encouraging and disconcerting. Encouraging because we have identified and measured potent predictors and contributions of the therapist that can be taught and implemented. Disconcerting because of the large number of potent relational behaviors that are highly intercorrelated and are without much organization or rationale.

Several researchers have clamored for a more coherent organization of relationship behaviors that could guide practice and training. One proposal would arrange the relational elements in a conceptual hierarchy of helping relationships (Horvath et al., 2016). Superordinate, high-level *Descriptive Constructs* describe the way of therapy. Featured here are the alliance, cohesion, and empathy as global ways of being in therapy. The following are *Strategies* for managing the relationship, such as positive regard, self-disclosure, managing emotional expression, promoting credibility, collecting formal feedback, and resolving ruptures. Then there are *Therapist Qualities*—more about the person than a strategy or skill. Exemplars are flexibility, congruence, and reactivity in responding to countertransference. The Strategies and the Therapist Qualities overlap of course, for example, in the personal quality of reactivity in responding to countertransference and in the Strategy of managing countertransference. Finally, on the bottom of the hierarchy come *Client Contributions*. These describe the client's attachment style, preferences, expectations, coping styles, culture, reactance level, and diagnosis (all these may serve as reliable markers to adapt therapy and are featured in the second volume). Horvath and colleague's (2016) four-level structure of the helping relationship provides greater organization and perhaps clarity.

That organization will assuredly benefit from multivariate meta-analyses conducted on several relationship constructs simultaneously. However, too few studies exist to allow meta-analytic reviews of multiple relationship elements (e.g., measures of the therapeutic alliance, therapist empathy, and client expectations for improvement). Future multivariate meta-analyses could elevate the expectations for future scholarship since most of these relationship variables share substantial variance and could inform conceptual schemes on their interrelations.

As the evidence base of therapist relationship behaviors develop, we will know more about their effectiveness for particular circumstances and conditions. A case in point is the meta-analysis on collecting and delivering client feedback (Chapter 17, this volume). The evidence is quite clear that adding formal feedback helps clinicians effectively treat patients at risk for deterioration ($d = .49$), while it is not needed in cases that are progressing well (Table 18.1). How well, then, does relationship feedback work in psychotherapy? It depends on the purpose and circumstances.

The strength of the therapy relationship also depends in some instances on the client's main disorder, as outlined in Chapter 1 (this volume). The meta-analyses occasionally find some relationship elements less efficacious with some disorders, usually substance abuse, severe anxiety, and eating disorders. Most moderator analyses usually find the relationship equally effective across disorders, but that conclusion may be due to the relatively small number of studies for any single disorder and the resulting low statistical power to find actual differences. And, of course, it becomes more complicated as patients typically present with multiple, comorbid disorders.

Our point is that each context and patient needs something different. "We are differently organized," as Lord Byron wrote. Empathy is demonstrably effective in psychotherapy, but suspicious patients respond negatively to classic displays of empathy, requiring therapist responsiveness and idiosyncratic expressions of empathy. The need to adapt or personalize therapy to the individual patient is covered in detail in volume 2.

ON CAUSATION

We briefly addressed the matter of causation in the opening chapter, and we repeat here that, with a couple of exceptions (collecting and delivering feedback, repairing alliance ruptures), all of the meta-analyses in this volume reported the association and prediction of the relationship element to psychotherapy outcome. These were overwhelmingly correlational designs, showing that more of, say, collaboration, emotional expression, and positive regard were associated with improved patient success.

There is much confusion between relational factors related to outcome and those that can be classified as characteristics or actions of effective therapists. Consider the example of empathy. There are dozens of studies and several meta-analyses now (Chapter 8, this volume) that indicate that empathy, as expressed or perceived in a session, is related to outcome; this is called a total correlation. We do not know if that correlation is due to the patient (verbal and cooperative patients elicit empathy from their therapist and also get better) or the therapist (some therapists are generally more empathic than others, across patients, and these therapists achieve better outcomes). Of the 18 relationship behaviors reviewed in this first volume, only two (feedback, alliance ruptures) have addressed this disaggregation by means of randomized controlled trials (RCTs) and only one (alliance in individual therapy; Del Re et al., 2012) by other statistical means. And it turns out the evidence is strong that it is the therapist that is important—therapists who generally form stronger alliances generally have better outcomes but not vice versa (Del Re et al., 2012). It is largely the therapist's contribution, not the patient's contribution, that relates to therapy outcome (Baldwin et al., 2007; Wampold & Imel, 2015). Unfortunately, we do not know if this is true of empathy or most of the other relational elements.

Put differently, for many of these relationship elements, we know with certainty that they characterize, positively correlate with, and predict successful therapy. But that does not necessarily mean that they are therapist contributions. Another type of causal linkage is needed.

The RCT has been historically considered the "gold standard" to establish that causal link. Indeed, it does prove the gold standard for many research questions, but the question should obviously dictate the research design of choice. RCTs prove practically meaningless for answering many ethical, epidemiological, diagnostic, assessment, and process questions.

Proof of causality is being reconsidered in many sciences, as the requirement for an RCT is limited. In other sciences, we accept causality in the absence of RCTs because the converging streams of evidence are so strong. We are convinced that smoking causes cancer, that parental love causes better child development, that black holes cause gravitational shifts in the universe, that chronic traumas early in life cause later problems—all without a single RCT conducted with humans.

Wholesale discounting of evidence from other research designs is unwarranted and contrary to evidence-based practice principles (Norcross et al., 2017). Not all fundamental questions can or will be addressed by controlled research with human participants. This point was made in a published spoof of the more radical requirements in evidence-based medicine (Smith & Pell, 2003). Unable to locate a single RCT on the use of parachutes, the authors sarcastically deplored their routine use. They condemned people for relying solely on observational data and using parachutes without controlled trials attesting to their efficacy! Sometimes, converging evidence from years of close observation, clinical experience, and careful study other than RCTs can lead to tentative casual inferences.

In the preceding chapters, the authors appropriately waffled on the "causal impact" of the particular relationship quality being reviewed. Many authors made reasonable arguments for why some degree of causal relation with treatment outcome seemed likely even though it was not investigated with RCTs. Researchers pointed to methodological triangulation of sorts in which laboratory experiments (strong causal inferences but poor external validity) were combined with field studies (weak causal inferences but strong external validity) using advanced statistics (such as path analysis and structural equation modeling, which can control for temporality and partial out certain factors). Findings derived from a combination of field studies, lab experiments, and advanced statistical methods do allow for fairly strong causal inferences but not definitive casual conclusions.

The authors of the empathy chapter (Chapter 7, this volume) make similar arguments. They do not claim that their meta-analytic evidence by itself is sufficient to justify strong and generalizable causal inference that therapist empathy causes client outcome. On the other hand, they doubt any single kind of evidence brought to bear on the causal link between these two variables, including RCTs, would prove sufficient. For them, saying any single kind of evidence is sufficient for making causal inferences is dogma rather than science. Instead, they advocate for a general strategy that logically considers the kind of evidence needed to make generalizable causal inferences. They recommend combining several frameworks for doing so, which together provide an integrative model of causal inference, consisting of six conditions (i.e., precedence, plausibility, statistical conclusion validity, internal validity, construct validity, and external validity). The future will bring more of these inclusive, multidimensional frames for determining what proves causal in psychotherapy research.

WHAT DOESN'T WORK

Translational research is both prescriptive and proscriptive; it tells us what works and what does not. In the following section, we highlight those therapist relational behaviors that are ineffective, perhaps even hurtful, in psychotherapy.

One means of identifying ineffective qualities of the therapeutic relationship is to reverse the effective behaviors identified in these meta-analyses. Thus what does not work are poor alliances in adult, adolescent, child, couple, and family psychotherapy, as well as low levels of cohesion in group therapy. Paucity of collaboration, consensus, empathy, and positive regard predict treatment dropout and failure. The ineffective practitioner will not seek nor be receptive to formal methods of providing client feedback on progress and relationship, will ignore alliance ruptures, and will not be aware of his or her countertransference. Incongruent therapists, discredible treatments, and emotional-less sessions detract from patient success.

Another means of identifying ineffective qualities of the relationship is to scour the research literature and conduct polls of experts. The following are several behaviors to avoid according to that research (Duncan et al., 2010; Lambert, 2010) and Delphi polls (Koocher et al., 2014; Norcross et al., 2006).

- *Confrontations.* Controlled research trials, particularly in the addictions field, consistently find a confrontational style to prove ineffective. In one review (Miller et al., 2003, 2012), confrontation was ineffective in all 12 identified trials. And yet it persists, especially in addiction and psychiatry. By contrast, expressing empathy, rolling with resistance, developing discrepancy, and supporting self-efficacy characteristic of motivational interviewing have demonstrated large effects with a small number of sessions (Lundahl & Burke, 2009, 2010, 2013).
- *Negative processes.* Client reports and research studies converge in warning therapists to avoid comments or behaviors that are experienced by clients as hostile, pejorative, critical, rejecting, or blaming (Binder & Strupp, 1997; Lambert & Barley, 2002). Therapists who attack a client's dysfunctional thoughts or relational patterns need,

repeatedly, to distinguish between attacking the person versus his or her behavior. Simply stated, repairing alliance ruptures are among the most easily applied skills and strongest relationship behaviors documented in psychotherapy (Chapter 16, this volume).

♦ *Assumptions.* Psychotherapists who assume or intuit their client's perceptions of relationship satisfaction and treatment success frequently misjudge these aspects. By contrast, therapists who formally measure and respectfully inquire about their client's perceptions frequently enhance the alliance and prevent premature termination (Chapter 17, this volume).

♦ *Therapist-centricity.* A recurrent lesson from process–outcome research and these meta-analyses is that the client's measured perspective on the therapy relationship best predicts outcome. Psychotherapy practice that relies on the therapist's observational perspective, while valuable, does not predict outcome as well. Therefore, privileging and monitoring the client's experience of the alliance prove central.

♦ *Rigidity.* By inflexibly and excessively structuring treatment, the therapist risks empathic failures and inattentiveness to clients' experiences. Such a therapist is likely to overlook a breach in the relationship and mistakenly assume he or she has not contributed to that breach. Dogmatic reliance on particular relational or therapy methods, incompatible with the client, imperils treatment (Ackerman & Hilsenroth, 2001).

♦ *Cultural arrogance.* Psychotherapy is inescapably bound to the cultures in which it is practiced by clinicians and experienced by clients. Arrogant impositions of therapists' cultural beliefs in terms of gender, race/ethnicity, sexual orientation, and other intersecting dimensions of identity are culturally insensitive and demonstrably less effective (DeSoto et al., volume 2). By contrast, therapists' expressing cultural humility and tracking clients' satisfaction with cultural responsiveness markedly improve client engagement, retention, and eventual treatment outcome.

We can optimize therapy relationships by simultaneously using what works *and* studiously avoiding what does not work.

CONCLUDING REFLECTIONS

In the culture wars of mental health that pit the therapy relationship against the treatment method (Chapter 1, this volume), it is easy to chose sides, ignore disconfirming research, and lose sight of our superordinate commitment to patient benefit. Instead, we conclude by underscoring four incontrovertible but oft-neglected truths about psychotherapy relationships.

First, we initiated the Interdivisional Task Force to augment patient benefit. We continue to explore what works in the therapy relationship and, in volume 2, what works when we adapt that relationship to (nondiagnostic) patient characteristics. That remains our collective aim: improving patient outcomes, however measured and manifested in a given case. A dispassionate analysis of the avalanche of meta-analyses in this volume reveals that multiple relationship behaviors positively associate with, temporally predict, and perhaps causally contribute to client outcomes. This is reassuring news in a technology-driven and drug-filled world (Greenberg, 2016).

To repeat one of the Task Force's conclusions: The psychotherapy relationship makes substantial and consistent contributions to outcome independent of the type of treatment. Decades of research and experience converge: the relationship works!. These effect sizes concretely translate into healthier and happier people.

Second, that research knowledge serves little practical purpose if therapists do not know it and if they do not enact the specific behaviors to enhance these relationship elements. The meta-analyses are complete for now, but not the tasks of dissemination and implementation. Members of the Task Force plan to share these results widely in journal articles, public presentations, training workshops, and professional websites. A training initiative, as reviewed in Chapter 1, is also underway to train students to competency in these evidence-based therapy relationships.

Third, psychotherapy is at root a human relationship. Even when "delivered" via distance or on a mobile device, psychotherapy is an irreducibly human encounter. Both parties bring themselves—their origins, culture, personalities, psychopathology, expectations, biases, defenses, and strengths—to the human relationship. Some will judge that relationship is a precondition of change and others a process of change, but all agree that it is a relational enterprise.

Fourth and final, how we create and cultivate that powerful human relationship can be guided by the fruits of research. We have dedicated this volume to Carl Rogers (1980) and Edward Bordin (1979), both of whom compellingly demonstrated that there is no inherent tension between a relational approach and a scientific one. Research (buttressed with clinical expertise and patient values) can and should inform us about what works in psychotherapy—be it a treatment method, an assessment measure, a patient behavior, an adaptation method (volume 2), or, yes, a therapy relationship.

REFERENCES

Ackerman, S. J., & Hilsenroth, M. J. (2001). A review of therapist characteristics and techniques negatively impacting the therapeutic alliance. *Psychotherapy, 38,* 171–185.

Baldwin, S. A., Wampold, B. E., & Imel, Z. E. (2007). Untangling the allaince–outcome correlation: Exploring the relative importance of therapist and patient variability in the alliance. *Journal of Consulting and Clinical Psychology, 75,* 842–852.

Binder, J. L., & Strupp, H. H. (1997). "Negative process": A recurrently discovered and underestimated facet of therapeutic process and outcome in the individual psychotherapy of adults. *Clinical Psychology: Science and Practice, 4,* 121–139.

Bordin, E. S. (1979). The generalizability of the psychoanalytic concept of the working alliance. *Psychotherapy, 16,* 252–260.

Del Re, A. C., Flückiger, C., Horvath, A. O., Symonds, D., & Wampold, B. E. (2012). Therapist effects in the therapeutic alliance–outcome relationship: A restricted-maximum likelihood meta-analysis. *Clinical Psychology Review, 32*(7), 642–649.

Duncan, B. L., Miller, S. D., Wampold, B. E., & Hubble, M. A. (Eds.). (2010). *Heart & soul of change in psychotherapy* (2nd ed.). Washington, DC: American Psychological Association.

Greenberg, R. P. (2016). The rebirth of psychosocial importance in a drug-filled world. *American Psychologist, 71,* 781–791.

Horvath, A. O., Symonds, D. B., Flückiger, C., DelRe, A. C., & Lee, E. (2016, June). *Integration across professional domains: The helping relationship.* Address presented at the 32nd annual conference of the Society for the Exploration of Psychotherapy Integration, Dublin, Ireland.

Koocher, G. P., McMann, M. R., Stout, A. O., & Norcross, J. C. (2014). Discredited assessment and treatment methods used with children and adolescents: A Delphi poll. *Journal of Clinical Child & Adolescent Psychology, 44,* 722–729.

Kramer, U., & Stiles, W. B. (2015). The responsiveness problem in psychotherapy: A review of proposed solutions. *Clinical Psychology: Science and Practice, 22,* 277–295.

Lambert, M. J. (2010). *Prevention of treatment failure.* Washington, DC: American Psychological Association.

Lambert, M. J., & Barley, D. E. (2002). Research summary on the therapeutic relationship and psychotherapy outcome. In J. C. Norcross (Ed.), *Psychotherapy relationships that work* (pp. 17–32). New York, NY: Oxford University Press.

Luborsky, L., Diguer, L., Seligman, D. A., Rosenthal, R., Krause, E. D., Johnson, S., . . . Schweitzer, E. (1999). The researcher's own therapy allegiances: A "wild card" in comparisons of treatment efficacy. *Clinical Psychology: Science and Practice, 6,* 95–106.

Lundahl, B. W., & Burke, B. L. (2009). The effectiveness and applicability of motivational interviewing: A practice-friendly review of four meta-analyses. *Journal of Clinical Psychology, 65,* 1232–1245.

Lundahl, B. W., Kunz, C., Brownell, C., Tollefson, D., & Burke, B. L. (2010). A meta-analysis of motivational interviewing: Twenty-five years of empirical studies. *Research on Social Work Practice, 20,* 137–160.

Lundahl, B., Moleni, T., Burke, B. L., Butters, R., Tollefson, D., Butler, C., & Rollnick, S. (2013). Motivational interviewing in medical care settings: A systematic review and meta-analysis of randomized controlled trials. *Patient Education and Counseling, 93,* 157–168.

Miller, W. R., & Rollnick, S. (2012). *Motivational interviewing* (3rd ed.). New York, NY: Guilford.

Miller, W. R., Wilbourne, P. L., & Hettema, J. E. (2003). What works? A summary of alcohol treatment outcome research. In R. K. Hester & W. R. Miller (Eds.), *Handbook of alcoholism treatment approaches: Effective alternatives* (3rd ed., pp. 13–63). Boston, MA: Allyn & Bacon.

Mohr, D. C., Spring, B., Freedland, K. E., Beckner, V., Arean, P., Hollon, S. D., . . . Kaplan, R. (2009). The selection and design of control conditions for randomized controlled trials of psychological interventions. *Psychotherapy and Psychosomatics, 78,* 275–284.

Nienhuis, J. B., Owen, J., Valentine, J. C., Black, S. W., Halford, T. C., Parazak, S. E., . . . Hilsenroth, M. (2016). Therapeutic alliance, empathy, and genuineness in individual adult psychotherapy: A meta-analytic review. *Psychotherapy Research, 28*(4), 593–605.

Norcross, J. C. (Ed.). (2002). *Psychotherapy relationships that work.* New York, NY: Oxford University Press.

Norcross, J. C. (Ed.). (2011). *Psychotherapy relationships that work* (2nd ed.). New York, NY: Oxford University Press.

Norcross, J. C., Hogan, T. P., Koocher, G. P., & Maggio, L. A. (2017). *Clinician's guide to evidence-based practices: Behavioral health and addictions* (2nd ed.). New York: Oxford University Press.

Norcross, J. C., Koocher, G. P., & Garofalo, A. (2006). Discredited psychological treatments and tests: A Delphi poll. *Professional Psychology: Research & Practice, 37*, 515–522.

Norcross, J. C., & Lambert, M. J. (2014). Relationship science and practice in psychotherapy: Closing commentary. *Psychotherapy, 51*, 398–403.

Rogers, C. R. (1980). *A way of being.* Boston, MA: Houghton Mifflin.

Smith, G. C. S., & Pell, J. P. (2003). Parachute use to prevent death and major trauma related to gravitational challenge: Systematic review of randomised controlled trials. *British Journal of Medicine, 327*, 1459–1461.

Stiles, W. B., Honos-Webb, L., & Surko, M. (1998). Responsiveness in psychotherapy. *Clinical Psychology: Science and Practice, 5*, 439–458.

Tolin, D. F., McKay, D., Forman, E. M., Klonsky, E. D., & Thombs, B. D. (2015). Empirically supported treatment: Recommendations for a new model. *Clinical Psychology: Science and Practice, 22*, 317–338.

Wampold, B. E., Flückiger, C., Del Re, A. C., Yulish, N. E., Frost, N. D., Pace, B. T., . . . Hilsenroth, M. J. (2017). In pursuit of truth: A critical examination of meta-analyses of cognitive behavior therapy. *Psychotherapy Research, 27*, 14–32. https://www.doi.org/10.1080/10503307.2016.1249433

Wampold, B. E., & Imel, Z. E. (2015). *The great psychotherapy debate* (2nd ed.). Mahwah, NJ: Erlbaum.

Wampold, B. E., Imel, Z. E., Laska, K. M., Benish, S., Miller, S. D., Flückiger, C., . . . Budge, S. (2010). Determining what works in the treatment of PTSD. *Clinical Psychology Review, 8*, 923–933.

Watson, J. C., & Geller, S. (2005). An examination of the relations among empathy, unconditional acceptance, positive regard and congruence in both cognitive-behavioral and process-experiential psychotherapy. *Psychotherapy Research, 15*, 25–33.

INDEX

Page numbers followed by *f* and *t* refer to figures and tables, respectively.

Achievement of Therapeutic Objectives
    Scale (ATOS), 427
Ackerman, S. J., 386, 448
actor-partner interdependence model
    (APIM), 127, 214–15
adolescents. *See* alliance in child and
    adolescent psychotherapy
affect, 423–24
affective attitude, 292–93
affective simulation, 267–68
affirmation, 289, 310. *See also* positive
    regard; therapist, affirmation of
AFT (alliance-focused training),
    568–69, 572–73
Against Empathy (Bloom), 246
age
    and alliance-impeding behaviors, 87
    and alliance in child/adolescent
        psychology, 97
    alliance–outcome affected by, 146
    and congruence, 340–41
    and emotional expression, 450
    and group cohesion, 218
    and outcome expectations, 479
    of therapist and congruence, 340
    and treatment credibility, 508, 511
Agnew, R. M., 560
Agnew Relationship Measure, 551
Agnew Relationship Measure–Partnership
    Scale, 170
alcohol abuse, 7–8
alexithymia, 424–25
allegiance, researcher, 15, 620
alliance, 25–62
    causality, evidence for, 55–58
    clinical examples, 29–31

defined, 25, 119–20, 549–50
developing, 102, 107
diversity considerations with, 60
historical background, 25–27
landmark studies, 31–34
measures of, 28–29
meta-analytic review, 36, 37–56*f*, 39*t*
moderators of, 35*t*, 49–55
patient contributions to, 58–59
as PsycINFO keyword, 24
relationship elements and outcome
    statistically related in, 638
research approaches to, 27–28
research limitations, 59–60
split (*See* split alliance)
and therapeutic practices, 61–62
Third Interdivisional Task Force on, 632
training implications for, 60–61
alliance-focused training (AFT),
    568–69, 572–73
alliance in child and adolescent
    psychotherapy, 79–107
    causality, evidence for, 99–100
    clinical examples, 84–85
    definitions related to, 80–82
    diversity considerations with, 103–4
    landmark studies, 86–87
    measures of, 82–83, 106
    meta-analytic review, 88–96, 91*t*
    moderators of, 97–99
    patient contributions to, 100–2
    research limitations, 102–3
    therapeutic practices, 106–7
    Third Interdivisional Task Force on, 631
    training implications for, 104–5
    unique challenges of, 79–80

alliance in couple and family
  therapy, 117–58
  causality, evidence for, 148–49
  client contributions to, 149–52
  clinical examples, 123–26
  definitions related to, 119–20
  diversity considerations with, 154–55
  landmark studies, 126–30
  measures of, 120–23
  mediators of, 141
  meta-analytic review, 131–41
  moderators of, 141–47
  research limitations, 152–54
  therapeutic practices, 156–58
  Third Interdivisional Task Force on, 632
  training implications for, 155–56
  unique challenges of, 117–18
Alliance Negotiation Scale, 551
alliance–outcome
  adult gender affecting, 146, 149
  age of problem youth affecting, 146
  in CFT, 156
  in family-involved treatment, 130–31
  treatment characteristics affecting, 146–47
alliance repair, defined, 120
alliance ruptures, 549–73
  causality, evidence for, 568–69
  in CFT, 120, 123–24, 157
  clinical examples, 556–59
  definitions of, 549–50
  diversity considerations with, 570
  landmark studies, 559–60
  measures of, 550–56
  meta-analytic review, 561–68
  patient contributions to, 569–70
  research limitations, 571–72
  therapeutic practices, 573
  Third Interdivisional Task Force
    on, 632
  training implications, 572–73
  withdrawal vs. confrontation, 550
alliance training, 155–56
alyexithymia, 424–25
ambivalence, 549–50
American Group Psychotherapy
  Association, 234

American Psychological Association
  (APA), 2, 582, 621
Anker, M. G., 128–29, 149, 595–96, 618
anxiety, 16, 526–27, 528
APA. See American Psychological
  Association (APA)
APA Division of Clinical Psychology, 2
APA Division of Counseling Psychology, 2
APA Division of Psychotherapy, 2, 18
APIM (actor-partner interdependence
  model), 127, 214–15
appraisal process, 424
Aristotle, 156
ASC. See Assessment for Signal Cases (ASC)
Asian Americans, 414, 514
Aspland, H., 560
Assessment for Signal Cases (ASC), 585–87,
  589f, 623
assessments, using in-session and post-
  session measures, 634
Assimilation of Problemtic Experiences
  Scale, 174–75
Association of State & Provincial Psychology
  Boards, 621
assumptions, of therapists, 643
ATOS (Achievement of Therapeutic
  Objectives Scale), 427
at-risk cases, in OQ-System vs. PCOMS, 602
attachment
  and alliance, 25
  and cohesion–outcome, 216
  and real relationship, 355, 367–68, 368f
attunement, shared communicative, 272
Auszra, L., 427
authenticity. See congruence (genuineness)
automatic appraisal, 424
avoidance, 527
awareness-oriented role plays, 572–73

Bachelor, A., 174, 271–72
Baldwin, S. A., 33
Balfour, L., 216
Bambling, M., 563
Barkham, M., 7
Barrett, M. S., 391
Barrett-Lennard, G. T., 248–49, 254, 272

and congruence, 324
and relationship inventory, 326
University of Chicago study
   by, 332–33
Barrett-Lennard Relationship Inventory
   (BLRI), 249–50, 251–52, 292, 293, 300,
   326, 327t
BDI. See Beck Depression Inventory
Beard, C., 500–1
Beck Depression Inventory (BDI), 54, 193,
   430–31, 583–84
behaviors
   paralinguistic, 268, 297
   therapist (See therapist behaviors)
Benjamin, L., 294
Bennett, D., 560
Berenson, B., 249
Bergin, A. E., 8–9
Berman, J. S., 391, 511
Berman, M., 412–13
Bhatia, A., 535t
bias, 34–35, 343. See also publication bias
bipolar disorder, 172–74
Bissada, H., 216
Bloom, P, 246
BLRI (Barrett-Lennard Relationship
   Inventory), 326, 327t
Body-Centered Countertransference
   Scale, 527
Bordin, E. S., 26, 49–50, 57, 81, 82–83,
   118, 591–92, 644
Borenstein, M., 435
Borkovec, T. D., 497–98, 499–500
Bormann, B., 207–10
Bowen, M., 151
Burlingame, G., 217–18
Byron, Lord, 640

California Psychotherapy Alliance Scales
   (CALPAS)
   alliance measured with, 28,
     50–52, 51f
   collaboration measured through,
     169–70, 193
   goal consensus measured through, 169,
     174, 193

CALPAS. See California Psychotherapy
   Alliance Scales
Capps, K. L., 448
Carkhuff, R. R., 249, 293–94
Carlier, I. V., 598
Carryer, J. R., 429–30
Cash, S. K., 560
Caspar, Franz, 636
Catherall, D., 119
causal inferences, 15
causality, evidence for
   with alliance ruptures, 568–69
   in alliance studies, 55–58, 58f
   in child/adolescent
     psychotherapy, 99–100
   with client feedback, 619
   for congruence, 341–42
   with countertransference, 536
   for emotions, 446–47
   with empathy, 268–71
   in CFT, 99–100
   in goal consensus/collaboration
     studies, 194
   in group therapy studies, 229–31
   in outcome expectations, 477–79
   and positive regard, 310
   real relationship, 369–70
   from research, 152
   with treatment credibility, 510–11
   for TSD, 412
causation, 640–42
CBT (cognitive-behavioral therapy),
   565, 568
CEAS-III (Client Expressed Emotional
   Arousal Scale-III-R), 426, 429–30
CEPS-R (Client Emotional Productivity
   Scale-Revised), 426
CEQ. See Credibility/Expectancy
   Questionnaire (CEQ)
CFI (Countertransference Factors
   Inventory), 527–28
challenges to alliance, 549–50
Chen, C. P., 312
Chen, R., 560, 568
child psychotherapy, negative outcomes
   of, 580–81

children. *See* alliance in child and adolescent psychotherapy

chronic countertransference, 526. *See also* countertransference

CIS (Collaborative Interaction Scale), 555–56

classical definition of countertransference, 523–24, 525

Clemence, A. J., 388

Client-based therapy, 266–67

client contributions
  to alliance ruptures, 569–70
  in CFT, 151–52
  to client feedback, 619
  to congruence, 342
  to countertransference, 539
  to emotions, 447–49
  to empathy, 271–72
  future research on, 634
  to immediacy, 412–13
  to positive regard, 310–11
  to real relationship, 367–69
  to treatment credibility, 511–12
  to TSD, 412–13

client emotional expression, 437–41, 442, 445–46

Client Emotional Productivity Scale–Revised (CEPS-R), 426

Client Expressed Emotional Arousal Scale–III-R (CEAS-III), 426, 429–30

client feedback, 580–624
  causality of, 619
  clinical examples, 587–91
  diversity considerations with, 620–21
  landmark studies, 593–97
  OQ psychotherapy quality management system for collecting, 583–91
  and outcome management, 583
  patient contributions to, 619
  PCOMS system for collecting, 591–93
  research limitations, 620
  research on, 640
  systemic and meta-analytic review of, 601–18
  and therapeutic practices, 622–24
  Third Interdivisional Task Force on, 632
  training implications, 621–22

client improvement, 530–31, 631

client perceptions, of TSDs, 384–85

clients
  future research with culturally diverse, 634
  monitoring of, 633
  role of, in psychotherapy success, 13, 14
  self-esteem of, and empathy, 272

Clinical Outcomes in Routine Evaluation (CORE) system, 583

clinical supervision, 543

Clinical Support Tool (CST), 584–85, 586*f*, 587, 599–600, 611–12, 623

cognitive-behavioral therapy (CBT), 7–8, 248
  and alliance in child/adolescent psychology, 86–87
  and group therapy training, 235
  and rupture resolution, 565, 568

cognitive therapy, countertransference in, 525–26

Cohen, J., 602

Cohen's *d*, 9

cohesion
  defining, 232
  temporala changes in, 229–30
  vertical, defined, 206
  See also cohesion in group therapy

cohesion in group therapy, 205–36
  causality, evidence for, 229–31
  clinical examples, 210–14
  defined, 205–6
  diversity considerations with, 233–34
  landmark studies, 214–18
  measures of, 206–10, 208*t*
  mediators/moderators of, 225–29, 226*t*
  meta-analytic review, 219–24, 220*t*, 223*t*
  patient contributions to, 232
  research limitations, 232–33
  similarity to therapeutic relationship, 205
  therapeutic practices, 235–36
  Third Interdivisional Task Force on, 632
  training implications for, 234–35

Cohesion Scale Revised, 206–7

Cohesion subscale, 206–7

collaboration, 167–96
  and alliance reconceptualization, 26
  causality, evidence for, 194

clinical examples, 172–74
defined, 168
diversity considerations with, 195
landmark studies, 174–75
measures of, 169–72
mediators/moderators of, 186*t*,
    188*t*, 192–93
meta-analytic review, 176, 184–86*f*
patient contributions to, 194
related constructs, 168
research limitations, 194–95
and therapeutic practices, 196
training implications for, 195–96
and treatment success, 167–68
See also goal consensus
Collaborative Interaction Scale
    (CIS), 555–56
Collaborative Research Network,
    about, 33
collectivist cultures, 344
communicative attunement, 248, 253, 254
Comparative Psychotherapy Process
    Scale, 382
COMPASS Treatment Outcome System, 583
competency-based training, 633, 634
complementary definition of
    countertransference, 523–25
components of treatment credibility
    perception, 496–97
conceptualizing ability, 528
conditions of worth, 290
conflict, unresolved, 525
confrontation ruptures
    clinical example, 557–58
    defined, 550
    landmark studies, 559–60
    therapeutic practices, 573
    See also alliance ruptures
confrontations, as ineffective relationship
    element, 642
congruence (genuineness), 323–46
    causality, evidence for, 341–42
    client contributions to, 342
    clinical examples, 329–32
    definitions, 323–25
    diversity considerations with, 343–44

elements of, 323–24
landmark studies, 332–35
measures, 325–29
mediators/moderators of, 339–41
meta-analytic review, 335–38, 337*t*
research limitations, 342–43
therapeutic practices, 346
Third Interdivisional Task Force on, 632
training implications, 344–45
connected knowing, and empathy, 247
Constantino, Michael, 18
construct validity (as condition for
    generalizable causal inference), 270
contextualized feedback theory, 581, 613
Contract Rating Scale, 170
Cooper, H., 363
coordination scale, 555–56
Cordaro, M., 312
CORE (Clinical Outcomes in Routine
    Evaluation) system, 583
correlational coefficients *(r)*, 9, 503
countertransference, 522–43
    and alliance ruptures, 549–50
    causality, evidence for, 536
    chronic vs. acute, 526
    clinical examples, 528–29
    definitions of, 523–27
    diversity considerations with, 540
    integrative definition of, 524–26
    landmark studies, 530–31
    managing, 374
    measures of, 527–28
    meta-analytic review, 532–36
    patient contributions to, 539
    recent developments in, 522–23
    research limitations, 539–40
    structural model of, 530
    therapeutic practices, 542–43
    Third Interdivisional Task Force on, 632
    training implications, 541–42
    training of, 373
    and work of Sigmund Freud, 522
countertransference behavior,
    526–27, 530–31
Countertransference Factors Inventory
    (CFI), 527–28

countertransference management, 530–31, 532, 537t
  and CT reactions, 536
  measures of, 527–28
  reflective practice for, 541
  therapeutic practices for, 542
  training in, 541–42
  and treatment outcomes, 536, 538t
Countertransference Management Scale, 528
countertransferetial feelings, 268
couple/family therapy (CFT). See alliance in couple and family therapy
couples therapy. See alliance in couple and family therapy
credibility
  enhancement strategies for, 515
  and outcome expectation, 462
  therapist, 495, 496, 512–13, 515–16
  treatment (See treatment credibility)
Credibility/Expectancy Questionnaire (CEQ), 463, 497–98, 499–500, 502–3
CST. See Clinical Support Tool (CST)
CT. See countertransference
CT Interaction Hypothesis, 539
Cuijpers, P., 13–14
cultural arrogance, 643
cultural background, and congruence, 344. See also diversity
Curtis, R., 361
customized approaches, 13
Cutler, R. L., 535t

Daly, A.-M., 560
Daniels, D., 295
Davidsen, A. H., 617–18
De Jong, K., 613, 618
deliberate practice, 5
depression, 13–14
Descriptive Constructs (organization of relationship behaviors), 639
Devilly, G. J., 500
Diener, M. J., 433, 445, 446
DiGiuseppe, R., 81, 87
direct measures, of alliance rupture, 550–51, 566

direct resolution strategies (alliance rupture), 550, 573
disorder-specific treatment, 16, 640
distal outcomes of psychotherapy, 5, 532–33
distress, relational, 150
diversity
  in alliance in child/adolescent psychotherapy, 103–4
  and alliance ruptures, 570
  in alliance studies, 60
  in CFT studies, 153, 154–55
  and client feedback, 620–21
  in cohesion in group therapy studies, 233–34
  with congruence, 343–44
  continual assessment and adaptation for, 633
  and countertransference, 540
  with emotional expression, 449–50
  and empathy, 274–75
  future research including, 634
  in goal consensus/collaboration studies, 195
  lack of attention to, 643
  and outcome expectations, 481
  and positive regard, 312–13
  with real relationship, 371–72
  training in assessing and honoring, 634
  and treatment credibility, 514
  with TSD, 414
Doolin, E. M., 301–2, 312
Dowell, N. M., 511
Duncan, B. L., 591–92, 593, 601, 603
Duquette, Patrice, 358–59

Eating Disorder Examination Interview, 617–18
EBP. See evidence-based practice (EBP)
EBPP (evidence-based practice in psychology), 2
Edbrooke-Childs, J., 621–22
education. See training
educational attainment, 340
effect sizes, 9, 10t, 17, 638
  and publication bias, 133t, 138t, 139–41
  variability of, in alliance studies, 49

Ekman, P., 450
EMFACS (Emotion Facial Action Coding
   System), 426–27
emotion(s)
   and affect, 423–24
   and alyexithymia, 424–25
   and appraisal process, 424
   causality, evidence for, 446–47
   client contributions to, 447–49
   clinical examples, 428–29
   defined, 422–23
   diversity considerations with, 449–50
   inclusion criteria, 434
   landmark studies, 429–32
   measures of, 425–27
   meta-analytic review, 433, 436–42t
   moderators of, 445–46
   and mood, 424
   preparation of data, 435
   productive vs. negative, 424
   therapeutic practices, 451
   training implications, 450
emotional CT reactions, 526–27
emotional processing, 425
emotional regulation, 247
emotional tone, 81, 86
emotion coaching, 451
Emotion Facial Action Coding System
   (EMFACS), 426–27
empathic accuracy, 248–49, 250
empathic reflection, 252
empathic resonance, 248
empathy, 245–77
   in alliance repair, 573
   causality, evidence for, 268–71
   on CFI, 528
   client contributions to, 271–72
   clinical examples, 252–54
   defined, 246–48
   different client responses to, 640
   diversity considerations with, 274–75
   history within psychotherapy, 245
   landmark studies, 254–57
   measures of, 248–52
   mediators/moderators of, 265–68
   meta-analytic review, 257–64
   and real relationship, 374

   research limitations, 273–74
   therapeutic practices, 275–77
   Third Interdivisional Task Force on, 632
   total correlation of, 640–41
   training implications for, 275
employment status, patient, 511
engagement
   in CFT, 117–18, 156, 157–58
   in child/adolescent psychotherapy, 79
   in SOFTA assessment, 122
ethnic minorities. See diversity
etiological beliefs, 499
Eubanks, C. F., 562
Eugster, S. L., 355–56, 359–60
evidence-based practice (EBP), 2, 4
evidence-based practice in psychology
   (EBPP), 2
evidence-based psychotherapy
   relationships, 1–2, 19
   development of criteria for assessment
   of, 634
   interdivisional task force on, 631–32
   used with evidence-based treatments, 633
evidence-based treatments, 6
   codification of, 6
   criteria for, 636
   criteria in study of, 636–38
   and psychotherapy relationship, 631
   used with evidence-based psychotherapy
   relationships, 633
evocative reflections, 253
EXP (Experiencing Scale), 426
expected treatment response,
   OQ-System, 584
Experiencing Scale (EXP), 426
expertness, practitioner, 495
expressive resolution strategies (alliance
   rupture), 550, 556–57, 558–59
external validity (as condition for
   generalizable causal inference), 270
extratherapeutic change, 11–12

family alliances, unbalanced. See unbalanced
   family alliances, 150
family therapy. See alliance in couple and
   family therapy
Farber, B. A., 301–2, 312

Fatter, D. M., 537*t*
Fauth, J., 538*t*
feedback
    client (*see* client feedback)
    cohesion, 217–18, 230–31, 231*t*, 235
    trainee, on CT reactions, 541–42
feedback theory, 601
feelings, conveying positive, 314. *See also*
    emotion(s)
feminist therapy, 525–26
Fisher's *r* to *z* transformation, 263, 503–4
Forester, C., 537*t*
Fortney, J. C., 599
Frank, J. D., 461
Freud, Anna, 80, 351–52
Freud, Sigmund, 25, 289, 522, 523–24
funnel plots, identifying publication bias
    with, 612–13

GAD. *See* generalized anxiety
    disorder (GAD)
Gallagher, M. E., 216
Gelso, C. J., 323, 324, 325, 326–28, 535*t*,
    537*t*, 538*t*, 540
gender
    and CFT alliance, 149, 154
    and congruence, 341
    and countertransference, 540
    and emotional expression, 449–50
    and outcome expectations, 479
generalized anxiety disorder (GAD),
    466, 477
generic inverse variance model (GIVM), 603
genuineness, 291, 324, 374. *See also*
    congruence (genuineness)
GES (Group Environment Scale), 206–7
GIVM (generic inverse variance model), 603
goal consensus, 14, 167–96
    causality, evidence for, 194
    clinical examples, 172–74
    defined, 168
    diversity considerations with, 195
    landmark studies, 174–75
    measures of, 169, 170–72
    mediators/moderators of, 188–82*t*,
        188–82*t*, 192, 193

meta-analytic review, 171*t*, 176, 180
with parents and children/adolescents, 82
patient contributions to, 194
related constructs, 168
research limitations, 194–95
therapeutic practices, 196
Third Interdivisional Task Force on, 632
training implications for, 195–96
and treatment success, 167
See also collaboration
Gondeck, D., 599
GQ (Group Questionnaire), 207–10
Greenberg, L. S., 268, 423, 429–30
Greenson, R. R., 25–26, 352, 353–54, 357
Grizzell, S., 608–9, 612–13
Gross, J. J., 425
group alliance, 119, 233–34
Group Atmosphere Scale, 206–7
group characteristics
    cohesion affected by, 218, 228–29
    members influenced by, 230
Group Climate Questionnaire
    (GCQ), 206–7
Group Cohesion, 206–7
Group Entitativity Measure–Group
    Psychotherapy, 207
Group Environment Scale (GES), 206–7
Group Questionnaire (GQ), 207–10,
    217, 232
groups, and member
    cohesion–outcome, 214–16
Group Session Rating Scale, 207
group therapy. *See* cohesion in group
    therapy
growth curve studies, 15–16
Gullo, S., 215, 230

Halkides, G., 325–26
Hamilton Rating Scale for Depression
    (HRSD), 53, 193
Hansson, H., 613
HAQ. *See* Helping Alliance Questionnaire
HAQ II, 28, 50–52, 51*f*
Hardy, G. E., 500
Harmon, S. C., 593–94
Harvard Group Cohesiveness Scale, 206–7

Hawley, K. M., 86

Hayes, J. A., 325, 355, 530–31, 535*t*, 537*t*, 538*t*, 539

Hedges, L. V., 435

Hedges' *g*, 9, 303

Heimberg, R. G., 480

Heinonen, E., 33–34

helping alliance, 24. *See also* alliance

Helping Alliance Questionnaire (HAQ), 28, 50–52, 51*f*, 174

Helping Alliance Questionnaire II, 591–92

Henretty, J. R., 386–87

Henry, D., 500

Hill, Clara E., 636

Hilsenroth, M. J., 386, 448

Hoehn-Saric, R., 465–66, 477–78

Holt, C. S., 480

homework compliance, 99, 102, 169–70, 188*t*

hope, 462–63, 479

Hopes and Expectations for Treatment Record Form, 464

horizontal cohesion, 206

hostage, therapy, 118

Hovarth, A. O., 639

Howard, K. I., 249, 300–301, 343

HRSD (Hamilton Rating Scale for Depression), 53, 193

humanism, 525–26

humanistic-experiential therapy tradition, 275

human performance, feedback and, 597

humility, 5

humor, therapist, 5

immediacy (Im), 379–417
  causality, evidence for, 412
  client contributions to, 412–13
  clinical examples, 383
  controversy surrounding, 379
  defined, 380
  diversity considerations with, 414
  landmark studies, 383–84, 385–86
  measures of, 381–82
  moderator analyses of, 402–12, 406*t*, 408*t*, 409*t*, 410*t*
  previous reviews of, 386–87

qualitative meta-analytic review of, 387–402, 390*t*, 393*t*, 401*t*, 405–10*t*
  research limitations, 413–14
  therapeutic practice, 415–17
  Third Interdivisional Task Force on, 632
  training implications, 414–15
  See also therapist self-disclosure (TSD)

immediate resolution strategies (alliance rupture), 550, 556–57

impasses, 412, 549–50

indirect measures, of alliance rupture, 551, 566

indirect resolution strategies (alliance rupture), 550, 573

individual psychotherapy, CFT vs., 117

influence, credibility and, 495

Ingram, K. M., 537*t*

in-session assessments, 634

Integrative Alliance Scales, 120–21

Integrative Alliance Scales for couples (CTAs), 120–21

Integrative Alliance Scales for familiy (FTAs), 120–21

internal countertransference, 527

internal validity (as condition for generalizable causal inference), 270

Internet-based psychotherapy, 8

interpersonal functioning, and child/ adolescent psychotherapy, 101

intraclass correlation coefficient, 214

Inventory of Interpersonal Problems, 53, 583–84

I^2 statistic, 265–66, 307, 504, 534, 604

Iwakabe, S., 431

Jacobson, N. S., 603, 617

Janse, P. D., 616–17, 618

Johnson, J. E., 207–10

Jolkovski, M. P., 537*t*

Jourard, S. M., 311

Jung, Carl, 522

Karver, M., 87

Kholocci, H., 537*t*

Kim, B., 414

Kim, S. S., 535*t*

Kirsch, I., 500
Klein, D. N., 15–16
Knaup, C., 598
Knox, S., 361
Kolden, G. G., 335, 340
Kragelohm C. U., 598

Ladany, N., 391
Lambert, J. E., 127, 129–30
Lambert, M. J., 8–9, 600
Lamers, A., 105
Lane, J. S., 301
language, as research limitation, 103, 447
Latts, M. G., 538t
Lease, Suzanne H., 636
Leidenfrost, C. M., 538t
Leijssen, M., 334–35
Lemoire, S. J., 312
Lichtenberg, James W., 636
Lietaer, G., 325
Ligiéro, D., 535t
limbic system, 247
Linehan, M. M., 292–93
Lingiardi, V., 175
Lipner, L., 562
Lipsey, M. W., 132
love, parental, 15–16
Lubitz, J., 562
Luborsky, L., 26, 541

managed care, 6, 18
manualized treatment, 508
Markin, Rayna, 18
Markin, Rayna D., 636
Martin, D. G., 272
McCracken, L. M., 501
McLeod, B. D., 88
MCO (multicultural orientation), 371–72.
    See also diversity
meditation, 543
Meeks, John, 80
member–leader relationship, 206
mental health problems, 499, 598–99, 640
meta-analysis, importance of, 32
Meta-Analysis Reporting Standards, 5
metacommunication, 570
MI (motivational interviewing), 466

microaggressions, 570
Miller, S. D., 591–92, 603
Miller, W., 255
Milwaukee Psychotherapy Expectations
    Questionnaire (MPEQ), 463–64
mindfulness training, 572–73
Minnesota Multiphasic Personality
    Inventory-2, 583–84
misattunements, 549–50
mistrust, 106
Mohr, J. J., 272, 535t
Monte Carlo simulations, 8
motivation, 79, 462–63, 585–87
motivational interviewing (MI), 466
Moyers, T. B., 255
MPEQ (Milwaukee Psychotherapy
    Expectations Questionnaire), 463–64
Multicenter Collaborative Study for the
    Treatment of Panic Disorder, 7–8
multicultural competence, 274
multicultural orientation (MCO), 371–72.
    See also diversity
multilevel modeling, about, 360
multilevel random effects model, 138
Multitheoretical List of Therapeutic
    Interventions, 382
multivariate meta-analyses, of relationship
    constructs, 639–40
Muran, J. C., 387–88, 559, 560, 563, 569
Myers, D., 535t
Myers, S., 255–56, 268

National Institute of Mental Health
    Treatment of Depression Collaborative
    Research Program (TDCRP), 16, 300,
    465, 480
National Registry of Evidence-based
    Programs and Practices, 636
Nau, S. D., 497–98, 499–500
NDST (nondirective supportive
    therapy), 13–14
negative feelings, attribution of, 569, 573
negative processes, as ineffective relationship
    element, 642–43
negative treatment outcomes, 580–82
nondirective supportive therapy
    (NDST), 13–14

nonlinguistic behavior, 268
nonpossessive warmth, 290
nonverbal communication, 517
Norcross, John C., 636
Norway Couple Project, 127

observational perspectives
    on effectiveness of relationship, 634
    therapist-centric, 643
observer-based measures, of alliance
        rupture, 551–56, 566
OE. *See* outcome expectation (OE)
Olkin, I., 435
OQ (psychotherapy quality management
        system), 583–91
OQ-Analyst application, 584–85, 585*f*, 587
OQ-45 measure, 583–84, 591, 601, 603,
        605*t*
OQ-System, 582
    causality, evidence for, 619
    clinical example, 587–91
    landmark studies, 593–95
    measures, 583–87
    meta-analyses, current, 604–14
    meta-analyses, previous, 599–600
    patient contributions, 619
    PCOMS vs., 591, 601–2, 623
ordering, temporal, 15–16
Orlinsky, D. E., 4, 249, 300–1, 312,
        343, 432–33
Ormhaug, S. M., 81
ORS. *See* Outcome Rating Scale (ORS)
Orwin's fail-safe *N* analysis, 307
outcome expectation (OE), 461–84
    causality, evidence for, 477–79
    clinical examples, 464–65
    on Credibility/Expectancy
        Questionnaire, 498
    credibility vs., 462
    definition of, 462–63
    diversity considerations with, 481
    landmark studies, 465–66
    measures of, 463–64
    mediators, 476–77
    meta-analytic review, 467–76, 471*t*, 475*f*
    and motivation, 462–63

patient contributions, 479–80
    research limitations, 480–81
    training implications, 481–82
    and treatment credibility, 496–97, 509
outcome management systems, 583. *See also*
        OQ-System
Outcome Rating Scale (ORS), 591, 592, 601,
        603, 612*f*, 615*t*, 616–17
outcomes. *See* treatment outcomes
Owen, Jesse, 636

paralinguistic behavior, 268, 297
parent alliance, and youth outcome, 99
parental love, 15–16
Parent Expectations for Therapy Scale, 464
parent management training, 81–82
parents, alliance with, 81–82
Parker, 424–25
Partners for Change Outcome Management
        (PCOMS) system, 582, 591–93,
        592*f*, 615*t*
    causality, evidence for, 619
    clinical example, 593
    landmark studies, 595–97
    measures, 591–92
    meta-analyses, current, 614–18
    meta-analyses, previous, 600–1
    OQ-System vs., 591, 601–2, 623
    patient contributions, 619
Pascual-Leone, A., 433, 445
PATHEV (Patients' Therapy Expectation
        and Evaluation), 464
patient contributions
    to alliance, 58–59
    to alliance in child/adolescent
        psychotherapy, 100–2
    to cohesion in group therapy, 232
    for goal consensus/collaboration, 194
    to outcome expectation, 479–80
    to real relationship, 353, 367–69, 368*f*
patient diagnosis, and alliance, 50, 51*f*
Patient Reported Outcome Measurement
        (PROM), 582, 583, 598–99,
        619, 621–22
Patients' Therapy Expectation and
        Evaluation (PATHEV), 464

PCOMS system. *See* Partners for Change
  Outcome Management system
Peabody, S. A., 537*t*, 538*t*
Pearson correlation, 259–62
PEPR (psychotherapist expressions of
  positive regard), 294–95
Perez-Rojas, A. E., 537*t*
personal distress, 150–51
personality disorder diagnosis, clients with,
  565, 566–68, 569
personal therapy, for therapist, 543
person-centered therapy, 290
person empathy, 248, 254
perspective-taking, 267–68
Persuasion and Healing (Frank), 461
Pinsof, W. B., 119
placebo controls, 497
plausibility (as condition for generalizable
  causal inference), 269–70
policy recommendations, of Third
  Interdivisional Task Force, 635
positive alliance, defined, 80
Positive and Negative Affect Schedule
  (PANAS), 427
positive regard, 4, 288–315
  causality, evidence for, 310
  client contributions to, 310–11
  clinical examples, 295–99
  defined by Rogers, Carl, 299–300
  definitions of, 289–93
  diversity considerations with, 312–13
  and genuineness, 291
  landmark studies, 299–300
  measures of, 293–95
  meta-analytic review, 302–8
  moderators, 308–9
  and reinforcement, 291
  and related terms, 289, 290
  research limitations, 311–12
  therapeutic practices, 314–15
  Third Interdivisional Task Force on, 632
  training implications for, 313–14
  unconditional positive regard vs., 291–93
  and work of Sigmund Freud, 289
  and work of Carl Rogers, 288–89, 290
Post-Session Questionnaire
  (PSQ), 550–51

poverty, 155. *See also* socioeconomic status,
  alliance formation and
practice recommendations, of Third
  Interdivisional Task Force, 633
practice standards, 6, 19
precedence (as condition for generalizable
  causal inference), 269
predictive validity, of Rupture Resolution
  Rating System, 555–56
preferences, psychotherapy, 497
primary emotions, 423
Project COMBINE, 255
Project MATCH, 7–8
PROM. *See* Patient Reported Outcome
  Measurement (PROM)
promoting treatment credibility. *See*
  treatment credibility
Prosser, M., 251
proximate outcomes of
  psychotherapy, 532–33
PSQ (Post-Session Questionnaire), 550–51
psychodynamic therapy, 565, 568
psychotherapist expressions of positive
  regard (PEPR), 294–95
psychotherapy
  adaptation of, 633
  adaptation of, and relationship, 634
  alliance in (*See* alliance)
  competency-based training in adaptation
    of, 634
  deprofessionalizing of, 19
  future of, 19
  future research on adaptations to, 634
  immediacy in, 385–86
  multiple factors affecting, 632
  outcome studies of, 176, 177*f*
  testing, 33
psychotherapy preferences, treatment
  credibility vs., 497
Psychotherapy Q-Set, 382
psychotherapy quality management system
  (OQ), 583–91
psychotherapy relationship
  affect of individual vs. combined elements
    of, 638–39
  defined, 1
  as human relationship, 644

ineffective qualities of, 642–43
meta-analysis of outcomes and, 636–40, 637*t*
and outcomes, 644
as primary aim of treatment, 633
techniques vs., 3
publication bias, 139–41, 178
in child/adolescent studies, 96, 97*f*
in cohesion studies, 223*t*, 224
identifying, with funnel plots, 612–13
PubMed, 467

QEEE (Questionnaire for Emotional
Expression Events), 432
Q statistic, 265–66, 307, 504, 534, 604
Questionnaire for Emotional Expression
Events (QEEE), 432

race. *See* diversity
random-effects model, 503–4
randomized controlled trials (RCTs),
560, 641
Rasting, M., 427
RCI (Reliable Change Index), 603
RCTs. *See* randomized controlled trials (RCTs)
realism, in real relationship, 333, 354–55
real relationship, 351–75
attachment and, 355
causality, evidence for, 369–70
client/therapist contributions to, 367–69
clinical examples, 356–59
definitions of, 333, 352–55
diversity considerations with, 371–72
landmark studies, 359–61
measures of, 355–56
meta-analytic review, 361, 364
research limitations, 370–71
therapeutic practices, 373–75
Third Interdivisional Task Force on, 632
training implications, 372–73
transference and, 354–55
Real Relationship Inventory (RRI), 326–28,
327*t*, 334
Reese, R. J., 593, 596–97, 601
reflective practice, for countertransference
management, 541
regulation of therapist emotion, 267–68
reinforcement, and positive regard, 291

relational distress, and CFT alliance, 150
relational patterns
adapting, to clients, 639
and alliance ruptures, 571–72
assessment of, 633
future research on, 634
relational style, countertransference and, 524
relationship, real. *See* real relationship
relationship, therapeutic. *See* therapeutic
relationship
Reliable Change Index (RCI), 603
REML (restricted maximum likelihood), 263
remoralization, 461
repairing alliance ruptures, 412
See also alliance ruptures
Research Consortium of Counseling and
Psychological Services, 33
researcher allegiance, 15, 343
responsibility, for alliance rupture, 573
responsiveness, to low treatment
credibility, 515, 516–17
restricted maximum likelihood (REML), 263
retention, in CFT, 117–18, 156
RI (role induction), 465–66
Ribeiro, E., 174–75
rigidity, in therapist behaviors, 643
Riker, J. B., 537*t*
Ritchie, K., 216
Robbins, M. S., 127–28
Robbins, S. B., 537*t*
Robins, M. S., 127
Rodriguez, Melanie M. Domenech, 636
Rogerian facilitative conditions, 293–94,
302–3, 313
Rogers, Carl, 17, 18
and congruence, 323, 325, 329
and empathic understanding, 247
on empathy, 245, 247
and empathy training, 275
and positive regard, 288–89, 290
on positive regard, 291–92
and positive regard/affirmation, 295,
310–11, 644
on unconditional positive regard, 291
Wisconsin Study by, 332
role expectation, treatment credibility and, 497
role induction (RI), 465–66

ROM. *See* routine outcome monitoring; Routine Outcome Monitoring (ROM)

Rosenberger, E. W., 535*t*, 538*t*

Rosenthal, R., 435

Rosenzweig, S., 26, 32

Rossberg, J. I., 535*t*

routine outcome monitoring (ROM), 582, 583, 619, 621–22

for cohesion, 217–18, 230–31, 231*t*, 233

RRI. *See* Real Relationship Inventory

Rupture Resolution Rating System (3RS), 551–55, 554*t*

rupture resolution training, and treatment outcome, 566–68, 567*f*

ruptures, alliance. *See* alliance ruptures

Ryan, A., 538*t*

safety within the therapeutic system, 119–20, 122, 158

Safran, J. D., 387–88, 559

Saiz, C. C., 86

same-sex couples, and CFT studies, 154. *See also* sexual-minorities

Sapyta, J., 598

schizophrenia, 329–30

Schuman, D. L., 596–97

SCL-90-R (Symptom Checklist-90-Revised), 583–84

Scnellbacher, J., 334–35

secondary emotions, 423

selection bias, in alliance studies, 34–35

self-awareness, and countertransference, 542

self-care, for therapists, 543

self-disclosure, therapist. *See* therapist self-disclosure (TSD)

self-doubt, 5

Self-Harm Inventory, 617–18

self-insight, countertransference and, 528, 542

self-integration, countertransference and, 528, 542, 543

Self Integration Regulation subscale, 528

self-report measures, 551, 556, 581

Session Rating Scale (SRS), 591–92, 615*t*

Session Rating Scale Version 3 (SRS V.3.0), 120–21, 128–29

sex, participant, 508, 511, 514

sexual-minorities, 104, 372. *See also* diversity

sexual orientation, and countertransference, 540

SFS (Strength of Feeling Scale-Revised), 431–32

shared sense of purpose, 122. *See also* within-family alliance (Integrative Psychotherapy Alliance)

Sheehan Disability Scale, 617–18

Shimokawa, K., 599–600

Shostrom, E. L., 290

Singer, B. A., 541

Social Adjustment Scale, 583–84

social behavior, structural analysis of, 294, 569

social influence theory, 495

socialization processes, and countertransference, 525–26

social support, in Assessment for Signal Cases, 585–87

Society for the Advancement of Psychotherapy, 18

Society of Psychotherapy Research (SPR), 33

socioeconomic status, alliance formation and, 104

Socrates, 542

SOFTA. *See* System for Observing Family Therapy Alliances

somatic CT reactions, 526–27

"Some Implicit Common Factors in Diverse Methods of Psychotherapy," Rosenzweig, 32

split alliance

and CFT, 118, 148, 152–53

in CFT, 123–24, 157

and family role, 150

and outcomes, 139*t*, 139

SPR (Society of Psychotherapy Research), 33

SRS. *See* Session Rating Scale; Session Rating Scale (SRS)

State Anxiety Inventory, 527

State-Trait Anxiety Inventory, 583–84

Sterba, R. F., 25–26

Stevens, C. L., 563

Strauss, B., 207–10

Strength of Feeling Scale–Revised (SFS), 431–32

Strong, S. R., 495

structural analysis of social behavior, 294, 569

structural model of countertransference, 530

Strupp, Hans, 3–4

Subcommittee on Research-Supported Treatments, 636

substance abuse, 16

Sue, D. W., 313

supervisory alliance, 572

support, 4, 585–87

Suri, G., 425

Suzuki, J., 313

Swank, L. E., 560

Symonds, B. D., 32–33, 34

Symptom Check List–90 (SCL-90), 53, 193, 617

Symptom Checklist-90-Revised (SCL-90-R), 583–84

symptom severity, 479, 511–12

System for Observing Family Therapy Alliances, 119–20, 122, 129–30, 555–56

TAS-20 (Toronto Alexithymia Scale-20), 427

TASC (Therapeutic Alliance Scale for Children), 80, 82–83

Tasca, G. A., 216

TASC-R (Therapeutic Alliance Scale for Children-Revised), 80

task analysis, for rupture resolution process, 559–60, 572

Taylor Manifest Anxiety Scale, 583–84

TCC (Therapist's Confident Collaboration), 170, 175

TDCRP. See National Institute of Mental Health Treatment of Depression Collaborative Research Program

Teaching and Learning Evidence-Based Relationships (initiative), 18

techniques, relationships vs., 3

temporal ordering, 15–16

TFI (Therapeutic Factor Inventory), 206–7

therapeutic alliance, 3, 24

  in Assessment for Signal Cases, 585–87

  defined, 25–26

  feedback on, 601

  and treatment credibility, 509

  See also alliance; alliance ruptures

Therapeutic Alliance Scale for Children (TASC), 80, 82–83

Therapeutic Alliance Scale for Children-Revised (TASC-R), 80

Therapeutic Collaboration Coding System, 175, 555–56

Therapeutic Factor Inventory (TFI), 206–7

therapeutic relationship

  and cohesion in group therapy, 205

  defined, 3

  fostering emotional expression, 422

  in groups, 212t

  in Session Rating Scale, 591–92

  treatment method vs., 1–2

therapist

  affirmation of, 290, 300–1

  behaviors of (See therapist behaviors)

  contributions of (See therapist contributions)

  credibility of, 495, 496, 512–13, 515–16

  effects of, 7, 512–13

  emotional expression by, 437, 440

  experience level of, 411–12

  experience of, and alliance rupture, 565

  reactions of, and countertransference, 523–24

  self-disclosure by (See therapist self-disclosure (TSD)

Therapist Appraisal Questionnaire, 527

therapist behaviors

  continual adaptations in, 639

  practice and treatment guidelines for, 631

  research on effectiveness of adapting, 643–44

  rigidity in, 643

  and treatment credibility, 511

  and youth outcome, 99–100

therapist-centricity, 643

therapist contributions

  to alliance–outcome relation, 33

  to congruence, 323–24

  future research on, 634

  to real relationship, 353, 367–69

  research on importance of, 640–41

therapist humor, 5

Therapist's Confident Collaboration (TCC), 170, 175

therapist self-disclosure (TSD), 379–417
  causality, evidence for, 412
  client contributions to, 412–13
  clinical example, 382–83
  controversy surrounding, 379
  defined, 379–80
  diversity considerations with, 414
  landmark studies, 383–85
  measures of, 381–82
  moderator analyses of, 402–12, 403t, 405t
  previous reviews of, 386–87
  qualitative meta-analytic review of, 387–402, 390t, 393t, 401t
  and real relationship, 373, 374
  research limitations, 413–14
  therapeutic practice, 415–17
  Third Interdivisional Task Force on, 632
  training implications, 414–15
  See also immediacy (Im)

therapist support, 300–1

Therapist Understanding and Involvement (TUI), 170, 175, 188t

Therapy Process Observational Coding System–Alliance Scale (TPOCS-A), 83

Therapy Process Observational Coding System–Group Cohesion scale, 207

therapy relationship, ix, 6–9
  establishing inclusion/exclusion criteria for, 4
  and person of therapist, 7–8
  and therapeutic relationship, 8–9

Third Interdivisional APA Task Force on Evidence-Based Relationships and Responsiveness, 2, 3–6, 16
  conclusions of, 631–32
  evaluation methods of, 635
  frequently asked questions, 16–19
  general recommendations, 633
  limitations of, 14–16
  members of, 635–36
  policy recommendations, 635
  practice recommendations, 633
  research recommendations, 634–35
  training recommendations, 633–34

3RS (Rupture Resolution Rating System), 551–55, 554t

Toronto Alexithymia Scale-20 (TAS-20), 427

totalistic definition of countertransference, 523–24, 525, 532

Town, J. M., 446

TPOCS-A (Therapy Process Observational Coding System-Alliance Scale), 83

training, 17
  for alliance in child/adolescent psychotherapy, 104–5
  for alliance in treatment, 60–61
  and alliance ruptures, 572–73
  and client feedback, 621–22
  for congruence, 344–45
  and countertransference, 541–42
  for emotional expression, 450
  and empathy, 275
  for group therapy, 234–35
  for immediacy, 414–15
  and outcome expectations, 481–82
  and positive regard, 313–14
  for real relationship, 372–73
  recommendations of Third Interdivisional Task Force on, 633–34
  rupture resolution, 566–68, 567f
  and treatment credibility, 515–16
  for TSD, 414–15

training implications
  for congruence, 344–45
  with emotional expression, 450
  for immediacy, 414–15
  for real relationship, 372–73
  for TSD, 414–15

transference
  countertransference as reaction to, 523–24, 525
  and real relationship, 354–55, 366, 367f
  training of, 373

translational research, 635, 642

transparency, 325

treatment credibility, 495–517
  causality, evidence for, 510–11
  clinical examples, 498–99
  definitions of, 495–97
  diversity considerations with, 514
  landmark studies, 499–501

measures of, 497–98
mediators of, 509–10
meta-analytic review, 501–8
moderators of, 508–9
outcome expectation vs., 497
patient contributions to, 511–12
research limitations, 512–14
therapeutic practices, 516–17
Third Interdivisional Task Force on, 632
training implications, 515–16
treatment expectations, credibility vs., 497
treatment methods, 1–2, 16
treatment outcomes
    accounting for, 11–14
    and client feedback, 594, 595–97
    cohesion moderators affecting, 218,
        225–29, 235–36
    and countertransference management,
        536, 538t
    and countertransference reactions, 531,
        534, 535t
    data sources of, 54
    defined, 5
    enhancing, 196
    future research on relationships and, 634
    improving, 13
    measures of, 53–54
    meta-analysis of relationship elements
        and, 636–40, 637t
    negative, 580–82
    positive, 580, 582
    and psychotherapy relationship, 644
    and real relationship, 370
    and relationship behavior, 15
    and rupture repair, 556, 560–61, 563–66
    and rupture resolution training, 566–68
    specificity of, 54
    and treatment credibility, 500, 501, 504–8, 509
    variance in, 11f, 11–12, 12f
treatment rationale, delivery of, 516
trim and fill procedure, 504–8
Truax, C. B., 249, 293–94, 299–300, 326
Truax, P., 603, 617
Truax Self-Congruence Scale, 326
trust, in child/adolescent psychotherapy, 106
TSD. See therapist self-disclosure; therapist
    self-disclosure (TSD)

TUI. See Therapist Understanding and
    Involvement

unbalanced family alliances, 127–28,
    150, 152–53
unconditional positive regard, 291–93.
    See also positive regard
Understanding Self and Client
    subscale, 528
universal emotions, 423
unresolved conflict, 525

valence, defined, 352
validation, 4, 292–93
Vandebilt Therapeutic Alliance Scale–
    Revised (VTAS-R), 120–21, 122
Vanderbilt Psychotherapy Process Scale
    (VPPS), 28, 294
VanWagoner, S. L., 538t
verbal response modes (VRMs), 381
videotape analysis, 572–73
Vîslă, A., 477
VPPS (Vanderbilt Psychotherapy Process
    Scale), 28, 294
VRMs (verbal response modes), 381
VTAS-R (Vandebilt Therapeutic Alliance
    Scale-Revised), 120–21, 122

WAI. See Working Alliance Inventory
WAI–A (Working Alliance
    Inventory-Adolescent), 80, 81
WAI-Co (WAI couple version), 120–21
WAI couple version (WAI-Co), 120–21
WAI-S (Working Alliance Inventory short
    version), 82–83
Walling, S. M., 233–34
Wampold, B. E., 355–56, 359–60, 636
Watson, J. C., 251, 268
weakenings of alliance, 549–50
weighted correlations, 9, 266–67
Weisz, J. R., 86
Westra, H. A., 535t
Williams, E. N., 537t, 538t
Willis, A., 621
Wilson, D. B., 132
Winnicott, D. W., 310
Wisconsin Project, 310–11, 326

withdrawal, as countertransference
 reaction, 527
withdrawal ruptures
 clinical example, 557–58
 defined, 550
 identifying, 551
 landmark studies, 559–60
 therapeutic practices, 573
 See also alliance ruptures
within-family alliance, 119, 129–30, 156–57
 problematic, 129–30
within-system alliance, 119
Wittenborn, A. K., 560
Woodhouse, S. S., 272
working alliance, 24
 Bordin conceptualization of, 26
 in real relationship, 353–54, 365–66, 366*f*
 therapeutic vs., 25–26
 See also alliance

Working Alliance Inventory
 (WAI), 120–21
 for alliance in child/adolescent
  therapy, 82–83
 alliance measured with, 28, 50–52, 51*f*
 emotional expression measured
  through, 431–32
 for goal consensus measurement, 169, 174
Working Alliance Inventory-Adolescent
 (WAI–A), 80, 81
Working Alliance Inventory short version
 (WAI-S), 82–83

Yalom, I., 358
Yeh, Y., 535*t*
Yeryomenko, N., 433, 445

Zetzel, E. R., 25–26
Zung Depression Scale, 583–84